D0173058

CALIFORNIA CAMPING

The Complete Guide to More Than 50,000 Campsites for Tenters, RVers, and Car Campers

Tom Stienstra

Foghorn
Press
BOOKS BUILDING COMMUNITY™

ISBN 1-57354-053-6

9 781573 540537

52095

California Chapter Reference Map

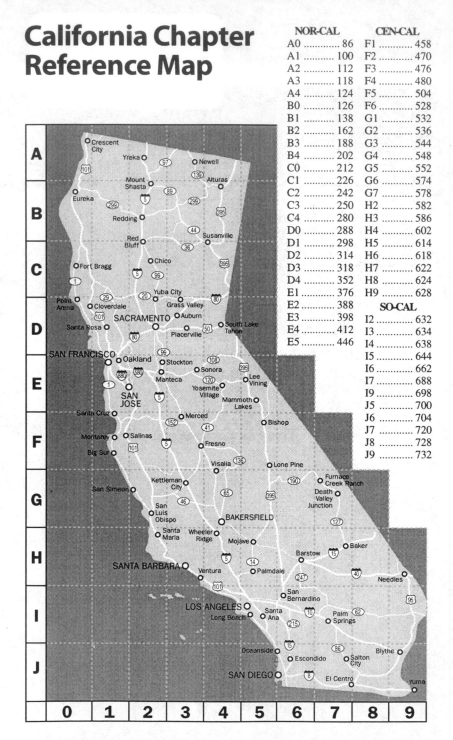

California Camping

The Complete Guide to More Than 50,000 Campsites for Tenters, RVers, and Car Campers

Contents

Central California Campgrounds 457

Southern California Campgrounds 631

Introduction

A lot of people would like to know what heaven looks like, but they aren't real eager to make the trip. It turns out there may be another way to get a glimpse or two of the promised land without ever having to leave the natural world.

I've always felt that camping is like religion: many paths, one truth . . . Like waking up at Santa Rosa Island in your tent, poking your head out, and feeling as if you have the entire world all to yourself . . . or at Buckhorn campground near Mt. Waterman in Angeles National Forest, making the hike down to gorgeous Cooper Canyon Falls, where all is tranquil and divine . . . or at Upper Soda Springs along the San Joaquin River near Devils Postpile, set high at 8,400 feet in the eastern Sierra, flyfishing for small brook trout, rainbow trout, and sometimes even golden trout, and hiking the trail to pristine Thousand Island Lake at the foot of Ritter and Banner peaks . . . or at Panther Meadows at the foot of Mount Shasta.

These adventures are slices of wonder and sensation that attract campers to some of the most beautiful places on earth. California has over 1,500 campgrounds, featuring 383 drive-to lakes, 185 major streams, 20 million acres of national forest, and 18 million acres of land controlled by the Bureau of Land Management—including many little-known, still largely secret places. I have made it a mission to find every one of these, and over the past year in a complete reworking of *California Camping,* I ventured to every section of the state, explored all 58 counties, and discovered countless new places.

With this book, you'll never get stuck again! You will always be able to find a spot to camp for the night.

Rarely has there been a more perfect time to take a trip, with every lake and stream filled, and projected to stay filled even through late summer as the snowpack in the high Sierra melts off. Everything is aligned for the best of the outdoors: camping, boating, hiking, fishing, or watching the sun rise at one of your special places on this planet.

The new edition of *California Camping* is completely reworked, with every listing faxed, checked, and personally reviewed by me and hundreds of experts, to put California's great outdoors right in the palm of your hand.

—Tom Stienstra

How to Use This Book

Finding a Campground

You can search for your ideal camping spot in two ways:

1) If you know the name of the campground you'd like to visit, or the nearest town or geographical feature (national or state forest, national or state park, lake, river, mountain, etc.), refer to it in the index beginning on page 736 and turn to the corresponding page. If you are looking for a specific camp, you'll find that page numbers for all camping areas listed in this book appear in the index in boldface type.

2) If you'd like to camp in a particular part of the state, and want to find out what camps are available there, use the California state foldout map on the inside back cover of this book. Find the zone where you'd like to camp (such as E1 for the San Fran-cisco Bay Area or H3 for Santa Barbara), then turn to the corresponding pages in the book.

This book is conveniently divided into Northern, Central, and Southern California. These sections are further divided into individually mapped grids to allow for greater detail.

Northern California, pages 85–456 (maps AØ–E5)

Central California, pages 457–630 (maps F1–H9)

Southern California, pages 631–735 (maps I2–J9)

• See the bottom of every page for a reference to corresponding maps.

• See the next page for an explanation of campground ratings and symbols.

Every effort has been made to ensure that the information in *California Camping* is as up-to-date as possible. However, details such as fees and telephone numbers are subject to change. Please contact the campgrounds you plan to visit for current information.

What the Ratings Mean

Every camping spot in this book is designated with a scenic beauty rating of ① through ⑩. The ratings are based on the scenic beauty of the area only and do not reflect quality issues such as the camp's cleanliness or the management's temperament, which can change from day to day.

What the Symbols Mean

Listings in this book feature activity symbols that represent the recreational offerings and side trip possibilities at or near the camp. They also indicate whether or not a camp has any wheelchair facilities or wheelchair-accessible areas. (Always phone ahead to be sure that the management's definition of wheelchair access matches your needs.)

Every listing also has easy-to-spot symbols that denote whether the camp is for RVers, tenters, or both.

The 5 Percent Club

Approximately 100 of the camps in *California Camping* are marked with the "5 Percent Club" symbol: 5%. It has been documented that 95 percent of American vacationers use only 5 percent of the available recreation areas. Campgrounds that display 5% are for the other 5 percent of us—those who want to escape the crowds and camp in California's hard-to-reach, hidden sites.

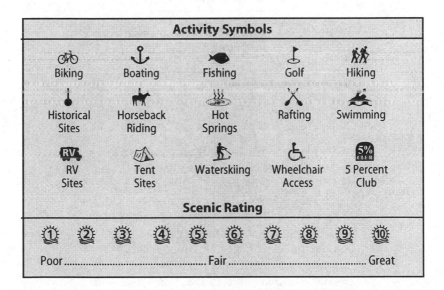

Activity Symbols

Biking	Boating	Fishing	Golf	Hiking
Historical Sites	Horseback Riding	Hot Springs	Rafting	Swimming
RV Sites	Tent Sites	Waterskiing	Wheelchair Access	5 Percent Club

Scenic Rating

① ② ③ ④ ⑤ ⑥ ⑦ ⑧ ⑨ ⑩

Poor..Fair..Great

Foghorn Press congratulates

Vicki DeSmet

of Sonoma for winning

California Camping's

Outdoor Gourmet Contest

with her excellent recipe for
BBQ Chicken Pitas!

Vicki won a Matchless Camp
Kitchen produced by Century and
a four-day camping trip to Caspar
Beach RV Park in Mendocino.

Her recipe was submitted
as follows:

BBQ Chicken Pitas

4 boneless, skinless chicken breasts
1-15 oz. can black beans
1 onion
1 red bell pepper
1 green bell pepper
1 jar BBQ sauce
pita bread

Slice onion and peppers into strips. Cut chicken up into bite-size chunks. Sauté chicken in pan with a little oil until meat is no longer pink. Add BBQ sauce. Remove from pan and cover with foil to keep warm. Sauté onions and peppers in pan for 5-10 minutes until tender. Add cooked chicken and can of drained, black beans. Mix altogether and add additional BBQ sauce if desired. Serve in pita bread. Serves 4-6 adults.

Camping Tips

Food and Cooking Gear

It was a warm, crystal clear day, the kind of day when if you had ever wanted to go skydiving, you would go skydiving. That was exactly the case for my old pal Foonsky, who had never before tried the sport. But a funny thing happened after he jumped out of the plane and pulled on the rip cord: his parachute didn't open.

In total free fall, Foonsky watched the earth below getting closer and closer. Not one to panic, he calmly pulled the rip cord on the emergency parachute. Again, nothing happened. No parachute, no nothing.

The ground was getting ever closer, and as he tried to search for a soft place to land, Foonsky detected a small object shooting up toward him, growing larger as it approached. It looked like a camper.

Figuring this was his last chance, Foonsky shouted as they passed in midair, "Hey, do you know anything about parachutes?"

The other fellow just yelled back as he headed off into space, "Do you know anything about lighting camping stoves?"

Well, Foonsky got lucky and his parachute opened. As for the other guy, well, he's probably in orbit like a NASA weather satellite. If you've ever had a mishap while lighting a camping stove, you know exactly what I'm talking about.

When it comes to camping, all gear is not created equal. Nothing is more important than lighting your stove easily and having it reach full heat without feeling like you're playing with a short fuse to a miniature bomb. If your stove does not work right, your trip can turn into a disaster, regardless of how well you have planned the other elements. In addition, a bad stove will add an underlying sense of foreboding to your day. You will constantly have the inner suspicion that your darn stove is going to foul up again.

Camping Stoves

If you are buying a camping stove, remember this one critical rule: Do not leave the store with a new stove unless you have been shown exactly how to use it.

Know what you are getting. Many stores that specialize in outdoor recreation equipment now provide experienced campers/employees who will demonstrate the use of every stove they sell and, while they're at it, describe their respective strengths and weaknesses.

An innovation by Peak 1 is a two-burner backpacking stove, allowing you to boil water and heat a pot of food simultaneously. While that has long been standard for car campers using Coleman's legendary camp stove, it is previously unheard of for wilderness campers in high-elevation areas. Another recent invention is the flameless stove (no kidding), which allows campers to cook in a tent safely for the first time.

A stove that has developed a cultlike following is the little Sierra, which burns small twigs and pinecones, then uses a tiny battery-driven fan to develop increased heat and cooking ability. It's an excellent alternative for long-distance backpacking trips, as it solves the problem of carrying a fuel bottle, especially on expeditions for which large quantities of fuel would otherwise be needed. Some tinkering with the flame (a very hot one) is required, and they are legal and functional only in the alpine zone where dry wood is available. Also note that in years with high fire danger, the Forest Service will enact rules prohibiting open flames, and fires are also often prohibited above an elevation of 10,000 feet.

I prefer a small, lightweight stove that uses white gas so I can closely gauge fuel consumption. My pal Foonsky uses one with a butane bottle because it lights so easily. We have contests to see who can boil a pot of water faster, and the difference is usually negligible. Thus, other factors are important when choosing a stove.

Of these, ease of cleaning the burner is the most important. If you camp often, especially with a smaller stove, the burner holes will eventually become clogged. Some stoves have a built-in cleaning needle; a quick twist of the knob and you're in business. Others require disassembly and a protracted session using special cleaning tools. If a stove is difficult to clean, you will tend to put off doing it, and your stove will sputter and pant while you feel humiliated watching the cold pot of water sitting there.

Before making a purchase, have the salesperson show you how to clean the burner head. Except in the case of large, multiburner family camping stoves, which rarely require cleaning, this test can do more to determine the long-term value of a stove than any other factor.

Fuels for camping stoves

White gas and butane have long been the most popular camp fuels, but a newly developed fuel could dramatically change that.

LPG (liquid petroleum gas) comes in cartridges for easy attachment to a stove or lantern. At room temperature, LPG is delivered in a combustible gaseous form. When you shake the cartridge, the contents sound liquid; that is because under pressure, the gas liquefies, which is why it is so easy to use. Large amounts of fuel are compressed into small canisters.

While convenience has always been the calling card for LPG, recent innovations have allowed it to become a suitable choice for winter and high-altitude mountaineering expeditions, coming close to matching white gas performance specs. For several years now, MSR, Epi (Coleman), Coleman, Primus, Camping Gaz, Markill, and other makers have been mixing propanes, butanes, and isobutanes to improve performance capabilities.

Two important obstacles that stood in the way of LPG's popularity were recently overcome. Coleman, working in cooperation with the U.S. Postal Service, has developed a program in which three-packs of 170-gram Coleman Max fuel cartridges can be shipped by mail to any address or post office in the 50 states and Puerto Rico. Also, each Coleman Max fuel cartridge is now made of aluminum and comes with a special device that allows the consumer to safely puncture the cartridge once the fuel is gone and then toss it into any aluminum can recycling container.

The following details the benefits and drawbacks of other available fuels:

White gas: White gas is the most popular camp fuel because it can be purchased at most outdoor recreation stores and many supermarkets, is inexpensive, and effective. It burns hot, has virtually no smell, and evaporates quickly when spilled. If you are caught in wet, miserable weather and can't get a fire going, you can use white gas as an emergency fire starter; however, if you do so, use it sparingly and never on an open flame.

White gas is a popular fuel both for car campers who use the large, two-burner stoves equipped with a fuel tank and a pump, and for hikers who carry a lightweight backpacking stove. On the latter, lighting can require priming with a gel called priming paste, which some people dislike. Another problem with white gas is that it can be extremely explosive.

As an example, I once almost burned my beard completely off in a mini explosion while lighting one of the larger stoves designed for car camping. I was in the middle of cooking dinner when the flame suddenly shut down. Sure enough, the fuel tank was empty, and after refilling it, I pumped the tank 50 or 60 times to regain pressure. When I lit a match, the sucker ignited from 3 feet away. The resulting explosion was like a stick of dynamite going off, and immediately the smell of burning beard was in the air. In a flash, my once thick, dark beard had been reduced to a mass of little yellow burned curlicues.

My error? After filling the tank I forgot to shut the fuel cock off while pumping up the pressure in the tank. As a result, when I pumped the tank the stove burners were slowly producing the gas/air mixture, filling the air above the stove. Then, strike a match from even a few feet away and ka-boom!

Butane: That problem can be solved by using stoves that burn bottled butane fuel. Butane requires no pouring, pumping, or priming, and butane stoves are the easiest to light. Just turn a knob and light—that's it. On the minus side, because it comes in bottles, you never know precisely how much fuel you have left. And when a bottle is empty, you have a potential piece of litter. (Never litter. Ever.)

The other problem with butane is that it just plain does not work well in cold weather or when there is little fuel left in the cartridge. Since you cannot predict mountain weather in spring or fall, you can wind up using more fuel than originally projected. That can be frustrating, particularly if your stove starts wheezing when there are still several days left to go. In addition, with most butane cartridges, if there is any chance of the temperature falling below freezing, you often have to sleep with the cartridge to keep it warm, or forget about using it come morning.

Coleman Max Performance Fuel: This new fuel offers the most unique approach to solving the consistent burn challenge facing all pressurized gas cartridges: operating at temperatures at or below 0 degrees Fahrenheit. Using a standard propane/butane blend for high-octane performance, Coleman gets around the drop-off in performance other cartridges experience by utilizing a version of fuel injection. A hose inside the cartridge pulls liquid fuel into the stove where it vaporizes, a switch from the standard approach of pulling only a gaseous form of the fuel into a stove. By drawing liquid out of the cartridge, Coleman gets around the tendency of propane to burn off first and allows each cartridge to deliver a consistent mix of propane and butane to the stove's burners throughout the cartridge's life.

Butane/Propane: This blend offers higher octane performance than butane alone, solving the cold temperature doldrums somewhat. However, propane burns off before butane so there will be a performance drop as the fuel level in the cartridge lowers.

Propane: Now available for single-burner stoves using larger, heavier cartridges to accommodate higher pressures, propane offers the very best performance of any of the pressurized gas canister fuels.

Primus Tri-Blend: This blend is made up of 20 percent propane, 70 percent butane, and 10 percent isobutane and is designed to burn with more consistent heat and efficiency than standard propane/butane mixes.

Denatured alcohol: Though this fuel burns cleanly and quietly and is virtually explosion-proof, it generates much less heat than pressurized or liquid gas fuels.

Kerosene: Never buy a stove that uses kerosene for fuel. Kerosene is smelly and messy, generates low heat, needs priming, and is virtually obsolete as a camp fuel in the United States. As a test, I once tried using a kerosene stove. I could scarcely boil a pot of water. In addition, some kerosene leaked out when the stove was packed, ruining everything it touched. The smell of kerosene never did go away. Kerosene remains popular in Europe only because most campers there haven't yet heard much about white gas. When they do, they will demand it.

Building Fires

One summer expedition took me to the Canadian wilderness in British Columbia for a 75-mile canoe trip on the Bowron Lake Circuit, a chain of 13 lakes, six rivers, and seven portages. It is one of the truly great canoe trips in the world, a loop that ends just a few hundred feet from its starting point. But at the first camp at Kibbee Lake, my stove developed a fuel leak at the base of the burner and the nuclear-like blast that followed just about turned Canada into a giant crater.

As a result, the final 70 miles of the trip had to be completed without a stove, cooking on open fires each night. The problem was compounded by the weather. It rained eight of the 10 days. Rain? In Canada, raindrops the size of silver dollars fall so hard they actually bounce on the lake surface. We had to stop paddling a few times in order to empty the rainwater out of the canoe. At the end of the day, we'd make camp and then face the test: Either make a fire or go to bed cold and hungry.

With an ax, at least we had a chance for success. As soaked as all the downed wood was, I was able to make my own fire-starting tinder from the chips of split logs; no matter how hard it rains, the inside of a log is always dry.

In miserable weather, matches don't stay lit long enough to get the tinder started. Instead, we used either a candle or the little waxlike fire-starter cubes that remain lit for several minutes. From those, we could get the tinder going. Then we added small, slender strips of wood that had been axed from the interior of the logs. When the flame reached a foot high, we added the logs, their dry interiors facing in. By the time the inside of the logs had caught fire, the outside would be drying from the heat. It wasn't long before a royal blaze was brightening the rainy night.

That's a worst-case scenario, and hopefully you will never face anything like it. Nevertheless, being able to build a good fire and cook on it can be one of the more satisfying elements of a camping trip. At times, just looking into the flames can provide a special satisfaction at the end of a good day.

However, never expect to build a fire for every meal, or in some cases, even to build one at all. Many state and federal campgrounds have been picked clean of downed wood, or forest fire danger forces rangers to prohibit fires altogether during the fire season. In either case, you must use your camp stove or go hungry.

But when you can build a fire, and the resources for doing so are available, it will enhance the quality of your camping experience. Of the campgrounds listed in this book, those where you are permitted to build fires will usually have fire rings. In primitive areas where you can make your own fire, you should dig a ring 8 inches deep, line the edges with rock, and clear all the needles and twigs in a five-foot radius. The next day, when the fire is dead, you can discard the rocks, fill over the black charcoal with dirt, then scatter pine needles and twigs over it. Nobody will even know you camped there. That's the best way I know to keep a secret spot a real secret.

When you start to build a campfire, the first thing you will notice is that no matter how good your intentions, your fellow campers will not be able to resist moving the wood around. Watch. You'll be getting ready to add a key piece of wood at just the right spot, and your companion will stick his mitts in, confidently believing he has a better idea. He'll shift the fire around and undermine your best thought-out plans.

So I enforce a rule on camping trips: One person makes the fire while everybody else stands clear or is involved with other camp tasks such as gathering wood, getting water, putting up tents, or planning dinner. Once the fire is going strong, then it's fair game; anyone adds logs at their discretion. But in the early, delicate stages of the campfire, it's best to leave the work to one person.

Before a match is ever struck, you should gather a complete pile of firewood. Then start small, with the tiniest twigs you can find, and slowly add larger twigs as you go, crisscrossing them like a miniature tepee. Eventually you will get to the big chunks that will produce high heat. The key is to get one piece of wood burning into another, which then burns into another, setting off what I call the "chain of flame." Conversely, single pieces of wood, set apart from each other, will not burn.

On a dry summer evening, at a campsite where plenty of wood is available, about the only way you can blow the deal is to get impatient and try to add the big pieces too quickly. Do that and you'll get smoke, not flames, and it won't be long before every one of your fellow campers is poking at your fire. It will drive you crazy, but they just won't be able to help it.

Cooking Gear

I like traveling light, and I've found that all I need for cooking is a pot, small frying pan, metal pot grabber, fork, knife, cup, and matches. If you want to keep the price of food low and also cook customized dinners each night, a small pressure cooker can be just the ticket. (See "Keeping the Price Down" on page 18.) I store all my gear in one small bag that fits into my pack. If I'm camping out of my four-wheel-drive rig, the little bag of cooking gear is easy to keep track of. Going simple, not complicated, is the key to keeping a camping trip on the right track.

You can get more elaborate by purchasing complete kits with plates, a coffeepot, large pots, and other cookware, but what really counts is having a single pot that makes you happy. It needs to be just the right size, not too big or small, and stable enough so it won't tip over, even if it is at a slight angle on a fire, full of water at a full boil. Mine is just 6 inches wide and 4.5 inches deep. It holds better than a quart of water and has served me well for several hundred camp dinners.

The rest of your cook kit is easy to complete. The frying pan should be small, light gauge aluminum, Teflon-coated, with a fold-in handle so it's no hassle to store. A pot grabber is a great addition. It's a little aluminum gadget that clamps to the edge of pots and allows you to lift them and pour water with total control, without burning your fingers. For cleanup, take a plastic scrubber and a small bottle filled with dish cleaner, and you're in business.

A Sierra Cup, a wide aluminum cup with a wire handle, is an ideal item to carry because you can eat out of it as well as use it for drinking. This means no plates to scrub after dinner, so cleanup is quick and easy. In addition, if you go for a hike, you can clip it to your belt with its handle.

If you want a more formal setup, complete with plates, glasses, silverware, and the like, you can end up spending more time preparing and cleaning up from meals than you do enjoying the country you are exploring. In addition, the more equipment you bring, the more loose ends you will have to deal with, and loose ends can cause plenty of frustration. If you have a choice, go simple.

And remember what Thoreau said: "A man is rich in proportion to what he can do without."

Food and Cooking Tricks

On a trip to the Bob Marshall Wilderness in western Montana, I woke up one morning, yawned, and said, "What've we got for breakfast?"

The silence was ominous. "Well," finally came the response, "we don't have any food left."

"What!?"

"Well, I figured we'd catch trout for meals every other night."

On the return trip, we ended up eating wild berries, buds, and, yes, even roots (not too tasty). When we finally landed the next day at a suburban pizza parlor, we nearly ate the wooden tables.

Running out of food on a camping trip can do more to turn reasonable people into violent grumps than any other event. There's no excuse for it, not when a system for figuring meals can be outlined with precision and little effort. You should not go out and buy a bunch of food, throw it in your rig, and head off for yonder. That leaves too much to chance. And if you've ever been in the woods and real hungry, you'll know it's worth taking a little effort to make sure a day or two of starvation will not occur. Here's a three-step solution:

1—Draw up a general meal-by-meal plan and make sure your companions like what's on it.

2—Tell your companions to buy any specialty items (like a special brand of coffee) on their own and not to expect you to take care of everything.

3—Put all the food on your living room floor and literally plan out every day of your trip, meal by meal, putting the food in plastic bags as you go. That way you will know exact food quotas and will not go hungry.

Fish for your dinner? There's one guarantee as far as that goes: If you expect to catch fish for meals, you will most certainly get skunked. If you don't expect to catch fish for meals, you will probably catch so many they'll be coming out of your ears. I've seen it a hundred times.

Keeping the Price Down

"There must be some mistake," I said with a laugh. "Who ever paid $750 for camp food?"

But the amount was as clear as the digital numbers on the cash register: $753.27.

"How is this possible?" I asked the clerk.

"Just add it up," she responded, irritated.

Then I started figuring. The freeze-dried backpack dinners cost $6 apiece. A small pack of beef jerky went for $2, the beef sticks for 75 cents, granola bars for 50 cents. Multiply it all by four hungry men, including Foonsky, for 21 days. This food was to sustain us on a major expedition—four guys hiking 250 miles over three weeks from Mount Whitney to Yosemite Valley.

The dinners alone cost close to $500. Add in the usual goodies—jerky, granola bars, soup, dried fruit, oatmeal, Tang, candy, and coffee—and I felt like an earthquake had struck when I saw the tab.

A lot of campers have received similar shocks. In preparation for their trips, campers shop with enthusiasm. Then they pay the bill in horror.

Well, there are solutions, lots of them. You can eat gourmet style in the outback without having your wallet cleaned out. But it requires do-it-yourself cooking, more planning, and careful shopping. It also means transcending the push-button "I-want-it-now" attitude that so many people can't leave behind when they go to the mountains.

The secret is to bring along a small pressure cooker. A reader, Mike Bettinger of San Francisco, passed this tip on to me. Little pressure cookers weigh about two pounds, which may sound like a lot to backpackers and backcountry campers. But when three or four people are on a trip, it actually saves weight.

The key is that it allows campers to bring items that are difficult to cook at high altitudes, such as brown and white rice; red, black, pinto, and lima beans; and lentils. You pick one or more for a basic staple and then add a variety of freeze-dried ingredients to make a complete dish. Available are packets of meat, vegetables, onions, shallots, and garlic. Sun-dried tomatoes, for instance, reconstitute wonderfully in a pressure cooker. Add herbs, spices, and maybe a few rainbow trout and you will be eating better out of a backpack than most people do at home.

"In the morning, I have used the pressure cooker to turn dried apricots into apricot sauce to put on the pancakes we made with sourdough starter," Bettinger said. "The pressure cooker is also big enough for washing out cups and utensils. The days when backpacking meant eating terrible freeze-dried food are over. It doesn't take a gourmet cook to prepare these meals, only some thought beforehand."

Now when Foonsky, Mr. Furnai, Rambob, and I sit down to eat such a meal, we don't call it "eating." We call it "hodgepacking" or "time to pack your hodge." After a particularly long day on the trail, you can do some serious hodgepacking.

If your trip is a shorter one, say for a weekend, you can bring more fresh food to add some sizzle to the hodge. You can design a hot soup/stew mix that is good enough to eat at home.

Start by bringing a pot of water to a full boil, then adding pasta, ramen noodles, or macaroni. While it simmers, cut in a potato, carrot, onion, and garlic clove, and cook for about 10 minutes. When the vegetables have softened, add in a soup mix or two, maybe some cheese, and you are just about in business. But you can still ruin it and turn your hodge into slodge. Make sure you read the directions on the soup mix to determine cooking time. It can vary widely. In addition, make sure you stir the whole thing up; otherwise you will get these hidden dry clumps of soup mix that can taste like garlic sawdust.

How do I know? Well, it was up near Kearsage Pass in the Sierra Nevada, where, feeling half-starved, I dug into our nightly hodge. I will never forget that first bite—I damn near gagged to death. Foonsky laughed at me, until he took his first bite (a nice big one), then turned green.

Another way to trim food costs is to make your own beef jerky, the trademark staple of campers for more than 200 years. A tiny packet of beef jerky costs $2, and for that 250-mile expedition, I spent $150 on jerky alone. Never again. Now we make our own and get big strips of jerky that taste better than anything you can buy.

Foonsky settled on the following recipe, starting with a couple pieces of meat, lean top round, sirloin, or tri-tip. At home, cut it into $3/16$-inch strips across the grain, trimming out the membrane, gristle, and fat. Marinate the strips for 24 hours in a glass dish. The fun begins in picking a marinade. Try two-thirds teriyaki sauce, one-third Worcestershire. You can customize the recipe by adding pepper, ground mustard, bay leaf, red wine vinegar, garlic, and, for the brave, Tabasco sauce. After a day or so, squeeze out each strip of meat with a rolling pin, lay them in rows on a cooling rack over a cookie sheet, and dry them in the oven at 125 degrees for 12 hours. Thicker pieces can take as long as 18 to 24 hours.

That's it. The hardest part is cleaning the cookie sheet when you're done. The easiest part is eating your own home-made jerky while sitting at a lookout on a mountain ridge. The do-it-yourself method for jerky may take a day or so, but it is cheaper and can taste better than any store-bought jerky.

If all this still doesn't sound like your idea of a gourmet but low-cost camping meal, well, you are forgetting the main course: rainbow trout. Remember: If you don't plan on catching them for dinner, you'll probably snag more than you can finish in one night's hodgepacking.

Some campers go to great difficulties to cook their trout, bringing along frying pans, butter, grills, tinfoil, and more, but all you really need is some seasoned salt and a campfire.

Rinse the gutted trout, and while it's still wet, sprinkle on a good dose of seasoned salt, both inside and out. Clear any burning logs to the side of the campfire, then lay the trout right on the coals, turning it once so both sides are cooked. Sound ridiculous? Sound like you are throwing the fish away? Sound like the fish will burn up? Sound like you will have to eat the campfire ash? Wrong on all counts. The fish cooks perfectly, the ash doesn't stick, and after cooking trout this way, you may never fry trout again.

But if you can't convince your buddies, who may insist the trout should be fried, then make sure you have butter to fry them in, not oil. Also make sure you cook them all the way through, so the meat strips off the backbone in two nice, clean fillets. The fish should end up looking like Sylvester the Cat just drew it of his mouth, leaving only the head, tail, and a perfect skeleton.

You can supplement your eats with sweets, nuts, freeze-dried fruits, and drink mixes. In any case, make sure you keep the dinner menu varied. If you and your buddies look into your dinner cups and groan, "Ugh, not this again," you will soon start dreaming of cheeseburgers and french fries instead of hiking, fishing, and finding beautiful campsites.

If you are car camping and have a big ice chest, you can bring virtually anything to eat and drink. If you are on the trail and don't mind paying the price, the newest premade freeze-dried dinners provide another option.

Some of the biggest advances in the outdoors industry have come in the freeze-dried dinners now available to campers. Some of them are almost good enough to serve in restaurants. Sweet-and-sour pork over rice, tostadas, Burgundy chicken . . . it sure beats the poopy goop we used to eat, like the old, soupy chili mac dinners that tasted bad and looked so unlike "food" that consumption was near impossible, even for my dog, Rebel. Foonsky usually managed to get it down, however, but just barely.

To provide an idea of how to plan a menu, consider what my companions and I ate while hiking 250 miles on California's John Muir Trail:

• Breakfast—instant soup, oatmeal (never get plain), one beef or jerky stick, coffee or hot chocolate.

• Lunch—one beef stick, two jerky sticks, one granola bar, dried fruit, half cup of pistachio nuts, Tang, one small bag of M&Ms.

• Dinner—instant soup, one freeze-dried dinner, one milk bar, rainbow trout.

What was that last item? Rainbow trout? Right! Lest you plan on it, you can catch them every night.

Clothing and Weather Protection

What started as an innocent pursuit of a perfect campground evolved into one heck of a predicament for Foonsky and me.

We had parked at the end of a logging road and then bushwhacked our way down a canyon to a pristine trout stream. On my first cast, a little flip into the plunge pool of a waterfall, I caught a 16-inch rainbow trout, a real beauty that jumped three times. Magic stuff.

Then just across the stream, we saw it: The Perfect Camping Spot. On a sandbar on the edge of the forest, there lay a flat spot, high and dry above the river. Nearby was plenty of downed wood collected by past winter storms that we could use for firewood. And, of course, this beautiful trout stream was bubbling along just 40 yards from the site.

But nothing is perfect, right? To reach it, we had to wade across the river, although it didn't appear to be too difficult. The cold water tingled a bit, and the river came up surprisingly high, just above the belt. But it would be worth it to camp at The Perfect Spot.

Once across the river, we put on some dry clothes, set up camp, explored the woods, and fished the stream, catching several nice trout for dinner. But late that afternoon, it started raining. What? Rain in the summertime? Nature makes its own rules. By the next morning, it was still raining, pouring like a Yosemite waterfall from a solid gray sky.

That's when we noticed The Perfect Spot wasn't so perfect. The rain had raised the river level too high for us to wade back across. We were marooned, wet and hungry.

"Now we're in a heck of a predicament," said Foonsky, the water streaming off him.

Getting cold and wet on a camping trip with no way to warm up is not only unnecessary and uncomfortable, it can be a fast ticket to hypothermia, the number one killer of campers in the woods. By definition, hypothermia is a condition in which body temperature is lowered to the point where it causes illness. It is particularly dangerous because the afflicted are usually unaware it is setting in. The first sign is a sense of apathy, then a state of confusion, which can lead eventually to collapse (or what appears to be sleep), then death.

You must always have a way to get warm and dry in short order, regardless of any conditions you may face. If you have no way of getting dry, then you must take emergency steps to prevent hypothermia. Those steps are detailed in the first-aid section on page 39.

But you should never reach that point. For starters, always have spare sets of clothing tucked away, so no matter how cold and wet you might get, you have something dry to put on. On hiking trips, I always carry a second set of clothes, sealed to stay dry, in a plastic garbage bag. I keep a third set waiting back at the truck.

If you are car camping, your vehicle can

cause an illusory sense of security. But with an extra set of dry clothes stashed safely away, there is no illusion. The security is real. And remember, no matter how hot the weather is when you start your trip, always be prepared for the worst. Foonsky and I learned the hard way.

So both of us were soaking wet on that sandbar, and with no other choice, we tried holing up in the tent for the night. A sleeping bag with Quallofil, or another polyester fiberfill, can retain warmth even when wet, because the fill is hollow and maintains its loft. So as miserable as it was, we made it through the night.

The rain finally stopped the next day and the river dropped a bit, but it was still rolling big and angry. Using a stick as a wading staff, Foonsky crossed about 80 percent of the stream before he was dumped, but he made a jump for it and managed to scramble to the riverbank. He waved for me to follow. "No problem," I thought.

It took me 20 minutes to reach nearly the same spot where Foonsky had been dumped. The heavy river current was above my belt and pushing hard. Then, in the flash of an instant, my wading staff slipped on a rock. I teetered in the river current and was knocked over like a bowling pin. I became completely submerged. I went tumbling down the river, heading right toward the waterfall. While underwater, I looked up at the surface, and I can remember how close it seemed, yet how out of control I was. Right then, this giant hand appeared, and I grabbed it. It was Foonsky. If it wasn't for that hand, I would have sailed right over the waterfall.

My momentum drew Foonsky right into the river, and we scrambled in the current, but I suddenly sensed the river bottom under my knees. On all fours, the two of us clambered ashore. We were safe.

"Thanks ol' buddy," I said.

"Man, we're wet," he responded. "Let's get to the rig and get some dry clothes on."

The Art of Layering

The most important element in enjoying the outdoor experience in any condition is to stay dry and warm. There is no substitute. You must stay dry, and you must stay warm.

Thus comes the theory behind layering, which suggests that as your body temperature fluctuates or the weather shifts, you simply peel off or add available layers as needed—and have a waterproof shell available in case of rain.

The introduction of a new era of outdoor clothing has made it possible for the next generation of campers to turn choosing clothes into an art form. Like art, it comes much more expensive than throwing on a pair of blue jeans, a T-shirt, and some flannel, but for many it is worth the price.

In putting together your ideal layering system there are some general considerations. What you need to do is create a system that effectively combines elements of breathability, wicking, rapid drying, insulation, durability, wind-resistance, and water-repellence while still being lightweight and offering the necessary freedom of movement, all with just a few garments.

The basic intent of a base layer is to manage moisture. Your base layer will be the first article of clothing you put on, and the last to come off. Since your own skin will be churning out the perspiration, the goal of this "second skin" is to manage the moisture and move it away from you without trapping your body's heat. The only time that cotton should become a part of your base layer is if you wish to keep cool, not warm, such as in a hot desert climate where evaporative cooling becomes your friend, not your enemy.

That is why the best base layer available is from bicomponent knits, that is, blends of polyester and cotton, which work to provide wicking and insulative properties in one layer. The way it works is that the side facing your skin is water-hating, while the side away from your skin is water-loving; thus it pulls or "wicks" moisture through. You'll stay dry and happy, even with only one layer on, something not possible with old single-function weaves. The best include Thermax, Capilene, Driclime, Lifa, and Polartec 100.

Stretch fleece and microdenier pile also provide a good base layer, though they can be used as a second layer as well. Microdenier pile can be worn alone, or layered under or over other pieces, and it has excellent wicking capability as well as more windproof potential.

The next layer should be a light cotton shirt or a long-sleeved cotton/wool shirt, or both, depending on the coolness of the day. For pants, many just wear blue jeans when camping, but blue jeans can be hot, tight, and once wet, they tend to stay that way. Putting on wet blue jeans on a cold morning is a torturous way to start the day. I can tell you from experience since I have suffered that fate a number of times. A better choice are pants made from a cotton/canvas mix, which are available at outdoors stores. They are light, have a lot of give, and dry quickly. If the weather is quite warm, shorts that have some room to them can be the best choice.

Finally, you'll top the entire ensemble off with a thin windproof, water-resistant layer. You want this layer to breathe like crazy, yet not be so porous that rain runs through it like floodwaters through a leaking dike. Patagonia's Velocity shell is one of the best. Its outer fabric is DWR-treated, and the coating is by Gore. Patagonia calls it Pneumatic (Gore now calls it Activent, while Marmot, Moonstone, and North Face all offer their own versions). Though condensation will still build up inside, it manages to get rid of enough moisture.

It is critical to know the difference between "water-resistant" and "waterproof." This is covered later in the chapter under the "Rain Gear" section.

But hey, why does anybody need all this fancy stuff just to go camping? Fair question. Like the introduction of Gore-Tex years ago, all this fabric and fiber mumbo jumbo has its skeptics, myself included. You don't have to opt for this aerobic function, fashion statement; it is unnecessary on many camping trips. But the fact is, when you venture into the outdoors, you must be ready for anything. And the truth is, the new era of outdoor clothing works and it works better than anything that has come before.

Regardless of what you choose, weather should never be a nuisance or cause discomfort, regardless of what you experience. Instead it should provide a welcome change of pace.

About Hats

One final word of advice: Always pack along a warm hat for those times when you need to seal in warmth. You lose a large percentage of heat through your head. I almost always wear a wide-brimmed hat, something like the legendary outlaws wore 150 years ago. There's actually logic behind it: My hat is made out of kangaroo skin (waterproof), is rigged with a lariat (can be cinched down when it's windy), and has a wide brim that keeps the tops of my ears from being sunburned (years ago, they once were burned to a red crisp on a trip where I was wearing a baseball hat). But to be honest, I like how it looks, kind of like my pal Waylon Jennings.

Vests and Parkas

In cold weather, you should take the layer system one step further with a warm vest and a parka jacket. Vests are especially useful because they provide warmth without the bulkiness of a parka. The warmest vests and parkas are either filled with down or Quallofil, or are made with a cotton/wool mix. Each has its respective merits and problems. Down fill provides the most warmth for the amount of weight, but becomes useless when wet, closely resembling a wet dishrag. Quallofil keeps much of its heat-retaining quality even when wet, but is expensive. Vests made of cotton/wool mixes are the most attractive and also are quite warm, but they can be as heavy as a ship's anchor when wet.

Sometimes the answer is combining the two. One of my best camping companions wears a good-looking cotton/wool vest and a parka filled with Quallofil. The vest never gets wet, so weight is not a factor.

Rain Gear

One of the most miserable nights I ever spent in my life was on a camping trip where I didn't bring my rain gear or a tent. Hey, it was early August, the temperature had been in the 90s for weeks, and if anybody had said it was going to rain, I would have told them to consult a brain doctor. But rain it did. And as I got wetter and wetter, I kept saying to myself, "Hey, it's summer, it's not supposed to rain." Then I remembered one of the Ten Commandments of Camping: Forget your rain gear and you can guarantee it will rain.

To stay dry, you need some form of water-repellent shell. It can be as simple as a $5 poncho made out of plastic or as elaborate as a Gore-Tex rain jacket and pants set that costs $300. What counts is not how much you spend, but how dry you stay.

The most important thing to realize is that waterproof and water-resistant are completely different things. In addition, there is no such thing as rain gear that is "waterproof" and "breathable" on equal planes. The more waterproof a jacket is, the less it breathes. Conversely, the more breathable a jacket is, the less waterproof it becomes.

If you wear water-resistant rain gear in a downpour, you'll get soaked. Water-resistant rain gear is appealing because it breathes and will keep you dry in the light stuff, such as mist, fog, even a little splash from a canoe paddle. But in rain? Forget it.

So what is the solution?

I've decided that the best approach is a set of fairly light, but 100 percent waterproof, rain gear. I recently bought a hooded jacket and pants from Coleman, and my assessment is that it is the most cost-efficient rain gear I've ever had. All I can say is, hey, it works: I stay dry, it doesn't weigh much, and it didn't cost a fortune.

You can also stay dry with any of the waterproof plastics and even heavy-duty rubber-coated outfits made for commercial fishermen. But these are uncomfortable during anything but a heavy rain. Because they are heavy and don't breathe, you'll likely get soaked anyway, even if it isn't raining hard—soaked, that is, from your own sweat.

On backpacking trips, I still stash a super lightweight water-repellent slicker for day hikes, and a poncho, which I throw over my pack at night to keep it dry. But otherwise, I never go anywhere—anywhere!—without my rain gear.

Some do just fine with a cheap poncho, and note that ponchos can serve other uses in addition to a raincoat. Ponchos can be used as a ground tarp, as a rain cover for supplies or a backpack, or can be roped up to trees in a pinch to provide a quick storm ceiling if you don't have a tent. The problem with ponchos is that in a hard rain, you just don't stay dry. First your legs get wet, then they get soaked. Then your arms follow the same pattern. If you're wearing cotton, you'll find that once part of the garment gets wet, the water will spread until, alas, you are dripping wet, poncho and all. Before long you start to feel like a walking refrigerator.

One high-cost option is buying a Gore-Tex rain jacket and pants. Gore-Tex is actually not a fabric, as is commonly believed, but a laminated film that coats a breathable fabric. The result is lightweight, water-repellent, breathable jackets and pants. They are perfect for campers, but they cost a fortune.

Some hiking buddies of mine have complained that the older Gore-Tex rain gear loses its water-repellent quality over time. However, manufacturers insist that this is the result of water seeping through seams, not leaks in the jacket. At each seam, tiny needles have pierced through the fabric, and as tiny as the holes are, water will find a way through. An application of Seam Lock, especially at major seams around the shoulders of a jacket, can usually fix the problem.

If you don't want to spend the big bucks for Gore-Tex rain gear, but want more rain protection than a poncho affords, a coated nylon jacket is the compromise that many choose. They are inexpensive, have the highest water-repellency of any rain gear, and are warm, providing a good outer shell for your layers of clothing. But they are not without fault. These jackets don't breathe at all, and if you zip them up tight, you can sweat like an Eskimo.

My brother Rambob gave me a nylon jacket prior to a mountain climbing expedition. I wore that $20 special all the way to the top with no complaints; it's warm and 100 percent waterproof. The one problem with nylon is when temperatures drop below freezing. It gets so stiff that it feels like you are wearing a straightjacket. But at $20, it seems like a treasure, especially compared to a $180 Gore-Tex jacket.

There's one more jacket-construction term to know: DWR, or durable water-repellent finish. All of the top-quality jackets these days are DWR-treated. The DWR causes water to bead up on the shell. When it wears off, even a once-waterproof jacket will feel like a wet dishrag.

Also note that ventilation is the key to coolness. The only ventilation on most shells is often the zipper. But water-proof jackets need additional openings. Look for mesh-backed pockets and underarm zippers, as well as cuffs, waists, and hems that can be adjusted to open wide. Storm flaps (the baffle over the zipper) that close with hook-and-loop material or snaps let you leave the zipper open for airflow into the jacket.

Other Gear ... and a Few Tips

What are the three items most commonly forgotten on a camping trip? A hat, sunglasses, and lip balm.

A hat is crucial, especially when you are visiting high elevations. Without one you are constantly exposed to everything nature can give you. The sun will dehydrate you, sap your energy, sunburn your head, and in worst cases, cause sunstroke. Start with a comfortable hat. Then finish with sunglasses, lip balm, and sunscreen for additional protection. They will help protect you from extreme heat.

To guard against extreme cold, it's a good idea to keep a pair of thin ski gloves stashed away with your emergency clothes, along with a wool ski cap. The gloves should be thick enough to keep your fingers from stiffening up, but pliable enough to allow full movement, so you don't have to take them off to complete simple tasks, like lighting a stove. An alternative to gloves are glovelets, which look like gloves with no fingers. In any case, just because the weather turns cold doesn't mean that your hands have to.

And if you fall into a river like Foonsky and I did, well, I hope you have a set of dry clothes waiting back at your rig. Oh, and a hand reaching out to you.

Hiking and Foot Care

We had set up a nice little camp in the woods, and my buddy, Foonsky, was strapping on his hiking boots, sitting against a big Douglas fir.

"New boots," he said with a grin. "But they seem pretty stiff."

We decided to hoof it down the trail for a few hours, exploring the mountain wildlands that are said to hide Bigfoot and other strange creatures. After just a short while on the trail, a sense of peace and calm seemed to settle in. The forest provides you the chance to be purified with clean air and the smell of trees, freeing you from all troubles.

But it wasn't long before a look of trouble was on Foonsky's face. And no, it wasn't from seeing Bigfoot.

"Got a hot spot on a toe," he said.

Immediately we stopped. He pulled off his right boot, then socks, and inspected the left side of his big toe. Sure enough, a blister had bubbled up, filled with fluid, but hadn't popped. From his medical kit, Foonsky cut a small piece of moleskin to fit over the blister, then taped it to hold it in place. A few minutes later, we were back on the trail.

A half hour later, there was still no sign of Bigfoot. But Foonsky stopped again and pulled off his other boot. "Another hot spot." On the little toe of his left foot was another small blister, over which he taped a Band-Aid to keep it from further chafing against the inside of his new boot.

In just a few days, ol' Foonsky, a strong, 6-foot-5, 200-plus-pound guy, was walking around like a sore-hoofed horse that had been loaded with a month's worth of supplies and then ridden over sharp rocks. Well, it wasn't the distance that had done Foonsky in; it was those blisters. He had them on 8 of his 10 toes and was going through Band-Aids, moleskin, and tape like he was a walking emergency ward. If he used any more tape, he would've looked like a mummy from an Egyptian tomb.

If you've ever been in a similar predicament, you know the frustration of wanting to have a good time, wanting to hike and explore the area where you have set up a secluded camp, only to be turned gimp-legged by several blisters. No one is immune—all are created equal before the blister god. You can be forced to bow to it unless you get your act together.

That means wearing the right style boots for what you have in mind and then protecting your feet with carefully selected socks. And then, if you are still so unfortunate as to get a blister or two, it means knowing how to treat them fast so they don't turn your walk into a sore-footed endurance test.

What causes blisters? In almost all cases, it is the simple rubbing of your foot against the rugged interior of your boot. That can be worsened by several factors:

1—A very stiff boot, or one in which your foot moves inside as you walk, instead of the boot flexing as if it were another layer of skin.

2—Thin, ragged, or dirty socks. This is the fastest route to blisters. Thin socks will allow your feet to move inside of your boots, ragged socks will allow your skin to chafe directly against the boot's interior, and dirty socks will wrinkle and fold, also rubbing against your feet instead of cushioning them.

3—Soft feet. By themselves, soft feet will not cause blisters, but in combination with a stiff boot or thin socks, they can cause terrible problems. The best way to toughen up your feet is to go barefoot. In fact, some of the biggest, toughest-looking guys you'll ever see, from Hell's Angels to pro football players, have feet that are as soft as a baby's butt. Why? Because they never go barefoot and don't hike much.

Selecting the Right Boots

One summer I hiked 400 miles, including 250 miles in three weeks, along the crest of California's Sierra Nevada, and another 150 miles over several months in an earlier general training program. In that span, I got just one blister, suffered on the fourth day of the 250-miler. I treated it immediately and suffered no more. One key is wearing the right boot, and for me, that means a boot that acts as a thick layer of skin that is flexible and pliable to my foot. I want my feet to fit snugly in them, with no interior movement.

There are three kinds of boots: mountaineering boots, hiking boots, and canvas walking shoes. Select the right one for you or pay the consequences.

The stiffest of the lot is the mountaineering boot. These boots are often identified by mid-range tops, laces that extend almost as far as the toe area, and ankle areas that are as stiff as a board. The lack of "give" is what endears them to mountaineers. Their stiffness is preferred when rock climbing, walking off-trail on craggy surfaces, or

hiking down the edge of streambeds where walking across small rocks can cause you to turn your ankle. Because these boots don't give on rugged, craggy terrain, they reduce ankle injuries and provide better traction.

The drawback to stiff boots is that if you don't have the proper socks and your foot starts slipping around in the boot, you will get a set of blisters that would raise even Foonsky's eyebrows. But if you just want to go for a walk, or a good tromp with a backpack, then hiking shoes or backpacking boots will serve you better.

Canvas walking shoes are the lightest of all boots, designed for day walks or short backpacking trips. Some of the newer models are like rugged tennis shoes, designed with a canvas top for lightness and a lug sole for traction. These are perfect for people who like to walk but rarely carry a backpack. Because they are flexible, they are easy to break in, and with fresh socks they rarely cause blister problems. And because they are light, general hiking fatigue is greatly reduced.

On the negative side, because canvas shoes have shallow lug soles, traction can be far from good on slippery surfaces. In addition, they provide less than ideal ankle support, which can be a problem in rocky areas, such as along a stream where you might want to go trout fishing. Turn your ankle and your trip can be ruined.

My preference is for a premium backpacking boot, the perfect medium between the stiff mountaineering boot and the soft canvas hiking shoe. The deep lug bottom provides traction, the high ankle coverage provides support, yet the soft, waterproof leather body gives each foot a snug fit. Add it up and that means no blisters. On the negative side, they can be quite hot, weigh a ton, and, if they get wet, take days to dry.

There are a zillion styles, brands, and price ranges to choose from. If you wander about, comparing all their many features, you will get as confused as a kid in a toy store. Instead, go into the store with your mind clear about what you want, then find it and buy it. If you want the best, expect to spend $60 to $80 for canvas walking shoes, from $100 to $140 and sometimes more for hiking or mountaineering boots. This is one area where you don't want to scrimp, so try not to yelp about the high cost. Instead, walk out of the store believing you deserve the best, and that's exactly what you just paid for.

If you plan on using the advice of a shoe salesperson, first look at what kind of boots he is wearing. If he isn't even wearing boots, then any advice he might tender may not be worth a plug nickel. Most people I know who own quality boots, including salespeople, will wear them almost daily if their job allows, since boots are the best footwear available. However, even these well-meaning folks can offer sketchy advice. Every hiker I've ever met will tell you he wears the world's greatest boot.

Instead, enter the store with a precise use and style in mind. Rather than fish for suggestions, tell the salesperson exactly what you want, try two or three brands of the same style, and always try on both boots in a pair simultaneously so you know exactly how they'll feel. If possible, walk up and down stairs with them. Are they too stiff? Are your feet snug yet comfortable, or do they slip? Do they have that "right" kind of feel when you walk?

If you get the right answers to those questions, then you're on your way to blister-free, pleasure-filled days of walking.

Socks

The poor gent was scratching his feet like ants were crawling over them. I looked closer. Huge yellow calluses had covered the bottom of his feet, and at the ball and heel, the calluses were about a quarter-inch thick, cracking and sore.

"I don't understand it," he said. "I'm on my feet a lot, so I bought a real good pair of hiking boots. But look what they've done to my feet. My feet itch so much I'm going crazy."

People can spend so much energy selecting the right kind of boot that they virtually overlook wearing the right kind of socks. One goes with the other.

Your socks should be thick enough to cushion your feet, as well as fit snugly. Without good socks, you might try to get the bootlaces too tight—and that's like putting a tourniquet on your feet. You should have plenty of clean socks on hand, or plan on washing what you have on your trip. As socks are worn, they become compressed, dirty, and damp. Any one of those factors can cause problems.

My camping companions believe I go overboard when it comes to socks, that I bring too many and wear too many. But it works, so that's where the complaints stop. So how many do I wear? Well, would you believe three socks on each foot? It may sound like overkill, but each has its purpose, and like I said, it works.

The interior sock is thin, lightweight, and made of polypropylene or silk synthetic materials designed to transport moisture away from your skin. With a poly interior sock, your foot stays dry when it sweats. Without a poly sock, your foot can get damp and mix with dirt, which can cause a "hot spot" to start on your foot. Eventually you get blisters, lots of them.

The second sock is for comfort and can be cotton, but a thin wool-based composite is ideal. Some made of the latter can wick moisture away from the skin, much like polypropylene does. If wool itches your feet, a thick cotton sock can be suitable, though cotton collects moisture and compacts more quickly than other socks. If you're on a short hike though, cotton will do just fine.

The exterior sock should be made of high-quality, thick wool—at least 80 percent wool. It will cushion your feet, provide that "just right" snug fit in your boot, and give you some additional warmth and insulation in cold weather. It is critical to keep the wool sock clean. If you wear a dirty wool sock over and over again, it will compact and lose its cushion and start wrinkling while you hike, then your feet will catch on fire from the blisters that start popping up.

A Few More Tips

If you are like most folks—that is, the bottom of your feet are rarely exposed and quite soft—you can take additional steps in their care. The best tip is keeping a fresh foot pad made of sponge rubber in your boot. Another cure for soft feet is to get out and walk or jog on a regular basis prior to your camping trip.

If you plan to use a foot pad and wear three socks, you will need to use these items when sizing boots. It is an unforgiving error to wear thin cotton socks when buying boots, then later trying to squeeze all this stuff, plus your feet, into them. There just won't be enough room.

The key to treating blisters is fast work at the first sign of a hot spot. But before you remove your socks, first check to see if the sock has a wrinkle in it, a likely cause of the problem. If so, either change socks or pull them tight, removing the tiny folds, after taking care of the blister. Cut a piece of moleskin to cover the offending toe, securing the moleskin with white medical tape. If moleskin is not available, small Band-Aids can do the job, but these have to be replaced daily, and sometimes with even more frequency. At night, clean your feet and sleep without socks.

Two other items that can help your walking is an Ace bandage and a pair of gaiters.

For sprained ankles and twisted knees, an Ace bandage can be like an insurance policy to get you back on the trail and out of trouble. Over the years, I have had serious ankle problems and have relied on a good wrap with a four-inch bandage to get me home. The newer bandages come with the clips permanently attached, so you don't have to worry about losing them.

Gaiters are leggings made of plastic, nylon, or Gore-Tex that fit from just below your knees, over your calves, and attach under your boots. They are of particular help when walking in damp areas, or in places where rain is common. As your legs brush against ferns or low-lying plants, gaiters will deflect the moisture. Without them, your pants will be soaking wet in short order.

Should your boots become wet, a good tip is never to try to force-dry them. Some well-meaning folks will try to dry them quickly at the edge of a campfire or actually put the boots in an oven. While this may dry the boots, it can also loosen the glue that holds them together, ultimately weakening them until one day they fall apart in a heap.

A better bet is to treat the leather so the boots become water repellent. Silicone-based liquids are the easiest to use and least greasy of the treatments available.

A final tip is to have another pair of lightweight shoes or moccasins that you can wear around camp, and in the process give your feet the rest they deserve.

Sleeping Gear

One mountain night in the pines on an eve long ago, my dad, brother, and I had rolled out our sleeping bags and were bedded down for the night. After the pre-trip excitement, a long drive, an evening of trout fishing, and a barbecue, we were like three tired doggies who had played too much.

But as I looked up at the stars, I was suddenly wide awake. The kid was still wired. A half hour later? No change—wide awake.

And as little kids can do, I had to wake up ol' dad to tell him about it. "Hey, Dad, I can't sleep."

"This is what you do," he said. "Watch the sky for a shooting star and tell yourself that you cannot go to sleep until you see at least one. As you wait and watch, you will start getting tired, and it will be difficult to keep your eyes open. But tell yourself you must keep watching. Then you'll start to really feel tired. When you finally see a shooting star, you'll go to sleep so fast you won't know what hit you."

Well, I tried it that night and I don't even remember seeing a shooting star, I went to sleep so fast.

It's a good trick, and along with having a good sleeping bag, ground insulation, maybe a tent, or a few tricks for bedding down in a pickup truck or motor home, you can get a good night's sleep on every camping trip.

More than 20 years after that camping episode with my dad and brother, we made a trip to the planetarium at the Academy of Sciences in San Francisco to see a show on Halley's Comet. The lights dimmed, and the ceiling turned into a night sky, filled with stars and a setting moon. A scientist began explaining phenomena of the heavens.

After a few minutes, I began to feel drowsy. Just then, a shooting star zipped across the planetarium ceiling. I went into a deep sleep so fast it was like I was in a coma. I didn't wake up until the show was over, the lights were turned back on, and the people were leaving.

Feeling drowsy, I turned to see if ol' Dad had liked the show. Oh yeah? Not only had he gone to sleep too, but he apparently had no intention of waking up, no matter what. Just like a camping trip.

Sleeping Bags

Question: What could be worse than trying to sleep in a cold, wet sleeping bag on a rainy night without a tent in the mountains?

Answer: Trying to sleep in a cold, wet sleeping bag on a rainy night without a tent in the mountains when your sleeping bag is filled with down.

Water will turn a down-filled sleeping bag into a mushy heap. Many campers do not like a high-tech approach, but the state-of-the-art polyfiber sleeping bags can keep you warm even when wet. That factor, along with temperature rating and weight, is key when selecting a sleeping bag.

A sleeping bag is a shell filled with heat-retaining insulation. By itself, it is not warm. Your body provides the heat, and the sleeping bag's ability to retain that heat is what makes it warm or cold.

The old-style canvas bags are heavy, bulky, cold, and, when wet, useless. With other options available, their use is limited. Anybody who sleeps outdoors or backpacks should choose otherwise. Instead, buy and use a sleeping bag filled with down or one of the quality poly-fills. Down is light, warm, and aesthetically pleasing to those who don't think camping and technology mix. If you choose a down bag, be sure to keep it double wrapped in plastic garbage bags on your trip in order to keep it dry. Once wet, you'll spend your nights howling at the moon.

The polyfiber-filled bags are not necessarily better than those filled with down, but they can be. Their one key advantage is that even when wet, some poly-fills can retain up to 85 percent of your body heat. This allows you to sleep and get valuable rest even in miserable conditions. And my camping experience is that no matter how lucky you may be, there comes a time when you will get caught in an unexpected, violent storm and everything you've got will get wet, including your sleeping bag. That's when a poly-fill bag becomes priceless. You either have one and can sleep, or you don't have one and suffer. It is that simple. Of the synthetic fills, Quallofil made by Dupont is the industry leader.

But as mentioned, just because a sleeping bag uses a high-tech poly-fill doesn't necessarily make it a better bag. There are other factors.

The most important are a bag's temperature rating and weight. The temperature rating of a sleeping bag refers to how cold it can get before you start actually feeling cold. Many campers make the mistake of thinking, "I only camp in the summer, so a bag rated at 30 or 40 degrees should be fine." Later, they find out it isn't so fine, and all it takes is one cold night to convince them of that. When selecting the right temperature rating, visualize the coldest weather you might ever confront, and then get a bag rated for even colder weather.

For instance, if you are a summer camper, you may rarely experience a night in the low 30s or high 20s. A sleeping bag rated at 20 degrees would be appropriate, keeping you snug, warm, and asleep. For most campers, I advise bags rated at zero or 10 degrees.

If you buy a poly-filled sleeping bag, never leave it squished in your stuff sack between camping trips. Instead, keep it on a hanger in a closet or use it as a blanket. One thing that can reduce a poly-filled bag's heat-retaining qualities is if you lose the loft out of the tiny hollow fibers that make up the fill. You can avoid this with proper storage.

The weight of a sleeping bag can also be a key factor, especially for backpackers. When you have to carry your gear on your back, every ounce becomes important. To keep your weight to a minimum, sleeping bags that weigh just 3 pounds are available, although they are expensive. But if you hike much, it's worth the price. For an overnighter you can get away with a 4- or 4.5-pound bag without much stress. However, bags weighing 5 pounds and up should be left back at the car.

I have two sleeping bags: a 7-pounder that feels like I'm in a giant sponge, and a little 3-pounder. The heavy-duty model is for pickup truck camping in cold weather and doubles as a blanket at home. The lightweight bag is for hikes. Between the two, I'm set.

Insulation Pads

Even with the warmest sleeping bag in the world, if you just lay it down on the ground and try to sleep, you will likely get as cold as a winter cucumber. That is because the cold ground will suck the warmth right out of your body. The solution is to have a layer of insulation between you and the ground. For this you can use a thin Insulite pad, a lightweight Therm-a-Rest inflatable pad, or an air mattress. Here is a capsule summary of all three:

•**Insulite pads:** They are light, inexpensive, roll up quickly for transport, and can double as a seat pad at your camp. The negative side is that in one night, they will compress, making you feel like you are sleeping on granite.

•**Therm-a-Rest pads:** These are a real luxury, because they do everything an Insulite pad does, but also provide a cushion. The negative side is that they are expensive by comparison, and if they get a hole in them, they become worthless without a patch kit.

•**Air mattress:** These are okay for car campers, but their bulk, weight, and the amount of effort necessary to blow them up make them a nuisance.

A Few Tricks

When surveying a camp area, the most important consideration should be to select a good spot to sleep. Everything else is secondary. Ideally, you want a flat spot that is wind-sheltered, on ground soft enough to drive stakes into. Yeah, and I want to win the lottery, too.

Sometimes that ground will have a slight slope to it. In that case, always sleep with your head on the uphill side. If you sleep parallel to the slope,

every time you roll over, you'll find yourself rolling down the hill. If you sleep with your head on the downhill side, you'll get a headache that feels like an ax is embedded in your brain.

When you've found a good spot, clear it of all branches, twigs, and rocks, of course. A good tip is to dig a slight indentation in the ground where your hip will fit. Since your body is not flat, but has curves and edges, it will not feel comfortable on flat ground. Some people even get severely bruised on the sides of their hips when sleeping on flat, hard ground. For that reason alone, they learn to hate camping. Instead, bring a spade, dig a little depression in the ground for your hip, and sleep well.

In wilderness, where leave-no-trace ethics should always be heeded, never dig such a depression. With a Therm-a-Rest pad it will be unnecessary anyway.

After the ground is prepared, throw a ground cloth over the spot, which will keep much of the morning dew off you. In some areas, particularly where fog is a problem, morning dew can be heavy and get the outside of your sleeping bag quite wet. In that case, you need overhead protection, such as a tent or some kind of roof, like that of a poncho or tarp with its ends tied to trees.

Tents and Weather Protection

All it takes is to get caught in the rain once without a tent and you will never go anywhere without one again. A tent provides protection from rain, wind, and mosquito attacks. In exchange, you can lose a starry night's view, though some tents now even provide moon roofs.

A tent can be as complex as a four-season, tubular-jointed dome with a rain fly, or as simple as two ponchos snapped together and roped up to a tree. They can be as cheap as a $10 tube tent, which is nothing more than a hollow piece of plastic, or as expensive as a $500 five-person deluxe expedition dome model. They vary greatly in size, price, and put-up time. If you plan on getting a good one, then plan on doing plenty of shopping and asking lots of questions. The key ones are: Will it keep me dry? How hard is it to put up? Is it roomy enough? How much does it weigh?

With a little bit of homework, you can get the right answers to these questions.

• **Will it keep me dry?** On many one-person and two-person tents, the rain fly does not extend far enough to keep water off the bottom sidewalls of the tent. In a driving rain, water can also drip from the rain fly and to the bottom sidewalls of the tent. Eventually the water can leak through to the inside, particularly through the seams where the tent has been sewed together.

You must be able to stake out your rain fly so it completely covers all of the tent. If you are tent shopping and this does not appear possible, then don't buy the tent. To prevent potential leaks, use a seam waterproofer such as Seam Lock, a gluelike substance, to close potential leak areas on tent seams. For large umbrella tents, keep a patch kit handy.

Another way to keep water out of your tent is to store all wet garments outside the tent, under a poncho. Moisture from wet clothes stashed in the tent will condense on the interior tent walls. If you bring enough wet clothes in the tent, by the next morning you can feel like you're camping in a duck blind.

• **How hard is it to put up?** If a tent is difficult to erect in full sunlight, you can just about forget it at night. Some tents can go up in just a few minutes, without requiring help from another camper. This might be the kind of tent you want.

The way to compare put-up time of tents when shopping is to count the number of connecting points from the tent poles to the tent, and also the number of stakes required. The fewer, the better. Think simple. My tent has seven connecting points and, minus the rain fly, requires no stakes. It goes up in a few minutes. If you need a lot of stakes, it is a sure tip-off to a long put-up time. Try it at night or in the rain, and you'll be ready to cash your chips and go for broke.

Another factor is the tent poles themselves. Some small tents have poles that are broken into small sections that are connected by bungee cords. It takes only an instant to convert them to a complete pole.

Some outdoor shops have tents on display on their showroom floor. Before buying the tent, have the salesperson take the tent down and put it back up. If it takes him more than five minutes, or he says he "doesn't have time," then keep looking.

• **Is it roomy enough?** Don't judge the size of a tent on floor space alone. Some tents small on floor space can give the illusion of roominess with a high ceiling. You can be quite comfortable in them and snug.

But remember that a one-person or

two-person tent is just that. A two-person tent has room for two people plus gear. That's it. Don't buy a tent expecting it to hold more than it is intended to.

• **How much does it weigh?** If you're a hiker, this becomes the preeminent question. If it's much more than 6 or 7 pounds, forget it. A 12-pound tent is bad enough, but get it wet and it's like carrying a piano on your back. On the other hand, weight is scarcely a factor if you camp only where you can take your car. My dad, for instance, used to have this giant canvas umbrella tent that folded down to this neat little pack that weighed about 500 pounds.

Family Tents

It is always worth spending the time and money to purchase a tent you and your family will be happy with.

Though many good family tents are available for $125 to $175, particularly from Coleman, here is a synopsis of four of the best tents available anywhere, without regard to cost:

Sierra Designs Mondo 5CD

(800) 736-8551

$495

10.14 pounds

82 square feet / 20-square-foot vestibule / Inside peak height: 5 feet, 5 inches

If you've got a family that likes to head for distant camps, then this is your tent. It's light enough to pack along, yet big enough to accommodate a family of four. Using speed clips, this tent is by far the easiest and quickest to set up of any family tent I've used. A generous rain fly and vestibule (new adjustment features allow various awning configurations) mean more than adequate protection from the elements, no matter how hard they are pelting down.

Kelty Domolite 6

(800) 423-2320

$350

16.4 pounds

81.5 square feet / Inside peak height: 5 feet, 7 inches

Using three 18-foot-long fiberglass poles, the Domolite boasts a sleek, low profile that slips the wind very nicely. Each pole slides easily through continuous pole sleeves, thanks to rubber-tipped ends, making set-up a snap. Kelty has an optional vestibule ($95) since without it, the tent is barely adequate shelter should you have to weather a deluge in cramped quarters. Floor seams are taped for added waterproofness. A great package.

Eureka! Space III

(800) 848-3673

$590

29 pounds

100 square feet / Inside peak height: 7 feet

This tent practically reeks of traditional design, and that's the beauty of it. It's a cabin tent by all appearances, with modern design applications intended to improve set-up convenience and make it essentially freestanding. The rigid side poles snap into four curved units that hook to a hub at the top of the tent and then attach to pins at each of the tent's four corners. From there it is a simple matter to hook the tent to the poles with clips attached to the tent body. Huge windows, a giant door, and high ceiling mean plenty of flow-through ventilation and wonderful interior space. At 29 pounds, you won't be wanting to move it around too much, but then who cares. With a tent like this, you're camping long-term anyway.

Quest Nomad

(800) 875-6901

$445

24.6 pounds

81 square feet + 50-square-foot screen porch / Inside peak height: 6 feet, 7 inches

If you are seeking bomb-proof construction, maximum insect protection, and ease of set-up coupled with plenty of space to spread out, then look no further. Using a patented Sportiva hub, the set-up is simplified as fiberglass poles extend like spider's legs, connecting into place with simple efficiency to rigid steel side poles. The screened porch makes this tent seem more like a mountain chalet. The tent's only weak point that I could find is a lack of tub floor. Puddles have a tendency to collect in many campgrounds I have frequented, and seams that rest on the ground, like the Nomad's, are an invitation to eventual leakage, even if well seam-sealed.

Bivouac Bags

If you like going solo and choose not to own a tent at all, a bivvy bag, short for bivouac bag, can provide the weather protection you require. A bivvy bag is a water-repellent shell in which your sleeping bag fits. It is light and tough, and for some is the perfect alternative to a heavy tent. On the downside, however, there is a strange sensation when you try to ride out a rainy night in one. You can hear the rain hitting you, and sometimes even feel the pounding of the drops through the bivvy bag. It can be unsettling to try and sleep under such circumstances.

Pickup Truck Campers

If you own a pickup truck with a camper shell, you can turn it into a self-contained campground with a little work. This can be an ideal way to go: it's fast, portable, and you are guaranteed a dry environment.

But that does not necessarily mean it is a warm environment. In fact, without insulation from the metal truck bed, it can be like trying to sleep on an iceberg. That is because the metal truck bed will get as cold as the air temperature, which is often much colder than the ground temperature. Without insulation, it can be much colder in your camper shell than it would be on the open ground.

When I camp in my rig, I use a large piece of foam for a mattress and insulation. The foam measures 4 inches thick, 48 inches wide, and 76 inches long. It makes for a bed as comfortable as anything one might ask for. In fact, during the winter, if I don't go camping for a few weeks because of writing obligations, I sometimes will throw the foam on the floor, lay down the old sleeping bag, light a fire, and camp right in my living room. It's in my blood, I tell you.

RVs

The problems RVers encounter come from two primary sources: lack of privacy and light intrusion.

The lack of privacy stems from the natural restrictions of where a "land yacht" can go. Without careful use of this book's guide portion, motor home owners can find themselves in parking lot settings, jammed in with plenty of neighbors. Because RVs often have large picture windows, you lose your privacy, causing some late nights; then, come daybreak, light intrusion forces an early wake-up. The result is you get shorted on your sleep.

The answer is to always carry inserts to fit over the inside of your windows. This closes off the outside and ensures your privacy. And if you don't want to wake up with the sun at daybreak, you don't have to. It will still be dark.

First Aid and Insect Protection

The mountain night could not have been more perfect, I thought, as I lay in my sleeping bag.

The sky looked like a mass of jewels and the air tasted sweet and smelled of pines. A shooting star fireballed across the sky, and I remember thinking, "It just doesn't get any better."

Just then, as I was drifting into sleep, this mysterious buzz appeared from nowhere and deposited itself inside my left ear. Suddenly awake, I whacked my ear with the palm of my hand, hard enough to cause a minor concussion. The buzz disappeared. I pulled out my flashlight and shined it on my palm, and there, lit in the blackness of night, lay the squished intruder: a mosquito, dead amid a stain of blood.

Satisfied, I turned off the light, closed my eyes, and thought of the fishing trip planned for the next day. Then I heard them. It was a squadron of mosquitoes, flying landing patterns around my head. I tried to grab them with an open hand, but they dodged the assault and flew off. Just 30 seconds later another landed in my left ear. I promptly dispatched the invader with a rip of the palm.

Now I was completely awake, so I got out of my sleeping bag to retrieve some mosquito repellent. But while en route, several of the buggers swarmed and nailed me in the back and arms. Later, after applying the repellent and settling snugly again in my sleeping bag, the mosquitoes would buzz a few inches from my ear. After getting a whiff of the poison, they would fly off. It was like sleeping in a sawmill.

The next day, drowsy from little sleep, I set out to fish. I'd walked but 15 minutes when I brushed against a bush and felt this stinging sensation on the inside of my arm, just above the wrist. I looked down: A tick had his clamps in me. I ripped it out before he could embed his head into my skin.

After catching a few fish, I sat down against a tree to eat lunch and just watch the water go by. My dog, Rebel, sat down next to me and stared at the beef jerky I was munching as if it were a T-bone steak. I finished eating, gave him a small piece, patted him on the head, and said, "Good dog." Right then, I noticed an itch on my arm where a mosquito had drilled me. I unconsciously scratched it. Two days later, in that exact spot, some nasty red splotches started popping up. Poison oak. By petting my dog and then scratching my arm, I had transferred the oil residue of the poison oak leaves from Rebel's fur to my arm.

On returning back home, Foonsky asked me about the trip.

"Great," I said. "Mosquitoes, ticks, poison oak. Can hardly wait to go back."

"Sorry I missed out," he answered.

Mosquitoes, No-See-Ums, Gnats, and Horseflies

On a trip to Canada, Foonsky and I were fishing a small lake from the shore when suddenly a black horde of mosquitoes could be seen moving across the lake toward us. It was like when the French Army looked across the Rhine and saw the Wehrmacht coming. There was a buzz in the air.

We fought them off for a few minutes, then made a fast retreat to the truck and jumped in, content the buggers had been fooled. But somehow, still unknown to us, the mosquitoes gained entry to the truck. In 10 minutes we squished 15 of them while they attempted to plant their oil derricks in our skin. Just outside the truck, the black horde waited for us to make a tactical error, like rolling down a window. It finally took a miraculous hailstorm to foil the attack.

When it comes to mosquitoes, no-see-ums, gnats, and horseflies, there are times when there is nothing you can do. However, in most situations you can muster a defense to repel the attack.

The first key with mosquitoes is to wear clothing too heavy for them to drill through. Expose a minimum of skin, wear a hat, and tie a bandanna around your neck, preferably one that has been sprayed with repellent. If you try to get by with just a cotton T-shirt, you will be declared a federal mosquito sanctuary.

So first your skin must be well covered, exposing only your hands and face. Second, you should have your companion spray your clothes with repellent. Third, you should dab liquid repellent directly on your skin.

Taking vitamin B1 and eating garlic are reputed to act as natural insect repellents, but I've met a lot of mosquitoes that are not convinced. A better bet is to examine the contents of the repellent in question. The key is the percentage of the ingredient non-diethyl-metatoluamide. That is the poison, and the percentage of it in the container must be listed and will indicate that brand's effectiveness. Inert ingredients are just excess fluids used to fill the bottles.

At night the easiest way to get a good sleep without mosquitoes buzzing in your ear is to sleep in a bug-proof tent. If the nights are warm and you want to see the stars, new tent models are available that have a skylight covered with mosquito netting. If you don't like tents on summer evenings, mosquito netting rigged with an air space at your head can solve the problem. Otherwise prepare to get bit, even with the use of mosquito repellent.

If your problems are with no-see-ums or biting horseflies, then you need a slightly different approach.

No-see-ums are tiny black insects that look like nothing more than a sliver of dirt on your skin. Then you notice something stinging, and when you rub the area, you scratch up a little no-see-um. The results are similar to mosquito bites, making your skin itch, splotch, and, when you get them bad, swell. In addition to using the techniques described to repel mosquitoes, you should go one step further.

The problem is, no-see-ums are tricky little devils. Somehow they can actually get under your socks and around your ankles where they will bite to their heart's content all night long while you sleep, itch, sleep, and itch some more. The best solution is to apply a liquid repellent to your ankles, then wear clean socks.

Horseflies are another story. They are rarely a problem, but when they get their dander up, they can cause trouble you'll never forget.

One such episode occurred when Foonsky and I were paddling a canoe along the shoreline of a large lake. This giant horsefly, about the size of a fingertip, started dive-bombing the canoe. After 20 minutes, it landed on Foonsky's thigh. He immediately slammed it with an open hand, then let out a bloodcurdling "yeeeee-ow!" that practically sent ripples across the lake. When Foonsky whacked it, the horsefly had somehow turned around and bit him in the hand, leaving a huge red welt.

In the next 10 minutes, that big fly strafed the canoe on more dive-bomb runs. I finally got my canoe paddle, swung it as if it was a baseball bat, and nailed that horsefly like I'd hit a home run. It landed about 15 feet from the boat, still alive and buzzing in the water. While I was trying to figure what it would take to kill this bugger, a large rainbow trout surfaced and snatched it out of the water, finally avenging the assault.

If you have horsefly or yellow jacket problems, you'd best just leave the area. One, two, or a few can be dealt with. More than that and your fun camping trip will be about as fun as being roped to a tree and stung by an electric shock rod.

On most trips, you will spend time doing everything possible to keep from getting bit by mosquitoes or no-see-ums. When that fails, you must know what to do next, and fast, if you are among those ill-fated campers who get big, red lumps from a bite inflicted from even a microscopic mosquito.

A fluid called After Bite or a dab of ammonia should be applied immediately to the bite. To start the healing process, apply a first-aid gel, not a liquid, such as Campho-Phenique.

A Discussion About DEET

What is DEET? You're not likely to find the word DEET on any repellent label. That's because DEET stands for N,N-diethyl-m-toluamide. If the label contains this scientific name, the repellent contains DEET. Despite fears of DEET-associated health risks and the increased attention given natural alternatives, DEET-based repellents are still acknowledged as by far the best option when serious insect protection is required.

What are the health risks associated with using DEET? A number of deaths and a number of medical problems have been attributed in the press to DEET in recent years—events that those in the DEET community vehemently deny as being specifically DEET related, pointing to reams of scientific documentation as evidence. It does seem logical to assume that if DEET can peel paint, melt nylon, destroy plastic, wreck wood finishes, and damage fishing line, then it must be hell on the skin—perhaps worse.

On one trip, I had a small bottle of mosquito repellent in the same pocket as a Swiss army knife. Guess what happened? The mosquito repellent leaked a bit and literally melted the insignia right off the knife. DEET will also melt synthetic clothes. That is why in bad mosquito country, I'll expose a minimum of skin, just hands and face (with full beard), and apply the repellent only to the back of my hands and cheeks, perhaps wear a bandanna sprinkled with a few drops as well. That does the trick with a minimum of exposure to the repellent.

Although nothing definitive has been published, there is a belief among a growing number in the scientific community that repeated applications of products containing low percentages of DEET can be potentially dangerous. It is theorized that this actually puts consumers at a greater risk for absorbing high levels of DEET into the body than if they had just used one application of a 30 to 50 percent DEET product with an efficacy of 4 to 6 hours. Also being studied is the possibility that low levels of DEET, which might not otherwise be of toxicological concern, may become hazardous if they are formulated with solvents or dilutents (considered inert ingredients) that may enhance the absorption rate.

Are natural alternatives a safer choice? To imply that essential oils are completely safe because they are a "natural" product is not altogether accurate. Essential oils, while derived from plants that grow naturally, are chemicals too. Some are potentially hazardous if ingested, and most are downright painful if they find their way into the eyes or onto mucus membranes. For example, pennyroyal is perhaps the most toxic of the essential oils used to repel insects, and can be deadly if taken internally. Other oils used include citronella (perhaps the most common, it's extracted from an aromatic grass indigenous to Southern Asia), eucalyptus, cedarwood, and peppermint.

Three citronella-based products, Buzz Away (manufactured by Quantum), Avon's Skin-So-Soft, and Natrapel (manufactured by Tender), have received EPA registration and approval for sale as repellents for use in controlling mosquitoes, flies, gnats, and midges.

How effective are natural repellents? While there are numerous studies cited by those on the DEET and citronella sides of the fence, the average effective repelling time of a citronella product appears to range from 1.5 to 2 hours. Tests conducted at Cambridge University, England, comparing Natrapel to DEET-based Skintastic (a low-percentage DEET product) found citronella to be just as effective in repelling mosquitoes. The key here is effectiveness and the amount of time until reapplication.

Citronella products work for up to 2 hours and then require reapplication (the same holds true for other natural formulations). Products using a low-percentage level of DEET also require reapplication every 2 hours to remain effective. So, if you're going outside for only a short period in an environment where insect bites are more an irritant than a hazard, you would do just as well to "go natural."

What other chemical alternatives are there? Another line of defense against insects is the chemical permethrin, used on clothing, not on skin. Permethrin-based products are designed to repel and kill arthropods or crawling insects, making them a preferred repellent for ticks. The currently available civilian products will remain effective, repelling and killing mosquitoes, ticks, and chiggers, for two weeks and through two launderings.

Ticks

Ticks are nasty little vermin that will wait in ambush, jump on unsuspecting prey, and then crawl to a prime location before filling their bodies with their victim's blood.

I call them Dracula Bugs, but by any name they can be a terrible camp pest.

Ticks rest on grass and low plants and attach themselves to those who brush against the vegetation (dogs are particularly vulnerable). Typically, they are no more than 18 inches above ground, and if you stay on the trails, you can usually avoid them.

There are two common species of ticks. The common coastal tick is larger, brownish in color, and prefers to crawl around prior to putting its clamps on you. The latter habit can give you the creeps, but when you feel it crawling, you can just pick it off and dispatch it. The coastal tick's preferred destination is usually the back of your neck, just where the hairline starts. The other species, the wood tick, is small and black, and when he puts his clamps in, it's immediately painful. When a wood tick gets into a dog for a few days, it can cause a large red welt. In either case, ticks should be removed as soon as possible.

If you have hiked in areas infested with ticks, it is advisable to shower as soon as possible, washing your clothes immediately. If you just leave your clothes in a heap, a tick can crawl out and invade your home. They like warmth, and one way or another, they can end up in your bed. Waking up in the middle of the night with a tick crawling across your chest can really give you the creeps.

Once a tick has its clampers on you, you must decide how long it has been there. If it has been a short time, the most painless and effective method for removal is to take a pair of sharp tweezers and grasp the little devil, making certain to isolate the mouth area, then pull him out. Reader Johvin Perry sent in the suggestion to coat the tick with Vaseline, which will cut off its oxygen supply, after which it may voluntarily give up the hunt.

If the tick has been in longer, you may wish to have a doctor extract it. Some people will burn a tick with a cigarette, or poison it with lighter fluid, but this is not advisable. No matter how you do it, you must take care to remove all of it, especially its clawlike mouth.

The wound, however small, should then be cleansed and dressed. This is done by applying liquid peroxide, which cleans and sterilizes, and then applying a dressing coated with a first-aid gel such as First-Aid Cream, Campho-Phenique, or Neosporin.

Lyme disease, which can be transmitted by the bite of the deer tick, is rare but common enough to warrant some attention. To prevent tick bites, some people tuck their pant legs into their hiking socks and spray tick repellent, called Permamone, on their pants.

The first symptom of Lyme disease is that the bite area will develop a bright red, splotchy rash. Other possible early symptoms include headache, nausea, fever, and/or a stiff neck. If this happens, or if you have any doubts, you should see your doctor immediately. If you do get Lyme disease, don't panic. Doctors say it is easily treated in the early stages with simple antibiotics. If you are nervous about getting Lyme disease, carry a small plastic bag with you when you hike. If a tick manages to get his clampers into you, put it in the plastic bag after you pull it out. Then give it to your doctor for analysis to see if the tick is a carrier of the disease.

During the course of my hiking and camping career, I have removed ticks from my skin hundreds of times without any problems. However, if you are really worried about ticks, you can purchase a tick removal kit from any outdoors store. These kits allow you to remove ticks in such a way that their toxins are guaranteed not to enter your bloodstream.

If you are particularly wary of ticks, or perhaps even have nightmares of them, then wear long pants that are tucked into the socks as well as long-sleeved shirts tucked securely into the pants and held with a belt. Clothing should be light in color, making it easier to spot ticks, and tightly woven so ticks have trouble hanging on. On one hike with my mom, Eleanor, on the central California coast, I brushed more than 100 ticks off my blue jeans in less than an hour, while she did not pick up a single one on her polyester pants.

Perform tick checks regularly, especially on the back of the neck. The combination of DEET insect repellents applied to the skin and permethrin repellents applied directly to clothing is considered to be the most effective line of defense against ticks.

Poison Oak

After a nice afternoon hike, about a five-miler, I was concerned about possible exposure to poison oak, so I immediately showered and put on clean clothes. Then I settled into a chair with my favorite foamy elixir to watch the end of a baseball game. The game went 18 innings; meanwhile, my dog, tired from the hike, went to sleep on my bare ankles.

A few days later I had a case of poison oak. My feet looked like they had been on fire and put out with an ice pick. The lesson? Don't always trust your dog, give him a bath as well, and beware of extra-inning ball games.

You can get poison oak only from direct contact with the oil residue from the leaves. It can be passed in a variety of ways, as direct as skin-to-leaf contact or as indirect as leaf to dog, dog to sofa, sofa to skin. Once you have it, there is little you can do but itch yourself to death. Applying Caladryl lotion or its equivalent can help because it contains antihistamines, which attack and dry the itch.

A tip that may sound crazy but seems to work is advised by my pal Furniss. You should expose the afflicted area to the hottest water you can stand, then suddenly immerse it in cold water. The hot water opens the skin pores and gets the "itch" out, and the cold water then quickly seals the pores.

In any case, you're a lot better off if you don't get poison oak to begin with. Remember the old Boy Scout saying: "Leaves of three, let them be." Also remember that poison oak can disguise itself. In the spring it is green, then it gradually turns reddish in the summer. By fall it becomes a bloody, ugly-looking red. In the winter it loses its leaves altogether and appears to be nothing more than barren, brown sticks of small plant. However, at any time and in any form, skin contact can quickly lead to infection.

Some people are more easily afflicted than others, but if you are one of the lucky few who aren't, don't cheer too loudly. While some people can be exposed to the oil residue of poison oak with little or no effect, the body's resistance can gradually be worn down with repeated exposure. At one time I could practically play in the stuff and the only symptom would be a few little bumps on the inside of my wrist. Now, over 15 years later, my resistance has broken down. If I merely rub against poison oak, in a few days the exposed area can look like it was used for a track meet.

So regardless of whether you consider yourself vulnerable or not, you should take heed to reduce your exposure. That can be done by staying on trails when you hike and making sure your dog does the same. Remember, the worst stands of poison oak are usually brush-infested areas just off the trail. Protect yourself also by dressing so your skin is completely covered, wearing long-sleeved shirts, long pants, and boots. If you suspect you've been exposed, immediately wash your clothes, then wash yourself with aloe vera, rinsing with a cool shower.

And don't forget to give your dog a bath as well.

Sunburn

The most common injury suffered on camping trips is sunburn, yet some people wear it as a badge of honor, believing that it somehow enhances their virility. Well, it doesn't. Neither do suntans. And too much sun can lead to serious burns or sunstroke.

It is easy enough to avoid. Use a high-level sunscreen on your skin, apply lip balm with sunscreen, and wear sunglasses and a hat. If any area gets burned, apply first-aid cream, which will soothe and provide moisture for your parched, burned skin.

The best advice is not to get even a suntan. Those who do are involved in a practice that can be eventually ruinous to their skin and possibly lead to cancer.

A Word About Giardia and Cryptosporidium

You have just hiked in to your backwoods spot, you're thirsty and a bit tired, but you smile as you consider the prospects. Everything seems perfect—there's not a stranger in sight, and you have nothing to do but relax with your pals.

You toss down your gear, grab your cup and dip it into the stream, and take a long drink of that ice-cold mountain water. It seems crystal pure and sweeter than anything you've ever tasted. It's not till later that you find out it can be just like drinking a cup of poison.

Whether you camp in the wilderness or not, if you hike, you're going to get thirsty. And if your canteen runs dry, you'll start eyeing any water source. Stop! Do not pass Go. Do not drink.

By drinking what appears to be pure mountain water without first treating it, you can ingest a microscopic protozoan called *Giardia lamblia.* The pain of the ensuing abdominal cramps can make you feel like your stomach and intestinal tract are in a knot, ready to explode. With that comes long-term diarrhea that is worse than even a bear could imagine.

Doctors call the disease *giardiasis,* or Giardia for short, but it is difficult to diagnose. One friend of mine who contracted Giardia was told he might have stomach cancer before the proper diagnosis was made.

Drinking directly from a stream or lake does not mean you will get Giardia, but you are taking a giant chance. There is no reason to assume such a risk, potentially ruining your trip and enduring weeks of misery.

A lot of people are taking that risk. I made a personal survey of campers in the Yosemite National Park wilderness, and found that roughly only one in 20 were equipped with some kind of water-purification system. The result, according to the Public Health Service, is that an average of 4 percent of all backpackers and campers suffer giardiasis. According to the Parasitic Diseases Division of the Center for Infectious Diseases, the rates range from 1 percent to 20 percent across the country.

But if you get Giardia, you are not going to care about the statistics. "When I got Giardia, I just about wanted to die," said Henry McCarthy, a California camper. "For about 10 days it was the most terrible thing I have ever experienced. And through the whole thing, I kept thinking, 'I shouldn't have drunk that water, but it seemed all right at the time.'"

That is the mistake most campers make. The stream might be running free, gurgling over boulders in the high country, tumbling into deep, oxygenated pools. It looks pure. Then in a few days, the problems suddenly start. Drinking untreated water from mountain streams is a lot like playing Russian roulette. Sooner or later, the gun goes off.

• **Filters:** There's really no excuse for going without a water filter: Handheld filters are getting more compact, lighter, easier to use, and often less expensive. Having to boil water or endure chemicals that leave a bad taste in the mouth has been all but eliminated.

With a filter, you just pump and drink. Filtering strains out microscopic contaminants, rendering the water clear and somewhat pure. How pure? That depends on the size of the filter's pores—what manufacturers call pore-size efficiency. A filter with a pore-size efficiency of one micron or smaller will remove protozoa like giardia and cryptosporidium, as well as parasitic eggs and larva, but it takes a pore-size efficiency of less than 0.4 microns to remove bacteria. All but one of the filters recommended here do that.

A good backcountry water filter weighs less than 20 ounces, is easy to grasp, simple to use, and a snap to clean and maintain. At the very least, buy one that will remove protozoa and bacteria. (A number of cheap, pocket-size filters remove only giardia and cryptosporidium. That, in my book, is risking your health to save money.) Consider the flow rate, too: a liter per minute is good.

All filters will eventually clog—it's a sign that they've been doing their job. If you force water through a filter that's becoming difficult to pump, you risk injecting a load of microbial nasties into your bottle. Some models can be backwashed, brushed, or, as with ceramic elements, scrubbed to extend their useful lives. And if the filter has a prefilter to screen out the big stuff, use it: It will give your filter a boost in mileage, which can then top out at about 100 gallons per disposable element. Any of the filters reviewed here will serve well on an outing into the wilds, providing you always play by the manufacturer's rules.

First Need Deluxe $70

The 15-ounce First Need Deluxe from General Ecology does something no other handheld filter will do: it removes protozoa, bacteria, and viruses without using chemicals. Such effectiveness is the result of a fancy three-stage matrix system. Unfortunately, if you drop the filter and unknowingly crack the cartridge, all the little nasties can get through. General Ecology's solution is to include a bottle of blue dye that indicates breaks. The issue hasn't scared off too many folks, though: the First Need has been around since 1982. Additional cartridges cost $30. A final note: The filter pumps smoothly and puts out more than a liter per minute. A favorite of mine.

Sweetwater Guardian +Plus $80

The Guardian was new in 1995 and quickly earned praise for its scant weight (11 ounces) and first-rate, fingertip-light pump action. The filter removes protozoa and bacteria—and chemicals, too, by way of the activated charcoal in the element. Add the 4-ounce ViralGuard cartridge (included) and the Guardian protects against viruses, too, making it a suitable choice for international travel. At its lower price, the Guardian compares favorably with the more expensive PUR Explorer and MSR WaterWorks II.

PentaPure Oasis $35

The PentaPure Oasis Water Purification System from WTC/Ecomaster offers drinkable water with a twist: you squeeze and sip instead of pumping. Weighing 6.5 ounces, the system packages a three-stage filter inside a 21-ounce-capacity sport bottle with an angled and sealing drinking nozzle, ideal for mountain bikers. The filter removes and/or kills protozoa, bacteria, and viruses, so it's also suitable for world travel. It's certainly conve-

nient: Just fill the bottle with untreated water, screw on the cap, give it a firm squeeze (don't expect the easy flow of a normal sport bottle; there's more work being done), and sip. The Oasis only runs into trouble if the water source is shallow; you'll need a cup for scooping.

Basic Designs Ceramic $32

The Basic Designs Ceramic Filter Pump weighs 8 ounces and is as stripped-down a filter as you'll find. The pump is simple, easy to use, and quite reliable. The ceramic filter effectively removes protozoa and bacteria, making it ideal and cost-effective for back-packing—but it won't protect against viruses. Also, the filter element is too bulbous to work directly from a shallow water source; like the PentaPure, you'll have to contaminate a pot, cup, or bottle to transfer your unfiltered water. It's a great buy, though, for anyone worried only about giardia and cryptosporidium.

SweetWater WalkAbout $35

The WalkAbout is perfect for the day hiker or backpacker who obsesses on lightening the load. The filter weighs just 8.5 ounces, is easily cleaned in the field, and removes both protozoa and bacteria: a genuine bargain. There are some trade-offs, however, for its diminutiveness. Water delivery is a tad slow at just under a liter per minute, but redesigned filter cartridges ($12.50) are now good for up to 100 gallons. Although the WalkAbout is lighter and a bit more compact than SweetWater's Guardian (see above), I prefer the more expensive sibling because the Guardian can be effecti√ against all waterborne dangers ar cartridges last twice as long.

MSR MiniWorks $59

Like the WalkAbout, the bargain-priced MiniWorks has a bigger and more expensive water-filtering brother. But in this case the differences are harder to discern: The new 14.3-ounce MiniWorks looks similar to the $140 WaterWorks II, and like the WaterWorks is fully field-maintainable while guarding against protozoa, bacteria, and chemicals. But the Mini is arguably the best-executed, easiest-to-use ceramic filter on the market, and it attaches directly to a standard one-quart Nalgene water bottle. Too bad it takes 90 seconds to filter that quart.

PUR Explorer $130

The Explorer offers protection from all the bad guys—viruses as well as protozoa and bacteria—by incorporating an iodine matrix into the filtration process. An optional carbon cartridge ($20) neutralizes the iodine's noxious taste. The Explorer is also considered a trusty veteran among water filters because of its smooth pumping action and nifty backwashing feature: With a quick twist, the device switches from filtering mode to self-cleaning mode. It may be on the heavy side (20 ounces) and somewhat pricey, but the Explorer works very well on iffy water anywhere.

Katadyn U.S.A. Mini Filter $130

The Mini Filter is a much more compact version of Katadyn's venerable Pocket Filter. This one weighs just 8 ounces, ideal for the minimalist backntry traveler, and it effectively re- protozoa and bacteria. A palm- nd-size filter, however, lenging to put any kind of e pump's tiny handle, ter comes through

at a paltry half-liter per minute. It also requires more cleaning than most filters—though the good news is that the element is made of long-lasting ceramic. Ironically, one option lets you purchase the Mini Filter with a carbon element instead of the ceramic: The pumping is easier, the flow rate is better, and the price is way down ($99), but I'd only go that route if you'll be pumping from clear mountain streams.

MSR WaterWorks II Ceramic $140

At 17.4 ounces the WaterWorks II isn't light, but for the same price as the Katadyn you get a better flow rate (90 seconds per liter), an easy pumping action, and—like the original Mini Filter—a long-lasting ceramic cartridge. This filter is a good match for the person who encounters a lot of dirty water—its three-stage filter weeds out protozoa, bacteria, and chemicals—and is mechanically inclined: The MSR can be completely disassembled afield for troubleshooting and cleaning. (If you're not so endowed, take the filter apart at home only, as the potential for confusion is somewhat high.) By the way, the company has corrected the clogging problem that plagued a previous version of the WaterWorks.

The big drawback with filters is that if you pump water from a mucky lake, the filter can clog in a few days. Therein lies the weakness. Once plugged up, it is useless and you have to replace it or take your chances.

One trick to extend the filter life is to fill your cook pot with water, let the sediment settle, then pump from there. As an added insurance policy, always have a spare filter canister on hand.

48

• **Boiling water:** Except for water filtration, this is the only treatment that you can use with complete confidence. According to the federal Parasitic Diseases Division, it takes a few minutes at a rolling boil to be certain you've killed *Giardia lamblia.* At high elevations, boil for three to 5 minutes. A side benefit is that you'll also kill other dangerous bacteria that live undetected in natural waters.

But to be honest, boiling water is a thorn for most people on backcountry trips. For one thing, if you boil water on an open fire, what should taste like crystal-pure mountain water tastes instead like a mouthful of warm ashes. If you don't have a campfire, it wastes stove fuel. And if you are thirsty *now,* forget it. The water takes hours to cool.

The only time boiling always makes sense, however, is when you are preparing dinner. The ash taste will disappear in whatever freeze-dried dinner, soup, or hot drink you make.

• **Water-purification pills:** Pills are the preference for most backcountry campers, and this can get them in trouble. At just $3 to $8 per bottle, which can figure up to just a few cents per canteen, they do come cheap. In addition, they kill most of the bacteria, regardless of whether you use iodine crystals or potable aqua iodine tablets.

The problem is they just don't always kill *Giardia lamblia,* and that is the one critter worth worrying about on your trip. That makes water-treatment pills unreliable and dangerous.

Another key element is the time factor. Depending on the water's temperature, organic content, and pH level, these pills can take a long time to do the job. A minimum wait of 20 minutes is advised. Most people don't like waiting that long, especially when they're hot and thirsty after a hike and thinking, "What the heck, the water looks fine."

And then there is the taste. On one trip, my water filter clogged and we had to use the iodine pills instead. It doesn't take long to get tired of the iodine-tinged taste of the water. Mountain water should be one of the greatest tasting beverages of the world, but the iodine kills that.

• **No treatment:** This is your last resort and, using extreme care, can be executed with success. One of my best hiking buddies, Michael Furniss, is a nationally renowned hydrologist, and on wilderness trips he has showed me the difference between "safe" and "dangerous" water sources.

Long ago, people believed that just finding water running over a rock used to be a guarantee of its purity. Imagine that. What we've learned is that the safe water sources are almost always small springs located in high, craggy mountain areas. The key is making sure no one has been upstream from where you drink.

Furniss mentioned that another potential problem in bypassing water treatment is that even in settings free of Giardia, you can still ingest other bacteria that can cause stomach problems.

The only sure way to beat the problem is to filter or boil your water before drinking, eating, or brushing your teeth. And the best way to prevent the spread of Giardia is to bury your waste products at least 8 inches deep 100 feet away from natural w

Hypothermia

No matter how well planned your trip might be, a sudden change in weather can turn it into a puzzle for which there are few answers. Bad weather or an accident can set in motion a dangerous chain of events.

Such a chain of episodes occurred for my brother Rambob and me on a fishing trip one fall day just below the snow line. The weather had suddenly turned very cold, and ice was forming along the shore of the lake. Suddenly, the canoe became terribly imbalanced and just that quick, it flipped. The little life vest seat cushions were useless, and using the canoe as a paddleboard, we tried to kick our way back to shore where my dad was going crazy at the thought of his two sons drowning before his eyes.

It took 17 minutes in that 38-degree water, but we finally made it to shore. When they pulled me out of the water, my legs were dead, not strong enough even to hold up my weight. In fact, I didn't feel so much cold as tired, and I just wanted to lie down and go to sleep.

I closed my eyes, and my brother-in-law, Lloyd Angal, slapped me in the face several times, then got me on my feet and pushed and pulled me about.

In the celebration over making it to shore, only Lloyd had realized that hypothermia was setting in. Hypothermia is the condition in which the temperature of the body is lowered to ___t that it causes poor reason-___ and collapse. It can look ___d person is just tired ___ but that sleep can ___d a coma.

___r and I shared

what little dry clothing remained. Then we began hiking around to get muscle movement, creating internal warmth. We ate whatever munchies were available because the body produces heat by digestion. But most important, we got our heads as dry as possible. More body heat is lost through wet hair than any other single factor.

A few hours later we were in a pizza parlor replaying the incident, talking about how only a life vest can do the job of a life vest. We decided never again to rely on those little flotation seat cushions that disappear when the boat flips.

Almost by instinct we had done everything right to prevent hypothermia: Don't go to sleep, start a physical activity, induce shivering, put dry clothes on, dry your head, and eat something. That's how you fight hypothermia. In a dangerous situation, whether you fall in a lake or a stream or get caught unprepared in a storm, that's how you can stay alive.

After being in that ice-bordered lake for almost 20 minutes and then finally pulling ourselves to the shoreline, we discovered a strange thing. My canoe was flipped right-side up and almost all of its contents were lost: tackle box, flotation cushions, and cooler. But remaining was one paddle and one fishing rod, the trout rod my grandfather had given me for my 12th birthday.

Lloyd gave me a smile. "This means that you are meant to paddle and fish again," he said with a laugh.

Getting Unlost

You could not have been more lost. But there I was, a guy who is supposed to know about these things, transfixed by confusion, snow, and hoofprints from a big deer.

I discovered it is actually quite easy to get lost. If you don't get your bearings, getting found is the difficult part. This occurred on a wilderness trip where I'd hiked in to a remote lake and then set up a base camp for a deer hunt.

"There are some giant bucks up on that rim," confided Mr. Furnai, who lives near the area. "But it takes a mountain man to even get close to them."

That was a challenge I answered. After four-wheeling it to the trailhead, I tromped off with pack and rifle, gut-thumped it up 100 switchbacks over the rim, and then followed a creek drainage up to a small, but beautiful, lake. The area was stark and nearly treeless, with bald granite broken only by large boulders. To keep from getting lost, I marked my route with piles of small rocks to act as directional signs for the return trip.

But at daybreak the next day, I stuck my head out of my tent and found 8 inches of snow on the ground. I looked up into a gray sky filled by huge, cascading snowflakes. Visibility was about 50 yards, with fog on the mountain rim. "I better get out of here and get back to my truck," I said to myself. "If my truck gets buried at the trailhead, I'll never get out."

After packing quickly, I started down the mountain. But after 20 minutes, I began to get disoriented. You see, all the little piles of rocks I'd stacked to mark the way were now buried in snow, and I had only a smooth white blanket of snow to guide me. Everything looked the same, and it was snowing even harder now.

I started chewing on some jerky to keep warm 5 minutes later, then sud-denly stopped. Where was I? Where was the creek drainage? Isn't this where I was supposed to cross over a creek and start the switchbacks down the mountain?

Right then I looked down and saw the tracks of a huge deer, the kind Mr. Furnai had talked about. What a pre-dicament: I was lost and snowed in, and seeing big hoofprints in the snow. Part of me wanted to abandon all safety and go after that deer, but a little voice in the back of my head won out. "Treat this as an emergency," it said.

The first step in any predicament is to secure your present situation, that is, to make sure it does not get any worse. I unloaded my rifle (too easy to slip, fall, and have a misfire), took stock of my food (three days worth), camp fuel (plenty), and clothes (rain gear keeping me dry). Then I wondered, "Where the hell am I?"

I took out my map, compass, and al-timeter, then opened the map and laid it on the snow. It immediately began collecting snowflakes. I set the com-pass atop the map and oriented it to north. Because of the fog, there was no way to spot landmarks, such as promi-nent mountaintops, to verify my posi-tion. Then I checked the altimeter, which read 4,900 feet. Well, the eleva-tion at my lake was 5,320 feet. That was critical information.

I scanned the elevation lines on the map and was able to trace the approxi-mate area of my position, somewhere downstream from the lake, yet close to a 4,900-foot elevation. "Right here," I said, pointing to a spot on the map with a finger. "I should pick up the switchback trail down the mountain somewhere off to the left, maybe just

40 or 50 yards away."

Slowly and deliberately, I pushed through the light, powdered snow. In 5 minutes, I suddenly stopped. To the left, across a 10-foot depression in the snow, appeared a flat spot that veered off to the right. "That's it! That's the crossing."

In minutes I was working down the switchbacks, on my way, no longer lost. I thought of the hoofprints I had seen, and now that I knew my position, I wanted to head back and spend the day hunting. Then I looked up at the sky, saw it filled with falling snow-flakes, and envisioned my truck buried deep in snow. Alas, this time logic won out over dreams.

In a few hours, now trudging through more than a foot of snow, I was at my truck at a spot called Doe Flat, and next to it was a giant, all-terrain Forest Service vehicle and two rangers.

"Need any help?" I asked them.

They just laughed. "We're here to help you," one answered. "It's a good thing you filed a trip plan with our district office in Gasquet. We wouldn't have known you were out here."

"Winter has arrived," said the other. "If we don't get your truck out now, it will be stuck here until next spring. If we hadn't found you, you might have been here until the end of time."

They connected a chain from the rear axle of their giant rig to the front axle of my truck and started towing me out, back to civilization. On the way to pavement, I figured I had gotten some of the more important lessons of my life. Always file a trip plan and have plenty of food, fuel, and a camp stove you can rely on. Make sure your clothes, weather gear, sleeping bag, and tent will keep you dry and warm. Always carry a compass, altimeter, and map with elevation lines, and know how to use them, practicing in good weather to get the feel of it.

And if you get lost and see the hoof-prints of a giant deer, well, there are times when it is best to pass them by.

Catching Fish, Avoiding Bears, and Having Fun

Feet tired and hot, stomachs hungry, we stopped our hike for lunch beside a beautiful little river pool that was catching the flows from a long, but gentle, waterfall. My brother Rambob passed me a piece of jerky. I took my boots off, then slowly dunked my feet into the cool, foaming water.

I was gazing at a towering peak across a canyon, when suddenly, Wham! There was a quick jolt at the heel of my right foot. I pulled my foot out of the water to find that, incredibly, a trout had bitten it.

My brother looked at me like I had antlers growing out of my head. "Wow!" he exclaimed. "That trout almost caught himself an outdoors writer!"

It's true that in remote areas trout sometimes bite on almost anything, even foot. On one high country trip, I have caught limits of trout using nothing but a bare hook. The only problem is that the fish will often hit the splitshot sinker instead of the hook. Of course, fishing isn't usually that easy. But it gives you an idea of what is possible.

America's wildlands are home to a remarkable abundance of fish and wildlife. Deer browse with little fear of man, bears keep an eye out for your food, and little critters like squirrels and chipmunks are daily companions. Add in the fishing and you've got yourself a camping trip.

Your camping adventures will evolve into premium outdoor experiences if you can work in a few good fishing trips, avoid bear problems, and occasionally add a little offbeat fun with some camp games.

Trout and Bass

He creeps up on the stream as quiet as an Indian scout, keeping his shadow off the water. With his little spinning rod, he'll zip his lure within an inch or two of its desired mark, probing along rocks, the edges of riffles, pocket water, or wherever he can find a change in river habitat. Rambob is trout fishing, and he's a master at it.

In most cases, he'll catch a trout on his first or second cast. After that it's time to move up the river, giving no spot much more than five minutes due. Stick and move, stick and move, stalking the stream like a bobcat zeroing in on an unsuspecting rabbit. He might keep a few trout for dinner, but mostly he releases what he catches. Rambob doesn't necessarily fish for food. It's the feeling that comes with it.

Fishing can give you a sense of exhilaration, like taking a hot shower after being coated with dust. On your walk back to camp, the steps come easy. You suddenly understand what John Muir meant when he talked of developing a oneness with nature, because you have it. That's what fishing can provide.

You don't need a million dollars worth of fancy gear to catch fish. What you need is the right outlook, and that can be learned. That goes regardless of whether you are fishing for trout or bass, the two most popular fisheries in the United States. Your fishing tackle selection should be as simple and clutter-free as possible.

At home, I've got every piece of fishing tackle you might imagine, more than 30 rods and many tackle boxes, racks and cabinets filled with all kinds of stuff. I've got one lure that looks like a chipmunk and another that resembles a miniature can of beer with hooks. If I hear of something new, I want to try it and usually do. It's a result of my lifelong fascination with the sport.

But if you just want to catch fish, there's an easier way to go. And when I go fishing, I take that path. I don't try to bring everything. It would be impossible. Instead, I bring a relatively small amount of gear. At home I will scan my tackle boxes for equipment and lures, make my selections, and bring just the essentials. Rod, reel, and tackle will fit into a side pocket of my backpack or a small carrying bag.

So what kind of rod should be used on an outdoor trip? For most camper/anglers, I suggest the use of a light, multipiece spinning rod that will break down to a small size. One of the best deals on the fishing market is the six-piece Daiwa 6.5-foot pack rod, No. 6752. It retails for as low as $30, yet is made of a graphite/glass composite that gives it the quality of a much more expensive model. And it comes in a hard plastic carrying tube for protection. Other major rod manufacturers, such as Fenwick, offer similar premium rods. It's tough to miss with any of them.

The use of graphite/glass composites in fishing rods has made them lighter and more sensitive, yet stronger. The only downside to graphite as a rod material is that it can be brittle. If you rap your rod against something, it can crack or cause a weak spot. That weak spot can eventually snap when under even light pressure, like setting a hook or casting. Of course, a bit of care will prevent that from ever occurring.

If you haven't bought a fishing reel in some time, you will be surprised at the quality and price of micro spinning reels on the market. The reels come tiny and strong, with rear-control drag systems. Sigma, Shimano, Cardinal, Abu, and others all make premium reels. They're worth it. With your purchase, you've just bought a reel that will last for years and years.

The one downside to spinning reels is that after long-term use, the bail spring will weaken. The result is that after casting and beginning to reel, the bail will sometimes not flip over and allow the reel to retrieve the line. Then you have to do it by hand. This can be incredibly frustrating, particularly when stream fishing, where instant line pickup is essential. The solution is to have a new bail spring installed every few years. This is a cheap, quick operation for a tackle expert.

You might own a giant tackle box filled with lures, but on your fishing trip you are better off to fit just the essentials into a small container. One of the best ways to do that is to use the Plano Micro-Magnum 3414, a tiny two-sided tackle box for trout anglers that fits into a shirt pocket. In mine, I can fit 20 lures in one side of the box and 20 flies, splitshot, and snap swivels in the other. For bass lures, which are bigger, you need a slightly larger box, but the same principle applies.

There are more fishing lures on the market than you can imagine, but a few special ones can do the job. I make sure these are in my box on every trip. For trout, I carry a small black Panther Martin spinner with yellow spots, a small gold Kastmaster, a yellow Roostertail, a gold Z-Ray with red spots, a Super Duper, and a Mepps Lightning spinner.

You can take it a step further using insider's wisdom. My old pal Ed "the Dunk" showed me his trick of taking a tiny Dardevle spoon, then spray painting it flat black and dabbing five tiny red dots on it. It's a real killer, particularly in tiny streams where the trout are spooky.

The best trout catcher I've ever used on rivers is a small metal lure called a Met-L Fly. On days when nothing else works, it can be like going to a shooting gallery. The problem is that the lure is near impossible to find. Rambob and I consider the few we have remaining so valuable that if the lure is snagged on a rock, a cold swim is deemed mandatory for its retrieval. These lures are as hard to find in tackle shops as trout can be to catch without one.

For bass you can also fit all you need into a small plastic tackle box. I have fished with many bass pros and all of them actually use just a few lures: a white spinner bait, a small jig called a Gits-It, a surface plug called a Zara Spook, and plastic worms. At times like when the bass move into shoreline areas during the spring, shad minnow imitations like those made by Rebel or Rapala can be dynamite. My favorite is the one-inch blue-silver Rapala. Every spring, as the lakes begin to warm and the fish snap out of their winter doldrums, I like to float and paddle around in my small raft. I'll cast that little Rapala along the shoreline and catch and release hundreds of bass, bluegill, and sunfish. The fish are usually sitting close to the shoreline, awaiting my offering.

Fishing Tips

There's an old angler's joke about how you need to "think like a fish." But if you're the one getting zilched, you may not think it's so funny.

The irony is that it is your mental approach, what you see and what you miss, that often determines your fishing luck. Some people will spend a lot of money on tackle, lures, and fishing clothes, and that done, just saunter up to a stream or lake, cast out, and wonder why they are not catching fish. The answer is their mental outlook. They are not attuning themselves to their surroundings.

You must live on nature's level, not your own. Try this and you will become aware of things you never believed even existed. Soon you will see things that will allow you to catch fish. You can get a head start by reading about fishing, but to get your degree in fishing, you must attend the University of Nature.

On every fishing trip, regardless what you fish for, try to follow three hard-and-fast rules:

1. Always approach the fishing spot so you will be undetected.

2. Present your lure, fly, or bait in a manner so it appears completely natural, as if no line was attached.

3. Stick and move, hitting one spot, working it the best you can, then move to the next.

Here's a more detailed explanation.

Approach: No one can just walk up to a stream or lake, cast out, and start catching fish as if someone had waved a magic wand. Instead, give the fish credit for being smart. After all, they live there.

Your approach must be completely undetected by the fish. Fish can sense your presence through sight and sound, though this is misinterpreted by most people. By sight, this rarely means the fish actually see you; more likely, they will see your shadow on the water, or the movement of your arm or rod while casting. By sound, it doesn't mean they hear you talking, but that they will detect the vibrations of your footsteps along the shore, kicking a rock, or the unnatural plunking sound of a heavy cast hitting the water. Any of these elements can spook them off the bite. In order to fish undetected, you must walk softly, keep your shadow off the water, and keep your casting motion low. All of these keys become easier at sunrise or sunset, when shadows are on the water. At midday, a high sun causes a high level of light penetration in the water, which can make the fish skittish to any foreign presence.

Like hunting, you must stalk the spots. When my brother Rambob sneaks up on a fishing spot, he is like a burglar sneaking through an unlocked window.

Presentation: Your lure, fly, or bait must appear in the water as if no line was attached, so it looks as natural as possible. My pal Mo Furniss has skin-dived in rivers to watch what the fish see when somebody is fishing.

"You wouldn't believe it," he said. "When the lure hits the water, every trout within 40 feet, like 15, 20 trout, will do a little zigzag. They all see the lure and are aware something is going on. Meanwhile, onshore the guy casting doesn't get a bite and thinks there aren't any fish in the river."

If your offering is aimed at fooling a fish into striking, it must appear as part of its natural habitat, as if it is an insect just hatched or a small fish looking for a spot to hide. That's where you come in.

After you have snuck up on a fishing spot, you should zip your cast upstream, then start your retrieve as soon as it hits the water. If you let the lure sink to the bottom, then start the retrieve, you have no chance. A minnow, for instance, does not sink to the bottom then start swimming. On rivers the retrieve should be more of a drift, as if the "minnow" is in trouble and the current is sweeping it downstream.

When fishing on trout streams, always hike and cast upriver, then retrieve as the offering drifts downstream in the current. This is effective because trout will sit almost motionless, pointed upstream, finning against the current. This way they can see anything coming their direction, and if a potential food morsel arrives, all they need to do is move over a few inches, open their mouths, and they've got an easy lunch. Thus you must cast upstream.

Conversely, if you cast downstream, your retrieve will bring the lure from behind the fish, where he cannot see it approaching. And I've never seen a trout that had eyes in its tail. In addition, when retrieving a downstream lure, the river current will tend to sweep your lure inshore to the rocks.

Finding spots: A lot of fishermen don't catch fish, and a lot of hikers never see any wildlife. The key is where they are looking.

The rule of the wild is that fish and wildlife will congregate wherever there is a distinct change in the habitat. This is where you should begin your search. To find deer, for instance, forget probing a thick forest, but look for where it breaks into a meadow or a clear-cut has splayed a stand of trees. That's where the deer will be.

In a river, it can be where a riffle pours into a small pool, a rapid that plunges into a deep hole and flattens, a big boulder in the middle of a long riffle, a shoreline point, a rock pile, a submerged tree. Look for the changes. Conversely, long, straight stretches of shoreline will not hold fish—the habitat is lousy.

On rivers, the most productive areas are often where short riffles tumble into small oxygenated pools. After sneaking up from the downstream side and staying low, you should zip your cast so the lure plops gently in the white water just above the pool. Starting your retrieve instantly, the lure will drift downstream and plunk into the pool. Bang! That's where the trout will hit. Take a few more casts, then head upstream to the next spot.

With a careful approach and lure presentation, and by fishing in the right spots, you have the ticket to many exciting days on the water.

Of Bears and Food

The first time you come nose-to-nose with a bear, it can make your skin quiver.

Even the sight of mild-mannered black bears, the most common bear in America, can send shock waves through your body. They range from 250 to 400 pounds, and have large claws and teeth that are made to scare campers. When they bound, the muscles on their shoulders roll like ocean breakers.

Bears in camping areas are accustomed to sharing the mountains with hikers and campers. They have become specialists in the food-raiding business. As a result, you must be able to make a bear-proof food hang, or be able to scare the fellow off. Many campgrounds provide bear- and raccoon-proof food lockers. You can also stash your food in your vehicle, but that limits the range of your trip.

If you are staying at one of the easy backpack sites listed in this book, there will be no food lockers available. Your car will not be there, either. The solution is to make a bear-proof food hang, suspending all of your food wrapped in a plastic garbage bag from a rope in midair, 10 feet from the tree trunk and 20 feet off the ground. (Counterbalancing two bags with a rope thrown over a tree limb is very effective, but finding an appropriate limb can be difficult.)

This is accomplished by tying a rock to a rope, then throwing it over a high but sturdy tree limb. Next, tie your food bag to the rope and hoist it in the air. When you are satisfied with the position of the food bag, tie off the end of the rope to another tree. In an area frequented by bears, a good food bag is a necessity—nothing else will do.

I've been there. On one trip, my pal Foonsky and my brother Rambob had left to fish, and I was stoking up an evening campfire when I felt the eyes of an intruder on my back. I turned around and this big bear was heading straight for our camp. In the next half hour, I scared the bear off twice, but then he got a whiff of something sweet in my brother's pack.

The bear rolled into camp like a semi truck, grabbed the pack, ripped it open, and plucked out the Tang and the Swiss Miss. The 350-pounder then sat astride a nearby log and lapped at the goodies like a thirsty dog drinking water.

Once a bear gets his mitts on your gear, he considers it his. I took two steps toward the pack and that bear jumped off the log and galloped across the camp right at me. Scientists say a man can't outrun a bear, but they've never seen how fast I can go up a granite block with a bear on my tail.

Shortly thereafter, Foonsky returned to find me perched on top of the rock, and demanded to know how I could let a bear get our Tang. It took all three of us, Foonsky, Rambob, and myself, charging at once and shouting like madmen, to clear the bear out of camp and send him off over the ridge. We learned never to let food sit unattended.

The Grizzly

When it comes to grizzlies, well, my friends, you need what we call an "attitude adjustment." Or that big ol' bear may just decide to adjust your attitude for you, making your stay at the park a short one.

Grizzlies are nothing like black bears. They are bigger, stronger, have little fear, and take what they want. Some people believe there are many different species of this critter, like Alaskan brown, silvertip, cinnamon, and Kodiak, but the truth is they are all grizzlies. Any difference in appearance has to do with diet, habitat, and life habits, not speciation. By any name, they all come big.

The first thing you must do is determine if there are grizzlies in the area where you are camping. That can usually be done by asking local rangers. If you are heading into Yellowstone or Glacier National Park, or the Bob Marshall Wilderness of Montana, well, you don't have to ask. They're out there, and they're the biggest and potentially most dangerous critters you could run into.

One general way to figure the size of a bear is from his footprint. Take the width of the footprint in inches, add one to it—and you'll have an estimated length of the bear in feet. For instance, a 9-inch footprint equals a 10-foot bear. Any bear that big is a grizzly, my friends. In fact, most grizzly footprints average about 9 to 10 inches across, and black bears (though they may be brown in color) tend to have footprints only 4.5 to 6 inches across.

If you are hiking in a wilderness area that may have grizzlies, it becomes a necessity to wear bells on your pack. That way, the bear will hear you coming and likely get out of your way. Keep talking, singing, or maybe even debating the country's foreign policy, but whatever, do not fall into a silent hiking vigil. And if a breeze is blowing in your face, you must make even more noise (a good excuse to rant and rave about the government's domestic affairs). Noise is important, because your smell will not be carried in the direction you are hiking. As a result, the bear will not smell you coming.

If a bear can hear you and smell you, it will tend to get out of the way and let you pass without your knowing it was even close by. The exception is if you are carrying fish or lots of sweets in your pack, or if you are wearing heavy, sweet deodorants or makeup. All of these are bear attractants.

Most encounters with grizzlies occur when hikers fall into a silent march in the wilderness with the wind in their faces, and they walk around a corner and right into a big, unsuspecting grizzly. If you do this and see a big hump just behind its neck, well, don't think twice: it's a grizzly.

And then what should you do? Get up a tree, that's what. Grizzlies are so big that their claws cannot support their immense weight, and thus they cannot climb trees. And although their young can climb, they rarely want to get their mitts on you.

If you do get grabbed, every instinct in your body will tell you to fight back. Don't believe it. Play dead. Go limp. Let the bear throw you around a little, because after awhile you become unexciting play material and the bear will get bored. My grandmother was grabbed by a grizzly in Glacier National Park and after a few tosses and hugs, was finally left alone to escape.

Some say it's a good idea to tuck your head under his chin, since that way, the bear will be unable to bite your head. I'll take a pass on that one. If you are taking action, any action, it's a signal that you are a force to be reckoned with, and he'll likely respond with more aggression. And bears don't lose many wrestling matches.

What grizzlies really like to do, believe it or not, is to pile a lot of sticks and leaves on you. Just let them, and keep perfectly still. Don't fight them; don't run. And when you have a 100 percent chance (not 98 or 99) to dash up a nearby tree, that's when you let fly. Once safely in a tree, you can hurl down insults and let your aggression out.

In a wilderness camp, there are special precautions you should take. Always hang your food at least 100 yards downwind of camp and get it high—30 feet is reasonable. In addition, circle your camp with rope and hang the bells from your pack on it. Thus, if a bear walks into your camp, he'll run into the rope, the bells will ring, and everybody will have a chance to get up a tree before ol' griz figures out what's going on. Often, the unexpected bell ringing is enough to send him off in search of a quieter environment.

You see, more often than not, grizzlies tend to clear the way for campers and hikers. So, be smart, don't act like bear bait, and always have a plan if you are confronted by one.

My pal Foonsky had such a plan during a wilderness expedition in Montana's northern Rockies. On our second day of hiking, we started seeing scratch marks on the trees, 13 to 14 feet off the ground.

"Mr. Griz made those," Foonsky said. "With spring here, the grizzlies are coming out of hibernation and using the trees like a cat uses a scratch board to stretch the muscles."

The next day, I noticed Foonsky had a pair of track shoes tied to the back of his pack. I just laughed.

"You're not going to outrun a griz," I said. "In fact, there's hardly any animal out here in the wilderness that man can outrun."

Foonsky just smiled.

"I don't have to outrun a griz," he said. "I just have to outrun you!"

Fun and Games

"Now what are we supposed to do?" the young boy asked his dad.

"Yeah, Dad, think of something," said another son.

Well, Dad thought hard. This was one of the first camping trips he'd taken with his sons and one of the first lessons he received was that kids don't appreciate the philosophic release of mountain quiet. They want action, and lots of it. With a glint in his eye, Dad searched around the camp and picked up 15 twigs, breaking them so each was 4inches long. He laid them in three separate rows, three twigs in one row, five twigs in another, and seven in the other.

"OK, this game is called 3-5-7," said Dad. "You each take turns picking up sticks. You are allowed to remove all or as few as one twig from a row, but here's the catch: You can only pick from one row per turn. Whoever picks up the last stick left is the loser."

I remember this episode well because those two little boys were my brother Bobby, as in Rambobby, and me. And to this day, we still play 3-5-7 on campouts, with the winner getting to watch the loser clean the dishes. What I have learned in the time span since that original episode is that you age does not matter: campers need options for camp fun.

Some evenings, after a long hike or ride, you are likely to feel too worn-out to take on a serious romp downstream to fish, or a climb up to a ridge for a view. That is especially true if you have been in the outback for a week or more. At that point a lot of campers will spend their time resting and gazing at a map of the area, dreaming of the next day's adventure, or just take a seat against a rock, watching the colors of the sky and mountain panorama change minute by minute. But kids in the push-button video era, and a lot of adults too, want more. After all, "I'm on vacation; I want some fun."

There are several options, like the 3-5-7 twig game, and they should be just as much a part of your pre-trip planning as arranging your gear.

For kids, plan on games, the more physically challenging the competition, the better. One of the best games is to throw a chunk of wood into a lake, then challenge the kids to hit it by throwing rocks. It wreaks havoc on the fishing, but it can keep kids totally absorbed for some time. Target practice with a wrist-rocket slingshot is also all-consuming for kids, firing rocks away at small targets like pinecones set on a log.

You can also set kids off on little missions near camp, such as looking for the footprints of wildlife, searching out good places to have a "snipe hunt," picking up twigs to get the evening fire started, or having them take the water purifier to a stream to pump some drinking water into a canteen. The latter is an easy, fun, yet important task that will allow kids to feel a sense of equality they often don't get at home.

For adults, the appeal should be more to the intellect. A good example is star and planet identification, and while you are staring into space, you're bound to spot a few asteroids, or shooting stars. A star chart can make it easy to locate and identify many distinctive stars and constellations, such as Pleiades (the Seven Sisters), Orion, and others from the zodiac, depending on the time of year. With a little research, this can add a unique perspective to your trip. You could point to Polaris, one of the most easily identified of all stars, and note that navigators in the 1400s used it to find their way. Polaris, of course, is the North Star and is at the end of the Little Dipper's handle. Pinpointing Polaris is quite easy. First find the Big Dipper and then locate the outside stars of the ladle of the Big Dipper. They are called the "Pointer Stars" because they point right at Polaris.

A tree identification book can teach you a few things about your surroundings. It is also a good idea for one member of the party to research the history of the area you have chosen and another to research the geology. With shared knowledge, you end up with a deeper love of wild places.

Another way to add some recreation into your trip is to bring a board game, a number of which have been miniaturized for campers. The most popular are chess, checkers, and cribbage. The latter comes with an equally miniature set of playing cards. And if you bring those little cards, that opens a vast set of other possibilities. With kids along, for instance, just take the Queen of Clubs out of the deck and you can instantly play Old Maid.

But there are more serious card games and they come with high stakes. Such occurred on one high country trip where Foonsky, Rambob, and myself sat down for a late afternoon game of poker. In a game of seven-card stud, I caught a straight on the sixth card and felt like a dog licking on a T-bone. Already, I had bet several Skittles and peanut M&Ms on this promising hand.

Then I examined the cards Foonsky had face up. He was showing three sevens, and acting as happy as a grizzly with a pork chop, like he had a full house. He matched my bet of two peanut M&Ms, then raised me three SweetTarts, one Starburst, and one sour apple Jolly Rancher. Rambob folded, but I matched Foonsky's bet and hoped for the best as the seventh and final card was dealt.

Just after Foonsky glanced at that last card, I saw him sneak a look at my grape stick and beef jerky stash.

"I raise you a grape stick," he said.

Rambob and I both gasped. It was the highest bet ever made, equivalent to a million dollars laid down in Las Vegas. Cannons were going off in my chest. I looked hard at my cards. They looked good, but were they good enough?

Even with a great hand like I had, a grape stick was too much to gamble, my last one with 10 days of trail ahead of us. I shook my head and folded my cards. Foonsky smiled at his victory.

But I still had my grape stick.

Old Tricks Don't Always Work

Most people are born honest, but after a few camping trips, they usually get over it.

I remember some advice I got from Rambob, normally an honest soul, on one camping trip. A giant mosquito had landed on my arm and he alerted me to some expert advice.

"Flex your arm muscles," he commanded, watching the mosquito fill with my blood. "He'll get stuck in your arm, then he'll explode."

For some unknown reason, I believed him. We both proceeded to watch the mosquito drill countless holes in my arm.

Alas, the unknowing face sabotage from their most trusted companions on camping trips. It can arise at any time, usually in the form of advice from a friendly, honest-looking face, as if to say, "What? How can you doubt me?" After that mosquito episode, I was a little more skeptical of my dear old brother. Then, the next day, when another mosquito was nailing me in the back of the neck, out came this gem:

"Hold your breath," he commanded. I instinctively obeyed. "That will freeze the mosquito," he said, "then you can squish him."

But in the time I wasted holding my breath, the little bugger was able to fly off without my having the satisfaction of squishing him. When he got home, he probably told his family, "What a dummy I got to drill today!"

Over the years, I have been duped numerous times with dubious advice:

On a grizzly bear attack: "If he grabs you, tuck your head under the grizzly's chin, then he won't be able to bite you in the head." This made sense to me until the first time I looked face-to-face with a nine-foot grizzly, 40 yards away. In seconds, I was at the top of a tree, which suddenly seemed to make the most sense.

On coping with animal bites: "If a bear bites you in the arm, don't try to jerk it away. That will just rip up your arm. Instead force your arm deeper into his mouth. He'll lose his grip and will have to open it to get a firmer hold, and right then you can get away." I was told this in the Boy Scouts, and when I was 14, I had a chance to try it out when a friend's dog bit me after I tried to pet it. What happened? When I shoved my arm deeper into his mouth, he bit me about three extra times.

On cooking breakfast: "The bacon will curl up every time in a camp frying pan. So make sure you have a bacon stretcher to keep it flat." As a 12-year-old Tenderfoot, I spent two hours looking for the bacon stretcher until I figured out the camp leader had forgotten it. It wasn't for several years until I learned that there is no such thing.

On preventing sore muscles: "If you haven't hiked for a long time and you are facing a rough climb, you can keep from getting sore muscles in your legs, back, and shoulders by practicing the 'Dead Man's Walk.' Simply let your entire body go slack, and then take slow, wobbling steps. This will clear your muscles of lactic acid, which causes them to be so sore after a rough hike." Foonsky pulled this one on me. Rambob and I both bought it, then tried it while we were hiking up Mount Whitney, which requires a 6,000-foot elevation gain in six miles. In one 45-minute period, about 30 other hikers passed us and looked at us as if we were suffering from some rare form of mental aberration.

Fish won't bite? No problem: "If the fish are not feeding or will not bite, persistent anglers can still catch dinner with little problem. Keep casting across the current, and eventually, as they hover in the stream, the line will feed across their open mouths. Keep reeling and you will hook the fish right in the side of the mouth. This technique is called 'lining.' Never worry if the fish will not bite, because you can always line 'em." Of course, heh, heh, heh, that explains why so many fish get hooked in the side of the mouth.

How to keep bears away: "To keep bears away, urinate around the borders of your campground. If there are a lot of bears in the area, it is advisable to go right on your sleeping bag." Yeah, surrrrrre.

What to do with trash: "Don't worry about packing out trash. Just bury it. It will regenerate into the earth and add valuable minerals." Bears, raccoons, skunks, and other critters will dig up your trash as soon as you depart, leaving one huge mess for the next camper. Always pack out everything.

Often the advice comes without warning. That was the case after a fishing trip with a female companion, when she outcaught me two-to-one, the third such trip in a row. I explained this to a shopkeeper, and he nodded, then explained why.

"The male fish are able to detect the female scent on the lure, and thus become aroused into striking."

Of course! That explains everything!

Getting Revenge

I was just a lad when Foonsky pulled the old snipe-hunt trick on me. It took nearly 30 years to get revenge.

You probably know about snipe hunting. That is where the victim is led out at night in the woods by a group, then is left holding a bag.

"Stay perfectly still and quiet," Foonsky explained. "You don't want to scare the snipe. The rest of us will go back to camp and let the woods settle down. Then when the snipe are least expecting it, we'll form a line and charge through the forest with sticks, beating bushes and trees, and we'll flush the snipe out right to you. Be ready with the bag. When we flush the snipe out, bag it. But until we start our charge, make sure you don't move or make a sound or you will spook the snipe and ruin everything."

I sat out there in the woods with my bag for hours, waiting for the charge. I waited, waited, and waited. Nothing happened. No charge, no snipe. It wasn't until well past midnight that I figured something was wrong. When I finally returned to camp, everybody was sleeping.

Well, I tell ya, don't get mad at your pals for the tricks they pull on you. Get revenge. Some 25 years later, on the last day of a camping trip, the time finally came.

"Let's break camp early," Foonsky suggested to Mr. Furnai and me. "Get up before dawn, eat breakfast, pack up, then be on the ridge to watch the sun come up. It will be a fantastic way to end the trip."

"Sounds great to me," I replied. But when Foonsky wasn't looking, I turned his alarm clock ahead three hours. So when the alarm sounded at the appointed 4:30 a.m. wake-up time, Mr. Furnai and I knew it was actually only 1:30 a.m.

Foonsky clambered out of his sleeping bag and whistled with a grin. "Time to break camp."

"You go ahead," I answered. "I'll skip breakfast so I can get a little more sleep. At the first sign of dawn, wake me up, and I'll break camp."

"Me, too," said Mr. Furnai.

Foonsky then proceeded to make some coffee, cook a breakfast, and eat it, sitting on a log in the black darkness of the forest, waiting for the sun to come up. An hour later, with still no sign of dawn, he checked his clock. It now read 5:30 A.M. "Any minute now we should start seeing some light," he said.

He made another cup of coffee, packed his gear, and sat there in the middle of the night, looking up at the stars, waiting for dawn. "Anytime now," he said. He ended up sitting there all night long.

Revenge is sweet. Prior to a fishing trip at a lake, I took Foonsky aside and explained that the third member of the party, Jimbobo, was hard of hearing and very sensitive about it. "Don't mention it to him," I advised. "Just talk real loud."

Meanwhile, I had already told Jimbobo the same thing. "Foonsky just can't hear very good."

We had fished less than 20 minutes when Foonsky got a nibble.

"GET A BITE?" shouted Jimbobo.

"YEAH!" yelled back Foonsky, smiling. "BUT I DIDN'T HOOK HIM!"

"MAYBE NEXT TIME!" shouted Jimbobo with a friendly grin.

Well, they spent the entire day yelling at each other from the distance of a few feet. They never did figure it out. Heh, heh, heh.

That is, I thought so, until we made a trip salmon fishing. I got a strike that almost knocked my fishing rod out of the boat. When I grabbed the rod, it felt like Moby Dick was on the other end. "At least a 25-pounder," I said. "Maybe bigger."

The fish dove, ripped off line, and then bulldogged. "It's acting like a 40-pounder," I announced, "Huge, just huge. It's going deep. That's how the big ones fight."

Some 15 minutes later, I finally got the "salmon" to the surface. It turned out to be a coffee can that Foonsky had clipped on the line with a snap swivel. By maneuvering the boat, he made the coffee can fight like a big fish.

This all started with a little old snipe hunt years ago. You never know what your pals will try next. Don't get mad. Get revenge!

Camping Options

Boat-in Seclusion

Most campers would never think of trading in their car, pickup truck, or RV for a boat, but people who go by boat on a camping trip enjoy virtually guaranteed seclusion and top-quality outdoor experiences.

Camping with a boat is a do-it-yourself venture in living under primitive circumstances. Yet, at the same time, you can bring along any luxury item you wish, from giant coolers, stoves, and lanterns to portable gasoline generators. Weight is almost never an issue.

If you want to create your own boat-in camp, perhaps near a special fishing spot, this is a go-for-it deal that provides the best way possible to establish your own secret campsite. But most people who set out freelance style forget three critical items for boat-in camping: a shovel, a sunshade, and an ax. Here is why these items can make a key difference in your trip:

Shovel: Many lakes and virtually all reservoirs have steep, sloping banks. At reservoirs subject to drawdowns, what was lake bottom in the spring can be a campsite in late summer. If you want a flat area for a tent site, the only answer is to dig one out yourself. A shovel gives you that option.

Sunshade: The flattest spots to camp along lakes often have a tendency to support only sparse tree growth. As a result, a natural shield from sun and rain is rarely available. What? Rain in the summer? Oh yeah, don't get me started. A light tarp, set up with poles and staked ropes, solves the problem.

Ax: Unless you bring your own firewood, which is necessary at some sparsely wooded reservoirs, there is no substitute for a good, sharp ax. With an ax, you can almost always find dry firewood, since the interior of an otherwise wet log will be dry. When the weather turns bad is precisely when you will most want a fire. You may need an ax to get one going.

In the search to create your own personal boat-in campsite, you will find that the flattest areas are usually the tips of peninsulas and points, while the protected back ends of coves are often steeply sloped. At reservoirs the flattest areas are usually near the mouths of the feeder streams, and the points are quite steep. On rivers there are usually sandbars on the inside of tight bends that make for ideal campsites.

Almost all boat-in campsites developed by government agencies are free of charge, but you are on your own. Only in extremely rare cases is piped water available.

Any way you go, by canoe, skiff, or power cruiser, you end up with a one-in-a-million campsite you can call your own.

Desert Outings

It was a cold, snowy day in Missouri when 10-year-old Rusty Ballinger started dreaming about the vast deserts of the West.

"My dad was reading aloud from a Zane Grey book called *Riders of the Purple Sage*," Ballinger said. "He would get animated when he got to the passages about the desert. It wasn't long before I started to have the same feelings."

That was in 1947. Ballinger, now in his 60s, has spent a good part of his life exploring the West, camping along the way. "The deserts are the best part. There's something about the uniqueness of each little area you see," Ballinger said. "You're constantly surprised. Just the time of day and the way the sun casts a different color. It's like the lady you care about. One time she smiles, the next time she's pensive. The desert is like that. If you love nature, you can love the desert. After awhile, you can't help but love it."

A desert adventure is not just an antidote for a case of cabin fever in the winter. Whether you go by RV, pickup truck, car, or on foot, it provides its own special qualities.

If you go camping in the desert, your approach has to be as unique as the setting. For starters, don't plan on any campfires, but bring a camp stove instead. And unlike in the mountains, do not camp near a water hole. That's because an animal such as a badger, coyote, or desert bighorn might be desperate for water, and if you set up camp in the animal's way, you may be forcing a confrontation.

In some areas, there is a danger of flash floods. An intense rain can fall in one area, collect in a pool, then suddenly burst through a narrow canyon. If you are in its path, you could be injured or drowned. The lesson? Never camp in a gully.

"Some people might wonder, 'What good is this place?'" Ballinger said. "The answer is that it is good for looking at. It is one of the world's unique places."

Camp Politics and Ethics

The perfect place to set up a base camp turned out to be not so perfect. In fact, according to Doug Williams of California, it did not even exist.

Williams and his son, James, had driven deep into Angeles National Forest, prepared to set up camp and then explore the surrounding area on foot. But when they reached their destination, no campground existed.

"I wanted a primitive camp in a national forest where I could teach my son some basics," said the senior Williams. "But when we got there, there wasn't much left of the camp and it had been closed. It was obvious that the area had been vandalized."

It turned out not to be an isolated incident. A lack of outdoor ethics practiced by a few people using the nonsupervised campgrounds available on national forestland has caused the U.S. Forest Service to close a few of them, and make extensive repairs to others.

"There have been sites closed, especially in Angeles and San Bernardino national forests in Southern California," said David Flohr, regional campground coordinator for the Forest Service. "It's an urban type of thing, affecting forests near urban areas, and not just Los Angeles. They get a lot of urban users and they bring with them a lot of the same ethics they have in the city. They get drinking and they're not afraid to do things. They vandalize and run. Of course, it is a public facility, so they think nobody is getting hurt."

But somebody is getting hurt, starting with the next person who wants to use the campground. And if the ranger district budget doesn't have enough money to pay for repairs, the campground is then closed for the next arrivals. Just ask Doug and James Williams.

In an era of considerable fiscal restraint for the Forest Service, vandalized campgrounds could face closure instead of repair in the next few years. Williams had just a taste of it, but Flohr, as camping coordinator, gets a steady diet.

"It starts with behavior," Flohr said. "General rowdiness, drinking, partying, and then vandalism. It goes all the way from the felt tip pen things (graffiti) to total destruction, blowing up toilet buildings with dynamite. I have seen toilets destroyed totally with shotguns. They burn up tables, burn barriers. They'll burn up signs for firewood, even the shingles right off the roofs of the bathrooms. They'll shoot anything—garbage cans, signs. It can get a little hairy. A favorite is to remove the stool out of a toilet building. We've had people fall in the open hole."

The National Park Service had a similar problem some years back, especially with rampant littering. Park Director Bill Mott responded by creating an interpretive program that attempts to teach visitors the wise use of natural areas, and to have all park workers set examples by picking up litter and reminding others to do the same.

The Forest Service has responded with a similar program, with brochures available that detail the wise use of national forests. The four most popular brochures are titled: "Rules for Visitors to the National Forest," "Recreation on the National Forests," "Is the Water Safe?" and "Backcountry Safety Tips." These include details on campfires, drinking water from lakes or streams, hypothermia, safety, and outdoor ethics. They are available for free by writing to Public Affairs, U.S. Forest Service, 630 Sansome Street, San Francisco, CA 94111.

Flohr said even experienced campers sometimes cross over the ethics line unintentionally. The most common example, he said, is when campers toss garbage into the outhouse toilet, rather than packing it out in a plastic garbage bag.

"They throw it in the vault toilet bowls, which just fills them up," Flohr said. "That creates an extremely high cost to pump it. You know why? Because some poor guy has to pick that stuff out piece by piece. It can't be pumped."

At most backcountry sites, the Forest Service has implemented a program called "Pack it in, pack it out," even posting signs that remind all visitors to do so. But a lot of people don't do it, and others may even uproot the sign and burn it for firewood.

On a trip to a secluded lake near Carson Pass in the Sierra Nevada, I arrived at a small, little-known camp where the picnic table had been spray-painted and garbage had been strewn about. A pristine place, the true temple of nature, had been defiled.

Then I remembered back 30 years to a story my dad told me: "There are two dogs inside of you," he said, "a good one, and a bad one. The one you feed is the one that will grow. Always try to feed the good dog."

Getting Along with Fellow Campers

The most important thing about a camping, fishing, or hunting trip is not where you go, how many fish you catch, or how many shots you fire. It often has little to do with how beautiful the view is, how easy the campfire lights, or how sunny the days are.

Oh yeah? Then what is the most important factor? The answer: the people you are with. It is that simple.

Who would you rather camp with? Your enemy at work or your dream mate in a good mood? Heh, heh. You get the idea. A camping trip is a fairly close-knit experience, and you can make lifetime friends or lifelong enemies in the process. That is why your choice of companions is so important. Your own behavior is equally consequential.

Yet most people spend more time putting together their camping gear than considering why they enjoy or hate the company of their chosen companions. Here are 10 behavior rules for good camping mates:

1—No whining: Nothing is more irritating than being around a whiner. It goes right to the heart of adventure, since often the only difference between a hardship and an escapade is simply whether or not an individual has the spirit for it. The people who do can turn a rugged day in the outdoors into a cherished memory. Those who don't can ruin it with their incessant sniveling.

2—Activities must be agreed upon: Always have a meeting of the minds with your companions over the general game plan. Then everybody will possess an equal stake in the trip's outcome. This is absolutely critical. Otherwise they will feel like merely an addendum to your trip, not an equal participant, and a whiner will be born (see No. 1).

3—Nobody's in charge: It is impossible to be genuine friends if one person is always telling another what to do, especially if the orders involve simple camp tasks. You need to share the space on the same emotional plane, and the only way to do that is to have a semblance of equality, regardless of differences in experience. Just try ordering your mate around at home for a few days. You'll quickly see the results, and they aren't pretty.

4—Equal chances at the fun stuff: It's fun to build the fire, fun to get the first cast at the best fishing spot, and fun to hoist the bagged food for a bear-proof food hang. It is not fun to clean the dishes, collect firewood, or cook every night. So obviously, there must be an equal distribution of the fun stuff and the not-fun stuff, and everybody on the trip must get a shot at the good and the bad.

5—No heroes: No awards are bestowed for achievement in the outdoors, yet some people treat mountain peaks, big fish, and big game as if they are prizes in a trophy competition. Actually, nobody cares how wonderful you are, which is always a surprise to trophy chasers. What people care about is the heart of the adventure, the gut-level stuff.

6—Agree on a wake-up time: It is a good idea to agree on a general wake-up time before closing your eyes for the night, and that goes regardless of whether you want to sleep in late or get up at dawn. Then you can proceed on course regardless of what time you crawl out of your sleeping bag in the morning, without the risk of whining (see No. 1).

7—Think of the other person: Be self-aware instead of self-absorbed. A good test is to count the number of times you say, "What do you think?" A lot of potential problems can be solved quickly by actually listening to the answer.

8—Solo responsibilities: There are a number of essential camp duties on all trips, and while they should be shared equally, most should be completed solo. That means that when it is time for you to cook, you don't have to worry about me changing the recipe on you. It means that when it is my turn to make the fire, you keep your mitts out of it.

9—Don't let money get in the way: Of course everybody should share equally in trip expenses, such as the cost of food, and it should be split up before you head out yonder. Don't let somebody pay extra, because that person will likely try to control the trip. Conversely, don't let somebody weasel out of paying their fair share.

10—Accordance on the food plan: Always have complete agreement on what you plan to eat each day. Don't figure that just because you like Steamboat's Sludge, everybody else will, too, especially youngsters. Always, always, always check for food allergies such as nuts, onions, or cheese, and make sure each person brings their own personal coffee brand. Some people drink only decaffeinated; others might gag on anything but Burma monkey beans.

Obviously, it is difficult to find companions who will agree on all of these elements. This is why many campers say that the best camping buddy they'll ever have is their mate, someone who knows all about them and likes them anyway.

Outdoors with Kids

How do you get a boy or girl excited about the outdoors? How do you compete with the television and remote control? How do you prove to a kid that success comes from persistence, spirit, and logic, which the outdoors teaches, and not from pushing buttons?

The answer is in the Ten Camping Commandments for Kids. These are lessons that will get youngsters excited about the outdoors, and will make sure adults help the process along, not kill it. Some are obvious, some are not, but all are important:

1. Take children to places where there is a guarantee of action. A good example is camping in a park where large numbers of wildlife can be viewed, such as squirrels, chipmunks, deer, and even bears. Other good choices are fishing at a small pond loaded with bluegill, or hunting in a spot where a kid can shoot a .22 at pinecones all day. Boys and girls want action, not solitude.

2. Enthusiasm is contagious. If you aren't excited about an adventure, you can't expect a child to be. Show a genuine zest for life in the outdoors and point out everything as if it is the first time you have ever seen it.

3. Always, always, always be seated when talking to someone small. This allows the adult and child to be on the same level. That is why fishing in a small boat is perfect for adults and kids. Nothing is worse for youngsters than having a big person look down at them and give them orders. What fun is that?

4. Always *show* how to do something, whether it is gathering sticks for a campfire, cleaning a trout, or tying a knot. Never tell—always show. A button usually clicks to "off" when a kid is lectured. But they can learn behavior patterns and outdoor skills by watching adults, even when the adults are not aware they are being watched.

5. Let kids be kids. Let the adventure happen, rather than trying to force it within some preconceived plan. If they get sidetracked watching pollywogs, chasing butterflies, or sneaking up on chipmunks, let them be. A youngster can have more fun turning over rocks and looking at different kinds of bugs that sitting in one spot, waiting for a fish to bite.

6. Expect short attention spans. Instead of getting frustrated about it, use it to your advantage. How? By bringing along a bag of candy and snacks. Where there is a lull in the camp activity, out comes the bag. Don't let them know what goodies await, so each one becomes a surprise.

7. Make absolutely certain the child's sleeping bag is clean, dry, and warm. Nothing is worse than discomfort when trying to sleep, but a refreshing sleep makes for a positive attitude the next day. In addition, kids can become quite scared of animals at night. A parent should not wait for any signs of this, but always play the part of the outdoor guardian, the one who will "take care of everything."

8. Kids quickly relate to outdoor ethics. They will enjoy eating everything they kill, building a safe campfire, and picking up all their litter, and they will develop a sense of pride that goes with it. A good idea is to bring extra plastic garbage bags to pick up any trash you come across. Kids long remember when they do something right that somebody else has done wrong.

9. If you want youngsters hooked on the outdoors for life, take a close-up photograph of them holding up fish they have caught, blowing on the camp-fire, or completing other camp tasks. Young children can forget how much fun they had, but they never forget if they have a picture of it.

10. The least important word you can ever say to a kid is "I." Keep track of how often you are saying "Thank you" and "What do you think?" If you don't say them very often, you'll lose out. Finally, the most important words of all are, "I am proud of you."

Predicting Weather

Foonsky climbed out of his sleeping bag, glanced at the nearby meadow, and scowled hard.

"It doesn't look good," he said. "Doesn't look good at all."

I looked at my adventure companion of 20 years, noting his discontent. Then I looked at the meadow and immediately understood why: *"When the grass is dry at morning light, look for rain before the night."*

"How bad you figure?" I asked him.

"We'll know soon enough, I reckon," Foonsky answered. "Short notice, soon to pass. Long notice, long it will last."

When you are out in the wild, spending your days fishing and your nights camping, you learn to rely on yourself to predict the weather. It can make or break you. If a storm hits the unprepared, it can quash the trip and possibly endanger the participants. But if you are ready, a potential hardship can be an adventure.

You can't rely on TV weather forecasters, people who don't even know that when all the cows on a hill are facing north, it will rain that night for sure. God forbid if the cows are all sitting. But what do you expect from TV's talking heads?

Foonsky made a campfire, started boiling some water for coffee and soup, and we started to plan the day. In the process, I noticed the smoke of the campfire: It was sluggish, drifting and hovering.

"You notice the smoke?" I asked, chewing on a piece of homemade jerky.

"Not good," Foonsky said. "Not good."

He knew that sluggish, hovering smoke indicates rain.

"You'd think we'd have been smart enough to know last night that this was coming," Foonsky said. "Did you take a look at the moon or the clouds?"

"I didn't look at either," I answered. "Too busy eating the trout we caught."

You see, if the moon is clear and white, the weather will be good the next day. But if there is a ring around the moon, the number of stars you can count inside the ring equals the number of days until the next rain. As for clouds, the high, thin clouds called cirrus indicate a change in the weather.

We were quiet for a while, planning our strategy, but as we did so, some terrible things happened: a chipmunk scampered past with his tail high, a small flock of geese flew by very low, and a little sparrow perched on a tree limb quite close to the trunk.

"We're in for trouble," I told Foonsky.

"I know, I know," he answered. "I saw 'em, too. And come to think of it, no crickets were chirping last night either."

"Damn, that's right!"

These are all signs of an approaching storm. Foonsky pointed at the campfire smoke and shook his head as if he had just been condemned. Sure enough, now the smoke was blowing toward the north, a sign of a south wind. *"When the wind is from the south, the rain is in its mouth."*

"We'd best stay hunkered down until it passes," Foonsky said.

I nodded. "Let's gather as much firewood now as we can, get our gear covered up, then plan our meals."

"Then we'll get a poker game going."

As we accomplished these camp tasks, the sky clouded up, then darkened. Within an hour, we had gathered enough firewood to make a large pile, enough wood to keep a fire going no matter how hard it rained. The day's meals had been separated out of the food bag, so it wouldn't have to be retrieved during the storm. We buttoned two ponchos together, staked two of the corners with ropes to the ground, and tied the other two with ropes to different tree limbs to create a slanted roof/shelter.

As the first raindrop fell with that magic sound on our poncho roof, Foonsky was just starting to shuffle the cards.

"Cut for deal," he said.

Just as I did so, it started to rain a bit harder. I pulled out another piece of beef jerky and started chewing on it. It was just another day in paradise. . . .

Weather lore can be valuable. Small signs provided by nature and wildlife can be translated to provide a variety of weather information. Here is the list I have compiled over the years:

When the grass is dry at morning light,

Look for rain before the night.

Short notice, soon to pass.

Long notice, long it will last.

When the wind is from the east,

'Tis fit for neither man nor beast.

When the wind is from the south,

The rain is in its mouth.

When the wind is from the west,

Then it is the very best.

Red sky at night, sailors' delight.

Red sky in the morning, sailors take warning.

When all the cows are pointed north,

Within a day rain will come forth.

Onion skins very thin, mild winter coming in.

Onion skins very tough, winter's going to be very rough.

When your boots make the squeak of snow,

Then very cold temperatures will surely show.

If a goose flies high, fair weather ahead.

If a goose flies low, foul weather will come instead.

A thick coat on a woolly caterpillar means a big, early snow is coming.

Chipmunks will run with their tails up before a rain.

Bees always stay near their hives before a rainstorm.

When the birds are perched on large limbs near tree trunks, an intense but short storm will arrive.

On the coast, if groups of seabirds are flying a mile inland, look for major winds.

If crickets are chirping very loudly during the evening, the next day will be clear and warm.

If the smoke of a campfire at night rises in a thin spiral, good weather is assured for the next day.

If the smoke of a campfire at night is sluggish, drifting and hovering, it will rain the next day.

If there is a ring around the moon,

count the number of stars inside the ring, and that is how many days until the next rain.

If the moon is clear and white, the weather will be good the next day.

High, thin clouds, or cirrus, indicate a change in the weather.

Oval-shaped lenticular clouds indicate high winds.

Two levels of clouds moving in different directions indicate changing weather soon.

Huge, dark, billowing clouds called cumulonimbus, suddenly forming on warm afternoons in the mountains, mean that a short but intense thunderstorm with lightning can be expected.

When squirrels are busy gathering food for extended periods, it means good weather is ahead in the short term, but a hard winter is ahead in the long term.

And God forbid if all the cows are sitting down. . . .

Camping Gear Checklist

- **Cooking Gear**
  Matches stored in zip-lock bags
  Fire-starter cubes or candle
  Camp stove
  Camp fuel
  Pot, pan, cup
  Pot grabber
  Knife, fork
  Dish soap and scrubber
  Salt, pepper, spices
  Itemized food
  Plastic spade

- **Optional Cooking Gear**
  Ax or hatchet
  Wood or charcoal for barbecue
  Ice chest
  Spatula
  Grill
  Tinfoil
  Dustpan
  Tablecloth
  Whisk broom
  Clothespins
  Can opener

- **Camping Clothes**
  Polypropylene underwear
  Cotton shirt
  Long-sleeved cotton/wool shirt
  Cotton/canvas pants
  Vest
  Fleece shirt or jacket
  Parka

Rain jacket, pants, or poncho
Hat
Sunglasses

- **Optional Clothing**
  Shorts
  Swimsuit
  Gloves
  Ski cap
  Seam Lock (for repairs)

- **Hiking Gear**
  Quality hiking boots
  Backup lightweight shoes
  Polypropylene socks
  Thick cotton socks
  80 percent wool socks
  Strong bootlaces
  Innersole or foot cushion
  Moleskin and medical tape
  Gaiters
  Water-repellent boot treatment

- **Sleeping Gear**
  Sleeping bag
  Insulite or Therm-a-Rest pad
  Ground tarp
  Tent or bivouac sack

- **Optional Sleeping Gear**
  Air pillow
  Mosquito netting
  Foam pad for truck bed
  Windshield light screen for RV
  Catalytic heater

- **First Aid**
  Band-Aids
  Sterile gauze pads
  Roller gauze
  Athletic tape
  Moleskin
  Thermometer
  Aspirin
  Ace bandage
  Mosquito repellent
  After-Bite or ammonia
  Campho-Phenique gel
  First-Aid Cream
  Sunscreen
  Neosporin
  Caladryl
  Biodegradable soap
  Towelettes
  Tweezers

- **Optional First Aid**
  Water purification system
  Coins for emergency phone calls
  Extra set of matches
  Mirror for signaling

- **Fishing/ Recreational Gear**
  Fishing rod
  Fishing reel with fresh line

Small tackle box with lures, splitshot, snap swivels
Pliers
Knife

- **Optional Recreation Gear**
  Stargazing chart
  Tree identification handbook
  Deck of cards
  Backpacking cribbage board
  Knapsack for each person

- **Miscellaneous**
  Maps
  Flashlight
  Lantern and fuel
  Nylon rope for food hanging
  Lip balm
  Handkerchief
  Camera and film
  Plastic garbage bags
  Toilet paper
  Toothbrush and toothpaste
  Compass
  Watch
  Feminine hygiene products

- **Optional Miscellaneous**
  Binoculars
  Notebook and pen
  Towel

Resource Guide

Now you're ready to join the 5 Percent Club, that is, the 5 percent of campers who know the secret spots where they can camp, fish, and hike, and have the time of their lives doing it. To aid in that pursuit, here are a number of contacts, map sources, and reservation systems available for your use:

National Forests

The Forest Service provides many secluded camps and allows camping anywhere except where it is specifically prohibited. If you ever want to clear the cobwebs from your head and get away from it all, this is the way to go.

Many Forest Service campgrounds are quite remote and have no potable water. You don't need to check in or make reservations, and there is no fee. At many Forest Service campgrounds that provide piped water, the camping fee is often only a few dollars, with payment made on the honor system. Because most of these camps are in mountain areas, they are subject to winter closure due to snow or mud. More popular Forest Service camps cost from $8 to $18. Group sites, accommodating up to 100 people, are available on a reservation basis and usually cost $50 to $100 per night.

National Forest Adventure Pass: Angeles, Cleveland, Los Padres, and San Bernardino National Forests require a recreation pass for each parked vehicle. Daily passes cost $5; annual passes are available for $30. You will not need an Adventure Pass while traveling through these forests, nor when you've paid other types of fees such as camping, trail, or ski pass fees. The new charges are use fees, not entrance fees covered by Golden Age, Golden Access, and Golden Eagle Passports; campers with these cards can purchase the Adventure Pass at a 50 percent discount at national forest offices.

Dogs are permitted in national forests with no extra charge and no hassle. Conversely, in state and national parks, dogs are not allowed on trails and must be leashed. Always carry documentation of current vaccinations.

Some of the more popular camps in national forests are on a reservation system, approximately 150 of 800 Forest Service campgrounds accessible by car. The phone number to reserve a site at these camps is (877) 444-6777. The fee to make a reservation for a campground in a national forest is usually $8.65. Reservations may also be made through a website: www.reserveusa.com

Maps for national forests are among the best you can get. They detail all backcountry streams, lakes, hiking trails, and logging roads for access. They cost $4, sometimes more for wilderness maps, and can be obtained by writing to the USDA-Forest Service, Office of Information, at the address on page 79.

Forest Service personnel are most helpful for obtaining camping or hiking trail information. Unless you are buying a map, it is advisable to phone, not write, to get the best service. For specific information on a national forest, contact the offices on page 79.

USDA–Forest Service, Office of Information, Pacific Southwest Region, 1323 Club Drive, Vallejo, CA 94592; (707) 562-USFS/8737; website: www.r5.fs.fed.us.

Angeles National Forest, 701 North Santa Anita Avenue, Arcadia, CA 91006; (626) 574-1613 or fax (626) 574-5233.

Cleveland National Forest, 10845 Rancho Bernardo Road, Suite 200, San Diego, CA 92127; (619) 673-6180 or fax (619) 673-6192.

Eldorado National Forest, 100 Forni Road, Placerville, CA 95667; (530) 622-5061 or fax (530) 621-5297.

Inyo National Forest, 873 North Main Street, Bishop, CA 93514; (760) 873-2400 or fax (760) 873-2458.

Klamath National Forest, 1312 Fairlane Road, Yreka, CA 96097; (530) 842-6131 or fax (530) 842-6327.

Lake Tahoe Basin Management Unit, 870 Emerald Bay Road, Suite 1, South Lake Tahoe, CA 96150; (530) 573-2600 or fax (530) 573 2603.

Lassen National Forest, 55 South Sacramento Street, Susanville, CA 96130; (530) 257-2151 or fax (530) 252-6428.

Los Padres National Forest, 6144 Calle Real, Goleta, CA 93117; (805) 683-6711 or fax (805) 681-2729.

Mendocino National Forest, 825 North Humboldt Avenue, Willows, CA 95988; (530) 934-3316 or fax (530) 934-7384.

Modoc National Forest, 800 West 12th Street, Alturas, CA 96101; (530) 233-5811 or fax (530) 233-8709.

Plumas National Forest, 159 Lawrence Street, PO Box 11500, Quincy, CA 95971; (530) 283-2050 or fax (530) 283-4156.

San Bernardino National Forest, 1824 South Commercenter Circle, San Bernardino, CA 92408-3430; (909) 383-5588 or fax (909) 383-5770.

Sequoia National Forest, 900 West Grand Avenue, Porterville, CA 93257; (559) 784-1500 or fax (559) 781-4744.

Shasta-Trinity National Forest, 2400 Washington Avenue, Redding, CA 96001; (530) 244-2978 or fax (530) 242-2233.

Sierra National Forest, 1600 Tollhouse Road, Clovis, CA 93611-0532; (559) 297-0706 or fax (559) 294-4809.

Six Rivers National Forest, 1330 Bayshore Way, Eureka, CA 95501-3834; (707) 442-1721 or fax (707) 442-9242.

Stanislaus National Forest, 19777 Greenley Road, Sonora, CA 95370; (209) 532-3671 or fax (209) 533-1890.

Tahoe National Forest, 631 Coyote Street, Nevada City, CA 95959-2250; (530) 265-4531 or fax (530) 478-6109.

Humboldt-Toiyabe National Forest, 1200 Franklin Way, Sparks, NV 89431; (775) 355-5317 or fax (775) 355-5399.

State Parks

The California State Parks system provides many popular camping spots. These campgrounds include drive-in numbered sites, tent spaces, and picnic tables, with showers and bathrooms provided nearby. Reservations are often necessary during the summer months. Although some parks are well known, there are still some little-known gems in the state parks system where campers can enjoy seclusion, even in the summer.

Reservations can be obtained toll-free from anywhere in California by calling (800) 444-PARK/7275. There is a charge of $7.50 for camp reservations, plus a separate camping fee. Most state parks charge from $16 to $29 per night for a campsite, less for walk-in sites, often more for beachfront sites. There may be additional fees for pets ($1) and, in some rare cases, premium sites. Discounts are available for campers 62 and older.

Reservations at state parks are available up to seven months in advance. For instance, in January reservations can be made for July. That means that campers who plan their vacations well in advance will have a significant advantage in obtaining quality campsites.

Because of a budget shortage, many state park telephones are no longer staffed. For this reason, the district office phone numbers have been added to state park listings in this book. District offices can usually provide any information visitors may require about state parks.

For general information about California State Parks, write to California State Parks, Office of Information, PO Box 942896, Sacramento, CA 94296-0001; (916) 653-6995.

National Parks

California's national parks are natural wonders, ranging from the spectacular yet crowded Yosemite Valley to the remote and rugged Lava Beds National Monument. Reservations for campsites are available three months in advance at approximately 75 percent of the national parks in California. The remainder are first come, first served. For Yosemite National Park reservations, phone (800) 436-PARK/7275. For all other national parks, phone (800) 365-CAMP/2267.

Cabrillo National Monument, 1800 Cabrillo Memorial Drive, San Diego, CA 92106-3601; (619) 557-5450 or fax (619) 557-5469.

Channel Islands National Park, 1901 Spinnaker Drive, Ventura, CA 93001; (805) 658-5730 or fax (805) 658-5799.

Death Valley National Park, PO Box 579, Death Valley, CA 92338; (760) 786-2331 or fax (760) 786-3283.

Golden Gate National Recreation Area, San Francisco Headlands, Building 201, Fort Mason, San Francisco, CA 94123; (415) 556-0560 or fax (415) 561-4320.

Joshua Tree National Park, 74485 National Park Drive, Twentynine Palms, CA 92277; (760) 367-5500 or fax (760) 367-6392.

King Range National Conservation Area, Bureau of Land Management, Arcata Field Office, 1695 Heindon Road, Arcata, CA 95521-4573; (707) 825-2300 or fax (707) 825-2301.

Klamath Basin National Wildlife Refuge, Route 1, Box 74, Tulelake, CA 96134; (530) 667-2231 or fax (530) 667-3299.

Lassen Volcanic National Park, PO Box 100, Mineral, CA 96063-0100; (530) 595-4444 or fax (530) 595-3262.

Lava Beds National Monument, PO Box 867, Tulelake, CA 96134; (530) 667-2282 or fax (530) 667-2737.

Marin Headlands, Golden Gate National Recreation Area, Building 948, Fort Barry, Sausalito, CA 94965; (415) 331-1540.

Pinnacles National Monument, 5000 Highway 146, Paicines, CA 95043; (831) 389-4485 or fax (831) 389-4489.

Point Reyes National Seashore, Point Reyes, CA 94956-9799; (415) 663-1092 or fax (415) 663-8132.

Redwood National and State Parks, 1111 Second Street, Crescent City, CA 95531; (707) 464-6101 or fax (707) 464-1812.

San Francisco Bay National Wildlife Refuge, PO Box 524, Newark, CA 94560; (510) 792 4275 or fax (510) 792-5828; website: www.fws.gov.

Santa Monica Mountains National Recreation Area, 30401 Agoura Road, Suite 100, Agoura Hills, CA 91301; (818) 597-9192 or fax (818) 597-8357.

Sequoia and Kings Canyon National Parks, Ash Mountain, Three Rivers, CA 93271; (209) 565-3341 or fax (209) 565-3730.

Smith River National Recreation Area, PO Box 228, Gasquet, CA 95543; (707) 457-3131 or fax (707) 457-3794.

Whiskeytown National Recreation Area, PO Box 188, Whiskeytown, CA 96095; (530) 241-6584 or fax (530) 246-5154.

Yosemite National Park, PO Box 577, Yosemite National Park, CA 95389; (209) 372-0265 or (209) 372-0200 for 24-hour recorded message.

State and Federal Offices

California Department of Boating and Waterways, 1629 S Street, Sacramento, CA 95814-7291; (916) 445-6281 or fax (916) 327-7250.

California Department of Fish and Game, 1416 Ninth Street, Sacramento, CA 95814; (916) 653-6420 or fax (916) 653-1856.

California State Parks, Office of Information, PO Box 942896, Sacramento, CA 94296-0001; (916) 653-6995.

US Geological Survey, Information Services, PO Box 25286, Federal Center, Denver, CO 80225; (303) 202-4700 or fax (303) 202-4693.

US Bureau of Land Management, California State Office, 2135 Butano Drive, Sacramento, CA 95825; (916) 978-4400 or fax (916) 978-4416.

County/Regional Park Departments

City of Arcata, 736F Street, Arcata, CA 95521; (707) 822-8184 or fax (707) 822-8018.

Blue Sky Ecological Preserve, PO Box 724, Poway, CA 92074; (619) 679-5469.

Carbon Canyon Regional Park, 4442 Carbon Canyon Road, Brea, CA 92823; (714) 996-5252 or fax (714) 996-5178.

Caspers Wilderness Park, PO Box 395, San Juan Capistrano, CA 92675; (949) 831-2174 or fax (949) 728-0346.

Del Norte County Parks, 840 Ninth Street, Crescent City, CA 95531; (707) 464-7230.

Devil's Punchbowl County Regional Park, 28000 Devil's Punchbowl Road, Pearblossom, CA 93553; (661) 944-2743 or fax (661) 944-6924.

East Bay Regional Park District, 2950 Peralta Oaks Court, PO Box 5381, Oakland, CA 94605-0381; (510) 635-0135 extension 2200 or fax (510) 569-4319.

Featherly Regional Park, 24001 Santa Ana Canyon Road, Anaheim, CA 92808; (714) 637-0210 or fax (714) 637-9317.

Humboldt County Parks, 1106 Second Street, Eureka, CA 95501; (707) 445-7652 or fax (707) 445-7409.

Irvine Regional Park, 1 Irvine Park Road, Orange, CA 92669; (714) 633-8072.

Jalama County Park, (805) 736-6316 (recorded message).

Lake Poway Recreation Area, PO Box 789, Poway, CA 92074; (619) 695-1400 or fax (619) 748-3153.

The Living Desert, 47900 Portola Avenue, Palm Desert, CA 92260; (760) 346-5694 or fax (760) 568-9685.

Los Coyotes Indian Reservation, PO Box 189, Warner Springs, CA 92086; (760) 782-0711 or fax (760) 782-2701.

Marin Municipal Water District, 220 Nellen Avenue, Corte Madera, CA 94925; (415) 924-4600 or fax (415) 927-4953.

Midpeninsula Regional Open Space District, 330 Distel Circle, Los Altos, CA 94022; (650) 691-1200 or fax (650) 691-0485.

Placerita Canyon County Park, 19152 Placerita Canyon Road, Newhall, CA 91321; (661) 259-7721 or fax (661) 254-1426.

San Diego County Parks and Recreation Department, 5201 Ruffin Road, Suite P, San Diego, CA 92123; (619) 694-3049 or fax (619) 495-5841.

City of San Diego Parks and Recreation Department, Northern Parks Division, 1250 Sixth Avenue, 4th floor, Mail Station 804A; San Diego, CA 92101-4215; (619) 685-1350 or fax (619) 685-1362.

San Mateo County Parks and Recreation Department, 455 County Center, 4th floor, Redwood City, CA 94063-1646; (650) 363-4020 or fax (650) 599-1721.

Santa Clara County Parks and Recreation, 298 Garden Hill Drive, Los Gatos, CA 95030; (408) 358-3741 or fax (408) 358-3245.

Santiago Oaks Regional Park, 2145 North Windes Drive, Orange, CA 92869; (714) 538-4400 or fax (714) 538-5036.

Vasquez Rocks County Park, 10700 West Escondido Canyon Road, Agua Dulce, CA 91350; (661) 268-0840 or fax (661) 268-1343.

RV Parks

The charge for hookups at RV parks varies from $10 to $20 per night. In populated areas, the charge often climbs beyond the $20 range. Many RV parks, particularly those in rural counties, must be contacted by phone for reservations. Many require a deposit with reservations, which is usually just an advance payment for your first night's stay. No reservation service is available for privately operated parks.

Information Services

Bodega Bay Chamber of Commerce, PO Box 146, Bodega Bay, CA 94923; (707) 875-3422.

Catalina Camping Reservations, PO Box 737, Avalon, CA 90704; (310) 510-2500 or fax (310) 510-7254.

Grassland Water District, 22759 South Mercey Springs Road, Los Banos, CA 93635; (209) 826-5188 or fax (209) 826-4984.

Lake County Visitor Information Center, 875 Lakeport Boulevard, Lakeport, CA 95453; (800) 525-3743, (707) 263-9544, or fax (707) 263-9564.

Lassen County Chamber of Commerce, 84 North Lassen Street, PO Box 338, Susanville, CA 96130; (530) 257-4323 or fax (530) 251-2561.

Mammoth Lakes Visitors Bureau, PO Box 48, Mammoth Lakes, CA 93546; (800) 367-6572 or fax (760) 934-7066; website: www.visitmammoth.com.

Fort Bragg-Mendocino Coast Chamber of Commerce, PO Box 1141, Fort Bragg, CA 95437; (707) 961-6300 or fax (707) 964-2056.

The Nature Conservancy, 201 Mission Street, 4th floor, San Francisco, CA 94105; (415) 777-0487.

The Nature Conservancy, Carrizo Plain Natural Area, US Bureau of Land Management, 3801 Pegasus Drive, Bakersfield, CA 93308; (661) 391-6000, (805) 475-2131*, or fax (661) 391-6040.

Plumas County Chamber of Commerce, PO Box 4120, Quincy, CA 95971; (800) 326-2247, (530) 283-6345, or fax (530) 283-5465.

Shasta-Cascade Wonderland Association, 1699 Highway 273, Anderson, CA 96007; (800) 474-2782, (530) 365-7500, or fax (530) 365-1258.

Trinidad Chamber of Commerce, PO Box 357, Trinidad, CA 95570; (707) 677-3448.

Map Companies

Earthwalk Press, 5432 La Jolla Hermosa Avenue, La Jolla, CA 92037; (800) 828-MAPS/6277.

Map Link, 30 South La Patera Lane, Unit 5, Santa Barbara, CA 93117; (805) 692-6777 or fax (800) 627-7768.

Olmsted Brothers, PO Box 5351, Berkeley, CA 94705; (510) 658-6534.

Tom Harrison Cartography, 2 Falmouth Cove, San Rafael, CA 94901; (415) 456-7940; website: www. tomharrisonmaps.com.

Wilderness Press, 2440 Bancroft Way, Berkeley, CA 94704; (510) 843-8080 or fax (510) 548-1355.

Maps are also available from the US Forest Service (see page 79) and the US Geologic Survey (see page 81).

Northern
California

Map A0

One inch equals approximately 10.7 miles.
See inside back cover for California state map.

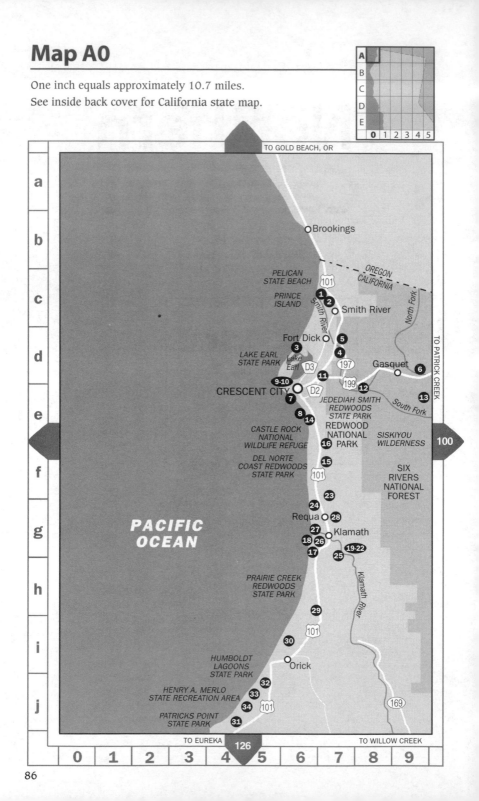

Chapter AØ features:

---

❶ Salmon Harbor Resort

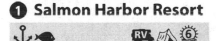

Location: On the Smith River; map AØ, grid c7.

Campsites, facilities: There are 98 sites for tents or RVs, 88 with full hookups and cable TV. Picnic tables, fire grills, flush toilets, showers, and a recreation room are provided. A coin laundry, ice, gas, a restaurant, a bar, and a bait and tackle shop are available within three miles. Leashed pets are permitted.

Reservations, fees: Reservations are accepted; $15 per night.

Contact: Salmon Harbor Resort, (707) 487-3341.

Directions: From Crescent City, drive north on US 101 for 13 miles to the town of Smith River. Continue three miles north on US 101 to the Salmon Harbor Road exit. Turn left on Salmon Harbor Road, drive two blocks, and look for Salmon Harbor Resort at the end of the road.

Trip notes: If location is everything, then this privately operated campground rates high for salmon fishermen in the fall months. It is set near the mouth of the Smith River, where salmon enter and school in the deep river holes in October. The fish are big, occasionally even surpass-

ing 40 pounds. Year-round this is a good layover for RV cruisers looking for a spot near the Oregon border. It is actually an RV parking area with hookups, set within a mobile home park. Salmon Harbor Resort overlooks the ocean, with good beachcombing and driftwood and agate hunting nearby.

---

❷ Ship Ashore Best Western RV Park

Location: On the Smith River; map AØ, grid c7.

Campsites, facilities: There are 200 RV sites, most with full hookups, and a separate area for tents. Tables, flush toilets, showers, recreation room, boat dock and ramp, and some patios are provided. A coin laundry, LP gas, groceries, and boat rentals are available. Leashed pets are permitted.

Reservations, fees: Reservations are accepted; $10 for two people for the first night, $15 per night thereafter.

Contact: Ship Ashore Best Western RV Park, (707) 487-3141 extension 6 or fax (707) 487-7070.

Directions: From Crescent City, drive north on

US 101 for 16 miles, three miles past the town of Smith River, to the Ship Ashore sign at Chinook Street. At Chinook Street, turn left and drive a short distance (less than half a block) to the camp store at the campground entrance.

Trip notes: This is a famous spot for Smith River fishermen, where the tales get taller as the evening gets late. The park is set on five acres of land adjacent to the lower Smith River. The salmon and steelhead seem to come in one size here—giant—but they can be as elusive as Bigfoot. If you want to hear how big, just check into the Ship Ashore Restaurant any fall or winter evening. In the summer, the resort has become quite popular with people cruising the coast on US 101.

---

❸ Lake Earl/Talawa State Park

🚲 ⚓ 🎣 🥾 🐎　　🏔 ⑨

Location: Near Crescent City; map AØ, grid d6.

Campsites, facilities: There are six primitive sites and a ride-in horse camp with 16 individual corrals and food lockers. There is no piped water, but picnic tables and composting toilets are provided. Fire rings are provided for the walk-in sites and fire pits for the horse camp. Leashed pets are permitted.

Reservations, fees: No reservations; $7 per night for walk-in sites. In the horse camp, there is a $4 fee per night per horse and rider, with a group rate of $50 per night for 13 or more riders. Registration is required at either Del Norte Coast Redwoods State Park or Jedediah Smith Redwoods State Park.

Contact: Redwood National and State Parks, (707) 464-6101 extension 5151.

Directions: In Crescent City, drive on US 101 to the lighted intersection at Northcrest Drive. Turn left (northwest) and drive about five miles (Northcrest becomes Lake Earl Drive) to Lower Lake Road. Turn left and drive 2.5 miles. Turn left on Kellogg Road and drive about a mile. A small metal gate, for which the combination is given at registration, and parking area large enough for a few cars is the access point on the right side of the road.

For the horse camp: In Crescent City, turn northwest on Northcrest Drive and drive five miles to Lower Lake Road. At Lower Lake Road, turn left and drive about seven miles to Palo Road. At Palo Road, turn left and drive to the parking area. The horse camp is about a half mile southwest of the Palo Road parking lot.

For trail and walk-in beach access: In Crescent City, turn northwest on Northcrest Drive and continue 1.5 miles to Old Mill Road. Turn west (left) on Old Mill Road and drive three miles to Sand Hill Road. For the state park trailhead, turn left at Sand Hill Road and drive 0.25 mile to the trail entrance. For Fish and Game trail and walk-in beach access, continue on Old Mill Road to the locked gate at the road's end (about 100 yards past the Sand Hill Road turnoff). The gate combination is given at registration.

For the Lake Earl boat launch: In Crescent City, turn northwest on Northcrest Drive and drive about 3.5 miles to Lake View Road. At Lake View Road, turn left and drive a mile to the road's end at Lake Earl.

For the drive-in beach access: From Crescent City, turn northwest on Northcrest Drive and drive north for about five miles to Lower Lake Road. At Lower Lake Road, turn left and drive 2.5 miles to Kellogg Road. At Kellogg Road, turn left and drive 1.5 miles to the beach parking lot at the end of the road.

For picnicking and bird-watching: In Crescent City, turn northwest on Northcrest Drive and drive north for about five miles to Lower Lake Road. At Lower Lake Road, turn left and drive about seven miles to Palo Road on the left.

Trip notes: This campground is one of the great discoveries available to people who love the outdoors. The walk-in sites are extremely secluded, quiet, and sheltered, set off little spur trails from the main access trail/road. With rolling hills, a benign climate, and a combination of marshes, sandy soil, and proximity to the ocean, the Smith River and Lake Earl are not only pretty and pleasant, but attract a wide variety of bird life. The access trail provides an outstanding bicycle trip. The campgrounds are not set near Lake Earl, but the lake is accessible with a short drive. Lakes Earl and Talawa are one and the same, Talawa to the west and Earl to the east, connected by a curving piece of water. Talawa borders coastal sand dunes, and after heavy rainfall, sometimes runs into the ocean. That is how sea-run cutthroat trout and flounder enter the brackish waters, caught rarely at the narrows between the lakes. Lakes Earl and Talawa offer 7.5 miles of ocean frontage, 15 miles of horseback riding trails, numerous hiking trails, opportunities for canoeing and kayaking, and the bonus of having the Smith River nearby to the north. Guided walks are conducted by state park volunteers in July and August.

❹ Ramblin' Rose Resort

Location: Near the Smith River; map AØ, grid d7.

Campsites, facilities: There are 110 RV sites, most with full hookups. Rest rooms, showers, picnic tables, and a recreation hall are provided. A gift store, groceries, ice, a coin laundry, and a sanitary disposal station are also available. The dance hall and sites are wheelchair accessible. Leashed pets are permitted.

Reservations, fees: Reservations are accepted; $17 per night.

Contact: Ramblin' Rose Resort, (707) 487-4831.

Directions: From Crescent City, take US 101 north for five miles to the junction of US 199. Continue north on US 101 for another six miles to the campground, which is located at 6701 US 101 North, in Crescent City.

Trip notes: Ramblin' Rose is an RV park set amid redwood trees, some of them giant. The big trees are the highlight of the area, of course, with Redwood National Park and Jedediah Smith Redwoods State Park just to the east on US 199. Nearby attractions include the beach to the immediate west and the Smith River to the north.

❺ Crescent City Redwoods KOA

Location: On the Smith River; map AØ, grid d7.

Campsites, facilities: There are 44 tent sites and 50 sites for RVs with full hookups. Cabins are also available. A sanitary disposal station, flush toilets, showers, picnic tables, a coin laundry, fire grills, and a playground are provided. LP gas, groceries, ice, and wood are also avail-

able. Leashed pets are permitted.

Reservations, fees: Reservations are accepted; $19 per night ($42 for cabins).

Contact: Crescent City Redwoods KOA, (707) 464-5744.

Directions: From Crescent City, take US 101 north for five miles to the junction of US 101 and US 199. Continue north on US 101 for one mile and look for the campground entrance on the right (east) side of the road.

Trip notes: This KOA camp is located on the edge of a recreation wonderland, a perfect jump-off spot for a vacation. The camp itself includes those little KOA Kamping Kabins, which are cute log cabins with electricity and heat; just make sure you bring your sleeping bag and pillows. In addition, there are two nine-hole golf courses nearby. The camp is only a 10-minute drive to Redwood National Park, Jedediah Smith Redwoods State Park, and the Smith River National Recreation Area. It is also only a 10-minute drive to the beach and Lake Earl to the east, and to Crescent City Harbor to the south.

❻ Panther Flat

Location: On the Smith River in Six Rivers National Forest; map AØ, grid d9.

Campsites, facilities: There are 39 sites for tents, trailers up to 40 feet long, and RVs up to 35 feet long. Piped water, flush toilets, hot showers, fire grills, and picnic tables are provided. Propane gas, groceries, and a coin laundry are available nearby. Several campsites are wheelchair accessible. Leashed pets are permitted.

Reservations, fees: Reservations are recommended; phone (800) 280-2267 ($8.65 reservation fee); $14 per night, $5 fee for extra vehicles. Open year-round.

Contact: Smith River National Recreation Area, Six Rivers National Forest, PO Box 228, Gasquet, CA 95543; (707) 457-3131 or fax 707 457-3794.

Directions: From Crescent City, drive north on US 101 for five miles to the junction with US 199. At US 199, turn east and drive 15 miles to Gasquet. From Gasquet, continue for 2.3 miles east on US 199 and look for the entrance to the campground on the left side of the highway.

Trip notes: This is an ideal alternative to the often crowded Jedediah Smith Redwoods State Park. The park provides easy road access since it is set right along US 199, the two-laner that runs aside the Smith River. This is one of the feature campgrounds in the Smith River National Recreation Area, with excellent prospects for salmon and steelhead fishing in the fall and winter, respectively, and outstanding hiking and backpacking in the summer. A great nearby hike is the Stoney Creek Trail, an easy walk along the North Fork Smith River; the trailhead is in nearby Gasquet on Stoney Creek Road. Redwood National Park is a short drive to the west. The Siskiyou Wilderness is a short drive to the southeast via forest roads detailed on Forest Service maps. The wild and scenic Smith River system provides swimming, sunbathing, kayaking for experts, and beautiful scenery.

❼ Sunset Harbor RV Park

Location: In Crescent City; map AØ, grid e6.

Campsites, facilities: There are 69 RV-only sites with full hookups. Picnic tables, flush toilets, and showers are provided. A coin laundry, grocery store, and a recreation room are available. Rest rooms and showers are wheelchair accessible. Leashed pets are permitted.

Reservations, fees: Reservations are accepted; $16 to $18 per night.

Contact: Sunset Harbor RV Park, (707) 464-3423.

Directions: In Crescent City on US 101, drive to King Street. At King Street, turn east and drive one block to the park entrance.

Trip notes: People camp here with their RVs in order to be close to the action in Crescent City and the nearby harbor and beach frontage. For starters, drive a few minutes to the northwest side of town, where the sea is sprinkled with gigantic rocks and boulders, for dramatic ocean views and spectacular sunsets. For finishers, go down to the west side of town for great walks along the ocean parkway or south to the harbor and adjacent beach, which is long and expansive.

❽ Harbor RV Anchorage

Location: In Crescent City; map AØ, grid e6.

Campsites, facilities: There are 123 RV-only sites with full hookups. Picnic tables, flush toilets, showers, and a sanitary disposal station are provided. A coin laundry and cable TV hookups are available. Leashed pets are permitted.

Reservations, fees: Reservations are accepted; $16 per night.

Contact: Harbor RV Anchorage, (707) 464-1724.

Directions: From US 101 at the southern end of Crescent City, turn west at Anchor Way and drive a short distance to Starfish Way. At Starfish Way, turn north and drive to the campground.

Trip notes: The Crescent City Harbor, restaurants, and a beach walk are all within close walking distance. The beach walk, located immediately to the south, is spectacular during low tides for beachcombing, especially for driftwood. Get the picture? Right—this park is right on the ocean, complete with salt air. If you don't mind the largely asphalt surroundings, more of a parking lot than anything else, you can get yourself a classic setup right on the edge of the sea.

❾ Bayside RV Park

Location: In Crescent City; map AØ, grid e6.

Campsites, facilities: There are 100 RV sites with full hookups. Picnic tables, flush toilets, and showers are provided. A coin laundry is available. Leashed pets are permitted.

Reservations, fees: Reservations are accepted; $15 per night.

Contact: Bayside RV Park, (707) 464-9482 or fax (707) 464-2625.

Directions: From US 101 at the southern end of Crescent City, turn west at Citizen Dock Road and drive a very short distance to the campground.

Trip notes: If you are towing a boat you just found your own personal heaven. That is because this RV park is located directly adjacent to the boat docking area in Crescent City Harbor. There are several walks in the immediate area, including exploring the harbor and ocean frontage. For a quick change of scenery, it is only a 15-minute drive to Redwood National Park and Jedediah Smith Redwoods State Park along US 199 to the north.

⑩ Village Camper Inn

Location: In Crescent City; map AØ, grid e6.

Campsites, facilities: There are 135 RV sites, most with full hookups, and a separate area for tents. Picnic tables, a sanitary disposal station, flush toilets, and showers are provided. A coin laundry and cable TV hookups are available. Leashed pets are permitted.

Reservations, fees: Reservations are accepted; $13 to $18 per night.

Contact: Village Camper Inn, (707) 464-3544.

Directions: From the north end of Crescent City on US 101, turn left on Washington Boulevard and drive one block to Parkway Drive. Turn left and drive one block to 1543 Parkway Drive on the right side of the road.

Trip notes: Woods and water, that's what attracts visitors to California's north coast. Village Camper Inn provides nearby access to big woods and big water. This RV park is located on 20 acres of wooded land, with the giant redwoods along US 199 about a 10 minute drive away. In addition, you find some premium beachcombing for driftwood and agates a mile away on the spectacular rocky beaches just west of town.

⑪ Hiouchi Hamlet RV Resort

Location: Near the Smith River; map AØ, grid d7.

Campsites, facilities: There are 120 sites for tents or RVs, most with full hookups. Flush toilets, showers, and a sanitary disposal station are provided. A coin laundry, LP gas, groceries, and a golf course are available within three miles. The facilities are wheelchair accessible. Pets are permitted.

Reservations, fees: Reservations are accepted; $15 to $22 per night.

Contact: Hiouchi Hamlet RV Resort, (707) 458-3321 or fax (707) 458-3033.

Directions: From Crescent City, drive five miles north on US 101 to US 199. Turn east on US 199 and drive about five miles (just past the entrance to Jedediah Smith State Park) to the town of Hiouchi. In Hiouchi, turn left at the well-signed campground entrance.

Trip notes: The folks who run this outfit are among the nicest you'll ever find, and hey, the fried chicken at the Hamlet is always good for a quick hit. The park is out of the wind and fog you get on the coast and set instead in the heart of the forest country. It makes a good base camp for a steelhead trip in winter. An excellent side trip is to drive just east of Hiouchi on US 199, turn right, and cross over two bridges, where you will reach a fork in the road. Turn left for a great scenic drive along the South Fork Smith River or turn right to get backdoor (and free) access to Jedediah Smith Redwoods State Park and three great trailheads for hiking in the redwoods. My favorite of the latter is the Boy Scout Tree Trail.

⑫ Jedediah Smith Redwoods State Park

Location: On the Smith River; map AØ, grid e8.

Campsites, facilities: There are 108 sites for tents or RVs up to 30 feet long and several hike-in/bike-in sites. Piped water, flush toilets, showers, picnic tables, fire grills, and a sanitary disposal station are provided. Propane gas, groceries, and a coin laundry are available within one mile. Leashed pets are permitted.

Reservations, fees: Reserve via phone at (800) 444-PARK/7275 ($7.50 reservation fee) or website www.cal-parks.ca.gov; $12 to $16 per night.

Contact: Redwood National and State Parks, (707) 464-6101 extension 5112.

Directions: From Crescent City, drive north on US 101 for five miles to the junction with US 199. Turn east at US 199 and drive nine miles. Turn right at the well-signed entrance station.

Trip notes: This is a beautiful redwood park set along the Smith River, where the campsites are sprinkled amid a grove of redwoods. During the summer months reservations are usually a necessity. The park has hiking trails that lead right out of the campground; one is routed along the beautiful Smith River, and another heads through forest, across US 199, and hooks up with the Simpson-Reed Interpretive Trail. In the summer, guided walks are available. There is also a good put-in spot at the park for river access in a drift boat, canoe, or raft. The fishing is best for steelhead from mid-January through March. An excellent side trip is available on the opposite bank of the Smith River; for access, see the trip notes for Hiouchi Hamlet RV Resort (campground number 11).

⑬ Big Flat

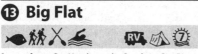

Location: On Hurdygurdy Creek in Six Rivers National Forest; map AØ, grid e9.

Campsites, facilities: There are 28 sites for tents or RVs up to 22 feet long. Vault toilets, picnic tables, and fire grills are provided, but there is no garbage service. There is no piped water, so bring your own. Leashed pets are permitted.

Reservations, fees: No reservations; $6 per night, $5 for each extra vehicle. Open year-round with limited services (like just about nothing) in the fall and winter.

Contact: Smith River National Recreation Area, Six Rivers National Forest, PO Box 228, Gasquet, CA 95543; (707) 457-3131 or fax (707) 457-3794.

Directions: From Crescent City, drive north on US 101 for five miles to the junction with US 199, turn east on US 199, and drive five miles to Hiouchi. Continue just past Hiouchi, turn right at South Fork Road, and cross two bridges. At the Y, turn left on South Fork Road and drive about 14 miles to Big Flat Road/County Road 405. At Big Flat Road, turn left and drive one-quarter mile. Look for the campground entrance on the left side of the road.

Trip notes: This camp provides an ideal setting for those who know of it, which is why it gets quite a bit of use for a relatively remote camp. Set along Hurdygurdy Creek, near where

the creek enters the South Fork of the Smith River, it provides nearby access to the South Kelsey Trail, an outstanding hiking route whether you are walking for a few hours or backpacking for days. From January through March, this is also an ideal base camp for a steelhead fishing trip, if you don't mind the inevitable rain, with a good stretch of water located within walking distance of the camp. In the summer, it is a good layover for rafters or kayakers paddling the South Fork of the Smith River.

⑭ Nickel Creek Walk-In

Location: In Redwood National Park; map AØ, grid e6.

Campsites, facilities: There are five hike-in tent sites. There is no piped water, but picnic tables, fire grills, and composting toilets are provided. No pets are allowed.

Reservations, fees: No reservations; $3 per night. Open year-round.

Contact: Redwood National and State Parks, 1111 Second Street, Crescent City, CA 95531; (707) 464-6101.

Directions: From Crescent City, drive south on US 101 for two miles to Enderts Beach Road, turn right on Enderts Beach Road, and drive about a mile to the trailhead at the end of the road. From the trailhead, hike in a half mile to the campground.

Trip notes: This camp is set 100 yards from the beach on a bluff, right near the mouth of Nickel Creek. One of the least-known national park campgrounds in the whole state, Nickel Creek Walk-In provides a backpacking-type experience, yet requires only a short walk. In return for the effort, you get seclusion and beach frontage, with seashore walks and tide pool exploration available.

⑮ De Martin

Location: In Redwood National Park; map AØ, grid f7.

Campsites, facilities: There are 10 tent sites. Composting toilets and caches for food storage are provided, but there is no piped water. No pets are allowed.

Reservations, fees: No reservations; no fee. Open year-round.

Contact: Redwood National and State Parks, 1111 Second Street, Crescent City, CA 95531; (707) 464-6101.

Directions: From Crescent City, drive south for approximately 18 miles on US 101 to Wilson Creek Road. At Wilson Creek Road, turn left and drive a quarter mile to the trailhead at the end of the road. From the trailhead, hike in about 2.5 miles to the campground.

Trip notes: This camp is primarily used by overnighters who are hiking the Pacific Coastal Trail. It is set in a grassy prairie area on a bluff overlooking the ocean along the De Martin section of the trail, right aside Wilson Creek. Sound good? You can chase the waves, hike the Coastal Trail, or just hunker down and let the joy of a peaceful spot renew your spirit.

⑯ Del Norte Coast Redwoods State Park

Location: Near Crescent City; map AØ, grid f7.

Campsites, facilities: There are 38 tent sites and 107 sites for tents or RVs up to 31 feet long. Hike-in/bike-in sites are also available. Piped water, sanitary disposal station, flush toilets, showers, fire grills, and picnic tables are provided. Leashed pets are permitted.

Reservations, fees: Reserve via phone (800) 444-PARK/7275 ($7.50 reservation fee) or website www.cal-parks.ca.gov; $12 to $16 per night; $3 for hike-in/bike-in sites. Open May through September.

Contact: Del Norte Coast Redwoods State Park, (707) 464-6106 extension 5101.

Directions: From Crescent City, drive nine miles south on US 101 to a signed access road for Del Norte Coast Redwoods State Park. Turn left at the park entrance.

Trip notes: The campsites are set in a series of loops in the forest, so while there are a lot of camps, you still feel a sense of privacy here. In addition to redwoods, there are also good stands of alders, along with a rambling stream fed by

several creeks. It makes for a very pretty setting, with a good loop hike available right out of the camp. One reason for the lush growth is what rangers call the "nurturing" coastal climate. Nurturing, in this case, means rain like you wouldn't believe in the winter and lots of fog in the summer. Evening ranger programs are conducted here.

⑰ Riverwoods Campground

Location: On the Klamath River; map AØ, grid g6.

Campsites, facilities: There are 74 RV sites, many with full hookups, and a separate area for tents. Piped water, picnic tables, fire grills, flush toilets, showers, and a sanitary disposal station are provided. Ice and wood are available. Satellite TV is available with full-hookup sites. A few rental trailers are available. A convenience store and fishing tackle store are located at the campground. Rest rooms and sites are wheelchair accessible. Leashed pets are permitted.

Reservations, fees: Reservations are accepted; $12 to $16 per night. Open year-round.

Contact: Riverwoods Campground, (707) 482-5591.

Directions: From the town of Klamath, drive a mile south on US 101 to Klamath Beach Road. Turn right on Klamath Beach Road and drive two miles. Look for the campground entrance on the right side of the road.

Trip notes: Riverwoods Campground provides direct access to the Klamath River, with pretty sites located in a grove of alder trees. Although the camp is set beside the Klamath, it is actually very close to the ocean as well, so the river is often more like a big lagoon. From mid-August through September, salmon will enter the Klamath and hold here, becoming acclimated to changes in salinity and water temperature. In the spring, usually late March and April, lampreys will enter this area and provide unusual shoreline fishing prospects. Nearby hiking is available on the Coastal Trail, with a trailhead a five-minute drive to the west on Klamath Beach Road, taking you to a spectacular ocean bluff.

⑱ Flint Ridge Walk-In

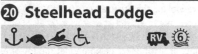

Location: In Redwood National Park; map AØ, grid g6.

Campsites, facilities: There are 10 hike-in tent sites. Composting toilets are provided, but there is no piped water. No pets are allowed.

Reservations, fees: No reservations; no fee.

Contact: Redwood National and State Parks, 1111 Second Street, Crescent City, CA 95531; (707) 464-6101.

Directions: From Eureka, drive north on US 101 to the Klamath River. Just before reaching the bridge at the Klamath River, take the Coastal Drive exit and head west up the hill for four miles to a dirt parking area on the right side of the road. Park here. The campground trailhead is adjacent to the parking area on the east side of the road. Hike five minutes to the camp.

Trip notes: This little-known camp is located on a grassy bluff overlooking the ocean, along the Flint Ridge section of the Pacific Coastal Trail. From the parking area at the trailhead, it's only a five-minute walk to reach a meadow surrounded by a thicket of wild blackberries, alders, and redwoods, with the ocean looming huge to the west. The parking area, by the way, is an excellent perch to watch for the "puff-of-smoke" spouts from passing whales. A hike out of camp is routed into the forest, a two-mile climb to reach a hill filled solid with redwoods. The only problem is that there is no real destination; just in, then back.

⑲ Crivelli's Trailer Park

Location: Near the Klamath River; map AØ, grid g7.

Campsites, facilities: There are 31 RV sites with full hookups. Facilities are wheelchair accessible. Flush toilets and showers are provided. A coin laundry, restaurant, and a lounge are available. Leashed pets are permitted.

Reservations, fees: Reservations are accepted; $10 to $15 per night. Open year-round.

Contact: Crivelli's Trailer Park, (707) 482-3713.

Directions: From Eureka, drive north on US 101 to Klamath and the junction with Highway 169. Turn east on Highway 169 and drive 2.5 miles to the trailer park entrance.

Trip notes: Crivelli's Trailer Park is adjacent to a motel, surrounded by trees, and only a mile away from the Klamath River. It's a good base camp for a salmon fishing trip during the fall run so when the salmon arrive en masse, it can be difficult to get a reservation. Some regulars show up every year, same time, same place, staying for a week or more and fishing daily for salmon in the lower river. A cafe and lounge are available

⑳ Steelhead Lodge

Location: On the Klamath River; map AØ, grid g7.

Campsites, facilities: There are 36 RV sites (10 drive-through) with full hookups. Picnic tables, flush toilets, and showers are provided. Ice is available. A bar, restaurant, and motel are also available. Bar and restaurant are wheelchair accessible. Leashed pets are permitted.

Reservations, fees: Reservations are accepted; $15 per night. Open year-round.

Contact: Steelhead Lodge, (707) 482-8145. For a fishing report, phone (707) 482-7775.

Directions: From Eureka, drive north on US 101 to Klamath and the junction with Highway 169. Turn east on Highway 169 and drive 3.2 miles to Terwer Riffle Road. Turn south on Terwer Riffle Road and drive a block to Steelhead Lodge.

Trip notes: Many anglers use this park as headquarters when the salmon and steelhead get going in August. The park has grassy sites near the Klamath River.

㉑ Redwood Rest

Location: On the Klamath River; map AØ, grid g7.

Campsites, facilities: There are 100 sites for

tents or RVs (30 drive-through) with full or partial hookups. Picnic tables, flush toilets, and showers are provided. Wood is available. Leashed pets are permitted.

Reservations, fees: Reservations are accepted; $12 to $14 per night. Open May through October.

Contact: Redwood Rest, (707) 482-5033 or fax (707) 482-5033.

Directions: From Eureka, drive north on US 101 to Klamath and the junction with Highway 169. Turn east on Highway 169 and drive 3.5 miles to the park.

Trip notes: While there are quite a few privately operated parks on the lower Klamath River, Redwood Rest is the only park with redwood trees actually in the campground and a 20-foot-tall wooden Indian at the entrance. Reservations are advised during summer and are a necessity when salmon fishing picks up in mid-August.

22 Terwer Park

Location: On the Klamath River; map AØ, grid g7.

Campsites, facilities: There are 98 RV sites with full hookups. Picnic tables, flush toilets, and hot showers are provided. A coin laundry, cable TV, and a dock with fee boat launching are available. Leashed pets are permitted.

Reservations, fees: Reservations are accepted; $16 per night. Open year-round.

Contact: Terwer Park, (707) 482-3855.

Directions: From Eureka, drive north on US 101 to Klamath and the junction with Highway 169. Turn east on Highway 169 and drive 3.5 miles to Terwer Riffle Road. Turn right on Terwer Riffle Road and drive seven blocks (about a half mile) to the park, located at 641 Terwer Riffle Road.

Trip notes: This RV park is situated near the Terwer Riffle, one of the better shore-fishing spots for steelhead and salmon on the lower Klamath River. You get grassy sites, river access, and some fair trails along the Klamath. When the salmon arrive in late August and September, Terwer Riffle can be loaded with fish,

as well as boaters and shore anglers—a wild scene.

23 Camp Marigold

Location: Near the Klamath River; map AØ, grid f7.

Campsites, facilities: There are 40 sites for tents or RVs with full hookups. Picnic tables, barbecues, cable TV, rest rooms, hot showers, and a coin laundry are provided. Cabins (with fully equipped kitchenettes and bedding, for two to six people) and a group lodge (with kitchen, for up to 15 people) are also available. Small leashed pets are permitted.

Reservations, fees: Reservations are recommended; $10 to $15 per night; cabins rent for $38.50 to $60 per night; the lodge rents for $150 per night for the first 10 people, $5 for each additional person (maximum 15).

Contact: Camp Marigold, (800) 621-8513; email: campmar@tlk.net.

Directions: From Eureka, drive 60 miles north on US 101 to the campground at 16101 US 101, four miles north of the Klamath River Bridge, on the right side of the road. The camp is a mile south of the Trees of Mystery.

Trip notes: Camp Marigold is surrounded by Redwood National Park, towering redwoods, Pacific Ocean beaches, driftwood, agates, fossilized rocks, blackberries, Fern Canyon, Lagoon Creek Park, and the Trees of Mystery. It also has world-famous fishing nearby for chinook and silver salmon, steelhead, sturgeon, trout, red tail perch, and candlefish. The camp has 3.5 acres of landscaped gardens with hiking trails . . . get the idea? Well, there's more: it is only two miles to the Klamath River, in case you can't find enough to do already.

24 Mystic Forest RV Park

Location: Near the Klamath River; map AØ, grid g6.

Campsites, facilities: There are 30 RV sites, many with full hookups (15 are drive-through), and a separate area for tents. Picnic tables, fire rings, piped water, flush toilets, showers, playground, and a solar-heated pool are provided. A coin laundry and wood are available. Some facilities are wheelchair accessible. Leashed pets are permitted.

Reservations, fees: Reservations are accepted; $14 to $16 per night.

Contact: Mystic Forest RV Park, (707) 482-4901 or fax (707) 482-0704.

Directions: From Eureka, drive north on US 101 to Klamath and continue north for 3.2 miles. Look for the entrance sign on the left side of the road. If you reach the Trees of Mystery, you have gone a mile too far north.

Trip notes: Yes, Paul Bunyan exists. After all, how do you think the Mojave got turned into a desert? Babe, the giant blue ox, is still around too, as you will discover at the Trees of Mystery north of Klamath, where a dinosaur-size Paul Bunyan guards the parking lot. Less than a mile away is the Mystic Forest RV Park. Though Mystic Forest and the Trees of Mystery are not associated commercially, the link is obvious as soon as you arrive.

㉕ Blackberry Patch

Location: On the Klamath River; map AØ, grid g7.

Campsites, facilities: There are 35 RV sites with full hookups and a cabin for rent. Flush toilets, showers, and picnic tables are provided. A coin laundry is available. Leashed pets are permitted.

Reservations, fees: Reservations are accepted; $15 per night; cabin rental is $35 per night. Open year-round.

Contact: Blackberry Patch, (707) 482-4782; email: blkbry@ns1.tlk.net.

Directions: From Eureka, drive north on US 101 to Klamath and the junction with Highway 169. Turn east on Highway 169 and drive 3.2 miles to Terwer Riffle Road. At Terwer Riffle Road, turn right and drive 0.25 mile to the campground entrance on the right side of the road.

Trip notes: It's no secret how this RV park got its name: there are tons of blackberry bushes in the park, and guests are allowed to pick to their

heart's content during the berry season from mid- to late summer. The Klamath River is a few blocks away, with the Terwer Riffle, a great salmon spot in September.

㉖ Camper Corral

Location: On the Klamath River; map AØ, grid g7.

Campsites, facilities: There are 140 sites for tents or RVs, many with full hookups. Flush toilets, showers, picnic tables, fire grills, recreation hall, and a playground are provided. A sanitary disposal station, LP gas, coin laundry, cable TV, ice, and a bait and tackle shop are available. Leashed pets are permitted.

Reservations, fees: Reservations are accepted; $14 to $20 per night. Open April through October.

Contact: Camper Corral, (707) 482-5741 or fax (707) 482-6625; website: www.campgrounds .com/campercorral.

Directions: From Eureka, drive north on US 101 to Klamath. Just after crossing the Klamath River Bridge, take the Terwer Valley Road exit. Drive a short distance west to the campground.

Trip notes: This resort offers 3,000 feet of Klamath River frontage, grassy tent sites, berry picking, access to the ocean, and hiking trails nearby. And, of course, in the fall it has salmon, the main attraction on the lower Klamath.

㉗ Chinook RV Resort

Location: On the Klamath River; map AØ, grid g7.

Campsites, facilities: There are 72 RV sites with full hookups. Picnic tables, fire grills, flush toilets, showers, a playground, coin laundry, and recreation room are provided. LP gas, groceries, RV supplies, boat ramp, and a tackle shop are available. Leashed pets are permitted.

Reservations, fees: Reservations are accepted; $17 per night. Open year-round.

Contact: Chinook RV Resort, (707) 482-3511.

Directions: From Eureka, drive north on US 101 to Klamath. After crossing the bridge at the Klamath River, continue north on US 101 for a mile to the campground.

Trip notes: Chinook RV Resort is another of the more well-known parks on the lower Klamath. A boat ramp, fishing supplies, and all the advice you can ask for are available. The camping area consists of grassy RV sites that overlook the river.

㉘ Riverside RV Park

Location: On the Klamath River; map AØ, grid g7.

Campsites, facilities: There are 93 RV sites with full hookups (30 drive-through). Flush toilets, showers, and a recreation room are provided. Boat rentals and a dock are available. Leashed pets are permitted.

Reservations, fees: Reservations are accepted; $5 to $17 per night. Open April through October.

Contact: Riverside RV Park, (707) 482-2523.

Directions: From Eureka, drive north on US 101 to Klamath and the junction with Highway 169. Continue north on US 101 for 1.5 miles to the campground.

Trip notes: This is one in a series of RV parks located near the town of Klamath along the lower Klamath River. It provides an option for RV cruisers looking for a layover spot on a US 101 tour or a base of operations for a Klamath River fishing trip. There's good salmon fishing during the fall run on the Klamath River.

㉙ Elk Prairie

Location: In Prairie Creek Redwoods State Park; map AØ, grid h6.

Campsites, facilities: There are 75 sites for tents, RVs up to 27 feet long, or trailers up to 24 feet long. Piped water, flush toilets, coin-operated showers, picnic tables, and fire grills are provided. The facilities are wheelchair accessible. Leashed pets are permitted.

Reservations, fees: Reserve via phone at (800) 444-PARK/7275 ($7.50 reservation fee) or website www.cal-parks.ca.gov; $12 to $16 per night, $1 pet fee.

Contact: Prairie Creek Redwoods State Park, (707) 445-6547 or (707) 464-6101 extension 5301.

Directions: From Eureka, drive 41 miles north on US 101 to Orick. At Orick, continue north on US 101 for six miles to the Newton B. Drury Scenic Parkway. Take the exit for the Newton B. Drury Scenic Parkway and drive north for a mile to the park. Turn left at the park entrance.

Trip notes: Herds of Roosevelt elk wander free in this remarkable park. Great opportunities for photographs abound, often right beside the highway. Where there are meadows, there are elk; it's about that simple. An elky here, an elky there, making this one of the best places to see wildlife in California. The park also has excellent hiking and some mountain biking, including a trailhead for a great bike ride at the campground. There are many additional trailheads and a beautiful tour of giant redwoods along the Drury Scenic Parkway.

㉚ Gold Bluff Beach

Location: In Prairie Creek Redwoods State Park; map AØ, grid i6.

Campsites, facilities: There are 25 primitive sites for tents or RVs up to 20 feet long (no trailers or vehicles wider than seven feet). Piped water, flush toilets, solar showers, fire grills, and tables are provided. Leashed pets are permitted.

Reservations, fees: No reservations; $12 to $16 per night, $1 pet fee. Open year-round, weather permitting.

Contact: Prairie Creek Redwoods State Park, (707) 445-6547 or (707) 464-6101 extension 5301.

Directions: From Eureka, drive north on US 101 for 41 miles to Orick. At Orick, continue north on US 101 for three miles to Davison Road. Turn left (west) on Davison Road and drive four miles to the campground. Note: No trailers are allowed on Davison Road, which is narrow and very bumpy.

Trip notes: The campsites here are set in a sandy, exposed area with man-made windbreaks, at the head of a huge, expansive beach. You can walk for miles at this beach, often without seeing another soul. In addition, the Fern Canyon Trail, one of the best 10-minute hikes in California, is located at the end of Davison Road. Hikers walk along a stream in a narrow canyon, its vertical walls covered with magnificent ferns. There are some herds of elk in the area, often right along the access road. These camps are rarely used in the winter because of the region's heavy rain and winds.

③ Patricks Point State Park

Location: Near Trinidad; map AØ, grid j4.

Campsites, facilities: There are 124 sites for tents or RVs up to 31 feet long. Piped water, flush toilets, coin-operated showers, fire grills, and picnic tables are provided. The facilities are wheelchair accessible. Leashed pets are permitted at the camp but not on trails or beaches.

Reservations, fees: Reserve via phone at (800) 444-PARK/7275 ($7.50 reservation fee) or website www.cal-parks.ca.gov; $12 to $16 per night, $1 pet fee.

Contact: Patricks Point State Park, (707) 677-3570 or (707) 445-6547.

Directions: From Eureka, drive north on US 101 for 22 miles to Trinidad. At Trinidad, continue north on US 101 for 2.5 miles and take the well-signed exit. At the stop sign, turn left and drive a short distance to the park entrance.

Trip notes: This pretty park is filled with Sitka spruce, dramatic coastal lookouts, and several beautiful beaches, including one with agates, one with tide pools, and another with an expansive stretch of beachfront leading to a lagoon. You can best see all of it on the Rim Trail, which has many little cut-off routes to the lookouts and down to the beaches. The campground is sheltered in the forest, and while it is often foggy and damp in the summer, it is always beautiful. Plan on making reservations.

③ Stone Lagoon Boat-In

Location: In Humboldt Lagoons State Park; map AØ, grid j5.

Campsites, facilities: There are six primitive tent sites accessible by boat only. There is no piped water, but pit toilets, picnic tables, and fire rings are provided. No pets are allowed.

Reservations, fees: No reservations; $7 per night. Open year-round.

Contact: Humboldt Lagoons State Park, (707) 488-2041.

Directions: From Eureka, drive 41 miles north on US 101 (15 miles north of Trinidad) to Stone Lagoon. At Stone Lagoon, turn left at the visitor information center. The boat-in campground is located in a cove directly across the lagoon from the visitor center. The campsites are dispersed in an area covering about 300 yards in the landing area.

Trip notes: Virtually nobody knows about this ideal spot for canoeists. While Stone Lagoon is located directly adjacent to US 101, the camp is set in a cove that is out of sight of the highway. That makes it a secret spot for many. It is a great place to explore by canoe or kayak, especially paddling upstream to the lagoon's inlet creek. After setting up camp, it is possible to hike to a secluded sand spit and stretch of beachfront. You may see elk in this area on the rare occasion. The water is usually calm in the morning but often gets choppy from afternoon winds. Translation: Get your paddling done early on Stone Lagoon. There is also good fishing for cutthroat trout here.

③ Dry Lagoon Walk-In

Location: In Humboldt Lagoons State Park; map AØ, grid j5.

Campsites, facilities: There are six primitive tent sites. There is no piped water, but pit toilets, fire rings, and picnic tables are provided. No pets are allowed.

Reservations, fees: No reservations; $7 per night.

Contact: Humboldt Lagoons State Park, (707) 488-2041.

Directions: From Eureka, drive north on US 101 for 22 miles to Trinidad. At Trinidad, continue north on US 101 for 13 miles to the campground parking entrance at milepost 114.5. After parking, walk 200 yards to the camp.

Trip notes: This is a walk-in camp; that is, you need to walk about 200 yards from the parking area to reach the campsites. This makes it a dream for members of the 5 Percent Club, because many tourists are unwilling to walk at all. It is beautiful here, set in the woods, with ocean views and beach access.

③ Big Lagoon County Park

Location: Overlooking the Pacific Ocean; map A∅, grid j5.

Campsites, facilities: There are 26 sites for tents or RVs. Piped water, flush toilets, fire grills, and picnic tables are provided. A boat ramp is available. Pets are permitted.

Reservations, fees: No reservations; $12 per night, $1 pet fee. Open year-round.

Contact: Humboldt County Parks, (707) 445-7651.

Directions: From Eureka, drive 22 miles north on US 101 to Trinidad. At Trinidad, continue north on US 101 for eight miles to Big Lagoon Park Road. Turn left (west) at Big Lagoon Park Road and drive two miles to the park.

Trip notes: This is a remarkable, huge lagoon that borders the Pacific Ocean. It provides good boating, excellent exploring, fair fishing, and good duck hunting in the winter. It's a good spot to paddle a canoe around on a calm day. A lot of out-of-towners cruise by, note the lagoon's proximity to the ocean, and figure it must be salt water. Wrong! Not only is it fresh water, but it provides a long shot for anglers trying for rainbow trout. One reason not many RV drivers stop here is that most of them are drawn farther north (another eight miles) to Freshwater Lagoon, where there is a wide shoulder along the highway that allows them to line up their rigs, like a convoy parking parade—an unbelievable sight.

Map A1

One inch equals approximately 10.7 miles.
See inside back cover for California state map.

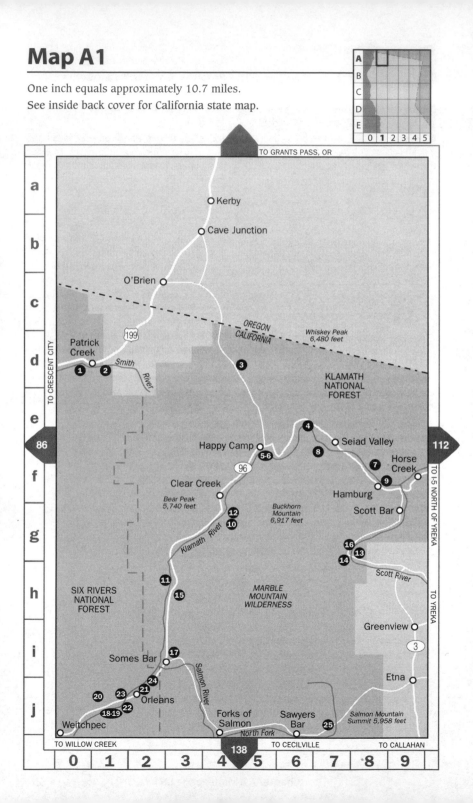

Chapter A1 features:

❶ Grassy Flat

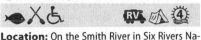

Location: On the Smith River in Six Rivers National Forest; map A1, grid d0.

Campsites, facilities: There are five tent sites and 14 sites for tents or RVs up to 22 feet long. Piped water, vault toilets, fire grills, and picnic tables are provided. Propane gas, groceries, and a coin laundry are available nearby. Some facilities are wheelchair accessible. Leashed pets are permitted.

Reservations, fees: Reservations are accepted via phone at (877) 444-6777 ($8.65 reservation fee) or website www.reserveusa.com; $10 per night, $5 for each extra vehicle. Open May through mid-September.

Contact: Smith River National Recreation Area, Six Rivers National Forest, PO Box 228, Gasquet, CA 95543; (707) 457-3131 or fax (707) 457-3794.

Directions: From Crescent City, drive north on US 101 for three miles to the junction with US 199, turn east on US 199 and drive 15 miles to Gasquet. From Gasquet, continue east on US 199 for 4.4 miles and look for the campground entrance on the right side of the road.

Trip notes: This is one in a series of three easy-to-reach Forest Service camps set near US 199 along the beautiful Smith River. It's a classic wild river, popular in the summer with kayakers, and the steelhead come huge in the winter for the crafty few. The camp itself is set directly across from a CalTrans waste area, and if you hit it when the crews are working, it can be noisy here. Most of the time, however, it is peaceful and quiet. In the winter when the camp is closed, fishermen will often park at the piped gate, and then walk past the camp to access a good steelhead spot.

❷ Patrick Creek

Location: In Six Rivers National Forest; map A1, grid d1.

Campsites, facilities: There are 13 sites for tents and RVs. Piped water, flush toilets, picnic tables, and fire grills are provided. Rest rooms and water spigots are wheelchair accessible. Leashed pets are permitted.

Reservations, fees: Reservations are accepted via phone at (877) 444-6777 ($8.65 reservation fee) or website www.reserveusa.com; $12 per night, $5 for each extra vehicle. Open May through mid-September.

Contact: Smith River National Recreation Area, Six Rivers National Forest, PO Box 228, Gasquet, CA 95543; (707) 457-3131 or fax (707) 457-3794.

Directions: From Crescent City, drive north on

US 101 for three miles to the junction with US 199, turn east on US 199, and drive 15 miles to Gasquet. From Gasquet, continue east on US 199 for 7.5 miles and look for the campground entrance on the right side of the road.

Trip notes: This is one of the prettiest spots along US 199, where Patrick Creek enters the upper Smith River. This section of the Smith looks something like a large trout stream, rolling green past a boulder-lined shore, complete with forest canopy. There are no trout of course, but rather salmon and steelhead in the fall and winter, and only their little smolts pooling up in the summer months. A big plus for this camp is its nearby access to excellent hiking in the Siskiyou Wilderness, especially the great day hike to Buck Lake. It is essential to have a map of Six Rivers National Forest, both for driving directions to the trailhead and for the hiking route. Maps are available for $3 at the information center for the Smith River National Recreation Area on the north side of US 199 in Gasquet. An option at this camp is Patrick Creek Lodge, located on the opposite side of the highway from the campground, which has a fine restaurant and bar.

❸ West Branch

Location: In Klamath National Forest; map A1, grid d5.

Campsites, facilities: There are 15 sites for tents or RVs. Piped water, vault toilets, picnic tables, and fire grills are provided. There are sanitary disposal stations in Happy Camp at the Elk Creek Campground and the Happy Camp Open Dump. Pack out your garbage. Leashed pets are permitted.

Reservations, fees: No reservations; $3 per night. Open May through October.

Contact: Klamath National Forest, Happy Camp Ranger District, (530) 493-2243 or fax (530) 493-2212.

Directions: From Happy Camp on Highway 96, turn north on Indian Creek Road (a paved road) and drive 14.5 miles to the camp on the right side of the road.

Trip notes: This is a virtually unknown, no-charge camp, set in a canyon near Indian Creek, deep in Klamath National Forest. It is a 20-minute drive from the town of Happy Camp at 2,200 feet in elevation. The best side trip here is the winding four-mile drive on a bumpy dirt road to Kelly Lake, little known and little used. A remote Forest Service station is located on the opposite side of Indian Creek Road from the campground.

❹ Fort Goff

Location: In Klamath National Forest; map A1, grid e6.

Campsites, facilities: There are five tent sites. Vault toilets, picnic tables, and fire grills are provided, but there is no piped water and you must pack out your garbage. Supplies are available in Seiad Valley. Leashed pets are permitted.

Reservations, fees: No reservations; no fee.

Contact: Klamath National Forest, Happy Camp Ranger District, (530) 493-2243 or fax (530) 493-2212.

Directions: From Yreka, drive north on Interstate 5 to the junction with Highway 96. At Highway 96, turn west and drive to Seiad Valley. At Seiad Valley, continue west on Highway 96 for five miles to the campground on the left side of the road.

Trip notes: This small, primitive campground is set right along the Klamath River, an ideal location for both fishing and rafting. Many of the most productive shoreline fishing spots on the Klamath River are in this area, with fair trout fishing in summer, good steelhead fishing in the fall and early winter, and a wild card for salmon in late September. There are pullouts along Highway 96 for parking, with short trails/scrambles down to the river. This is also a good spot for rafting, especially in inflatable kayaks, and commercial rafting operations have trips available on this stretch of river. On the opposite side of Highway 96 (within walking distance to the west) is a trailhead for a hike that is routed along Little Fort Goff Creek, an uphill tromp for five miles to Big Camp and the Boundary National Recreation Trail. The creek also runs near the camp.

❺ Elk Creek Campground

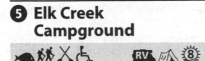

Location: On the Klamath River; map A1, grid f5.

Campsites, facilities: There are 78 RV sites, many with full or partial hookups, and a separate area for tents. Rest rooms, hot showers, recreation room, beach, picnic tables, and fire grills are provided. Coin laundry, sanitary disposal station, ice, propane, and wood are available. Leashed pets are permitted.

Reservations, fees: Reservations are accepted; $7 per person for tent campers, $18 to $20 for RVs.

Contact: Elk Creek Campground, (530) 493-2208.

Directions: From Highway 96 in the town of Happy Camp, turn south on Elk Creek Road and drive one mile to the campground.

Trip notes: Elk Creek Campground is a year-round RV park set where Elk Creek pours into the Klamath River. It is a beautiful facility, with sites right on the water in a pretty, wooded setting. The section of the Klamath River nearby is perfect for inflatable kayaking and light rafting. While demure enough to keep rafters completely safe, it is still wild enough to make things exciting. In addition, the water is quite warm in the summer months and flows are maintained throughout the year, making it ideal for water sports.

❻ Curly Jack

Location: On the Klamath River in Klamath National Forest; map A1, grid f5.

Campsites, facilities: There are 17 sites for tents or RVs up to 22 feet and two group sites. Piped water, vault toilets and fire grills are available. Some facilities are wheelchair accessible. Leashed pets are permitted.

Reservations, fees: Reservations required for group camps only; phone (877) 444-6777 ($8.65 reservation fee); $7 per night, $20 per night for a group camp site. Open year-round,

but services available only from May through September.

Contact: Klamath National Forest, Happy Camp Ranger District, (530) 493-2243 or fax (530) 493-2212.

Directions: From the town of Happy Camp on Highway, turn south on Elk Creek Road and drive about one mile. Turn right on Curly Jack Road and drive one block to the campground entrance.

Trip notes: This campground is set at 1,075 feet in elevation on the Klamath River, providing opportunities for fishing, light rafting, and kayaking. What's special about Curly Jack, though, is that the water is generally warm enough through the summer months for swimming.

❼ O'Neil Creek

Location: In Klamath National Forest; map A1, grid f8.

Campsites, facilities: There are 18 sites for tents or RVs up to 22 feet. Vault toilets, piped water, picnic tables, and fire grills are provided. Pack out your garbage. Supplies can be obtained in Seiad Valley. Leashed pets are permitted.

Reservations, fees: No reservations; $6 per night.

Contact: Klamath National Forest, Happy Camp Ranger District, (530) 493-2243 or fax (530) 493-2212.

Directions: From Yreka drive, north on Interstate 5 to the junction with Highway 96. Turn west on Highway 96 and drive past Hamburg, continuing west for three miles to the campground.

Trip notes: This camp is set near O'Neil Creek, and though not far from the Klamath River, access to the river is not easy. To fish or raft, most people will use this as a base camp, then drive out for recreation during the day. That creates a predicament for RV owners, who lose their campsites every time they drive off. During the fall hunting season, this is a good base camp for hunters branching out into the surrounding national forest. There are also historic mining sites nearby.

⑧ Grider Creek

Location: In Klamath National Forest; map A1, grid f7.

Campsites, facilities: There are 10 sites for tents or RVs up to 16 feet long. Vault toilets, picnic tables, and fire grills are provided, but there is no piped water, so bring your own. Pack out your garbage. Leashed pets are permitted.

Reservations, fees: No reservations; no fee.

Contact: Klamath National Forest, Happy Camp Ranger District, (530) 493-2243 or fax (530) 493-2212.

Directions: From Yreka, drive north on Interstate 5 to the junction with Highway 96. At Highway 96, turn west and drive to Walker Creek Road/Forest Service Road 46N64, located one mile before Seiad Valley. Turn left to enter Walker Creek Road and stay to the right as it runs adjacent to the Klamath River to Grider Creek Road. At Grider Creek Road, turn left and drive south for three miles to the camp entrance.

Trip notes: This obscure little camp is used primarily by hikers, since a trailhead for the Pacific Crest Trail is available, and by deer hunters in the fall. The camp is set at 1,700 feet along Grider Creek. From here, the Pacific Crest Trail is routed uphill along Grider Creek into the Marble Mountain Wilderness, about an 11-mile ripper to Huckleberry Mountain at 6,303 feet. There are no lakes along the route, only small streams and feeder creeks.

⑨ Sarah Totten

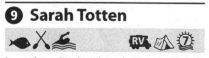

Location: On the Klamath River in Klamath National Forest; map A1, grid f8.

Campsites, facilities: There are 12 tent sites, five sites for tents and RVs up to 22 feet long, and a group site. Piped water, vault toilets, picnic tables, and fire grills are provided. There's a small grocery store nearby. Leashed pets are permitted.

Reservations, fees: Reservations for the group site only; phone (877) 444-6777; $6 per night for family sites, $20 per night for the group site.

Contact: Klamath National Forest, Happy Camp Ranger District, (530) 493-2243 or fax (530) 493-2212.

Directions: From Yreka, drive north on Interstate 5 to the junction with Highway 96. At Highway 96, turn west and drive to Horse Creek, continuing west for five miles to the campground on the right side of the road. If you reach the town of Hamburg, you have gone a half mile too far.

Trip notes: This is one of the more popular Forest Service camps on the Klamath River, and it's no mystery why. In the summer, its placement is perfect for rafters, who camp here and use it as a put-in spot. In fall and winter, fishermen arrive for the steelhead run. It's located in the "banana belt," or good weather area of the Klamath, in a pretty grove of oak trees. Fishing is often good here for salmon in early October and for steelhead from November through spring, providing there are fishable water flows.

⑩ Norcross

Location: Near Happy Camp in Klamath National Forest; map A1, grid g4.

Campsites, facilities: There are eight sites for tents or RVs. Vault toilets, picnic tables and fire pits are available, but there is no potable water. Leashed pets are permitted.

Reservations, fees: No reservations, no fee. Open year-round.

Contact: Klamath National Forest, Happy Camp Ranger District, (530) 493-2243 or fax (530) 493-2212.

Directions: From Yreka on Interstate 5, drive west on Highway 96 to the town of Happy Camp. In Happy Camp, turn south onto Elk Creek Road and drive 16 miles to the campground.

Trip notes: Set at 2,400 feet in elevation, this camp serves as a staging area for various trails that provide access into the Marble Mountain Wilderness. There is also access to the popular Kelsey Trail and to swimming and fishing activities.

⑪ Dillon Creek

Location: On the Klamath River in Klamath National Forest; map A1, grid h2.

Campsites, facilities: There are 10 tent sites and 11 RV sites. Piped water, vault toilets, picnic tables, and fire grills are provided. There is a sanitary disposal station in Happy Camp 25 miles north of the campground and at Aikens Creek Campground 13 miles west of the town of Orleans. Leashed pets are permitted.

Reservations, fees: No reservations; $6 fee per night. Open year-round.

Contact: Klamath National Forest, Ukonom Ranger District, (530) 627-3291 or fax (530) 627-3401.

Directions: From Yreka on Interstate 5, turn west on Highway 96 and drive to the town of Happy Camp. Continue west from Happy Camp for 35 miles and look for the campground on the right side of the road. Coming from the west, from Somes Bar, drive 15 miles north on Highway 96.

Trip notes: This is a prime base camp for a rafting or steelhead fishing trip. A put-in spot for rafting is located adjacent to the camp, with an excellent river run available from here on down past Presido Bar to the takeout at Ti Bar. If you choose to go on, make absolutely certain to pull out at Somes Bar, or risk death at Ishi Pishi Falls. The water is warm here in the summer, and there are also many excellent swimming holes in the area. In addition, this is a good stretch of water for steelhead fishing in September and October, best from Dillon Beach to Ti-Bar. The elevation is 800 feet.

⑫ Sulphur Springs

Location: On Elk Creek in Klamath National Forest; map A1, grid g4.

Campsites, facilities: There are several walk-in tent sites with vault toilets. Picnic tables and fire grills are provided, but there's no piped water, so bring your own. Pack out your garbage. Leashed pets are permitted.

Reservations, fees: No reservations; no fee.

Contact: Klamath National Forest, Happy Camp Ranger District, (530) 493-2243 or fax (530) 493-2212.

Directions: From Yreka, drive north on Interstate 5 to the junction with Highway 96. At Highway 96, turn west and drive to Happy Camp. In Happy Camp, turn south on Elk Creek Road and drive 14 miles to the campground.

Trip notes: This hidden spot is set along Elk Creek on the border of the Marble Mountain Wilderness. The camp is at a trailhead that provides access to miles and miles of trails that follow streams into the backcountry of the wilderness area. It is a 12-mile backpack trip one way and largely uphill to Spirit Lake, one of the prettiest lakes in the entire wilderness. Sulphur Springs Camp is set at 3,100 feet. The nearby hot springs (which are actually lukewarm) provide a side attraction. There are also some swimming holes nearby in Elk Creek, but these aren't hot springs, so expect the water to be cold.

⑬ Bridge Flat

Location: In Klamath National Forest; map A1, grid g8.

Campsites, facilities: There are four sites for tents or RVs up to 22 feet long. There is no piped water. Vault toilets, fire grills, and picnic tables are provided. Leashed pets are permitted.

Reservations, fees: No reservations; no fee.

Contact: Klamath National Forest, Scott River Ranger District, (530) 468-5351 or fax (530) 468-5654.

Directions: From Redding, drive north on Interstate 5 to Yreka. In Yreka, turn southwest on Highway 3 and drive 16.5 miles to Fort Jones. In Fort Jones, turn right on Scott River Road and drive 21 miles to the campground on the right side of the road.

Trip notes: This camp is set at 2,000 feet along the Scott River. Though commercial rafting trips are only rarely available here, the river is accessible during the early spring for skilled rafters and kayakers, with a good put-in and take-out spot located four miles downriver. For backpackers a trailhead for the Kelsey Trail is nearby, leading into the Marble Mountain Wilderness.

⑭ Lovers Camp

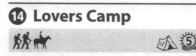

Location: In Klamath National Forest; map A1, grid g7.

Campsites, facilities: There are five walk-in sites. Vault toilets, fire grills, and picnic tables are provided. There are also facilities for stock unloading and a corral. The only water available is for stock, so bring your own drinking water. Leashed pets are permitted.

Reservations, fees: No reservations; no fee. Open June through October.

Contact: Klamath National Forest, Scott River Ranger District, (530) 468-5351 or fax (530) 468-5654.

Directions: From Redding, drive north on Interstate 5 to Yreka. In Yreka, turn southwest on Highway 3 and drive to Fort Jones. In Fort Jones, turn right and drive 18 miles on Scott River Road to Forest Service Road 43N45. Turn south on Forest Service Road 43N45 and drive nine miles to the campground at the end of the road.

Trip notes: Lovers Camp isn't set up for lovers at all, but for horses and backpackers. This is a trailhead camp set at 4,300 feet at the edge of the Marble Mountain Wilderness, one of the best in the entire wilderness for packers with horses. The trail here is routed up along Canyon Creek to the beautiful Marble Valley at the foot of Black Marble Mountain. The most common destination is the Sky High Lakes, a good one-day huff-and-puff away. Now there's a place for lovers.

⑮ Marble Mountain Ranch

Location: Near the Klamath River; map A1, grid h3.

Campsites, facilities: There are 30 tent sites, 11 cabins, two houses, and 30 RV sites with full hookups. Rest rooms, hot showers, recreation room, picnic tables, fire grills, horseshoe pits, and volleyball and basketball courts are pro-

vided. Coin laundry, ice, and wood are available. Leashed pets are permitted.

Reservations, fees: Reservations are accepted; $5 to $14 per night, $30 per night for cabins, $50 per night for houses.

Contact: Marble Mountain Ranch, (530) 469-3322 or (800) KLAMATH/552-6284.

Directions: From the junction of US 101 and Highway 299 near Arcata, turn east on Highway 299 and drive to Willow Creek. In Willow Creek, turn north on Highway 96 and drive to Somes Bar. At Somes Bar, continue for 7.5 miles to Marble Mountain Ranch.

Trip notes: The lodge is set just across the road from the Klamath River, an ideal location as headquarters for a rafting trip in the summer or a steelhead fishing trip in the fall. Commercial rafting trips are available here, as this piece of river is beautiful and fresh with lots of wildlife and birds, yet not dangerous. However, be absolutely certain to take out at Somes Bar before reaching Ishi Pishi Falls, which cannot be run. If you like privacy and comfort, the cabin rentals available here are a nice bonus.

⑯ Indian Scotty

Location: On the Scott River in Klamath National Forest; map A1, grid g7.

Campsites, facilities: There are 28 sites and a group site for tents or RVs up to 22 feet long. Piped water, vault toilets, fire grills, and picnic tables are provided. There is a playground in the group-use area. Leashed pets are permitted.

Reservations, fees: Reservations are accepted; $6 per night, $30 per night for the group site.

Contact: Klamath National Forest, Scott River Ranger District, (530) 468-5351 or fax (530) 468-5654.

Directions: From Redding, drive north on Interstate 5 to Yreka. In Yreka, turn southwest on Highway 3 and travel 16.5 miles to Fort Jones. In Fort Jones, turn right on Scott River Road and drive 18 miles to a concrete bridge and the adjacent signed campground entrance.

Trip notes: This is a popular camp that provides direct access to the adjacent Scott River.

Because it is easy to reach (no gravel roads) and shaded, it gets a lot of use. The camp is set at 2,400 feet. The levels, forces, and temperatures on the Scott River fluctuate greatly from spring to fall. In the spring, it can be a raging cauldron, cold from snowmelt. Come summer it quiets, with some deep pools providing swimming holes. By fall, it can be reduced to a trickle. Keep your expectations flexible according to the season.

⑰ Oak Bottom on the Salmon River

Location: In Klamath National Forest; map A1, grid i3.

Campsites, facilities: There are 26 sites for tents and RVs and some group sites. Piped water, vault toilets, picnic tables, and fire grills are provided. There is a sanitary disposal station at the Elk Creek Campground in Happy Camp and at Aikens Creek (campground number 18), 13 miles west of the town of Orleans. Supplies are available in Somes Bar. Leashed pets are permitted.

Reservations, fees: No reservations; $7 per night. Open year-round.

Contact: Klamath National Forest, Ukonom Ranger District, (530) 627-3291 or fax (530) 627-3401.

Directions: From the junction of US 101 and Highway 299 near Arcata, turn east on Highway 299 and drive to Willow Creek. At Willow Creek, turn north on Highway 96 and drive to Somes Bar. At Somes Bar, turn right on Somes Bar–Etna Road and drive three miles to the campground on the left side of the road.

Trip notes: This camp is just far enough off Highway 96 that it gets missed by zillions of out-of-towners every year. It is set across the road from the lower Salmon River, a pretty, clean, and cold stream that pours out of the surrounding wilderness high country. Swimming is very good in river holes, though the water is cold, especially when nearby Wooley Creek is full of snowmelt pouring out of the Marble Mountains to the north. In the fall, there is good shoreline fishing for steelhead, though the canyon bottom is shaded almost all day and gets very cold.

⑱ Aikens Creek

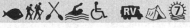

Location: On the Klamath River in Six Rivers National Forest; map A1, grid j1.

Campsites, facilities: There are 10 sites for tents only and 19 sites for RVs up to 35 feet long. Piped water, flush toilets, picnic tables, fire grills, and a sanitary disposal station are provided. Facilities are wheelchair accessible. Leashed pets are permitted.

Reservations, fees: No reservations; $7 per night.

Contact: Six Rivers National Forest, Orleans Ranger District, (530) 627-3291 or fax (530) 627-3401.

Directions: From the junction of US 101 and Highway 299 near Arcata, turn east on Highway 299 and drive to Willow Creek. In Willow Creek, turn north on Highway 96 and drive to Weitchpec, continuing on Highway 96 for five miles to the campground on the right side of the road.

Trip notes: The Klamath River is warm and green here in summer, and this camp provides an ideal put-in spot for a day of easy rafting, especially for newcomers in inflatable kayaks. The camp is set at 340 feet in elevation on Aikens Creek, a feeder stream a short distance from the Klamath. From here to Weitchpec is an easy paddle, with the takeout on the right side of the river just beyond Muddy Creek. The river is set in a beautiful canyon with lots of birds and enters the Hoopa Valley Indian Reservation. The steelhead fishing can be good in this area from August through mid-November, and best downstream at Johnson's Bar from a boat, boondogging Glo Bugs. Highway 96 is a scenic but slow cruise.

Special note: This camp may be closed due to flooding. Check status before planning your trip.

⑲ E-Ne-Nuck

Location: In Six Rivers National Forest; map A1, grid j1.

Campsites, facilities: There are 11 campsites for tents or RVs up to 22 feet long. Piped water, vault toilets, picnic tables, and cast iron, fire box stoves are available. Leashed pets are permitted.

Reservations, fees: No reservations; $8 per night, $5 per additional vehicle. Open July through November 5.

Contact: Six Rivers National Forest, Orleans Ranger District, (530) 627-3291 or fax (530) 627-3401.

Directions: From the junction of US 101 and Highway 299 near Arcata, turn east on Highway 299 and drive to Willow Creek. In Willow Creek, turn north on Highway 96 and drive to Weitchpec, continuing on Highway 96 for about five miles to the campground. E-Ne-Nuck is just beyond Aikens Creek campground.

Trip notes: The campground gets its name from a Karuk Indian chief who lived in the area in the late 1800s. It's a popular spot for fisherman; Bluff Creek and the Klamath are within walking distance and Fish Lake is eight miles to the west. Other attractions are the bald eagles and osprey that can be spotted here.

⓴ Fish Lake

Location: In Six Rivers National Forest; map A1, grid j1.

Campsites, facilities: There are 10 sites for tents and 14 sites for tents or RVs up to 35 feet long. Potable water is available from a common location but is not provided at each site. Vault toilets, picnic tables, and fire grills are provided. Leashed pets are permitted.

Reservations, fees: No reservations; $8 per night. Open May through September.

Contact: Six Rivers National Forest, Orleans Ranger District, (530) 627-3291 or fax (530) 627-3401.

Directions: From Interstate 5 in Redding, turn west on Highway 299 and drive to Willow Creek. At Willow Creek, turn north on Highway 96 and drive to Weitchpec, continuing seven miles north on Highway 96 to Fish Lake Road. Turn left on Fish Lake Road and drive five miles (stay to the right at the Y) to Fish Lake.

Trip notes: This is a pretty little lake that provides good fishing for stocked rainbow trout

from the season opener on Memorial Day weekend through July. The camp gets little pressure in other months. It's located in the heart of Bigfoot country, with numerous Bigfoot sightings occurring near Bluff Creek. No powerboats are permitted on the lake, but it's too small for that anyway, being better suited for a float tube, raft, or pram. The elevation is 1,800 feet. The presence here of Port Orford cedar root disease, spread by spores in the mud, forces closure in the months from October through April.

㉑ The Pines Trailer Park

Location: On the Klamath River; map A1, grid j2.

Campsites, facilities: There are 25 RV sites, all with full hookups, and a separate area for tents. Picnic tables, rest rooms, showers, and a sanitary disposal station are provided. A coin laundry is available. Leashed pets are permitted.

Reservations, fees: Reservations are accepted; $12 per night. Open year-round.

Contact: The Pines Trailer Park, (530) 627-3425.

Directions: From the junction of US 101 and Highway 299 near Arcata, drive east on Highway 299 to Willow Creek. At Willow Creek, turn north on Highway 96, drive past Weitchpec, and continue to Orleans. In Orleans, look for the park entrance on the left side of the road.

Trip notes: This is an option for RV cruisers touring Highway 96, looking for a stopover in Orleans. The steelhead fishing is good in this area in the fall. The campground is located in a wooded setting, across the highway from the Klamath River.

㉒ Sivshaneen

Location: On the Klamath River; map A1, grid j1.

Campsites, facilities: There are 25 RV sites, all with full hookups. Rest rooms, showers, a coin laundry, and sanitary disposal station are available. Leashed pets are permitted.

Reservations, fees: Reservations are accepted; $12 per night. Open Memorial Day through October.

Contact: Sivshaneen, (530) 627-3354.

Directions: From the junction of US 101 and Highway 299 near Arcata, drive east on Highway 299 to Willow Creek. At Willow Creek, turn north on Highway 96, drive past Weitchpec, and continue to Orleans. In Orleans, turn south on Red Cap Road and drive 1.5 miles to the campground.

Trip notes: This makes a good base camp for a Klamath River fishing trip from August to December. That is when the steelhead and the "half-pounders," actually juvenile steelhead in the 12- to 16-inch class, arrive in huge numbers in this stretch of river. In the summer, the river is warm, with a good put-in spot for rafters available nearby.

㉓ Klamath Riverside RV Park and Camp

Location: On the Klamath River; map A1, grid j1.

Campsites, facilities: There are 48 RV sites with full hookups and a separate area for tents. Picnic tables, rest rooms, showers, and a small store are provided. A coin laundry is available. Horseback riding, river rafting services, and seasonal drift boat fishing are available within nine miles. Leashed pets are permitted.

Reservations, fees: Reservations are accepted; phone (800) 627-9779; $9 to $19 per night. Open year-round.

Contact: Klamath Riverside RV Park and Camp, (530) 627-3239 or fax (530) 627-3755; email: klamathrv@aol.com.

Directions: From the junction of US 101 and Highway 299 near Arcata, drive east on Highway 299 to Willow Creek, turn north on Highway 96, and drive past Weitchpec to Orleans. This campground is located at the west end of the town of Orleans on Highway 96.

Trip notes: Klamath Riverside RV Park and Camp is an option for RV cruisers touring Highway 96 and looking for a place in Orleans to tie up the horse for the night. The camp has large grassy sites set amid pine trees, right on the

river. There are spectacular views of Mount Orleans and the surrounding hills.

㉔ Pearch Creek

Location: On the Klamath River in Six Rivers National Forest; map A1, grid j2.

Campsites, facilities: There are nine sites for tents and two sites for tents or RVs up to 22 feet long. Piped water, vault toilets, picnic tables, and fire grills are provided. A grocery store, coin laundry, and propane gas are available within one mile. Leashed pets are permitted.

Reservations, fees: No reservations; $8 per night. Open year-round.

Contact: Six Rivers National Forest, Orleans Ranger District, (530) 627-3291 or fax (530) 627-3401.

Directions: From Interstate 5 in Redding, turn west on Highway 299 and drive to Willow Creek. In Willow Creek, turn north on Highway 96, drive past Weitchpec, and continue to Orleans. In Orleans, continue for one mile and look for the campground entrance on the right side of the road.

Trip notes: This is one of the premium Forest Service camps on the Klamath River because of its easy access from the highway and easy access to the river. The camp is set on Pearch Creek, about a quarter mile from the Klamath at a deep bend in the river. It is open year-round and has fish smokers available, which is either a sign of optimism or a true indication of how good the fishing can be. Indeed, the fishing is excellent for 1- to 5-pound steelhead from August through November. The elevation is 400 feet.

㉕ Idlewild

Location: On the North Fork of the Salmon River in Klamath National Forest; map A1, grid j7.

Campsites, facilities: There are 23 sites, including two group sites, for tents or RVs up to 22 feet long. Piped water, vault toilets, fire grills, and picnic tables are provided. Leashed pets are permitted.

Reservations, fees: No reservations; $6 per night. Open June through October.

Contact: Klamath National Forest, Salmon River Ranger District, (530) 467-5757 or fax (530) 468-1290.

Directions: From Redding, drive north on Interstate 5 to Yreka. In Yreka, turn southwest on Highway 3 and drive to Etna. In Etna, turn west on Etna–Somes Bar Road (Main Street in town) and drive about 16 miles to the campground on the right side of the road. Note: A shorter but more complete route on Gazelle-Callahan Road, north of Weed, is also available.

Trip notes: This is one of the prettiest drive-to camps in the region, set near the confluence of the Salmon River and its south fork, a beautiful, cold, clear stream and a major tributary to the Klamath River. Most campers are using the camp for its nearby trailhead (two miles north on a dirt Forest Service road out of camp). The hike here is routed to the north, climbing alongside the Salmon River for miles into the Marble Mountain Wilderness (wilderness permits are required). It's a rugged 10-mile, all-day climb to Lake of the Island with several other lakes (highlighted by Hancock Lake) to the nearby west, accessible on weeklong trips.

Map A2

One inch equals approximately 10.7 miles.

See inside back cover for California state map.

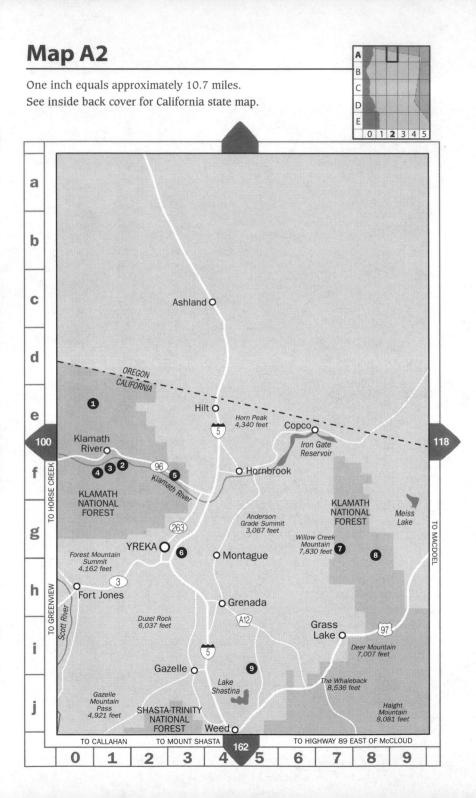

TO HORSE CREEK

TO GREENVIEW

100

118

162

a

b

c
Ashland ○

d
OREGON
CALIFORNIA

e
❶
Hilt ○
Horn Peak
4,340 feet
Copco ○
Iron Gate
Reservoir

Klamath
River ○

f
❹ ❸ ❷
96
❺
Klamath River
Hornbrook ○
KLAMATH
NATIONAL
FOREST
KLAMATH
NATIONAL
FOREST
Meiss
Lake

g
263
YREKA ○ ❻
Montague ○
Anderson
Grade Summit
3,067 feet
Willow Creek
Mountain
7,830 feet ❼
❽
Forest Mountain
Summit
4,162 feet

TO MACDOEL

h
3
Fort Jones ○
Grenada ○
Scott River

i
Duzel Rock
6,037 feet
A12
Grass
Lake ○
97
Deer Mountain
7,007 feet
5

j
Gazelle ○
❾
Lake
Shastina
The Whaleback
8,536 feet
Gazelle
Mountain
Pass
4,921 feet
SHASTA-TRINITY
NATIONAL
FOREST
Weed ○
Haight
Mountain
8,081 feet

TO CALLAHAN   TO MOUNT SHASTA   TO HIGHWAY 89 EAST OF McCLOUD

0   1   2   3   4   5   6   7   8   9

Chapter A2 features:

① Beaver Creek

Location: In Klamath National Forest; map A2, grid e1.

Campsites, facilities: There are eight sites for tents or small RVs. Piped water, vault toilets, picnic tables, and fire grills are provided. Leashed pets are permitted.

Reservations, fees: No reservations; no fee.

Contact: Klamath National Forest, Scott River Ranger District, (530) 468-5351 or fax (530) 468-5654.

Directions: From Redding, drive north on Interstate 5 to Highway 96. Turn west on Highway 96 and drive approximately 15 miles (if you reach the town of Klamath River, you have gone a half mile too far) to Beaver Creek Road. Turn right on Beaver Creek Road/Forest Service Road 11 and drive four miles to the campground.

Trip notes: This camp is set along Beaver Creek, a feeder stream to the nearby Klamath River, with two small creeks entering Beaver Creek on the far side of the river near the campground. It is quiet and pretty. There are several historic mining sites in the area; you'll need a map of Klamath National Forest (available for $4 at the district office) in order to find them. In the fall, this campground is usually taken by deer hunters.

② Klamath River Trailer Park

Location: On the Klamath River; map A2, grid f1.

Campsites, facilities: There are 17 RV sites with full hookups. Rest rooms, hot showers, and a coin laundry are provided. Leashed pets are permitted.

Reservations, fees: Reservations are accepted; $10 per night. Open year-round.

Contact: Klamath River Trailer Park, (530) 465-2324.

Directions: From Redding, drive north on Interstate 5 to Highway 96. Turn west on Highway 96 and drive approximately 15 miles (if you reach the town of Klamath River, you have gone a mile too far) to the campground entrance.

Trip notes: This privately operated RV park is located in one of the prettiest areas of the Klamath River. There's a good piece of river here for summer rafting or fall steelhead fishing. For rafting, the river is sprinkled with Class II and III rapids, ideal for inflatable kayaks, and several commercial rafting companies operate in this area. Every site has a view of the river and the beautiful Siskiyou Mountains.

③ Quigley's General Store and Trailer Park

Location: On the Klamath River; map A2, grid f1.

Campsites, facilities: There are 20 RV sites with full hookups. Tables, rest rooms, and hot showers are provided. A store and coin laundry are available. Leashed pets are permitted.

Reservations, fees: Reservations are accepted; $15 per night. Open year-round.

Contact: Quigley's General Store and Trailer Park, (530) 465-2224 or fax (530) 465-2422.

Directions: From Redding, drive north on Interstate 5 to Highway 96. Turn west on Highway 96 and drive approximately 15 miles to the town of Klamath River. Look for the campground entrance along the road.

Trip notes: This year-round, privately operated park is set along the Klamath River. Many of the parking sites have clear views of the river, as well as good mountain views. Quigley's General Store is well stocked for such a remote little shop, and you can usually get reliable fishing information here, too.

❹ The Oaks RV Park

Location: On the Klamath River; map A2, grid f1.

Campsites, facilities: There are 10 sites for tents and 12 sites for RVs. Picnic tables, fire grills, rest rooms, hot showers, snack bar, and coin laundry are available. A restaurant and lounge are available within walking distance. Groceries can be obtained within three miles in the town of Klamath River. Leashed pets are permitted.

Reservations, fees: Reservations are accepted; $10 to $12 per night.

Contact: The Oaks RV Park, (530) 465-2323.

Directions: From Redding, drive north on Interstate 5 to Highway 96. Turn west on Highway 96 and drive approximately 15 miles to the town of Klamath River. Look for the park entrance across from the town post office.

Trip notes: Fishing? Rafting? Canoeing? Hiking? This camp provides a good headquarters for all of these adventures. This stretch of the Klamath is ideal for boating, with summer flows warm and often at perfect levels for rafting and canoeing. Fishing is best in the fall, when salmon, and later steelhead, migrate through the area.

❺ Tree of Heaven

Location: In Klamath National Forest; map A2, grid f3.

Campsites, facilities: There are 10 tent sites and 11 sites for moderate-sized RVs. Piped water, vault toilets, picnic tables, and fire grills are provided. A boat ramp is available. Leashed pets are permitted.

Reservations, fees: No reservations; $8 per night.

Contact: Klamath National Forest, Scott River

Ranger District, (530) 468-5351 or fax (530) 468-5654.

Directions: From Redding, drive north on Interstate 5 to Highway 96. Turn west on Highway 96 and drive seven miles to the campground entrance on the left side of the road.

Trip notes: This is an outstanding riverside campground that provides excellent access to the Klamath River for fishing, rafting, and hiking. The best deal is to put in your raft, canoe, or drift boat upstream at the ramp below Iron Gate Reservoir, then make the all-day run down to the takeout at Tree of Heaven. This section of river is an easy paddle and also provides excellent steelhead fishing in the winter. There is also a trail out of the camp that is routed along the river and probes through vegetation, ending at a fair fishing spot (a better spot is nearby at the mouth of the Shasta River). On the drive in from the highway, you can watch the landscape turn from high chaparral to forest.

❻ Waiiaka Trailer Haven

Location: Near Yreka; map A2, grid g3.

Campsites, facilities: There are 60 RV sites with full hookups. Rest rooms, showers, playground, and a recreation room are provided. A coin laundry and propane gas are available. Leashed pets are permitted.

Reservations, fees: Reservations are accepted; $22 per night. Open year-round.

Contact: Waiiaka Trailer Haven, (530) 842-4500.

Directions: From Redding, drive north on Interstate 5 to Yreka, take the Fort Jones exit, and drive one block east to Fairlane Road. At Fairlane Road, turn north and drive to Sharps Road. At Sharps Road, turn east and drive one block to the RV park, which is just past the fairgrounds parking lot.

Trip notes: If it's late, you're tired, and you're hunting for a spot to hunker down for the night, this is your only bet in the immediate Yreka vicinity. A string of fast-food restaurants is available nearby on the west side of the highway. The campground is not exactly paradise, but the view of Mount Shasta to the south is beautiful. The best side trip is heading north on Interstate 5 to the Klamath River; an exit with river access is available at the Interstate 5 bridge.

❼ Martins Dairy

Location: On the Little Shasta River in Klamath National Forest; map A2, grid g7.

Campsites, facilities: There are eight sites for tents or small RVs and a horse camp site. Piped water, vault toilets, picnic tables, and fire grills are provided. Leashed pets are permitted.

Reservations, fees: No reservations; $6 per night.

Contact: Klamath National Forest, Goosenest Ranger District, (530) 398-4391 or fax (530) 398-4599.

Directions: From Redding, drive north on Interstate 5 to Weed. In Weed, turn north on US 97 and drive to Grass Lake. Continue about seven miles to Forest Service Road 70/46N10 (if you reach Hebron Summit, you have driven about a mile too far). Turn left, drive about 10 miles to a Y, take the left fork, and drive three miles (including a very sharp right turn) to the campground on the right side of the road. A map of Klamath National Forest is advised.

Trip notes: This camp is set at 6,000 feet, where the deer get big and the country seems wide open. A large meadow is nearby, located directly across the road from this remote camp, with fantastic wildflower displays in late spring. This is one of the prettiest camps around in the fall, with dramatic color from aspens and other hardwoods. It also makes a good base camp for hunters in the fall. Before heading into the surrounding backcountry, obtain a map of Klamath National Forest, available for $3 at the Goosenest Ranger Station on Highway 97, on your way in to camp.

❽ Juanita Lake

Location: In Klamath National Forest; map A2, grid g8.

Campsites, facilities: There are 12 tent sites, 11 sites for RVs up to 32 feet, and a group site that can accommodate 50 people. Piped water, vault toilets, picnic tables, and fire grills are provided. Boating is allowed, but no motorboats are permitted on the lake. This lake is wheelchair accessible. Leashed pets are permitted.

Reservations, fees: No reservations; $8 per night, group site is $15 per night. Open May through October.

Contact: Klamath National Forest, Goosenest Ranger District, (530) 398-4391 or fax (530) 398-4599.

Directions: From Redding, drive north on Interstate 5 to Weed. In Weed, turn north on US 97 and drive approximately 37 miles. Turn left on Ball Mountain Road and drive 2.5 miles, veer right at the fork, and continue to the campground entrance at the lake.

Trip notes: Small and relatively little known, this camp is set along the shore of Juanita Lake at 5,100 feet. It is stocked with rainbow trout and brown trout, but a problem with golden shiners has cut into the lake's fishing productivity. It's a small lake and forested, set near the Butte Valley Wildlife Area in the plateau country just five miles to the northeast. The latter provides an opportunity to see waterfowl and, in the winter, bald eagles. Campers will discover a network of Forest Service roads in the area, providing an opportunity for mountain biking. There is also a paved trail around the lake that is wheelchair accessible and spans approximately 1.25 miles.

❾ Lake Shastina

Location: Near Klamath National Forest and Weed; map A2, grid i5.

Campsites, facilities: There is a small primitive area designated for camping. There is no piped water. A chemical toilet and boat launch are available. Supplies can be obtained five miles away in Weed. Leashed pets are permitted.

Reservations, fees: No reservations; no fee.

Contact: Siskiyou County Public Works, (530) 842-8250.

Directions: From Redding, drive north on Interstate 5 to Weed. In Weed, turn north on US 97 and drive about five miles to Big Springs Road.

Turn left (west) on Big Springs Road and drive about one mile to Jackson Ranch Road. Turn left (west) on Jackson Ranch Road and drive a half mile to an unpaved access road (watch for the signed turnoff). Turn left and drive to the campground.

Trip notes: Lake Shastina is set at the northern foot of Mount Shasta, offering spectacular views, good swimming on hot summer days, and a chance at crappie and trout fishing. One reason the views of Mount Shasta are so good is that this is largely high sagebrush country with few trees. As such, it can get very dusty, windy, and in the winter, nasty cold. When the lake is full and the weather is good, there are few complaints. This is one of the few lakes in Northern California that has property with lakeside housing, consisting of several small developments. Alas, the water slide, once offering great fun for kids, is now off-limits to the public.

Map A3

One inch equals approximately 10.7 miles.
See inside back cover for California state map.

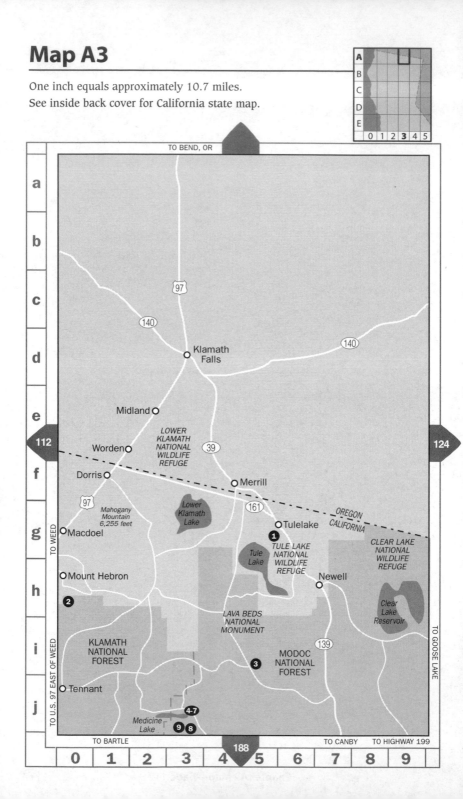

Chapter A3 features:

① Shady Lane Trailer Park

Location: In Tulelake; map A3, grid g5.

Campsites, facilities: There are 60 RV sites with full hookups. Rest rooms, showers, and patios are provided. A coin laundry is available. Leashed pets are permitted.

Reservations, fees: Reservations are accepted; $15 per night.

Contact: Shady Lane Trailer Park, 795 Modoc Avenue, PO Box 297, Tulelake, CA 96134; (530) 667-2617.

Directions: From Redding, turn east on Highway 299 and drive to the junction with Highway 139 at Canby. At Highway 139 turn north and drive 52 miles to Tulelake. At Tulelake take the south exit of East West Road, drive to Modoc Avenue, turn left, and drive to the trailer park.

Trip notes: There isn't much shade in Modoc County, but this private park manages to provide some. Good side trips include the Tulelake Game Refuge, one of the best places in America (during the winter months) to see bald eagles and a good bet year-round for bird-watching. Nearby is Lava Beds National Monument, whose northern edge is an excellent place to see deer in late fall and early winter.

② Shafter

Location: In Klamath National Forest; map A3, grid h0.

Campsites, facilities: There are 14 sites for tents or small RVs. Piped water, vault toilets, picnic tables, and fire grills are provided. Pack out your own garbage. Pets must be controlled.

Reservations, fees: No reservations; $4 per night.

Contact: Klamath National Forest, Goosenest Ranger District, (530) 398-4391 or fax (530) 398-4599.

Directions: From Redding, drive north on Interstate 5 to Weed, turn north on Highway 97, and drive 40 miles to Ball Mountain Road. At Ball Mountain Road, turn right and drive two miles to where the road dead-ends at an unnamed road. Turn right and drive seven miles (crossing railroad tracks after a quarter mile) to the campground on the right side of the road.

Trip notes: This is a little-used camp with trout fishing at nearby Butte Creek for small rainbows, primarily six- to eight-inchers. Little Orr Lake, located about a 10-minute drive away on the southwest flank of Orr Mountain, provides fishing for larger rainbow trout, 10- to 12-inchers, as well as a sprinkling of smaller brook trout. This camp is primitive and not well known, set in a juniper- and sage-filled landscape. A great side trip is to the nearby Orr Mountain Lookout, where there are spectacular views of Mount Shasta.

③ Indian Well

Location: In Lava Beds National Monument; map A3, grid i5.

Campsites, facilities: There are 40 sites for tents, pickup campers, or small trailers. Picnic tables, fire rings, and cooking grills are provided. From Memorial Day to Labor Day, water and flush toilets are available. During the winter, the water is turned off and only pit toilets are available. However, water and flush toilets are always available at the visitor center. The town of Tulelake (30 miles north) is the nearest supply station. Leashed pets are permitted.

Reservations, fees: No reservations; $6 per night in winter, $10 in summer.

Contact: Lava Beds National Monument, (530) 667-2282 or fax (530) 667-2737.

Directions: From Redding, drive east on Highway 299 to Canby and the junction with Highway 139. Turn left and drive about 30 miles to Forest Service Road 97 on the left (signed Lava Beds National Monument). Turn left and drive three miles to Forest Service Road 10. Bear right and drive 15 miles to the visitor center and the campground entrance road on the right. Turn right and drive a quarter mile to the campground.

Trip notes: This is a one-in-a-million spot with 20 lava tube caves, a cinder cone (climbable), Mammoth Crater, Native American pictographs, and wildlife overlooks at Tule Lake. After winter's first snow, this is one of the best places in the west to photograph deer. Nearby Klamath National Wildlife Refuge is the largest bald eagle wintering area in the lower 48. If you are new to the outdoors, an interpretive center is available to explain it all to you.

❹ Medicine Lake

Location: On Medicine Lake in Modoc National Forest; map A3, grid j3.

Campsites, facilities: There are 22 sites for tents or RVs up to 22 feet long. Piped water, vault toilets, picnic tables, and fire grills are provided. A boat ramp is available nearby. Supplies can be obtained in Bartle. Leashed pets are permitted.

Reservations, fees: No reservations; $7 per vehicle per night. Open late May through early October, weather permitting.

Contact: Modoc National Forest, Tule Lake Ranger District, (530) 667-2246 or fax (530) 667-4808.

Directions: From Redding, drive north on Interstate 5 past Dunsmuir to Highway 89. Go east on Highway 89 and drive 28 miles to Bartle. Just past Bartle, turn left on Forest Service Road 49 and drive 31 miles (it becomes Medicine Lake Road) to the lake. From Bartle, the route is signed.

Trip notes: Lakeside campsites tucked away in conifers make this camp a winner. Medicine Lake was formed in the crater of an old volcano and is surrounded by sugar pine and fir trees. The lake is stocked with rainbow and brook trout in the summer, gets quite cold in the fall, and freezes over in winter. Many side trips are possible, including nearby Blanche Lake and Ice Caves (both signed and off the access road) and Lava Beds National Monument just 15 miles north. At 6,700 feet, temperatures can turn cold in summer and the season is short.

❺ A. H. Hogue

Location: On Medicine Lake in Modoc National Forest; map A3, grid j3.

Campsites, facilities: There are 24 sites for tents or RVs. Picnic tables, fire grills, piped water, and vault toilets are provided. A boat ramp is available nearby. Supplies can be obtained in Bartle. Leashed pets are permitted.

Reservations, fees: No reservations; $7 per vehicle per night.

Contact: Modoc National Forest, Tule Lake Ranger District, (530) 667-2246 or fax (530) 667-4808.

Directions: From Redding, drive north on Interstate 5 past Dunsmuir to Highway 89. Turn east on Highway 89 and drive 28 miles to Bartle. Just past Bartle, turn left on Forest Service Road 49 and drive 31 miles (it becomes Medicine Lake Road) to the lake. From Bartle, the route is signed.

Trip notes: This camp was created in 1990 when the original Medicine Lake Campground was divided in half. For more information, see the trip notes for Medicine Lake (campground number four).

❻ Hemlock

Location: On Medicine Lake in Modoc National Forest; map A3, grid j3.

Campsites, facilities: There are 19 sites for tents or RVs up to 22 feet long. Piped water, vault toilets, picnic tables, and fire grills are provided. A boat ramp is available nearby. Supplies can be obtained in Bartle. Leashed pets are permitted.

Reservations, fees: No reservations; $7 per vehicle per night.

Contact: Modoc National Forest, Tule Lake Ranger District, (530) 667-2246 of fax (530) 667-4808.

Directions: From Redding, drive north on Interstate 5 past Dunsmuir to Highway 89. Turn east on Highway 89 and drive 28 miles to Bartle. Just past Bartle, turn left on Forest Service Road 49 and drive 31 miles (it becomes Medicine Lake Road) to the lake. From Bartle, the route is signed.

Trip notes: This is one in a series of campgrounds on Medicine Lake operated by the Forest Service. A special attraction at Hemlock is the natural sand beach. For more information, see the trip notes for Medicine Lake (campground number four).

➐ Headquarters

Location: On Medicine Lake in Modoc National Forest; map A3, grid j3.

Campsites, facilities: There are 10 sites for tents and RVs. Piped water, vault toilets, picnic tables, and fire grills are provided. A boat ramp is available nearby. Supplies can be obtained in Bartle. Leashed pets are permitted.

Reservations, fees: No reservations; $7 per vehicle per night.

Contact: Modoc National Forest, Tule Lake Ranger District, (530) 667-2246 or fax (530) 667-4808.

Directions: From Redding, drive north on Interstate 5 past Dunsmuir to Highway 89. Go east on Highway 89 and drive 28 miles to Bartle. Just past Bartle, turn left on Forest Service Road 49 and drive 31 miles (it becomes Medicine Lake Road) to the lake. From Bartle, the route is signed.

Trip notes: This is one of four campgrounds set beside Medicine Lake. For more information, see the trip notes for Medicine Lake (campground number four).

➑ Bullseye Lake

Location: Near Medicine Lake in Modoc National Forest; map A3, grid j3.

Campsites, facilities: There are a few primitive campsites, but no piped water or other facilities are available. Supplies are available in McCloud; limited supplies can be obtained at the Bartle Lodge. Leashed pets are permitted.

Reservations, fees: No reservations; no fee.

Contact: Modoc National Forest, Tule Lake Ranger District, (530) 667-2246 or fax (530) 667-4808.

Directions: From Redding, drive north on Interstate 5 past Dunsmuir to Highway 89. Go east on Highway 89 and drive 28 miles to Bartle. Just past Bartle, turn left on Forest Service Road 49 and drive 30 miles (if you reach Medicine Lake, you have gone about two miles too far). Turn right at the Bullseye Lake access road and drive a short distance to the lake.

Trip notes: This tiny lake gets overlooked every year, mainly because of its proximity to nearby Medicine Lake. Bullseye Lake is shallow, but because snow keeps it locked up until late May or early June, the water stays plenty cold for small trout through July. It is stocked with just 750 six- to eight-inch rainbow trout, not much to crow about—or to catch, for that matter. Nearby are some ice caves, created by ancient volcanic action, which are fun to poke around in and explore. The place is small, quiet, and pretty, but most of all, small.

➒ Payne Springs

Location: Near Medicine Lake in Modoc National Forest; map A3, grid j3.

Campsites, facilities: There are a few, dispersed and primitive campsites. There is no piped water, but a vault toilet is available. Supplies are available in McCloud. Leashed pets are permitted.

Reservations, fees: No reservation; no fee. Open year-round, but inaccessible in some winter months.

Contact: Modoc National Forest, Doublehead Ranger District, (530) 667-2246 or fax (530) 667-4808.

Directions: From Redding, on Interstate 5 drive past Dunsmuir to Highway 89. Turn east on Highway 89 and drive 28 miles. Just past Bartle, turn left on Forest Service Road 49 and drive 30 miles. A quarter mile past the Bullseye Lake access road, turn left onto the Payne Springs access road. (If you reach Medicine Lake, you have gone too far.)

Trip notes: This camp is set by a small spring, (a natural reservoir) in a very pretty riparian area. It's small, but it is special.

Map A4

One inch equals approximately 10.7 miles.
See inside back cover for California state map.

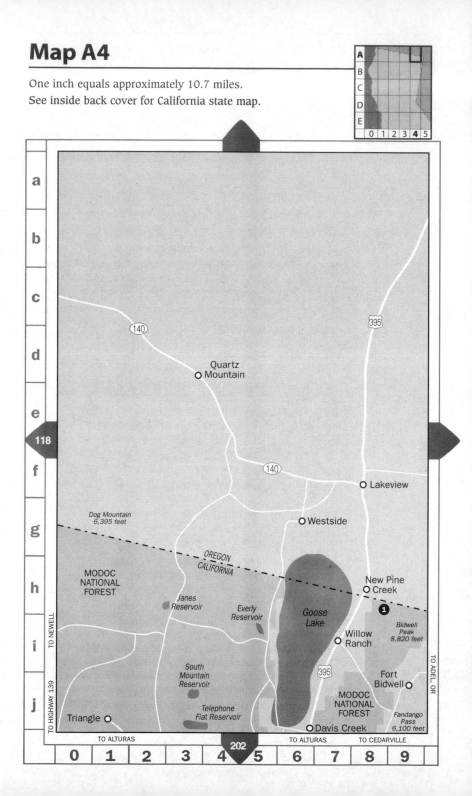

Chapter A4 features:

1 Cave Lake

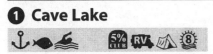

Location: In Modoc National Forest; map A4, grid h8.

Campsites, facilities: There are six sites for tents or RVs up to 15 feet long; trailers are not advised due to the steep access road. Piped water, vault toilets, fire grills, and picnic tables are provided. A boat ramp is available for small boats, but all motors are prohibited on the lake, including electric. Supplies are available in New Pine Creek, Fort Bidwell, and Davis Creek. Leashed pets are permitted.

Reservations, fees: No reservations; no fee. Open July through September.

Contact: Modoc National Forest, Warner Mountain Ranger District, PO Box 220, Cedarville, CA 96104; (530) 279-6116 or fax (530) 279-6107.

Directions: From Redding, turn east on Highway 299 and drive 146 miles to Alturas. In Alturas, turn north on US 395 and drive 40 miles to Forest Service Road 2 (if you reach the town of New Pine Creek on the Oregon/California border, you have driven a mile too far). Turn right on Forest Service Road 2 (a steep dirt road—trailers are not recommended) and drive six miles to the campground entrance on the left side of the road, just beyond the Lily Lake picnic area.

Trip notes: A pair of lakes can be discovered out here in the middle of nowhere, with Cave Lake on one end and Lily Lake on the other. Together they make a nice set, very quiet, extremely remote, with good fishing for rainbow trout and brook trout. Of the two lakes, it is nearby Lily Lake that is prettier and provides the better fishing. Cave Lake is set at 6,600 feet. By camping here, you become a member of the 5 Percent Club; that is, the five percent of campers who know of secret, isolated little spots such as this one.

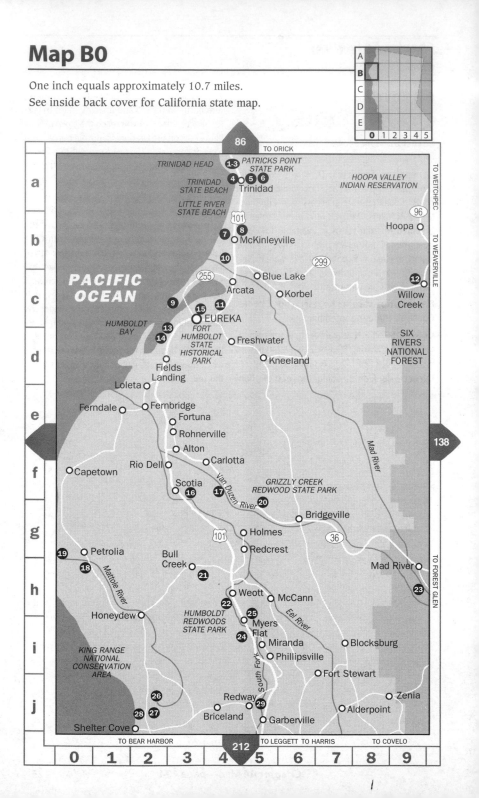

Map B0

One inch equals approximately 10.7 miles.
See inside back cover for California state map.

TO ORICK

86

PACIFIC OCEAN

TRINIDAD HEAD
PATRICKS POINT STATE PARK
1-3
TRINIDAD STATE BEACH
4 5 6
Trinidad
LITTLE RIVER STATE BEACH

HOOPA VALLEY INDIAN RESERVATION

101

7 8 McKinleyville

10

255
Blue Lake

Arcata
Korbel

96
Hoopa

299

12
Willow Creek

9 15 11
EUREKA
FORT HUMBOLDT STATE HISTORICAL PARK
13
14
Freshwater

HUMBOLDT BAY
Kneeland

SIX RIVERS NATIONAL FOREST

Fields Landing

Loleta

Ferndale Fernbridge
Fortuna
Rohnerville
Alton
Rio Dell Carlotta
Scotia
16 17

Capetown

GRIZZLY CREEK REDWOOD STATE PARK
20
Bridgeville

Mad River

101
Holmes
Redcrest

36

19 Petrolia
18
Bull Creek
21

Mad River
23

Mattole River

Weott
McCann
22
25
Myers Flat
24
Miranda
Blocksburg
Honeydew

HUMBOLDT REDWOODS STATE PARK

Eel River

Phillipsville
Fort Stewart

KING RANGE NATIONAL CONSERVATION AREA

South Fork

26
Redway
29
Zenia

28 27
Briceland
Garberville
Alderpoint

Shelter Cove

Van Duzen River

138

TO WEITCHPEC
TO WEAVERVILLE
TO FOREST GLEN
TO BEAR HARBOR TO LEGGETT TO HARRIS TO COVELO

212

0 1 2 3 4 5 6 7 8 9

A B C D E
0 1 2 3 4 5

1

Chapter BØ features:

❶ Sounds of the Sea

Location: In Trinidad; map BØ, grid a4.

Campsites, facilities: There are 52 RV sites with full hookups. Picnic tables, fire rings, rest rooms, showers, and a sanitary disposal station are provided. RV storage, a coin laundry, grocery store, gift shop, cable TV, and ice are available. The facilities are wheelchair accessible. Leashed pets are permitted.

Reservations, fees: Reservations are accepted; $21 per night.

Contact: Sounds of the Sea, (707) 677-3271.

Directions: From Eureka, drive north on US 101 to Trinidad. In Trinidad, continue north on US 101 for 2.5 miles to the Patricks Point exit. Take the Patricks Point exit, turn left, and drive a half mile to the campground.

Trip notes: The Trinidad area, located about 20 miles north of Eureka, is one of the great places on this planet. Nearby Patricks Point State Park is one of the highlights, with a Sitka spruce forest, beautiful coastal lookouts, a great easy hike on the Rim Trail, and access to several se-

cluded beaches. To the nearby south at Trinidad Head is a small harbor and dock, with deep-sea and salmon fishing trips available. A breezy beach is located to the immediate north of the Seascape Restaurant. A bonus at this privately operated RV park is good berry picking.

❷ Sylvan Harbor RV Park and Cabins

Location: In Trinidad; map BØ, grid a4.

Campsites, facilities: There are 73 RV sites with full hookups and three cabins for rent. Rest rooms, showers, and a sanitary disposal station are provided. A coin laundry and LP gas are available. Leashed pets are permitted.

Reservations, fees: No reservations except for cabins; $12 to $15 per night for RV sites; call for cabin fees. Open year-round.

Contact: Sylvan Harbor RV Park and Cabins, (707) 677-9988.

Directions: From Eureka, drive north on US 101 to Trinidad. Take the Trinidad exit, turn left at the stop sign, and drive a short distance under the freeway to Patricks Point Drive. Turn right and drive one mile to the campground.

Trip notes: This is one of several privately operated parks in the Trinidad area, offering a choice of shaded or open sites near the ocean. For more information about recreation options nearby, see the trip notes for Sounds of the Sea (campground number one).

❸ View Crest Campground

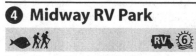

Location: In Trinidad; map B0, grid a4.

Campsites, facilities: There are 25 RV sites (nine drive-through) with full hookups, and a separate area for tents. Picnic tables, fire rings, rest rooms, showers, playground, and a sanitary disposal station are provided. Cable TV, RV storage, a coin laundry, and wood are available. Leashed pets are permitted.

Reservations, fees: Reservations are accepted; $14 to $20 per night.

Contact: View Crest Campground, (707) 677-3393 or fax (707) 677-9363.

Directions: From Eureka, drive 40 miles north on US 101 to Trinidad. At the Trinidad exit, turn left at the stop sign on Seawood Drive and drive a short distance under the freeway to Patricks Point Drive. Turn right on Patricks Point Drive and drive two miles to the campground on the right.

Trip notes: View Crest Campground is one of the premium spots in Trinidad, with pretty cottages available as well as campsites for RVs and tenters. A bonus here is the remarkable flights of swallows, many of which have nests at the cottages. Recreation options include deep-sea and salmon fishing at Trinidad Harbor to the nearby south, and outstanding easy hiking at Patricks Point State Park to the nearby north.

❹ Midway RV Park

Location: In Trinidad; map B0, grid a4.

Campsites, facilities: There are 65 RV sites with full hookups. Picnic tables, restrooms, showers, cable TV, club room, and a playground are provided. RV storage is available. Leashed pets are permitted.

Reservations, fees: Reservations are recommended in the summer; $16 to $20 per night.

Contact: Midway RV Park, (707) 677-3934.

Directions: From Eureka, drive north on US 101 to Trinidad. Take the Trinidad exit, turn left at the stop sign, and drive a short distance under the freeway to Patricks Point Drive. Turn right on Patricks Point Drive and drive a half mile to the campground.

Trip notes: This is one of several privately developed campgrounds in Trinidad. In the summer, salmon fishing can be excellent just off Trinidad Head. In the fall, rockfishing is the way to go, and in winter, crabbing is tops. Patricks Point State Park provides a nearby side trip option to the north.

❺ Hidden Creek

Location: In Trinidad; map B0, grid a5.

Campsites, facilities: There are 56 RV sites (six drive-through) with full or partial hookups, and four tent sites. Several group sites are also available. Picnic tables, patios, rest rooms, showers, LP gas, and a sanitary disposal station are available. Leashed pets are permitted.

Reservations, fees: Reservations are recommended in the summer; $12 to $19 per night.

Contact: Hidden Creek, (707) 677-3775 or fax (707) 677-3886.

Directions: From Eureka, drive north on US 101 to Trinidad. Take the Trinidad exit, turn left at the stop sign, drive under the freeway, and continue on Main Street to 199 North Westhaven.

Trip notes: To tell you the truth, there really isn't much hidden about this RV park, but you might be hard-pressed to find year-round Parker Creek. Regardless, it is still in a very pretty location in Trinidad, with the Trinidad pier, adjacent harbor, restaurants, and beach all within a drive of just a minute or two. Some of California's best deep-sea fishing for salmon, lingcod, and rockfish is available on boats out of Trinidad Harbor, and there are annual lingcod and halibut derbies. Crab and albacore tuna are also caught here, and there's beachcombing for agates and driftwood on the beach to the immediate north.

⑥ Emerald Forest

Location: In Trinidad; map BØ, grid a5.

Campsites, facilities: There are 107 sites for tents or RVs (two drive-through), some with full or partial hookups. There are also 15 cabins with kitchens. Picnic tables, fire rings, barbecues, rest rooms, showers, free cable TV in RV and tent sites, and a playground are provided. A mini-mart, ice, wood, meeting hall with kitchen and fireplace (seats about 40), and LP gas are available. Leashed pets are permitted, except in the tent sites.

Reservations, fees: Reservations are recommended in the summer; $17 to $22 per night, $1 pet fee; call for cabin fees.

Contact: Emerald Forest, (707) 677-3554 or fax (707) 677-0963.

Directions: From Eureka, drive north on US 101 to Trinidad. Take the Trinidad exit, turn left at the stop sign, and drive a short distance under the freeway to Patricks Point Drive. Turn right on Patricks Point Drive and drive about two miles north to the campground on the right side of the road.

Trip notes: This campground is set on nine acres of redwoods, often dark and wet, with the ocean at Trinidad Head only about a five-minute drive away. This campground has new owners, a new name, and a new commitment to ensuring a welcoming experience for visitors.

⑦ Clam Beach County Park

Location: Near McKinleyville; map BØ, grid b4.

Campsites, facilities: There are 50 sites for tents and RVs. Piped water and vault toilets are provided. Propane gas, grocery store, and a coin laundry are in McKinleyville. Pets are permitted.

Reservations, fees: No reservations; $8 per night.

Contact: Clam Beach County Park, (707) 445-7652.

Directions: From Eureka, drive north on US 101 to McKinleyville. Just past McKinleyville, turn west at the sign for Clam Beach and drive two blocks to the campground, which is adjacent to Little River State Beach.

Trip notes: Here awaits a beach that seems to stretch on forever, one of the great places to bring a lover, dog, children, or, hey, all three. While the campsites are a bit exposed, making winds out of the north a problem in the spring, the direct beach access largely makes up for it. The park gets its name from the good clamming that is available, but you must come equipped with a clam gun or special clam shovel, and then be out when minus low tides arrive at daybreak. Most people just enjoy playing tag with the waves, taking long romantic walks, or throwing sticks for the dog.

⑧ Widow White Creek RV Park

Location: In McKinleyville; map BØ, grid b5.

Campsites, facilities: There are 40 RV sites with full hookups and a separate area for tents. Picnic tables, rest rooms, showers, playground, and a sanitary disposal station are provided. A coin laundry is available. The facilities are wheelchair accessible. Leashed pets are permitted.

Reservations, fees: Reservations are accepted; $12.50 to $18 per night.

Contact: Widow White Creek RV Park, (707) 839-1137; website: www.campgrounds.com/widowwhite.

Directions: From Eureka, drive north on US 101 and continue for 4.5 miles past the junction with Highway 299 to the Murray Road exit. Take the exit, head east on Murray Road, and drive one-half block to the campground.

Trip notes: This privately operated park provides extremely easy access from the highway. Nearby recreation options include the Mad River, where there is a nice picnic site near the hatchery, productive steelhead fishing in the winter, and good perch fishing in the surf where the Mad River enters the ocean. The park offers horseshoes, volleyball, badminton, and get this—nearby are the "world's largest totem poles." They'll tell you all about it.

⑨ Samoa Boat Launch County Park

Location: On Humboldt Bay; map BØ, grid c3.

Campsites, facilities: There are 10 tent sites and 40 RV sites. Picnic tables, fire grills, piped water, and flush toilets are provided. A boat ramp, grocery store, LP gas, and a coin laundry are available in Eureka (about five miles away). Leashed pets are permitted.

Reservations, fees: No reservations; $10 per night, $1 pet fee. Open year-round.

Contact: Samoa Boat Launch County Park, (707) 445-7652 or fax (707) 445-7409.

Directions: From US 101 in Eureka, turn west on Highway 255 and drive two miles until it dead-ends at New Navy Base Road. At New Navy Base Road, turn left and drive five miles to the end of the Samoa Peninsula and the campground entrance.

Trip notes: The nearby vicinity of the boat ramp, with access to Humboldt Bay and the Pacific Ocean, makes this a star attraction for campers towing their fishing boats. At the park you get good beachcombing and clamming at low tides and a chance to see a huge variety of seabirds, highlighted by egrets and herons. There's a reason: directly across the bay is the Humboldt Bay National Wildlife Refuge. This park is set near the famed all-you-can-eat, logger-style Samoa Cookhouse.

⑩ Mad River Rapids RV Park

Location: In Arcata; map BØ, grid b4.

Campsites, facilities: There are 92 RV sites (40 drive-through) with full hookups. Patios, picnic tables, fire grills, rest rooms, showers, sanitary disposal station, recreation room, tennis courts, fitness room, playground, swimming pool, and a spa are provided. Cable TV, VCR rentals, grocery store, and coin laundry are available. Some facilities are wheelchair accessible. Leashed pets are permitted.

Reservations, fees: Reservations are ac-

cepted; $22 to $29 per night.

Contact: Mad River Rapids RV Park, (707) 822-7275 or fax (707) 822-7286.

Directions: From the junction of US 101 and Highway 299 in Arcata, drive a quarter mile north on US 101 to the Guintoli Lane exit. At the exit, turn west on Janes Road and drive two blocks west to the campground.

Trip notes: This camp is near the farmlands on the outskirts of town, in a pastoral, quiet setting. There is a great bike ride nearby on a trail routed along the Mad River, and it is also excellent for taking a dog for a walk. Nearby Arcata is a unique town, a bit of the old and a bit of the new, and the Arcata Marsh at the north end of Humboldt Bay provides a scenic and easy bicycle trip, as well as an excellent destination for hiking, sight-seeing, and bird-watching.

⑪ Eureka KOA

Location: In Eureka; map BØ, grid c4.

Campsites, facilities: There are eight bike-in/hike-in sites, 26 tent sites, and 140 RV sites (42 drive-through with full hookups and some partial hookups). Group sites and 10 camping cabins are also available. Piped water, flush toilets, showers, fire pits, picnic tables, playground, and a recreation room are provided. A heated swimming pool, two hot tubs, grocery store, coin laundry, sanitary disposal station, LP gas, ice, and wood are available. Pets are permitted.

Reservations, fees: Reservations are accepted; $20 to $25 per night. Cabins are $35 per night for two people.

Contact: Eureka KOA, (707) 822-4243.

Directions: From Eureka, drive north on US 101 for four miles and look for the KOA sign on the right side of the highway at 4050 north US 101.

Trip notes: This is a year-round KOA camp for US 101 cruisers looking for a layover spot in Eureka. A bonus here is a few of those little KOA Kamping Kabins, the log-style jobs that win on cuteness alone. The closest significant recreation option is the Arcata Marsh on Humboldt Bay, a richly diverse spot with good trails for biking and hiking or just parking and looking at the water. Another option is excellent salmon fishing in June, July, and August, with party boats available just south of Eureka at King Salmon Charters.

⑫ Boise Creek

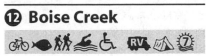

Location: In Six Rivers National Forest; map BØ, grid c9.

Campsites, facilities: There are several sites for bicyclists and hikers and 17 sites for tents or RVs up to 40 feet long. Piped water, vault toilets, picnic tables, and fire grills are provided. A grocery store, coin laundry, and propane gas are available nearby. Leashed pets are permitted.

Reservations, fees: No reservations; $8 per night, $5 for an extra vehicle. Open year-round.

Contact: Six Rivers National Forest, Lower Trinity Ranger District, (530) 629-2118 or fax (530) 629-2102.

Directions: From the intersection of US 101 and Highway 299 near Arcata, drive 39 miles east on Highway 299 and look for the campground entrance on the left side of the road. If you reach the town of Willow Creek, you have gone 1.5 miles too far.

Trip notes: This camp features a quarter-mile-long trail down to Boise Creek and nearby access to the Trinity River. If you have ever wanted to see Bigfoot, you can do it while camping here because there's a giant wooden Bigfoot on display in front of the Flame restaurant in nearby Willow Creek. After your Bigfoot experience, your best bet during summer is to head north on nearby Highway 96 (turn north in Willow Creek) to the campground at Tish Tang, where there is excellent river access, swimming, and inner tubing in the late summer's warm flows. The Trinity River also provides good salmon and steelhead fishing during fall and winter, respectively, with the best nearby access upriver along Highway 299 at Burnt Ranch.

⑬ E-Z Landing RV Park and Marina

Location: On Humboldt Bay; map BØ, grid d3.

Campsites, facilities: There are 55 RV sites (20 drive-through) with full hookups. Patios, flush toilets, and showers are provided. A sanitary disposal station, marine gas, ice, coin laundry, boat docks, boat launch, party boat rentals, bait, and tackle are available. Pets must be controlled.

Reservations, fees: Reservations are accepted; $20 per night.

Contact: E-Z Landing RV Park and Marina, (707) 442-1118.

Directions: From Eureka, drive 3.5 miles south on US 101. Turn west on King Salmon Avenue (it becomes Buhne Drive) and drive for a half mile. Turn south on Buhne Drive and go a half mile to 1875 Buhne Drive.

Trip notes: This is a good base camp for salmon trips in July and August when big schools of king and coho salmon often teem just west of the entrance of Humboldt Bay. A boat ramp with access to Humboldt Bay and party boat fishing trips is available out of E-Z Landing. It's not the prettiest camp in the world, with quite a bit of asphalt, but most people use this camp as a simple parking spot for sleeping and getting down to the business of the day: fishing. This spot is ideal for ocean fishing, clamming, beachcombing, and boating.

⑭ Johnny's Marina and RV Park

Location: On Humboldt Bay; map BØ, grid d3.

Campsites, facilities: There are 53 RV sites (four drive-through) with full hookups. Patios, rest rooms, showers, and a sanitary disposal station are provided. A coin laundry and boat dock are available. Pets must be controlled.

Reservations, fees: Reservations are accepted; $18 per night. Open year-round.

Contact: Johnny's Marina and RV Park, (707) 442-2284.

Directions: From Eureka, drive 3.5 miles south on US 101. Turn west on King Salmon Avenue (it becomes Buhne Drive). Continue about a half mile to 1821 Buhne Drive.

Trip notes: This is a good base camp for salmon fishing during the peak season in June, July, and

August. Boat rentals are available along with launching and mooring for private boats. Other recreation activities include beachcombing, clamming, and perch fishing from shore. Charter fishing trips are available from King Salmon Charters.

⑮ Ebb Tide Park

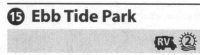

Location: In Eureka; map BØ, grid c3.

Campsites, facilities: There are 81 RV sites (58 drive-through) with full or partial hookups. Rest rooms, showers, picnic tables, and patios are provided. A sanitary dump station, RV storage, and coin laundry are available. Pets must be controlled.

Reservations, fees: Reservations are accepted; $11 to $22 per night.

Contact: Ebb Tide Park, (707) 445-2273.

Directions: In Eureka, drive north on US 101, take the Mall 101 exit. Look for the park on the east side of the road. Driving south on US 101, take the V Street exit and drive to the first stoplight. Turn left and drive to Sixth Street. Turn left on Sixth Street and drive into Mall 101 and straight ahead to the park.

Trip notes: This year-round RV park provides easy access off the highway and to stores and movie theaters—not exactly a primitive spot in pristine wilderness. It is what it is: a place to park the rig for the night.

⑯ Stafford RV Park

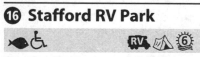

Location: Near Scotia; map BØ, grid f3.

Campsites, facilities: There are 50 RV sites (14 drive-through) with full or partial hookups and 30 tent sites. Group sites are available. Piped water, flush toilets, showers, fire grills, and picnic tables are provided. A coin laundry, playground, and store are available. Some facilities are wheelchair accessible. Leashed pets are permitted.

Reservations, fees: Reservations are accepted; $10 to $20 per night, $2 pet fee.

Contact: Stafford RV Park, (707) 764-3416 or fax (707) 764-3226.

Directions: From Eureka, drive south on US 101 to Scotia. At Scotia, continue south for three miles to Stafford Road. Turn right on Stafford Road and at the first stop sign, turn left under the overpass, and drive a short distance to North Road. At North Road, turn right and drive a quarter mile to 385 North Road.

Trip notes: This is a privately operated park for RVs that provides several side trip options: a tour of the giant sawmill in Scotia, a tour of giant redwoods on the Avenue of the Giants, access to the nearby Eel River, and best of all, the nearby Redwood National Park. One of the better park information centers in California is here, with maps and information about hikes, bike rides, and driving tours.

⑰ Van Duzen County Park

Location: On the Van Duzen River; map BØ, grid f4.

Campsites, facilities: There are 30 sites for tents or RVs. Piped water, flush toilets, showers, fire grills, and picnic tables are provided. A grocery store and coin laundry are available nearby. Pets are permitted.

Reservations, fees: No reservations; $12 per night, $1 pet fee. Open year-round.

Contact: Van Duzen County Park, (707) 445-7652 or fax (707) 445-7409.

Directions: From Eureka, drive south on US 101 to the junction of Highway 36 at Alton. Turn east on Highway 36 and drive 12 miles to the campground.

Trip notes: This campground is set at the headwaters of the Van Duzen River, one of the Eel River's major tributaries. The river is subject to tremendous fluctuations in flows and height, so low in the fall that it is often temporarily closed to fishing by the Department of Fish and Game, so high in the winter that only fools would stick their toes in. For a short period in late spring, it provides a benign run for rafting and canoeing, putting in at Grizzly Creek and taking out at Van Duzen. In October, an excellent salmon fishing spot is where the Van Duzen enters the Eel.

⑱ A.W. Way County Park

🐟🏃🚶 🚐 ⛺ 8️⃣

Location: On the Mattole River; map BØ, rid hØ.

Campsites, facilities: There are 30 sites for tents or RVs. Piped water, flush toilets, showers, fire grills, and picnic tables are provided. A grocery store, coin laundry, and propane gas are available nearby. Pets are permitted.

Reservations, fees: No reservations; $10 per night, $1 pet fee.

Contact: A.W. Way County Park, (707) 445-7652 or fax (707) 445-7409.

Directions: From Garberville, drive north on US 101 to the South Fork–Honeydew exit. Turn west on South Fork–Honeydew Road and drive 31 miles (the road alternates between pavement, gravel, dirt, then pavement again) to the park entrance on the left side of the road. The park is located 7.5 miles south of the town of Petrolia.

Trip notes: This secluded camp provides a home for visitors to the "Lost Coast," the beautiful coastal stretch of California located far from any semblance of urban life. The highlight here is the Mattole River, a great steelhead stream when flows are suitable between January and mid-March. Nearby is excellent hiking in the King Range National Conservation Area. For the great hike out to the abandoned Punta Gorda Lighthouse, drive to the trailhead on the left side of Lighthouse Road (see next listing). This area is typically bombarded with monsoon-level rains in winter.

⑲ Mouth of the Mattole

🐟🏃🚶 5%🚐 ⛺ 8️⃣

Location: On the Pacific Ocean; map BØ, grid gØ.

Campsites, facilities: There are 14 sites for tents or RVs up to 15 feet long. Piped water, vault toilets, fire grills, and tables are provided. Leashed pets are permitted.

Reservations, fees: No reservations; $8 per night with a two-day limit. Open year-round.

Contact: Bureau of Land Management, Arcata Field Office, (707) 825-2300 or fax (707) 825-2301.

Directions: From US 101 north of Garberville, take the South Fork–Honeydew exit and drive west to Honeydew. At Honeydew, turn right on Mattole Road and drive toward Petrolia. At the second bridge over the Mattole River, one mile before Petrolia, turn west on Lighthouse Road and drive five miles to the campground at the end of the road.

Trip notes: This is a little-known camp set at the mouth of the Mattole River, right where it pours into the Pacific Ocean. It is beautiful and isolated. An outstanding hike is available to the Punta Gorda Lighthouse. Hike from the campground to the ocean and head south. It's a level walk, and at low tide, there's a chance to observe tide pool life. Perch fishing is good where the Mattole flows into the ocean, best during low tides. In the winter, the Mattole often provides excellent steelhead fishing. Check the Department of Fish and Game regulations for closed areas. Be sure to have a full tank on the way out—the nearest gas station is quite distant.

⑳ Grizzly Creek Redwoods State Park

🏃🚶 ♿ 🚐 ⛺ 7️⃣

Location: Near Bridgeville; map BØ, grid g5.

Campsites, facilities: There are nine tent sites and 21 sites for RVs up to 30 feet long or trailers up to 18 feet. Piped water, flush toilets, showers, fire grills, and picnic tables are provided. A coin laundry and grocery store are available within 12 miles. The facilities are wheelchair accessible. Leashed pets are permitted.

Reservations, fees: Reserve via phone at (800) 444-PARK/7275 ($7.50 reservation fee) or website www.cal-parks.ca.gov; $12 to $16 per night, $1 pet fee. Open year-round.

Contact: Grizzly Creek Redwoods State Park, (707) 777-3683, (707) 946-2409, or (707) 445-6547.

Directions: From Eureka, drive south on US 101 to the junction of Highway 36 at Alton. Turn east on Highway 36 and drive about 17 miles to the campground.

Trip notes: Most summer vacationers hit the campgrounds on the Redwood Highway, that is, US 101. However, this camp is just far enough off the beaten path to provide some semblance of seclusion. It is set in redwoods, quite beautiful, with fair hiking and good access to the adjacent Van Duzen River. In the winter one of the better holes for steelhead fishing is accessible here.

㉑ Albee Creek

Location: In Humboldt Redwoods State Park; map BØ, grid h3.

Campsites, facilities: There are 21 sites for tents and 18 sites for tents or RVs up to 24 feet long. Piped water, flush toilets, showers, fire grills, and picnic tables are provided. Leashed pets are permitted.

Reservations, fees: Reserve via phone at (800) 444-PARK/7275 ($7.50 reservation fee) or website www.cal-parks.ca.gov; $12 to $16 per night, $1 pet fee. Open May through September.

Contact: Humboldt Redwoods State Park, (707) 946-2409 or (707) 445-6547.

Directions: From Eureka, drive south on US 101 about 11 miles to the Honeydew exit (if you reach Weott, you have gone two miles too far). At Mattole Road, turn west and drive five miles to the campground.

Trip notes: Humboldt Redwoods State Park is known for some unusual giant trees in the Federation Grove and Big Tree Area. A series of excellent hikes, both short and long, is available here. The camp is set in a redwood grove, and the smell of these trees has a special magic. Nearby Albee Creek, a benign trickle most of the year, can flood in the winter after heavy rains.

㉒ Burlington

Location: In Humboldt Redwoods State Park; map BØ, grid h4.

Campsites, facilities: There are 57 sites for tents or RVs up to 33 feet long or trailers up to 24 feet; one site is wheelchair accessible. Piped water, flush toilets, showers, fire grills, and picnic tables are provided. Leashed pets are permitted.

Reservations, fees: Reserve via phone at (800) 444-PARK/7275 ($7.50 reservation fee) or

website www.cal-parks.ca.gov; $12 to $16 per night, $1 pet fee. Open year-round.

Contact: Humboldt Redwoods State Park, (707) 946-2409.

Directions: From Eureka, drive south on US 101 for 45 miles to the Weott/Newton Road exit. Turn right on Newton Road and continue to the T junction where Newton Road meets the Avenue of the Giants. Turn left on the Avenue of the Giants and drive two miles to the campground entrance on the left.

Trip notes: This camp is often at capacity during the tourist months. You get shady campsites with big redwood stumps that kids can play on. There's good hiking on trails routed through the redwoods, and in winter, steelhead fishing is often good on the nearby Eel River. The park has 100 miles of trails, but it is the little half-mile Founders Grove Nature Trail that has the quickest payoff and requires the least effort.

㉓ Mad River

Location: In Six Rivers National Forest; map BØ, grid h9.

Campsites, facilities: There are 40 sites, a few of which are for RVs up to 22 feet long or trailers up to 30 feet long. Piped water is available from approximately mid-May to mid-October. Vault toilets, picnic tables, and fire grills are provided. Leashed pets are permitted.

Reservations, fees: No reservations; $12 per night, $5 per extra vehicle. Open year-round.

Contact: Six Rivers National Forest, Mad River Ranger District, (707) 574-6233 or fax (707) 574-6273.

Directions: From Eureka, drive south on US 101 to Alton. Turn east on Highway 36 and drive about 50 miles to the town of Mad River. Turn southeast on Lower Mad River Road and drive four miles to the camp on the right side of the road.

Trip notes: This Forest Service campground is set in a hot, remote section of Six Rivers National Forest at an elevation of 2,600 feet. The headwaters of the Mad River pour right past the campground, about two miles downstream from the Ruth Lake Dam. People making weekend trips to Ruth Lake often end up at this camp.

Ruth Lake is the only major recreation lake within decent driving range of Eureka, offering a small marina with boat rentals and a good boat ramp for access to trout fishing, bass fishing, and waterskiing.

㉔ Giant Redwoods RV Camp

Location: On the Eel River; map BØ, grid i4.

Campsites, facilities: There are 25 tent sites and 57 RV sites (34 drive-through), many with full or partial hookups. Picnic tables, fire rings, rest rooms, showers, and a sanitary disposal station are provided. A store, ice, LP gas, coin laundry, playground, and a recreation room are available. Pets are allowed.

Reservations, fees: Reservations are recommended in the summer; $18 to $25 per night. Open year-round.

Contact: Giant Redwoods RV Camp, (707) 943-3198 or fax (707) 943-3559; email: rathj@humboldt.net; website: www. campgrounds. com/giantredwoods.

Directions: From Eureka, drive south 50 miles on US 101 to the Myers Flat/Avenue of the Giants exit. Turn right on Avenue of the Giants and make a quick left onto Myers Avenue. Drive a quarter mile on Myers Avenue to the campground entrance.

Trip notes: This privately operated park is set in a grove of redwoods and covers 23 acres, much of it fronting the Eel River. Trip options include the scenic drive on Avenue of the Giants.

㉕ Hidden Springs

Location: In Humboldt Redwoods State Park; map BØ, grid h5.

Campsites, facilities: There are 112 sites for tents or RVs up to 33 feet long or trailers up to 24 feet. Piped water, flush toilets, showers, fire grills, and picnic tables are provided. A grocery store, coin laundry, and LP gas are available within one mile in Myers Flat. Leashed pets are permitted.

Reservations, fees: Reserve via phone at

(800) 444-PARK/7275 ($7.50 reservation fee) or website www.cal-parks.ca.gov; $12 to $16 per night, $1 pet fee.

Contact: Humboldt Redwoods State Park, (707) 946-2409 or (707) 445-6547.

Directions: From Eureka, drive south 50 miles on US 101 to the Myers Flat/Avenue of the Giants exit. Continue south and drive less than a mile to the campground entrance.

Trip notes: This camp gets heavy use from May through September, but the campgrounds have been situated in a way that offers relative seclusion. Side trips include good hiking on trails routed through redwoods and a touring drive on Avenue of the Giants. The park has more than 100 miles of hiking trails, many of them amidst spectacular giant redwoods, including the Bull Creek Flats Trail and Founders Grove Nature Trail. In winter, nearby High Rock on the Eel River is one of the better shoreline fishing spots for steelhead.

㉖ Horse Mountain

Location: In the King Range; map BØ, grid j2.

Campsites, facilities: There are nine sites for tents or RVs up to 20 feet long. Piped water, vault toilets, fire grills, and picnic tables are provided. Leashed pets are permitted.

Reservations, fees: No reservations; $8 per night. Open year-round.

Contact: Bureau of Land Management, Arcata Field Office, (707) 825-2300.

Directions: From Eureka, drive 60 miles south on US 101. Take the Redway/Shelter Cove exit onto Redwood Drive in the town of Redway. Look on the right for the King Range Conservation Area sign. Turn right on Briceland-Thorne Road (which will become Shelter Cove Road) and drive 18 miles to Kings Peak Road. Turn right and continue seven miles to the campground on the right.

Trip notes: Few people know of this spot. The campground is set along the northwest flank of Horse Mountain. A primitive road (Saddle Mountain Road) leads west from the camp and then goes left at the Y, up to Horse Mountain (1,929 feet), which offers spectacular ocean and coastal views on clear days. If you turn right at the Y, the road leads to the trailhead for the King Crest Trail near Saddle Mountain (3,290 feet). This hike is an ambitious climb to Kings Peak (4,087 feet), rewarding hikers with a fantastic panorama, including Mount Lassen poking up above the Yolla Bolly Wilderness to the east.

㉗ Shelter Cove

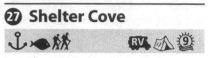

Location: Overlooking the Pacific Ocean; map BØ, grid j2.

Campsites, facilities: There are 105 sites for tents or RVs (15 drive-through), many with full hookups. Picnic tables, fire rings, rest rooms, showers, and a sanitary disposal station are provided. A coin laundry, grocery store, deli, LP gas, ice, RV supplies, and a boat ramp are available. Leashed pets are permitted.

Reservations, fees: Reservations are recommended; $15 to $25 per night. Open year-round.

Contact: Shelter Cove, (707) 986-7474; email: ladydi12@juno.com.

Directions: From Eureka, drive 60 miles south on US 101 to the Redway/Shelter Cove exit. Drive 2.5 miles north on Redwood Road to Briceland–Shelter Cove Road. Turn west and drive 24 miles (following the truck/RV route signs) to Upper Pacific Drive. Turn south on Upper Pacific Drive and proceed a half mile.

Trip notes: This is a prime oceanside spot to set up a base camp for deep-sea fishing, whale watching, tide pooling, beachcombing, and hiking. A relatively new six-lane boat ramp makes it perfect for campers who have trailered boats and don't mind the long drive. Reservations are strongly advised here. The park's backdrop is the King Range National Conservation Area, offering spectacular views. The deli is world famous for its fish-and-chips. The salmon fishing is quite good here in July and August, crabbing in December, clamming during winter's low tides, and hiking in the King Mountain Range during the summer. There is heavy rain in winter.

㉘ Tolkan

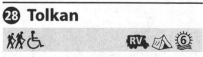

Location: In the King Range; map BØ, grid j2.

Campsites, facilities: There are nine sites for tents or RVs up to 20 feet long. Piped water, vault toilets, fire grills, and picnic tables are provided. The facilities are wheelchair accessible. Leashed pets are permitted.

Reservations, fees: No reservations; $8 per night.

Contact: Bureau of Land Management, Arcata Field Office, (707) 825-2300 or fax (707) 825-2301.

Directions: From Eureka, drive 60 miles south on US 101 to the Redway exit. Take the Redway/ Shelter Cove exit onto Redwood Drive into the town of Redway. Look on the right for the King Range Conservation Area sign, turn right on Briceland-Thorne Road (which will become Shelter Cove Road), and drive 18 miles to Kings Peak Road. Turn right on Kings Peak Road and continue five miles to the campground on the right.

Trip notes: This remote camp is set at 1,840 feet, a short drive south of Horse Mountain. For nearby side trip options, see the trip notes for Horse Mountain (campground number 26).

㉙ Dean Creek Resort

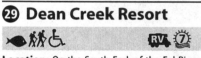

Location: On the South Fork of the Eel River; map BØ, grid j5.

Campsites, facilities: There are 64 RV sites with full or partial hookups and 12 drive-through sites. Picnic tables, fire grills, rest rooms, showers, and a recreation room are provided. A coin laundry, store, RV supplies, wood, ice, giant spa, sauna, pool, sanitary dump station, and a playground are available. Leashed pets are permitted.

Reservations, fees: Reservations are recommended in the summer; $14 to $22 per night, $1 pet fee.

Contact: Dean Creek Resort, (707) 923-2555 or fax (707) 923-2547; email: deancrk@ humboldt.net;website: www.campgrounds .com/deancreek.

Directions: From Eureka, drive 60 miles south on US 101 to the Redway/Shelter Cove exit. Exit onto Redwood Drive and continue about one block to the campground entrance on the right.

Trip notes: This year-round RV park is set on

the South Fork of the Eel River. In the summer, it makes a good base camp for a redwood park adventure, with the adjacent Humboldt Redwoods State Park providing 100 miles of hiking trails, many routed through awesome stands of giant trees. In the winter heavy rains feed the South Fork Eel, inspiring steelhead upstream on their annual winter journey. Fishing is good in this area, best by shore at nearby High Rock. Bank access is good at several other spots, particularly upstream near Benbow and in Cooks Valley. An excellent side trip is to drive on Avenue of the Giants, a tour through giant redwood trees three miles from the park. The campground also offers volleyball, shuffleboard, badminton, and horseshoes. You get the idea.

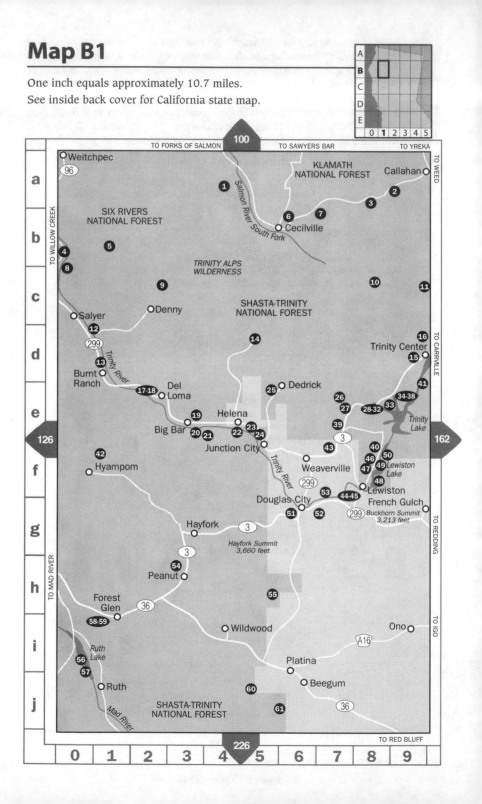

Chapter B1 features:

1 Matthews Creek

Location: On the Salmon River in Klamath National Forest; map B1, grid a4.

Campsites, facilities: There are seven sites for tents or RVs up to 16 feet long and seven sites for tents only. Piped water, vault toilets, fire grills, and picnic tables are provided. Leashed or controlled pets are permitted.

Reservations, fees: No reservations; $6 per night.

Contact: Klamath National Forest, Salmon River Ranger District, (530) 468-5351 or fax (530) 468-1290.

Directions: From the junction of US 101 and

Highway 299 near Arcata, head east on Highway 299 and drive to Willow Creek. In Willow Creek, turn north on Highway 96 and drive past Orleans to Somes Bar. At Somes Bar, turn east on Salmon River Road/Forest Service Road 2B01 and drive to the town of Forks of Salmon. Turn right on Cecilville Road/Forest Service Road 1002/ and drive about nine miles to the campground. Cecilville Road is very narrow.

Trip notes: This camp is set in a dramatic river canyon, with the beautiful South Fork of the Salmon River nearby. Rafters call it the "Cal Salmon," and good put-in and takeout spots are found every few miles all the way to the confluence with the Klamath. In early summer the water is quite cold from snowmelt, but by summer it warms up significantly. The best fishing for steelhead on the Salmon is in December in the stretch of river downstream from Forks of Salmon (check regulations for closed areas). In winter the mountain rims shield the canyon floor from sunlight and it gets so cold you'll feel like a human glacier. The elevation is 1,700 feet.

❷ Carter Meadows Horse Camp

Location: In Klamath National Forest; map B1, grid a8.

Campsites, facilities: There is one group equestrian site for tents or RVs, with three large horse corrals. Piped water and vault toilets are available. Group BBQs and picnic tables are provided. Stock water troughs are also available.

Reservations, fees: Reservations required, phone (800) 444-6777 ($8.65 reservation fee); $30 per night. Open mid-June to mid-October, weather permitting.

Contact: Klamath National Forest, Scott River Ranger District, (530) 468-5351 or fax (530) 468-1290.

Directions: From Redding, drive north on Interstate 5 past Weed. Take the Edgewood exit, turn left at the stop sign, and drive a short distance. Turn right on Old Stage Road, drive to Gazelle, turn left on Gazelle-Callahan Road, and continue to Callahan. In Callahan turn southwest on Cecilville Road and drive 11 miles to the campground.

Trip notes: Carter Meadows offers an extensive trail network for riding and hiking. The Pacific Crest National Scenic Trail passes through the area and serves as access to the Russian Wilderness to the north and the Trinity Alps Wilderness to the south. Stream fishing is another option here. Trail Creek and East Fork are nearby.

❸ Trail Creek

Location: In Klamath National Forest; map B1, grid a8.

Campsites, facilities: There are seven sites for tents or RVs up to 22 feet long and eight sites for tents only. Piped water, vault toilets, fire grills, and picnic tables are provided. Pets are permitted on leashes or otherwise restrained.

Reservations, fees: No reservations; $6 per night. Open May through October.

Contact: Klamath National Forest, Scott River Ranger District, (530) 468-5351 or fax (530)468-1290.

Directions: From Redding, drive north on Interstate 5 past Weed to the Edgewood exit. Take the Edgewood exit, turn left at the stop sign, and drive a short distance to another stop sign at Old Stage Road. Turn right at Old Stage Road and drive to Gazelle. In Gazelle, turn left on Gazelle-Callahan Road and continue to Callahan. In Callahan, turn southwest on Cecilville Road and drive 17 miles to the campground.

Trip notes: This simple and quiet camp is set beside Trail Creek, a small tributary to the upper Salmon River, at an elevation of 4,700 feet. A trailhead is located about a mile to the south, accessible via a Forest Service road, providing access to a two mile trail routed along Fish Creek and leading to little Fish Lake. From Fish Lake the trail climbs steeply, switchbacking at times, for another two miles to larger Trail Gull Lake, a very pretty spot set below Deadman Peak (7,741 feet).

❹ East Fork Willow Creek

Location: On Willow Creek; map B1, grid b0.

Campsites, facilities: There are 13 sites for tents and RVs. Picnic tables, fire rings, and vault toilets with wheelchair access are provided. No piped water is available. Leashed pets are permitted.

Reservations, fees: No reservations; $6 per night, $5 for each additional vehicle.

Contact: Six Rivers National Forest, Lower Trinity Ranger District, (530) 629-2118 or fax (530) 629-2102. For a map send $4 to US Forest Map Sales, US Forest Service, 1323 Club Drive, Vallejo, CA 94592, (707) 562-USFS/8737, and ask for the Six Rivers National Forest area.

Directions: From the junction of US 101 and Highway 299 near Arcata, turn east on Highway 299 and drive to Willow Creek. From Willow Creek continue six miles east on Highway 299, then look for the camp's signed turnoff on the south side of the road.

Trip notes: This is a beautiful spot along Willow Creek. Set at a 2,000-foot elevation, it's one of the prettiest campgrounds in the area. In August and September the river is often quite warm, ideal for swimming or inner tubing. In the winter it is one of the better camps for shoreline steelhead fishing. Way back in the 1950s and early 1960s this was one of the better-known campgrounds in the area, but the flood of 1964 wiped it out. Only recently have rehabilitation efforts restored it to life.

❺ Mill Creek Lake Hike-In

Location: On the border of the Trinity Alps Wilderness; map B1, grid b1.

Campsites, facilities: There are three primitive tent sites at locations around the lake. Fire rings are provided. No piped water is available. No pets are allowed.

Reservations, fees: No reservations; no fee. A free wilderness permit is required from the US Forest Service.

Contact: Six Rivers National Forest, Lower Trinity Ranger District, (530) 629-2118 or fax (530) 629-2102. For a map send $4 to US Forest Map Sales, US Forest Service, 1323 Club Drive, Vallejo, CA 94592, (707) 562-USFS/8737, and ask for the Six Rivers National Forest area.

Directions: From the junction of US 101 and Highway 299 near Arcata, turn east on Highway 299 and drive to Willow Creek. In Willow Creek

turn north on Highway 96, drive into the Hoopa Valley, turn east on Big Hill Road, and drive 12 miles to the national forest boundary. Turn right on Forest Road 10N02 and drive about 3.5 miles, where you will reach another junction. Turn right at the signed junction to the Mill Creek Lake Trailhead and drive a short distance to the parking area. A one-hour walk is then required to reach the lake.

Trip notes: Mill Creek Lake is a secret three-acre lake set at 5,000 feet on the edge of the Trinity Alps Wilderness. Reaching it requires a two-mile hike from the wilderness boundary, with the little lake set just north of North Trinity Mountain (6,362 feet). This is a rare chance to reach a wilderness lake with such a short walk, backpacking without having to pay the penalty of days of demanding hiking. The lake features excellent swimming, with warmer water than in higher and more remote wilderness lakes, and decent fishing for rainbow trout. It is stocked with fingerlings yearly by airplane.

❻ East Fork

Location: On the Salmon River in Klamath National Forest; map B1, grid b6.

Campsites, facilities: There are six tent sites and three sites for RVs up to 16 feet long. Vault toilets, fire grills, and picnic tables are provided. No piped water is provided, so bring your own. Pets are permitted on leashes.

Reservations, fees: No reservations; no fee.

Contact: Klamath National Forest, Scott River Ranger District, (530) 468-5351 or fax (530) 468-1290.

Directions: From Redding, drive north on Interstate 5 past Weed to the Edgewood exit. Take the Edgewood exit, turn left at the stop sign, and drive a short distance to another stop sign at Old Stage Road. Turn right at Old Stage Road, drive to Gazelle, turn left on Gazelle-Callahan Road, and drive to Callahan. In Callahan, turn southwest on Cecilville Road and drive about 30 miles to the campground on the right side of the road. If you reach the town of Cecilville, you have gone two miles too far.

Trip notes: This is one of the more spectacular areas in the fall when the leaves turn different shades of gold. It's set at 2,400 feet along the Salmon River, just outside the town of Cecilville. Directly adjacent to the camp is Forest Service Road 37N02, which leads to a Forest Service station four miles away, and a trailhead for the Trinity Alps Wilderness three miles beyond that. Note to steelhead anglers: Check the Department of Fish and Game regulations for closed areas on the Salmon River.

❼ Shadow Creek

Location: In Klamath National Forest; map B1, grid b7.

Campsites, facilities: There are five tent sites and five sites for RVs up to 16 feet long. Vault toilets, fire grills, and picnic tables are provided. No piped water is available, so remember to bring your own. Leashed pets are permitted.

Reservations, fees: No reservations; no fee. Open year-round.

Contact: Klamath National Forest, Salmon River Ranger District, (530) 468-5351 or fax (530) 468-1290.

Directions: From Redding, drive north on Interstate 5 past Weed to the Edgewood exit. Take the Edgewood exit, turn left at the stop sign, and drive a short distance to another stop sign at Old Stage Road. Turn right at Old Stage Road, drive to Gazelle, turn left on Gazelle-Callahan Road, and drive to Callahan. In Callahan, turn southwest on Cecilville Road and drive about 25 miles to the campground on the left side of the road.

Trip notes: This tiny spot, secluded and quiet, is along little Shadow Creek where it enters the East Fork Salmon River, adjacent to a deep bend in the road. An unusual side trip is to take the Forest Service road out of camp (turn north off Cecilville Road) and follow it as it winds back and forth, finally arriving at Grouse Point, 5,409 feet in elevation, for a view of the western slopes of the nearby Russian and Trinity Alps Wilderness Areas. There are three trailheads six miles to the east of the camp: Fish Creek, Long Gulch, and Trail Gulch. Note: The river adjacent to the campground is a spawning area and is closed to salmon and steelhead fishing, but you can take trout.

❽ Tish Tang

Location: In Six Rivers National Forest; map B1, grid c0.

Campsites, facilities: There are 21 sites for tents and 19 sites for tents or RVs up to 30 feet long and trailers up to 22 feet long. Piped water, vault toilets, picnic tables, and fire grills are provided. Leashed pets are permitted.

Reservations, fees: No reservations; $10 per night, $4 for each additional vehicle, $15 per night for multiple-family sites. Open late May to late October.

Contact: Hoopa Valley Tribe, Forestry Department, (530) 625-4284 or fax (530) 625-4230.

Directions: From the junction of US 101 and Highway 299 near Arcata, turn east on Highway 299 and drive to Willow Creek. In Willow Creek, turn north on Highway 96 and drive eight miles north to the campground entrance on the right side of the road.

Trip notes: This campground is located adjacent to one of the best swimming holes in all of Northern California. By late July the adjacent Trinity River is warm and slow, perfect for inner tubing, falling in "by accident," and paddling a canoe. There is a large gravel beach, and some people will bring along their shorty lawn chairs and just take a seat on the edge of the river in a few inches of water. Though Tish Tang is a good put-in spot for rafting in the late spring and early summer, taking the river north into the Hoopa Valley, it is too easy for most rafters to even ruffle a feather during the summer months. The elevation is 400 feet.

❾ Denny

Location: On the New River in Shasta-Trinity National Forest; map B1, grid c2.

Campsites, facilities: There are 16 tent sites and six sites for tents or RVs up to 25 feet long. No piped water is available. Vault toilets, picnic tables, and fire grills are provided. Leashed pets are permitted. Supplies are available about one hour away in Salyers Bar.

Reservations, fees: No reservations; no fee. Open year-round.

Contact: Shasta-Trinity National Forest, Big Bar Ranger Station, (530) 623-6106 or (530) 623-6123.

Directions: From the junction of US 101 and Highway 299 near Arcata, turn east on Highway 299 and drive to Willow Creek. In Willow Creek, continue east on Highway 299 and, after reaching Salyer, continue for four miles to Denny Road/County Road 402. Turn north on Denny Road and drive about 14 miles on a paved but very windy road to the campground.

Trip notes: This is a secluded and quiet campground located along the New River, a tributary to the Trinity River and a designated Wild and Scenic River. Trout fishing is decent, but the fish are small in the five miles of river near the campground. The stream here is OK for swimming, but too cold to even dip a toe in until late summer. If you drive north from the camp on Denny Road, you will find several trailheads for trips into the Trinity Alps Wilderness. The best of them is at the end of the road, where there is a good parking area, with a trail that is routed along the East Fork New River up toward Limestone Ridge. The campground is set at 1,400 feet.

⑩ Goldfield

Location: In Shasta-Trinity National Forest; map B1, grid c8.

Campsites, facilities: There are six tent sites. Vault toilets, picnic tables, hitching posts for horses, and fire grills are provided, but there is no piped water, so bring your own. Leashed pets are permitted.

Reservations, fees: No reservations; no fee.

Contact: Shasta-Trinity National Forest, Weaverville Ranger Station, (530) 623-2121 or fax (530) 623-6010.

Directions: From Redding, head east on Highway 299 and drive to Weaverville. Turn north on Highway 3 and drive just past the north end of Trinity Lake to Coffee Creek Road/Forest Service Road 104, adjacent to a Forest Service ranger station. Turn left on Coffee Creek Road and drive 6.5 miles to the campground on the left side of the road.

Trip notes: For hikers, this camp makes a perfect first stop after a long drive. You wake up, get your gear organized, then take the trailhead to the south. It is routed along Boulder Creek, and with a left turn at the junction (about four miles in), will take you to Boulder Lake (another two miles), set inside the edge of the Trinity Alps Wilderness. Former 49er coach George Seifert first told me about the beauty of this place, and how perfectly this campground is located for the hike. Campground elevation is 3,000 feet.

⑪ Big Flat

Location: On Coffee Creek in Klamath National Forest; map B1, grid c9.

Campsites, facilities: There are nine sites for tents or RVs up to 16 feet long. There is no piped water, but vault toilets, fire grills, and picnic tables are provided. Trash must be packed out. Leashed pets are permitted.

Reservations, fees: No reservations; no fee.

Contact: Klamath National Forest, Salmon River Ranger District, (530) 468-5351 or fax (530) 468-1290.

Directions: From Redding, turn east on Highway 299 and drive to Weaverville. In Weaverville, turn north on Highway 3 and drive just past the north end of Trinity Lake to Coffee Creek Road/Forest Service Road 104, adjacent to a Forest Service ranger station. Turn left on Coffee Creek Road and drive 21 miles to the campground at the end of the road.

Trip notes: This is a great jump-off spot for a wilderness backpacking trip into the adjacent Trinity Alps. An 11-mile hike will take you into the beautiful Caribou Lakes Basin for lakeside campsites, excellent swimming, dramatic sunsets, and fair trout fishing. The trail is routed out of camp, crosses the stream, then rises up a series of switchbacks to the ridge. From here it gets easier, rounding a mountain and depositing you in the basin. Bypass Little Caribou, Lower Caribou, and Snowslide Lakes, and instead head all the way to Caribou, the biggest and best of the lot. Big Flat is set at 5,000 feet in elevation along Coffee Creek, and on the drive in, you'll see big piles of boulders along the stream, evidence of past gold mining activity.

⑫ Grays Falls

Location: On the Trinity River in Six Rivers National Forest; map B1, grid d0.

Campsites, facilities: There are 17 tent sites and 16 sites for tents or RVs up to 35 feet long and trailers up to 40 feet long. Piped water, flush toilets, picnic tables, and fire grills are provided. One facility is wheelchair accessible. Leashed pets are permitted.

Reservations, fees: No reservations; $10 per night, $5 for each additional vehicle. Open May to mid-September.

Contact: Six Rivers National Forest, Lower Trinity Ranger District, (530) 629-2118 or fax (530) 629-2102.

Directions: From the junction of US 101 and Highway 299 near Arcata, turn east on Highway 299 and drive to Willow Creek. In Willow Creek, continue east on Highway 299 for 12 miles to the campground.

Trip notes: This is a prime summer spot to do absolutely nothing but enjoy the warm weather and cool water, and watch the adjacent Trinity River flow past. It is a good put-in spot for a short trip on an inner tube or inflatable kayak, with the water warm and benign by late summer. A nature trail is also nearby. Grays Falls isn't actually much of a waterfall, but rather a short coursing piece of water over rocks that salmon have to leap over during their run upstream in mid-September. This is a good spot for fishing, not only for salmon, but for steelhead in late November and early December. The elevation is 1,000 feet.

⑬ Burnt Ranch

Location: On the Trinity River in Shasta-Trinity National Forest; map B1, grid d1.

Campsites, facilities: There are 16 sites for tents or RVs up to 25 feet long. Piped water, vault toilets, picnic tables, and fire grills are provided. Supplies can be obtained in Hawkins Bar about one hour away. Leashed pets are permitted.

Reservations, fees: No reservations; $6 to $10 per night in season, free in winter when water is not available. Open year-round.

Contact: Shasta-Trinity National Forest, Big Bar Ranger Station, (530) 623-6106 or fax (530) 623-6123.

Directions: From Redding, take Highway 299 west and drive past Weaverville to Burnt Ranch. In Burnt Ranch, continue a half mile and look for the campground entrance on the right side of the road.

Trip notes: This campground is set on a bluff above the Trinity River and is one of its most compelling spots. Burnt Ranch Falls isn't much of a waterfall, but provides a fantastic spot to watch salmon and steelhead leap like greyhounds to make it past the falls and into a calm pool above. The peak migration periods are in mid-September for salmon and in early winter and early spring for steelhead. On their migratory route, the fish will hold below the falls, gaining strength for their upriver surge, making it a natural fishing spot. This section of river is very pretty, with deep, dramatic canyons nearby. The elevation is 1,000 feet.

⑭ Hobo Gulch

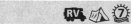

Location: On the North Fork of the Trinity River in Shasta-Trinity National Forest; map B1, grid d5.

Campsites, facilities: There are 10 sites for tents or RVs. Vault toilets, picnic tables, and fire grills are provided, but there is no piped water, so bring your own. Supplies can be obtained in Junction City, about one hour away. Leashed pets are permitted.

Reservations, fees: No reservations; $10 per night in season, free in winter when water is not available.

Contact: Shasta-Trinity National Forest, Big Bar Ranger Station, (530) 623-6106 or fax (530) 623-6123.

Directions: From Redding, turn west on Highway 299, drive past Weaverville, and continue 13 miles to Helena. In Helena, turn right and drive four miles on County East Fork Road to Hobo Gulch Road. At Hobo Gulch Road, turn north and drive 16 miles to the end of the road at the campground.

Trip notes: Only the ambitious need apply. This is a trailhead camp set on the edge of the

Trinity Alps Wilderness, and the reason only the ambitious show up is that it is a 20-mile uphill haul all the way to Grizzly Lake, set at the foot of the awesome Thompson Peak (8,663 feet), with no other lakes available en route. The camp is set at 2,900 feet along the North Fork of the Trinity River. The adjacent slopes of the wilderness are known for little creeks, woods, and a few pristine meadows, and are largely devoid of lakes.

⓯ Preacher Meadow

Location: In Shasta-Trinity National Forest; map B1, grid d9.

Campsites, facilities: There are 45 sites for tents or RVs up to 32 feet long. Piped water, vault toilets, picnic tables, and fire grills are provided. Supplies, a coin laundry, and a small airport are available nearby. Leashed pets are permitted.

Reservations, fees: No reservations; $8 per night.

Contact: Shasta-Trinity National Forest, Weaverville Ranger Station, (530) 623-2121 or fax (530) 623-6010.

Directions: From Redding, turn west on Highway 299 and drive to Weaverville at Highway 3. Head north on Highway 3 and drive to Trinity Lake. Continue toward Trinity Center and look for the campground entrance on the left side of the road (if you reach Trinity Center you have gone two miles too far).

Trip notes: The best thing about Preacher Meadow Camp is its good view of the Trinity Alps, providing you seek out the right vantage point. Otherwise, compared to all the other camps in the area located so close to Trinity Lake, it has trouble matching up in the quality department. If the lakeside camps are full, this camp provides an overflow option.

⓰ Wyntoon Resort

Location: On Trinity Lake; map B1, grid d9.

Campsites, facilities: There are 78 tent sites and 136 full-hookup sites for trailers or RVs. Piped water, picnic tables, fire rings, rest rooms, showers, and a coin laundry are provided. A playground, pool, sanitary dump station, gasoline, hardware store, grocery store, bicycle rentals, fish cleaning area, boat rentals, slips, and a boat launch are available. Trailers and cottages are also available for rent. The facilities are wheelchair accessible. Leashed pets are permitted.

Reservations, fees: Reservations are accepted; $18 to $24 per night; call for trailer and cottage rental rates.

Contact: Wyntoon Resort, (530) 266-3337 or fax (530) 266-3820.

Directions: From Redding, turn west on Highway 299 and drive to Weaverville at Highway 3. Turn north on Highway 3 and drive to Trinity Lake. At Trinity Center, continue a half mile north on Highway 3 to the resort.

Trip notes: This huge resort is an ideal family vacation destination. Set in a wooded area on the north shore of Trinity Lake, it provides opportunities for fishing, boating, swimming, and waterskiing, with access within walking distance. The lake sits at the base of the dramatic Trinity Alps, one of the most beautiful regions in the state.

⓱ Del Loma RV Park and Campground

Location: On the Trinity River; map B1, grid e2.

Campsites, facilities: There are 43 RV sites with full or partial hookups. Picnic tables, fire grills, flush toilets, hot showers, and a sanitary dump station are provided. A grocery store, RV supplies, firewood, coin laundry, recreation room, volleyball, and horseshoe pits are available. Leashed pets are permitted.

Reservations, fees: Reservations are accepted; phone (800) 839-0194; $18.75 per night. Open year-round.

Contact: Del Loma RV Park and Campground, (530) 623-2834.

Directions: From the junction of US 101 and Highway 299 in Arcata, turn east on Highway 299 and drive to Burnt Ranch. From Burnt Ranch, continue 10 miles east on Highway 299 to the town of Del Loma and look for the campground entrance along the road.

Trip notes: RV cruisers looking for a layover spot near the Trinity River will find just that at Del Loma. Shady sites and sandy beaches are available here along the Trinity. Rafting and inner tube trips are popular in this area during the summer months. Salmon fishing is best in the fall, steelhead fishing in the winter.

⑱ Hayden Flat

Location: On the Trinity River in Shasta-Trinity National Forest; map B1, grid e2.

Campsites, facilities: There are 20 sites for tents or RVs up to 25 feet long and five sites for RVs up to 35 feet in length. Piped water, vault toilets, picnic tables, and fire grills are provided. Leashed pets are permitted.

Reservations, fees: No reservations; $6 to $10 per night in season, free in winter. Open year-round.

Contact: Shasta-Trinity National Forest, Big Bar Ranger Station, (530) 623-6106 or fax (530) 623-6123.

Directions: From the junction of US 101 and Highway 299 in Arcata, head east on Highway 299 and drive to Burnt Ranch. From Burnt Ranch, continue 10 miles east on Highway 299 and look for the campground entrance along the left side of the road. If you reach the town of Del Loma, you have gone a half mile too far.

Trip notes: This campground is split into two pieces, with most of the sites grouped in a large, shaded area across the road from the river and a few on the river side. A beach is available along the river; it is a good spot for swimming as well as a popular put-in and takeout for rafters. The elevation is 1,200 feet.

⑲ Big Flat

Location: On the Trinity River in Shasta-Trinity National Forest; map B1, grid e3.

Campsites, facilities: There are 10 sites for tents or RVs up to 25 feet long. Piped water,

vault toilets, picnic tables, and fire grills are provided. Leashed pets are permitted.

Reservations, fees: No reservations; $6 to $10 per night in season, free in winter.

Contact: Shasta-Trinity National Forest, Big Bar Ranger Station, (530) 623-6106 or fax (530) 623-6123.

Directions: From Redding, turn west on Highway 299, drive past Weaverville, Junction City, and Helena, and continue for about seven miles. Look for the campground entrance on the right side of the road. If you reach the town of Big Bar, you have gone three miles too far.

Trip notes: This level campground is set off Highway 299, just across the road from the Trinity River. The sites are close together, and it can be hot and dusty in midsummer. No problem. That is when you will be on the Trinity River, taking the lowest-priced rafting trip available anywhere in the West—as low as $25 to rent an inflatable kayak from Trinity River Rafting in nearby Big Bar, which includes shuttle service. It's fun, exciting, easy (newcomers are welcome), and cheap.

⑳ Big Bar

Location: Near the Trinity River in Shasta-Trinity National Forest; map B1, grid e3.

Campsites, facilities: There are three tent sites. Piped water, vault toilets, picnic tables, and fire grills are provided. Supplies are available within one mile. Leashed pets are permitted.

Reservations, fees: No reservations; no fee.

Contact: Shasta-Trinity National Forest, Big Bar Ranger Station, (530) 623-6106 or fax (530) 623-6123.

Directions: From Redding, turn west on Highway 299 and drive past Weaverville, Junction City, and Helena to the town of Big Bar. In Big Bar, turn left at R Street and drive one mile to the campground on the right side of the road.

Trip notes: You name it, you got it—a quiet, small campground with easy access, good fishing nearby (in the fall), and piped water. In addition, there is a good put-in spot for inflatable kayaks and rafts. It is an ideal piece of water for newcomers, with Trinity River Rafting offering inflatable rentals for as low as $25, including shuttle service. The elevation is 1,200 feet. If the shoe fits. . . .

㉑ Skunk Point Group Camp

Location: On the Trinity River in Shasta-Trinity National Forest; map B1, grid e4.

Campsites, facilities: There are two group sites that hold up to 30 people each. Vault toilets, picnic tables, and fire grills are provided, but there is no piped water. Leashed pets are permitted.

Reservations, fees: Reservations are required via phone at (877) 444-6777 ($8.65 reservation fee) or website www.reserveusa.com; $20 per night for 10 or fewer campers, $2 each additional camper to a maximum of 30 people. Open year-round.

Contact: Shasta-Trinity National Forest, Big Bar Ranger Station at (530) 623-6106 or fax (530) 623-6123.

Directions: From Redding, head west on Highway 299, driving past Weaverville, Junction City, and Helena, and continue for about seven miles. Look for the campground entrance on the left side of the road. If you reach the town of Big Bar, you have gone two miles too far.

Trip notes: This is an ideal site for groups on rafting trips. You get easy access to the nearby Trinity River with a streamside setting and privacy for the group. A beach on the river is nearby. In the spring, this section of river offers primarily Class II rapids (only more difficult during high water), but most of it is rated Class I. By late summer, the water is warm and benign, ideal for families. Guided rafting trips and inflatables are available for hire and rent in nearby Big Bar. The camp elevation is 1,200 feet.

㉒ Pigeon Point

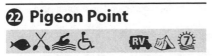

Location: On the Trinity River in Shasta-Trinity National Forest; map B1, grid e4.

Campsites, facilities: There are 10 sites for tents or RVs up to 25 feet long. Vault toilets,

picnic tables, and fire grills are provided. There's no piped water, so bring your own. Supplies can be obtained within 10 miles in Big Bar or Junction City. The facilities are wheelchair accessible. Leashed pets are permitted.

Reservations, fees: No reservations; $6 to $10 per night. Open May through October.

Contact: Shasta-Trinity National Forest, Big Bar Ranger Station, (530) 623-6106 or fax (530) 623-6123.

Directions: From Redding, head west on Highway 299 and drive to Weaverville. Continue west on Highway 299 to Helena and continue a half mile to the campground on the left (south) side of the road.

Trip notes: In the good old days, huge flocks of bandtail pigeons flew the Trinity River Canyon, swooping and diving in dramatic shows. Nowadays you don't see too many pigeons, but this camp still keeps its namesake. It is better known for its access to the Trinity River, with a large beach for swimming. The camp is not right on the Trinity, however; the highway runs between the camp and the river. The Forest Service road from the camp is routed north past several old mines on the way up to the Hobo Gulch Trailhead for the Trinity Alps. The elevation is 1,100 feet.

㉓ Bigfoot Campground and RV Park

Location: On the Trinity River; map B1, grid e5.

Campsites, facilities: There are 45 RV sites with full or partial hookups, a separate area for tent camping, and two cabins. From December 1 to May 1 only self-contained vehicles are allowed. Flush toilets, hot showers (for a fee), a coin laundry, grocery store, sanitary dump station, television, propane gas, swimming pool, and horseshoe pits are available. Facilities are wheelchair accessible. Leashed pets are permitted.

Reservations, fees: Reservations are recommended from July through October; $14 to $18 per night; cabins are $69.50 per night.

Contact: Bigfoot Campground and RV Park, (530) 623-6088 or fax (530) 623-3573.

Directions: From Redding, turn west on Highway 299 and drive to Junction City. Continue west on Highway 299 for three miles to the camp.

Trip notes: This private RV park has excellent access to the nearby Trinity River. It is a popular layover for Highway 299 cruisers but provides the option for longer stays with rafting, gold panning, and in the fall and winter, fishing for salmon and steelhead, respectively.

㉔ Junction City Camp

Location: On the Trinity River in Shasta-Trinity National Forest; map B1, grid e5.

Campsites, facilities: There are 26 sites for RVs up to 30 feet long. Piped water (available only from the pump house from November through April), vault toilets, picnic tables, and fire grills are provided. Groceries and propane gas are available within two miles in Junction City. Leashed pets are permitted.

Reservations, fees: No reservations; $8 per night from May through October.

Contact: Bureau of Land Management, Redding Field Office, (530) 224-2100.

Directions: From Redding, turn west on Highway 299 and drive to Junction City. At Junction City, continue west on Highway 299 for 1.5 miles to the camp.

Trip notes: Some of the Trinity River's best fall salmon fishing is in this area in September and early October, with steelhead following from mid-October into the winter. That makes it an ideal base camp for a fishing or camping trip.

㉕ Ripstein

Location: On Canyon Creek in Shasta-Trinity National Forest; map B1, grid e6.

Campsites, facilities: There are 10 tent sites. Vault toilets, picnic tables, and fire grills are provided, but there's no piped water, so bring your own. Supplies can be obtained 45 minutes away in Junction City. Leashed pets are permitted.

Reservations, fees: No reservations; $6 to $10 per night in season, free in winter. Open year-round.

Contact: Shasta-Trinity National Forest, Big Bar Ranger Station, (530) 623-6106 or fax (530) 623-6123.

Directions: From Redding, head west on Highway 299 and drive to Junction City. At Junction City, turn right on Canyon Creek Road and drive 15 miles to the campground on the left side of the road.

Trip notes: This is one of the great trailhead camps for the neighboring Trinity Alps. It is set at 2,600 feet on the southern edge of the wilderness and is a popular spot for a late-night arrival followed by a backpacking trip the next morning. Waiting are the Canyon Creek Lakes via a six-mile uphill hike along Canyon Creek. The destination is extremely beautiful—two alpine lakes set in high granite mountains. The route passes Canyon Creek Falls, a set of two different waterfalls, about 3.5 miles out.

㉖ Bridge Camp

Location: On Stuarts Fork in Shasta-Trinity National Forest; map B1, grid e7.

Campsites, facilities: There are 10 sites for tents or trailers up to 12 feet long. Piped water (spring, summer, and fall only), vault toilets, picnic tables, and fire grills are provided. Horse corrals are available. Leashed pets are permitted.

Reservations, fees: No reservations; $8 per night, free in winter. Open year-round, weather permitting.

Contact: Shasta-Trinity National Forest, Weaverville Ranger Station, (530) 623-2121 or fax (530) 623-6010.

Directions: From Redding, head west on Highway 299 and drive to Weaverville. In Weaverville, turn north on Highway 3 and drive 17 miles to Trinity Alps Road (at Stuarts Fork of Trinity Lake). At Trinity Alps Road, turn left and drive about 2.5 miles to the campground on the right side of the road.

Trip notes: This remote spot is an ideal jump-off point for backpackers. It's located at the head of Stuarts Fork Trail, about two miles from the western shore of Trinity Lake. The trail leads into the Trinity Alps Wilderness, along Stuarts Fork, past Oak Flat and Morris Meadows, and up to Emerald Lake and the Sawtooth Ridge. It is a long and grueling climb, but fishing is excellent at Emerald Lake as well as at neighboring Sapphire Lake. There's a great view of the Alps from this camp. It is set at 2,700 feet and remains open year-round, but there's no piped water in the winter and it gets mighty cold up here.

㉗ Pinewood Cove Campground

Location: On Trinity Lake; map B1, grid e7.

Campsites, facilities: There are 42 RV sites with full or partial hookups and 37 tent sites. Picnic tables and fire grills are provided. Rest rooms, showers, a coin laundry, sanitary disposal station, RV supplies, free movies three nights a week, recreation room, pinball and video machines, grocery store, ice, fishing tackle, library, boat dock with 32 slips, beach, and boat rentals are available. Pets must be controlled.

Reservations, fees: Reservations are recommended in the summer; $18 to $24 per night. Open mid-April through October.

Contact: Pinewood Cove Campground, (530) 286-2201; website www.campgrounds.com/pinewood.

Directions: From Redding, turn west on Highway 299 and drive to Weaverville. In Weaverville, turn north on Highway 3 and drive 14 miles to the campground entrance.

Trip notes: This is a privately operated camp with full boating facilities at Trinity Lake. If you don't have a boat but want to get on Trinity Lake, this can be a good starting point. A reservation is advised during the peak summer season. The elevation is 2,300 feet.

㉘ Ridgeville Island Boat-In Camp

Location: On Trinity Lake in Shasta-Trinity National Forest; map B1, grid e8.

Campsites, facilities: There are three tent sites. Vault toilets, picnic tables, and fire grills are provided. There is no piped water, so bring your own. Boat ramps can be found near Clark Springs Campground, Alpine View Campground, or farther north at Trinity Center. Leashed pets are permitted.

Reservations, fees: No reservations; no fee.

Contact: Shasta-Trinity National Forest, Weaverville Ranger Station, (530) 623-2121 or fax (530) 623-6010.

Directions: From Redding, head west on Highway 299 and drive to Weaverville. In Weaverville, turn north on Highway 3 and drive seven miles to the Stuarts Fork arm of Trinity Lake. Boat launches are located at Stuarts Fork. After launching, drive your boat to the mouth of Stuarts Fork; the campground is set on a small island here.

Trip notes: This is one of the 100 featured campgrounds in my book *Easy Camping in Northern California*. Why? Well, how would you like to be on a deserted island for a week? You'll learn the answer from this tiny, little-known island with a great view of the Trinity Alps. It is one of several boat-in camps in the Trinity Lake region. The elevation is 2,500 feet.

㉙ Ridgeville Boat-In Camp

Location: On Trinity Lake in Shasta-Trinity National Forest; map B1, grid e8.

Campsites, facilities: There are 11 tent sites. Vault toilets, picnic tables, and fire grills are provided. There is no piped water, so bring your own. Boat ramps can be found near Clark Springs (campground number 36), Alpine View (campground number 41), or farther north at Trinity Center. Leashed pets are permitted.

Reservations, fees: No reservations; no fee.

Contact: Shasta-Trinity National Forest, Weaverville Ranger Station, (530) 623-2121 or fax (530) 623-6010.

Directions: From Redding, head west on Highway 299 and drive to Weaverville. In Weaverville, turn north on Highway 3 and drive seven miles to the Stuarts Fork arm of Trinity Lake. Boat launches are located at Stuarts Fork. After launching, drive your boat to the mouth of Stuarts Fork. The campground is set on the western shore at the end of a peninsula at the entrance to that part of the lake.

Trip notes: This is one of the ways to get a camping spot to call your own—go by boat. The camp is exposed on a peninsula, providing beautiful views. Good prospects for waterskiing and trout or bass fishing make for a highlight film. The early part of the season is the prime time here for boaters, prior to the furnace heat of full summer, with both trout and bass on the bite. A great view of the Trinity Alps is a bonus. The only downer is the typical lake drawdown at the end of summer and beginning of fall, when this boat-in camp is left a long traipse from water's edge.

㉚ Hayward Flat

Location: On Trinity Lake in Shasta-Trinity National Forest; map B1, grid e8.

Campsites, facilities: There are 94 sites for tents or RVs up to 40 feet long and four multi-family sites. Piped water, flush toilets, picnic tables, and fire grills are provided. Supplies and a boat ramp are available nearby. Leashed pets are permitted.

Reservations, fees: Reserve via phone at (877) 444-6777 ($8.65 reservation fee) or website www.reserveusa.com; $12 to $18 per night, $5 for each additional vehicle. Open mid-May through mid-September.

Contact: Shasta-Trinity National Forest, Weaverville Ranger Station, (530) 623-2121 or fax (530) 623-6010.

Directions: From Redding, head west on Highway 299 and drive to Weaverville. In Weaverville, turn north on Highway 3 and drive about 20 miles, approximately three miles past the Mule Creek Ranger Station. Turn right at the signed access road for Hayward Flat and drive about three miles to the campground at the end of the road.

Trip notes: When giant Trinity Lake is full of water, Hayward Flat is one of the prettiest places you could ask for. The camp has become one of the most popular Forest Service campgrounds on Trinity Lake because it sits right along the shore and offers a "private"

beach for Hayward Flat campers only. The elevation is 2,400 feet.

㉛ Minersville

Location: On Trinity Lake in Shasta-Trinity National Forest; map B1, grid e8.

Campsites, facilities: There are 21 sites for tents or RVs up to 18 feet long. Piped water (spring, summer, and fall only; no piped water in the winter), flush toilets, picnic tables, fire grills, and a low-water boat ramp are provided. Leashed pets are permitted.

Reservations, fees: No reservations; $10 to $17 per night, free in winter. Open year-round, but note that there is no piped water in the winter.

Contact: Shasta-Trinity National Forest, Weaverville Ranger Station, (530) 623-2121 or fax (530) 623-6010.

Directions: From Redding, head west on Highway 299 to Weaverville. Turn north on Highway 3 and drive about 18 miles (if you reach the Mule Creek Ranger Station, you have gone a half mile too far). Turn right at the signed campground access road and drive a half mile to the camp.

Trip notes: This is a good camp for boaters, with a boat ramp located in the cove a short distance to the north. The setting is near lakeside, quite beautiful when Trinity Lake is fullest in the spring and early summer. The elevation is 2,500 feet.

㉜ Stoney Point

Location: On Trinity Lake in Shasta-Trinity National Forest; map B1, grid e8.

Campsites, facilities: There are 22 tent sites. Piped water, flush toilets, picnic tables, and fire grills are provided. Leashed pets are permitted.

Reservations, fees: No reservations; $10 per night in season, free in winter. Open year-round, weather permitting.

Contact: Shasta-Trinity National Forest, Weaverville Ranger Station, (530) 623-2121 or fax (530) 623-6010.

Directions: From Redding, head west on Highway 299 and drive to Weaverville. In Weaverville, turn north on Highway 3 and drive 14 miles (about a quarter mile past the Stuarts Fork Bridge) to the campground.

Trip notes: This is a popular spot at Trinity Lake, easily discovered and easily reached. Set near the inlet of Stuarts Fork, it often fills up, but two other campgrounds close by provide overflow options. The elevation is 2,400 feet.

33 Tannery Gulch

Location: On Trinity Lake in Shasta-Trinity National Forest; map B1, grid e8.

Campsites, facilities: There are 83 sites for tents or RVs up to 40 feet long and four multi-family sites. Piped water, flush and vault toilets, picnic tables, boat ramp, and fire grills are provided. A grocery store is available nearby. Leashed pets are permitted.

Reservations, fees: Reserve via phone at (877) 444-6777 ($8.65 reservation fee) or website www.reserveusa.com; $12 to $18 per night, $5 for an extra vehicle.

Contact: Shasta-Trinity National Forest, Weaverville Ranger Station at (530) 623-2121 or fax (530) 623-6010.

Directions: From Redding, head west on Highway 299 and drive to Weaverville. In Weaverville, turn north on Highway 3 and drive 13.5 miles north to County Road 172. Turn right on County Road 172 and drive 1.5 miles to the campground on the left side of the road.

Trip notes: This is one of the more popular Forest Service camps on the southwest shore of huge Trinity Lake. There's a nice beach near the campground, provided the infamous Bureau of Reclamation hasn't drawn the lake level down too far. It can be quite low in the fall. The elevation is 2,400 feet.

34 Stoney Creek Group Camp

Location: On Trinity Lake in Shasta-Trinity National Forest; map B1, grid e9.

Campsites, facilities: This group campground can hold up to 50 people. Sites are for tents only. Piped water (spring, summer, and fall only; no piped water in the winter), flush toilets, picnic tables, and fire grills are provided. Leashed pets are permitted.

Reservations, fees: Reservations are required via phone at (877) 444-6777 ($8.65 reservation fee) or website www.reserveusa.com; $50 per night. Open year-round, but there's no piped water in the winter.

Contact: Shasta-Trinity National Forest, Weaverville Ranger Station, (530) 623-2121 or fax (530) 623-6010.

Directions: From Redding, turn west on Highway 299 and drive to Weaverville. In Weaverville, turn north on Highway 3 and drive 14.5 miles (about a half mile past the Stuarts Fork Bridge) to the campground.

Trip notes: A series of camps is located on the northern shore of the Stuarts Fork arm of Trinity Lake. This is one of two designed for groups (the other is Bushy Tail), and it is clearly the better. It is set along the Stoney Creek arm, a cove with a feeder creek, with the camp large but relatively private. A swimming beach nearby is a bonus. The elevation is 2,400 feet.

35 Bushy Tail Group Camp

Location: On Trinity Lake in Shasta-Trinity National Forest; map B1, grid e9.

Campsites, facilities: This group campground can hold up to 200 people. Sites are for tents or RVs up to 22 feet long. Piped water, flush toilets, picnic tables, and fire grills are provided. Supplies and a boat ramp are available nearby. Leashed pets are permitted.

Reservations, fees: Reservations are required via phone at (877) 444-6777 ($8.65 reservation fee) or website www.reserveusa.com; $60 group fee per night. Open May through September.

Contact: Shasta-Trinity National Forest, Weaverville Ranger Station, (530) 623-2121 or fax (530) 623-6010.

Directions: From Redding, head west on Highway 299 and drive to Weaverville. In Weaverville, turn north on Highway 3 and drive about

16 miles (approximately 3.5 miles past the Stuarts Fork Bridge) to the campground entrance road on the right. Turn right and drive a short distance to the camp on the left side of the road.

Trip notes: This is a huge group camp at Trinity Lake, the kind of place where you might want to have a political convention. Then you could tell some politician to go jump in a lake. (Haven't you always wanted to do that?) What the heck, it's pretty enough to want to jump in yourself, and with a boat launch nearby, you get a bonus. The elevation is 2,500 feet.

36 Clark Springs

Location: On Trinity Lake in Shasta-Trinity National Forest; map B1, grid e9.

Campsites, facilities: There are 21 tent sites. Piped water (spring, summer, and fall only; no piped water in the winter), flush toilets, picnic tables, and fire grills are provided. A grocery store and boat ramp are nearby. Leashed pets are permitted.

Reservations, fees: No reservations; $8 per night. Open year-round, but there's no piped water in the winter.

Contact: Shasta-Trinity National Forest, Weaverville Ranger Station, (530) 623-2121 or fax (530) 623-6010.

Directions: From Redding, head west on Highway 299 and drive to Weaverville. In Weaverville, turn north on Highway 3 and drive 16.5 miles (about four miles past the Stuarts Fork Bridge) to the campground entrance road on the right.

Trip notes: This used to be a day-use-only picnic area, but due to popular demand, the Forest Service has opened it for camping. That makes sense because people were bound to declare it a campground anyway, since it has a nearby boat ramp and a beach. The elevation is 2,400 feet.

37 Mariners Roost Boat-In Camp

Location: On Trinity Lake in Shasta-Trinity National Forest; map B1, grid e9.

Campsites, facilities: There are seven tent

sites. Vault toilets, picnic tables, and fire grills are provided. There is no piped water, so bring your own. Boat ramps can be found near Clark Springs Campground, Alpine View Campground, or farther north at Trinity Center. Leashed pets are permitted.

Reservations, fees: No reservations; no fee.

Contact: Shasta-Trinity National Forest, Weaverville Ranger Station, (530) 623-2121 or fax (530) 623-6010.

Directions: From Redding, head west on Highway 299 and drive to Weaverville. In Weaverville, turn north on Highway 3 and drive seven miles to the Stuarts Fork arm of Trinity Lake. Boat launches are located at Stuarts Fork. After launching, drive your boat to the mouth of Stuarts Fork and look for the camp on the peninsula, just east and on the opposite shore of Ridgeville Island Boat-In Camp.

Trip notes: A perfect boat camp? This comes close at Trinity since it's positioned perfectly for boaters, with spectacular views of the Trinity Alps to the west, and is an ideal spot for water-skiers. That is because it is located on the western side of the lake's major peninsula, topped by Bowerman Ridge. Secluded and wooded, this area is set at 2,400 feet elevation.

38 Fawn Group Camp

Location: On Trinity Lake in Shasta-Trinity National Forest; map B1, grid e9.

Campsites, facilities: This group campground can hold up to 300 people. Sites are for tents or RVs up to 37 feet long. Piped water, flush toilets, picnic tables, and fire grills are provided. Leashed pets are permitted.

Reservations, fees: Reservations are required via phone at (877) 444-6777 ($8.65 reservation fee) or website www.reserveusa.com; $60 group fee per night. Open May through September.

Contact: Shasta-Trinity National Forest, Weaverville Ranger Station, (530) 623-2121 or fax (530) 623-6010.

Directions: From Redding, head west on Highway 299 and drive to Weaverville. In Weaverville, turn north on Highway 3 and drive 15 miles to the campground.

Trip notes: If you want Trinity Lake all to yourself, one way to do it is to get a group together and then reserve this camp near the shore of Trinity Lake. The elevation is 2,500 feet.

㊴ Rush Creek

Location: In Shasta-Trinity National Forest, north of Weaverville; map B1, grid e7.

Campsites, facilities: There are 10 sites for tents only. Picnic tables and fire pits are provided. Vault toilets are available. No piped water is available. No trash facilities are provided, so bring a garbage bag to pack out all refuse.

Reservations, fees: No reservations; $5 per night.

Contact: Shasta-Trinity National Forest, Weaverville Ranger Station at (530) 623-2121 or fax (530) 623-6010.

Directions: From Redding, go west on Highway 299 and drive to Weaverville. In Weaverville, turn north on Highway 3 and drive about eight miles to the signed turnoff on the left side of the road. Turn left and drive a quarter mile on the short spur road to the campground on the left side of the road. If you get to Forest Service Road 113, you've gone too far.

Trip notes: This small, primitive camp provides overflow space during busy holiday weekends when the camps at Lewiston and Trinity Lakes are near capacity. It may not be much, but hey, at least if you know about Rush Creek you'll never get stuck for a spot. The camp borders Rush Creek and is secluded, but again, it's nearly five miles to the nearest access point to Trinity Lake.

㊵ Captain's Point Boat-In Camp

Location: On Trinity Lake in Shasta-Trinity National Forest; map B1, grid f8.

Campsites, facilities: There are three tent sites. Vault toilets, picnic tables, and fire grills are provided. There's no piped water, so bring your own. Boat ramps can be found near Clark Springs and Alpine View (campground numbers 36 and 41), or farther north at Trinity Center. Leashed pets are permitted.

Reservations, fees: No reservations; no fee.

Contact: Shasta-Trinity National Forest, Weaverville Ranger Station, (530) 623-2121 or fax (530) 623-6010.

Directions: From Redding, head west on Highway 299 and drive to Weaverville. In Weaverville, turn north on Highway 3 and drive about seven miles to the signed turnoff on the right side of the road for the Trinity Alps Marina. Turn right and drive approximately 10 miles to the marina and boat ramp. Launch your boat and cruise north about four miles up the main Trinity River arm of the lake. Look for Captain's Point on the left side of the lake.

Trip notes: The Trinity River arm of Trinity Lake is a massive piece of water, stretching north from the giant Trinity Dam for nearly 20 miles. This camp is the only boat-in camp along this entire stretch of shore, and it is situated at a prominent spot, where a peninsula juts well out into the main lake body. This is a perfect boat-in site for water-skiers or fishermen. The fishing is often excellent for smallmouth bass in the cove adjacent to Captain's Point, using grubs. The elevation is 2,400 feet.

㊶ Alpine View

Location: On Trinity Lake in Shasta-Trinity National Forest; map B1, grid e9.

Campsites, facilities: There are 66 sites for tents or RVs up to 32 feet long. Piped water, flush toilets, picnic tables, and fire grills are provided. The Bowerman Boat Ramp is next to the camp. Leashed pets are permitted.

Reservations, fees: No reservations; $12 to $18 per night, $5 for an extra vehicle. Open mid-May through mid-September (rarely, it is closed temporarily when lake levels are extremely low).

Contact: Shasta-Trinity National Forest, Weaverville Ranger Station, (530) 623-2121 or fax (530) 623-6010.

Directions: From Redding, turn west on Highway 299 and drive to Weaverville. In Weaverville, turn north on Highway 3 and drive to Covington Mill (six miles south of Trinity Center). Turn right (south) on Guy Covington Road and drive three miles to the camp (one mile past Bowerman Boat Ramp) on the right side of the road.

Trip notes: This is an attractive area, set on the shore of Trinity Lake at a creek inlet, and is again open after a temporary closure due to a major restoration project. The boat ramp nearby provides a bonus. It's a very pretty spot, with views to the west across the lake arm and to the Trinity Alps, featuring Granite Peak. The Forest Service also runs tours from the campground to historic Bowerman Barn, which was built in 1894. The elevation is 2,400 feet.

⓸ Big Slide

Location: On the South Fork of the Trinity River in Shasta-Trinity National Forest; map B1, grid f1.

Campsites, facilities: There are four tent sites and four sites for tents or RVs. There is no piped water. Vault toilets, picnic tables, and fire grills are provided. Leashed pets are permitted.

Reservations, fees: No reservations; no fee. Open April through November.

Contact: Shasta-Trinity National Forest, Hayfork Ranger Station, (530) 628-5227 or fax (530) 628-5212.

Directions: From Redding, head west on Highway 299 and drive over the Buckhorn Summit to the junction with Highway 3 near Douglas City. Turn south on Highway 3 and drive to Hayfork. From Hayfork, turn right on County Road 301 and drive about 20 miles to the town of Hyampom. In Hyampom, turn right on Lower South Fork Road /County Road 311 and drive five miles on County Road 311.

Trip notes: This camp is literally out in the middle of nowhere. Free? Of course it's free. Otherwise, someone would actually have to show up now and then to collect. It's a tiny, secluded, little-visited spot set along the South Fork of the Trinity River. The elevation is 1,200 feet.

⓹ East Weaver

Location: On the east branch of Weaver Creek in Shasta-Trinity National Forest; map B1, grid f7.

Campsites, facilities: There are eight tent sites and seven sites for tents or RVs up to 16 feet long. Piped water (spring, summer, and fall only), vault toilets, picnic tables, and fire grills are provided. Supplies and a coin laundry are available in Weaverville. Leashed pets are permitted.

Reservations, fees: No reservations; $8 per night. Open year-round, but there's no piped water in the winter.

Contact: Shasta-Trinity National Forest, Weaverville Ranger Station, (530) 623-2121 or fax (530) 623-6010.

Directions: From Redding, go west on Highway 299 and drive to Weaverville. In Weaverville, turn north on Highway 3 and drive about two miles to East Weaver Road. Turn left on East Weaver Road and drive 3.5 miles to the campground.

Trip notes: This camp is set along East Weaver Creek. Another mile to the west on East Weaver Road, the road dead-ends at a trailhead, a good side trip. From here, the hiking trail is routed four miles, a significant climb, to tiny East Weaver Lake, set to the southwest of Monument Peak (7,771 feet elevation). The elevation at East Weaver is 2,700 feet.

⓻ Old Lewiston Bridge RV Resort

Location: On the Trinity River; map B1, grid f7.

Campsites, facilities: There are 52 RV sites with full hookups and a separate area for tents. Rest rooms, hot showers, a coin laundry, and picnic tables are provided. A grocery store and propane gas refills are available. A group picnic area is available by reservation. Supplies can be obtained within walking distance in Lewiston. Leashed pets are permitted.

Reservations, fees: Reservations are accepted; $21 per night.

Contact: Old Lewiston Bridge RV Resort, (530) 778-3894.

Directions: From Redding, head west on Highway 299, drive over Buckhorn Summit, and continue for five miles to County Road 105. Turn right on County Road 105, drive four miles to

Lewiston, and continue north to the junction of Rush Creek Road and Trinity Dam Road. Turn west on Rush Creek Road and drive three-quarters of a mile to the resort.

Trip notes: Though much of the water from Trinity and Lewiston Lakes is diverted via tunnel to Whiskeytown Lake (en route to the valley and points south), enough escapes downstream to provide a viable fishery on the stretch of river near the town of Lewiston. This upstream portion below Lewiston Lake is prime in the early summer for trout, particularly the chance for a huge brown trout (special regulations in effect). In the winter, the stretch near Steelbridge is often good for steelhead. The campground is in a hilly area but has level sites, with nearby Lewiston Lake a major attraction.

㊺ Trinity River Lodge RV Resort

Location: On the Trinity River; map B1, grid f7.

Campsites, facilities: There are 60 RV sites, all with full hookups, and five tent sites. Rest rooms, hot showers, a coin laundry, cable TV, recreation room, lending library, club house, recreation field, propane gas, camp store, ice, wood, furnished trailer rentals, boat and trailer storage, and horseshoes are available. There is lake fishing less than 10 minutes away. Leashed pets are permitted.

Reservations, fees: Reservations are recommended; $14 to $21 per night. Open April through October.

Contact: Trinity River Lodge RV Resort, (530) 778-3791; email: trinityriver@snowcrest.net; website www. campgrounds.com/trinityriver.

Directions: From Redding, go west on Highway 299, drive over Buckhorn Summit, and continue for five miles to County Road 105. Turn right on County Road 105 and drive four miles to Lewiston. Turn right at Trinity Dam Boulevard and drive six miles, crossing the Trinity River. Just after the bridge, turn left on Rush Creek Road and drive to the campground on the left.

Trip notes: For many, this privately operated

park has an ideal location. You get level, grassy sites with shade trees along the Trinity River, yet it is just a short drive north to Lewiston Lake or a bit farther to giant Trinity Lake. Lake or river, take your pick.

㊻ Ackerman

Location: On Lewiston Lake in Shasta-Trinity National Forest; map B1, grid f8.

Campsites, facilities: There are 66 sites for tents or RVs up to 40 feet long. Piped water (spring, summer, and fall only; no piped water in the winter), flush toilets, picnic tables, and fire grills are provided. A sanitary dump station is available. Leashed pets are permitted.

Reservations, fees: No reservations; $5 to $10 per night. Open year-round, but there's no piped water in the winter.

Contact: Shasta-Trinity National Forest, Weaverville Ranger Station, (530) 623-2121 or fax (530) 623-6010.

Directions: From Redding, head west on Highway 299, drive over Buckhorn Summit, and continue for five miles to County Road 105. Turn right on County Road 105 and drive four miles to Lewiston. Continue north on County Road 105 (Buckeye Creek Road) for eight miles to the campground.

Trip notes: Of the camps and parks at Lewiston Lake, Ackerman is located closest to the lake's headwaters. This stretch of water below Trinity Dam is the best area for trout fishing on Lewiston Lake. Nearby Pine Cove boat ramp, located two miles south of the camp, offers the only boat launch on Lewiston Lake with docks and a fish-cleaning station—a popular spot for fishermen. When the Trinity powerhouse is running, trout fishing is excellent in this area. The elevation is 2,000 feet.

㊼ Lakeview Terrace Resort

Location: On Lewiston Lake; map B1, grid f8.

Campsites, facilities: There are 35 RV sites

with full hookups, and cabins with one to five bedrooms. Rest rooms, hot showers, laundry room, dump station, heated pool, propane gas, and boat rentals are available. Supplies are available within five miles. Leashed pets are permitted.

Reservations, fees: Reservations are accepted; $18 per night; cabins are $50 to $100 per night.

Contact: Lakeview Terrace Resort, (530) 778-3803.

Directions: From Redding, go west on Highway 299, drive over Buckhorn Summit, and continue for five miles to County Road 105. Turn right on County Road 105 , drive four miles to Lewiston, and continue north on Trinity Dam Boulevard for five miles to the resort on the left side of the road.

Trip notes: This might be your Golden Pond. It's a terraced RV park—with cabin rentals also available—that overlooks Lewiston Lake, one of the prettiest drive-to lakes in the region. Fishing for trout is excellent from Lakeview Terrace on upstream toward the dam. Lewiston Lake is perfect for fishing, with a 10 mph speed limit in effect (all the hot boats go to nearby Trinity Lake), along with excellent prospects for rainbow and brown trout. The topper is that Lewiston Lake is always full to the brim, just the opposite of the up-and-down nightmare of its neighboring big brother, Trinity.

48 Mary Smith

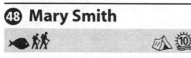

Location: On Lewiston Lake in Shasta-Trinity National Forest; map B1, grid f8.

Campsites, facilities: There are 18 tent sites. Piped water, flush and vault toilets, picnic tables, and fire grills are provided. Supplies and a coin laundry are available in Lewiston. Leashed pets are permitted.

Reservations, fees: No reservations; $9 per night. Open April through October.

Contact: Shasta-Trinity National Forest, Weaverville Ranger Station, (530) 623-2121 or fax (530) 623-6010.

Directions: From Redding, head west on Highway 299, drive over Buckhorn Summit, and con-

tinue for five miles to County Road 105. Turn right on County Road 105/Buckeye Creek Road, drive four miles to Lewiston, and then continue 2.5 miles north on County Road 105/Buckeye Creek Road to the campground.

Trip notes: This is one of the prettiest spots you'll ever see, set along the southwestern shore of Lewiston Lake. When you wake up and peek out of your sleeping bag, the natural beauty of this serene lake so nearby can take your breath away. Hand-launched boats, such as canoes, are ideal here. Trolling for trout is only fair in this end of the lake; most of the fish are below the Trinity Dam. Bird-watching is good, however. The elevation is 2,000 feet.

49 Cooper Gulch

Location: On Lewiston Lake in Shasta-Trinity National Forest; map B1, grid f8.

Campsites, facilities: There are five sites for tents or RVs up to 16 feet long. Vault toilets, picnic tables, and fire grills are provided, but there's no piped water, so bring your own. Supplies and a coin laundry are available in Lewiston. Some facilities are wheelchair accessible. Leashed pets are permitted.

Reservations, fees: No reservations; $10 per night. Open April through November.

Contact: Shasta-Trinity National Forest, Weaverville Ranger Station, (530) 623-2121 or fax (530) 623-6010.

Directions: From Redding, head west on Highway 299, drive over Buckhorn Summit, and continue for five miles to County Road 105/Buckeye Creek Road. Turn right on County Road 105/Buckeye Creek road, drive four miles to Lewiston, and then continue another four miles north on County Road 105/Buckeye Creek Road to the campground.

Trip notes: Here is a nice spot along a beautiful lake, featuring a short trail to Baker Gulch, where a pretty creek enters Lewiston Lake. The trout fishing is good on the upper end of the lake (where the current starts) and upstream. The lake was recently designated as a wildlife viewing area, with large numbers of waterfowl and other birds often spotted near the tules off the shore of Lakeview Terrace. Bring all of your own supplies and plan on hunkering down here for a while.

⑤⓪ Tunnel Rock

Location: On Lewiston Lake in Shasta-Trinity National Forest; map B1, grid f8.

Campsites, facilities: There are six tent sites. Vault toilets, picnic tables, and fire grills are provided, but there is no piped water, so bring your own. Leashed pets are permitted.

Reservations, fees: No reservations; $5 per night. Open year-round.

Contact: Shasta-Trinity National Forest, Weaverville Ranger Station, (530) 623-2121 or fax (530) 623-6010.

Directions: From Redding, go west on Highway 299, drive over Buckhorn Summit, and continue for five miles to County Road 105/Buckeye Creek Road. Turn right on County Road 105/Buckeye Creek Road, drive four miles to Lewiston, and then continue another seven miles north on County Road 105/Buckeye Creek Road to the campground.

Trip notes: This is a very small, primitive alternative to the Ackerman (campground number 46), which is more developed and located another mile up the road to the north. The proximity to the Pine Cove boat ramp and fish-cleaning station, located less than two miles to the south, is a primary attraction. The elevation is 1,900 feet.

⑤① Douglas City

Location: On the Trinity River; map B1, grid g6.

Campsites, facilities: There are 18 sites for tents or RVs up to 30 feet long. Piped water, rest rooms, picnic tables, and fire grills are provided. Supplies are available within one mile in Douglas City. Leashed pets are permitted.

Reservations, fees: No reservations; $10 per night. Open May through October.

Contact: Bureau of Land Management, Redding Field Office, (530) 224-2100.

Directions: From Redding, go west on Highway 299 and continue over the bridge at the Trinity River near Douglas City to Steiner Flat Road. Turn left on Steiner Flat Road and drive a half mile to the campground.

Trip notes: If you want to camp along this stretch of the main Trinity River, this camp is your best bet. It is set off the main road, near the river, with good bank fishing access (the prime season being from mid-August through winter for salmon and steelhead). There's paved parking and a nice beach. This can be a good base camp for an off-season fishing trip on the Trinity River or a lounging spot during the summer. The elevation is 2,000 feet.

⑤② Indian Creek RV Park

Location: On the Trinity River; map B1, grid g7.

Campsites, facilities: There are 12 RV sites with full hookups. Water, showers, flush toilets, picnic tables, and a coin laundry are provided. Supplies are available in Douglas City. Leashed pets are permitted.

Reservations, fees: Reservations are accepted; $18 per night. Open year-round.

Contact: Indian Creek RV Park, (530) 623-6332.

Directions: From Redding, drive west on Highway 299 for 36 miles to the Indian Creek Park sign on the left. Turn left at the sign, drive a short distance, and look for the park entrance on the right.

Trip notes: This privately operated RV park is set in the heart of Trinity River country across the road from the Trinity River. The elevation is 1,650 feet.

⑤③ Steelbridge

Location: On the Trinity River; map B1, grid f7.

Campsites, facilities: There are eight sites for tents or small RVs. There is no piped water, but pit toilets, picnic tables, and fire grills are provided. Supplies are available within three miles in Douglas City. Leashed pets are permitted.

Reservations, fees: No reservations; $5 per night. Open year-round.

Contact: Bureau of Land Management, Redding Field Office, (530) 224-2100.

Directions: From Redding, head west on Highway 299, drive over Buckhorn Summit, and continue toward Douglas City to Steel Bridge Road (if you reach Douglas City, you have gone 2.3 miles too far). At Steel Bridge Road, turn right and drive about four miles to the campground at the end of the road.

Trip notes: Very few campers know of this spot, primarily because it is operated by the publicity-shy Bureau of Land Management. But it is a prime spot for anglers and campers. It's one of the better stretches of water in the area for steelhead, with good shore fishing access. The prime time is from October through December. In the summer, the shade of conifers will keep you cool. Don't forget to bring your own water. The elevation is 2,000 feet.

54 Philpot

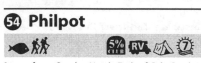

Location: On the North Fork of Salt Creek in Shasta-Trinity National Forest; map B1, grid h3.

Campsites, facilities: There are six sites for tents or RVs. No piped water is available. Vault toilets, picnic tables, and fire grills are provided. Leashed pets are permitted.

Reservations, fees: No reservations; no fee. Open April through November.

Contact: Shasta-Trinity National Forest, Hayfork Ranger Station, (530) 628-5227 or fax (530) 628-5212.

Directions: From Redding, turn west on Highway 299, drive over the Buckhorn Summit, and continue to the junction with Highway 3 near Douglas City. Turn south on Highway 3 and drive to Hayfork. From Hayfork, continue south on Highway 3 for about six miles to Plummer Lookout Road in Peanut. Turn right on Plummer Lookout Road and drive one mile to the campground.

Trip notes: It's time to join the 5 Percent Club; that is, the five percent of the people who know the little-used, beautiful spots in California. This is one of those places, set on the North Fork of Salt Creek on national forest land. The elevation is 2,600 feet. Remember: 95 percent of the people use just five percent of the available open

space. Why would anyone come here? To join the 5 Percent Club, that's why.

55 Deerlick Springs

Location: On Browns Creek in Shasta-Trinity National Forest; map B1, grid h5.

Campsites, facilities: There are 13 sites for tents or RVs up to 20 feet long. Vault toilets, picnic tables, and fire grills are provided. Leashed pets are permitted.

Reservations, fees: No reservations; no fee. Open May through November.

Contact: Shasta-Trinity National Forest, Yolla Bolla Ranger Station, (530) 352-4211 or fax (530) 352-4312.

Directions: From Red Bluff, turn west on Highway 36 (very twisty) and drive to the Forest Service ranger station in Platina. In Platina, turn north on Harrison Gulch Road and drive 10 miles to the campground.

Trip notes: It's a long, twisty drive to this remote and primitive camp set on the edge of the Chanchelulla Wilderness, located in the transition zone where the valley's oak grasslands give way to conifers. This quiet little spot is set along Browns Creek. A trailhead just north of camp provides a streamside walk. The elevation is 3,100 feet.

56 Bailey Cove

Location: On Ruth Lake in Six Rivers National Forest; map B1, grid i0.

Campsites, facilities: There are 25 sites, a few of which are for RVs up to 22 feet long. Piped water, vault toilets, picnic tables, and fire grills are provided. A boat ramp and small marina are available nearby. Leashed pets are permitted.

Reservations, fees: No reservations; $12 per night, $5 for an extra vehicle. Open May through October.

Contact: Six Rivers National Forest, Mad River Ranger District, (707) 574-6233 or fax (707) 574-6273.

Directions: From Eureka, drive south on US 101 to Alton and the junction with Highway 36. Turn east on Highway 36 and drive about 50 miles to the town of Mad River. Turn right at the sign for Ruth Lake/Lower Mad River Road and drive 13 miles to the campground on the right side of the road.

Trip notes: Ruth Lake is the only major lake within a reasonable driving distance of US 101, although some people might argue with you over how reasonable this twisty drive is. Regardless, you end up at a camp along the east shore of Ruth Lake, where fishing for trout or bass and waterskiing are popular. What really wins out is that it is hot and sunny all summer, the exact opposite of the fogged-in Humboldt coast. The elevation is 2,600 feet.

(57) Fir Cove

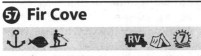

Location: On Ruth Lake in Six Rivers National Forest; map B1, grid i0.

Campsites, facilities: There are 19 single and 3 group sites. Several sites can accommodate RVs up to 22 feet long. Piped water, vault toilets, picnic tables, and fire grills are provided. Leashed pets are permitted.

Reservations, fees: The campground is available for single family camping on summer weekends only, from Friday after 2 P.M. to Monday at 2 P.M. No reservations for single sites; $12 per night during the week and $17 per night on weekends. This is a group camp the rest of the year; reserve group sites through the Mad River Ranger Station at (707) 574-6233; $35 to $45 per night. Open May through October.

Contact: Six Rivers National Forest, Mad River Ranger District, (707) 574-6233 or fax (707) 574-6273.

Directions: From Eureka, drive south on US 101 to Alton and the junction with Highway 36. Turn east on Highway 36 and drive about 50 miles to the town of Mad River. Turn right at the sign for Ruth Lake/Lower Mad River Road and drive 12 miles to the campground on the right side of the road.

Trip notes: This spot is situated along Ruth Lake adjacent to Bailey Cove (campground number 56). It's a unique setup for groups only (and individual families on weekends). The elevation is 2,600 feet.

(58) Hell Gate

Location: On the South Fork of the Trinity River in Shasta-Trinity National Forest; map B1, grid i1.

Campsites, facilities: There are 17 tent sites and seven sites for tents or RVs up to 15 feet long. Piped water, vault toilets, picnic tables, and fire grills are provided. The facilities are wheelchair accessible. Supplies are available in Forest Glen. Leashed pets are permitted. If Hell Gate is full, there are 10 additional campsites that will take tents and RVs up to 20 feet long, just a half mile beyond this campground at Scott's Flat Campground.

Reservations, fees: No reservations; $4 per night. Open April through November.

Contact: Shasta-Trinity National Forest, Hayfork Ranger Station, (530) 628-5227 or fax (530) 628-5212.

Directions: From Red Bluff, turn west on Highway 36 (very twisty) and drive past Platina to the junction with Highway 3. Continue west on Highway 36 for 10 miles to the campground entrance on the left side of the road. If you reach Forest Glen, you have gone a mile too far.

Trip notes: This is a pretty spot bordering the South Fork of the Trinity River that is visited by virtually no one. The prime feature is for hikers. The South Fork National Recreation Trail begins at the campground and follows the river for many miles. Additional trails branch off and up into the South Fork Mountains. This area is extremely hot in summer. The elevation is 2,300 feet.

(59) Forest Glen

Location: On the South Fork of the Trinity River in Shasta-Trinity National Forest; map B1, grid i1.

Campsites, facilities: There are 15 sites for

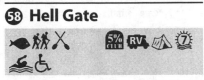

tents or RVs up to 15 feet long. No piped water is available. Vault toilets, picnic tables, and fire grills are provided. The facilities are wheelchair accessible. Supplies can be obtained in Forest Glen. Leashed pets are permitted.

Reservations, fees: No reservations; $4 per night. Open April through November.

Contact: Shasta-Trinity National Forest, Hayfork Ranger Station, (530) 628-5227 or fax (530) 628-5212.

Directions: From Red Bluff, turn west on Highway 36 (very twisty) and drive past Platina to the junction with Highway 3. Continue west on Highway 36 for 11 miles to Forest Glen. The campground is at the west end of town on the right side of the road.

Trip notes: If you get stuck for a spot in this region, this camp almost always has sites open, even during three-day weekends. It is on the edge of a forest near the South Fork of the Trinity River.

---

⑥⓪ Basin Gulch

Location: In Shasta-Trinity National Forest; map B1, grid j5.

Campsites, facilities: There are 13 sites for tents or RVs up to 20 feet. No piped water is available. Vault toilets, picnic tables, and fire grills are provided. Leashed pets are permitted.

Reservations, fees: No reservations; no fee. Open April through November.

Contact: Shasta-Trinity National Forest, Yolla Bolla Ranger Station, (530) 352-4211 or fax (530) 352-4312.

Directions: From Red Bluff, drive about 45 miles west on Highway 36 to the Yolla Bolly District Ranger Station. From the ranger station, turn south on Stuart Gap Road and drive two miles to the campground.

Trip notes: This is one of three little-known campgrounds in the vicinity that rarely gets much use. A trail out of this camp climbs Noble Ridge, eventually rising to a good lookout at 3,933 feet, providing sweeping views of the north valley. Of course, you could also just drive there, taking a dirt road out of Platina. There are many backcountry Forest Service roads in the area so your best bet is to get a Shasta-Trinity National Forest map, which details the roads. The elevation is 2,600 feet.

⑥① Beegum Gorge

Location: In Shasta-Trinity National Forest; map B1, grid j5.

Campsites, facilities: There is no piped water, but vault toilets, picnic tables, and fire grills are provided. Leashed pets are permitted.

Reservations, fees: No reservations; no fee. Open April through November.

Contact: Shasta-Trinity National Forest, Yolla Bolla Ranger Station, (530) 352-4211 or fax (530) 352-4312.

Directions: From Red Bluff, turn west on Highway 36 and drive to Platina. In Platina, turn south on Forest Service Road 29N06 and drive 6.5 miles to the campground.

Trip notes: If you want to get the heck away from anything and everything, this spot should be your calling. The camp is set along little Beegum Creek. The road to this camp dead-ends another mile down the road (west), at a trailhead for a hike that is routed along the creek for nearly five miles to North Fork Beegum Campground. Another route heads up nearby Little Red Mountain, but it involves a 2,000-foot climb, often across dry, hot terrain. The payoffs include incredible views of the Yolla Bolly–Middle Eel Wilderness and spectacular wildflower displays in the spring. The elevation at the camp is 2,200 feet.

Map B2

One inch equals approximately 10.7 miles.
See inside back cover for California state map.

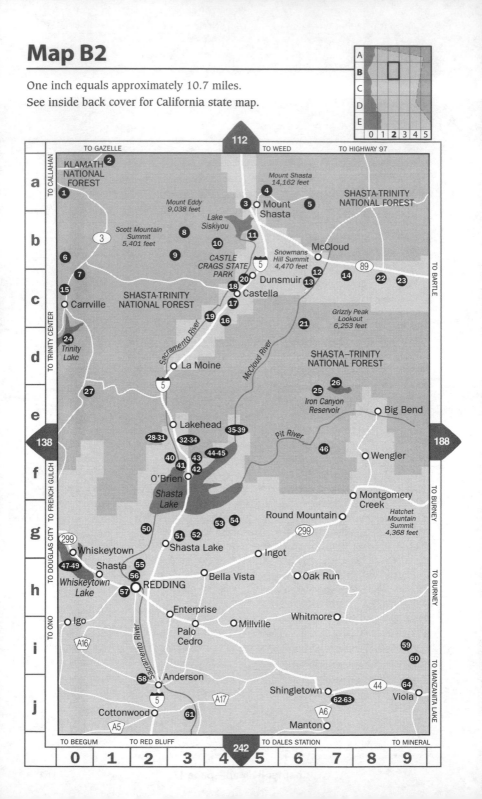

Chapter B2 features:

❶ Scott Mountain

Location: In Shasta-Trinity National Forest; map B2, grid a0.

Campsites, facilities: There are seven tent sites. Vault toilets, picnic tables, and fire grills are provided, but there is no piped water, so bring your own. Leashed pets are permitted.

Reservations, fees: No reservations; no fee. Open year-round.

Contact: Shasta-Trinity Naional Forest, Weaverville Ranger Station, (530) 623-2121 or fax (530) 6010.

Directions: From Redding, drive north on Interstate 5 just past Weed and take the Edgewood turnoff. At the stop sign, turn left and drive a short distance to the stop sign at Old Stage Road. Turn right on Old Stage Road and drive six miles to Gazelle. In Gazelle, turn left at Gazelle-Callahan Road and drive to Callahan. In Callahan, turn south on Highway 3 and drive to Scott Mountain Summit and look for the campground on the right side of the road.

Trip notes: This camp is a jump-off point for hikers, with the Pacific Crest Trail passing right by here. If you hike southwest, it leads into the Scott Mountains and skirts the northern edge of the Trinity Alps Wilderness. Another option here is driving on Forest Service Road 40N08, which begins directly across from camp and Highway 3. On this road, it's only two miles to Big Carmen Lake, a small, largely unknown and pretty little spot. Campground elevation is 5,400 feet.

❷ Kangaroo Lake Walk-In

Location: In Klamath National Forest; map B2, grid a1.

Campsites, facilities: There are 13 drive-in sites for RVs or trailers up to 25 feet and five walk-in sites for tents. Piped water, vault toilets, fire grills, and picnic tables are provided. A fishing pier is available. Facilities are wheelchair accessible. Pets must be controlled.

Reservations, fees: No reservations; $8 per night.

Contact: Klamath National Forest, Scott River Ranger Station, (530) 468-5351 or fax (530) 468-1290.

Directions: From Redding, drive north on Interstate 5 just past Weed and take the Edgewood turnoff. At the stop sign, turn left and drive a short distance to the stop sign at Old Stage Road. Turn right on Old Stage Road and drive six miles to Gazelle. In Gazelle, turn left at Gazelle-Callahan Road and drive over the summit. From the summit, continue about five miles to Rail Creek Road. Turn left at Rail Creek Road and drive approximately five miles to where the road dead-ends at Kangaroo Lake Walk-In.

Trip notes: A remote paved road leads right to Kangaroo Lake, set at 6,050 feet, providing a genuine rarity: a beautiful and pristine mountain lake with a walk-in campground, good fishing for brook and rainbow trout, and an excellent trailhead for hikers. The walk to the campsites is very short, five minutes tops, with many sites located within a minute's walk. Reaching the lake requires another five minutes, but a paved wheelchair-accessible trail is available. In addition, a switchbacked ramp for wheelchairs makes it one of the best wheelchair-accessible fishing areas in California. For hiking, a trail rises up steeply out of the campground and connects to the Pacific Crest Trail, from which you turn left to gain a dramatic lookout of Northern California peaks as well as the lake below.

❸ KOA Mount Shasta

Location: In Mount Shasta; map B2, grid a5.

Campsites, facilities: There are 41 RV sites with full hookups, four camping cabins, and 89 additional sites for tents or RVs (partial hookups). Rest rooms, showers, fire grills, picnic tables, and a playground are provided. Propane gas, a grocery store, and coin laundry are available. Leashed pets are permitted.

Reservations, fees: Reservations are accepted via phone at (800) 562-3617; $18 to $25 per night. Cabins are $31 to $39 per night.

Contact: KOA Mount Shasta, (530) 926-4029.

Directions: From Redding, drive north on Interstate 5 to the town of Mount Shasta. Continue past the first Mount Shasta exit and take the Central Mount Shasta exit. Turn right at the stop sign and drive to the stoplight at Mount Shasta Boulevard. Turn left and drive a half mile to East Hinckley Boulevard. Turn right on East Hinckley, drive a very short distance, then turn left at the entrance to the extended driveway for Mount Shasta KOA.

Trip notes: Despite this KOA camp's relative proximity to the town of Mount Shasta, the extended driveway, wooded grounds, and view of Mount Shasta offer some feeling of seclusion. A bonus here is that those cute little KOA log cabins are available, providing additional privacy. There are many excellent side trips. The best is driving up Everitt Memorial Highway, which rises up the slopes of Mount Shasta to tree line at Bunny Flat, where you can take outstanding, short day hikes with great views to the south of the Sacramento River Canyon and Castle Crags. In the winter, you can play in the snow.

❹ McBride Springs

Location: In Shasta-Trinity National Forest; map B2, grid a6.

Campsites, facilities: There are 10 sites for tents or RVs. Maximum length allowed for RVs is 10 feet. Piped water, vault toilets, picnic tables, and fire grills are provided. Supplies and a coin laundry are available in the town of Mount Shasta. Leashed pets are permitted.

Reservations, fees: No reservations; $12 per night. Open May through October.

Contact: Shasta-Trinity National Forest, Mount Shasta Ranger District, (530) 926-4511 or fax (530) 926-5120.

Directions: From Redding drive north on Interstate 5 to the town of Mount Shasta and take the Central Mount Shasta exit. Turn right and continue on Lake Street through town; once out of town, it turns to the left and becomes Everitt Memorial Highway. Continue on Everitt Memorial Highway for four miles to the campground entrance on the left side of the road.

Trip notes: This camp is set on the slopes of the awesome Mount Shasta (14,162 feet), California's most majestic mountain. Stargazing is fantastic here, and during full moons, an eerie glow is cast on the adjoining high mountain slopes. A good side trip is to drive to the end of Everitt Memorial Highway, which tops out above 7,000 feet. You get great lookouts to the west and a jump-off point for a Shasta expedition or day hike to Panther Meadows.

❺ Panther Meadows Walk-In

Location: In Shasta-Trinity National Forest; map B2, grid a7.

Campsites, facilities: There are 10 walk-in tent sites (trailers not recommended). Vault toilets, picnic tables, and fire grills are provided, but there is no piped water. Supplies are available in the town of Mount Shasta. Leashed pets are permitted.

Reservations, fees: No reservations; no fee.

Contact: Shasta-Trinity National Forest, Mount Shasta Ranger District, (530) 926-4511 or fax (530) 926-5120.

Directions: From Redding, drive north on Interstate 5 to the town of Mount Shasta and take the Central Mount Shasta exit. Turn right and continue on Lake Street through town; once out of town, Lake Street turns to the left and becomes Everitt Memorial Highway. Continue on Everitt Memorial Highway for about 10 miles to the Bunny Flat parking area (where the road is gated). Park, walk past the gate, and continue for one mile to the campground entrance on the right side of the road. Note: When the gate is open, the walk takes only a few minutes.

Trip notes: This quiet site, located on the slopes of Mount Shasta at 7,400 feet, features access to the pristine Panther Meadows, a high mountain meadow set just below tree line. It's a sacred place, regardless of your religious orientation. The hiking is excellent here, with a short hike out to Gray Butte (8,108 feet) for a perfect look to the south of Castle Crags, Mount Lassen, and the Sacramento River Canyon.

❻ Horse Flat

Location: On Eagle Creek in Shasta-Trinity National Forest; map B2, grid b0.

Campsites, facilities: There are five tent sites and 11 sites for tents or RVs up to 16 feet long. Vault toilets, picnic tables, and fire grills are provided, but there is no piped water, so bring your own. Leashed pets are permitted. Horse corrals are available.

Reservations, fees: No reservations; no fee.

Contact: Shasta-Trinity National Forest, Weaverville Ranger Station, (530) 623-2121 or fax (530) 623-6010.

Directions: From Redding, drive west on Highway 299 to Weaverville and Highway 3. Turn north on Highway 3 and drive to Trinity Center at the north end of Trinity Lake. From Trinity Center, continue north on Highway 3 for 16.5 miles to Eagle Creek Campground (on the right) and Forest Service Road 38N27 on the left. Turn left on Forest Service Road 38N27 and drive two miles to the campground.

Trip notes: This camp is used by commercial pack operations as well as horse owners preparing for trips into the Trinity Alps. The camp even has a corral, though it was unused on our visit. A trail starts right out of camp and is routed deep into the Trinity Alps Wilderness. It starts at 3,200 feet in elevation, then climbs all the way along Eagle Creek to Eagle Peak, where it intersects with the Pacific Crest Trail, then drops over the ridge to little Telephone Lake, a nine-mile hike. Note: Horse owners should call for the condition of the corral prior to making the trip.

❼ Eagle Creek

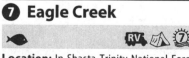

Location: In Shasta-Trinity National Forest; map B2, grid b0.

Campsites, facilities: There are five tent sites and 12 sites for tents or RVs up to 27 feet long. Piped water (spring, summer, and fall only), vault toilets, picnic tables, and fire grills are provided. Leashed pets are permitted.

Reservations, fees: No reservations; $8 per night. Open year-round.

Contact: Shasta-Trinity National Forest, Weaverville Ranger Station, (530) 623-2121 or fax (530) 623-6010.

Directions: From Redding, drive west on Highway 299 to Weaverville and Highway 3. Turn north on Highway 3 and drive to Trinity Center at the north end of Trinity Lake. From Trinity Center, continue north on Highway 3 for 16.5 miles to the campground on the right side of the road.

Trip notes: This campground is set where little Eagle Creek enters the north Trinity River. Some campers use it as a base camp for a fishing trip, with the rainbow trout often abundant but predictably small in this stretch of water. The campground is open year-round, but there is no piped water in the winter. The elevation is 2,800 feet.

❽ Toad Lake Walk-In

Location: In Shasta-Trinity National Forest; map B2, grid b3.

Campsites, facilities: There are six walk-in tent sites. Vault toilets are provided, but there is no piped water. Leashed pets are permitted.

Reservations, fees: No reservations; no fee. Access roads may be closed due to flooding; call ahead for status. Open May through October, weather permitting.

Contact: Shasta-Trinity National Forest, Mount Shasta Ranger District, (530) 926-4511 or fax (530) 926-5120.

Directions: From the town of Mount Shasta on Interstate 5, take the Central Mount Shasta exit and drive to the stop sign. Turn left, cross over the highway, and go a short distance to Old Stage Road. Turn right and drive a half mile to a Y at W. A. Barr Road. Turn left, drive past Box Canyon Dam and the entrance to Lake Siskiyou, and continue up the mountain (the road becomes Forest Service Road 26). Just past a concrete bridge, turn right, drive a very short distance, then turn left on a dirt Forest Service road and continue for 10 miles to the parking area. The road is extremely bumpy and twisty, and the final quarter mile to the trailhead is rough. High-clearance, four-wheel-drive vehicles are recommended.

Trip notes: If you want the remote beauty and splendor of an alpine lake on the Pacific Crest Trail, yet don't want to walk far to get there, this is the place. Little Toad Lake is no easy trick to get to, with a bone-jarring ride for the last half hour, followed by a 15-minute walk, but it's worth the effort. It's a beautiful little lake in the Mount Eddy Range, with lakeside sites, excellent swimming, fair fishing for small trout, and great hiking. The best of the latter is a 45-minute hike out of the Toad Lake Basin (follow the trail counterclockwise around the lake and up to the ridge) to Porcupine Lake, a pristine mountain lake.

⑨ Gumboot Lake

Location: In Shasta-Trinity National Forest; map B2, grid b3.

Campsites, facilities: There are four sites for tents or RVs up to 10 feet long, and across the creek there are four tent sites. Vault toilets and picnic tables are provided, but there is no piped water. Leashed pets are permitted.

Reservations, fees: No reservations; no fee. Open May through October.

Contact: Shasta-Trinity National Forest, Mount Shasta Ranger District, (530) 926-4511 or fax (530) 926-5120.

Directions: From the town of Mount Shasta on Interstate 5, take the Central Mount Shasta exit and drive to the stop sign. Turn left, cross over the highway, and continue a short distance to Old Stage Road. Turn left and drive a half mile to a Y at W. A. Barr Road. Veer right on W. A. Barr Road and drive past Box Canyon Dam and the Lake Siskiyou Campground entrance. Continue two miles to the Red Hill Road detour. Turn left on Red Hill Road and drive six miles. Turn left on Forest Service Road 26 and drive three miles. Veer left on Gumboot Lake Road and drive a half mile to the lake.

Trip notes: This pretty spot provides a few small camps set beside a small yet beautiful high mountain lake, the kind of place many think you can only reach with long hikes. Not so with Gumboot. In addition, the fishing is good here, with rainbow trout in the 12-inch class. The lake is small, almost too small for even a canoe, and

better suited to a pram, raft, or float tube. When the fishing gets good, it can get crowded, with both out-of-towners and locals making casts from the shoreline. An excellent hike is available here, tromping off-trail up the back slope of the lake to the Pacific Crest Trail, then turning left and scrambling to a great lookout of Mount Shasta in the distance and Gumboot in the foreground.

⑩ Castle Lake

Location: In Shasta-Trinity National Forest; map B2, grid b4.

Campsites, facilities: There are six sites for tents or RVs up to 16 feet long. There is no piped water, but vault toilets, picnic table, and a fire grill are provided. Leashed pets are permitted.

Reservations, fees: No reservations; no fee. Open mid-May through October.

Contact: Shasta-Trinity National Forest, Mount Shasta Ranger District, (530) 926-4511 or fax (530) 926-5120.

Directions: From the town of Mount Shasta on Interstate 5, take the Central Mount Shasta exit and drive to the stop sign. Turn left, cross over the highway, and continue a short distance to Old Stage Road. Turn left and drive a half mile to a Y at W. A. Barr Road. Veer right on W. A. Barr Road and drive past Box Canyon Dam. Turn left at Castle Lake Road and drive seven miles to the campground access road on the left. Turn left and drive a short distance to the campground. Note: Castle Lake is another quarter mile up the road; there are no legal campsites along the lake's shoreline.

Trip notes: Castle Lake is a beautiful spot, a deep blue lake set in a granite bowl with a spectacular wall on the far side. The views of Mount Shasta are great, fishing is good (especially ice fishing in winter), canoeing or floating around on a raft is a lot of fun, and there is a terrific hike that loops around the left side of the lake, rising to the ridge overlooking the lake for dramatic views. The campground is not right beside the lake, to ensure the pristine clear waters remain untouched, but is rather just a short distance downstream along Castle Lake Creek. The elevation is 5,450 feet.

⑪ Lake Siskiyou Campground and Marina

Location: Near Mount Shasta; map B2, grid b5.

Campsites, facilities: There are 150 RV sites (25 with partial and 125 with full hookups) and 225 additional sites for tents, four of which are group areas. There are also 11 RV rentals available. Piped water, flush toilets, fire grills, picnic tables, showers, playground, propane, grocery store, gift shop, deli, coin laundry, and a sanitary disposal station are all available for campers' use. There are also marinas, boat rentals (canoes, kayaks, motorized boats), free boat launching, fishing dock, fish-cleaning station, beach, and a banquet room. A free movie plays every night in the summer. Some facilities are wheelchair accessible. Leashed pets are permitted.

Reservations, fees: Reservations are accepted; $14 to $22 per night. RVs rent for $50 to $80 per night. A $1 day-use fee is charged at the entrance station.

Contact: Lake Siskiyou Campground and Marina, (530) 926-2618.

Directions: From the town of Mount Shasta on Interstate 5, take the Central Mount Shasta exit and drive to the stop sign. Turn left, cross over the highway, and continue a short distance to Old Stage Road. Turn left and drive a half mile to a Y at W. A. Barr Road. Veer right on W. A. Barr Road and drive past Box Canyon Dam. Two miles farther, turn right at the entrance road for Lake Siskiyou Campground and Marina and drive a short distance to the entrance station.

Trip notes: This true gem of a lake, virtually in the shadow of Mount Shasta, is almost always full and offers a variety of recreation options. The campground complexes are huge, yet they are tucked into the forest so visitors don't get their style cramped. The lake is located within walking distance, but fishermen will want to drive since a good boat ramp is available. The 10 mph speed limit is strictly enforced. There is an excellent beach and swimming area, the latter protected by a buoy line.

⑫ Dance Country RV Park

Location: In McCloud; map B2, grid c7.

Campsites, facilities: There are 120 sites for RVs of any length, 83 with full and 37 with partial hookups. Piped water, rest rooms with hot showers, and picnic tables are provided. A central barbecue area, two campfire areas, cable TV, laundry room, fish-cleaning station, and two pet walks are available. Leashed pets are permitted.

Reservations, fees: Reservations are recommended; $12 to $19 per night for two people, $1.50 for each additional child from six to 12 years old, and $3 for each additional camper 13 years of age or older. Open April through October.

Contact: Dance Country RV Park, PO Box 686, McCloud, CA 96057; (530) 964-2252.

Directions: From Redding, drive north on Interstate 5 and continue just past Dunsmuir to the junction with Highway 89. Turn east on Highway 89 and drive 12 miles to McCloud. Turn right on Squaw Valley Road and then turn immediately left into the park entrance.

Trip notes: Dance Country RV Park is very popular with square dancers in the summer. The town of McCloud is the home of Dance Country and two large dance halls dedicated to square and round dancing activities. McCloud River's three waterfalls are accessible from the McCloud River Loop, five miles south of the park on Highway 89. Mount Shasta Ski Park also offers summer activities such as biking, mountain climbing, and chairlift rides to great views of the surrounding forests. The ski park access road is located six miles west of McCloud off Highway 89 at Snowman's Hill Summit. The McCloud River Railroad runs an excursion and a dinner train on summer weekends out of McCloud; reservations are available in town. If you're lucky you might see "Old Engine No. 25," one of the few remaining steam engines in service. For more information, see Fowler's Camp (campground number 14).

⑬ Friday's

Location: Near McCloud; map B2, grid c7.

Campsites, facilities: There are 30 sites for RVs of any length with full hookups, and a large, grassy area for dispersed tent camping. Piped water, rest rooms with hot showers and flush toilets, fire pits, and picnic tables are provided. Cable TV, laundry room, pay phone, propane gas, and a recreation room are available. There is a one-acre stocked fish pond for the youngsters, another three-acre pond with wild and stocked trout, and a scheduled fly-fishing school. No fishing license is required on the premises. Leashed pets are permitted.

Reservations, fees: Reservations are advised; $12 to $16 per night for two people, $3 for each additional camper; weekly rates are $73 to $90. Open mid-April through October, weather permitting.

Contact: Friday's, (530) 964-2878.

Directions: From Redding, drive north on Interstate 5 and continue just past Dunsmuir to the junction with Highway 89. Turn east on Highway 89 and drive 12 miles to McCloud. Turn right at Squaw Valley Road and drive six miles to the park entrance on the right.

Trip notes: With two fishing ponds, a fishable stream running through the camp, and the nearby McCloud River's wild trout section a half-hour drive to the south, Friday's offers great fishing opportunities for every member of the family. The park covers 400 wooded and grassy acres with nearby access to the Pacific Crest Trail for hiking. Also available is a public golf course on Squaw Valley Road, plus the dinner and excursion train that runs out of McCloud on summer weekends. See Ah-Di-Na (campground number 21) and Dance Country RV Park (campground number 12) for other information and side trip options.

⑭ Fowler's Camp

Location: On the McCloud River in Shasta-Trinity National Forest; map B2, grid c7.

Campsites, facilities: There are 39 sites for tents or RVs up to 30 feet long. Piped water, vault toilets, picnic tables, and fire grills are provided. The facilities are wheelchair accessible. Leashed pets are permitted.

Reservations, fees: No reservations; $12 per night.

Contact: Shasta-Trinity National Forest, McCloud Ranger District, (530) 964-2184 or fax (530) 964-2938.

Directions: From Redding, drive north on Interstate 5 and continue just past Dunsmuir to the junction with Highway 89. Turn east on Highway 89 and drive 12 miles to McCloud. From McCloud, drive five miles southeast on Highway 89 to the campground entrance road on the right. Turn right and drive a short distance to a Y, then turn left at the Y to the campground.

Trip notes: This campground is set beside the beautiful McCloud River, providing the chance for an easy hike to two waterfalls, including one of the most dramatic in Northern California. From the camp, the trail is routed upstream through forest, a near-level walk for only 15 minutes, then arrives at awesome Middle Falls, a wide-sweeping and powerful cascade best viewed in April. By summer, the flows subside and warm to the point that some people will swim in the pool at the base of the falls. Another trail is routed from camp downstream to Lower Falls, an outstanding swimming hole in midsummer. Fishing the McCloud River here is fair, with trout stocks suspended to protect native species of redband trout. If this camp is full, Cattle Camp (campground number 22) and Algoma (campground number 23) offer overflow areas.

⑮ Trinity River

Location: In Shasta-Trinity National Forest; map B2, grid c0.

Campsites, facilities: There are seven sites for tents or RVs up to 32 feet long. Piped water (spring, summer, and fall only), vault toilets, picnic tables, and fire grills are provided. Leashed pets are permitted.

Reservations, fees: No reservations; $8 per night. Open year-round, but there's no piped water in the winter.

Contact: Shasta-Trinity National Forest, Weaverville Ranger Station, (530) 623-2121 or fax (530) 623-6010.

Directions: From Redding, drive west on Highway 299 to Weaverville and Highway 3. Turn north on Highway 3 and drive to Trinity Center at the north end of Trinity Lake. From Trinity Center, continue north on Highway 3 for 9.5 miles to the campground on the left side of the road.

Trip notes: This camp offers easy access off Highway 3, yet is fairly secluded and provides streamside access to the upper Trinity River. It's a good base camp for a trout fishing trip when the upper Trinity is loaded with small trout. The elevation is 2,500 feet.

⑯ Sims Flat

Location: On the Sacramento River; map B2, grid c4.

Campsites, facilities: There are 19 sites for tents or RVs up to 16 feet. Piped water, flush and vault toilets, picnic tables, and fire grills are provided. A grocery store is nearby. The campground is wheelchair accessible. Leashed pets are permitted.

Reservations, fees: No reservations; $12 per night. Open March through October.

Contact: Shasta-Trinity National Forest, Mount Shasta Ranger District, (530) 926-4511 or fax (530) 926-5120.

Directions: From Redding, drive north on Interstate 5 for about 40 miles to the Sims Road exit. Take the Sims Road exit (on the east side of the highway) and drive south for a mile to the campground.

Trip notes: The upper Sacramento River is again becoming one of the best trout streams in America with direct access off an interstate highway. This camp is an example of the best of it. Sitting beside the upper Sacramento River, it provides access to some of the better spots for trout fishing, particularly from mid-May through July. The trout population has largely recovered since the devastating spill from a train derailment that occurred in 1991. There is a wheelchair-accessible interpretive trail. If you want to literally get away from it all, there is a trailhead about three miles east on Sims Flat Road which

climbs along South Fork, including a terrible, steep, one-mile section near the top, eventually popping out at Tombstone Mountain.

⑰ Crag View Valley Camp

Location: On the Sacramento River; map B2, grid c4.

Campsites, facilities: There are 10 sites (four drive-through), most with full hookups. There is a separate area for tents only. Picnic tables, fire grills, rest rooms, and hot showers are provided. A coin laundry is available. Leashed pets are permitted.

Reservations, fees: Reservations are accepted; $11 to $17 fee per night. Open year-round.

Contact: Crag View Valley Camp, (530) 235-0081 or fax (530) 235-2486.

Directions: From Redding, drive north on Interstate 5 for 44 miles to the Castella exit. Turn right on the frontage road on the east side of the highway and drive three-quarters of a mile to the campground.

Trip notes: This camp is situated on the Sacramento River, below nearby Castle Crags State Park, and also near Castle Creek. There is access for trout fishing and good views of Castle Crags directly to the west and Mount Shasta to the north.

⑱ Castle Crags State Park

Location: On the Sacramento River; map B2, grid c4.

Campsites, facilities: There are 64 sites for tents or RVs up to 27 feet. Picnic tables, fire grills, piped water, hot showers, and flush toilets are provided. Wood is available. Pets are permitted.

Reservations, fees: Reservations are accepted via phone at (800) 444-PARK/7275 ($7.50 reservation fee) or website www.cal-parks.ca.gov; $16 per night. Open year-round.

Contact: Castle Crags State Park, (530) 235-2684.

Directions: From Redding, drive north on Interstate 5 for 45 miles to the Castle Crags State

Park exit. Turn west and drive to the well-signed park entrance on the right side of the road.

Trip notes: Ancient granite spires tower 6,000 feet above the park, and beyond to the north is the giant Mount Shasta, making for a spectacular natural setting. The campsites are set in forest, shaded, very pretty, and sprinkled along a paved access road. At the end of the access road is a parking area for the two-minute walk to the Crags Lookout, a beautiful view. Nearby is the trailhead (at 2,500 feet elevation) for hikes up the Crags, featuring a six-mile round-trip that rises to Castle Dome at 4,966 feet, the leading spire on the crag's ridge. Trout fishing is good in the nearby Sacramento River, but requires driving, walking, and exploring to find the best spots. This is a popular state park, with reservations often required in summer months, but with your choice of any campsite even in late spring.

⑲ Best in the West Resort

Location: Near Dunsmuir; map B2, grid c4.

Campsites, facilities: There are 16 RV sites, most with full hookups. Five cabins are also available. Picnic tables are provided. Rest rooms, hot showers, cable TV, ice, coin laundry, playground, and horseshoes are available. Leashed pets are permitted.

Reservations, fees: Reservations are accepted; $15 per night. Call for cabin fees.

Contact: Best in the West Resort, (530) 235-2603.

Directions: From Redding, drive north on Interstate 5 for about 40 miles to the Sims Road exit. Take the Sims Road exit and drive one block west on Sims Road to the campground on the left.

Trip notes: This is a good layover spot for RV cruisers looking to take a break. The proximity to Castle Crags State Park, the Sacramento River, and Mount Shasta make the location a winner.

⑳ Railroad Park Campground

Location: On the Sacramento River; map B2, grid c5.

Campsites, facilities: There are 60 sites, many with full hookups, and a separate area for tents only. Rest rooms, hot showers, satellite TV hookups, grocery store, ice, laundry room, restaurant, recreation room, playground, and horseshoes are available. Leashed pets are permitted.

Reservations, fees: Deposit required with reservation; $13 to $18 fee per night.

Contact: Railroad Park Campground, (530) 235-0420.

Directions: From Redding, drive north on Interstate 5 for 45 miles to Railroad Park Road. Turn west and drive a half mile to the campground.

Trip notes: This camp was designed in the spirit of the railroad, when steam trains ruled the rails. The property features old stage cars (available for overnight lodging) and a steam locomotive. Many good side trips are available in the area, including excellent hiking and sightseeing at Castle Crags State Park (where there is a series of awesome granite spires) and outstanding trout fishing on the upper Sacramento River.

㉑ Ah-Di-Na

Location: On the McCloud River in Shasta-Trinity National Forest; map B2, grid c6.

Campsites, facilities: There are 16 tent sites. Piped water, flush toilets, picnic tables, and fire grills are provided. Leashed pets are permitted.

Reservations, fees: No reservations; $8 per night.

Contact: Shasta-Trinity National Forest, McCloud Ranger District, (530) 964-2184 or fax (530) 964-2938.

Directions: From Redding, drive north on Interstate 5 past Dunsmuir to the junction with Highway 89. Turn right and drive to McCloud. In McCloud, turn right on Squaw Valley Road and drive to Lake McCloud. Turn right at Lake McCloud and continue along the lake to a signed turnoff on the right side of the road (at a deep cove in the lake). Turn right (the road turns to dirt) and drive four miles to the campground entrance on the left side of the road.

Turn left and drive a short distance to the campground.

Trip notes: This is the perfect base camp for trout fishing on the lower McCloud River, with campsites just a cast away from one of the prettiest streams in California. Downstream of the camp is a special two-mile stretch of river governed by the Nature Conservancy, where all fish must be released, no bait is permitted, single, barbless hooks are mandated, and only 10 rods are allowed on the river at any one time. Wildlife is abundant in the area, the Pacific Crest Trail passes adjacent to the camp, and an excellent nature trail is also available along the river in the McCloud Nature Conservancy.

㉒ Cattle Camp

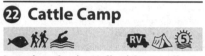

Location: On the McCloud River in Shasta-Trinity National Forest; map B2, grid c8.

Campsites, facilities: There are 20 sites for tents or RVs. Piped water is available, and vault toilets, picnic tables, and fire grills are provided. Leashed pets are permitted.

Reservations, fees: No reservations; $8 to $12 per night.

Contact: Shasta-Trinity National Forest, McCloud Ranger District, (530) 964-2184 or fax (530) 964-2938.

Directions: From Redding, drive north on Interstate 5 and continue just past Dunsmuir to the junction with Highway 89. Turn east on Highway 89 and drive to McCloud. From McCloud, drive 11 miles east on Highway 89 to the campground entrance road on the right. Turn right and drive a half mile to the campground on the left side of the road.

Trip notes: This primitive campground is ideal for RV campers who want a rustic setting, or as an overflow area if the more attractive Fowler's Camp is filled. One of the best swimming holes in the McCloud River is located near the camp, although the water is typically cold. There are several good side trips in the area, including fishing on the nearby McCloud River, visiting the three waterfalls near Fowler's Camp, and exploring the north slopes of Mount Shasta (a map of Shasta-Trinity National Forest details the back roads).

㉓ Algoma

Location: On the McCloud River in Shasta-Trinity National Forest; map B2, grid b9.

Campsites, facilities: There are eight sites for tents or RVs. There is no piped water, but vault toilets, picnic tables, and fire grills are provided. Leashed pets are permitted.

Reservations, fees: No reservations; no fee.

Contact: Shasta-Trinity National Forest, McCloud Ranger District, (530) 964-2184 or fax (530) 964-2938.

Directions: From Redding, drive north on Interstate 5 and continue just past Dunsmuir to the junction with Highway 89. Turn east on Highway 89 and drive to McCloud. From McCloud, drive 14 miles east on Highway 89 to the campground entrance road on the right. Turn right and drive one mile to the campground on the right side of the road.

Trip notes: This little-known, undeveloped spot along the McCloud River is quite dusty in August. It is an alternative to Fowler's Camp (campground number 14) and Cattle Camp (campground number 22). See the trip notes for those places for side trip options. A dirt road out of camp (turn right at the junction) follows along the headwaters of the McCloud River, past Cattle Camp to Upper Falls. There is a parking area for a short walk to view Middle Falls and on to Fowler's Camp and Lower Falls.

㉔ Jackass Springs

Location: On Trinity Lake in Shasta-Trinity National Forest; map B2, grid d0.

Campsites, facilities: There are 21 sites for tents or RVs up to 32 feet long. Piped water (spring, summer, and fall only), vault toilets, picnic tables, and fire grills are provided. Leashed pets are permitted.

Reservations, fees: No reservations; no fee. Open year-round, but there is no piped water in the winter.

Contact: Shasta-Trinity National Forest, Weaverville Ranger Station, (530) 623-2121 or fax (530) 623-6010.

Directions: From Redding head west on Highway 299 and drive to Weaverville and the junction with Highway 3. Turn north on Highway 3 and drive 29 miles to Trinity Center. Continue five miles past Trinity Center to County Road 106. Turn right on County Road 106 and drive 12 miles to the Jackass Springs/County Road 119 turnoff. Turn right on County Road 119 and drive four miles to the campground at the end of the road.

Trip notes: If you're poking around for a more secluded campsite on this end of the lake, halt your search and pick the best spot you can find at this campground, since it's the only one in this area of Trinity Lake. The camp is set on the remote east shore in a large, beautiful cove, complete with a little island just offshore. The only downer is that when the lake level is down, the water is a steep tromp from the campground. The elevation is 2,500 feet.

㉕ Hawkins Landing

Location: On Iron Canyon Reservoir; map B2, grid d7.

Campsites, facilities: There are 10 sites for tents or RVs up to 30 feet long. Piped water, vault toilets, picnic tables, and fire grills are provided. A boat ramp is available. Supplies can be obtained in Big Bend. Leashed pets are permitted.

Reservations, fees: No reservations; $10 per night, $1 pet fee.

Contact: PG&E Building and Land Services, (916) 386-5164.

Directions: From Redding, drive east on Highway 299 for 37 miles to Big Bend Road. At Big Bend Road turn left and drive 15.2 miles to the town of Big Bend. Continue for five miles to the lake, veering right at the T intersection, and continue for a mile to the boat launch/campground turnoff. Turn left and drive a quarter mile to the campground.

Trip notes: The adjacent boat ramp makes Hawkins Landing the better of the two camps at Iron Canyon Reservoir for campers with trailered boats (though Deadlun is far more secluded). Iron Canyon provides good fishing for trout, has a resident bald eagle or two, and also has nearby hot springs in the town of Big Bend. One problem with this lake is the annual drawdown in late fall, which causes the shoreline to be extremely muddy in the spring. The lake usually rises high enough to make the boat ramp functional by mid-April.

㉖ Deadlun

Location: On Iron Canyon Reservoir in Shasta-Trinity National Forest; map B2, grid d7.

Campsites, facilities: There are 30 sites for tents or RVs up to 24 feet long. There is no piped water, so bring your own. Vault toilets, picnic tables, and fire grills are provided. A boat ramp is available one mile from the camp. Leashed pets are permitted.

Reservations, fees: No reservations; no fee.

Contact: Shasta-Trinity National Forest, Shasta Lake Ranger District, (530) 275-1587 or fax (530) 275-1512.

Directions: From Redding, drive east on Highway 299 for 37 miles to Big Bend Road. At Big Bend Road, turn left and drive 15.2 miles to the town of Big Bend. Continue for five miles to the lake, veering right at the T intersection, and continue for two miles (past the boat launch turnoff) to the campground turnoff on the left side of the road. Turn left and drive one mile to the campground.

Trip notes: Deadlun is a pretty campground set in the forest, shaded and quiet, with a five-minute walk or one-minute drive to the Deadlun Creek arm of Iron Canyon Reservoir. Drive? If you have a canoe to launch or fishing equipment to carry, driving is the choice. Trout fishing is good here, both in April and May, then again in October and early November. One downer is that the shoreline is often very muddy here in March and early April. Because of an engineering error with the dam, the lake never fills completely, causing the lakeshore to be strewn with stumps and quite muddy after spring rains and snowmelt.

㉗ Clear Creek

Location: In Shasta-Trinity National Forest; map B2, grid e0.

Campsites, facilities: There are two tent sites

and six sites for tents or RVs up to 22 feet long. Vault toilets, picnic tables, and fire grills are provided, but there is no piped water, so bring your own. Leashed pets are permitted.

Reservations, fees: No reservations; no fee.

Contact: Shasta-Trinity National Forest, Weaverville Ranger District, (530) 623-2121 or fax (530) 623-6010.

Directions: From Redding, turn west on Highway 299 and drive 17 miles to Trinity Lake Road (just west of Whiskeytown Lake). Turn north on Trinity Lake Road and continue past the town of French Gulch for about 12 miles to the Trinity Mountain Ranger Station. Turn right on County Road 106/East Side Road (gravel) and drive north for about 11 miles to the campground access road (dirt) on right. Turn right on the access road and drive two miles to the campground.

Trip notes: This is a primitive, little-known camp that gets extremely little use. It is set near Clear Creek at 3,500 feet elevation. In fall months hunters will occasionally turn it into a deer camp, with the adjacent slopes of Blue Mountain and Damnation Peak in the Trinity Divide country providing fair numbers of large bucks, three points or better. Trinity Lake is located only seven miles to the west, but it seems like it's in a different world. That's because it is.

28 Lakeshore Villa RV Park and Camp

Location: On Shasta Lake; map B2, grid e2.

Campsites, facilities: There are 92 sites for RVs only, with partial or full hookups. Picnic tables are provided. Rest rooms, hot showers, sanitary disposal station, cable TV, coin laundry, playground, recreation room, and a boat dock are available. Leashed pets are permitted.

Reservations, fees: A deposit is required with reservation; $15.50 to $19.50 per night.

Contact: Lakeshore Villa RV Park and Camp, (530) 238-8688.

Directions: From Redding, drive north on Interstate 5 for 24 miles to the Lakeshore-Antlers Road exit in Lakehead. Take that exit, turn left at the stop sign, and drive under the freeway to Lakeshore Drive. Turn left on Lakeshore Drive and drive a half mile to the campground on the right.

Trip notes: This is a large campground with level, shaded sites for RVs, set near the northern Sacramento River arm of giant Shasta Lake. Prime time is from April through July, when lake levels are highest and the bass are on the bite.

29 Lakeshore

Location: On Shasta Lake; map B2, grid e2.

Campsites, facilities: There are 35 RV sites with partial and full hookups and 10 cabins. Picnic tables are provided. Rest rooms, hot showers, swimming pool, video arcade, bar, restaurant, and a small grocery store are available. Live music is scheduled most weekends. A marina and boat rentals are nearby. Leashed pets are permitted.

Reservations, fees: Reservations are recommended; $16 to $18 per night; single cabins are $65 per night, double cabins are $85 per night.

Contact: Lakeshore, (530) 238-2004 or fax (530) 238-2832.

Directions: From Redding, drive north on Interstate 5 for 24 miles to the Lakeshore-Antlers Road exit in Lakehead. Take that exit, turn left at the stop sign, and drive under the freeway to Lakeshore Drive. Turn left on Lakeshore Drive and drive one mile to the campground.

Trip notes: Shasta Lake is a boater's paradise, and an ideal spot for campers with boats, with a boat ramp and private marina available. It is located on the Sacramento River arm of Shasta Lake.

30 Shasta Lake RV Resort and Camp

Location: On Shasta Lake; map B2, grid e2.

Campsites, facilities: There are 21 tent sites and 53 RV sites with full hookups. Picnic tables, barbecues, and fire rings are provided. Rest rooms, hot showers, grocery store, wood, coin laundry, playground, and a swimming pool are available. There is also a private dock with 36 boat slips. Pets are permitted.

Reservations, fees: A deposit is required with reservation; $14 to $21 per night.

Contact: Shasta Lake RV Resort and Camp, (530) 238-2370.

Directions: From Redding, drive north on Interstate 5 for 24 miles to the Lakeshore-Antlers Road exit in Lakehead. Take that exit, turn left at the stop sign, and drive under the freeway to Lakeshore Drive. Turn left on Lakeshore Drive and drive 1.5 miles to the campground.

Trip notes: Shasta Lake RV Resort and Camp is one of a series located on the upper end of Shasta Lake with easy access off Interstate 5 by car, then easy access by boat to premium trout or bass fishing as well as waterskiing.

㉛ Lakeshore East

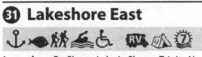

Location: On Shasta Lake in Shasta-Trinity National Forest; map B2, grid e2.

Campsites, facilities: There are 36 sites for tents or RVs up to 30 feet long. Piped water, flush toilets, picnic tables, and fire grills are provided. A boat ramp, grocery store, and coin laundry are nearby. Some facilities are wheelchair accessible. Leashed pets are permitted.

Reservations, fees: Reservations are accepted via phone at (877) 444-6777 ($8.65 reservation fee) or website www.reserveusa.com; $15 to $25 per night. Open May through September.

Contact: Shasta-Trinity National Forest, Shasta Lake Ranger District, (530) 275-1587 or fax (530) 275-1512; Shasta Recreation Company, (530) 238-2824.

Directions: From Redding, drive north on Interstate 5 for 24 miles to the Antlers exit at Lakehead. Take the Antlers exit, turn left at the stop sign, and drive under the freeway to Lakeshore Drive. Turn left on Lakeshore Drive and drive three miles. Look for the campground entrance on the left side of the road.

Trip notes: Lakeshore East is near the full-service community of Lakehead and is located on the Sacramento arm of Shasta Lake. It's a nice spot, with a good boat ramp and marina nearby at Antlers or Sugarloaf.

㉜ Antlers RV Resort and Campground

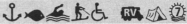

Location: On Shasta Lake; map B2, grid e3.

Campsites, facilities: There are 36 tent sites and 70 RV sites, many with full hookups, and a separate area for tents. Rest rooms, hot showers, snack bar, seasonal grocery store, ice, laundry room, recreation room, playground, volleyball court, swimming pool, propane gas, boat rental, houseboats, moorage, and a complete marina are available. Pets are permitted.

Reservations, fees: A deposit is required with reservation; $11 to $26.50 per night.

Contact: Antlers RV Resort and Campground, (530) 238-2322.

Directions: From Redding, drive north on Interstate 5 for 24 miles to the Lakeshore-Antlers Road exit in Lakehead. Take that exit, turn left at the stop sign, and drive a short distance to Antlers Road. At Antlers Road, turn right and drive 1.5 miles south to the campground.

Trip notes: Antlers Resort is set along the Sacramento River arm of Shasta Lake at 1,215 feet. The prime time to visit is from March through June when the lake levels are highest. This is a full-service spot for campers, boaters, and anglers.

㉝ Gregory Creek

Location: On Shasta Lake in Shasta-Trinity National Forest; map B2, grid e3.

Campsites, facilities: There are five tent sites and 13 sites for tents or RVs up to 24 feet long. Piped water, flush toilets, picnic tables, and fire grills are provided. Leashed pets are permitted.

Reservations, fees: No reservations; $12 per night, $5 for each additional vehicle. Open May through September.

Contact: Shasta-Trinity National Forest, Shasta Lake Ranger District, (530) 275-1587 or fax (530) 275-1512; Shasta Recreation Company, (530) 238-2824 or email: shastacrec@snowcrest.net.

Directions: From Redding, drive north on Interstate 5 for 21 miles to the Salt Creek exit. Take the Salt Creek exit and head east, driving four miles north on Gregory Creek Road to the camp-ground at the end of the road.

Trip notes: This is one of the more secluded Forest Service campgrounds on Shasta Lake. It is set just above lakeside, on the eastern shore of the northern Sacramento River arm of the lake. When the lake is fullest in the spring and early summer, this is a great spot.

34 Antlers

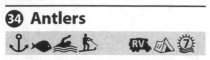

Location: On Shasta Lake in Shasta-Trinity National Forest; map B2, grid e3.

Campsites, facilities: There are 41 single sites and 18 double sites for tents or RVs up to 30 feet long. Piped water, flush and vault toilets, picnic tables, and fire grills are provided. A boat ramp, grocery store, and coin laundry are nearby. Leashed pets are permitted.

Reservations, fees: Reservations are accepted via at phone (877) 444-6777 ($8.65 reservation fee) or website www.reserveusa.com; $15 to $25 per night, $5 for an extra vehicle. Open April through September.

Contact: Shasta-Trinity National Forest, Shasta Lake Ranger District, (530) 275-1587 or fax (530) 275-1512; Shasta Recreation Company, (530) 238-2824 or email: shastarec@snowcrest.net.

Directions: From Redding, drive north on Interstate 5 for 24 miles to the Lakeshore-Antlers Road exit in Lakehead. Take that exit, turn left at the stop sign, and drive a short distance to Antlers Road. At Antlers Road, turn right and drive one mile south to the campground.

Trip notes: This spot is set on the primary Sacramento River inlet of giant Shasta Lake. Antlers is a well-known spot that attracts returning campers and boaters year after year. It is the farthest upstream marina/camp on the lake. Because of that, lake levels can fluctuate greatly from spring through fall, and the operators will move their docks to compensate. Easy access off Interstate 5 is a big plus for boaters.

35 Moore Creek

Location: On Shasta Lake in Shasta-Trinity National Forest; map B2, grid e4.

Campsites, facilities: There are 12 sites for tents or RVs up to 16 feet long. Piped water, vault toilets, picnic tables, and fire grills are provided. Leashed pets are permitted.

Reservations, fees: No reservations; $12 per night, $5 for each additional vehicle. Open May through September.

Contact: Shasta-Trinity National Forest, Shasta Lake Ranger District, (530) 275-1587 or fax (530) 275-1512; Shasta Recreation Company, (530) 238-2824 or email: shastarec@snowcrest.net.

Directions: From Redding, drive north on Interstate 5 for about 20 miles to the Gilman exit. Take Gilman Road/County Road 7H009 and drive northeast for 11 miles to the campground on the right side of the road.

Trip notes: The McCloud arm of Shasta Lake is the most beautiful of the five arms at Shasta, with its emerald green waters and limestone canyon towering overhead to the east. That beautiful setting is taken advantage of at this camp, with a good view of the lake and limestone, along with good trout fishing on the adjacent section of water.

36 Dekkas Rock Group Camp

Location: On Shasta Lake in Shasta-Trinity National Forest; map B2, grid e4.

Campsites, facilities: There are four sites for tents or RVs up to 16 feet long. Piped water, vault toilets, picnic tables, and fire grills are provided. A grocery store is nearby. Leashed pets are permitted.

Reservations, fees: Reservations are required via at phone (877) 444-6777 ($8.65 reservation fee) or website www.reserveusa.com; $90 per night per group site, each of which can accommodate up to 60 campers.

Contact: Shasta-Trinity National Forest, Shasta Lake Ranger District, (530) 275-1587 or fax (530) 275-1512; Shasta Recreation Company, (530) 238-2824 or email: shastarec@snowcrest.net.

Directions: From Redding, drive north on Interstate 5 for about 20 miles to the Gilman exit. Take Gilman Road/County Road 7H009 and drive northeast for 11 miles to the campground on the right side of the road.

Trip notes: The few people who know about this camp love this little spot. It is an ideal group camp, set on a flat above the McCloud arm of Shasta Lake, shaded primarily by bays and oaks, with a boat ramp located two miles to the south at Hirz Bay. The views are pretty here, looking across the lake at the limestone ridge that borders the McCloud arm. In late summer and fall when the lake level drops, it can be a hike from the camp down to water's edge.

❸❼ Ellery Creek

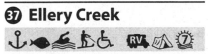

Location: On Shasta Lake in Shasta-Trinity National Forest; map B2, grid e4.

Campsites, facilities: There are 19 sites for tents or RVs up to 30 feet long. Piped water, vault toilets, picnic tables, and fire grills are provided. Toilet facilities are wheelchair accessible. Leashed pets are permitted.

Reservations, fees: Reservations are accepted via phone at (877) 444-6777 ($8.65 reservation fee) or website www.reserveusa.com; $12 per night, $5 for each additional vehicle. Open year-round, with limited winter facilities.

Contact: Shasta-Trinity National Forest, Shasta Lake Ranger District, (530) 275-1587 or fax (530) 275-1512; Shasta Recreation Company, (530) 238-2824 or email: shastarec@snowcrest.net.

Directions: From Redding, drive north on Interstate 5 for about 20 miles to the Gilman exit. Take Gilman Road/County Road 7H009 and drive northeast for 15 miles to the campground on the right side of the road.

Trip notes: This camp is set at a pretty spot where Ellery Creek empties into the upper McCloud arm of Shasta Lake. This stretch of water is excellent for trout fishing in the summer, with bank-fishing access available two miles upstream at the McCloud Bridge. In the spring, there are tons of small spotted bass along the shore from the camp on upstream to the inlet of the McCloud River. Boat launching facilities are available five miles south at Hirz Bay.

❸❽ Pine Point

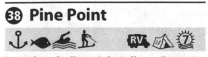

Location: On Shasta Lake in Shasta-Trinity Na-

tional Forest; map B2, grid e4.

Campsites, facilities: There are 14 sites for tents or RVs up to 24 feet. Piped water, vault toilets, picnic tables, and fire rings are provided. Leashed pets are permitted.

Reservations, fees: No reservations; $12 per night, $5 for each additional vehicle. Open April through September.

Contact: Shasta-Trinity National Forest, Shasta Lake Ranger District, (530) 275-1587 or fax (530) 275-1512; Shasta Recreation Company, (530) 238-2824 or email: shastarec@snowcrest.net.

Directions: From Redding, drive north on Interstate 5 for about 20 miles to the Gilman exit. Take Gilman Road/County Road 7H009 and drive northeast for 17 miles to the campground entrance road on the right. Turn right and drive a short distance to the campground.

Trip notes: Pine Point is a pretty little camp, set on a ridge above the McCloud arm of Shasta Lake amid oak trees and scattered ponderosa pines. The view is best in spring, when lake levels are generally highest. Boat launching facilities are available at Hirz Bay; boaters park their boats at shore below the camp while the rest of their party arrives at the camp by car. That provides a chance not only for camping, but for boating, swimming, waterskiing, and fishing as well.

❸❾ McCloud Bridge

Location: On Shasta Lake in Shasta-Trinity National Forest; map B2, grid e4.

Campsites, facilities: There are 20 sites for tents or RVs up to 16 feet long. Piped water, vault toilets, picnic tables, and fire grills are provided. Leashed pets are permitted.

Reservations, fees: Reservations are accepted via phone at (877) 444-6777 ($8.65 reservation fee) or website www.reserveusa.com; $15 to $25 per night, $5 for each additional vehicle. Open April through September.

Contact: Shasta-Trinity National Forest, Shasta Lake Ranger District, (530) 275-1587 or fax (530) 275-1512; Shasta Recreation Company, (530) 238-2824 or email: shastarec@snowcrest.net.

Directions: From Redding, drive north on Interstate 5 for about 20 miles to the Gilman exit. Take Gilman Road/County Road 7H009 and drive northeast for 19 miles to the campground.

Trip notes: Even though reaching this camp requires a long drive, it remains popular. That is because the best shore-fishing access at the lake is available at the nearby McCloud Bridge. It is common to see 15 or 20 people shore fishing here for trout on weekends. In the fall, big brown trout migrate through this section of lake en route to their upstream spawning grounds.

⑩ Salt Creek RV Park and Campground

Location: Near Shasta Lake; map B2, grid f3.

Campsites, facilities: There are 56 sites, many with full hookups, and one cabin. Picnic tables and fire grills are provided. Rest rooms, hot showers, sanitary disposal station, grocery store, wood, laundry room, playground, video game room, heated pool, horseshoes, and a volleyball court are available. Leashed pets are permitted.

Reservations, fees: Reservations are accepted; $15.50 to $20.50 per night. Open year-round.

Contact: Salt Creek RV Park and Campground, (530) 238-8500.

Directions: From Redding, drive north on Interstate 5 for about 20 miles to the Salt Creek Road exit. Take that exit, look for the signs, and drive a half mile to the campground.

Trip notes: This camp is located on a ridge across the highway from Shasta Lake. The sites are wooded and offer a view of the lake when the water level is high. There's boating, waterskiing, swimming, and fishing on the upper end of Shasta Lake. Some private, shaded RV sites are available.

⑪ Nelson Point

Location: On Shasta Lake in Shasta-Trinity National Forest; map B2, grid f3.

Campsites, facilities: There are eight sites for tents or RVs up to 16 feet long. Vault toilets, picnic tables, and fire grills are provided. No piped water is provided, so bring your own. A grocery store and coin laundry are nearby. Leashed pets are permitted.

Reservations, fees: No reservations; $8 per night, $5 for each additional vehicle. Open May through September.

Contact: Shasta-Trinity National Forest, Shasta Lake Ranger District, (530) 275-1587 or fax (530) 275-1512; Shasta Recreation Company, (530) 238-2824 or email: shastacrec@snowcrest.net.

Directions: From Redding, drive north on Interstate 5 for about 20 miles to the Salt Creek Road exit. Take that exit, turn left, and drive one mile west to the campground.

Trip notes: This is an easy-to-reach campground, located only a few minutes from Interstate 5. It's set beside the Salt Creek inlet of Shasta Lake, deep in a cove. In low water years, or when the lake level is low in the fall and early winter, this camp can seem quite distant from water's edge.

⑫ Holiday Harbor

Location: On Shasta Lake; map B2, grid f3.

Campsites, facilities: There 27 RV sites with full hookups. Rest rooms, hot showers, picnic tables, and barbecues are provided. A grocery store, coin laundry, boat moorage, playground, propane gas, and boat rentals are available. Leashed pets are permitted.

Reservations, fees: Reservations are accepted; $14 per night for two people, $3 for each additional camper, and $6.50 for boat moorage.

Contact: Holiday Harbor, (530) 238-2383 or (800) 776-2628.

Directions: From Redding, drive 18 miles north on Interstate 5 to the Shasta Caverns Road exit. Turn right at Shasta Caverns Road and drive about one mile to the campground entrance on the right.

Trip notes: This camp is one of the more popular year-round, all-service resorts on Shasta Lake. It is set on the lower McCloud arm of the lake, which is extremely beautiful with a limestone mountain ridge off to the east. It is an ideal jump-off for all water sports, especially houseboating and fishing. A good boat ramp, boat rentals, and store with all the goodies are bonuses. Another plus is the side trip to Shasta Caverns, a privately guided adventure (fee charged) into limestone caves.

④ Trail In RV Campground

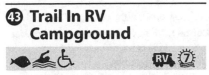

Location: On Shasta Lake; map B2, grid f3.

Campsites, facilities: There are 39 sites, some pull-through, with full hookups. Picnic tables and fire grills are provided. Rest rooms, hot showers, TVs, sanitary disposal station, swimming pool, grocery store, ice, wood, and coin laundry are available. The facilities are wheelchair accessible. Pets are permitted.

Reservations, fees: A deposit is required with reservation; $16.50 per night.

Contact: Trail In RV Campground, (530) 238-8533.

Directions: From Redding, drive 22 miles north on Interstate 5. Take the Gilman Road/Salt Creek Road exit and drive a short distance west on Gilman Road to Gregory Creek Road. Turn north on Gregory Creek Road and drive one mile to the campground.

Trip notes: This is a privately operated campground near the Salt Creek arm of giant Shasta Lake. Open, level sites are available. The lake is about three miles away and offers fishing, boating, and swimming. Its proximity to Interstate 5 makes this a popular spot, fast and easy to reach, which is extremely attractive for drivers of RVs and trailers who want to avoid the many twisty roads surrounding Shasta Lake.

④ Hirz Bay Group Camp

Location: On Shasta Lake in Shasta-Trinity National Forest; map B2, grid f4.

Campsites, facilities: There are four group sites for tents and RVs up to 24 feet long. Piped water, vault toilets, picnic tables, and fire grills are provided. Leashed pets are permitted.

Reservations, fees: Reservations are accepted via phone at (877) 444-6777 ($8.65 reservation fee) or website www.reserveusa.com; Camp One accommodates up to 120 people at a

rate of $90 per night; Camp Two accommodates up to 80 people at a rate of $65 per night. Open from May through September.

Contact: Shasta-Trinity National Forest, Shasta Lake Ranger District, (530) 275-1587 or fax (530) 275-1512.

Directions: From Redding, drive north on Interstate 5 for about 20 miles to the Gilman exit. Take Gilman Road/County Road 7H009 and drive northeast for 10 miles to the campground/boat launch access road. Turn right and drive a half mile to the camp on the left side of the road.

Trip notes: This is the spot for your own private party—providing you get a reservation—set on a point at the entrance of Hirz Bay on the McCloud River arm of Shasta Lake. A boat ramp is located only a half mile away on the camp access road, giving access to the McCloud River arm. This is an excellent spot to make a base camp for a fishing trip, with great trolling for trout in this stretch of the lake.

④ Hirz Bay

Location: On Shasta Lake in Shasta-Trinity National Forest; map B2, grid f4.

Campsites, facilities: There are 38 single sites and 10 double sites for tents or RVs up to 30 feet long. Piped water, flush toilets, picnic tables, and fire grills are provided. A boat ramp is nearby. The facilities are wheelchair accessible. Leashed pets are permitted.

Reservations, fees: Reservations are accepted via phone at (877) 444-6777 ($8.65 reservation fee) or website www.reserveusa.com; $15 to $25 per night, $5 for an extra vehicle. Reduced rates and services in the winter. Open May through September.

Contact: Shasta-Trinity National Forest, Shasta Lake Ranger District, (530) 275-1587 or fax (530) 275-1512; Shasta Recreation Company, (530) 238-2824 or email: shastacrec@snowcrest.net.

Directions: From Redding, drive north on Interstate 5 for about 20 miles to the Gilman exit. Take Gilman Road/County Road 7H009 and drive northeast for 10 miles to the campground/boat launch access road. Turn right and drive a half mile to the camp on the left side of the road.

Trip notes: This is one of two camps in the immediate area (the other is Hirz Bay Group Camp) that provides nearby access to a boat ramp (a half mile down the road) and the McCloud River arm of Shasta Lake. The camp is set on a point at the entrance of Hirz Bay. This is an excellent spot to make a base camp for a fishing trip, with great trolling for trout in this stretch of the lake.

46 Madrone Camp

Location: On Squaw Creek in Shasta-Trinity National Forest; map B2, grid f7.

Campsites, facilities: There are 13 sites for tents or RVs up to 16 feet long. There is no piped water, but vault toilets, picnic tables, and fire grills are provided. Pets are permitted on leashes.

Reservations, fees: No reservations; no fee.

Contact: Shasta-Trinity National Forest, Shasta Lake Ranger District, (530) 275-1587 or fax (530) 275-1512.

Directions: From Redding, drive 29 miles east on Highway 299 to the town of Montgomery Creek. Turn left on Fenders Ferry Road/Forest Service Road 27 and drive 22 miles to the camp (the road starts as gravel and then becomes dirt).

Trip notes: Tired of people? Then you've come to the right place. This remote camp is set along Squaw Creek, a feeder stream of Shasta Lake to the southwest. It's way out there, far away from anybody. Even though Shasta Lake is relatively close, about 10 miles away, it is literally in another world. A network of four-wheel-drive roads provides a recreation option, detailed on a map of Shasta-Trinity National Forest.

47 Brandy Creek

Location: On Whiskeytown Lake; map B2, grid h0.

Campsites, facilities: There are 46 RV sites for self-contained vehicles up to 30 feet long. A dump station and piped water (except in winter) are available. Leashed pets are permitted.

Reservations, fees: No reservations; $7 to $14 per night (rate depends upon water availability). Open Memorial Day through Labor Day.

Contact: Whiskeytown National Recreation Area, (530) 241-6584 or fax (530) 246-5154.

Directions: From Redding, drive 10 miles west on Highway 299. Turn left at the visitor center (Kennedy Memorial Drive) and drive five miles to the campground entrance road on the right. Turn right and drive a short distance to the camp.

Trip notes: For campers with boats, this is the best place to stay at Whiskeytown Lake, with a boat ramp located less than a quarter mile away. Whiskeytown is popular for sailing and windsurfing, getting a lot more wind than other lakes in the region. Fishing for kokanee salmon is good in the early morning prior to the wind coming up.

48 Oak Bottom

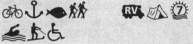

Location: On Whiskeytown Lake; map B2, grid h0.

Campsites, facilities: There are 101 walk-in tent sites with picnic tables and fire grills. There are 50 RV sites in the large parking area near the launch ramp and rest rooms. Piped water, flush toilets, coin-operated showers, groceries, ice, wood, sanitary dump station, boat ramp, and boat rentals are available. Some facilities are wheelchair accessible. Leashed pets are permitted.

Reservations, fees: No reservations in the off-season; reservations are required in the summer. Reserve via phone at (877) 444-6777 ($8.65 reservation fee) or website www.reserveusa.com; $7 to $18 per night.

Contact: Whiskeytown National Recreation Area, (530) 241-6584 or fax (530) 246-5154.

Directions: From Redding, drive 15 miles west on Highway 299 (past the visitor center) to the campground entrance road on the left. Turn left and drive a short distance to the campground.

Trip notes: The prettiest hiking trails at Whiskeytown Lake are at the far western end of the reservoir, and this camp provides excellent access to them. One hiking and biking trail skirts the north shoreline of the lake and is routed to the lake's inlet at the Judge Carr Powerhouse. The other, with the trailhead just a short drive to the west, is routed along Mill Creek, a pristine, clear-running stream with the trail jumping over the water many times—the kind of place you may never want to leave. The campground sites seem a little close, but the location is next to a beach area with a self-guided nature trail nearby. There are junior ranger programs for kids six to 12 years old, and evening ranger seminars at the Oak Bottom Amphitheater are available every night from mid-June through Labor Day.

㊾ Dry Creek Group Camp

Location: On Whiskeytown Lake; map B2, grid h0.

Campsites, facilities: There are two group sites that can accommodate 80 people each. Piped water, pit toilets, picnic tables, and fire grills are provided. Leashed pets are permitted.

Reservations, fees: Reservations are required and, because the camp is very popular, should be made the first working day of the year to reserve any date through the summer. Reserve via phone at (877) 444-6777 ($8.65 reservation fee) or website www.reserveusa.com; group fee is $50 to $100 per night for single group sites and $150 for both; maximum stay is seven days.

Contact: Whiskeytown National Recreation Area, (530) 241-6584 extension 221 or fax (530) 246-5154.

Directions: From Redding, drive 10 miles west on Highway 299. Turn left at the visitor center (Kennedy Memorial Drive) and drive six miles to the campground on the right side of the road.

Trip notes: If you're in a group and take the time to reserve this spot, you'll be rewarded with some room and the quiet that goes along with it. This is the most remote drive-to camp at Whiskeytown Lake. A boat ramp is located about two miles away (to the east) at Brandy Creek. You'll pass it on the way in.

㊿ Shasta

Location: On the Sacramento River in Shasta-Trinity National Forest; map B2, grid g2.

Campsites, facilities: There are 30 sites for tents or RVs up to 24 feet long. Piped water, vault toilets, picnic tables, and fire rings are provided. A boat ramp is nearby. Groceries and bait are available in Summit City. Leashed pets are permitted.

Reservations, fees: No reservations; $10 per night, $5 for each additional vehicle. Open year-round.

Contact: Shasta-Trinity National Forest, Shasta Lake Ranger District, (530) 275-1587 or fax (530) 275-1512.

Directions: From Interstate 5 just north of Redding, take the exit for the town of Shasta Lake City/Shasta Dam. Turn west on Shasta Dam Boulevard and drive three miles. Turn right on Lake Boulevard and drive two miles. Cross Shasta Dam and follow the signs to the campground.

Trip notes: This campground is located between Shasta Dam and the Sacramento River, and adjacent to an off-highway-vehicle staging area. Get the idea? Right, this place is for ATVs and dirt bikes, loud and wild, and hey, it's a perfect spot for them. It's barren and there isn't much to look at.

⑤ Wonderland Mobile Home & RV Park

Location: Near Shasta Lake; map B2, grid g3.

Campsites, facilities: There are 36 RV sites, many with full hookups. Rest rooms, showers, coin laundry, cable TV, seasonally-heated swimming pool, and horseshoes are available. Leashed pets are permitted.

Reservations, fees: Reservations are required with a deposit; $10 to $14.50 per night. Open year-round.

Contact: Wonderland Mobile Home & RV Park, (530) 275-1281.

Directions: From Redding, drive north on Interstate 5 for 11 miles to the Fawndale exit. Exit west onto Wonderland Boulevard and drive a quarter mile to 15203 Wonderland Boulevard.

Trip notes: This RV park is located within a mobile home park south of Shasta Lake. The tour of Shasta Caverns is a recreation option, via a short drive to Holiday Harbor. Other options include the city of Redding's extensive visitor center, the Carter House Natural History Museum in Caldwell Park, public golf courses, and the Sacramento River trails, which are paved, making them accessible for wheelchairs and bikes.

⑤ Bear Mountain RV Resort

Location: Near Shasta Lake; map B2, grid g3.

Campsites, facilities: There are 17 tent sites and 97 RV sites with full or partial hookups. Piped water, flush toilets, laundry room, store, dump station, picnic tables, and fire rings are provided, as are a pool, recreation hall, arcade, and horseshoe pit. Within three miles, there is a free boat launch ramp. Leashed pets are permitted.

Reservations, fees: Reservations are accepted; $12 to $16 per night.

Contact: Bear Mountain RV Resort, (530) 275-4728, (800) 952-0551, or fax (530) 275-8459.

Directions: From Redding, drive north on Interstate 5 for three miles to the Oasis Road exit. Turn right on Oasis Road/Old Oregon Trail and drive 3.5 miles. Turn right on Bear Mountain Road and drive 3.5 miles to the campground.

Trip notes: This is a privately operated park set up primarily for RVs in the remote Jones Valley area along Shasta Lake.

⑤ Jones Inlet

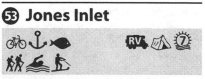

Location: On Shasta Lake in Shasta-Trinity National Forest; map B2, grid g4.

Campsites, facilities: There is an area for dispersed, primitive camping for tents or RVs up to 30 feet long. There is no piped water, but vault toilets are provided. A boat ramp is two miles from camp. Leashed pets are permitted.

Reservations, fees: No reservations; $6 per vehicle per night, $4 fee for each additional vehicle.

Contact: Shasta-Trinity National Forest, Shasta Lake Ranger District, (530) 275-1587 or fax (530) 275-1512.

Directions: From Redding, turn east on Highway 299 and drive 7.5 miles just past the town of Bella Vista. At Dry Creek Road turn left and drive nine miles to a Y in the road. Veer right at the Y (left will take you to Silverthorn Resort) and drive a short distance to the campground entrance on the left side of the road.

Trip notes: This is one of the few primitive camp areas on Shasta Lake, set on the distant Pit River arm of the lake. It is an ideal camp for hiking and biking, with the nearby Clickipudi Trail routed for miles along the lake's shore, in and out of coves, and then entering the surrounding foothills and oak/bay woodlands. The camp is pretty, if a bit exposed, with two nearby resorts, Jones Valley and Silverthorn, providing boat rentals and supplies.

⑤ Upper and Lower Jones Valley Camps

Location: On Shasta Lake in Shasta-Trinity National Forest; map B2, grid g4.

Campsites, facilities: There are 27 sites for tents or RVs up to 16 feet long in two adjacent campgrounds. Picnic tables, fire grills, piped water, and vault toilets are provided. A boat ramp is two miles from camp. Leashed pets are permitted.

Reservations, fees: Reservations are accepted via phone at (877) 444-6777 ($8.65 reservation fee) or website www.reserveusa.com; Upper sites are $12 per night, Lower sites are $15 for a single site and $25 for a double, $5 for each additional vehicle.

Contact: Shasta-Trinity National Forest, Shasta Lake Ranger District, (530) 275-1587 or fax (530) 275-1512.

Directions: From Redding, turn east on Highway 299 and drive 7.5 miles just past the town of Bella Vista. At Dry Creek Road, turn left and drive nine miles to a Y in the road. Veer right at the Y (left will take you to Silverthorn Resort) and drive a short distance to the campground entrances, on the left side for Lower Jones and on the right side for Upper Jones.

Trip notes: Lower Jones is a small, pretty camp sheltered by oaks and bays along a deep cove in the remote Pit River arm of Shasta Lake. There is a trailhead at camp that provides access to the Clickipudi Trail, a great hiking and biking trail that traces the lake's shore, routed through pretty woodlands. Two nearby resorts, Jones Valley and Silverthorn, provide boat rentals and supplies.

---

55 KOA of Redding

Location: In Redding; map B2, grid h1.

Campsites, facilities: There are 111 RV sites, 53 with full hookups, 22 with partial hookups, and a separate area for tents. Piped water, flush toilets, showers, playground, swimming pool, laundry room, dump station, picnic tables, and fire grills are provided. A grocery store and propane gas are also available. Leashed pets are permitted.

Reservations, fees: Reservations are accepted; $19.50 to $24.50 per night.

Contact: KOA of Redding, (530) 246-0101 or (800) 562-0899.

Directions: In Redding, drive north on Interstate 5 to the Lake Boulevard/Burney-Alturas exit. Turn west on Lake Boulevard and drive a quarter mile to North Boulder Drive. Turn north on North Boulder Drive and drive one block to the campground.

Trip notes: If you're stuck with no place to go, this large park could be your savior, but expect very hot weather in the summer. Nearby recreation options include the waterslide park across the road, the Sacramento River which runs through town, Whiskeytown Lake to the west, and Shasta Lake to the north.

---

56 Twin View Terrace RV Park

Location: Near Redding; map B2, grid h2.

Campsites, facilities: There are 48 drive-through RV sites with full hookups. Rest rooms, showers, a coin laundry, and swimming pool are available. Leashed pets are permitted.

Reservations, fees: No reservations; $17 per night.

Contact: Twin View Terrace RV Park, (530) 243-8114.

Directions: In Redding, take the Twin View exit off Interstate 5. Turn south on Twin View and drive one mile on Twin View Boulevard to the RV park.

Trip notes: This is one of several RV parks open year-round in the Redding area. It is located within a mobile home park.

---

57 Marina RV Park

Location: On the Sacramento River; map B2, grid h1.

Campsites, facilities: There are 42 RV sites with full or partial hookups. Rest rooms, hot showers, a coin laundry, general store, snack bar, swimming pool, whirlpool, boat ramp, and dump station are on park grounds. Pets are permitted.

Reservations, fees: Reservations are accepted; $20.90 per night. Open year-round.

Contact: Marina RV Park, (530) 241-4396.

Directions: In Redding turn west on Highway 299 and drive to Park Marina Drive. At Park Marina Drive turn south and drive one mile to the park.

Trip notes: The riverside setting is a highlight here, with the Sacramento River providing relief from the dog days of summer. An easy, paved walking and bike trail is available nearby at the Sacramento River Parkway, providing river views and sometimes a needed breeze on hot summer evenings. A miniature golf course is located nearby.

---

58 Sacramento River RV Park

Location: South of Redding; map B2, grid i2.

Campsites, facilities: There are 20 tent sites

and 140 RV sites with full hookups. Rest rooms, hot showers, grocery store, coin laundry, dump station, cable TV, bait and tackle shop, propane gas, boat launch and 30 slips, two tennis courts, and a large swimming pool are available. Leashed pets are permitted.

Reservations, fees: Reservations are accepted; $14 to $21 per night. All discount coupons are honored for RVs.

Contact: Sacramento River RV Park, (530) 365-6402 or fax (530) 365-2601.

Directions: From Redding, drive south on Interstate 5 for five miles to the Knighton Road exit. Turn west and drive a short distance to Riverland Drive. Turn right on Riverland Drive and drive two miles to the end of the road.

Trip notes: This makes a good headquarters for a fall fishing trip on the Sacramento River, where the salmon come big from August through October. In the summer trout fishing is very good from this area as well, but a boat is a must. No problem; there's a boat ramp at the park. In addition, you can hire fishing guides who launch from here daily. The park is open year-round, and if you want to stay close to home, a three-acre pond is available at the park. You also get great views of Mount Shasta and Mount Lassen.

⑤⑨ Old Cow Meadows

Location: In Latour Demonstration State Forest; map B2, grid i9.

Campsites, facilities: There are three sites for tents or RVs. There is no piped water, but picnic tables, fire grills, and pit toilets are provided. Pets are permitted.

Reservations, fees: No reservations; no fee. Open June through October.

Contact: Latour Demonstration State Forest, (530) 225-2505 or (530) 225-2438.

Directions: In Redding, turn east on Highway 44 and drive about 9.5 miles to Millville Road. Turn left on Millville Road and drive a half mile to the intersection of Millville Road and Whitmore Road. Turn right on Whitmore Road and drive 13 miles, through Whitmore, until Whitmore Road becomes Tamarac Road. Con-

tinue for one mile to a fork at Bateman Road. Take the right fork on Bateman Road, drive 3.5 miles (where the road turns to gravel), and then continue 12 miles to the entrance to the campground.

Trip notes: Nobody finds this campground without this book. You want quiet? You don't want to be bugged by anybody? You want piped water, too? Well, two out of three ain't bad. This tiny camp, virtually unknown, is set at 5,900 feet in a wooded area along Old Cow Creek. Recreation options include off-road-vehicle use and walking the dirt roads that crisscross the area.

⑥⓪ South Cow Creek Meadows

Location: In Latour Demonstration State Forest; map B2, grid i9.

Campsites, facilities: There are two sites for tents or RVs. Creek water is available. Pit toilets, picnic tables, and fire grills are provided. Pets are allowed.

Reservations, fees: No reservations; no fee. Open June through October.

Contact: Latour Demonstration State Forest, (530) 225-2505 or (530) 225-2438.

Directions: In Redding, turn east on Highway 44 and drive about 9.5 miles to Millville Road. Turn left on Millville Road and drive one-half mile to the intersection of Millville Road and Whitmore Road. Turn right on Whitmore Road and drive 13 miles, through Whitmore, until Whitmore Road becomes Tamarac Road. Continue for one mile to the fork at Bateman Road. Take the right fork on Bateman Road, drive 3.5 miles (where the road turns to gravel), and then continue for 11 miles to the entrance to the campground.

Trip notes: This camp is set in a pretty, wooded area next to a small meadow along South Cow Creek. It's mostly used in the fall for hunting, with off-highway-vehicle use on the surrounding roads in the summer. The camp is set at 5,600 feet. If you want to get away from it all without leaving your vehicle, this is one way to do it.

⑥ Reading Island Group Camp

Location: On the Sacramento River; map B2, grid j3.

Campsites, facilities: One group site for tents or RVs up to 30 feet long can accommodate up to 100 people. Piped water, vault toilets, picnic tables, and fire grills are provided. A boat ramp, groceries, propane gas, and a coin laundry are available within 15 minutes. Leashed pets are permitted.

Reservations, fees: Reservations are required; $75 per night or $2 per camper, whichever is greater.

Contact: Bureau of Land Management, Redding Field Office, (530) 224-2100 or fax (530) 224-2172.

Directions: From Redding, drive 15 miles south on Interstate 5 to Cottonwood. In Cottonwood, turn east on Balls Ferry Road and drive five miles to Adobe Road. Take Adobe Road to the campground entrance.

Trip notes: This is a prime spot along the Sacramento River amid the best stretch of river for salmon. The state record 88-pounder was caught near here at the mouth of Old Battle Creek (the "Barge Hole"). The average salmon ranges from 12 to 25 pounds, best from mid-August through October. The river is usually too high and too cold for swimming, even when temperatures are in the 100s in the summer months. Inner tubers without life jackets will be ticketed and taken off the water by the Shasta County sheriff's patrol boat. The Coleman Fish Hatchery offers a nearby side trip.

⑥ KOA Lassen/ Shingletown

Location: Near Lassen Volcanic National Park; map B2, grid j7.

Campsites, facilities: There are 50 sites for tents or RVs; some are drive-through sites with full or partial hookups. Picnic tables, fire grills, piped water, flush toilets, hot showers, play-

ground, heated pool, and a dump station are provided. Groceries, ice, wood, coin laundry, and propane gas are available. Pets must be controlled.

Reservations, fees: Phone (800) 562-3403. A deposit is required with reservation; $18 to $22 per night. Open year-round.

Contact: KOA Lassen/Shingletown, (530) 474-3133.

Directions: From Redding, turn east on Highway 44 and drive to Shingletown. In Shingletown, continue east for four miles and look for the KOA sign.

Trip notes: This popular KOA camp is 14 miles from the entrance of Lassen Volcanic National Park and has pretty, wooded sites. Location is always the critical factor on vacations, and this park is set up perfectly for launching trips to the nearby east. Mill Creek provides trout fishing along Highway 44, and just inside the Highway 44 entrance station at Lassen Park is Manzanita Lake, providing good fishing and hiking.

⑥ Mill Creek Park

Location: Near Shingletown; map B2, grid j7.

Campsites, facilities: There are 34 sites for tents or RVs; some are drive through sites with full or partial hookups. Picnic tables, fire grills, piped water, flush toilets, dump station, and a laundry room are available. A fishing pond and creek are also available. Leashed pets are permitted.

Reservations, fees: A deposit is required with reservation; $16 to $20 per night.

Contact: Mill Creek Park, (530) 474-5384 or fax (530) 474-1236.

Directions: From Redding, drive east on Highway 44 to Shingletown. In Shingletown, continue east on Highway 44 for two miles to the campground.

Trip notes: This year-round park is set up primarily for RVs, but has sites for tenters. The elevation is 4,000 feet, and it's set amid conifers on the western slopes of Mount Lassen. The proximity to Lassen Volcanic National Park is a key attraction.

64 McCumber Reservoir

Location: On McCumber Reservoir; map B2, grid j9.

Campsites, facilities: There are seven sites for tents or RVs and five walk-in sites. Piped water, vault toilets, picnic tables, and fire grills are provided. Leashed pets are permitted.

Reservations, fees: No reservations; $13 per night, $1 pet fee.

Contact: PG&E Building and Land Services, (916) 386-5164.

Directions: In Redding, turn east on Highway 44 and drive toward Viola to Lake McCumber Road (if you reach Viola, you have gone four miles too far). At Lake McCumber Road, turn left and drive two miles to the reservoir and campground.

Trip notes: Here's a small lake, easy to reach from Redding, that is little known and rarely visited. McCumber Reservoir is set at 3,500 feet and is stocked with 6,000 rainbow trout each year, providing fair fishing. No gas motors are permitted here. That's fine—it guarantees quiet, calm water, ideal for cartop boats: prams, canoes, rafts, and small aluminum boats.

Map B3

One inch equals approximately 10.7 miles.
See inside back cover for California state map.

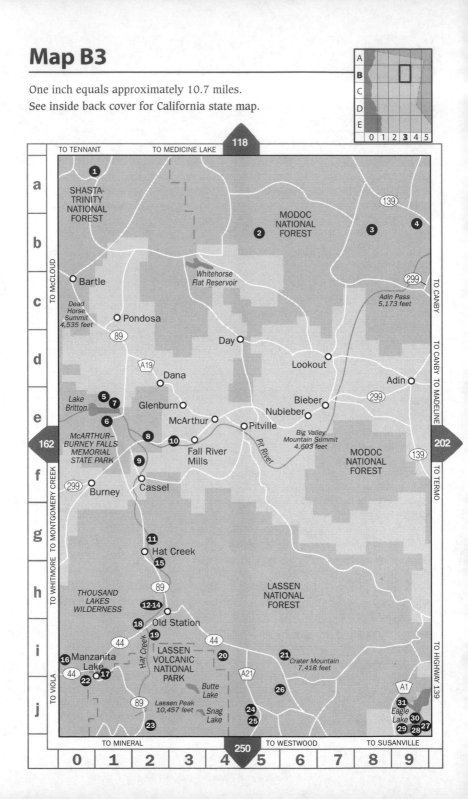

Chapter B3 features:

1 Harris Springs

Location: In Shasta-Trinity National Forest; map B3, grid a1.

Campsites, facilities: There are 15 sites for tents or RVs up to 32 feet long. Piped water, vault toilets, picnic tables, and fire grills provided. Leashed pets are permitted.

Reservations, fees: No reservations; no fee.

Contact: Shasta-Trinity National Forest, McCloud Ranger District, (530) 964-2184 or fax (530) 964-2938.

Directions: From Redding, drive north on Interstate 5 past Dunsmuir to the junction with Highway 89. Turn east on Highway 89, drive to McCloud, and then continue on Highway 89 for 17 miles just past the town of Bartle. Turn left (north) on Medicine Lake Road and drive about five miles to the Y intersection. Turn left at the Y on Harris Springs Road/Forest Service Road 15 and drive 12 miles. Turn right at a Forest Service road signed for the Harris Springs Ranger Station, drive a short distance, and look for the campground entrance on the right side of the road.

Trip notes: This camp is a hidden spot in remote Shasta-Trinity National Forest, nestled in the long, mountainous ridge that runs east from Mount Shasta to the Lava Beds National Monument. The camp is set at 4,800 feet, with a ranger station located within a quarter mile on the opposite side of the access road. The area is best explored by four-wheel drive, venturing to a series of small buttes, mountaintops, and lookouts in the immediate area. A map of Shasta-Trinity National Forest is a must.

2 Lava Camp

Location: In Modoc National Forest; map B3, grid b5.

Campsites, facilities: There are 12 sites for tents or RVs up to 32 feet long. Vault toilets, tables, and fire grills are provided. No piped water is available. Leashed pets are permitted.

Reservations, fees: No reservations; no fee. Open May through October.

Contact: Modoc National Forest, Big Valley Ranger District, (530) 299-3215 or fax (530) 299-3210.

Directions: From Redding, take Highway 299 east to Bieber (about 90 miles). Continue just past Bieber to County Road 91, turn left (north), and drive seven miles to the town of Lookout. After crossing the Pit River, turn right on County Road 91 and drive about 13 miles to Forest Service Road 42N03. Turn left on Forest Service Road 42N03 and drive seven miles to the junction with Forest Service Road 42N23. Turn right and drive five miles to the campground on the right side of the road. A map of Modoc Forest is a must.

Trip notes: Modoc country is "old country." It feels like it hasn't changed since the beginning of time. If that's what you are looking for, this camp is for you. It's virtually unknown, yet is in a prime spot in the area, on the outskirts of Long Bell State Game Refuge. Glass Mountain and nearby lava flows offer good side trips. The elevation is 4,400 feet, set below Sugar Pine Ridge. In the fall, it's a good base camp for a hunting trip.

❸ Cottonwood Flat

Location: In Modoc National Forest; map B3, grid b8.

Campsites, facilities: There are 10 sites for tents or RVs up to 22 feet long. Potable spring-water, vault toilets, fire grills, and picnic tables are provided. Supplies are available within five miles in Canby. Leashed pets are permitted.

Reservations, fees: No reservations; no fee. Open June through September.

Contact: Modoc National Forest, Devil's Garden Ranger District, (530) 233-5811 or fax (530) 233-5817.

Directions: From Redding, drive east on Highway 299 for about 100 miles to Adin. Continue on Highway 299 for about 20 miles to the Canby Bridge at the Pit River and the junction with Forest Service Road 84. Turn left on Forest Service Road 84 and drive about eight miles to Forest Service Road 42N95. Turn right and drive a half mile to the campground entrance on the left side of the road.

Trip notes: The camp is wooded and shady, set at 4,700 feet in elevation in the rugged and remote Devil's Garden area of Modoc National Forest. The region is known for large mule deer,

and Cottonwood Flat is well situated as a base camp for a hunting trip in the fall. Temperatures can get extremely cold early and late in the season.

❹ Howard's Gulch

Location: Near Duncan Reservoir in Modoc National Forest; map B3, grid b9.

Campsites, facilities: There are 11 sites for tents or RVs up to 22 feet long. Piped water, vault toilets, tables, and fire grills are provided. One toilet is wheelchair accessible. Supplies are available within five miles in Canby. Leashed pets are permitted.

Reservations, fees: No reservations; $6 per night. Open May through October.

Contact: Modoc National Forest, Devil's Garden Ranger District, (530) 233-5811 or fax (530) 233-5817.

Directions: From Redding, drive east on Highway 299 for about 100 miles to Adin. Continue on Highway 299 for about 25 miles. Turn left (northwest) on Highway 139 and drive six miles to the campground on the left side of the road.

Trip notes: This is the nearest campground to Duncan Reservoir, located three miles to the north, which is stocked with trout each year by the Department of Fish and Game. The camp is set in the typically sparse woods of Modoc National Forest, but a beautiful grove of aspen is located three miles to the west on Highway 139, on the left side of the road. By the way, Highway 139 isn't much of a highway at all, but it is paved and will get you there. The elevation is 4,700 feet.

❺ McArthur–Burney Falls State Park

Location: In McArthur–Burney Falls Memorial State Park; map B3, grid e1.

Campsites, facilities: There are 128 sites for tents or RVs up to 35 feet long. Piped water, flush toilets, hot showers, sanitary dump station, picnic tables, and fire grills are provided. The rest rooms are wheelchair accessible. A grocery store and boat rentals are available in the summer. Leashed pets are permitted, except on the trails and the beach.

Reservations, fees: Reserve via phone at (800) 444-PARK/7275 ($7.50 reservation fee) or website www.cal-parks.ca.gov; $14 to $16 per night, $1 pet fee.

Contact: McArthur–Burney Falls State Park, (530) 335-2777.

Directions: From Redding, drive east on Highway 299 to Burney and then continue for five miles to the junction with Highway 89. At Highway 89, drive north for six miles to the campground entrance on the left side of the road.

Trip notes: The 129-foot waterfall here, Burney Falls, is a beautiful cascade, split at the top by a little grove of trees, with small trickles oozing and falling out of the adjacent moss-lined wall. Since it is fed primarily by a spring, it runs strong and glorious most of the year. The Headwaters Trail provides an outstanding hike, both to see the waterfall and Burney Creek, as well as for an easy adventure and fishing access to the stream. There are other stellar recreation options at this state park. At the end of the campground access road is a boat ramp for Lake Britton, with rentals available for canoes and paddleboats. This is a beautiful lake, with awesome canyon walls on its upper end, and good trout and crappie fishing. There is also a good swimming beach. The Pacific Crest Trail is routed right through the park and provides an additional opportunity for a day hike, best explored downstream from the dam. Reservations for sites are essential during the summer months.

➏ Northshore

Location: On Lake Britton; map B3, grid e1.

Campsites, facilities: There are 30 sites for tents or RVs up to 30 feet long. Piped water, vault toilets, picnic tables, and fire grills are provided. An unimproved boat ramp is available at the camp and an improved boat ramp is available in Burney Falls State Park (about four miles away). Supplies can be obtained in Fall River Mills or Burney. Leashed pets are permitted.

Reservations, fees: No reservations; $13 per night, $1 pet fee.

Contact: PG&E Building and Land Services, (916) 386-5164.

Directions: From Redding, drive east on Highway 299 to Burney and then continue for five miles to Highway 89. Turn north and drive 9.7 miles (past the state park entrance and over the Lake Britton Bridge) to Clark Creek Road. Turn left (west) and drive about a mile to the camp access road. Turn left and drive to the camp.

Trip notes: This peaceful campground is set among the woodlands near the shore of Lake Britton, directly across the lake from McArthur–Burney Falls Memorial State Park (see the trip notes for campground number five). Boating and fishing are popular here, and once the water warms up in midsummer, swimming is also a winner. The best trout fishing in the area is on the Pit River near Powerhouse No. 3, but skilled and aggressive wading is required. A hot spring is available in Big Bend, about a 30-minute drive from camp.

➐ Dusty Campground

Location: On Lake Britton; map B3, grid e1.

Campsites, facilities: There are seven primitive sites for tents or RVs up to 20 feet long and two primitive group sites that can accommodate up to 25 people each. There is no piped water, so bring your own. Vault toilets and fire rings are provided. Leashed pets are permitted.

Reservations, fees: No reservations; $6 per night, $1 pet fee; group sites are $12 per night.

Contact: PG&E Building and Land Services, (916) 386-5164.

Directions: From Redding, drive east on Highway 299 to Burney and continue for five miles to the junction with Highway 89. At Highway 89, turn left (north) and drive 9.7 miles (past the state park entrance and over the Lake Britton Bridge) to Clark Creek Road. Turn left (west) on Clark Creek Road and drive about 7.5 miles to the camp access road on the left. Turn right and drive three-quarters of a mile to the campground directly ahead.

Trip notes: This is one in a series of campgrounds near the north shore of Lake Britton. See the trip notes for Northshore (campground number six) for more information.

⑧ Burney Falls Trailer Resort

⚓🐟🚶🏊 🚐 ⑤

Location: Near Lake Britton; map B3, grid e2.

Campsites, facilities: There are 28 RV sites with full hookups. Rest rooms, hot showers, a coin laundry, horseshoes, and a swimming pool are on the premises. Leashed pets are permitted.

Reservations, fees: Reservations are accepted; $16 per night.

Contact: Burney Falls Trailer Resort, (530) 335-2781.

Directions: From Redding, drive east on Highway 299 to Burney and continue for five miles to the junction with Highway 89. At Highway 89, turn north and drive seven miles to Clark Creek Road. Turn left on Clark Creek Road and drive a short distance to the campground entrance.

Trip notes: This is a year-round RV park located near Lake Britton, Burney Creek, and the Pit River. McArthur–Burney Falls Memorial State Park, with its spectacular waterfall, is within a five-minute drive. The region is loaded with adventure, with Lassen Volcanic National Park, Hat Creek, and Fall River all within a 30-minute drive.

⑨ Cassel

⚓🐟 🚐 ⑧

Location: On Hat Creek; map B3, grid f2.

Campsites, facilities: There are 27 sites for tents or RVs up to 30 feet long. Piped water, vault toilets, picnic tables, and fire grills are provided. Leashed pets are permitted.

Reservations, fees: No reservations; $13 per night, $1 pet fee.

Contact: PG&E Building and Land Services, (916) 386-5164.

Directions: From Redding, drive east on Highway 299 to Burney and continue for five miles to the junction with Highway 89. At the junction, continue straight on Highway 299 for two miles to Cassel Road. At Cassel Road, turn right and drive 3.6 miles to the campground entrance on the left.

Trip notes: This is an outstanding location for a fishing trip base camp, with nearby Crystal Lake, Baum Lake, and Hat Creek (all set in the Hat Creek Valley) providing trout fishing. This section of Hat Creek is well known for its challenging fly-fishing, typically with an excellent evening hatch and surface rise. Long leaders and very small flies are critical. A good source of fishing information is Vaughn's Sporting Goods in Burney. Baum Lake is ideal for cartop boats with electric motors.

⑩ Pit River

🐟🚶 🚐 🏕 ⑥

Location: On the Pit River; map B3, grid e3.

Campsites, facilities: There are 10 sites for tents or RVs. There is no piped water, but vault toilets, picnic tables, and fire grills are provided. There are supplies and a coin laundry in Fall River Mills. Pets are permitted.

Reservations, fees: No reservations; no fee.

Contact: Bureau of Land Management, Alturas Resource Area, (530) 233-4666 or fax (530) 233-5696.

Directions: From Redding, drive east on Highway 299 to Burney and continue for five miles to the junction with Highway 89. At the junction, continue straight on Highway 299, cross the Pit River Bridge, and drive about three miles to Pit One Powerhouse Road on the right. Turn right and drive along the river for about a mile to the campground.

Trip notes: Very few out-of-towners know about this hidden and primitive campground set along the Pit River. It can provide a good base camp for a fishing trip adventure. The best stretch of trout water on the Pit is near Powerhouse No. 3. In addition to fishing there are many other recreation options. A parking area and trail along Hat Creek are available where the Highway 299 bridge crosses Hat Creek. Baum Lake, Crystal Lake, and the Cassel section of Hat Creek are all within five miles of this camp.

⑪ Hat Creek Hereford Ranch Campground

🐟 🚐 🏕 ⑧

Location: Near Hat Creek; map B3, grid g2.

Campsites, facilities: There are 40 tent sites

and 40 RV sites with full or partial hookups. Rest rooms, hot showers, sanitary dump station, coin laundry, playground, and a grocery store are on the premises. No pets are allowed.

Reservations, fees: Reservations are recommended; $14.95 to $17.95 per night. Open April through October.

Contact: Hat Creek Hereford Ranch Campground, (530) 335-7171.

Directions: From Redding, drive east on Highway 299 to Burney and continue for five miles to the junction with Highway 89. Turn south on Highway 89 and drive 12 miles to the second Doty Road exit and the entrance to the campground.

Trip notes: This privately operated campground is set in a working cattle ranch, so if you go for a stroll, watch where you plant your Vibrams. Fishing is available in Hat Creek or in the nearby stocked trout pond. Sight-seeing is excellent with Burney Falls, Lassen Volcanic National Park, and Subway Caves all within 30 miles.

⑫ Cave Camp

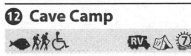

Location: On Hat Creek in Lassen National Forest; map B3, grid h2.

Campsites, facilities: There are 46 sites for tents or RVs up to 22 feet long. Piped water, vault toilets, picnic tables, and fire grills are provided. Some facilities are wheelchair accessible. Supplies can be obtained in Old Station. Leashed pets are permitted.

Reservations, fees: No reservations; $12 per night. Open May through October.

Contact: Lassen National Forest, Hat Creek Ranger District, (530) 336-5521 or fax (530) 336-5758.

Directions: From Redding, drive east on Highway 299 to Burney and continue for five miles to the junction with Highway 89. Turn right (south) on Highway 89 and drive 23 miles to the campground entrance on the right side of the road. If you reach Old Station, you have gone one mile too far.

Trip notes: Cave Camp is set right along Hat Creek, with both easy access off Highway 89 and an anglers' trail available along the stream. This

stretch of Hat Creek is planted with rainbow trout twice per month by the Department of Fish and Game, and for campers hoping to fish, the prospects are all or nothing: all after a plant, nothing the rest of the time. Nearby side trips include Lassen Volcanic National Park, located about a 15-minute drive to the south on Highway 89, and Subway Caves (turn left at the junction just across the road from the campground). A rare bonus at this camp is that wheelchair-accessible fishing is available.

⑬ Bridge Camp

Location: On Hat Creek in Lassen National Forest; map B3, grid h2.

Campsites, facilities: There are 25 sites for tents or RVs up to 22 feet long. Piped water, vault toilets, picnic tables, and fire grills are provided. A grocery store and propane gas are also available nearby. Leashed pets are permitted.

Reservations, fees: No reservations; $11 per night.

Contact: Lassen National Forest, Hat Creek Ranger District, (530) 336-5521 or fax (530) 336-5758.

Directions: From Redding, drive east on Highway 299 to Burney and continue for five miles to the junction with Highway 89. Turn south on Highway 89 and drive 19 miles to the campground entrance on the right side of the road. If you reach Old Station, you have gone five miles too far.

Trip notes: This camp is one of four along Highway 89 in the area along Hat Creek. It is set at 3,800 feet elevation, with shaded sites and the stream within very short walking distance. Trout are stocked on this stretch of the creek, with fishing access available out of camp, as well as at Rocky and Cave Camps to the south and Honn to the north. In one weekend, fishermen might hit all four. See the trip notes for Cave Camp (campground number 12) for more information.

⑭ Rocky Camp

Location: On Hat Creek in Lassen National Forest; map B3, grid h2.

Campsites, facilities: There are eight tent sites. There is no piped water, but vault toilets, picnic tables, and fire grills are provided. A grocery store and propane gas are also available nearby. Leashed pets are permitted.

Reservations, fees: No reservations; $8 per night.

Contact: Lassen National Forest, Hat Creek Ranger District, (530) 336-5521 or fax (530) 336-5758.

Directions: From Redding, drive east on Highway 299 to Burney and continue for five miles to the junction with Highway 89. Turn right (south) on Highway 89 and drive 20 miles to the campground entrance on the right side of the road. If you reach Old Station, you have gone four miles too far.

Trip notes: This is a small, primitive camp located along Hat Creek on Highway 89. It's usually a second choice for campers if nearby Cave and Bridge Camps are full. Streamside fishing access is a plus here, with this section of stream stocked with rainbow trout. See the trip notes for Cave Camp (campground number 12) for more information.

⓯ Honn

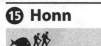

Location: On Hat Creek in Lassen National Forest; map B3, grid h2.

Campsites, facilities: There are six tent sites. There is no piped water, but vault toilets, picnic tables, and fire grills are provided. A grocery store, coin laundry, and propane gas are also available nearby. Leashed pets are permitted.

Reservations, fees: No reservations; $8 per night.

Contact: Lassen National Forest, Hat Creek Ranger District, (530) 336-5521 or fax (530) 336-5758.

Directions: From Redding, drive east on Highway 299 to Burney and continue for five miles to the junction with Highway 89. Turn south on Highway 89 and drive 15 miles to the campground entrance on the left side of the road.

Trip notes: This primitive, tiny campground is set near the point where Honn Creek enters Hat Creek, at 3,400 feet elevation in Lassen National Forest. The creek is extremely pretty here, shaded by trees and flowing emerald green. The camp provides streamside access for trout fishing, though this stretch of creek is sometimes overlooked by the Department of Fish and Game in favor of stocking the creek at the more popular Cave and Bridge Campgrounds. See the trip notes for Cave Camp (campground number 12) for more information.

⓰ North Battle Creek Reservoir

Location: On Battle Creek Reservoir; map B3, grid i0.

Campsites, facilities: There are 10 sites for tents or RVs and five walk-in tent sites. Piped water, vault toilets, picnic tables, and fire grills are provided. A cartop boat launch is available. Leashed pets are permitted.

Reservations, fees: No reservations; $11 per night, $1 pet fee.

Contact: PG&E Building and Land Services, (916) 386-5164.

Directions: From Redding, drive east on Highway 44 to Viola. From Viola, continue east for 3.5 miles to Forest Service Road 32N17. Turn left on Forest Service Road 32N17 and drive five miles. Turn left on Forest Service Road 32N31 and drive four miles. Turn right on Forest Service Road 32N18 and drive a half mile to the reservoir and the campground on the right side of the road.

Trip notes: This little-known lake is set at 5,600 feet in elevation, largely surrounded by Lassen National Forest. No gas engines are permitted on the lake, making it ideal for canoes, rafts, and cartop aluminum boats equipped with electric motors. When the lake level is up in early summer, it is a pretty setting with good trout fishing.

⓱ Crags Camp

Location: In Lassen Volcanic National Park; map B3, grid i1.

Campsites, facilities: There are 45 sites for tents or RVs up to 35 feet long. Piped water, pit toilets, picnic tables, and fire grills are provided. Leashed pets are permitted.

Reservations, fees: Reservations required via phone at (877) 444-6777 ($8.65 reservation fee) or website www.reserveusa.com; $12 per night and a $2 dump fee. Open March to mid-September, weather permitting.

Contact: Lassen Volcanic National Park, (530) 595-4444 or fax (530) 595-3262.

Directions: From Redding, drive east on Highway 44 for 42 miles to the junction with Highway 89. At Highway 89, turn right and drive to the entrance station at Lassen Volcanic National Park. Continue on Highway 89 for about six miles to the campground on the left side of the road.

Trip notes: Crags Camp is sometimes overlooked as a prime spot at Lassen Volcanic National Park because there is no lake nearby. No problem, because even though this camp is small compared to the giant complex at Manzanita Lake, the campsites are more spacious, a lot more private, and many are backed by forest. In addition, the Emigrant Trail runs out of camp, routed east and meeting up with pretty Lost Creek after a little over a mile, a great short hike. Directly across from Crags Camp are the towering Chaos Crags, topping out at 8,503 feet. The camp is set at 5,720 feet.

⑱ Hat Creek

Location: On Hat Creek in Lassen National Forest; map B3, grid i2.

Campsites, facilities: There are 73 sites for tents or RVs up to 22 feet long and three group camp loops, each of which accommodates from 15 to 20 vehicles. Piped water, flush toilets, sanitary dump station, picnic tables, and fire grills are provided. A grocery store, coin laundry, and propane gas are also available nearby. Leashed pets are permitted.

Reservations, fees: Reservations required via phone at (877) 444-6777 ($8.65 reservation fee) or website www.reserveusa.com; $12 per night for family sites; $50 per night for each group camp loop. Open May through October.

Contact: Lassen National Forest, Hat Creek Ranger District, (530) 336-5521 or fax (530) 336-5758.

Directions: From Redding, drive east on Highway 44 to the junction with Highway 89 (near the entrance to Lassen Volcanic National Park). Turn north on Highway 89 and drive about 12 miles to the campground entrance on the left side of the road. (If you reach Old Station, you have gone one mile too far.) Turn left and drive a short distance to the campground.

Trip notes: This is one in a series of Forest Service camps set beside beautiful Hat Creek, a good trout stream stocked regularly by the Department of Fish and Game. The elevation is 4,400 feet. The proximity to Lassen Volcanic National Park to the south is a big plus. Supplies are available in the little town of Old Station one mile to the north.

⑲ Big Pine Camp

Location: On Hat Creek in Lassen National Forest; map B3, grid i2.

Campsites, facilities: There are 19 sites for tents or RVs up to 22 feet long. Two hand pumps provide water. Vault toilets, picnic tables, and fire grills are provided. A sanitary disposal station, grocery store, and propane gas are nearby. Leashed pets are permitted.

Reservations, fees: No reservations; $10 per night.

Contact: Lassen National Forest, Hat Creek Ranger District, (530) 336-5521 or fax (530) 336-5758.

Directions: From Redding, drive east on Highway 44 to the junction with Highway 89 (near the entrance to Lassen Volcanic National Park). Turn north on Highway 89 and drive about eight miles (one mile past the vista point) to the campground entrance on the right side of the road. Turn right and drive a half mile to the campground.

Trip notes: This campground is set on the headwaters of Hat Creek, a pretty spot amid lodgepole pines. A dirt road out of camp parallels Hat Creek, providing access for trout fishing. A great vista point is set on the highway, a mile south of the campground entrance road. It is only a 10-minute drive south to the Highway 44 entrance station for Lassen Volcanic National Park.

⑳ Butte Creek

Location: In Lassen National Forest; map B3, grid i4.

Campsites, facilities: There are 10 unimproved sites for tents or RVs up to 22 feet long. No piped water is available. Vault toilets, fire grills, and tables are provided. Leashed pets are permitted.

Reservations, fees: No reservations; no fee. Open May through October.

Contact: Lassen National Forest, Eagle Lake Ranger District, (530) 257-4188 or fax (530) 257-4150.

Directions: From Redding, drive east on Highway 44 to the junction with Highway 89 (near the entrance to Lassen Volcanic National Park). Turn north on Highway 89 and drive to Highway 44. Turn east on Highway 44 and drive 11 miles to Forest Service Road 18. Turn right at Forest Service Road 18 and drive three miles to the campground on the left side of the road.

Trip notes: This primitive, little-known spot is just three miles from the northern boundary of Lassen Volcanic National Park, set on little Butte Creek. It is a four-mile drive south out of camp on Forest Service Road 18 to Butte Lake in Lassen Park, as well as to the trailhead for a great hike up to the Cinder Cone (6,907 feet), with dramatic views of the Lassen wilderness.

㉑ Crater Lake

Location: In Lassen National Forest; map B3, grid i6.

Campsites, facilities: There are 17 sites for tents. Well water is available. Vault toilets, fire grills, and picnic tables are provided. Leashed pets are permitted.

Reservations, fees: No reservations; $11 per night. Open June through October.

Contact: Lassen National Forest, Eagle Lake Ranger District, (530) 257-4188 or fax (530) 257-4150.

Directions: From Redding, drive east on Highway 44 to the junction with Highway 89 (near the entrance to Lassen Volcanic National Park). Turn north on Highway 89 and drive to Highway 44. Turn east on Highway 44 and drive to the Bogard Work Center and adjacent rest stop. Turn left at Forest Service Road 32N08 (signed Crater Lake) and drive one mile to a T intersection. Bear right and continue on Forest Service Road 32N08 for six miles (including two hairpin left turns) to the campground on the left side of the road.

Trip notes: This camp is set near Crater Lake at 6,800 feet in remote Lassen National Forest, just below Crater Mountain (that's it up there to the northeast at 7,420 feet). This primitive hideaway provides fishing, boating, and, if you can stand the ice-cold water, a quick dunk on warm summer days.

㉒ Manzanita Lake

Location: In Lassen Volcanic National Park; map B3, grid j0.

Campsites, facilities: There are 179 sites for tents or RVs up to 35 feet long and 31 sites for tents only. Piped water, flush toilets, showers, dump station, picnic tables, and fire grills are provided. Propane gas, groceries, and a coin laundry are available nearby. Pets must be controlled.

Reservations, fees: No reservations; $14 per night.

Contact: Lassen Volcanic National Park, (530) 595-4444 or fax (530) 595-3262.

Directions: From Redding, drive east on Highway 44 to the junction with Highway 89. Turn south on Highway 89 and drive one mile to the entrance station to Lassen Volcanic National Park. Continue a short distance on Highway 89, turn right at the campground entrance road, and drive a half mile to the campground.

Trip notes: Manzanita Lake, set at 5,890 feet, is one of the prettiest lakes in Lassen Volcanic National Park and has good catch-and-release trout fishing for experienced fly fishers in prams and other nonpowered boats. This is no place for a dad and a youngster to fish from shore with Power Bait. Because of the great natural beauty of the lake, the campground is often crowded—a drawback as the sites are closer together than at other camps in the park. Evening walks around the lake are very beautiful. A major visitor center and small store are available nearby.

㉓ Summit Lake, North and South

Location: In Lassen Volcanic National Park; map B3, grid j2.

Campsites, facilities: There are 94 sites for tents or RVs up to 30 feet long. Piped water, flush and pit toilets (flush toilets on the north side, pit toilets on the south side), picnic tables, and fire grills are provided. Leashed pets are permitted.

Reservations, fees: No reservations; $14 per night.

Contact: Lassen Volcanic National Park, (530) 595-4444 or fax (530) 595-3262.

Directions: From Redding, drive east on Highway 44 to the junction with Highway 89. Turn south on Highway 89 and drive one mile to the entrance station to Lassen Volcanic National Park. Continue on Highway 89 for 12 miles to the campground entrance on the left side of the road.

Trip notes: Summit Lake is a beautiful spot where deer often visit each evening on the adjacent meadow just east of the campground. The lake is small, and since trout plants were suspended, it has been just about fished out. Evening walks around the lake are perfect for families. A more ambitious trail is routed out of camp and leads past lavish wildflower displays in early summer to a series of wilderness lakes.

㉔ Silver Bowl

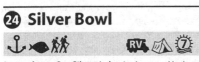

Location: On Silver Lake in Lassen National Forest; map B3, grid j5.

Campsites, facilities: There are 18 sites for tents or RVs. Piped water, vault toilets, fire grills, and picnic tables are provided. Leashed pets are permitted.

Reservations, fees: No reservations; $10 per night. Open May through September.

Contact: Lassen National Forest, Almanor Ranger District, (530) 258-2141 or fax (530) 258-3491.

Directions: From Red Bluff, drive east on Highway 36 to the junction with Highway 89. Continue east on Highway 89/36 past Lake Almanor to Westwood. In Westwood, turn left on County Road A21 and drive 12.5 miles to Silver Lake Road. Turn left on Silver Lake Road/County Road 110 and drive 8.5 miles north to Silver Lake. At Silver Lake, turn right and drive a short distance to the campground.

Trip notes: Silver Lake is a pretty lake set at 6,400 feet elevation at the edge of the Caribou Wilderness. It is stocked with 9,000 Eagle Lake trout and 900 brown trout each year and provides a good summer fishery for campers. There is an unimproved boat ramp at the southern end of the lake. A trailhead from adjacent Caribou Lake is routed west into the wilderness, with routes available both to Emerald Lake to the northwest, and Betty, Trail, and Shotoverin Lakes nearby to the southeast.

㉕ Bogard

Location: In Lassen National Forest; map B3, grid j5.

Campsites, facilities: There are 21 sites for tents or RVs up to 28 feet long. Water, vault toilets, tables, and fire grills are provided. Leashed pets are permitted.

Reservations, fees: No reservations; $9 per night. Open May through September.

Contact: Lassen National Forest, Eagle Lake Ranger District, (530) 257-4188 or fax (530) 257-4150.

Directions: From Redding, drive east on Highway 44 to the junction with Highway 89 (near the entrance to Lassen Volcanic National Park). Turn north on Highway 89 and drive to Highway 44. Turn east on Highway 44 and drive to the Bogard Work Center (about seven miles past Poison Lake) and the adjacent rest stop. Continue east on Highway 44 for two miles to a gravel road on the right side of the road (Forest Service Road 31N26). Turn right on Forest Service Road 31N26 and drive two miles. Turn right on Forest

Service Road 31N21 and drive a half mile to the campground at the end of the road.

Trip notes: This little camp is set along Pine Creek, which flows through Pine Creek Valley at the foot of the Bogard Buttes. It is a relatively obscure camp that gets missed by many travelers. To the nearby west is a network of Forest Service roads, and beyond is the Caribou Wilderness.

㉖ Rocky Knoll

Location: On Silver Lake in Lassen National Forest; map B3, grid j6.

Campsites, facilities: There are seven tent sites and 11 sites for RVs up to 27 feet long. Piped water, vault toilets, fire grills, and picnic tables are provided. Leashed pets are permitted.

Reservations, fees: No reservations; $10 per night. Open May through September.

Contact: Lassen National Forest, Almanor Ranger District, (530) 258-2141 or fax (530) 258-3491.

Directions: From Red Bluff, drive east on Highway 36 to the junction with Highway 89. Continue east on Highway 89/36 past Lake Almanor to Westwood. In Westwood, turn left on County Road A21 and drive 12.5 miles to Silver Lake Road. Turn left (west) on Silver Lake Road/County Road 110 and drive 8.5 miles north to Silver Lake. At Silver Lake, turn left and drive a short distance to the campground.

Trip notes: This is one of two camps at pretty Silver Lake, set at 6,400 feet elevation at the edge of the Caribou Wilderness. The other camp is Silver Bowl to the nearby north, which is larger and provides better access for hikers. This camp, however, is located closer to the boat ramp, which is set at the south end of the lake. Silver Lake provides a good summer fishery for campers.

㉗ Aspen Grove

Location: On Eagle Lake in Lassen National Forest; map B3, grid j9.

Campsites, facilities: There are 26 tent sites.

Picnic tables, fire grills, piped water, phone, and flush toilets are provided. A boat ramp is available. Leashed pets are permitted

Reservations, fees: No reservations; $11 per night. Open May through September.

Contact: Lassen National Forest, Eagle Lake Ranger District, (530) 257-4188 or fax (530) 257-4150.

Directions: From Red Bluff, drive east on Highway 36 toward Susanville. Three miles before Susanville, turn left on Eagle Lake Road/County Road A1 and drive 15.5 miles to County Road 231. Turn right on County Road 231 and drive two miles to the campground on the left side of the road.

Trip notes: Eagle Lake is one of the great trout lakes in California, producing the fast-growing and often huge Eagle Lake trout, which are common in the 18- to 22-inch class. This camp is one of three located at the south end of the lake and is a popular choice for anglers, with a boat ramp available adjacent to the campground. The one problem with Eagle Lake is the wind, which can whip the huge but shallow lake into a froth in the early summer. It is imperative that anglers/boaters get on the water early, and then get back to camp early, with the fishing for the day often done by 10:30 A.M. A bonus here is a good chance to see bald eagles and osprey.

㉘ Eagle

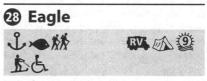

Location: On Eagle Lake in Lassen National Forest; map B3, grid j9.

Campsites, facilities: There are 49 sites for tents or RVs up to 32 feet long. Piped water, flush toilets, picnic tables, and fire grills are provided. The facilities are wheelchair accessible. There is a boat launch nearby at Aspen Grove. Leashed pets are permitted.

Reservations, fees: Reserve via phone at (877) 444-6777 ($8.65 reservation fee) or website www.reserveusa.com; $13 per night. Open May through September.

Contact: Lassen National Forest, Eagle Lake Ranger District, (530) 257-4188 or fax (530) 257-4150.

Directions: From Red Bluff, drive east on Highway 36 toward Susanville. Three miles before Susanville, turn left on Eagle Lake Road/County Road A1 and drive 15.5 miles to County Road 231. Turn right and drive a half mile to the campground on the left side of the road.

Trip notes: Eagle is set just up the road from Aspen Grove; the latter is more popular because of the adjacent boat ramp. For information about Eagle Lake, see the trip notes for Aspen Grove (campground number 27).

㉙ West Eagle Group Camps

Location: On Eagle Lake in Lassen National Forest; map B3, grid j9.

Campsites, facilities: There are two group camps for tents and RVs up to 35 feet long. Piped water, flush toilets, tables, and picnic areas are provided. The facilities are wheelchair accessible. A grocery store and boat ramp are nearby. The campground capacity is limited to 100 people for camp one and 75 people for camp two. Leashed pets are permitted.

Reservations, fees: Reservations are required via phone at (877) 444-6777 ($8.65 reservation fee) or website www.reserveusa.com; $70 to $110 per night for camp one, $70 to $100 per night for camp two.

Contact: Lassen National Forest, Eagle Lake Ranger District, (530) 257-4188 or fax (530) 257-4150.

Directions: From Red Bluff, drive east on Highway 36 toward Susanville. Three miles before Susanville, turn left on Eagle Lake Road/County Road A1 and drive 15.5 miles to County Road 231. Turn right on County Road 231 and drive a quarter mile to the campground on the left side of the road.

Trip notes: If you are coming in a big group to Eagle Lake, you'd better get on the horn first and reserve this camp. Then you can have your own private slice of solitude along the southern shore of Eagle Lake. Bring your boat. The Aspen boat ramp is only about a mile away.

㉚ Merrill

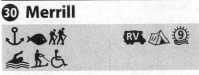

Location: On Eagle Lake in Lassen National Forest; map B3, grid j9.

Campsites, facilities: There are 180 sites for tents or RVs up to 32 feet long. Piped water, flush toilets, picnic tables, and fire grills are provided. A sanitary disposal station is available. The facilities are wheelchair accessible. A grocery store and boat ramp are nearby. Leashed pets are permitted.

Reservations, fees: Reservations accepted for 30 lakeside sites only; reserve via phone at (877) 444-6777 ($8.65 reservation fee) or website www.reserveusa.com; $13 to $15 per night. Open May through November.

Contact: Lassen National Forest, Eagle Lake Ranger District, (530) 257-4188 or fax (530) 257-4150.

Directions: From Red Bluff, drive east on Highway 36 toward Susanville. Three miles before Susanville, turn left on Eagle Lake Road/County Road A1 and drive 15.5 miles to County Road 231. Turn right on County Road 231 and drive one mile to the campground on the right side of the road.

Trip notes: This is one of the largest, most developed Forest Service campgrounds in the entire county. It is set along the southern shore of huge Eagle Lake at 5,100 feet. The nearest boat launch is adjacent to Aspen Grove; see the trip notes for campground number 27.

㉛ Christie

Location: On Eagle Lake in Lassen National Forest; map B3, grid j9.

Campsites, facilities: There are 69 sites for tents or RVs up to 50 feet long. Piped water, flush toilets, fire grills, and picnic tables are provided. The facilities are wheelchair accessible. A grocery store is nearby. A disposal station is two miles away at Merrill (campground number 30). Leashed pets are permitted.

Reservations, fees: Reservations accepted for lakeside sites only; reserve via phone at (877) 444-6777 ($8.65 reservation fee) or website www.reserveusa.com; $13 per night. Open May through September.

Contact: Lassen National Forest, Eagle Lake Ranger District, (530) 257-4188 or fax (530) 257-4150.

Directions: From Red Bluff, drive east on Highway 36 toward Susanville. Three miles before Susanville turn left on Eagle Lake Road/County Road A1 and drive 15.5 miles to County Road 231. Turn right on County Road 231 and drive four miles to the campground on the right side of the road.

Trip notes: This camp is set along the southern shore of Eagle Lake at 5,100 feet. Eagle Lake is well known for its big trout (yea) and big winds (boo). The camp offers some protection from the north winds. Its location is also good for seeing osprey, with the Osprey Management Area, which covers a six-mile stretch of shoreline, located just two miles to the north above Wildcat Point. A nearby resort is a bonus. The nearest boat ramp is at Aspen Grove (see the trip notes for campground 27).

Note: For more campgrounds at Eagle Lake, see chapter B4.

Map B4

One inch equals approximately 10.7 miles.
See inside back cover for California state map.

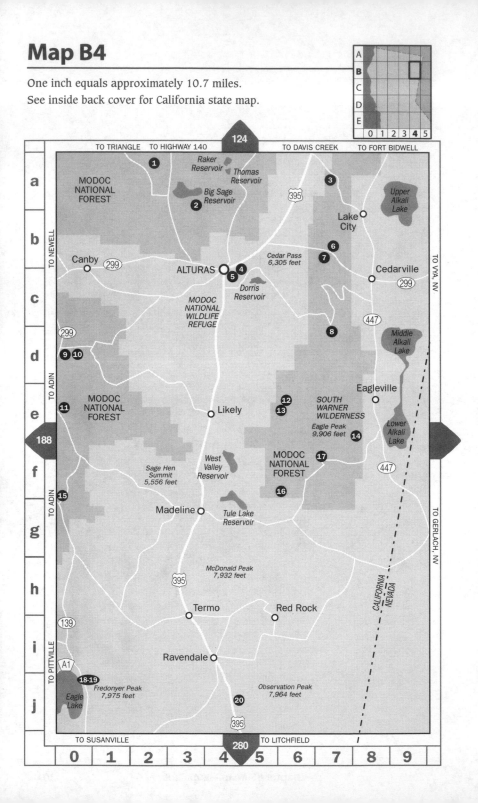

Chapter B4 features:

1 Reservoir C

Location: Near Alturas in Modoc National Forest; map B4, grid a2.

Campsites, facilities: There are six primitive sites. There is no piped water. A vault toilet and picnic tables are provided. Leashed pets are permitted.

Reservations, fees: No reservations; no fee. Open May through September.

Contact: Modoc National Forest, Devil's Garden Ranger District, (530) 233-5811 or fax (530) 233-5817.

Directions: From Alturas drive west on Highway 299 for three miles to Crowder Flat Road/County Road 73. Turn right on Crowder Flat Road and drive 9.5 miles to Triangle Ranch Road/Forest Service Road 43N18. Turn left on Triangle Ranch Road and drive seven miles to Forest Service Road 44N32. Turn right on Forest Service Road 44N32, drive a half mile, turn right on the access road for the lake and campground, and drive a half mile to the camp at the end of the road.

Trip notes: It is a hell of an adventure to explore the "alphabet lakes," located in the remote Devil's Garden area of Modoc County. Reservoir C and Reservoir F provide the best of the lot, but the success can go up and down like a yo-yo, just like the water levels in the lakes. Reservoir C is stocked with both Eagle Lake trout and brown trout. A sidelight to this area is the number of primitive roads that are routed through Modoc National Forest, perfect for four-wheel-drive cowboys.

2 Big Sage Reservoir

Location: In Modoc National Forest; map B4, grid a3.

Campsites, facilities: There are primitive, dispersed sites for tents or RVs of any length. Vault toilets and picnic tables are provided. No piped water is available, so bring your own. Pack out your garbage. A boat ramp is available. Supplies can be obtained in Alturas, about eight miles away. Leashed pets are permitted.

Reservations, fees: No reservations; no fee. Open May through September.

Contact: Modoc National Forest, Devil's Garden Ranger District, (530) 233-5811 or fax (530) 233-5817.

Directions: From Alturas, drive west on Highway 299 for three miles to Crowder Flat Road/County Road 73. Turn right on Crowder Flat Road and drive about five miles to County Road 180. Turn right on County Road 180 and drive four miles. Turn left at the access road for the campground and boat ramp and drive a short distance to the camp on the left side of the road.

Trip notes: This is a do-it-yourself camp; that is, pick your own spot, bring your own water, and don't expect to see any Forest Service rangers or, for that matter, anybody else. This camp is set along Big Sage Reservoir—that's right, sagebrush country at 4,900 feet elevation. It is a big lake, covering 5,000 acres, and a boat ramp is located adjacent to the campground. This is one of the better bass lakes in Modoc County. Catfishing is also available here.

❸ Plum Valley

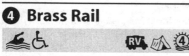

Location: Near the South Fork of Davis Creek in Modoc National Forest; map B4, grid a7.

Campsites, facilities: There are 15 sites for tents or RVs up to 15 feet long. Vault toilets, fire grills, and picnic tables are provided. No piped water is available. Supplies are available in Davis Creek, about 3.5 miles away. Leashed pets are permitted.

Reservations, fees: No reservations; no fee. Open May through September.

Contact: Modoc National Forest, Warner Mountain Ranger District, (530) 279-6116 or fax (530) 279-6107.

Directions: From Alturas drive north on US 395 for 18 miles to the town of Davis Creek. Turn right on County Road 11 and drive two miles to a Y. Bear right on Forest Service Road 45N35 and drive one mile to the signed entrance to the campground on the left side of the road.

Trip notes: This secluded and primitive camp is set near the South Fork of Davis Creek, at 5,600 feet elevation. Davis Creek provides for catch-and-release, barbless hook, no-bait fishing. You can, however, keep the brown trout. There are no other campgrounds within 15 miles.

❹ Brass Rail

Location: Near Alturas; map B4, grid c5.

Campsites, facilities: There are 70 RV sites, some with full hookups, and a separate tent area. Picnic tables are provided. Hot showers, flush toilets, sanitary disposal station, coin laundry, ice, propane gas, playground, tennis court, and swimming pool are available. Supplies can be obtained in Alturas, less than a mile away. Leashed pets are permitted.

Reservations, fees: Reservations are accepted; $8 to $14 per night. Open March through October.

Contact: Brass Rail Campground, (530) 233-2906.

Directions: In Alturas at the junction of Highway 299 and US 395, turn east on US 395 and drive a half mile to the signed campground entrance on the right.

Trip notes: This private RV park has easy access from the highway. The elevation is 4,400 feet. Alturas is the biggest "small town" in Modoc County and offers a nice city park with a playground, museum, old-time saloon, and just south of town, the Modoc National Wildlife Refuge. The Warner Mountains to the distant east provide a backdrop.

❺ Sully's Trailer Lodge

Location: Near Alturas; map B4, grid c4.

Campsites, facilities: There are 15 RV sites, some with full hookups. Hot showers, flush toilets, coin laundry, and horseshoe pits are available. Cable TV is available for an extra fee. Supplies can be obtained in Alturas, several blocks away. Leashed pets are permitted.

Reservations, fees: Reservations are accepted; $10.40 to $14.40 per night. Open year-round.

Contact: Sully's Trailer Lodge, (530) 233-2253.

Directions: In Alturas, at the junction of Highway 299 and US 395, turn south on US 395 and drive a half mile (look for the steam engine) to County Road 56. Turn east on County Road 56 and drive one block to the campground.

Trip notes: This privately operated park is located next to the playground, the city park, and the Modoc County Museum, which details the history of the area. The surrounding Modoc National Wildlife Refuge is only a short drive away, either a mile southwest of town along the Pit River, or three miles east of town at Dorris Reservoir. Big Sage Reservoir (see campground number two) provides another getaway option.

❻ Stowe Reservoir

Location: In Modoc National Forest; map B4, grid b7.

Campsites, facilities: There are eight sites for tents or RVs up to 22 feet long. Piped water, vault toilets, picnic tables, and fire grills are provided. Supplies can be obtained in Cedarville, six miles away. Leashed pets are permitted.

Reservations, fees: No reservations; no fee. Open May to October.

Contact: Modoc National Forest, Warner Mountain Ranger District, (530) 279-6116 or fax (530) 279-6107.

Directions: From Redding, drive east on Highway 299 to Alturas. In Alturas, continue north on Highway 299/US 395 for five miles. Turn right on Highway 299 and drive about 12 miles (just past Cedar Pass). Look for the signed entrance road on the left side of the road. Turn left and drive one mile to the campground on the right side of the road.

Trip notes: Stowe Reservoir looks like a large country pond where cattle might drink. You know why? Because it once actually was a cattle pond on a family ranch that has since been converted to Forest Service property. It is located in the north Warner Mountains (not to be confused with the South Warner Wilderness), which features many back roads and remote four-wheel-drive routes.

Special note: You may find this campground named "Stough Reservoir" on some maps and in previous editions of this book. The name is now officially spelled "Stowe Reservoir," after the family that originally owned the property.

❼ Cedar Pass

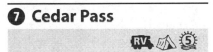

Location: On Cedar Pass in Modoc National Forest; map B4, grid b7.

Campsites, facilities: There are 17 sites for tents or RVs up to 22 feet long. Vault toilets, picnic tables, and fire grills are provided. No piped water is available, so bring your own. Pack out your garbage. Supplies can be obtained in Cedarville or Alturas. Leashed pets are permitted.

Reservations, fees: No reservations; no fee. Open May through September.

Contact: Modoc National Forest, Warner Moun-

tain Ranger District, (530) 279-6116 or fax (530) 279-6107.

Directions: From Redding drive east on Highway 299 to Alturas. In Alturas continue north on Highway 299/US 395 for five miles. Turn right on Highway 299 and drive about nine miles. Look for the signed entrance road on the right side of the road.

Trip notes: Cedar Pass is at 5,900 feet, set on the ridge between Cedar Mountain (8,152 feet) to the north and Payne Peak (7,618) to the south, high in the north Warner Mountains. Bear Creek enters Thomas Creek adjacent to the camp, both small streams, but a pretty spot.

❽ Pepperdine

Location: In Modoc National Forest; map B4, grid d7.

Campsites, facilities: There are five sites for tents or RVs up to 22 feet long. Piped water, vault toilets, picnic tables, and fire grills are provided. Corrals are available with stock watering facilities. Pack out your garbage. Supplies are available in Cedarville or Alturas. Leashed pets are permitted.

Reservations, fees: No reservations; no fee. Open July through October.

Contact: Modoc National Forest, Warner Mountain Ranger District, (530) 279-6116 or fax (530) 279-6107.

Directions: In Alturas, drive south on US 395 to the southern end of town and County Road 56. Turn left on County Road 56 and drive 13 miles to the Modoc Forest boundary and the junction with Parker Creek Road. Bear left on Parker Creek Road and continue for six miles to the signed campground access road on the right. Turn right and drive a half mile to the campground on the right side of the road.

Trip notes: This camp is outstanding for hikers planning a backpacking trip into the adjacent South Warner Wilderness. The camp is at 6,680 feet, set along the south side of tiny Porter Reservoir, with a horse corral located within walking distance. A trailhead out of camp provides direct access to the Summit Trail, the best hike in the South Warner Wilderness.

❾ Lower Rush Creek

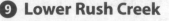

Location: In Modoc National Forest; map B4, grid d0.

Campsites, facilities: There are five sites for tents and five sites for RVs up to 22 feet long. Piped water, vault toilets, picnic tables, and fire grills are provided. Supplies are available in Canby. Leashed pets are permitted.

Reservations, fees: No reservations; $6 per night. Open May through September.

Contact: Modoc National Forest, Big Valley Ranger District, (530) 299-3215 or fax (530) 299-3210.

Directions: From Redding, turn east on Highway 299 and drive to Adin. Continue east on Highway 299 for about seven miles to a signed campground turnoff on the right side of the road. Turn right and drive one mile to the campground.

Trip notes: This is one of two obscure campgrounds set a short distance from Highway 299 off Rush Creek in southern Modoc County. Lower Rush Creek is the first camp you will come to, with flat campsites surrounded by an outer fence and set along Rush Creek. This camp is better suited for trailers than the one at Upper Rush Creek. It is little known and little used. It's set at 4,400 feet in elevation.

❿ Upper Rush Creek

Location: In Modoc National Forest; map B4, grid d0.

Campsites, facilities: There are 13 sites for tents or RVs up to 22 feet long, but Lower Rush Creek (campground number nine) is better for trailers. Piped water, vault toilets, fire grills, and tables are provided. Supplies can be obtained in Adin or Canby. Leashed pets are permitted.

Reservations, fees: No reservations; $6 per night. Open May through September.

Contact: Modoc National Forest, Big Valley Ranger District, (530) 299-3215 or fax (530) 299-3210.

Directions: From Redding, turn east on Highway 299 and drive to Adin. Continue east on Highway 299 for about seven miles to a signed campground turnoff on the right side of the road. Turn right and drive 2.5 miles to the campground at the end of the road.

Trip notes: Upper Rush Creek is a pretty campground, set along Rush Creek, a quiet, wooded spot that gets little use. It sits in the shadow of nearby Manzanita Mountain (7,036 feet elevation) to the east, where there is an old Forest Service lookout for a great view. To reach the lookout, drive back toward Highway 299, and just before reaching the highway, turn left on Forest Service Road 22. A mile from the summit, turn left at a four-way junction and drive to the top. You get dramatic views of the Warm Springs Valley to the north and the Likely Flats to the east, looking across miles and miles of open country.

⓫ Ash Creek

Location: In Modoc National Forest; map B4, grid e0.

Campsites, facilities: There are seven sites for tents only. Vault toilets, tables, and fire grills are provided, but there's no piped water. Pack out your garbage. Supplies can be obtained in Adin. Leashed pets are permitted.

Reservations, fees: No reservations; no fee. Open May through September.

Contact: Modoc National Forest, Big Valley Ranger District, (530) 299-3215 or fax (530) 299-3210.

Directions: From Redding, turn east on Highway 299 and drive to Adin. In Adin, turn right on Ash Valley Road/County Road 88/527 and drive eight miles. Turn left at a signed entrance road and drive a mile to the campground on the right side of the road.

Trip notes: This remote camp has stark beauty and is set along Ash Creek, a stream with small trout. This region of Modoc National Forest has an extensive network of backcountry roads, popular with deer hunters in the fall. Summer comes relatively late out here, and it can be cold and wet even in early June. Stash some extra clothes, just in case. That will probably guarantee nice weather.

⑫ Soup Springs

Location: In Modoc National Forest; map B4, grid e6.

Campsites, facilities: There are eight tent sites and six sites for tents or RVs up to 22 feet long. Piped water, vault toilets, picnic tables, and fire grills are provided. Corrals are available. Supplies can be obtained in Likely. Leashed pets are permitted.

Reservations, fees: No reservations; $6 per night. Open June through September.

Contact: Modoc National Forest, Warner Mountain Ranger District, (530) 279-6116 or fax (530) 279-6107.

Directions: From Alturas, drive south on US 395 for 17 miles to the town of Likely. Turn left on Jess Valley Road/County Road 64 and drive nine miles to the fork. Bear left on West Warner Road/Forest Service Road 5 and go 4.5 miles to Soup Loop Road. Turn right on Soup Loop Road/Forest Service Road 40N24 and continue on that gravel road for six miles to the campground entrance on the right.

Trip notes: This is a beautiful, quiet, wooded campground at a trailhead into the South Warner Wilderness. Soup Creek originates at Soup Springs in the meadow adjacent to the campground. The trailhead here is routed two miles into the wilderness, where it junctions with the Mill Creek Trail. From here, turn left for a beautiful walk along Mill Creek and into Mill Creek Meadow, an easy yet pristine stroll that can provide a serene experience. The elevation is 6,800 feet.

⑬ Mill Creek Falls

Location: In Modoc National Forest; map B4, grid e6.

Campsites, facilities: There are 11 sites for tents and eight sites for tents or RVs up to 22 feet long. Piped water, vault toilets, tables, and fire grills are provided. Supplies are available in Likely. Leashed pets are permitted.

Reservations, fees: No reservations; $6 per night. Open May through October.

Contact: Modoc National Forest, Warner Mountain Ranger District, (530) 279-6116 or fax (530) 279-6107.

Directions: From Alturas drive 17 miles south on US 395 to the town of Likely. Turn left on Jess Valley Road/County Road 64 and drive nine miles to the fork. Bear left on West Warner Road/Forest Service Road 5 for 2.5 miles, turn right on Forest Service Road 40N46, and proceed two miles to the campground entrance at the end of the road.

Trip notes: This nice, wooded campground is a good base camp for a wilderness backpacking trip into the South Warner Wilderness. The camp is set on Mill Creek at 5,700 feet in elevation. To see Mill Creek Falls take the trail out of camp and bear left at the Y. To enter the interior of the South Warner Wilderness, bear right at the Y, after which the trail passes Clear Lake, heads on to Poison Flat and Poison Creek, and then reaches a junction. Left will take you to the Mill Creek Trail, right will take you up to the Summit Trail. Take your pick. You can't go wrong.

⑭ Emerson

Location: In Modoc National Forest; map B4, grid e8.

Campsites, facilities: There are four sites for tents or RVs up to 16 feet long. Vault toilets, picnic tables, and fire grills are provided. No piped water is available, so bring your own. Supplies can be obtained in Eagleville. Leashed pets are permitted.

Reservations, fees: No reservations; no fee. Open July through September.

Contact: Modoc National Forest, Warner Mountain Ranger District, (530) 279-6116 or fax (530) 279-6107.

Directions: From Alturas, drive north on US 395/Highway 299 for about five miles to the junction with Highway 299. Turn right on Highway 299 and drive to Cedarville. From Cedarville, drive 15 miles south on County Road 1 to Eagleville. From Eagleville, continue one mile south on County Road 1 to County Road 40. Turn right on County Road 40 and drive three miles to the campground at the end of the road. The access road is steep and very slick in wet weather. Trailers are not recommended.

Trip notes: This tiny camp is virtually unknown, nestled at 6,000 feet on the eastern boundary of the South Warner Wilderness. Big alkali lakes and miles of the Nevada flats can be seen on the other side of the highway as you drive along the entrance road to the campground. This primitive setting is used by backpackers hitting the trail, a steep, sometimes wrenching climb for 4.5 miles to North Emerson Lake (poor to fair fishing). For many, this hike is a true butt-kicker.

⓯ Willow Creek

Location: In Modoc National Forest; map B4, grid f0.

Campsites, facilities: There are eight sites for tents or RVs up to 32 feet long. Piped water, vault toilets, tables, and fire grills are provided. A wheelchair-accessible toilet is located across from the picnic area. Leashed pets are permitted.

Reservations, fees: No reservations; $6 per night. Open May through October.

Contact: Modoc National Forest, Big Valley Ranger District, (530) 299-3215 or fax (530) 299-3210.

Directions: From Redding, drive east on Highway 299 to Adin. From Adin, turn right on Highway 139 and drive to the campground on the left side of the road.

Trip notes: This remote camp and picnic area is set along little Willow Creek amid pine, aspen, and willows. On the north side of the campground is Lower McBride Springs. To the southwest is a state game refuge, with access available by vehicle, and with several four-wheel-drive routes near its border.

⓰ Blue Lake

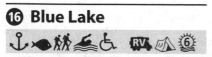

Location: In Modoc National Forest; map B4, grid f6.

Campsites, facilities: There are 48 sites for tents or RVs up to 25 feet long. Piped water, vault toilets, tables, and fire grills are provided.

A paved boat launch is available on the lake. A wheelchair-accessible fishing pier is also available. Obtain supplies in Likely. Leashed pets are permitted.

Reservations, fees: No reservations; $7 per night. Open June through October.

Contact: Modoc National Forest, Warner Mountain Ranger District, (530) 279-6116 or fax (530) 279-6107.

Directions: From Alturas, drive south on US 395 for seven miles to the town of Likely. In Likely, turn left on Jess Valley Road/County Road 64 and drive nine miles to the fork. At the fork, bear right on Forest Service Road 64 and drive seven miles to Forest Service Road 38N60. Turn right on Forest Service Road 38N60 and drive two miles to the campground.

Trip notes: This is a wooded campground with some level sites near the shore of Blue Lake. The lake, which covers 160 acres, provides fishing for brown trout and rainbow trout. A 5 mph speed limit assures quiet water for small boats and canoes. A trail circles the lake and takes less than an hour to hike. The elevation is 6,000 feet. A pair of nesting bald eagles lives here; over the last several years there have been three fledged chicks. While their presence negates year-round use of six campsites otherwise available, the trade-off is an unprecedented opportunity to view the national bird.

⓱ Patterson

Location: In Modoc National Forest; map B4, grid f7.

Campsites, facilities: There are five sites for tents or RVs up to 20 feet long. Piped water, vault toilets, tables, and fire grills are provided. Pack out your garbage. Supplies are available in Likely or Eagleville. Leashed pets are permitted.

Reservations, fees: No reservations; no fee. Open late June through September, weather permitting.

Contact: Modoc National Forest, Warner Mountain Ranger District, (530) 279-6116 or fax (530) 279-6107.

Directions: From Alturas drive 17 miles south on US 395 to the town of Likely. Turn left on Jess

Valley Road/County Road 64 and drive nine miles to the fork. Bear right on Forest Service Road 64 and drive for 16 miles to the campground.

Trip notes: This quiet, wooded campground is set across the road from Patterson Meadow at 7,200 feet in elevation. It's an ideal jump-off spot for a backpacking trip into the South Warner Wilderness, with a trailhead at the camp providing access to the southern wilderness boundary. A great hike from here is the East Creek Loop, a 15-miler that can be completed in a weekend, providing an encapsulated look at the amazing contrasts of the Warners, from small pristine streams to high, barren mountain rims. The camp is rarely open before July.

⑱ Eagle Lake RV Park

Location: Near Susanville; map B4, grid j0.

Campsites, facilities: There are 30 tent sites and 69 RV sites, most with full or partial hookups. There is a separate area for tents only. Picnic tables and fire grills are provided. Rest rooms, showers, coin laundry, sanitary disposal station, grocery store, propane gas, RV supplies, wood, recreation room, and a boat ramp are available. Leashed pets are permitted.

Reservations, fees: Reservations are recommended; $15 to $20 per night.

Contact: Eagle Lake RV Park, (530) 825-3133.

Directions: From Red Bluff, drive east on Highway 36 toward Susanville. Just before reaching Susanville, turn left on County Road A1 and drive to County Road 518 near Spalding Tract. Turn right on County Road 518 and drive through a small neighborhood to the lake frontage road (look for The Strand). Turn right on Palmetto Way and drive eight blocks to the store at the RV park entrance at 687-125 Palmetto Way.

Trip notes: Eagle Lake RV Park has become something of a headquarters for anglers in pursuit of Eagle Lake trout, which typically range 18 to 22 inches. A nearby boat ramp provides access to Pelican Point and Eagle Point, where the fishing is often best in the summer. In the fall months, the north end of the lake provides better prospects (see North Eagle Lake, campground number 19). This RV park has all the amenities, including a small store. That means no special

trips into town, just vacation time, lounging beside Eagle Lake, maybe catching a big trout now and then. One downer: the wind typically howls here most summer afternoons. Resident deer can be like pets here on late summer evenings.

⑲ North Eagle Lake

Location: On Eagle Lake; map B4, grid j0.

Campsites, facilities: There are 20 sites for tents or RVs. Piped water, vault toilets, picnic tables, and fire grills are provided. A private sanitary dump station and boat ramp are available within two miles. Leashed pets are permitted.

Reservations, fees: No reservations; $6 per night. Open Memorial Day through December 31.

Contact: Bureau of Land Management, Eagle Lake Field Office, (530) 257-5381.

Directions: From Red Bluff, drive east on Highway 36 to Susanville. In Susanville, turn left (north) on Highway 139 and drive 29 miles to County Road A1. Turn left at County Road A1 and drive a half mile to the campground.

Trip notes: This camp provides direct access in the fall months to the best fishing area of huge Eagle Lake. When the weather turns cold, the population of big Eagle Lake trout migrate to their favorite haunts just outside the tules, often in water only five to eight feet deep. From shore, try fishing with inflated night crawlers near the lake bottom, just outside the tules. A boat ramp is located about two miles south. From there, troll a Needlefish along the tules, or anchor or tie up and use a night crawler for bait. In the summer months this area is quite exposed and can be hammered by north winds, which typically howl from midday to sunset. The elevation is 5,100 feet.

⑳ Ramhorn Springs

Location: South of Ravendale; map B4, grid j4.

Campsites, facilities: There are 12 sites for tents or RVs up to 28 feet long. There is no potable water. Vault toilets, picnic tables, and fire grills are provided. Leashed pets are permitted.

Reservations, fees: No reservations; no fee.

Contact: Bureau of Land Management, Eagle Lake Field Office, (530) 257-0456.

Directions: From Red Bluff, drive east on Highway 36 to Susanville. In Susanville, turn north on US 395 and drive 45 miles to Post Camp Road. Turn right on Post Camp Road and drive 2.5 miles east to the campground.

Trip notes: This very remote, little-known spot, is set in an area with good numbers of antelope. Though being drawn for tags is nearly an impossibility, the lucky few hunters can use this camp for their base. It is located way out in Nowhere Land, near the flank of Shinn Peak (7,562 feet).

Map C0

One inch equals approximately 10.7 miles.
See inside back cover for California state map.

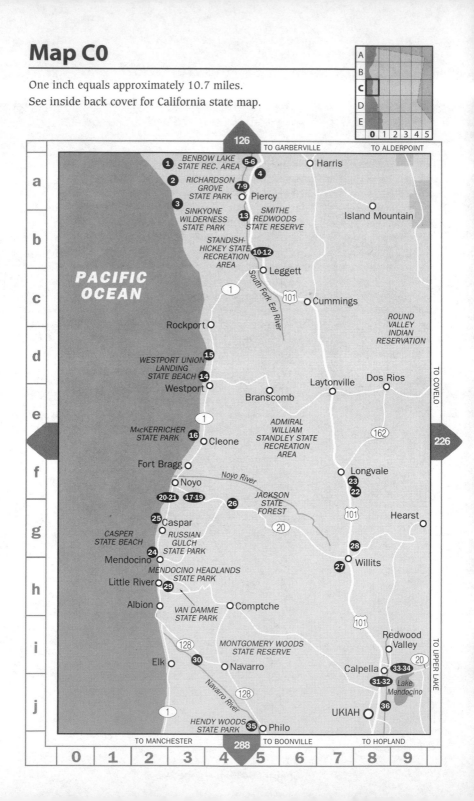

Chapter CØ features:

❶ Nadelos

Location: In the King Range; map CØ, grid a3.

Campsites, facilities: There are eight single tent sites and one group site. Piped water, vault toilets, picnic tables, and fire grills are provided. Some facilities are wheelchair accessible. Leashed pets are permitted.

Reservations, fees: No reservations; $8 per night.

Contact: Bureau of Land Management, Arcata Field Office, (707) 825-2300 or fax (707) 825-2301; website: www.ca.blm.gov/arcata.

Directions: From US 101 north of Garberville, take the Redway exit, turn west on Shelter Cove Road, and drive 17 miles to Chemise Mountain Road. Turn left on Chemise Mountain Road and drive one mile to the campground on the right.

Trip notes: Nadelos Campground is set at 1,840 feet near the South Fork Bear Creek, located at the southern end of the King Range National Conservation Area. This provides access to a rare geographic dynamic, where mountains and coast adjoin. Nearby Chemise Mountain, elevation 2,598 feet, is one of the highest points in California within two miles of the sea. You can hike to the top of this mountain from a trailhead, which provides a dramatic lookout on clear days.

❷ Wailaki

Location: In the King Range; map CØ, grid a3.

Campsites, facilities: There are 13 sites for tents or RVs up to 21 feet long. Piped water, vault toilets, picnic tables, and fire grills are provided. Some facilities are wheelchair accessible. Leashed pets are permitted.

Reservations, fees: No reservations; $8 per night. Open year-round.

Contact: Bureau of Land Management, Arcata Field Office, (707) 825-2300 or fax (707) 825-2301.

Directions: From US 101 north of Garberville, take the Redway exit, turn west on Shelter Cove Road, and drive about 17 miles to Chemise Mountain Road. Turn left on Chemise Mountain Road and drive 1.5 miles to the campground on the right.

Trip notes: This is the southernmost camp in the King Range National Conservation Area, just a half mile down the road from Nadelos (campground number one). A trailhead from this camp is routed via a short connector link to the Lost Coast Trail, and from there hikers can venture south to the Sinkyone Wilderness and the coast, or make the day trip to Chemise Mountain (2,598 feet). The camp is set at 1,840 feet.

❸ Sinkyone Wilderness

Location: In Sinkyone Wilderness State Park; map CØ, grid a3.

Campsites, facilities: There are 15 tent sites, each with a fire ring and a picnic table, at Usal Beach. There is no potable piped water, but water is available if you purify it. Pit toilets are provided. Between Bear Harbor and Jones Beach there are 25 primitive tent sites, some of which have tables, fire rings, and pit toilets. You can drive within three-quarters of a mile of Bear Harbor and park at Orchard Creek, provided the weather is good and the gate is open at Needle Rock Ranch House. Leashed pets are permitted, except on the trails.

Reservations, fees: No reservations; $7 to $11 per night, $1 pet fee.

Contact: Sinkyone Wilderness State Park, (707) 986-7111, (707) 247-3318, or fax (707) 247-3300.

Directions: To reach the northern boundary of the Sinkyone Wilderness from US 101 north of Garberville, take the Redway exit, turn west on Briceland Road, and drive 17 miles to Whitethorn. From Whitethorn continue six more miles to the four corners fork. Take the middle left fork and drive four miles on a gravel road to the Needle Rock Ranger Station.

To reach the southern boundary of the Sinkyone Wilderness from Leggett on US 101 turn southwest on Highway 1 (toward Fort Bragg) and drive 14.66 miles to milepost 90.88 at County Road 431. Turn right on County Road 431 (a dirt road, often unsigned) and drive six miles to the Usal Beach Campground. Note: the roads can be quite rough; four-wheel-drive recommended.

Trip notes: This is a great jump-off point for a backpacking trip in the Sinkyone Wilderness on the Lost Coast, one of the few wilderness areas where a trip can be made any month of the year. The terrain is primitive, steep, and often wet, but provides a rare coastal wilderness experience. Starting at the northern trailhead at Orchard Camp, or the southern trailhead at the Usal Beach Campground, it's an ambitious weekend tromp of 17 miles.

❹ Madrone

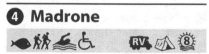

Location: In Richardson Grove State Park; map CØ, grid a5.

Campsites, facilities: There are 40 sites for tents or RVs up to 30 feet long. Piped water, flush toilets, coin-operated showers, fire grills, and picnic tables are provided. A grocery store and sanitary disposal station (five miles away) are available. The facilities are wheelchair accessible. Leashed pets are permitted.

Reservations, fees: Reservations are recommended for the May through September season; reserve via phone at (800) 444-PARK/7275 ($7.50 reservation fee) or website www.cal-parks.ca.gov; $12 to $16 per night, $5 per additional vehicle, $1 pet fee.

Contact: Richardson Grove State Park, (707) 247-3318 or (707) 445-6547.

Directions: From the junction of US 101 and Highway 1 in Leggett, drive north on US 101 past Piercy to the park entrance along the west side of the road.

Trip notes: The highway cuts a swath right through Richardson Grove State Park, and everyone slows to gawk at the giant trees, one of the most impressive groves of redwoods you can drive through in California. To explore further, there are several campgrounds available at the park, as well as a network of outstanding hiking trails. The best of these are the short Red-wood Exhibit Trail, Settlers Loop, and Toumey Trail.

⑤ Benbow Lake State Recreation Area

Location: On the Eel River; map CØ, grid a5.

Campsites, facilities: There are 75 sites for tents or RVs up to 30 feet long. Piped water, flush toilets, coin-operated showers, fire grills, and picnic tables are provided. A boat ramp (no motors) and boat rentals are available. There is a dump station at the park entrance. Supplies and a coin laundry are available in Garberville. Leashed pets are permitted.

Reservations, fees: Reservations are recommended for the May through September season; reserve via phone at (800) 444-PARK/7275 ($7.50 reservation fee) or website www.cal-parks.ca.gov; $12 to $21 per night, $5 for each additional vehicle, $1 pet fee. Open April through October, weather permitting.

Contact: Benbow Lake State Recreation Area, (707) 923-3238 or (707) 247-3318.

Directions: From the junction of US 101 and Highway 1 in Leggett, drive north on US 101 past Richardson Grove State Park to the park entrance (two miles south of Garberville).

Trip notes: This camp is set along the South Fork of the Eel River, with easy access from US 101. It gets heavy use in the summer. The river is dammed each summer, which temporarily creates Benbow Lake, an ideal spot for swimming and light boating. In the winter, this stretch of river can be quite good for steelhead fishing.

⑥ Benbow Valley Resort

Location: On the Eel River; map CØ, grid a5.

Campsites, facilities: There are 112 RV sites (60 drive-through) with full hookups and picnic tables. Cable TV, rest rooms, showers, coin laundry, grocery store, LP gas, restaurant, playground, recreation room, heated swimming pool, whirlpool, RV supplies, and a nine-hole golf course are available. A boat dock and boat rent-als (in summer) are available within 100 feet at Benbow Lake. Leashed pets are permitted.

Reservations, fees: Reservations are accepted; $29 to $33 per night. Open year-round.

Contact: Benbow Valley Resort, (707) 923-2777 or fax (707) 923-2821; email: benbowrv @humboldt.net; website: www.campgrounds. com/benbow.

Directions: From the junction of US 101 and Highway 1 in Leggett, drive north on US 101 past Richardson Grove State Park to Benbow Drive (two miles south of Garberville). Turn north on Benbow Drive and travel a short distance to the campground.

Trip notes: This is an RV park set along US 101 and the South Fork Eel River, with both a small golf course and little Benbow Lake providing nearby recreation. It takes on a dramatically different character in the winter, when the highway is largely abandoned, the river comes up, and steelhead migrate upstream to the stretch of water here. Cooks Valley and Benbow provide good shorefishing access.

⑦ Huckleberry

Location: In Richardson Grove State Park; map CØ, grid a5.

Campsites, facilities: There are 36 sites for tents or RVs up to 30 feet. Piped water, flush toilets, coin-operated showers, fire grills, and picnic tables are provided. A grocery store and sanitary disposal station (five miles away) are available. The facilities are wheelchair accessible. Leashed pets are permitted.

Reservations, fees: Reservations are recommended for the May through September season; reserve via phone at (800) 444-PARK/7275 ($7.50 reservation fee) or website www.cal-parks.ca.gov or website www.cal-parks.ca.gov; $12 to $16 per night, $5 for each additional vehicle, $1 pet fee.

Contact: Richardson Grove State Park, (707) 247-3318 or (707) 445-6547.

Directions: From the junction of US 101 and Highway 1 in Leggett, drive north on US 101 past Piercy to the park entrance on the west side of the road.

Trip notes: This camp is set in a grove of giant coastal redwoods, the tallest trees in the world. The park is one of the prettiest and most popular state parks, making reservations a necessity from Memorial Day through Labor Day. There is good hiking and sight-seeing, but it is often crowded near the visitor center in the summer months. It's a good base camp in the winter for steelhead fishing in the South Fork of the Eel River.

❽ Richardson Grove Campground

Location: On the Eel River; map CØ, grid a4.

Campsites, facilities: There are 91 sites for tents or RVs (28 drive-through), many with full or partial hookups, and two cabins. Picnic tables, fire rings, rest rooms, showers, sanitary disposal station, and playground are provided. A coin laundry, grocery store, LP gas, and ice are available. Leashed pets are permitted.

Reservations, fees: Reservations are recommended; $13.50 to $18 per night for individual sites, $27 per night for cabin rentals. Open year-round.

Contact: Richardson Grove Campground, (707) 247-3380.

Directions: From the junction of US 101 and Highway 1 in Leggett, drive north on US 101 one mile past Richardson Grove State Park to the camp entrance on the west side of the road.

Trip notes: This private camp provides a nearby alternative to Richardson Grove State Park, complete with cabin rentals. The state park, with its grove of giant redwoods and excellent hiking, is the primary attraction. The adjacent South Fork Eel River may look like a trickle in the summer, but it is an excellent steelhead stream providing good shore fishing access here as well as to the south in Cooks Valley.

❾ Oak Flat

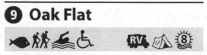

Location: In Richardson Grove State Park; map CØ, grid a5.

Campsites, facilities: There are 94 sites for tents or RVs up to 30 feet long. Piped water, flush toilets, coin-operated showers, fire grills, and picnic tables are provided. A grocery store, sanitary disposal station (five miles away), and propane gas are available nearby. Leashed pets are permitted.

Reservations, fees: Reservations are recommended for the May through September season; reserve via phone at (800) 444-PARK/7275 ($7.50 reservation fee) or website www.cal-parks.ca.gov; $12 to $16 per night, $5 for each additional vehicle, $1 pet fee.

Contact: Richardson Grove State Park, (707) 247-3318 or (707) 445-6547.

Directions: From the junction of US 101 and Highway 1 in Leggett, drive north on US 101 past Piercy to the park entrance on the west side of the road.

Trip notes: Oak Flat is located on the eastern side of the Eel River in the shade of forest and provides easy access to the river. The campground is open only in the summer. For side trip information, see the trip notes for Madrone (campground number four) and Huckleberry (campground number seven).

❿ Redwood Campground

Location: On the Eel River in Standish-Hickey State Recreation Area; map CØ, grid b5.

Campsites, facilities: There are 63 sites for tents or RVs up to 18 feet long. Piped water, coin-operated showers, flush toilets, picnic tables, and fire rings are provided. Some facilities are wheelchair accessible. Leashed pets are permitted.

Reservations, fees: Reserve via phone at (800) 444-PARK/7275 ($7.50 reservation fee) or website www.cal-parks.ca.gov; $14 to $16 per night, $5 for each additional vehicle, $1 pet fee. Open Memorial Day weekend through Labor Day weekend, weather permitting.

Contact: Standish-Hickey State Recreation Area, (707) 925-6482, (707) 445-6547, or fax (707) 247-3300.

Directions: From the junction of US 101 and Highway 1 in Leggett, drive north on US 101 for one mile to the park entrance.

Trip notes: This is one of three camps in Standish-Hickey State Recreation Area, and it is by far the most unusual. To reach Redwood Campground requires driving over a temporary "summer bridge," which provides access to a pretty spot along the South Fork Eel River. In the winter, out comes the bridge and up comes the river. The elevation is 800 feet.

⑪ Rock Creek

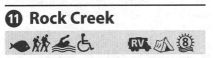

Location: On the Eel River in Standish-Hickey State Recreation Area; map CØ, grid b5.

Campsites, facilities: There are 36 sites for tents or RVs up to 27 feet long and trailers to 24 feet long. Piped water, coin-operated showers, flush toilets, picnic tables, and fire rings are provided. Some facilities are wheelchair accessible. Leashed pets are permitted.

Reservations, fees: Reserve via phone at (800) 444-PARK/7275 ($7.50 reservation fee) or website www.cal-parks.ca.gov; $14 to $16 per night, $5 for each additional vehicle, $1 pet fee.

Contact: Standish-Hickey State Recreation Area, (707) 925-6482, (707) 445-6547, or fax (707) 247-3300.

Directions: From the junction of US 101 and Highway 1 in Leggett, drive north on US 101 for one mile to the park entrance on the west side of the road.

Trip notes: This is one of two main campgrounds set in a redwood grove at Standish-Hickey State Recreation Area (the other is Hickey, campground number 12). It is the classic state park camp, with numbered sites, flat tent spaces, picnic tables, and food lockers. Hiking is only fair in this park, but most people enjoy the short tromp down to the nearby South Fork Eel River. In the winter, steelhead migrate through the area.

⑫ Hickey

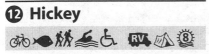

Location: On the Eel River in Standish-Hickey State Recreation Area; map CØ, grid b5.

Campsites, facilities: There are 65 sites for tents or RVs up to 27 feet long and trailers to 24 feet long. There are also several hike-in/bike-in sites. Piped water, showers, flush toilets, picnic tables, and fire rings are provided. A grocery store and coin laundry are nearby. Some facilities are wheelchair accessible. Leashed pets are permitted.

Reservations, fees: Reserve via phone at (800) 444-PARK/7275 ($7.50 reservation fee) or website www.cal-parks.ca.gov; $14 to $16 per night, $5 for each additional vehicle, $1 pet fee.

Contact: Standish-Hickey State Recreation Area, (707) 925-6482, (707) 445-6547, or fax (707) 247-3300.

Directions: From the junction of US 101 and Highway 1 in Leggett, drive north on US 101 for one mile to the park entrance on the left.

Trip notes: This is an ideal layover for US 101 cruisers yearning to spend a night in the redwoods. The park is best known for its camps set amid redwoods and for the nearby South Fork Eel River with its steelhead fishing in the winter. The elevation is 800 feet.

⑬ Redwoods River Resort

Location: On the Eel River; map CØ, grid b5.

Campsites, facilities: There are 14 tent sites and 27 RV sites (nine drive-through) with full hookups, eight cabins, and eight lodge rooms. Cabins and lodge rooms have fully furnished kitchenettes and private bathrooms. Lodge rooms have decks with barbecues and picnic tables. Cabins have wood-burning stoves. Fire rings and picnic tables are provided in the campsites. Rest rooms, hot showers, heated pool, playground, recreation room, mini-mart, coin laundry, group kitchen, dump station, and an evening campfire are among the amenities offered here. Leashed pets are permitted.

Reservations, fees: Reservations are recommended in the summer; campsites are $16 to $24 per night, cabin rentals are $60 to $65 per night, and lodge rooms are $55 to $60 per night. Open year-round.

Contact: Redwoods River Resort, (707) 925-

6249 or fax (707) 925-6413; website: www. campgrounds.com/redwoodriver.

Directions: From the junction of US 101 and Highway 1 in Leggett, drive north on US 101 for seven miles to the campground entrance.

Trip notes: This resort is situated in a 20-acre grove of redwoods on US 101. Many of the campsites are shaded. It is one in a series of both public and private campgrounds located along the highway between Leggett and Garberville. Steelhead and salmon fishing are popular here in the winter, and the resort provides nearby access to state parks. The elevation is 700 feet.

⑭ Wages Creek Beach Campground

Location: Overlooking the Pacific Ocean; map CØ, grid d3.

Campsites, facilities: There are 175 sites for tents or RVs. Piped water, fire grills, picnic tables, and flush toilets are provided. Coin-operated hot showers, sanitary disposal station, wood, and ice are available. Leashed pets are permitted.

Reservations, fees: Reservations are accepted; reserve via phone at (800) 444-PARK/7275 ($7.50 reservation fee) or website www.cal-parks.ca.gov; $10 to $17 per night. Open March through November.

Contact: Wages Creek Beach Campground, (707) 964-2964 or fax (707) 964-8185.

Directions: From Fort Bragg, drive north on Highway 1 to Westport. In Westport, continue north on Highway 1 for a half mile to the campground entrance.

Trip notes: Wages Creek Beach Campground is set above the beach near the mouth of Wages Creek, with creekside sites available, some offering glimpses of the ocean. You will notice as you venture north from Fort Bragg that the number of vacationers in the area falls way off, providing a chance for quiet beaches and serene moments. The best nearby hiking is to the north out of the trailhead for the Sinkyone Wilderness (see directions and trip notes for campground number three).

⑮ Westport Union Landing State Beach

Location: Overlooking the Pacific Ocean; map CØ, grid d4.

Campsites, facilities: There are 100 primitive sites for tents or RVs up to 35 feet long. Piped water, chemical toilets, fire grills, and picnic tables are provided. A grocery store is nearby. Pets are permitted.

Reservations, fees: No reservations; $10 to $12 per night, $1 pet fee. Open year-round.

Contact: Westport Union Landing State Beach, (707) 937-5804, (707) 865-2391, or fax (707) 937-2953.

Directions: From Fort Bragg, drive north on Highway 1 to Westport. In Westport, continue north on Highway 1 for three miles to the campground entrance.

Trip notes: The northern Mendocino coast is remote, beautiful, and gets far less people pressure than the Fort Bragg area. That is the key to its appeal. The campsites are on an ocean bluff, relatively sheltered from coastal winds.

⑯ MacKerricher State Park

Location: Overlooking the Pacific Ocean; map CØ, grid e3.

Campsites, facilities: There are 142 sites for tents or RVs up to 35 feet long and 10 walk-in sites. Piped water, showers, flush toilets, dump station, picnic tables, and fire grills are provided. The facilities are wheelchair accessible. Pets are permitted.

Reservations, fees: Reserve via phone at (800) 444-PARK/7275 ($7.50 reservation fee) or website www.cal-parks.ca.gov; $14 to $16 per night, $1 pet fee. Open year-round.

Contact: MacKerricher State Park, (707) 937-5804, (707) 865-2391, or fax (707) 937-2953.

Directions: From Fort Bragg, drive north on Highway 1 for three miles to the campground entrance on the left side of the road.

Trip notes: MacKerricher is a beautiful park on

the Mendocino coast, a great destination for adventure and exploration. The camps are set in a coastal forest, with gorgeous walk-in sites. Nearby is a small beach, great tide pools, a rocky point where harbor seals hang out in the sun, a small lake (Cleone) with trout fishing, a great bike trail, and outstanding short hikes. The short jaunt around little Cleone Lake has many romantic spots, often tunneling through vegetation, then emerging for lake views. The coastal walk to the point to see seals and tide pools is equally captivating, and if you can't get a kiss here, you're in trouble.

⑰ Wildwood

Location: Near Fort Bragg; map CØ, grid f3.

Campsites, facilities: There are 65 sites for tents or RVs, many with full or partial hookups. Rest rooms, picnic tables, fire rings, hot showers, and a sanitary disposal station are provided. A coin laundry and wood are available. No pets are permitted.

Reservations, fees: Reservations are recommended; $16 to $20 per night, $5 fee for dump use.

Contact: Wildwood, (707) 964-8297.

Directions: Near Fort Bragg at the junction of Highway 1 and Highway 20, turn east on Highway 20 and drive 3.5 miles to the campground.

Trip notes: The drive from Willits to Fort Bragg on Highway 20 is always a favorite, a curving two-laner through redwoods, not too slow, not too fast, best seen from the saddle of a Harley-Davidson. At the end of it is the coast, and just three miles out is this privately operated campground in the sunbelt, said to be out of the fog by breakfast. Within short drives are Noyo Harbor in Fort Bragg, Russian Gulch State Park, Mendocino to the south, and MacKerricher State Park to the north. In fact, there's so much in the area, you could explore for days.

⑱ Fort Bragg Leisure Time RV Park

Location: In Fort Bragg; map CØ, grid f3.

Campsites, facilities: There are 82 sites for tents or RVs, many with full or partial hookups. Rest rooms, picnic tables, cable TV, fire rings, hot showers (coin-operated), and sanitary disposal station are provided. A coin laundry is available. The facilities are wheelchair accessible. Leashed pets are permitted.

Reservations, fees: Reservations are accepted; $16.50 to $22.50 per night.

Contact: Fort Bragg Leisure Time RV Park, (707) 964-5994.

Directions: In Fort Bragg at the junction of Highway 1 and Highway 20, turn east on Highway 20 and drive 2.5 miles to the campground entrance on the right side of the road.

Trip notes: This privately operated park offers volleyball, horseshoes, and badminton. You get the idea. See the trip notes for Wildwood (campground number 17) for side trip options.

⑲ Pomo Campground and RV Park

Location: In Fort Bragg; map CØ, grid f3.

Campsites, facilities: There are 30 sites for tents and 94 RV sites with full or partial hookups. Rest rooms, hot showers (coin-operated), cable TV hookups, store, wood, ice, RV supplies, propane gas, coin laundry, sanitary disposal station, fish cleaning table, horseshoe pits, and large grass playing field are available. Picnic tables and fire rings are at each campsite. Leashed pets are permitted.

Reservations, fees: Reservations are recommended in the summer; $18 to $24 per night.

Contact: Pomo Campground and RV Park, (707) 964-3373 or fax (707) 964-0619.

Directions: In Fort Bragg at the junction of Highway 1 and Highway 20, drive south on Highway 1 for one mile to Tregoning Lane. Turn east and drive a short distance to 17999 Tregoning Lane.

Trip notes: This park covers 17 acres of lush, native vegetation near the ocean, one of several camps located on the Fort Bragg and Mendocino coast. Nearby Noyo Harbor offers busy restaurants, deep-sea fishing, a boat ramp, harbor, and a nice walk out to the Noyo

Harbor jetty. Huckleberry picking is also an option.

⑳ Woodside RV Park and Campground

Location: In Fort Bragg; map CØ, grid f3.

Campsites, facilities: There are 18 sites for tents only and 86 sites for tents or RVs with full or partial hookups. Group sites are available. Picnic tables, fire rings, rest rooms, showers, recreation room, sauna, and sanitary disposal station are provided. Cable TV, RV supplies, ice, wood, and a fish cleaning table are available. Boating and fishing access are within one mile. Leashed pets are permitted.

Reservations, fees: Reservations are accepted; $15 to $21 per night.

Contact: Woodside RV Park and Campground, (707) 964-3684 or fax (707) 964-3684.

Directions: In Fort Bragg at the junction of Highway 1 and Highway 20, drive south on Highway 1 for one mile to the campground.

Trip notes: This privately operated park is set up primarily for RVs. It covers nine acres, is somewhat wooded, and provides access to nearby Fort Bragg and the ocean.

㉑ Dolphin Isle Marina

Location: On the Noyo River in Fort Bragg; map CØ, grid f3.

Campsites, facilities: There are 83 RV sites with full or partial hookups. Rest rooms, picnic tables, hot showers (coin-operated), and a sanitary disposal station are provided. A coin laundry, delicatessen, propane gas, boat ramp, and a dock are available. The facilities are wheelchair accessible. Leashed pets are permitted.

Reservations, fees: Reservations are accepted; $12 to $21 per night.

Contact: Dolphin Isle Marina, (707) 964-4113.

Directions: In Fort Bragg at the junction of Highway 1 and Highway 20, drive east on Highway 20 for a quarter mile to South Harbor Drive. Turn left on South Harbor Drive and drive a quarter mile to Basin Street. Turn right on Basin Street and drive one mile to the campground.

Trip notes: Noyo Harbor is the headquarters of Fort Bragg—the place where everything begins. For vacationers that includes wharfside restaurants, fishing trips, boat docks, and a chance for a nice stroll out to the Noyo Harbor jetty. This RV park is right at the marina, providing an ideal jump-off point for all of those adventures. Beach access is available one mile away.

㉒ Hidden Valley Campground

Location: North of Willits; map CØ, grid f7.

Campsites, facilities: There are 50 sites for tents or RVs, some with modem access and with full or partial hookups. Picnic tables, fire grills, rest rooms, ice, horseshoes, basketball, a coin laundry, dump station and showers are provided. Leashed pets are permitted.

Reservations, fees: Reservations are accepted; $15 to $17 per night for two campers, $2 each additional camper over four years of age; $5 per additional vehicle. Open year-round.

Contact: Hidden Valley Campground, (707) 459-2521 or fax (707) 459-3396; website: www.campgrounds.com/hiddenvalley.

Directions: From Willits on US 101, drive north for 6.5 miles on US 101 to the campground on the east side of the road.

Trip notes: The privately operated park is located in a pretty valley, primarily oak/bay woodlands with a sprinkling of conifers. The most popular nearby recreation option is taking the Skunk Train in Willits for the ride out to the coast at Fort Bragg.

㉓ Sleepyhollow RV Park

Location: North of Willits; map CØ, grid f7.

Campsites, facilities: There are six sites for tents and 24 RV sites (six drive-through) with full or partial hookups. Picnic tables, rest rooms, showers, pond, recreation room, and a sanitary dump station are provided. Leashed pets are permitted.

Reservations, fees: Reservations are accepted; $10 to $15 per night.

Contact: Sleepyhollow RV Park, (707) 459-0613.

Directions: From Willits on US 101, drive north for eight miles to the 55.5 mile marker (two-tenths of a mile beyond the Shimmins Ridge Road sign). At the beginning of the divided four-lane highway, turn right at the signed campground access road and drive to the entrance.

Trip notes: This year-round, privately operated park provides easy access off the highway. A nearby recreation option is the Skunk Train in Willits.

㉔ Russian Gulch State Park

🚲🎣🏃‍♀️♿   🚐🏕️⑨

Location: Near the Pacific Ocean; map CØ, grid g2.

Campsites, facilities: There are 30 sites for tents or RVs up to 27 feet long. Hike-in/bike-in sites are also available. Piped water, showers, flush toilets, picnic tables, and fire grills are provided. The facilities are wheelchair accessible. Pets must be controlled.

Reservations, fees: Reserve via phone at (800) 444-7275 ($7.50 reservation fee); $14 to $16 per night, $1 pet fee. Open mid-March to mid-October.

Contact: Russian Gulch State Park, (707) 937-5804, (707) 865-2391, or fax (707) 937-2953.

Directions: From Mendocino, drive two miles north on Highway 1 to the campground.

Trip notes: Russian Gulch State Park is set near some of California's most beautiful coastline, but the camp speaks to the woods, not the water, with the campsites set in a wooded canyon. They include some of the prettiest and secluded drive-in sites available on the Mendocino coast. There is a great hike here, an easy hour-long walk to Russian Gulch Falls, a wispy 35-foot waterfall that falls into a rock basin. While it's always pretty, it's awesome in late winter. Much of the route is accessible by bicycle, with a rack available where the trail narrows and turns to dirt.

㉕ Caspar Beach RV Park

🎣   🚐🏕️⑧

Location: Near Mendocino; map CØ, grid g2.

Campsites, facilities: There are 23 sites for tents only and 59 RV sites with full or partial hookups. Picnic tables, barbecues, fire pits, cable TV hookups, flush and pit toilets, showers (coin-operated), and a sanitary disposal station are provided. A store, wood, playground, video arcade, convenience store, and a coin laundry are available. Leashed pets are permitted.

Reservations, fees: Reservations are accepted; $17.50 to $25 per night. Open year-round.

Contact: Caspar Beach RV Park, (707) 964-3306 or fax (707) 964-0526; website: www.casparbeach .com

Directions: From Mendocino on Highway 1, drive north for 3.5 miles to the Point Cabrillo exit. Turn west on Point Cabrillo Drive and continue three-quarters of a mile to the campground on the left.

From Fort Bragg on Highway 1, drive south for 4.5 miles. Turn right on Point Cabrillo Drive and continue three-quarters of a mile to the campground.

Trip notes: This privately operated park has ocean frontage and opportunities for beachcombing, fishing, abalone and scuba diving, and good lookouts for whale watching. The park is somewhat wooded, with a small, year-round creek running behind it. The nearby village of Mendocino is an interesting side trip.

㉖ Jackson Demonstration State Forest

🏃‍♀️🚶🏇   5%🚐🏕️⑥

Location: Near Fort Bragg; map CØ, grid g4.

Campsites, facilities: There are 18 primitive tent or RV sites. No piped water is available, but pit toilets, picnic tables, and fire rings are provided. Two equestrian campsites are also available. Leashed pets are permitted.

Reservations, fees: No reservations; no fee.

A camping permit is required and a campground map is needed. Both can be obtained in advance from the State Department of Forestry office at 802 North Main Street (Highway 1) in Fort Bragg, or with a reservation from the campground host in Jackson Demonstration State Forest. Open year-round, but subject without notice to closure for maintenance as required. Call ahead for status.

Contact: Jackson Demonstration State Forest, (707) 964-5674 or (707) 964-0941.

Directions: From Willits on US 101, turn west on Highway 20 and drive 17 miles. At the 16.9 mile marker, turn left into the Jackson State Forest entrance and Dunlop Campground. Obtain a camping permit and a map from the camp host on the premises at Dunlop Camp.

Trip notes: Primitive campsites set in a vast forest of redwoods and Douglas fir are the prime attraction here. Even though Highway 20 is a major connecting link to the coast in the summer months, these camps get bypassed because they are primitive and largely unknown. Why? Because reaching them requires driving on dirt roads sometimes frequented by logging trucks, and there are no campground signs along the highway. A highlight of the area is a 50-foot waterfall on Chamberlain Creek. Set in a steep canyon amid giant firs and redwoods, it can be reached with a 10-minute walk. The elevation is in the 2,000-foot range. What to do first? Get a map from the State Forestry Department. The roads are extremely dusty in summer and muddy in winter.

㉗ Willits KOA

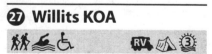

Location: Near Willits; map CØ, grid h7.

Campsites, facilities: There are 21 sites for tents and 50 RV sites (27 drive-through) with full or partial hookups. Group sites and six cabins are available. Piped water, flush toilets, showers, and picnic tables are provided. A playground, swimming pool, horseback riding facilities, hayrides, miniature golf, basketball, volleyball, fishing pond, grocery store, RV supplies, coin laundry, and a sanitary dump station are available. Leashed pets are permitted.

Reservations, fees: Reservations are ac-

cepted; $21 to $26.50 per night. Open year-round.

Contact: Willits KOA, (707) 459-6179 or fax (707) 459-1489.

Directions: From Willits at the junction of US 101 and Highway 20, turn west on Highway 20 and drive 1.5 miles to the campground.

Trip notes: This is an ideal spot to park your RV if you plan on taking the Skunk Train west to Fort Bragg. A depot for the train is within walking distance of the campground. The campground also offers nightly entertainment and weekend barbecues. The elevation is 1,377 feet.

㉘ Quail Meadows

Location: In Willits; map CØ, grid g8.

Campsites, facilities: There are 49 RV sites, most with full or partial hookups. There is a separate section for tents only. Patios, picnic tables, fire grills, rest rooms, showers, and a sanitary disposal station are provided. A small convenience store, coin laundry, propane gas, ice, and TV hookups are available. Leashed pets are permitted.

Reservations, fees: Reservations are accepted; $14 to $20 per night.

Contact: Quail Meadows Campground, (707) 459-6006.

Directions: In Willits at the junction of U.S. 101 and Highway 20, drive north on US 101 for one mile to the campground.

Trip notes: This is one of several RV parks in the Willits area. Nearby is Lake Emily, set near the Brook Trails development, which is stocked in the spring and early summer with trout by the Department of Fish and Game. It's like a backyard fishing hole for the folks around here. Another recreation option is the Skunk Train, which runs from Willits to Fort Bragg.

㉙ Van Damme State Park

Location: Near Mendocino; map CØ, grid h2.

Campsites, facilities: There are 74 sites for tents or RVs up to 35 feet long, 10 primitive hike-in sites, and one group campsite. Piped water, flush toilets, sanitary disposal station, showers, picnic tables, and fire grills are provided. A grocery store, coin laundry, and propane gas are available nearby. Pets are permitted.

Reservations, fees: Reserve via phone at (800) 444-PARK/7275 ($7.50 reservation fee) or website www.cal-parks.ca.gov; $14 to $16 per night, $1 pet fee. Open year-round.

Contact: Van Damme State Park, (707) 937-5804 or (707) 865-2391.

Directions: From Mendocino on Highway 1, drive south for three miles to the town of Little River and the park entrance road on the left side of the road.

Trip notes: The campsites at Van Damme are extremely popular, usually requiring reservations, but with a bit of planning your reward is a base of operations in a beautiful park with redwoods and a remarkable fern understory. The hike-in sites on the Fern Canyon Trail are perfectly situated for those wishing to take one of the most popular hikes in the Mendocino area, with the trail crossing the Little River several times and weaving among old trees. Just across from the entrance of the park is a small but beautiful coastal bay with a pretty beach, ideal for launching sea kayaks.

---

③⓪ Paul M. Dimmick Wayside State Camp

Location: On the Navarro River in Navarro River Redwoods State Park; map CØ, grid i3.

Campsites, facilities: There are 28 sites for tents or RVs up to 30 feet long. Piped water (summer only), vault toilets, fire grills, and picnic tables are provided. Pets are permitted.

Reservations, fees: No reservations; $10 to $12 per night, $1 pet fee. Open year-round.

Contact: Paul M. Dimmick Wayside State Camp, (707) 937-5804, (707) 865-2391, or fax (707) 937-2953.

Directions: From Cloverdale on US 101 turn north on Highway 128 and drive 49 miles. Look for the signed campground entrance on the left side of the road.

Trip notes: A pretty grove of redwood trees and the nearby Navarro River are the highlights of this campground. It's a nice spot but, alas, lacks any significant hiking trails that could make it an overall spectacular destination; all the trailheads along Highway 128 turn out to be just little spur routes from the road to the river.

---

③① Che-Ka-Ka

Location: At Lake Mendocino; map CØ, grid j8.

Campsites, facilities: There are 22 sites for tents or RVs up to 35 feet long. Piped water, vault toilets, picnic tables, and fire grills are provided. A boat ramp is adjacent to the campground. Leashed pets are permitted.

Reservations, fees: No reservations; $8 per night. Open year-round.

Contact: US Army Corps of Engineers, Lake Mendocino, (707) 462-7581.

Directions: From Ukiah, drive north on US 101 to the Highway 20 turnoff. Drive east on Highway 20 to Lake Mendocino Drive. Exit right on Lake Mendocino Drive and continue to the first stoplight. Turn left on North State Street and drive to the next stoplight. Turn right (which will put you back on Lake Mendocino Drive) and drive about one mile to the signed entrance to the campground at Coyote Dam.

Trip notes: This campground sits beside the dam at the south end of Lake Mendocino, the lake with the leg-biting catfish. What? Right: the Department of Fish and Game installed "catfish condominiums" in the lake; that is, homes for catfish on the lake bottom. When swimmers started wading out and stepping on them, the catfish would come out and chomp them in the legs. Lake Mendocino is also known for good striped bass fishing, waterskiing, and boating. Nearby, upstream of the lake, is Potter Valley and the East Fork Russian River (also called Cold Creek), which provides trout fishing in the summer. A boat ramp located at the corner of the dam is a bonus. The elevation is 750 feet.

32 Ky-En

Location: At Lake Mendocino; map CØ, grid j8.

Campsites, facilities: There are 103 sites for tents or RVs up to 35 feet long. Rest rooms, showers, playground (in the adjacent day-use area), sanitary dump station, picnic tables, and fire grills are provided. A boat ramp, boat rentals, and limited supplies are available at the nearby marina. Some sites are wheelchair accessible. Leashed pets are permitted.

Reservations, fees: Reservations are available for 43 of the family sites; phone the Ky-En Ranger Station, (707) 485-1427. For group and wheelchair site information and reservations, phone the US Army Corps of Engineers, (707) 462-7581; $14 to $16 per night for family sites.

Contact: US Army Corps of Engineers, Lake Mendocino, (707) 462-7581.

Directions: From Ukiah, drive north on US 101 to the Highway 20 turnoff. Drive east on Highway 20 to Marina Drive. Turn right and drive to the north end of the lake and the campground.

Trip notes: This camp is located on the north shore of Lake Mendocino. With the access road off Highway 20 instead of US 101 (as with Che-Ka-Ka), it can be overlooked by newcomers. A nearby boat ramp makes it especially attractive. For more information see the trip notes for Che-Ka-Ka (campground number 31).

33 Miti Boat-In/Hike-In

Location: On Lake Mendocino; map C0, i9.

Campsites, facilities: There are 15 sites for tents only. Vault toilets, fire rings and picnic tables are available, but there is no piped water. Garbage must be carried out. Leashed pets are permitted.

Reservations, fees: No reservations; $5 per night, one-time $2 boat launch fee. Open April through September, weather permitting. (Some sites may be flooded in the spring.)

Contact: US Army Corps of Engineers, Lake Mendocino, (707) 462-7581.

Directions: From Ukiah, drive north on US 101 to the Highway 20 turnoff. For boat-in campers: Drive east on Highway 20 to Marina Drive. Turn right and drive to the north ramp of the lake. The campground is approximately one mile by water.

For hike-in campers: Drive five miles east on Highway 20. Just after crossing the Russian River bridge, turn left (Inlet Road) and drive approximately one mile to the campground parking lot (which will be the Bu-Shay campground parking lot). The campground is two miles from the parking area.

Trip notes: One of several campgrounds on the north end of Lake Mendocino, this one has the added advantage of having a boat launch facility. The North Boat Ramp (Marina Drive off Highway 20) is open 24 hours; the south ramp closes at night.

34 Bu-Shay

Location: At Lake Mendocino; map CØ, grid j9.

Campsites, facilities: There are 164 sites for tents or RVs up to 35 feet long. There are three group sites for up to 120 people each. Rest rooms, showers, playground (in the adjacent day-use area), sanitary dump station, picnic tables, and fire grills are provided. The boat ramp is two miles from camp near Ky-En Campground. Some sites are wheelchair accessible. Leashed pets are permitted.

Reservations, fees: Reservations accepted for group and wheelchair sites only; $14 per night for individual sites, $120 per night for groups. Open April through September.

Contact: US Army Corps of Engineers, Lake Mendocino, (707) 462-7581.

Directions: From Ukiah, drive north on US 101 to the Highway 20 turnoff. Drive five miles east on Highway 20. Just after crossing the Russian River bridge, turn left (Inlet Road) and drive approximately one mile to the campground parking lot.

Trip notes: Bu-Shay, on the northeast end of Lake Mendocino, is set on a point that provides a pretty southern exposure when the lake is full.

The lake is about three miles long and one mile wide. It offers fishing for striped bass and bluegill, as well as waterskiing and power boating. A nearby visitor center features exhibits of local Native American history. The elevation is 750 feet. For more information about Lake Mendocino, see the trip notes for Che-Ka-Ka (campground number 31).

35 Hendy Woods State Park

Location: Near Boonville; map CØ, grid j5.

Campsites, facilities: There are 92 sites for tents or RVs up to 35 feet long. Piped water, flush toilets, showers, sanitary disposal station, picnic tables, and fire grills are provided. A grocery store and propane gas station are available nearby. The facilities are wheelchair accessible. Leashed pets are permitted.

Reservations, fees: Reserve via phone at (800) 444-PARK/7275 ($7.50 reservation fee) or website www.cal-parks.ca.gov; $14 to $16 per night, $1 pet fee. Open year-round.

Contact: Hendy Woods State Park, (707) 937-5804, (707) 865-2391, or fax (707) 937-2953.

Directions: From Cloverdale on US 101, turn northwest on Highway 128 and drive about 35 miles to Philo Greenwood Road. Turn left on Philo Greenwood Road and drive a short distance to the park entrance.

Trip notes: This is a remarkable setting where the flora changes from open valley grasslands and oaks to a cloaked redwood forest with old growth, as if you had waved a magic wand. The camps are set in the forest, with a great trail routed amid the old redwoods and up to the Hermit Hut, where a hobo lived for 18 years in a few giant tree stumps covered with branches. Note: It is illegal to fish in the park's river.

36 Manor Oaks Overnighter Park

Location: In Ukiah; map CØ, grid j8.

Campsites, facilities: There are 53 RV sites (15 drive-through) with full hookups. Picnic tables, fire grills, rest rooms, showers, and a swimming pool (in summer) are provided. A coin laundry and ice are available. The camp is wheelchair accessible. Leashed pets are permitted.

Reservations, fees: Reservations are accepted; $20 per night. Open year-round.

Contact: Manor Oaks Overnighter Park, (707) 462-0529.

Directions: From US 101 in Ukiah, take the Central Ukiah/Gobbi Street exit and drive east for a short distance to 700 East Gobbi Street on the left.

Trip notes: Manor Oaks Overnighter Park is an RV park in an urban setting for US 101 motor home cruisers. Nearby Lake Mendocino provides a side trip option, with access to boating, waterskiing, and fishing.

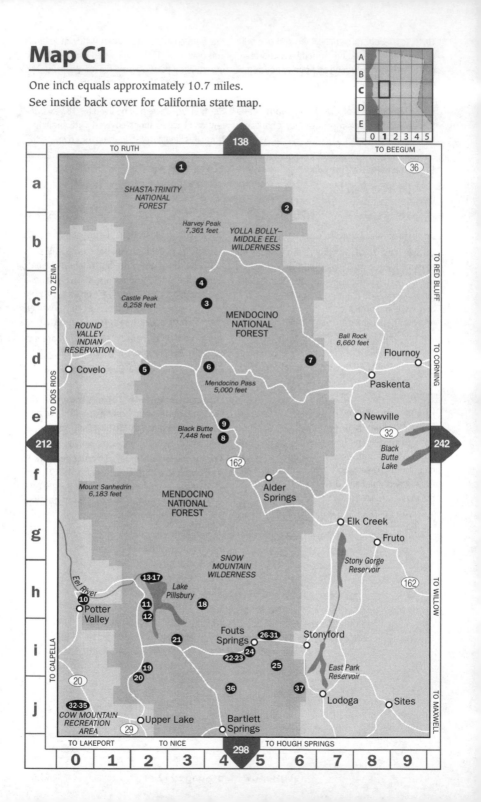

Map C1

One inch equals approximately 10.7 miles.
See inside back cover for California state map.

Chapter C1 features:

❶ Tomhead Saddle

Location: In Shasta-Trinity National Forest; map C1, grid a3.

Campsites, facilities: There are five sites for tents or RVs. There is no piped water, so bring your own. Vault toilets, picnic tables, and fire grills are provided. A horse corral is available. Pets are permitted.

Reservations, fees: No reservations; no fee.

Contact: Shasta-Trinity National Forest, Yolla Bolla Ranger Station, (530) 352-4211 or fax (530) 352-4312.

Directions: From Interstate 5 in Red Bluff, turn west on Highway 36 and drive about 13 miles. Turn left on Cannon Road and drive about five miles to Pettyjohn Road. Turn west on Pettyjohn Road, drive to Saddle Camp, turn south on Forest Service Road 27N06, and drive three miles to the campground. It is advisable to obtain a map of Shasta-Trinity National Forest.

Trip notes: This one is way out there in booger country. Little known and rarely visited, it's primarily a jump-off point for ambitious backpackers. The camp is located on the edge of the Yolla Bolly–Middle Eel Wilderness. A trailhead here is routed to the South Fork of Cottonwood Creek, a trek that entails hiking eight miles in dry, hot terrain. The elevation is 5,700 feet.

❷ White Rock

Location: In Shasta-Trinity National Forest; map C1, grid a6.

Campsites, facilities: There are three tent sites. Vault toilets, picnic tables, and fire grills are provided. Leashed pets are permitted.

Reservations, fees: No reservations; no fee.

Contact: Shasta-Trinity National Forest, Yolla Bolla Ranger Station, (530) 352-4211 or fax (530) 352-4312.

Directions: From Red Bluff, drive about 45 miles west on Highway 36 to the Yolla Bolla ranger office. Continue west for about eight miles to Wild Mad River Road/Forest Service

Road 30. Turn left on Forest Service Road 30 and drive nine miles to Pine Ridge Saddle Road/ Forest Service Road 35. Turn left and drive nine miles (on a gravel road, very twisty) to the campground.

Trip notes: There's a reason why there's no charge to camp here: usually nobody's around. It's primitive, little known, and likely to be empty. If you don't want to see anybody, you've found the right place. The big attraction here is watching the turtles swim at nearby White Rock Pond. A trailhead is available nearby out of Stuart Gap, which provides access to the North Yolla Bolly Mountains.

❸ Little Doe

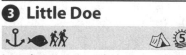

Location: Near Howard Lake in Mendocino National Forest; map C1, grid c4.

Campsites, facilities: There are 13 tent sites. No piped water is available. Fire pits are provided. Supplies are available in Covelo, 12 miles away. Leashed pets are permitted.

Reservations, fees: No reservations; $6 per night. Open June through October.

Contact: Mendocino National Forest, Covelo Ranger District, (707) 983-6118 or fax (707) 983-8004. For a map send $4 to USDA Forest Service, US Forest Map Sales, 1323 Club Drive, Vallejo, CA 94592; (707) 562-USFS/8737; website: www.r5.fs.fed.us.

Directions: From Willits, drive north on US 101 for 13 miles to Longvale and the junction with Highway 162. Turn northeast on Highway 162 and drive to Covelo. Continue east on Highway 162 to the Eel River Bridge. Turn left at the bridge on Forest Service Road M1 and drive about 11 miles to the campground at the north end of the lake.

Trip notes: Little Howard Lake is tucked deep in the interior of Mendocino National Forest between Espee Ridge to the south and Little Doe Ridge to the north, at elevation 3,600 feet. For a drive-to lake, it is surprisingly remote and provides fair trout fishing, primitive camping, and an opportunity for cartop boating. Side trips include Hammerhorn Lake, about six miles away, and several four-wheel-drive roads that allow you to explore the area.

❹ Hammerhorn Lake

Location: Near Covelo in Mendocino National Forest; map C1, grid c3.

Campsites, facilities: There are eight sites for tents or RVs up to 16 feet long. Piped water, picnic tables, fire grills, and vault toilets are provided. There are two wheelchair-accessible campsites, a rest room, piers, and a trail. Supplies are available in Covelo. Leashed pets are permitted.

Reservations, fees: No reservations; $6 per night. Open June through October.

Contact: Mendocino National Forest, Covelo Ranger District, (707) 983-6118 or fax (707) 983-8004. For a map send $4 to USDA Forest Service, US Forest Map Sales, 1323 Club Drive, Vallejo, CA 94592; (707) 562-USFS/8737; website: www.r5.fs.fed.us.

Directions: From Willits, drive north on US 101 for 13 miles to Longvale and the junction with Highway 162. Turn northeast on Highway 162 and drive to Covelo. Continue east on Highway 162 to the Eel River Bridge. Turn left at the bridge on Forest Service Road M1 and drive about 17 miles to the campground at the north end of the lake.

Trip notes: Obscure and hidden, this is a veritable dot of a lake, just five acres, set at 3,500 feet in Mendocino National Forest. But it gets stocked with good-sized trout and can provide good fishing, camping, and adventuring. The lake is set near the border of the Yolla Bolly Wilderness, with the trailhead located nearby to the northeast. A great side trip is the drive up to Hammerhorn Mountain Lookout.

❺ Eel River

Location: In Mendocino National Forest; map C1, grid d2.

Campsites, facilities: There are 16 sites for tents or RVs. Piped water, vault toilets, picnic tables, and fire grills are provided. You must pack out your garbage. Leashed pets are permitted.

Reservations, fees: No reservations; $6 per night. Open May through October.

Contact: Mendocino National Forest, Covelo Ranger District, (707) 983-6118 or fax (707) 983-8004.

Directions: From Willits, drive north on US 101 for 13 miles to Longvale and the junction with Highway 162. Turn northeast on Highway 162 and drive to Covelo. Continue east on Highway 162 for 13 miles to the campground.

Trip notes: This is a little-known spot, set in oak woodlands at the confluence of the Middle Fork of the Eel River and the Black Butte River. The elevation is 1,500 feet, and it's often extremely hot in summer. But at no cost, the price is right. Eel River, an ancient Native American campsite, is a major archaeological site. For this reason restoration has been limited and at times the camp is overgrown and weedy. Who cares, though. After all, you're camping.

❻ Wells Cabin

Location: In Mendocino National Forest; map C1, grid d4.

Campsites, facilities: There are 25 sites for tents or RVs up to 22 feet long. There is no piped water in the winter. Vault toilets, picnic tables, and fire grills are provided. You must pack out your own garbage. Leashed pets are permitted.

Reservations, fees: No reservations; no fee. Open July through October.

Contact: Mendocino National Forest, Corning Ranger District, (530) 824-5196 or fax (530) 824-6034.

Directions: From Corning on Interstate 5, turn west on County Road A9 and drive 20 miles to Paskenta. In Paskenta turn left on County Road 55 and drive into Mendocino National Forest (where the road becomes Forest Service Road M4). Continue on Forest Service Road M4 all the way near the ridge at Government Flat at Forest Service Road 24N02. Turn left on Forest Service Road 24N02 and drive two miles to the campground.

Trip notes: You'll join the 5 Percent Club when you reach this spot. It is situated one mile from Anthony Peak Lookout (6,900 feet) where, on a clear day, you can get great views all the way to the Pacific Ocean and sweeping views of the

Sacramento Valley to the east. This campground is hardly used during the summer and often provides a cool escape from the heat of the valley. The elevation is 6,300 feet.

❼ Whitlock

Location: In Mendocino National Forest; map C1, grid d6.

Campsites, facilities: There are three sites for tents or RVs up to 22 feet long. Piped water, vault toilets, picnic tables, and fire grills are provided. You must pack out your own garbage. Leashed pets are permitted.

Reservations, fees: No reservations; no fee. Open June through October.

Contact: Mendocino National Forest, Corning Ranger District, (530) 824-5196 or fax (530) 824-6034.

Directions: From Corning on Interstate 5, turn west onto County Road A9/Corning Road and drive 20 miles to Paskenta. Turn north on Toomes Camp Road/County Road 122 and drive 14 miles to the campground.

Trip notes: This obscure Forest Service camp is often empty or close to empty. It is set at 4,300 feet, where conifers have taken over from the valley grasslands to the nearby east. The camp is situated amid good deer range and makes a good hunting base camp in the fall, with a network of Forest Service roads in the area. It is advisable to obtain a Forest Service map.

❽ Plaskett Meadows

Location: In Mendocino National Forest; map C1, grid e4.

Campsites, facilities: There are 32 sites for tents or RVs up to 16 feet long. Piped water, vault toilets, fire grills, and picnic tables are provided. Leashed pets are permitted.

Reservations, fees: No reservations; $5 per night. Open July through October.

Contact: Mendocino National Forest, Stonyford Work Station, (530) 963-3128 or fax (530) 963-3173.

Directions: In Willows on Interstate 5, turn west on Highway 162 and drive toward the town of Elk Creek. Just after crossing the Stony Creek Bridge, turn north on County Road 306 and drive four miles. Turn left on Alder Springs Road/Forest Service Road 7 and drive 31 miles to the campground.

Trip notes: This is a little-known camp in the mountains near Plaskett Lakes, a pair of connected dot-size mountain lakes that form the headwaters of little Plaskett Creek. Trout fishing is best at the westernmost of the two lakes. No motors or swimming are permitted in the lakes.

⑨ Masterson Group Camp

Location: Near Plaskett Lakes in Mendocino National Forest; map C1, grid e4.

Campsites, facilities: This group camp can accommodate up to 100 people, with 20 tent sites, piped water, vault toilets, fire grills, and picnic tables provided. Leashed pets are permitted.

Reservations, fees: Reservations are required; $35 group fee per night. Open mid-May through mid-October.

Contact: Mendocino National Forest, Grindstone Ranger District, Stonyford Work Station, (530) 963-3128 or fax (530) 963-3173.

Directions: In Willows on Interstate 5, turn west on Highway 162 and drive toward the town of Elk Creek. Just after crossing the Stony Creek Bridge, turn north on County Road 306 and drive four miles. Turn left on Alder Springs Road/Forest Service Road 7 and drive 31 miles to the camp on the right.

Trip notes: This is a group camp only. It is located just a mile away from the Plaskett Lakes, two small lakes set at 6,000 feet and surrounded by mixed conifer forest. No swimming or motors are permitted at either lake. It is advisable to obtain a map of Mendocino National Forest, which details nearby streams, lakes, and hiking trails. One notable trail is the Black Butte Trail. For more information see the trip notes for Plaskett Meadows (campground number eight).

⑩ Trout Creek

Location: Near East Van Arsdale Reservoir; map C1, grid h0.

Campsites, facilities: There are 15 sites for tents or RVs. Piped water, picnic tables, fire grills, and vault toilets are provided. Leashed pets are permitted.

Reservations, fees: No reservations; $10 per night, $1 pet fee. Open May through October.

Contact: PG&E Building and Land Services, (916) 386-5164.

Directions: From Ukiah on US 101, drive north to the junction with Highway 20. Turn east on Highway 20 and drive five miles. Turn northwest on County Road 240/Potter Valley/Lake Pillsbury Road toward Lake Pillsbury. From the Eel River Bridge, drive two miles to the campground entrance.

Trip notes: This is a spot that relatively few campers know about. Most others looking over this area are setting up shop at nearby Lake Pillsbury to the east. But if you like to watch the water roll by, this could be your port of call since it is located at the confluence of Trout Creek and the Eel River (not far from the East Van Arsdale Reservoir). Insider's note: Nearby in Potter Valley to the south, the East Fork Russian River (Cold Creek) is stocked with trout during the summer months. The elevation is 1,500 feet.

⑪ Fuller Grove

Location: On Lake Pillsbury in Mendocino National Forest; map C1, grid h2.

Campsites, facilities: There are 30 sites for tents or RVs. Picnic tables and fire grills are provided. Piped water and vault toilets are available. A boat ramp is nearby. Leashed pets are permitted.

Reservations, fees: No reservations; $10 per night for a maximum of six campers, $3 per extra vehicle, $1 pet fee.

Contact: Mendocino National Forest, Upper Lake Ranger District, (707) 275-2361 or fax (707) 275-0676.

Directions: From Ukiah on US 101, drive north

to the junction with Highway 20. Turn east on Highway 20 and drive five miles. Turn northwest on County Road 240/Potter Valley/Lake Pillsbury Road and drive to the Eel River Information Kiosk at Lake Pillsbury. Continue for one mile, turn right at the campground access road, and drive a quarter mile to the campground.

Trip notes: This is one of several campgrounds bordering Lake Pillsbury, which at 2,000 acres, is by far the largest lake in Mendocino National Forest. It has lakeside camping, good boat ramps, and in the spring, good fishing for trout. This camp is set along the northwest shore of the lake, with a boat ramp located only about a quarter mile away to the north. There are numerous backcountry roads in the area, which provide access to a state game refuge to the north and the Snow Mountain Wilderness to the east.

⑫ Lake Pillsbury Resort

Location: On Lake Pillsbury; map C1, grid h2.

Campsites, facilities: There are 34 sites for tents or RVs, with no hookups. There are also eight cabins for rent. A snack bar, rest rooms, showers, boat rentals, fuel, dock, fishing supplies, and pier are available. Leashed pets are permitted.

Reservations, fees: Reservations are recommended; $14 to $15 per night. Small cabins are $47 per night, large cabins are $60 per night. Open May through November.

Contact: Lake Pillsbury Resort, (707) 743-1581 or fax (707) 743-2666.

Directions: From Ukiah on US 101, drive north to the junction with Highway 20. Turn east on Highway 20 and drive five miles. Turn northwest on County Road 240/Potter Valley/Lake Pillsbury Road and drive to Lake Pillsbury and Forest Service Road 301F. Turn right at Forest Service Road 301F and drive two miles to the resort.

Trip notes: This is a pretty spot beside the shore of Lake Pillsbury in the heart of Mendocino National Forest. It can be headquarters for a vacation involving boating, fishing, waterskiing, or exploring the surrounding national forest. A boat ramp, small marina, and full facilities make this place a prime attraction in a relatively remote location. This is the only resort on the lake that

accepts reservations, and it has some lakefront sites.

⑬ Pogie Point

Location: On Lake Pillsbury in Mendocino National Forest; map C1, grid h2.

Campsites, facilities: There are 50 sites for tents or RVs. Piped water is provided, except in winter. Picnic tables and fire grills are provided. Vault toilets are available. Two campsites are wheelchair accessible. Leashed pets are permitted.

Reservations, fees: No reservations; $10 per night, $3 per extra vehicle, $1 pet fee. Open year-round.

Contact: Mendocino National Forest, Upper Lake Ranger District, (707) 275-2361 or fax (707) 275-0676.

Directions: From Ukiah on US 101, drive north to the junction with Highway 20. Turn east on Highway 20 and drive five miles. Turn northwest on County Road 240/Potter Valley/Lake Pillsbury Road and drive 26 miles to the Eel River Information Kiosk at Lake Pillsbury. Continue for two miles, turn right at the campground access road, and drive a short distance to the campground.

Trip notes: This camp is set beside Lake Pillsbury in Mendocino National Forest, located in the back of a cove at the lake's northwest corner. When the lake is full, this spot is quite pretty. When the lake level is way down, well, you can't win 'em all. A boat ramp is located about a quarter mile to the south, a bonus. The elevation is 1,900 feet.

⑭ Sunset Campground

Location: On Lake Pillsbury in Mendocino National Forest; map C1, grid h2.

Campsites, facilities: There are 54 sites for tents or RVs. Piped water (except in the winter), picnic tables, fire grills, and vault toilets are provided. A boat ramp is nearby. Leashed pets are permitted.

Reservations, fees: No reservations; $10 per night, $3 per extra vehicle, $1 pet fee. Open year-round.

Contact: Mendocino National Forest, Upper Lake Ranger District, (707) 275-2361 or fax (707) 275-0676.

Directions: From Ukiah on US 101, drive north to the junction with Highway 20. Turn east on Highway 20 and drive five miles. Turn northwest on County Road 240/Potter Valley/Lake Pillsbury Road and drive 26 miles to the Eel River Information Kiosk at Lake Pillsbury. Continue for five miles around the north end of the lake and look for the camp entrance on the right side of the road.

Trip notes: This camp is located on the northeast corner of Lake Pillsbury, with a boat ramp available at the mouth of Squaw Creek Cove less than a quarter mile to the south. The adjacent designated nature trail along the shore of the lake here is another attraction. The surrounding national forest offers side trip possibilities.

⑮ Oak Flat

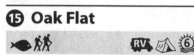

Location: On Lake Pillsbury in Mendocino National Forest; map C1, grid h2.

Campsites, facilities: There are 12 primitive sites for tents or RVs, used primarily as an overflow area. There is no piped water, but picnic tables, fire grills, and vault toilets are provided. Leashed pets are permitted.

Reservations, fees: No reservations; no fee. Open year-round.

Contact: Mendocino National Forest, Upper Lake Ranger District, (707) 275-2361 or fax (707) 275-0676.

Directions: From Ukiah on US 101, drive north to the junction with Highway 20. Turn east on Highway 20 and drive five miles. Turn northwest on County Road 240/Potter Valley/Lake Pillsbury Road and drive 26 miles to the Eel River Information Kiosk at Lake Pillsbury. Continue for four miles around the north end of the lake and look for the camp entrance on the right side of the road.

Trip notes: This primitive camp is used primarily by riders of off-road motorcycles and as an overflow area if Lake Pillsbury's other camps are full. It is set at 1,850 feet near the north shore of Lake Pillsbury in the heart of Mendocino National Forest. Nearby trails leading into the backcountry are detailed on a Forest Service map.

⑯ Navy

Location: On Lake Pillsbury in Mendocino National Forest; map C1, grid h2.

Campsites, facilities: There are 20 sites for tents or RVs. Picnic tables are provided. Piped water and vault toilets are available, and a boat ramp is nearby. Facilities are wheelchair accessible. Leashed pets are permitted.

Reservations, fees: No reservations; $8 per night, $1 pet fee.

Contact: Mendocino National Forest, Upper Lake Ranger District, (707) 275-2361 or fax (707) 275-0676. For a map send $4 to Upper Lake Ranger Station, 10025 Elk Mountain Road, Upper Lake, CA 95485, and ask for Mendocino National Forest area.

Directions: From Ukiah on US 101, drive north to the junction with Highway 20. Turn east on Highway 20 and drive five miles. Turn northwest on County Road 240/Potter Valley/Lake Pillsbury Road and drive 26 miles to the Eel River Information Kiosk at Lake Pillsbury. Continue for four miles around the north end of the lake and look for the campground entrance on the right side of the road. The campground is on the north shore, just west of Oak Flat Camp.

Trip notes: When Lake Pillsbury is full of water, this is one of the most attractive of the many camps here. It is set in the lake's north cove, sheltered from north winds. Surrounded by forest, the camp is in quite a pretty setting. However, when the lake level is down, such as is common in the fall, it can seem like the camp is on the edge of a dust bowl.

⑰ Fuller Group Camp

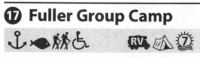

Location: On Lake Pillsbury in Mendocino National Forest; map C1, grid h2.

Campsites, facilities: This group campsite can accommodate up to 60 people in tents or RVs. Group cooking and eating facilities are provided. Piped water and vault toilets are available, and a boat ramp is nearby. Facilities are wheelchair accessible. Leashed pets are permitted.

Reservations, fees: Reservations are required

via phone at (877) 444-6777 ($8.65 reservation fee) or website: www.reserveusa.com.

Contact: Mendocino National Forest, Upper Lake Ranger District, (707) 275-2361 or fax (707) 275-0676. For a map, send $4 to Upper Lake Ranger Station, 10025 Elk Mountain Road, Upper Lake, CA 95485, and ask for Mendocino National Forest area.

Directions: From Ukiah on US 101, drive north to the junction with Highway 20. Turn east on Highway 20 and drive five miles. Turn northwest on County Road 240/Potter Valley/Lake Pillsbury Road and drive 26 miles to the Eel River Information Kiosk at Lake Pillsbury. Continue for one mile, turn right at the campground access road, and drive a quarter mile to the campground.

Trip notes: With a giant group camp, you can have your own personal party headquarters. Every year there are groups that do exactly that at this camp set on the northwest shore of Lake Pillsbury. Unlike many other group camps, this one actually comes equipped with facilities designed for a large number of people, a giant grill being one of the main features. A boat ramp is available about a half mile to the north.

---

⑱ Lower Nye

Location: In Mendocino National Forest; map C1, grid h3.

Campsites, facilities: There are six sites for tents or RVs. There is no piped water, but picnic tables, fire grills, and vault toilets are provided. Leashed pets are permitted.

Reservations, fees: No reservations; no fee. Open May to mid-September.

Contact: Mendocino National Forest, Upper Lake Ranger District, (707) 275-2361 or fax (707) 275-0676.

Directions: From Ukiah on US 101, drive north to the junction of Highway 20. Turn east on Highway 20 and drive to the town of Upper Lake and to Elk Mountain Road. Turn left on Elk Mountain Road (which becomes Forest Service Road 1N02) and drive 17 miles. Turn right on Forest Service Road 18N01/Bear Creek Road and drive seven miles. Turn north on Forest Service Road 18N04/Rice Creek Road and drive 14 miles to the campground.

Trip notes: This camp is on the northern border of the Snow Mountain Wilderness. It is a good jump-off point for backpackers, or a spot for folks who don't want to be bugged by anybody to hunker down for a while. It is set at 3,300 feet on Skeleton Creek near the Eel River. It is advisable to obtain a detailed USGS topographic map.

---

⑲ Deer Valley Campground

Location: In Mendocino National Forest; map C1, grid i2.

Campsites, facilities: There are 13 sites for tents or RVs. There is no piped water, but picnic tables, fire grills, and vault toilets are provided. Leashed pets are permitted.

Reservations, fees: No reservations; no fee. Open April through October.

Contact: Mendocino National Forest, Upper Lake Ranger District, (707) 275-2361 or fax (707) 275-0676.

Directions: From Ukiah on US 101, drive north to the junction of Highway 20. Turn east on Highway 20 and drive to the town of Upper Lake and to Elk Mountain Road. Turn left on Elk Mountain Road (which becomes Forest Service Road 1N02) and drive 12 miles (the latter section is extremely twisty). Turn right on Forest Service Road 16N01 and drive about three miles to the campground.

Trip notes: This one is out there in booger country. It is used primarily in the fall by deer hunters. It is set at 3,700 feet in Deer Valley, about five miles from the East Fork of Middle Creek.

---

⑳ Middle Creek Campground

Location: In Mendocino National Forest; map C1, grid i2.

Campsites, facilities: There are 23 sites for tents or small RVs. Piped water, picnic tables, and fire grills are provided. Vault toilets are available. Leashed pets are permitted.

Reservations, fees: No reservations; $4 per

night, $3 for an extra vehicle. Open year-round.

Contact: Mendocino National Forest, Upper Lake Ranger District, (707) 275-2361 or fax (707) 275-0676.

Directions: From Ukiah on US 101, drive north to the junction with Highway 20. Turn east on Highway 20 and drive to the town of Upper Lake. Turn left on Mendenhall Avenue (which becomes Forest Service Road 1N02) and drive eight miles to the camp on the right side of the road.

Trip notes: This camp is not widely known, but known well enough. It's an off highway vehicle staging area and sometimes there's a problem with noise in the area. That ruins an otherwise quiet spot, which is set at 2,000 feet at the confluence of the West and East Forks of Middle Creek. This campground was refurbished in late 1997.

21 Bear Creek Campground

Location: In Mendocino National Forest; map C1, grid i3.

Campsites, facilities: There are 16 sites for tents or small RVs. There is no piped water, but picnic tables, fire grills, and vault toilets are provided. Leashed pets are permitted.

Reservations, fees: No reservations; no fee. Open May to mid-October.

Contact: Mendocino National Forest, Upper Lake Ranger District, (707) 275-2361 or fax (707) 275-0676. Call for road conditions.

Directions: From Ukiah on US 101, drive north to the junction with Highway 20. Turn east on Highway 20 and drive to the town of Upper Lake. Turn left on Mendenhall Avenue (which becomes Forest Service Road 1N02) and drive 17 miles (the latter stretch is extremely twisty). Turn east on Forest Service Road 301C/Bear Creek Road and drive eight miles to the campground on the right side of the road.

Trip notes: Bet you didn't know about this one—a primitive spot out in the boondocks of Mendocino National Forest, set at 2,000 feet. It's a pretty spot, too, set beside Bear Creek near its confluence with Blue Slides Creek. Trout fishing can be good here. It's about a 10-minute drive

to the Summit Springs Trailhead at the southern end of the Snow Mountain Wilderness. There are also numerous OHV roads in this region, detailed on a map of Mendocino National Forest.

22 Letts Lake Complex

Location: In Mendocino National Forest; map C1, grid i4.

Campsites, facilities: There are 42 sites for tents or RVs up to 26 feet long. Piped water, vault toilets, picnic tables, and fire rings are provided. A wheelchair-accessible fishing pier is available. There is also an 11-unit picnic area with tables and barbecues on the left side of the lake, open during the day only. Leashed pets are permitted.

Reservations, fees: No reservations; $8 per night; 14-day limit. Open mid-April through October.

Contact: Mendocino National Forest, Stonyford Work Station, (530) 963-3128 or fax (530) 963-3173.

Directions: From Interstate 5 at Maxwell, turn west on Maxwell-Sites Road and drive to Sites. Bear right on Sites-Lodoga Road and continue to Lodoga. Turn right on Lodoga-Stonyford Road and loop around East Park Reservoir to reach Stonyford. From Stonyford, turn west on Fouts Springs Road/Forest Service Road M10 and drive about 17 miles into national forest (where the road becomes Forest Service 17N02) to the campground on the east side of Letts Lake.

Trip notes: Not too many folks know about Letts Lake, a 30-acre, spring-fed lake set in a mixed conifer forest at 4,500 feet just south of the Snow Mountain Wilderness. There are three camps on the east side of the lake, so take your pick. No motors are allowed on the water, making it ideal for canoes, rafts, and float tubes. This lake is stocked with rainbow trout in the early summer and is known also for black bass and catfish. It's a designated historical landmark, the site where the homesteaders known as the Letts brothers were murdered. While that may not impress you, the views to the north of the Snow Mountain Wilderness will. In addition, there are several natural springs that can be fun to hunt up. By the way, after such a long drive to get here, don't let your eagerness cause you to stop at Lily Pond (on the left, one mile before reaching Letts Lake), because there are no trout in it.

㉓ Mill Valley

Location: Near Letts Lake in Mendocino National Forest; map C1, grid i5.

Campsites, facilities: There are 15 sites for tents or RVs up to 18 feet long. Seasonal piped water, vault toilets, picnic tables, and fire grills are provided. Leashed pets are permitted.

Reservations, fees: No reservations; fees range from free to $5 per night, depending upon water availability. Open mid-April through October, weather permitting.

Contact: Mendocino National Forest, Stonyford Work Station, (530) 963-3128 or fax (530) 963-3173.

Directions: From Interstate 5 at Maxwell, turn west on Maxwell-Sites Road and drive to Sites. Turn left on Sites-Lodoga Road and continue to Lodoga. Turn right on Lodoga-Stonyford Road and loop around East Park Reservoir to reach Stonyford. From Stonyford, turn west on Fouts Springs Road/Forest Service Road M10 and drive about 17 miles into national forest (where the road becomes Forest Service 17N02) to the camp access road on the left. Turn left and drive a half mile to the camp.

Trip notes: This camp is set beside Lily Pond, a little, teeny guy, with larger Letts Lake just a mile away. Since Lily Pond does not have trout and Letts Lake does, this camp gets far less traffic than its counterpart. The area is crisscrossed with numerous creeks, four-wheel-drive routes, and Forest Service roads, making it a great adventure for owners of four-wheel drives. The elevation is 4,200 feet.

㉔ Dixie Glade Horse Camp

Location: Near the Snow Mountain Wilderness in Mendocino National Forest; map C1, grid i5.

Campsites, facilities: This group campsite can accommodate up to 50 people in tents or RVs. A horse corral, troughs, picnic tables, and fire grills are provided. Piped water is available for horse troughs only. There is no potable water. Leashed pets are permitted.

Reservations, fees: No reservations; no fee.

Contact: Mendocino National Forest, Stonyford Work Station, (530) 963-3128 or fax (530) 963-3173. For a map, send $4 to USDA Forest Service, US Forest Map Sales, 1323 Club Drive, Vallejo, CA 94592, and ask for Mendocino National Forest area; (707) 562-USFS/8737; website: www.r5.fs.fed.us.

Directions: From Interstate 5 at Maxwell, turn west on Maxwell-Sites Road and drive to Sites. Turn left on Sites-Lodoga Road and continue to Lodoga. Turn right on Lodoga-Stonyford Road and loop around East Park Reservoir to reach Stonyford. From Stonyford, turn west on Fouts Springs Road/County Road M10 and drive 13 miles to the camp on the left side of the road.

Trip notes: Got a horse who likes to tromp? No? Then take a pass on this one. Yes? Then sign right up, because this is a trailhead camp for people preparing to head north by horseback into the adjacent Snow Mountain Wilderness.

㉕ Old Mill

Location: Near Mill Creek in Mendocino National Forest; map C1, grid I5.

Campsites, facilities: There are eight sites for tents and two sites for tents or RVs up to 16 feet long. (However, the access road to the campground is narrow.) There is no piped water, but toilets, picnic tables, and fire grills are provided. Leashed pets are permitted.

Reservations, fees: No reservations; no fee. Open May through October.

Contact: Mendocino National Forest, Stonyford Work Station, (530) 963-3128 or fax (530) 963-3173.

Directions: From Interstate 5 at Maxwell, turn west on Maxwell-Sites Road and drive to Sites. Turn left on Sites-Lodoga Road and continue to Lodoga. Turn right on Lodoga-Stonyford Road and loop around East Park Reservoir to reach Stonyford. From Stonyford, turn west on Fouts Springs Road/County Road M10 and drive about six miles. Turn left on Forest Service Road M5/ Trough Springs Road and drive 7.5 miles on a narrow road to the campground on your right.

Trip notes: Little known and little used, this camp is set at 3,700 feet amid a mature stand of pine and fir on Trough Spring Ridge. It's located at the site of—guess what? An old mill. Expect some OHV company.

㉖ Mill Creek

Location: In Mendocino National Forest; map C1, grid i5.

Campsites, facilities: There are six tent sites. There is no piped water, but vault toilets, picnic tables, and fire grills are provided. Leashed pets are permitted.

Reservations, fees: No reservations; no fee. Open year-round.

Contact: Mendocino National Forest, Stonyford Work Station, (530) 963-3128 or fax (530) 963-3173.

Directions: From Interstate 5 at Maxwell, turn west on Maxwell-Sites Road and drive to Sites. Turn left on Sites-Lodoga Road and continue to Lodoga. Turn right on Lodoga-Stonyford Road and loop around East Park Reservoir to reach Stonyford. From Stonyford, turn west on Fouts Springs Road/Forest Service Road M10 and drive about 8.5 miles to the campground entrance on the right.

Trip notes: This tiny, pretty, secluded camp is set beside Mill Creek near Fouts Springs at the southeastern boundary of the Snow Mountain Wilderness. A nearby trailhead, a mile to the west, provides a hiking route into the wilderness that connects along Trout Creek, a great little romp. Mill Creek is quite pretty in the late spring, but by late summer the flow drops way down. The elevation is 1,700 feet. Expect heavy off-highway-vehicle use from October through May; Fouts Springs/Davis Flat is an OHV staging area.

㉗ North Fork

Location: On Stony Creek in Mendocino National Forest; map C1, grid i5.

Campsites, facilities: There are six tent sites. There is no piped water, but a vault toilet, picnic tables, and fire grills are provided. Leashed pets are permitted.

Reservations, fees: No reservations; no fee. Open year-round.

Contact: Mendocino National Forest, Stonyford Work Station, (530) 963-3128 or fax (530) 963-3173.

Directions: From Interstate 5 at Maxwell, turn west on Maxwell-Sites Road and drive to Sites. Turn left on Sites-Lodoga Road and continue to Lodoga. Turn right on Lodoga-Stonyford Road and loop around East Park Reservoir to reach Stonyford. From Stonyford, turn west on Fouts Springs Road/Forest Service Road M10 and drive about eight miles. Turn right on Forest Service Road 18N03 and drive two miles to the campground.

Trip notes: This primitive camp, quiet from June through September when motorcycle use is infrequent, is set at 1,700 feet in a grove of oak trees at the confluence of the north, south, and middle forks of Stony Creek. There are many trailheads for hiking in the area, located within a few miles of the Snow Mountain Wilderness, but none at this camp. There are great views of St. John Mountain and Snow Mountain. See the trip notes for Mill Creek (campground number 25) for additional information. The elevation is 1,700 feet.

㉘ Fouts Campground

Location: On Stony Creek in Mendocino National Forest; map C1, grid i5.

Campsites, facilities: There are 11 dispersed sites for tents or RVs up to 16 feet long. Piped water, vault toilet, picnic tables, and fire grills are provided. Leashed pets are permitted.

Reservations, fees: No reservations; no fee. Open year-round.

Contact: Mendocino National Forest, Stonyford Work Station, (530) 963-3128 or fax (530) 963-1373.

Directions: From Interstate 5 at Maxwell, turn west on Maxwell-Sites Road and drive to Sites. Turn left on Sites-Lodoga Road and continue to

Lodoga. Turn right on Lodoga-Stonyford Road and loop around East Park Reservoir to reach Stonyford. From Stonyford, turn west on Fouts Springs Road/County Road M10 and drive about eight miles. Turn right (north) on Forest Service Road 18N03 and drive one mile to the campground on your right.

Trip notes: Fouts Campground camp is located in a brushy area shaded by digger pines. It is set beside Stony Creek near Davis Flat and Fouts Springs. Several other four-wheel-drive trails are nearby—North Fork, South Fork, and Mill Creek. To the west is the Snow Mountain Wilderness and excellent hiking trails; to the south is an extensive Forest Service road and OHV trail network that provides access for four-wheel-drive vehicles and dirt bikes. The elevation is 1,700 feet.

㉙ Gray Pine Group Camp

Location: In Mendocino National Forest; map C1, grid i5.

Campsites, facilities: There is one group site that can accommodate 15 to 75 campers with tents or RVs up to 16 feet long. Piped water, rest rooms, picnic tables, fire rings and group BBQ grill are provided. An amphitheater is also available. Leashed pets are permitted.

Reservations, fees: Reservations are required via phone at (800) 444-6777 ($8.65 reservation fee); no fee. Open year-round.

Contact: Mendocino National Forest, Stonyford Work Station, (530) 963-3128 or fax (530) 963-1373.

Directions: From Interstate 5 at Maxwell, turn west on Maxwell-Sites Road and drive to Sites. Turn left on Sites-Lodoga Road and continue to Lodoga. Turn right on Lodoga-Stonyford Road and loop around East Park Reservoir to reach Stonyford. From Stonyford, turn west on Fouts Springs Road/County Road M10 and drive about eight miles. Turn right on Forest Service Road 18N03 and drive less than a mile to the campground on your right.

Trip notes: Similar to Fouts Campground, Gray Pine is located in an area of digger pines with four-wheel-drive trails nearby. It is near, but not on, Stony Creek. See Fouts Campground

(campground number 28) for additional information.

㉚ South Fork

Location: On the South Fork of Stony Creek in Mendocino National Forest; map C1, grid i5.

Campsites, facilities: There are five dispersed tent sites. A vault toilet, picnic tables, and fire rings are provided. There is no piped water. Leashed pets are permitted.

Reservations, fees: No reservations; no fee. Open year-round.

Contact: Mendocino National Forest, Stonyford Work Station, (530) 963-3128 or fax (530) 963-3173.

Directions: From Interstate 5 at Maxwell, turn west on Maxwell-Sites Road and drive to Sites. Turn left on Sites-Lodoga Road and continue to Lodoga. Turn right on Lodoga-Stonyford Road and loop around East Park Reservoir to reach Stonyford. From Stonyford, turn west on Fouts Springs Road/County Road M10 and drive about eight miles. Turn right on Forest Service Road 18N03 and drive one mile to the campground on your right.

Trip notes: This camp is set on the South Fork of Stony Creek near Fouts Campground (number 28) and Davis Flat (campground number 31). These camps are located in a designated off-highway-vehicle area and are used primarily by dirt bikers, so if you're looking for quiet, this probably isn't your camp. The elevation is 1,700 feet.

㉛ Davis Flat

Location: In Mendocino National Forest; map C1, grid i5.

Campsites, facilities: There are 70 dispersed sites for tents or RVs of any length. Piped water, vault toilets, fire rings, and picnic tables are provided. Leashed pets are permitted.

Reservations, fees: No reservations; no fee. Open year-round.

Contact: Mendocino National Forest, Stonyford Work Station, (530) 963-3128 or fax (530) 963-3173.

Directions: From Interstate 5 at Maxwell, turn west on Maxwell-Sites Road and drive to Sites. Turn left on Sites-Lodoga Road and continue to Lodoga. Turn right on Lodoga-Stonyford Road and loop around East Park Reservoir to reach Stonyford. From Stonyford, turn west on Fouts Springs Road/County Road M10 and drive about eight miles. Turn right on Forest Service Road 18N03 and drive one mile to the campground on your left.

Trip notes: This camp is located across the road from Fouts and South Fork Campgrounds. All three are in a designated off-highway-vehicle area, so expect OHVers, especially in the winter months. This isn't the quietest camp around, but there is some good hiking in the area to the immediate west in the Snow Mountain Wilderness. The elevation is 1,700 feet.

㉜ Le Trianon Resort

Location: On Lower Blue Lake; map C1, grid j0.

Campsites, facilities: There are 200 sites for tents or RVs with water and electric hookups, and 17 cabins for rent. Picnic tables are provided. Flush toilets, showers, sanitary disposal station, playground, boat ramp, boat rentals, fishing supplies, coin laundry, snack bar, and grocery store are available. Leashed pets are permitted.

Reservations, fees: No reservations; $25 per night. Open April through October.

Contact: Le Trianon Resort, (707) 275-2262 or fax (707) 275-9416.

Directions: From Ukiah, drive north on US 101 for five miles to the junction with Highway 20. Turn east on Highway 20 and drive 12 miles to 5845 West Highway 20.

Trip notes: Le Trianon Resort is the biggest of the camps on the Blue Lakes, the overlooked lakes not far from giant Clear Lake. It is an angler's special with good trout fishing in spring and no waterskiing permitted. The better fishing is in Upper Blue Lake, which is stocked with 28,000 trout per year and where the water is much clearer than at the lower lake. The best fishing is in the spring, in April, May, and June. A plus at this park is a few lakeside campsites.

㉝ Mayacmus

Location: Near Ukiah; map C1, grid j0.

Campsites, facilities: There are nine tent sites. Piped water, vault toilets, picnic tables, and fire grills are provided. Leashed pets are permitted.

Reservations, fees: No reservations; no fee. Stay limit is 14 days.

Contact: Bureau of Land Management, Ukiah District, (707) 468-4000.

Directions: From US 101 in Ukiah, turn east on Talmage Road and drive 1.5 miles to Eastside Road. Turn right and drive a third of a mile to Mill Creek Road. Turn left and drive three miles. Just beyond Mill Creek County Park, look for the North Cow Mountain sign on the left. Make a left there and drive seven miles to the campground.

Trip notes: This campground is set within the Cow Mountain Recreation Area on the slopes of Cow Mountain, the oft overlooked wild region east of Ukiah. The primitive area is ideal for hiking and horseback riding. In the fall, it is a popular hunting area as well, for the few who know of it. This section of the rec area is quiet, with hiking on the Mayacmus Trail providing access to Willow Creek, Mill Creek, and several overlooks of Clear Lake to the south. The flora is chaparral and oak/bay grasslands, and the weather is extremely hot in the summer. By the way, off-road vehicles frequent the southern portion of the rec area, but not this immediate region.

㉞ Pine Acres Blue Lake Resort

Location: On Upper Blue Lake; map C1, grid j0.

Campsites, facilities: There are 32 RV sites, most with full or partial hookups, and 12 tent sites. Picnic tables and fire grills are provided. Flush toilets, showers, sanitary disposal station, boat rentals, boat launching, moorings, boat ramp, grocery store, fishing supplies, and lake frontage sites are available. Leashed pets are permitted.

Reservations, fees: Reservations are accepted; $17 to $20 per night. Open year-round.

Contact: Pine Acres Blue Lake Resort, (707) 275-2811 or fax (707) 275-9549.

Directions: From Ukiah, drive north on US 101 for five miles to the junction with Highway 20. Turn east on Highway 20 and drive about 13 miles to Irvine Street. Turn right on Irvine Street and drive one block to Blue Lakes Road. Turn right and drive two blocks to the resort.

Trip notes: Because of their proximity to Clear Lake, the Blue Lakes are often overlooked. But these lovely lakes offer good fishing for trout, especially in spring and early summer on Upper Blue Lake. With a speed limit in place, quiet boating is the rule. Swimming is good here. No waterskiing is permitted.

35 Narrows Lodge Resort

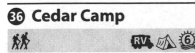

Location: On Upper Blue Lake; map C1, grid j0.

Campsites, facilities: There are 28 sites for tents or RVs, with full or partial hookups. Picnic tables are provided. Flush toilets, showers, sanitary disposal station, recreation room, boat rentals, pier, boat ramp, fishing supplies, propane, and ice are available. A motel and cabins are also available. Pets are allowed on leashes, but not in some motel rooms or cabins.

Reservations, fees: Reservations are accepted; $19 to $21 per night. Open year-round.

Contact: Narrows Lodge Resort, (707) 275-2718; website: www.gram@pacific.net.

Directions: From Ukiah, drive north on US 101 for five miles to the junction with Highway 20. Turn east on Highway 20 and drive about 11.5 miles to Blue Lakes Road. Turn right and drive to 5690 Blue Lakes Road.

Trip notes: This is one of four campgrounds in the immediate vicinity. The Blue Lakes are often overlooked because of their proximity to Clear Lake, but they are a quiet and pretty alternative, with good trout fishing in the spring and early summer.

36 Cedar Camp

Location: In Mendocino National Forest; map C1, grid j4.

Campsites, facilities: There are five sites for tents or small RVs (the access road is poor for trailers). There is no piped water, but vault toilets, picnic tables, and fire rings are provided. Leashed pets are permitted.

Reservations, fees: No reservations; no fee. Open mid-June through mid-October.

Contact: Mendocino National Forest, Stonyford Work Station, (530) 963-3128 or fax (530) 963-3173.

Directions: From Interstate 5 at Maxwell, turn west on Maxwell-Sites Road and drive to Sites. Turn left on Sites-Lodoga Road and continue to Lodoga. Turn right on Lodoga-Stonyford Road and loop around East Park Reservoir to reach Stonyford. From Stonyford, turn west on Fouts Springs Road/County Road M10 and drive about six miles. Turn left on County Road M5 (Trough Springs Road) and drive 13 miles to the campground on your right.

Trip notes: This camp is set at 4,300 feet elevation, just below Goat Mountain (6,121 feet), to the west about a mile away. Why did anybody decide to build a campground way out here? Because a small spring starts nearby, creating a trickle that runs into the nearby headwaters of Little Stony Creek.

37 Little Stony Campground

Location: On Little Stony Creek in Mendocino National Forest; map C1, grid j6.

Campsites, facilities: There are seven sites for tents or small RVs. There is no piped water, but vault toilets, picnic tables, and fire grills are provided. Leashed pets are permitted.

Reservations, fees: No reservations; no fee.

Contact: Mendocino National Forest, Stonyford Work Station, (530) 963-3128 or fax (530) 963-3173.

Directions: From Interstate 5 at Maxwell, turn west on Maxwell-Sites Road and drive to Sites. Turn left on Sites-Lodoga Road and continue to where the road crosses Stony Creek. Just after the bridge, turn left on Goat Mountain Road and drive four miles (a rough county road) to the campground on the left.

Trip notes: This pretty spot is set in Little Stony Canyon, beside Little Stony Creek at 1,500 feet. Very few people know of the place, and you will find it is appropriately named: it is little, it is stony, and the little trout amid the stones fit right in. The camp provides streamside access and, with Goat Mountain Road running along most of the stream, it is easy to fish much of this creek in an evening. Expect heavy OHV use from fall through spring.

Special note: This campground is scheduled for restoration; check status before planning a visit.

Map C2

One inch equals approximately 10.7 miles.
See inside back cover for California state map.

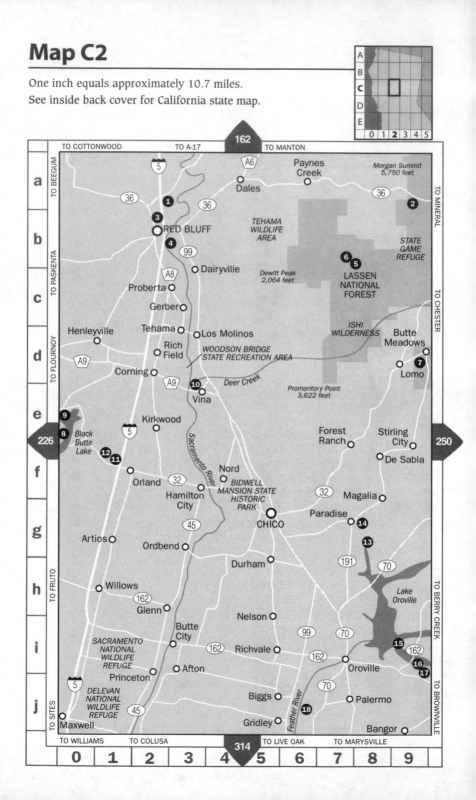

Chapter C2 features:

1 Bend RV Park and Fishing Resort

Location: On the Sacramento River; map C2, grid a2.

Campsites, facilities: There are 18 sites for RVs with full or partial hookups. In addition, there is a separate area for tents only. Piped water, showers, flush toilets, and picnic tables are provided. A grocery store, bait and tackle shop, boat ramp, boat dock, coin laundry, and a sanitary dump station are also available. Some facilities are wheelchair accessible. Leashed pets are permitted.

Reservations, fees: Reservations are accepted; $14 to $20 per night. Open year-round.

Contact: Bend RV Park and Fishing Resort, (530) 527-6289.

Directions: From Interstate 5 in Red Bluff, drive four miles north on Interstate 5 to the Jelly's Ferry Road exit. Turn northeast on Jelly's Ferry Road and drive 2.5 miles to the resort at 21795 Bend Ferry Road.

Trip notes: Here's a spot for all you RV cruisers to tie up your horse for a while. Big Bend RV Park and Fishing Resort is open year-round and is set beside the Sacramento River. The salmon average 15 to 25 pounds in this area, and anglers typically have the best results from mid-August through October. In recent years, the Bureau of Reclamation has been raising the gates of the Red Bluff Diversion Dam in early September. When that occurs, huge numbers of salmon charge upstream from Red Bluff to Anderson, holding in each deep river hole. Expect very hot weather in July and August.

2 Battle Creek

Location: On Battle Creek in Lassen National Forest; map C2, grid a9.

Campsites, facilities: There are 12 tent sites and 38 sites for tents or RVs. Piped water, picnic tables, and fire grills are provided. Flush toilets are available. Supplies can be obtained in the town of Mineral. Leashed pets are permitted.

Reservations, fees: No reservations; $12 per night. Open May through October.

Contact: Lassen National Forest, Almanor Ranger District, (530) 258-2141 or fax (530) 258-3491.

Directions: From Red Bluff, turn east on Highway 36 and drive 41 miles to the campground (if you reach Mineral, you have gone two miles too far).

Trip notes: This pretty spot offers easy access and streamside camping along Battle Creek. The trout fishing can be good in May, June, and early July, when the creek is stocked by the Department of Fish and Game, which plants 23,000 rainbow trout and 2,000 smaller brook trout. Many people drive right by without knowing there is a stream here and that the fishing can be good. The elevation is 4,800 feet.

❸ O'Nite Park

Location: Near the Sacramento River; map C2, grid b2.

Campsites, facilities: There are 74 RV sites with full hookups. Picnic tables, rest rooms, showers, and swimming pool are provided. A coin laundry, propane gas, and ice are available. Leashed pets are permitted.

Reservations, fees: Reservations are accepted; $11 to $19 per night.

Contact: O'Nite Park, (530) 527-5868.

Directions: From Interstate 5 and the junction of Highways 99 and 36 (in Red Bluff), drive west on Highway 36/Antelope Boulevard for one block to Gilmore Road. Turn south on Gilmore Road and drive one block to the camp.

Trip notes: Easy access from the highway, nearby supermarkets and restaurants, and many side trips make this spot a winner. The park is only one block from the Sacramento River, which gets a big salmon run from mid-August through October. It's about a 45-minute drive east to Lassen Park. The elevation is approximately 300 feet and temperatures are typically in the 100s from mid-June through August.

❹ Lake Red Bluff

Location: On the Sacramento River near Red Bluff; map C2, grid b2.

Campsites, facilities: There are 30 sites with no hookups for tents or RVs (Sycamore Camp), and a group camp (Camp Discovery) with six screened cabins that can accommodate a maximum of 48 campers. Some facilities are wheelchair accessible. Piped water, showers, vault and flush toilets, picnic areas, two boat ramps, and a fish viewing plaza are available. There are two large barbecues, electrical outlets, lockable storage, five large picnic tables, comfort station with showers and sinks, and an amphitheater in the group camp area. Leashed pets are permitted.

Reservations, fees: Reservations are required

only for the group camp; $10 per night for individual sites; group camp fee per night is $100 for 50 people, $150 for 51 to 75 people, and $200 for 76 to 100 people.

Contact: Mendocino National Forest, Corning Work Station, (530) 824-5196 or fax (530) 824-8004.

Directions: From Interstate 5 at Red Bluff, take the Highway 99/Lassen Park exit. Turn right at Sale Lane and drive about two miles south to the campground.

Trip notes: Lake Red Bluff is created by the Red Bluff Diversion Dam on the Sacramento River, and waterskiing, bird-watching, hiking, and fishing are the most popular activities. It has become a backyard swimming hole for local residents in the summer when the temperatures reach the high 90s and low 100s almost every day. In early September, the Bureau of Reclamation raises the gates at the diversion dam in order to allow migrating salmon an easier course on the upstream journey, and in the process, Lake Red Bluff reverts to its former self as the Sacramento River.

❺ Black Rock

Location: On the eastern edge of the Ishi Wilderness; map C2, grid c8.

Campsites, facilities: There are four tent sites. Picnic tables and fire pits are provided, and a vault toilet is available. There is no piped water. Mill Creek is adjacent to the camp and is a viable water source through early summer. Leashed pets are permitted.

Reservations, fees: No reservations; $8 per night.

Contact: Lassen National Forest, Almanor Ranger District, (530) 258-2141 or fax (530) 258-5194. For a map send $4 to USDA Forest Service, US Forest Map Sales, 1323 Club Drive, Vallejo, CA 94592, and ask for Lassen National Forest area; (707) 562-USFS/8737; website: www.r5.fs.fed.us.

Directions: From Red Bluff, drive east on Highway 36 for about 35 miles to the town of Paynes Creek. In Paynes Creek, turn right on Little Giant Mill Road and continue about five miles to Plum Creek Road. Turn right and drive two miles to Ponderosa Way. Turn right and continue for about 20 miles to the campground on the right. Note: Only vehicles with high clearance are advised. No RVs or trailers are allowed.

Trip notes: This remote, primitive camp is set at the base of the huge, ancient Black Rock, one of the oldest geological points in Lassen National Forest. A bonus is that Mill Creek runs adjacent to the sites, providing a water source. This is the edge of the Ishi Wilderness, where remote hiking in solitude is possible without a wilderness permit and without venturing to high mountain elevations. A trailhead is available right out of the camp. The trail here is routed downstream along Mill Creek, extending five miles into the Ishi Wilderness, downhill all the way.

⑥ South Antelope

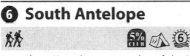

Location: Near the eastern edge of the Ishi Wilderness; map C2, grid c7.

Campsites, facilities: There are four sites for tents only. Picnic tables and fire pits are provided. A vault toilet is available. There is no piped water. Leashed pets are permitted.

Reservations, fees: No reservations; no fee.

Contact: Lassen National Forest, Almanor Ranger District, (530) 258-2141 or fax (530) 258-5194. For a map send $4 to USDA Forest Service, US Forest Map Sales, 1323 Club Drive, Vallejo, CA 94592, and ask for Lassen National Forest area; (707) 562-USFS/8737; website: www.r5.fs.fed.us.

Directions: From Red Bluff, drive east on Highway 36 for about 35 miles to the town of Paynes Creek. In Paynes Creek, turn right on Little Giant Mill Road and continue for five miles to Plum Creek Road. Turn right and drive two miles to Ponderosa Way. Turn right and continue for about nine miles on a very rough road recommended for high clearance vehicles only to the campground on the right. No RVs or trailers are advised.

Trip notes: This primitive campsite is for visitors who want to explore the Ishi Wilderness

without an extensive drive (compared to other camps in the wilderness here). The South Fork of Antelope Creek runs west from the camp and provides an off-trail route for the ambitious. For easier hikes, trailheads along Ponderosa Way provide access into the eastern flank of the Ishi. The best nearby trail is the Lower Mill Creek Trail, with the trailhead located eight miles south at Black Rock (campground number five).

⑦ Butte Meadows

Location: On Butte Creek in Lassen National Forest; map C2, grid d9.

Campsites, facilities: There are 12 sites for tents or RVs. Piped water, vault toilets, fire grills, and picnic tables are provided. Supplies are available in Butte Meadows. Leashed pets are permitted.

Reservations, fees: No reservations; $9 per night. Open May through October.

Contact: Lassen National Forest, Almanor Ranger District, (530) 258-2141 or fax (530) 258-5194.

Directions: From Chico, drive about 15 miles north on Highway 32 to the town of Forest Ranch. Continue on Highway 32 for another nine miles. Turn right on Humboldt Road and drive five miles to Butte Meadows.

Trip notes: On hot summer days, when a cold stream sounds even better than a cold beer, Butte Meadows provides a hideout in the national forest east of Chico. This is a summer camp situated along Butte Creek, which is stocked with 5,000 rainbow trout by the Department of Fish and Game. Nearby Doe Mill Ridge and the surrounding Lassen National Forest can provide a good side trip adventure. The camp elevation is 4,600 feet.

⑧ Orland Buttes

Location: On Black Butte Lake; map C2, grid e0.

Campsites, facilities: There are four tent sites and 35 sites for tents or RVs up to 35 feet long. Piped water, rest rooms, showers, fire grills, picnic tables, boat-launch ramp, and a sanitary disposal station are provided. Leashed pets are permitted.

Reservations, fees: No reservations; $10 to $12 per night. Open March through Labor Day.

Contact: US Army Corps of Engineers, Black Butte Lake, (530) 865-4781.

Directions: From Interstate 5 in Orland, take the Black Butte Lake exit. Drive west on Road 200/Newville Road for eight miles to the east shore of the lake.

Trip notes: Black Butte Lake isn't far from Interstate 5, but a lot of campers zoom right by it. The prime time to visit is in late spring and early summer, when the bass and crappie fishing can be quite good. There's a boat launch nearby. Expect very hot weather in the summer when this part of the state turns into a hellhole for campers.

⑨ Buckhorn

Location: On Black Butte Lake; map C2, grid e0.

Campsites, facilities: There are 92 sites for tents or RVs up to 35 feet long. Piped water, picnic tables, fire grills, flush toilets, sanitary dump station, showers, and a playground are provided. A boat ramp, propane gas, and a grocery store are within walking distance. Leashed pets are permitted.

Reservations, fees: No reservations; $10 to $12 per night. Open year-round.

Contact: US Army Corps of Engineers, Black Butte Lake, (530) 865-4781.

Directions: From Interstate 5 in Orland, take the Black Butte Lake exit. Drive about 12 miles west on Road 200/Newville Road to Buckhorn Road. Turn left and drive a short distance to the campground on the north shore of the lake.

Trip notes: Black Butte Lake is set in the foothills of the north valley at 500 feet. It is one of the 10 best lakes in Northern California for crappie, best in spring. Recreation options include boating and hiking (an interpretive trail is available below the dam). For dirt bikers, an off-road motorcycle park is available at the Buckhorn Recreation Area.

⑩ Woodson Bridge State Recreation Area

Location: On the Sacramento River; map C2, grid e3.

Campsites, facilities: There are 41 sites for tents or RVs up to 31 feet long. One group site is available. Piped water, picnic tables, and fire grills are provided. Showers, flush toilets, and boat launch (across the street) are available. Some facilities are wheelchair accessible, but the rest rooms are not. Leashed pets are permitted.

Reservations, fees: Reserve via phone at (800) 444-PARK/7275 ($7.50 reservation fee) or website www.cal-parks.ca.gov; $10 to $14 per night, $1 pet fee.

Contact: Woodson Bridge State Recreation Area, (530) 839-2112; Bidwell Mansion, (530) 895-6144.

Directions: From Interstate 5 in Corning, take the South Avenue exit and drive nine miles east to the campground.

Trip notes: This campground features direct access to the Sacramento River, and a boat ramp makes it an ideal spot for campers with trailered boats. In June, the nearby Tehama Riffle is one of the best spots on the entire river for shad. By mid-August, salmon start arriving, en route to their spawning grounds.

⑪ Old Orchard RV Park

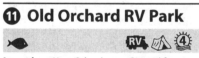

Location: Near Orland; map C2, grid f1.

Campsites, facilities: There are 52 RV sites with partial or full hookups and a separate site for tents only. Showers, sanitary disposal station, propane, coin laundry, and a store are available. Leashed pets are permitted.

Reservations, fees: Reservations are accepted; $12 to $20 per night.

Contact: Old Orchard RV Park, 4490 County Road HH, Orland, CA 95963; (530) 865-5335.

Directions: From Interstate 5 at Orland, take the Chico/Highway 32 exit, head one block west, and turn right on County Road HH. The park is one block down.

Trip notes: Most folks use this as a layover spot while on long trips up or down Interstate 5 in the Central Valley. If you're staying longer than a night, there are two side trips that have appeal for anglers. Nearby Black Butte Lake to the west, with crappie in the early summer, and the Sacramento River to the east, with salmon in the late summer and early fall, can add some spice to your trip. The elevation is 250 feet.

⑫ Green Acres RV Park

Location: Near Orland; map C2, grid f1.

Campsites, facilities: There are 68 RV sites with partial or full hookups and 24 tent sites. A store, coin laundry, sanitary dump station, barbecues, recreation room, swimming pool, and ice are available. Leashed pets are permitted.

Reservations, fees: Reservations are recommended; $15 to $19 per night.

Contact: Green Acres RV Park, 4515 County Road H, Orland, CA 95963; (530) 865-9188.

Directions: From Orland on Interstate 5, take the Highway 32 exit and drive a half mile west to the campground.

Trip notes: This is a layover spot near Interstate 5 in the Central Valley, set in the heart of olive and almond country. It's a restful setting, but hot in summer, at times unbearable without air conditioning. Salmon fishing is available on the nearby Sacramento River, best from mid-August through October.

⑬ Quail Trails Village

Location: Near Paradise; map C2, grid g8.

Campsites, facilities: There are 20 RV sites with full hookups (all are drive-through) and five tent sites. Picnic tables are provided. Rest rooms, hot showers, and coin laundry are available. Leashed pets are permitted.

Reservations, fees: Reservations are accepted; $10.60 to $15.90 per night. Open year-round.

Contact: Quail Trails Village, (530) 877-6581 or fax (530) 876-0516.

Directions: From Highway 99 in Chico, take the Paradise turnoff (Skyway). Turn right at the first signal in Paradise (Pearson Road). Go about 4.5 miles all the way to the end of the road and turn right on Pentz Magalia Highway. Drive 1.5 miles south to the park at 5110 Pentz Road.

Trip notes: This is a rural motor home campground, set near the west branch of the Feather River, with nearby Lake Oroville as the feature attraction. The Lime Saddle section of the Lake Oroville State Recreation Area is nearby, with a beach, boat launching facilities, and concessions.

⑭ Pine Ridge RV Park

Location: In Paradise; map C2, grid g8.

Campsites, facilities: There are 44 RV sites with partial hookups. Piped water, flush toilets, showers, and coin laundry are available. Leashed pets are permitted.

Reservations, fees: Reservations are accepted; $17 per night. Open year-round.

Contact: Pine Ridge RV Park, (530) 877-0677.

Directions: From Highway 191 in Paradise (at the south end of town), turn east on Pearson Road and drive two miles. Turn south on Pentz Road and go one mile to 5084 Pentz Road.

Trip notes: This privately operated motor home park offers shaded sites in the pines and is set at 1,700 feet, in the transition zone where the foothill country with oak and bay grasslands starts to give way to pines and other conifers. A good side trip is to the northernmost part of the Lake Oroville State Recreation Area, the Lime Saddle Area. It offers a beach, boat ramp, concessions, and picnic area.

⑮ Bidwell Canyon

Location: On Lake Oroville; map C2, grid i9.

Campsites, facilities: There are 70 sites for tents or RVs up to 40 feet long and trailers up to 31 feet long (including boat trailers), all with full hookups. Piped water, flush toilets, showers, tables, and fire grills are provided. A coin laundry, grocery store, and propane gas are available. Leashed pets are permitted, except on trails or beaches; pets must be enclosed at night.

Reservations, fees: Reserve via phone at (800) 444-PARK/7275 ($7.50 reservation fee) or website www.cal-parks.ca.gov; $16 to $20 per night, $1 pet fee.

Contact: Lake Oroville State Recreation Area, (530) 538-2200.

Directions: From Oroville, drive eight miles east on Highway 162. Turn north on Kelly Ridge Road and drive 1.5 miles to the campground on the right.

Trip notes: Bidwell Canyon is a major destination at giant Lake Oroville as the campground is located near a major marina and boat ramp. It is set along the southern shore of the lake, on a point directly adjacent to the massive Oroville Dam to the west. Many campers use this spot for boating headquarters. It is popular for waterskiing, as the water is warm enough in the summer for all water sports, and there is enough room for both fishermen and water-skiers. Recent habitat work has given the bass fishing a big help, with 30- and 40-fish days possible in the spring, casting plastic worms in the backs of coves where there is floating wood debris. What a lake—there are even floating outhouses here (imagine that!). It is very hot in midsummer.

⓰ Loafer Creek

Location: On Lake Oroville; map C2, grid i9.

Campsites, facilities: There are 137 sites for tents and RVs up to 40 feet long and trailers to 31 feet long (including boat trailers). A sanitary disposal station, piped water, flush toilets, showers, fire grills, and tables are provided. A boat ramp is available. The facilities are wheelchair accessible. Propane, groceries, and a coin laundry are available nearby. Leashed pets are permitted, but not on trails or beaches.

Reservations, fees: Reserve via phone at (800) 444-PARK/7275 ($7.50 reservation fee) or website www.cal-parks.ca.gov; $10 to $14 per night, $1 pet fee. Open mid-March through October.

Contact: Lake Oroville State Recreation Area, (530) 538-2200; California State Parks, Northern Buttes District, (530) 538-2200.

Directions: From Oroville, drive east on Highway 162 about two miles past the Kelly Ridge Road turnoff to the signed campground entrance on the left.

Trip notes: Loafer Creek Campground is set directly adjacent to a boat ramp on a deep cove at Lake Oroville, just across the water from Bidwell Canyon. Campers come here to avoid the high number of people at Bidwell Marina, but hey, this spot is no secret, believe me. It's a primary option for campers with boats. The fishing is best for bass and trout in the spring and early summer.

⓱ Loafer Creek Group Camps

Location: On Lake Oroville; map C2, grid i9.

Campsites, facilities: There are six group camps that can accommodate up to 25 people each. The sites can be combined to accommodate up to 150 people. RV parking is limited and the maximum length is 20 feet; no trailers are permitted. Piped water, flush toilets, showers, fire grills, and picnic tables are provided. A coin laundry, grocery store, and propane gas are available nearby. A large boat-in group camp is also available; call Lake Oroville State Recreation Area at the number below for more information. Leashed pets are permitted, except on trails or beaches; pets must be enclosed at night.

Reservations, fees: Reserve via phone at (800) 444-PARK/7275 ($7.50 reservation fee) or website www.cal-parks.ca.gov; $40 per night for groups, $60 per night for the boat-in group, and $1 pet fee. Open April through October.

Contact: Lake Oroville State Recreation Area, (530) 538-2200; California State Parks, Northern Buttes District, (530) 538-2200.

Directions: From Oroville, drive east on Highway 162 about two miles past the Kelly Ridge Road turnoff to the signed campground entrance on the left.

Trip notes: This is an ideal base camp for Scout

troops and other large groups that need some privacy and a spot to call their own at Lake Oroville. It is located adjacent to Loafer Creek (campground number 16). A lakeside setting (pretty much), a beach, and a nearby boat ramp are the primary attractions.

⑱ Dingerville USA

⚓🐟⛵🥾🏊♿ 🚐③

Location: Near Oroville; map C2, grid j6.

Campsites, facilities: There are 29 sites for RVs with full hookups. Picnic tables are provided. Rest rooms, showers, swimming pool, coin laundry, horseshoe pit, and a nine-hole executive golf course are available. Facilities are wheelchair accessible. Leashed pets are permitted.

Reservations, fees: Reservations are recommended; $20 per night. Open year-round.

Contact: Dingerville USA, 5813 Pacific Heights Road, Oroville, CA 95965; (530) 533-9343.

Directions: From Oroville and north, drive south on Highway 70. Turn right at the second Pacific Heights Road turnoff and continue on Pacific Heights Road to the campground. From Highway 70 and south, turn left at Palermo-Welsh Road and continue north on Pacific Heights Road for a half mile to camp.

Trip notes: You're right, they thought of this name all by themselves, needed no help. It is an RV park set in the Oroville foothill country—hot, dry, and sticky in the summer, but with a variety of side trips available nearby. It is located adjacent to a wildlife area and the Feather River and within short range of Lake Oroville and the Thermalito Afterbay for boating, water sports, and fishing. In the fall, the Duck Club in nearby Richvale is one of the few privately owned properties that offers duck hunting on a single-day basis. The RV park is a clean, quiet campground with easy access from the highway.

Map C3

One inch equals approximately 10.7 miles.
See inside back cover for California state map.

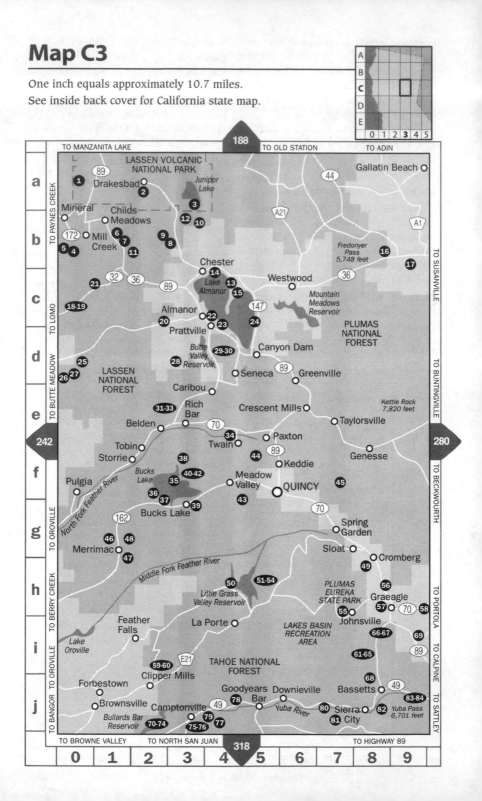

Chapter C3 features:

➊ Southwest Walk-In

![hiking] ![tent ⑧]

Location: In Lassen Volcanic National Park; map C3, grid a0.

Campsites, facilities: There are 21 walk-in tent sites. Picnic tables, fire pits, piped water, and flush toilets are available. Leashed pets are permitted.

Reservations, fees: No reservations; $12 per night.

Contact: Lassen Volcanic National Park, (530) 595-4444 or fax (530) 595-3262.

Directions: From Red Bluff, take Highway 36 east for 44 miles to the junction with Highway 89. Turn left on Highway 89 and drive to the park's entrance. Just after passing through the park entrance gate, look for the camp parking area on the east side of the road.

Trip notes: Just taking the short walk required to reach this camp will launch you into an orbit beyond most of the highway cruisers visiting Lassen. In addition, the nearby trail for Bumpass Hell will put you into a different universe; it is located about five miles north on Highway 89 on the right side of the road. The route will take you past steam vents, boiling mud pots, and hot springs, all set in prehistoric-looking volcanic rock.

➋ Warner Valley

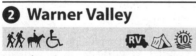

Location: On Hot Springs Creek in Lassen Volcanic National Park; map C3, grid a2.

Campsites, facilities: There are 18 tent or RV sites. Trailers are not recommended due to road conditions. Piped water, pit toilets, fire grills, and picnic tables are provided. Leashed pets are permitted.

Reservations, fees: No reservations; $12 per night. Open May through September.

Contact: Lassen Volcanic National Park, (530) 595-4444 or fax (530) 595-3262.

Directions: From Red Bluff, take Highway 36 east for 44 miles to the junction with Highway 89. Continue east on Highway 36/89 to Chester. In Chester turn left (north) on Warner Valley Road/County Road 312 (a dirt road; RVs not rec-

ommended) and drive 16 miles to the campground.

Trip notes: Lassen is one of the great national parks of the West, yet it gets surprisingly little use compared to Yosemite, Sequoia, and Kings Canyon National Parks. This camp gets overlooked because of its remote access out of Chester. The camp is set along Hot Springs Creek at 5,650 feet. A highlight here is a great 2.5-mile trail with an 800-foot climb to pretty Drake Lake. Another trail, about the same distance and flatter, is routed out to the unique Devil's Kitchen Geothermal Area, a great hike. It's also a good horseback riding area. The Drakesbad Resort, where reservations are about as difficult to get as finding Bigfoot, is located near the campground.

➌ Juniper Lake

![hiking]

Location: In Lassen Volcanic National Park; map C3, grid a34.

Campsites, facilities: There are 18 sites for tents. Fire pits and pit toilets are provided. No piped water is available. Leashed pets are permitted.

Reservations, fees: No reservations; $10 per night.

Contact: Lassen Volcanic National Park, (530) 595-4444 or fax (530) 595-3262.

Directions: From Red Bluff, take Highway 36 east for 44 miles to the junction with Highway 89. Continue east on Highway 36/89 to Chester. In Chester, turn left (north) on Warner Valley Road/County Road 312 and drive one mile to the Y and the junction for County Road 318. Bear right (marked for Juniper Lake) on County Road 318 and drive 11 miles to the campground on the east side of the lake. Note: This is a very rough dirt road; RVs and trailers are not recommended.

Trip notes: This pretty spot is on the eastern shore of Juniper Lake, at an elevation of 6,792 feet. It is far distant from the busy Highway 89 corridor that is routed through central Lassen Volcanic National Park. From the north end of the lake, a great side trip is to make the half-mile, 400-foot climb to Inspiration Point, which provides a panoramic view of the park's backcountry. A wilderness trailhead is located adjacent to the Juniper Lake Ranger Station. Since no piped water is provided, it is critical to bring a water purification pump or plenty of bottled water.

❹ Mill Creek Resort

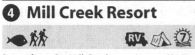

Location: On Mill Creek near Lassen National Forest; map C3, grid b0.

Campsites, facilities: There are 16 sites for tents or RVs up to 22 feet long, eight with full hookups. Nine one- and two-bedroom cabins are also available. Picnic tables, fire grills, piped water, and vault toilets are provided. Showers, coin laundry, small grocery store, and a coffee shop are available. Pets are permitted.

Reservations, fees: Reservations are accepted; $10 per night; cabins are $50 to $80 per night. Campsites are open May through October; cabins are available year-round.

Contact: Mill Creek Resort, (530) 595-4449.

Directions: From Red Bluff, drive 43 miles east on Highway 36 to the town of Mineral and the junction with Highway 172. Turn right and drive six miles to the town of Mill Creek. In Mill Creek, look for the sign for Mill Creek Resort on the right side of the road.

Trip notes: This is a great spot, surrounded by Lassen National Forest and within close range of the southern Highway 89 entrance to Lassen Volcanic National Park. It is set at 4,800 feet along oft-bypassed Highway 172. A highlight here is Mill Creek (to reach it, turn south on the Forest Service road in town and drive to a parking area at the end of the road along the stream), where there is a great easy walk along the stream and fair trout fishing.

❺ Hole-In-the-Ground

Location: On Mill Creek in Lassen National Forest; map C3, grid b0.

Campsites, facilities: There are four tent sites and nine sites for tents or RVs. Piped water, vault toilets, picnic tables, and fire grills are provided. Supplies are available in Mineral. Leashed pets are permitted.

Reservations, fees: No reservations; $10 per night. Open May through October.

Contact: Lassen National Forest, Almanor Ranger District, (530) 258-2141 or (530) 258-3491.

Directions: From Red Bluff, drive 43 miles east on Highway 36 to the town of Mineral and the junction with Highway 172. Turn right on Highway 172 and drive six miles to the town of Mill Creek. In Mill Creek, turn south onto a Forest Service road (signed) and drive five miles to the campground access road. Turn left and drive a quarter mile to the camp.

Trip notes: This is one of two campgrounds set along Mill Creek at 4,300 feet. Take your pick. The highlight here is a trail that follows along Mill Creek for many miles, which provides good fishing access. The stream is stocked with 2,000 rainbow trout each summer, joining residents and holdovers. Another option is to drive two more miles to the end of the Forest Service road, where there is a parking area for a trail that is routed downstream along Mill Creek and into a state game refuge. To keep things easy, obtain a map of Lassen National Forest that details the recreational opportunities.

❻ Gurnsey Creek Group Camp

Location: In Lassen National Forest; map C3, grid b1.

Campsites, facilities: This group campground can accommodate up to 100 people, with 20 sites for tents or RVs. Piped water, vault toilets, picnic tables, and fire grills are provided. A large community fireplace is centrally located for group use. Supplies are available in Mineral or Chester. Leashed pets are permitted.

Reservations, fees: Reservations are required; $75 per night with a 50 percent deposit. The deposit is refundable if cancellation notice is given 10 days prior to the reservation date. Open May through September.

Contact: Lassen National Forest, Almanor Ranger District, (530) 258-2141 or (530) 258-3491.

Directions: From Red Bluff, drive east on Highway 36 for 55 miles (five miles east of Childs Meadow). Turn left at the campground entrance road and drive a short distance to the campground.

Trip notes: This group camp is an ideal spot for a Scout troop. For more information, see the trip notes for the adjacent Gurnsey Creek (campground number seven).

---

❼ Gurnsey Creek

Location: In Lassen National Forest; map C3, grid b1.

Campsites, facilities: There are 32 sites for tents or RVs. Piped water, vault toilets, picnic tables, and fire grills are provided. Supplies are available in Mineral. Leashed pets are permitted.

Reservations, fees: No reservations; $10 per night. Open May through October.

Contact: Lassen National Forest, Almanor Ranger District, (530) 258-2141 or (530) 258-3491.

Directions: From Red Bluff, drive east on Highway 36 for 55 miles (five miles east of Childs Meadow). Turn left at the campground entrance road and drive a short distance to the campground.

Trip notes: This camp is set at 5,000 feet in Lassen National Forest, with extremely easy access off Highway 36. The camp is on the headwaters of little Gurnsey Creek, a highlight of the surrounding Lost Creek Plateau. Gurnsey Creek runs downstream and pours into Deer Creek, a good trout stream with access along narrow, winding Highway 32 to the nearby south.

---

❽ High Bridge

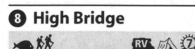

Location: On the North Fork of the Feather River in Lassen National Forest; map C3, grid b3.

Campsites, facilities: There are 12 sites for tents or RVs. Nonpiped water, vault toilets, picnic tables, and fire grills are provided. Groceries and propane gas are available nearby. Leashed pets are permitted.

Reservations, fees: No reservations; $10 per night. Open June through September.

Contact: Lassen National Forest, Almanor Ranger District, (530) 258-2141 or (530) 258-3491.

Directions: From Red Bluff, take Highway 36 east for 44 miles to the junction with Highway 89. Continue east on Highway 36/89 to Chester. In Chester, turn left on Warner Valley Road (a dirt road, RVs not recommended) and drive five miles to the campground entrance road on the left.

Trip notes: This camp is ideal for many people. It is just far enough off pavement that it is missed by thousands of campers wishing for such a spot. The payoff includes a pretty, adjacent trout stream, the headwaters of the North Fork Feather. Trout fishing is often good here, including some rare large brown trout, a surprise considering the relatively small size of the stream. Nearby access to the Warner Valley/Drakesbad entrance of Lassen Volcanic National Park provides a must-do side trip. The area is wooded and the road dusty.

---

❾ Domingo Springs

Location: In Lassen National Forest; map C3, grid b3.

Campsites, facilities: There are nine sites for tents and nine sites for tents or RVs. Piped water, vault toilets, picnic tables, and fire grills are provided. Leashed pets are permitted.

Reservations, fees: No reservations; $10 per night. Open May through October.

Contact: Lassen National Forest, Almanor Ranger District, (530) 258-2141 or (530) 258-3491.

Directions: From Red Bluff, take Highway 36 east for 44 miles to the junction with Highway 89. Continue east on Highway 36/89 to Chester. In Chester, turn left on Warner Valley Road (a dirt road, RVs not recommended) and drive six miles to the Y with Red Bluff Road/Forest Service Road 311. Bear left on Forest Service Road 311 and drive two miles to the campground entrance road on the left.

Trip notes: This camp is named after a spring located adjacent to the site. It is a small fountain that pours into the headwaters of the North Fork Feather River, a good trout stream. The Pacific

Crest Trail is routed from this camp north for four miles to Little Willow Lake and the southern border of Lassen Volcanic National Park. The elevation is 5,200 feet.

⑩ Benner Creek

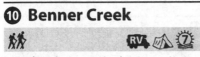

Location: On Benner Creek in Lassen National Forest; map C3, grid b3.

Campsites, facilities: There are nine sites for tents or RVs up to 20 feet long. Fire grills, picnic tables, and vault toilets are provided. Leashed pets are permitted.

Reservations, fees: No reservations; $8 per night.

Contact: Lassen National Forest, Almanor Ranger District, (530) 258-2141 or (530) 258-3491.

Directions: In Chester on Highway 36, turn west on Juniper Lake Road and drive seven miles to Benner Creek Campground on the right.

Trip notes: Benner Creek is just outside the remote eastern border of Lassen Volcanic National Park and its stellar but primitive Juniper Lake Campground. If that national park camp is full, this provides a nearby option. For drivers of RVs, this camp is preferable to navigating the rough road to Juniper Lake. In the fall, the camp gets occasional use by deer hunters.

⑪ Willow Springs

Location: Near Lost Creek Spring in Lassen National Forest; map C3, grid b2.

Campsites, facilities: There are 15 primitive sites for tents. Picnic tables and fire grills are provided. A vault toilet is available. No piped water is available.

Reservations, fees: No reservations; $8 per night.

Contact: Lassen National Forest, Almanor Ranger District, (530) 258-2141 or (530) 258-3491. For a map, send $4 to the USDA Forest Service, US Forest Map Sales, 1323 Club Drive, Vallejo, CA 94592, and ask for the Lassen National Forest area; (707) 562-USFS/8737; website www.r5.fs.fed.us.

Directions: From Red Bluff, drive east on High-

way 36 for about 55 miles. About two miles past Childs Meadows parking area, turn left on Wilson Lake Road/Forest Road 29N19 and drive 1.5 miles to Forest Service Road 29N19. Turn right on Forest Service Road 29N19 and drive about 3.5 miles to the campground on the left side of the road.

Trip notes: This is a primitive, undeveloped camp set on the southwest flank of North Stover Mountain (6,035 feet), used primarily by hunters during the fall deer season and ignored the rest of the time. A network of Forest Service roads in the area provides vehicle access. Though there is no piped water available, Lost Creek Spring to the east of camp and Lost Creek are viable water sources during wet years. The headwaters of Lost Creek run by the camp, flowing downstream into nearby Deer Creek to the south.

⑫ Warner Creek

Location: In Lassen National Forest; map C3, grid b3.

Campsites, facilities: There are 13 sites for tents or RVs up to 22 feet long. There is no piped water, but vault toilets, picnic tables, and fire grills are provided. Leashed pets are permitted.

Reservations, fees: No reservations; $8 per night. Open June through September.

Contact: Lassen National Forest, Almanor Ranger District, (530) 258-2141 or (530) 258-3491.

Directions: From Red Bluff, take Highway 36 east for 44 miles to the junction with Highway 89. Continue east on Highway 36/89 to Chester. In Chester, turn left on Warner Valley Road/County Road 312 (a dirt road; RVs are not recommended) and drive seven miles to the campground on the right side of the road.

Trip notes: Some people find this camp by accident. They are driving to the Warner/Drakesbad entrance of Lassen Volcanic National Park and discover the small, primitive camp on the way in, always an option during crowded weekends. It is set at 5,000 feet in elevation along little Warner Creek, a tributary to the North Fork Feather River. Warner Valley is located two miles to the north, and the entrance to Lassen Park is another six miles.

⑬ Last Chance Creek

Location: Near Lake Almanor; map C3, grid c4.

Campsites, facilities: There are 12 sites for tents or RVs up to 30 feet long, and 13 group campsites. Piped water, vault toilets, picnic tables, and fire grills are provided. Leashed pets are permitted.

Reservations, fees: Reservations are required for the group camp, phone (916) 386-5164; $13 per night for individual sites, $20 for group sites, $1 pet fee.

Contact: PG&E Building and Land Services, (916) 386-5164.

Directions: From Red Bluff, take Highway 36 east for 44 miles to the junction with Highway 89. Continue east on Highway 36/89 to Chester and continue for two miles over the causeway at the north end of Lake Almanor. About a quarter mile after crossing the causeway, turn left and drive about four miles to the campground.

Trip notes: This secluded camp is adjacent to where Last Chance Creek empties into the north end of Lake Almanor. It is an unpublicized PG&E facility that is known primarily by locals and gets missed almost every time by out-of-towners. The adjacent lake area is a breeding ground in the spring for white pelicans, and the beauty of these birds in large flocks can be extraordinary.

⑭ Northshore Campground

Location: On Lake Almanor; map C3, grid c4.

Campsites, facilities: There are 94 RV sites, many with partial hookups, and 34 tent sites. Piped water, picnic tables, fire grills, flush toilets, and showers are provided. A boat ramp and a dock are available. Leashed pets are permitted.

Reservations, fees: Reservations are accepted; $15 to $18 per night. Open April through October.

Contact: Northshore Campground, (530) 258-3376 or fax (530) 258-2838.

Directions: From Red Bluff, take Highway 36 east for 44 miles to the junction with Highway

89. Drive east on Highway 36/89; the camp is two miles past Chester.

Trip notes: This large, privately developed park on the northern shoreline of beautiful Lake Almanor is primarily for RVs.

⑮ Ponderosa RV Park

Location: Near Lake Almanor; map C3, grid b4.

Campsites, facilities: There are eight large sites for RVs or fifth wheels up to 40 feet long, all with full hook-ups, including cable TV and phone. Restaurants and stores are nearby. Leashed pets are permitted.

Reservations, fees: Reservations accepted; $20 per night; monthly rentals available. Open May through October.

Contact: Ponderosa RV Park, (530) 596-3781 or (530) 346-8624.

Directions: From Red Bluff, take Highway 36 and drive about six miles past Chester. Turn right on State Route A13 and drive three miles. Turn right on Peninsula Drive, then right again on Big Cove Drive, and drive one block. Turn left and drive to 408 Ponderosa Drive.

Trip notes: This small park in the tall pines, with big spaces and all the hook-up amenities, has the convenience of nearby stores and restaurants. The lake is only two blocks away. If this is what you're looking for, you've found it.

⑯ Goumaz

Location: On the Susan River in Lassen National Forest; map C3, grid b8.

Campsites, facilities: There are five sites for tents or RVs up to 30 feet long. Vault toilets, picnic tables, and fire rings are provided. There is no piped water. Pets must be controlled.

Reservations, fees: No reservations; $6 per night. Open May through September.

Contact: Lassen National Forest, Eagle Lake Ranger District, (530) 257-4188 or fax (530) 257-4150.

Directions: From Red Bluff, drive east on Highway 36 past Lake Almanor to the junction with llighway 44. Turn west on llighway 44 and drive six miles (one mile past the Worley Ranch) to Goumaz Road/Forest Service Road 30N08. Turn left on Goumaz Road and drive about five miles to the campground entrance road on the right.

Trip notes: This camp is set beside the Susan River, adjacent to the historic Bizz Johnson Trail, a former route for a rail line that has been converted to a 25-mile trail. The trail runs from Susanville to Westwood, but this section provides access to many of its prettiest and most remote stretches as it runs in a half circle around Pegleg Mountain (7,112 feet) to the east. It is an outstanding route for biking, hiking, and horseback riding in the summer and cross-country skiing in the winter.

⑰ Roxie Peconom

Location: In Lassen National Forest; map C3, grid b9.

Campsites, facilities: There are 10 tent sites. Piped water, vault toilet, picnic tables, and fire rings are provided. Leashed pets are permitted.

Reservations, fees: No reservations; no fee. Open May through September.

Contact: Lassen National Forest, Eagle Lake Ranger District, (530) 257-4188 or fax (530) 257-4150.

Directions: From Red Bluff, drive east on Highway 36 past Lake Almanor and continue past Fredonyer Pass for three miles to Forest Service Road 29N03 on the right. Turn right and drive two miles to the campground on the left.

Trip notes: This small camp is set next to Willard Creek, a seasonal stream in eastern Lassen National Forest. It's shaded and quiet. The best nearby recreation is the Bizz Johnson Trail, with a trailhead located on Highway 44 (two miles east) at a parking area on the left side of the highway. This is an outstanding biking and hiking route.

⑱ Alder

Location: On Deer Creek in Lassen National Forest; map C3, grid c0.

Campsites, facilities: There are five tent sites. There is no piped water. Vault toilets, picnic tables, and fire grills are provided. Leashed pets are permitted.

Reservations, fees: No reservations; $8 per night. Open April through October.

Contact: Lassen National Forest, Almanor Ranger District, (530) 258-2141 or (530) 258-3491.

Directions: From Red Bluff, take Highway 36 east for 44 miles to the junction with Highway 89. Continue east on Highway 36/89 to the junction with Highway 32. Turn south on Highway 32 and drive eight miles to the campground on the right side of the road. Trailers are not recommended.

Trip notes: Deer Creek is a great little trout stream that runs along Highway 32. Alder is one of four camps set along Highway 32 with streamside access; this one is at 3,900 feet elevation, set near where both Alder Creek and Round Valley Creek pour into Deer Creek. The stream's best stretch of trout water is from here on upstream to Elam (campground number 21).

⑲ Potato Patch

Location: On Deer Creek in Lassen National Forest; map C3, grid c0.

Campsites, facilities: There are 20 sites for tents and 12 sites for tents or RVs. Piped water, vault toilets, picnic tables, and fire grills are provided. Leashed pets are permitted.

Reservations, fees: No reservations; $10 per night. Open May through October.

Contact: Lassen National Forest, Almanor Ranger District, (530) 258-2141 or (530) 258-3491.

Directions: From Red Bluff, take Highway 36 east for 44 miles to the junction with Highway 89. Continue east on Highway 36/89 to the junction with Highway 32. Turn south on Highway 32 and drive 11 miles to the campground on the right side of the road. Trailers are not recommended.

Trip notes: You get good hiking and fishing at this camp. It is set beside Deer Creek, 3,400 feet elevation, with good access for trout fishing, best in May and June. In early summer, a side trip adventure is heading two miles up Highway 32 to find Deer Creek Falls.

⑳ Soldier Meadow

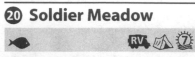

Location: On Soldier Creek in Lassen National Forest; map C3, grid c2.

Campsites, facilities: There are 15 sites for tents or RVs. Vault toilets, picnic tables, and fire rings are provided. There is no piped water. Leashed pets are permitted.

Reservations, fees: No reservations; $8 per night.

Contact: Lassen National Forest, Almanor Ranger District, (530) 258-2141 or (530) 258-3491.

Directions: From Chester, drive south on Highway 89 to Humboldt Road. Turn right on Humboldt Road and drive one mile, bear right at the fork, and continue five more miles to the intersection at Fanani Meadows. Turn right and drive one mile to the campground on the left.

Trip notes: This camp is little known and primitive and is used primarily by fishermen and hunters in season. The campsites here are shaded, set in forest on the edge of meadows, and near a stream. The latter is Soldier Creek, which is stocked with trout by the Department of Fish and Game. In the fall, early storms can drive deer through this area on their annual migration to their wintering habitat in the valley, making this a decent base camp for hunters. However, no early storms often mean no deer.

㉑ Elam

Location: On Deer Creek in Lassen National Forest; map C3, grid c0.

Campsites, facilities: There are 15 sites for tents or RVs. Piped water, vault toilets, picnic tables, and fire grills are provided. Leashed pets are permitted.

Reservations, fees: No reservations; $11 per night. Open May through September.

Contact: Lassen National Forest, Almanor Ranger District, (530) 258-2141 or (530) 258-3491.

Directions: From Red Bluff, take Highway 36 east for 44 miles to the junction with Highway 89. Continue east on Highway 36/89 to the junction with Highway 32. Turn south on Highway 32 and drive three miles to the campground on the right side of the road. Trailers are not recommended.

Trip notes: Of the campgrounds set on Deer Creek along Highway 32, Elam gets the most use. It is the first stopping point visitors arrive at while heading west on narrow, curvy Highway 32, and it has an excellent day-use picnic area available. The stream here is stocked with rainbow trout in late spring and early summer, with good access for fishing. It is a pretty area, set where Elam Creek enters Deer Creek. A Forest Service Information Center is nearby. If the camp has too many people to suit your style, consider other more distant and primitive camps located downstream on Deer Creek. The elevation here is 4,600 feet.

㉒ Lake Almanor Campground

Location: On Lake Almanor; map C3, grid c4.

Campsites, facilities: There are 130 sites for tents or RVs up to 30 feet long. Piped water, vault toilets, picnic tables, and fire grills are provided. A sanitary disposal station is available. Leashed pets are permitted.

Reservations, fees: No reservations; $13 per night, $1 pet fee. Open May through September.

Contact: PG&E Building and Land Services, (916) 386-5164.

Directions: From Red Bluff, take Highway 36 east for 44 miles to the junction with Highway 89. Continue east on Highway 36/89 to Lake Almanor and the next junction with Highway 89 (two miles before reaching Chester). Turn right on Highway 89 and drive about 10 miles to the southeast end of Lake Almanor. Turn left at your choice of four campground entrances.

Trip notes: What you get here is a series of

four campgrounds along the southwest shore of Lake Almanor provided by PG&E as mitigation for their hydroelectric activities on the Feather River system. The camps are set upstream from the dam, with boat ramps available on each side of the dam. This is a pretty spot, with giant Almanor ringed by lodgepole pine and firs. The lake is usually full, or close to it, well into summer, with Mount Lassen set in the distance to the north—bring your camera. Though it can take a day or two to locate the fish, once that effort is made, fishing is good for large trout and salmon in the spring and fall, and for smallmouth bass in the summer.

㉓ Almanor

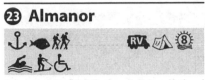

Location: On Lake Almanor in Lassen National Forest; map C3, grid c4.

Campsites, facilities: There are 15 sites for tents and 86 sites for tents or RVs. Piped water, vault toilets, picnic tables, and fire grills are provided. A boat ramp is available nearby. Leashed pets are permitted.

Reservations, fees: No reservations; $12 per night. Open May through October.

Contact: Lassen National Forest, Almanor Ranger District, (530) 258-2141 or (530) 258-3491.

Directions: From Red Bluff, take Highway 36 east for 44 miles to the junction with Highway 89. Continue east on Highway 36/89 to Lake Almanor and the next junction with Highway 89 (two miles before reaching Chester). Turn right on Highway 89 and drive six miles to County Road 310. Turn left on County Road 310 and drive one mile to the campground.

Trip notes: This is one of Lake Almanor's best-known and most popular Forest Service campgrounds. It is set along the western shore of beautiful Almanor, 4,519 feet elevation, directly across from the famous Almanor Peninsula. There is an excellent view of Mount Lassen to the north, along with gorgeous sunrises. This section of the lake provides good fishing for smallmouth bass in the summer, best using live crickets for bait.

㉔ Lassen View Resort

Location: At Lake Almanor east of Red Bluff; map C3, grid c5.

Campsites, facilities: There are 13 cabins and 59 tent and RV sites with full or partial hookups. Piped water, a rest room with showers, fire pits, and picnic tables are provided. A small store, fishing equipment, boat rentals, boat dock, and a fish-cleaning facility are also available. A fishing guide can be hired through the store.

Reservations, fees: Reservations are recommended; $17 to $19 per night; cabins are $60 to $95. Open May through October.

Contact: Lassen View Resort, (530) 596-3437 or fax (530) 596-4437.

Directions: From Red Bluff, take Highway 36 east for 44 miles to the junction with Highway 89. Continue east on Highway 36/89 to Chester and drive through Chester to the junction with County Road A13. Turn right (south) and drive about four miles to the junction with Highway 147. Turn right on Highway 147 and drive one mile to the well-signed camp entrance on the right.

Trip notes: This is one of the few classic fishing camps in California, designed from start to finish with fishing in mind. Its location is near one of the best fishing spots on the entire lake, Big Springs, at the mouth of the Hamilton Branch. After launching a boat or renting one at Lassen View, Big Springs is just a five-minute ride, "right around the corner," as they say here. This is where salmon congregate in the spring, and big brown and rainbow trout show up in the fall to feed on the lake's huge supply of pond smelt. The camp is rustic but friendly, and the folks here can help put you on to the fish. Lake Almanor, of course, is a big, beautiful lake set at 4,600 feet, ringed by conifers, and kept full most of the year.

㉕ Cherry Hill

Location: On Butte Creek in Lassen National Forest; map C3, grid d0.

Campsites, facilities: There are 13 walk-in tent sites and 12 sites for tents or RVs. Picnic tables, fire grills, piped water, and vault toilets are provided. Supplies are available in the town of Butte Meadows. Leashed pets are permitted.

Reservations, fees: No reservations; $10 per night. Open May through September.

Contact: Lassen National Forest, Almanor Ranger District, (530) 258-2141 or (530) 258-3491.

Directions: From Chico, drive about 15 miles north on Highway 32 to the town of Forest Ranch. Continue on Highway 32 for another nine miles to the junction with Humboldt Road. Turn right and drive five miles to Butte Meadows. Continue on Humboldt Road for three miles to the campground on the right side of the road.

Trip notes: The camp is set along little Butte Creek at the foot of Cherry Hill, just downstream from the confluence of Colby Creek and Butte Creek. It is also on the western edge of the alpine zone in Lassen National Forest. A four-mile drive to the north, much of it along Colby Creek, will take visitors to the Colby Mountain Lookout at 6,002 feet for a dramatic view of the Ishi Wilderness to the west. Nearby to the south is Philbrook Reservoir (see campground number 26).

26 Philbrook Reservoir

Location: In Lassen National Forest; map C3, grid d0.

Campsites, facilities: There are 20 sites for tents or RVs up to 30 feet long. Picnic tables, fire grills, piped water, and vault toilets are provided. Trailer and cartop boat launches are available. Leashed pets are permitted.

Reservations, fees: No reservations; $11 per night, $1 pet fee. Open May through September.

Contact: PG&E Building and Land Services, (916) 386-5164.

Directions: At Orland on Interstate 5, take the Highway 32/Chico exit and drive to Chico and the junction with Highway 99. Turn south on Highway 99 and drive to Skyway Road/Paradise (in south Chico). Turn east on Skyway Road, drive through Paradise, and continue for 27 miles to

Humbug Summit Road. Turn right and drive two miles to Philbrook Road. Turn right and drive four miles to the campground at the north end of the lake.

Trip notes: Philbrook Reservoir is set at 5,500 feet on the western mountain slopes above Chico, on the southwest edge of Lassen National Forest. It is a pretty lake, though subject to late season drawdowns, with a scenic lookout located a short distance from camp. The lake is loaded with small trout—a dink here, a dink there, a dink everywhere.

27 West Branch

Location: On the Feather River in Lassen National Forest; map C3, grid d0.

Campsites, facilities: There are eight sites for tents and seven sites for tents or RVs. Picnic tables, fire grills, piped water, and vault toilets are provided. Leashed pets are permitted.

Reservations, fees: No reservations; $9 per night. Open June through September.

Contact: Lassen National Forest, Almanor Ranger District, (530) 258-2141 or (530) 258-3491.

Directions: At Orland on Interstate 5, take the Highway 32/Chico exit and drive to Chico and the junction with Highway 99. Turn south on Highway 99 and drive to Skyway Road/Paradise (in south Chico). Turn east on Skyway Road and drive through Paradise and continue for 27 miles to Humbug Summit Road. Turn right and drive two miles to Philbrook Road and the campground access road on the right. Turn right and drive a half mile to the campground.

Trip notes: This is a small and remote campground set on the West Branch Feather River, 5,000 feet elevation, just upstream from where Philbrook Creek joins the Feather. It is set on the western edge of Lassen National Forest, with a network of backcountry roads in the area. Nearby destinations include Spring Valley Lake, Snag Lake, and Snow Mountain; several roads are accessible only to four-wheel-drive vehicles. Because of its proximity to Philbrook Reservoir, located two miles to the east, this camp is often overlooked.

28 Yellow Creek

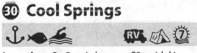

Location: In Humbug Valley; map C3, grid d3.

Campsites, facilities: There are 10 sites for tents or RVs. Piped water, vault toilets, picnic tables, and fire grills are provided. Pets are permitted.

Reservations, fees: No reservations; $11 per night, $1 pet fee. Open May through September.

Contact: PG&E Building and Land Services, (916) 386-5164.

Directions: From Oroville, drive north on Highway 70 to Belden. At Belden, turn left on Forest Service Road 26N26 and drive north about 11 miles to the campground entrance road on the left side of the road.

From Red Bluff, take Highway 36 east for 44 miles to the junction with Highway 89. Continue east on Highway 36/89 to Lake Almanor and the junction with Highway 89 (two miles before reaching Chester). Turn right on Highway 89 and drive about five miles to Humbug Road/County Road 308/309. Turn right (west) and drive a mile to the junction of County Road 308 and 309. Bear left on County Road 309 and drive two miles to the junction with County Road 307. Bear right on County Road 307 and drive about five miles to a Y. Bear left at the Y and drive 1.2 miles to the campground entrance on the right.

Trip notes: Yellow Creek is one of Cal Trout's pet projects. It's a beautiful stream for fly fishers, demanding the best from skilled anglers: approaching with complete stealth, making delicate casts with long leaders and small dry flies during the evening rise. This camp is set at 4,400 feet in Humbug Valley and provides access to this stretch of water. An option is to fish Butt Creek, much easier fishing for small planted rainbow trout, with access available along the road on the way in.

29 Ponderosa Flat

Location: On Butt Lake; map C3, grid d4.

Campsites, facilities: There are 63 sites for tents or RVs. Piped water, vault toilets, picnic tables, and fire grills are provided. A boat ramp is available. Leashed pets are permitted.

Reservations, fees: No reservations; $11 per night, $1 pet fee. Open May through October, weather permitting.

Contact: PG&E Building and Land Services, (916) 386-5164.

Directions: From Red Bluff, take Highway 36 east for 44 miles to the junction with Highway 89. Continue east on Highway 36/89 to Lake Almanor and the next junction with Highway 89 (two miles before reaching Chester). Turn right on Highway 89 and drive about seven miles to Butt Valley Road. Turn right on Butt Valley Road and drive 3.2 miles to the campground on the right side of the road.

Trip notes: This camp is set at the north end of Butt Lake, the little brother to nearby Lake Almanor. It is a fairly popular camp, with the boat ramp a prime attraction, allowing campers/anglers on vacation a lakeside spot with easy access. Technically, Butt is the "afterbay" for Almanor, fed by a four-mile-long pipe with water from Almanor. What occurs is that pond smelt from Almanor get ground up in the Butt Lake powerhouse, providing a huge amount of feed for trout at the head of the lake; that's why the trout often get huge at Butt Lake. The one downer here is that lake drawdowns are common, exposing tree stumps.

30 Cool Springs

Location: On Butt Lake; map C3, grid d4.

Campsites, facilities: There are 30 sites for tents or RVs. Piped water, vault toilets, picnic tables, and fire grills are provided. A boat ramp is available. Leashed pets are permitted.

Reservations, fees: No reservations; $11 per night, $1 pet fee. Open May through October, weather permitting.

Contact: PG&E Building and Land Services, (916) 386-5164.

Directions: From Red Bluff, take Highway 36 east for 44 miles to the junction with Highway 89. Continue east on Highway 36/89 to Lake Almanor and the next junction with Highway 89 (two miles before reaching Chester). Turn right on Highway 89 and drive about seven miles to Butt Valley Road. Turn right on Butt Valley Road and drive five miles to the campground on the right side of the road.

Trip notes: One of two camps at Butt Lake, Cool Springs is set about midway down the lake on its eastern shore, two miles south of Ponderosa Flat. Cool Springs Creek enters the lake near the camp. For more information about Butt Lake, see the trip notes for Ponderosa Flat (campground number 29).

㉛ Queen Lily

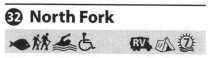

Location: On the North Fork of the Feather River in Plumas National Forest; map C3, grid e2.

Campsites, facilities: There are 12 sites for tents or RVs up to 16 feet long. Piped water, flush toilets, fire grills, and picnic tables are provided. A grocery store and coin laundry are available within three miles. Leashed pets are permitted.

Reservations, fees: No reservations; $11 per night. Open May through September.

Contact: Plumas National Forest, Mount Hough Ranger District, (530) 283-0555 or fax (530) 283-1821.

Directions: From Oroville, drive north on Highway 70 to Caribou Road (two miles past Belden at Gansner Ranch Ranger Station). Turn left on Caribou Road and drive about three miles to the campground on the left side of the road.

Trip notes: The North Fork Feather River is a prime destination for camping and trout fishing, especially for families. This is one of three camps along the river on Caribou Road. This stretch of river is well stocked. Insider's note: the first 150 yards of river below the dam at Caribou typically have large but elusive trout.

㉜ North Fork

Location: On the North Fork of the Feather River in Plumas National Forest; map C3, grid e2.

Campsites, facilities: There are 20 sites for tents or RVs up to 32 feet long. Piped water, flush toilets, fire grills, and picnic tables are provided. A grocery store and coin laundry are available within three miles. Leashed pets are permitted.

Reservations, fees: No reservations; $11 per night. Open May through September.

Contact: Plumas National Forest, Mount Hough Ranger District, (530) 283-0555 or fax (530) 283-1821.

Directions: From Oroville, drive north on Highway 70 to Caribou Road (two miles past Belden at Gansner Ranch Ranger Station). Turn left on Caribou Road and drive about two miles to the campground on the left side of the road.

Trip notes: This camp is between Queen Lily (campground number 31) to the nearby north and Gansner Bar (campground number 33) to the nearby south, all three set on the North Fork Feather River. The elevation is 2,600 feet. Fishing access is good and trout plants are decent, making for a good fishing/camping trip. Note: All three camps are extremely popular on summer weekends.

㉝ Gansner Bar

Location: On the North Fork of the Feather River in Plumas National Forest; map C3, grid e2.

Campsites, facilities: There are 14 sites for tents or RVs up to 32 feet long. Piped water, flush toilets, fire grills, and picnic tables are provided. A grocery store and coin laundry are available within one mile. Facilities are wheelchair accessible. Leashed pets are permitted.

Reservations, fees: No reservations; $11 per night. Open April through October.

Contact: Plumas National Forest, Mount Hough Ranger District, (530) 283-0555 or fax (530) 283-1821.

Directions: From Oroville, drive north on Highway 70 to Caribou Road (two miles past Belden at Gansner Ranch Ranger Station). Turn left on Caribou Road and drive a short distance to the campground on the left side of the road.

Trip notes: Gansner Bar is the first of three camps along Caribou Road, which runs parallel to the North Fork Feather River. Of the three, this one receives the highest trout stocks of rainbow trout in the 10- to 12-inch class. Caribou Road runs upstream to Caribou Dam, with stream and fishing access along almost all of it. The camps often fill on summer weekends.

➌ Hallsted

Location: On the North Fork of the Feather River in Plumas National Forest; map C3, grid e4.

Campsites, facilities: There are 20 sites for tents or RVs up to 22 feet long. Piped water, flush toilets, picnic tables, and fire grills are provided. A grocery store is available within a quarter mile. Leashed pets are permitted.

Reservations, fees: Reserve via phone at (877) 444-6777 ($8.65 reservation fee) or website www.reserveusa.com; $9 per night. Open May through September.

Contact: Plumas National Forest, Mount Hough Ranger District, (530) 283-0555 or fax (530) 283-1821.

Directions: From Oroville, drive northeast on Highway 70 to Belden. Continue past Belden for about 12 miles to the campground entrance on the right side of the road. Turn right and drive a quarter mile to the campground.

Trip notes: Easy highway access and a pretty trout stream right alongside have made this an extremely popular campground. It typically fills on summer weekends. Hallsted is set on the East Branch North Fork River, 2,800 feet elevation. The river is stocked with trout by the Department of Fish and Game.

➎ Lower Bucks

Location: On Lower Bucks Lake in Plumas National Forest; map C3, grid f3.

Campsites, facilities: There are six sites for RVs only up to 26 feet long. No piped water or toilet facilities are provided. Picnic tables and fire rings are available. Leashed pets are permitted.

Reservations, fees: No reservations; $6 per night. Open May through October.

Contact: Plumas National Forest, Mount Hough Ranger District, (530) 283-0555 or fax (530) 283-1821.

Directions: From Oroville, drive north on Highway 70 to the junction with Highway 89. Turn

south on Highway 89/70 and drive 11 miles to Quincy. In Quincy, turn right at Bucks Lake Road and drive 17 miles to Bucks Lake and the junction with Bucks Lake Dam Road/Forest Service Road 33. Turn right and drive four miles around the lake, cross over the dam, drive a quarter mile, and then turn left on the campground entrance road.

Trip notes: This camp is located on Lower Bucks Lake, which is actually the afterbay for Bucks Lake, set below the Bucks Lake Dam. It is a small, primitive, and quiet spot that is often overlooked because it is not located on the main lake.

➏ Grizzly Creek

Location: Near Bucks Lake in Plumas National Forest; map C3, grid f2.

Campsites, facilities: There are eight sites for tents or RVs up to 35 feet long. Piped water, vault toilets, picnic tables, and fire grills are provided. A boat ramp is available at Bucks Lake. A grocery store and coin laundry are available within five miles. Leashed pets are permitted.

Reservations, fees: No reservations; $9 per night. Open June through October.

Contact: Plumas National Forest, Mount Hough Ranger District, (530) 283-0555 or fax (530) 283-1821.

Directions: From Oroville, drive north on Highway 70 to the junction with Highway 89. Turn south on Highway 89/70 and drive 11 miles to Quincy. In Quincy, turn right at Bucks Lake Road and drive 17 miles to Bucks Lake and the junction with Bucks Lake Dam Road/Forest Service Road 33. Turn right and drive one mile to the junction with Oroville-Quincy Road/Forest Service Road 36. Bear left and drive one mile to the campground on the right side of the road.

Trip notes: This is an alternative to the more developed, more crowded campgrounds at Bucks Lake. It is a small, primitive camp set near Grizzly Creek at 5,400 feet in elevation. Nearby Bucks Lake provides good trout fishing, resorts, and boat rentals.

㊲ Haskins Valley

Location: On Bucks Lake; map C3, grid f2.

Campsites, facilities: There are 65 sites for tents or RVs. Piped water, vault toilets, picnic tables, and fire grills are provided. A sanitary disposal station and boat ramp are available. Leashed pets are permitted.

Reservations, fees: No reservations; $11 per night, $1 pet fee. Open May through October, weather permitting.

Contact: PG&E Building and Land Services, (916) 386-5164.

Directions: From Oroville, drive north on Highway 70 to the junction with Highway 89. Turn south on Highway 89/70 and drive 11 miles to Quincy. In Quincy, turn right at Bucks Lake Road and drive 16.5 miles to the campground entrance on the right side of the road.

Trip notes: This is the biggest and most popular of the campgrounds at Bucks Lake, a pretty alpine lake with excellent trout fishing and clean campgrounds. A boat ramp is available to the nearby north, along with Bucks Lodge. This camp is set deep in a cove at the extreme south end of the lake, where the water is quiet and sheltered from north winds. Bucks Lake, 5,200 feet elevation, is well documented for excellent fishing for rainbow and Mackinaw trout, with high catch rates of rainbow trout and lake records in the 16-pound class.

㊳ Silver Lake

Location: In Plumas National Forest; map C3, grid f3.

Campsites, facilities: There are eight tent sites. There is no piped water, but vault toilets, picnic tables, and fire grills are provided. Leashed pets are permitted.

Reservations, fees: No reservations; no fee. Open May through October.

Contact: Plumas National Forest, Mount Hough Ranger District, (530) 283-0555 or fax (530) 283-1821.

Directions: From Oroville, drive north on Highway 70 to the junction with Highway 89. Turn south on Highway 89/70 and drive 11 miles to Quincy. In Quincy, turn right at Bucks Lake Road and drive west for nine miles to Silver Lake Road. Turn right and drive seven miles to the campground at the north end of the lake

Trip notes: While tons of people go to Bucks Lake for the great trout fishing and lakeside camps, nearby Silver Lake gets little attention despite great natural beauty, good hiking, decent trout fishing, and a trailhead to the Bucks Lake Wilderness. The camp is located at the north end of the lake, 5,800 feet elevation, a primitive and secluded spot. No powerboats (or swimming) are allowed on Silver Lake, which makes it ideal for canoes and rafts. The lake has lots of small brook trout. The Pacific Crest Trail is routed on the ridge above the lake, skirting past Mount Pleasant (6,924 feet) to the nearby west.

㊴ Whitehorse

Location: Near Bucks Lake in Plumas National Forest; map C3, grid g3.

Campsites, facilities: There are 20 sites for tents or RVs up to 43 feet long. Piped water, vault toilets, fire grills, and picnic tables are provided. A grocery store and coin laundry are available within five miles. Leashed pets are permitted.

Reservations, fees: No reservations; $12 per night. Open June through September.

Contact: Plumas National Forest, Mount Hough Ranger District, (530) 283-0555 or fax (530) 283-1821.

Directions: From Oroville, drive north on Highway 70 to the junction with Highway 89. Turn south on Highway 89/70 and drive 11 miles to Quincy. In Quincy, turn right at Bucks Lake Road and drive 14.5 miles to the campground entrance on the right side of the road.

Trip notes: This campground is set along Bucks Creek, about two miles from the boat ramps and south shore concessions at Bucks Lake. The trout fishing can be quite good at Bucks Lake, particularly on early summer evenings. The elevation is 5,200 feet. For more information, see the trip notes for Haskins Valley (campground number 37).

⑩ Sundew

Location: On Bucks Lake in Plumas National Forest; map C3, grid f3.

Campsites, facilities: There are 19 sites for tents or RVs up to 22 feet long. Piped water, vault toilets, fire grills, and picnic tables are provided. Leashed pets are permitted. There is a boat ramp two miles north of the camp.

Reservations, fees: No reservations; $12 per night.

Contact: Plumas National Forest, Mount Hough Ranger District, (530) 283-0555 or fax (530) 283-1821.

Directions: From Oroville, drive north on Highway 70 to the junction with Highway 89. Turn south on Highway 89/70 and drive 11 miles to Quincy. In Quincy, turn right at Bucks Lake Road and drive 17 miles to Bucks Lake and the junction with Bucks Lake Dam Road/Forest Service Road 33. Turn right, drive around the lake, cross over the dam, continue for a half mile, and turn right at the campground access road.

Trip notes: Sundew Camp is set on the northern shore of Bucks Lake, just north of Bucks Lake Dam. A boat ramp is located about two miles north in the Mill Creek Cove, providing access to one of the better trout spots on the lake. You want fish? At Bucks Lake you can get fish—it's one of the state's top mountain trout lakes. Sunrises are often spectacular from this camp, with the light glowing on the lake's surface.

⑪ Mill Creek

Location: At Bucks Lake in Plumas National Forest; map C3, grid f3.

Campsites, facilities: There are eight sites for tents or RVs up to 58 feet long and two walk-in tent sites. Piped water, vault toilets, fire grills, and picnic tables are provided. Groceries are available within five miles. Leashed pets are permitted.

Reservations, fees: No reservations; $12 per night.

Contact: Plumas National Forest, Mount

Hough Ranger District, (530) 283-0555 or fax (530) 283-1821.

Directions: From Oroville, drive north on Highway 70 to the junction with Highway 89. Turn south on Highway 89/70 and drive 11 miles to Quincy. In Quincy, turn right at Bucks Lake Road and drive 17 miles to Bucks Lake and the junction with Bucks Lake Dam Road/Forest Service Road 33. Turn right, drive around the lake, cross over the dam, and continue for about three miles to the campground.

Trip notes: When Bucks Lake is full, this is one of the prettiest spots on the lake. The camp is set deep in Mill Creek Cove, adjacent to where Mill Creek enters the northernmost point of Bucks Lake. A boat ramp is located a half mile away to the south, providing boat access to one of the better trout fishing spots at the lake. Unfortunately, when the lake level falls, this camp is left high and dry, some distance from the water. The elevation is 5,200 feet.

⑫ Hutchins Group Camp

Location: Near Bucks Lake in Plumas National Forest; map C3, grid f3.

Campsites, facilities: There are three group sites for tents or RVs, each with a 25-person maximum. Piped water, vault toilets, picnic tables, and fire grills are provided. A boat ramp is available. Leashed pets are permitted.

Reservations, fees: Reservations are required; $43.60 group fee per night. Open May through October.

Contact: Plumas National Forest, Mount Hough Ranger District, (530) 283-0555 or fax (530) 283-1821.

Directions: From Oroville, drive north on Highway 70 to the junction with Highway 89. Turn south on Highway 89/70 and drive 11 miles to Quincy. In Quincy, turn right at Bucks Lake Road and drive 17 miles to Bucks Lake and the junction with Bucks Lake Dam Road/Forest Service Road 33. Turn right, drive around the lake, cross over the dam, continue for a short distance, and turn right. Drive a half mile, cross the stream (passing an intersection), and continue straight for a half mile to the campground.

Trip notes: This is a prime spot for a Scout outing or for any other large group that would like a pretty spot. An amphitheater is available. It is set at 5,200 feet near Bucks and Lower Bucks Lakes. For more information, see the trip notes for Lower Bucks (campground number 35), Haskins Valley (campground number 37), and Sundew (campground number 40).

㊸ Deanes Valley

Location: On Rock Creek in Plumas National Forest; map C3, grid f4.

Campsites, facilities: There are seven sites for tents or RVs. There is no piped water, but vault toilets, picnic tables, and fire grills are provided. Leashed pets are permitted.

Reservations, fees: No reservations; no fee. Open April through October.

Contact: Plumas National Forest, Mount Hough Ranger District, (530) 283-0555 or fax (530) 283-1821.

Directions: From Oroville, drive north on Highway 70 to the junction with Highway 89. Turn south on Highway 89/70 and drive 11 miles to Quincy. In Quincy, turn right at Bucks Lake Road and drive 3.5 miles to Forest Service Road 24N28. Turn left and drive seven miles to the campground.

Trip notes: This secret spot is set on South Fork Rock Creek, deep in a valley in Plumas National Forest. The trout here are very small natives. If you want a pure, quiet spot, great. If you want great fishing, not great. The surrounding region has a network of backcountry roads, including routes passable only by four-wheel-drive vehicles; to explore these roads, get a map of Plumas National Forest.

㊹ Snake Lake

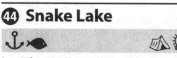

Location: In Plumas National Forest; map C3, grid f5.

Campsites, facilities: There are seven tent sites. There is no piped water, but vault toilets, picnic tables, and fire grills are provided. Leashed pets are permitted.

Reservations, fees: No reservations; no fee. Open May through October.

Contact: Plumas National Forest, Mount Hough Ranger District, (530) 283-0555 or fax (530) 283-1821.

Directions: From Oroville, drive north on Highway 70 to the junction with Highway 89. Turn south on Highway 89/70 and drive 11 miles to Quincy. In Quincy, turn right at Bucks Lake Road and drive five miles to County Road 422. Turn right and drive two miles to the Snake Lake access road. Turn right and drive one mile to the campground.

Trip notes: Snake Lake is a rarity in the northern Sierra, a mountain lake that has bass, catfish, and bluegill. That is because it is a shallow lake, set at 4,200 feet in Plumas National Forest. The camp is located on the west shore. A road that circles the lake provides a good bicycle route for youngsters. A side trip to the nearby north is Smith Lake, about a five-minute drive, with the Butterfly Valley Botanical Area bordering it.

㊺ Brady's Camp

Location: On Pine Creek in Plumas National Forest; map C3, grid f7.

Campsites, facilities: There are four tent sites. There is no piped water, but vault toilets, picnic tables, and fire grills are provided. Leashed pets are permitted.

Reservations, fees: No reservations; no fee. Open May through October.

Contact: Plumas National Forest, Mount Hough Ranger District, (530) 283-0555 or fax (530) 283-1821.

Directions: From Oroville, drive north on Highway 70 to the junction with Highway 89. Turn south on Highway 89/70 and drive 11 miles to Quincy. In Quincy, continue on Highway 89/70 for six miles to Squirrel Creek Road. Turn left and drive seven miles (after two miles bear right at the Y) to Forest Service Road 25N29. Turn left and drive one mile to the campground on the right side of the road.

Trip notes: Don't expect any company here. This is a tiny, little-known, primitive camp near Pine Creek, at roughly 7,000 feet in elevation. A side trip is to make the half-mile drive up to Argentine Rock (7,209 feet) for a lookout onto this remote forest country. To the east are many miles of national forest, accessible by vehicle, although there is significant logging activity in portions of the forest.

⑯ Rogers Cow Camp

Location: In Plumas National Forest; map C3, grid g1.

Campsites, facilities: There are five sites for tents or RVs. Tables, fire grills, and vault toilets are provided, but no piped water is available. Leashed pets are permitted.

Reservations, fees: No reservations; no fee. Open May through September.

Contact: Plumas National Forest, Feather River Ranger District, (530) 534-6500 or fax (530) 532-1210.

Directions: In Oroville, drive east on Highway 162 /Oroville-Quincy Highway for 26.5 miles to the Brush Creek Ranger Station. Continue on Oroville-Quincy Highway for eight miles to the campground entrance road on the left side of the road. Turn left and drive a short distance to the camp.

Trip notes: First note that the Oroville-Quincy "Highway" is actually a bumpy, twisty dirt Forest Service road, a backcountry route that connects Oroville to Quincy and passes Lake Oroville and Bucks Lake in the process. That puts this camp way out there in no-man's-land, set in Plumas National Forest at 4,000 feet. You want quiet, you get it. You want water, you bring it yourself. The camp is set near the headwaters of Coon Creek. There are no other natural destinations in the area, and I'm not saying Coon Creek is anything to see. It's advisable to obtain a map of Plumas National Forest, which details all backcountry roads. There has been logging activity in the area.

⑰ Milsap Bar

Location: On the Middle Fork of the Feather River in Plumas National Forest; map C3, grid g1.

Campsites, facilities: There are 20 sites for tents or RVs up to 16 feet long. There is no piped water, but tables, fire grills, and vault toilets are provided. Leashed pets are permitted.

Reservations, fees: No reservations; no fee. Open May through September.

Contact: Plumas National Forest, Feather River Ranger District, (530) 534-6500 or fax (530) 532-1210.

Directions: In Oroville, drive east on Highway 162/Oroville-Quincy Highway for 26.5 miles to the Brush Creek Ranger Station. Turn right on Bald Rock Road and drive for about a half mile to Forest Service Road 22N62/Milsap Bar Road. Turn left and drive eight miles to the campground (a narrow, steep, mountainous dirt road).

Trip notes: Among white-water river rafters, Milsap Bar is a well-known access point to the Middle Fork Feather River. This river country features a deep canyon, beautiful surroundings, and is formally recognized as the Feather Falls Scenic Area (named after the 640-foot waterfall), with trips offered by several rafting companies. The elevation is 1,600 feet.

⑱ Little North Fork

Location: On the Middle Fork of the Feather River in Plumas National Forest; map C3, grid g1.

Campsites, facilities: There are eight sites for tents or RVs up to 16 feet long. There is no piped water, but vault toilets, tables, and fire grills are provided. Leashed pets are permitted.

Reservations, fees: No reservations; no fee. Open May through October.

Contact: Plumas National Forest, Feather River Ranger District, (530) 534-6500 or fax (530) 532-1210.

Directions: From Oroville, turn east on Highway 162/Oroville-Quincy Highway and drive 26.5 miles to the Brush Creek Ranger Station. Continue northeast on Oroville-Quincy Highway for about six miles to Forest Service Road 60. Turn right and drive about eight miles to the campground entrance road on the left side of the road. Turn left and drive a quarter mile to the campground. Note: This route is long, twisty, bumpy, and narrow for most of the way.

Trip notes: Guaranteed quiet? You got it. This is a primitive camp in the outback that few know of. It is set along the Little North Fork of the Middle Fork of the Feather River at 2,700 feet. The surrounding backcountry of Plumas National Forest features an incredible number of roads, giving four-wheel-drive owners a chance to get so lost they'll need this camp. Instead, get a map of Plumas National Forest before venturing out.

49 Golden Coach Trailer Resort

Location: Near the Feather River; map C3, grid g8.

Campsites, facilities: There are 60 RV sites with full hookups. Rest rooms, showers, picnic tables, and fire grills are provided. A coin laundry, wood, store, cafe, and LP gas are also available. Leashed pets are permitted.

Reservations, fees: Reservations are recommended in July and August; $15 to $19 per night. Open May through mid-October.

Contact: Golden Coach Trailer Resort, (530) 836-2426; email: gcoach@thegrid.net.

Directions: In Truckee, at the junction of Highway 80 and Highway 89, take Highway 89 north to the junction with Highway 70. Drive north on Highway 89/Highway 70 for 6.5 miles to Cromberg and look for the signed entrance to the campground at 59704 Highway 70.

Trip notes: This is a good layover spot for RV cruisers looking to hole up for the night. The park is wooded and set near the Feather River. You'll find mostly older adults here.

50 Black Rock

Location: On Little Grass Valley Reservoir in Plumas National Forest; map C3, grid h4.

Campsites, facilities: There are 10 walk-in tent sites and 20 sites for tents or RVs up to 22 feet long. Piped water, vault toilets, picnic tables, and fire grills are provided. A sanitary dump station, boat ramp, and grocery store are nearby. Leashed pets are permitted.

Reservations, fees: No reservations; $10 per night. Open June through October.

Contact: Plumas National Forest, Feather River Ranger District, (530) 534-6500 or fax (530) 532-1210.

Directions: From Oroville, drive east on Highway 162 for about eight miles to the junction signed Challenge/LaPorte. Bear right and drive east past Challenge and Strawberry Valley to LaPorte. Continue two miles past LaPorte to the junction with County Road 514/Little Grass Valley Road. Turn left and drive about five miles to the campground access road on the west side of the lake. Turn right on the access road and drive a quarter mile to the campground.

Trip notes: This is the only campground on the west shore of Little Grass Valley Reservoir, with an adjacent boat ramp making it an attractive choice for anglers. The lake is set at 5,000 feet in Plumas National Forest and provides lakeside camping and decent fishing for rainbow trout and kokanee salmon. If you don't like the company, there are four other camps to choose from at the lake, all on the opposite eastern shore.

51 Running Deer

Location: On Little Grass Valley Reservoir in Plumas National Forest; map C3, grid h5.

Campsites, facilities: There are 40 sites for tents or RVs. Piped water, flush toilets, picnic tables, and fire grills are provided. A boat ramp, grocery store, and sanitary dump station are nearby. Leashed pets are permitted.

Reservations, fees: No reservations; $12 to $14 per night. Open June through September.

Contact: Plumas National Forest, Feather River Ranger District, (530) 534-6500 or fax (530) 532-1210.

Directions: From Oroville, drive east on Highway 162 for about eight miles to the junction signed Challenge/LaPorte. Bear right and drive east past Challenge and Strawberry Valley to LaPorte. Continue two miles past LaPorte to the junction with County Road 514/Little Grass Valley Road. Turn left and drive one mile to a junction. Turn right and drive three miles to the campground on the left side of the road.

Trip notes: Little Grass Valley Reservoir is a pretty mountain lake set at 5,000 feet in Plumas National Forest, providing lakeside camping, boating, and fishing for rainbow trout and kokanee salmon. One of four campgrounds on the eastern shore, this one is on the far northeastern end of the lake. Looking straight north from the camp is a spectacular view, gazing across the water and up at Bald Mountain, 6,255 feet in elevation. A trailhead for the Pacific Crest Trail is available nearby, located at little Fowler Lake about four miles north of Little Grass Valley Reservoir.

52 Wyandotte

Location: On Little Grass Valley Reservoir in Plumas National Forest; map C3, grid h5.

Campsites, facilities: There are 28 sites for tents or RVs up to 22 feet long. Piped water, flush toilets, picnic tables, and fire grills are provided. A sanitary dump station, boat ramp, and grocery store are nearby. Leashed pets are permitted.

Reservations, fees: No reservations; $12 to $18 per night. Open May through September.

Contact: Plumas National Forest, Feather River Ranger District, (530) 534-6500 or fax (530) 532-1210.

Directions: From Oroville, drive east on High way 162 for about eight miles to the junction signed Challenge/LaPorte. Bear right and drive east past Challenge and Strawberry Valley to LaPorte. Continue two miles past LaPorte to the junction with County Road 514/Little Grass Valley Road. Turn left and drive one mile to a junction. Turn left and drive one mile to the campground entrance road on the right.

Trip notes: Of the five camps on Little Grass Valley Reservoir, this is the favorite. It is set on a small peninsula that extends well into the lake, with a boat ramp nearby. For more information, see the trip notes for Running Deer (campground number 51).

53 Little Beaver

Location: On Little Grass Valley Reservoir in Plumas National Forest; map C3, grid h5.

Campsites, facilities: There are 120 sites for tents or RVs. Piped water, flush toilets, picnic tables, and fire grills are provided. A grocery store, sanitary dump station, and boat ramp are nearby. Leashed pets are permitted.

Reservations, fees: No reservations; $12 to $14 per night. Open June through October.

Contact: Plumas National Forest, Feather River Ranger District, (530) 534-6500 or fax (530) 532-1210.

Directions: From Oroville, drive east on Highway 162 for about eight miles to the junction signed Challenge/LaPorte. Bear right and drive east past Challenge and Strawberry Valley to LaPorte. Continue two miles past LaPorte to the junction with County Road 514/Little Grass Valley Road. Turn left and drive one mile to a junction. Turn right and drive two miles to the campground entrance road on the left.

Trip notes: This is one of five campgrounds on Little Grass Valley Reservoir, set at 5,000 feet. Take your pick. For more information, see the trip notes for Running Deer (campground number 51).

54 Red Feather Camp

Location: On Little Grass Valley Reservoir in Plumas National Forest; map C3, grid h5.

Campsites, facilities: There are 60 sites for tents or RVs up to 22 feet long. Piped water, flush toilets, picnic tables, and fire grills are provided. A sanitary dump station, boat ramp, and grocery store are nearby. Leashed pets are permitted.

Reservations, fees: Reserve via phone at (877) 444-6777 ($8.65 reservation fee) or website www.reserveusa.com; $12 to $14 per night. Open June through October.

Contact: Plumas National Forest, Feather River Ranger District, (530) 534-6500 or fax (530) 532-1210.

Directions: From Oroville, drive east on Highway 162 for about eight miles to the junction signed Challenge/LaPorte. Bear right and drive east past Challenge and Strawberry Valley to LaPorte. Continue two miles past LaPorte to the junction with County Road 514/Little Grass Valley Road. Turn left and drive one mile to a junction. Turn right and drive three miles to the campground entrance road on the left.

Trip notes: This camp is well developed and popular, set on the eastern shore of Little Grass Valley Reservoir, just south of Running Deer (campground number 51) and just north of Little Beaver (campground number 53). For more information, see the trip notes for Running Deer.

55 Plumas-Eureka State Park

Location: Near Graeagle; map C3, grid h7.

Campsites, facilities: There are 67 sites for tents, trailers, or RVs up to 30 feet long. Piped water, showers, flush toilets, sanitary dump station, picnic tables, and fire grills are provided. A grocery store, coin laundry, and propane gas are available within five miles. Leashed pets are permitted.

Reservations, fees: No reservations; $12 to 16 per night, $1 pet fee. Open June through September.

Contact: Plumas-Eureka State Park, (530) 836-2380 or fax (530) 836-0498.

Directions: In Truckee, drive north on Highway 89 to Graeagle. Just after passing Graeagle (one mile from the junction of Highway 70) turn left on County Road A14/Graeagle-Johnsville Road and drive west for about five miles to the park entrance.

Trip notes: Plumas-Eureka State Park is a beautiful chunk of parkland, featuring great hiking, a pretty lake, and this well-maintained campground. For newcomers to the area, Jamison Camp at the southern end of the park makes for an excellent first stop. So does the nearby hike to Grass Lake, a first-class tromp that takes about two hours and features a streamside walk along Jamison Creek, with the chance to take a five-minute cutoff to see 40-foot Jamison Falls. Other must-see destinations in the park include Eureka Lake, and from there, the 1,100-foot climb up to Eureka Peak, 7,447 feet, for a dramatic view of all the famous peaks in this region. Camp elevation is 5,200 feet.

56 Little Bear RV Park

Location: On the Feather River; map C3, grid h8.

Campsites, facilities: There are 95 RV sites, 80 with full hookups. Rest rooms, showers, picnic tables, and fire pits are provided. A coin laundry, grocery store, and ice are also available. Leashed pets are permitted.

Reservations, fees: Reservations are accepted; $20 to $22 per night, $1 pet fee. Open mid-April through October.

Contact: Little Bear RV Park, (530) 836-2774.

Directions: In Truckee, drive north on Highway 89 to Blairsden and the junction with Highway 70. Turn north and drive one mile to Little Bear Road. Turn left on Little Bear Road and drive a short distance to the campground.

Trip notes: This is a privately operated RV park set near the Feather River. Nearby destinations include Plumas-Eureka State Park and the Lakes Basin Recreation Area. The elevation is 4,300 feet.

57 Movin' West Trailer Ranch

Location: Near Graeagle; map C3, grid h8.

Campsites, facilities: There are 32 RV sites with full or partial hookups. Piped water, picnic tables, fire grills, flush toilets, showers, and a coin laundry are provided. Propane gas is available nearby. Leashed ets are permitted.

Reservations, fees: Reservations are accepted; $20 per night. Open May through October.

Contact: Movin' West Trailer Ranch, (530) 836-2614.

Directions: From Truckee, drive northwest on Highway 89 about 50 miles to Graeagle. Continue just past Graeagle to County Road A14. Turn left and drive a quarter mile northwest to the campground.

Trip notes: This RV area is set within a mobile home park. If that's what you want, you've found it. The elevation is 4,300 feet.

58 Sierra Springs Trailer Resort

Location: Near Blairsden; map C3, grid h9.

Campsites, facilities: There are 40 RV sites, 30 with full hookups. Piped water, showers, flush toilets, picnic tables, and fire grills are provided. A dump station, coin laundry , cable TV, playground, recreation room, and volleyball net are available. Leashed pets are permitted.

Reservations, fees: Reservations are accepted; $18 per night. Open April through October.

Contact: Sierra Spring Trailer Resort, (530) 836-2747 or fax (530) 836-2559.

Directions: From Truckee, drive northwest on Highway 89 about 50 miles to Blairsden and the junction with Highway 70. Turn right and drive 3.5 miles east to Sierra Springs Drive. Turn left on Sierra Springs Drive and drive a quarter mile to 70099 Sierra Springs Road on the left.

Trip notes: This privately operated park provides all the amenities. Possible side trips include the Feather River Park, located four miles away in the town of Blairsden. The elevation is 5,000 feet.

59 Strawberry

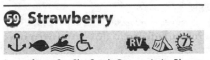

Location: On Sly Creek Reservoir in Plumas National Forest; map C3, grid i2.

Campsites, facilities: There are 17 sites for tents, trailers, or RVs. Piped water, vault toilets, picnic tables, and fire grills are provided. A cartop boat launch is available on Sly Creek Reservoir. Leashed pets are permitted.

Reservations, fees: No reservations; $10 per night.

Contact: Plumas National Forest, Feather River Ranger District, (530) 534-6500 or fax (530) 532-1210.

Directions: From Oroville, drive east on Highway 162 for about eight miles to the junction signed Challenge/LaPorte. Bear right and drive east on LaPorte Road past Challenge and continue for about 14 miles to a signed turnoff on

the left for Sly Creek Reservoir. Turn left and drive one mile to the campground on the eastern end of the lake.

Trip notes: Sly Creek Reservoir is a long, narrow lake set in western Plumas National Forest. There are two campgrounds on opposite ends of the lake, with different directions to each. This camp is set in the back of a cove on the lake's eastern arm, with a nearby boat ramp available. This is a popular lake for trout fishing in the summer.

60 Sly Creek

Location: On Sly Creek Reservoir in Plumas National Forest; map C3, grid i2.

Campsites, facilities: There are 21 sites for tents, trailers, or RVs. Five walk-in tent cabins are also available. Piped water, vault toilets, picnic tables, and fire grills are provided. A cartop boat launch is available on Sly Creek Reservoir. Leashed pets are permitted.

Reservations, fees: No reservations; $12 per night.

Contact: Plumas National Forest, Feather River Ranger District, (530) 534-6500 or fax (530) 532-1210.

Directions: From Oroville, drive east on Highway 162 for about eight miles to the junction signed Challenge/LaPorte. Bear right and drive east on LaPorte Road past Challenge and continue for 10 miles to Forest Service Road 16 (a signed turnoff on the left). Turn left and drive 4.5 miles to the campground.

Trip notes: Sly Creek Camp is set on Sly Creek Reservoir's southwestern shore near Lewis Flat, with a boat ramp located about a mile to the north. Both camps are well situated for campers/anglers. This camp provides direct access to the lake's main body, with good trout fishing well upstream on the main lake arm. You get quiet water and decent fishing.

61 Diablo

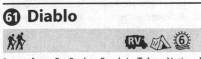

Location: On Packer Creek in Tahoe National Forest; map C3, grid i8.

Campsites, facilities: This is an undeveloped, designated camping area for tents and RVs. There is no piped water, but vault toilets are provided. Supplies are available in Bassetts and Sierra City. Pets must be controlled.

Reservations, fees: No reservations; no fee.

Contact: Tahoe National Forest, North Yuba/Downieville Ranger District, (530) 288-3231 or fax (530) 288-0727.

Directions: From Truckee, turn north on Highway 89 and drive 20 miles to Sierraville. At Sierraville, turn left on Highway 49 and drive about 10 miles to the Bassetts Store. Turn right on Gold Lake Road and drive 1.5 miles to Packer Lake Road. Turn left, drive a short distance, bear right at the fork, and drive one mile to the campground on the right side of the road.

Trip notes: This is a primitive camping area set on Packer Creek, about two miles from Packer Lake. This area is extremely beautiful with several lakes nearby, including the Sardine Lakes and Packer Lake, and this camp provides an overflow area when the more developed campgrounds have filled.

⑥ Salmon Creek

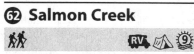

Location: In Tahoe National Forest; map C3, grid i8.

Campsites, facilities: There are 31 sites for tents or RVs up to 22 feet long. Piped water, vault toilets, picnic tables, and fire grills are provided. Supplies and a coin laundry are available in Sierra City. Pets must be controlled.

Reservations, fees: No reservations; $10 per night. Open June through October.

Contact: Tahoe National Forest, North Yuba/Downieville Ranger District, (530) 288-3231 or fax (530) 288-0727.

Directions: From Truckee, turn north on Highway 89 and drive 20 miles to Sierraville. At Sierraville, turn left on Highway 49 and drive about 10 miles to the Bassetts Store. Turn right on Gold Lake Road and drive two miles to the campground on the left side of the road.

Trip notes: This campground is set at the confluence of Packer and Salmon Creeks, 5,800 feet in elevation, with easy access off the Gold Lakes

Highway. It is on the edge of the Lakes Basin Recreation Area, with literally dozens of lakes located within 15 miles, plus great hiking, fishing, and low-speed boating.

⑥ Packsaddle

Location: Near Packer Lake in Tahoe National Forest; map C3, grid i8.

Campsites, facilities: There are 12 sites for tents or RVs. There is no piped water, but vault toilets are provided. Pack and saddle stock are permitted. Corrals and hitching rails are available. Supplies are available in Bassetts and Sierra City. Pets must be controlled.

Reservations, fees: No reservations; $10 per night. Open June through October.

Contact: Tahoe National Forest, North Yuba/Downieville Ranger District, (530) 288-3231 or fax (530) 288-0727.

Directions: From Truckee, turn north on Highway 89 and drive 20 miles to Sierraville. At Sierraville, turn left on Highway 49 and drive about 10 miles to the Bassetts Store. Turn right on Gold Lake Road and drive 1.5 miles to Packer Lake Road. Turn left, drive a short distance, bear right at the fork, and drive 2.5 miles to the campground.

Trip notes: Packsaddle is a primitive spot, located about a half mile from Packer Lake, with an additional 15 lakes within a five-mile radius, and one of America's truly great hiking trails available nearby. The trail to the Sierra Buttes features a climb of 2,369 feet over the course of five miles. It is highlighted by a stairway with 176 steps that literally juts out into open space, and crowned by an astounding view for hundreds of miles in all directions. Packer Lake, 6,218 feet, is located at the foot of the dramatic Sierra Buttes and has lakefront log cabins, good trout fishing, and low-speed boating.

⑥ Berger Creek

Location: In Tahoe National Forest; map C3, grid i8.

Campsites, facilities: There are 10 sites for

tents or RVs up to 16 feet long. There is no piped water, but vault toilets, picnic tables, and fire grills are provided. Supplies are available in Bassetts and Sierra City. Pets must be controlled.

Reservations, fees: No reservations; no fee. Open June through October.

Contact: Tahoe National Forest, North Yuba/Downieville Ranger District, (530) 288-3231 or fax (530) 288-0727.

Directions: From Truckee, turn north on Highway 89 and drive 20 miles to Sierraville. At Sierraville, turn left on Highway 49 and drive about 10 miles to the Bassetts Store. Turn right on Gold Lake Road and drive 1.5 miles to Packer Lake Road. Turn left, drive a short distance, bear right at the fork, and drive two miles to the campground.

Trip notes: Berger Creek, primitive and undeveloped, provides an overflow alternative to nearby Diablo (campground number 61), which is also extremely primitive. On busy summer weekends, when an open campsite can be difficult to find at a premium location in the Lakes Basin Recreation Area, these two camps provide a safety valve to keep you from being stuck for the night. Nearby is Packer Lake, the trail to the Sierra Buttes, Sardine Lakes, and Sand Pond, all excellent destinations. The elevation is 5,900 feet.

65 Snag Lake

Location: In Tahoe National Forest; map C3, grid i8.

Campsites, facilities: There are 16 sites for tents or RVs up to 16 feet long. There is no piped water, but vault toilets, picnic tables, and fire grills are provided. Only hand boat launching is allowed. Supplies are available in Bassetts and Sierra City. Pets must be controlled.

Reservations, fees: No reservations; no fee. Open June through October.

Contact: Tahoe National Forest, North Yuba/Downieville Ranger District, (530) 288-3231 or fax (530) 288-0727.

Directions: From Truckee, turn north on Highway 89 and drive 20 miles to Sierraville. At Sierraville, turn left on Highway 49 and drive about 10 miles to the Bassetts Store. Turn right on Gold

Lake Road and drive five miles to the campground.

Trip notes: Snag Lake is an ideal little lake for camping anglers with canoes. There are no boat ramps and you can have the place virtually to yourself. It is set at 6,600 feet in elevation, an easy-to-reach lake in the Lakes Basin Recreation Area. Trout fishing is only fair, as in fair numbers and fair size, mainly rainbow trout in the 10- to 12-inch class. This is a primitive camp, so bring everything you will need, including water.

66 Lakes Basin Group Camp

Location: In Plumas National Forest; map C3, grid i8.

Campsites, facilities: This group tent camp can accommodate up to 25 people. Piped water, vault toilets, picnic tables, and fire grills are provided. Supplies are available in Graeagle. Leashed pets are permitted.

Reservations, fees: Reserve via phone at (877) 444-6777 ($8.65 reservation fee) or website www.reserveusa.com; $45 group fee per night.

Contact: Plumas National Forest, Beckwourth Ranger District, (530) 836-2575 or fax (530) 836-0493.

Directions: From Truckee, drive north on Highway 89 toward Graeagle to the Gold Lake Highway (one mile before reaching Graeagle). Turn left on the Gold Lake Highway and drive about seven miles to the campground.

Trip notes: This is a Forest Service group camp that is ideal for Boy and Girl Scouts. It is set at 6,400 feet in elevation, just a short drive from the trailhead to beautiful Frazier Falls, and also near Gold Lake, Little Bear Lake, and some 15 lakes set below nearby Mount Elwell.

67 Lakes Basin

Location: In Plumas National Forest; map C3, grid i8.

Campsites, facilities: There are 24 sites for tents or small RVs. Piped water, vault toilets, picnic tables, and fire grills are provided. Supplies are available in Graeagle. Leashed pets are permitted.

Reservations, fees: Reservations are accepted via phone at (877) 444-6777 ($8.65 reservation fee) or website www.reserveusa.com; $10 per night. Open June through October.

Contact: Plumas National Forest, Beckwourth Ranger District, (530) 836-2575 or fax (530) 836-0493.

Directions: From Truckee, drive north on Highway 89 toward Graeagle to the Gold Lake Highway (one mile before reaching Graeagle). Turn left on the Gold Lake Highway and drive about seven miles to the campground.

Trip notes: Since its renovation in 1996, this camp is now far more accessible to small RVs and trailers, and is a great location for a base camp to explore the surrounding Lakes Basin Recreation Area. From nearby Gold Lake or Elwell Lodge, there are many short hikes available to small pristine lakes. A must-do trip is the easy hike to Frazier Falls, only a mile round-trip to see the spectacular 176-foot waterfall, though the trail is crowded during the middle of the day. The camp elevation is 6,400 feet.

68 Sardine Lake

Location: In Tahoe National Forest; map C3, grid j8 .

Campsites, facilities: There are 29 sites for tents or RVs up to 22 feet long. Piped water, vault toilets, picnic tables, and fire grills are provided. Limited supplies are available at the Sardine Lake Lodge or in Bassetts. Pets must be controlled.

Reservations, fees: No reservations; $10 per night. Open June through October.

Contact: Tahoe National Forest, North Yuba/Downieville Ranger District, (530) 288-3231 or fax (530) 288-0727.

Directions: From Truckee, drive north on Highway 89 for 20 miles to Sierraville. Turn left on Highway 49 and drive about 10 miles to the Bassetts Store. Turn right on Gold Lake Road and drive 1.5 miles to Packer Lake Road. Turn left, drive a short distance, then bear left at the fork and drive a half mile to the campground.

Trip notes: Lower Sardine Lake is a jewel set below the Sierra Buttes, one of the prettiest settings in California. The campground is actually about a mile east of the lake. Nearby is the beautiful Sand Pond Interpretive Trail. A great hike is routed along the shore of Lower Sardine Lake to a hidden waterfall (in spring) that feeds the lake, and ambitious hikers can explore beyond and discover Upper Sardine Lake. Trout fishing is excellent in Lower Sardine Lake, with a primitive boat ramp available for small boats. The speed limit and small size of the lake keeps boaters slow and quiet. A small marina and boat rentals are available.

69 Clio's River's Edge

Location: On the Feather River; map C3, grid i9.

Campsites, facilities: There are 220 RV sites with full hookups. Piped water, showers (coin operated), picnic tables, flush toilets, laundry room, and cable TV are provided. A grocery store is within four blocks. Leashed pets are permitted.

Reservations, fees: Reservations are accepted; $20 per night. Open mid-April through mid-October.

Contact: Clio's River's Edge, (530) 836-2375.

Directions: From Truckee, drive north on Highway 89 toward Graeagle and Blairsden. Near Clio (3.5 miles south of Highway 70 at Blairsden), look for the campground entrance.

Trip notes: This is a giant RV park set adjacent to a pretty and easily accessible stretch of the Feather River. There are many possible side trip destinations, including Plumas-Eureka State Park, Lakes Basin Recreation Area, and several nearby golf courses. The elevation is about 4,500 feet.

70 Garden Point Boat-In

Location: On Bullards Bar Reservoir; map C3, grid j2.

Campsites, facilities: There are 16 sites (four single and four double sites) accessible by boat only. There is no piped water, but picnic tables, fire grills, and vault toilets are provided. You must burn or pack out your garbage. Supplies are available in Emerald Cove Marina. Leashed pets are permitted.

Reservations, fees: Reservations are required; $14 per night.

Contact: Emerald Cove Resort and Marina, (530) 692-3200 or fax (530) 692-3202.

Directions: From Marysville, drive northeast on Highway 20 to Marysville Road. Turn north at Marysville Road (signed Bullards Bar Reservoir) and drive about 10 miles to Old Marysville Road. Turn right and drive 14 miles to reach the Cottage Creek Launch Ramp and the marina (turn right just before the dam).

To reach the ramp at the Dark Day Walk-In, continue over the dam and drive four miles, turn left on Garden Valley Road, and continue to the ramp. From the boat launch, continue to the campground on the northwest side.

Trip notes: Bullards Bar Reservoir is one of the few lakes in the Sierra Nevada to offer boat-in camping at developed boat-in sites and to allow boaters to create their own primitive sites anywhere along the lake's shoreline. A chemical toilet is required gear. Garden Point Boat-In is located on the western shore of the northern Yuba River arm. This lake provides plenty of recreation options, including good fishing for kokanee salmon, waterskiing, and many coves for playing in the water.

⑦ Dark Day Walk-In

Location: On Bullards Bar Reservoir; map C3, grid j2.

Campsites, facilities: There are 16 walk-in tent sites. Picnic tables and fire pits are provided. Piped water and flush and vault toilets are available. A boat ramp is available nearby, and supplies are available at Emerald Cove Marina. Pets must be controlled.

Reservations, fees: Reservations are required; $14 per night. Open year-round.

Contact: Emerald Cove Resort and Marina, (530) 692-3200 or fax (530) 692-3202.

Directions: From Marysville, drive northeast on Highway 20 to Marysville Road. Turn north at

Marysville Road (signed Bullards Bar Reservoir) and drive about 10 miles to Old Marysville Road. Turn right, drive 14 miles, and continue over the dam to Garden Valley Road. Turn left and drive past the boat launch to the campground on the northwest side of the lake.

Trip notes: Along with Schoolhouse, this is the only car-accessible camping area at Bullards Bar Reservoir with direct shoreline access. You park in a central area and then walk a short distance to the campground. The lake is a very short walk beyond that. Bullards Bar is a great camping lake, pretty and large with several lake arms and good fishing for kokanee salmon (as long as you have a boat). It is set at 2,000 feet in the foothills, like a silver dollar in a field of pennies. A bonus at Bullards Bar is that there is never a charge for day use, parking, or boat launching.

⑦ Shoreline Camp Boat-In

Location: On Bullards Bar Reservoir; map C3, grid j2.

Campsites, facilities: Boaters may choose their own primitive campsite anywhere on the shore of Bullards Bar Reservoir. You must burn or pack out your garbage. Supplies are available at Emerald Cove Marina. Pets must be controlled.

Reservations, fees: Reservations and a shoreline camping permit are required; $14 per night. Note: A portable chemical toilet is required for boat-in campers.

Contact: Emerald Cove Resort and Marina, (530) 692-3200 or fax (530) 692-3202.

Directions: From Marysville, turn east on Highway 20 and drive 12 miles. Turn left on Marysville Road (look for the sign for Bullards Bar Reservoir) and drive 10 miles. Turn right on Old Marysville Road and drive 14 miles to the Cottage Creek Launch Ramp (turn right just before the dam). To reach the boat launch, continue to the campgrounds on the west side.

Trip notes: There are two boat-in campgrounds on Bullards Bar Reservoir, but another option is to throw all caution to the wind and just head out on your own, camping wherever you want. It is critical to bring a shovel to dig a flat site for sleeping, a large tarp for sun protection, and of course, plenty of water or a water purification pump. This is a big, beautiful lake, with good trolling for kokanee salmon. Note: a portable chemical toilet is required.

⑦ Madrone Cove Boat-In

Location: On Bullards Bar Reservoir; map C3, grid j2.

Campsites, facilities: There are 10 sites, accessible by boat only. There is no piped water, but picnic tables, fire grills, and vault toilets are provided. You must burn or pack out your garbage. Supplies are available at the marina. Pets must be controlled.

Reservations, fees: Reservations are required; $14 per night.

Contact: Emerald Cove Resort and Marina, (530) 692-3200 or fax (530) 692-3202.

Directions: From Marysville, drive 12 miles east on Highway 20. Turn left at the sign for Bullards Bar Reservoir (Marysville Road). Drive 10 miles north, turn right on Old Marysville Road, and drive 14 miles to reach the Cottage Creek Launch Ramp and the marina (turn right just before the dam). To reach the ramp continue over the dam, drive four miles, turn left on Garden Valley Road, and continue to the ramp. From the boat launch, continue to the campground on the west side.

Trip notes: This is one of several boat-in campgrounds at Bullards Bar Reservoir. It is set on the main Yuba River arm of the lake, along the western shore. This is a premium boat-in site. The elevation is 2,000 feet.

⑦ Schoolhouse

Location: On Bullards Bar Reservoir; map C3, grid j2.

Campsites, facilities: There are 56 sites (one triple, 11 double, and 44 single sites) for tents or RVs. Single sites accommodate six people, double sites accommodate 12, and triple sites hold up to 18 people. Picnic tables, fire grills, piped water, and flush and vault toilets are provided. A boat ramp is nearby. Supplies are available in North San Juan, Camptonville, Dobbins, and at the marina. Pets must be controlled.

Reservations, fees: Reservations are required; $14 per night. Open year-round with limited winter facilities.

Contact: Emerald Cove Resort and Marina, (530) 692-3200 or fax (530) 692-3202.

Directions: From Marysville, turn east on Highway 20 and drive 12 miles. Turn left on Marysville Road (look for the sign for Bullards Bar Reservoir) and drive 10 miles. Turn right on Old Marysville Road, drive 14 miles to the dam, and continue for another three miles to the campground entrance road on the left.

Trip notes: Bullards Bar Reservoir is one of the better lakes in the Sierra Nevada for camping, primarily because the lake levels tend to be higher here than at many other lakes. The camp is set on the southeast shore, with a trail available out of the camp to a beautiful lookout of the lake. Bullards Bar is known for good fishing for trout and kokanee salmon, waterskiing, and all water sports. A three-lane concrete boat ramp is located to the south at Cottage Creek. Boaters should consider the special boat-in camps at the lake. The elevation is 2,200 feet.

⑦ Fiddle Creek

Location: On the North Yuba River in Tahoe National Forest; map C3, grid j3.

Campsites, facilities: There are 15 tent sites. Piped water, vault toilets, picnic tables, and fire pits are provided. Limited supplies are available nearby at the Indian Valley Outpost. Facilities are wheelchair accessible, including a paved trail to the Yuba River. Pets must be controlled.

Reservations, fees: No reservations; $10 per night. Open year-round.

Contact: Tahoe National Forest, North Yuba/Downieville Ranger District, (530) 288-3231 or fax (530) 288-0727.

Directions: From Auburn, take Highway 49 north to Nevada City and continue (the road jogs left, then narrows) to Camptonville. Drive 9.5 miles to the campground entrance.

Trip notes: This camp is situated on the North Yuba River in a quiet, forested area. This is a beautiful stream, one of the prettiest to flow westward out of the Sierra Nevada, with deep pools and miniature waterfalls. It is popular for rafting out of Goodyears Bar, and if you can stand the cold water, there are many good swimming holes along Highway 49. Fiddle Bow Trail leads out from the camp to Halls Ranch Station or Indian Rock. Bring your own drinking water or a water purifier. It's set at 2,200 feet. There are a series of campgrounds located on this stretch of the Yuba River.

76 Cal-Ida/Carlton Flat

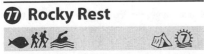

Location: On the North Yuba River in Tahoe National Forest; map C3, grid j3.

Campsites, facilities: There are two undeveloped camping areas. Piped water, picnic tables, barbecues, and vault toilets are provided (one is wheelchair accessible). Some supplies are available at the Indian Valley Outpost nearby. Leashed pets are permitted.

Reservations, fees: No reservations; $10 per night, $5 each additional vehicle.

Contact: Tahoe National Forest, North Yuba/ Downieville Ranger District, (530) 288-3231 or fax (530) 288-0727.

Directions: From Auburn, take Highway 49 north to Nevada City and continue (the road jogs left, then narrows) to Camptonville. Drive nine miles to the campground entrance. The camping area at Lower Carlton Flat is located one mile northeast of the Highway 49 bridge at Indian Valley. The camping area at Upper Carlton Flat is located behind the Indian Valley Outpost on the Cal-Ida Road.

Trip notes: Lower Carlton is on the North Yuba River, and Cal-Ida is across the road. Both are right next door to Fiddle Creek. For more information, see the trip notes for Fiddle Creek (campground number 75).

77 Rocky Rest

Location: On the North Yuba River in Tahoe National Forest; map C3, grid j4.

Campsites, facilities: There are 10 dispersed

camping sites. Piped water, picnic tables, barbecues, and vault toilets are provided. Limited supplies are available at the Indian Valley Outpost nearby. Leashed pets are permitted.

Reservations, fees: No reservations; $10 per night.

Contact: Tahoe National Forest, North Yuba/ Downieville Ranger District, (530) 288-3231 or fax (530) 288-0727.

Directions: From Auburn, take Highway 49 north to Nevada City and continue (the road jogs left, then narrows) to Camptonville. Drive 10 miles north to the campground entrance.

Trip notes: This is one in a series of campgrounds set at streamside on the North Yuba River. The elevation is 2,200 feet. A newly constructed footbridge is now available that crosses the North Yuba and provides an outstanding seven-mile hike.

78 Ramshorn

Location: On the North Yuba River in Tahoe National Forest; map C3, grid j4.

Campsites, facilities: There are a total of 16 sites, nine for tents and seven for RVs up to 22 feet long. Piped water, vault toilets, picnic tables, and fire pits are provided. Supplies are available in Downieville. Leashed pets are permitted.

Reservations, fees: No reservations; $10 per night. Open year-round.

Contact: Tahoe National Forest, North Yuba/ Downieville Ranger District, (530) 288-3231 or fax (530) 288-0727.

Directions: From Auburn, take Highway 49 north to Nevada City and continue (the road jogs left, then narrows) to Camptonville. Drive 15 miles north to the campground entrance.

Trip notes: This camp is set on Ramshorn Creek, just across the road from the North Yuba River. It's one in a series of camps on this stretch of the beautiful North Yuba River. A short distance downstream is a picnic area with a trailhead for the Hallsranch Fiddle Ridge Trail. Goodyears Bar, located one mile east, is a famous access point for white-water rafting trips on the Yuba. The camp's elevation is 2,600 feet.

⑲ Indian Valley

Location: On the North Yuba River in Tahoe National Forest; map C3, grid j4.

Campsites, facilities: There are a total of 17 sites, nine for tents and eight for RVs up to 22 feet long. Piped water, vault toilets, picnic tables, and fire pits are provided. Limited supplies are available nearby at the Indian Valley Outpost. Pets must be controlled.

Reservations, fees: No reservations; $14 per night. Open year-round.

Contact: Tahoe National Forest, North Yuba/ Downieville Ranger District, (530) 288-3231 or fax (530) 288-0727.

Directions: From Auburn, take Highway 49 north to Nevada City and continue (the road jogs left, then narrows) to Camptonville. Drive 10 miles to the camp entrance.

Trip notes: This is an easy-to-reach spot set at 2,200 feet beside the North Yuba River. Highway 49 runs adjacent to the Yuba for miles eastward, providing easy access to the river in many areas. There are several other camps in the immediate area; see the trip notes for Fiddle Creek (campground number 75) and Cal-Ida (campground number 76), both located within a mile.

⑳ Union Flat

Location: On the North Yuba River in Tahoe National Forest; map C3, grid j7.

Campsites, facilities: There are 11 sites for tents or RVs up to 35 feet long. Piped water, vault toilets, picnic tables, and fire pits are provided. Facilities are wheelchair accessible. Supplies are available in Downieville. Leashed pets are permitted.

Reservations, fees: No reservations; $10 per night. Open May through October.

Contact: Tahoe National Forest, North Yuba/ Downieville Ranger District, (530) 288-3231 or fax (530) 288-0727.

Directions: From Auburn, take Highway 49 north to Nevada City and continue (the road jogs left, then narrows) to Downieville. Drive six miles east to the campground entrance.

Trip notes: Of all the campgrounds on the North Yuba River along Highway 49, this one has the best swimming. The camp is set near Quartz Point and Granite Mountain and has a nice swimming hole next to it if you can stand the cold. Recreational mining is also an attraction here. The elevation is 3,400 feet.

㉑ Loganville

Location: On the North Yuba River in Tahoe National Forest; map C3, grid j7.

Campsites, facilities: There are 20 sites for tents or RVs up to 22 feet long. Piped water, vault toilets, and picnic tables are provided. Supplies and a coin laundry are available in Sierra City. Pets must be controlled.

Reservations, fees: No reservations; $10 per night. Open May through October.

Contact: Tahoe National Forest, North Yuba/ Downieville Ranger District, (530) 288-3231 or fax (530) 288-0727.

Directions: From Auburn, take Highway 49 north to Nevada City and continue (the road jogs left, then narrows) to Downieville. Drive 12 miles east to the campground entrance on the right (2 miles west of Sierra City).

Trip notes: Nearby Sierra City is only two miles away, meaning you can make a quick getaway for a prepared meal or any food or drink you may need to add to your camp. Loganville is set on the North Yuba River, elevation 4,200 feet. It offers a good stretch of water in this region for trout fishing, with many pools set below miniature waterfalls.

㉒ Wild Plum

Location: On Haypress Creek in Tahoe National Forest; map C3, grid j8.

Campsites, facilities: There are a total of 47 sites, 26 for tents and 21 for RVs up to 22 feet long. Piped water, vault toilets, picnic tables, and fire pits are provided. Supplies and a coin laundry are available in Sierra City. Pets must be controlled.

Reservations, fees: No reservations; $10 per

night. Open May through October.

Contact: Tahoe National Forest, North Yuba/ Downieville Ranger District, (530) 288-3231 or fax (530) 288-0727.

Directions: From Auburn, take Highway 49 north to Nevada City and continue (the road jogs left, then narrows) past Downieville to Sierra City at Wild Plum Road. Turn right on Wild Plum Road and drive two miles to the campground entrance road on the right.

Trip notes: This popular Forest Service camp is set on Haypress Creek at 4,400 feet. There are several hidden waterfalls in the area, which makes this a well-loved camp for the people who know of them. There's a scenic hike up the Haypress Trail, which goes past a waterfall to Haypress Valley. Two other nearby waterfalls are Loves Falls (on the North Yuba on Highway 49 two miles east of Sierra City) and Hackmans Falls (remote, set in a ravine one mile south of Sierra City; no road access).

⑧ Chapman Creek

Location: On the North Yuba River in Tahoe National Forest; map C3, grid j9.

Campsites, facilities: There are a total of 29 sites, 15 for tents and 14 for RVs up to 22 feet long. Piped water, vault toilets, picnic tables, and fire pits are provided. Supplies are available in Bassetts. Leashed pets are permitted.

Reservations, fees: No reservations; $10 per night. Open June through October.

Contact: Tahoe National Forest, North Yuba/ Downieville Ranger District, (530) 288-3231 or fax (530) 288-0727.

Directions: From Truckee, turn north on Highway 89 and drive 20 miles to Sierraville. At Sierraville, turn left on Highway 49, drive over Yuba

Pass, and continue for four miles to the campground on the right.

Trip notes: This camp is set along Chapman Creek at 6,000 feet, just across the highway from where it enters the North Yuba River. A good side trip is to hike the Chapman Creek Trail, which leads out of camp to Beartrap Meadow or to Haskell Peak (8,107 feet).

⑧ Sierra

Location: On the North Yuba River in Tahoe National Forest; map C3, grid j9.

Campsites, facilities: There are nine sites for tents and seven sites for tents or RVs up to 22 feet long. There is no piped water, but vault toilets, picnic tables, and fire pits are provided. Supplies are available in Bassetts. Pets must be controlled.

Reservations, fees: No reservations; $10 per night. Open June through October.

Contact: Tahoe National Forest, North Yuba/ Downieville Ranger District, (530) 288-3231 or fax (530) 288-0727.

Directions: From Truckee, turn north on Highway 89 and drive 20 miles to Sierraville. At Sierraville, turn left on Highway 49 and drive over Yuba Pass. Continue for five miles to the campground on the left side of the road.

Trip notes: This is a primitive and easy-to-reach spot set along the North Yuba River, used primarily as an overflow area from nearby Chapman Creek (located a mile upstream). Nearby recreation options include the Chapman Creek Trail (see the trip notes for Chapman Creek, campground number 83), several waterfalls (see Wild Plum, campground number 82), and the nearby Lakes Basin Recreation Area to the north off the Gold Lake Highway. The elevation is 5,600 feet.

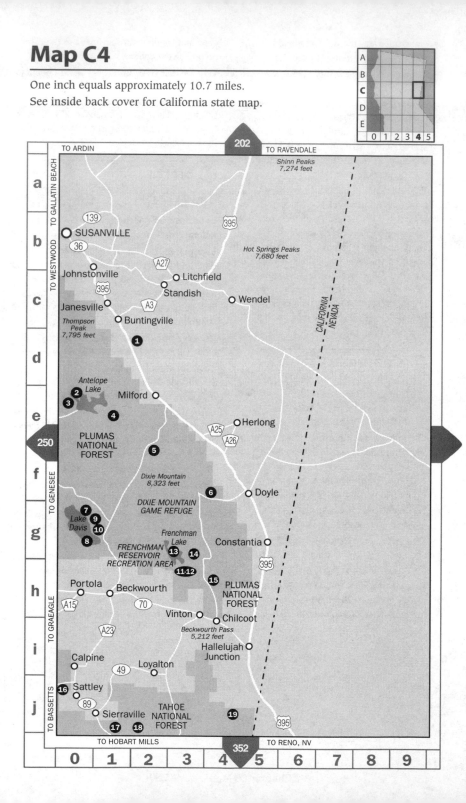

Map C4

One inch equals approximately 10.7 miles.
See inside back cover for California state map.

TO ARDIN
TO RAVENDALE

202

TO GALLATIN BEACH

Shinn Peaks
7,274 feet

a

139

b
TO WESTWOOD
SUSANVILLE
36
395
Hot Springs Peaks
7,680 feet
A27

Johnstonville
Litchfield
395
Standish

c
Janesville
A3
Wendel
Buntingville

Thompson
Peak
7,795 feet

1

CALIFORNIA
NEVADA

d

Antelope
Lake
2
Milford
3
4

e
TO GENESEE
250
PLUMAS
NATIONAL
FOREST
Herlong
A25
A26

5

Dixie Mountain
8,323 feet

DIXIE MOUNTAIN
GAME REFUGE
6
Doyle

f

7
Lake
Davis
9
10
8
FRENCHMAN
RESERVOIR
RECREATION AREA
Frenchman
Lake
13
14
11-12
15
Constantia
395

g

h
TO GRAEAGLE
Portola
Beckwourth
A15
70
Vinton
Chilcoot
PLUMAS
NATIONAL
FOREST

A23
Beckwourth Pass
5,212 feet
Hallelujah
Junction

i
TO BASSETTS
Calpine
Loyalton
49

Sattley
16
89
Sierraville
TAHOE
NATIONAL
FOREST
19
395

j
17
18
352
TO HOBART MILLS
TO RENO, NV

Chapter C4 features:

❶ Honey Lake Campground

Location: Near Milford; map C4, grid d2.

Campsites, facilities: There are 50 sites for tents or RVs, most with full or partial hookups. Picnic tables are provided. Rest rooms, showers, laundry room, sanitary disposal station, propane gas, grocery store, playground, ice, wood, and a game room are available. Leashed pets are permitted.

Reservations, fees: Reservations are accepted; $12.50 to $16.50 per night.

Contact: Honey Lake Campground, (530) 253-2508.

Directions: From Susanville on US 395, drive 19 miles south (if you reach Milford, you have gone two miles too far) to the campground.

Trip notes: For newcomers, Honey Lake is a strange looking place—a vast, flat alkali lake with not much around. It sits in a huge basin that, from a distance, looks almost moonlike. The campground is set at 4,300 feet and covers 27 acres, most of it overlooking the lake. There are a lot of junipers and scraggly aspens nearby, and a waterfowl management area is located along the north shore of the lake.

❷ Boulder Creek

Location: At Antelope Lake in Plumas National Forest; map C4, grid e0.

Campsites, facilities: There are 70 sites for tents or RVs. Piped water, vault toilets, picnic tables, and fire grills are provided. A sanitary dump station, boat ramp, and grocery store are nearby. Leashed pets are permitted.

Reservations, fees: Reserve via phone at (877) 444-6777 ($8.65 reservation fee) or website www.reserveusa.com; $13 per night, lakeshore sites are $15 per night; $3 for an extra vehicle. Open May through October.

Contact: Plumas National Forest, Mount Hough Ranger District, (530) 283-0555 or fax (530) 283-1821.

Directions: From Red Bluff, drive east on Highway 36 to Susanville and US 395. Turn south on US 395 and drive about 10 miles (one mile past Janesville) to County Road 208. Turn right on County Road 208 (signed Antelope Lake) and drive about 15 miles to a Y (one mile before Antelope Lake). Turn left at the Y and drive four miles to the campground entrance on the right side of the road (on the northwest end of the lake).

Trip notes: Antelope Lake is a pretty mountain lake circled by conifers with nice campsites and good trout fishing. It is set at 5,000 feet in remote eastern Plumas National Forest, far enough away so the marginally inclined never make the trip. Campgrounds are located at each end of the lake (this one is just north of Lone Rock at the north end), with a boat ramp at Lost Cove on the east side of the lake. The lake isn't huge, but it is big enough, with 15 miles of shoreline and little islands, coves, and peninsulas to give it an intimate feel.

③ Lone Rock

Location: At Antelope Lake in Plumas National Forest; map C4, grid e0.

Campsites, facilities: There are 86 sites for tents or RVs up to 45 feet long. Piped water, vault toilets, picnic tables, and fire grills are provided. A sanitary dump station, boat ramp, and grocery store are nearby. Leashed pets are permitted.

Reservations, fees: Reserve via phone at (877) 444-6777 ($8.65 reservation fee) or website www.reserveusa.com; $13 to $15 per night, $3 for an extra vehicle. Open May through October.

Contact: Plumas National Forest, Mount Hough Ranger District, (530) 283-0555 or fax (530) 283-1821.

Directions: From Red Bluff, drive east on Highway 36 to Susanville and US 395. Go south on US 395 and drive about 10 miles (one mile past Janesville) to County Road 208. Turn right on County Road 208 (signed Antelope Lake) and drive about 15 miles to a Y (one mile before Antelope Lake). Turn left at the Y and drive three miles to the campground entrance on the right side of the road (on the northwest end of the lake).

Trip notes: This camp provides an option to nearby Boulder Creek, located to the immediate north at the northwest shore of Antelope Lake. For more information, see the trip notes for Boulder Creek (campground number two). The elevation is 5,000 feet. Campfire programs are offered in the summer at the on-site amphitheater.

④ Long Point

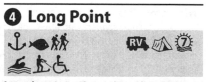

Location: At Antelope Lake in Plumas National Forest; map C4, grid e1.

Campsites, facilities: There are 38 single sites and four group sites for tents or RVs up to 50 feet long. Piped water, vault toilets, picnic tables, and fire grills are provided. A grocery store, boat ramp, and sanitary dump station are nearby. Leashed pets are permitted.

Reservations, fees: Reserve via phone at (877) 444-6777 ($8.65 reservation fee) or website www.reserveusa.com; $12 to $14 per night; group sites are $20 to $33 per night. Open May through October.

Contact: Plumas National Forest, Greenville Work Center, Mount Hough Ranger District, (530) 284-7126 or fax (530) 284-6211.

Directions: From Red Bluff, drive east on Highway 36 to Susanville and US 395. Go south on US 395 and drive about 10 miles (one mile past Janesville) to County Road 208. Turn right on County Road 208 (signed Antelope Lake) and drive about 15 miles to a Y (one mile before Antelope Lake). Turn right at the Y and drive one mile to the campground entrance on the left side of the road.

Trip notes: Long Point is a pretty camp set on a peninsula that extends well into Antelope Lake, facing Lost Cove. There are actually two camps here, with a bonus group camp set on the east side of the main campground. The lake's boat ramp is at Lost Cove, a three-mile drive around the northeast shore. Trout fishing is often good here, with a wide variety of sizes, from the little stocked Slim Jim rainbow trout on up to some large brown trout. A wheelchair-accessible nature trail and fishing pier are available.

⑤ Conklin Park

Location: On Willow Creek in Plumas National Forest; map C4, grid f2.

Campsites, facilities: There are nine sites for tents or RVs up to 22 feet long. There is no piped water, but vault toilets, picnic tables, and fire grills are provided. Leashed pets are permitted.

Reservations, fees: No reservations; no fee. Open May through October.

Contact: Plumas National Forest, Beckwourth Ranger District, (530) 836-2575 or fax (530) 836-0493.

Directions: From Susanville on US 395, drive south for 24 miles to Milford. In Milford turn right (east) on County Road 336 and drive about four miles to a Y. Bear to the left on Forest Service Road 70/26N70 and drive three miles. Turn right at the bridge at Willow Creek, turn left on Forest Service Road 70 (now paved), and drive three miles to the camp entrance road on the left side.

Trip notes: This camp is located along little Willow Creek on the northeastern border of the Dixie Mountain State Game Refuge. Much of the area is recovering from a fire that burned during the summer of 1989. Although the area has greened up, there remains significant evidence of the fire. The campground is little known, primitive, rarely used, and is not likely to change any time soon. The elevation is 5,900 feet.

❻ Meadow View

Location: Near Little Last Chance Creek in Plumas National Forest; map C4, grid f4.

Campsites, facilities: There are six sites for tents or RVs. There is no piped water, but vault toilets, picnic tables, and fire grills are provided. Leashed pets are permitted.

Reservations, fees: No reservations; no fee. Open May through October.

Contact: Plumas National Forest, Beckwourth Ranger District, (530) 836-2575 or fax (530) 836-0493.

Directions: From Reno, drive north on US 395 for 43 miles to Doyle. At Doyle, turn west on Doyle Grade Road/County Road 331 (a dirt road most of the way) and drive 7.5 miles to the campground.

Trip notes: This little-known, primitive camp is set along the headwaters of Little Last Chance Creek, along the eastern border of the Dixie Mountain State Game Refuge. The access road continues along the creek and connects with primitive roads that enter the interior of the game refuge. Side trip options include Frenchman Lake to the south, and the drive up to Dixie Mountain, at 8,323 feet in elevation. The elevation is 6,100 feet.

❼ Lightning Tree

Location: On Lake Davis in Plumas National Forest; map C4, grid g0.

Campsites, facilities: There are 38 sites for RVs. There is no piped water. Vault toilets, sanitary dump station, and a cartop boat launch are nearby. Leashed pets are permitted.

Reservations, fees: Reservations are accepted for some sites, reserve via phone at (877) 444-6777 ($8.65 reservation fee) or website www. reserveusa.com; $6 per night, $10 for a double site.

Contact: Plumas National Forest, Beckwourth Ranger District, (530) 836-2575 or fax (530) 836-0493.

Directions: From Truckee, turn north on Highway 89 and drive to Sattley and County Road A23. Turn right on County Road A23 and drive 13 miles to Highway 70. Turn left on Highway 70 and drive one mile to Grizzly Road. Turn right on Grizzly Road and drive about six miles to Lake Davis. Continue north on Lake Davis Road along the lake's east shore and drive about five miles to the campground entrance on the left side of the road.

Trip notes: Lake Davis is one of the top mountain lakes for fishing in California, with large rainbow trout in the early summer and fall, and an improving bass fishery in the summer. This camp is perfectly situated for a fishing trip. It is located at Lightning Tree Point on the lake's remote northeast shore, directly across the lake from Freeman Creek, one of the better spots for big trout. A boat launch is available on the north side of the camp, a great bonus. Davis is a good-sized lake, with 30 miles of shoreline, set high in the northern Sierra at 5,775 feet, so it gets lots of snow and often freezes over in the winter.

❽ Grizzly

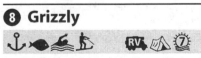

Location: On Lake Davis in Plumas National Forest; map C4, grid g0.

Campsites, facilities: There are 55 sites for tents or RVs up to 32 feet long. Piped water, flush toilets, picnic tables, and fire grills are provided. A boat ramp, grocery store, and sanitary dump station are nearby. Leashed pets are permitted.

Reservations, fees: Reservations are accepted for some sites; $13 per night. Open May through October.

Contact: Plumas National Forest, Beckwourth Ranger District, (530) 836-2575 or fax (530) 836-0493.

Directions: From Truckee, turn north on Highway 89 and drive to Sattley and County Road A23. Turn right on County Road A23 and drive 13 miles to Highway 70. Turn left on Highway 70 and drive one mile to Grizzly Road. Turn right on Grizzly Road and drive about six miles to Lake Davis. Continue north on Lake Davis Road for less than a mile to the campground entrance on the left side of the road.

Trip notes: This is one of the better developed campgrounds at Lake Davis and is a popular spot for camping anglers. Its proximity to the Grizzly Store, located just over the dam to the south, makes getting last-minute supplies a snap. In addition, a boat ramp is located to the north in Honker Cove, providing access to the southern reaches of the lake, including the island area, where trout trolling is good in early summer and fall.

⑨ Grasshopper Flat

Location: On Lake Davis in Plumas National Forest; map C4, grid g0.

Campsites, facilities: There are 70 sites for tents or RVs up to 32 feet long. Piped water, flush toilets, picnic tables, and fire grills are provided. A boat ramp, grocery store, and sanitary dump station are nearby. Leashed pets are permitted.

Reservations, fees: Reservations are accepted for some sites; $13 per night. Open May through October.

Contact: Plumas National Forest, Beckwourth Ranger District, (530) 836-2575 or fax (530) 836-0493.

Directions: From Truckee, turn north on Highway 89 and drive to Sattley and County Road A23. Turn right on County Road A23 and drive 13 miles to Highway 70. Turn left on Highway 70 and drive one mile to Grizzly Road. Turn right on Grizzly Road and drive about six miles to Lake Davis. Continue north on Lake Davis Road for a mile (just past Grizzly, campground number eight) to the campground entrance on the left side of the road.

Trip notes: Grasshopper Flat provides a nearby alternative to Grizzly at Lake Davis, with the nearby boat ramp at adjacent Honker Cove a primary attraction for campers with trailered boats for fishing. The camp is on the southeast end of the lake, at 5,800 feet elevation. Lake Davis is known for its large rainbow trout that bite best in early summer and fall.

⑩ Crocker

Location: In Plumas National Forest; map C4, grid g1.

Campsites, facilities: There are 10 sites for tents or RVs up to 32 feet long. There is no piped water, but vault toilets, picnic tables, and fire grills are provided. Leashed pets are permitted.

Reservations, fees: No reservations; no fee. Open May through October.

Contact: Plumas National Forest, Beckwourth Ranger District, (530) 836-2575 or fax (530) 836-0493.

Directions: From Reno, drive north on US 395 to the junction with Highway 70. Turn west on Highway 70 and drive to Beckwourth and County Road 111/Beckwourth-Genessee Road. Turn right on County Road 111 and drive six miles to the campground on the left side of the road.

Trip notes: Even though this camp is located just four miles east of Lake Davis, it is little known and little used since there are three lakeside camps close by. This camp is set in Plumas National Forest at 5,800 feet elevation, and it is about a 15-minute drive north to the border of the Dixie Mountain State Game Refuge.

⑪ Frenchman

Location: On Frenchman Lake in Plumas National Forest; map C4, grid h3.

Campsites, facilities: There are 38 sites for tents or RVs. Piped water, vault toilets, picnic tables, and fire grills are provided. A sanitary dump station and boat ramp are nearby. Leashed pets are permitted.

Reservations, fees: Reserve via phone at

(877) 444-6777 ($8.65 reservation fee) or website www.reserveusa.com; $12 per night. Open May through October.

Contact: Plumas National Forest, Beckwourth Ranger District, (530) 836-2575 or fax (530) 836-0493.

Directions: From Reno, drive north on US 395 to the junction with Highway 70. Turn west on Highway 70 and drive to Chilcoot and the junction with Frenchman Lake Road. Turn right on Frenchman Lake Road and drive nine miles to the lake and to a Y. At the Y, turn right and drive 1.5 miles to the campground on the left side of the road.

Trip notes: Frenchman Lake is set at 5,500 feet in elevation, on the edge of high desert to the east and forest to the west. This camp is on the southeast end of the lake, where there are four other campgrounds, including a group camp and a boat ramp. The lake provides good fishing for stocked rainbow trout. The best fishing is in the cove near the campgrounds and the two inlets, one along the west shore and one at the head of the lake. The proximity to Reno, only 35 miles away, keeps gambling in the back of the minds of many anglers. Because of water demands downstream, the lake often drops significantly by the end of summer.

---

⑫ Cottonwood Springs

Location: Near Frenchman Lake in Plumas National Forest; map C4, grid h3.

Campsites, facilities: There are 20 sites for tents or RVs up to 50 feet long and two group camping areas which can accommodate up to 25 and 50 people, respectively. Piped water, flush toilets, picnic tables, and fire grills are provided. A boat ramp and sanitary dump station are nearby. Leashed pets are permitted.

Reservations, fees: Reserve via phone at (877) 444-6777 ($8.65 reservation fee) or website www.reserveusa.com; $12 per night, $44 to $87 per night for groups. Open May through October.

Contact: Plumas National Forest, Beckwourth Ranger District, (530) 836-2575 or fax (530) 836-0493.

Directions: From Reno, drive north on US 395 to the junction with Highway 70. Turn west on Highway 70 and drive to Chilcoot and the junction with Frenchman Lake Road. Turn right on Frenchman Lake Road and drive nine miles to the lake and to a Y. At the Y, turn left and drive 1.5 miles to the campground on the left side of the road.

Trip notes: Cottonwood Springs, elevation 5,700 feet, is largely an overflow camp at Frenchman Lake. The more popular Frenchman, Big Cove, and Spring Creek (campground numbers 11, 13, and 14) are located along the southeast shore of the lake near a boat ramp. Cottonwood Springs, on the other hand, is set on a creek about two miles from the dam. However, there is a great side trip here, taking Forest Service Road 24N52 out of camp to the southwest and driving through the Little Last Chance Canyon Scenic Area; the road dead-ends about seven miles in.

---

⑬ Big Cove

Location: At Frenchman Lake in Plumas National Forest; map C4, grid g3.

Campsites, facilities: There are 38 sites for tents or RVs up to 50 feet long (19 are multiple-family units; 10 are wheelchair accessible). Piped water, flush toilets, picnic tables, and fire grills are provided. A boat ramp, sanitary dump station, grocery store, and propane gas are available nearby. Pets are permitted.

Reservations, fees: Reserve via phone at (877) 444-6777 ($8.65 reservation fee) or website www.reserveusa.com; $12 to $22 per night. Open May through September.

Contact: Plumas National Forest, Beckwourth Ranger District, (530) 836-2575 or fax (530) 836-0493.

Directions: From Reno, drive north on US 395 to the junction with Highway 70. Turn west on Highway 70 and drive to Chilcoot and the junction with Frenchman Lake Road. Turn right on Frenchman Lake Road and drive nine miles to the lake and to a Y. At the Y, turn right and drive two miles to Forest Service Road 24N01. Turn left and drive a short distance to the campground entrance on the left side of the road.

Trip notes: Big Cove is one of four camps at the southeastern end of Frenchman Lake, with a boat ramp available about a mile away near the Frenchman and Spring Creek camps. See the trip notes for Frenchman (campground number 11) for more information. A trail from the campground leads to the lakeshore.

⑭ Spring Creek

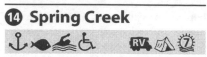

Location: On Frenchman Lake in Plumas National Forest; map C4, grid g3.

Campsites, facilities: There are 35 sites for tents or RVs up to 55 feet long. Piped water, vault toilets, picnic tables, and fire grills are provided. A boat ramp and sanitary dump station are nearby. Leashed pets are permitted.

Reservations, fees: Reserve via phone at (877) 444-6777 ($8.65 reservation fee) or website www.reserveusa.com; $12 per night.

Contact: Plumas National Forest, Beckwourth Ranger District, (530) 836-2575 or fax (530) 836-0493.

Directions: From Reno, drive north on US 395 to the junction with Highway 70. Turn west on Highway 70 and drive to Chilcoot and the junction with Frenchman Lake Road. Turn right on Frenchman Lake Road and drive nine miles to the lake and to a Y. At the Y, turn right and drive two miles to the campground on the left side of the road.

Trip notes: Frenchman Lake is set at 5,500 feet elevation, on the edge of high desert to the east and forest to the west. This camp is on the southeast end of the lake, where there are four other campgrounds, including a group camp and a boat ramp. The lake provides good fishing for stocked rainbow trout, best in the cove near the campgrounds.

⑮ Chilcoot

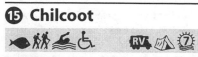

Location: On Little Last Chance Creek in Plumas National Forest; map C4, grid h4.

Campsites, facilities: There are five walk-in sites for tents and 35 sites for tents or RVs up to 45 feet long. Two sites are wheelchair acces-

sible. Piped water, flush toilets, picnic tables, and fire grills are provided. A boat ramp, grocery store, and sanitary dump station are nearby. Leashed pets are permitted.

Reservations, fees: Reserve via phone at (877) 444-6777 ($8.65 reservation fee) or website www.reserveusa.com; $12 per night. Open May through October.

Contact: Plumas National Forest, Beckwourth Ranger District, (530) 836-2575 or fax (530) 836-0493.

Directions: From Reno, drive north on US 395 to the junction with Highway 70. Turn west on Highway 70 and drive to Chilcoot and the junction with Frenchman Lake Road. Turn right on Frenchman Lake Road and drive six miles to the campground on the left side of the road.

Trip notes: This small camp is set along Little Last Chance Creek at 5,400 feet in elevation, about three miles downstream from Frenchman Lake. The stream once provided excellent trout fishing, but it is now largely overgrown with brush, making fishing access very difficult.

⑯ Yuba Pass

Location: In Tahoe National Forest; map C4, grid j0.

Campsites, facilities: There are 20 sites for tents or RVs up to 22 feet long. Piped water, vault toilets, picnic tables, and fire grills are provided. Supplies are available at Bassetts. Pets must be controlled.

Reservations, fees: No reservations; $10 per night. Open late June through October.

Contact: Tahoe National Forest, Sierraville Ranger District, (530) 994-3401 or fax (530) 994-3143.

Directions: From Truckee, drive north on Highway 89 past Sattley to the junction with Highway 49. Turn west on Highway 49 and drive about six miles to the campground on the left side of the road.

Trip notes: This camp is set right at Yuba Pass at an elevation of 6,700 feet. In the winter, the surrounding area is a sno-park, which gives it an unusual look in summer months. Yuba Pass is a popular bird-watching area in the summer.

⑰ Cottonwood Creek

Location: In Tahoe National Forest; map C4, grid j1.

Campsites, facilities: There are 21 sites for tents and 28 sites for tents or RVs up to 22 feet long. There is also a group camp that can accommodate up to 125 people. Piped water, vault toilets, picnic tables, and fire grills are provided. Supplies are available in Sierraville. Pets must be controlled.

Reservations, fees: Reserve via phone at (877) 444-6777 ($8.65 reservation fee) or website www.reserveusa.com; $9 per night, $5 for each additional vehicle; group camp is $206.25 per night. Open May through October.

Contact: Tahoe National Forest, Sierraville Ranger District, (530) 994-3401 or fax (530) 994-3143.

Directions: From Truckee, drive north on Highway 89 for about 20 miles to the campground entrance road on the right (a half mile past Cold Creek Camp). Turn right and drive a quarter mile to the campground.

Trip notes: This camp sits beside Cottonwood Creek at 5,800 feet elevation. An interpretive trail starts at the camp and makes a short loop, and there are several nearby side trip options, including trout fishing on the Little Truckee River to the nearby south, visiting the Sierra Valley Hot Springs out of Sierraville to the nearby north, or venturing into the surrounding Tahoe National Forest.

⑱ Bear Valley

Location: On Bear Valley Creek in Tahoe National Forest; map C4, grid j2.

Campsites, facilities: There are 10 tent and/or trailer sites. Piped water, vault toilets, picnic tables, and fire grills are provided. Supplies are available in Sierraville. Pets must be controlled.

Reservations, fees: No reservations; no fee. Open June through October.

Contact: Tahoe National Forest, Sierraville Ranger District, (530) 994-3401 or fax (530) 994-3143.

Directions: From Truckee, drive north on Highway 89 about 17 miles. Turn right on County Road 451 and drive northeast about six miles to the campground entrance.

Trip notes: The surrounding national forest land was largely burned by the historic Cottonwood Fire of 1994, but the camp itself was saved. It is set on the headwaters of Bear Valley Creek, 6,700 feet in elevation, with a spring adjacent to the campground. The road leading southeast out of camp is routed to Sardine Peak (8,134 feet), where there is a dramatic view of the burned region. There is an 18-mile loop OHV trail across the road from the campground.

⑲ Lookout

Location: In Humboldt-Toiyabe National Forest; map C4, grid j4.

Campsites, facilities: There are 15 sites for tents and four sites for tents or RVs up to 22 feet long, plus a group campground that can accommodate up to 16 people. Pit toilets, picnic tables, and fire grills are provided. No piped water is available. Pets must be controlled.

Reservations, fees: No reservations; $5 per night. Open May through September.

Contact: Humboldt-Toiyabe National Forest, Carson Ranger District, (702) 882-2766.

Directions: From Truckee on Interstate 80, drive east across the state line into Nevada to Verdi. Take the Verdi exit and drive north through town to Old Dog Valley Road. Drive north on Old Dog Valley Road for 11 miles to the campground.

Trip notes: This primitive camp is set in remote country near the California/Nevada border at 6,700 feet. It is a former mining site, and the highlight here is a quartz crystal mine a short distance from the campground. Stampede Reservoir provides a side trip option, about 10 miles to the southwest, over the rough dirt Henness Pass Road.

Special Note: The campground may be closed for removal of timber debris; call for status.

Map D0

One inch equals approximately 10.7 miles.
See inside back cover for California state map.

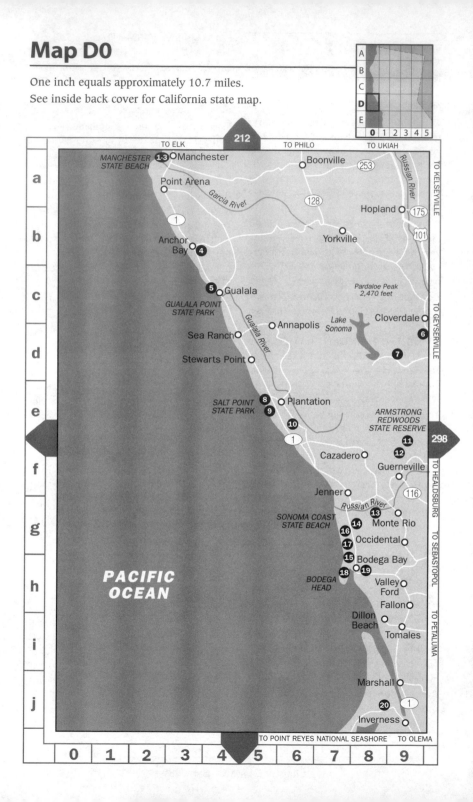

Chapter DØ features:

1 Manchester State Beach

Location: Near Point Arena; map DØ, grid a2.

Campsites, facilities: There are 46 sites for tents or RVs up to 35 feet long. Piped water, chemical toilets, picnic tables, and fire grills are provided. A sanitary dump station is available. Leashed pets are permitted.

Reservations, fees: No reservations; $12 per night, $1 pet fee. Open year-round.

Contact: Manchester State Beach, (707) 937-5804.

Directions: From Santa Rosa on US 101, turn west on Highway 12 (it becomes Highway 116 at Forestville) and drive to Highway 1 at Jenner. Turn north on Highway 1 and drive 55 miles to Point Arena. From Point Arena, continue about two miles north to the park on the left side of the road.

Trip notes: Manchester State Beach is a beautiful park on the Sonoma coast, set near the Garcia River with the town of Point Arena to the nearby north providing a supply point. If you hit it during one of the rare times when the skies are clear and the wind is down, the entire area will seem aglow in magical sunbeams. The Alder Creek Trail is a great hike here, routed north along beachfront to the mouth of Alder Creek and its beautiful coastal lagoon. This is where the San Andreas Fault heads off from land and into the sea.

2 Manchester Beach KOA

Location: North of Point Arena at Manchester State Beach; map DØ, grid a2.

Campsites, facilities: There are 63 sites for RVs, some with full or partial hookups. There are also 18 cabins and 48 tent sites. Rest rooms, showers, heated pool (seasonal), hot tub and spa, recreation room, playground, dump station, picnic tables, and fire grills are provided. A grocery store, ice, wood, a coin laundry, and propane gas are available. Pets are permitted.

Reservations, fees: Reservations are accepted; $28 to $35 per night for two people; each additional child (17 and under) is $3, each additional adult (18 and over) is $5. Cabins are $41 to $49 per night. Open year-round.

Contact: Manchester Beach KOA, PO Box 266, Manchester, CA 95459; (707) 882-2375 or fax (707) 882-3104; website www.mcn.org/a/mendokoa.

Directions: From Santa Rosa on US 101, turn west on Highway 12 (it becomes Highway 116 at Forestville) and drive to Highway 1 at Jenner. Turn north on Highway 1 and drive 55 miles to Point Arena. From Point Arena, continue north for about two miles to the park on the left side of the road.

Trip notes: This is a privately operated KOA park set beside Highway 1 and near the beautiful Manchester State Beach. A great plus here is the cute little log cabins, complete with electric heat. They can provide a great sense of privacy, and after a good sleep, campers are ready to explore the adjacent state park.

❸ Rollerville Junction

Location: Near Point Arena; map DØ, grid a2.

Campsites, facilities: There are 51 sites for tents or RVs (12 are drive-through), 41 with full hookups. Rest rooms, hot showers, hot tub, heated swimming pool, clubhouse with full kitchen, playground, cable TV hookups, sanitary dump station, picnic tables, and fire grills are provided. Laundry facilities, small store, and propane gas are available. Facilities are wheelchair accessible. Leashed pets are permitted.

Reservations, fees: Reservations are accepted; $23 to $27 per night. Open year-round.

Contact: Rollerville Junction, (707) 882-2440 or fax (707) 882-3049; website www.campgrounds.com/rollerville.

Directions: From Santa Rosa on US 101, turn west on Highway 12 (it becomes Highway 116 at Forestville) and drive to Highway 1 at Jenner. Turn north on Highway 1 and drive 55 miles to Point Arena. From Point Arena continue north for two miles to the campground.

Trip notes: This privately operated campground has gone through recent renovation, with more future improvements anticipated. Its location makes it an attractive spot, with the beautiful Manchester State Beach, Alder Creek, and Garcia River all available nearby on one of California's most attractive stretches of coastline. The elevation of the camp is 220 feet.

❹ Anchor Bay Campground

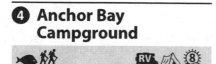

Location: Near Gualala; map DØ, grid b3.

Campsites, facilities: There are 25 sites for tents or RVs, many with water and electrical hookups. Rest rooms, hot showers, sanitary dump station, picnic tables, and fire grills are provided. Leashed pets are permitted.

Reservations, fees: Reservations are accepted; $25 to $27 per night. Open year-round.

Contact: Anchor Bay Campground, (707) 884-4222.

Directions: From Santa Rosa on US 101, turn west on Highway 12 (it becomes Highway 116 at Forestville) and drive to Highway 1 at Jenner. Turn north on Highway 1 and drive 38 miles to Gualala. From Gualala, continue four miles north on Highway 1 to the campground on the left side of the road.

Trip notes: This is a quiet and beautiful stretch of California coast. The campground is located on the ocean side of Highway 1 north of Gualala, with sites set on an ocean bluff as well as amid trees—take your pick. Nearby Gualala Regional Park provides an excellent easy hike, the headlands-to-beach loop with coastal views, a lookout of the Gualala River, and many giant cypress trees. In winter, the nearby Gualala River attracts large but elusive steelhead.

❺ Gualala Point

Location: At Sonoma County Regional Park; map DØ, grid c4.

Campsites, facilities: There are 18 sites for tents and RVs up to 30 feet long, five walk-in tent sites, and two hike-in/bike-in sites. Rest rooms, coin-operated showers, sanitary dump station, picnic tables, and fire grills are provided. Wood is available. The facilities are wheelchair accessible. Leashed pets are permitted.

Reservations, fees: No reservations; $15 per night, $3 per night for hike-in/bike-in sites, $5 per extra vehicle, $1 pet fee.

Contact: Gualala Point, (707) 785-2377.

Directions: From Santa Rosa on US 101, turn west on Highway 12 (it becomes Highway 116 at Forestville) and drive to Highway 1 at Jenner. Turn north on Highway 1 and drive 38 miles to Gualala. Turn right at the park entrance (a day-use area is located on the west side of the highway).

Trip notes: This is a dramatic spot right on the ocean, adjacent to the mouth of the Gualala River. A trail along the bluff provides an easy hiking adventure; on the west side of the highway other trails to the beach are available.

6 Dutcher Creek RV Park and Camp

Location: Near Lake Sonoma; map DØ, grid d9.

Campsites, facilities: There are 10 tent sites and 38 RV sites (two are drive-through), five with full and many with partial hookups. Picnic tables are provided. Flush toilets, showers, sanitary disposal station, pay phone, and coin laundry are available. Leashed pets are permitted.

Reservations, fees: Reservations are accepted; $12 to $20 per night. Open year-round.

Contact: Dutcher Creek RV Park and Camp, (707) 894-4829.

Directions: From Santa Rosa, drive north on US 101 beyond Healdsburg to the Dutcher Creek exit (just south of Cloverdale). Take the Dutcher Creek exit, drive west on Theresa Drive under the freeway, continue a half mile to the end of Theresa Drive, and follow signs to the park office at 230 Theresa Drive.

Trip notes: This privately operated camp provides a layover for US 101 cruisers. It has both native and seasonal plant displays, exceptional opportunities for native bird-watching, and the nearby Asti Vineyard provides a side trip. Lake Sonoma is located seven miles to the west, with the best access provided to the south out of Dry Creek Road (see listing for Lake Sonoma, campground number seven). The elevation is 385 feet.

7 Lake Sonoma Recreation Area

Location: Near Healdsburg; map DØ, grid d9.

Campsites, facilities: There are 15 primitive boat-in sites around the lake, and 113 tent sites and two group sites at Liberty Glen Campground located 2.5 miles from the lake. Picnic tables, fire grills, and portable toilets are provided at the primitive sites, but no piped water is available. Piped water, flush toilets, solar-heated showers, and a sanitary disposal station are available in Liberty Glen. A boat ramp and boat rentals are available. Saturday night campfire talks are held at the two amphitheaters during the summer. Campsites have limited facilities in winter. Leashed pets are permitted.

Reservations, fees: No reservations; $8 per night, $7 for each additional vehicle. A permit is required from the visitor center. Liberty Glen fees are $14 per night; call for group fees and reservations. Open year-round.

Contact: US Army Corps of Engineers, Lake Sonoma, (707) 433-9483.

Directions: From Santa Rosa, drive north on US 101 to Healdsburg. In Healdsburg, take the Dry Creek Road exit, turn left, and drive northwest for 11 miles. After crossing a small bridge, the visitor center will be on your right.

Trip notes: Lake Sonoma is rapidly becoming one of the best weekend vacation sites for Bay Area campers. The developed campground (Liberty Glen) is fine for car campers, but the boat-in sites are ideal for folks who desire a quiet and pretty lakeside setting. This is a big lake, extending nine miles north on the Dry Creek arm and four miles west on the Warm Springs Creek arm. There is an adjacent 8,000-acre wildlife area with 40 miles of hiking trails. The water-skier versus angler conflict has been resolved by limiting high-speed boats to specified areas. Laws are strictly enforced, making this lake excellent for either sport. The best fishing is in the protected coves of the Warm Springs and Dry Creek arms of the lake; use live minnows for bass, which are available at the Dry Creek Store located on the access road south of the lake. The visitor center is adjacent to a public fish hatchery. Salmon and steelhead come to spawn from the Russian River between October and March.

8 Salt Point State Park

Location: Near Fort Ross; map DØ, grid e5.

Campsites, facilities: There are 109 sites for tents or RVs up to 31 feet long, 20 walk-in tent sites, 10 hike-in/bike-in sites, and a group site. Picnic tables, fire grills, and piped water are provided. Flush and pit toilets and a sanitary disposal station are available. The picnic areas and some hiking trails are wheelchair accessible. Leashed pets are permitted, except on trails.

Reservations, fees: Reserve via phone at (800) 444-PARK/7275 ($7.50 reservation fee) or website www.cal-parks.ca.gov; $16 per night. Open year-round.

Contact: Salt Point State Park, (707) 847-3221 or (707) 865-2391.

Directions: From Santa Rosa on US 101, turn west on Highway 12 (it becomes Highway 116 at Forestville) and drive to Highway 1 at Jenner. Turn north on Highway 1 and drive about 20 miles to the park entrance at Gerstle Cove.

Trip notes: This is a gorgeous piece of Sonoma coast, highlighted by Fisk Mill Cove, inshore kelp beds, outstanding short hikes, and abalone diving. Great hikes include the Bluff Trail and Stump Beach Trail (great views but crowded). During abalone season, this is one of the best and most popular spots on the Northern California coast. Camp reservations are advised.

9 Ocean Cove Campground

Location: Near Fort Ross; map DØ, grid e5.

Campsites, facilities: There are 125 sites for tents or RVs. Piped water, picnic tables, fire grills, coin-op showers, and chemical toilets are provided. A boat launch, grocery store, fishing supplies, and diving gear sales are available. Pets are permitted.

Reservations, fees: No reservations; $12 per night, $1 pet fee. Open April through November.

Contact: Ocean Cove Campground, (707) 847-3422 or fax (707) 847-3624.

Directions: From Santa Rosa on US 101, turn west on Highway 12 (it becomes Highway 116 at Forestville) and drive to Highway 1 at Jenner. Turn north on Highway 1 and drive 17 miles north on Highway 1 (five miles north of Fort Ross) to the campground entrance.

Trip notes: The highlights here are the campsites on a bluff overlooking the ocean. Alas, it can be foggy during the summer. A good side trip is to Fort Ross, with a stellar easy hike available on the Fort Ross Trail, which features a walk through an old colonial fort as well as great coastal views, excellent for whale watching. There is also excellent hiking at Stillwater Cove Regional Park, located just a mile to the south off Highway 1.

10 Stillwater Cove Regional Park

Location: Near Fort Ross; map DØ, grid e6.

Campsites, facilities: There are 23 sites for tents or RVs up to 35 feet long, and a hike-in/bike-in site. Picnic tables, fire grills, and piped water are provided. Flush toilets, showers, firewood for purchase, and a sanitary disposal station are available. Supplies can be obtained in Ocean Cove (one mile north) and Fort Ross. The facilities are wheelchair accessible. Leashed pets are permitted.

Reservations, fees: No reservations; $15 per night, $5 for each additional vehicle, $3 per night for the hike-in/bike-in site, $1 pet fee. Open year-round.

Contact: Stillwater Cove Regional Park, (707) 847-3245.

Directions: From Santa Rosa on US 101, turn west on Highway 12 (it becomes Highway 116 at Forestville) and drive to Highway 1 at Jenner. Turn north on Highway 1 and drive 16 miles north on Highway 1 (four miles north of Fort Ross) to the park entrance.

Trip notes: Stillwater Cove has a dramatic rock-strewn cove and sits on a classic chunk of Sonoma coast. The campground is sometimes overlooked, since it is a county-operated park and not on the state park reservation system. One of the region's great hikes is available here, the Stockoff Creek Loop, with the trailhead located at the day-use parking lot. In a little over a mile, the trail is routed through forest with both firs and redwoods, and then along a pretty stream. To get beach access, you will need to cross Highway 1 and then drop down to the cove.

11 Austin Creek State Recreation Area

Location: Near the Russian River; map DØ, grid e9.

Campsites, facilities: There are 23 sites for tents or RVs up to 20 feet long and four hike-in sites. No trailers are allowed. (The access road is very narrow.) Picnic tables, fire grills, piped water, and flush toilets are provided. Pets are permitted on leashes in the main campground. There are also four primitive, hike-in, backcountry campsites with tables, fire rings, and pit toilets, but no piped water is available and no pets are permitted. The camps are 2.5 to four miles from the main campground. Obtain a backcountry camping permit from the office.

Reservations, fees: No reservations; $10 to $12 per night, $7 for hike-in sites; $1 pet fee.

Contact: Austin Creek State Recreation Area, (707) 869-2015 or (707) 869-5629.

Directions: From Santa Rosa on US 101, turn west on Highway 12 (it becomes Highway 116 at Forestville) to Guerneville. At Armstrong Woods Road, turn right and drive 2.5 miles to the entrance of Armstrong Redwoods State Park. Continue 3.5 miles through Armstrong Redwoods to Austin Creek State Recreation Area to the campground.

Trip notes: Austin Creek State Recreation Area and Armstrong Redwoods State Park are actually coupled, forming 5,000 acres of continuous parkland. Most visitors prefer the redwood park. The highlight at the recreation area is a system of hiking trails that lead to a series of small creeks: Stonehouse Creek, Gilliam Creek, and Austin Creek. They involve pretty steep climbs, and in the summer it's hot here. There are many attractive side trip possibilities, including the adjacent Armstrong Redwoods, of course, but also canoeing on the Russian River, fishing (smallmouth bass in summer, steelhead in winter), and wine tasting.

⑫ Faerie Ring Campground

Location: Near the Russian River; map DØ, grid f9.

Campsites, facilities: There are 32 sites for tents or RVs up to 42 feet long, nine with full hookups. Picnic tables and fire grills are provided. Piped water, flush toilets, showers, and a sanitary disposal station are available. Leashed pets are permitted.

Reservations, fees: Reservations are accepted; $20 per night (adults), $3 for kids.

Contact: Faerie Ring Campground, (707) 869-2746.

Directions: From Santa Rosa on US 101, turn west at the Guerneville/River Road exit (it becomes Highway 116 at Forestville) and drive 15 miles to Guerneville. At Armstrong Woods Road, turn right and drive 1.5 miles to the campground on the right.

Trip notes: If location is everything, then this privately operated campground is set right in the middle of the best of it in the Russian River region. It is one mile north of the Russian River and less than a mile south of Armstrong Redwoods State Park.

⑬ Casini Ranch Family Campground

Location: On the Russian River; map DØ, grid g8.

Campsites, facilities: There are 225 sites for tents and RVs (28 drive-through), many with full or partial hookups. Picnic tables and fire grills are provided. Flush toilets, showers, playground, sanitary disposal station, coin laundry, cable TV, video arcade, game arcade, boat and canoe rentals, propane gas, and a grocery store are available. Some facilities are wheelchair accessible. Leashed pets are permitted.

Reservations, fees: Reservations are recommended; $19 to $25 per night. Open year-round.

Contact: Casini Ranch Family Campground, (707) 865-2255 or (800) 451-8400 for reservations, or fax (707) 865-2046.

Directions: From Santa Rosa on US 101, turn west on Highway 12 (it becomes Highway 116 at Forestville) to Duncan Mills. In Duncan Mills, turn southeast on Moscow Road and drive a half mile to the campground.

Trip notes: Woods and water—this campground has both, with sites set near the Russian River in both sun-filled and shaded areas. Its location on the lower river makes a side trip to the coast easy, with the Sonoma Coast State Beach about a 15-minute drive to the nearby west.

⑭ Pomo Canyon Walk-In

Location: In Sonoma Coast State Beach; map DØ, grid g8.

Campsites, facilities: There are 21 walk-in tent sites. Picnic tables and fire grills are provided. Piped water and pit toilets are available. No pets are permitted. Closed from December 1 through March 31, weather depending.

Reservations, fees: No reservations; $10 per night, $5 per night for each additional vehicle.

Contact: Sonoma Coast State Beach, 3095 Highway 1, Bodega Bay, CA 94923; (707) 875-3483 or fax (707) 865-2046.

Directions: From San Francisco, drive north on US 101 to Petaluma. In Petaluma, take the East Washington exit and turn left (This street becomes Bodega Avenue). Drive through Petaluma for 26 miles to Bodega Bay, where the road merges with Highway 1. Continue north on Highway 1 past Bodega Bay for about 10 miles. Turn right on Willow Creek Road and drive about three miles to the campground. Reaching the campsites requires a one- to five-minute walk.

Trip notes: This is a gorgeous camp, well hidden, and offering a great trailhead and nearby beach access. The camp is actually not on the coast at all, but on the east-facing slope of Pomo Canyon (just over the ridge from the coast), where the campsites are set within a beautiful second-growth redwood forest. A trail is routed through the redwoods (with many cathedral trees) and up to the ridge, where there are divine views of the mouth of the Russian River, Goat Rock, and the beautiful Sonoma coast. The trail continues for two miles, all the way to Shell Beach, where you can spend hours poking around and beachcombing. The camp's seclusion and proximity to the Bay Area make it a rare winner.

⑮ Bodega Dunes Campground

Location: In Sonoma Coast State Beach; map DØ, grid g7.

Campsites, facilities: There are 90 sites for tents or RVs up to 31 feet long, with a limit of eight people per site. Picnic tables, fire grills, and piped water are provided. Flush toilets, showers, and a sanitary disposal station are available. Laundry facilities, supplies, and horse rentals are available within one mile. Leashed pets are permitted, except on the trails.

Reservations, fees: Reserve via phone at (800) 444-PARK/7275 ($7.50 reservation fee) or website www.cal-parks.ca.gov; $16 per night, $5 for each additional car, $1 pet fee.

Contact: Sonoma Coast State Beach, (707) 875-3483 or (707) 865-2391.

Directions: From Petaluma on US 101, take the East Washington exit, drive west through Petaluma (it becomes Bodega Avenue), and continue to Highway 1. Turn north on Highway 1 and drive to Bodega Bay. In Bodega Bay, drive one mile north to the campground entrance.

Trip notes: Sonoma Coast State Beach features several great campgrounds, and if you like the beach, this one rates high. It is set at the end of a beach that stretches for miles, providing stellar beach walks and excellent beachcombing during low tides. To the nearby south is Bodega Bay, including a major deep-sea sportfishing operation with excellent salmon fishing in June and July, and outstanding prospects for rockfish and lingcod from August through November. The town of Bodega Bay offers a full marina and restaurants.

⑯ Wrights Beach Campground

Location: In Sonoma Coast State Beach; map DØ, grid g7.

Campsites, facilities: There are 30 sites for tents or RVs up to 27 feet long, with a limit of eight people per site. Picnic tables, fire grills, piped water, and flush toilets are provided. Pets must be controlled.

Reservations, fees: Reserve via phone at (800) 444-PARK/7275 ($7.50 reservation fee) or website www.cal-parks.ca.gov; $18 to $20 per night, $5 for each additional vehicle, $1 pet fee.

Contact: Sonoma Coast State Beach, (707) 875-3483 or (707) 865-2391.

Directions: From Petaluma on US 101, take

the East Washington exit, drive west through Petaluma (it becomes Bodega Avenue), and continue to Highway 1. Turn north on Highway 1 and drive to Bodega Bay. In Bodega Bay, drive six miles north to the campground entrance.

Trip notes: This state park campground is at the north end of a beach that stretches south for several miles, yet to the north, it is steep and rocky. There are many excellent side trips. The best is to the north, where you can explore dramatic Shell Beach (the turnoff is on the west side of Highway 1), or take the Pomo-Ohlone Trail (the trailhead is on the east side of the highway, across from Shell Beach) up the adjacent foothills for sweeping views of the coast.

⑰ Bodega Bay RV Park

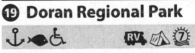

Location: In Bodega Bay; map DØ, grid h7.

Campsites, facilities: There are 85 sites for RVs, 70 with full hookups. Picnic tables, fire grills, piped water, flush toilets, and showers are provided. Laundry facilities, volleyball, and horseshoes are available. Pets are permitted.

Reservations, fees: Reservations are recommended; $25 per night for two people, $2 for each additional person.

Contact: Bodega Bay RV Park, 2000 Highway 1, PO Box 96, Bodega Bay, CA 94923; (707) 875-3701 or fax (707) 875-9811.

Directions: From Petaluma on US 101, take the East Washington exit, drive west through Petaluma (it becomes Bodega Avenue), and continue to Highway 1. Turn north on Highway 1 and drive to Bodega Bay. In Bodega Bay, continue north for two miles past the Union 76 station to the RV park.

Trip notes: Bodega Bay RV Park is one of the oldest RV parks in the state, and there are few coastal destinations better than Bodega Bay. Excellent seafood restaurants are available within five minutes, and some of the best deep-sea fishing is available out of Bodega Bay Sportfishing. In addition, there is a great view of the ocean at nearby Bodega Head to the west. What more could you want?

⑱ Westside Regional Park

Location: On Bodega Bay; map DØ, grid h7.

Campsites, facilities: There are 47 sites for tents or RVs. Piped water, picnic tables, and fire grills are provided. Flush toilets, showers, sanitary disposal station, fish-cleaning station, and a boat ramp are available. Supplies can be obtained in Bodega Bay, less than one mile away. Leashed pets are permitted.

Reservations, fees: No reservations; $15 per night, $1 pet fee. Open year-round.

Contact: Sonoma County Parks Department, (707) 875-3540.

Directions: From Petaluma on US 101, take the East Washington exit, drive west through Petaluma (it becomes Bodega Avenue), and continue to Highway 1. Turn north on Highway 1 and drive to Bodega Bay. In Bodega Bay, continue north to Bay Flat Road. Turn left on Bay Flat Road and drive two miles (looping around the bay) to the campground on the right.

Trip notes: This campground is located on the west shore of Bodega Bay. One of the greatest boat launches on the coast is nearby to the south, providing access to prime fishing waters. Salmon fishing is excellent from mid-June through August. A small, protected beach (for kids to dig in the sand and wade) is available at the end of the road beyond the campground.

⑲ Doran Regional Park

Location: On Bodega Bay; map DØ, grid h8.

Campsites, facilities: There are 10 sites for tents and 124 sites for tents or RVs. Picnic tables, fire grills, and piped water are provided. Flush toilets, showers, sanitary disposal stations, fish-cleaning station, and a boat ramp are available. Supplies can be obtained in Bodega Bay. Leashed pets are permitted.

Reservations, fees: No reservations; $15 per night, $1 pet fee. Open year-round.

Contact: Sonoma County Parks Department, (707) 875-3540.

Directions: From Petaluma on US 101, take the East Washington exit, drive west through Petaluma (it becomes Bodega Avenue), and continue to Highway 1. Turn north on Highway 1 toward Bodega Bay and look for the campground entrance on the right. If you reach the town of Bodega Bay, you have gone a mile too far.

Trip notes: This campground is set beside Doran Beach on Bodega Bay, which offers complete fishing and marina facilities. In season, it's also a popular clamming and crabbing spot. Salmon fishing is often excellent during the summer months at the Whistle Buoy offshore from Bodega Head, and rockfishing is good year-round at Cordell Bank. Fishing is also available off the rock jetty in the park.

⑳ Tomales Bay State Park Walk-In

Location: Near Inverness; map DØ, grid j8.

Campsites, facilities: There are six tent sites for hikers and bicyclists only. Piped water is provided. No pets are allowed.

Reservations, fees: No reservations; $5 day use fee, $3 per person per night, two-night maximum stay.

Contact: Tomales Bay State Park Walk-In, (415) 669-1140 or (415) 456-1286.

Directions: From Marin on US 101, take the Sir Francis Drake Boulevard exit. Turn west and drive about 20 miles to the town of Olema. Turn right on Highway 1, drive about four miles, turn left at Sir Francis Drake Boulevard, and drive north for seven miles to Pierce Point Road. Turn right and drive 1.2 miles to the access road for Tomales Bay State Park. Turn right and drive 1.5 miles to the park entrance.

Trip notes: Few know of this tiny campground, including the many bicyclists touring Highway 1 who are looking for exactly such a spot. This camp is for hikers and bikers only. The park is on the secluded western shore of Tomales Bay, pretty, quiet, and protected from the coastal winds. The park offers good hiking, picnicking, and during low tides, clamming (make sure you have a fishing license). There are several excellent hikes in this park, including the Johnstone Trail, which ranges from Heart's Desire Beach to Shell Beach and beyond, and the Indian Nature Trail.

Map D1

One inch equals approximately 10.7 miles.
See inside back cover for California state map.

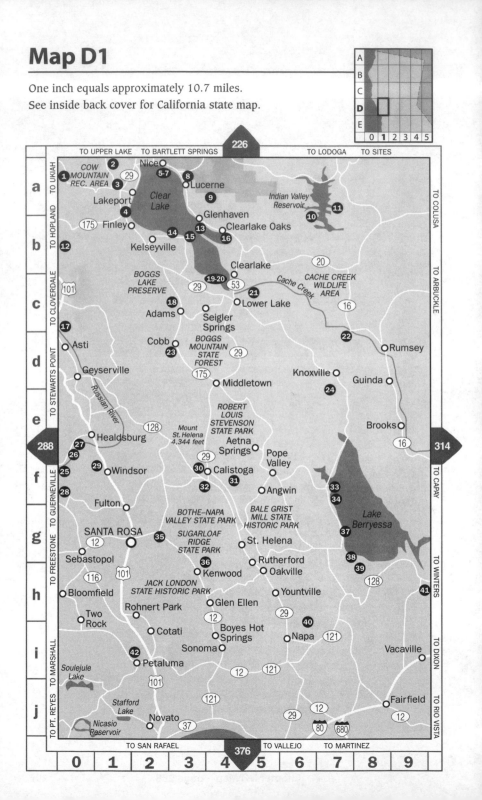

Chapter D1 features:

❶ Red Mountain

Location: Near Ukiah; map D1, grid a0.

Campsites, facilities: There are 10 tent sites. Piped water, vault toilets, picnic tables, and fire grills are provided. Pets must be controlled.

Reservations, fees: No reservations; no fee.

Contact: Bureau of Land Management, Ukiah District, (707) 468-4000 or fax (707) 468-4027.

Directions: From Ukiah on US 101, drive to Talmage Road. Turn east and drive 1.5 miles to Eastside Road. Turn right and drive a short distance to Mill Creek Road. Turn left and drive nine miles to the campground.

Trip notes: Like Mayacmus in chapter C1, this camp is also set in the Cow Mountain area east of Ukiah. But be forewarned: It is a popular spot for off-road motorcycles. If you don't like bikes, go to the other camp. Besides motorcycle trails, there are opportunities for hiking, horseback riding, and hunting.

❷ Kelly's Kamp

Location: On Scotts Creek near Clear Lake; map D1, grid a1.

Campsites, facilities: There are 75 sites for tents or RVs, many with partial hookups. Picnic tables and fire grills are provided. Flush toilets, showers, sanitary disposal station, coin laundry, ice, and a small camp store are available. Leashed pets are permitted.

Reservations, fees: Reservations are accepted; $16 to $18.50 per night. Open April through October.

Contact: Red Mountain, (707) 263-5754.

Directions: From Ukiah on US 101, drive north to the junction with Highway 20. Turn east and drive 14 miles (five miles from Upper Lake) to Scotts Valley Road. Turn south and drive to the park at 8220 Scotts Valley Road.

Trip notes: This privately operated park is set beside Scotts Creek, within short driving range of Blue Lakes to the north on Highway 20 and the north end of Clear Lake to the south.

❸ U-Wanna Camp

Location: Near Clear Lake; map D1, grid a1.

Campsites, facilities: There are 30 sites for tents or RVs (four drive-through) with partial hookups. Picnic tables, fire grills, rest rooms, showers, sanitary disposal station, coin laundry, playground, and a recreation room are provided. Leashed pets are permitted.

Reservations, fees: Reservations are accepted; $18 per night, $1 pet fee. Open year-round.

Contact: U-Wanna Camp, (707) 263-6745.

Directions: From Highway 29 in Lakeport, go to 11th Street. Turn west and drive a half mile to Riggs Road. Turn left and go 0.75 of a mile to Scotts Creek Road. Turn right and go 0.75 of a mile to 2699 Scotts Creek Road.

Trip notes: Whether U-Wanna or not, this could be where you end up if you're hunting for a site on a good-weather summer weekend. The camp is set about two miles from Clear Lake, with a boat ramp at nearby Lakeport. A small fishing pond for kids here is a plus.

❹ Will-O-Point Resort

Location: On Clear Lake; map D1, grid a1.

Campsites, facilities: There are 113 sites for tents, 10 RV sites with full hookups, and 10 cab-

ins. Rest rooms, showers, boat ramp, jet ski rentals, fishing supplies, restaurant, and a snack bar are available. Leashed pets are permitted.

Reservations, fees: Reservations are accepted; $18 to $20 per night, cabins are $60 to $71 per night. Open year-round.

Contact: Will-O-Point Resort, (707) 263-5407 or fax (707) 263-7072.

Directions: In Lakeport on Highway 29, take the Lakeport exit onto Main Street and drive to First Street. The camp is on the corner of First and Main Streets.

Trip notes: Will-O-Point Resort is an attractive spot on Clear Lake, with a public park nearby that offers picnic facilities and a children's playground. There are two beaches within walking distance of the campsites. Tent cabins are available. Possible side trips include visiting the nearby Chateau du Lac/Kendall-Jackson Winery. The nearby shore is a good area for bass fishing, and the resort occasionally hosts fishing tournaments.

❺ Sandpiper Shores

Location: On Clear Lake; map D1, grid a2.

Campsites, facilities: There are 30 RV sites with full or partial hookups. Picnic tables, rest rooms, showers, and a boat ramp are provided. Moorings, pier, coin laundry, and propane gas are available. Leashed pets are permitted.

Reservations, fees: Reservations are accepted; $17 to $21 per night.

Contact: Sandpiper Shores, (707) 274-4448.

Directions: From Ukiah on US 101, drive north to the junction with Highway 20. Turn east on Highway 20 and drive to the town of Nice and Hammond Avenue. Turn right on Hammond and drive a half mile to Lakeshore Boulevard. Turn left and drive to 2630 Lakeshore Boulevard.

Trip notes: Sandpiper Shores provides boating access to the northern end of Clear Lake. Fishing for catfish is good near here, both in Rodman Slough and just outside the mouth of the slough. This is where the legendary Catfish George Powers caught 4,000 to 5,000 catfish per year, using dead minnows for bait. In addition, the old submerged pilings in this area provide good bass fishing for boaters casting spinner baits. Several beaches are also available at the north end of the lake.

⑥ North Shore Resort and Marina

Location: On Clear Lake; map D1, grid a2.

Campsites, facilities: There are 10 sites with full or partial hookups for tents or RVs. Picnic tables and fire grills are provided. Rest rooms, showers, coin laundry, boat ramp, pier, and a bookstore are available. Leashed pets are permitted.

Reservations, fees: Reservations are accepted; $18 per night.

Contact: North Shore Resort and Marina, (707) 274-7771.

Directions: From Ukiah on US 101, drive north to the junction with Highway 20. Turn east on Highway 20 and drive toward the town of Nice to Hammond Avenue. Turn left on Hammond Avenue and drive a half mile to Lakeshore Boulevard. Turn right and drive to 2345 Lakeshore Boulevard.

Trip notes: This is one of a half dozen privately run parks in the immediate vicinity.

⑦ Holiday Harbor RV Park

Location: On Clear Lake; map D1, grid a2.

Campsites, facilities: There are 30 RV sites with full or partial hookups. An enclosed marina with 150 boat slips, boat ramp, and an adjacent beach are available. Picnic tables, rest rooms, showers, recreation room, and a sanitary disposal station are provided. A coin laundry and ice are available. Leashed pets are permitted.

Reservations, fees: Reservations are accepted; $16 to $17.50 per night.

Contact: Holiday Harbor RV Park, (707) 274-1136.

Directions: From north of Ukiah on US 101, drive north to the junction with Highway 20. Turn east on Highway 20 and drive toward the town of Nice to Hammond Avenue. Turn left on

Hammond Avenue and drive a half mile to Lakeshore Boulevard. Turn left and drive to 3605 Lakeshore Boulevard.

Trip notes: This is one of the most popular resorts at the north end of Clear Lake. It is ideal for boaters, with a full-service marina and a major docking complex. Fishing for bass is good in this area, along old docks and submerged pilings. Waterskiing just offshore is also good, with the north end of the lake often more calm than the water to points south. The elevation is about 2,000 feet.

⑧ Arrow RV Park and Marina

Location: On Clear Lake; map D1, grid a3.

Campsites, facilities: There are 24 sites for RVs, many with full or partial hookups. Rest rooms, showers, coin laundry, boat rentals, moorings, fishing supplies, boat ramp, grocery store, beer, wine, and ice are available. Leashed pets are permitted.

Reservations, fees: Reservations are accepted; $18 per night.

Contact: Arrow RV Park and Marina, PO Box 1735, Lucerne, CA 95458; (707) 274-7715.

Directions: From north of Ukiah on US 101, or from Williams on Interstate 5, turn on Highway 20 and drive to Clear Lake and the town of Lucerne. Look for the campground at 6720 East Highway 20.

Trip notes: Lucerne is known for its harbor and its long stretch of well-kept public beaches along the shore of Clear Lake. The town offers a shopping district, restaurants, and cafes. In summer months, crappie fishing is good at night from the boat docks, as long as there are bright lights to attracts gnats, which in turn attract minnows, the prime food for crappie.

⑨ Lakeview Campground

Location: Near Clear Lake in Mendocino National Forest; map D1, grid a4.

Campsites, facilities: There are nine sites for tents or RVs. There is no piped water, but picnic tables, fire grills, and vault toilets are provided. Pets must be controlled.

Reservations, fees: No reservations; no fee. Open May to mid-October.

Contact: Mendocino National Forest, Upper Lake Ranger District at (707) 275-2361 or fax (707) 275-0676.

Directions: From north of Ukiah on US 101, or from Williams on Interstate 5, turn west on Highway 20 and drive to Clear Lake. Drive two miles north of the town of Lucerne to Bartlett Springs Road/Forest Service Road 8. Turn east on Bartlett Springs Road and drive five miles to High Valley Road/Forest Service Road 15N09. Turn southwest and drive three miles to the camp.

Trip notes: When Clear Lake is packed to the rafters with campers, this spot offers a perfect alternative, if you don't mind roughing it a bit. It is set at 3,400 feet (above the town of Lucerne) overlooking the lake. A trail from camp leads down to the town; it's a two-mile hike, but most folks wouldn't want to make the uphill return trip, especially on a hot summer day. Options include fishing and boating at Clear Lake, of course, but also venturing east on Bartlett Springs Road to the north end of remote Indian Valley Reservoir, where there is excellent fishing for bass.

⑩ Blue Oak

Location: At Indian Valley Reservoir; map D1, grid a6.

Campsites, facilities: There are six sites for tents or RVs. Picnic tables and fire rings are provided. Piped water and pit toilets are available. Pets must be controlled.

Reservations, fees: No reservations; no fee; 14-day stay limit.

Contact: Bureau of Land Management, Clear Lake Resource Area, 2550 North State Street, Ukiah, CA 95482; (707) 468-4000. A detailed map is available from the BLM.

Directions: From Williams on Interstate 5, turn west on Highway 20 and drive 25 miles into the foothills to Walker Ridge Road. Turn north on

Walker Ridge Road (a dirt road) and drive north for about four miles to a "major" intersection of two dirt roads. Turn left and drive about 2.5 miles toward the Indian Valley Dam. The Blue Oak campground is located just off the road to your right, about 1.5 miles from Indian Valley Reservoir.

Trip notes: Indian Valley Reservoir is kind of like an ugly dog that you love more than anything because inside beats a heart that will never betray you. The camp is out in the middle of nowhere in oak woodlands, about a mile from the dam. It is primitive and little known. For many, that kind of isolation is perfect. While there are good trails nearby, it is the outstanding fishing for bass and bluegill at the lake every spring and early summer that is the key reason to make the trip.

⑪ Wintun

Location: Near Indian Valley Reservoir; map D1, grid a7.

Campsites, facilities: There is a primitive tent site with a picnic table and a fire ring. Piped water and pit toilets are available.

Reservations, fees: No reservations; no fee.

Contact: Bureau of Land Management, Ukiah Field Office, 2550 North State Street, Ukiah, CA 95482; (707) 468-4000. A detailed map is available from the BLM.

Directions: From Williams on Interstate 5, turn west on Highway 20 and drive 25 miles into the foothills to Walker Ridge Road. Turn north on Walker Ridge Road (a dirt road) and drive north for about four miles to a "major" intersection of two dirt roads. Continue straight on Walker Ridge Road for another five miles. At the sign for Wintun, turn left and drive about a mile on a spur road that dead-ends at the campground. Note: To reach Indian Valley Reservoir from Wintun, you must backtrack a mile, turn left on Walker Ridge Road, and drive eight or nine miles to the north end of the lake.

Trip notes: If you want to feel like you are out in the middle of nowhere without being out in the middle of nowhere, then this camp answers your call. Wintun is the smallest and most obscure camp anywhere, yet it has excellent trails nearby for hiking and biking and is about a 20-minute drive from the north end of Indian Valley Reservoir (which has outstanding bass fishing). Note: Summer temperatures can burn you into a crispy chimichanga, so bring a tarp that you can rig for shade cover.

⑫ Sheldon Creek

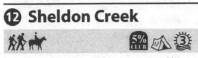

Location: Near Hopland; map D1, grid b0.

Campsites, facilities: There are six sites for tents. Piped water, vault toilets, picnic tables, and fire grills are provided. Pets must be controlled.

Reservations, fees: No reservations; no fee.

Contact: Bureau of Land Management, Ukiah Field Office, 2550 North State Street, Ukiah, CA 95482; (707) 468-4000.

Directions: From Santa Rosa on US 101, drive north to Hopland and the junction with Highway 175. Turn east on Highway 175 and drive three miles to Old Toll Road. Turn right on Old Toll Road and drive eight miles to the camp.

Trip notes: Only the locals know about this spot, and hey, there aren't a lot of locals around. The camp is set amid rolling hills, grasslands, and oaks along little Sheldon Creek. It is pretty and quiet in the spring when the hills have greened up, but hot in the summer. Recreational possibilities include hiking, horseback riding (bring your own horse, pardner), and in the fall, hunting.

⑬ Glenhaven Beach Camp and Marina

Location: On Clear Lake; map D1, grid b3.

Campsites, facilities: There are 21 sites with full or partial hookups for RVs up to 26 feet long. Picnic tables, fire grills, rest rooms, showers, and a recreation room are provided. A boat ramp and boat rentals are available. Leashed pets are permitted.

Reservations, fees: Reservations are accepted; $16 to $18 per night. Open February through November.

Contact: Glenhaven Beach Camp and Marina, (707) 998-3406.

Directions: From north of Ukiah on US 101, or Interstate 5 at Williams, turn on Highway 20 and drive to Clear Lake and the town of Glenhaven (four miles northwest of Clearlake Oaks). In Glenhaven, drive to the camp at 9625 East Highway 20.

Trip notes: This makes a good base camp for all boaters, water-skiers, and anglers. It is set on a peninsula on the eastern shore of Clear Lake, with nearby Indian Beach providing a good recreation and water-play spot. In addition, it is a short boat ride out to Anderson Island, Weekend Island, and Buckingham Point, where bass fishing can be excellent along shaded tules.

⑭ Clear Lake State Park

Location: In Kelseyville; map D1, grid b3.

Campsites, facilities: There are 147 sites for tents or RVs, located in four campgrounds, and several primitive hike-in sites. Picnic tables, fire grills, rest rooms, showers, sanitary disposal station, and a boat ramp are available. A grocery store, coin laundry, and propane gas are available within 1.5 miles. The boat ramp, picnic area, and some campsites are wheelchair accessible. Pets are permitted.

Reservations, fees: Reserve via phone at (800) 444-PARK/7275 ($7.50 reservation fee) or website www.cal-parks.ca.gov; $20 per night for "lakeside premium" sites, $16 per night for other sites, $3 per night for hike-in/bike-in sites, $1 pet fee.

Contact: Clear Lake State Park, (707) 279-4293.

Directions: From Vallejo, drive north on Highway 29 to Lower Lake. Turn left on Highway 29 and drive eight miles to Soda Bay Road. Turn right on Soda Bay Road and drive about 10 miles to the park entrance on the right side of the road.

From Kelseyville on Highway 29, take the Kelseyville exit and turn north on Main Street. Drive a short distance to State Street. Turn north and drive to Gaddy Lane. Continue north on Gaddy Lane for about two miles to Soda Bay Road. Turn right and drive a half mile to the park entrance on the left.

Trip notes: If you have fallen in love with Clear Lake and its surrounding oak woodlands, it is difficult to find a better spot than at Clear Lake State Park. It is set on the western shore of Clear Lake, and though the oak woodlands flora means you can seem quite close to your camping neighbors, the proximity to quality boating, water sports, and fishing makes the lack of privacy worth it. Reservations are a necessity in summer months. That stands to reason, with excellent bass fishing from boats beside a tule-lined shoreline near the park and good catfishing in the sloughs that run through the park. Some campsites have water frontage. A few short hiking trails are also available. Rangers here are friendly, helpful, and provide reliable fishing information. The elevation is 2,000 feet.

ⓕ Edgewater Resort and RV Park

Location: On Clear Lake; map D1, grid b3.

Campsites, facilities: There are 61 RV sites with full hookups and six cabins with air conditioning and heat, kitchenettes, color TV, and cable. Picnic tables, fire grills, rest rooms, showers, and a boat ramp are provided. A game room, general store, swimming pool, fishing pier, horseshoes, volleyball, Ping-Pong, charter boats, and watercraft rentals are available. Wood is available for purchase. Leashed pets are permitted. There is a dog run at the beach.

Reservations, fees: Reservations are accepted; $25 per night, $65 for cabins.

Contact: Edgewater Resort and RV Park, (707) 279-0208 or fax (707) 279-0138.

Directions: In Kelseyville on Highway 29, take the Merritt Road exit and drive on Merritt for two miles (it becomes Gaddy Lane) to Soda Bay Road. Turn right on Soda Bay Road and drive three miles to the campground entrance on the left.

Trip notes: Soda Bay is one of Clear Lake's prettiest and most intimate spots, and this camp provides excellent access. Both waterskiing and fishing for bass and bluegill are excellent in this part of the lake, sheltered from north winds for quiet water, with a tule-lined shore from Henderson Point all the way around to Dorn

Bay—nearly three miles of prime fishing territory. This resort specializes in groups and gatherings.

⓰ M & M Campgrounds

Location: On Clear Lake; map D1, grid b4.

Campsites, facilities: There are 36 RV sites. Flush toilets, showers, and a boat ramp are provided. Boat rentals and a grocery store are available within a quarter mile. Leashed pets are allowed.

Reservations, fees: Reservations are required; $12.50 per night, $5 launch fee. Open year-round.

Contact: M & M Campgrounds, (707) 998-9943.

Directions: From north of Ukiah on US 101, or at Williams on Interstate 5, turn on Highway 20 and drive to Clearlake Oaks and Island Drive. Turn south (the only way you can turn) on Island Drive and drive two blocks to 13050 Island Drive.

Trip notes: This park has a unique setting, located on an island in the shaded lagoons and waterways that lead from Clear Lake into the town of Clearlake Oaks. That means the boat ramp is extremely sheltered from wakes. Fishing for bass and catfish is good in the immediate area, with an excellent catfish hole located off nearby Rattlesnake Island.

⓱ Cloverdale KOA

Location: Near the Russian River; map D1, grid c0.

Campsites, facilities: There are 47 sites for tents, 104 RV sites (11 drive-through), most with full hookups, and eight cabins. Picnic tables and fire grills are provided. Flush toilets, showers, swimming pool, playground, sanitary disposal station, coin laundry, recreation room, mini-golf, nature trails, catch-and-release fish pond, nightly entertainment on weekends in the summer, and a grocery and gift store are available. Pets must be controlled.

Reservations, fees: Reservations are accepted; $25 to $45 per night, cabins are $40 per night. Open year-round.

Contact: Cloverdale KOA, (707) 894-3337. Reserve via phone at (800) 368-4558.

Directions: From Cloverdale on US 101, take the Central Cloverdale exit, which puts you on Asti Road. Drive straight on Asti Road to First Street. Turn east and drive a short distance to River Road. Turn south and drive four miles to KOA Road. Turn left and drive to the campground entrance.

In summer/fall: South of Cloverdale on US 101, take the Asti exit and drive east a block to Asti Road. Turn south and drive a short distance to Washington School Road. Turn east and drive 1.5 miles to KOA Road. Turn right and drive to the campground entrance. (Note: This route is open May 15 to December 15, when a seasonal bridge is in place.) Both routes are well signed.

Trip notes: This KOA campground is set just above the Russian River in the Alexander Valley wine country, just south of Cloverdale. Since new owners took over in 1994 the place has undergone considerable renovation and is now both rustic and tidy, with adorable little camping cabins a great bonus. In addition, a fishing pond is stocked with largemouth bass, bluegill, catfish, and, when water temperatures are cool enough, trout. The nearby Russian River is an excellent beginner's route in an inflatable kayak or canoe. The nearby winery in Asti makes for a popular side trip.

⑱ Loch Lomond Park

Location: Near Middletown; map D1, grid c3.

Campsites, facilities: There are 10 RV sites with full or partial hookups and 17 tent sites. Picnic tables, fire grills, rest rooms, and showers are provided. There is a swimming pool and grocery store across the street. Leashed pets are permitted.

Reservations, fees: Reservations are accepted; $10 to $12 per night. Open year-round.

Contact: Loch Lomond Park, (707) 928-5044.

Directions: From Vallejo, drive north on Highway 29 past Calistoga to Middletown and the junction with Highway 175. Turn north on Highway 175 and drive 12 miles to the park entrance on the left side of the road.

Trip notes: This park is located midway between Clear Lake and the Napa Valley and is favored primarily by seniors with RVs. Though the Highway 29 corridor gets tons of vacation traffic, you can escape most of it here on little Highway 175. The valley setting is pretty in the spring when everything is still green, with Cobb Mountain nearby.

⑲ Shaw's Shady Acres

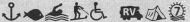

Location: On Cache Creek; map D1, grid c4.

Campsites, facilities: There are 13 sites for tents or RVs, many with partial or full hookups. Picnic tables and fire grills are provided. Rest rooms, showers, sanitary disposal station, pier, boat rentals, boat ramp, coin laundry, swimming pool, recreation patio, beer and wine bar, fishing supplies, and a grocery store are available. Pets must be leashed and may not be left unattended in camp.

Reservations, fees: Reservations are recommended; $16 per night, 50¢ pet fee.

Contact: Shaw's Shady Acres, (707) 994-2236.

Directions: From the town of Lower Lake, drive north on Highway 53 for 1.3 miles to Old Highway 53. Turn left (a frontage road) and drive a quarter mile to the park entrance.

Trip notes: This is one of several privately operated campgrounds set beside Cache Creek, just south of Clear Lake. The fishing for catfish is often quite good on summer nights in Cache Creek, a deep green, slow-moving water that looks more like a slough in a Mississippi bayou than a creek. Waterfront campsites with scattered walnut, ash, and oak trees are available. Clear Lake is a short drive to the north.

⑳ Garners' Resort

Location: On Cache Creek; map D1, grid c4.

Campsites, facilities: There are 25 sites for tents and 40 full-hookup RV sites. Flush toilets, showers, dump station, boat rentals, pier, boat ramp, recreation room, swimming pool, wading pool, fishing supplies, coin laundry, and a store are available. Leashed pets are permitted.

Reservations, fees: Reservations are accepted; $15 to $16 per night. Open year-round.

Contact: Garners' Resort, (707) 994-6267 or fax (707) 994-3470.

Directions: From the town of Lower Lake, drive north on Highway 53 for 1.3 miles to Old Highway 53. Turn left (a frontage road) and drive 1.5 miles to the resort entrance on the left.

Trip notes: This is one of several privately operated parks in the immediate area along Cache Creek just south of Clear Lake. The park offers sites for tents as well as RVs, many near Cache Creek, which actually looks more like a slough—deep, wide, green, and slow moving.

㉑ Aztec RV Park

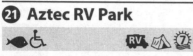

Location: On Cache Creek; map D1, grid c5.

Campsites, facilities: There are 30 RV sites with full or partial hookups and six tent sites. This is an "adult park" (no children allowed). Rest rooms, showers, pier, boat ramp, coin laundry, and river frontage sites are available. Propane gas is available within 1.5 miles. Small pets are permitted and must be controlled.

Reservations, fees: Reservations are recommended; $15 per night. Open year-round.

Contact: Aztec RV Park, (707) 994-4377.

Directions: From the town of Lower Lake, drive north on Highway 29 for a mile to Dam Road. Turn right and drive across the bridge. Turn left on Tish-a-Tang Road and continue to the campground at 16150 Tish-a-Tang Road.

Trip notes: This is an adults-only RV park set near Cache Creek, just south of Clear Lake.

㉒ Cache Creek Canyon Regional Park

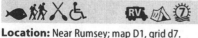

Location: Near Rumsey; map D1, grid d7.

Campsites, facilities: There are 45 sites for tents or RVs and three group sites that can accommodate 20 to 30 people. Picnic tables, fire grills, and piped water are provided. Flush toilets and a sanitary disposal station are available. Leashed pets are permitted.

Reservations, fees: No reservations; $13 to $15 per night, $2 fee for pets. Open year-round.

Contact: Cache Creek Canyon Regional Park, (530) 666-8115 or fax (530) 666-8117.

Directions: From Vacaville on Interstate 80, turn north on Interstate 505 and drive 21 miles to Madison and the junction with Highway 16. Turn north on Highway 16 and drive northwest for about 45 miles to the town of Rumsey. From Rumsey, continue west on Highway 16 for five miles to the park entrance.

Trip notes: This is the best campground in Yolo County, yet it's known by few out-of-towners. It is set at 1,300 feet beside Cache Creek, which is the closest river to the Bay Area that provides white-water rafting opportunities. This section of river features primarily Class I and II water, ideal for inflatable kayaks and overnight trips. Occasionally, huge catfish are caught in this area.

㉓ Yogi Bear Beaver Creek Campground

Location: Near Cobb Mountain; map D1, grid d3.

Campsites, facilities: There are 10 tent sites and 97 sites for RVs up to 40 feet long. Most sites are pull-through, and all have full hookups. Piped water is provided. Picnic tables, fire rings, rest rooms, showers, group area, coin laundry, pool, kayaks and paddleboats, boating pond, playground, horseshoes, recreation hall, and a store are available. Some facilities are wheelchair accessible. Leashed pets are permitted.

Reservations, fees: Reservations are recommended; $19 to $22 per night.

Contact: Beaver Creek RV Park, 14417 Bottle Rock Road, PO Box 49, Cobb Mountain, CA 95426; (707) 928-4322, (800) 307-CAMP/2267 or fax (707) 928-5341; website: www.campyogi.com.

Directions: From Vallejo, drive north on Highway 29 past Calistoga to Middletown and the junction with Highway 175. Turn north on Highway 175 and drive 8.5 miles to Bottle Rock Road. Turn left and drive three miles to the campground entrance on the left side of the road.

Trip notes: This camp has a trout creek, a pond

with canoes and kayaks in summer, plus plenty of hiking and birding opportunities. In addition, horseback riding and hot air balloon rides are available nearby. This camp is set near Highway 175 between Middletown and Clear Lake, and while there is a parade of vacation traffic on Highway 29, relatively few people take the longer route on Highway 175. Cobb Mountain looms nearby.

㉔ Lower Hunting Creek

Location: Near Lake Berryessa; map D1, grid d7.

Campsites, facilities: There are five sites for tents or RVs. Piped water, picnic tables, fire grills, shade shelters, and vault toilets are provided. Pets must be controlled.

Reservations, fees: No reservations; no fee. Open year-round.

Contact: Bureau of Land Management, Clear Lake Field Office, (707) 468-4000.

Directions: In Lower Lake on Highway 29, turn southeast on Morgan Valley Road/Berryessa-Knoxville Road and drive 15 miles to Devilhead Road. Turn south and drive two miles to the campground.

Trip notes: This little-known camp might seem like it's out in the middle of nowhere for the folks who wind up here accidentally (like we did), and it turns out that it is. If you plan on spending a few days here, it's advisable to get information or a map of the surrounding area from the Bureau of Land Management prior to your trip. There are some 25 miles of trails for off-highway-vehicle exploration on the surrounding lands. In the fall, the area provides access for deer hunting with generally poor to fair results.

㉕ Mirabel Trailer Park and Camp

Location: On the Russian River; map D1, grid f0.

Campsites, facilities: There are 125 sites for tents or RVs, many with full or partial hookups.

Picnic tables and fire grills are provided. Flush toilets, showers, playground, coin laundry, sanitary disposal station, horseshoes, shuffleboard, and canoe and kayak rentals are available. Leashed pets, except pit bulls, are allowed.

Reservations, fees: Reservations are recommended; $15 to $18 per night. Open March through October.

Contact: Mirabel Trailer Park and Camp, (707) 887-2383.

Directions: North of Santa Rosa on US 101, take the River Road exit and head west. Drive eight miles to the campground at 7600 River Road.

Trip notes: The big attraction here during the summer is swimming and paddling around in canoes. This privately operated park is set near the Russian River, but in the summer the "river" is actually a series of small lakes, with temporary dams stopping most of the water flow. In winter, out come the dams, up comes the water, and in come the steelhead, migrating upstream past this area. Armstrong Redwoods State Park just north of Guerneville provides a nearby side trip.

㉖ Schoolhouse Canyon Campground

Location: Near the Russian River; map D1, grid f0.

Campsites, facilities: There are 65 sites for tents or RVs, some with partial hookups. Picnic tables and fire grills are provided. Piped water, flush toilets, showers, and wood are available. Leashed pets are permitted.

Reservations, fees: Reservations are accepted; $20 per night for two people, $5 for each additional person, $4 pet fee. Open May through October.

Contact: Schoolhouse Canyon Campground, (707) 869-2311.

Directions: From Santa Rosa, drive north on US 101 about 2.5 miles and take the River Road/Guerneville exit. Drive to the stop sign, turn left on River Road, and drive 12.5 miles to the campground entrance.

Trip notes: This campground comprises 210

acres and features a mile of sandy swimming beach along the Russian River, campsites in a grove of large redwoods, and a parklike setting on land originally homesteaded in the 1850s. A one-mile scenic hiking trail is available, routed up to a ridge for some nice views of the countryside.

㉗ Burke's Resort and Canoe Trips

Location: On the Russian River; map D1, grid f0.

Campsites, facilities: There are 60 sites for tents or RVs. Picnic tables and fire grills are provided. Flush toilets, showers, wood, and canoe rentals are available. Pets are not allowed.

Reservations, fees: Reservations are required; $12 to $16 per night. Open April through October.

Contact: Burke's Resort and Canoe Trips, (707) 887-1222.

Directions: In Marin, drive north on US 101 to Rohnert Park and the junction with Highway 116. Turn north on Highway 116 and drive 14 miles to Forestville and Mirabel Road. Turn right and drive a mile until it dead-ends at the Russian River and the campground.

Trip notes: Burke's is the long-established canoe rental service and campground on the Russian River. The favorite trip is the 10-miler from Burke's in Forestville to Guerneville, which is routed right through the heart of the area's redwoods, about a 3.5-hour trip with plenty of time for sunbathing, swimming, or anything else you can think of. The cost is $30, including a return by shuttle. Many other trips are available.

㉘ Hilton Park

Location: On the Russian River; map D1, grid f0.

Campsites, facilities: There are 20 tent sites and five RV sites with no hookups. Picnic tables, fire rings, showers, rest rooms, beach, coin laundry, dishwashing area, playground, firewood,

and ice are available. Canoe rentals are available within three miles. Leashed pets are permitted.

Reservations, fees: Reservations are recommended; $20 to $25 per night. Open year-round.

Contact: Hilton Park, (707) 887-9206.

Directions: From US 101 north of Santa Rosa, take the River Road/Guerneville exit. Drive west for 11.5 miles (shortly after the bridge) to the campground on the left side of the road just behind the Russian River Pub.

Trip notes: This lush, wooded park is set on the banks of the Russian River, with a choice of open or secluded sites. The highlight of the campground is a large, beautiful beach that offers access for swimming, fishing, and canoeing. The folks here are very friendly, and you get a choice of many recreation options in the area.

㉙ Windsorland RV Park

Location: Near Santa Rosa; map D1, grid f0.

Campsites, facilities: There are 55 RV sites with full hookups. Patios are provided. Flush toilets, showers, swimming pool, sanitary disposal station, coin laundry, recreation room, and a playground are available. Pets must be controlled.

Reservations, fees: Reservations are accepted; $22.50 to $25 per night. No credit cards. Open year-round.

Contact: Windsorland RV Park, (707) 838-4882.

Directions: From Santa Rosa on US 101, drive north for nine miles to Windsor. Take the Windsor exit, turn north on Old Redwood Highway, and drive a half mile to 9290 Old Redwood Highway.

Trip notes: This developed park is located close to the Russian River, the wine country to the east, redwoods to the west, and Lake Sonoma to the northwest. But with a swimming pool, playground, and recreation room, many visitors are content to stay right here, spend the night, then head out on their vacation.

㉚ Napa County Fairgrounds

Location: In Calistoga; map D1, grid f3.

Campsites, facilities: There are 50 RV sites (all drive-through and with hookups) and a lawn area for tents. Group sites are available by reservation only. Rest rooms, showers, and a sanitary disposal station are available. No fires are permitted. A nine-hole golf course is adjacent to the campground area. Leashed pets are permitted.

Reservations, fees: No reservations (except for groups); $10–18 per night.

Contact: Napa County Fairgrounds, (707) 942-5111 or fax (707) 942-5125.

Directions: From Napa on Highway 29, drive north to Calistoga, turn right on Lincoln Avenue, and drive four blocks to Fairway. Turn left and drive to the end of the road to the campground.

Trip notes: What this really is, folks, is just the county fairgrounds, converted to an RV park for 11 months each year. It is closed to camping from mid-June through mid-July, but what the heck, you can stick around and try to win a stuffed animal. What is more likely, of course, is that you have come here for the health spas, with great natural hot springs, mud baths, and assorted goodies at the health resorts in Calistoga. Nearby parks for hiking include Bothe-Napa Valley and Robert Louis Stevenson State Parks.

③ Calistoga Ranch Campground

Location: Near Calistoga; map D1, grid f4.

Campsites, facilities: There are 60 sites for tents, 84 RV sites with full or partial hookups, four cabins, and two trailers. There is a limit of four people per site. Picnic tables and barbecue grills are provided. Flush toilets, showers, sanitary disposal station, coin laundry, lake, swimming pool, and a snack bar are available. Leashed pets are permitted.

Reservations, fees: Reservations are accepted; $19 to $25 per night, $54 per night for cabins, $98 per night for trailers, $2 pet fee. Open year-round.

Contact: Calistoga Ranch Campground, (707) 942-6565 or fax (707) 942-6902.

Directions: From Napa on Highway 29, drive north through St. Helena and continue for about five miles to Larkmead Lane. Turn right and drive a short distance to the Silverado Trail. Turn left and drive about 200 yards to Lommel Road. Turn right and drive a quarter mile to the campground.

Trip notes: This is a large, privately run camp set in the heart of the wine country, about a 15-minute drive from the famous Calistoga spas and mud baths. The elevation is 600 feet.

③ Bothe–Napa Valley State Park

Location: Near Calistoga; map D1, grid f3.

Campsites, facilities: There are 50 sites for tents or RVs up to 31 feet long. Picnic tables, fire grills, and piped water are provided. Flush toilets, showers, coin-operated showers, and a swimming pool (in the summer) are available. The facilities are wheelchair accessible. Supplies can be obtained in Calistoga or St. Helena, about three miles away. Pets must be controlled.

Reservations, fees: Reservations are recommended April through October; reserve via phone at (800) 444-PARK/7275 ($7.50 reservation fee) or website www.cal-parks.ca.gov; $15 to $16 per night, $1 pet fee. Open April through October.

Contact: Bothe–Napa Valley State Park, (707) 942-4575.

Directions: From Napa on Highway 29, drive north to St. Helena and continue north for five miles (one mile past the entrance to Bale Grist Mill State Park) to the park entrance road on the left.

Trip notes: It's always a stunner for newcomers to discover this beautiful park with redwoods and a pretty stream so close to the Napa Valley wine and spa country. Though the campsites are relatively exposed, they are set beneath a pretty oak/bay/madrone forest, with trailheads for hiking nearby. One trail is routed south for 1.2 miles to the restored Bale Grist Mill, a giant mill wheel on a pretty creek. Another, more scenic route heads up Ritchey Canyon, amid redwoods and along Ritchey Creek, beautiful and intimate.

㉝ Rancho Monticello Resort

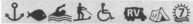

Location: On Lake Berryessa; map D1, grid f7.

Campsites, facilities: There are 59 sites for tents and 45 RV sites with full hookups. Picnic tables, fire grills, and piped water are provided. Rest rooms, showers, snack bar, complete marina facilities, ice, propane gas, and groceries are available. Leashed pets are permitted.

Reservations, fees: No reservations; $14 to $27 per night. Open year-round.

Contact: Rancho Monticello Resort, (707) 966-2188 or fax (707) 963-2440.

Directions: From Vallejo, drive north on Interstate 80 to the Suisun Valley Road exit. Take Suisun Valley Road north to Highway 121. Turn north on Highway 121 and drive five miles to Highway 128. Turn north on Highway 128, drive five miles to Berryessa-Knoxville Road, and continue 10 miles to 6590 Knoxville Road.

Trip notes: This is a fully developed, privately operated park set on the shore of Lake Berryessa. Berryessa is the third largest man-made lake in Northern California, smaller than only Shasta and Oroville. It is a popular spot for waterskiing and fishing for trout and bass. The elevation is 475 feet.

㉞ Putah Creek Park

Location: On Lake Berryessa; map D1, grid f7.

Campsites, facilities: There are 200 tent and 55 RV sites, many with full or partial hookups. Rest rooms, showers, sanitary disposal station, coin laundry, boat ramp, rowboat rentals, snack bar, motel, cocktail lounge, restaurant, propane gas, ice, and groceries are available. Leashed pets are permitted.

Reservations, fees: Reservations are recommended; reserve via phone at (707) 966-0794; $21 to $26 per night. Open year-round.

Contact: Putah Creek Park, (707) 966-2116 or (707) 966-0794, or fax (707) 966-0593.

Directions: From Vallejo, drive north on Interstate 80 to the Suisun Valley Road exit. Take Suisun Valley Road and drive north to Highway 121. Turn north on Highway 121 and drive five miles to Highway 128. Turn left on Highway 128, drive five miles to Berryessa-Knoxville Road, and continue 13 miles to 7600 Knoxville Road.

Trip notes: This campground is set at 400 feet elevation on the northern end of Lake Berryessa. The Putah Creek arm provides very good bass fishing in the spring and trout trolling in the summer. The north end of the lake has a buoy line that keeps powerboats out, but it can still be explored by paddling a canoe, which allows you to fish in relatively untouched waters and see deer during the evening on the eastern shore. In the fall, usually by mid-October, the trout come to the surface and provide excellent fishing at the mouth of Pope Creek or Putah Creek for anglers drifting live minnows. The resort also has some apartment-style rentals.

㉟ Spring Lake Regional Park

Location: In Santa Rosa; map D1, grid g2.

Campsites, facilities: There are 30 sites for tents or RVs of any length. Picnic tables, fire grills, and piped water are provided. Flush toilets, showers, sanitary disposal station, boat ramp (no gas-powered motorboats), summer boat rentals, and bike paths are available. A grocery store, coin laundry, wood, and propane gas are available within five minutes. Leashed pets are permitted with proof of rabies vaccination.

Reservations, fees: Reservations are accepted; reserve via phone at (707) 539-8092; $14 per night, $1 pet fee and proof of rabies vaccination, $5 for the second vehicle. Note: The limit is eight people and two vehicles per campsite. Open daily from mid-May through mid-September and on weekends and holidays only during off-season.

Contact: Spring Lake Regional Park, (707) 539-8082.

Directions: From Santa Rosa on US 101, turn east on Highway 12 (it will become Hoen Avenue) and continue to Newanga Avenue. Turn left and drive to the park at the end of the road.

Trip notes: Spring Lake is one of the few lakes in the greater Bay Area that provides lakeside camping. Not only that, Spring Lake is stocked twice each month in late winter and spring with rainbow trout by the Department of Fish and Game. Only nonpowered boats are permitted on this small, pretty lake, which keeps things fun and quiet for everybody. An easy trail along the west shore of the lake to the dam, then into adjoining Howarth Park, provides a pleasant evening stroll.

36 Sugarloaf Ridge State Park

Location: Near Santa Rosa; map D1, grid g3.

Campsites, facilities: There are 49 sites for tents or RVs up to 27 feet long. Picnic tables, fire grills, piped water, and flush toilets are provided. Leashed pets are permitted, except on the trails.

Reservations, fees: Reserve via phone at (800) 444-PARK/7275 ($7.50 reservation fee) or website www.cal-parks.ca.gov; $12 to $16 per night, $1 pet fee. Open year-round.

Contact: Sugarloaf Ridge State Park, (707) 833-5712.

Directions: From Santa Rosa on US 101, turn east on Highway 12 and drive seven miles to Adobe Canyon Road. Turn north and drive three miles to the park entrance.

Trip notes: Sugarloaf Ridge State Park is a perfect example of a place that you can't make a final judgment about from your first glance. Your first glance will lead you to believe that this is just hot foothill country, with old ranch roads set in oak woodlands for horseback riding and sweaty hiking or biking. A little discovery here, however, is that the Canyon Trail (the trailhead is located on the south side of the park access road) will lead you to a rock-studded, 25-foot waterfall, beautifully set in a canyon, complete with a redwood canopy. In all, there are 21 miles of trail here. It will launch your perspective and your camping trip into a new dimension.

37 Lake Berryessa Marina Resort

Location: On Lake Berryessa; map D1, grid g7.

Campsites, facilities: There are 70 sites for tents and 53 RV sites with water and electrical hookups. Flush toilets, showers, sanitary disposal station, coin laundry, snack bar, complete marina facilities (including boat repair), RV supplies, and groceries are available. Leashed pets are permitted.

Reservations, fees: Reservations are recommended; $15 to $24 per night, $1 pet fee. Open year-round.

Contact: Lake Berryessa Marina Resort, (707) 966-2161 or fax (707) 966-0761.

Directions: From Vallejo, drive north on Interstate 80 to the Suisun Valley Road exit. Take Suisun Valley Road and drive north to Highway 121. Turn north on Highway 121 and drive five miles to Highway 128. Turn left on Highway 128, drive five miles to Berryessa Knoxville Road, turn right, and continue nine miles to 5800 Knoxville Road.

Trip notes: Lake Berryessa is the Bay Area's backyard water recreation headquarters, the number one lake (in the greater Bay Area) for waterskiing, loafing, and fishing. This resort is set on the west shore of the main lake, one of several resorts at the lake.

38 Spanish Flat Resort

Location: On Lake Berryessa; map D1, grid g7.

Campsites, facilities: There are 120 sites for tents or RVs, a few with partial hookups. Picnic tables, fire grills, and piped water are provided. Flush toilets, showers, boat launch, complete marina facilities, boat rentals, and groceries are available. Coin laundry, restaurant, post office, and RV supplies are available within 1.5 miles. The facilities are wheelchair accessible. Leashed pets are permitted.

Reservations, fees: Reservations are accepted; $20 to $23 per night. Open year-round.

Contact: Spanish Flat Resort, (707) 966-7700 or fax (707) 966-7704.

Directions: From Vallejo, drive north on Interstate 80 to the Suisun Valley Road exit. Take Suisun Valley Road and drive north to Highway 121. Turn north on Highway 121 and drive five miles to Highway 128. Turn north on Highway 128 and drive five miles. Turn right on Berryessa-Knoxville Road and continue four miles to 4290 Knoxville Road.

Trip notes: This is one of several lakeside camps at Lake Berryessa. Berryessa, considered the Bay Area's backyard fishing hole, is the third largest man-made lake in Northern California (Lakes Shasta and Oroville are larger). It is a popular lake for powerboating, waterskiing, and fishing. Trout fishing is good, trolling deep in the summer or drifting with minnows in fall and winter. The elevation is approximately 500 feet.

㊴ Pleasure Cove Resort

Location: On Lake Berryessa; map D1, grid h8.

Campsites, facilities: There are 105 sites for tents or RVs (20 have water and electrical hookups). Picnic tables and fire grills are provided. Rest rooms, showers, ice, restaurant, bar, boat ramp, propane gas, and groceries are available. Leashed pets are permitted.

Reservations, fees: Reservations are accepted; $16 to $18 per night, $2 pet fee.

Contact: Pleasure Cove Resort, (707) 966-2172 or fax (707) 966-0320.

Directions: From Vallejo, drive north on Interstate 80 about 10 miles to the Suisun Valley Road exit. Take Suisun Valley Road and drive north another 10 miles to Highway 121. Turn north right on Highway 121 and drive about eight miles to the end of Highway 121 and the junction with Highway 128. Bear southeast on Highway 128 and proceed four miles to Wragg Canyon Road. Turn left and continue three miles to the resort entrance.

Trip notes: Pleasure Cove is set on the south end of Lake Berryessa, an excellent area for trout and bass fishing. Top spots that are nearby include the Monticello Dam, the narrows, and Skier's Cove for trout, and the back of the coves of the Markley Cove arm for bass. This park is family oriented.

㊵ Napa Town and Country Fairgrounds

Location: In Napa; map D1, grid h6.

Campsites, facilities: There are 100 RV sites, many with electrical and water hookups, and an open area with space for 400 self-contained units. Rest rooms, showers, coin laundry, and a sanitary disposal station are provided. A grocery store and restaurant are within walking distance. Leashed pets are permitted.

Reservations, fees: No reservations except for groups of 15 or more; $15 per night.

Contact: Napa Town and Country Fairgrounds, (707) 253-4900 or fax (707) 253-4943; email: nvexpo.aol.com.

Directions: From Napa on Highway 29, drive to the Napa/Lake Berryessa exit. Turn east and drive to Third Street. Turn right and drive to Burnell Street and the campground entrance.

Trip notes: This campground is actually the parking area for the Napa Fairgrounds. When the fair is in operation in early August, it is closed temporarily. The rest of the year it is simply a large parking lot near Napa.

㊶ Lake Solano County Park

Location: Near Lake Berryessa; map D1, grid h9.

Campsites, facilities: There are 90 sites for tents or RVs up to 35 feet long, 40 sites with full hookups. Piped water, fire grills, and tables are provided. A sanitary disposal station, flush toilets, showers, boat ramp, and boat rentals are available. A grocery store is within walking distance. Some facilities are wheelchair accessible. Leashed pets are accepted with proof of vaccination.

Reservations, fees: Reservations are accepted; $15 to $18 per night, $1 pet fee. Open year-round.

Contact: Lake Solano County Park, (530) 795-2990 or fax (530) 795-1408.

Directions: In Vacaville, turn north on Interstate 505 and drive 11 miles to the junction of

Highway 128. Turn west on Highway 128 and drive about five miles (past Winters) to Pleasant Valley Road. Turn left on Pleasant Valley Road and drive to the park at 8685 Pleasant Valley Road.

Trip notes: Lake Solano provides a low-pressure option to nearby Lake Berryessa. It is a long, narrow lake set below the outlet at Monticello Dam at Lake Berryessa, technically called the afterbay. Compared to Berryessa, life here moves at a much slower pace and some people prefer it. The lake has fair trout fishing in the spring. The camp can also be used as an overflow area if the camps at Berryessa fill on popular weekends.

㊷ San Francisco North/ Petaluma KOA

Location: Near Petaluma; map D1, grid i2.

Campsites, facilities: There are 312 sites for tents or RVs (161 drive-through), many with full or partial hookups, and 34 cabins. Picnic tables and fire grills are provided. Flush toilets, showers, cable TV hookups, sanitary disposal station, playground, recreation rooms, swimming pool, whirlpool, petting zoo, shuffleboard, coin laundry, propane gas, and a grocery store are available. Some facilities are wheelchair accessible. Leashed pets are permitted.

Reservations, fees: Reservations are recommended; $29 to $40 per night, cabins are $39 per night. Open year-round.

Contact: San Francisco North/Petaluma KOA, (707) 763-1492 or fax (707) 763-2668; website: www. koakampgrounds.com

Directions: From Petaluma on US 101, take the Penngrove exit and drive west for a quarter mile on Petaluma Boulevard to Stony Point Road. Turn north on Stony Point Road and drive to Rainsville Road. Turn west on Rainsville Road and drive to 20 Rainsville Road.

Trip notes: This campground is less than a mile from US 101, yet it has a rural feel. It's a good base camp for folks who require some quiet mental preparation before heading south to the Bay Area or to the nearby wineries, redwoods, and the Russian River. The big plus here is that this KOA has the cute log cabins called "Kamping Kabins," providing privacy for those who want it.

Map D2

One inch equals approximately 10.7 miles.
See inside back cover for California state map.

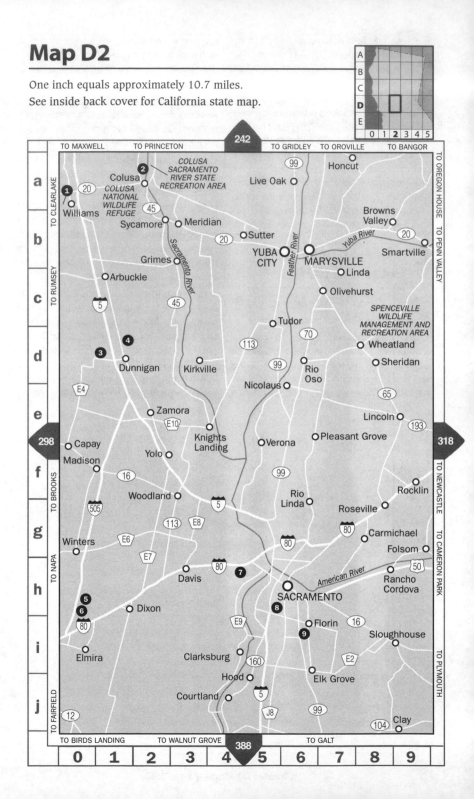

TO MAXWELL   TO PRINCETON   242   TO GRIDLEY   TO OROVILLE   TO BANGOR

TO CLEARLAKE
TO RUMSEY
TO BROOKS
TO NAPA
TO FAIRFIELD

TO OREGON HOUSE
TO PENN VALLEY
TO NEWCASTLE
TO CAMERON PARK
TO PLYMOUTH

298   318

TO BIRDS LANDING   TO WALNUT GROVE   388   TO GALT

Colusa
COLUSA SACRAMENTO RIVER STATE RECREATION AREA
Live Oak
Honcut
Williams
20
COLUSA NATIONAL WILDLIFE REFUGE
Sycamore
45
Meridian
Sutter
Browns Valley
20
Grimes
20
YUBA CITY
Feather River
Yuba River
MARYSVILLE
Smartville
Arbuckle
Linda
45
Olivehurst
5
Tudor
SPENCEVILLE WILDLIFE MANAGEMENT AND RECREATION AREA
113
70
Wheatland
Dunnigan
Kirkville
99
Rio Oso
Sheridan
Nicolaus
E4
65
Zamora
E10
Lincoln
193
Capay
Yolo
Knights Landing
Verona
Pleasant Grove
Madison
16
99
Woodland
5
Rio Linda
Rocklin
505
113
E8
Roseville
Winters
E6
80
Carmichael
E7
80
Folsom
Davis
80
7
American River
50
5
Rancho Cordova
Elmira
Dixon
SACRAMENTO
8
E9
Florin
16
9
Sloughhouse
Clarksburg
160
E2
Hood
Elk Grove
Courtland
5
J8
99
Clay
12
104

Chapter D2 features:

1 Almond Grove Mobile Home Park

Location: In Williams; map D2, grid a0.

Campsites, facilities: There are seven pull-through RV sites with full hookups. Picnic tables, rest rooms, and showers are provided. Cable TV and a coin laundry are available. A store is nearby (within six blocks). Pets must be controlled.

Reservations, fees: Reservations are accepted; $14 per night. Open year-round.

Contact: Almond Grove Mobile Home Park, (530) 473-5620.

Directions: From the Central Valley on Interstate 5, drive to Williams and the Central Williams exit. Take that exit and drive west on E Street for eight blocks. Turn left on 12th Street and drive three blocks to the entrance at 880 12th Street.

Trip notes: The town of Williams is set in the middle of the Sacramento Valley, a popular spot to stop and grab a bite at its outstanding delicatessen (Granzella's), where there is a gigantic stuffed polar bear.

2 Colusa–Sacramento River State Recreation Area

Location: Near Colusa; map D2, grid a2.

Campsites, facilities: There are 14 sites for tents or RVs up to 30 feet long. Rest rooms, hot showers, sanitary dump station, picnic tables, and fire grills are provided. A grocery store and coin laundry are nearby (within three blocks). A boat ramp is available. Leashed pets are permitted.

Reservations, fees: No reservations; $10 to $14 per night, $4 boat fee, $5 fee per extra vehicle. Open year-round.

Contact: Colusa–Sacramento River State Recreation Area, (530) 458-4927 or (530) 538-2200.

Directions: In Williams, at the junction of Interstate 5 and Highway 20, drive east on Highway 20 for 10 miles to the town of Colusa. Turn north on 10th Street and drive a short distance, just over the levee, to the park.

Trip notes: This region of the Sacramento Valley is well known as a high-quality habitat for birds. Nearby Delevan National Wildlife Refuge is an outstanding destination for wildlife viewing, and provides good duck hunting in December. In summer months the nearby Sacramento River is a bonus with shad fishing in June and July, salmon fishing from August through October, sturgeon fishing in the winter, and striped bass fishing in the spring.

3 Campers Inn

Location: Near Dunnigan; map D2, grid d1.

Campsites, facilities: There are 13 tent sites and 72 RV sites (44 drive-through) with full or partial hookups. Flush toilets, picnic tables, showers, heated pool, clubhouse, horseshoes, nine-hole golf course, coin laundry, propane gas, ice, and groceries are available. The facilities are wheelchair accessible. Leashed pets are permitted.

Reservations, fees: Reservations are accepted; $15 to $21 per night. Open year-round.

Contact: Campers Inn, (530) 724-3350, or fax (530) 724-3110.

Directions: From Interstate 5, take the Dunnigan exit (just north of the Interstate 505 cutoff). Drive west on County Road E-4 for a mile to County Road 88. Turn north and drive for 1.5 miles to the park.

Trip notes: This private park has a rural valley

atmosphere and provides a layover for drivers cruising Interstate 5. The Sacramento River, located to the east, is the closest body of water, but this section of river is hardly a premium side trip destination. There are no nearby lakes.

❹ Happy Time RV Park

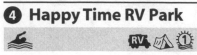

Location: Near Dunnigan; map D2, grid d1.

Campsites, facilities: There are eight tent sites and 30 RV sites (18 drive-through) with full hookups. Flush toilets, showers, picnic tables, playground, coin laundry, and a swimming pool are available. Leashed pets are permitted.

Reservations, fees: Reservations are accepted; $18 to $20 per night. Open year-round.

Contact: Happy Time RV Park, (530) 724-3336.

Directions: From Interstate 5 near the Interstate 505 intersection, take the County Road 8 exit. Drive east on County Road 8 for a short distance to Road 99W. Turn left on Road 99W and drive a block to the campground.

Trip notes: If you are cruising Interstate 5 and are exhausted, or need to take a deep breath before hitting the Bay Area or Sacramento, this private park can provide a respite and, to be honest, not a whole lot more. Restaurants are available in nearby Dunnigan.

❺ Neil's Vineyard RV Park

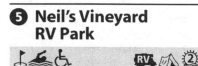

Location: Near Vacaville; map D2, grid h0.

Campsites, facilities: There are 10 tent sites and 110 RV sites (20 drive-through) with full hookups. Flush toilets, showers, picnic tables, swimming pool, coin laundry, sanitary disposal station, putting green, pay phones, and ice are available. Pets are permitted.

Reservations, fees: Reservations are recommended; $18 to $25 per night, $1 pet fee. Open year-round.

Contact: Neil's Vineyard RV Park, 4985 Midway Road, Vacaville, CA 95688; (707) 447-8797.

Directions: From Sacramento, drive west on Interstate 80 and take the Midway exit. Turn left

on Frontage Road and drive to Midway Road. Turn right on Midway and drive 2.5 miles to the park.

From Vacaville on Interstate 80, turn north on Interstate 505 and drive three miles to Midway Road. Turn east on Midway Road and travel a half mile to the campground on the left.

Trip notes: This is one of two privately operated parks in the area set up primarily for RVs. It is in a eucalyptus grove, with clean, well-kept sites. If you are heading to the Bay Area, it is late in the day, and you don't have your destination set, this spot offers a chance to hole up for the night and formulate your travel plans.

❻ Gandy Dancer

Location: Near Vacaville; map D2, grid h0.

Campsites, facilities: There are 51 RV sites, all drive-through with full hookups. Flush toilets, showers, picnic tables, swimming pool, children's pool, coin laundry, and ice are available. Pets are permitted.

Reservations, fees: Reservations are recommended; $18 per night. Open year-round.

Contact: Gandy Dancer, (707) 446-7679.

Directions: From Vacaville on Interstate 80, turn north on Interstate 505 and drive three miles to Midway Road. Turn east on Midway Road and travel a quarter mile to the campground.

Trip notes: This layover spot for RV cruisers is near Vacaville. Six Flags Marine World in Vallejo is located within a half-hour drive.

❼ Sacramento-Metro KOA

Location: West of Sacramento; map D2, grid h4.

Campsites, facilities: There are 27 tent sites and 95 RV sites with full or partial hookups. Ten cabins are also available. Flush toilets, showers, playground, swimming pool, coin laundry, propane gas, and groceries are available. Pets are permitted.

Reservations, fees: Reservations are recommended; $23 to $29 per night, cabins are $36 per night. Open year-round.

Contact: Sacramento-Metro KOA, (916) 371-6771 or (800) 545-KAMP/5267.

Directions: From Sacramento, drive west on Interstate 80 about four miles to the West Capitol Avenue exit. Exit and turn left onto West Capitol Avenue, going under the freeway to the first stoplight and the intersection with Lake Road. Turn left onto Lake Road and continue a half block to the camp on the left at 3951 Lake Road.

Trip notes: This is the choice of car and RV campers touring California's capital and looking for a layover spot. It is located in downtown Sacramento near the Capitol building and the railroad museum.

⑧ Stillman Trailer Park

🛶🏊♿   🚐 ①

Location: In Sacramento; map D2, grid h5.

Campsites, facilities: There are 65 RV sites with full hookups. Flush toilets, showers, coin laundry, clubhouse, and a swimming pool are available. Adults only. Small pets are permitted.

Reservations, fees: Reservations are accepted; $28 per night. Open year-round.

Contact: Stillman Trailer Park, (916) 392-2820.

Directions: In Sacramento on Highway 99, take the 47th Avenue West exit and go to the first light at Stillman Park Circle. Turn right and the park will be just ahead at 3880 Stillman Park Circle.

Trip notes: This is an adults-only RV park located in downtown Sacramento near the Capitol and the railroad museum. It's a popular layover spot in summer months.

⑨ 99 Trailer Park

🚐 ②

Location: Near Sacramento; map D2, grid i6.

Campsites, facilities: There are 26 RV sites with full hookups, including phone. There are no rest room facilities. Weekly residents preferred. A grocery store, coin laundry, and propane gas are within 300 feet. Leashed pets are permitted.

Reservations, fees: Reservations are accepted; $18 per night.

Contact: 99 Trailer Park, (916) 423-4078.

Directions: From Sacramento, drive south on Highway 99 to the Sheldon Road exit. Turn west and drive to Stockton Boulevard (frontage road). Make a hard right on Stockton Boulevard and drive a short distance to the park.

Trip notes: This is a popular RV park for folks touring Sacramento because it's about a five-minute drive from the city. Most of the sites are tree shaded and that's a good thing, since Sacramento does a good job of imitating a furnace in the summer. Maybe it's all the hot air emanating from the mouths of politicians. Side trips include all the sights of California's capital city, of course, and the nearby Consumnes River.

Map D3

One inch equals approximately 10.7 miles.
See inside back cover for California state map.

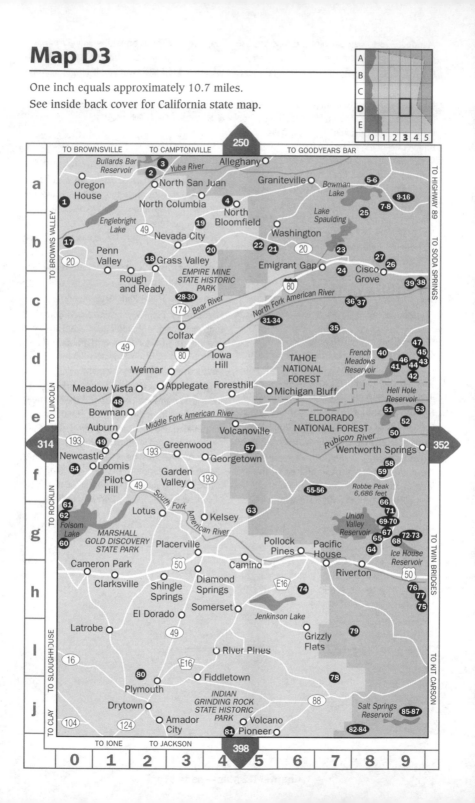

Chapter D3 features:

① Collins Lake Recreation Area

Location: Near Marysville on Collins Lake; map D3, grid a0.

Campsites, facilities: There are 159 sites for tents or RVs (29 drive-through), many with partial hookups (52 are located along the lakefront). There are also three group picnic areas. Picnic tables, fire grills, and piped water are provided. A large open camping area is nearby, which requires no reservations and has piped water and chemical toilets. Flush toilets, sanitary disposal station, coin-operated showers, boat ramp, boat rentals, sandy swimming beach, volleyball, marina, grocery store, coin laundry, wood, ice, and propane gas are available. Many facilities are wheelchair accessible. Leashed pets are permitted.

Reservations, fees: Reservations are recommended; $15 to $24 per night. Open year-round.

Contact: Collins Lake Recreation Area, (530) 692-1600 or fax (530) 692-1607.

Directions: From Marysville, drive east on Highway 20 for about 12 miles to Marysville Road. Turn north and drive approximately eight miles to the recreation area entrance road on the right. Turn right, drive a mile to the entrance station, and then continue to the campground on the left side of the road.

Trip notes: Collins Lake is set in the foothill country east of Marysville at 1,200 feet in elevation, ideal in spring and early summer for the camper, boater, and angler. The lake has 12 miles of shoreline and is quite pretty in the spring.

Fishing is good for trout until late June and, after that, the warm water makes the lake exceptional for waterskiing. There is a marina adjacent to the campground, and farther south is a swimming beach and boat ramp.

② Moonshine Campground

Location: Near the Yuba River and Bullards Bar Reservoir; map D3, grid a2.

Campsites, facilities: There are 25 sites for tents or RVs, all with partial hookups. Picnic tables, fire rings, and piped water are provided. Vault toilets, ice, and firewood are available. A grocery store and propane gas are available about three miles away in North San Juan. Leashed pets are permitted.

Reservations, fees: Reservations are required; $20 to $25 per night. Open May through October 5.

Contact: Moonshine Campground, (530) 288-3585.

Directions: From Auburn, drive north on Highway 49 to Nevada City and continue for 17 miles through the town of North San Juan. Continue on Highway 49 and cross a bridge over the Middle Fork Yuba to Moonshine Road. Turn left on Moonshine Road and drive three-quarters of a mile to the campground.

Trip notes: This campground features shaded sites and a swimming hole on the nearby Middle Fork Yuba River. Both are needed, with the weather hot here in the summer, at roughly 2,400 feet in the Sierra foothills. It's a seven-mile drive to a three-lane boat ramp at Dark Day Picnic Area at Bullards Bar Reservoir, the feature side trip.

❸ Hornswoggle Group Camp

Location: On Bullards Bar Reservoir in Tahoe National Forest; map D3, grid a2.

Campsites, facilities: There are four 25-person group sites and one 50-person group site. Picnic tables, fire grills, piped water, and flush and vault toilets are provided. A boat ramp is nearby. Supplies are available at the marina. Leashed pets are permitted.

Reservations, fees: Reservations are required; phone Emerald Cove Marina, (530) 692-3200; $25 to $50 per night. Open year-round.

Contact: Tahoe National Forest, North Yuba/Downieville Ranger District, (530) 288-3231 or fax (530) 692-3200.

Directions: From Auburn, drive north on Highway 49 to Nevada City and continue for 17 miles through the town of North San Juan. Continue on Highway 49 and cross a bridge over the Middle Fork Yuba to Moonshine Road. Turn left on Moonshine Road and drive five miles to Marysville Road. Turn north and drive about a mile to the campground on the right.

Trip notes: This camp is designed for group use. A three-lane concrete boat ramp is located two miles north at the Dark Day Picnic Area. For information about family campgrounds and boat-in sites, see the listings for Bullards Bar Reservoir in chapter C3.

❹ Malakoff Diggins State Historic Park

Location: Near Nevada City; map D3, grid a4.

Campsites, facilities: There are 30 sites for tents or RVs up to 24 feet long. Piped water, flush toilets (except mid-November through February), picnic tables, and fire grills are provided. A small grocery store is nearby (within seven miles). Pets must be controlled.

Reservations, fees: Reserve for Memorial Day through Labor Day via phone at (800) 444-PARK/7275 ($7.50 reservation fee) or website www.cal-parks.ca.gov; $10 per night, $5 for an extra vehicle, $1 pet fee. Open year-round.

Contact: California State Parks, Goldrush District, (530) 265-2740.

Directions: From Auburn, drive north on Highway 49 to Nevada City and continue 11 miles to the junction of Tyler Foote Crossing Road (it will become Cruzon Grade). Turn right and drive 16 miles (the last two are quite steep) to the entrance.

Trip notes: This camp is set near a small lake in the park, but the main attraction of the area is the gold mining history. Tours of the numerous historic sites are available during the summer months. The elevation is 3,400 feet.

❺ Jackson Creek

Location: Near Bowman Lake in Tahoe National Forest; map D3, grid a8.

Campsites, facilities: There are 14 primitive tent sites. There is no piped water, but vault toilets, picnic tables, and fire grills are provided. Pack out your garbage. Leashed pets are permitted.

Reservations, fees: No reservations; no fee. Open June through September, weather permitting.

Contact: Tahoe National Forest, Nevada City Ranger District, (530) 265-4531 or fax (530) 478-6109.

Directions: From Sacramento, drive east on Interstate 80 past Emigrant Gap to Highway 20. Head west on Highway 20 and drive to Bowman Road/County Road 18. Turn right and drive about 12 miles to Bowman Lake (much of the road is quite rough), then continue for a mile east of the lake to the campground on the left.

Trip notes: This primitive campground is located at 5,600 feet, adjacent to Jackson Creek, a primary feeder stream to Bowman Lake to the nearby west. There are several lakes within a five-mile radius, including Bowman Lake, Jackson Meadow Reservoir, Sawmill Lake (private), and Faucherie Lake. A trailhead is available a mile south (on the right side of the road) at the north end of Sawmill Lake. The trail is routed to a series of pretty Sierra lakes to the west of Haystack Mountain (7,391 feet).

❻ Bowman Lake

Location: In Tahoe National Forest; map D3, grid a8.

Campsites, facilities: There are seven primitive tent sites. There is no piped water, but vault toilets are provided. Pack out your garbage. Leashed pets are permitted.

Reservations, fees: No reservations; no fee.

Contact: Tahoe National Forest, Nevada City Ranger District, (530) 265-4531 or fax (530) 478-6109.

Directions: From Sacramento, drive east on Interstate 80 past Emigrant Gap to Highway 20. Head west on Highway 20 and drive to Bowman Road/County Road 18. Turn right and drive about 12 miles (much of the road is quite rough) to Bowman Lake and the campground on the right side of the road at the head of the lake.

Trip notes: Bowman is a sapphire jewel set in Sierra granite at 5,568 feet, extremely pretty and ideal for campers with cartop boats. There is no boat ramp (you wouldn't want to trailer a boat on the access road anyway), but there are lots of small rainbow trout that are eager to please during the evening bite. The camp is set on the eastern end of the lake, just below where Jackson Creek pours in. The lake is flanked by Bowman Mountain (7,392 feet) and Red Hill (7,075 feet) to the south and Quartz Hill (7,025 feet) to the north.

❼ Faucherie Lake Group Camp

Location: Near Bowman Lake in Tahoe National Forest; map D3, grid a8.

Campsites, facilities: There is a large group camp for tents or RVs up to 22 feet long. The camp accommodates up to 25 campers. There is no piped water, but vault toilets, picnic tables, and fire grills are provided. Pack out your garbage. Leashed pets are permitted.

Reservations, fees: Reserve via phone at (877) 444-6777 ($8.65 reservation fee) or website www.reserveusa.com; $30 per night. Open June through October.

Contact: Tahoe National Forest, Nevada City Ranger District, (530) 265-4531 or fax (530) 478-6109.

Directions: From Sacramento, drive east on Interstate 80 past Emigrant Gap to Highway 20. Head west on Highway 20 and drive to Bowman Road/County Road 18. Turn right and drive about 12 miles (much of the road is quite rough) to Bowman Lake and continue a mile to a Y. Bear right at the Y and drive about three miles to the campground at the end of the road.

Trip notes: Faucherie Lake is the kind of place that most people believe can only be reached by long, difficult hikes with a backpack. Guess again: here it is, set in Sierra granite at 6,100 feet in elevation, quiet and pristine, a classic alpine lake. It is ideal for cartop boating and has decent fishing for both rainbow and brown trout. This is a group camp on the lake's northern shore, a prime spot, with the outlet creek nearby. Note: Road washouts may require four-wheel drive.

❽ Canyon Creek

Location: Near Faucherie Lake in Tahoe National Forest; map D3, grid a8.

Campsites, facilities: There are 20 sites for tents. There is no piped water, but vault toilets, picnic tables, and fire grills are provided. Pack out your garbage. Leashed pets are permitted.

Reservations, fees: No reservations; no fee. Open June through October.

Contact: Tahoe National Forest, Nevada City Ranger District, (530) 265-4531 or fax (530) 478-6109.

Directions: From Sacramento, drive east on Interstate 80 to Emigrant Gap. Take the off-ramp and head north on the short connector road to Highway 20. Turn west on Highway 20 and drive four miles to Bowman Road/County Road 18. Turn right and drive about 12 miles (nine of these miles are paved, but the rest is quite rough) to Bowman Lake and continue a mile to a Y. Bear right at the Y and drive about two miles to the campground on the right side of the road.

Trip notes: This pretty spot is at 6,000 feet in Tahoe National Forest, a mile from Sawmill Lake (which you pass on the way in) and a mile from pretty Faucherie Lake. It is set along Canyon Creek, the stream that connects those two lakes. Of the two, Faucherie provides better fishing and, because of that, there are fewer people at Sawmill. Take your pick. A trailhead is available at the north end of Sawmill Lake with a hike to several small alpine lakes, a great day or overnight backpacking trip.

⑨ Silver Tip Group Camp

Location: At Jackson Meadow Reservoir in Tahoe National Forest; map D3, grid a9.

Campsites, facilities: There are two 25-person group sites for tents or RVs up to 22 feet long. Piped water, vault toilets, picnic tables, and fire grills are provided. Obtain supplies in Truckee or Sierraville. A boat ramp is nearby. Leashed pets are permitted.

Reservations, fees: Reserve via phone at (877) 444-6777 ($8.65 reservation fee) or website www.reserveusa.com; $37.50 group fee per night. Open late June through October.

Contact: Tahoe National Forest, Sierraville Ranger District, (530) 944-3401 or fax (530) 994-3143; California Land Management (530) 582-0120.

Directions: From Truckee, drive north on Highway 89 for 17.5 miles to Forest Service Road 7. Turn left on Forest Service Road 7 and drive 16 miles to Jackson Meadow Reservoir. At the lake, continue across the dam around the west shoreline and then turn left at the campground access road. The entrance is on the right just before the Woodcamp boat ramp.

Trip notes: This group camp is set on the southwest edge of Jackson Meadow Reservoir at 6,200 feet, in a pretty area with pine forest, high meadows, and the trademark granite look of the Sierra Nevada. A boat ramp and swimming beach are located nearby at Woodcamp. For more information, see the trip notes for Woodcamp (campground number 10).

⑩ Woodcamp

Location: At Jackson Meadow Reservoir in Tahoe National Forest; map D3, grid a9.

Campsites, facilities: There are 10 sites for tents and 10 sites for tents or RVs up to 22 feet long. Piped water, flush toilets, picnic tables, and fire grills are provided. Supplies are available in Truckee or Sierraville. A boat ramp is adjacent to the camp. Leashed pets are permitted.

Reservations, fees: Reservations are accepted; $11 per night, $5 for each additional vehicle. Open June through October.

Contact: Tahoe National Forest, Sierraville Ranger District, (530) 944-3401 or fax (530) 994-3143; California Land Management, (530) 582-0120.

Directions: From Truckee, drive north on Highway 89 for 17.5 miles to Forest Service Road 7. Turn left on Forest Service Road 7 and drive 16 miles to Jackson Meadow Reservoir. At the lake, continue across the dam around the west shoreline and then turn left at the campground access road. The entrance is on the right just before the Woodcamp boat ramp.

Trip notes: Woodcamp and Pass Creek (see campground number 11) are the best camps for boaters at Jackson Meadow Reservoir because each is directly adjacent to a boat ramp. That is critical because fishing is far better by boat here than from shore, with a good mix of both rainbow and brown trout. The camp is set at 6,100 feet along the lake's southwest shore, in a pretty spot with a swimming beach and short interpretive hiking trail nearby. This is a beautiful lake in the Sierra Nevada, complete with pine forest and a classic granite backdrop.

⑪ Pass Creek

Location: At Jackson Meadow Reservoir in Tahoe National Forest; map D3, grid a9.

Campsites, facilities: There are 15 sites for tents and 15 sites for RVs up to 22 feet long. Piped water, sanitary dump station, vault and flush toilets, picnic tables, and fire grills are provided. A boat ramp is nearby. Supplies are available in Truckee or Sierraville. Leashed pets are permitted.

Reservations, fees: Reserve via phone at (877) 444-6777 ($8.65 reservation fee) or website www.reserveusa.com; $11 per night, $5 for an extra vehicle. Open June through October.

Contact: Tahoe National Forest, Sierraville Ranger District, (530) 944-3401 or fax (530) 994-3143; California Land Management, (530) 582-0120.

Directions: From Truckee, drive north on Highway 89 for 17.5 miles to Forest Service Road 7. Turn left on Forest Service Road 7 and drive 16 miles to Jackson Meadow Reservoir; the campground is on the left at the north end of the lake.

Trip notes: This is the premium campground at Jackson Meadow Reservoir, a developed site with water, concrete boat ramp, swimming beach nearby at Aspen Creek Picnic Area, and access to the Pacific Crest Trail a half mile to the east (you'll pass it on the way in). This lake has the trademark look of the high Sierra, and the bonus here is that lake levels are often kept higher than at other reservoirs on the western slopes of the Sierra Nevada. Trout stocks are excellent, with 85,000 rainbow and brown trout planted each summer after ice-out. The elevation is 6,100 feet.

⑫ Fir Top

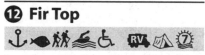

Location: At Jackson Meadow Reservoir in Tahoe National Forest; map D3, grid a9.

Campsites, facilities: There are 12 sites for tents or RVs up to 22 feet long. Piped water, sanitary dump station, flush toilets, picnic tables, and fire grills are provided. Supplies are available in Truckee or Sierraville. A boat ramp is nearby. Some facilities are wheelchair accessible. Leashed pets are permitted.

Reservations, fees: Reserve via phone at (877) 444-6777 ($8.65 reservation fee) or website www.reserveusa.com; $12 per night, $5 for an extra vehicle. Open June through November.

Contact: Tahoe National Forest, Sierraville Ranger District, (530) 944-3401 or fax (530) 994-3143; California Land Management, (530) 582-0120.

Directions: From Truckee, drive north on Highway 89 for 17.5 miles to Forest Service Road 7. Turn left on Forest Service Road 7 and drive 16 miles to Jackson Meadow Reservoir. Continue across the dam and around the lake to the west side. Turn left at the campground access road. The campground entrance is on the right across from the entrance to the Woodcamp Picnic Area.

Trip notes: Jackson Meadow is a great destination for a short vacation, and that's why there are so many campgrounds available; it's not exactly a secret. This camp is set on a cove on the lake's southwest shore, less than a mile from a boat ramp near Woodcamp. See the trip notes for Woodcamp (campground number 10) and Pass Creek (campground number 11) for more information. The elevation is 6,200 feet.

⑬ Findley

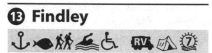

Location: At Jackson Meadow Reservoir in Tahoe National Forest; map D3, grid a9.

Campsites, facilities: There are 15 sites for tents or RVs up to 22 feet long. Piped water, flush toilets, picnic tables, and fire grills are provided. Supplies are available in Truckee or Sierraville. A boat ramp is nearby. The facilities are wheelchair accessible. Leashed pets are permitted.

Reservations, fees: Reserve via phone at (877) 444-6777 ($8.65 reservation fee) or website www.reserveusa.com; $12 per night, $5 for an extra vehicle. Open late June through October.

Contact: Tahoe National Forest, Sierraville Ranger District, (530) 944-3401 or fax (530) 994-3143; California Land Management, (530) 582-0120.

Directions: From Truckee, drive north on Highway 89 for 17.5 miles to Forest Service Road 7. Turn left on Forest Service Road 7 and drive 16 miles to Jackson Meadow Reservoir. Continue across the dam around the lake to the west side. Turn left at the campground access road and drive about a quarter mile to the entrance on the left.

Trip notes: Findley is set near Woodcamp Creek, a quarter mile from where it pours into Jackson Meadow Reservoir. Though it is not a lakeside camp, it is quite pretty just the same, and within a half mile of the boat ramp near

Woodcamp. It is set at 6,200 feet. This is one of several camps at the lake.

⑭ Jackson Point Boat-In

Location: At Jackson Meadow Reservoir in Tahoe National Forest; map D3, grid a9.

Campsites, facilities: There are 10 tent sites. There is no piped water, but vault toilets, picnic tables, and fire grills are provided. Supplies are available in Truckee or Sierraville. Leashed pets are permitted.

Reservations, fees: No reservations; no fee. Open late June through September.

Contact: Tahoe National Forest, Sierraville Ranger District, (530) 944-3401 or fax (530) 994-3143; California Land Management, (530) 582-0120.

Directions: From Truckee, drive north on Highway 89 for 17.5 miles to Forest Service Road 7. Turn left on Forest Service Road 7 and drive 16 miles to Jackson Meadow Reservoir. Drive to Pass Creek and boat launch (on the left at the north end of the lake). Launch your boat and cruise a half mile south to Jackson Point and the boat-in campsites.

Trip notes: This is one of the few boat-in camps available anywhere in the high Sierra. The gorgeous spot is situated on the end of a peninsula that extends from the east shore of Jackson Meadow Reservoir. Small and primitive, it's the one place at the lake where you can gain entry into the 5 Percent Club. From the point, there is a spectacular view of the Sierra Buttes. Because the lake levels are kept near full all summer, this boat-in camp is doubly appealing. The elevation is 6,100 feet.

⑮ East Meadow

Location: At Jackson Meadow Reservoir in Tahoe National Forest; map D3, grid a9.

Campsites, facilities: There are 20 tent sites and 26 sites for tents or RVs. (Some sites can accommodate RVs 40 feet in length, most can accommodate 22 feet). Piped water, flush toilets, picnic tables, and fire grills are provided. A sanitary dump station and boat ramp are available at Pass Creek. Supplies are available in Truckee or Sierraville. Some facilities are wheelchair accessible. Leashed pets are permitted.

Reservations, fees: Reserve via phone at (877) 444-6777 ($8.65 reservation fee) or website www.reserveusa.com; $13 per night, $5 for an extra vehicle. Open late June through October.

Contact: Tahoe National Forest, Sierraville Ranger District, (530) 944-3401 or fax (530) 994-3143; California Land Management, (530) 582-0120.

Directions: From Truckee, drive north on Highway 89 for 17.5 miles to Forest Service Road 7. Turn left on Forest Service Road 7 and drive 15 miles to the campground entrance road on the left (if you reach Pass Creek, you have gone too far). Turn left and drive a mile to the campground on the right.

Trip notes: This camp is in a beautiful setting on the east side of Jackson Meadow Reservoir, on the edge of a sheltered cove. The Pacific Crest Trail passes right by camp, providing access for a day trip, though no stellar destinations are on this stretch of the PCT. The nearest boat ramp is at Pass Creek , two miles away. The elevation is 6,100 feet.

⑯ Aspen Group Camp

Location: At Jackson Meadow Reservoir in Tahoe National Forest; map D3, grid a9.

Campsites, facilities: There are two 25-person group sites and a 50-person group site for tents or RVs up to 22 feet long. Piped water, vault toilets, sanitary dump station, picnic tables, fire grills, and a campfire circle are provided. There is a boat ramp nearby at Pass Creek. Supplies are available in Truckee or Sierraville. Leashed pets are permitted.

Reservations, fees: Reserve via phone by (877) 444-6777 ($8.65 reservation fee) or website www.reserveusa.com; $55 to $110 group fee per night. Open June through October.

Contact: Tahoe National Forest, Sierraville Ranger District,(530) 944-3401 or fax (530) 994-3143; California Land Management, (530) 582-0120.

Directions: From Truckee, drive north on Highway 89 for 17.5 miles to Forest Service Road 7. Turn left on Forest Service Road 7 and drive 16 miles (a mile past Pass Creek) to the campground entrance on the right.

Trip notes: A swimming beach, boat ramp, and easy access to adjacent Jackson Meadow Reservoir make this a premium group camp. The elevation is 6,100 feet.

---

⑰ Englebright Lake Boat-In

Location: Near Marysville; map D3, grid b0.

Campsites, facilities: There are 100 boat-in sites along the shores of Englebright Lake and a group camping area that accommodates 40 people (by reservation only). Picnic tables, fire grills, and pit toilets are provided. Two boat ramps are available on either side of Skippers Cove (and more boat-in campsites). Boat rentals (including houseboats), mooring, fuel dock, and groceries are available. Leashed pets are permitted.

Reservations, fees: No reservations (except group-use area); $6 per night, $2 boat-launch fee from May to October. Open year-round.

Contact: US Army Corps of Engineers, Englebright Lake, (530) 639-2342; Skippers Cove concessionaire, (530) 639-2272 or fax (530) 639-0610.

Directions: From Auburn, drive north on Highway 49 to Grass Valley and the junction with Highway 20. Turn west on Highway 20 and drive to Mooney Flat Road (if you reach Smartville, you have gone a mile too far). Turn right on Mooney Flat and drive three miles to a fork. Turn left at the fork and drive a mile to park headquarters and the boat ramp just east of the dam.

Trip notes: Englebright Lake is an outstanding destination for boat-in camping, fishing, and waterskiing. Remember this place. It always seems to have plenty of water, and there are more developed boat-in campsites than at any other lake in California. The lake looks like a huge water snake, long and narrow, set in the Yuba River Canyon at 520 feet in elevation. Trout fishing is good in the spring, when waterskiing is prohibited on the upper end of the lake. In sum-

mer, it is a waterskiing mecca, with warm and calm water.

⑱ Nevada County Fairgrounds

Location: At the fairgrounds near Grass Valley; map D3, grid b2.

Campsites, facilities: There are 120 sites for RVs, all with hookups. Two sanitary dump stations, showers, and flush toilets are available. Leashed pets are permitted.

Reservations, fees: Reservations are accepted; $15 per night. A 14-day limit is enforced. Open year-round.

Contact: Nevada County Fairgrounds, PO Box 2687, Grass Valley, CA 95945; (530) 273-6217 or fax (530) 273-1146.

Directions: From Auburn, drive north on Highway 49 to Grass Valley. Take either the McKnight Way or Empire Street exit and follow the signs to the Nevada County Fairgrounds.

Trip notes: The motto here is "California's Most Beautiful Fairgrounds," and they're right. The area is set at 2,300 feet in the Sierra foothills, with a good number of pines sprinkled about. The park is located adjacent to the fairgrounds, and even though the fair runs for a few weeks every summer, the park is open year-round. A caretaker at the park is available to answer any questions. Kids can fish at a small lake nearby.

⑲ South Yuba

Location: Near the Yuba River; map D3, grid b3.

Campsites, facilities: There are 16 sites for tents or RVs up to 27 feet long. Piped water, pit toilets, picnic tables, and fire grills are provided. Leashed pets are permitted.

Reservations, fees: No reservations; $5 per night. Open March through October.

Contact: The Bureau of Land Management, Folsom Field Office, (916) 985-4474.

Directions: From Auburn, turn north on Highway 49, drive to Nevada City, and then continue a short distance to North Bloomfield Road. Turn right and drive 10 miles to the campground on the right side of the road (the road becomes quite rough).

Alternate route for RVs or vehicles with trailers: From Auburn turn north on Highway 49 to Nevada City and continue to Tyler Foote Crossing Road. Turn right and drive to Grizzly Hills Road (just past North Columbia). Turn right and drive three miles to North Bloomfield Road. Turn left and drive to the campground on the right.

Trip notes: This little-known BLM camp is set next to where little Kenebee Creek enters the Yuba River. The Yuba is about a mile away, with some great swimming holes to explore. A good side trip is to nearby Malakoff Diggins State Historic Park and the town of North Bloomfield (about a 10-minute drive to the northeast on North Bloomfield Road), which is being completely restored to its 1850s character. Hopefully, that does not include the food. The elevation is 2,600 feet.

⑳ Scotts Flat Lake Recreation Area

Location: Near Grass Valley; map D3, grid b4.

Campsites, facilities: There are 187 sites for tents or RVs up to 35 feet long. Restrooms, showers, and a sanitary dump station are provided. A general store, bait and tackle shop, boat rentals, boat ramp, and a playground are also available. Most facilities are wheelchair accessible. Leashed pets are permitted.

Reservations, fees: Reservations are recommended in the summer; $18 to $23 per night. Open year-round, weather permitting.

Contact: Scotts Flat Lake Recreation Area, (530) 265-5302.

Directions: From Auburn, drive north on Highway 49 to Grass Valley and the junction with Highway 20. Turn right and drive five miles to Scotts Flat Road. Turn right and drive four miles (three miles paved, a mile gravel) to the camp entrance road on the right (on the north shore of the lake).

Trip notes: Scotts Flat Reservoir (at 3,100 feet in elevation) is shaped like a large teardrop, one of the prettier lakes in the Sierra foothills, with 7.5 miles of shoreline circled by forest. The camp is set on the lake's north shore, largely protected from spring winds and within short range of the marina and one of the lake's two boat launches. Trout fishing is good here in the spring and early summer. When the lake heats up, waterskiing and powerboating become more popular.

㉑ Skillman Group Camp

Location: In Tahoe National Forest; map D3, grid b5.

Campsites, facilities: This group campsite can accommodate up to 8 campers in one area and 25 in another. Piped water, vault toilets, picnic tables, and fire grills are provided. Horse corrals, tie rails and troughs are available. Leashed pets are permitted.

Reservations, fees: Reserve via phone at (877) 444-6777 ($8.65 reservation fee) or website www.reserveusa.com; $15 to $50 per night. Open May through November, weather permitting.

Contact: Tahoe National Forest, Nevada City Ranger District, (530) 265-4531 or fax (530) 478-6109; Sierra Recreation Managers, (209) 295-4512.

Directions: From Sacramento, drive east on Interstate 80 past Emigrant Gap to Highway 20. Turn west on Highway 20 and drive 12 miles to the campground entrance on the left.

Trip notes: Skillman Group Camp is set at 4,400 feet, on a loop access road just off of Highway 20, and the historic Pioneer Trail runs right through it. See the trip notes for White Cloud (campground number 22) for more information.

㉒ White Cloud

Location: In Tahoe National Forest; map D3, grid b5.

Campsites, facilities: There are 46 sites for tents or RVs up to 22 feet long. Piped water, vault and flush toilets, picnic tables, and fire grills are provided. Leashed pets are permitted.

Reservations, fees: Reservations required;

reserve via phone at (877) 444-6777 ($8.65 reservation fee) or website www.reserveusa.com; $10 per night. Open June through October.

Contact: Tahoe National Forest, Nevada City Ranger District, (530) 265-4531 or fax (530) 478-6109; Sierra Recreation Managers, (209) 295-4512.

Directions: From Sacramento, drive east on Interstate 80 to Emigrant Gap. Take the off-ramp and then head north on the short connector road to Highway 20. Turn west on Highway 20 and drive about 15 miles to the campground entrance on the left.

Trip notes: This camp is set along the historic Pioneer Trail, which has turned into one of the top mountain bike routes in the Sierra Nevada, easy and fast. The trail traces the route of the first wagon road opened by emigrants and gold seekers in 1850. It is best suited for mountain biking, with a lot of bikers taking the one-way downhill ride (with an extra car for a shuttle ride) from Bear Valley to Lone Grave. The Omega Overlook is the highlight, with dramatic views of granite cliffs and the Yuba River. The elevation is 4,200 feet.

㉓ Lake Spaulding

Location: Near Emigrant Gap; map D3, grid b8.

Campsites, facilities: There are 25 sites for tents or RVs up to 20 feet long. Piped water, picnic tables, fire grills, and vault toilets are provided. A boat ramp is available. Supplies are available in Nevada City. Leashed pets are permitted.

Reservations, fees: No reservations; $13 per night, $1 pet fee.

Contact: PG&E Building and Land Services, (916) 386-5164.

Directions: From Sacramento, drive east on Interstate 80 past Emigrant Gap to Highway 20. Drive west on Highway 20 to Lake Spaulding Road. Turn right on Lake Spaulding Road and travel a half mile to the lake.

Trip notes: Lake Spaulding is set at 5,000 feet in the Sierra Nevada, complete with huge boulders and a sprinkling of conifers. Its clear, pure, very cold water has startling effects on swim-

mers. The lake is extremely pretty, with the Sierra granite backdrop looking as if it has been cut, chiseled, and smoothed. The drive here is nearly a straight shot up Interstate 80, the boat ramp is fine for small aluminum boats, and if there is any problem here, it is that there will be plenty of company at the campground. Fishing for kokanee salmon and rainbow trout is often good, as well as fishing for trout at the nearby South Fork Yuba River. There are many other lakes set in the mountain country to the immediate north that can make for excellent side trips, including Bowman, Weaver, and Faucherie Lakes.

㉔ Lodgepole

Location: On Lake Valley Reservoir in Tahoe National Forest; map D3, grid b7.

Campsites, facilities: There are 18 sites for tents or RVs up to 20 feet long. Piped water, picnic tables, fire grills, and vault toilets are provided. A boat ramp is available nearby. Supplies can be obtained off Interstate 80. Leashed pets are permitted.

Reservations, fees: No reservations; $13 per night, $1 pet fee.

Contact: PG&E Building and Land Services, (916) 386-5164.

Directions: From Interstate 80, take the Yuba Gap exit and drive south for a quarter mile to Lake Valley Road. Turn right on Lake Valley Road and drive for a mile until the road forks. Bear right and continue for 1.5 miles to the campground entrance road to the right on another fork.

Trip notes: Lake Valley Reservoir is set at 5,786 feet and covers 300 acres. It is gorgeous when full, its shoreline sprinkled with conifers and boulders. The lake provides decent results for anglers, who have the best luck while trolling. A speed limit prohibits waterskiing and jet skiing, and that keeps the place quiet and peaceful. The camp is about a quarter mile from the lake's southwest shore and two miles from the boat ramp on the north shore. A trailhead from camp leads south up Monumental Ridge and to Monumental Creek (three miles, one way) on the northwestern flank of Quartz Mountain (6,931 feet).

25 Grouse Ridge

Location: Near Bowman Lake in Tahoe National Forest; map D3, grid a8.

Campsites, facilities: There are nine sites for tents only. No piped water. Vault toilets, picnic tables, and fire grills are provided. Pack out your garbage. Leashed pets are permitted.

Reservations, fees: No reservations; no fee. Open June through October.

Contact: Tahoe National Forest, Nevada City Ranger District, (530) 265-4531 or fax (530) 478-6109.

Directions: From Sacramento, drive east on Interstate 80 past Emigrant Gap to Highway 20. Turn west on Highway 20 and drive to Bowman Road/County Road 18. Turn north on Bowman Road and drive five miles to Grouse Ridge Road. Turn right on Grouse Ridge Road and drive six miles on rough gravel to the campground.

Trip notes: Grouse Ridge is set at 7,400 feet at the gateway to some beautiful hiking country filled with small high Sierra lakes. The camp is primarily used as a trailhead and jump-off point, not as a destination itself. The closest hike is the half-mile tromp up to the Grouse Ridge Lookout, 7,707 feet, which provides a spectacular view to the north of this area and its many small lakes. Hiking north, the trail passes Round Lake (to the left) in the first mile and Middle Lake (on the right) two miles later, with opportunities to take cutoff trails on either side of the ridge to visit numerous other lakes.

26 Woodchuck

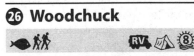

Location: On Rattlesnake Creek in Tahoe National Forest; map D3, grid b8.

Campsites, facilities: There are eight sites for tents or RVs up to 16 feet long. There is no piped water, but vault toilets, picnic tables, and fire grills are provided. A grocery store and propane gas are also available nearby. Leashed pets are permitted.

Reservations, fees: No reservations; no fee. Open June through October.

Contact: Tahoe National Forest, Nevada City Ranger District, (530) 265-4531 or fax (530) 478-6109.

Directions: From Sacramento, drive east on Interstate 80 to Yuba Pass and continue for about four miles to the Cisco Grove exit north. Take that exit, turn left on the frontage road, and drive a short distance to Rattlesnake Road (just prior to reaching Thousand Trails). Turn right on Rattlesnake Road (gravel, steep, and curvy; trailers not recommended) and drive three miles to the campground on the right.

Trip notes: This small camp is only a few miles from Interstate 80, but it is quite obscure and little known to most travelers. It is set on Rattlesnake Creek at 6,300 feet in Tahoe National Forest, at the threshold of some great backcountry and four-wheel-drive roads that access many beautiful lakes. To explore, a map of Tahoe National Forest is a must.

27 Indian Springs

Location: Near the Yuba River in Tahoe National Forest; map D3, grid b8.

Campsites, facilities: There are 35 sites for tents or RVs up to 25 feet long. Piped water, vault toilets, picnic tables, and fire grills are provided. A grocery store and propane gas are also available nearby. Leashed pets are permitted.

Reservations, fees: No reservations; $11 per night, $5 for each additional vehicle. Open May through October.

Contact: Tahoe National Forest, Nevada City Ranger District, (530) 265-4531 or fax (530) 478-6109; Sierra Recreation Managers, (209) 295-4512.

Directions: From Sacramento, drive east on Interstate 80 to Yuba Pass and continue for about three miles to the Eagle Lakes exit. Head north on Eagle Lakes Road for a mile to the campground on the left side of the road.

Trip notes: The camp is easy to reach from Interstate 80, yet is in a beautiful setting at 5,600 feet along the South Fork Yuba River. This is a gorgeous stream, running deep blue-green and pure through a granite setting, complete with giant boulders and beautiful pools. Trout fishing is fair. There is a small beach nearby where you can go swimming, though the water is cold. There are also several lakes in the vicinity.

28 Long Ravine

Location: On Rollins Lake; map D3, grid c3.

Campsites, facilities: There are 84 sites for tents or RVs. Flush toilets, picnic tables, and barbecues or fire pits are provided. Hot showers, parking pads, hiking trails, and a dump station are available. A full-service marina with floating gas dock, stores, restaurant, and boat rentals is nearby. Pets must be controlled.

Reservations, fees: Reservations are recommended; $18 to $25 per night.

Contact: Long Ravine, (530) 346-6166.

Directions: From Auburn, drive northeast on Interstate 80 for about 20 miles. Turn north on Highway 174 (a winding, two-lane road) and drive about two miles. Turn right on Rollins Lake Road and drive to the campground at 26909 Rollins Lake Road.

Trip note: Long Ravine is one of three campgrounds at Rollins Lake, a popular lake for fishing (bass and trout) and waterskiing. The lake, in the Sierra foothills at 2,100 feet, has two extensive lake arms covering 26 miles of shoreline. It also has long stretches of open water near the lower end of the lake, making it excellent for waterskiing, with water surface temperatures ranging from 75 to 80 degrees in the summer.

29 Orchard Springs

Location: On Rollins Lake; map D3, grid c3.

Campsites, facilities: There are 80 sites with full hookups for tents or RVs. Picnic tables, fire rings, and barbecues are provided. Rest rooms, showers, launch ramp, floating gas dock, swimming beach, group picnic area, and a store are available. Leashed pets are permitted.

Reservations, fees: Reservations are accepted; $16 to $25 per night, $2 pet fee.

Contact: Orchard Springs, PO Box 270, Colfax,

CA 95713; (530) 346-2212; email: orchard@gv.net.

Directions: From Auburn, drive northeast on Interstate 80 for about 20 miles. Turn north on Highway 174 (a winding, two-lane road) and drive about 3.5 miles. Turn right on Orchard Springs Road and drive a half mile to the road's end. Turn right at the gatehouse and continue to the campground.

Trip notes: Orchard Springs is set on the shore of Rollins Lake in the Sierra Nevada foothills among pine, oak, and cedar trees. The summer heat makes the lake excellent for waterskiing, boating, and swimming, and the spring and fall are great for trout and bass fishing.

30 Peninsula Campground

Location: On Rollins Lake; map D3, grid c3.

Campsites, facilities: There are 78 sites for tents or RVs up to 38 feet long. Piped water, modem access, fire rings, and picnic tables are provided. Rest rooms with flush toilets and hot showers, dump station, boat rentals, boat launch ramp, swim beach, and a country store are available. Leashed pets are permitted.

Reservations, fees: Reservations are accepted; $18 to $30 per night with a maximum of six campers and a vehicle per site.

Contact: Peninsula Campground, PO Box 344, Chicago Park, CA 95712; (530) 477-9413; email: pencamp@oro.net; website www.rollins-lake resort.com.

Directions: From Auburn, drive northeast on Interstate 80 for about 20 miles. Turn north on Highway 174 (a winding, two-lane road) and drive about six miles. Turn right on You Bet Road, drive 4.3 miles (turning right again to stay on You Bet Road), and continue another 3.1 miles to the campground entrance at 21597 You Bet Road.

Trip notes: Peninsula Campground is set on a point that extends into Rollins Lake, flanked on each side by two sprawling lake arms. If you like boating, waterskiing, or swimming, you'll definitely like this place in the summer. If you want trout, prospects are best in April and May. After that the fast boats take over, though there is a good bass bite at dawn and dusk.

㉛ Forbes Creek Group Camp

Location: On Sugar Pine Reservoir in Tahoe National Forest; map D3, grid c5.

Campsites, facilities: There are two group campsites, Madrone and Rocky Ridge, each of which can accommodate up to 50 people in tents or RVs up to 30 feet long. Piped water, vault toilets, picnic tables, and fire grills are provided. All facilities are wheelchair accessible. A campfire circle, central parking area, sanitary dump station, and a boat ramp are available nearby. Supplies can be obtained in Foresthill. Leashed pets are permitted.

Reservations, fees: Reserve via phone at (877) 444-6777 ($8.65 reservation fee) or website www.reserveusa.com; $55 per night.

Contact: Tahoe National Forest, Foresthill Ranger District, (530) 367-2224 or fax (530) 367-2992; L & L, Inc., (800) 342-2267.

Directions: From Sacramento, drive east on Interstate 80 to the north end of Auburn and the Foresthill Road exit. Take that exit and drive east for eight miles to Sugar Pine Road. Turn left and drive seven miles to a fork (just before reaching the lake). Turn right and drive two miles around the south end of the lake to the campground on the left.

Trip notes: The boat launch is nearby, but note: a 10 mph speed limit is the law. That makes for quiet water, perfect for anglers, canoeists, and other small boats. A paved trail circles the lake. For more information see Giant Gap (campground number 32).

㉜ Giant Gap

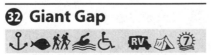

Location: On Sugar Pine Reservoir in Tahoe National Forest; map D3, grid c5.

Campsites, facilities: There are 30 sites for tents or RVs up to 30 feet long. Piped water,

vault toilets, picnic tables, and fire grills are provided. Some facilities are wheelchair accessible. A sanitary dump station and boat ramp are available on the south shore. Supplies can be obtained in Foresthill. Leashed pets are permitted.

Reservations, fees: Reserve via phone at (877) 444-6777 ($8.65 reservation fee) or website www.reserveusa.com; $10 to $27 per night.

Contact: Tahoe National Forest, Foresthill Ranger District, (530) 367-2224 or fax (530) 367-2992; L & L, Inc., (800) 342-2267.

Directions: From Sacramento, drive east on Interstate 80 to the north end of Auburn and the Foresthill Road exit. Take that exit, drive east to Foresthill, and continue for eight miles to Sugar Pine Road. Turn left and drive seven miles to a fork (just before reaching the lake). Turn left and drive for about a mile to the campground on the right.

Trip notes: This is a lakeside spot along the western shore of Sugar Pine Reservoir at 3,500 feet in elevation in Tahoe National Forest. For boaters, there is a ramp on the south shore. Note that a 10 mph speed limit is the law, making this lake ideal for anglers in search of quiet water. Other recreation notes: There's a little less than a mile of paved trail which goes through the day-use area. Big Reservoir, located five miles to the east, is the only other lake in the region and also has a campground. The trout fishing at Sugar Pine is fair, but much better than that at Big Reservoir.

㉝ Big Reservoir

Location: On Big Reservoir in Tahoe National Forest; map D3, grid c5.

Campsites, facilities: There are 100 sites for tents or RVs up to 25 feet long. Piped water, vault toilets, showers, picnic tables, and fire grills are provided. Firewood is limited. Supplies are available in Foresthill. Leashed pets are permitted.

Reservations, fees: Reservations are accepted; $15 per night. Open May through October.

Contact: Tahoe National Forest, Foresthill Ranger District, (530) 367-2224 or fax (530) 367-

2992; De Anza Placer Gold Mining Company, (530) 367-2129.

Directions: From Sacramento, drive east on Interstate 80 to the north end of Auburn and the Foresthill Road exit. Take that exit, drive east to Foresthill, and then continue for eight miles to Sugar Pine Road. Turn left and drive about three miles to Forest Service Road 24 (signed Big Reservoir). Bear right on Forest Service Road 24 and drive about five miles to the campground entrance road on the right.

Trip notes: Here's a quiet lake where no boat motors are allowed. That makes it ideal for canoeists, row boaters, and tube floaters who don't like the idea of having to dodge water-skiers or fishermen for that matter, because the fishing is zilch here. The lake is quite pretty and a nice beach is available not far from the resort. The elevation is 4,000 feet.

③④ Shirttail Creek

Location: On Sugar Pine Reservoir in Tahoe National Forest; map D3, grid c5.

Campsites, facilities: There are 30 sites for tents or RVs up to 30 feet long (double and triple sites are available). Piped water, vault toilets, picnic tables, and fire grills are provided. Some facilities are wheelchair accessible. A sanitary dump station and boat ramp are available on the south shore. Supplies can be obtained in Foresthill. Leashed pets are permitted.

Reservations, fees: Reserve via phone at (877) 444-6777 ($8.65 reservation fee) or website www.reserveusa.com; $10 per night.

Contact: Tahoe National Forest, Foresthill Ranger District, (530) 367-2224 or fax (530) 367-2992; L & L, Inc., (800) 342-2267.

Directions: From Sacramento, drive east on Interstate 80 to the north end of Auburn and the Foresthill Road exit. Take that exit, drive east to Foresthill, and then continue for eight miles to Sugar Pine Road. Turn left and drive seven miles to a fork (just before reaching the lake). Turn left and drive approximately three miles to the campground on the right.

Trip notes: This camp is set near the little creek that feeds into the north end of Sugar Pine Res-

ervoir. The boat ramp is located all the way around the other side of the lake in Sugar Pine Cove near Forbes Creek Group Camp. For recreation information, see the trip notes for Giant Gap (campground number 32).

③⑤ Secret House

Location: In Tahoe National Forest; map D3, grid c7.

Campsites, facilities: There are two tent sites. There is no piped water, but vault toilets, picnic tables, and fire grills are provided. Pack out your garbage. Supplies are available in Foresthill. Leashed pets are permitted.

Reservations, fees: No reservations; no fee. Open May through October.

Contact: Tahoe National Forest, Foresthill Ranger District, (530) 367-2224 or fax (530) 367-2992.

Directions: From Sacramento, drive east on Interstate 80 to the north end of Auburn and the Foresthill Road exit. Take that exit and drive east to Foresthill and Foresthill Divide Road. Continue northeast (the road eventually turns to gravel and is narrow and curvy) and drive 19 miles to the campground on the right side of the road.

Trip notes: Foresthill Divide Road is set on a mountain ridge with a series of trailheads on the left side of the road. They provide access to old mining trails that lead down to the North Fork American River. These are some of the steepest hiking trails in California, with 2,000-foot drops over the course of two miles typical for all the routes, but the payoff is a series of secluded and pristine streamside hikes and fishing spots. The camp itself is perched in forest on the flank of Whiskey Hill. The nearest trailhead is less than two miles up the road on the left. The elevation is 5,400 feet.

③⑥ North Fork

Location: On the North Fork of the American River in Tahoe National Forest; map D3, grid c7.

Campsites, facilities: There are 17 sites for tents or RVs up to 16 feet long. Piped water, vault toilets, picnic tables, and fire grills are provided. Supplies are available at Emigrant Gap, Cisco Grove, and Soda Springs. Leashed pets are permitted.

Reservations, fees: No reservations; $11 per night. Open May through October.

Contact: Tahoe National Forest, Nevada City Ranger District, (530) 265-4531 or fax (530) 478-6109.

Directions: From Sacramento, drive east on Interstate 80 to the Emigrant Gap exit. Take that exit and drive south for a quarter mile to Texas Hill Road/County Road 19. Turn right and drive about five miles to the camp on the right.

Trip notes: This is gold mining country, and this camp is set along the Little North Fork of the North Fork American River at 4,400 feet in elevation, where you might still find a few magic gold flecks. Unfortunately, they are probably fool's gold, not the real stuff. This feeder stream is small and pretty, and the camp is fairly remote and overlooked by most. It is set on the edge of a network of backcountry Forest Service roads. To explore them, a map of Tahoe National Forest is a must.

㊲ Tunnel Mill Group Camp

Location: On the North Fork of the American River in Tahoe National Forest; map D3, grid c8.

Campsites, facilities: There are two group sites for tents or RVs up to 16 feet long. Each camp can accommodate up to 50 people. There is no piped water, but vault toilets, picnic tables, and fire grills are provided. Supplies are available at the Nyack exit of Emigrant Gap. Leashed pets are permitted.

Reservations, fees: Reservations are required via phone at (877) 444-6777 ($8.65 reservation fee) or website www.reserveusa.com; call for fees. Open from June through October.

Contact: Tahoe National Forest, Nevada City Ranger District, (530) 265-4531 or fax (530) 478-6109.

Directions: From Sacramento, drive east on Interstate 80 to the Emigrant Gap exit. Drive south for a quarter mile to Texas Hill Road/County Road 19. Turn right and drive about

seven miles to the campground on the right side of the road.

Trip notes: This is a good spot for a Boy or Girl Scout camp out. It's a rustic, quiet group camp set all by itself along the (take a deep breath) East Fork of the North Fork of the North Fork of the American River (whew). See North Fork (campground number 36) for more recreation information. The elevation is 4,400 feet.

㊳ Kidd Lake Group Camp

Location: West of Truckee; map D3, grid c9.

Campsites, facilities: This group site will accommodate up to 100 people in tents only. Piped water, picnic tables, fire grills, and rest rooms are provided. An unimproved boat ramp is available. Supplies are available in Truckee. Leashed pets are permitted.

Reservations, fees: Reservations are required; $15 per night, $2 pet fee.

Contact: PG&E Building and Land Services, PO Box 1148, Auburn, CA 95603; (916) 386-5164.

Directions: From Sacramento, drive east on Interstate 80 toward Truckee. Take the Norden exit, drive a short distance, turn south on Soda Springs Road, and drive a mile to Pahatsi Road. Turn right and drive two miles. When the road forks, bear right and drive a mile to the campground entrance road on the left.

Trip notes: Kidd Lake is one of four lakes bunched in a series along the access road just south of Interstate 80. It is set in the northern Sierra's high country, at 6,500 feet, and gets loaded with snow every winter. In late spring and early summer, always call ahead for conditions on the access road. The fishing is frustrating, consisting of a lot of tiny brook trout. Only cartop boats are permitted on Kidd Lake. The camp is set just northeast of the lake, within walking distance of the shore.

㊴ Hampshire Rocks

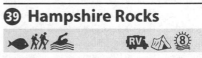

Location: On the Yuba River in Tahoe National Forest; map D3, grid c9.

Campsites, facilities: There are 31 sites for tents or RVs up to 22 feet long. Piped water, vault toilets, picnic tables, and fire grills are provided. A grocery store, restaurant, and propane gas are available nearby. Leashed pets are permitted.

Reservations, fees: Reserve via phone at (877) 444-6777 ($8.65 reservation fee) or website www.reserveusa.com; $11 per night, $5 per additional vehicle. Open May through October.

Contact: Tahoe National Forest, Nevada City Ranger District, (530) 265-4531 or fax (530) 478-6109.

Directions: From Sacramento, drive east on Interstate 80 to Cisco Grove and continue for a mile to the Big Bend exit. Take that exit (remaining just south of the highway), then turn left on the frontage road and drive east for 1.5 miles to the campground.

Trip notes: This camp sits along the South Fork of the Yuba River at 5,900 feet in elevation, with easy access off Interstate 80 and a nearby Forest Service visitor information center. Fishing for trout is fair. There are some swimming holes, but the water is often very cold. Nearby lakes that can provide side trips include Sterling and Fordyce Lakes (drive-to) to the north, and the Loch Leven Lakes (hike-to) to the south.

40 Robinson Flat

Location: Near French Meadows Reservoir in Tahoe National Forest; map D3, grid d8.

Campsites, facilities: There are five tent sites. There is no piped water, but vault toilets, picnic tables, and fire grills are provided. Pack out your garbage. Supplies are available in Foresthill. Leashed pets are permitted.

Reservations, fees: No reservations; no fee. Open May through October.

Contact: Tahoe National Forest, Foresthill Ranger District, (530) 367-2224 or fax (530) 367-2992.

Directions: From Sacramento, drive east on Interstate 80 to the north end of Auburn and the Foresthill Road exit. Take that exit and drive east to Foresthill and Foresthill Divide Road. Continue northeast (the road is narrow and curvy) and drive 27 miles to the junction with County Road

43. The campground is located at the junction.

Trip notes: This camp is set at 6,800 feet in remote Tahoe National Forest, on the eastern flank of Duncan Peak (7,116 feet), with a two-mile drive south to Duncan Peak Lookout (7,182 feet). A trail out of camp follows along a small stream, a fork to Duncan Creek, in Little Robinsons Valley. French Meadows Reservoir is located to the nearby southeast.

41 Poppy Hike-In, Boat-In

Location: On French Meadows Reservoir in Tahoe National Forest; map D3, grid d9.

Campsites, facilities: There are 12 tent sites, accessible by boat or by a mile-long foot trail from McGuire Boat Ramp. There is no piped water, but vault toilets, picnic tables, and fire grills are provided. Supplies are available in Foresthill. Leashed pets are permitted.

Reservations, fees: No reservations; no fee.

Contact: Tahoe National Forest, Foresthill Ranger District, (530) 367-2224 or fax (530) 367-2992; L & L, Inc., (800) 342-2267.

Directions: From Sacramento, drive east on Interstate 80 to the north end of Auburn and the Foresthill Road exit. Take that exit and drive east to Foresthill and Mosquito Ridge Road. Turn east and drive 36 miles (curvy) to a dirt road on the left (a mile before reaching Anderson Dam). Turn left and drive three miles to the end of the road. Park and hike a mile to the camp. Note: The trailhead access road is sometimes blocked by a locked gate, making it a three-mile hike to the campground. An option if the gate is locked is to drive around the lake and hike in a mile from the McGuire Picnic Area.

Trip notes: This camp is located on the north side of French Meadows Reservoir, about midway along the lake's shore. It can be reached only by boat or on foot, supplying a great degree of privacy compared to the other camps on this lake. A trail that is routed along the north shore of the reservoir runs right through the camp, providing two different trailhead access points, as well as a good side trip hike. The lake is quite big, covering nearly 2,000 acres when full, at 5,300 feet in elevation on a dammed-up section of the Middle Fork American River. It is stocked with rainbow trout but also has prime habitat for brown trout, and big ones are sometimes caught by surprise.

㊷ French Meadows

Location: On French Meadows Reservoir in Tahoe National Forest; map D3, grid d9.

Campsites, facilities: There are 75 sites for tents or RVs up to 35 feet long. Piped water, flush toilets, picnic tables, and fire grills are provided. A concrete boat ramp is nearby. Supplies are available in Foresthill. Leashed pets are permitted.

Reservations, fees: Reserve via phone at (877) 444-6777 ($8.65 reservation fee) or website www.reserveusa.com; $10 per night. Open June through October.

Contact: Tahoe National Forest, Foresthill Ranger District, (530) 367-2224 or fax (530) 367-2992; L & L, Inc., (800) 342-2267.

Directions: From Sacramento, drive east on Interstate 80 to the north end of Auburn and the Foresthill Road exit. Take that exit and drive east to Foresthill and Mosquito Ridge Road. Turn east, drive 36 miles (curvy) to Anderson Dam, and then continue along the southern shoreline of French Meadows Reservoir for four miles to the campground.

Trip notes: The nearby boat launch makes this the choice for boating campers. The camp is on French Meadows Reservoir at 5,300 feet. It is set on the lake's southern shore, with the boat ramp located about a mile to the south (you'll see the entrance road on the way in). This is a big lake set in remote Tahoe National Forest in the North Fork American River Canyon with good trout fishing. The lake level often drops in late summer, then a lot of stumps and boulders start poking through the lake surface. This creates navigational hazards for boaters, but it also makes it easier for the fishermen to know where to find the fish. If the fish don't bite here, boaters should make the nearby side trip to pretty Hell Hole Reservoir to the south.

㊸ Gates Group Camp

Location: On the North Fork of the American River in Tahoe National Forest; map D3, grid d9.

Campsites, facilities: There are two 25-person group sites and a 75-person group site for tents or RVs up to 35 feet long. Piped water, vault toilets, picnic tables, fire grills, central parking, and a campfire circle are provided. Obtain supplies in Foresthill. Leashed pets are permitted.

Reservations, fees: Reserve via phone at (877) 444-6777 ($8.65 reservation fee) or website www.reserveusa.com; $40 to $55 fee per night. Open June through October.

Contact: Tahoe National Forest, Foresthill Ranger District, (530) 367-2224 or fax (530) 367-2992; L & L, Inc., (800) 342-2267.

Directions: From Sacramento, drive east on Interstate 80 to the north end of Auburn and the Foresthill Road exit. Take that exit and drive east to Foresthill and Mosquito Ridge Road. Turn east, drive 36 miles (curvy) to Anderson Dam, and then continue for five miles along the southern shoreline to French Meadows Reservoir and a fork at the head of the lake. Bear right at the fork and drive a mile to the camp at the end of the road.

Trip notes: This group camp is well secluded along the North Fork American River, just upstream from where it pours into French Meadows Reservoir. For recreation options, see the trip notes for French Meadows (campground number 42), Lewis (campground number 46); Coyote Group Camp (campground number 44).

㊹ Coyote Group Camp

Location: On French Meadows Reservoir, in Tahoe National Forest; map D3, grid d9.

Campsites, facilities: There are three 25-person group sites and a 50-person group site for tents or RVs up to 35 feet long. Piped water, vault toilets, picnic tables, and fire grills are provided. A campfire circle and central parking area are also provided. Supplies are available in Foresthill. Leashed pets are permitted.

Reservations, fees: Reserve via phone at (877) 444-6777 ($8.65 reservation fee) or website www.reserveusa.com; $40 to $55 group fee per night or $1 per person. Open June through October.

Contact: Tahoe National Forest, Foresthill Ranger District, (530) 367-2224 or fax (530) 367-2992; L & L, Inc., (800) 342-2267.

Directions: From Sacramento, drive east on Interstate 80 to the north end of Auburn and the Foresthill Road exit. Take that exit and drive east to Foresthill and Mosquito Ridge Road. Turn east and drive 36 miles (curvy) to Anderson Dam, then continue for five miles along the southern shoreline to French Meadows Reservoir and a fork at the head of the lake. Bear left at the fork and drive a half mile to the camp on the left side of the road.

Trip notes: This group camp is set right at the head of French Meadows Reservoir, at 5,300 feet in elevation. A boat ramp is located two miles to the south, just past Lewis (campground number 46) on the lake's north shore. For recreation options, see the trip notes for Poppy Hike-In, Boat-In (campground number 41) and French Meadows (campground number 42).

⑤ Ahart

Location: Near French Meadows Reservoir in Tahoe National Forest; map D3, grid d9.

Campsites, facilities: There are 12 sites for tents or RVs up to 22 feet long. There is no piped water, but vault toilets, picnic tables, and fire grills are provided. Supplies are available in Foresthill. Leashed pets are permitted.

Reservations, fees: No reservations; $7 per night. Open June through October.

Contact: Tahoe National Forest, Foresthill Ranger District, (530) 367-2224 or fax (530) 367-2992; L & L, Inc., (800) 342-2267.

Directions: From Sacramento, drive east on Interstate 80 to the north end of Auburn and the Foresthill Road exit. Take that exit and drive east to Foresthill and Mosquito Ridge Road. Turn east, drive 36 miles (curvy) to Anderson Dam, and then continue for five miles along the southern shoreline to French Meadows Reservoir and a fork at the head of the lake. Bear left at the fork and drive 1.5 miles to the campground.

Trip notes: This camp is located a mile north of French Meadows Reservoir near where the Middle Fork of the American River enters the

lake. It is primarily used as an overflow camp if lakeside camps are filled. This is bear country in the summer.

⑥ Lewis

Location: On French Meadows Reservoir in Tahoe National Forest; map D3, grid d9.

Campsites, facilities: There are 40 sites for tents or RVs up to 35 feet long. Piped water, flush toilets, picnic tables, and fire grills are provided. A concrete boat ramp is nearby. Supplies are available in Foresthill. Leashed pets are permitted.

Reservations, fees: Reserve via phone at (877) 444-6777 ($8.65 reservation fee) or website www.reserveusa.com; $10 per night. Open May through October.

Contact: Tahoe NationalForest, Foresthill Ranger District, (530) 367-2224 or fax (530)367-2992; L & L, Inc., (800) 342-2267.

Directions: From Sacramento, drive east on Interstate 80 to the north end of Auburn and the Foresthill Road exit. Take that exit and drive east to Foresthill and Mosquito Ridge Road. Turn east, drive 36 miles (curvy) to Anderson Dam, and then continue for five miles along the southern shoreline to French Meadows Reservoir and a fork at the head of the lake. Bear left at the fork and drive a half mile to the campground entrance road on the left. Turn left and drive a mile to the camp on the right.

Trip notes: This camp is not right at lakeside but is just across the road from French Meadows Reservoir. It is still quite pretty, set along a feeder creek near the lake's northeast shore. A boat ramp is available only a half mile to the south, and the adjacent McGuire Picnic Area has a trailhead that is routed along the lake's northern shoreline. This lake is big (2,000 acres) and pretty, created by a dam on the Middle Fork American River, with good fishing for rainbow trout.

⑦ Talbot

Location: On the Middle Fork of the American River in Tahoe National Forest; map D3, grid d9.

Campsites, facilities: There are five tent sites. There is no piped water, but vault toilets, picnic tables, and fire grills are provided. Supplies are available in Foresthill. The camp is within a state game refuge, so no firearms are permitted. Leashed pets are permitted.

Reservations, fees: No reservations; no fee. Open June through October.

Contact: Tahoe National Forest, Foresthill Ranger District, (530) 367-2224 or fax (530) 367-2992.

Directions: From Sacramento, drive east on Interstate 80 to the north end of Auburn and the Foresthill Road exit. Take that exit and drive east to Foresthill and Mosquito Ridge Road. Turn east, drive 36 miles (curvy) to French Meadows Reservoir, and continue to the head of the lake to a fork. Bear left at the fork and continue for 6 miles to the campground.

Trip notes: Talbot camp is set at 5,600 feet along the Middle Fork of the American River, primarily used as a trailhead camp for backpackers heading into the Granite Chief Wilderness. The trail is routed along the Middle Fork American River, turning south into Picayune Valley, flanked by Needle Peak (8,971 feet), Granite Chief (9,886 feet), and Squaw Peak to the east, then beyond to connect with the Pacific Crest Trail. The camp has 10 stalls for horses and pack stock trailer parking. Hitching rails are available at the trailhead.

⓽ Auburn KOA

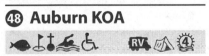

Location: Near Auburn; map D3, grid e1.

Campsites, facilities: There are 10 tent sites and 66 RV sites, all with hookups. There are also two cabins and a rental trailer. Picnic tables, fire grills, flush toilets, showers, and a sanitary dump station are provided. A playground, swimming pool, whirlpool, recreation room, fishing pond, badminton, horseshoes, volleyball, grocery store, coin laundry, and propane gas are available. Leashed pets are permitted.

Reservations, fees: Reservations are accepted; $21 to $28 per night, $36 per night for a cabin and $50 per night for the trailer.

Contact: Auburn KOA, (530) 885-0990.

Directions: From Auburn, drive north on Highway 49 for 3.5 miles to Rock Creek Road (one block past Bell Road). Turn right on Rock Creek Road and follow the signs to 3550 KOA Way.

Trip notes: This year-round KOA park is set at 1,250 feet and has all the amenities. What the heck, it even has a swimming pool.

⓽ Auburn State Recreation Area

Location: Near Auburn; map D3, grid e1.

Campsites, facilities: There are 53 tent sites, 21 boat-in sites, and a group site. Pit toilets, picnic tables, and fire rings are provided. There is no piped water. Leashed pets are permitted.

Reservations, fees: Reserve boat-in sites via phone at (800) 444-PARK/7275 ($7.50 reservation fee) or website www.cal-parks.ca.gov; $7 to $13 per night. Open May 26 through September 4.

Contact: Auburn State Recreation Area, (530) 885-4527, (916) 988-0205; PO Box 3266, Auburn, CA 95604.

Directions: From Auburn, turn south on Highway 49 and drive a mile to the park entrance. The campsites are dispersed throughout the park. For directions to a specific campsite, contact the park office.

Trip notes: This 42,000-acre state park is a jewel in the valley foothill country, at 500 feet in elevation. It is located in the scenic American River Canyon, just far enough out of Sacramento to make visitors feel like they're escaping the city treadmill. The American River runs through the park, offering visitors opportunities to fish, boat, and raft. In addition, there are over 50 miles of hiking and horseback riding trails.

⓾ Middle Meadows Group Camp

Location: On Long Canyon Creek in Eldorado National Forest; map D3, grid e8.

Campsites, facilities: There are two group sites for tents or small RVs. Piped water, vault toilets, and picnic tables are provided. Supplies can be obtained in Foresthill. Leashed pets are permitted.

Reservations, fees: Reserve via phone at (877) 444-6777 ($8.65 reservation fee) or website www.reserveusa.com; $50 per night. Open June through September.

Contact: Eldorado National Forest, Georgetown Ranger District, (530) 333-4312 or fax (530) 333-5522.

Directions: From Sacramento, drive east on Interstate 80 to the north end of Auburn. Take the Elm Avenue exit and turn left at the first stoplight onto Elm Avenue. Drive 0.1 mile, turn left on High Street, and continue through the signal where High Street merges with Highway 49. Travel on Highway 49 for about 3.5 miles, turn right over the bridge, and drive about 2.5 miles into the town of Cool. Turn left on Georgetown Road/Highway 193 and drive about 14 miles into Georgetown. At the four-way stop turn left on Main Street (which becomes Wentworth Springs/Forest Service Road 1) and drive about 25 miles. Turn left on Forest Service Road 2 and drive 19 miles to the campground on the right.

Trip notes: This group camp is within range of several adventures. To the nearby east is Hell Hole Reservoir (you'll need a boat here to do it right), and to the nearby north is French Meadows Reservoir (you'll drive past the dam on the way in). Unfortunately, there isn't a heck of a lot to do at this camp other than watch the water flow by on adjacent Long Canyon Creek.

⑤ Big Meadows

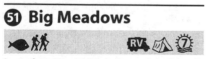

Location: Near Hell Hole Reservoir in Eldorado National Forest; map D3, grid e8.

Campsites, facilities: There are 54 sites for tents or RVs up to 22 feet long. Piped water, vault toilets, picnic tables, and fire grills are provided. Supplies are available in Foresthill. Leashed pets are permitted.

Reservations, fees: No reservations; $8 per night. Open May through November.

Contact: Eldorado National Forest, Georgetown Ranger District, (530) 333-4312 or fax (530) 333-5522.

Directions: From Sacramento, drive east on Interstate 80 to the north end of Auburn. Take the Elm Avenue exit and turn left at the first stoplight onto Elm Avenue. Drive 0.1 mile, turn left on High Street, and continue through the signal where High Street merges with Highway 49. Travel on Highway 49 for about 3.5 miles, turn right over the bridge, and drive about 2.5 miles into the town of Cool. Turn left on Georgetown Road/Highway 193 and drive about 14 miles into Georgetown. At the four-way stop turn left on Main Street (which becomes Wentworth Springs/Forest Service Road 1) and drive about 25 miles. Turn left on Forest Service Road 2 and drive 21 miles to the campground on the left.

Trip notes: This camp sits on a meadow near the ridge above Hell Hole Reservoir (which is about two miles away). For more information, see the trip notes for Hell Hole (campground number 52).

⑤ Hell Hole

Location: Near Hell Hole Reservoir in Eldorado National Forest; map D3, grid e9.

Campsites, facilities: There are 10 sites for tents or RVs. Piped water, vault toilets, picnic tables, and fire grills are provided. Supplies can be obtained in Foresthill. A boat launch is available nearby at the reservoir. Leashed pets are permitted.

Reservations, fees: No reservations; $8 per night.

Contact: Eldorado National Forest, Georgetown Ranger District, (530) 333-4312 or fax (530) 333-5522.

Directions: From Sacramento, drive east on Interstate 80 to the north end of Auburn. Take the Elm Avenue exit and turn left at the first stoplight onto Elm Avenue. Drive 0.1 mile, turn left on High Street, and continue through the signal where High Street merges with Highway 49. Travel on Highway 49 for about 3.5 miles, turn right over the bridge, and drive about 2.5 miles into the town of Cool. Turn left on Georgetown Road/Highway 193 and drive about 14 miles into Georgetown. At the four-way stop turn left on Main Street (which becomes

Wentworth Springs/Forest Service Road 1) and drive about 25 miles. Turn left on Forest Service Road 2 and drive about 22 miles to the campground on the left.

Trip notes: Hell Hole is a mountain temple with sapphire blue water. For the most part, there is limited bank access because of its granite-sculpted shore, and that's why there are no lakeside campsites. This is the closest drive-to camp at Hell Hole Reservoir, about a mile away with a boat launch nearby. Be sure to bring a boat and then enjoy the scenery while you troll for kokanee salmon, brown trout, Mackinaw trout, and a sprinkling of rainbow trout. This is a unique fishery compared to the put-and-take rainbow trout at so many other lakes. The lake elevation is 4,700 feet; the elevation is 5,200 feet.

---

⑤③ Upper Hell Hole Walk-In

Location: On Hell Hole Reservoir in Eldorado National Forest; map D3, grid e9.

Campsites, facilities: There are 15 tent sites, accessible by trail or boat only. There is no piped water, but pit toilets, picnic tables, and fire grills are provided. A boat launch is available at the reservoir. Supplies can be obtained in Foresthill. Leashed pets are permitted.

Reservations, fees: No reservations; no fee. Open May through October.

Contact: Eldorado National Forest, Georgetown Ranger District, (530) 333-4312 or fax (530) 333-5522.

Directions: From Sacramento, drive east on Interstate 80 to the north end of Auburn. Take the Elm Avenue exit and turn left at the first stoplight onto Elm Avenue. Drive 0.1 of a mile, turn left on High Street, and continue through the signal where High Street merges with Highway 49. Travel on Highway 49 for about 3.5 miles, turn right over the bridge, and drive about 2.5 miles into the town of Cool. Turn left on Georgetown Road/Highway 193 and drive about 14 miles into Georgetown. At the four-way stop turn left on Main Street (which becomes Wentworth Springs/Forest Service Road 1) and drive about 25 miles. Turn left on Forest Service Road 2 and drive about 23 miles (a mile past the Hell Hole Campground access road) to the parking area at the boat ramp. From the trailhead hike 3.5 miles to the camp.

Trip notes: This is a beautiful spot, set on the southern shore at the upper end of Hell Hole Reservoir in remote national forest seen by relatively few people. Getting here requires a 3.5-mile walk on a trail routed along the southern edge of the lake overlooking Hell Hole. The trail's short rises and falls can tire you out on a hot day—bring plenty of water. You arrive at this little trail camp, ready to explore onward the next day into the Granite Chief Wilderness, or just do nothing except enjoy adjacent Buck Meadow, the lake's headwaters, and the paradise you have discovered.

---

⑤④ Loomis KOA

Location: In Loomis; map D3, grid f0.

Campsites, facilities: There are 74 RV sites (many with hookups), a separate tent area, and two cabins. Picnic tables, fire grills, flush toilets, showers, and a sanitary dump station are provided. A playground, swimming pool, recreation room, volleyball, horseshoes, grocery store, coin laundry, and propane gas are available. Leashed pets are permitted.

Reservations, fees: (000) 562 3312. Reservations are accepted; $21 to $28 per night, $34 cabin fee per night.

Contact: Loomis KOA, (916) 652-6737.

Directions: From Sacramento, drive east on Interstate 80 to Loomis and the junction of Sierra College Boulevard. Drive north on Sierra College Boulevard for a half mile to Taylor Road. Turn east and drive a half block to the camp.

Trip notes: This KOA park is set in the Sierra foothills, which are known for hot summer weather. The sites are on level gravel and some are shaded. The elevation is 1,200 feet.

---

⑤⑤ Black Oak Group Camp

Location: Near Stumpy Meadows Lake in Eldorado National Forest; map D3, grid f6.

Campsites, facilities: There are four group sites for tents or RVs up to 16 feet long. Piped water, vault toilets, picnic tables, and fire grills are provided. A boat ramp is nearby. Leashed pets are permitted.

Reservations, fees: Reserve via phone at (877) 444-6777 ($8.65 reservation fee) or website www.reserveusa.com; $50 group-use fee. Open April through November.

Contact: Eldorado National Forest, Georgetown Ranger District, (530) 333-4312 or fax (530) 333-5522.

Directions: From Sacramento on Interstate 80, drive east to the north end of Auburn. Turn left on Elm Avenue and drive about 0.1 of a mile. Turn left on High Street and drive through the signal that marks the continuation of High Street as Highway 49. Drive 3.5 miles on Highway 49, turn right over the bridge, and drive 2.5 miles into the town of Cool. Turn left on Georgetown Road/Highway 193 and drive 14 miles into Georgetown. At the four-way stop, turn left on Main Street, which becomes Georgetown-Wentworth Springs Road/Forest Service Road 1. Drive about 18 miles to Stumpy Meadows Lake, and then continue for two miles to the north shore of the lake and the campground entrance road on the right.

Trip notes: This group camp is set directly adjacent to Stumpy Meadows Campground. For more information, see the listing for Stumpy Meadows (campground number 56). The boat ramp for the lake is located just south of the Mark Edson Dam, near the picnic area. The elevation is 4,400 feet.

56 Stumpy Meadows

Location: On Stumpy Meadows Lake in Eldorado National Forest; map D3, grid f6.

Campsites, facilities: There are 40 sites for tents or RVs up to 16 feet long. Piped water, vault toilets, picnic tables, and fire grills are provided. A boat ramp is nearby. Leashed pets are permitted.

Reservations, fees: Reserve via phone at (877) 444-6777 ($8.65 reservation fee) or website www.reserveusa.com; $10 per night, $15 for two-family sites. Open April through November.

Contact: Eldorado National Forest, Georgetown Ranger District, (530) 333-4312 or fax (530) 333-5522.

Directions: From Sacramento on Interstate 80, drive east to the north end of Auburn. Turn left on Elm Avenue and drive about 0.1 of a mile. Turn left on High Street and drive through the signal that marks the continuation of High Street as Highway 49. Drive 3.5 miles on Highway 49, turn right over the bridge, and drive 2.5 miles into the town of Cool. Turn left on Georgetown Road/Highway 193 and drive 14 miles into Georgetown. At the four-way stop, turn left on Main Street, which becomes Georgetown-Wentworth Springs Road/Forest Service Road 1. Drive about 18 miles to Stumpy Meadows Lake. Continue about a mile and turn right into Stumpy Meadows campground.

Trip notes: This is the camp of choice for visitors to Stumpy Meadows Lake. The first thing visitors notice is the huge ponderosa pine trees, noted for their distinctive mosaic-like bark. The lake is set at 4,400 feet in Eldorado National Forest and covers 320 acres with water that is cold and clear. The lake has both rainbow and brown trout, and in the fall provides good fishing for big browns (they move up into the head of the lake, near where Pilot Creek enters).

57 Dru Barner Equestrian Camp

Location: Near Georgetown in Eldorado National Forest; map D3, grid f6.

Campsites, facilities: There are 47 sites for tents or RVs up to 35 feet long. Piped water, vault toilets, picnic tables, two stock troughs, and fire grills are provided. Leashed pets are permitted.

Reservations, fees: No reservations; $6 per night. Open year-round.

Contact: Eldorado National Forest, Georgetown Ranger District, (530) 333-4312 or fax (530) 333-5522.

Directions: From Sacramento on Interstate 80, drive east to the north end of Auburn. Turn left on Elm Avenue and drive about 0.1 mile. Turn left on High Street and drive through the signal that marks the continuation of High Street as Highway 49. Drive 3.5 miles on Highway 49, turn right over the bridge, and drive 2.5 miles into the town of Cool. Turn left on Georgetown Road/Highway 193 and drive 14 miles into Georgetown. At the four-way stop, turn left on Main Street, which becomes Georgetown-Wentworth Springs Road/Forest Service Road 1, and drive 5.5 miles. Turn left on Bottle Hill Bypass Road and drive about a mile to the campground on the left.

Trip notes: This camp, set at 3,200 feet in an area of pine and fir, is ideal for horses; there are miles of equestrian trails. For more information see the listing for Stumpy Meadows (campground number 56) and Black Oak Group Camp (campground number 55).

58 Gerle Creek

Location: On Gerle Creek Reservoir in Eldorado National Forest; map D3, grid f8.

Campsites, facilities: There are 50 sites for tents or RVs up to 22 feet long. Piped water, vault toilets, picnic tables, wheelchair-accessible trails, fire grills, and fishing pier are provided. Leashed pets are permitted.

Reservations, fees: Reserve via phone at (877) 444-6777 ($8.65 reservation fee) or website www.reserveusa.com; $10 per night. Open June through October.

Contact: Eldorado National Forest, Georgetown Ranger District, (530) 333-4312 or fax (530) 333-5522.

Directions: From Sacramento, drive east on US 50 to Riverton and the junction with Ice House Road/Soda Springs–Riverton Road. Turn north and drive about 30 miles (past Union Valley Reservoir) to a fork with Forest Service Road 30. Turn left, drive two miles, bear left on the campground entrance road, and drive a mile to the campground.

Trip notes: This is a small, pretty, but limited spot set along the northern shore of little Gerle Creek Reservoir at 5,231 feet in elevation. The lake is ideal for canoes or other small boats because no motors are permitted and no boat ramp is available. That makes for quiet water. It is set

in the Gerle Creek Canyon, which feeds into the South Fork Rubicon River. No trout plants are made at this lake, and fishing is correspondingly poor. A network of Forest Service roads to the north can provide great exploring. A map of Eldorado National Forest is a must.

59 South Fork

Location: On the South Fork of the Rubicon River in Eldorado National Forest; map D3, grid f8.

Campsites, facilities: There are 17 sites for tents or RVs up to 22 feet long. There is no piped water, but vault toilets, picnic tables and fire grills are provided. Leashed pets are permitted.

Reservations, fees: No reservations; no fee. Open June through October.

Contact: Eldorado National Forest, Placerville Ranger District, (530) 644-6048 or fax (530) 295-5624.

Directions: From Sacramento, drive east on US 50 Riverton and the junction with Ice House Road/Soda Springs–Riverton Road. Turn north and drive about 25 miles to the junction with Forest Service Road 13N28 (3.5 miles past Union Valley Reservoir). Bear left on Forest Service Road 13N28 and drive two miles to the campground entrance on the right.

Trip notes: This primitive national forest camp sits alongside the South Fork Rubicon River, just over a mile downstream from the outlet at Gerle Creek Reservoir. Trout fishing is fair, the water tastes extremely sweet (always pump filter with a water purifier), and there are several side trips available. These include Loon Lake (eight miles to the northeast), Gerle Creek Reservoir (to the nearby north), and Union Valley Reservoir (to the nearby south).

60 Peninsula

Location: In Folsom Lake State Recreation Area; map D3, grid g0.

Campsites, facilities: There are 100 sites for tents or RVs. Picnic tables, fire grills, and piped water are provided. Flush toilets, showers, and a bike path are available. Boat rentals, moorings, snack bar, ice, and bait and tackle are available at the Folsom Lake Marina. Pets are permitted.

Reservations, fees: Reserve via phone at (800) 444-PARK/7275 ($7.50 reservation fee) or website www.cal-parks.ca.gov; $14 to $16 per night, $1 pet fee.

Contact: Folsom Lake State Recreation Area, (916) 988-0205.

Directions: From Placerville, drive east on US 50 to the Spring Street/Highway 49 exit. Turn north on Highway 49 (toward the town of Coloma) and continue 8.3 miles into the town of Pilot Hill and Rattlesnake Bar Road. Turn left on Rattlesnake Bar Road and drive nine miles to the end of the road and the park entrance.

Trip notes: This is one of the big camps at Folsom Lake, but it is also more remote than the other camps, requiring a circuitous drive. It is set on the peninsula on the northeast shore, right where the North Fork American River arm of the lake enters the main lake area. A nearby boat ramp, marina, and boat rentals make this a great weekend spot. Fishing for bass and trout is often quite good in spring and early summer, and waterskiing is popular in the hot summer months.

⑥ Negro Bar Group Camp

Location: In Folsom Lake State Recreation Area; map D3, grid g0.

Campsites, facilities: There are three group sites that can accommodate from 25 to 50 people each. Picnic tables, fire grills, and piped water are provided. Flush toilets, showers, and a bike path are available. A grocery store and coin laundry are nearby. There are boat rentals, moorings, a snack bar, ice, and bait and tackle available at the Folsom Lake Marina.

Reservations, fees: Reserve via phone at (916) 988-0205; $37.50 to $75 per night.

Contact: Folsom Lake State Recreation Area, (916) 988-0205.

Directions: From Interstate 80 north of Sacra-

mento, take the Douglas Boulevard exit and head east for five miles to Auburn-Folsom Road. Turn right on Auburn-Folsom Road and drive south for six miles until the road dead-ends into Greenback Lane. Turn right on Greenback Lane and merge immediately into the left lane. The park entrance is approximately 0.2 mile on the left.

Trip notes: Lake Natoma is the afterbay for Folsom Lake, but it is nothing like Folsom Lake. Natoma is comparatively small (500 acres), very narrow instead of wide, with cold water instead of warm. This camp is set at the head of the lake on the northern shore, with an adjacent boat ramp available. Negro Bar used to have family sites but these were eliminated when the bridge crossing at Lake Natoma was built. Beal's Point (see campground number 62) increased its family sites in compensation.

⑥ Beal's Point

Location: In Folsom Lake State Recreation Area; map D3, grid g0.

Campsites, facilities: There are 69 sites for tents or RVs up to 31 feet long. Picnic tables, fire grills, and piped water are provided. Flush toilets, showers, dump station, bike path, and horseback riding facilities are available. Camping, picnicking, and fishing areas are wheelchair accessible. There are boat rentals, moorings, snack bar, ice, and bait and tackle available at the Folsom Lake Marina. Pets are permitted.

Reservations, fees: Reserve via phone at (800) 444-PARK/7275 ($7.50 reservation fee) or website www.cal-parks.ca.gov; $14 to $16 per night, $1 pet fee. Open year-round.

Contact: Folsom Lake State Recreation Area, (916) 988-0205.

Directions: From Sacramento, drive east on US 50 to the Folsom Boulevard exit. Turn left at the stop sign and continue on Folsom Boulevard for 3.5 miles, following the road as it curves onto Leidesdorff Street. Head east on Leidesdorff Street for a half mile, dead-ending into Riley Street. Turn left onto Riley Street and proceed over the bridge, turning right on Folsom-Auburn Road. Head north on Folsom-Auburn Road for

3.5 miles to the park entrance on the right.

Trip notes: Folsom Lake is Sacramento's backyard vacation spot, a huge lake covering some 12,000 acres with 75 miles of shoreline, which means plenty of room for boating, waterskiing, fishing, and suntanning. This camp is set on its southwest side, just north of the dam, with a boat ramp nearby at Granite Bay. The lake has a productive trout fishery in the spring, a fast-growing population of kokanee salmon, and good prospects for bass in late spring and early summer. By summer water-skiers usually take over the lake each day by about 10 A.M. One problem with this lake is that a minor water drawdown can cause major amounts of shoreline to become exposed on its upper arms.

⑥③ Finnon Lake Resort

Location: Near Placerville; map D3, grid g5.

Campsites, facilities: There are 35 sites for tents or RVs. Piped water, chemical toilets, picnic tables, and fire grills are provided. Pets are permitted.

Reservations, fees: No reservations; $8 per night. Open year-round.

Contact: Finnon Lake Resort, (530) 622-9314.

Directions: From Sacramento, drive east on US 50 to Placerville. Turn north on Highway 49 and drive a mile to the junction with Highway 193. Drive four miles north on Highway 193 to Rock Creek Road. Turn right on Rock Creek Road and drive nine miles to the lake.

Trip notes: Not many out-of-towners head to Finnon Lake, a little county recreation lake set up for small boats that are hand launched and paddle powered. But it does provide lakeside camping and fair fishing for a light mix of bass, sunfish, and bluegill, with warm water for swimming. It is set at 2,200 feet in the foothills, a few miles north of the South Fork American River.

⑥④ Silver Creek

Location: Near Ice House Reservoir in Eldorado National Forest; map D3, grid g8.

Campsites, facilities: There are 11 tent sites.

There is no piped water, but vault toilets, picnic tables, and fire grills are provided. Leashed pets are permitted.

Reservations, fees: No reservations; no fee. Open June through October.

Contact: Eldorado National Forest, Placerville Ranger District, (530) 644-6048 or fax (530) 295-5624.

Directions: From Sacramento, drive east on US 50 to Riverton and the junction with Ice House Road/Soda Springs–Riverton Road. Turn left and drive about seven miles to the campground entrance road on the left (if you reach the junction with Forest Service Road 3, you have gone a quarter mile too far). Turn left and drive a quarter mile to the campground.

Trip notes: Silver Creek might be a pretty spot at 5,200 feet in elevation, but it is rarely the destination of campers. Rather, it is primarily used as an overflow spot if the camps at nearby Ice House Reservoir are full. Ice House is only two miles north, and Union Valley Reservoir is four miles north.

⑥⑤ Jones Fork

Location: On Union Valley Reservoir in Eldorado National Forest; map D3, grid g8.

Campsites, facilities: There are 10 sites for tents or RVs up to 25 feet long. Vault toilets, picnic tables, fire rings, and grills are provided. There is no piped water. Leashed pets are permitted.

Reservations, fees: No reservations; $5 per night, $5 for a third vehicle. Open June through October.

Contact: Eldorado National Forest, Pacific Ranger District, (530) 644-2349 or fax (530) 647-5405.

Directions: From Sacramento, drive east on U.S. 50 to Riverton and the junction with Ice House Road/Soda Springs–Riverton Road. Turn left and drive 14 miles to the campground entrance road on the left (at the south end of Union Valley Reservoir). Turn left and drive a half mile to the campground.

Trip notes: The Crystal Basin Recreation Area is the most popular backcountry region for campers from the Sacramento area, and Union Valley Reservoir is the centerpiece. The area gets its name from the prominent granite Sierra ridge, which looks like crystal when it is covered with frozen snow. This is a big lake, set at 4,900 feet in elevation, with four lakeside campgrounds and three boat ramps providing access. This is the first camp you will arrive at, set at the mouth of the Jones Fork Cove, and is the only camp that is free and without a developed water source.

66 Yellowjacket

Location: On Union Valley Reservoir in Eldorado National Forest; map D3, grid f8.

Campsites, facilities: There are 40 sites for tents or RVs up to 22 feet long. Piped water, vault and flush toilets, picnic tables, and fire grills are provided. A boat ramp is nearby. Leashed pets are permitted.

Reservations, fees: Reserve via phone at (877) 444-6777 ($8.65 reservation fee) or website www.reserveusa.com; $13 for a single site per night, $20 for a double; $5 for a third vehicle. Open June through October.

Contact: Eldorado National Forest, Pacific Ranger District, (530) 644-2349 or fax (530) 647-5405.

Directions: From Sacramento, drive east on US 50 to Riverton and the junction with Ice House Road/Soda Springs–Riverton Road. Turn left and drive 21 miles to Wolf Creek Road (at the head of Union Valley Reservoir). Turn left and drive a mile to the campground entrance road. Turn left and drive a mile to the campground.

Trip notes: The camp, set at 4,900 feet, is located on the north shore of the reservoir. A boat launch adjacent to the camp makes this an ideal destination for trout-angling campers with boats. Union Valley Reservoir, a popular weekend destination for campers from the Central Valley, is stocked with brook trout and rainbow trout by the Department of Fish and Game.

67 Sunset

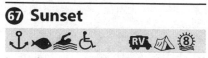

Location: On Union Valley Reservoir in

Eldorado National Forest; map D3, grid g8.

Campsites, facilities: There are 131 sites for tents or RVs up to 22 feet long and 30 walk-in tent sites. Piped water, vault toilets, picnic tables, and fire grills are provided. A boat ramp and sanitary disposal station are available. One site is wheelchair accessible. Leashed pets are permitted.

Reservations, fees: Reserve via phone at (877) 444-6777 ($8.65 reservation fee) or website www.reserveusa.com; $13 for a single site per night, $20 for a double; $5 for a third vehicle. Open June through October.

Contact: Eldorado National Forest, Pacific Ranger District, (530) 644-2349 or fax (530) 647-5405.

Directions: From Sacramento, drive east on US 50 to Riverton and the junction with Ice House Road/Soda Springs–Riverton Road. Turn left and drive 15 miles to the campground entrance road (a mile past the turnoff for Jones Fork Camp). Turn left and drive 1.5 miles to the campground at the end of the road.

Trip notes: This is the prettiest of all the camps at Union Valley Reservoir, set at the eastern tip of the peninsula that juts out into the lake at the mouth of Jones Fork. A nearby boat ramp (you'll see it on the left on the way in) is a big plus, along with a picnic area and beach. The lake has decent trout fishing, with both brook trout and rainbow trout. The place is gorgeous, set at 4,900 feet in the Sierra Nevada.

68 Ice House

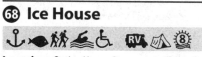

Location: On Ice House Reservoir in Eldorado National Forest; map D3, grid g9.

Campsites, facilities: There are 17 sites for tents and 66 sites for tents or RVs up to 22 feet long. Three sites are wheelchair accessible. Piped water, vault toilets, picnic tables, and fire grills are provided. A boat ramp and sanitary disposal station are available. Leashed pets are permitted.

Reservations, fees: Reservations are accepted via phone at (877) 444-6777 ($8.65 reservation fee) or website www.reserveusa.com; $13 for a single site per night, $20 for a double; $5 for a third vehicle. Open June through October.

Contact: Eldorado National Forest, Pacific Ranger District, (530) 644-2349 or fax (530) 647-5405.

Directions: From Sacramento, drive east on US 50 to Riverton and the junction with Ice House Road/Soda Springs–Riverton Road. Turn left and drive about 11 miles to the junction with Forest Service Road 3 and Ice House Road. Turn right on Ice House Road and drive two miles to the campground access road on the right.

Trip notes: Along with Loon Lake and Union Valley Reservoir, Ice House Reservoir is a feature destination in the Crystal Basin Recreation Area. Ice House gets most of the fishermen and Union Valley gets most of the campers. The camp here is set on the lake's northwestern shore, 5,500 feet in elevation, just up from the dam and adjacent to the lake's boat ramp. The lake was created by a dam on South Fork Silver Creek and covers 650 acres, with the deepest spot about 130 feet deep. It is stocked with rainbow trout, brook trout, and brown trout.

⑥⑨ Azalea Cove Hike-In/Boat-In

Location: On Union Valley Reservoir in Eldorado National Forest; map D3, grid g9.

Campsites, facilities: There are 10 sites for tents only. There is no piped water. Vault toilets, picnic tables, and fire grills are available. Leashed pets are permitted.

Reservations, fees: No reservations; no fee. Open June through September.

Contact: Eldorado National Forest, Pacific Ranger District, (530) 644-2349 or fax (530) 647-5405.

Directions: From Sacramento, drive east on US 50 to Riverton and the junction with Ice House Road/Soda Springs–Riverton Road. Turn left and drive about 17 miles to the campground entrance road (three miles past the turnoff for Sunset Camp).

Trip notes: On the shores of Union Valley Reservoir at 4,900 feet in elevation, there is access to 4.5 miles of bike trail in addition to boating and fishing activities. For additional informa-

tion, see the trip notes for Wench Creek (campground number 71) and Sunset (campground number 67).

⑦⓪ Big Silver Group Camp

Location: On Union Valley Reservoir in Eldorado National Forest; map D3, grid g9.

Campsites, facilities: There is a large group site for tents or RVs up to 22 feet in length. Piped water, vault toilets, picnic tables, and fire rings are available. There is also a group kitchen area with pedestal grills. Some facilities are wheelchair accessible. Leashed pets are permitted.

Reservations, fees: Reservations are required via phone at (877) 444-6777 ($8.65 reservation fee) or website www.reserveusa.com; $50 per night. Open June through September.

Contact: Eldorado National Forest, Pacific Ranger District, (530) 644-2349 or fax (530) 647-5405.

Directions: From Sacramento, drive east on US 50 to Riverton and the junction with Ice House Road/Soda Springs–Riverton Road. Turn left and drive about 17 miles to the campground entrance road (three miles past the turnoff for Sunset Camp).

Trip notes: Like its neighboring campgrounds Wench Creek, Sunset, and Azalea Cove, this camp sits at 4,900 feet in elevation on the shores of Union Valley Reservoir and offers multiple activities, including mountain biking. See neighboring campgrounds for additional information.

⑦① Wench Creek

Location: On Union Valley Reservoir in Eldorado National Forest; map D3, grid g9.

Campsites, facilities: There are 100 sites for tents or RVs up to 22 feet long. There are also two group sites. Piped water, flush toilets, vault toilets, picnic tables, and fire grills are provided. A boat ramp is three miles away at the campground at Yellowjacket. Leashed pets are permitted.

Reservations, fees: No reservations for family sites; $13 for a single site per night, $20 for a double, $5 for a third vehicle. Reserve group sites via phone at (877) 444-6777 ($8.65 reservation fee) or website www.reserveusa.com; $60 group fee. Open June through October.

Contact: Eldorado National Forest, Pacific Ranger District, (530) 644-2349 or fax (530) 647-5405.

Directions: From Sacramento, drive east on US 50 to Riverton and the junction with Ice House Road/Soda Springs–Riverton Road. Turn left and drive 19 miles to the campground entrance road (four miles past the turnoff for Sunset Camp). Turn left and drive a mile to the campground at the end of the road.

Trip notes: Wench Creek is on the northeast shore of Union Valley Reservoir, one of four camps at the lake. For more information, see the trip notes for Jones Fork (campground number 65) and Sunset (campground number 67). The elevation is 4,900 feet.

(72) Northwind

Location: On Ice House Reservoir in Eldorado National Forest; map D3, grid g9.

Campsites, facilities: There are 10 sites for tents or RVs up to 25 feet long. Vault toilets, picnic tables, fire rings, and grills are provided. There is no piped water. Leashed pets are permitted.

Reservations, fees: No reservations; $5 per night, $5 for a third vehicle. Open June through October.

Contact: Eldorado National Forest, Pacific Ranger District, (530) 644-2349 or fax (530) 647-5405.

Directions: From Sacramento, drive east on US 50 to Riverton and the junction with Ice House Road/Soda Springs–Riverton Road. Turn left and drive about 11 miles to the junction with Forest Service Road 3 and Ice House Road. Turn right on Ice House Road and drive about three miles (two miles past the boat ramp) to the campground access road on the right.

Trip notes: This camp sits on the north shore of Ice House Reservoir, one of two rare free campgrounds on the shore of the lake (the other is Strawberry Point). It is located slightly above the reservoir, offering prime views. See the trip notes for Ice House (campground number 68) for more information.

(73) Strawberry Point

Location: On Ice House Reservoir in Eldorado National Forest; map D3, grid g9.

Campsites, facilities: There are 10 sites for tents or RVs up to 25 feet long. Vault toilets, picnic tables, fire rings, and grills are provided. There is no piped water. Leashed pets are permitted.

Reservations, fees: No reservations; $5 per night, $5 for a third vehicle. Open March through December, weather permitting.

Contact: Eldorado National Forest, Pacific Ranger District, (530) 644-2349 or fax (530) 647-5405.

Directions: From Sacramento, drive east on US 50 to Riverton and the junction with Ice House Road/Soda Springs–Riverton Road. Turn left and drive about 11 miles to the junction with Forest Service Road 3 and Ice House Road. Turn right on Ice House Road and drive about four miles (three miles past the boat ramp) to the campground access road on the right.

Trip notes: This camp is one of two free camps on the north shore of Ice House Reservoir, 5,400 feet in elevation. For more information, see the trip notes for Ice House (campground number 68).

(74) Sly Park Recreation Area

Location: On Jenkinson Lake; map D3, grid h6.

Campsites, facilities: There are 159 sites with no hookups for tents or RVs up to 32 feet long. Picnic tables, fire grills, piped water, pit toilets, and two boat ramps are provided. Some facilities are wheelchair accessible. There are five group sites that can accommodate 50 to 100 people and an equestrian camp called Black Oak, which has 15 sites and two youth-group sites. A grocery store, snack bar, bait, and propane gas are available nearby. Firewood is sold on site.

Leashed pets are permitted.

Reservations, fees: Reservations are recommended; (530) 644-2792; $15 per night; $110 minimum group fee for the first 50 people, $1.50 for each additional camper; $1.50 pet fee; $9 for each additional vehicle; $5 boat-launch fee. Open year-round.

Contact: Sly Park Recreation Area, (530) 644-2545.

Directions: From Sacramento, drive east on US 50 to Pollock Pines and take the exit for Sly Park Road. Drive south for five miles to Jenkinson Lake and the campground access road. Turn left and drive a half mile to the campground on the left.

Trip notes: Jenkinson Lake is set at 3,500 feet in elevation in the lower reaches of Eldorado National Forest, with a climate that is perfect for waterskiing and fishing. Participants of both sports get along, with most water-skiers motoring around the lake's main body, while anglers head upstream into the Hazel Creek arm of the lake for trout (in the spring) and bass (in the summer). This is one of the better lakes in the Sierra for brown trout. The boat ramp is located in a cove on the southwest end of the lake, about two miles from the campground. The area also has several hiking trails, and the lake is good for swimming. A group camp is available for visitors with horses, complete with riding trails, hitching posts, and corrals. A horse trail circles the 640-acre lake.

⑦ Silver Fork

Location: On the Silver Fork of the American River in Eldorado National Forest; map D3, grid h9.

Campsites, facilities: There are 35 sites for tents or RVs up to 22 feet long and five double-family sites. One of the sites is wheelchair accessible. Piped water, vault toilets, picnic tables, and fire grills are provided. Leashed pets are permitted.

Reservations, fees: No reservations; $10 per night, $14 for double-family sites. Open May through October.

Contact: Eldorado National Forest, Placerville Ranger District, (530) 644-6048 or fax (530) 295-5624.

Directions: From Sacramento, drive east on US 50 to Kyburz and Silver Fork Road. Turn right and drive eight miles to the campground on the right side of the road.

Trip notes: The tons of vacationers driving US 50 along the South Fork American River always get frustrated when they try to fish or camp, because there are precious few opportunities for either, with about zero trout and camps alike. But, just 10 minutes off the beaten path, you can find both at Silver Fork Camp. The access road provides many fishing opportunities and is stocked with rainbow trout by the state. The camp is set right along the river, at 5,500 feet in elevation, in Eldorado National Forest.

⑦ Sand Flat

Location: On the South Fork of the American River in Eldorado National Forest; map D3, grid h9.

Campsites, facilities: There are 29 sites for tents or RVs up to 22 feet long. Piped water, vault toilets, picnic tables, and fire grills are provided. Groceries, restaurant, and gas are available nearby. Leashed pets are permitted.

Reservations, fees: No reservations; $11 per night. Open year-round.

Contact: Eldorado National Forest, Placerville Ranger District, (530) 644-6048 or fax (530) 295-5624.

Directions: From Sacramento, drive east on US 50 to Placerville and then continue 28 miles to the campground on the right.

Trip notes: This first-come, first-served campground often gets filled up by US 50 travelers. And why not? You get easy access, a well-signed exit, and a nice setting on the South Fork of the American River. The elevation is 3,900 feet. The river is very pretty here, but fishing is often poor. In winter the snow level usually starts just a few miles uphill.

⑦ China Flat

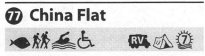

Location: On the Silver Fork of the American River in Eldorado National Forest; map D3, grid h9.

Campsites, facilities: There are 23 sites for tents or RVs up to 22 feet long. Piped water, vault toilets, picnic tables, and fire grills are provided. Leashed pets are permitted.

Reservations, fees: No reservations; $11 per night. Open May through October.

Contact: Eldorado National Forest, Placerville Ranger District, (530) 644-6048 or fax (530) 295-5624.

Directions: From Sacramento, drive east on US 50 to Kyburz and Silver Fork Road. Turn right and drive three miles to the campground on the left side of the road.

Trip notes: China Flat sits across the road from the Silver Fork American River, with a nearby access road that is routed along the river for a mile. This provides access for fishing, swimming, gold panning, and exploring. The camp feels far off the beaten path, even though it is only five minutes from that parade of traffic on US 50.

⑦ Pi Pi

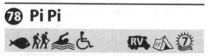

Location: On the Middle Fork of the Consumnes River in Eldorado National Forest; map D3, grid i7.

Campsites, facilities: There are 51 sites for tents or RVs up to 22 feet long (three double-family sites). Piped water, vault toilets, picnic tables, and fire grills are provided. There is wheelchair access to some camping areas, rest rooms, and pathways. Leashed pets are permitted.

Reservations, fees: Reserve via phone at (877) 444-6777 ($8.65 reservation fee) or website www.reserveusa.com; $11 to $18 per night. Open May through November.

Contact: Eldorado National Forest, Amador Ranger District, (209) 295-4251 or fax (209) 295-5994.

Directions: From Jackson, drive east on Highway 88 to Pioneer and continue for nine miles to Omo Ranch Road. Turn left and drive a mile to North-South Road/Forest Service Road 6. Turn right and drive 5.5 miles to the campground on the left side of the road.

Trip notes: This place is far enough out of the way to get missed by most campers. It is beside the Middle Fork of the Consumnes River at 4,100 feet. There are some good swimming holes in the area, but the water is cold in early summer (after all, it's snowmelt). A nature trail/boardwalk along the river is wheelchair accessible. Several sites border a pretty meadow in the back of the camp. This is also the gateway to a vast network of Forest Service roads to the north in Eldorado National Forest.

⑦ Capps Crossing

Location: On the North Fork of the Consumnes River in Eldorado National Forest; map D3, grid i8.

Campsites, facilities: There are 11 tent sites. Piped water, vault toilets, picnic tables, and fire grills are provided. Leashed pets are permitted.

Reservations, fees: No reservations; $11 per night. Open June through October.

Contact: Eldorado National Forest, Placerville Ranger District, (530) 644-6048 or fax (530) 295-5624.

Directions: From Sacramento, drive east on US 50 to Placerville and continue for 12 miles to the Sly Park Road exit. Turn right and drive about six miles to the Mormon Emigrant Trail/Forest Service Road 5. Turn left on Mormon Emigrant Trail and drive about 13 miles to North-South Road/Forest Service Road 6. Turn right (south) on North-South Road and drive about six miles to the campground on the left side of the road.

Trip notes: Here's a candidate for the Five Percent Club. It's set out in the middle of nowhere along the North Fork of the Consumnes River. It's a primitive spot that doesn't get much use. This camp is in the western reaches of a vast number of backcountry Forest Service roads. A map of Eldorado National Forest is a must to explore them. The elevation is 5,200 feet.

⑧ Far Horizons 49er Trailer Village

Location: In Plymouth; map D3, grid j2.

Campsites, facilities: There are 329 sites for RVs only, with full hookups. Flush toilets, sanitary disposal station, showers, playground, two swimming pools, hot tub, recreation room, pool room, TV lounge, coin laundry, delicatessen, propane gas, and a general store are available. Leashed pets are permitted.

Reservations, fees: Reservations are recommended; $25 to $33 per night. Open year-round.

Contact: Far Horizons 49er Trailer Village, (209) 245-6981 or (800) 339-6981.

Directions: From Sacramento, drive east on US 50 for a short distance to the junction with Highway 16. Turn east on Highway 16 and drive to Highway 49. Turn north on Highway 49 and drive a mile to the campground on the left side of the road at 18265 Highway 49. Note: This is a mile south of Main Street in Plymouth.

Trip notes: This is the granddaddy of RV parks, set in the heart of the gold country 40 miles east of Stockton and Sacramento. It is rarely crowded and offers warm pools, a huge spa, and a friendly staff.

⑧ Indian Grinding Rock State Historic Park

Location: Near Jackson; map D3, grid j4.

Campsites, facilities: There are 23 sites for tents or RVs, some up to 27 feet long. Picnic tables, fire grills, and piped water are provided. Flush toilets and coin-operated hot showers are available. Facilities are wheelchair accessible. Leashed pets are permitted.

Reservations, fees: No reservations; $12 to $17 per night, $1 pet fee. Open year-round.

Contact: Indian Grinding Rock State Historic Park, (209) 296-7488.

Directions: From Jackson, drive east on Highway 88 for 11 miles to Pine Grove–Volcano Road. Turn left on Pine Grove–Volcano Road and drive 1.5 miles to the park.

Trip notes: Visiting this park, located about three miles from Sutter Creek, is like entering a time machine. It offers a reconstructed Miwok village with petroglyphs, bedrock mortars, a cultural center, and interpretive talks for groups, by reservation. The camp is set at 2,500 feet in the Sierra foothills.

㊆ White Azalea

Location: On the Mokelumne River in Eldorado National Forest; map D3, grid j8.

Campsites, facilities: There are six tent sites. Vault toilets are provided. There is no piped water, so bring your own. Leashed pets are permitted.

Reservations, fees: No reservations; no fee. Open May through October.

Contact: Eldorado National Forest, Amador Ranger District, (209) 295-4251 or fax (209) 295-5624.

Directions: From Jackson, drive east on Highway 88 to Pioneer and then continue for about 20 miles to Ellis Road/Forest Service Road 92, at a signed turnoff for Lumberyard Campground. Turn right on Forest Service Road 92 and drive about eight miles. Cross the Bear River and drive a short distance to a turnoff for Forest Service Road 9. Turn right and drive three miles (past Mokelumne) to the campground. The road is steep, narrow, and winding in spots—not good for RVs or trailers.

Trip notes: Out here in the remote Mokelumne River Canyon are three primitive camps set on the Mokelumne's North Fork. White Azalea, 3,500 feet in elevation, is the closest of the three to Salt Springs Reservoir, the prime recreation destination. It's about a three-mile drive to the dam and an adjacent parking area for a wilderness trailhead for the Mokelumne Wilderness. This trail makes a great day hike, routed for four miles along the north shore of Salt Springs Reservoir to Blue Hole at the head of the lake.

㊓ Moore Creek

Location: On the Mokelumne River in Eldorado National Forest; map D3, grid j8.

Campsites, facilities: There are eight tent sites. Vault toilets are provided. There is no piped water, so bring your own. Leashed pets are permitted.

Reservations, fees: No reservations; no fee. Open May through October.

Contact: Eldorado National Forest, Amador Ranger District, (209) 295-4251 or fax (209) 295-5624.

Directions: From Jackson, drive east on Highway 88 to Pioneer and then continue for about 20 miles to Ellis Road/Forest Service Road 92, at a signed turnoff for Lumberyard Campground. Turn right on Forest Service Road 92 and drive about eight miles. Cross the Bear River and drive a short distance to a turnoff for Forest Service Road 9. Turn right and drive two miles (past Mokelumne) to the campground access road on the right. Turn right and drive a quarter mile to the campground on the right. The road is steep, narrow, and winding in spots—not good for RVs or trailers.

Trip notes: This camp is set at 3,200 feet elevation on little Moore Creek, a feeder stream to the nearby North Fork Mokelumne River. It's one of three primitive camps within two miles. See the trip notes for White Azalea (campground number 82) for more information.

84 Mokelumne

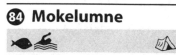

Location: On the Mokelumne River in Eldorado National Forest; map D3, grid j8.

Campsites, facilities: There are eight tent sites. Vault toilets are provided. There is no piped water. Leashed pets are permitted.

Reservations, fees: No reservations; no fee. Open May through October.

Contact: Eldorado National Forest, Amador Ranger District, (209) 295-4251 or fax (209) 295-5624.

Directions: From Jackson, drive east on Highway 88 to Pioneer and then continue for about 20 miles to Ellis Road/Forest Service Road 92, at a signed turnoff for Lumberyard Campground. Turn right on Forest Service Road 92 and drive about eight miles. Cross the Bear River and drive a short distance to a turnoff for Forest Service Road 9. Turn right and drive two miles to the campground on the left side of the road.

Trip notes: This primitive spot is set beside the Mokelumne River at 3,200 feet in elevation, one of three primitive camps in the immediate area. See the trip notes for White Azalea (campground number 82) for more information. There

are some good swimming holes nearby. Fishing is fair, with the trout on the small side.

85 South Shore

Location: On Bear River Reservoir in Eldorado National Forest; map D3, grid j9.

Campsites, facilities: There are 13 sites for tents and nine sites for tents or RVs. There are four two-family sites. Picnic tables, fire grills, piped water, and vault toilets are provided. A boat ramp, grocery store, boat rentals, and propane gas are available at nearby Bear River Lake Resort. Leashed pets are permitted.

Reservations, fees: No reservations; $10 per night, $18 per night for two-family sites. Open June through October.

Contact: Eldorado National Forest, Amador Ranger District, (209) 295-4251 or fax (209) 295-5624.

Directions: From Stockton, drive east on Highway 88 for about 80 miles to the lake entrance on the right side of the road. Turn right and drive four miles (past the dam) to the campground entrance on the right side of the road.

Trip notes: Bear River Reservoir is set at 5,900 feet, which means it becomes ice-free earlier in the season each spring than its uphill neighbors to the east, Silver Lake and Caples Lake. It is a good-sized lake—725 acres—and cold and deep, too. It gets double-barreled trout stocks, receiving fish from the state and from the operator of the lake's marina and lodge. This campground is on the lake's southern shore, just east of the dam. Explorers can drive south for five miles to Salt Springs Reservoir, which has a trailhead and parking area on the north side of the dam for a great day hike along the lake.

86 Bear River Group Camp

Location: On Bear River Reservoir in Eldorado National Forest; map D3, grid j9.

Campsites, facilities: There are three group sites for tents; two sites can accommodate 25 people each and one site can accommodate 50 people. Picnic tables, fire grills, piped water, and vault toilets are provided. A grocery store, boat ramp, boat rentals, and propane gas are available nearby. Leashed pets are permitted.

Reservations, fees: Reservations are required; $50 to $100 per night. Open June through October.

Contact: Eldorado National Forest, Amador Ranger District, (209) 295-4251 or fax (209) 295-5624.

Directions: From Stockton, drive east on Highway 88 for about 80 miles to the lake entrance on the right side of the road. Turn right and drive five miles (past the dam) to the campground entrance on the left side of the road.

Trip notes: This is a group camp set near Bear River Reservoir, a pretty lake that provides power boating and trout fishing. See the trip notes for South Shore (campground number 85), which is located just a mile from this camp.

---

87 Bear River Lake Resort

Location: On Bear River Reservoir; map D3 grid j9.

Campsites, facilities: There are 127 sites for tents or RVs, all with partial hookups. Picnic tables, fire grills, and piped water are provided. Rest rooms, showers, sanitary disposal station, boat ramp, boat rentals, firewood, ice, propane gas, coin laundry, post office, telephone, restaurant and cocktail lounge, and a grocery store are available. Pets are permitted.

Reservations, fees: Reservations are recommended; $20 per night. Open year-round.

Contact: Bear River Reservoir, (209) 295-4868 or fax (209) 295-4585.

Directions: From Stockton, drive east on Highway 88 for about 80 miles to the lake entrance on the right side of the road. Turn right and drive four miles to a junction (if you pass the dam, you have gone a quarter mile too far). Turn left and drive a half mile to the campground entrance on the right side of the road.

Trip notes: Bear River Lake Resort is a complete vacation service lodge, with everything you could ask for. A lot of people have been asking in recent years, making this a popular spot that often requires a reservation. The resort also sponsors fishing derbies in the summer, and sweetens the pot considerably by stocking exceptionally large rainbow trout. The resort is set at 6,000 feet. For more information about Bear River Reservoir, see the trip notes for South Shore (campground number 85).

Map D4

One inch equals approximately 10.7 miles.
See inside back cover for California state map.

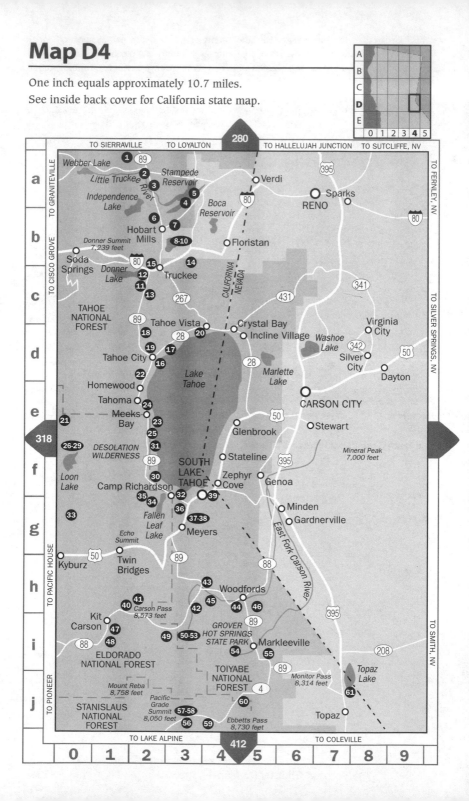

Chapter D4 features:

❶ Cold Creek

🐟 🥾 ♨️   🆁🆅 ⛺ ⑧

Location: In Tahoe National Forest; map D4, grid a1.

Campsites, facilities: There are 13 sites for tents or RVs up to 22 feet long. Piped water, vault toilets, picnic tables, and fire grills are pro-

vided. Supplies are available in Sierraville. Leashed pets are permitted.

Reservations, fees: Reserve via phone at (877) 444-6777 ($8.65 reservation fee) or website www.reserveusa.com; $10 per night, $5 for an extra vehicle. Open May through October.

Contact: Tahoe National Forest, Truckee Ranger

District, (530) 587-3558 or fax (530) 587-6914; California Land Management, (530) 582-0120.

Directions: From Truckee, drive north on Highway 89 for about 16 miles to the campground on the left side of the road. If you reach Sierraville, you have gone five miles too far.

Trip notes: There are four small campgrounds along Highway 89 between Sierraville and Truckee, all within close range of side trips to Webber Lake, Independence Lake, and Campbell Hot Springs in Sierraville. Cold Creek is set just downstream of the confluence of Cottonwood Creek and Cold Creek, at 5,800 feet in elevation.

❷ Upper Little Truckee

Location: On the Little Truckee River in Tahoe National Forest; map D4, grid a2.

Campsites, facilities: There are 26 sites for tents or RVs up to 22 feet long. Piped water, vault toilets, picnic tables, and fire grills are provided. Supplies are available in Sierraville. Leashed pets are permitted.

Reservations, fees: Reserve via phone at (877) 444-6777 ($8.65 reservation fee) or website www.reserveusa.com; $10 per night, $5 for an extra vehicle. Open May through October.

Contact: Tahoe National Forest, Truckee Ranger District, (530) 587-3558 or fax (530) 587-6914; California Land Management, (530) 582-0120.

Directions: From Truckee, drive north on Highway 89 for about 11 miles to the campground on the left, a short distance beyond Lower Little Truckee Camp.

Trip notes: This camp is set along the Little Truckee River at 6,100 feet, two miles from Stampede Reservoir. The Little Truckee is a pretty trout stream, with easy access not only from this campground, but also from another three miles northward along Highway 89, then from another seven miles to the west along Forest Service Road 7, the route to Webber Lake. It is only about a 10-minute drive from this camp to reach Stampede Reservoir to the east or Independence Lake to the west.

❸ Lower Little Truckee

Location: On the Little Truckee River in Tahoe National Forest; map D4, grid a2.

Campsites, facilities: There are 15 sites for tents or RVs up to 22 feet long. Piped water, vault toilets, picnic tables, and fire grills are provided. Supplies are available in Sierraville. Leashed pets are permitted.

Reservations, fees: Reserve via phone at (877) 444-6777 ($8.65 reservation fee) or website www.reserveusa.com; $10 per night, $5 for an extra vehicle. Open May through October.

Contact: Tahoe National Forest, Truckee Ranger District, (530) 587-3558 or fax (530) 587-6914; California Land Management, (530) 582-0120.

Directions: From Truckee, drive north on Highway 89 for about 11 miles to the campground on the left. If you reach Upper Little Truckee Camp, you have gone a quarter mile too far.

Trip notes: This pretty camp is set along Highway 89 and the Little Truckee River at 6,000 feet, about two miles from Stampede Reservoir and about a quarter mile from Lower Little Truckee. For more information, see the trip notes for Upper Little Truckee (campground number two).

❹ Logger

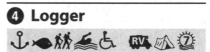

Location: At Stampede Reservoir in Tahoe National Forest; map D4, grid a3.

Campsites, facilities: There are 252 sites for tents or RVs up to 32 feet long. Piped water, sanitary dump station, vault and flush toilets, picnic tables, and fire grills are provided. A concrete boat ramp is available one mile from camp. A grocery store is within seven miles. The facilities are wheelchair accessible. Leashed pets are permitted.

Reservations, fees: Reserve via phone at (877) 444-6777 ($8.65 reservation fee) or website www.reserveusa.com; $13 per night, $5 for an extra vehicle. Open May through October.

Contact: Tahoe National Forest, Truckee Ranger District, (530) 587-3558 or fax (530) 587-6914;

California Land Management, (530) 582-0120.

Directions: From Truckee, drive east on Interstate 80 for seven miles to the Boca-Hirschdale/County Road 270 exit. Take that exit and drive north on County Road 270 for about seven miles (past Boca Reservoir) to the junction with County Road S261 on the left. Turn left and drive 1.5 miles to the campground on the right.

Trip notes: Stampede is a huge lake by Sierra standards, covering 3,400 acres, the largest lake in the region after Lake Tahoe. It is set at 6,000 feet, surrounded by classic Sierra granite and pines, and is big and beautiful. The campground is also huge, set about a half mile from the lake near its southern shore, a few minutes drive from the Captain Roberts Boat Ramp. This camp is ideal for campers, boaters, and anglers. The lake is becoming one of the top fishing lakes in California for kokanee salmon (catchable only by trolling), and also has some large Mackinaw trout and a sprinkling of planter-sized rainbow trout. One problem at Stampede is receding water levels from midsummer through fall, a real pain, which puts the campsites some distance from the lake. However, the boat ramp has been extended to assist boaters during drawdowns.

❺ Emigrant Group Camp

Location: At Stampede Reservoir in Tahoe National Forest; map D4, grid a3.

Campsites, facilities: There are two 25-person group sites and two 50-person group sites for tents or RVs up to 32 feet long. Piped water, flush and vault toilets, picnic tables, and fire grills are provided. Bring your own firewood. A three-lane concrete boat ramp is available. The facilities are wheelchair accessible. Leashed pets are permitted.

Reservations, fees: Reserve via phone at (877) 444-6777 ($8.65 reservation fee) or website www.reserveusa.com; $55 to $110 group fee per night. Open May through September.

Contact: Tahoe National Forest, Truckee Ranger District, (530) 587-3558 or fax (530) 587-6914; California Land Management, (530) 582-0120.

Directions: From Truckee, drive east on Interstate 80 for seven miles to the Boca-Hirschdale/County Road 270 exit. Take that exit and drive north on County Road 270 for about seven miles (past Boca Reservoir) to the junction with County Road S261 on the left. Turn left and drive 1.5 miles to the campground access road on the right. Turn right and drive one mile to the camp on the left.

Trip notes: Emigrant Group Camp is set at a beautiful spot on Stampede Reservoir, near a point along a cove on the southeastern corner of the lake. There is a beautiful view of the lake from the point, and a boat ramp is located two miles to the east. Elevation is 6,000 feet. See the trip notes for Logger (campground number four) for more information.

❻ Sage Hen Creek

Location: In Tahoe National Forest; map D4, grid b2.

Campsites, facilities: There are 10 sites for tents or RVs up to 16 feet long. There is no piped water, but vault toilets are provided. Pack out your garbage. Leashed pets are permitted.

Reservations, fees: No reservations; no fee. Open June through October.

Contact: Tahoe National Forest, Truckee Ranger District, (530) 587-3558 or fax (530) 587-6914.

Directions: From Truckee, drive nine miles north on Highway 89 to Sagehen Summit Road on the left. Turn left and drive two miles to the campground. A gate on the road a short distance from the camp is sometimes locked early and late in the season.

Trip notes: This is a small, primitive camp set at 6,500 feet beside little Sage Hen Creek, just north of a miniature mountain range called the Sagehen Hills, which tops out at 7,707 feet. This camp is only five miles from the undeveloped southwestern shore of Stampede Reservoir. It is popular with hunters and with campers who want to avoid the crowds. Sage Hen Creek is primarily used as an overflow site on popular weekends when the camps along Highway 89 and at Stampede, Boca, and Prosser Creek have filled.

❼ Lakeside

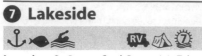

Location: On Prosser Creek Reservoir in Tahoe National Forest; map D4, grid b3.

Campsites, facilities: There are 30 sites for tents or RVs up to 33 feet long and one group site. Piped water and vault toilets are provided. A boat ramp is available nearby. Leashed pets are permitted.

Reservations, fees: No reservations; $8 per night. Open June through October.

Contact: Tahoe National Forest, Truckee Ranger District, (530) 587-3558 or fax (530) 587-6914.

Directions: From Truckee, drive north on Highway 89 for three miles to the campground entrance road on the right. Turn right and drive less than a mile to the campground.

Trip notes: This primitive camp is in a deep cove in the northwestern end of Prosser Creek Reservoir, near the lake's headwaters. It is a gorgeous lake, set at 5,741 feet, and a 10 mph speed limit keeps the fast boats out. The adjacent shore is decent for hand-launched, cartop boats, providing the lake level is up, and a concrete boat ramp is located a mile down the road. Lots of trout are stocked here every year, including 100,000 rainbow trout fingerlings added in an experiment by the Department of Fish and Game to see how fast they will grow. The trout fishing is often quite good after the ice breaks up in late spring; the lake is also popular with ice fishermen in the winter.

❽ Boyington Mill

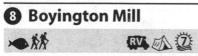

Location: On the Little Truckee River in Tahoe National Forest; map D4, grid b3.

Campsites, facilities: There are 10 sites for tents or RVs up to 32 feet long. There is no piped water, but vault toilets and picnic tables are provided. Leashed pets are permitted.

Reservations, fees: No reservations; $10 per night, $5 for an extra vehicle. Open May through October.

Contact: Tahoe National Forest, Truckee Ranger District, (530) 587-3558 or fax (530) 587-6914; California Land Management, (530) 582-0120.

Directions: From Truckee, go east on Interstate 80 for seven miles. Take the Boca-Hirschdale exit and drive north on County Road 270 for four miles (past Boca Reservoir) to the campground.

Trip notes: Boyington Mill is a little Forest Service camp set between Boca Reservoir to the nearby south and Stampede Reservoir to the nearby north, along a small inlet creek to the adjacent Little Truckee River. It comes in use as an overflow camp when lakeside campsites at Boca, Stampede, and Prosser have already filled. The elevation is 5,700 feet.

❾ Boca Rest Campground

Location: On Boca Reservoir in Tahoe National Forest; map D4, grid b3.

Campsites, facilities: There are 25 sites for tents or RVs up to 22 feet long. Piped water, vault toilets, picnic tables, and fire rings are provided. A hand-launch boat ramp is available. A concrete boat ramp is three miles away on the southwest shore of Boca Reservoir. Truckee is the nearest place for telephones and supplies. Leashed pets are permitted.

Reservations, fees: No reservations; $8 per night, $5 for an extra vehicle. Open May through October.

Contact: Tahoe National Forest, Truckee Ranger District, (530) 587-3558 or fax (530) 587-6914; California Land Management, (530) 582-0120.

Directions: From Truckee, travel east on Interstate 80 for seven miles to the Boca-Hirschdale exit. Take that exit and drive north on County Road 270 for about 2.5 miles to the campground on the right side of the road.

Trip notes: The Boca Dam faces Interstate 80, so the lake is out of sight of the zillions of highway travelers who would otherwise certainly stop here. Those who do stop find that the lake is very pretty, set at 5,700 feet in elevation and covering 1,000 acres with deep, blue water. This camp is located on the lake's northeastern shore, not far from the inlet to the Little Truckee River. The boat ramp is some distance away (see next listing).

⑩ Boca Springs Campground

Location: On Boca Reservoir in Tahoe National Forest; map D4, grid b3.

Campsites, facilities: There are 20 sites for tents or RVs up to 16 feet long. Piped water, portable toilets, and fire grills are provided. A concrete boat ramp is north of the campground on Boca Reservoir. Truckee is the nearest place for telephones and supplies. Leashed pets are permitted.

Reservations, fees: No reservations; $10 per night, $5 for an extra vehicle. Open May through October.

Contact: Tahoe National Forest, Truckee Ranger District, (530) 587-3558 or fax (530) 587-6914; California Land Management, (530) 582-0120.

Directions: From Truckee, travel east on Interstate 80 for seven miles to the Boca-Hirschdale exit. Take that exit and drive north for a short distance to County Road 73 and continue for one mile to the campground on the right side of the road.

Trip notes: Boca Reservoir is known for being a "big fish factory," with some huge but rare brown trout and rainbow trout sprinkled among a growing fishery for kokanee salmon. The lake is set at 5,700 feet, a Sierra gem within a few miles of Interstate 80. The camp is the best choice for anglers/boaters, with a launch ramp set just down from the campground.

⑪ Granite Flat

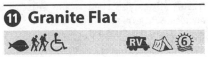

Location: On the Truckee River in Tahoe National Forest; map D4, grid c2.

Campsites, facilities: There are 65 sites for tents or RVs and 10 walk-in tent sites. Piped water, vault toilets, fire grills, and picnic tables are provided. The facilities are wheelchair accessible. Leashed pets are permitted.

Reservations, fees: Reserve via phone at (877) 444-6777 ($8.65 reservation fee) or website www.reserveusa.com; $12 per night, $5 for an extra vehicle. Open May through October.

Contact: Tahoe National Forest, Truckee Ranger

District, (530) 587-3558 or fax (530) 587-6914; California Land Management, (530) 582-0120.

Directions: From Truckee, drive south on Highway 89 for 1.5 miles to the campground entrance on the right.

Trip notes: This camp is set along the Truckee River at 5,800 feet, in an area known for a ton of traffic on adjacent Highway 89, as well as decent trout fishing and, in the spring and early summer, rafting. It is about a 15-minute drive to Squaw Valley or Lake Tahoe. A bike route is also available along the Truckee River out of Tahoe City.

⑫ Donner Memorial State Park

Location: On Donner Lake; map D4, grid c2.

Campsites, facilities: There are 154 sites for tents or RVs up to 28 feet long. Piped water, flush toilets, showers, picnic tables, and fire grills are provided. Supplies are available about one mile away in Truckee. Facilities are wheelchair accessible. Leashed pets are permitted.

Reservations, fees: Reserve via phone at (800) 444-PARK/7275 ($7.50 reservation fee) or website www.cal-parks.ca.gov; $15 to $17 per night, $1 pet fee.

Contact: Donner Memorial State Park, (530) 582-7892, (530) 582-7894 or fax (530) 583-7893.

Directions: From Auburn, drive east on Interstate 80 just past Donner Lake to the Donner State Park exit. Turn south on Donner Pass Road and drive a half mile to the park entrance and the southeast end of the lake.

Trip notes: The remarkable beauty of Donner Lake often evokes a deep, heartfelt response. The lake is big, three miles long and three-quarters of a mile wide, gemlike blue, and set near the Sierra crest at 5,900 feet. The area is well developed, with a number of cabins and access roads, and this state park is the feature destination. Located along the southeastern end of the lake, it is extremely pretty. Fishing is good here (typically only in the early morning), trolling for kokanee salmon or rainbow trout, with big Mackinaw and brown trout providing wild cards. In the summer a wind often comes up in the early afternoon. In the winter a good cross-country ski trail is available. One last note: Please bring plenty of food. You know why.

⑬ Goose Meadows

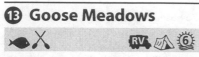

Location: On the Truckee River in Tahoe National Forest; map D4, grid c2.

Campsites, facilities: There are 25 sites for tents or RVs up to 30 feet long. Hand-pumped water is available. Vault toilets, fire grills, and picnic tables are provided. Supplies are available in Truckee and Tahoe City. Leashed pets are permitted.

Reservations, fees: Reserve via phone at (877) 444-6777 ($8.65 reservation fee) or website www.reserveusa.com; $10 per night, $5 for an extra vehicle. Open May through October.

Contact: Tahoe National Forest, Truckee Ranger District, (530) 587-3558 or fax (530) 587-6914; California Land Management, (530) 582-0120.

Directions: From Truckee, drive south on Highway 89 for four miles to the campground entrance on the left (river) side of the highway.

Trip notes: There are three campgrounds set along the Truckee River off Highway 89 between Truckee and Tahoe City. Goose Meadows provides good fishing access with decent prospects, despite the high number of vehicles roaring past on the adjacent highway. This stretch of river is also popular for rafting. The elevation is 5,800 feet.

⑭ Martis Creek Lake

Location: Near Truckee; map D4, grid c3.

Campsites, facilities: There are 25 sites for tents or RVs up to 30 feet long; two sites are wheelchair accessible. Piped water, vault toilets, picnic tables, and fire grills are provided. Supplies are available six minutes away in Truckee. Leashed pets are permitted.

Reservations, fees: No reservations except for wheelchair-accessible sites; $10 per night.

Open year-round, fees payable May through October.

Contact: US Army Corps of Engineers, Martis Creek Lake, (530) 639-2342 or fax (530) 639-2175; email: englebright@usace.mil.

Directions: From Truckee, drive south on Highway 267 for about three miles (past the airport) to the entrance road to the lake on the left. Turn left and drive another 2.5 miles to the campground at the end of the road.

Trip notes: If only this lake weren't so often windy in the afternoon, it would be heaven to fly fishers in float tubes, casting out with sinking lines and leech patterns, using a strip retrieve. To some it's heaven anyway, with Lahontan cutthroat trout ranging to 25 inches here. This is a special catch-and-release fishery where anglers are permitted to use only artificial lures with single barbless hooks. The setting is somewhat sparse and open, a small lake on the eastern edge of the Martis Valley. No motors are permitted at the lake, making it ideal (when the wind is down) for float tubes or prams. The elevation is 5,800 feet.

⑮ Coachland RV Park

Location: In Truckee; map D4, grid c2.

Campsites, facilities: There are 131 sites for trailers or RVs up to 40 feet long. Picnic tables, rest rooms, showers, coin laundry, cable TV, and propane are available. The facilities are wheelchair accessible. Leashed pets are permitted.

Reservations, fees: Reservations are recommended; $25 per night. Open year-round.

Contact: Coachland RV Park, 10500 Highway 89 North, Unit 35, Truckee, CA 96161; (530) 587-3071 or fax (530) 587-6976.

Directions: From Truckee, drive north on Highway 89 for a short distance to the park at 10500 Highway 89 on the left side of the road.

Trip notes: Truckee is the gateway to recreation at North Tahoe. Within minutes are Donner Lake, Prosser Creek Reservoir, Boca Reservoir, Stampede Reservoir, and the Truckee River. Squaw Valley is a short distance to the south off Highway 89, and Northstar is the same off Highway 267. The park is set in a wooded area near the junction of Interstate 80 and Highway 89, providing easy access. The downtown Truckee area (with restaurants) is nearby. This is one of the only parks in the area that is open year-round. The elevation is 6,000 feet.

⑯ William Kent

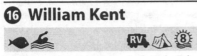

Location: Near Lake Tahoe in the Lake Tahoe Basin; map D4, grid d2.

Campsites, facilities: There are 55 tent sites and 40 sites for RVs up to 24 feet long. Piped water, flush toilets, sanitary dump station, picnic tables, and fire grills are provided. A grocery store, coin laundry, and propane gas are available nearby. Pets are permitted.

Reservations, fees: Reserve via phone at 9877) 444-6777 ($8.65 reservation fee) or website www.reserveusa.com; $14 per night. Open June through September.

Contact: US Forest Service, (530) 573-2600, or William Kent, (530) 544-5994.

Directions: From Truckee, drive south on Highway 89 to Tahoe City. Turn south on Highway 89 and drive three miles to the campground entrance on the right side of the road.

Trip notes: William Kent camp is a little pocket of peace set near the busy traffic of Highway 89 on the western shore corridor. It is on the west side of the highway, meaning visitors have to cross the highway in order to get lakeside access. The elevation is 6,300 feet, and the camp is wooded with primarily lodgepole pines. The drive here is awesome or ominous, depending on how you look at it, with the view of incredible Lake Tahoe to the east, the deepest blue in the world. But you often have a lot of time to look at it, since traffic rarely moves quickly.

⑰ Lake Forest Campground

Location: On Lake Tahoe; map D4, grid d3.

Campsites, facilities: There are 20 sites for tents or RVs up to 20 feet long. Piped water, flush toilets, and picnic tables are provided. A boat ramp is available. A grocery store, coin laun-

dry, and propane gas are available within 2.5 miles.

Reservations, fees: No reservations; $12 per night. Open April through October.

Contact: Lake Forest Campground, (530) 583-3796 extension 29 or fax (530) 583-1475.

Directions: From Truckee, drive south on Highway 89 through Tahoe City. Turn north on Highway 28 and drive two miles to the campground entrance road (Lake Forest Road).

Trip notes: The northwest shore of Lake Tahoe provides beautiful lookouts and excellent boating access. The latter is a highlight of this camp, with a boat ramp nearby. From here it is a short cruise to Dollar Point and around the corner north to Carnelian Bay, one of the better stretches of water for trout fishing. The elevation is 6,200 feet.

⑱ Silver Creek

Location: On the Truckee River in Tahoe National Forest; map D4, grid d2.

Campsites, facilities: There are 20 sites for tents or RVs up to 10 feet long and eight walk-in sites. Hand-pumped, piped water, vault toilets, picnic tables, and fire grills are provided. Supplies are available in Truckee and Tahoe City. Leashed pets are permitted.

Reservations, fees: Reserve via phone at (877) 444-6777 ($8.65 reservation fee) or website www.reserveusa.com; $10 per night, $5 for an extra vehicle. Open June through September.

Contact: Tahoe National Forest, Truckee Ranger District, (530) 587-3558 or fax (530) 587-6914.

Directions: From Truckee, drive south on Highway 89 for six miles to the campground entrance on the river side of the highway.

Trip notes: This pretty campground is set near where Deer Creek enters the Truckee River. The trout fishing is often good in this area, and side trips include a good hike up the trail that runs along Deer Creek, with the trailhead right at the camp. This is one of three campgrounds along Highway 89 and the Truckee River, between Truckee and Tahoe City. The elevation is 5,800 feet.

⑲ Tahoe State Recreation Area

🛥️ 🎣 🐎 ✕ 🏊 🚐 ⛺ ⑨

Location: On Lake Tahoe; map D4, grid d2.

Campsites, facilities: There are 38 sites for tents or RVs up to 24 feet long. Piped water, coin-operated showers, flush toilets, picnic tables, and fire grills are provided. Firewood, other supplies, and a coin laundry are available within walking distance. Leashed pets are permitted.

Reservations, fees: Reserve via phone at (800) 444-PARK/7275 ($7.50 reservation fee) or website www.cal-parks.ca.gov; $14 to $16 per night, $5 for each additional vehicle, $1 pet fee.

Contact: Tahoe State Recreation Area, (530) 583-3074 or (530) 525-7232.

Directions: From Truckee, drive south on Highway 89 through Tahoe City. Turn north on Highway 28 and drive to the campground entrance on the left side of the road.

Trip notes: This is a popular summer-only campground at the northwest side of Lake Tahoe. The Tahoe State Recreation Area covers a large area just west of Highway 28 near Tahoe City, with the opportunity for hiking and horseback riding. A boat ramp is located two miles to the northwest at nearby Lake Forest, and bike rentals are available in Tahoe City for rides along Highway 89 near the shore of the lake.

⑳ Sandy Beach Campground

🛥️ 🎣 🏊 🚐 ⛺ ⑧

Location: On Lake Tahoe; map D4, grid d3.

Campsites, facilities: There are 44 sites with full or partial hookups for tents or RVs up to 35 feet long. Piped water, showers, flush toilets, laundry room, picnic tables, and barbecues are provided. A free public boat ramp is available half a block away. A grocery store and propane gas are available nearby. Leashed pets are permitted.

Reservations, fees: Reservations are accepted; $15 to $20 per night, $1.50 pet fee (two dog limit). Open May through October, weather permitting.

Contact: Sandy Beach Campground, PO Box 6868, Tahoe City, CA 96145; (530) 546-7682.

Directions: From Truckee, drive south on Highway 89 through Tahoe City. Turn north on Highway 89, which becomes Highway 28, and drive seven miles east to the campground (signed) on the left side of the road.

Trip notes: Sandy Beach Campground is set at 6,200 feet near the northwest shore of Lake Tahoe. A nearby boat ramp provides access to one of the better fishing areas of the lake for Mackinaw trout. The water in Tahoe is always cold, and though a lot of people will get suntans on beaches next to the lake, swimmers need to be members of the Polar Bear Club. A short drive to the east will take you past the town of Kings Beach and into Nevada, where there are some small casinos near the shore of Crystal Bay.

㉑ Wentworth Springs

🐟 🥾 ⛺ ⑦

Location: Near Loon Lake in Eldorado National Forest; map D4, grid e0.

Campsites, facilities: There are eight tent sites. There is no piped water, but vault toilets, picnic tables, and fire grills are provided. Access is recommended for off-road motorcycles or four-wheel-drive vehicles only. Leashed pets are permitted.

Reservations, fees: No reservations; no fee. Open June through October.

Contact: Eldorado National Forest, Placerville Ranger District, (530) 644-6048 or fax (530) 295-5624.

Directions: From Sacramento, drive east on US 50 to Riverton and the junction with Ice House Road/Soda Springs–Riverton Road on the left. Turn left and drive 30 miles to the junction with Forest Service Road 30. Bear left and drive 3.5 miles to Forest Service Road 33. Turn right and drive seven miles to the campground on the left side of the road. (The access road is suitable for four-wheel-drive vehicles and off-road motorcycles only.)

Trip notes: There is one reason people come here: to set up a base camp for an OHV adventure, whether they are the owners of four-wheel drives, all-terrain vehicles, or dirt bikes. A network of roads lead from this camp, passable only by these vehicles, roads that would flat-out destroy your average car. The camp is set deep in Eldorado National Forest, at 6,200 feet in elevation. While the north end of Loon Lake is located a mile to the east, the road there is extremely rough (perfect, right?). The road is gated along the lake, preventing access to this camp for those who drive directly to Loon Lake.

㉒ Sugar Pine Point State Park

Location: On Lake Tahoe; map D4, grid d2.

Campsites, facilities: There are 175 sites for tents or RVs up to 30 feet long. There are also 10 group sites available. Piped water, coin-operated showers (except in winter), flush toilets, sanitary dump station, picnic tables, and fire grills are provided. A grocery store, coin laundry, and propane gas are available nearby. There is wheelchair access to picnic areas. Leashed pets are permitted.

Reservations, fees: Reserve via phone at (800) 444-PARK/7275 ($7.50 reservation fee) or website www.cal-parks.ca.gov; $12 to $16 per night, $1 pet fee. Open year-round.

Contact: Sugar Pine Point State Park, (530) 525-7982 or (530) 525-7232.

Directions: From Truckee, drive south on Highway 89 through Tahoe City. Continue south on Highway 89 and drive 10 miles to the campground (signed) on the west side of the road.

Trip notes: This is one of three beautiful and popular state parks on the west shore of Lake Tahoe. It is just north of Meeks Bay on General Creek, with almost two miles of lake frontage available, though the campground is located on the opposite side of Highway 89. A pretty trail is routed four miles along the creek up to Lost Lake, just outside the northern boundary of the Desolation Wilderness. The elevation is 6,200 feet.

㉓ Meeks Bay

Location: On Lake Tahoe; map D4, grid e2.

Campsites, facilities: There are 40 sites for tents or RVs up to 20 feet long. Piped water, flush toilets, picnic tables, and fire grills are provided. Coin laundry and groceries are available nearby. Pets are permitted.

Reservations, fees: Reserve via phone at (877) 444-6777 ($8.65 reservation fee) or website www.reserveusa.com; $14 per night. Open May through September.

Contact: Tahoe National Forest, Lake Tahoe Basin, (530) 583-3642; California Land Management, (530) 583-3642.

Directions: In South Lake Tahoe at the junction of Highway 89 and US 50, turn north on Highway 89 and drive 17 miles to the campground.

Trip notes: Meeks Bay is a beautiful spot along the western shore of Lake Tahoe. A bicycle trail is available nearby and is routed along the lake's shore, but it requires occasionally crossing busy Highway 89.

㉔ Kaspian

Location: On Lake Tahoe; map D4, grid e2.

Campsites, facilities: There are eight sites for tents. RVs may use the parking lot on a space-available basis. Piped water, flush toilets, picnic tables, and fire grills are provided. A grocery store, coin laundry, and propane gas are available nearby. Leashed pets are permitted.

Reservations, fees: No reservations; $10 per night. Open May through September.

Contact: California Land Management, (530) 583-3642.

Directions: From Truckee, drive south on Highway 89 to Tahoe City. Turn south on Highway 89 and drive four miles to the campground (signed) on the east side of the road.

Trip notes: As gorgeous and as huge as Lake Tahoe is, there are relatively few camps or even restaurants with lakeside settings. This is one of the few. Kaspian is set along the west shore of the lake at 6,235 feet in elevation, near the little town of Tahoe Pines. A Forest Service road (03) is available adjacent to the camp on the west side of Highway 89, routed west into national forest (becoming quite rough) to a trailhead. From there you can hike up to Barker Peak (8,166 feet) for incredible views of Lake Tahoe, as well as access to the Pacific Crest Trail.

㉕ Meeks Bay Resort & Marina

Location: On Lake Tahoe; map D4, grid e2.

Campsites, facilities: There are 28 sites for RVs, 10 with full hookups. Showers, flush toilets, picnic tables, and fire grills are provided. Coin laundry, snack bar, gift shop, and groceries are available. A boat ramp and boat slips are available. No pets are allowed.

Reservations, fees: Reservations are accepted; $18 to $26 per night, $5 day-use fee, $20 per night for boat slips. Open June through September.

Contact: Meeks Bay Resort & Marina, (530) 525-6942 or (877) 326-3357.

Directions: In South Lake Tahoe at the junction of Highway 89 and US 50, turn north on Highway 89 and drive 17 miles to the campground.

Trip notes: Prime access for boating makes this a camp of choice for the boater/camper at Lake Tahoe. A boat launch is not only nearby, but access to Rubicon Bay and beyond to breathtaking Emerald Bay is possible, a six-mile trip one way for boats large enough and fast enough to make it. The resort is adjacent to a 20-mile paved bike trail.

㉖ Red Fir Group Camp

Location: On Loon Lake in Eldorado National Forest; map D4, grid f0.

Campsites, facilities: This group site will accommodate up to six vehicles and 25 people. Piped water, vault toilets, fire rings, and grills are provided. Leashed pets are permitted.

Reservations, fees: Reserve via phone at (877) 444-6777 ($8.65 reservation fee) or website www.reserveusa.com; $35 per night, $5 for an extra vehicle. Open June through September.

Contact: Eldorado National Forest, Pacific Ranger District, (530) 644-2349 or fax (530) 644-5405.

Directions: From Sacramento, drive east on US 50 to Riverton and the junction with Ice House Road/Soda Springs–Riverton Road on the left. Turn left and drive 34 miles to a fork at the foot of Loon Lake. Turn left and drive three miles to the campground (just beyond the Loon Lake Northshore Camp).

Trip notes: This is a pretty, wooded camp, ideal for medium-sized groups. It is across the road from the water, offering a secluded, quiet spot. Lake access is a short hike away. See the trip notes for Loon Lake Northshore (campground number 27) for more information. The elevation is 6,500 feet.

㉗ Loon Lake Northshore

Location: On Loon Lake in Eldorado National Forest; map D4, grid f0.

Campsites, facilities: There are 15 sites for tents or self-contained RVs. No piped water is available. Vault toilets, picnic tables, fire rings, and grills are provided. Leashed pets are permitted.

Reservations, fees: No reservations; $5 per night, $5 for an extra vehicle. Open June through September.

Contact: Eldorado National Forest, Pacific Ranger District, (530) 644-2349 or fax (530) 644-5405.

Directions: From Sacramento, drive east on US 50 to Riverton and the junction with Ice House Road/Soda Springs–Riverton Road on the left. Turn left and drive 34 miles to a fork at the foot of Loon Lake. Turn left and drive three miles to the campground.

Trip notes: This camp is set on the northwestern shore of Loon Lake, where the waterfront sites provide an extremely pretty setting, even though there are few facilities and no boat ramp. (The boat ramp is located near the Loon Lake campground and picnic area at the south end of the lake.) For more information about Loon Lake, see the trip notes for Pleasant Hike-In, Boat-In (campground number 28) and Loon Lake (campground number 29).

㉘ Pleasant Hike-In, Boat-In

Location: On Loon Lake in Eldorado National Forest; map D4, grid f0.

Campsites, facilities: There are 10 boat-in or hike-in tent sites. There is no piped water, but pit toilets, picnic tables, and fire grills are provided. The camp is accessible by boat or trail only. Leashed pets are permitted.

Reservations, fees: No reservations; no fee. Open June through October.

Contact: Eldorado National Forest, Pacific Ranger District, (530) 644-2349 or fax (530) 644-5405.

Directions: From Sacramento, drive east on US 50 to Riverton and the junction with Ice House Road/Soda Springs–Riverton Road on the left. Turn left and drive 34 miles to a fork at the foot of Loon Lake. Turn right and drive a mile to the Loon Lake Picnic Area or boat ramp. Either hike or boat 2.5 miles to the campground on the northeast shore of the lake.

Trip notes: This premium Sierra camp, hike-in or boat-in only, is set on the remote northeast shore of Loon Lake at 6,378 feet in elevation. In many ways this makes for a perfect short vacation. After reaching the camp a trail is available routed east for four miles past Buck Island Lake (6,436 feet) and Rockbound Lake (6,529 feet), set just inside the northern border of the Desolation Wilderness. When the trail is clear of snow, this makes for a fantastic day hike; a wilderness permit is required if staying overnight inside the wilderness boundary.

㉙ Loon Lake

Location: In Eldorado National Forest; map D4, grid f0.

Campsites, facilities: There are 53 sites for tents or RVs up to 22 feet long. Piped water, vault toilets, picnic tables, and fire grills are provided. A boat ramp and swimming beach are nearby. Leashed pets are permitted.

Reservations, fees: Reserve via phone at

(877) 444-6777 ($8.65 reservation fee) or website www.reserveusa.com; $13 per night (single), $20 per night double, $5 for a third vehicle. Open June through September.

Contact: Eldorado National Forest, Pacific Ranger District, (530) 644-2349 or fax (530) 644-5405.

Directions: From Sacramento, drive east on US 50 to Riverton and the junction with Ice House Road/Soda Springs–Riverton Road on the left. Turn left and drive 34 miles to a fork at the foot of Loon Lake. Turn right and drive one mile to the Loon Lake Picnic Area or boat ramp.

Trip notes: Loon Lake is set near the Sierra crest at 6,400 feet, covering 600 acres with depths up to 130 feet. This is the lake's primary campground, and it is easy to see why, with a picnic area, beach (includes a small unit to change your clothes in), and boat ramp located adjacent to the camp. The lake provides good trout fishing, and once the access road is clear of snow, the lake can be stocked every week of summer. Afternoon winds drive anglers off the lake but are cheered by sailboarders. An excellent trail is also available here, with the hike routed along the lake's eastern shore to Pleasant Hike-In, Boat-In (a trailhead for the Desolation Wilderness is available at Pleasant Hike-In, Boat-In (campground number 28).

㉚ Emerald Bay State Park

Location: On Lake Tahoe; map D4, grid f2.

Campsites, facilities: There are 100 sites for tents or RVs up to 21 feet long and trailers up to 18 feet long. Piped water, coin-operated showers, flush toilets, picnic tables, and fire grills are provided. There are also 20 boat-in sites available on the north side of the bay with water and toilets provided. Leashed pets are permitted except on the beach.

Reservations, fees: Reserve via phone at (800) 444-PARK/7275 ($7.50 reservation fee) or website www.cal-parks.ca.gov; $14 to $16 per night, $1 pet fee. No reservations for boat-in sites; $10 to $12 per night. Open June through September.

Contact: Emerald Bay State Park, (530) 541-3030, (530) 525-7277, or (530) 525-7232.

Directions: In South Lake Tahoe at the junction of Highway 89 and US 50, turn north on Highway 89 and drive 6.5 miles to the state park turnoff on the right side of the road. Turn east and drive a mile to the park entrance.

Trip notes: This is one of the most beautiful and popular state parks on the planet Earth. It is set at Eagle Point, near the mouth of Emerald Bay on Lake Tahoe, a place of rare, divine beauty. Although the high number of people at Lake Tahoe, and at this park in particular, present an inevitable problem, the 20 boat-in sites provide a remarkable solution. There may be no more beautiful place anywhere to run a boat than in Emerald Bay, with its deep cobalt-blue waters, awesome surrounding ridgelines, glimpses of Lake Tahoe out the mouth of the bay, and even a little island. The park also has several short hiking trails.

㉛ D. L. Bliss State Park

Location: On Lake Tahoe; map D4, grid f2.

Campsites, facilities: There are 168 sites for tents or RVs up to 18 feet long and trailers up to 15 feet long. Piped water, showers, flush toilets, picnic tables, and fire grills are provided. Leashed pets are permitted.

Reservations, fees: Reserve via phone at (800) 444-PARK/7275 ($7.50 reservation fee) or website www.cal-parks.ca.gov; $16 to $20 per night, $1 pet fee. Open June through mid-October.

Contact: D. L. Bliss State Park, (530) 525-7277 or (530) 525-7232.

Directions: In South Lake Tahoe at the junction of Highway 89 and US 50, turn north on Highway 89 and drive 10.5 miles to the state park turnoff on the right side of the road. Turn east and drive to the park entrance.

Trip notes: D. L. Bliss State Park is set on one of Lake Tahoe's most beautiful stretches of shoreline, from Emerald Point at the mouth of Emerald Bay on northward to Rubicon Point, spanning some three miles. The camp is located at the north end of the park, the sites nestled amid pine trees, with the lake about a quarter mile away. A trail from the camp is routed south to Emerald Point (6,232 feet), where there is a beautiful view of the lake and beyond to the surrounding mountain rim, an awesome sight in early summer when it is still covered with snow.

㉜ Camp Richardson Resort

Location: On Lake Tahoe; map D4, grid f3.

Campsites, facilities: There are 223 sites for tents and 112 sites for RVs, some with full or partial hookups. Piped water, showers, flush toilets, sanitary dump station, playground, picnic tables, and fire pits are provided. A boat ramp, boat rentals, groceries, and propane gas are also available. No pets are allowed.

Reservations, fees: Reservations are recommended; $17 to $25 per night. Open June through October.

Contact: Camp Richardson Resort, (530) 541-1801 or (800) 544-1801.

Directions: In South Lake Tahoe at the junction of Highway 89 and US 50, turn north on Highway 89 and drive 2.5 miles to the resort on the right side of the road.

Trip notes: Camp Richardson Resort is within minutes of boating, biking, gambling and, in the winter, skiing. It's a take-your-pick deal. With cabins and a hopping restaurant and nightclub also on the property, this is a place that offers one big package. The campsites are set in the woods, not on the lake itself. From here you can gain access to an excellent bike route that runs for three miles, then loops around by the lake for another three miles, most of it flat and easy, all of it beautiful. Expect company. The elevation is 6,300 feet.

㉝ Wrights Lake

Location: In Eldorado National Forest; map D4, grid g0.

Campsites, facilities: There are 35 sites for tents and 36 sites for tents or RVs up to 22 feet long. Piped water, vault toilets, picnic tables, and fire grills are provided. Leashed pets are permitted.

Reservations, fees: Reserve via phone at (877) 444-6777 ($8.65 reservation fee) or website www.reserveusa.com; $13 per night (single), $20 per night (double), $5 for a third vehicle. Open June through October.

Contact: Eldorado National Forest Information Center, (530) 644-6048 or fax (530) 644-3034.

Directions: From Sacramento, drive east on US 50 about 20 miles beyond Placerville. Turn left on Ice House Road and drive north 11.5 miles to Ice House Reservoir. Turn east on Road 32 and drive 10 miles. Turn left on Wrights Lake Road and drive two miles to the campground on the right side of the road.

Trip notes: This high mountain lake (7,000 feet) has shoreline camping and good fishing and hiking. There is no boat ramp, plus rules do not permit motors, so it is ideal for canoes, rafts, prams, and people who like quiet. Fishing is fair for both rainbow trout and brown trout. It is a classic alpine lake, though small (65 acres), with a trailhead for the Desolation Wilderness located at its north end. From here it is only a three-mile hike to the beautiful Twin Lakes and Island Lake, set on the western flank of Mount Price (9,975 feet).

㉞ Fallen Leaf Campground

Location: In the Lake Tahoe Basin; map D4, grid g2.

Campsites, facilities: There are 75 sites for tents and 130 sites for tents or RVs up to 40 feet long. Piped water, flush toilets, picnic tables, and fire grills are provided. A boat ramp, coin laundry, and supplies are available nearby. Leashed pets are permitted.

Reservations, fees: Reserve via phone at (877) 444-6777 ($8.65 reservation fee) or website www.reserveusa.com; $15 per night. Open May through October, weather permitting.

Contact: California Land Management, (530) 544-0426.

Directions: In South Lake Tahoe at the junction of US 50 and Highway 89, turn north on

Highway 89 and drive two miles to the Fallen Leaf Lake turnoff. Turn left and drive 1.5 miles to the campground.

Trip notes: This is a large "tent city" near the north shore of Fallen Leaf Lake, set at 6,337 feet. The lake is almost as deep blue as nearby Lake Tahoe. It's a big lake, three miles long, and also quite deep, 430 feet at its deepest point. The campground is operated by the concessionaire, which provides a variety of recreational opportunities, including a boat ramp and horseback riding rentals. Fishing is best in the fall for kokanee salmon. Because Fallen Leaf Lake is circled by forest and much of it is private property, you will need a boat to fish or explore the lake. A visitor center is available north of the Fallen Leaf Lake turnoff on Highway 89.

㉟ Camp Shelley

Location: Near Lake Tahoe in the Lake Tahoe Basin; map D4, grid g2.

Campsites, facilities: There are 26 sites for tents or RVs up to 22 feet long. Piped water, flush toilets, showers, picnic tables and fire grills are provided. A boat ramp, groceries and propane gas are available nearby at Camp Richardson. Leashed pets are permitted.

Reservations, fees: Reservations can be made in person, Monday through Friday, 8 A.M. to 5 P.M. at the Livermore Recreation and Park District Office, 71 Trevarno Road, Livermore, CA 94550. Reservations can also be made at the campground office, which is intermittently staffed during the season; $23 fee per night, ($17 for Livermore residents). Open mid-June through Labor Day.

Contact: Livermore Area Recreation and Park District, (925) 373-5700.

Directions: In South Lake Tahoe at the junction of US 50 and Highway 89, turn north on Highway 89, drive 2.5 miles to Camp Richardson, and then continue for 1.3 miles to the sign for Mount Tallac. Turn left on Mount Tallac Trailhead Road and drive to the campground on the right.

Trip notes: This privately owned campground is set near South Lake Tahoe, within close range of an outstanding bicycle trail. Nearby to the west is the drive to Inspiration Point and the incredible lookout of Emerald Bay, as well as the parking area for the short hike to Eagle Falls. Nearby to the east is Fallen Leaf Lake and the south shore of Lake Tahoe.

36 Chris Haven Mobile Home and RV Park

Location: Near South Lake Tahoe; map D4, grid g3.

Campsites, facilities: There are 30 RV sites with full hookups. Patios, rest rooms, showers, and a coin laundry are provided. Leashed pets are permitted.

Reservations, fees: Reservations are recommended; $26 per night. Open year-round.

Contact: Chris Haven Mobile Home and RV Park, (530) 541-1895 or fax (530) 541-0525.

Directions: Entering South Lake Tahoe on US 50, drive east to E Street (a half mile south of the junction of US 50 and Highway 89). Turn east on E Street and drive one block to the park on the right.

Trip notes: This is an RV-only park that is set within the boundaries of a mobile home park, within close range of the casinos to the east.

37 KOA South Lake Tahoe

Location: Near Lake Tahoe; map D4, grid g3.

Campsites, facilities: There are 16 sites for tents and 52 sites with full hookups for RVs up to 30 feet long. Picnic tables, fire grills, rest rooms, showers, sanitary dump station, recreation room, swimming pool, and a playground are on the premises. (Rest rooms, showers, and pool are not available in very cold weather.) Coin laundry, groceries, RV supplies, and propane gas are also available. Pets are permitted.

Reservations, fees: Reservations are recommended; $25 to $29.75 per night, $3.50 pet fee. Open April through December.

Contact: KOA South Lake Tahoe, (530) 577-3693; website www.laketahoekoa.com.

Directions: Entering South Lake Tahoe on US

50, look for the KOA sign along the road (located five miles south of the junction of US 50 and Highway 89).

Trip notes: Like so many KOA camps, this one is located on the outskirts of a major destination area, in this case, South Lake Tahoe. It is within close range of gambling, fishing, hiking, bike rentals and, in winter, good skiing. The camp is set at 6,300 feet.

38 Tahoe Valley Campground

Location: Near Lake Tahoe; map D4, grid g3.

Campsites, facilities: There are 77 sites for tents and 305 sites with full or partial hookups for RVs. Rest rooms, sanitary dump station, picnic tables, fire grills, coin laundry, heated swimming pool, playground, grocery store, RV supplies, propane gas, ice, firewood, cable TV, and a recreation room are all provided. Leashed pets are permitted (limit of two animals).

Reservations, fees: Reservations are recommended; $22 to $30 per night, $2 pet fee. Open mid-April through mid-October.

Contact: Tahoe Valley Campground, (530) 541-2222.

Directions: Entering South Lake Tahoe on US 50, drive east on US 50 to Meyers. Continue on US 50 about five miles beyond Meyers to the signed entrance on the right.

Trip notes: This is a massive privately operated park near South Lake Tahoe. The nearby attractions include five golf courses, horseback riding, casinos and, of course, "the Lake."

39 Campground by the Lake

Location: Near Lake Tahoe; map D4, grid g4.

Campsites, facilities: There are 170 sites for tents or RVs up to 32 feet long. Piped water, flush toilets, showers, sanitary dump station, playground, picnic tables, and fire grills are provided. A boat ramp is also available. Supplies and a coin laundry are nearby. Pets are permitted with proof of vaccinations.

Reservations, fees: Reservations are accepted; $11 to $20 per night (two-night minimum on weekends and holidays), $1 pet fee. Open April through September.

Contact: Campground by the Lake, (530) 542-6096 or (530) 542-6055.

Directions: Entering South Lake Tahoe on US 50, drive east on US 50 to Rufus Allen Boulevard. Turn right and drive a quarter mile to the campground on the right side of the road.

Trip notes: This city-operated campground at South Lake Tahoe is set at 6,200 feet and is primarily designed for RV drivers on tour.

⑩ Kirkwood Lake

Location: In Eldorado National Forest; map D4, grid h1.

Campsites, facilities: There are 12 tent sites. Piped water, vault toilets, picnic tables, and fire rings are provided. Leashed pets are permitted.

Reservations, fees: No reservations; $10 per night. Open June through October.

Contact: Eldorado National Forest, Amador Ranger District, (209) 295-4251 or fax (209) 295-5624.

Directions: From Jackson, drive east on Highway 88 for 60 miles (four miles past Silver Lake) to the campground entrance road on the left (if you reach the sign for Kirkwood Ski Resort, you have gone a half mile too far). Turn left and drive a quarter mile (road not suitable for trailers or RVs) to the campground.

Trip notes: Little Kirkwood Lake is in a beautiful Sierra setting, with good shoreline access, fishing for small rainbow trout, and quiet water. Despite that, it is often overlooked in favor of nearby Silver Lake and Caples Lake along Highway 88. Nearby Kirkwood Ski Resort stays open all summer and offers excellent opportunities for horseback riding, hiking, and meals. The elevation is 7,600 feet.

④ Caples Lake

Location: In Eldorado National Forest; map D4, grid h2.

Campsites, facilities: There are 20 sites for tents and 15 sites for tents or RVs up to 22 feet long. Piped water, vault toilets, picnic tables, and fire rings are provided. Groceries, propane gas, boat ramp, and boat rentals are nearby. Leashed pets are permitted.

Reservations, fees: No reservations; $11 per night. Open June through October.

Contact: Eldorado National Forest, Amador Ranger District, (209) 295-4251 or fax (209) 295-5624.

Directions: From Jackson, drive east on Highway 88 for 63 miles (one mile past the entrance road to Kirkwood Ski Area) to the camp entrance road on the left.

Trip notes: Caples Lake, here in the high country at 7,800 feet, is a pretty lake right along Highway 88. It covers 600 acres, has a 10 mph speed limit, and provides good trout fishing and excellent hiking terrain. The camp is set across the highway (a little two-laner) from the lake, with the Caples Lake Resort and boat rentals nearby. There is a parking area at the west end of the lake, and from here you can access a great 3.5-mile hike to Emigrant Lake, located in the Mokelumne Wilderness on the western flank of Mount Round Top (10,310 feet).

④ Hope Valley

Location: Near the Carson River in Humboldt-Toiyabe National Forest; map D4, grid h3.

Campsites, facilities: There are 20 sites for tents or RVs up to 22 feet long and a group area for up to 16 people. Piped water, vault toilets, picnic tables, and fire grills are provided. Leashed pets are permitted.

Reservations, fees: Reserve via phone at (887) 444-6777 ($8.65 reservation fee); $9 per night, $16 group camp fee per night. Open June through September.

Contact: Humboldt-Toiyabe National Forest, Carson Ranger District, (702) 882-2766 or fax (702) 884-8199.

Directions: From Sacramento, drive east on US 50 to the junction with Highway 89. Turn south on Highway 89 and drive over Luther Pass to the junction with Highway 88. Turn right (west) and drive two miles to Blue Lakes Road. Turn left (south) and drive 1.5 miles to the campground on the right side of the road.

From Jackson, drive east on Highway 88 over Carson Pass and continue east for five miles to Blue Lakes Road. Turn right (south) and drive 1.5 miles to the campground on the right side of the road.

Trip notes: The West Fork of the Carson River runs right through Hope Valley, a pretty trout stream with a choice of four streamside campgrounds. Trout stocks are made near the campgrounds during summer. The campground at Hope Valley is just east of Carson Pass, at 7,300 feet in elevation, in a very pretty area. A trailhead for the Pacific Crest Trail is located three miles south of the campground. The primary nearby destination is Blue Lakes, about a 10-minute drive away. An insider's note is that little Tamarack Lake, set just beyond the turnoff for Lower Blue Lake, is excellent for swimming.

㊸ Kit Carson

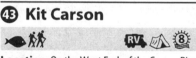

Location: On the West Fork of the Carson River in Humboldt-Toiyabe National Forest; map D4, grid h4.

Campsites, facilities: There are 12 sites for tents or RVs up to 22 feet long. Piped water, vault toilets, picnic tables, and fire grills are provided. Leashed pets are permitted.

Reservations, fees: Reserve via phone at (877) 444-6777 ($8.65 reservation fee) or website www.reserveusa.com; $9 per night. Open mid-May through mid-September.

Contact: Humboldt-Toiyabe National Forest, Carson Ranger District, (702) 882-2766 or fax (702) 884-8199.

Directions: From Sacramento, drive east on US 50 to the junction with Highway 89. Turn south on Highway 89 and drive over Luther Pass to the junction with Highway 88. Turn left and drive a mile to the campground on the left side of the road.

From Jackson, drive east on Highway 88 over Carson Pass and to the junction with Highway 89 and then continue for a mile to the campground on the left side of the road.

Trip notes: This is one in a series of pristine,

high Sierra camps set along the West Fork of the Carson River. There's good trout fishing, thanks to regular stocks from the Department of Fish and Game. This is no secret, however, and the area from the Highway 89 bridge on downstream gets a lot of fishing pressure. The elevation is 6,600 feet.

㊹ Crystal Springs

Location: On the West Fork of the Carson River in Humboldt-Toiyabe National Forest; map D4, grid h4.

Campsites, facilities: There are 20 sites for tents or RVs up to 22 feet long. Piped water, vault toilets, picnic tables, and fire grills are provided. Leashed pets are permitted.

Reservations, fees: Reserve via phone at (877) 444-6777 ($8.65 reservation fee) or website www.reserveusa.com; $9 per night. Open late April through September.

Contact: Humboldt-Toiyabe National Forest, Carson Ranger District, (702) 882-2766 or fax (702) 884-8199.

Directions: From Sacramento, drive east on US 50 to the junction with Highway 89. Turn south on Highway 89 and drive over Luther Pass to the junction with Highway 88. Turn left (east) and drive 4.5 miles to the campground on the right side of the road.

From Jackson, drive east on Highway 88 over Carson Pass to the junction with Highway 89 and continue for 4.5 miles to the campground on the right side of the road.

Trip notes: For many people, this camp is an ideal choice. It is set at an elevation of 6,000 feet, right alongside the West Fork of the Carson River. This stretch of water is stocked with trout by the Department of Fish and Game. Crystal Springs is easy to reach, just off Highway 88, and supplies can be obtained in nearby Woodfords or Markleeville. Grover Hot Springs State Park makes a good side trip destination.

㊺ Snowshoe Springs

Location: On the West Fork of the Carson River

in Humboldt-Toiyabe National Forest; map D4, grid h4.

Campsites, facilities: There are 13 tent sites. Piped water, vault toilets, picnic tables, and fire grills are provided. Leashed pets are permitted.

Reservations, fees: No reservations; $9 per night. Open June through September.

Contact: Humboldt-Toiyabe National Forest, Carson Ranger District, (702) 882-2766 or fax (702) 884-8199.

Directions: From Sacramento, drive east on US 50 to the junction with Highway 89. Turn south on Highway 89 and drive over Luther Pass to the junction with Highway 88. Turn left (east) and drive two miles to the campground on the right side of the road.

From Jackson, drive east on Highway 88 over Carson Pass to the junction with Highway 89 and continue for two miles to the campground on the right side of the road.

Trip notes: Take your pick of this or the other three streamside camps on the West Fork of the Carson River. This one is at 6,600 feet. Trout are plentiful but rarely grow very large.

㊽ Turtle Rock Park

Location: Near Woodfords; map D4, grid h5.

Campsites, facilities: There are 28 sites for tents or RVs up to 30 feet long. Piped water, pit toilets, picnic tables, and fire grills are provided. Coin laundry, groceries, and propane gas are available within two miles. Leashed pets are permitted.

Reservations, fees: No reservations; $8 per night, $3 for each additional vehicle. Open May to mid-October, weather permitting.

Contact: Alpine County Parks, (530) 694-2140.

Directions: From Sacramento, drive east on US 50 to the junction with Highway 89. Turn south on Highway 89 and drive over Luther Pass to the junction with Highway 88. Turn left (east) and drive to Woodfords and the junction with Highway 89. Turn south and drive 4.5 miles to the park entrance on the right side of the road.

Trip notes: This pretty, wooded campground, set at 6,000 feet, gets missed by a lot of folks. That's because it is administered at the county

level and also because most vacationers want the more pristine beauty of the nearby camps along the Carson River. (If it snows, they close, so call ahead if you're planning an autumn visit.) Nearby side trips include Grover Hot Springs and the hot springs in Markleeville.

㊼ Silver Lake West

Location: On Silver Lake; map D4, grid i1.

Campsites, facilities: There are 37 sites for tents or RVs up to 30 feet long. Picnic tables and fire pits are provided. Piped water and vault toilets are available. Leashed pets are permitted.

Reservations, fees: No reservations; $13 per night. Open May through October, weather permitting.

Contact: PG&E Building and Land Services, (916) 386-5164.

Directions: From Jackson, drive east on Highway 88 for 50 miles (to the north end of Silver Lake) to the campground entrance road on the left.

Trip notes: The Highway 88 corridor provides access to three excellent lakes: Lower Bear River Reservoir, Silver Lake, and Caples Lake. Silver Lake is difficult to pass by, with cabin rentals, pretty campsites, decent trout fishing, and excellent hiking. The lake is set at 7,200 feet in a classic granite cirque just below the Sierra ridge. This camp is on the west side of Highway 88, across the road from the lake. A great hike starts at the trailhead on the east side of the lake, a two-mile tromp to little Hidden Lake, one of several nice hikes in the area.

㊽ East Silver Lake

Location: In Eldorado National Forest; map D4, grid i1.

Campsites, facilities: There are 28 sites for tents and 34 sites for tents or RVs. Picnic tables, fire grills, vault toilets, and piped water are provided. A grocery store, boat rentals, boat ramp, and propane gas are nearby. Leashed pets are permitted.

Reservations, fees: Reserve via phone at

(877) 444-6777 ($8.65 reservation fee) or website www.reserveusa.com; $12 per night. Open June through October.

Contact: Eldorado National Forest, Amador Ranger District, (209) 295-4251 or fax (209) 295-5624.

Directions: From Jackson, drive east on Highway 88 for 50 miles (to the north end of Silver Lake) to the campground entrance road on the right.

Trip notes: Silver Lake is an easy-to-reach alpine lake set at 7,200 feet, which provides a beautiful setting, good trout fishing, and hiking. This camp is on the northeast side of the lake, with a boat ramp located nearby. See the trip notes for Silver Lake West (campground number 47) for more information.

㊾ Woods Lake

Location: In Eldorado National Forest; map D4, grid i2.

Campsites, facilities: There are 25 tent sites and a multiple-family unit. Hand-pumped water, vault toilets, picnic tables, and fire rings are provided. Groceries and propane gas are available within five miles. Leashed pets are permitted.

Reservations, fees: No reservations; $11 to $18 per night. Open June through October.

Contact: Eldorado National Forest, Amador Ranger District, (209) 295-4251 or fax (209) 295-5624.

Directions: From Jackson, drive east on Highway 88 to Caples Lake and continue for a mile to the Woods Lake turnoff on the right (two miles west of Carson Pass). Turn south and drive a mile to the campground on the right (trailers and RVs are not recommended).

Trip notes: Woods Lake is only two miles from Highway 88, yet it can provide campers the feeling of visiting a far-off land. It is a small but beautiful lake in the granite backdrop of the high Sierra, set at 8,200 feet near Carson Pass. Boats with motors are not permitted, making it ideal for canoes and rowboats. Trout fishing is fair. A great trailhead is available here, a three-mile loop hike to little Round Top Lake and Winnemucca Lake (twice the size of Woods Lake) and back. They are set on the northern flank of Mount Round Top (10,310 feet).

㊿ Lower Blue Lake

Location: Near Carson Pass; map D4, grid i3.

Campsites, facilities: There are 16 sites for tents or RVs. Piped water, vault toilets, picnic tables, and fire grills are provided. Leashed pets are permitted.

Reservations, fees: No reservations; $13 per night, $1 pet fee. Open June through September, weather permitting.

Contact: PG&E Building and Land Services, (916) 386-5164.

Directions: From Sacramento, drive east on US 50 to the junction with Highway 89. Turn south on Highway 89 and drive over Luther Pass to the junction with Highway 88. Turn right and drive two miles to Blue Lakes Road. Turn left and drive 11 miles to a junction at the south end of Lower Blue Lake. Turn right and drive a short distance to the campground on the left side of the road.

From Jackson, drive east on Highway 88 over Carson Pass and continue east for five miles to Blue Lakes Road. Turn right (south) and drive 11 miles (seven paved, four gravel) to a junction at the south end of Lower Blue Lake. Turn right and drive a short distance to the campground on the left.

Trip notes: This is the high country, 8,200 feet, where the terrain is stark and steep and edged by volcanic ridgelines, and where the deep blue-green hue of lake water brightens the landscape. Lower Blue Lake provides a popular trout fishery, with rainbow trout, brook trout, and cutthroat trout all stocked regularly. The boat ramp is located adjacent to the campground. The access road crosses the Pacific Crest Trail, providing a route to a series of small, pretty hike-to lakes just outside the edge of the Mokelumne Wilderness.

(51) Middle Creek

Location: Near Carson Pass and Blue Lakes; map D4, grid i3.

Campsites, facilities: There are five sites for tents or RVs. Piped water, vault toilets, picnic tables, and fire grills are provided. Leashed pets are permitted.

Reservations, fees: No reservations; $13 per night, $1 pet fee. Open June through September, weather permitting.

Contact: PG&E Building and Land Services, (916) 386-5164.

Directions: From Sacramento, drive east on US 50 to the junction with Highway 89. Turn south on Highway 89 and drive over Luther Pass to the junction with Highway 88. Turn right and drive two miles to Blue Lakes Road. Turn left and drive 11 miles to a junction at the south end of Lower Blue Lake. Turn right and drive 1.5 miles to the campground on the left side of the road.

From Jackson, drive east on Highway 88 over Carson Pass and continue east for five miles to Blue Lakes Road. Turn right (south) and drive 11 miles (seven paved, four gravel) to a junction at the south end of Lower Blue Lake. Turn right and drive 1.5 miles to the campground on the left side of the road.

Trip notes: This is a tiny, captivating spot set along the creek that connects Upper and Lower Blue Lakes, providing a take your pick deal for anglers. See the trip notes for Lower Blue Lake (campground number 50) for more information. The elevation is 8,200 feet.

52 Upper Blue Lake

Location: Near Carson Pass; map D4, grid i3.

Campsites, facilities: There are 32 sites for tents. Piped water, vault toilets, picnic tables, and fire grills are provided. Leashed pets are permitted.

Reservations, fees: No reservations; $13 per night, $1 pet fee. Open June through September, weather permitting.

Contact: PG&E Building and Land Services, (916) 386-5164.

Directions: From Sacramento, drive east on US 50 to the junction with Highway 89. Turn south on Highway 89 and drive over Luther Pass to the junction with Highway 88. Turn right and drive two miles to Blue Lakes Road. Turn left and

drive 11 miles to a junction at the south end of Lower Blue Lake. Turn right and drive three miles to the campground on the left side of the road.

From Jackson, drive east on Highway 88 over Carson Pass and continue east for five miles to Blue Lakes Road. Turn right (south) and drive 11 miles (seven paved, four gravel) to a junction at the south end of Lower Blue Lake. Turn right and drive three miles to the campground on the left side of the road.

Trip notes: This is one of two camps set along Upper Blue Lake and one of four camps in the immediate area. The trout fishing is usually quite good here in early summer. See the trip notes for Lower Blue Lake (campground number 50) for more information. The elevation is 8,200 feet.

53 Upper Blue Lake Dam

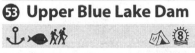

Location: Near Carson Pass; map D4, grid i3.

Campsites, facilities: There are 25 tent sites. Piped water, vault toilets, picnic tables, and fire grills are provided. Leashed pets are permitted.

Reservations, fees: No reservations; $13 per night, $1 pet fee. Open June through September, weather permitting.

Contact: PG&E Building and Land Services, (916) 386-5164.

Directions: From Sacramento, drive east on US 50 to the junction with Highway 89. Turn south on Highway 89 and drive over Luther Pass to the junction with Highway 88. Turn right and drive two miles to Blue Lakes Road. Turn left and drive 11 miles to a junction at the south end of Lower Blue Lake. Turn right and drive three miles to the campground next to the dam.

From Jackson, drive east on Highway 88 over Carson Pass and continue east for five miles to Blue Lakes Road. Turn right and drive 11 miles (seven paved, four gravel) to a junction at the south end of Lower Blue Lake. Turn right and drive three miles to the campground next to the dam.

Trip notes: This is one of four camps at the Blue Lakes, at 8,200 feet in elevation south of Carson Pass. A boat ramp is located near this camp. For recreation options, see the trip notes for Lower Blue Lake (campground number 50).

54 Grover Hot Springs State Park

Location: Near Markleeville; map D4, grid i4.

Campsites, facilities: There are 26 sites for tents, 13 sites for RVs, and 37 sites for tents or RVs up to 27 feet long. Piped water, flush toilets, coin-operated showers (except in the winter), hot springs pool with wheelchair access, swimming pool, picnic tables, and fire grills are provided. A grocery store and coin laundry are nearby. Leashed pets are permitted.

Reservations, fees: Reserve via phone at (800) 444-PARK/7275 ($7.50 reservation fee) or website www.cal-parks.ca.gov; $15 to $17 per night, $1 pet fee; pool fees are $4 per adult, $2 per child seven or under. Open year-round.

Contact: Grover Hot Springs State Park, (530) 694-2248, (530) 694-2649, or (530) 525-7232.

Directions: From Sacramento, drive east on US 50 to the junction with Highway 89. Turn south on Highway 89 and drive over Luther Pass to the junction with Highway 88. Turn left and drive to Woodfords and the junction with Highway 89. Turn south and drive six miles to Markleeville and the junction with Hot Springs Road. Turn west and drive four miles to the park entrance.

Trip notes: This is a famous spot for folks who like the rejuvenating powers of a hot spring. Some say they feel a glow about them for weeks. When touring the South Tahoe/Carson Pass area, many vacationers take part of a day to make the trip to the hot springs. Side trip options include a nature trail in the park and driving to the Carson River (where the water is a mite cooler) and fishing for trout. The elevation is 5,800 feet.

55 Markleeville

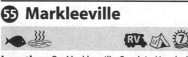

Location: On Markleeville Creek in Humboldt-Toiyabe National Forest; map D4, grid i5.

Campsites, facilities: There are 10 sites for tents or RVs up to 20 feet long. Trailers are prohibited due to road conditions. Piped water, a vault toilet, picnic tables, and fire grills are provided. A grocery store and restaurant are nearby. Leashed pets are permitted.

Reservations, fees: No reservations; $9 per night. Open late April through September.

Contact: Humboldt-Toiyabe National Forest, Carson Ranger District, (702) 882-2766 or fax (702) 884-8199.

Directions: From Sacramento, drive east on US 50 to the junction with Highway 89. Turn south on Highway 89 and drive over Luther Pass to the junction with Highway 88. Turn left and drive to Woodfords and the junction with Highway 89. Turn south, drive six miles to Markleeville, and continue for a half mile to the campground on the left side of the highway.

Trip notes: This is a pretty, streamside camp set at 5,500 feet along Markleeville Creek, a mile from the East Fork of the Carson River. The trout here are willing, but alas, are dinkers. This area is the transition zone where high mountains to the west give way to the high desert to the east. The hot springs in Markleeville and Grover Hot Springs State Park provide good side trips.

56 Pacific Valley

Location: Overlooking Pacific Creek in Stanislaus National Forest; map D4, grid j3.

Campsites, facilities: There are 15 sites for tents and a large area for dispersed camping. Trailers are not recommended due to road conditions. There is no piped water, but picnic tables, fire rings, and vault toilets are provided. Leashed pets are permitted.

Reservations, fees: No reservations; no fee. A free campfire permit is required from the district office. Open June through September.

Contact: Stanislaus National Forest, Calaveras Ranger District, (209) 795-1381 or fax (209) 795-6849. For a map send $4 to the USDA Forest Service, US Forest Map Sales, 1323 Club Drive, Vallejo, CA 94592, and ask for Stanislaus National Forest area.

Directions: From Angels Camp, drive east on Highway 4 to Lake Alpine and continue for about seven miles to the campground on the right side of the road.

Trip notes: This is a do-it-yourself special; that is, more of a general area for camping than a campground, set up for backpackers heading out on expeditions into the Carson-Iceberg Wilderness to the south. It is set at 7,600 feet along Pacific Creek, a tributary to the Mokelumne River. The trail from camp is routed south and reaches three forks within two miles. The best is routed deep into the wilderness, flanking Hiram Peak (9,760 feet), Airola Peak (9,938 feet), and Iceberg Peak (9,720 feet).

☞ Hermit Valley

Location: In Stanislaus National Forest; map D4, grid j3.

Campsites, facilities: There is a large area for dispersed camping. There is no piped water, but vault toilets are provided. Leashed pets are permitted.

Reservations, fees: No reservations; no fee. A free campfire permit is required from the district office. Open June through September.

Contact: Stanislaus National Forest, Calaveras Ranger District, (209) 795-1381 or fax (209) 795-6849. For a map send $4 to the USDA Forest Service, US Forest Map Sales, 1323 Club Drive, Vallejo, CA 94592, and ask for Stanislaus National Forest area.

Directions: From Angels Camp, drive east on Highway 4 to Lake Alpine and continue for about nine miles to the campground on the left side of the road.

Trip notes: This tiny, remote, little known spot is set near the border of the Mokelumne Wilderness near where Grouse Creek enters the Mokelumne River, at 7,500 feet in elevation. Looking north, there is a good view into Deer Valley. A primitive road, located a half mile west of camp, is routed through Deer Valley north for six miles to the Blue Lakes. On the opposite (south) side of the road from the camp there is a little-traveled hiking trail that is routed up Grouse Creek to Milk Ranch Meadow at the border of the Carson-Iceberg Wilderness.

☞ Mosquito Lake

Location: At Mosquito Lake in Stanislaus National Forest; map D4, grid j3.

Campsites, facilities: There are a few primi-

tive, undesignated sites for tents. Picnic tables and a vault toilet are provided. No piped water is available. Leashed pets are permitted.

Reservations, fees: No reservations; $5 per night. A free campfire permit is required from the district office.

Contact: Stanislaus National Forest, Calaveras Ranger District, (209) 795-1381 or fax (209) 795-6849. For a map send $4 to the USDA Forest Service, US Forest Map Sales, 1323 Club Drive, Vallejo, CA 94592, and ask for Stanislaus National Forest area.

Directions: From Angels Camp, drive east on Highway 4 to Lake Alpine and continue for about six miles to the campground on the left side of the road.

Trip notes: Mosquito Lake is in a pristine Sierra setting at 8,260 feet, presenting remarkable beauty for a place that can be reached by car. Most people believe that Mosquito Lake is for day-use only, and that's why they get crowded into nearby Alpine Campground (see chapter E4). But it's not just for day use, and this camp is often overlooked because it is about a mile west of the little lake, and on the opposite side of the road. The lake is small, a pretty emerald green, and even has a few small trout in it.

☞ Bloomfield

Location: In Stanislaus National Forest; map D4, grid j4.

Campsites, facilities: There are five sites for tents or RVs. Trailers are not recommended due to road conditions. Piped water, vault toilets, picnic tables, and fire rings are provided. A grocery store, propane gas, and coin laundry are available nearby. Leashed pets are permitted.

Reservations, fees: No reservations; $8 per night. A free campfire permit is required from the district office. Open June through October.

Contact: Stanislaus National Forest, Calaveras Ranger District, (209) 795-1381 or fax (209) 795-6849. For a map send $4 to the USDA Forest Service, US Forest Map Sales, 1323 Club Drive, Vallejo, CA 94592, and ask for Stanislaus National Forest area.

Directions: From Angels Camp, drive east on Highway 4 to Lake Alpine and continue for about 15 miles to Forest Service Road 8N01 on the right side of the road (1.5 miles west of Ebbetts Pass). Turn right and drive two miles to the campground on the right side of the road.

Trip notes: This is a primitive and little-known camp set at 7,800 feet near Ebbetts Pass. The North Fork Mokelumne River runs right by the camp, with good stream access for about a mile on each side of the camp. The access road continues south to Highland Lakes, a destination that provides cartop boating, fair fishing, and trailheads for hiking into the Carson-Iceberg Wilderness.

⑥⓪ Silver Creek

Location: In Humboldt-Toiyabe National Forest; map D4, grid j5.

Campsites, facilities: There are 22 sites for tents or RVs up to 22 feet long. Piped water, vault toilets, picnic tables, and fire grills are provided. Leashed pets are permitted.

Reservations, fees: Reserve via phone at (877) 444-6777 ($8.65 reservation fee) or website www.reserveusa.com; $9 per night. Open June through October.

Contact: Humboldt-Toiyabe National Forest, Carson Ranger District, (702) 882-2766 or fax (702) 884-8199.

Directions: From Angels Camp, drive east on Highway 4 all the way over Ebbetts Pass and continue for about six miles to the campground.

From Markleeville, drive south on Highway 89 to the junction with Highway 4. Turn west on Highway 4 (steep and winding) and drive about five miles to the campground.

Trip notes: This pretty spot, set near Silver Creek, has easy access from Highway 4 and, in years without washouts, good fishing in early summer for small trout. It is in the remote high Sierra, east of Ebbetts Pass. A side trip to Ebbetts Pass features Kinney Lake, PCT access, and a trailhead at the north end of the lake (on the west side of Highway 4) for a mile hike to Lower Kinney Lake. No bikes are permitted on the trails. The elevation is 6,800 feet.

⑥① Topaz Lake RV Park

Location: On Topaz Lake, near Markleeville; map D4, grid j7.

Campsites, facilities: There are 54 RV sites with full hookups, cable TV, and picnic tables. Rest rooms, showers, coin laundry, propane gas, and a boat ramp are available. Leashed pets are permitted.

Reservations, fees: Reservations are accepted; $18 to $20 per night. Open March through mid-October, weather permitting; owners request a call prior to visits in the off-season.

Contact: Topaz Lake RV Park, (530) 495-2357 or fax (530) 495-2118.

Directions: From Carson City, drive south on US 395 for 45 miles to Topaz Lake and the campground on the left side of the road.

From Bridgeport, drive north on US 395 for 45 miles to the campground on the right side of the road.

Trip notes: Topaz Lake, set at 5,000 feet, is one of the hidden surprises for California anglers. The surprise is the size of the rainbow trout, with one of the highest rates of 15- to 18-inch trout of any lake in the mountain country. The setting is hardly pretty; a good-sized lake on the edge of the barren high desert country which also serves as the border between California and Nevada. Wind is a problem for small boats, especially in the early summer. The RV park is adjacent to Topaz Lake Marina, which offers boat rentals, as well as a tackle shop and snack bar.

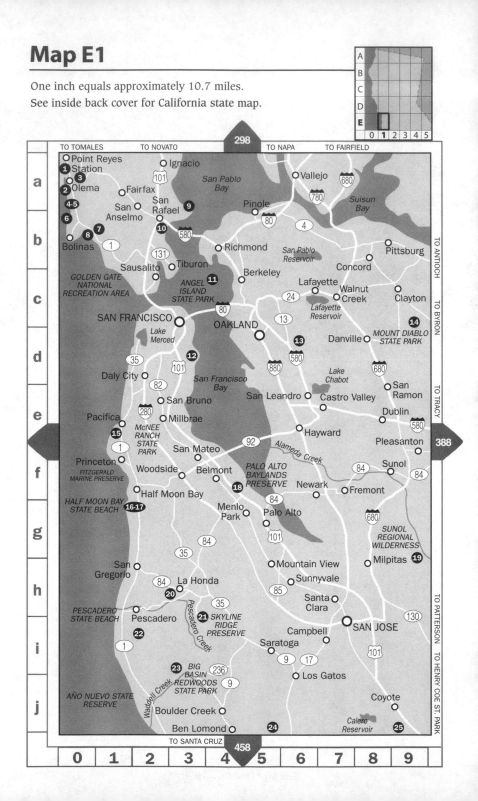

Map E1

One inch equals approximately 10.7 miles.
See inside back cover for California state map.

Chapter E1 features:

❶ Olema Ranch Campground

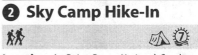

Location: In Olema; map E1, grid a0.

Campsites, facilities: There are 200 sites for tents or RVs, some with full or partial hookups. Picnic tables are provided. Piped water, rest rooms, showers, sanitary disposal station, coin laundry, and a recreation hall (for groups of 25 or more only) are available. Leashed pets are permitted.

Reservations, fees: Reservations are accepted; $18 to $25 per night. Open year-round.

Contact: Olema Ranch Campground, (415) 663-8001 or fax (415) 663-8832.

Directions: From US 101 in Marin, take the Sir Francis Drake Boulevard exit and drive west for about 20 miles to Highway 1 at Olema. Turn north on Highway 1 and drive a half mile to the campground.

Trip notes: This large, private park is in a perfect location for a Point Reyes adventure. Olema is a beautiful country town set in a valley amid Marin's coastal foothills. It borders the Point Reyes National Seashore to the west and the Golden Gate National Recreation Area to the

east, with Tomales Bay to the nearby north. There are several excellent trailheads available within a 10-minute drive along Highway 1 to the south. Though a wildfire on nearby Inverness Ridge and adjacent western slopes ravaged an old-growth forest of Bishop pine in the fall of 1995, the land's regeneration has become a beautiful spectacle.

❷ Sky Camp Hike-In

Location: In Point Reyes National Seashore; map E1, grid a0.

Campsites, facilities: There are 11 individual sites and a group site (walk-in only) which can accommodate up to eight campers. Piped water is available but potability is not assured; campers are advised to carry water purification equipment. Pit toilets are provided, as are fire grills for use with charcoal, but no wood fires are permitted in the park. No vehicles or pets are allowed.

Reservations, fees: Reservations are required; $10 per night, $30 per night for the group site (maximum of 25 people); four-day maximum stay.

Contact: Sky Camp Hike-In, (415) 663-8054.

Directions: From US 101 in Marin, take the Sir Francis Drake Boulevard exit and drive west for about 20 miles to Highway 1 at Olema. Turn north on Highway 1 and drive a very short distance. Turn left on Bear Valley Road and drive north for 0.7 mile. Turn left at the "Seashore Information" sign and drive to the park headquarters parking lot and the Bear Valley Trailhead.

Trip notes: Sky Camp is set on the western flank of Mount Wittenberg on Inverness Ridge, right at the edge of the area in Point Reyes National Seashore that burned in the fall 1995 wildfire. In fact, this hike-in camp was right at the edge of the firebreak and was partially burned. To reach the camp, take the Bear Valley Trail from park headquarters and walk a mile to the Meadow Trail. Turn right (north) on the Meadow Trail and hike 1.5 miles to the Sky Trail, cross it, and continue a half mile to the campground. From here you get a dramatic view of the burned area and the adjacent Marin coast. No open fires and no pets are permitted. You must have a backcountry permit from the Bear Valley Visitor Center to camp here.

❸ Samuel P. Taylor State Park

Location: Near San Rafael; map E1, grid a0.

Campsites, facilities: There are 25 sites for tents and 35 sites for tents or RVs up to 27 feet long. Piped water, fire grills, tables, flush toilets, showers (coin operated), and food lockers are provided. There is a small store two miles away in Lagunitas. Two campsites are wheelchair accessible. Pets are permitted on leashes in the campground only; they are not permitted on trails.

Reservations, fees: Reserve by phoning (800) 444-PARK/7275 ($7.50 reservation fee) or website www.cal-parks.ca.gov; $12 to $16 per night, $1 pet fee. Open year-round.

Contact: Samuel P. Taylor State Park, (415) 488-9897; California State Parks, Marin District, (415) 893-1580 or fax (415) 893-1583.

Directions: From US 101 in Marin, take the Sir Francis Drake Boulevard exit and drive west for about 15 miles to the park entrance on the left side of the road.

Trip notes: This is a beautiful park, with campsites set amid redwoods, complete with a babbling brook running nearby. Hikers will find 20 miles of hiking trails, a hidden waterfall, and some good mountain biking routes on service roads. The paved bike path that runs through the park and parallels Sir Francis Drake Boulevard is a terrific, easy ride.

❹ Coast Camp Hike-In

Location: In Point Reyes National Seashore; map E1, grid a0.

Campsites, facilities: There are 12 individual and two group hike-in sites, with piped water and pit toilets. Backpacking stoves are required for cooking. No vehicles or pets are permitted.

Reservations, fees: Reservations are required; $10 per night; four-day maximum stay.

Contact: Coast Camp Hike-In, (415) 663-8054.

Directions: From US 101 in Marin, take the Sir Francis Drake Boulevard exit and drive about 20 miles to Highway 1 at Olema. Turn right on Highway 1 and drive a very short distance. Turn left at Bear Valley Road and drive north for two miles to Limantour Road. Turn left at Limantour Road and drive six miles to the access road for the Point Reyes Hostel. Turn left and drive 0.2 mile to the trailhead on the right side of the road.

Trip notes: This is a classic ocean-bluff setting, a hike-in camp set just above Santa Maria Beach on the Point Reyes National Seashore, providing an extended tour into a land of charm. It is a 2.8-mile hike to get here, the northernmost camp on the Coast Trail. (The complete Coast Trail is a 19-mile trip that is one of the best hikes in the Bay Area.) From Coast Camp, the trail contours south along the bluffs above the beach for 1.4 miles to Sculptured Beach, where there is a series of odd geologic formations, including caves, tunnels, and sea stacks. Reservations and a backcountry permit are required. Note: This camp is set on the edge of the area that burned in the fall 1995 wildfire.

❺ Wildcat Camp Hike-In

🚶🚶   ⛺ 🔟

Location: In Point Reyes National Seashore; map E1, grid a0.

Campsites, facilities: There are nine individual and three group hike-in sites with piped water and pit toilets. (The three group sites can hold 25 people each.) Fire grills are provided for use with charcoal, but no wood fires are permitted in the park. No vehicles or pets are permitted.

Reservations, fees: Reservations are required; $10 per night, group sites are $30 per night; four-day maximum stay.

Contact: Wildcat Camp Hike-In, (415) 663-8054.

Directions: From US 101 in Marin, take the Sir Francis Drake Boulevard exit and drive west for about 20 miles to Highway 1 at Olema. Turn south on Highway 1 and drive about 10 miles south to Olema-Bolinas Road (often unsigned). Turn right and drive 2.1 miles to Mesa Road. Turn right and drive 5.8 miles to the Palomarin Trailhead. It is a 5.6-mile hike to the campground on the Coast Trail.

Trip notes: This backpack camp sits in a grassy meadow near a small stream that flows to the ocean, just above remote Wildcat Beach. Getting there takes you on a fantastic hike that crosses some of the Bay Area's most beautiful wildlands. The trail is routed along the ocean for about a mile, heads up in the coastal hills, turns left, and skirts past Bass Lake, Crystal Lake, and Pelican Lake and, ultimately, heads past Alamere Creek with its dramatic 40-foot waterfall, one of the rare ocean bluff waterfalls anywhere.

❻ Glen Camp Hike-In

🚶🚶   ⛺ 🔟

Location: In Point Reyes National Seashore; map E1, grid b0.

Campsites, facilities: There are 12 hike-in sites with pit toilets. Well water is available, but may not be potable; bring water purification equipment. Backpacking stoves are required for cooking. No pets are permitted.

Reservations, fees: Reservations are required; $10 per night; four-day maximum stay.

Contact: Glen Camp Hike-In, (415) 663-8054.

Directions: From US 101 in Marin, take the Sir Francis Drake Boulevard exit and drive about 20 miles to Highway 1 at Olema. Turn north on Highway 1 and drive a very short distance. Turn left on Bear Valley Road and drive north for 0.7 mile. Turn left at the "Seashore Information" sign and drive to the park headquarters parking lot and the Bear Valley Trailhead. It is a 4.6-mile hike to the camp.

Trip notes: Glen Camp Hike-In is set in the coastal foothills of Point Reyes National Seashore, right at the edge of where forest gives way to grasslands. The hike to it starts at the Bear Valley Visitor Center, where you can obtain your backcountry permits and hiking information, and is routed on the popular Bear Valley Trail, a wide road made out of compressed rock. It is 1.6 miles to Divide Meadow, with a modest 215-foot climb, then another 1.6 miles through Bear Valley to the Glen Camp Trail. Turn left and hike 1.4 miles, with the trail lateralling in and out of two canyons to reach the camp. It is secluded and quiet. Get a map, a reservation, and bring everything you need.

❼ Pantoll Campground Walk-in

🐟🚶🚶🕴🐴   ⛺ 🔟

Location: In Mount Tamalpais State Park; map E1, grid b1.

Campsites, facilities: There are 16 walk-in tent sites. Piped water, flush toilets, fire grills, food lockers, and tables are provided. Firewood is available to purchase. Leashed pets are permitted.

Reservations, fees: No reservations; $15 to $16 per night, $1 pet fee.

Contact: Pantoll Campground, (415) 388-2070; California State Parks, Marin District, (415) 893-1580 or fax (415) 388-2968.

Directions: From US 101 in Marin, take the Stinson Beach/Highway 1 exit. Drive west to the stoplight at the T intersection (Highway 1). Turn south and drive about four miles uphill to the Panoramic Highway. Bear to the right on Panoramic Highway and continue for 5.5 miles (past the turnoff to Muir Woods). Turn left at the Pantoll parking area and ranger station. A 100-

foot walk is required to reach the campground.

Trip notes: When camping at Pantoll, you are within close range of the divine, including some of the best hiking, best lookouts, and just plain best places to be anywhere in the Bay Area. The camp is set in the woods on the western slopes of Mount Tamalpais, which some say is a place of special power. The Steep Ravine Trail is routed out of camp to the west into a wondrous gorge filled with redwoods and a stream with miniature waterfalls. After a good rain, when everything is oozing with moisture, this can be one of the most romantic places on Earth. Another hike, on the Matt Davis/Coast Trail, provides breathtaking views of the coast. Another must is the nearby drive to the East Peak Lookout, where the entire world seems within reach.

❽ Steep Ravine Environmental Campsites

Location: In Mount Tamalpais State Park; map E1, grid b0.

Campsites, facilities: There are six walk-in sites for tents and 10 primitive cabins, each with a wood stove, picnic table, and a flat wood surface for sleeping. Pit toilets, fire grills, and tables are provided. Piped water is nearby, and wood is available to purchase. No pets are permitted.

Reservations, fees: Reserve by phoning (800) 444-PARK/7275 ($7.50 reservation fee) or website www.cal-parks.ca.gov; $7 to $9 per night.

Contact: Steep Ravine Environmental Campsites, (415) 388-2070; California State Parks, (415) 893-1580 of fax (415) 388-2968.

Directions: From US 101 in Marin, take the Stinson Beach/Highway 1 exit and drive north on Highway 1 about 11 miles to the gated access road on the left side of the highway. (The gate lock combination will be provided when reservations are made.)

Trip notes: This is one of the most remarkable spots on the California coast, with primitive cabin/wood shacks set on a bluff on Rocky Point overlooking the ocean. It is primitive but dramatic, with passing ships, fishing boats, lots of marine birds, occasionally even whales, and a chance for heart-stopping sunsets. There is an easy walk to the north down to Redrock Beach,

which is very secluded, and just across the road (with a short jog to the right) is a trailhead for the Steep Ravine Trail on the slopes of Mount Tamalpais. After a while you'll feel like you're a million miles from civilization.

❾ China Camp State Park Walk-In

Location: On San Pablo Bay near San Rafael; map E1, grid a3.

Campsites, facilities: There are 30 walk-in tent sites. Picnic tables and fire grills are provided. Piped water, showers, and a rest room are available. Leashed pets are permitted.

Reservations, fees: Reserve by phoning (800) 444-PARK/7275 ($7.50 reservation fee) or website www.cal-parks.ca.gov; $15 to $16 per night, $5 for each additional vehicle.

Contact: China Camp State Park Walk-In, (415) 456-0766; California State Parks, Marin District, (415) 893-1580 or fax (415) 388-2968.

Directions: From San Francisco, drive north on US 101 to San Rafael and take the North San Pedro Road exit. Drive west on North San Pedro Road for five miles to the park entrance station at Back Ranch Meadows. Shortly after passing through the entrance station, bear right and drive a short distance to the campground parking lot. Reaching the sites requires a one-minute walk.

Trip notes: This is one of the Bay Area's prettiest campgrounds. It is set in woodlands with a picturesque creek running past. The camps are shaded and sheltered. Directly adjacent to the camp is a meadow, marshland, and then San Pablo Bay. Deer can seem as tame as chipmunks. Hiking is outstanding here, either taking the Shoreline Trail for a pretty walk to the edge of San Pablo Bay, or the Bay View Trail for the climb up the ridge that borders the park, in the process gaining spectacular views of the bay and miles of charm.

❿ Marin Park, Inc.

Location: Near San Rafael; map E1, grid b2.

Campsites, facilities: There are 89 RV sites

with full hookups. Showers, coin laundry, swimming pool, and RV supplies are available. Pets are permitted.

Reservations, fees: Reservations are accepted with a deposit; $28 per night.

Contact: Marin Park, Inc., (415) 461-5199.

Directions: From US 101 in Marin, take the Lucky Drive exit (just south of San Rafael). Make an immediate left under the freeway and drive on Tamal Vista Avenue to the first stoplight. Turn left on Wornum and drive to Redwood Highway. Turn left and drive four blocks to the park at 2140 Redwood Highway.

Trip notes: For out-of-towners with RVs, this can make an ideal base camp for Marin County adventures. To the west is Mount Tamalpais State Park, Muir Woods National Monument, Samuel P. Taylor State Park, and Point Reyes National Seashore. To the nearby east is the Loch Lomond Marina on San Pablo Bay, where fishing trips can be arranged for striped bass and sturgeon; phone (415) 456-0321. The park offers complete sight-seeing information and easy access to buses and ferry service to San Francisco.

⑪ Angel Island State Park Walk-In

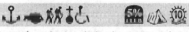

Location: On Angel Island; map E1, grid c4.

Campsites, facilities: There are nine walk-in sites with piped water, toilets, fire grills, and tables provided. No pets are permitted. A cafe is available on the island.

Reservations, fees: Reserve via phone at (800) 444-PARK/7275 ($7.50 reservation fee) or website www.cal-parks.ca.gov; $12 per night (limit eight people per site).

Contact: Angel Island State Park, (415) 435-1915; California State Parks, Marin District, (415) 893-1580 or fax (415) 893-1583.

Directions: Angel Island is in northern San Francisco Bay and can be reached by ferry from Pier 41 in San Francisco (for schedule information, call 415-773-1188), Tiburon (for schedule information, call 415-435-2131), and Vallejo (for schedule information, call 707-64-FERRY).

Trip notes: Camping at Angel Island is one of the most unique adventures in the Bay Area, with the only catch being that getting to the campsites requires a walk of up to two miles. The payoff comes at 4:30 P.M., when all the park's day visitors and most of the staff depart for the mainland, leaving the entire island to you. From start to finish, it's a great trip, featuring a ferry boat ride, a great hike in, and a private campsite, often with spectacular views of San Francisco Bay. The tromp up to 781-foot Mount Livermore includes a short, very steep stretch but in return furnishes one of the most spectacular urban lookouts in America.

⑫ Candlestick RV Park

Location: In San Francisco; map E1, grid d3.

Campsites, facilities: There are 118 sites for trailers or RVs, all with full hookups. Rest rooms and showers are provided. Coin laundry, grocery store, game room, and propane are available. Shuttles and bus tours are also available. The facilities are wheelchair accessible. Small leashed pets are permitted.

Reservations, fees: Reservations are recommended; phone (800) 888-CAMP/2267; $34–36 per night.

Contact: Candlestick RV Park, (415) 822-2299 or fax (415) 822-7638.

Directions: From San Francisco on US 101 south, take the Candlestick Park (3COM) exit. Turn east on the stadium entrance road and drive around the parking lot to the far end of the stadium (Gate 4). During games, campers are advised to take the Third Street exit in order to avoid traffic.

Trip notes: If you are arriving from out of town to see the Giants play baseball or the 49ers play football, this park is your calling, set adjacent to the Candlestick Park, I mean 3COM Park (that will always sound ridiculous), parking lot. The location is four miles from downtown San Francisco. It is an ideal destination for out-of-towners who want to explore the city without having to drive, because the park offers tours and inexpensive shuttles to the downtown area.

⑬ Anthony Chabot Regional Park

Location: Near Castro Valley; map E1, grid d6.

Campsites, facilities: There are 65 tent and RV sites, some with partial hookups, and 10 walk-in tent sites. Fire rings and picnic tables are provided. Piped water, flush toilets, hot showers, and a sanitary disposal station are available. Leashed pets are permitted.

Reservations, fees: Reservations are accepted; phone (510) 562-2267 ($5 reservation fee); $15 to $20 per night, $5 per night for each additional vehicle, $1 pet fee.

Contact: Anthony Chabot Regional Park, (510) 639-4751/4752 or fax (510) 636-0751.

Directions: From Interstate 580 in the Oakland hills, take the 35th Avenue exit. Turn east on 35th Avenue and drive up the hill and straight across Skyline Boulevard, where 35th Avenue becomes Redwood Road. Continue on Redwood Road for six miles to the park entrance on the right.

Trip notes: The campground at Chabot Regional Park is set on a hilltop sheltered by eucalyptus, with good views and trails available. The best campsites are the walk-in units, requiring a walk of only a minute or so. Several provide views of Lake Chabot to the south a half mile away. The lake provides good trout fishing in the winter and spring, and a chance for huge but elusive largemouth bass. The Huck Trail is routed down from the campground (near walk-in site 20) to the lake at Honker Bay, a good fishing area. There is also a good 12-mile bike ride around the lake. Boat rentals at a small marina are available.

⑭ Mount Diablo State Park

Location: East of Oakland; map E1, grid c9.

Campsites, facilities: There are 60 sites for tents or RVs up to 24 feet long (in three campgrounds). There are four group sites. Piped water, vault or flush toilets, fire grills, and tables are provided. Leashed pets are permitted.

Reservations, fees: Reserve via phone at (800) 444-PARK/7275 ($7.50 reservation fee) or website www.cal-parks.ca.gov; $15 per night, $1 pet fee. Call for group site fee information.

Contact: Mount Diablo State Park, (925) 837-2525 or (415) 330-6300; website: www.mdia.org.

Directions: From Danville on Interstate 680, take the Diablo Road exit. Follow Diablo Road for 1.5 miles to Mount Diablo Scenic Boulevard. Turn left (it eventually becomes Blackhawk Road) and drive to South Gate Road. Turn left and drive four miles to the park entrance.

Trip notes: Mount Diablo, elevation 3,849 feet, provides one of the most all-encompassing lookouts anywhere in America. On crystal clear days you can see the Sierra Nevada and its white, snowbound crest. With binoculars, some claim to have seen Half Dome in Yosemite. The drive to the summit is a must-do trip, and the interpretive center right on top of the mountain is one of the best in the Bay Area. The camps at Mount Diablo are set in foothill/oak grassland country, with some shaded sites. Winter and spring are good times to visit, when the weather is still cool enough for good hiking trips. Most of the trails require long hikes, often including significant elevation gains and losses. In late summer the park is sometimes closed to camping due to fire danger. No alcohol is permitted in the park.

⑮ Pacific Park RV Resort

Location: In Pacifica; map E1, grid e1.

Campsites, facilities: There are 257 RV sites with full hookups. Rest rooms, showers, heated swimming pool, spa, and a recreation room are provided. Cable TV, grocery store, coin laundry, and propane gas are available. Leashed pets are permitted.

Reservations, fees: Reservations are recommended; $32 to $36 per night, $1 pet fee.

Contact: Pacific Park RV Resort, (800) 992-0554 or fax (650) 355-7102.

Directions: From San Francisco, drive south on US 101 to Highway 1 into Pacifica. Take the Manor Drive exit and drive to the stop sign (you will be on the west side of the highway). Continue straight ahead (the road becomes Palmetto

Avenue) for about a mile and look for the entrance to the park on the right side of the road at 700 Palmetto.

From the south, drive north on Highway 1 into Pacifica. Take the Manor Drive exit. At the stop sign, turn left on the frontage road (you will be on the east side of the highway) and drive a block to another stop sign. Turn left, drive a short distance over the highway to a stop sign at Manor/Palmetto, and turn left. Drive about a mile to the park on the right.

Trip notes: This has become the best RV park in the Bay Area. It is set on the bluffs just above the Pacific Ocean, complete with beach access, nearby fishing pier, and sometimes excellent surf fishing. There is also a nearby golf course and the chance for dramatic ocean sunsets. The park is relatively new, kept clean and in good shape, and though there is too much asphalt, the proximity to the beach overcomes it. It is only 20 miles from San Francisco.

⑯ Half Moon Bay State Beach

Location: At Half Moon Bay; map E1, grid g1.

Campsites, facilities: There are 56 sites for tents or RVs up to 36 feet long. Piped water, fire rings and grills, barbecues, and picnic tables are provided. A sanitary disposal station and flush toilets are available. Leashed pets are permitted.

Reservations, fees: No reservations; $16 per night, $5 for each additional vehicle, $1 pet fee.

Contact: Half Moon Bay State Beach, (650) 726-8820 or (415) 330-6300.

Directions: In Half Moon Bay, at the junction of Highway 1 and Highway 92, turn south on Highway 1 and drive about a mile to Kelly Avenue. Turn right on Kelly Avenue and drive two miles to the park entrance.

Trip notes: During summer months, this park often fills to capacity with campers touring Highway 1. The campground has level, grassy sites for tents, a clean parking area for RVs, and a state beach available just a short walk away. Side trips include Princeton and Pillar Point Marina, seven miles north on Highway 1, where fishing and whale watching trips are possible.

⑰ Pelican Point RV Park

Location: In Half Moon Bay; map E1, grid g1.

Campsites, facilities: There are 75 RV sites with full hookups and patios. Picnic tables, rest rooms, showers, coin laundry, propane gas, small store, clubhouse, and a sanitary disposal station are provided. Leashed pets are permitted.

Reservations, fees: Reservations are recommended; $29 to $32 per night, $1 pet fee. Open year-round.

Contact: Pelican Point RV Park, (650) 726-9100.

Directions: In Half Moon Bay, at the junction of Highway 1 and Highway 92, turn south on Highway 1 and drive 2.5 miles to Miramontes Point Road. Turn right and drive a short distance to the park entrance.

Trip notes: This park is in a rural setting on the southern outskirts of the town of Half Moon Bay, set on an extended bluff near the ocean. All facilities are available nearby, with restaurants available in Half Moon Bay and 10 miles north in Princeton at Pillar Point Harbor. The harbor has an excellent boat launch, a fish-cleaning station, party boat trips for salmon and rockfish and, in the winter, whale watching trips.

⑱ Trailer Villa

Location: In Redwood City; map E1, grid f4.

Campsites, facilities: There are 50 RV sites with full hookups. Rest rooms, showers, coin laundry, and a sanitary disposal station are available. Pets must be controlled.

Reservations, fees: Reservations are required; $25 per night. Open year-round.

Contact: Trailer Villa, (650) 366-7880 or fax (650) 366-7948.

Directions: In Redwood City on US 101, take the Seaport Boulevard exit east. Drive a short distance to East Bayshore Road. Turn right and drive a mile to 3401 East Bayshore Road.

Trip notes: The Peninsula can seem like a zoo on parade when driving the "Bayshore Freeway," but a short drive to Trailer Villa provides a quick return to some semblance of sanity. It is located near the Redwood City Harbor, a pretty spot adjacent to the unusual Leslie Salt site on the shore of the Bay, where there is often an unbelievably high pile of salt. A boat launch is available at the harbor, providing access to South San Francisco Bay.

⑲ Sunol Regional Wilderness

Location: South of Sunol; map E1, grid g9.

Campsites, facilities: There are four tent sites. Piped water, picnic tables, fire grills, and vault toilets are provided. Leashed pets are permitted.

Reservations, fees: Reservations are required; phone (925) 636-1684 ($5 reservation fee); $11 per night, $1 pet fee.

Contact: East Bay Regional Park District, (510) 635-0135 extension 2200; Sunol Regional Wilderness, (510) 862-2244.

Directions: In the East Bay on Interstate 680, south drive to Sunol and take the Calaveras Road exit. Turn south on Calaveras and drive four miles to Geary Road. Turn left on Geary Road and drive two miles to the park entrance.

Trip notes: Sunol Regional Wilderness is an outstanding park for off-season hiking and camping. In the spring and early summer, it is one of the best of the 250 parks in the Bay Area to see wildflowers. In addition, Alameda Creek in Little Yosemite forms several miniature pool-and-drop waterfalls in the spring and early summer. The park is set in rolling oak/bay grasslands. In addition to the drive-in campsites, there are also a few trail camps available, the closest requiring a 3.4-mile hike from park headquarters. It is extremely quiet and secluded, with a nearby spring developed to provide drinking water. No alcohol is permitted in the park, and it is subject to temporary closures in late summer due to fire danger.

⑳ Memorial County Park

Location: Near La Honda; map E1, grid h2.

Campsites, facilities: There are 156 sites for tents or RVs up to 35 feet long. Fire grills, picnic tables, piped water, showers, and flush toilets are provided. A sanitary disposal station is available from May through October. No pets are allowed.

Reservations, fees: No reservations; $15 per night, $5 for each additional vehicle. Open year-round.

Contact: Memorial County Park, San Mateo County Parks and Recreation, (650) 363-4021.

Directions: In Half Moon Bay, at the junction of Highway 1 and Highway 92, drive south on Highway 1 for 18 miles to the Pescadero Road exit. Turn left on Pescadero Road and drive about 10 miles to the park entrance.

Trip notes: This beautiful redwood park is set on the western slopes of the Santa Cruz Mountains, tucked in a pocket between the tiny towns of La Honda and Loma Mar. The campground features access to a nearby network of 50 miles of trails, with the best hike along the headwaters of Pescadero Creek. In late winter, it is sometimes possible to see steelhead spawn (no fishing permitted, of course). The trails link up with others in nearby Portola State Park and Sam McDonald County Park, providing access to a vast recreation land. The camp is often filled on summer weekends, but the sites are spaced so it won't cramp your style.

㉑ Portola Redwoods State Park

Location: Near Skyline Ridge; map E1, grid h3.

Campsites, facilities: There are 59 sites for tents or RVs up to 24 feet long. Piped water, fire rings, and tables are provided. Toilets, coin-operated showers, ice, and firewood are available. There are nature hikes and campfire programs scheduled from Memorial Day through Labor Day. The nearest gas is 13 miles away. Pets are permitted on paved surfaces only.

Reservations, fees: Reserve via phone at (800) 444-PARK/7275 ($7.50 reservation fee) or website www.cal-parks.ca.gov; $14 to $18 per night, $10 hike-in fee. $1 pet fee. Closed in December; no reservations October through mid-May.

Contact: Portola Redwoods State Park, (650) 948-9098 or fax (650) 948-0137; California State Parks, Santa Cruz District , (831) 429-2851 or fax (831) 429-2876.

Directions: From Palo Alto on Interstate 280, turn west on Page Mill Road and drive (slow and twisty) to Skyline Boulevard/Highway 35. Cross Skyline and continue west on Alpine Road (very twisty) for about three miles to Portola State Park Road. Turn left on Portola State Park Road and drive about three miles to the park entrance.

Trip notes: Portola State Park is very secluded, the result of visitors being required to travel on an extremely slow and winding series of roads to reach it. The park features redwoods and foothill grasslands on the western slopes of the Santa Cruz Mountains, the headwaters of Pescadero Creek, and 18 miles of hiking trails. A four-mile hike links up to nearby Memorial Park. At times in the summer, a low fog will move in along the San Mateo coast, and from lookouts near Skyline, visitors can peer to the west at what seems like a pearlescent sea with little islands (hilltops) poking through.

㉒ Butano State Park

Location: Near Pescadero; map E1, grid i2.

Campsites, facilities: There are 21 sites for tents or RVs and 18 walk-in sites with pit toilets. Piped water, fire grills, and picnic tables are provided. A rest room with flush toilets is available. Pets are permitted.

Reservations, fees: Reserve via phone at (800) 444-PARK/7275 ($7.50 reservation fee) or website www.cal-parks.ca.gov; $12 to $16 per night, $1 pet fee.

Contact: Butano State Park, (650) 879-2040; California State Parks, Bay Area District, (415) 330-6300 or fax (415) 330-6312.

Directions: In Half Moon Bay, at the junction of Highway 1 and Highway 92, drive south on Highway 1 for 18 miles to the Pescadero Road exit. Turn left on Pescadero Road and drive past the town of Pescadero to Cloverdale Road. Turn right and drive about five miles to the park entrance on the left.

Trip notes: The campground at Butano is set in a redwood forest, so pretty and with such good hiking that it has become popular enough to make reservations a must. It is the favorite campground of former State Parks Director Don Murphy. The reason is that there is a series of exceptional hikes, including one to the Año Nuevo Lookout (pick a clear day), the Mill Ox Loop and, for the ambitious, the 11-mile Butano Rim Loop. The latter has a backpack camp in the park's most remote area, where no water is available.

㉓ Big Basin Redwoods State Park

Location: Near Santa Cruz; map E1, grid j3.

Campsites, facilities: There are 111 sites for tents or RVs up to 27 feet long, 38 walk-in sites, 36 tent cabins (reservations required), and 10 hike-in campsites. Piped water, picnic tables, and fire grills are provided. Rest rooms, coin-operated showers, sanitary disposal station, and groceries are available. Some campsites and facilities are wheelchair accessible. Leashed pets are allowed in campsites only.

Reservations, fees: Reserve via phone at (800) 444-PARK/7275 ($7.50 reservation fee) or website www.cal-parks.ca.gov; $14 to $18 per night, $1 pet fee. For tent cabin fees and reservations, phone (800) 874-8368.

Contact: Big Basin Redwoods State Park, (831) 338-8861; California State Parks, Santa Cruz District, (831) 429-2851 or fax (831) 429-2876.

Directions: From Santa Cruz, turn north on Highway 9 and drive 12 miles to Boulder Creek. Turn west on Highway 236 and drive nine miles to the park headquarters.

Trip notes: Big Basin is one of the best state parks in California, featuring giant redwoods near the park headquarters, secluded campsites set in forest, and rare opportunities to stay in a tent cabin or a backpacking trail site. It is a great park for hikers, with two waterfalls, one close and one far, making for stellar destinations. The close one is Sempervirens Falls, a long, narrow, silvery stream, an easy 1.5-hour round trip on the Sequoia Trail. The far one is the famous Berry Creek Falls, a spectacular 70-foot cascade set in a beautiful canyon, framed by redwoods. For hikers in good condition, figure two hours (4.7 miles) to reach Berry Creek Falls, five hours for the round-trip in-and-out, and six hours for the complete loop (12 miles) that extends into the park's most remote areas. There is also an easy nature loop trail near the park headquarters in the valley floor that is routed past several mammoth redwoods.

㉔ Carbonero Creek Trailer Park

Location: Near Scotts Valley; map E1, grid j5.

Campsites, facilities: There are 10 sites for tents and 104 RV sites with full or partial hookups. Rest rooms, showers, cable TV, coin laundry, recreation room, hot tub, whirlpool, and a seasonal swimming pool are available. Leashed pets are permitted at the RV sites only.

Reservations, fees: Reservations are recommended; $21 to $29 per night. Open year-round.

Contact: Carbonero Creek Trailer Park, (831) 438-1288, (800) 546-1288, or fax (831) 438-2877.

Directions: From Santa Cruz, at the junction of Highways 1 and 17 north, turn east on Highway 17 north and drive four miles to the Mount Hermon/Big Basin exit. Take that exit north onto Mount Hermon Road and drive to Scotts Valley Drive. Turn right and drive to Disc Drive. Turn right and continue to 917 Disc Drive.

Trip notes: This camp is just a short hop from Santa Cruz and the shore of Monterey Bay. There are many side trip options, making this a prime location for vacationers cruising the California coast. In Santa Cruz there are several quality restaurants, plus fishing trips and boat rentals at Santa Cruz Wharf, as well as the famous Santa Cruz Boardwalk and amusement park.

㉕ Parkway Lakes RV Park

Location: Near Morgan Hill; map E1, grid j9.

Campsites, facilities: There are 113 RV sites with electricity and piped water. Rest rooms, showers, sanitary disposal station, coin laundry, and a recreation room are available. Leashed pets are permitted.

Reservations, fees: Reservations are required; $25 to $27 per night.

Contact: Parkway Lakes RV Park, (408) 779-0244 or fax (408) 778-7647.

Directions: From San Jose, drive south about 12 miles on US 101 to the Cochrane-Monterey Road exit. Turn right on Cochrane Road and continue about 1.5 miles to the Monterey Highway turnoff. Drive south (right) on Monterey Highway about 3.5 miles to Ogier Road. Turn right on Ogier Road and drive to 100 Ogier Road on the right.

Trip notes: This RV park provides a spot to park on the southern outskirts of the San Francisco Bay Area. It gets its name from nearby Parkway Lake, a pay-to-fish lake where for $10 you get a chance to catch rainbow trout up to 10 pounds in the winter and spring, and catfish and sturgeon in the summer. There are several other reservoirs in the nearby foothills, including Coyote, Anderson, Chesbro, Uvas, and Calero. The best nearby source for fishing and recreation is Coyote Discount Bait and Tackle at (408) 463-0711.

Note: For Del Valle Regional Park, Joseph Grant County Park, and Henry W. Coe State Park, see chapter E2.

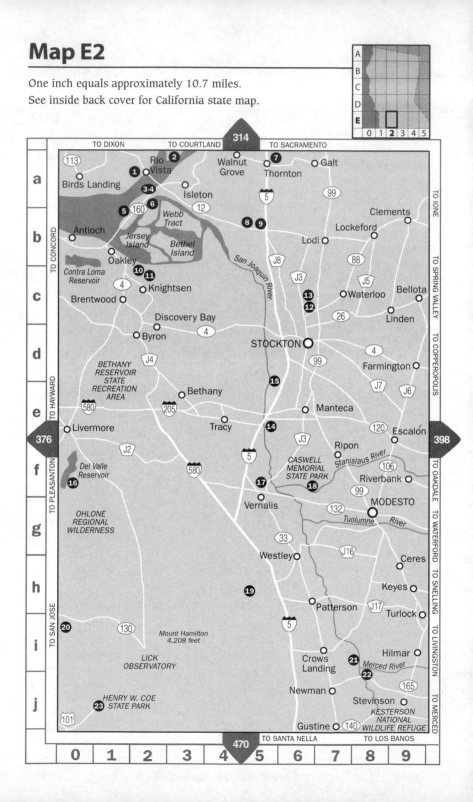

Map E2

One inch equals approximately 10.7 miles.
See inside back cover for California state map.

Chapter E2 features:

1 Sandy Beach County Park

Location: On the Sacramento River; map E2, grid a2.

Campsites, facilities: There are 42 sites for tents or RVs. Electricity, picnic tables, fire grills, and piped water are provided. Flush toilets, showers, playground, sanitary disposal station, and a boat ramp are available. The facilities are wheelchair accessible. Supplies can be obtained nearby (within a mile). Pets are permitted with proof of rabies vaccination.

Reservations, fees: Reservations are accepted; $10 to $15 per night, $1 pet fee. Open year-round.

Contact: Solano County Parks, (707) 374-2097 or fax (707) 374-4972.

Directions: From Interstate 80 in Fairfield, take the Highway 12 exit and drive southeast for 14 miles to Rio Vista and the intersection with Main Street. Turn right on Main Street and drive a short distance to Second Street. Turn right and drive a half mile to Beach Drive. Continue on Beach Drive to the park.

Trip notes: This is a surprisingly little-known park, especially considering it provides beachside access to the Sacramento River. It is a popular spot for sunbathers in hot summer months, but in winter, it is one of the few viable spots where you can fish from the shore for sturgeon. It also provides outstanding boating access to the Sacramento River, including one of the best fishing spots for striped bass in the fall, the Rio Vista Bridge.

2 Snug Harbor Marina and RV Camp/Park

Location: Near Rio Vista; map E2, grid a3.

Campsites, facilities: There are 45 waterfront sites for RVs or tents with docks and full hookups and 15 inland sites with water hookups only. There are also five rental cabins. Rest rooms, hot showers, sanitary disposal station, convenience store, barbecue, swimming beach, children's play area, boat launch, paddle boat rentals, propane gas, and a full-service marina are available.

Reservations, fees: Reservations recommended; $20 to $25 per night and fees.

Contact: Snug Harbor Marina and RV Camp/ Park, (916) 775-1455 or fax (916) 775-1594; email: sunshine@i-cafe.net.

Directions: From Sacramento, drive 26 miles south on Interstate 5 to Highway 12. Drive west on Highway 12 about 20 miles to Rio Vista and then turn north on Route 84 for two miles to the Real McCoy Ferry to Ryer Island. Take the ferry across the Sacramento River (cars are allowed). On Ryer Island, drive four miles on the levee road to Snug Harbor.

Trip notes: This year-round resort is an ideal resting place for families who enjoy waterskiing, boating, biking, swimming, and fishing. Anglers will find good prospects for striped bass, black bass, blue gill, and catfish. The waterfront sites with docks give Snug Harbor the feel of a Louisiana bayou.

❸ Duck Island RV Park

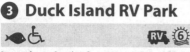

Location: On the Sacramento River; map E2, grid a2.

Campsites, facilities: There are 51 RV sites with full hookups. Picnic tables are provided. A laundry and recreation room with a kitchen are available. Supplies can be obtained in Rio Vista. The facilities are wheelchair accessible. Adults only. Leashed pets are permitted.

Reservations, fees: Reservations are accepted; $20 per night. Reservation and deposit are required for groups.

Contact: Duck Island RV Park, (916) 777-6663.

Directions: In Fairfield on Interstate 80, take the Highway 12 exit and drive 14 miles southeast to Rio Vista and continue to Highway 160 (at the signal before the bridge). Turn right on Highway 160 and drive just under a mile to the RV park.

Trip notes: This pleasant rural park, set up for adults only, has riverside access that provides an opportunity for bank fishing on the Sacramento River. A boat ramp is available at the end of Main Street in Rio Vista. Both Hap's and The Trap provide reliable fishing information as well as all gear needed for fishing.

❹ Delta Marina RV Resort

Location: On the Sacramento River Delta; map E2, grid a2.

Campsites, facilities: There are 25 RV sites with full hookups. Picnic tables and fire grills are provided. Rest rooms, showers, coin laundry, playground, boat ramp, ice, and propane gas are available. Leashed pets (one pet per vehicle) are permitted.

Reservations, fees: Reservations are accepted; $18 to $25 per night. Open year-round.

Contact: Delta Marina RV Resort, (707) 374-2315 or fax (707) 374-6471.

Directions: From Fairfield on Interstate 80, take the Highway 12 exit and drive southeast for 14 miles to Rio Vista and the intersection with Main Street. Take the Main Street exit, drive a short distance, turn right on Second Street, left on Marina Drive, and continue another short distance to the harbor.

Trip notes: This is a prime spot for boat campers. Summers are hot and breezy, and waterskiing is popular on the nearby Sacramento River. From November to March, the striped bass fishing is quite good, often as close as just a half mile upriver at the Rio Vista Bridge. The boat launch at the harbor is a bonus.

❺ New Hope Landing

Location: On the Mokelumne River north of Stockton; map E2, grid a1.

Campsites, facilities: There are 25 sites for tents or RVs, some with hookups. Piped water is provided. Rest rooms, showers, ice, bait, propane gas, and full-service marina are available. Leashed pets are permitted.

Reservations, fees: Reservations are accepted; $15 per night for two people, $3 for each additional person.

Contact: New Hope Landing, (209) 794-2627.

Directions: From Stockton on Interstate 5, drive north for 25 miles to the Thornton exit. Take that exit, turn west on Walnut Grove Road, and drive 3.3 miles to the campground entrance on the left.

Trip notes: New Hope Landing is a privately operated resort set along the Mokelumne River in the upper San Joaquin Delta. There's a marina available, which gives you access to 1,000 miles of Delta waterways via the Mokelumne River. The Lower Mokelumne is often an excellent area to troll for striped bass in April, and to water ski in summer. In late summer, water hyacinth is sometimes a problem farther upstream.

❻ Eddo's Harbor and RV Park

Location: On the San Joaquin River Delta; map E2, grid a2.

Campsites, facilities: There are 40 sites with full hookups for RVs and three tent sites. Picnic tables and piped water are provided. Flush toilets, hot showers, launch ramp, boat storage, fuel dock, coin laundry, and a small grocery store are available. Leashed pets are permitted.

Reservations, fees: Reservations are recommended; $17 to $20 per night.

Contact: Eddo's Harbor and RV Park, (925) 757-5314 or fax (925) 757-6246; email: eddo1@aol.com.

Directions: In Fairfield on Interstate 80, take the Highway 12 exit and drive 14 miles southeast to Rio Vista and continue three miles to Highway 160 (at the signal before the bridge). Turn left on Highway 160 and drive five miles to the campground along the San Joaquin River. Note: If arriving by boat, the camp is located adjacent to Light 21.

Trip notes: This is an ideal spot for campers with boats. Eddo's is set on the San Joaquin River, upstream of the Antioch Bridge, in an outstanding region for fishing, powerboating, and waterskiing. In summer months, boaters have access to 1,000 miles of Delta waterways, with the best of them in a nearby spiderweb of rivers and sloughs off the San Joaquin to False River, Frank's Tract, and Old River. Hot weather and sheltered sloughs make this ideal for waterskiing. In the winter, a nearby fishing spot called Eddo's Bar, as well as the mouth of the False River, attract striped bass.

❼ Brannan Island State Recreation Area

Location: On the Sacramento River; map E2, grid a5.

Campsites, facilities: There are 102 sites for tents or RVs up to 36 feet long. Picnic tables and fire grills are provided. Rest rooms, showers (at the boat launch site), sanitary disposal station, and a boat launch are available. Several sites have a total of 32 boat berths. Facilities are wheelchair accessible. Supplies can be obtained three miles away in Rio Vista. Pets are permitted.

Reservations, fees: Reserve via phone at (800) 444-PARK/7275 ($7.50 reservation fee) or website www.cal-parks.ca.gov; $14 to $16 per night, $1 pet fee.

Contact: Brannan Island State Recreation Area, (916) 777-6671; Goldrush District Office, (916) 445-7373.

Directions: In Fairfield on Interstate 80, take the Highway 12 exit, drive 14 miles southeast to Rio Vista, and continue to Highway 160 (at the signal before the bridge). Turn right on Highway 160 and drive three miles to the park entrance.

Trip notes: This state park is perfectly designed for boaters, set in the heart of the Delta's vast waterways. You get year-round adventure: waterskiing and fishing for catfish are popular in the summer, and in the winter the immediate area is often good for striped bass fishing. The proximity of the campgrounds to the boat launch deserves a medal. What many people do is tow a boat here, launch it, and keep it docked, then return to their site and set up; this allows them to come and go as they please, boating, fishing, and exploring in the Delta.

❽ Tower Park Marina and Resort

Location: Near Stockton; map E2, grid b5.

Campsites, facilities: There are 500 sites for tents or RVs, most with full hookups (tent sites are closed in the winter months). Picnic tables and barbecues are provided. Rest rooms, showers, sanitary disposal station, pavilion, boat rentals, overnight boat slips, elevator boat launch, playground, restaurant, coin laundry, gift shop, grocery store, and propane gas are available. Leashed pets are permitted.

Reservations, fees: Reservations are recommended; $16 to $26 per night. Open year-round.

Contact: Tower Park Marina and Resort, (209) 369-1041 or fax (209) 943-5656.

Directions: In Stockton, head north on Interstate 5 for 14 miles to the Lodi/Highway 12 exit. Turn west on Highway 12 and drive about five miles to 14900 Highway 12.

Trip notes: This huge resort is ideal for boat-in campers who desire a full-facility marina. The camp is set on Little Potato Slough near the Mokelumne River. In the summer, this is a popular waterskiing area. Some hot weekends are like a continuous party.

---

⑨ Westgate Landing County Park

Location: In the San Joaquin River Delta near Stockton; map E2, grid b5.

Campsites, facilities: There are 14 sites for tents or RVs. Piped water, barbecues, and picnic tables are provided. Flush toilets are available. Groceries and propane gas are nearby. There are 24 boat slips available. Leashed pets are permitted.

Reservations, fees: No reservations; $9 per night, boat slips are $10, $1 pet fee. Open year-round.

Contact: County Parks Department, (209) 953-8800.

Directions: In Stockton at the junction of Interstate 5 and Highway 4, head north on Interstate 5 for 14 miles to the Lodi/Highway 12 exit. Turn left (west) on Highway 12 and drive about five miles to Glasscock Road. Turn right and drive about a mile to the park.

Trip notes: Summer temperatures typically reach the high 90s and low 100s here, and this county park provides a little shade and boating access to the South Fork Mokelumne River. On hot summer nights, some campers will stay up late and night fish for catfish. Between storms in winter months, the area typically gets smothered in dense fog.

⑩ Island Park

Location: On the San Joaquin River Delta; map E2, grid c2.

Campsites, facilities: There are 80 RV sites with full hookups. Rest rooms, showers, coin laundry, recreation room, cable TV, and a swimming pool are available. Small leashed pets are permitted.

Reservations, fees: Reservations are accepted; $19 per night.

Contact: Island Park, (925) 684-2144 or fax (925) 684-0889.

Directions: From Antioch, turn east on Highway 4 and drive to Oakley and Cypress Road. Turn right on Cypress Road, drive over the Bethel Island Bridge, and continue a half mile to Gateway Road. Turn right and drive a half mile to Island Park.

Trip notes: This privately operated RV park is set on the edge of the San Joaquin Delta's boating paradise, with more than 1,000 miles of waterways available. Nearby Frank's Tract, Old River, False River, and the lower Mokelumne River are all spots that provide good waterskiing in the summer.

⑪ Delta Resort

Location: On the San Joaquin River Delta; map E2, grid c2.

Campsites, facilities: There are 76 RV sites with full hookups. Rest rooms, laundry room, showers, sanitary disposal station, propane gas, playground, boat ramp, and full restaurant and bar are available. Leashed pets are permitted.

Reservations, fees: Reservations and deposit are required; $10 to $18 per night, $96 weekly rate.

Contact: Delta Resort, PO Box 455, Bethel Island, CA 94511; (925) 684-9351.

Directions: From Antioch, turn east on Highway 4 and drive to Oakley and Cypress Road.

Turn right on Cypress Road, drive over the Bethel Island Bridge, and continue a half mile to Gateway Road. Turn right on Gateway Road, drive two miles, then turn left into the park at 6777 River View Road.

Trip notes: This park is set on Bethel Island in the heart of the San Joaquin Delta. The boat ramp here provides immediate access to an excellent area for waterskiing, and it turns into a playland on hot summer days. In the fall and winter, the area often provides good striper fishing at nearby Frank's Tract, False River, and San Joaquin River. Catfishing in surrounding slough areas is good year-round. The Delta Sportsman Shop at Bethel Island has reliable fishing information.

⑫ Sahara Mobile Park

Location: In Stockton; map E2, grid c6.

Campsites, facilities: There are 187 RV sites with electric hookups. Rest rooms, showers, recreation room, heated swimming pool (seasonal), and coin laundry are available. A playground and grocery store are within several miles. Small leashed pets are permitted.

Reservations, fees: Reservations are accepted; $20 per night, $85 weekly rate, $250 monthly rate. Open year-round.

Contact: Sahara Mobile Park, (209) 464-9392.

Directions: In Stockton on Highway 99 north, take the Cherokee exit and drive west for about three miles to Sanguinetti Lane. Turn right and drive a mile to 2340 Sanguinetti Lane.

Trip notes: They play Bingo every Tuesday night here, and that should tell you everything you need to know about this spot.

⑬ Stockton-Lodi KOA

Location: In Stockton; map E2, grid c6.

Campsites, facilities: There are 102 sites for tents or RVs, many with full hookups. There are two cabins available. Picnic tables are provided. Rest rooms, showers, sanitary disposal station, grocery store, propane gas, coin laundry, recreation room, swimming pool, and a playground

are available. Leashed pets are permitted.

Reservations, fees: Reservations are accepted for cabins only; $19 to $24 per night for tent and RV sites, $34 per night for cabins. Open year-round.

Contact: Stockton-Lodi KOA, (209) 941-2573, (209) 334-0309, or fax (209) 941-2573.

Directions: From Stockton on Interstate 5 north, drive five miles north to Eight Mile Road. Turn east and drive five miles to the campground at 2851 East Eight Mile Road.

Trip notes: This KOA camp is in the heart of the San Joaquin Valley. The proximity to Interstate 5 and Highway 99 make it work for long-distance vacationers looking for a spot to park the rig for the night. The San Joaquin Delta is located 15 miles to the west, with best access provided off Highway 12 to Isleton and Rio Vista; it's also a pretty drive.

⑭ Dos Reis County Park

Location: On the San Joaquin River near Stockton; map E2, grid e6.

Campsites, facilities: There are 26 tent and RV sites with full hookups. Picnic tables and fire grills are provided. Rest rooms, showers, and a boat ramp are available. A grocery store, coin laundry, and propane gas can be found within several miles. Leashed pets are permitted.

Reservations, fees: Reservations are accepted and must be made at least three weeks in advance; $13 per night, $1 pet fee. Open year-round.

Contact: San Joaquin County Parks Department, (209) 953-8800.

Directions: From Stockton on Interstate 5, drive a short distance to the Lathrop exit. Turn northwest on Lathrop and drive a mile to Dos Reis Road. Turn toward the San Joaquin River and drive to the park on the east side of the river.

Trip notes: This is a 90-acre county park that has a quarter mile of San Joaquin River frontage, boat ramp, and nearby access to the eastern Delta near Stockton. The sun gets scalding hot here in the summer, branding everything in sight. That's why boaters make quick work of getting in the water, then cooling off with water sports. In the winter, this area often has zero visibility from tule fog.

⑮ Oakwood Lake Resort

Location: Near Stockton; map E2, grid d6.

Campsites, facilities: There are 111 tent sites, 74 tent or RV sites with partial hookups, and 196 RV-only sites with full hookups. Picnic tables are provided. Piped water, electrical connections, and sewer hookups are provided at most sites. Rest rooms, showers, dump station, grocery store, coin laundry, propane gas, swimming lagoon, water slides, organized activities, and a stocked 75-acre lake are available. The facilities are wheelchair accessible. Leashed pets are permitted.

Reservations, fees: Reservations are accepted; $21 to $27 per night, $2 pet fee. Open year-round.

Contact: Oakwood Lake Resort, (209) 239-9566 or fax (209) 239-2060; email: oakwoodlake@earthlink.net. Website: www.oakwoodlake.com.

Directions: In Manteca, turn east on Highway 120 and drive two miles to Airport Way. Turn south and drive a half mile to Woodward Way. Turn right and drive two miles to the park entrance.

Trip notes: This is a huge, privately operated "water theme" park that covers 375 acres and offers a wide array of water-related recreation activities. It is a great place for families to cool off and have fun on hot summer days, with youngsters lining up for trips down the water slides.

⑯ Del Valle Regional Park

Location: Near Livermore; map E2, grid f0.

Campsites, facilities: There are 150 sites for tents or RVs, 21 with partial hookups. Piped water, fire grills, and picnic tables are provided. A sanitary disposal station, flush toilets, hot showers, full marina, and a boat launch are available. Pets are permitted.

Reservations, fees: Reservations are required; phone (510) 562-2267 ($4 reservation fee); $15 to $18 per night, $1 pet fee.

Contact: East Bay Regional Park District, (510) 635-0135 extension 2200; Del Valle Regional Park, (925) 373-0332.

Directions: On Interstate 580, drive to Livermore and the North Livermore Avenue exit. Turn south and drive on North/South Livermore Road (this will turn into Tesla Road) to Mines Road. Turn right and drive south for three miles to Del Valle Road. Turn right and drive for three miles to the entrance to the park.

Trip notes: Of the 50 parks in the East Bay Regional Park District, it is Del Valle that provides the highest variety of recreation at the highest quality levels. Del Valle Reservoir is the centerpiece, a long narrow lake that fills a canyon, providing a good boat launch for powerboating and fishing for trout, striped bass, and catfish. The sites are somewhat exposed due to the grassland habitat, but they fill anyway on most weekends and three-day holidays. A trailhead south of the lake provides access to the Ohlone Wilderness Trail, and for the well conditioned, there is the 5.5-mile butt-kicker of a climb to Murietta Falls, gaining 1,600 feet in 1.5 miles. Murietta Falls is the Bay Area's highest waterfall, 100 feet tall, though its thin, silvery wisp is difficult to view directly and rarely evokes much emotional response after such an intense climb.

⑰ Orchard RV Park

Location: Near Stockton; map E2, grid f5.

Campsites, facilities: There are 12 tent sites and 88 drive-through RV sites with full hookups. Picnic tables and fire grills are provided. Rest rooms, showers, laundry room, sanitary disposal station, swimming pool, restaurant, and horseshoe pits are available. The facilities are wheelchair accessible. Groceries, propane gas, and a weekend flea market can be found within walking distance (less than a mile). Leashed pets are permitted.

Reservations, fees: Reservations are accepted; $20 per night.

Contact: Orchard RV Park, (209) 836-2090.

Directions: From Interstate 5 in Vernalis, turn east on Highway 132 and drive three miles to the signed campground entrance at 2701 East Highway 132.

Trip notes: The huge swimming pool and water slides here make this a popular campground for families. Temperatures in the 100-degree range in the summer months keep both in constant use. This privately operated park is set up primarily for owners of RVs. Its location near Interstate 5 makes it a winner for many of them.

⑱ Caswell Memorial State Park

Location: On the Stanislaus River near Stockton; map E2, grid f6.

Campsites, facilities: There are 64 sites for tents or RVs up to 24 feet long. Piped water, fire grills, and picnic tables are provided. Flush toilets, showers, wood, and a nature trail and exhibits are available. The exhibits are wheelchair accessible. Leashed pets are permitted.

Reservations, fees: Reserve via phone at (800) 444-PARK/7275 ($7.50 reservation fee) or website www.cal-parks.ca.gov; $12 per night, $1 pet fee; groups with up to 12 vehicles, $50 to $75 per night. Open year-round.

Contact: Caswell Memorial State Park, (209) 599-3810; California State Parks, Four Rivers District, (209) 826-1196 or fax (209) 826-0284.

Directions: From Manteca, drive south on Highway 99 for 1.5 miles to the Austin Road exit. Turn south and drive four miles to the park entrance.

Trip notes: Caswell Memorial State Park features shoreline frontage along the Stanislaus River, along with an additional 250 acres of parkland. The Stanislaus provides shoreline fishing for catfish on summer nights. Other recreation options here include a fine visitor center, an interpretive nature trail, and swimming.

⑲ Frank Raines Regional Park

Location: Near Modesto; map E2, grid h5.

Campsites, facilities: There are 34 tent or RV sites. Fire grills, picnic tables, piped water, electrical connections, and sewer hookups are provided. Rest rooms, showers, and a playground are available. Pets are permitted.

Reservations, fees: No reservations; $12 to $16 per night, $2 pet fee, $2 fee for rough terrain vehicles. Open year-round.

Contact: Frank Raines Regional Park, (408) 897-3127.

Directions: On Interstate 5 (south of the junction of Interstate 5 and Interstate 580), drive to the Patterson exit. Turn east and drive to Del Puerto Canyon Road. Turn west and drive 16 miles to the park.

Trip notes: This park is primarily a riding area for folks with dirt bikes and three- and four-wheel OHVs, who take advantage of the rough-terrain riding course available here. A side trip option is to visit Minniear Park, located directly to the east, which is a day-use wilderness park with hiking trails and a creek. This area is very pretty in the spring when the foothills are still green and many wildflowers are blooming.

⑳ Joseph Grant County Park

Location: Near San Jose; map E2, grid i0.

Campsites, facilities: There are 40 sites for tents or RVs up to 28 feet long. Fire grills and tables are provided. Piped water, hot showers, sanitary dump station, and toilets are available. Pets are permitted.

Reservations, fees: No reservations; $10 per night, $1 pet fee. Open weekends in March, then daily from April through November.

Contact: Santa Clara County Parks Department, (408) 274-6121 or fax (408) 270-4808.

Directions: In San Jose at the junction of Interstate 680 and US 101, take Interstate 680 north to the Alum Rock Avenue exit. Turn east and drive four miles to Mount Hamilton Road. Turn right and drive eight miles to the park headquarters entrance on the right side of the road.

Trip notes: Grant Ranch is a great wild playland covering 9,000 acres in the foothills of nearby Mount Hamilton to the east. It features 40 miles of hiking trails (horses permitted), 20 miles of old ranch roads that are perfect for mountain biking, a pretty lake (Grant Lake), and miles of foothills, canyons, and grasslands. The campground is set amid oak grasslands, is shaded, and can be used as a base camp for planning the day's recreation. The best hikes are to Halls Valley, especially in the winter and spring when there are many secret little creeks and miniature waterfalls in hidden canyons, and the Hotel Trail and Cañada de Pala Trail, which drops down to San Felipe Creek, the prettiest stream in the park. A great side trip is the slow, curvy drive east to Lick Observatory for great views of the Santa Clara Valley.

㉑ Fisherman's Bend River Camp

Location: On the San Joaquin River; map E2, grid i7.

Campsites, facilities: There are 20 sites for tents only and 38 RV sites with full hookups. Picnic tables and fire grills are provided. Piped water, rest rooms, showers, sanitary disposal station, laundry room, boat ramp, fish cleaning station, swimming pool, playground, and horseshoe pits are available. Leashed pets are permitted.

Reservations, fees: Reservations are accepted; $17 to $24 per night. Open year-round.

Contact: Fisherman's Bend River Camp, (209) 862-3731.

Directions: South of the junction of Interstate 5 and Interstate 580, take Interstate 5 south to the Newman/Stuhr Road exit. Turn east on County Road J18/Stuhr Road and drive 6.5 miles to Hills Ferry Road. Turn left and drive a mile to River Road. Turn left on River Road and drive to 26836 River Road.

Trip notes: This small, privately operated campground is set along the San Joaquin River on the southern outskirts of the San Joaquin Delta country. The park offers shaded sites and direct river access for boaters. This section of river provides fishing for catfish on hot summer nights.

㉒ George J. Hatfield State Recreation Area

Location: Near Newman; map E2, grid i8.

Campsites, facilities: There are 21 family sites and a large group site for tents or RVs up to 32 feet long. The group site can accommodate up to 40 people. Picnic tables, fire grills, and piped water are provided. Flush toilets are available. Supplies can be obtained in Newman, five miles away. Leashed pets are permitted.

Reservations, fees: Call ahead for group reservations; $12 per night, $60 per night for the group site, $1 pet fee. There is a $5 fee for each additional vehicle. Open year-round.

Contact: California State Parks, Four Rivers District Office, (209) 826-1196.

Directions: South of the junction of Interstate 5 and Interstate 580, take Interstate 5 south to the Newman/Stuhr Road exit. Turn east on County Road J18/Stuhr Road and drive to Newman and the junction with Highway 33. Turn right and drive a short distance to Hills Ferry Road. Turn left and drive five miles to the park entrance.

Trip notes: This is a small state park set in the heart of the San Joaquin Valley, near the confluence of the Merced River and the San Joaquin River, well known for hot summer days and foggy winter nights. Some folks say that if you eat enough catfish from this spot, you'll glow in the dark after a few years. It's advisable to throw them back.

㉓ Henry W. Coe State Park

Location: Near Gilroy; map E2, grid j1.

Campsites, facilities: There are seven sites for tents and 13 sites for tents or RVs. There are also eight horse camp sites, multiple hike-in sites and several group sites. Piped water, pit toilets, fire grills, and tables are provided. Leashed pets are permitted.

Reservations, fees: Reservations required for all but the horse and hike-in campsites; reserve via phone at (800) 444-PARK/7275 ($7.50 reservation fee) or website www.cal-parks.ca.gov; $8 per night, $3 for hike-in sites, $12 for horse campsites, $30 per night for the group site, $1 pet fee.

There is a $5 fee for each additional vehicle. Open year-round.

Contact: Henry W. Coe State Park, (408) 779-2728 or (408) 848-4006; California State Parks, Four Rivers District, (209) 826-1196. Website: www.coepark.parks.ca.gov.

Directions: From Morgan Hill on US 101, take the East Dunne Avenue exit, drive over the bridge at Anderson Lake, and continue another 13 miles (very twisty) to the park entrance.

Trip notes: This is the Bay Area's backyard wilderness, with 80,000 acres of wildlands, 100 lakes and ponds, and 150 miles of trails for hiking, biking, and wilderness-style camping. The drive-in campground is set on a hilltop, and because it is exposed, provides dramatic views and a good spot for stargazing. Before setting out for the outback, always consult with the rangers here—the ambitious plans of many hikers cause them to suffer dehydration and heatstroke. The park has excellent pond-style fishing, but requires extremely long hikes (typically 10- to 25-mile round trips) to reach the best lakes, including Mustang Pond, Coit Lake, Mississippi Lake, Kelly Lake, and Hoover Lake. Expect hot weather in the summer; spring and early summer are the prime times. Even though the park may appear to be 120 square miles of oak foothills, the terrain is sometimes steep, and there are many great secrets to be discovered here, including Rooster Comb and Coyote Creek. Bring a water purifier for hikes because there is no piped water in the outback.

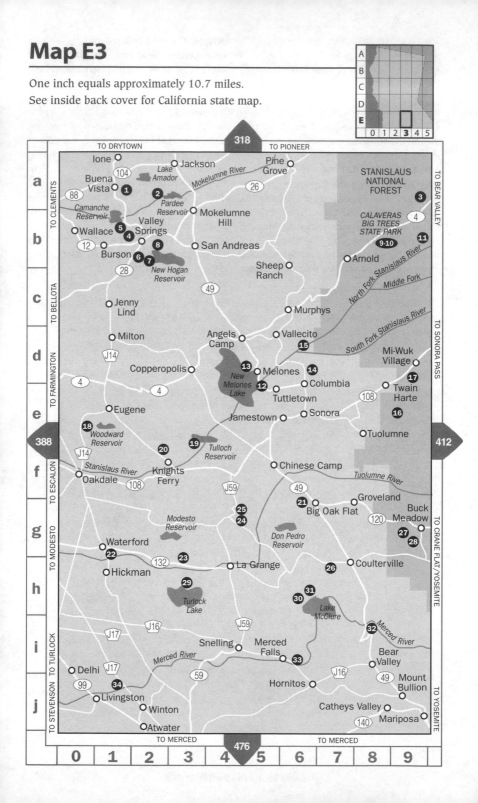

Chapter E3 features:

1 Lake Amador Recreation Area

Location: Near Stockton; map E3, grid a1.

Campsites, facilities: There are 150 sites for tents or RVs, 72 with full hookups, and 12 group sites. Picnic tables and fire grills are provided. Piped water, rest rooms, showers, sanitary disposal station, boat ramp, boat rentals, fishing supplies (including bait and tackle), restaurant, grocery store, propane gas, swimming pond, and a playground are available. Leashed pets are permitted.

Reservations, fees: Reservations are accepted seven days in advance in the summer; $18 to $23 per night. Open year-round.

Contact: Lake Amador Recreation Area, (209) 274-4739.

Directions: From Stockton, turn east on Highway 88 and drive 24 miles to Clements. Just east of Clements, continue straight on Highway 12 and drive 11 miles to Jackson Valley Road. Turn right (well signed) and drive 4 miles to Lake Amador Drive. Turn right and drive over the dam to the campground office.

Trip notes: Lake Amador is set in the foothill country east of Stockton at an elevation of 485 feet, covering 425 acres with 13 miles of shoreline. Everything here is set up for fishing, with large trout stocks from winter through late spring and the chance for huge bass; plus, waterskiing and jet skiing are prohibited. The largest two-man bass limit in California was caught here, 80 pounds, and the lake record weighed 15 pounds, 13 ounces. The Carson Creek arm and Jackson Creek arm are the top spots.

2 Pardee Recreation Area

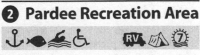

Location: On Pardee Reservoir; map E3, grid a2.

Campsites, facilities: There are 99 sites for

tents or RVs without hookups and 12 RV sites with full hookups. Picnic tables, fire grills, and piped water are provided. Rest rooms, showers (in the RV section), sanitary disposal station, boat ramp, boat rentals, coin laundry, grocery store, propane gas, RV and boat storage, wading pool, and a swimming pool are available. Leashed pets are permitted.

Reservations, fees: Reservations are accepted for full-hookup RV sites only; $14 to $19 per night, $1 pet fee. Open February through October.

Contact: Pardee Recreation Area, (209) 722-1472 or fax (209) 722-0985.

Directions: From Stockton, drive east on Highway 88 for 24 miles to the town of Clements. Just east of Clements, turn left on Highway 88 and drive 11 miles to Jackson Valley Road. Turn right and drive to a four-way stop sign at Buena Vista. Turn right and drive for three miles to Stony Creek Road on the left. Turn left and drive a mile to the campground.

Trip notes: Many people feel that Pardee is the prettiest lake in the Mother Lode country, a big lake covering 2,257 acres with 37 miles of shoreline. It is a beautiful sight in the spring when the lake is full and the surrounding hills are green and glowing. Waterskiing, jet skiing, and swimming are prohibited at the lake; it is set up expressly for fishing, with high catch rates for rainbow trout and kokanee salmon, best while trolling in the north arm of the lake.

❸ Golden Pines RV Resort and Camp

Location: Near Arnold; map E3, grid a9.

Campsites, facilities: There are 40 tent sites, 62 RV sites with full hookups, and four with partial hookups. Fire grills and picnic tables are provided. Piped water, rest rooms, showers, sanitary disposal station, recreation room, swimming pool, playground, grocery store, laundry room, and propane gas are available. Pets are permitted.

Reservations, fees: Reservations are recommended; $16 to $24 per night. Open year-round.

Contact: Golden Pines RV Resort and Camp,

(209) 795-2820 or fax (209) 7957432; email: goldenpine @cdepot.net; website: www .angelfire.com/biz/goldenpines/index/html.

Directions: From Angels Camp, turn northeast on Highway 4 and drive 22 miles to Arnold. Continue for seven miles to the campground entrance.

Trip notes: This is a privately operated park set at 5,800 feet on the slopes of the Sierra Nevada near Stanislaus National Forest, the North Stanislaus River, and Calaveras Big Trees State Park (three miles away). The latter features 150 giant sequoias, along with the biggest stump you can imagine, and two easy hikes, one routed through the North Grove, another through the South Grove.

❹ Lake Camanche South

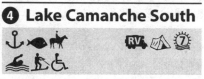

Location: On Camanche Reservoir; map E3, grid b1.

Campsites, facilities: There are 330 sites for tents or RVs, 120 with full hookups. There are also seven cottages. Picnic tables, fire grills, and piped water are provided. Rest rooms, showers, sanitary disposal station, trout pond, boat ramp, boat rentals, coin laundry, snack bar, and a grocery store are available. Leashed pets are permitted.

Reservations, fees: Reservations are required for group RV sites and cottages; RV site reservations are accepted for holidays only. RV sites are $20 per night, cottages are $75 to $95 per night. Open year-round.

Contact: Lake Camanche South, (209) 763-5178 or fax (209) 763-5724.

Directions: From Stockton, drive east on Highway 88 for 24 miles to Clements. Just east of Clements continue east on Highway 12 and drive six miles to South Camanche Parkway. Turn left and drive six miles to the entrance gate.

Trip notes: Camanche Reservoir is a huge, multifaceted facility, covering 7,700 acres with 53 miles of shoreline, set in the foothills east of Lodi at 325 feet in elevation. It is the No. 1 recreation lake for waterskiing and jet skiing (in specified areas), as well as swimming. In the spring and summer, it provides outstanding fishing for bass, trout, crappie, bluegill, and catfish. There are two campgrounds at the lake, and both have boat ramps nearby and all facilities. This one at South Shore has a large but exposed overflow area for camping, a way to keep from getting stuck for a spot on popular weekends.

⑤ Lake Camanche North

Location: On Camanche Reservoir; map E3, grid b1.

Campsites, facilities: There are 219 sites for tents or RVs, all without hookups. There are also 12 cottages and some motel rooms. Picnic tables, fire grills, and piped water are provided. Rest rooms, showers, sanitary disposal station, boat ramp, boat rentals, laundry room, grocery store, coffee shop/restaurant, and a playground are available. Leashed pets are permitted.

Reservations, fees: Reservations are required for group RV sites and cottages; RV site reservations are accepted for holidays only. RV sites are $15 per night, cottages are $75 to $95 per night, and motel rooms are $35 to $63 per night. There is a $6 boat launch fee. Open year round.

Contact: Lake Camanche North, 209) 763-5121 or fax (209) 763-5789.

Directions: From Stockton, drive east on Highway 88 for 24 miles to Clements. Just east of Clements, bear left on Highway 88 and drive six miles to Camanche Parkway. Turn right and drive seven miles to the Camanche North Shore entrance gate.

Trip notes: The sites at North Shore feature grassy spots with picnic tables set above the lake, and though there are few trees and the sites seem largely exposed, the lake view is quite pretty. The lake will beckon you for water sports and is excellent for boat owners. The warm, clean waters make for good waterskiing (in specified areas), and fishing for trout in spring, bass in early summer, and crappie, bluegill, and catfish in summer.

⑥ Acorn West

Location: At New Hogan Reservoir; map E3, grid b2.

Campsites, facilities: There are 59 sites for tents or RVs. Fire pits and picnic tables are provided. Piped water, flush toilets, showers, and a sanitary dump station are available. A four-lane paved boat ramp is located in adjacent Acorn East Campground. Groceries and propane gas are available within three miles. Leashed pets are permitted.

Reservations, fees: No reservations; $12 per night, $6 for each additional vehicle.

Contact: New Hogan Marina, (209) 772-1462; US Army Corps of Engineers, (209) 772-1343.

Directions: From Stockton, drive east on Highway 26 for about 35 miles to Valley Springs and Hogan Dam Road. Turn right and drive about four miles to the campground.

Trip notes: New Hogan is a big lake in the foothill country east of Stockton, covering 4,000 acres with 50 miles of shoreline. Acorn West is one of three campgrounds on the lake operated by the Army Corps of Engineers; the others are Acorn East and Oak Knoll. Boaters might also consider boat-in sites located near Deer Flat on the eastern shore. Boating and waterskiing are popular here. Fishing for largemouth bass is off-and-on, best in the spring up the Bear Creek and Whiskey Creek arms, and again in the fall when the striped bass come to life, chasing bait fish on the surface. An interpretive trail below the dam is worth checking out.

⑦ Acorn East

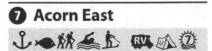

Location: At New Hogan Reservoir; map E3, grid b2.

Campsites, facilities: There are 69 sites for tents or RVs. Fire pits and picnic tables are provided. Piped water, flush toilets, showers, and a sanitary dump station are available. A four-lane paved boat ramp is located near the campground. Groceries and propane gas are available nearby. Leashed pets are permitted.

Reservations, fees: No reservations; $12 per night, $6 for each additional vehicle.

Contact: US Army Corps of Engineers, (209) 772-1343.

Directions: From Stockton, drive east on Highway 26 for about 35 miles to Valley Springs and Hogan Dam Road. Turn right and drive about four miles to the campground (just beyond Acorn West).

Trip notes: This is the campground of choice for boaters who prefer drive-to camps instead of the boat-in sites located on the east side of the lake near Deer Flat. A four-lane concrete boat ramp near this camp makes access easy. New Hogan is a big lake, and waterskiing and high-speed boating are popular here, along with fishing for largemouth bass in the spring and striped bass in the fall. See the trip notes for Acorn West (campground number six) for more information.

⑧ Oak Knoll

Location: At New Hogan Reservoir; map E3, grid b2.

Campsites, facilities: There are 50 sites for tents or RVs. Fire grills and picnic tables are provided. Piped water and vault toilets are available. Groceries, propane gas, sanitary dump station, and a four-lane boat ramp are available nearby. Leashed pets are permitted.

Reservations, fees: No reservations; $8 per night, $4 for each additional vehicle. Open April through September.

Contact: US Army Corps of Engineers, (209) 772-1343.

Directions: From Stockton, drive east on Highway 26 for about 35 miles to Valley Springs and Hogan Dam Road. Turn right and drive about four miles to the campground (adjacent to the Acorn camps).

Trip notes: This is one of three camps at New Hogan Reservoir and is basically only used as overflow camping during busy years. The reservoir was created by an Army Corps of Engineers dam project on the Calaveras River. See the trip notes for Acorn West (campground number six) for more information.

⑨ North Grove

Location: In Calaveras Big Trees State Park; map E3, grid b8.

Campsites, facilities: There are 36 sites for tents, 14 sites for RVs up to 18 feet long, 24 sites for RVs up to 30 feet long, and two sites designed for wheelchair use. A group campground is also available. Fire grills and picnic tables are provided. Piped water, flush toilets, firewood for purchase, coin-operated showers, and a sanitary disposal station are available. A nature trail and exhibits are wheelchair accessible. No bicycles are allowed on the paths, but they are permitted on fire roads. Leashed pets are permitted, except on trails.

Reservations, fees: Reserve via phone at (800) 444-PARK/7275 ($7.50 reservation fee) or website www.cal-parks.ca.gov; $16 per night, $150 group fee, $1 pet fee. Open year-round.

Contact: Calaveras Big Trees State Park, (209) 795-2334 or (209) 532-0150.

Directions: From Angels Camp, drive east on Highway 4 for 22 miles to Arnold and then continue another three miles to the park entrance.

Trip notes: This is one of two campgrounds at Calaveras Big Trees State Park, the state park known for its two groves of giant sequoias (mountain redwoods). The trailhead for a hike on the North Grove Loop is available here, an easy one-mile walk that is routed among 150 sequoias, where the sweet fragrance of the huge trees fills the air. These trees are known for their massive diameter, not for their height, as is the case with coastal redwoods. Another hike, a five-miler, is available in the South Grove, where the park's two largest sequoias (the Agassiz Tree and the Palace Hotel Tree) can be seen on a spur trail. A visitor center is open during peak periods, offering exhibits on the giant sequoia and natural history. The North Fork Stanislaus River runs near Highway 4, providing trout fishing access. In the winter this is a popular spot for cross-country skiing and snowshoeing. The elevation is 4,800 feet.

⑩ Oak Hollow

Location: In Calaveras Big Trees State Park; map E3, grid b8.

Campsites, facilities: There are 31 sites for tents only, 19 sites for RVs up to 18 feet long, and five sites for RVs up to 30 feet long. Fire rings and picnic tables are provided. Piped water, flush toilets, sanitary disposal station, and coin-operated showers are available. Supplies can be purchased in Dorrington. A nature trail and exhibits are wheelchair accessible. Leashed pets are permitted, except on trails.

Reservations, fees: Reserve via phone at (800) 444-PARK/7275 ($7.50 reservation fee) or website www.cal-parks.ca.gov; $15 to $17 per night, $1 pet fee. Open May through September.

Contact: Calaveras Big Trees State Park, (209) 795-2334 or (209) 532-0150.

Directions: From Angels Camp, drive east on Highway 4 for 22 miles to Arnold and then continue another four miles to the park entrance.

Trip notes: This is one of two campgrounds at Calaveras Big Trees State Park. See the trip notes for North Grove (campground number nine) for recreation information.

⑪ Boards Crossing

Location: On the North Fork of the Stanislaus River in Stanislaus National Forest; map E3, grid b9.

Campsites, facilities: There are five tent sites. Piped water, picnic tables, and vault toilets are available. Groceries and propane gas can be purchased nearby. Leashed pets are permitted.

Reservations, fees: No reservations; no fee; campfire permits required (free). Open June through September.

Contact: Stanislaus National Forest, Calaveras Ranger District, (209) 795-1381 or fax (209) 795-6849.

Directions: From Angels Camp, drive east on Highway 4 and pass Arnold to Dorrington and Boards Crossing Road on the right. Turn right and drive about two miles to the campground entrance road on the right. Turn right and drive

about a mile to the campground on the right.

Trip notes: One of the oldest campgrounds in the Western US, Boards Crossing is near a historic one-way bridge that crosses the North Fork Stanislaus River. It is a small, primitive camp set along the river at 3,800 feet in elevation, with Beaver Creek located three miles to the east (continue on the access road after crossing the bridge). This place is just far enough off Highway 4 to be overlooked by most campers.

⑫ Tuttletown Recreation Area

Location: At New Melones Lake; map E3, grid d5.

Campsites, facilities: There are 95 sites for tents or RVs and 60 RV-only sites. Picnic tables and fire grills are provided. Piped water, flush toilets, sanitary dump station, showers, playground, and a boat ramp are available. Leashed pets are permitted.

Reservations, fees: No reservations; $14 per night. Open year-round.

Contact: US Department of Reclamation, (209) 536-9094.

Directions: From Sonora, drive north on Highway 49 in Tuttletown to Reynolds Ferry Road. Turn left and drive about two miles to the campground on the left side of the road.

Trip notes: Here is one of two camps on New Melones Lake in the Sierra Nevada foothills. This is a huge reservoir that covers 12,250 acres and offers 100 miles of shoreline and good fishing. Waterskiing is permitted in specified areas; a boat ramp is located near camp. Although the lake's main body is huge, the better fishing is well up the lake's Stanislaus River arm (for trout) and in its coves (for bass and bluegill), where there are submerged trees providing perfect aquatic habitat. The lake level often drops dramatically in the fall.

⑬ Glory Hole

Location: At New Melones Lake; map E3, grid d5.

Campsites, facilities: There are 144 sites for tents or RVs. Picnic tables and fire grills are provided. Piped water, flush toilets, sanitary dump station, showers, marina, boat rentals, volleyball net, baseball diamond, and a playground are available. Leashed pets are permitted.

Reservations, fees: No reservations; $14 per night. Open year-round.

Contact: US Department of Reclamation, (209) 536-9094.

Directions: From Sonora, drive north on Highway 49 for about 15 miles (Glory Hole Market will be on the left side of the road) to Glory Hole Road. Turn left and drive five miles to the campground, with sites on both sides of the road.

Trip notes: This is one of two camps on New Melones Lake in the Sierra Nevada foothills, a popular spot with a boat ramp nearby for access to outstanding waterskiing and fishing. See the trip notes for Tuttletown Recreation Area (campground number 12).

⑭ Marble Quarry RV Park

Location: Near Columbia; map E3, grid d6.

Campsites, facilities: There is a small area for tents and 85 sites for RVs (26 have full hookups, 59 have partial hookups). Piped water and picnic tables are provided. Rest rooms, showers, swimming pool, coin laundry, store, sanitary dump station, playground, two clubhouses, lounge, two full kitchens, satellite TV, and propane gas are available. Some facilities are wheelchair accessible. Leashed pets are permitted.

Reservations, fees: Reservations are accepted; $18 to $26 per night. Open year-round.

Contact: Marble Quarry RV Park, (209) 532-9539.

Directions: From Sonora, turn north on Highway 49 for 2.5 miles to Parrotts Ferry Road. Bear right and drive two miles to Yankee Hill Road. Turn right and drive a half mile to the campground at 11551 Yankee Hill Road.

Trip notes: This RV park is set at 2,100 feet in the Mother Lode country, within nearby range of several adventures. Columbia State Historic

Park is located within walking distance, and the Stanislaus River arm of New Melones Lake is only five miles away.

⑮ 49er RV Ranch

Location: Near Columbia; map E3, grid d6.

Campsites, facilities: There are 45 sites for trailers and RVs, all with full hookups. Piped water, picnic tables, and barbecues are provided. Rest rooms, hot showers, laundry room, store, sanitary dump station, cable TV, propane gas, and a large barn for group or club activities are available. Leashed pets are permitted.

Reservations, fees: Reservations are accepted; $24.50 to $25.50 per night, $2.50 for each additional person. Group rates are available. Open year-round.

Contact: 49er RV Ranch, (209) 532-4978 or fax (209) 532-9978; email: 49rv@mlode.com.

Directions: From Sonora, turn north on Highway 49 for 2.5 miles to Parrots Ferry Road. Turn right and drive 1.7 miles to Columbia Street. Turn right and drive 0.4 mile to Pacific Street. Turn left and drive a block to Italian Bar Road. Turn right and drive a half mile to the campground on the right.

Trip notes: This historic ranch/campground was originally built in 1852 as a dairy farm. Several original barns are still standing. The place has been brought up to date, of course, with a small store on the property providing last-minute supplies. Location is a plus, with the Columbia State Historic Park only a half mile away, and the Stanislaus River arm of New Melones Lake within a five-minute drive. The elevation is 2,100 feet.

⑯ River Ranch Campground

Location: On the Tuolumne River; map E3, grid e9.

Campsites, facilities: There are 50 sites for tents or RVs. Piped water, fire grills, and picnic tables are provided. Rest rooms and showers are available. A grocery store, coin laundry, and propane gas are nearby. Leashed pets are permitted.

Reservations, fees: Group reservations are accepted; $14 per night. Open year-round.

Contact: River Ranch Campground, (209) 928-3708 or fax (209) 928-1606.

Directions: From Sonora, drive east on Highway 108 and exit right at Tuolumne Road. Drive to the end of Tuolumne Road and turn left on Carter Street. Drive four blocks and turn right on Buchanon Road. Drive another four miles and continue straight on Fish Hatchery Road for two miles to the campground exit on the right.

Trip notes: This pretty spot is at 2,700 feet, right where conifers begin to take over from the valley foothill grasslands. The campground is set near where Basin Creek enters the Tuolumne River, adding a peaceful element for campers, as well as a chance for trout fishing.

⑰ Sugarpine RV Park

Location: In Twain Harte; map E3, grid d9.

Campsites, facilities: There are 17 tent sites and 65 RV sites with full hookups. Piped water and picnic tables are provided. Rest rooms, showers, playground, pool, video games in summer, laundry room, guest lounge and a store are available. Leashed pets are permitted.

Reservations, fees: Reservations are accepted; $12 to $30 per night.

Contact: Sugarpine RV Park, (209) 586-4631 or (916) 987-9585.

Directions: From Sonora, drive east on Highway 108 for 17 miles to the park on the right side of the road.

Trip notes: Twain Harte is a beautiful little town, located right at the edge of the snow line in winter, and right where pines take over in the alpine landscape. This park is at the threshold of the mountain country, with Pinecrest, Dodge Ridge, and Beardsley Reservoir nearby. Note: Heading east out of Twain Harte, beware of the unannounced horseshoe turn at the town of Confidence. Some drivers are surprised by the turn and cross over into oncoming traffic.

⑱ Woodward Reservoir County Park

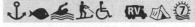

Location: Near Oakdale; map E3, grid e0.

Campsites, facilities: There are 155 sites for tents or RVs, 115 with partial hookups, 40 with full hookups and some equestrian facilities. Piped water, fire grills, and picnic tables are provided. Flush toilets, showers, sanitary disposal station, groceries, propane gas, three boat ramps, mooring, boat rentals, dry boat storage, bait, and fishing licenses are available. Leashed pets are permitted.

Reservations, fees: No reservations; $12 to $16 per night, $5 boat launch fee, $2 pet fee. Open year-round.

Contact: Woodward Reservoir County Park, (209) 847-3304 or (209) 525-6750.

Directions: From Manteca, drive east on Highway 120 (it becomes Highway 108) for 20 miles to Oakdale and the junction with County Road J14/26 Mile Road. Turn left and drive four miles to 14528 26 Mile Road at Woodward Reservoir.

Trip notes: Woodward Reservoir is a large lake covering 2,900 acres with 23 miles of shoreline, set in the rolling foothills just north of Oakdale. It is a good lake for both waterskiing and bass fishing, with minimal conflict between the two sports. That is because two large coves on the south and east ends of the lake, as well as the area behind Whale Island, are for low-speed boats only. That makes for good fishing, while the speedboats have the main lake body to let 'er rip.

⑲ Lake Tulloch RV Camp and Marina

Location: On the south shore of Lake Tulloch; map E3, grid f4.

Campsites, facilities: There are 130 sites for tents or RVs. Piped water, fire rings, and picnic tables are provided. Many sites have full hookups. There are five waterfront cabins with electricity; each sleeps six and each has its own dock. An additional large area is available for lakefront tent camping and self-contained-unit camping.

Flush toilets, hot showers, laundry room, store, propane gas, boat launch, and a boat ramp are provided. Many facilities are wheelchair accessible. Group sites and rates are available. Leashed pets are permitted.

Reservations, fees: Reservations are accepted; $17.50 to $27.50 per night for tent and RV sites, cabins are $75 per night or $400 per week. Open year-round.

Contact: Lake Tulloch RV Camp and Marina, 14448 Tulloch Dam Road, Jamestown, CA 95327; (209) 881-0107.

Directions: From Manteca, drive east on Highway 120 (it becomes Highway 108) for about 35 miles to Tulloch Road. Turn left and drive 4.6 miles to the campground entrance at the south shore of Lake Tulloch.

Trip notes: Unlike so many reservoirs in the foothill country, this one is nearly always full of water. In addition, it is one of the rare places where fishermen and water-skiers live in harmony. That is due to the many coves and a six-mile-long arm with an enforced 5 mph speed limit. It's a big lake, shaped like a giant "X" with extended lake arms adding up to 55 miles of shoreline. The campground features mature oak trees that provide shade to most of the developed sites. A secret at Tulloch is that fishing is also good for crawdads.

⑳ Knights Ferry Resort

Location: On the Stanislaus River; map E3, grid f2.

Campsites, facilities: There are 21 sites for tents or RVs. A community fire pit, rest rooms, showers, and a restaurant are available. Leashed pets are permitted.

Reservations, fees: Reservations are accepted with deposit; $20 to $23 per night, $3 pet fee. There is a two-night minimum stay on weekends and a three-night minimum on holidays.

Contact: Knights Ferry Resort, (209) 881-3349.

Directions: From Manteca, drive east on Highway 120 (it becomes Highway 108) for about 35 miles to Knights Ferry and Kennedy

Road. Turn left, drive to a bridge, cross the bridge, and continue a short distance to Sonora Road/Main Street. Turn left and drive to the Knights Ferry Restaurant at the entrance to the campground.

Trip notes: This is a privately run resort located in the small historic town of Knights Ferry. Side trips include tours of the covered bridge ("the longest west of the Mississippi") and several historic buildings and homes, all within walking distance of the park. River access and hiking trails are available at the east end of town. Raft and canoe rentals are also available nearby.

㉑ Moccasin Point

Location: At Don Pedro Reservoir; map E3, grid f6.

Campsites, facilities: There are 65 sites for tents and 15 sites with full hookups for RVs. Picnic tables, food lockers, and barbecue units are provided at all sites. Piped water, rest rooms, showers, store, sanitary dump station, propane gas, ice, snack bar, boat ramp, motorboat and houseboat rentals, fuel, moorings, and bait and tackle are available. Campfires are prohibited. No pets are permitted.

Reservations, fees: Reservations are accepted; $14 to $20 per night. Open year-round.

Contact: Moccasin Point, (209) 852-2396 or fax (209) 857-2780.

Directions: From Manteca, drive east on Highway 120 (it becomes Highway 108) for 30 miles to the Highway 120/Yosemite exit. Bear right on Highway 120 and drive 11 miles. Turn left on Jacksonville Road and drive a short distance to the campground on the right.

Trip notes: This camp is at the north end of Don Pedro Reservoir, adjacent to a boat ramp. Moccasin Point juts out well into the lake, directly across from where the major Tuolumne River arm enters the lake. Don Pedro is a giant lake, with nearly 13,000 surface acres and 160 miles of shoreline, but is subject to drawdowns from midsummer through early fall. At different times, fishing is excellent for salmon, trout, or bass. Houseboating and boat-in camping (bring sunscreen) provide options.

㉒ Big Bear Water Park

Location: On the Tuolumne River near Modesto; map E3, grid g1.

Campsites, facilities: There are 96 sites for tents and 116 RV sites, most with full hookups. Piped water, rest rooms, showers, sanitary disposal station, coin laundry, propane, ice, small store, three clubhouses, and a playground are available. A miniature train ride and a water slide operate from May to September. Leashed pets are permitted (RV section only).

Reservations, fees: Reservations are accepted; $17 to $21 per night, four campers per site. Open year-round.

Contact: Big Bear Water Park, (209) 874-1984 or fax (209) 874-4544.

Directions: From Modesto, drive east on Highway 132 for 12 miles to the town of Waterford (where the road becomes Yosemite Boulevard) and drive to the park at 13400 Yosemite Boulevard.

Trip notes: Big Bear Water Park is set at 2,500 feet in the foothill country east of Modesto. The park welcomes families with young children. The Tuolumne River runs right alongside the campground. Nearby side trips include Modesto Reservoir, Turlock Lake, and Don Pedro Reservoir.

㉓ Modesto Reservoir Regional Park

Location: On Modesto Reservoir; map E3, grid g3.

Campsites, facilities: There are 100 sites for tents or RVs with partial hookups. Piped water, fire grills, and picnic tables are provided. Flush toilets, dump station, showers, two boat ramps, waterskiing, fishing, marina, and a store are available. Propane gas is available within four miles. No pets are allowed.

Reservations, fees: No reservations; $12 to $16 per night. Open year-round.

Contact: Modesto Reservoir Regional Park,

(209) 874 9540 or fax (209) 874-4513.

Directions: From Modesto, drive east on Highway 132 for 16 miles past Waterford to Reservoir Road. Turn left and drive to the campground at 18139 Reservoir Road.

Trip notes: Modesto Reservoir is not well known, but it is a surprisingly big lake, at 2,700 acres with 31 miles of shoreline, set in the hot foothill country. Waterskiing is excellent here in the main lake body. Anglers head to the southern shore of the lake, which is loaded with submerged trees and coves and is also protected by a 5 mph speed limit. Fishing for bass is good, though the fish are often small.

㉔ Fleming Meadows

Location: On Don Pedro Reservoir; map E3, grid g4.

Campsites, facilities: There are 152 sites for tents or RVs and 89 RV sites with full hookups. Picnic tables, food lockers, and barbecue grills are provided. Rest rooms, showers, and sanitary dump station are available. A coin laundry, store, ice, snack bar, restaurant, tackle and bait, motorboat and houseboat rentals, boat ramp, berths, engine repairs, and propane gas are nearby. Campfires are prohibited. No pets are permitted.

Reservations, fees: Reservations are accepted; $14 to $20 per night. Open year-round.

Contact: Fleming Meadows, (209) 852-2396.

Directions: From Modesto, drive east on Highway 132 to La Grange. Turn left on La Grange/J59 and drive five miles. Turn right on Bonds Flat Road and drive two miles to the campground.

Trip notes: Fleming Meadows is set on the shore of Don Pedro Reservoir at its extreme south end, just east of the dam. A boat ramp is available in the campground on the southeast side of the dam. This is a big camp at the foot of a giant lake, where hot weather, warm water, waterskiing, and bass fishing make for weekend vacations. Don Pedro has many extended lake arms, providing 160 miles of shoreline and nearly 13,000 surface acres when full.

㉕ Blue Oaks

Location: At Don Pedro Reservoir; map E3, grid g4.

Campsites, facilities: There are 197 sites for tents and RVs. Piped water, picnic tables, food lockers, and barbecue units are provided. Flush toilets, showers, and sanitary disposal station are available. A grocery store, coin laundry, boat ramp, and propane gas are located nearby. Campfires are prohibited. No pets are permitted.

Reservations, fees: Reservations are accepted; $14 per night.

Contact: Blue Oaks, (209) 852-2396.

Directions: From Modesto, drive east on Highway 132 to La Grange. Turn left on LaGrange/J59 and drive five miles. Turn right on Bonds Flat Road and drive a mile to the campground on the shoreline.

Trip notes: Blue Oaks is located between the dam at Don Pedro Reservoir and Fleming Meadows. The on-site boat ramp to the east is a big plus here. See the trip notes for Fleming Meadows (campground number 24) and Moccasin Point (campground number 21) for more information.

㉖ Horseshoe Bend Recreation Area

Location: On Lake McClure; map E3, grid g7.

Campsites, facilities: There are 110 sites for tents or RVs, 35 with partial hookups. Picnic tables are provided. Rest rooms, showers, sanitary disposal station, and a boat ramp are available. A grocery store and coin laundry are nearby. Leashed pets are permitted.

Reservations, fees: Reservations are required, phone (800) 468-8889; $13 to $17 per night, $2 pet fee. Open year-round.

Contact: Horseshoe Bend Recreation Area, (209) 878-3452 or fax (209) 378-2519.

Directions: From Modesto, drive east on Highway 132 for 31 miles to La Grange and then continue for about 17 miles (toward Coulterville) to the north end of Lake McClure and the camp-

ground entrance road on the right side of the road. Turn right and drive a half mile to the campground.

Trip notes: Lake McClure is a unique, horseshoe-shaped lake in the foothill country west of Yosemite. It adjoins smaller Lake McSwain, connected by the Merced River. McClure is shaped like a giant "H," with its lake arms providing 81 miles of shoreline, warm water for waterskiing, and fishing for bass (on the left half of the "H" near Cotton Creek) and for trout (on the right half of the "H"). There is a boat launch adjacent to the campground. It's one of four lakes in the immediate area; the others are Don Pedro Reservoir to the north and Modesto Reservoir and Turlock Lake to the west. The elevation is 900 feet.

㉗ The Pines

Location: In Stanislaus National Forest; map E3, grid g9.

Campsites, facilities: There are 12 sites for tents or RVs up to 22 feet long. Piped water (May through October only), picnic tables, and fire grills are provided. Vault toilets are available. A grocery store is nearby. Leashed pets are permitted.

Reservations, fees: No reservations; $9 per night, $45 group fee. Open year-round.

Contact: Stanislaus National Forest, Groveland Ranger District, (209) 962-7825 or fax (209) 962-6406.

Directions: From Groveland, drive east on Highway 120 for eight miles (about a mile past the County Road J132 turnoff) to the signed campground entrance road on the right. Turn right onto the campground entrance road and drive a short distance to the camp.

Trip notes: The Pines Camp is set at 3,200 feet in elevation on the western edge of Stanislaus National Forest, only a half mile from the Buck Meadows Ranger Station and about five miles from the Tuolumne River (see Lumsden, chapter E4). A Forest Service road is routed south of camp for two miles, climbing to Smith Peak Lookout (3,877 feet) and providing sweeping views to the west of the San Joaquin Valley foothills.

㉘ Moore Creek Group Camp

Location: In Stanislaus National Forest; map E3, grid g9.

Campsites, facilities: There is a group campsite. Vault toilets and fire grills are provided. There is no piped water. Leashed pets are permitted.

Reservations, fees: Reservations are required; call for fees.

Contact: Stanislaus National Forest, Groveland Ranger District, (209) 962-7825 or fax (209) 962-6406.

Directions: From Groveland, drive east on Highway 120 about 12 miles to Forest Road 2S95. Turn right and drive 1.5 miles to the campground on the right.

Trip notes: This group camp is set at 2,800 feet, just past where the Sierra alpine zone takes over from foothill oak woodlands. It is set near the access route (Highway 120) to the Crane Flat entrance station to Yosemite National Park.

㉙ Turlock Lake State Recreation Area

Location: East of Modesto; map E3, grid h3.

Campsites, facilities: There are 66 sites for tents or RVs up to 27 feet long. Piped water, fire grills, and picnic tables are provided. Flush toilets, showers, and a boat ramp are available. The boat facilities are wheelchair accessible. Leashed pets are permitted.

Reservations, fees: Reserve via phone at (800) 444-PARK/7275 ($7.50 reservation fee) or website www.cal-parks.ca.gov; $14 to $16 per night, $5 boat launch fee.

Contact: Turlock Lake State Recreation Area, (209) 874-2008, (209) 874-2056, or fax (209) 874-2611.

Directions: From Modesto, go east on Highway 132 for 14 miles to Waterford. Turn right on Hickman Road and drive a mile. Turn left on Lake Road and drive 10 miles to the park.

Trip notes: Turlock Lake heats up like a big bathtub in the summer, just right for boating and all water sports. It covers 3,500 acres and offers 26 miles of shoreline. A boat ramp and small marina are available near the camp, making it ideal for boaters/campers. Bass fishing is fair in the summer. In the late winter and spring, the surprise here is that the water is quite cold, being fed by snowmelt from the Tuolumne River, providing a once-a-year chance for trout fishing. By early summer, forget trout and think bass. If they don't bite, just give up and literally jump in the lake.

㉚ Barrett Cove Recreation Area

Location: On Lake McClure; map E3, grid h6.

Campsites, facilities: There are 275 sites for tents or RVs. Piped water, electrical connections, and sewer hookups are provided at some sites. Picnic tables are provided. Rest rooms, showers, boat ramps, dump station, swimming lagoon, and a playground are available. A grocery store, coin laundry, boat and houseboat rentals, and propane gas are also available on site. Leashed pets are permitted.

Reservations, fees: Reservations are accepted; $13 to $17 per night, $2 pet fee. Open year-round.

Contact: Barrett Cove Recreation Area, (800) 468-8889 or (209) 378-2521.

Directions: From Modesto, drive east on Highway 132 for 31 miles to La Grange and then continue for about 11 miles (toward Coulterville) to Merced Falls Road. Turn right and drive three miles to the campground entrance on the left. Turn left and drive a mile to the campground on the left side of the road.

Trip notes: Lake McClure is shaped like a giant "H," with its lake arms providing 81 miles of shoreline. This camp is on the left side of the "H," that is, on the western shore, within a park that provides a good boat ramp. This is the largest in a series of camps on Lake McClure. See Horseshoe Bend Recreation Area (campground number 26), McClure Point Recreation Area (campground number 31), and Bagby Recreation Area (campground number 32) for more information.

③ McClure Point Recreation Area

Location: On Lake McClure; map E3, grid h6.

Campsites, facilities: There are 100 sites for tents or RVs up to 40 feet long. Piped water and electrical connections are provided at many sites. Picnic tables are provided. Rest rooms, showers, boat ramp, and a laundry room are available. A grocery store is nearby. Leashed pets are permitted.

Reservations, fees: Reservations are accepted; $13 to $17 per night, $2 pet fee. Open year-round.

Contact: McClure Point Recreation Area, (800) 468-8889 or (209) 378-2521.

Directions: From Turlock, drive east on County Road J16 for 19 miles to the junction with Highway 59. Continue east on Highway 59/County Road J16 for 4.5 miles to Snelling and bear right at Lake McClure Road. Drive seven miles to Lake McSwain Dam and continue for seven miles to the campground at the end of the road.

Trip notes: The campground at McClure Point Recreation Area is the one of choice for campers/boaters coming from the Turlock and Merced areas. It is a well-developed facility with an excellent boat ramp that provides access to the main body of Lake McClure. This is the best spot on the lake for waterskiing.

③ Bagby Recreation Area

Location: On upper Lake McClure; map E3, grid i8.

Campsites, facilities: There are 25 tent sites and several partial hookups available. Piped water, rest rooms with flush toilets and hot showers, small store, and a boat ramp are available. Leashed pets are permitted.

Reservations, fees: Reservations are accepted; $12 to $15 per night, $2 pet fee. Open year-round.

Contact: Bagby Recreation Area, (800) 468-8889 or (209) 378-2521.

Directions: From Modesto, drive east on Highway 132 for 31 miles to La Grange and then continue for 20 miles to Coulterville and the junction with Highway 49. Turn south on Highway 49, drive about 12 miles, cross the bridge, and look for the campground entrance on the left side of the road. Turn left and drive a quarter mile to the campground.

Trip notes: This is the most distant and secluded camp on Lake McClure. It is set near where the Merced River enters the lake, way up adjacent to the Highway 49 Bridge, nearly an hour's drive from the dam. Trout fishing is good in the area, and it makes sense; when the lake heats up in summer, the trout naturally congregate near the cool incoming flows of the Merced River.

③ Lake McSwain Recreation Area

Location: Near McSwain Dam on the Merced River; map E3, grid i6.

Campsites, facilities: There are 112 sites for tents or RVs up to 40 feet long. Piped water, electrical connections, picnic tables, and sewage disposal are provided. Rest rooms, showers, boat ramp, boat rentals, coin laundry, playground, and a dump station are available. A grocery store, boat rentals, and propane gas are nearby. Leashed pets are permitted.

Reservations, fees: Reservations are accepted; $13 to $17 per night, $2 pet fee. Open March to mid-October.

Contact: Lake McSwain Recreation Area, (800) 468-8889 or (209) 378-2521.

Directions: From Turlock, drive east on County Road J16 for 19 miles to the junction with Highway 59. Continue east on Highway 59/County Road J16 for 4.5 miles to Snelling and bear right at Lake McClure Road. Drive seven miles to the campground turnoff on the right.

Trip notes: Lake McSwain is actually the afterbay for adjacent Lake McClure, and this camp is located near the McSwain Dam on the Merced River. If you have a canoe or cartop boat, this lake is preferable to Lake McClure because waterskiing is not allowed. In terms of size McSwain is like a puddle compared to the giant McClure, but unlike McClure, the water levels are kept up almost year-round at McSwain. The water is cold here and trout stocks are good in the spring.

34 McConnell State Recreation Area

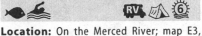

Location: On the Merced River; map E3, grid j1.

Campsites, facilities: There are 21 sites for tents or RVs up to 24 feet long and two group sites for tents only. Piped water, fire grills, and picnic tables are provided. Flush toilets and hot showers are available. Supplies can be obtained in Delhi, three miles away. Leashed pets are permitted.

Reservations, fees: Reserve via phone at (800) 444-PARK/7275 ($7.50 reservation fee) or website www.cal-parks.ca.gov for group fees and reservations; $15 per night for family sites, $1 pet fee. Open March through September.

Contact: Four Rivers District Office, (209) 826-1196.

Directions: From Modesto or Merced, drive on Highway 99 to Delhi and the Shanks Road exit. Turn east on El Capitan Way and drive five miles to Pepper Street. Turn right and drive to the park.

Trip notes: The weather gets scorching hot around these parts in the summer months, and a lot of out-of-towners would pay a bunch for a little shade and a river to sit next to. That's what this park provides, with the Merced River flowing past, along with occasional mermaids on the beach. In high-water years the Merced River attracts salmon (in the fall).

Map E4

One inch equals approximately 10.7 miles.
See inside back cover for California state map.

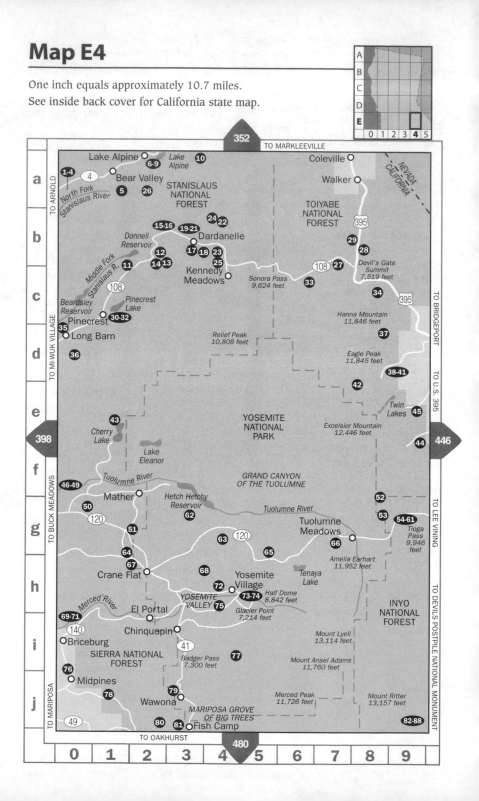

352 TO MARKLEEVILLE

TO ARNOLD

Lake Alpine ○ Lake Alpine **10**
1-4 ○ **4** **6-9**
North Fork Bear Valley
Stanislaus River **5** **26**

STANISLAUS
NATIONAL
FOREST

Coleville ○
Walker ○

TOIYABE
NATIONAL
FOREST

395

15-16 **24 22**
19-21 Dardanelle
Donnell **17 18 23**
Reservoir **12** **25**
14 13
Kennedy
Meadows

29 28
Devil's Gate
Summit
7,519 feet

108 **27**

Sonora Pass
9,624 feet

11

108

33

395

Beardsley
Reservoir Pinecrest
Lake **30-32**
Pinecrest
35 ○
Long Barn ○

Hanna Mountain
11,846 feet

34

TO MI-WUK VILLAGE

36

Relief Peak
10,808 feet

Eagle Peak
11,845 feet

37

38-41

TO BRIDGEPORT

42

43
Cherry
Lake

YOSEMITE
NATIONAL
PARK

Excelsior Mountain
12,446 feet

Twin
Lakes **45**

398

Lake
Eleanor

44

446

TO U.S. 395

46-49
Tuolumne River

GRAND CANYON
OF THE TUOLUMNE

TO BUCK MEADOWS

50
Mather ○
120

Hetch Hetchy
Reservoir **62**

Tuolumne River

52

53 **54-61**
Tioga
Pass
9,946
feet

51

63 **120**

Tuolumne
Meadows

65

66

64
67
Crane Flat ○

68

72

Yosemite
Village
73-74
YOSEMITE **75**
VALLEY

Amelia Earhart
11,952 feet

Tenaya
Lake

Half Dome
8,842 feet

Merced River

El Portal ○

Glacier Point
7,214 feet

INYO
NATIONAL
FOREST

TO LEE VINING

69-71
140
Briceburg ○

Chinquapin ○

41

SIERRA NATIONAL
FOREST

Badger Pass
7,300 feet

77

Mount Lyell
13,114 feet

Mount Ansel Adams
11,760 feet

TO MARIPOSA

76
Midpines ○

78

79
Wawona ○

MARIPOSA GROVE
OF BIG TREES

Merced Peak
11,726 feet

Mount Ritter
13,157 feet

49

80 **81**
Fish Camp ○

TO OAKHURST

82-88

TO DEVILS POSTPILE NATIONAL MONUMENT

480

NEVADA
CALIFORNIA

a
b
c
d
e
f
g
h
i
j

0 1 2 3 4 5 6 7 8 9

Chapter E4 features:

❶ Big Meadows Group Camp

Location: In Stanislaus National Forest; map E4, grid a0.

Campsites, facilities: There is a group campsite for tents or RVs. Piped water, picnic tables, and fire grills are provided. Vault toilets are available. Groceries, a coin laundry, and propane gas are nearby. Leashed pets are permitted.

Reservations, fees: Reserve via phone at (877) 444-6777 ($17.35 reservation fee); $30 per group of 25 people per night, $1 per additional camper. Open May through September.

Contact: Stanislaus National Forest, Calaveras Ranger District, (209) 795-1381 or fax (209) 795-6849.

Directions: From Angels Camp on Highway 49, turn east on Highway 4 and drive about 30 miles (three miles past Ganns Meadows) to the campground on the right.

Trip notes: Big Meadows Group Camp is set at 6,500 feet on the western slopes of the Sierra Nevada. There are a number of recreation attractions nearby, the most prominent being the North Fork Stanislaus River two miles to the south in national forest (see Sand Flat, campground number two), with access available from a four-wheel-drive road just east of camp, or on Spicer Reservoir Road (see Stanislaus River, campground number three). Lake Alpine, a pretty, popular lake for trout fishing, is located nine miles east on Highway 4.

❷ Sand Flat

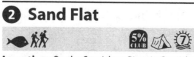

Location: On the Stanislaus River in Stanislaus National Forest; map E4, grid a0.

Campsites, facilities: There are four tent sites. Fire rings, picnic tables, and vault toilets are available. There is no piped water. Leashed pets are permitted.

Reservations, fees: No reservations; no fee. Free campfire permits are required. Open June through August.

Contact: Stanislaus National Forest, Calaveras Ranger District, (209) 795-1381 or fax (209) 795-6849.

Directions: From Angels Camp on Highway 49, turn east on Highway 4, drive about 30 miles (3.5 miles past Ganns Meadows), and then continue a half mile past Big Meadows Group Camp to a dirt/gravel road on the right. Turn right and drive two miles on a steep, unimproved road (four-wheel drive required).

Trip notes: This one is for four-wheel-drive cowboys who want to carve out a piece of the Sierra Nevada wildlands for themselves. It is set at 5,900 feet on the North Fork Stanislaus River, where there is decent fishing for small trout, with the fish often holding right where white water runs into pools. The tiny, primitive camp, where you won't get bugged by anyone, was named for the extensive sandy flat on the south side of the river.

❸ Stanislaus River

Location: In Stanislaus National Forest; map E4, grid a0.

Campsites, facilities: There are 25 sites for tents or RVs up to 16 feet long. Fire grills and picnic tables are provided. Piped water and vault toilets are available. Supplies are available in Tamarack. Leashed pets are permitted.

Reservations, fees: No reservations; $8 per night. Open June through September.

Contact: Stanislaus National Forest, Calaveras Ranger District, (209) 795-1381 or fax (209) 795-6849.

Directions: From Angels Camp on Highway 49, turn east on Highway 4 and drive about 32 miles (five miles past Ganns Meadows) to Spicer Reservoir Road on the right. Turn right and drive four miles to the campground on the right side of the road.

Trip notes: As you might figure from its name, this camp provides excellent access to the adjacent North Fork Stanislaus River, but it is also the closest drive-in campground to Utica Reservoir, Union Reservoir, and Spicer Reservoir, all located within seven miles to the east. Of the three, Spicer Meadow has the best trout fishing. The elevation is 6,200 feet, with timbered sites and the river just south of camp.

❹ Big Meadow

Location: Near the Stanislaus River in Stanislaus National Forest; map E4, grid a0.

Campsites, facilities: There are 65 sites for tents or RVs. Piped water, fire grills, and picnic tables are provided and vault toilets are available. Groceries, a coin laundry, and propane gas are nearby. Pets are permitted.

Reservations, fees: Reserve via phone at (877) 444-6777 ($8.65 reservation fee) or website www.reserveusa.com; $9 per night. Open June through October.

Contact: Stanislaus National Forest, Calaveras Ranger District, (209) 795-1381 or fax (209) 795-6849.

Directions: From Angels Camp on Highway 49, turn east on Highway 4 and drive about 30 miles (three miles past Ganns Meadows) to the campground on the right.

Trip notes: Big Meadow is set at 6,500 feet and features a number of nearby recreation options. The most prominent is the North Fork Stanislaus River, with access available at Sand Flat and Stanislaus River campgrounds. In addition, Lake Alpine is located nine miles to the east, and three mountain reservoirs, Spicer Meadow, Utica, and Union, are all within a 15-minute drive. Big Meadow is also a good base camp for hunters.

❺ Union Reservoir Walk-In

Location: Northeast of Arnold in Stanislaus National Forest; map E4, grid a1.

Campsites, facilities: There are 15 primitive walk-in tent sites. A rest room is available, along with a signboard explaining lake rules and camp policies. A boat ramp is available nearby.

Reservations, fees: No reservations; no fee.

Contact: Stanislaus National Forest, Calaveras Ranger District, (209) 795-1381 or fax (209) 795-6849. For a map send $4 to the US Forest Service, US Forest Map Sales, 1323 Club Drive, Vallejo, CA 94592, and ask for Stanislaus National Forest area.

Directions: From Angels Camp, drive east on Highway 4 for about 32 miles to Spicer Reservoir Road. Turn right and travel east for about seven miles to Forest Service Road 7N75. Turn left and drive three miles to Union Reservoir. There are four designated parking areas for the walk-in camps along the road.

Trip notes: Union Reservoir is set in Sierra granite at 6,850 feet, a beautiful and quiet lake that is kept that way with rules that mandate a 5 mph speed limit and walk-in camping only. Most of the sites provide lakeside views. Fishing is often good, trolling for kokanee salmon, but you need a boat. The setting is great, especially for canoes or other small boats. This camp is not well known, and those who visit usually keep quiet so everybody can enjoy a pristine experience.

❻ Pine Marten

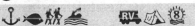

Location: Near Lake Alpine in Stanislaus National Forest; map E4, grid a2.

Campsites, facilities: There are 33 sites for tents or RVs up to 22 feet long. Piped water, flush toilets, picnic tables, and fire grills are provided. A boat ramp is available. A grocery store, propane gas, and coin laundry are nearby. Leashed pets are permitted.

Reservations, fees: No reservations; $13 per night. A free campfire permit is required. Open June to mid-October.

Contact: Stanislaus National Forest, Calaveras Ranger District, (209) 795-1381 or fax (209) 795-6849.

Directions: From Angels Camp, drive east on Highway 4 to Arnold and continue for 29 miles to Lake Alpine. Drive to the northeast end of the lake to the campground entrance on the right side of the road.

Trip notes: Lake Alpine is a beautiful Sierra lake surrounded by granite and pines and set at 7,320 feet, just above where the snowplows stop in winter. This camp is on the northeast side, about a quarter mile from the shore. Fishing for rainbow trout is good in May and early June, prior to the summer crush. Despite the long drive to get here, the lake is becoming better known for its beauty, camping, and hiking. A trailhead available out of nearby Silver Valley Camp provides a two-mile hike to pretty Duck Lake and beyond into the Carson-Iceberg Wilderness.

❼ Silver Valley

Location: On Lake Alpine in Stanislaus National Forest; map E4, grid a2.

Campsites, facilities: There are 25 sites for tents or RVs up to 22 feet long. Piped water, flush toilets, picnic tables, and fire grills are provided. A boat launch is available. Facilities are wheelchair accessible. A grocery store, propane gas, and a coin laundry are nearby. Leashed pets are permitted.

Reservations, fees: No reservations; $13 per night. A free campfire permit is required. Open June through mid-October.

Contact: Stanislaus National Forest, Calaveras Ranger District, (209) 795-1381 or fax (209) 795-6849.

Directions: From Angels Camp, drive east on Highway 4 to Arnold and continue for 29 miles to Lake Alpine. Drive to the northeast end of the lake to the campground entrance on the right side of the road. Turn right and drive a half mile to the campground.

Trip notes: This is one of four camps at Lake Alpine. Silver Valley is on the northeast end of the lake at 7,400 feet in elevation, with a trailhead nearby that provides access to the Carson-Iceberg Wilderness. For recreation information, see the trip notes for Pine Marten (campground number six).

❽ Alpine Campground

Location: On Lake Alpine in Stanislaus National Forest; map E4, grid a2.

Campsites, facilities: There are five tent sites and 22 sites for RVs up to 22 feet long. Piped water, flush and vault toilets, showers, picnic tables, fire grills, and a boat launch are provided. A grocery store, propane gas, and a coin laundry are nearby. The facilities are wheelchair accessible. Leashed pets are permitted.

Reservations, fees: No reservations; $13 per night. Open June through October.

Contact: Stanislaus National Forest, Calaveras Ranger District, (209) 795-1381 or fax (209) 795-6849.

Directions: From Angels Camp, drive east on Highway 4 to Arnold and continue for 29 miles to Lake Alpine. Just before reaching the lake turn right and drive a quarter mile to the campground on the left.

Trip notes: This is the campground that is in the greatest demand at Lake Alpine, and it is easy to see why. It is very small, a boat ramp is located adjacent to the camp, you can get supplies at a small grocery store within walking distance, and during the evening rise you can often see the jumping trout from your campsite. Lake Alpine is one of the prettiest lakes you can drive to, set at 7,320 feet amid pines and Sierra granite. A trailhead out of nearby Silver Valley Camp provides a two-mile hike to pretty Duck Lake and beyond into the Carson-Iceberg Wilderness.

❾ Silver Tip

Location: Near Lake Alpine in Stanislaus National Forest; map E4, grid a2.

Campsites, facilities: There are 24 sites for tents or RVs up to 22 feet long. Piped water, flush toilets, picnic tables, and fire grills are provided. A boat launch is about a mile away. A grocery store, propane gas, and a coin laundry are nearby. Leashed pets are permitted.

Reservations, fees: No reservations; $13 per night.

Contact: Stanislaus National Forest, Calaveras Ranger District, (209) 795-1381 or fax (209) 795-6849.

Directions: From Angels Camp, drive east on Highway 4 to Arnold and continue for 29 miles to Lake Alpine. A mile before reaching the lake (adjacent to the Bear Valley/Mount Reba turnoff), turn right at the campground entrance on the right side of the road.

Trip notes: This camp is about two miles from the shore of Lake Alpine at an elevation of 7,300 feet. Why then would anyone camp here when there are campgrounds right at the lake? Two reasons: One, those lakeside camps are often full on summer weekends. Two, Highway 4 is snowplowed to this campground entrance, but not beyond. So in big snow years when the road is still closed in late spring and early summer, you can park your rig here to camp, then hike in to the lake. It also makes a good base camp for hunters. See the trip notes for Alpine Campground (campground number eight) for more information.

⑩ Upper and Lower Highland Lakes

Location: In Stanislaus National Forest; map E4, grid a3.

Campsites, facilities: There are 35 sites for tents or RVs. Piped water, vault toilets, picnic tables, and fire rings are provided. Leashed pets are permitted.

Reservations, fees: No reservations; $8 per night. Open mid-June through September.

Contact: Stanislaus National Forest, Calaveras Ranger District, (209) 795-1381 or fax (209) 795-6849.

Directions: From Angels Camp, drive east on Highway 4 to Arnold, past Lake Alpine, and continue for 14.5 miles to Forest Service Road 8N01 (one mile west of Ebbetts Pass). Turn right and drive 7.5 miles to the campground on the right side of the road. Trailers are not recommended.

Trip notes: This camp is set between Upper and Lower Highland Lakes, two beautiful alpine ponds that offer good fishing for small brook trout as well as spectacular panoramic views. Hiram Peak (9,760 feet) looms to the nearby south. A trail that starts at the north end of Highland Lakes (a parking area is available) is routed east for two miles to Wolf Creek Pass, where it connects with the Pacific Crest Trail; from there, turn left or right—you can't lose.

⑪ Cascade Creek

Location: In Stanislaus National Forest; map E4, grid b1.

Campsites, facilities: There are seven sites for tents or RVs up to 22 feet long. Picnic tables and pit toilets are provided. There is no piped water. Supplies are available in Dardanelle. Leashed pets are permitted.

Reservations, fees: No reservations; $0 to $5 per night. Open May through October.

Contact: Stanislaus National Forest, Summit Ranger District, (209) 965-3434 or fax (209) 965-3372.

Directions: From Sonora, drive east on Highway 108 to Strawberry and continue for eight miles to the campground on the left side of the road.

Trip notes: This tiny, rarely used spot along Cascade Creek is located at 6,000 feet in elevation. A Forest Service road, about a quarter mile west of camp on the south side of the highway, provides a side trip drive three miles up to Pikes Peak, at 7,236 feet.

⑫ Niagara Creek Off-Highway-Vehicle Camp

Location: In Stanislaus National Forest; map E4, grid b2.

Campsites, facilities: There are 10 sites for tents or RVs up to 22 feet long. Two double sites are available. Metal fire rings with adjustable grills and picnic tables are provided. Vault toilets are available. There is no piped water. A seasonal spring is nearby. Supplies can be purchased in Pinecrest about 10 miles away. Leashed pets are permitted.

Reservations, fees: No reservations; No fee. Open May through October, weather permitting.

Contact: Stanislaus National Forest, Summit Ranger District, (209) 965-3434 or fax (209) 965-3372.

Directions: From Sonora, drive east on Highway 108 to the town of Strawberry and continue for about 12 miles to Eagle Meadows Road/Forest Service Road 5N01 on the right. Turn right and drive a mile to the campground on the left.

Trip notes: This camp is set beside Niagara Creek at 6,600 feet, high in Stanislaus National Forest on the western slopes of the Sierra. It provides direct access to a network of backcountry roads in national forest, including routes to Double Dome Rock and another to Eagle Meadows. So if you have a four-wheel-drive vehicle or dirt bike, this is the place to come.

⑬ Niagara Creek

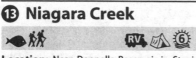

Location: Near Donnells Reservoir in Stanislaus National Forest; map E4, grid b2.

Campsites, facilities: There are nine sites for tents or RVs up to 22 feet long and three walk-in tent sites. Metal fire rings with adjustable grills and picnic tables are provided. Vault toilets are available. There is no piped water. Supplies can be purchased in Pinecrest about 10 miles away. Leashed pets are permitted.

Reservations, fees: No reservations; $5 per night, $2 per additional vehicle. Open May through October, weather permitting.

Contact: Stanislaus National Forest, Summit Ranger District, (209) 965-3434 or fax (209) 965-3372.

Directions: From Sonora, drive east on Highway 108 to Strawberry and continue for about 12 miles to Eagle Meadows Road/Forest Service Road 6N24 on the right. Turn right and drive a mile to the campground on the left.

Trip notes: This small, primitive camp, located adjacent to the preceding camp, was designed primarily for people with off-road vehicles.

⑭ Mill Creek Camp

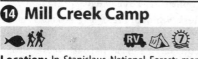

Location: In Stanislaus National Forest; map E4, grid b2.

Campsites, facilities: There are 17 sites for tents or RVs. Metal fire rings with adjustable

grills, picnic tables, vault toilets, and fire grills are provided. There is no piped water.

Reservations, fees: No reservations; $5 per night.

Contact: Stanislaus National Forest, Summit Ranger District, (209) 965-3434 or fax (209) 965-3372.

Directions: From Sonora, drive east on Highway 108 to Strawberry. From Strawberry continue east on Highway 108 about 11.5 miles; turn right on Forest Service Road 5N21 and drive 0.1 mile to the campground access road (Forest Service Road 5N26) on the left.

Trip notes: This pretty little camp is set at 6,200 feet in elevation, high in Stanislaus National Forest, near a variety of outdoor recreation options. The camp is near the Middle Fork Stanislaus River, which is stocked with trout near Donnells. For hiking there is an outstanding trailhead at Kennedy Meadow (east of Donnells). For fishing both Beardsley Reservoir (boat necessary) and Pinecrest Lake (shoreline prospects okay) provide two nearby alternatives.

⑮ Spicer Reservoir

Location: Near Spicer Reservoir in Stanislaus National Forest; map E4, grid b2.

Campsites, facilities: There are 60 family sites, two double-family sites, and a triple-family site, all suitable for tents or RVs. Piped water, vault toilets, phone, picnic tables, and fire grills are provided. Two sites are wheelchair accessible. A boat ramp is available nearby. Leashed pets are permitted.

Reservations, fees: No reservations; $10 per night.

Contact: Stanislaus National Forest, Calaveras Ranger District, (209) 795-1381 or fax (209) 795-6849. For a map send $4 to the USDA Forest Service, US Forest Map Sales, 1323 Club Drive, Vallejo, CA 94592.

Directions: From Angels Camp, drive east on Highway 4 for about 32 miles to Spicer Reservoir Road/Forest Service Road 7N01. Turn right, drive seven miles, bear right at a fork with a sharp right turn, and drive a mile to the campground at the west end of the lake.

Trip notes: Spicer Reservoir, set at 6,418 feet, isn't big by reservoir standards, covering 227 acres, but it is quite pretty from a boat and is surrounded by canyon walls. The beauty is compounded by good trout fishing, sometimes even excellent trout fishing. A boat ramp is available near the campground. A trail that leads around the reservoir has recently been completed. Note: This area can really get hammered with snow in big winters, so in the spring and early summer, always check for access conditions before planning a trip.

⑯ Fence Creek

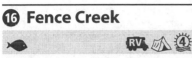

Location: Near the Middle Fork of the Stanislaus River in Stanislaus National Forest; map E4, grid b2.

Campsites, facilities: There are 34 sites for tents or RVs up to 22 feet long. Metal fire rings with adjustable grills and picnic tables are provided. Pit and vault toilets are available. There is no piped water. Supplies can be purchased in Pinecrest about 10 miles away. Leashed pets are permitted.

Reservations, fees: No reservations; $5 per night. Open May through October, weather permitting.

Contact: Stanislaus National Forest, Summit Ranger District, (209) 965-3434 or fax (209) 965-3372.

Directions: From Sonora, drive east on Highway 108 about 18 miles to Clark Ford Road. Turn left and drive a mile to Forest Service Road 6N06. Turn left again and drive a half mile to the campground on the right.

Trip notes: Fence Creek is a feeder stream to Clark Fork, which runs a mile downstream and joins with the Middle Fork Stanislaus River en route to Donnells Reservoir. The camp sits along little Fence Creek, 6,100 feet in elevation. Fence Creek Road continues east for another nine miles to an outstanding trailhead at Iceberg Meadow on the edge of the Carson-Iceberg Wilderness.

⑰ Pigeon Flat

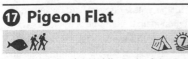

Location: On the Middle Fork of the Stanislaus River in Stanislaus National Forest; map E4, grid b3.

Campsites, facilities: There are seven walk-in tent sites. Metal fire rings with adjustable grills and picnic tables are provided, and a vault toilet is available. There is no piped water, so bring your own. Supplies can be purchased in Dardanelle. Leashed pets are permitted.

Reservations, fees: No reservations; $7 per night, $2 for an extra vehicle. Open May through October, weather permitting.

Contact: Stanislaus National Forest, Summit Ranger District, (209) 965-3434 or fax (209) 965-3372.

Directions: From Sonora, drive east on Highway 108 past the town of Strawberry to Dardanelle. Continue two miles east to the campground on the right side of the road, next to the Columns of the Giants Interpretive Site.

Trip notes: The prime attraction at Pigeon Flat is the short trail to Columns of the Giants, a rare example of columnar hexagonal rock, similar to the phenomenon at Devils Postpile near Mammoth Lakes. In addition, the camp is adjacent to the Middle Fork Stanislaus River; trout are small here and get fished hard. Supplies are available within walking distance in Dardanelle. The elevation is 6,000 feet.

⑱ Eureka Valley

Location: On the Middle Fork of the Stanislaus River in Stanislaus National Forest; map E4, grid b3.

Campsites, facilities: There are 27 sites for tents or RVs up to 22 feet long. Three hand pump wells, metal fire rings with adjustable grills, and picnic tables are provided. Vault toilets are available. Supplies can be purchased in Dardanelle. Pets are permitted.

Reservations, fees: No reservations; $10 per night, $2 for an extra vehicle. Open May through October, weather permitting.

Contact: Stanislaus National Forest, Summit Ranger District, (209) 965-3434 or fax (209) 965-3372.

Directions: From Sonora, drive east on Highway 108 past the town of Strawberry to Dardanelle. Continue three miles east to the campground on the right.

Trip notes: There are some half-dozen campgrounds on this stretch of the Middle Fork Stanislaus River near Dardanelle, at 6,100 feet in elevation. This stretch of river is planted with trout by the Department of Fish and Game, but it is hit pretty hard despite its relatively isolated location. A good short and easy hike is to Columns of the Giants, accessible on a quarter-mile-long trail out of Pigeon Flat, a mile to the west.

⑲ Boulder Flat

Location: Near the Middle Fork of the Stanislaus River in Stanislaus National Forest; map E4, grid b3.

Campsites, facilities: There are 23 sites for tents or RVs up to 22 feet long, plus a double site. Metal fire rings with adjustable grills and picnic tables are provided. Piped water and vault toilets are available. Supplies can be purchased in Dardanelle. Leashed pets are permitted.

Reservations, fees: No reservations; $10 per night, $2 for an extra vehicle. Open May through September.

Contact: Stanislaus National Forest, Summit Ranger District, (209) 965-3434 or fax (209) 965-3372.

Directions: From Sonora, drive east on Highway 108 past the town of Strawberry to Clark Fork Road. At Clark Fork Road, continue east on Highway 108 for a mile to the campground on the left side of the road.

Trip notes: You want camping on the Stanislaus River? Driving east on Highway 108, this is the first in a series of campgrounds along the Middle Fork Stanislaus. Boulder Flat is set at 5,600 feet and offers easy access off the highway. Here's another bonus: this stretch of river is stocked with trout.

⑳ Brightman Flat

Location: On the Middle Fork of the Stanislaus River in Stanislaus National Forest; map E4, grid b3.

Campsites, facilities: There are 33 sites for tents or RVs up to 22 feet long. Metal fire rings with adjustable grills and picnic tables are provided. Vault toilets are available. There is no piped water. Supplies can be purchased in Dardanelle. Leashed pets are permitted.

Reservations, fees: No reservations; $7 per night. Open May through October, weather permitting.

Contact: Stanislaus National Forest, Summit Ranger District, (209) 965-3434 or fax (209) 965-3372.

Directions: From Sonora, drive east on Highway 108 past the town of Strawberry to Clark Fork Road. At Clark Fork Road continue east on Highway 108 for two miles to the campground on the left side of the road.

Trip notes: This camp is located on the Middle Fork of the Stanislaus River at 5,600 feet elevation, a mile east of Boulder Flat (campground number 19) and two miles west of Dardanelle. For recreation options, see the trip notes for Pigeon Flat (campground number 17).

㉑ Dardanelle

Location: On the Middle Fork of the Stanislaus River in Stanislaus National Forest; map E4, grid b3.

Campsites, facilities: There are 28 sites for tents or RVs up to 22 feet long, plus three double sites. Piped water, metal fire rings with adjustable grills, and picnic tables are provided. Vault toilets are available. Supplies can be purchased in Dardanelle. Leashed pets are permitted.

Reservations, fees: No reservations; $12 per night for single sites, $16 per night for double sites, $2 for an extra vehicle. Open May through October, weather permitting.

Contact: Stanislaus National Forest, Summit Ranger District, (209) 965-3434 or fax (209) 965-3372.

Directions: From Sonora, drive east on Highway 108 past Strawberry to Dardanelle and the campground on the left side of the road.

Trip notes: This Forest Service camp is within walking distance of supplies in Dardanelle and is also located right alongside the Middle Fork

Stanislaus River. This section of river is stocked with trout by the Department of Fish and Game. The trail to see Columns of the Giants is just 1.5 miles to the east out of Pigeon Flat.

㉒ Sand Flat

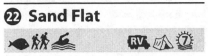

Location: On the Clark Fork of the Stanislaus River in Stanislaus National Forest; map E4, grid b4.

Campsites, facilities: There are 53 sites for tents or RVs and 15 walk-in sites. Metal fire rings with adjustable grills and picnic tables are provided. Six hand-pump wells and vault toilets are available. Supplies can be purchased in Dardanelle. Leashed pets are permitted.

Reservations, fees: No reservations; $7 per night per vehicle. Open May through September.

Contact: Stanislaus National Forest, Summit Ranger District, (209) 965-3434 or fax (209) 965-3372.

Directions: From Sonora, drive east on Highway 108 past the town of Strawberry to Clark Fork Road. Turn left on Clark Fork Road and drive six miles to the campground entrance on the right side of the road.

Trip notes: Sand Flat Campground, at 6,200 feet, is only three miles (by vehicle on Clark Fork Road) from an outstanding trailhead for the Carson-Iceberg Wilderness. The camp is used primarily by late-arriving backpackers who camp for the night, get their gear in order, then head off on the trail. The trail is routed out of Iceberg Meadow, with a choice of heading north to Paradise Valley (unbelievably green and loaded with corn lilies along a creek) and onward to the Pacific Crest Trail, or east to Clark Fork and upstream to Clark Fork Meadow below Sonora Peak. Two choices, both winners.

㉓ Baker

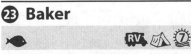

Location: On the Middle Fork of the Stanislaus River in Stanislaus National Forest; map E4, grid b4.

Campsites, facilities: There are 44 sites for tents or RVs up to 22 feet long. Piped water, fire grills, and picnic tables are provided. Vault toi-

lets are available. Supplies can be purchased in Dardanelle. Leashed pets are permitted.

Reservations, fees: No reservations; $9.50 per night, $4 for an extra vehicle. Open May to October, weather permitting.

Contact: Stanislaus National Forest, Summit Ranger District, (209) 965-3434 or fax (209) 965-3372.

Directions: From Sonora, drive east on Highway 108 past Strawberry to Dardanelle. From Dardanelle, continue six miles east to the campground on the right side of the road at the turnoff for Kennedy Meadow.

Trip notes: Baker lies at the turnoff for the well-known and popular Kennedy Meadow Trailhead for the Emigrant Wilderness. The camp is set along the Middle Fork Stanislaus River, 6,200 feet elevation, downstream a short ways from the confluence with Deadman Creek. The trailhead, with a nearby horse corral, is located another two miles farther on the Kennedy Meadow access road. From here it is a 1.5-mile hike to a fork in the trail; right will take you two miles to Relief Reservoir, 7,226 feet, and left will route you up Kennedy Creek for five miles to pretty Kennedy Lake, just north of Kennedy Peak (10,716 feet).

㉔ Clark Fork

Location: On the Clark Fork of the Stanislaus River in Stanislaus National Forest; map E4, grid b4.

Campsites, facilities: There are 88 sites for tents or RVs up to 22 feet long and a 14-site equestrian area with water troughs. Metal fire rings with adjustable grills and picnic tables are provided. Piped water, flush or vault toilets, and a sanitary disposal station are available. Some sites are wheelchair accessible. Supplies can be purchased in Dardanelle. Leashed pets are permitted.

Reservations, fees: No reservations; $10 to $11 per night for family sites, horse camp fee is $5 per night, $5 for an extra vehicle. Open May through October, weather permitting.

Contact: Stanislaus National Forest, Summit Ranger District, (209) 965-3434 or fax (209) 965-3372.

Directions: From Sonora, drive east on Highway 108 past the town of Strawberry to Clark Fork Road. Turn left, drive five miles, turn left again, and drive a half mile to the campground entrance on the right side of the road.

Trip notes: Clark Fork borders the Clark Fork of the Stanislaus River and is used both by drive-in vacationers and backpackers. A trailhead for hikers is located a quarter mile away on the north side of Clark Fork Road (a parking area is available here). From here the trail is routed up along Arnot Creek, skirting between Iceberg Peak on the left and Lightning Mountain on the right, for eight miles to Wolf Creek Pass and the junction with the Pacific Crest Trail. For another nearby trailhead, see the trip notes for Sand Flat (campground number 22).

25 Deadman

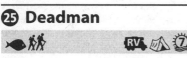

Location: On the Middle Fork of the Stanislaus River in Stanislaus National Forest; map E4, grid b4.

Campsites, facilities: There are 17 sites for tents or RVs up to 22 feet long. Piped water, fire grills, and picnic tables are provided. Flush and vault toilets are available. Supplies can be purchased in Dardanelle. Pets are permitted.

Reservations, fees: No reservations; $9.50 per night, $4 for an extra vehicle.

Contact: Stanislaus National Forest, Summit Ranger District, (209) 965-3434 or fax (209) 965-3372.

Directions: From Sonora, drive east on Highway 108 past the town of Strawberry to Dardanelle. From Dardanelle, continue six miles east to the Kennedy Meadow turnoff. Drive a mile on Kennedy Meadow Road to the campground, which is opposite the parking area for the Kennedy Meadow Trail.

Trip notes: This is a popular trailhead camp and an ideal jump-off point for backpackers heading into the adjacent Emigrant Wilderness. The camp is located a short distance from Baker; see the trip notes for campground number 23 for hiking destinations.

26 Spicer Reservoir Group Camp

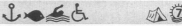

Location: Near Spicer Reservoir in Stanislaus National Forest; map E4, grid a2.

Campsites, facilities: There is one group site that can accommodate up to 50 people. Piped water, vault toilets, picnic tables, fire grills, food preparation area, primitive amphitheater, and a group parking area are provided. A boat ramp is available a mile away. Some facilities are wheelchair accessible. Leashed pets are permitted.

Reservations, fees: Reservations are required; phone (877) 444-6777 ($8.65 reservation fee); $90 per night.

Contact: Stanislaus National Forest, Calaveras Ranger District, (209) 795-1381 or fax (209) 795-6849. For a map, send $4 to the USDA Forest Service, US Forest Map Sales, 1323 Club Drive, Vallejo, CA 94592.

Directions: From Angels Camp, drive east on Highway 4 for about 32 miles to Spicer Reservoir Road/Forest Service Road 7N01. Turn right, drive seven miles, bear right at a fork with a sharp right turn, and drive a mile to the campground at the west end of the lake.

Trip notes: Set at 6,418 feet, Spicer Reservoir isn't big by reservoir standards, covering only 227 acres, but it is quite pretty from a boat and is surrounded by canyon walls. The beauty is compounded by good trout fishing. A boat ramp is available near the campground. A trail that leads around the reservoir has recently been completed. Note: This area can really get hammered with snow in big winters, so in the spring and early summer, always check for access conditions before planning a trip.

27 Sonora Bridge

Location: Near the Walker River in Humboldt-Toiyabe National Forests; map E4, grid b7.

Campsites, facilities: There are 23 sites for tents or RVs up to 40 feet long. Piped water, fire grills, and picnic tables are provided. Vault toilets are available. Leashed pets are permitted.

Reservations, fees: Reserve via phone at (877) 444-6777, ($8.65 reservation fee); $9 per night. Open May through mid-October.

Contact: Humboldt-Toiyabe National Forests, Bridgeport Ranger District, (760) 932-7070 or fax (760) 932-1299.

Directions: From north of Bridgeport, at the junction of US 395 and Highway 108, turn west on Highway 108 and drive two miles to the campground.

Trip notes: The West Walker River is a pretty stream, flowing over boulders and into pools, and each year this stretch of river is well stocked with rainbow trout by the Department of Fish and Game. One of several campgrounds located near the West Walker, Sonora Bridge is set at 6,800 feet, about a half mile from the river. The setting is in the transition zone from high mountains to high desert on the eastern edge of the Sierra Nevada.

㉘ Chris Flat

Location: On the Walker River in Humboldt-Toiyabe National Forests; map E4, grid b7.

Campsites, facilities: There are 15 sites for tents or RVs up to 40 feet long. Piped water, fire grills, and picnic tables are provided. Vault toilets are available. Leashed pets are permitted.

Reservations, fees: No reservations; $9 per night. Open May through October.

Contact: Humboldt-Toiyabe National Forests, Bridgeport Ranger District, (760) 932-7070 or fax (760) 932-1299.

Directions: From Carson City, drive south on US 395 to Coleville and then continue south for 15 miles to the campground on the east side of the road (located four miles north of the junction of US 395 and Highway 108).

Trip notes: This is one of two campgrounds set along US 395 next to the West Walker River, a pretty trout stream with easy access and good stocks of rainbow trout. The plants are usually made at two campgrounds, resulting in good prospects here at Chris Flat, and west on Highway 108 at Sonora Bridge (campground number 27). The elevation is 6,600 feet.

㉙ Bootleg

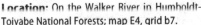

Location: On the Walker River in Humboldt-Toiyabe National Forests; map E4, grid b8.

Campsites, facilities: There are 63 paved sites for tents or RVs up to 45 feet long. Piped water, fire grills, and picnic tables are provided. Flush toilets are available. Leashed pets are permitted.

Reservations, fees: Reserve via phone at (877) 444-6777 ($8.65 reservation fee) or website www.reserveusa.com; $9 per night. Open mid-May to mid-September.

Contact: Humboldt-Toiyabe National Forests, Bridgeport Ranger District, (760) 932-7070.

Directions: From Carson City, drive south on US 395 to Coleville and then continue south for 13 miles to the campground on the west side of the highway (located six miles north of the junction of US 395 and Highway 108).

Trip notes: Location is always a key, and easy access off US 395, the adjacent West Walker River, and good trout stocks in summer make this a popular spot. See the trip notes for Chris Flat (campground number 28) and Sonora Bridge (campground number 27) for more information. Note that this camp is on the west side of the highway, and that anglers will have to cross the road in order to gain fishing access (which makes Chris Flat a better choice). The elevation is 6,600 feet.

㉚ Meadowview

Location: Near Pinecrest Lake in Stanislaus National Forest; map E4, grid c1.

Campsites, facilities: There are 100 sites for tents or RVs up to 22 feet long. Piped water, fire grills, and picnic tables are provided. Flush toilets and equestrian facilities are available. A grocery store, coin laundry, boat ramp, pay showers (in summer months only), and propane gas are nearby. Leashed pets are permitted.

Reservations, fees: No reservations; $12.50 per night. Open May to October.

Contact: Stanislaus National Forest, Summit

Ranger District, (209) 965-3434 or fax (209) 965-3372.

Directions: From Sonora, drive east on Highway 108 for about 25 miles to the town of Strawberry and the signed road for Pinecrest Lake. Turn right at the sign and drive a half mile to Pinecrest/Dodge Ridge Road. Turn right and drive about 100 yards to the campground entrance on the left side of the road.

Trip notes: No secret here, folks. This camp is located one mile from Pinecrest Lake, a popular weekend vacation area (and there's a trail that connects the camp with the town). Pinecrest Lake is set at 5,621 feet, covers 300 acres, is stocked with rainbow trout, and has a 20 mph speed limit for boaters. This is a family-oriented vacation center, and a popular walk is the easy hike around the lake. If you want something more ambitious, there is a cutoff on the north side of the lake that is routed one mile up to little Catfish Lake. The Dodge Ridge Ski Area is nearby, with many privately owned cabins in the area.

③① Pioneer Trail Group Camp

Location: Near Pinecrest Lake in Stanislaus National Forest; map E4, grid c1.

Campsites, facilities: There are three group sites here. Piped water, picnic tables, and fire grills are provided. Vault toilets are available. A grocery store, coin laundry, boat ramp, pay showers (in summer months only), and propane gas are nearby. Leashed pets are permitted.

Reservations, fees: Reserve via phone at (877) 444-6777 ($8.65 reservation fee) or website www.reserveusa.com; $50 to $65 group fee per night. Open April to October, weather permitting.

Contact: Stanislaus National Forest, Summit Ranger District, (209) 965-3434 or fax (209) 965-3372.

Directions: From Sonora, drive east on Highway 108 for about 25 miles to the town of Strawberry and the signed road for Pinecrest Lake. Turn right at the sign and drive a very short distance to the signed road for Pinecrest/Dodge Ridge. Turn right and drive about a mile to the

campground entrance on the left.

Trip notes: If you're going to Pinecrest Lake with a Scout troop, this is the spot since it is set up specifically for groups. You get beautiful creek and canyon views. For recreation information, see the trip notes for nearby Meadowview (campground number 30).

③② Pinecrest

Location: Near Pinecrest Lake in Stanislaus National Forest; map E4, grid c1.

Campsites, facilities: There are 200 sites for tents or RVs up to 22 feet long. Piped water, picnic tables, and metal fire rings with adjustable grills are provided. Vault toilets are available, and there are two winterized rest rooms with flush toilets and sinks. A grocery store, coin laundry, pay showers (in summer months only), equestrian facilities, boat ramp, and propane gas are nearby. Leashed pets are permitted.

Reservations, fees: No reservations; $15 per night. Open April to October, weather permitting.

Contact: Stanislaus National Forest, Summit Ranger District, (209) 965-3434 or fax (209) 965-3372.

Directions: From Sonora, drive east on Highway 108 for about 25 miles. Turn right at the sign for Pinecrest Lake. Go about 100 yards past the turnoff for Pinecrest and turn right on the access road for Pinecrest Camp.

Trip notes: This monster-sized Forest Service camp is set near Pinecrest Lake. In early summer, there is good fishing for stocked rainbow trout. A launch ramp is available, and a 20 mph speed limit is enforced on the lake. A trail circles the lake and also branches off to nearby Catfish Lake. The elevation is 5,800 feet. Winter camping is allowed near the Pinecrest Day-Use Area.

③③ Leavitt Meadows

Location: On the Walker River in Humboldt-Toiyabe National Forests; map E4, grid c6.

Campsites, facilities: There are 16 sites for tents or RVs up to 40 feet long. Piped water, fire grills, and picnic tables are provided. Vault toilets are available. Leashed pets are permitted.

Reservations, fees: No reservations; $9 per night. Open mid-April to mid-October, weather permitting.

Contact: Humboldt-Toiyabe National Forests, Bridgeport Ranger District, (760) 932-7070 or fax (760) 932-1299.

Directions: From the junction of Highway 108 and US 395 north of Bridgeport, turn west on Highway 108 and drive seven miles to the campground on the left side of the road.

Trip notes: While Leavitt Meadows sits right aside Highway 108, a little winding two-laner, there are several nearby off-pavement destinations that make this camp a winner. The camp is set in the high eastern Sierra, east of Sonora Pass at 7,000 feet in elevation, where Leavitt Creek and Brownie Creek enter the West Walker River. There is a pack station for horseback riding nearby. The most popular side trip is driving four miles west on Highway 108, then turning south and driving four miles to Leavitt Lake, where the trout fishing is sometimes spectacular, trolling a gold Cripplure.

㉞ Obsidian

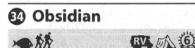

Location: On Molybdenite Creek in Humboldt-Toiyabe National Forests; map E4, grid c8.

Campsites, facilities: There are 14 sites for tents or RVs up to 30 feet long. Fire grills and picnic tables are provided. Vault toilets are available. There is no piped water, so bring your own. Leashed pets are permitted.

Reservations, fees: No reservations; $5 per night. Open early June to mid-October.

Contact: Humboldt-Toiyabe National Forests, Bridgeport Ranger District, (760) 932-7070.

Directions: At the junction of US 395 and Highway 108 (12 miles north of Bridgeport), drive south a short distance on US 395 to an improved dirt road and a sign that says "Forest Service Campground." Turn west and drive four miles to the campground.

Trip notes: This primitive, little-known camp at 7,800 feet in elevation is set up for backpackers, with an adjacent trailhead providing a jump-

off point into the wilderness. The trail here is routed up the Molybdenite Creek drainage and into the Hoover Wilderness.

㉟ Fraser Flat

Location: On the South Fork of the Stanislaus River in Stanislaus National Forest; map E4, grid d0.

Campsites, facilities: There are 32 sites for tents or RVs up to 22 feet long. Piped water, picnic tables, and fire grills are provided. Vault toilets are available. A grocery store and propane gas are nearby. A camping and fishing site for wheelchair use is provided. Leashed pets are permitted.

Reservations, fees: No reservations; $9 per night. Open May through October.

Contact: Stanislaus National Forest, Mi-Wok Ranger District, (209) 586-3234 or fax (209) 586-0643.

Directions: From Sonora, drive east on Highway 108 to Long Barn. Continue east for six miles to the campground entrance road on the left. Turn left and drive two miles to the campground on the left side of the road.

Trip notes: This camp is set along the South Fork of the Stanislaus River. If the fish aren't biting, a seven-mile side trip via Forest Service roads will route you north into the main canyon of the Middle Fork Stanislaus. A map of Stanislaus National Forest is required for this adventure. Fraser Flat also provides an overflow area if the camps at nearby Pinecrest Lake near Strawberry are filled.

㊱ Hull Creek

Location: In Stanislaus National Forest; map E4, grid d0.

Campsites, facilities: There are 20 sites for tents or RVs up to 22 feet long. Picnic tables and stoves are provided. Piped water and vault toilets are available. Leashed pets are permitted.

Reservations, fees: No reservations; $5 per night. Open May through October, weather permitting.

Contact: Stanislaus National Forest, Mi-Wok Ranger District, (209) 586-3234 or fax (209) 586-0643.

Directions: From Sonora, drive east on Highway 108 to Long Barn. Turn right and drive nine miles east on Road 31/Road 3N01 to the campground on the left side of the road.

Trip notes: This obscure camp borders little Hull Creek (too small for trout fishing), at 5,600 feet elevation in Stanislaus National Forest. This is a good spot for those wishing to test out four-wheel-drive vehicles, with an intricate set of Forest Service roads available to the east. To explore that area, a map of Stanislaus National Forest is essential.

③⑦ Buckeye

Location: Near Buckeye Creek in Humboldt-Toiyabe National Forests; map E4, grid d8.

Campsites, facilities: There are 65 paved sites for tents or RVs up to 30 feet long. There is one group site available. Piped water, fire grills, and picnic tables are provided. Flush toilets are available. Leashed pets are permitted.

Reservations, fees: Group site reservations are available via phone at (877) 444-6777 ($8.65 reservation fee) or website www.reserveus.com; $35 per night. No reservations for individual sites; $9 per night. Open mid-April to mid-October.

Contact: Humboldt-Toiyabe National Forests, Bridgeport Ranger District, (760) 932-7070.

Directions: On US 395, drive to Bridgeport and the junction with Twin Lakes Road. Turn west and drive seven miles to Buckeye Road. Turn north on Buckeye Road (dirt, often impassable when wet) and drive 3.5 miles to the campground.

Trip notes: Here's a little secret: A two-mile hike out of camp heads to Buckeye Hot Springs, an undeveloped hot springs. That is what inspires campers to bypass the fishing at nearby Robinson Creek (three miles away) and Twin Lakes (six miles away). The camp feels remote and primitive, set at 7,000 feet on the eastern slope of the Sierra near Buckeye Creek. Another secret is that brook trout are planted at the little bridge that crosses Buckeye Creek near the campground. A trail that starts near camp is routed through Buckeye Canyon and into the Hoover Wilderness.

③⑧ Honeymoon Flat

Location: On Robinson Creek in Humboldt-Toiyabe National Forests; map E4, grid d8.

Campsites, facilities: There are 35 sites for tents or RVs up to 45 feet long. Piped water, fire grills, and picnic tables are provided. Vault toilets are available. Leashed pets are permitted.

Reservations, fees: Reserve via phone at (877) 444-6777 ($8.65 reservation fee) or website www.reserveusa.com; $9 per night. Open mid-April through October.

Contact: Humboldt-Toiyabe National Forests, Bridgeport Ranger District, (760) 932-7070 or fax (760) 932-1299.

Directions: On US 395, drive to Bridgeport and the junction with Twin Lakes Road. Turn west and drive eight miles to the campground.

Trip notes: The camp is set aside Robinson Creek at 7,000 feet in elevation, in the transition zone between the Sierra Nevada range to the west and the high desert to the east. It is easy to reach, located on the access road to Twin Lakes, only three miles farther. The lake is famous for occasional huge brown trout. However, the fishing at Robinson Creek is also often quite good, thanks to the more than 50,000 trout planted each year by the Department of Fish and Game.

③⑨ Paha

Location: Near Twin Lakes in Humboldt-Toiyabe National Forests; map E4, grid d8.

Campsites, facilities: There are 22 paved sites for tents or RVs up to 40 feet long. Piped water, fire grills, and picnic tables are provided. Flush toilets are available. A boat launch, store, showers, and a coin laundry are available nearby. Leashed pets are permitted.

Reservations, fees: Reserve via phone at (877) 444-6777 ($8.65 reservation fee) or website www.reserveusa.com; $10 per night. Open mid-April to mid-October, weather permitting.

Contact: Humboldt-Toiyabe National Forests,

Bridgeport Ranger District, (760) 932-7070 or fax (760) 932-1299.

Directions: On US 395, drive to Bridgeport and the junction with Twin Lakes Road. Turn west and drive 10 miles to the campground.

Trip notes: This is one in a series of camps near Robinson Creek and within close range of Twin Lakes. The elevation at the camp is 7,000 feet. See the trip notes for Lower Twin Lake (campground number 42) and Honeymoon Flat (campground number 38) for more information.

④ Robinson Creek

Location: Near Twin Lakes in Humboldt-Toiyabe National Forests; map E4, grid d8.

Campsites, facilities: There are 54 paved sites for tents or RVs up to 45 feet long. Piped water, fire grills, and picnic tables are provided. There is also an amphitheater. Flush and vault toilets are available. Leashed pets are permitted.

Reservations, fees: Reserve via phone at (877) 444-6777 ($8.65 reservation fee) or website www.reserveusa.com; $10 per night. Open mid-April through October.

Contact: Humboldt-Toiyabe National Forests, Bridgeport Ranger District, (760) 932-7070 or fax (760) 932-1299.

Directions: On US 395, drive to Bridgeport and the junction with Twin Lakes Road. Turn west and drive 10 miles to the campground.

Trip notes: This campground, one of a series in the area, is set at 7,000 feet on Robinson Creek, not far from Twin Lakes. For recreation options, see the trip note for Lower Twin Lake (campground number 42) and Honeymoon Flat (campground number 38).

④ Crags Campground

Location: On Robinson Creek in Humboldt-Toiyabe National Forests; map E4, grid d8.

Campsites, facilities: There are 27 sites for tents or RVs up to 45 feet long. Picnic tables and fire grills are provided. Piped water, flush toilets, and lighted bathrooms are available. The campground is wheelchair accessible. A boat launch

(at Lower Twin Lake), store, a coin laundry, and showers are located within a half mile. Leashed pets are permitted.

Reservations, fees: No reservations; $9 per night.

Contact: Humboldt-Toiyabe National Forests, Bridgeport Ranger District, (760) 932-7070 or fax (760) 932-1299.

Directions: On US 395, drive to Bridgeport and the junction with Twin Lakes Road. Turn west and drive 11 miles to a road on the left (just before reaching Lower Twin Lake). Turn left and drive over the bridge at Robinson Creek to another road on the left. Turn left and drive a short distance to the campground.

Trip notes: Crags Camp is set at 7,000 feet in the Sierra, one of a series of campgrounds along Robinson Creek near Lower Twin Lake. While this camp does not offer direct access to Lower Twin, home of giant brown trout, it is very close. See the trip notes for Lower Twin Lake (campground number 42) and Honeymoon Flat (campground number 38).

④ Lower Twin Lake

Location: In Humboldt-Toiyabe National Forests; map E4, grid d8.

Campsites, facilities: There are 15 paved sites for tents or RVs up to 40 feet long. Piped water, fire grills, and picnic tables are provided. Flush toilets are available. A boat launch, store, showers, and a coin laundry are available nearby. Leashed pets are permitted.

Reservations, fees: Reserve via phone at (877) 444-6777 ($8.65 reservation fee) or website www.reserveusa.com; $10 per night. Open mid-April to mid-October, weather permitting.

Contact: Humboldt-Toiyabe National Forests, Bridgeport Ranger District, (760) 932-7070 or fax (760) 932-1299.

Directions: On US 395, drive to Bridgeport and the junction with Twin Lakes Road. Turn west and drive 11 miles to the campground.

Trip notes: The Twin Lakes are actually two lakes, of course, set high in the eastern Sierra at 7,000 feet. The best of the two is Lower Twin, where a full resort, marina, boat ramp, and some of the biggest brown trout in the West can be found. The state record brown was caught here, 26.5 pounds and, in 1991, 11-year-old Micah Beirle of Bakersfield caught one that weighed 20.5 pounds, one of the great fish catches by a youngster anywhere in America. Of course, most of the trout are your typical 10- to 12-inch planted rainbow trout, but nobody seems to mind, with the chance of a true monster-sized fish always in the back of the minds of anglers. An option for campers is an excellent trailhead for hiking near Mono Village at the head of Upper Twin Lake. Here you will find the Barney Lake Trail, which is routed up the headwaters of Robinson Creek, steeply at times, to little Barney Lake, an excellent day hike.

㊸ Cherry Valley

Location: On Cherry Lake in Stanislaus National Forest; map E4, grid e1.

Campsites, facilities: There are 46 sites for tents or RVs of any length. Piped water (only in summer months), picnic tables, and fire grills are provided. Vault toilets are available. A boat ramp is nearby. Leashed pets are permitted.

Reservations, fees: No reservations; $10 per night, $20 for double sites. Open April through October.

Contact: Stanislaus National Forest, Groveland Ranger District, (209) 962-7825 or fax (209) 962-6406.

Directions: From Groveland, drive east on Highway 120 for about 15 miles to Forest Service Road 1N07/Cherry Valley Road on the left side of the road. Turn left and drive 18 miles to the south end of Cherry Lake and the campground access road on the right. Turn right and drive one mile to the campground.

Trip notes: Cherry Lake is a mountain lake surrounded by national forest at 4,700 feet in elevation, just outside the western boundary of Yosemite National Park. It is much larger than most people anticipate and provides much better trout fishing than anything in Yosemite. The camp is on the southwest shore of the lake, a very pretty spot, about a mile ride to the boat launch on the west side of the Cherry Valley Dam. The lake is bordered to the east by Kibbie

Ridge; just on the other side is Yosemite Park and Lake Eleanor.

㊹ Trumbull Lake

Location: In Humboldt-Toiyabe National Forests; map E4, grid e9.

Campsites, facilities: There are 45 sites for tents or RVs up to 45 feet long. Piped water, fire grills, and picnic tables are provided. Vault toilets are available. A store is nearby at the resort. Leashed pets are permitted.

Reservations, fees: Reserve via phone at (877) 444-6777 ($8.65 reservation fee) or website www.reserveusa.com; $9 per night. Open mid-June to mid-October, weather permitting.

Contact: Humboldt-Toiyabe National Forests, Bridgeport Ranger District, (760) 932-7070 or fax (760) 932-1299.

Directions: From Bridgeport, drive south on US 395 for 13.5 miles to Virginia Lakes Road. Turn right on Virginia Lakes Road and drive 6.5 miles to the campground entrance road.

Trip notes: This is a high-mountain camp (9,600 feet) at the gateway to a beautiful Sierra basin. Little Trumbull Lake is the first lake on the north side of Virginia Lakes Road, with Virginia Lakes set nearby, along with the Hoover Wilderness and access to many other small lakes by trail. A trail is available that is routed just north of Blue Lake, then leads west to Frog Lake, Summit Lake, and beyond into a remote area of Yosemite National Park. If you don't want to rough it, cabins, boat rentals, and a restaurant are available at Virginia Lakes Resort.

㊺ Green Creek

Location: In Humboldt-Toiyabe National Forests; map E4, grid e9.

Campsites, facilities: There are 11 sites for tents or RVs up to 22 feet long and two group sites that can accommodate 20 and 25 people, respectively. Piped water, fire grills, and picnic tables are provided. Vault toilets are available. Pets are permitted.

Reservations, fees: Group site fees and reservations can be obtained via phone at (877) 444-6777 ($8.65 reservation fee) or website www.reserveusa.com; $9 per night per individual site. Open mid-May to early October, weather permitting.

Contact: Humboldt-Toiyabe National Forests, Bridgeport Ranger District, (760) 932-7070 or fax (760) 932-1299.

Directions: From Bridgeport, drive south on US 395 for four miles to Green Lakes Road (dirt). Turn right and drive seven miles to the campground.

Trip notes: This camp is ideal for backpackers or campers who like to fish for trout in streams. That is because it is set at 7,500 feet, with a trailhead that leads into the Hoover Wilderness and to several high mountain lakes, including Green Lake, West Lake, and East Lake; the ambitious can hike beyond in remote northeastern Yosemite National Park. The camp is set along Green Creek, a fair trout stream with small rainbow trout.

⑯ Lumsden

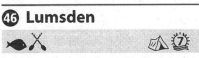

Location: On the Tuolumne River in Stanislaus National Forest; map E4, grid f0.

Campsites, facilities: There are 11 tent sites. Picnic tables and fire grills are provided. Vault toilets are available. There is no piped water. Leashed pets are permitted.

Reservations, fees: No reservations; no fee. Open April through October.

Contact: Stanislaus National Forest, Groveland Ranger District, (209) 962-7825 or fax (209) 962-6406.

Directions: From Groveland, drive east on Highway 120 for about eight miles (just under a mile beyond County Road J132) to a dirt road on the left side of the highway. Turn left and drive to a Forest Service road intersection. Jog left, then right, and continue for four miles to the camp on the right side of the road.

Trip notes: This is one of the great access points for white-water rafting on the wild and scenic Tuolumne River and its premium stretch between Hetch Hetchy Reservoir in Yosemite and Don Pedro Reservoir in the Central Valley foothills. Unless you are an expert rafter, you are advised to attempt running this stretch of river

only with a professional rafting company. The camp is set at 1,500 feet, just across the road from the river. The access road down the canyon is steep and bumpy. There are two other camps within a mile, South Fork and Lumsden Bridge.

⑰ Lumsden Bridge

Location: On the Tuolumne River in Stanislaus National Forest; map E4, grid f0.

Campsites, facilities: There are nine tent sites. Picnic tables and fire grills are provided. Vault toilets are available. There is no piped water. Leashed pets are permitted.

Reservations, fees: No reservations; no fee.

Contact: Stanislaus National Forest, Groveland Ranger District, (209) 962-7825 or fax (209) 962-6406.

Directions: From Groveland, drive east on Highway 120 for about eight miles (just under a mile beyond County Road J132) to a dirt road on the left side of the highway. Turn left and drive to a Forest Service road intersection. Jog left, then right, and continue for 5.5 miles to the campground on the left side of the road.

Trip notes: This is one of three camps along this immediate stretch of the Tuolumne River, one of the best white-water rafting rivers in California. The camp is set at 1,500 feet on the north side of the river, accessible just after crossing the Lumsden Bridge, hence the name. See the trip notes for Lumsden (campground number 46) for more information.

⑱ South Fork

Location: Near the Tuolumne River in Stanislaus National Forest; map E4, grid f0.

Campsites, facilities: There are eight tent sites. Picnic tables and fire grills are provided. Vault toilets are available. There is no piped water. Leashed pets are permitted.

Reservations, fees: No reservations; no fee. Open April through October.

Contact: Stanislaus National Forest, Groveland Ranger District, (209) 962-7825 or fax (209) 962-6406.

Directions: From Groveland, drive east on Highway 120 for about eight miles (just under a mile beyond County Road J132) to a dirt road on the left side of the highway. Turn left and drive to a Forest Service road intersection. Jog left, then right, and continue for five miles to the camp on the right side of the road.

Trip notes: South Fork Camp is located a half mile upstream from Lumsden and about a mile downstream from Lumsden Bridge (campground numbers 46 and 47). Why do we say "upstream" and "downstream" instead of east and west? Because this is a camp for white-water rafters, featuring the spectacular Tuolumne River and access to its most exciting stretches. You should only attempt to run this river with a professional rafting company. The elevation is 1,500 feet.

㊾ Lost Claim

Location: Near the Tuolumne River in Stanislaus National Forest; map E4, grid f0.

Campsites, facilities: There are 10 sites for tents or small RVs. Picnic tables and fire grills are provided. Vault toilets and hand-pumped well water are available. A grocery store is nearby. Leashed pets are permitted.

Reservations, fees: No reservations; $8 per night. Open May through Labor Day.

Contact: Stanislaus National Forest, Groveland Ranger District, (209) 962-7825 or fax (209) 962-6406.

Directions: From Groveland, drive east on Highway 120 for 14 miles (1.5 miles past the Buck Meadows Ranger Station) to the campground on left side of the road.

Trip notes: This is one in a series of easy-access camps off Highway 120 that provide overflow areas when all the sites are taken in Yosemite National Park to the east. A feeder stream to the Tuolumne River runs by the camp. The elevation is 3,100 feet.

㊿ Sweetwater

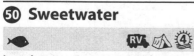

Location: Near the South Fork of the Tuolumne River in Stanislaus National Forest; map E4, grid g0.

Campsites, facilities: There are 13 sites for tents or RVs up to 22 feet long. Piped water, picnic tables, and fire grills are provided. Vault toilets are available. A grocery store is nearby. Leashed pets are permitted.

Reservations, fees: No reservations; $9 per night. Open April through October.

Contact: Stanislaus National Forest, Groveland Ranger District, (209) 962-7825 or fax (209) 962-6406.

Directions: From Groveland, drive east on Highway 120 for about 18 miles (four miles past the Buck Meadows Ranger Station) to the campground on the left side of the road.

Trip notes: This camp is set at 3,000 feet, near the South Fork Tuolumne River, one of several camps along Highway 120 that provides a safety valve for campers who can't find space in Yosemite National Park to the east.

(51) Dimond "O"

Location: In Stanislaus National Forest; map E4, grid g2.

Campsites, facilities: There are 38 sites suitable for trailers and RVs up to 33 feet long. Piped water and fire grills are provided. Vault toilets are available. Leashed pets are permitted.

Reservations, fees: No reservations; $11 per night. Open April through October.

Contact: Stanislaus National Forest, Groveland Ranger District, (209) 962-7825 or fax (209) 962-6406.

Directions: From Groveland, drive east on Highway 120 for 25 miles. Turn left on Evergreen Road and drive six miles to the campground.

Trip notes: Dimond "O" is set at 4,400 feet in elevation on the eastern side of Stanislaus National Forest—just two miles from the Yosemite National Park border.

(52) Saddlebag Lake

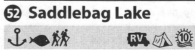

Location: In Inyo National Forest; map E4, grid f8.

Campsites, facilities: There are 20 sites for

tents or RVs up to 22 feet long. One group site can accommodate up to 25 people. Piped water, fire grills, and picnic tables are provided. Vault toilets, boat rentals, and a boat launch are available. A grocery store is nearby. Leashed pets are permitted.

Reservations, fees: Reservations for the group site only are accepted via phone at (877) 444-6777 ($8.65 reservation fee) or website www.reserveusa .com; $11 per night for single sites, $20 per night for the group site. Open July through September.

Contact: Inyo National Forest, Mono Lake Ranger District, (760) 647-3000 or fax (760) 647-3027.

Directions: On US 395, drive to just south of Lee Vining and the junction with Highway 120. Turn west and drive about 11 miles to Saddlebag Lake Road. Turn right and drive three miles to the campground.

From Merced, turn east on Highway 140, drive into Yosemite National Park, and continue toward Yosemite Valley to the junction with Highway 120. Turn north and drive about 65 miles through the Tioga Pass entrance station. Continue three miles to Saddlebag Lake Road. Turn left and drive three miles to the campground.

Trip notes: This camp is set in spectacular high country above tree line, the highest drive-to camp and lake in California, with Saddlebag Lake at 10,087 feet. The camp is about a quarter mile from the lake, within walking range of the little store, boat rentals, and a one-minute drive for launching a boat at the ramp. The scenery is stark, everything is granite, ice, or water, with only a few white bark and lodgepole pines managing precarious toeholds, sprinkled across the landscape on the access road. An excellent trailhead is available for hiking, with the best hike routed out past little Hummingbird Lake to Lundy Pass.

⑤③ Junction

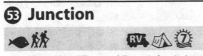

Location: Near Ellery and Tioga Lakes in Inyo National Forest; map E4, grid g8.

Campsites, facilities: There are 13 sites for tents or RVs up to 22 feet long. Fire grills and picnic tables are provided. Vault toilets are available. There is no piped water, so bring your own.

Leashed pets are permitted.

Reservations, fees: No reservations; $6 per night. Open June to October.

Contact: Inyo National Forest, Mono Lake Ranger District, (760) 647-3000 or fax (760) 647-3027.

Directions: On US 395, drive to just south of Lee Vining and the junction with Highway 120. Turn west on highway 120 and drive about 10 miles to Saddlebag Road and the campground on the right side of the road.

From Merced, turn east on Highway 140, drive into Yosemite National Park, and continue toward Yosemite Valley to the junction with Highway 120/Tioga Road. Turn north and drive about 65 miles through the Tioga Pass entrance station. Continue four miles to Saddlebag Road and the campground on the left side of the road.

Trip notes: Which way do you go? From Junction any way you choose, you can't miss. Two miles to the north is Saddlebag Lake, the highest drive-to lake (10,087 feet) in California. Directly across the road is Ellery Lake, and a mile to the south is Tioga Lake, two beautiful pristine waters with trout fishing. To the east is Mono Lake, and to the west is Yosemite National Park. Take your pick. Camp elevation is 9,600 feet.

⑤④ Lower Lee Vining Camp

Location: Near Lee Vining; map E4, grid g9.

Campsites, facilities: There are 60 sites for tents or RVs up to 40 feet long in four separate campgrounds located next to each other. Pit and portable toilets are available. There is no piped water. Supplies can be purchased in Lee Vining (about two miles away). Leashed pets are permitted.

Reservations, fees: No reservations; $7 per night. Open May through October.

Contact: Mono County Building and Parks Department, (760) 932-5231.

Directions: On US 395, drive to just south of Lee Vining and the junction with Highway 120. Turn west on Highway 120 and drive about 2.5 miles. Turn left into the campground entrance.

Trip notes: This camp and its neighboring camps—Cattleguard, Moraine, and Boulder—can be a godsend for vacationers who show up at Yosemite National Park and make the discovery that there are no sites left, a terrible experience for some late-night arrivals. But these county campgrounds provide a great safety valve, even if they are extremely primitive, in an edge-of-desert environment. Lee Vining Creek is the highlight, flowing right past the campgrounds, along Highway 120 bound for Mono Lake to the nearby east. It is stocked weekly during the fishing season. A must-do side trip is venturing to the south shore of Mono Lake to walk amid the bizarre yet beautiful tufa towers.

55 Cattleguard Camp

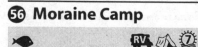

Location: Near Lee Vining; map E4, grid g9.

Campsites, facilities: There are 15 sites for tents or RVs up to 30 feet long in four separate campgrounds located next to each other. Portable toilets are available. There is no piped water, so bring your own. Supplies can be purchased in Lee Vining (about two miles away). Leashed pets are permitted.

Reservations, fees: No reservations; $7 per night. Open May through October.

Contact: Mono County Building and Parks Department, (760) 932-5231.

Directions: On US 395, drive to just south of Lee Vining and the junction with Highway 120. Turn west on Highway 120 and drive about three miles. Turn left into the campground entrance.

Trip notes: This camp is an alternative to Yosemite National Park. Though primitive, it has several advantages: It is quiet, gets more sun than the three neighboring camps (Lower Lee Vining, Moraine, and Boulder), and provides the best views of Dana Plateau. For more information, see the trip notes for Lower Lee Vining Camp (campground number 54).

56 Moraine Camp

Location: Near Lee Vining; map E4, grid g9.

Campsites, facilities: There are 30 sites for tents or RVs up to 30 feet long in four separate campgrounds located next to each other. Portable toilets are available. There is no piped water, so bring your own. Supplies can be purchased in Lee Vining (about two miles away). Leashed pets are permitted.

Reservations, fees: No reservations; $7 per night. Open May through October.

Contact: Mono County Building and Parks Department, (760) 932-5231.

Directions: On US 395, drive to just south of Lee Vining and the junction with Highway 120. Turn west on Highway 120 and drive 3.5 miles to Poole Power Plant Road. Exit left onto Poole Power Plant Road and drive a quarter mile to the campground entrance at the end of the road.

Trip notes: This camp provides an alternative to Yosemite National Park. For more information, see the trip notes for Lower Lee Vining Camp (campground number 54).

57 Boulder Camp

Location: Near Lee Vining; map E4, grid g9.

Campsites, facilities: There are 22 sites for tents or RVs up to 30 feet long in four separate campgrounds located next to each other. Portable toilets are available. There is no piped water, so bring your own. Supplies can be purchased in Lee Vining (about two miles away). Leashed pets are permitted.

Reservations, fees: No reservations; $7 per night. Open May through October.

Contact: Mono County Building and Parks Department, (760) 932-5231.

Directions: On US 395, drive to just south of Lee Vining and the junction with Highway 120. Turn west on Highway 120 and drive to Poole Power Plant Road. Exit left and then make a quick right on Poole Power Plant Road and drive a half mile to the campground entrance on the left.

Trip notes: This camp provides an alternative to Yosemite National Park. For more information, see the trip notes for Lower Lee Vining (campground number 54).

58 Big Bend

Location: On Lee Vining Creek in Inyo National Forest; map E4, grid g9.

Campsites, facilities: There are 17 water, fire grills, and picnic tables are provided. Vault toilets are available. Leashed pets are permitted.

Reservations, fees: No reservations; $11 per night. Open May to mid-October.

Contact: Inyo National Forest, Mono Lake Ranger District, (760) 647-3000 or fax (760) 647-3027.

Directions: On US 395, drive to just south of Lee Vining and the junction with Highway 120. Turn west on Highway 120 and drive about 3.5 miles to a county road. Turn right and drive three miles west to the campground access road on the left. Turn left and drive a short distance to the camp.

Trip notes: This camp is set in sparse but beautiful country along Lee Vining Creek at 7,800 feet elevation. It is an excellent bet for an overflow camp if Tuolumne Meadows in nearby Yosemite is packed. The view from the camp to the north features Mono Dome (10,614 feet) and Lee Vining Peak (11,691 feet).

59 Aspen Grove

Location: On Lee Vining Creek; map E4, grid g9.

Campsites, facilities: There are 56 sites for tents or RVs up to 20 feet long. Obtain potable water from a wellhead at the entrance to the camp. Pit and portable toilets are available. Supplies can be purchased in Lee Vining. Leashed pets are permitted.

Reservations, fees: No reservations; $7 per night. Open May through October.

Contact: Mono County Building and Parks Department, (760) 932-5231.

Directions: On US 395, drive to just south of Lee Vining and the junction with Highway 120. Turn west on Highway 120 and drive about 3.5 miles. Exit onto Poole Power Plant Road. Turn

left and drive about four miles west to the campground on the left.

Trip notes: This high-country, primitive camp is set along Lee Vining Creek at 7,500 feet, on the eastern slopes of the Sierra just east of Yosemite National Park. Take the side trip to moonlike Mono Lake, best seen at the south shore's Tufa State Reserve.

60 Tioga Lake

Location: In Inyo National Forest; map E4, grid g9.

Campsites, facilities: There are 13 tent sites. Piped water, picnic tables, and fire grills are provided. Vault toilets are available. Leashed pets are permitted.

Reservations, fees: No reservations; $11 per night. Open June through September.

Contact: Inyo National Forest, Mono Lake Ranger District, (760) 647-3000 or fax (760) 647-3027.

Directions: On US 395, drive to just south of Lee Vining and the junction with Highway 120. Turn west on Highway 120 and drive about 11 miles (just past Ellery Lake) to the campground on the left side of the road.

From Merced, turn east on Highway 140, drive into Yosemite National Park, and continue toward Yosemite Valley to the junction with Highway 120/Tioga Road. Turn north and drive about 65 miles through the Tioga Pass entrance station. Continue three miles to the campground on the right side of the road.

Trip notes: Tioga Lake is a dramatic sight, with gemlike blue waters encircled by Sierra granite at 9,700 feet in elevation. Together with adjacent Ellery Lake, it makes up a pair of gorgeous waters with near-lake camping, trout fishing (stocked with rainbow trout), and access to Yosemite National Park and Saddlebag Lake. See the trip notes for Ellery Lake (campground number 61) for more information.

61 Ellery Lake

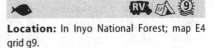

Location: In Inyo National Forest; map E4 grid g9.

Campsites, facilities: There are 14 sites for tents or RVs up to 22 feet long. Piped water, fire grills, and picnic tables are provided. Flush toilets are available. A grocery store is nearby. Leashed pets are permitted.

Reservations, fees: No reservations; $11 per night. Open June through September.

Contact: Inyo National Forest, Mono Lake Ranger District, (760) 647-3000 or fax (760) 647-3027.

Directions: On US 395, drive to just south of Lee Vining and the junction with Highway 120. Turn west on Highway 120 and drive about 10 miles to the campground on the left side of the road.

From Merced turn east on Highway 140, drive into Yosemite National Park, and continue toward Yosemite Valley to the junction with Highway 120/Tioga Road. Turn north and drive about 65 miles through the Tioga Pass entrance station. Continue four miles to the campground on the right side of the road.

Trip notes: Ellery Lake offers all the spectacular beauty of Yosemite but is two miles outside park borders. That means it is stocked with trout by the Department of Fish and Game (no lakes in Yosemite are planted, hence the lousy fishing). Just like at neighboring Tioga Lake, here are deep-blue waters set in rock in the 9,500-foot elevation range, one of the most pristine highway-access lake settings anywhere. Nearby Saddlebag Lake is a common side trip, the highest drive-to lake in California. Whenever Tuolumne Meadows (campground number 66) fills in Yosemite, this camp fills shortly thereafter. Camp elevation is 9,600 feet.

(62) White Wolf

Location: In Yosemite National Park; map E4, grid g3.

Campsites, facilities: There are 87 sites for tents or RVs up to 35 feet long. Piped water, fire rings, and picnic tables are provided. Flush toilets and evening ranger programs are available. A grocery store is nearby. Leashed pets are permitted in the campground but not on trails.

Reservations, fees: No reservations; $10 per night. Open June through mid-September.

Contact: Yosemite National Park, (209) 372-0200 for a recorded message, (209) 372-0265, or fax (209) 372-0371.

Directions: From Merced, drive east on Highway 140 to the El Portal entrance station at Yosemite National Park. Continue east on Highway 140 to the junction with Highway 120/Tioga Road (just before entering the valley). Turn left and drive to the junction with Highway 120. Turn right and drive 15 miles to White Wolf Road on the left. Turn left and drive a mile to the campground entrance road on the right.

Trip notes: This is one of Yosemite National Park's prime mountain camps for people who like to hike, either for great day hikes in the immediate area and beyond, or for overnight backpacking trips. The day hike to Lukens Lake is an easy two-mile trip, the payoff being this pretty little alpine lake set amid a meadow, pines, and granite. Just about everybody who camps at White Wolf makes the trip. Backpackers can make the overnight trip into the Ten Lakes Basin, set below Grand Mountain and Colby Mountain. Bears are common at this camp, so be certain to secure your food in the bear-proof lockers. The elevation is 8,000 feet.

(63) Yosemite Creek

Location: On Yosemite Creek in Yosemite National Park; map E4, grid g4.

Campsites, facilities: There are 75 tent sites. Picnic tables and fire pits are provided. Pit toilets are available. No piped water is available. Leashed pets are permitted.

Reservations, fees: No reservations; $6 to $8 per night. A 14-day stay limit is enforced.

Contact: Yosemite National Park, (209) 372-0200 for a recorded message, (209) 372-0265, or fax (209) 372-0371.

Directions: From Merced, drive east on Highway 140 to the Yosemite National Park entrance and continue toward Yosemite Valley to the junction with Highway 120/Tioga Road. Turn north and drive about 30 miles (just beyond the White Wolf turnoff on the left) to Yosemite

Creek Campground Road on the right. Turn right (RVs and trailers are not recommended) and drive five miles to the campground at the end of the road.

Trip notes: This is the most remote drive-to camp in Yosemite National Park, a great alternative to camping in the valley or at Tuolumne Meadows, and the rough, curvy access road keeps many out-of-state tourists away. It is set along Yosemite Creek at 7,659 feet, with poor trout fishing but a trailhead for a spectacular hike. If you arrange a shuttle ride, you can make a great one-way trip down to the north side of the Yosemite Canyon rim, skirting past the top of Yosemite Falls (a side trip to Yosemite Point is a must!), then tackling the unbelievable descent into the valley, emerging at Sunnyside Walk-In.

⑥④ Hodgdon Meadow

Location: In Yosemite National Park; map E4, grid g1.

Campsites, facilities: There are 105 family sites for tents or RVs up to 35 feet long. There are also four group sites for up to 30 people, and a few walk-in camps for tents only. Piped water, fire rings, and picnic tables are provided. Flush toilets are available. A grocery store and propane gas are nearby. Leashed pets are permitted in the campground but not on trails.

Reservations, fees: Reservations are required May through October. Phone (800) 436-PARK/7275; $15 per night, group campsite is $35 per night. Open year-round.

Contact: Yosemite National Park, (209) 372-0200 for a recorded message, (209) 372-0265, or fax (209) 372-0371.

Directions: From Groveland, drive east on Highway 120 to the Big Oak Flat entrance station for Yosemite National Park. Just after passing the entrance station, turn left and drive a short distance to the campground.

Trip notes: Hodgdon Meadow is on the outskirts of Yosemite, just inside the park's borders at the Highway 120 entrance station, at 4,900 feet in elevation. It is located near a small feeder creek to the South Fork Tuolumne River. It is

about a 20-minute drive on Highway 120 to a major junction, where a left turn takes you on Tioga Road and to Yosemite's high country, including Tuolumne Meadows, and a right turn routes you toward Yosemite Valley (25 miles from the camp).

⑥⑤ Porcupine Flat

Location: Near Yosemite Creek in Yosemite National Park; map E4, grid g5.

Campsites, facilities: There are 52 sites for tents or RVs up to 35 feet long. There is limited RV space. Fire rings and picnic tables are provided. Pit toilets are available. There is no piped water, so bring your own. No pets are allowed.

Reservations, fees: No reservations; $6 per night. Open June through September.

Contact: Yosemite National Park, (209) 372-0200 for a recorded message, (209) 372-0265, or fax (209) 372-0371.

Directions: From Merced, drive east on Highway 140 to the El Portal entrance station at Yosemite National Park. Continue east on Highway 140 to the junction with Highway 120/Tioga Road (just before entering the valley). Turn left and drive to the junction with Highway 120. Turn right and drive about 25 miles to the campground on the left side of the road (16 miles west from Tuolumne Meadows).

Trip notes: Porcupine Flat, set at 8,100 feet, is southwest of Mount Hoffman, one of the prominent nearby peaks along Tioga Road in Yosemite National Park. The trailhead for a hike to May Lake, set just below Mount Hoffman, is about five miles away on a signed turnoff on the north side of the road. There are several little peaks above the lake where hikers can gain great views, including one of the back side of Half Dome.

⑥⑥ Tuolumne Meadows

Location: In Yosemite National Park; map E4, grid g7.

Campsites, facilities: There are 314 sites for tents or RVs up to 35 feet long. Piped water, flush toilets, picnic tables, fire grills, and a dump station are provided, but there are no hookups. Showers and groceries are nearby. There are also an additional 25 hike-in sites available for backpackers (usually those hiking the Pacific Crest Trail, for which a wilderness permit is required), and eight group sites that can accommodate 30 people each. Leashed pets are permitted.

Reservations, fees: Reserve via phone at (800) 444-PARK/7275. Only half of the sites are available through reservations; the other half are first come, first served. There is a $15 fee per night for family sites, $3 per night for walk-in sites, and $35 per night for group sites. The 25 hike-in sites are free with a wilderness permit. Open June through mid-September.

Contact: Yosemite National Park, (209) 372-0200 for a recorded message, (209) 372-0265, or fax (209) 372-0371.

Directions: From Merced, drive east on Highway 140 to the El Portal entrance station at Yosemite National Park. Continue east on Highway 140 to the junction with Highway 120/Tioga Road (just before entering the valley). Turn left and drive to the junction with Highway 120. Turn right and drive 46 miles to the campground on the right side of the road.

From just south of Lee Vining at the junction of US 395 and Highway 120, turn west and drive to the Tioga Pass entrance station for Yosemite National Park. Continue for about 10 miles to the campground entrance on the left.

Trip notes: This is Yosemite's biggest camp, and for the variety of nearby adventures, it might also be the best. It is set in the high country, at 8,600 feet, and can be used as a base camp for fishing, hiking, and horseback riding, or as a jump-off point for a backpacking trip (wilderness permits required). There are two outstanding and easy day hikes from here, one heading north on the Pacific Crest Trail for the near-level walk to Tuolumne Falls, the other heading south up Lyell Fork, with good fishing for small brook trout. With a backpack, either route can be extended for as long as desired into remote and beautiful country. The campground is huge, and neighbors are guaranteed, but it is well wooded and feels somewhat secluded even with all the RVs and tents. There

are lots of food-raiding bears in the area, so use of the food lockers is required.

67 Crane Flat

Location: Near Tuolumne Grove of Big Trees in Yosemite National Park; map E4, grid h1.

Campsites, facilities: There are 166 sites for tents or RVs up to 35 feet long. Piped water, fire rings, and picnic tables are provided. Flush toilets, groceries, propane gas, and evening ranger programs are available. A gas station is nearby.

Reservations, fees: Reserve via phone at (800) 436-PARK/7275; $15 per night. Open May through October.

Contact: Yosemite National Park, (209) 372-0200 for a recorded message, (209) 372-0265, or fax (209) 372-0371.

Directions: From Groveland, drive east on Highway 120 to the Big Oak Flat entrance station for Yosemite National Park. After passing through the entrance station, drive about 10 miles to the campground entrance road on the right. Turn right and drive a half mile to the campground.

Trip notes: Crane Flat is located within a five-minute drive of the Tuolumne Grove of Big Trees, as well as the Merced Grove to the nearby west. This is the feature attraction in this part of Yosemite National Park, set near the western border in close proximity to the Highway 120 entrance station. The elevation is 6,200 feet. Yosemite Valley is about a 25-minute drive away.

68 Tamarack Flat

Location: On Tamarack Creek in Yosemite National Park; map E4, grid h3.

Campsites, facilities: There are 52 sites for tents or small RVs up to 24 feet long. Fire rings and picnic tables are provided. Pit toilets are available. No piped water is available, so bring your own. No pets are allowed.

Reservations, fees: No reservations; $6 per night. Open June through mid-October.

Contact: Yosemite National Park, (209) 372-0200 for a recorded message, (209) 372-0265, or fax (209) 372-0371.

Directions: From Merced, drive east on Highway 140 to the El Portal entrance station at Yosemite National Park. Continue east on Highway 140 to the junction with Highway 120/Tioga Road (just before entering the Valley). Turn left and drive to the junction with Highway 120. Turn right on Tioga Road and drive three miles to the campground entrance on the right side of the road. Turn right and drive 2.5 miles to the campground. Trailers and RVs are not advised.

Trip notes: The road to this campground looks something like the surface of the moon. Then you arrive and find one of the few primitive drive-to camps in Yosemite National Park, 6,300 feet in elevation. From the trailhead at camp, you can link up with the El Capitan Trail and then hike across Ribbon Meadow on up to the north valley rim at El Capitan, 7,569 feet. This is the largest single piece of granite in the world, and standing atop it for both the sensation and the divine view is a breathtaking experience. From camp, Yosemite Valley is 23 miles away.

⑥⑨ McCabe Flat

Location: On the Merced River east of Briceburg; map E4, grid i0.

Campsites, facilities: There are seven tent sites. Picnic tables and fire rings are provided. Vault toilets are available. Leashed pets are permitted.

Reservations, fees: No reservations; $10 for the first four people per night, $2 for each additional camper. There is a 14-day limit.

Contact: Bureau of Land Management, Folsom Resource Area, 63 Natoma Street, Folsom, CA 95630; (916) 985-4474.

Directions: From Merced, drive south on Highway 99 for just a few miles to its junction with Highway 140. Turn east on Highway 140 and drive through Mariposa and on to Briceburg. At the Briceburg Visitor Center, turn left at a road that is signed "BLM Camping Areas" (the road remains paved for about 150 yards). Drive over the suspension bridge and turn left, traveling downstream on the road, parallel to the river. Drive two miles to McCabe Flat.

Trip notes: What a spot: McCabe Flat is secluded on one of the prettiest sections of the

Merced River, where you can enjoy great hiking, swimming, and fishing, all on the same day. The access road out of camp leads downstream to the Yosemite Railroad Grade, which has been converted into a great trail. If you don't mind cold water, the Merced River's pools can provide relief from summer heat. Evening fly-fishing is good in many of the same spots through July.

⑦⓪ Willow Placer

Location: On the Merced River east of Briceburg; map E4, grid i0.

Campsites, facilities: There are five tent sites. Picnic tables and fire rings are provided. Vault toilets are available. Leashed pets are permitted.

Reservations, fees: No reservations; $10 for the first four people per night, $2 for each additional camper. There is a 14-day limit.

Contact: Bureau of Land Management, Folsom Resource Area, 63 Natoma Street, Folsom, CA 95630; (916) 985-4474.

Directions: From Merced, drive south on Highway 99 for just a few miles to its junction with Highway 140. Turn east on Highway 140 and drive through Mariposa and on to Briceburg. At the Briceburg Visitor Center, turn left at a road that is signed "BLM Camping Areas" (the road remains paved for about 150 yards). Drive over the suspension bridge and turn left, traveling downstream on the road, parallel to the river. Drive four miles (two miles past McCabe Flat) to Willow Placer.

Trip notes: Willow Placer is a small, beautiful campground that gets overlooked by many travelers streaming to Yosemite. Evening trout fishing is decent, and rafting and swimming can be outstanding in this stretch of the Merced. Just a quarter mile away, down the road leading out of camp, is the trailhead for the old Yosemite Railroad Grade, now a trail for hikers, bikers, and horseback riders.

⑦① Railroad Flat

Location: On the Merced River east of Briceburg; map E4, grid i0.

Campsites, facilities: There are eight tent sites. Picnic tables and fire rings are provided. Vault toilets are available. Leashed pets are permitted.

Reservations, fees: No reservations; $10 for the first four people per night, $2 for each additional camper. There is a 14-day limit.

Contact: Bureau of Land Management, Folsom Resource Area, 63 Natoma Street, Folsom, CA 95630; (916) 985-4474.

Directions: From Merced, drive south on Highway 99 for just a few miles to its junction with Highway 140. Turn east on Highway 140 and drive through Mariposa and on to Briceburg. At the Briceburg Visitor Center, turn left at a road that is signed "BLM Camping Areas" (the road remains paved for about 150 yards). Drive over the suspension bridge and turn left, traveling downstream on the road, parallel to the river. Drive for 4.5 miles to where the road dead-ends at Railroad Flat Campground, about a quarter mile past Willow Placer Camp.

Trip notes: The access road that leads to the three BLM camps on the Merced River—McCabe Flat, Willow Placer, and Railroad Flat—is actually part of the old Yosemite Railroad Grade. And the gate that blocks cars at Railroad Flat doesn't keep anybody else out—the old railroad is a great hiking, biking, and horseback riding route that runs all the way to Bagby. Access to the adjacent Merced River is good. It's a stretch of water that can be excellent for rafting and trout fishing. Insider's note: The spring wildflower display, which usually happens in April, is probably better at Red Hills (located just outside Chinese Camp) than anywhere in the Sierra foothills.

(72) Sunnyside Walk-In

Location: In Yosemite Valley in Yosemite National Park; map E4, grid h4.

Campsites, facilities: There are 35 walk-in tent sites. Each site must be shared with as many as six other campers. Picnic tables and fire pits are provided. Piped water and flush toilets are available. A parking area, showers, groceries, and a coin laundry are nearby. No pets are allowed.

Reservations, fees: No reservations; $6 per night, $5 park entrance fee. There is a seven-day limit.

Contact: Yosemite National Park, (209) 372-0200 for a recorded message, (209) 372-0265, or fax (209) 372-0371.

Directions: After entering Yosemite Valley, drive past the chapel and turn left at the first stop sign. Cross Sentinel Bridge, drive about a quarter mile, and then turn left at the next stop sign (at the sign for Yosemite Lodge). Drive a half mile past the base of Yosemite Falls and look for the large sign marking the parking area for Sunnyside Walk-in on the right.

Trip notes: The concept at Sunnyside was to provide a walk-in alternative to drive-in camps that sometimes resemble combat zones. Unfortunately, it doesn't really work, with the sites here jammed together. Regardless, the camp is in a great location, within walking distance of Yosemite Falls. It has a view of Leidig Meadow and the southern valley rim, with Sentinel Rock directly across the valley. A trail is routed from camp to Lower Yosemite Falls. In addition, the trailhead for the Yosemite Falls Trail is a short distance away, a terrible butt-kicking climb up Columbia Rock to the rim adjacent to the top of the falls, providing one of most incredible views in all the world.

(73) Upper Pines

Location: In Yosemite Valley in Yosemite National Park; map E4, grid h5.

Campsites, facilities: There are 238 sites for tents or RVs up to 40 feet long. Fire rings and picnic tables are provided. Piped water, flush toilets, and a sanitary disposal station are available. A grocery store, coin laundry, propane gas, recycling center, and bike rentals are available nearby. Leashed pets are permitted in the campground but not on trails.

Reservations, fees: Reserve via phone at (800) 436-PARK/7275; $15 per night. Open year-round.

Contact: Yosemite National Park, (209) 372-0200 for a recorded message, (209) 372-0265, or fax (209) 372-0371.

Directions: After entering Yosemite Valley,

drive past Curry Village (on the right) and Stoneman Meadow (on the left) to the campground entrance on the right side of the road (just before Clarks Bridge).

Trip notes: Of the campgrounds in Yosemite Valley, Upper Pines is located closest to the jump-off to paradise, providing you can get a campsite at the far south end of the camp. From here it is a short walk to the Happy Isles Trailhead and with it the chance to hike to Vernal Falls on the Mist Trail (steep), or beyond to Nevada Falls (very steep) at the foot of Liberty Cap. But crowded this camp is, and you'd best expect it. People come from all over the world to camp here. Sometimes it appears as if they are from other worlds as well. The elevation is 4,000 feet.

(74) North Pines

Location: In Yosemite Valley in Yosemite National Park; map E4, grid h5.

Campsites, facilities: There are 85 sites for tents or RVs up to 40 feet long. Piped water, fire grills, and picnic tables are provided. Flush toilets are available. A grocery store, coin laundry, recycling center, propane gas, and bike rentals are available nearby. No pets are allowed.

Reservations, fees: Reserve via phone at (800) 436-PARK/7275; $15 per night. Open April through September.

Contact: Yosemite National Park, (209) 372-0200 for a recorded message, (209) 372-0265, or fax (209) 372-0371.

Directions: After entering Yosemite Valley, drive past Curry Village (on the right) and Stoneman Meadow (on the left). Continue past Upper and Lower Pines Campgrounds, drive over Clarks Bridge, turn left (at the horse stables), and drive a short distance to the campground on the right.

Trip notes: North Pines is set along the Merced River. A trail out of camp heads east and links up the paved road/trail to Mirror Lake, a virtual parade of people. If you continue hiking past Mirror Lake you will get astounding views of Half Dome and then leave the masses behind as you enter Tenaya Canyon. The elevation is 4,000 feet.

(75) Lower Pines

Location: In Yosemite Valley in Yosemite National Park; map E4, grid h4.

Campsites, facilities: There are 40 sites for tents or RVs up to 40 feet long. Fire rings and picnic tables are provided. Piped water and flush toilets are available. A grocery store, coin laundry, propane gas, recycling center, and horse, bike, and cross-country ski rentals are available nearby. Pets are allowed from November through March only.

Reservations, fees: Reserve via phone at (800) 436-PARK/7275; $15 per night. Open April through November, weather permitting.

Contact: Yosemite National Park, (209) 372-0265, (209) 372-0200 for a recorded message.

Directions: After entering Yosemite Valley, drive past Curry Village (on the right) and Stoneman Meadow (on the left) to the campground entrance on the left side of the road (just before Clarks Bridge).

Trip notes: For combat-style camping, this is a pretty good place. Lower Pines sits right along the Merced River, quite pretty, in the center of Yosemite Valley. Of course, the tents and RVs are jammed in quite close together. Within walking distance is the trail to Mirror Lake (a zoo on parade), as well as the trailhead at Happy Isles for the hike up to Vernal Falls and Nevada Falls. The park's shuttle bus picks up riders near the camp entrance.

(76) Yosemite-Mariposa KOA

Location: Near Mariposa; map E4, grid i0.

Campsites, facilities: There are 40 tent sites and 50 RV sites, 30 with full hookups and 20 with partial hookups, plus 12 cabins. Picnic tables and barbecues are provided. Rest rooms, showers, sanitary disposal station, coin laundry, store, propane gas, recreation room, swimming pool, and a playground are available. Leashed pets are permitted.

Reservations, fees: Reservations are accepted; $25 to $36 per night, $42 per night for cabins.

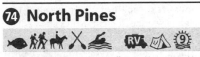

Contact: Yosemite-Mariposa KOA, (209) 966-2201 or (800) 562-9392.

Directions: From Merced, drive east on Highway 140 to Mariposa. Continue on Highway 140 for six miles to Midpines and 6323 Highway 140. Turn left at the campground entrance.

Trip notes: A little duck pond, cute log cabins, swimming pool, and proximity to Yosemite National Park make this one a winner. The RV sites are lined up along the entrance road, edged by grass. A 10 P.M. "quiet time" helps ensure a good night's sleep. It's a one-hour drive to Yosemite Valley, and your best bet is to get there early to enjoy the spectacular beauty before the park is packed with people.

(77) Bridalveil Creek

Location: Near Glacier Point in Yosemite National Park; map E4, grid i4.

Campsites, facilities: There are 110 sites for tents and RVs. Picnic tables and fire grills are provided. Piped water and flush toilets are available. Leashed pets are permitted.

Reservations, fees: No reservations; $10 per night. A 14-day stay limit is enforced. Open June through September, weather permitting.

Contact: Yosemite National Park, (209) 372-0200 for a recorded message, (209) 372-0265, or fax (209) 372-0371.

Directions: In Yosemite, drive toward Yosemite Valley and the junction of Highway 140 and Highway 41. Turn right on Highway 41/Wawona Road and drive about 10 miles to Glacier Point Road. Turn left on Glacier Point Road and drive about 25 miles (a few miles past Badger Pass Ski Area) to Peregoy Meadow and the campground access road on the right. Turn right and drive a short distance to the campground.

Trip notes: There may be no better view in the world than the one from Glacier Point, looking down into Yosemite Valley, where Half Dome stands like nature's perfect sculpture. Then there are the perfect views of Yosemite Falls, Nevada Falls, Vernal Falls, and several hundred square miles of Yosemite's wilderness backcountry. This is the closest camp to Glacier Point's drive-to vantage point, but it is also the closest camp to the best day hikes in the entire park. Along Glacier Point Road are trailheads to Sentinel Dome (incredible view of Yosemite Falls) and Taft Point (breathtaking drop, incredible view of El Capitan), and McGurk Meadow (one of the most pristine and romantic spots on Earth). At 7,200 feet, the camp is more than 3,000 feet higher than Yosemite Valley. A good day hike out of camp leads you to Ostrander Lake, just below Horse Ridge.

(78) Jerseydale

Location: In Sierra National Forest; map E4, grid j1.

Campsites, facilities: There are eight tent sites and two sites for tents or RVs up to 22 feet long. Piped water, fire grills, and picnic tables are provided. Vault toilets are available. Leashed pets are permitted.

Reservations, fees: No reservations; $10 per night. Open May through November.

Contact: Sierra National Forest, Mariposa Ranger District, (209) 683-4665 or fax (209) 683-7258.

Directions: From Mariposa, drive northeast on Highway 140 for about five miles to Triangle Road (if you reach Midpines, you have gone 1.5 miles too far). Turn right on Triangle Road and drive about six miles to Darrah and Jerseydale Road. Turn left and drive three miles to the campground on the left side of the road (adjacent to the Jerseydale Ranger Station).

Trip notes: This little camp gets overlooked by many visitors shut out of nearby Yosemite National Park simply because they don't realize it exists. Jerseydale is set southwest of the national park in Sierra National Forest, with two good side trips nearby. If you continue north on Jerseydale Road to its end (about six miles), you will come to a gated Forest Service road/trailhead that provides access east for miles along the South Fork of the Merced River, where there is often good fishing, swimming, and rafting. In addition, a dirt road from the camp is routed east for many miles into the Chowchilla Mountains.

California Map—see inside back cover

79 Wawona

Location: On the South Fork of the Merced River in Yosemite National Park; map E4, grid j3.

Campsites, facilities: There are 100 sites for tents or RVs up to 35 feet long and one group campsite. Piped water, fire rings, and picnic tables are provided. Flush toilets are available. A grocery store, propane gas, and horseback riding facilities are available nearby. Pets are permitted on leashes in the campground but not on trails. There are also some stock handling facilities for camping with pack animals; call for further information.

Reservations, fees: No reservations for family camping; $15 per night. For a group campsite write to Wawona Group Reservations, Wawona District Office, PO Box 2027, Yosemite National Park, CA 95389; $34 per night. Open year-round.

Contact: Yosemite National Park, (209) 372-0200 for a recorded message, (209) 372-0265, or fax (209) 372-0371.

Directions: From Oakhurst, drive north on Highway 41 to the Wawona entrance to Yosemite National Park. Continue north on Highway 41 past Wawona (golf course on the left) and drive one mile to the campground entrance on the left.

Trip notes: Wawona Camp is an attractive alternative to the packed camps in Yosemite Valley, providing you don't mind the relatively long drives to the best destinations. The camp is pretty, set along the South Fork Merced River, with the sites more spaciously situated than at most other drive to camps in the park. The nearest attraction is the Mariposa Grove of giant sequoias, but get your visit in early and be out by 9 A.M. because after that it turns into a zoo, complete with shuttle train. The best nearby hike is a strenuous eight-mile round-trip to Chilnualna Falls, the prettiest sight in the southern region of the park, with its trailhead located at the east end of the Redwoods in North Wawona. It's a 45-minute drive to either Glacier Point or Yosemite Valley.

80 Summit Camp

Location: In Sierra National Forest; map E4, grid j2.

Campsites, facilities: There are six tent sites. Piped water, fire grills, and picnic tables are provided. Vault toilets are available. Leashed pets are permitted.

Reservations, fees: No reservations; no fee. Open June through October.

Contact: Sierra National Forest, Mariposa Ranger District, (209) 683-4665 or fax (209) 683-7258.

Directions: From Oakhurst, drive north on Highway 41 toward the town of Fish Camp and the gravel Forest Service Road 5S09X a mile before Fish Camp on the left. Turn left and drive six twisty miles to the campground on the left side of the road.

Trip notes: The prime attraction of tiny Summit Camp is its proximity to the Wawona entrance of Yosemite National Park. It is located along a twisty Forest Service road, perched in the Chowchilla Mountains at 5,800 feet, about three miles from Big Creek. It's an extremely little-known alternative when the park campgrounds at Wawona are packed.

81 Summerdale

Location: On the South Fork of the Merced River in Sierra National Forest; map E4, grid j3.

Campsites, facilities: There are 30 tent sites and nine sites for tents or RVs up to 22 feet long. Piped water, fire grills, and picnic tables are provided. Vault toilets are available. A grocery store is nearby (within one mile). Leashed pets are permitted.

Reservations, fees: No reservations, but this camp usually fills by noon on Fridays; $12 per night. Open May through September.

Contact: Sierra National Forest, Mariposa Ranger District, (209) 683-4665 or fax (209) 683-7258.

Directions: From Oakhurst, drive north on Highway 41 to Fish Camp and continue for one mile to the campground entrance on the left side of the road.

Trip notes: You can't get much closer to Yosemite National Park. This camp is within a mile of the Wawona entrance to Yosemite, about a five-minute drive to the Mariposa Grove. If you don't mind its proximity to the highway, this is a pretty spot in its own right, set along Big Creek, a feeder stream to the South Fork Merced River. Some good swimming holes are in this area. The elevation is 5,000 feet.

(82) Minaret Falls

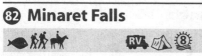

Location: On the San Joaquin River in Inyo National Forest; map E4, grid j9.

Campsites, facilities: There are 28 sites for tents or RVs, most of which can accommodate RVs up to 47 feet long and some up to 55 feet. Piped water, fire grills, and picnic tables are provided. Chemical toilets and horseback riding facilities are available within five miles. Supplies can be purchased in Mammoth Lakes. Leashed pets are permitted.

Reservations, fees: No reservations; $12 per night. Open mid-June to late September.

Contact: Inyo National Forest, Mammoth Lakes Ranger District, (760) 924-5500 or fax (760) 924-5537.

Directions: On US 395, drive to Mammoth Junction/Highway 203. Turn west on Highway 203 and drive four miles, through the town of Mammoth Lakes to Minaret Road (still Highway 203). Turn right and drive 5.4 miles to the Devils Postpile entrance kiosk (past the Mammoth Mountain Ski Area). Continue for six miles to the campground entrance road on the right. Turn right and drive a quarter mile to the campground.

Trip notes: This camp has one of the prettiest settings of the series of camps along the Upper San Joaquin River and near Devils Postpile National Monument. It is set at 7,700 feet near Minaret Creek, across from where beautiful Minaret Falls pours into the San Joaquin River. Devils Postpile National Monument, one of the best examples in the world of hexagonal, columnar rock, is less than a mile from camp, where there is also a trail to awesome Rainbow Falls. The Pacific Crest Trail runs right through this area as well, and if you hike to the south, there is excellent streamside fishing access.

Special note: Noncampers arriving between 7:30 A.M. and 5:30 P.M. are required to take a shuttle bus ($8 per person) from the Mammoth Mountain Ski Area to access this area.

(83) Devils Postpile National Monument

Location: Near the San Joaquin River; map E4, grid j9.

Campsites, facilities: There are 21 sites for tents or RVs. Piped water, fire grills, and picnic tables are provided. Flush toilets are available. Leashed pets are permitted.

Reservations, fees: No reservations; $12 per night. Open mid-June to late October.

Contact: National Park Service, (760) 934-2289.

Directions: On US 395, drive to Mammoth Junction/Highway 203. Turn west on Highway 203 and drive four miles, through the town of Mammoth Lakes to Minaret Road (still Highway 203). Turn right and drive 5.4 miles to the entrance kiosk (past the Mammoth Mountain Ski Area). Continue for 6.4 miles to the campground entrance road on the right.

Trip notes: Devils Postpile is a spectacular and rare example of hexagonal, columnar rock that looks like posts, hence the name. The camp is set at 7,600 feet in elevation and provides nearby access for the easy hike to the Postpile. If you keep walking, it is a 2.5-mile walk to Rainbow Falls, a breathtaking cascade that produces rainbows in its floating mist seen only from the trail alongside the waterfall looking downstream. The camp is also adjacent to the Upper San Joaquin River and the Pacific Crest Trail.

Special note: Noncampers arriving between 7:30 A.M. and 5:30 P.M. are required to take a shuttle bus ($8 per person) from the Mammoth Mountain Ski Area to access this area.

84 Red's Meadow

Location: In Inyo National Forest; map E4, grid j9.

Campsites, facilities: There are 54 sites for tents or RVs, most of which can accommodate RVs 30 feet in length and some up to 55 feet. Piped water, fire grills, and picnic tables are provided. Flush toilets, natural hot springs, shower house, and horseback riding facilities are available. Supplies can be purchased in Mammoth Lakes. Leashed pets are permitted.

Reservations, fees: No reservations; $12 per night. Open mid-June to late October.

Contact: Inyo National Forest, Mammoth Lakes Ranger District, (760) 924-5500 or fax (760) 924-5537.

Directions: On US 395, drive to Mammoth Junction/Highway 203. Turn west on Highway 203 and drive four miles, through the town of Mammoth Lakes to Minaret Road (still Highway 203). Turn right and drive 5.4 miles to the entrance kiosk (past the Mammoth Mountain Ski Area). Continue for 7.4 miles to the campground entrance on the left.

Trip notes: Red's Meadow has long been established as one of the best outfitters for horseback riding trips. To get the feel of it, five-mile round-trip rides are available to Rainbow Falls. Multiday trips into the Ansel Adams Wilderness on the Pacific Crest Trail are also available. A small restaurant is a bonus here, always a must-stop for long-distance hikers getting a shot to chomp their first hamburger in weeks, something like a bear finding a candy bar, quite a sight for the drive-in campers. The nearby Devils Postpile National Monument, Minaret Falls, and San Joaquin River provide recreation options.

Special note: Noncampers arriving between 7:30 A.M. and 5:30 P.M. are required to take a shuttle bus ($8 per person) from the Mammoth Mountain Ski Area to access this area.

85 Pumice Flat

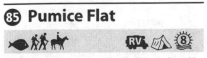

Location: On the San Joaquin River in Inyo National Forest; map E4, grid j9.

Campsites, facilities: There are 17 sites for tents or RVs, most of which can accommodate RVs 47 feet in length and some up to 55 feet. Piped water, fire grills, and picnic tables are provided. Flush toilets and horseback riding facilities are available. Supplies are available in Mammoth Lakes. Leashed pets are permitted.

Reservations, fees: No reservations; $12 per night. Open mid-June to late September.

Contact: Inyo National Forest, Mammoth Lakes Ranger District, (760) 924-5500 or fax (760) 924-5537.

Directions: On US 395, drive to Mammoth Junction/Highway 203. Turn west on Highway 203 and drive four miles, through the town of Mammoth Lakes to Minaret Road (still Highway 203). Turn right and drive 5.4 miles to the entrance kiosk (past the Mammoth Mountain Ski Area). Continue for 5.1 miles to the campground on the right side of the road.

Trip notes: Pumice Flat (7,700 feet in elevation) provides roadside camping within short range of several adventures. A trail out of camp links with the Pacific Crest Trail, where you can hike along the Upper San Joaquin River for miles, providing excellent access for fly-fishing, and head north into the Ansel Adams Wilderness. Devils Postpile National Monument is just two miles south, along with the trailhead for Rainbow Falls.

Special note: Noncampers arriving between 7:30 A.M. and 5:30 P.M. are required to take a shuttle bus ($8 per person) from the Mammoth Mountain Ski Area to access this area.

86 Upper Soda Springs

Location: On the San Joaquin River in Inyo National Forest; map E4, grid j9.

Campsites, facilities: There are 29 sites for tents or RVs, most of which can accommodate RVs 36 feet in length and some up to 55 feet. Piped water, fire grills, and picnic tables are provided. Flush toilets and horseback riding facilities are available. Supplies can be purchased in Mammoth Lakes. Leashed pets are permitted.

Reservations, fees: No reservations; $12 per night. Open mid-June to late September.

Contact: Inyo National Forest, Mammoth Lakes Ranger District, (760) 924-5500 or fax (760) 924-5537.

Directions: On US 395, drive to Mammoth Junction/Highway 203. Turn west on Highway 203 and drive four miles, through the town of Mammoth Lakes to Minaret Road (still Highway 203). Turn right and drive 5.4 miles to the entrance kiosk (past the Mammoth Mountain Ski Area). Continue for five miles to the campground entrance road on the right. Turn right and drive a quarter mile to the campground.

Trip notes: This is a premium location within earshot of the Upper San Joaquin River and within minutes of many first-class recreation options. The river is stocked with trout at this camp, with several good pools within short walking distance. Farther upstream, accessible by an excellent trail, are smaller wild trout that provide good fly-fishing prospects. Devils Postpile National Monument, a massive formation of ancient columnar rock, is only three miles to the south. The Pacific Crest Trail passes right by the camp, providing a trailhead for access to numerous lakes in the Ansel Adams Wilderness. The elevation is 7,700 feet.

Special note: Noncampers arriving between 7:30 A.M. and 5:30 P.M. are required to take a shuttle bus ($8 per person) from the Mammoth Mountain Ski Area to access this area.

87 Agnew Meadows

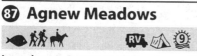

Location: In Inyo National Forest; map E4, grid j9.

Campsites, facilities: There are 22 sites for tents or RVs, most of which can accommodate RVs 46 feet in length and some up to 55 feet. A group camp is also available (reservations required for the group camp). Piped water, fire grills, and picnic tables are provided. Chemical toilets and horseback riding facilities are available (three family sites have hitching racks where horse camping is permitted). Supplies can be obtained in Mammoth Lakes. Leashed pets are permitted.

Reservations, fees: No reservations; $12 per night. Reservations are required for the group camp and recommended for horse camping

sites. Reserve via phone at (877) 444-6777 ($8.65 reservation fee) or website www.reserveusa.com; $15 to $30 per night. Open mid-June to early October.

Contact: Inyo National Forest, Mammoth Lakes Ranger District, (760) 924-5500 or fax (760) 924-5537.

Directions: On US 395, drive to Mammoth Junction/Highway 203. Turn west on Highway 203 and drive four miles, through the town of Mammoth Lakes to Minaret Road (still Highway 203). Turn right and drive 5.4 miles to the entrance kiosk (past the Mammoth Mountain Ski Area). Continue for 2.6 miles to the campground entrance road on the right. Turn right and drive just under a mile to the campground.

Trip notes: This is a perfect camp to use as a launching pad for a backpacking trip or day of fly-fishing for trout. It is set along the Upper San Joaquin River at 8,400 feet, with a trailhead for the Pacific Crest Trail available near the camp. From here you can hike six miles to the gorgeous Thousand Island Lake, a beautiful lake sprinkled with islands set below Banner and Ritter Peaks in the spectacular Minarets. For day hikes, another choice is walking the River Trail, which is routed from Agnew Meadows along the San Joaquin, providing excellent fishing, though the trout are small.

Special note: Noncampers arriving between 7:30 A.M. and 5:30 P.M. are required to take a shuttle bus ($8 per person) from the Mammoth Mountain Ski Area to access this area. There is also a shuttle stop on the paved road less than a mile from the campground.

88 Pumice Flat Group Camp

Location: On the San Joaquin River in Inyo National Forest; map E4, grid j9.

Campsites, facilities: There are four group sites for tents or RVs (check with ranger for information regarding acceptable RV lengths). Piped water, fire grills, and picnic tables are provided. Flush toilets and horseback riding facilities are available. Supplies can be purchased in Mammoth Lakes. Leashed pets are permitted.

Reservations, fees: Reserve via phone at (877) 444-6777 ($8.65 reservation fee); $40 to $100 per night per group. Open mid-June to late September.

Contact: Inyo National Forest, Mammoth Lakes Ranger District, (760) 924-5500 or fax (760) 924-5537.

Directions: On US 395, drive to Mammoth Junction/Highway 203. Turn west on Highway 203 and drive four miles, through the town of Mammoth Lakes to Minaret Road (still Highway 203). Turn right and drive 5.4 miles to the entrance kiosk (past the Mammoth Mountain Ski Area). Continue for 5.1 miles to the campground on the left side of the road.

Trip notes: Pumice Flat Group Camp is set at 7,700 feet in elevation near the Upper San Joaquin River, adjacent to Pumice Flat. For recreation information, see the trip notes for Pumice Flat (campground number 85).

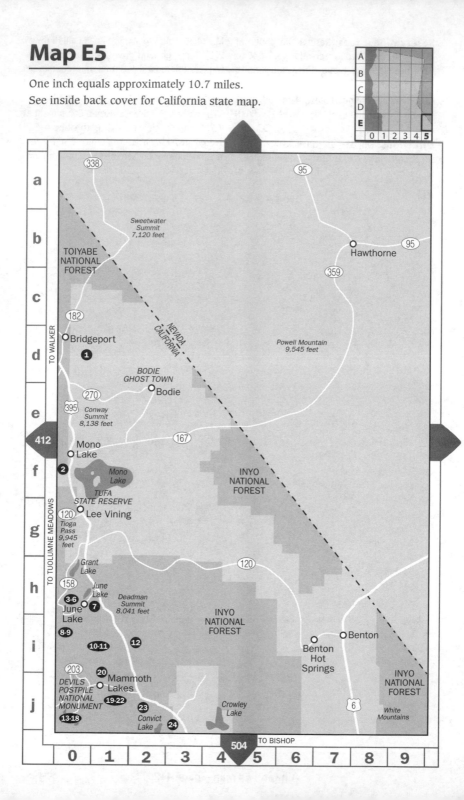

Map E5

One inch equals approximately 10.7 miles.
See inside back cover for California state map.

Chapter E5 features:

1 Willow Springs Trailer Park

Location: Near Bridgeport; map E5, grid d0.

Campsites, facilities: There are 25 RV sites with picnic tables and full hookups. Rest rooms, showers, trout pond, and coin laundry are available. Leashed pets are permitted.

Reservations, fees: Reservations are accepted; $18 per night. Open May through October.

Contact: Willow Springs Trailer Park, (760) 932-7725.

Directions: From Bridgeport on US 395, drive five miles south to the park.

Trip notes: Willow Springs Trailer Park is set at 6,800 feet along US 395, which runs along the eastern Sierra from Carson City south to Bishop and Independence. The country is stark here on the edge of the high Nevada desert, but there are many side trips that give the area life. The most popular destinations are to the nearby south: Mono Lake with its tufa towers and incredible populations of breeding gulls and waterfowl, and the ghost town of Bodie. For trout fishing, there's Bridgeport Reservoir to the north (good trolling) and downstream to the East Walker River (fly-fishing), both excellent destinations, as well as Twin Lakes to the west (huge brown trout). Ken's Sporting Goods in Bridgeport provides excellent information.

2 Lundy Canyon Campground

Location: Near Lundy Lake; map E5, grid f0.

Campsites, facilities: There are 54 sites for tents or RVs up to 24 feet long. Pit toilets are available. There is no piped water, so bring your own. Supplies can be purchased in Lee Vining, 8.5 miles away. Leashed pets are permitted.

Reservations, fees: No reservations; $7 per night. Open May through October.

Contact: Mono County Building and Parks Department, (760) 932-5231.

Directions: From Lee Vining, drive north on US 395 for seven miles to Lundy Lake Road. Turn left and drive a short distance to the campground.

Trip notes: This camp is set high in the eastern Sierra at 7,800 feet in elevation along pretty Lundy Creek, the mountain stream that feeds Lundy Lake and then runs downhill, eventually joining other creeks on its trip to nearby Mono Lake. Nearby Lundy Lake is a long, narrow lake with good fishing for rainbow trout and brown trout. There is a trailhead just west of the lake that is routed steeply up into the Hoover Wilderness to several small pretty lakes, passing two waterfalls about two miles in. A must-do side trip is visiting Mono Lake and its spectacular tufa towers, best done at the Mono Lake Tufa State Reserve along the southern shore of the lake.

❸ Pine Cliff Resort

Location: At June Lake; map E5, grid h0.

Campsites, facilities: There are 55 sites for tents and small trailers (18 feet or less) only, 17 partial-hookup sites for tents or RVs, and 154 RV sites with full or partial hookups. Fire rings, picnic tables, piped water, electrical connections, and sewer hookups are provided at most sites. Rest rooms, showers, coin laundry, store, and propane gas are available. A boat ramp, boat and tackle rentals, fish cleaning facilities, and fuel are available within two miles. Leashed pets are permitted.

Reservations, fees: Reservations are recommended; $8 to $16 per night. Open mid-April through October.

Contact: Pine Cliff Resort, (760) 648-7558.

Directions: From Lee Vining, drive south on US 395 (past the first Highway 158/June Lake Loop turnoff) to June Lake Junction (a gas station/store is on the west side of the road) and Highway 158. Turn west on Highway 158 and drive a mile to June Lake Beach Road. Turn right and drive a mile to the park entrance road on the right.

Trip notes: This camp is in a pretty setting along the north shore of June Lake (7,600 feet in elevation), the feature lake among four in the June Lake Loop. The 160-acre high-mountain lake sits below snowcapped peaks, and it gets large numbers of trout plants each summer, making it extremely popular with anglers. Of the lakes in the June Lake Loop, this is the one that has the most of everything—the most beauty, the most fish, the most developed accommodations and, alas, the most people.

❹ Silver Lake

Location: In Inyo National Forest; map E5, grid h0.

Campsites, facilities: There are 65 sites for tents or RVs up to 22 feet long. Piped water, fire grills, and picnic tables are provided. Flush toilets and horseback riding facilities are available. A grocery store, coin laundry, motorboat rent-

als, boat ramp, bait, snack bar, boat fuel, and propane gas are available nearby. Leashed pets are permitted.

Reservations, fees: No reservations; $12 per night. Open May through September.

Contact: Inyo National Forest, Mono Lake Ranger District, (760) 647-3000 or fax (760) 647-3027.

Directions: From Lee Vining on US 395, drive south to the first Highway 158/June Lake Loop turnoff. Turn west and drive nine miles (past Grant Lake) to Silver Lake. Just as you arrive at Silver Lake (a small store is on the right), turn left at the campground entrance.

Trip notes: Silver Lake is set at 7,600 feet, an 80-acre lake in the June Lake Loop with Carson Peak looming in the background. Boat rentals, fishing for trout at the lake, a beautiful trout stream (Rush Creek) next to the camp, and a nearby trailhead for wilderness hiking and horseback riding (rentals available) are the highlights. The camp is largely exposed and vulnerable to winds, the only downer. Within walking distance to the south is Silver Lake, always a pretty sight, especially when afternoon winds cause the lake surface to sparkle in crackling silvers. Just across the road from the camp is a great trailhead for the Ansel Adams Wilderness, with a two-hour hike available that climbs up to pretty Agnew Lake overlooking the June Lake basin.

❺ June Lake

Location: In Inyo National Forest; map E5, grid h0.

Campsites, facilities: There are 22 sites for tents or RVs up to 22 feet long. Piped water, fire grills, and picnic tables are provided. Flush toilets and boat ramp are available. A grocery store, coin laundry, boat and tackle rentals, moorings, and propane gas are available nearby. Leashed pets are permitted.

Reservations, fees: Reservations are accepted; $12 per night. Open mid-April through October.

Contact: Inyo National Forest, Mono Lake Ranger District, (760) 647-3000 or fax (760) 647-3027.

Directions: From Lee Vining, drive south on

US 395 (past the first Highway 158/June Lake Loop turnoff) to June Lake Junction (a gas station/store is on the west side of the road) and Highway 158. Turn west on Highway 158 and drive two miles to June Lake. Turn right and drive a short distance to the campground.

Trip notes: There are three campgrounds at pretty June Lake; this is one of the two operated by the Forest Service (the other is Oh! Ridge). This one is located on the northeast shore of the lake at 7,600 feet in elevation, a pretty spot with all supplies available just two miles to the south in the town of June Lake. The nearest boat launch is north of town. This is a good lake for trout fishing, receiving nearly 100,000 stocked trout per year.

⑥ Oh! Ridge

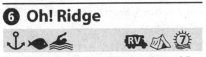

Location: On June Lake in Inyo National Forest; map E5, grid h0.

Campsites, facilities: There are 148 sites for tents or RVs up to 32 feet long. Piped water, fire grills, and picnic tables are provided. Flush toilets and a playground are available. A grocery store, coin laundry, boat ramp, boat and tackle rentals, swimming beach, moorings, and propane gas are available nearby. Leashed pets are permitted.

Reservations, fees: Reserve via phone at (877) 444-6777 ($8.65 reservation fee) or website www.reserveusa.com; $12 per night. Open mid-April through October.

Contact: Inyo National Forest, Mono Lake Ranger District, (760) 647-3000 or fax (760) 647-3027.

Directions: From Lee Vining, drive south on US 395 (past the first Highway 158/June Lake Loop turnoff) to June Lake Junction (a gas station/store is on the west side of the road) and Highway 158. Turn west on Highway 158 and drive two miles to Oh! Ridge Road. Turn right and drive a mile to the campground.

Trip notes: This is the largest of the campgrounds on June Lake. However, it is not the most popular since it is not right on the lakeshore, but back about a quarter mile or so from the north end of the lake. Regardless, it is a beautiful setting, with the ridge of the high Si-

erra providing a backdrop, along with good trout fishing. The elevation is 7,600 feet.

⑦ Hartley Springs

Location: In Inyo National Forest; map E5, grid h1.

Campsites, facilities: There are 20 sites for tents or RVs up to 40 feet long. Fire grills and picnic tables are provided. Vault toilets are available. There is no piped water, so bring your own. Leashed pets are permitted.

Reservations, fees: No reservations; no fee. Open June to mid-September.

Contact: Inyo National Forest, Mono Lake Ranger District, (760) 647-3000 or fax (760) 647-3027.

Directions: From Lee Vining, drive south on US 395 for 11 miles to June Lake Junction. Continue south for two miles to a dirt Forest Service road on the right. Turn right and drive two miles to the campground entrance road on the left.

Trip notes: Even though this camp is only a five-minute drive from US 395, those five minutes will take you into another orbit. It has the feel of a remote, primitive camp, set in a dusty, spartan high mountain environment at 8,400 feet in elevation. About two miles to the immediate north at elevation 8,611 feet is Obsidian Dome "Glass Flow," a craggy geologic formation that some people enjoy scrambling around and exploring; pick your access point carefully.

⑧ Reversed Creek

Location: In Inyo National Forest; map E5, grid i0.

Campsites, facilities: There are 17 sites for tents or RVs up to 22 feet long. Piped water, fire grills, and picnic tables are provided. Flush toilets are available. A grocery store, coin laundry, and propane gas are nearby. Boating is available at nearby Silver Lake, two miles away. Leashed pets are permitted.

Reservations, fees: No reservations; $12 per night. Open May through September.

Contact: Inyo National Forest, Mono Lake

Ranger District, (760) 647-3000 or fax (760) 647-3027.

Directions: From Lee Vining, drive south on US 395 (past the first Highway 158/June Lake Loop turnoff) to June Lake Junction (a gas station/store is on the west side of the road) and Highway 158. Turn west on Highway 158 and drive three miles to the campground on the left side of the road (across from Gull Lake).

Trip notes: This camp is set at 7,600 feet near pretty Reversed Creek, the only stream in the region that flows toward the mountains, not away from them. It is a small, tree-lined stream that provides decent trout fishing. There are also cabins available for rent near here. Directly opposite the camp, on the other side of the road, is Gull Lake and the boat ramp. Two miles to the west, on the west side of the road, is the trailhead for the hike to Fern Lake on the edge of the Ansel Adams Wilderness, a little butt-kicker of a climb.

❾ Gull Lake

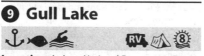

Location: In Inyo National Forest; map E5, grid i0.

Campsites, facilities: There are 11 sites for tents or RVs up to 22 feet long. Piped water, fire grills, and picnic tables are provided, and flush toilets are available. A grocery store, coin laundry, boat ramp, and propane gas are available nearby. Leashed pets are permitted.

Reservations, fees: No reservations; $12 per night. Open May through October.

Contact: Inyo National Forest, Mono Lake Ranger District, (760) 647-3000 or fax (760) 647-3027.

Directions: From Lee Vining, drive south on US 395 (past the first Highway 158/June Lake Loop turnoff) to June Lake Junction (a gas station/store is on the west side of the road) and Highway 158. Turn west on Highway 158 and drive three miles to the campground entrance on the right side of the road.

Trip notes: Little Gull Lake, just 64 acres, is the smallest of the lakes on the June Lake Loop, but to many it is the prettiest. It is set at 7,600 feet, just west of June Lake and, with Carson Peak

looming on the Sierra crest to the west, it is a dramatic and intimate setting. The lake is stocked with nearly 50,000 trout each summer, providing good fishing. A boat ramp is located on the lake's southwest corner.

❿ Glass Creek

Location: In Inyo National Forest; map E5, grid i1.

Campsites, facilities: There are 50 sites for tents or RVs up to 22 feet long. Fire grills and picnic tables are provided. Vault toilets are available. There is no piped water, so bring your own. Leashed pets are permitted.

Reservations, fees: No reservations; no fee. Open mid-May through October.

Contact: Inyo National Forest, Mono Lake Ranger District, (760) 647-3000 or fax (760) 647-3027.

Directions: From Lee Vining, drive south on US 395 for 11 miles to June Lake Junction. Continue south for six miles to a Forest Service road (Glass Creek Road) on the right side of the road. Turn right and drive a quarter mile to the camp access road on the right. Turn right and drive a half mile to the camp at the end of the road. (Note: If arriving from the south on US 395, you will pass the CalTrans Crestview Maintenance Station on the right. Continue north, make a U-turn when possible, and follow the above directions.)

Trip notes: This primitive camp is set along Glass Creek at 7,600 feet, about a mile from Obsidian Dome to the nearby west. A trail follows Glass Creek past the southern edge of the dome, a craggy, volcanic formation that tops out at 8,611 feet in elevation. That trail continues along Glass Creek, climbing to the foot of San Joaquin Mountain for a great view of the high desert to the east. Insider's note: The Department of Fish and Game stocks Glass Creek with trout just once each June, right at the camp.

⓫ Deadman

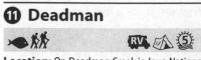

Location: On Deadman Creek in Inyo National Forest; map E5, grid i1.

Campsites, facilities: There are 30 sites for tents or RVs up to 22 feet long. A group camp is also available (reservations required). Fire grills and picnic tables are provided. Vault toilets are available. There is no piped water. Leashed pets are permitted.

Reservations, fees: Reservations are required for group sites only; reserve via phone at (877) 444-6777 ($8.65 reservation fee) or website www.reserveusa .com; $20 per night per group site, no fee for individual sites. Open June to mid-October.

Contact: Inyo National Forest, Mono Lake Ranger District, (760) 647-3000 or fax (760) 647-3027.

Directions: From Lee Vining, drive south on US 395 for 11 miles to June Lake Junction. Continue south for six miles to a Forest Service Road (Deadman Creek Road) on the right side of the road. Turn right and drive two miles to the camp access road on the right. Turn right and drive a half mile to the camp. (Note: If arriving from the south on US 395 and you reach the CalTrans Crestview Maintenance Station on the right, you have gone a mile too far.)

Trip notes: This little-known camp is set at 7,800 feet along little Deadman Creek. It is primitive and dusty in the summer, cold in the early summer and fall. From camp, hikers can drive west for three miles to the headwaters of Deadman Creek and to a trailhead for a route that runs past San Joaquin Mountain and beyond to little Yost Lake, a one-way hike of four miles.

⑫ Big Springs

Location: On Deadman Creek in Inyo National Forest; map E5, grid i2.

Campsites, facilities: There are 24 sites for tents or RVs up to 22 feet long. Fire grills and picnic tables are provided. Vault toilets are available. There is no piped water, so bring your own. Leashed pets are permitted.

Reservations, fees: No reservations; no fee. Open June through September.

Contact: Inyo National Forest, Mono Lake Ranger District, (760) 647-3000 or fax (760) 647-3027.

Directions: From Lee Vining, drive south on

US 395 for 11 miles to June Lake Junction. Continue south for about seven miles to Owens River Road. Turn left and drive two miles to a fork. Bear left at the fork and drive a quarter mile to the camp on the left side of the road.

Trip notes: Big Springs, at 7,300 feet, is set on the edge of the high desert on the east side of US 395. The main attractions are Deadman Creek, which runs right by the camp, and Big Springs, which is set just on the opposite side of the river. There are several hot springs in the area, best reached by driving south on US 395 to the Mammoth Lakes Airport and turning left on Hot Creek Road.

⑬ Horseshoe Lake Group Camp

Location: In Inyo National Forest; map E5, grid j0.

Campsites, facilities: There are six sites for tents or RVs. There is very limited parking space; check with the ranger for RV length limits. Piped water, fire grills, and picnic tables are provided. Flush toilets and a swimming beach are available. Supplies can be purchased in Mammoth Lakes. Leashed pets are permitted.

Reservations, fees: Reserve via phone at (877) 444-6777 ($8.65 reservation fee) or website www.reserveusa.com; $28 to $60 group fee per night. Open late June to mid-September.

Contact: Inyo National Forest, Mammoth Lakes Ranger District, (760) 924-5500 or fax (760) 924-5537.

Directions: From Lee Vining on US 395, drive south for 25 miles to Mammoth Junction and Highway 203/Minaret Summit Road. Turn west on Highway 203 and drive four miles to Lake Mary Road. Continue straight through the intersection and drive five miles (past Twin Lakes, Lake Mary, and Lake Mamie) to Horseshoe Lake. Follow the signs to the campground.

Trip notes: Horseshoe Lake is a beautiful little lake set at 8,900 feet, as pristine as any drive-to lake in the eastern Sierra. Unlike the other lakes in the Mammoth area, here there is no resort, no boat rentals, no boat ramp, and the fishing is only fair. But it is beautiful, and a trailhead is available on the northern side of the lake; it heads west up to Mammoth Pass and connects with the Pacific Crest Trail. There are numerous wilderness lakes in the region.

⑭ Twin Lakes

Location: In Inyo National Forest; map E5, grid j0.

Campsites, facilities: There are 95 sites for tents and RVs, most of which can accommodate RVs up to 38 feet long and some up to 55 feet. Picnic tables, fire grills, and piped water are provided. Flush toilets, boat launch, and horseback riding facilities are available. A grocery store, coin laundry, and propane gas are nearby. Leashed pets are permitted.

Reservations, fees: No reservations; $13 per night, seven-day limit. Open late May to late October.

Contact: Inyo National Forest, Mammoth Lakes Ranger District, (760) 924-5500 or fax (760) 924-5537.

Directions: From Lee Vining on US 395, drive south for 25 miles to Mammoth Junction and Highway 203/Minaret Summit Road. Turn west on Highway 203 and drive four miles to Lake Mary Road. Continue straight through the intersection and drive 2.3 miles to Twin Lakes Loop. Turn right and drive a half mile to the campground.

Trip notes: From Twin Lakes, you can look west and see pretty Twin Falls, a wide cascade that runs into the head of upper Twin Lake. There are actually two camps here, one on each side of the access road, at 8,600 feet. Lower Twin Lake is a favorite for fly fishers in float tubes.

⑮ Lake George

Location: In Inyo National Forest; map E5, grid j0.

Campsites, facilities: There are 16 sites for tents or RVs, most of which can accommodate RVs up to 18 feet long and some up to 25 feet. Piped water, fire grills, and picnic tables are provided. Flush toilets, boat launch, and horseback riding facilities are available. A grocery store,

coin laundry, and propane gas are available nearby. Leashed pets are permitted.

Reservations, fees: No reservations; $13 per night; seven-day limit. Open mid-June to early September.

Contact: Inyo National Forest, Mammoth Lakes Ranger District, (760) 924-5500 or fax (760) 924-5537.

Directions: From Lee Vining on US 395, drive south for 25 miles to Mammoth Junction and Highway 203/Minaret Summit Road. Turn west on Highway 203 and drive four miles to Lake Mary Road. Continue straight through the intersection and drive four miles to Lake Mary Loop Drive. Turn left and drive one-third of a mile to Lake George Road. Turn right and drive a half mile to the campground.

Trip notes: The sites here have views of Lake George, a beautiful lake in a rock basin set below the spectacular Crystal Crag. Lake George is at 9,000 feet in elevation, a small lake fed by creeks coming from both Crystal Lake and TJ Lake. Both of the latter make excellent short hiking trips; TJ Lake is only about a 20-minute walk from the campground. Trout fishing at Lake George is decent—not great, not bad, but decent.

⑯ Lake Mary

Location: In Inyo National Forest; map E5, grid j0.

Campsites, facilities: There are 51 sites for tents or RVs up to 30 feet long. Piped water, fire grills, and picnic tables are provided. Flush toilets and horseback riding facilities are available. A grocery store, coin laundry, and propane gas are nearby. Leashed pets are permitted.

Reservations, fees: No reservations; $13 per night; 14-day limit. Open mid-June to mid-September.

Contact: Inyo National Forest, Mammoth Lakes Ranger District, (760) 924-5500 or fax (760) 924-5537.

Directions: From Lee Vining on US 395, drive south for 25 miles to Mammoth Junction and Highway 203/Minaret Summit Road. Turn west on Highway 203 and drive four miles to Lake Mary Road. Continue straight through the intersection and drive four miles to Lake Mary Loop Drive. Turn left and drive a quarter mile to the campground entrance.

Trip notes: Lake Mary is the star of the Mammoth Lakes region. Of the 11 lakes in the area, this is the largest. It provides a resort, boat ramp, and boat rentals, and it receives the highest number of trout stocks. It is set at 8,900 feet in a place of incredible natural beauty, one of the few spots that literally has it all. Of course, that often includes quite a few other people. If there are too many for you, an excellent trailhead is available at nearby Coldwater (campground number 18).

⓱ Pine City

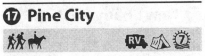

Location: Near Twin Lakes in Inyo National Forest; map E5, grid j0.

Campsites, facilities: There are 10 sites for tents or RVs, most of which can accommodate RVs up to 40 feet in length and some up to 50 feet. Piped water, fire grills, and picnic tables are provided. Flush toilets and horseback riding facilities are available. A grocery store, a coin laundry, and propane gas are available nearby. Leashed pets are permitted.

Contact: Inyo National Forest, Mammoth Lakes Ranger District, (760) 924-5500 or fax (760) 924-5537.

Directions: From Lee Vining on US 395, drive south for 25 miles to Mammoth Junction and Highway 203/Minaret Summit Road. Turn west on Highway 203 and drive four miles to Lake Mary Road. Continue straight through the intersection and drive 3.6 miles to Lake Mary Loop Drive. Turn left and drive a quarter mile to the campground.

Trip notes: This is one of two camps set amid the Twin Lakes. Of the 11 lakes in the region, Twin Lakes is the favorite of fly fishers in float tubes. From the water, it is a dramatic scene, looking west at pretty Twin Falls cascading into the head of upper Twin Lake. The elevation is 8,700 feet.

⓲ Coldwater

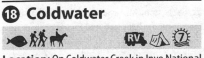

Location: On Coldwater Creek in Inyo National

Forest, map E5, grid j0.

Campsites, facilities: There are 78 sites for tents or RVs, most of which can accommodate RVs up to 37 feet in length and some up to 50 feet. Piped water, fire grills, and picnic tables are provided. Flush toilets and horseback riding facilities are available. Supplies can be purchased in Mammoth Lakes. Leashed pets are permitted.

Reservations, fees: No reservations; $13 per night; 14-day limit. Open mid-June to late September.

Contact: Inyo National Forest, Mammoth Lakes Ranger District, (760) 924-5500 or fax (760) 924-5537.

Directions: From Lee Vining on US 395, drive south for 25 miles to Mammoth Junction and Highway 203/Minaret Summit Road. Turn west on Highway 203 and drive four miles to Lake Mary Road. Continue straight through the intersection and drive 3.6 miles to Lake Mary Loop Drive. Turn left and drive six-tenths of a mile to the camp entrance road.

Trip notes: While this camp is not the first choice of many simply because there is no lake view, it has a special attraction all its own. First, it is a two-minute drive from the campground to Lake Mary, where there is a boat ramp, rentals, and good trout fishing. Second, at the end of the campground access road is a trailhead for two outstanding hikes. From the Y at the trailhead, if you head right, you will be routed up Coldwater Creek to Emerald Lake, a great little hike. If you head to the left, you will have a more ambitious trip to Arrowhead, Skelton, and Red Lakes, all within three miles. The elevation is 8,900 feet.

⓳ Mammoth Mountain RV Park

Location: Near Mammoth Lakes; map E5, grid j1.

Campsites, facilities: There are 185 sites for tents and RVs, some with full hookups. Piped water, electricity, picnic tables, and fire grills are provided. Rest rooms, hot showers, cable TV hookups, sanitary disposal station, coin laundry, swimming pool, RV supplies, and a whirlpool are available. The facilities are wheelchair accessible. Supplies can be obtained in Mammoth Lakes, a quarter mile away. Leashed pets are permitted.

Reservations, fees: Reservations are accepted; $27.50 per night. Open year-round.

Contact: Mammoth Mountain RV Park, (760) 934-3822 or fax (760) 934-1896; PO Box 288, Mammoth Lakes, CA 93546.

Directions: From Lee Vining on US 395, drive south for 25 miles to Mammoth Junction and Highway 203 . Turn west on Highway 203 and drive about two miles to the park.

From Bishop, drive 40 miles north on Highway 395 to Mammoth Lakes Exit. Turn west on Highway 203, go under the overpass, and drive 2.5 miles to the park.

Trip notes: This RV park is located just across the street from the Forest Service Visitor Center. Got a question? They've got an answer. This camp is open year-round, making it a great place to stay for a ski trip.

⑳ Pine Glen

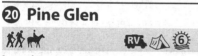

Location: In Inyo National Forest; map E5, grid j1.

Campsites, facilities: There are 11 family sites (used as overflow from Old Shady Rest and New Shady Rest Campgrounds) and six group sites for tents or RVs. Most family sites will accommodate RVs up to 51 feet in length and some up to 55 feet. Check with the ranger for RV length limits in the group sites. Piped water, fire grills, and picnic tables are provided. Flush toilets and a sanitary disposal station are available. A grocery store, coin laundry, propane gas, and horseback riding facilities are nearby in Mammoth Lakes. Leashed pets are permitted.

Reservations, fees: Reservations are required for group sites only. Reserve via phone at (877) 444-6777 ($8.65 reservation fee) or website www.reserveusa.com; $35 to $50 for group sites, $12 per night for family sites. Open June through September.

Contact: Inyo National Forest, Mammoth Lakes Ranger District, (760) 924-5500 or fax (760) 924-5537.

Directions: From Lee Vining on US 395, drive

south for 25 miles to Mammoth Junction and Highway 203/Minaret Summit Road. Turn west on Highway 203 and drive about three miles to the Forest Service Visitor Center. Just past the visitor center, turn right and drive a short distance to the campground.

Trip notes: This is a well-located base camp for several side trips. The most popular is the trip to Devils Postpile National Monument, with a shuttle ride from the Mammoth Ski Area. Other nearby trips include exploring Inyo Craters, Mammoth Lakes, and the hot springs near Mammoth Lakes Airport. The elevation is 7,800 feet.

㉑ New Shady Rest

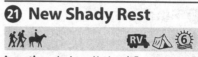

Location: In Inyo National Forest; map E5, grid j1.

Campsites, facilities: There are 95 sites for tents or RVs, most of which will accommodate RVs up to 38 feet in length and some up to 55 feet. Piped water, fire grills, and picnic tables are provided. Flush toilets, dump station, playground, and horseback riding facilities are available three-quarters of a mile away. A grocery store, coin laundry, and propane gas are nearby. Supplies can be obtained in Mammoth Lakes. Leashed pets are permitted.

Reservations, fees: No reservations; $12 per night; 14-day limit. Open when snowmelt allows.

Contact: Inyo National Forest, Mammoth Lakes Ranger District, (760) 924-5500 or fax (760) 924-5537.

Directions: From Lee Vining on US 395, drive south for 25 miles to Mammoth Junction and Highway 203/Minaret Summit Road. Turn west on Highway 203 and drive about three miles to the Forest Service Visitor Center. Just past the visitor center, turn right and drive a short distance to the campground.

Trip notes: This easy-to-reach camp is set at 7,800 feet, not far from the Mammoth Mountain Ski Area. The surrounding Inyo National Forest provides many side trip opportunities, including Devils Postpile National Monument (shuttles available from Mammoth), Upper San Joaquin River, and the Inyo National Forest backcountry trails, streams, and lakes. The camp is open for walk-in, tent-only camping during the winter.

㉒ Old Shady Rest

Location: In Inyo National Forest; map E5, grid j1.

Campsites, facilities: There are 51 sites for tents or RVs, most of which can accommodate RVs up to 40 feet in length and some up to 55 feet. Piped water, fire grills, and picnic tables are provided. Flush toilets, dump station, playground, and horseback riding facilities are available. A grocery store, coin laundry, and propane gas are nearby. Supplies can be obtained in Mammoth Lakes. Leashed pets are permitted.

Reservations, fees: No reservations; $12 per night; 14-day limit. Open mid-June through early September.

Contact: Inyo National Forest, Mammoth Lakes Ranger District, (760) 924-5500 or fax (760) 924-5537.

Directions: From Lee Vining on US 395, drive south for 25 miles to Mammoth Junction and Highway 203/Minaret Summit Road. Turn west on Highway 203 and drive about three miles to the Forest Service Visitor Center. Just past the visitor center turn right and drive 0.3 mile to the campground.

Trip notes: Names like "Old Shady Rest" are usually reserved for mom-and-pop RV parks. The Forest Service respected tradition in officially naming this park what the locals have called it all along. Like New Shady Rest (campground number 21), this camp is located near the Mammoth Visitor Center, with the same side trips available. It is one of three camps in the immediate vicinity. The elevation is 7,800 feet.

㉓ Sherwin Creek

Location: In Inyo National Forest; map E5, grid j2.

Campsites, facilities: There are 87 sites for tents or RVs, most of which can accommodate RVs up to 34 feet in length and some up to 50 feet. Fifteen sites are restricted to walk-in tent camping. Piped water, fire grills, and picnic tables are provided. Flush toilets are available. Horseback riding facilities are nearby. Supplies are

available in Mammoth Lakes. Leashed pets are permitted.

Reservations, fees: Reservations are accepted for 58 sites, including the 15 walk-in sites; $12 per night; 21-day limit. Open mid-May through mid-September.

Contact: Inyo National Forest, Mammoth Lakes Ranger District, (760) 924-5500 or fax (760) 924-5537.

Directions: From Lee Vining on US 395, drive south for 25 miles to Mammoth Junction and Highway 203/Minaret Summit Road. Turn west on Highway 203 and drive about three miles to the Forest Service Visitor Center and continue a short distance to Old Mammoth Road. Turn left and drive about a mile to Sherwin Creek. Turn south and drive two miles on largely unpaved road to the campground on the left side of the road.

Trip notes: This camp is set along little Sherwin Creek, at 7,600 feet in elevation, a short distance from the town of Mammoth Lakes. If you drive a mile east on Sherwin Creek Road, then turn right at the short spur road, you will find a trailhead for a hike that is routed up four miles to Valentine Lake in the John Muir Wilderness, set on the northwest flank of Bloody Mountain.

㉔ Convict Lake

Location: In Inyo National Forest; map E5, grid j3.

Campsites, facilities: There are 88 sites for tents or RVs, most of which can accommodate RVs up to 41 feet in length and some up to 55 feet. Rental cabins are also available. Piped water, fire grills, and picnic tables are provided. Flush toilets, dump station, boat ramp, and horseback riding facilities are available. Leashed pets are permitted.

Reservations, fees: No reservations; $10 per night; seven-day limit. Open late April through October.

Contact: Inyo National Forest, Mammoth Lakes Ranger District, (760) 924-5500 or fax (760) 924-5537.

Directions: From Lee Vining on US 395, drive south for 31 miles (5 miles past Mammoth Junction) to Convict Lake Road (adjacent to Mammoth Lakes Airport). Turn right on Convict Lake Road and drive three miles to Convict Lake. Cross the dam and drive a short distance to the campground entrance road on the left. Turn left and drive a quarter mile to the campground.

Trip notes: After driving in the stark desert on US 395 to get here, it is always astonishing to clear the rise and see Convict Lake (7,583 feet) and its gemlike waters set in a mountain bowl beneath a back wall of high, jagged wilderness peaks. The camp is about a half mile from the lake but is right beside Convict Creek, which provides surprisingly good trout fishing, including some rare monster-size brown trout in the fall below the Convict Lake outlet. Fishing is also good in Convict Lake, with a chance of hooking a 10- or 15-pound trout. A bonus is an outstanding resort with a boat launch, boat rentals, cabin rentals, small store, restaurant, and bar. Horseback rides and hiking are also available, with a trail routed along the north side of the lake, then along upper Convict Creek (a stream crossing is required about three miles in), and into the John Muir Wilderness. This is the most popular camp in the Mammoth area and is frequently full.

Central
California

Map F1

One inch equals approximately 10.7 miles.
See inside back cover for California state map.

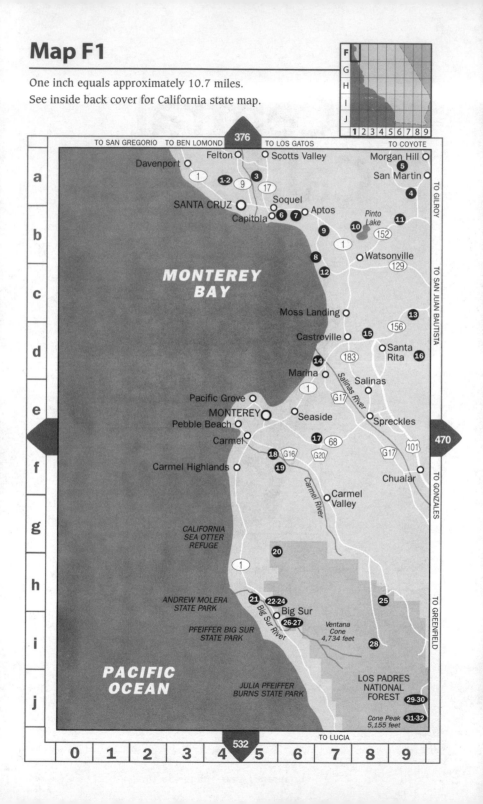

Chapter F1 features:

1 Cotillion Gardens RV Park

Location: Near Santa Cruz; map F1, grid a4.

Campsites, facilities: There are three sites for tents and 80 for RVs, many with full hookups. Picnic tables and fire grills are provided. Rest rooms, showers, cable TV hookups, recreation room, swimming pool, and a small store are available. Leashed pets are permitted.

Reservations, fees: Reservations are recommended; $27 to $29 per night.

Contact: Cotillion Gardens RV Park, 300 Old Big Trees, Felton, CA 95018; (831) 335-7669.

Directions: From Highway 17, five miles north of Santa Cruz, turn right at the Felton–Scotts Valley exit and drive 3.5 miles on Mount Hermon Road to the town of Felton. Turn left on Highway 9 and drive 1.5 miles to the park.

Trip notes: This is a pretty place with several possible side trips. It is set on the edge of the Santa Cruz Mountain redwoods, near Henry Cowell Redwoods State Park and the San Lorenzo River. Monterey Bay is only about a 10-minute drive from the park. Other side trips include the steam engine ride along the San Lorenzo River out of Roaring Camp Train Rides in Felton, and visiting Loch Lomond Reservoir near Ben Lomond for hiking, boat rentals, or fishing.

2 Smithwoods RV Park

Location: Near Santa Cruz; map F1, grid a4.

Campsites, facilities: There are 142 RV sites with full hookups. No tent camping is allowed. Picnic tables and fire pits are provided. Rest rooms, showers, a recreation room, a swimming pool, a playground, and a small store are available. Leashed pets are permitted.

Reservations, fees: Reservations are recommended; $29 per night (two people), $1 for each additional person.

Contact: Smithwoods RV Park, (831) 335-4321.

Directions: From Highway 17 five miles north

of Santa Cruz, turn right at the Felton–Scotts Valley exit and drive 3.5 miles on Mount Hermon Road to the town of Felton. Turn left on Highway 9 and drive about 1.5 miles to the campground.

Trip notes: You get a pretty redwood setting at this privately operated park with its many side trip possibilities. Henry Cowell Redwoods State Park (good) and Big Basin Redwoods State Park (better) are two nearby parks that provide hiking opportunities. The narrow-gauge train ride through the area is fun, too; it is located in Felton at Roaring Camp Train Rides.

❸ Henry Cowell Redwoods State Park

Location: Near Santa Cruz; map F1, grid a5.

Campsites, facilities: There are 112 sites for tents or RVs up to 35 feet long. Piped water, fire grills, and tables are provided. Coin-operated showers and flush toilets are available. Leashed pets are permitted.

Reservations, fees: The reservation service is closed from November through mid-March, but reservations are advisable the rest of the year. Reserve via phone at (800) 444-PARK/7275 ($7.50 reservation fee) or website www.cal-parks.ca.gov; $17 to $18 per night (maximum of eight people and one vehicle per campsite), $1 pet fee. Open mid-February through November.

Contact: Henry Cowell Redwoods State Park, (831) 335-4598, (831) 438-2396, or (831) 429-2850/2851.

Directions: In Scotts Valley on Highway 17, take the Mount Hermon Road exit and drive west toward Felton. Turn left on Lockwood Lane and drive about one mile. Turn left on Graham Hill Road and continue a half mile to the campground.

Trip notes: This is a quality redwood state park near Santa Cruz with good hiking, including a 15-minute walk to a great lookout over Santa Cruz and the Pacific Ocean; the trailhead is located near campsite 49. Another good hike is the Eagle Creek Trail, a three-mile walk that heads along Eagle Creek and the San Lorenzo River, running through a classic redwood canyon.

❹ Uvas Canyon County Park

Location: Near Morgan Hill; map F1, grid a9.

Campsites, facilities: There are 25 sites for tents only. There is a youth group area with five tent sites. Fire grills and tables are provided. Piped water and toilets are available. There is a boat ramp at the reservoir six miles away. Leashed pets are permitted.

Reservations, fees: No reservations for individual sites; phone (831) 358-3751 to reserve the youth group area; $10 per night, $5 for each additional vehicle, $1 pet fee.

Contact: Uvas Canyon County Park, (408) 779-9232 or fax (408) 779-3315.

Directions: From US 101 in San Jose, drive west on Bernal Avenue and then south on Santa Teresa Boulevard to Bailey Avenue. Drive west on Bailey Avenue to McKean Road. Go south on McKean Road, which becomes Uvas Road. Continue on Uvas Road to Croy Road. Turn right on Croy Road and drive 4.5 miles to the park.

Trip notes: This county park has a stunning array of waterfalls that can be reached with short hikes, including Triple Falls, Black Rock Falls, and several others, making for stellar hikes in winter and spring. But Uvas is even better known for its lake, Uvas Reservoir, which provides some of the better black bass and crappie fishing in the Bay Area. Prospects are best by far during the spring, when the lake is also stocked with rainbow trout. Call Coyote Discount Bait and Tackle at (408) 463-0711 for the latest fishing tips.

❺ Oak Dell

Location: Near Morgan Hill; map F1, grid a9.

Campsites, facilities: There are 57 RV sites, most with full hookups. Picnic tables, rest rooms, showers, and a sanitary disposal station are provided. Leashed pets are permitted.

Reservations, fees: Reservations are accepted; $19 per night for two people, $2 per night for each additional person. Open year-round.

Contact: Oak Dell, (408) 779-7779; 12790

Watsonville Road, Morgan Hill, CA 95037.

Directions: From US 101 in Morgan Hill, take the Tennant Road exit and drive west for a mile to Monterey Road. Turn left onto Monterey Road and drive a short distance to Watsonville Road. Turn right on Watsonville Road and drive 3.5 miles to the RV park on the left.

Trip notes: A highlight of this park is Anderson Dam and Coyote Lake, located on the east side of the Santa Clara Valley near Morgan Hill. Anderson (accessed from Dunne Avenue or Cochran Road off of US 101) is a large, beautiful lake, nearly 1,000 acres, providing waterskiing, fishing for bass, bluegill, crappie, and catfish, swimming, and general relief on the hot summer days here. Coyote Reservoir is Anderson's little brother to the south, a long, narrow lake that is stocked with trout in late winter and provides good bass fishing in early spring.

---

⑥ New Brighton State Beach

Location: Near Santa Cruz; map F1, grid b5.

Campsites, facilities: There are 112 sites for tents or RVs up to 31 feet long. Piped water, fire grills, and picnic tables are provided. A sanitary disposal station, toilets, coin-operated showers, propane gas, groceries, and coin laundry are available. Leashed pets are permitted in the campground but not on the beach.

Reservations, fees: Reservations are recommended from mid-March through October; reserve via phone at (800) 444-PARK/7275 ($7.50 reservation fee) or website www.cal-parks.ca.gov; $17 to $19 per night, $1 pet fee.

Contact: New Brighton State Beach, (831) 464-6329; California State Parks, Santa Cruz District, (831) 429-2851 or fax (831) 429-2876.

Directions: From Santa Cruz, drive south on Highway 1 for about five miles to the Capitola/New Brighton Beach exit. The park is just off the highway.

Trip notes: This is one in a series of state park camps set on the bluffs overlooking Monterey Bay. They are among the most popular and in-demand state campgrounds in California. Reservations are a necessity. The summer months are often foggy and cool, especially in the morning. Beachcombing and surf fishing for perch provide recreation options, and skiff rentals are available at the nearby Capitola Wharf. The San Lorenzo River enters the ocean nearby.

⑦ Seacliff State Beach

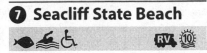

Location: Near Santa Cruz; map F1, grid b6.

Campsites, facilities: There are 26 sites with hookups for RVs up to 40 feet long. Fire grills and tables are provided. Rest rooms and coin-operated showers are available. Propane gas, groceries, and a coin laundry are available nearby. Some facilities are wheelchair accessible. Leashed pets are permitted in the camping area but not on the beach.

Reservations, fees: Reservations are recommended; reserve via phone at (800) 444-PARK/7275 ($7.50 reservation fee) or website www.cal-parks.ca.gov; $28 to $29 per night, $1 pet fee.

Contact: Seacliff State Beach, (831) 685-6000; California State Parks, Santa Cruz District, (831) 429-2851 or fax (831) 429-2876.

Directions: From Santa Cruz, drive south on Highway 1 about six miles to the Seacliff Beach exit. Turn west and drive to the park entrance.

Trip notes: Here is a very pretty spot on bluffs overlooking Monterey Bay. Beach walks are great, especially on clear evenings for dramatic sunsets. A structure named the "old cement ship" nearby provides some of the best shore fishing in Monterey Bay. An interpretive center is available in the summer months. This is a popular layover for vacationers touring Highway 1 in the summer, but the best weather is from mid-August to early October.

⑧ Manresa Beach State Park

Location: On the Pacific Ocean; map F1, grid b6.

Campsites, facilities: There are 64 walk-in tent sites. Piped water, picnic tables, rest rooms, coin-operated showers, food lockers, and fire rings are provided. Some facilities are wheelchair accessible. Leashed pets are permitted.

Reservations, fees: Reservations are recommended from mid-March through October; reserve via phone at (800) 444-PARK/7275 ($7.50 reservation fee) or website www.cal-parks.ca.gov; $17 to $18 per night. Open April through October.

Contact: Manresa Beach State Park, (831) 761-1795; California State Parks, Santa Cruz District, (831) 429-2851 or fax (831) 429-2876.

Directions: From Santa Cruz, drive 12 miles southeast on Highway 1 to the San Andreas Road exit. Drive five miles south on San Andreas Road to Sand Dollar Drive and follow the signs to the park entrance. The parking area is about 1,000 yards from the camping area.

Trip notes: This is a beautiful and extremely popular state park, with the campground set on a bluff overlooking the Pacific Ocean. Many sites have ocean views; others are set back in a secluded grove of pine and cypress trees. There is beach access for fishing, swimming, or beach-combing. Santa Cruz and Monterey are each a short drive away and offer endless recreation possibilities.

⑨ Santa Cruz KOA

Location: Near Watsonville; map F1, grid b7.

Campsites, facilities: There are 12 sites for tents only and 213 RV sites with full or partial hookups. There are also 50 camping cabins. Picnic tables and fire grills are provided. Rest rooms, showers, sanitary disposal station, swimming pool, hot tub, wading pool, playground, recreation room, bicycle rentals, miniature golf, mining sluice, store, and propane gas are available. Leashed pets are permitted.

Reservations, fees: Reservations are accepted; $49.95-$59.95 per two adult campers per night, $2 each child and $6 each additional adult. Open year-round.

Contact: Santa Cruz KOA, (831) 722-0551 or fax (831) 722-0989.

Directions: From Santa Cruz, drive 12 miles southeast on Highway 1. Take the San Andreas Road exit and head southwest for 3.5 miles to 1186 San Andreas Road.

Trip notes: Bike rentals and nearby access to Manresa Beach State Park make this KOA campground a winner. The little log cabins are quite cute, and security is first class. For those who have been here, it is a popular layover spot and weekend vacation destination. The only downer is the amount of asphalt, with everything paved right up to your cabin doorstep.

⑩ Pinto Lake Park

Location: Near Watsonville; map F1, grid b8.

Campsites, facilities: There are 28 RV sites with full hookups. Piped water, sewer hookups, and electricity are provided. A boat ramp and boat rentals are available in the summer. Leashed pets are permitted.

Reservations, fees: Reservations are accepted; $20 per night, $2 per child and per additional car, $2 pet fee.

Contact: Pinto Lake Park, (831) 722-8129.

Directions: From Santa Cruz, drive 17 miles south on Highway 1 to the Watsonville/Highway 152 exit and immediately turn left on Green Valley Road. Drive three miles (a half mile past the hospital) to the campground on the lake.

From Monterey, drive north on Highway 1, take a right at the Green Valley Road exit, and drive three miles (a half mile past the hospital) to the campground on the lake.

Trip notes: Pinto Lake can be a real find. Of the seven lakes in the nine Bay Area counties that offer camping, it is the only one where the RV campsites are actually near the lake. For the few who know about it, it's an offer that can't be refused. From winter to early summer, the Department of Fish and Game stocks the lake twice a month with rainbow trout. A 5 mph speed limit has been established for boaters, and no swimming is permitted.

⑪ Mount Madonna County Park

Location: Near Gilroy; map F1, grid b9.

Campsites, facilities: There are 117 sites for

tents or RVs. Piped water, fire grills, and tables are provided. Vault toilets are available. Leashed pets are permitted.

Reservations, fees: No reservations; $10 per night, $1 pet fee.

Contact: Call Mount Madonna County Park, (408) 842-2341 or fax (408) 842-6642.

Directions: From US 101 in Gilroy, take the Hecker Pass Highway/Highway 152 exit west. Drive approximately seven miles west to the park entrance.

From Highway 1 in Watsonville, turn east onto Highway 152 and drive about 12 miles to the park entrance.

Trip notes: It's a twisty son-of-a-gun road to reach the top of Mount Madonna, but the views on clear days of Monterey Bay to the west and Santa Clara Valley to the east always make it worth the trip. In addition, a small herd of white deer are kept protected in a pen near the parking area for a rare chance to see unique wildlife. There are many good hiking trails in the park; the best is the Bayview Loop. Elevation in the park reaches 1,896 feet.

⑫ Sunset State Beach

Location: Near Watsonville; map F1, grid c7.

Campsites, facilities: There are 90 sites for tents or RVs up to 31 feet long. Rest rooms, showers, fire grills, and picnic tables are provided. Leashed pets are permitted, except on the beach.

Reservations, fees: Reservations are recommended from mid-March through November; reserve via phone at (800) 444-PARK/7275 ($7.50 reservation fee) or website www.cal-parks.ca.gov; $17 to $18 per night, $1 pet fee.

Contact: Sunset State Beach, (831) 763-7063; California State Parks, Santa Cruz District, (831) 429-2851 or fax (831) 429-2876.

Directions: From Highway 1 near Watsonville, take the Riverside Drive exit toward the ocean to Beach Road. Drive 3.5 miles on Beach Road to the San Andreas Road exit. Turn right on San Andreas Road and drive about 4.5 miles to the beach.

Trip notes: On clear evenings, the sunsets here look like they are imported from Hawaii. The

camp is set on a bluff overlooking Monterey Bay, making it a short traipse for a beautiful beach walk. It is also a good spot for pismo clams during minus low tides. The best weather is in late summer and fall. Spring can be windy here, and early summer is often foggy. Reservations are often needed well in advance to secure a spot.

⑬ Monterey Vacation RV Park

Location: Near San Juan Bautista; map F1, grid c9.

Campsites, facilities: There are 88 sites for RVs with full hookups and a few tent sites. Flush toilets, showers, hot tub, swimming pool, coin laundry, and propane gas are available. Leashed pets are permitted.

Reservations, fees: Reservations are recommended for three-day holiday weekends; $20 per night.

Contact: Monterey Vacation RV Park, (831) 726-9118 or fax (831) 726-1841.

Directions: The park is located between Gilroy and Salinas, at 1400 Highway 101 (two miles south of the Highway 156/San Juan Bautista exit).

Trip notes: This RV park has an ideal location for many vacationers. It's a 10-minute drive to San Juan Bautista, 30 minutes to the Monterey Bay Aquarium, and 40 minutes to Monterey's Fisherman's Wharf. It's set in an attractive spot with some trees, but the nearby attractions are what make it a clear winner.

⑭ Marina Dunes RV Park

Location: Near Monterey Bay; map F1, grid d6.

Campsites, facilities: There are 65 RV sites, many with full or partial hookups. Piped water and picnic tables are provided. Rest rooms, showers, laundry room, cable TV, recreation room, and groceries are available. Leashed pets are permitted.

Reservations, fees: Reservations are recommended; $21 to $36 per night, $1 pet fee.

Contact: Marina Dunes RV Park, (831) 384-6914 or fax (831) 384-0285.

Directions: From Highway 1 in Marina, take the Reservation Road exit and drive one block west. Turn north onto Dunes Drive and drive to 3330 Dunes Drive.

Trip notes: This is a popular park for RV cruisers who are touring Highway 1 and want a layover spot near Monterey. This place fills the bill, being open all year and located in Marina, just a short drive from the many side trip opportunities available in Monterey and Carmel. It is set in the sand dunes, about 200 yards from the ocean.

⑮ Cabana Holiday

Location: Near Salinas; map F1, grid d8.

Campsites, facilities: There are 96 RV sites with full or partial hookups. Picnic tables are provided. Rest rooms, showers, recreation room, swimming pool, playground, coin laundry, and a snack bar are available. Leashed pets are permitted.

Reservations, fees: Reservations are recommended; $26.95 per night.

Contact: Cabana Holiday, (831) 663-2886 or fax (831) 663-1660.

Directions: From Salinas, drive north on US 101 for seven miles to the junction with Highway 156. This park is at the intersection at 8710 Prunedale North Road, which runs parallel to US 101.

Trip notes: If Big Sur, Monterey, and Carmel are packed, this spot provides some overflow space. It's about a half-hour drive from the Monterey area. Facilities are limited in the winter.

⑯ Fremont Peak State Park

Location: Near San Juan Bautista; map F1, grid d9.

Campsites, facilities: There are 25 primitive sites for tents or RVs up to 26 feet long and trailers up to 18 feet long. There are also a few group sites available. Picnic tables, fire rings, and piped water are provided. Pit toilets are available. Leashed pets are permitted.

Reservations, fees: No reservations; $7 to $12 per night, $1 pet fee. Call for group fees and reservation information.

Contact: Fremont Peak State Park, (831) 623-4255, (831) 649-2836, or fax (831) 649-2847.

Directions: From Highway 156 in San Juan Bautista, turn south on San Juan Canyon Road and drive 11 miles to the park.

Trip notes: Most vacationers in this region are heading to Monterey Bay and the surrounding environs. That's why Fremont Peak State Park is missed by a lot of folks. It is located on a ridge (2,900 feet) with great views of Monterey Bay available on the trail going up Fremont Peak. An observatory at the park is open to the public on specified Saturdays. Note: There is no access from this park to the adjacent Hollister Hills State Vehicular Recreation Area.

⑰ Laguna Seca Recreation Area

Location: Near Monterey; map F1, grid e6.

Campsites, facilities: There are 170 sites for tents or RVs, many with partial hookups. Picnic tables and fire grills are provided. Rest rooms, showers, sanitary disposal station, pond, rifle and pistol range, clubhouse, and group camping facilities are available. Leashed pets are permitted.

Reservations, fees: Reservations are accepted, phone (831) 755-4899; $18 to $22 per night, $1 pet fee. Open year-round.

Contact: Laguna Seca Recreation Area, (831) 758-3604, (888) 588-2267, or fax (831) 755-4914.

Directions: From Monterey, drive nine miles east on Highway 68 to the entrance.

Trip notes: This campground is just minutes away from the sights in Monterey and Carmel. It is situated in oak woodlands overlooking the world-famous Laguna Seca Raceway.

⑱ Carmel by the River RV Park

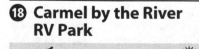

Location: On the Carmel River; map F1, grid f5.

Campsites, facilities: There are 35 RV sites

with full hookups and cable TV. Rest rooms, showers, recreational cabana, game room with pool tables, barbecue area, horseshoes, basketball courts, and a river beach are available. A grocery store, coin laundry, and propane gas are nearby. Leashed pets are permitted.

Reservations, fees: Reservations are accepted; $27-$40 per night for two people, $13 each additional camper over 14 years old, $1 pet fee. Open year-round.

Contact: Carmel by the River RV Park, (831) 624-9329 or fax (831) 624-8416.

Directions: In Carmel on Highway 1, take Carmel Valley Road and drive southeast for 4.5 miles to Schulte Road. Turn right and drive to the end of the road (27680 Schulte Road).

Trip notes: Location, location, location. That's what vacationers want. Well, this park is set on the Carmel River, minutes away from Carmel, Cannery Row, the Monterey Bay Aquarium, golf courses, and the beach. Each RV site is separated by hedges and flowers.

---

⑲ Saddle Mountain Recreation Park

Location: Near the Carmel River; map F1, grid f5.

Campsites, facilities: There are 25 tent sites and 25 full hookup sites for RVs. Piped water, picnic tables, barbecues, rest rooms, and showers are provided. A swimming pool, playground, horseshoe pits, volleyball net, basketball court, and a game room are available. The facilities are wheelchair accessible. Leashed pets are permitted in the RV area only.

Reservations, fees: Reservations are accepted; $25 to $35 per night.

Contact: Saddle Mountain Recreation Park, (831) 624-1617 or fax (831) 624-4470.

Directions: In Carmel, on Highway 1 take Carmel Valley Road and drive southeast 4.5 miles to Schulte Road. Turn right and drive to the park at the end of the road.

Trip notes: This pretty park is set about 100 yards from the Carmel River amid a grove of oak trees. The park offers hiking trails, and if you want to make a buyer's swing in Carmel, it's

only a five-mile drive. Note: The Carmel River is reduced to a trickle most of the year.

---

⑳ Bottcher's Gap Walk-In

Location: In Los Padres National Forest; map F1, grid g5.

Campsites, facilities: There are eight walk-in sites. Picnic tables and fire grills are provided. There is no piped water. Vault toilets are available. Leashed pets are permitted.

Reservations, fees: No reservations; $10 per night. Open year-round.

Contact: Parks Management Company at (805) 927-4622; Los Padres National Forest, Monterey Ranger District, (831) 385-5434 or fax (831) 385-0628.

Directions: From Carmel, drive south on Highway 1 for about 10 miles to Palo Colorado Road/County Road 5012. Turn left and drive nine miles to the campground.

Trip notes: Here is a surprise for all the Highway 1 cruisers who never leave the highway. Just inland is this little-known camp, set in beautiful Palo Colorado (redwood) Canyon. It's a good jump-off spot for a hiking trip; the trail leading out of camp is routed all the way into the Ventana Wilderness. Compared to the RV parks near Monterey and Carmel, this place is truly a world apart. The elevation is 2,100 feet.

㉑ Andrew Molera State Park Walk-In

Location: In Big Sur, map F1, grid h5.

Campsites, facilities: There is a 10-acre meadow with undesignated, primitive, walk-in sites. Fire rings, picnic tables, piped water, and chemical toilets are available. Bring your own wood. Leashed pets are permitted.

Reservations, fees: No reservations; $3 per night per person, $1 pet fee. There is a three-day limit.

Contact: Bottcher's Gap Walk-In, (831) 667-2315; California State Parks, Monterey District, (831) 649-2836.

Directions: From Carmel, drive 21 miles south on Highway 1 to the park on the right.

Trip notes: Considering the popularity and grandeur of Big Sur, some campers might find it hard to believe that any primitive campgrounds are available. Believe it. This park offers walk-in sites amid some beautiful coastal terrain. One of the highlights is a great trail that leads one mile to a beautiful beach. Park rangers often have a one-page flyer available on the best places to spot sea otters. One downer: The campsites are too close together.

㉒ Fernwood Park

Location: On the Big Sur River; map F1, grid h5.

Campsites, facilities: There are 38 sites for tents only and 28 RV sites with partial hookups. Fire grills and picnic tables are provided. Rest rooms with showers, grocery store, restaurant, and a bar are available. Leashed pets are permitted.

Reservations, fees: Reservations are accepted; $24 to $27 per night, $3 pet fee.

Contact: Fernwood Park, (831) 667-2422.

Directions: From Carmel, drive 28 miles south on Highway 1 to the campground on the right.

Trip notes: This motor home park is on the banks of the Big Sur River in the redwoods of the beautiful Big Sur coast. You can crown your trip with a first-class dinner at Nepenthe or the Ventana Inn (bring your bank with you).

㉓ Big Sur Campground and Cabins

Location: On the Big Sur River; map F1, grid h5.

Campsites, facilities: There are 40 RV sites with water and electrical hookups, 40 sites for tents or RVs, and 13 cabins. Piped water, fire grills, and picnic tables are provided. Rest rooms, showers, dump station, playground, small store, and a laundry room are available. Leashed pets are permitted, except in the cabins.

Reservations, fees: Reservations are recommended; $26 to $29 per night, $3 pet fee. Cabin fees are $80 to $160 for two people and $12 for each additional person.

Contact: Big Sur Campground and Cabins, (831) 667-2322 or fax (831) 667-0456.

Directions: From Carmel, drive 27 miles south on Highway 1 to the campground on the right side of the road.

Trip notes: This camp is located in the redwoods near the Big Sur River. Campers can stay near redwoods, hike on great trails through the forest, or explore nearby Pfeiffer Beach. Nearby Los Padres National Forest and Ventana Wilderness in the mountains to the east provide access to remote hiking trails with ridge-top vistas. Cruising Highway 1 south to Lucia and back offers endless views of breathtaking coastal scenery.

㉔ Riverside Campground

Location: On the Big Sur River; map F1, grid h5.

Campsites, facilities: There are 46 sites for tents or RVs, some with water and electrical hookups. Picnic tables and fire grills are provided. Rest rooms, showers, and a playground are available. Leashed pets are permitted.

Reservations, fees: Reservations are recommended; $24 to $27 per night, $3 pet fee. Open year-round, weather permitting.

Contact: Riverside Campground, (831) 667-2414.

Directions: From Carmel, drive 25 miles south on Highway 1 to the campground on the right.

Trip notes: This is one in a series of privately operated camps designed for Highway 1 cruisers touring the Big Sur area. This camp is set amid redwoods. Side trips include expansive beaches with sea otters playing on the edge of kelp beds (Andrew Molera State Park), redwood forests and waterfalls (Julia Pfeiffer Burns State Park), and several quality restaurants, including Nepenthe for those on a budget, and the Ventana Inn for those who can light cigars with $100 bills.

25 White Oaks

Location: On Chews Ridge in Los Padres National Forest; map F1, grid h8.

Campsites, facilities: There are eight tent sites. There is no piped water. Picnic tables and fire grills are provided. Vault toilets are available. Leashed pets are permitted.

Reservations, fees: No reservations; $5 daily fee per parked vehicle, or use an Adventure pass ($30 annual fee).

Contact: Los Padres National Forest, Monterey Ranger District, (831) 385-5434 or fax (831) 385-0628.

Directions: From Highway 1 in Carmel, turn east on Carmel Valley Road and drive about 22 miles. Turn right (south) on Tassajara Road/County Road 5007 and drive eight miles to the campground.

Trip notes: This camp is set at 4,200 feet, near Anastasia Creek, and there's a surprisingly remote feel to the area despite its relative proximity to Carmel Valley. You can get some unexpected adventures around here. On one trip, we kept meeting these bald guys and asking them about the hiking possibilities. They just shook their heads. Turns out they were from a religious cult on a one-week vigil of silence. Either that or they wanted to keep their favorite hikes secret. Well, we found a good one that starts about a mile from the camp and is routed into the Ventana Wilderness. Several backcountry trail camps are also available.

26 Ventana Campgrounds

Location: In Big Sur; map F1, grid i6.

Campsites, facilities: There are 70 sites for tents or RVs up to 22 feet. Piped water, fire rings, and picnic tables are provided. A rest room and showers are available. A small grocery store is nearby. Leashed pets are permitted.

Reservations, fees: Reservations are accepted; $25 per night, $5 pet fee. Open year-round.

Contact: Ventana Campgrounds, (831) 667-2688; PO Box 206, Big Sur, CA 93920.

Directions: From Carmel, drive 28 miles south on Highway 1 to the campground, on the left in Big Sur.

Trip notes: This rustic camp has wooded sites and is set in an ideal location for many. Premium side trips are available, highlighted by the beautiful beach at Andrew Molera State Park (a one-mile hike is necessary), the majestic redwoods, a creek hike, and a bluff-top waterfall in Julia Pfeiffer Burns State Park.

27 Pfeiffer Big Sur State Park

Location: In Big Sur; map F1, grid i6.

Campsites, facilities: There are 218 sites for tents or RVs up to 32 feet long and some primitive bike-in sites. Piped water, picnic tables, and fire grills are provided. Rest rooms, showers, coin laundry, groceries, and propane gas are available. Campgrounds, rest rooms, the grocery store, and food services are wheelchair accessible. Leashed pets are permitted.

Reservations, fees: Reserve via phone at (800) 444-PARK/7275 ($7.50 reservation fee) or website www.cal-parks.ca.gov; $20 to $23 per night, $1 pet fee, $3 per night for bike-in sites. Open year-round.

Contact: Pfeiffer Big Sur State Park, (831) 667-2315; California State Parks, Monterey District, (831) 649-2836.

Directions: From Carmel, drive 26 miles south on Highway 1 to the park on the left.

Trip notes: Pfeiffer Big Sur State Park is one of the most popular state parks in California, and it's easy to see why. You can have it all: fantastic coastal vistas along Highway 1, redwood forests and waterfalls in the Julia Pfeiffer Burns State Park, expansive beaches with sea otters playing on the edge of kelp beds in the (Andrew Molera State Park), great restaurants like the Nepenthe and Ventana Inn, and private, patrolled sites. Reservations are a necessity.

㉘ China Camp

Location: On Chews Ridge in Los Padres National Forest; map F1, grid i8.

Campsites, facilities: There are eight sites for tents only. There is no piped water. Picnic tables and fire grills are provided. Vault toilets are available. Leashed pets are permitted.

Reservations, fees: No reservations; $5 daily fee per parked vehicle or Adventure Pass ($30 annual fee). Open April through November, weather permitting.

Contact: Los Padres National Forest, Monterey Ranger District, (831) 385-5434 or fax (831) 385-0628.

Directions: From Highway 1 in Carmel, turn east on Carmel Valley Road and drive about 22 miles. Turn right (south) on Tassajara Road/County Road 5007 and drive 10 miles to the campground on the right.

Trip notes: A lot of folks might find it difficult to believe that a spot that feels so remote can be so close to the manicured Carmel Valley. But here it is, one of two camps on Tassajara Road. This one has a trail out of camp that is routed into the Ventana Wilderness. Tassajara Hot Springs is seven miles away at the end of Tassajara Road. And keep a lookout for the gents with shaved heads. They're good at keeping secrets; they never talk. The elevation is 4,300 feet.

㉙ Arroyo Seco

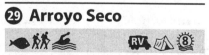

Location: Along Arroyo Seco Creek in Los Padres National Forest; map F1, grid j9.

Campsites, facilities: There are 51 sites for tents or RVs. Piped water, picnic tables, and fire grills are provided. Vault toilets and coin-operated showers are available. Leashed pets are permitted.

Reservations, fees: No reservations; $10 to $15 per night, $15 per night for multi-family sites. Open year-round.

Contact: Pyramid Enterprises, (805) 295-1378;

Los Padres National Forest, Monterey Ranger District, (831) 385-5434 or fax (831) 385-0628.

Directions: From US 101 in the town of Greenfield, turn west on Greenfield-Arroyo Seco Road/County Roads G16 and 3050 and drive 19 miles to the camp at the end of the road.

Trip notes: This pretty spot near Arroyo Seco Creek (900-foot elevation) is just outside the northern border of the Ventana Wilderness. Arroyo Seco Group Camp (see campground number 30) is available to keep the pressure off this campground.

㉚ Arroyo Seco Group Camp

Location: In Los Padres National Forest; map F1, grid j9.

Campsites, facilities: There is a group campsite for tents or RVs. Piped water, picnic tables, and fire grills are provided. Vault toilets are available. Leashed pets are permitted.

Reservations, fees: Reservations are required; reserve via phone at (877) 444-6777 ($8.65 reservation fee) or website www.reserveusa.com; $40 group fee per night. Open year-round.

Contact: Pyramid Enterprises, (805) 295-1378; Los Padres National Forest, Monterey Ranger District, (831) 385-5434 or fax (831) 385-0628.

Directions: From US 101 at the town of Greenfield, turn west on Greenfield-Arroyo Seco Road/County Roads G16 and 3050 and drive 19 miles to the camp.

Trip notes: If you have a larger group, give the folks at Arroyo Seco a break and use this adjoining spot instead. That way you'll get the privacy you desire. This camp is in a pretty spot, set near Arroyo Seco Creek near the northern border of the Ventana Wilderness.

㉛ Memorial Park

Location: In Los Padres National Forest; map F1, grid j9.

Campsites, facilities: There are eight tent sites. Picnic tables and fire grills are provided. Vault toilets are available. Leashed pets are permitted.

Reservations, fees: No reservations; $8 per night. Open year-round.

Contact: Pyramid Enterprises, (805) 295-1378; Los Padres National Forest, Monterey Ranger District, (831) 385-5434 or fax (831) 385-0628.

Directions: From US 101 in King City, turn south on County Route G14 and drive 18 miles. Turn north on Mission Road and drive six miles. Turn left on Del Venturi–Milpitas Road/County Road 4050 and drive 16 miles to the campground on the right.

Trip notes: This is one of two backcountry camps in the area. The camp has a trailhead that provides access to the Ventana Wilderness trail network. The elevation is 2,000 feet, which gives hikers a nice head start on the climb. Be sure to pack plenty of drinking water for the trail and, even in spring, expect warm, dry conditions.

㉜ Escondido

Location: In Los Padres National Forest; map F1, grid j9.

Campsites, facilities: There are nine tent sites. Picnic tables and fire grills are provided. Vault toilets are available. Leashed pets are permitted.

Reservations, fees: No reservations; $8 per night. Open April through November.

Contact: Pyramid Enterprises, (805) 295-1378; Los Padres National Forest, Monterey Ranger District, (831) 385-5434 or fax (831) 385-0628.

Directions: From US 101 in King City, turn south on County Route G14 and drive 18 miles. Turn north on Mission Road and drive six miles. Turn left on Del Venturi–Milpitas Road/Indian Road and drive 20 miles to the campground on the left.

Trip notes: This is a prime jump-off spot for backpackers heading into the Ventana Wilderness. The camp is set at 900 feet at a trailhead that connects to a network of other trails. The only catch is you have to plan on walking up, very steep at times, for a climb of more than a thousand feet to reach the ridge.

Map F2

One inch equals approximately 10.7 miles.
See inside back cover for California state map.

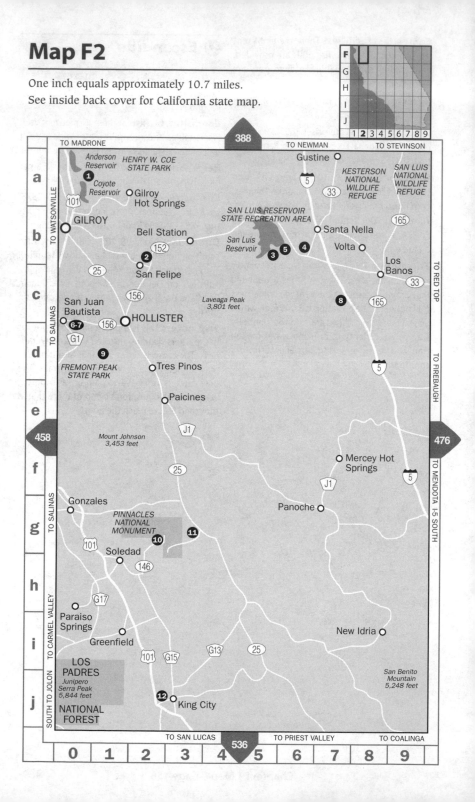

1 Coyote Lake County Park

Location: Near Gilroy; map F2, grid a1.

Campsites, facilities: There are 74 sites for tents. Picnic tables and fire grills are provided. Piped water, flush toilets, and a boat ramp are available. Leashed pets are permitted.

Reservations, fees: No reservations; $10 per night, $5 for a second vehicle.

Contact: Coyote Lake County Park, (408) 842-7800 or fax (408) 842-6439.

Directions: From US 101 in Gilroy, drive east on Leavesley Road to New Avenue. Turn left on New Avenue and drive to Roop Road. Turn right on Roop Road and drive to Coyote Lake Road. Turn left on Coyote Lake Road and drive to the campground. The park is a total of 5.5 miles from Gilroy.

Trip notes: Coyote Lake is a pretty surprise to newcomers, a long, narrow lake set in a canyon just over the ridge east of US 101. It covers 688 acres and is stocked with a total of 24,000 trout on a biweekly basis from late winter through spring; the lake also provides a decent fishery for bass. The campground is nestled in oaks, furnishing some much-needed shade. Note: If you continue east about four miles on the access road that runs past the lake to the Coe State Park Hunting Hollow entrance, you'll come to a remote trailhead into that park's wilderness.

2 Casa De Fruta Orchard Resort

Location: Near Pacheco Pass; map F2, grid b2.

Campsites, facilities: There are 300 RV sites, all with water and electric hookups (some also have sewer connections). Picnic tables and fire grills are provided. Also available are flush toilets, showers, sanitary disposal station, cable TV, satellite TV, coin laundry, playground, swimming pool, wading pool, outdoor dance floor, horseshoes, volleyball courts, baseball diamonds, wine and cheese tasting room, candy factory, bakery, fruit stand, petting zoo, 24-hour restaurant, gift shop, and a grocery store. Leashed pets are permitted.

Reservations, fees: Reservations are accepted; $23 to $24 per night.

Contact: Casa De Fruta Orchard Resort, (408) 842-9316 or fax (831) 637-1293.

Directions: From Gilroy, drive 13 miles east on Highway 152. Take the Casa De Fruta Parkway exit. You will see the entrance at 10031 Pacheco Pass Highway.

Trip notes: This 80-acre RV park has a festival-like atmosphere to it, with country music and dancing every weekend in the summer and barbecues on Sundays. Huge, but sparse, San Luis Reservoir is located 20 miles to the east.

3 Basalt

Location: On San Luis Reservoir; map F2, grid b5.

Campsites, facilities: There are 79 sites for tents or RVs. Piped water, fire grills, and picnic tables are provided. Flush toilets, showers, dump station, and a boat ramp are available. A grocery store, coin laundry, and propane gas are nearby (about 1.5 miles away). The facilities are wheelchair accessible. Leashed pets are permitted.

Reservations, fees: Reserve via phone at (800) 444-PARK/7275 ($7.50 reservation fee) or website www.cal-parks.ca.gov; $12 to $16 per night, $1 pet fee. Open year-round.

Contact: San Luis Reservoir State Recreation Area, (209) 826-1196 or fax (209) 826-0284.

Directions: From Los Banos, drive 12 miles west on Highway 152 to the entrance road. Turn left and drive 2.5 miles to the campground.

Trip notes: San Luis Reservoir is a huge, man-made lake, covering 13,800 acres with 65 miles of shoreline, developed among stark foothills to provide a storage facility along the California Aqueduct. It fills by late winter and is used primarily by anglers, water-skiers, and windsurfers. When the Sacramento River Delta water pumps take the water, they also take the fish, filling this lake up with both. Striped bass fishing is best in the fall when the stripers chase schools of bait fish on the lake surface. Spring and early summer can be quite windy, but that makes for good windsurfing. The adjacent O'Neill Forebay is the best recreation bet because of the developed marina and often good fishing. The elevation is 575 feet.

---

④ Madeiros

Location: On San Luis Reservoir; map F2, grid b6.

Campsites, facilities: There are 350 primitive sites for tents or RVs. Some shaded ramadas with fire grills and picnic tables are available. Piped water and chemical toilets are available. A boat ramp is nearby. Leashed pets are permitted.

Reservations, fees: No reservations; $7 to $10 per night, $1 pet fee. Open year-round.

Contact: San Luis Reservoir State Recreation Area, (209) 826-1196 or fax (209) 826-0284.

Directions: From Los Banos, drive 12 miles west on Highway 152 to the intersection with Highway 33. Turn north on Highway 33 and drive a short distance to the campground entrance.

Trip notes: This is a vast, primitive campground set on the stark expanse of foothill country near San Luis Reservoir. See the trip notes for Basalt (campground number 3) for more infor-

mation. It is best known for wind in the spring, hot weather in the summer, and low water levels in the fall. Striped bass fishing is best in the fall when the wind is down and stripers will corral schools of bait fish near the lake surface. The elevation is 225 feet.

⑤ San Luis Campground

Location: On San Luis Reservoir; map F2, grid b5.

Campsites, facilities: There are 53 sites for tents or RVs with electrical and water hookups. Fire pits, picnic tables, and pit toilets are provided. A dump station is nearby at Basalt Camp. Leashed pets are permitted.

Reservations, fees: Reservations are required; $15 per night, $1 pet fee.

Contact: San Luis Reservoir State Recreation Area, (209) 826-1196 or fax (209) 826-0284.

Directions: From Los Banos, drive 15 miles west on Highway 152 to the signed entrance on the right.

Trip notes: San Luis Campground is located on Los Banos Creek near San Luis Reservoir. It is one in a series of camps operated by the state in the San Luis Reservoir State Recreation Area, adjacent to the reservoir and O'Neill Forebay, home of the biggest striped bass in California, including the world record for landlocked stripers.

⑥ Mission Farm RV Park

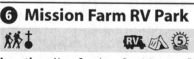

Location: Near San Juan Bautista; map F2, grid c0.

Campsites, facilities: There are four sites for tents and 165 RV sites with full hookups and picnic tables. Flush toilets, showers, barbecue area, sanitary disposal station, coin laundry, and propane gas are available. Leashed pets are permitted; a dog run is available.

Reservations, fees: Reservations are recommended; $10 to $22 per night.

Contact: Mission Farm RV Park, (831) 623-4456.

Directions: From US 101, drive three miles east on Highway 156. Turn right on The Alameda and drive a block. Turn left on San Juan–Hollister Road and drive a quarter mile to the campground at 400 San Juan–Hollister Road.

Trip notes: The primary appeal of this RV park is that it is within easy walking distance of San Juan Bautista. In addition, the park is set beside a walnut orchard, and in the fall you can pick walnuts for free and keep them.

❼ San Juan Bautista KOA

Location: Near San Juan Bautista; map F2, grid c0.

Campsites, facilities: There are 17 sites for tents only, 27 sites with partial hookups for tents or RVs, and 14 RV sites with full hookups. Two cabins are also available. Picnic tables and fire grills are provided. Flush toilets, showers, sanitary disposal station, recreation room, swimming pool, coin laundry, propane gas, and groceries are available. Some facilities are wheelchair accessible. Leashed pets are permitted.

Reservations, fees: Reservations are accepted; $21 to $26 per night, $35 per night for cabin rentals, and $4 for each additional adult.

Contact: San Juan Bautista KOA, (831) 623-4263.

Directions: From US 101, take the Highway 129 exit west and drive 100 feet. Turn left onto Searle Road (frontage road) and drive to the stop sign. Turn left again on Anzar and drive under the freeway to 900 Anzar Road.

Trip notes: This is the only privately operated campground in the immediate region that has any spots for tenters. The two camping cabins here look like miniature log cabins, quite cute and comfortable. Highlights of the park are its proximity to Mission San Juan Bautista and the relatively short drive to the Monterey-Carmel area.

❽ Los Banos Creek Reservoir

Location: Near Los Banos; map F2, grid c7.

Campsites, facilities: There are 25 sites for tents or RVs up to 30 feet long. Fire grills and picnic tables are provided. Pit toilets and a boat ramp are available. There is no piped water. Leashed pets are permitted.

Reservations, fees: No reservations; $7 to $10 per night, $1 pet fee. Open year-round.

Contact: San Luis Reservoir State Recreation Area, (209) 826-1196 or fax (209) 826-0284.

Directions: From Los Banos, go five miles west on Highway 152. Turn south on Volta Road and drive about a mile. Turn left on Pioneer Road and drive a mile. Turn south onto Canyon Road and go about five miles to the park.

Trip notes: Los Banos Creek Reservoir is set in a long, narrow valley, covering 410 acres and with 12 miles of shoreline. It provides a smaller, more low-key setting (a 5 mph speed limit is enforced) compared to the nearby giant, San Luis Reservoir. In spring, it can be quite windy and is a popular spot for sailboarding. The elevation is 400 feet.

❾ Hollister Hills State Vehicular Recreation Area

Location: Near Hollister; map F2, grid d1.

Campsites, facilities: There are 125 sites for tents or RVs. Some group sites are available. Picnic tables, fire grills, and piped water are provided. Flush toilets, showers, and a grocery store are available. Leashed pets are permitted.

Reservations, fees: No reservations; $6 per night. Open year-round.

Contact: Hollister Hills State Vehicular Recreation Area, (831) 637-3874, (831) 637-8186, or fax (831) 637-4725.

Directions: From Highway 156 northwest of Hollister, turn south on Union Road and drive three miles. Turn south on Cienega Road and drive five miles to the park on the right.

Trip notes: This unique park was designed for off-road-vehicle enthusiasts. It provides 80 miles of trails for motorcycles and 40 miles of trails for four-wheel-drive vehicles. All trails close at sunset. There is no direct access to the Fremont Peak State Park, bordering directly to the west. The elevation is about 1,500 feet.

⑩ Pinnacles National Monument

Location: South of Hollister; map F2, grid g2.

Campsites, facilities: There are 18 walk-in tent sites. There are two wheelchair-accessible sites near wheelchair-accessible rest rooms. Picnic tables, fire grills, and piped water are provided. Leashed pets are permitted, except on trails.

Reservations, fees: No reservations, but call ahead for status; may be closed due to repairs or improvements; $10 per night plus a $4 entrance fee, which is good for seven days. Closed on weekends from mid-February through May.

Contact: Pinnacles National Monument, (831) 389-4526 or fax (831) 389-4489.

Directions: From US 101 in Soledad, drive 11 miles northeast on Highway 146 to the campground.

Trip notes: The Pinnacles National Monument is like a different planet. It's a 16,000-acre park with volcanic clusters and strange caves, all great for exploring. This is one of two campgrounds at the Pinnacles, and don't get the two mixed up. This is the more primitive of the two, and far less visited. Does the shoe fit? If so, come prepared for hot weather and the chance of meeting up with a rattlesnake, and bring plenty of ice in a cooler to keep your drinks cold.

⑪ Pinnacles Campground

Location: Near Pinnacles National Monument; map F2, grid g3.

Campsites, facilities: There are 36 RV sites, 78 sites for tents or RVs, and 13 group sites. Picnic tables and fire grills are provided. Piped water, electricity, flush toilets, sanitary disposal station, showers, store, and a swimming pool are available. Bring your own firewood or purchase it at the campground. Leashed pets are permitted, except on trails.

Reservations, fees: Reservations are required for group sites; all others are on a first-come,

first-served basis; $7 per night per person for a family site, $6 per night per person for a group site with a $50 minimum, and a $10 leash deposit per pet.

Contact: Pinnacles Campground, (831) 389-4462 or fax (831) 637-2337; website: www.pincamp.com.

Directions: From Hollister, drive 32 miles south on Highway 25. Turn at the sign for the Pinnacles/Highway 146 and drive about 2.5 miles to the campground.

Trip notes: This is one of two camps at the Pinnacles National Monument. This private one gets a lot more traffic—it has more facilities, the access road is in better shape, and the campground is closer to Bear Gulch Caves, a prime destination. The jagged pinnacles for which the park was named were formed by the erosion of an ancient volcanic eruption. If you are planning to stay a weekend in the spring, arrive early on Friday evening to be sure you get a campsite. Beware of temperatures in the 90s and 100s in the summer.

⑫ San Lorenzo County Park

Location: In King City; map F2, grid j2.

Campsites, facilities: There are 119 sites for tents or RVs with partial hookups. Tables and fire grills are provided. A dump station, rest rooms, and showers are available. Leashed pets are permitted.

Reservations, fees: Reservations are accepted; $14 to $21 per night. Open year-round.

Contact: San Lorenzo County Park, (831) 385-5964.

Directions: From King City on US 101, turn left at the Broadway exit and drive to the park at 1160 Broadway.

Trip notes: A lot of folks cruising up and down the state on US 101 can underestimate their travel time and find themselves caught out near King City, a small city located about midpoint between Northern and Southern California. Well, don't sweat it, because San Lorenzo County Park offers a spot to overnight. It's set near the Salinas River, which isn't exactly the Mississippi, but it'll do.

Map F3

One inch equals approximately 10.7 miles.
See inside back cover for California state map.

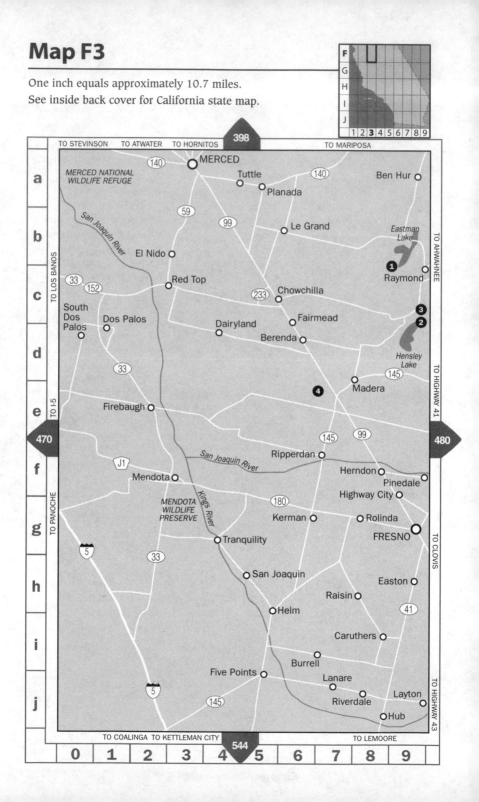

Chapter F3 features:

1 Cordorniz Recreation Area

Location: On Eastman Lake; map F3, grid b8.

Campsites, facilities: There are 62 sites for tents or RVs. Three group sites, providing for a maximum of 200 people, are also available. Piped water, fire grills, and picnic tables are provided. Flush toilets, showers, dump station, and a boat ramp are available. An equestrian staging area is available for overnight use, and there are seven miles of hiking, biking, and equestrian trails. Leashed pets are permitted.

Reservations, fees: No reservations for individual sites; $8 to $20 per night. Reservations are recommended for the group site; group fees range from $25 to $65 per night. Open year-round.

Contact: US Army Corps of Engineers, Eastman Lake, (559) 689-3255 or fax (559) 689-3408.

Directions: From Chowchilla, on Highway 99 take the Avenue 26 exit. Drive 17 miles east on Avenue 26. Turn north on County Road 29 and drive eight miles to the lake.

Trip notes: Eastman Lake may not look like paradise, but it is treated just the same by people seeking relief on your typical 100-degree summer day out here. It is tucked in the foothills of the San Joaquin Valley at an elevation of 650 feet and covers 1,800 surface acres. It makes a nice tub to take a dunk in, a favorite for waterskiing, swimming and, in the spring, fishing for big bass. Check fishing regulations, posted on all bulletin boards. The lake is also a designated "Watchable Wildlife" site with 163 species of birds, and it is home to a nesting pair of bald eagles.

Special note: The upper end of the lake is closed to boats, with the area marked by a keep-out buoy line. The reason is to prevent the spread of hydrilla, a weed that took over Eastman Lake in the late 1980s and caused the lake to be temporarily closed.

2 Hensley Group Site

Location: North of Fresno on Hensley Lake; map F3, grid c9.

Campsites, facilities: There is a group site. Piped water, fire grills, and picnic tables are provided. Flush toilets, showers, dump station, playground, and a boat ramp are available. Leashed pets are permitted.

Reservations, fees: Reservations are recommended for groups; reserve via phone at (877) 444-6777 ($8.65 reservation fee) or website www.reserveusa.com; $50 group fee per night (includes a $2 boat launch fee). Individual campers are welcome on an "as available" basis at $14 per night. Open year-round.

Contact: US Army Corps of Engineers, Hensley Lake, (559) 673-5151 or fax (559) 673-2044.

Directions: From Madera, drive northeast on Highway 145 for about six miles. Bear left on County Road 400 and left again on County Road 603 below the dam. Drive about two miles on County Road 603, turn right on County Road 407, and drive a half mile to the campground at the reservoir.

Trip notes: Hensley Lake is one of the two lakes just east of Madera (the other is Millerton Lake). Hensley covers 1,500 surface acres with 24 miles of shoreline and, as long as water levels are maintained, makes for a wonderful water playland. Swimming is good, with two beaches to choose from; the best spot is at Buck Ridge on the east side of the lake, where there are picnic tables and trees for shade. The reservoir was created by a dam on the Fresno River. The elevation is 500 feet.

3 Hidden View Campground

Location: North of Fresno on Hensley Lake; map F3, grid c9.

Campsites, facilities: There are 55 sites for tents or RVs; four sites have electrical hookups. Piped water, fire grills, and picnic tables are provided. Flush toilets, showers, dump station, and a boat ramp are available. Leashed pets are permitted.

Reservations, fees: No reservations; $6 to $14 per night, $2 additional for a site with an electrical hookup, $2 boat launch fee. Open year-round.

Contact: US Army Corps of Engineers, Hensley Lake, (559) 673-5151 or fax (559) 673-2044; website: www.wetland.usace.mil/ops/hensley .html.

Directions: From Madera, drive northeast on Highway 145 for about six miles. Bear left on County Road 400 and drive 12 miles to the campground at the reservoir.

Trip notes: This is the other camp at Hensley Lake set in the foothills northeast of Madera, a popular spot for water sports (see the trip notes for Hensley Group Site, campground number two). In the spring and early summer, fishing is good for bass, crappie, bluegill, and catfish, and in the winter months trout plantings provide good angling opportunities.

④ Country Living Mobile Home and RV Park

Location: In Madera; map F3, grid e6.

Campsites, facilities: There are 49 sites for RVs. Picnic tables, piped water, electrical connections, and sewer hookups are provided. Rest rooms, showers, and coin laundry are available. A swimming pool and hot tub are open in the summer only. A store is available within 1.5 miles. Leashed pets are permitted.

Reservations, fees: Reservations are accepted; $10 to $20 per night. Open year-round.

Contact: Country Living Mobile Home and RV Park, phone or fax (559) 674-5343.

Directions: In Madera, take the Avenue 16 exit west from Highway 99 and drive a quarter mile to the camp on the right at 24833 Avenue 16.

Trip notes: It can be a dry piece of life driving this country on a hot summer afternoon, when you're ready to stop but know of nowhere to go. This RV park gives you an option, one of the scant few on Highway 99 in this region of the San Joaquin Valley.

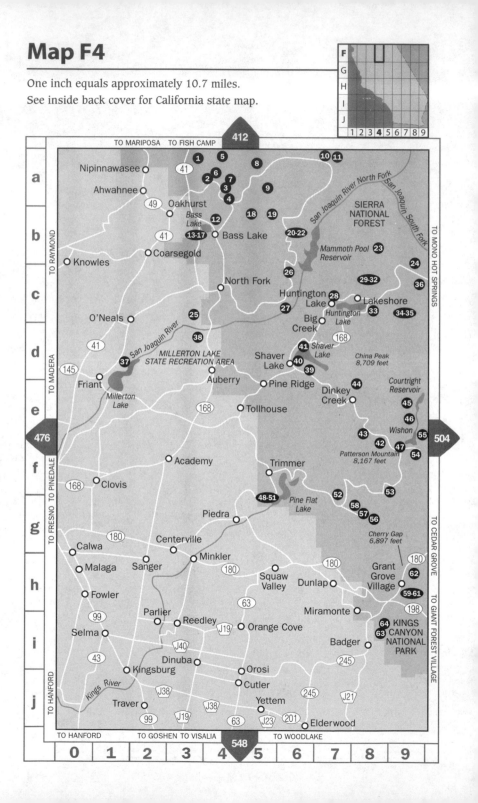

Map F4

One inch equals approximately 10.7 miles.
See inside back cover for California state map.

Chapter F4 features:

1 Big Sandy

Location: On Big Creek in Sierra National Forest; map F4, grid a3.

Campsites, facilities: There are 14 sites for tents only and four sites for tents or RVs up to 16 feet long. Picnic tables and fire grills are pro-vided. Vault toilets are available. There is no piped water. Leashed pets are permitted.

Reservations, fees: No reservations; $10 per night, $5 for each additional vehicle. Open from June through October.

Contact: Sierra National Forest, Mariposa-Minarets Ranger District, (559) 877-2218 or fax (559) 877-3108.

Directions: From Oakhurst on Highway 41, turn right on Jackson Road/Forest Service Road 6507 and drive about five miles north. Go northeast on County Road 632 for about 20 miles to the camp.

Trip notes: It's only six miles from the highway and just eight miles from the southern entrance to Yosemite National Park. Add that up: right, when Wawona is full in southern Yosemite, this camp provides a much-needed option. It's a pretty camp set on Big Creek in the Sierra National Forest, one of two camps in the immediate area. The elevation is 5,800 feet. If you head into Yosemite for the tour of giant sequoias in Wawona, get there early, by 7:30 or 8:30 A.M., when the grove is still quiet and cool, and you will have the old, mammoth trees practically to yourself.

② Grey's Mountain

Location: On Willow Creek in Sierra National Forest; map F4, grid a4.

Campsites, facilities: There are 26 sites for tents and RVs up to 22 feet long. Picnic tables and fire grills are provided. Pit toilets are available. No piped water is available. Leashed pets are permitted.

Reservations, fees: No reservations; $10 per night, $5 for each additional vehicle. Open June through October.

Contact: Sierra National Forest, Mariposa-Minarets Ranger District, (559) 877-2218 or fax (559) 877-3108.

Directions: From Fresno, drive north on Highway 41 about 60 miles to Jackson Road/Forest Service Road 6507. Turn right and drive four miles to the campground on the right.

Trip notes: This is a small, primitive campground to keep in mind when all the campgrounds are filled at nearby Bass Lake. It is one of a series of campgrounds located on Willow Creek. The elevation is 5,200 feet, set just below Sivels Mountain to the east at 5,813 feet.

③ Soquel

Location: On the North Fork of Willow Creek in Sierra National Forest; map F4, grid a4.

Campsites, facilities: There are 11 sites for tents and RVs up to 22 feet long. Fire grills and picnic tables are provided. Vault toilets are available. There is no piped water. Leashed pets are permitted.

Reservations, fees: Reserve via phone at (877) 444-6777 ($8.65 reservation fee) or website www.reserveusa.com; $10 per night, $5 for each additional vehicle. Open June through October.

Contact: Sierra National Forest, Mariposa-Minarets Ranger District, (559) 877-2218 or fax (559) 877-3108.

Directions: From Fresno, drive about 52 miles north on Highway 41 to Sky Ranch Road/County Road 632. Turn east on County Road 632 and drive about five miles. Turn right on Forest Service Road 6540 and drive about three-quarters of a mile to the campground.

Trip notes: Soquel is located at 5,400 feet in elevation on the North Fork of Willow Creek, an alternative to nearby Grey's Mountain (campground number two) in Sierra National Forest. When the camps are filled at Bass Lake, these two camps provide overflow areas as well as more primitive settings for those who are looking for more of a wilderness experience.

④ Nelder Grove

Location: In Sierra National Forest; map F4, grid a4.

Campsites, facilities: There are seven sites for tents or RVs up to 22 feet long. Fire grills and picnic tables are provided. Vault toilets are available. There is no piped water. Leashed pets are permitted.

Reservations, fees: No reservations; no fee. Open May through September.

Contact: Sierra National Forest, Mariposa-Minarets Ranger District, (559) 877-2218 or fax (559) 877-3108.

Directions: From Fresno, drive 46 miles north on Highway 41 to the town of Oakhurst. Continue north on Highway 41 for five miles to Sky Ranch Road/County Road 632. Drive northeast about eight miles to the campground.

Trip notes: Nelder Grove is a primitive spot,

also pretty, yet a camp that is often overlooked. It is set amid the Nelder Grove of giant sequoias, the majestic mountain redwoods. Since the southern entrance to Yosemite National Park is just 10 miles away, Nelder Grove is overshadowed by Yosemite's Wawona Grove. The elevation is 5,300 feet. A good option.

❺ Texas Flat Group Camp

Location: On the North Fork of Willow Creek in Sierra National Forest; map F4, grid a4.

Campsites, facilities: There are four sites for tents or RVs up to 22 feet long. Fire grills and picnic tables are provided. Vault toilets and stock handling facilities are available. There is no piped water. Leashed pets are permitted.

Reservations, fees: Reservations are accepted; reserve via phone at (877) 444-6777 ($8.65 reservation fee) or website www.reserveusa.com for reservations and fees. Open June through November.

Contact: Sierra National Forest, Mariposa-Minarets Ranger District, (559) 877-2218 or fax (559) 877-3108.

Directions: From Fresno, drive about 52 miles north on Highway 41. Turn east on Sky Ranch Road/County Road 632 and drive approximately five miles. Turn right on Forest Service Road 6540 and drive about three-quarters of a mile. Turn left on Forest Service Road 6538 and drive 2.5 miles to the campground.

Trip notes: If you are on your honeymoon, this definitely ain't the place. Unless you like the smell of horses, that is. It's a pretty enough spot, set along the North Fork of Willow Creek, but the camp is primitive and designed for groups with horses. This camp is 15 miles from the south entrance of Yosemite National Park and 15 miles north of Bass Lake. The elevation is 5,500 feet.

❻ Fresno Dome

Location: On Big Creek in Sierra National Forest; map F4, grid a4.

Campsites, facilities: There are 15 sites for tents or RVs up to 22 feet long. Picnic tables and fire grills are provided. Pit toilets are available. There is no piped water. Leashed pets are permitted.

Reservations, fees: No reservations; $10 per night, $5 for each additional vehicle.

Contact: Sierra National Forest, Mariposa-Minarets Ranger District, (559) 877-2218 or fax (559) 877-3108.

Directions: From Fresno, drive north on Highway 41 about 60 miles to Jackson Road/Forest Service Road 6507. Turn right and drive six miles to the campground on the left.

Trip notes: This camp is named after nearby Fresno Dome to the east, at 7,540 feet the dominating feature in the surrounding landscape. The trailhead for a mile hike to its top is located two miles curving down the road to the east. This camp is set at 6,400 feet on Big Creek in Sierra National Forest, a good option to nearby Yosemite National Park.

❼ Kelty Meadow

Location: On Willow Creek in Sierra National Forest; map F4, grid a4.

Campsites, facilities: There are 11 sites for tents and RVs up to 22 feet long. Fire grills and picnic tables are provided. Vault toilets and stock handling facilities are available. There is no piped water. Leashed pets are permitted.

Reservations, fees: Reservations are required for equestrians; reserve via phone at (877) 444-6777 ($8.65 reservation fee) or website www.reserveusa.com; $10 per night, $5 for each additional vehicle. Open June through October.

Contact: Sierra National Forest, Mariposa-Minarets Ranger District, (559) 877-2218 or fax (559) 877-3108.

Directions: From Oakhurst on Highway 41, drive five miles north to Sky Ranch Road/County Road 632. Drive northeast on County Road 632 about 10 miles to the campground.

Trip notes: This primitive campground is often used by campers with horses. It is located at Kelty Meadow by Willow Creek. Side trip options feature nearby Fresno Dome, the Nelder Grove of giant sequoias and, of course, the south-

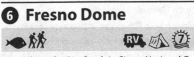

ern entrance to nearby Yosemite National Park. The elevation is 5,800 feet.

⑧ Upper Chiquito

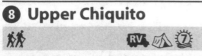

Location: On Chiquito Creek in Sierra National Forest; map F4, grid a5.

Campsites, facilities: There are 10 sites for tents only and 10 sites for tents or RVs up to 22 feet long. Picnic tables and fire grills are provided. Vault toilets are available. There is no piped water. Leashed pets are permitted.

Reservations, fees: No reservations; no fee. Open from June through September.

Contact: Sierra National Forest, Mariposa-Minarets Ranger District, (559) 877-2218 or fax (559) 877-3108.

Directions: From Fresno, drive 50 miles north on Highway 41 to Yosemite Forks. Turn right onto County Road 222 and drive six miles to Pines Village. Turn left onto Beasore Road and drive 16 miles to the campground.

Trip notes: Upper Chiquito is set at 6,800 feet on a major access road to Sierra National Forest and the western region of the Ansel Adams Wilderness, located about 15 miles to the east. The camp is set on Upper Chiquito Creek. About a mile down the road (southwest) is a Forest Service spur road (turn north) that provides access to a trail that is routed up Chiquito Creek for three miles to gorgeous Chiquita Lake (another route with a longer drive and shorter hike is available out of Fresno Dome, campground number six).

⑨ Lower Chiquito

Location: On Chiquito Creek in Sierra National Forest; map F4, grid a5.

Campsites, facilities: There are seven sites for tents or RVs up to 22 feet long. Fire grills and picnic tables are provided. Vault toilets are available. There is no piped water. Leashed pets are permitted.

Reservations, fees: No reservations; $10 per night, $5 for each additional vehicle. Open May through September.

Contact: Sierra National Forest, Mariposa-Mina-

rets Ranger District, (559) 877-2218 or fax (559) 877-3108.

Directions: From the town of North Fork (south of Bass Lake), drive east and south on Mammoth Pool Road/County Road 225, which becomes Minarets Road/Forest Service Road 4S81. Veer left (north) on Minarets Road/Forest Service Road 4S81. The drive is about 38 miles from North Fork. Turn left onto Forest Service Road 6S71 and drive three miles to the campground.

Trip notes: Lower Chiquito is a small, little-known, primitive camp in Sierra National Forest, located about eight miles from Mammoth Pool Reservoir. The elevation is 4,900 feet, with a very warm climate here in summer. Note that Lower Chiquito is a long distance (a twisting, 30- to 40-minute drive) from Upper Chiquito (see previous camp), despite the similarity in names and streamside settings along the same creek.

⑩ Clover Meadow

Location: On Granite Creek in Sierra National Forest; map F4, grid a7.

Campsites, facilities: There are seven sites for tents or RVs up to 16 feet long. Picnic tables and fire grills are provided. Piped water and vault toilets are available. Leashed pets are permitted.

Reservations, fees: No reservations; no fee. Open June through September.

Contact: Sierra National Forest, Mariposa-Minarets Ranger District, (559) 877-2218 or fax (559) 877-3108.

Directions: From the town of North Fork (south of Bass Lake), drive east and south on Mammoth Pool Road/County Road 225, which becomes Minarets Road/ Forest Service Road 4S81 and which will veer left (north) to the campground entrance road. The camp is adjacent to the Clover Meadow Ranger Station. The total distance from North Fork to the entrance road is about 63 miles—20 miles north of Mammoth Pool Reservoir on Minarets Road.

Trip notes: This is one of two excellent jump-off camps in the area for backpackers; the other is Granite Creek (campground number 11). The camp is set at 7,000 feet, adjacent to the Clover Meadow Ranger Station, where backcountry information is available. While a trail is available from camp heading east into the Ansel Adams Wilderness, most hikers drive about three miles farther northeast on Minarets Road to access a trailhead for a five-mile hike to Cora Lakes.

⑪ Granite Creek

Location: In Sierra National Forest; map F4, grid a7.

Campsites, facilities: There are 20 tent sites. Picnic tables and fire grills are provided. Pit toilets are available. There is no piped water. Leashed pets are permitted.

Reservations, fees: No reservations; no fee. Open June through September.

Contact: Sierra National Forest, Mariposa-Minarets Ranger District, (559) 877-2218 or fax (559) 877-3108.

Directions: From the town of North Fork (south of Bass Lake), drive east and south on Mammoth Pool Road/County Road 225, which becomes Minarets Road/Forest Service Road 4S81. Veer left on Minarets Road/Forest Service Road 4S81 and drive to the campground entrance road, which goes to the Clover Meadow Ranger Station. (The total distance from North Fork to the entrance road is about 61 miles—18 miles north of Mammoth Pool Reservoir on Minarets Road.) Drive 3.5 miles to the campground.

Trip notes: This camp is a good a jump-off point for backpackers since a trail from camp leads north for five miles to Cora Lakes in the Ansel Adams Wilderness, with the option of continuing onward to more remote wilderness. Note that nearby Clover Meadow (campground number 10) may be more desirable because it has both piped water to tank up your canteens and a ranger station to obtain the latest trail information. The elevation is 6,900 feet.

⑫ Chilkoot

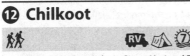

Location: Near Bass Lake in Sierra National Forest; map F4, grid b4.

Campsites, facilities: There are 14 sites for tents and RVs up to 22 feet long. Picnic tables and fire grills are provided. Vault toilets are avail-

able, but there is no piped water. Groceries and a coin laundry are available at Bass Lake. Leashed pets are permitted.

Reservations, fees: Reserve via phone at (877) 444-6777 ($8.65 reservation fee) or website www.reserveusa.com; $10 per night, $5 for each additional vehicle. Open May through August.

Contact: Sierra National Forest, Mariposa-Minarets Ranger District, (559) 877-2218 or fax (559) 877-3108.

Directions: From Fresno, drive 50 miles north on Highway 41 to Yosemite Forks. Turn right onto County Road 222 and drive six miles to the town of Bass Lake. Turn left onto Beasore Road and drive 4.5 miles to the campground.

Trip notes: A lot of people have heard of Bass Lake, but only the faithful know about Chilcoot Creek. That's where this camp is located, but it's just two miles from Bass Lake. It provides a primitive option to use either as an overflow area for Bass Lake or for folks who don't want to get jammed into one of the Bass Lake campgrounds on a popular weekend.

⑬ Forks

Location: On Bass Lake in Sierra National Forest; map F4, grid b3.

Campsites, facilities: There are 25 sites for tents only and six sites for tents or RVs up to 22 feet long. Fire grills and picnic tables are provided. Piped water and flush toilets are available. A grocery store and coin laundry are nearby. Leashed pets are permitted.

Reservations, fees: From Memorial Day through Labor Day, reserve via phone at (877) 444-6777 ($8.65 reservation fee) or website www.reserveusa.com; $16 per night, $5 for each additional vehicle. Open May through September.

Contact: Sierra National Forest, Mariposa-Minarets Ranger District, (559) 877-2218 or fax (559) 877-3108.

Directions: From Fresno, drive 50 miles north on Highway 41 to Yosemite Forks. Turn right onto County Road 222 and drive six miles, keeping right at each of two Ys in the road, to the campground on Bass Lake.

Trip notes: Bass Lake is set in a canyon. It's a long, narrow, deep lake that is popular for fishing in the spring and waterskiing in the summer. It's a pretty spot, set at 3,400 feet in the Sierra National Forest. This is one of several camps at the lake. Boats must be registered at the Bass Lake observation tower after launching. Note that the only camp on Bass Lake that is open year-round is Lupine-Cedar (campground number 15).

⑭ Crane Valley Group and Youth Camp

Location: On Bass Lake in Sierra National Forest; map F4, grid b3.

Campsites, facilities: There are four sites that hold 30 to 50 people each at Youth Group Camp and seven sites that hold 30 to 50 people each at Crane Valley Camp. Fire grills and picnic tables are provided. Piped water and flush toilets are available; there is no water at Crane Valley Camp. A grocery store is nearby. Leashed pets are permitted.

Reservations, fees: Reserve via phone at (877) 444-6777 ($17.35 reservation fee); $20 to $50 per night, $5 for each additional vehicle. (Note that the camp is open only to youth groups from May through Labor Day.)

Contact: Sierra National Forest, Mariposa-Minarets Ranger District, (559) 877-2218 or fax (559) 877-3108.

Directions: From Fresno, drive 50 miles north on Highway 41 to Yosemite Forks. Turn right onto County Road 222 and drive six miles to Bass Lake.

Trip notes: Bass Lake is a long, narrow mountain lake set in the Sierra foothills at 3,400 feet. It's especially popular in the summer for water-skiers.

⑮ Lupine-Cedar

Location: On Bass Lake in Sierra National Forest; map F4, grid b3.

Campsites, facilities: There are 113 sites for tents or RVs up to 40 feet long, and several double-family sites. Picnic tables and fire grills are provided. Piped water and flush toilets are available. Some facilities are wheelchair accessible. Groceries and a boat ramp are available nearby. Leashed pets are permitted.

Reservations, fees: Reserve via phone at (877) 444-6777 ($8.65 reservation fee) or website www.reserveusa.com; $16 per night, $30 per night for double-family sites, $5 for each additional vehicle. Open year-round.

Contact: Sierra National Forest, Mariposa-Minarets Ranger District, (559) 877-2218 or fax (559) 877-3108.

Directions: From Fresno, drive 50 miles north on Highway 41 to Yosemite Forks. Turn right onto County Road 222 and drive six miles, keeping to the right at each of two Ys in the road, to the campground on Bass Lake.

Trip notes: This is *the* camping headquarters at Bass Lake and the only camp open year-round. Bass Lake is a popular vacation spot, a pretty lake, long and narrow, covering 1,200 acres when full and surrounded by national forest. Most of the campgrounds are filled on weekends and three-day holidays. Fishing is best in the spring for rainbow trout and largemouth bass, and by mid-June water-skiers have usually taken over. Boats must be registered at the Bass Lake observation tower after launching.

⑯ Spring Cove

Location: On Bass Lake in Sierra National Forest; map F4, grid b3.

Campsites, facilities: There are 54 sites for tents only and 11 sites for RVs up to 30 feet long. Picnic tables and fire grills are provided. Piped water and flush toilets are available. Groceries and a boat ramp are available nearby. Leashed pets are permitted.

Reservations, fees: From Memorial Day through Labor Day, reserve via phone at (877) 444-6777 ($8.65 reservation fee) or website www.reserveusa.com; $16 per night. Open May through August.

Contact: Sierra National Forest, Mariposa-

Minarets Ranger District, (559) 877-2218 or fax (559) 877-3108.

Directions: From Fresno, drive 50 miles north on Highway 41 to Yosemite Forks. Turn right onto County Road 222 and drive six miles, bearing right at each Y, to the campground on Bass Lake.

Trip notes: This is one of the several camps beside Bass Lake, a long, narrow reservoir in the Sierra foothill country. Expect hot weather in the summer. Boats must be registered at the Bass Lake observation tower after launching. The elevation is 3,400 feet.

⓱ Wishon Point

Location: On Bass Lake in Sierra National Forest; map F4, grid b3.

Campsites, facilities: There are 47 sites for tents or RVs up to 30 feet long and several double-family sites. Picnic tables, fire grills, and piped water are provided. Flush toilets are available. Groceries and a boat ramp are nearby. Leashed pets are permitted.

Reservations, fees: From Memorial Day through Labor Day, reserve via phone at (877) 444-6777 ($8.65 reservation fee) or website www.reserveusa.com; $16 per night, $30 per night for double-family sites. Open June through September.

Contact: Sierra National Forest, Mariposa-Minarets Ranger District, (559) 877-2218 or fax (559) 877-3108.

Directions: From Fresno, drive 50 miles north on Highway 41 to Yosemite Forks. Turn right onto County Road 222 and drive six miles, bearing right at each Y, to the campground on Bass Lake.

Trip notes: This camp, located on Wishon Point, is the smallest, and many say the prettiest as well, of the camps at Bass Lake. The elevation is 3,400 feet.

⓲ Gaggs Camp

Location: In Sierra National Forest; map F4, grid b5.

Campsites, facilities: There are 12 sites for tents or RVs up to 16 feet long. Picnic tables and fire grills are provided. Pit toilets are available. There is no piped water. Leashed pets are permitted.

Reservations, fees: No reservations; no fee. Open June through October, weather permitting.

Contact: Sierra National Forest, Mariposa-Minarets Ranger District, (559) 877-2218 or fax (559) 877-3108.

Directions: From the town of North Fork (south of Bass Lake), drive 4.5 miles north on Mallum Ridge Road/County Road 274. Turn right onto Central Camp Road (a narrow, winding road) and drive 11.5 miles to the campground on the right.

Trip notes: The masses are not exactly beating a hot trail to this camp. It's a small, remote, and primitive spot, set along a little creek at 5,800 feet, deep in the interior of Sierra National Forest. A Forest Service map is advisable. With that in hand, you can make the three-mile drive to Little Shuteye Pass, where the road is gated; from here it is a three-mile hike to Shuteye Peak, 8,351 feet, where there is a lookout station with a drop-dead gorgeous view of the surrounding landscape.

⓳ Soda Springs

Location: On the West Fork of Chiquito Creek in Sierra National Forest; map F4, grid b5.

Campsites, facilities: There are 18 sites for tents or RVs up to 25 feet long. Fire grills and picnic tables are provided. Vault toilets are available. There is no piped water. A grocery store and boat ramp are nearby. Leashed pets are permitted.

Reservations, fees: No reservations; no fee. Open April through October, weather permitting.

Contact: Sierra National Forest, Mariposa-Minarets Ranger District, (559) 877-2218 or fax (559) 877-3108.

Directions: From the town of North Fork (south of Bass Lake), drive east and south on Mammoth Pool Road/County Road 225, which will become Minarets Road/ Forest Service Road 4S81 and will veer north to the campground. The total distance from North Fork is about 37 miles on narrow, winding roads.

Trip notes: Soda Springs is set at 4,400 feet on West Fork Chiquito Creek, about five miles from Mammoth Pool Reservoir, and is used primarily as an overflow area if the more developed camps with piped water have filled up. As long as you remember that the camp is primitive, it is a good overflow option.

⑳ Mammoth Pool

Location: Near Mammoth Pool Reservoir in Sierra National Forest; map F4, grid b6.

Campsites, facilities: There are 18 sites for tents only, 29 sites for tents or RVs up to 22 feet long, and five multifamily sites. Picnic tables and fire grills are provided. Piped water and vault toilets are available. A grocery store and boat ramp are within a mile. Leashed pets are permitted.

Reservations, fees: No reservations; $12 per night, $24 multifamily site fee, $5 for each additional vehicle. Open May through October.

Contact: Sierra National Forest, Mariposa-Minarets Ranger District, (559) 877-2218 or fax (559) 877-3108.

Directions: From the town of North Fork (south of Bass Lake), drive southeast on County Road 225, which becomes Minarets Road/Forest Service Road 4S81 and will veer north to the campground. The total distance from North Fork is about 42 miles on narrow, winding roads.

Trip notes: Mammoth Pool was created by a dam in the San Joaquin River gorge, a steep canyon, resulting in a long, narrow lake with steep, high walls. The lake seems much higher than its official elevation of 3,330 feet, but that is because of the high ridges. This is the only drive-in camp at the lake, though there is a boat-in camp, China Camp, on the lake's upper reaches. Trout fishing can be good in the spring and early summer, with waterskiing dominant during warm weather. Get this: Water sports are restricted from May 1 to June 15 due to deer migrating across the lake—that's right, swimming—but the campgrounds here are still open.

㉑ Placer

Location: Near Mammoth Pool Reservoir on Chiquito Creek in Sierra National Forest; map F4, grid b6.

Campsites, facilities: There are seven tent sites. Picnic tables and fire grills are provided. Vault toilets are available. There is no piped water. Leashed pets are permitted.

Reservations, fees: No reservations; $10 per night. Open April through October.

Contact: Sierra National Forest, Mariposa-Minarets Ranger District, (559) 877-2218 or fax (559) 877-3108.

Directions: From the town of North Fork (south of Bass Lake), drive east and south on Mammoth Pool Road/County Road 225, which becomes Minarets Road/Forest Service Road 4S81 and will veer north to the campground. The total distance from North Fork is about 39 miles on narrow, winding roads.

Trip notes: This little camp is located just three miles from Mammoth Pool Reservoir. With piped water and a pretty setting along Chiquito Creek, it is one of the better campgrounds that is used as an overflow area for Mammoth Pool visitors. The elevation is 4,100 feet. For more information, see the trip notes for Mammoth Pool (campground number 20).

㉒ Sweet Water

Location: Near Mammoth Pool Reservoir on Chiquito Creek in Sierra National Forest; map F4, grid b6.

Campsites, facilities: There are five sites for tents only and five sites for RVs up to 16 feet long. Picnic tables and fire grills are provided. Vault toilets are available. There is no piped water. A grocery store and boat ramp are within 1.5 miles. Leashed pets are permitted.

Reservations, fees: No reservations; $10 per night. Open April through October.

Contact: Sierra National Forest, Mariposa-Minarets Ranger District, (559) 877-2218 or fax (559) 877-3108.

Directions: From the town of North Fork (south of Bass Lake), drive southeast on County Road 225, which becomes Minarets Road/ Forest Service Road 4S81 and will veer north to the campground. The total distance from North Fork is about 41 miles on narrow, winding roads.

Trip notes: Sweet Water is small and primitive, but if the camp at Mammoth Pool Reservoir is filled up, this spot provides an alternative. It is set on Chiquito Creek, just a mile from the lake. The elevation is 3,800 feet. See the trip notes for Mammoth Pool (campground number 20) for more information.

㉓ Sample Meadow

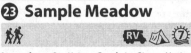

Location: On Kaiser Creek in Sierra National Forest; map F4, grid b8.

Campsites, facilities: There are 16 sites for tents or small RVs up to 16 feet long. Fire grills and picnic tables are provided. Vault toilets are available. There is no piped water. Leashed pets are permitted.

Reservations, fees: No reservations, no fee. Open June through September.

Contact: Sierra National Forest, Pineridge Ranger District, (559) 855-5360 or fax (559) 855-5375.

Directions: From the town of Shaver Lake, drive 21 miles north on Highway 168. Turn northeast on Kaiser Pass Road /Forest Service Road 80 and drive nine miles. Turn north on the entrance road (dirt) and drive five miles to the campground.

Trip notes: This is a pretty, secluded spot set at 7,800 feet along Kaiser Creek, with nearby trailheads available for backpackers. While there is a trail out of camp, most will drive a mile down Forest Service Road 80 to the Rattlesnake Parking Area. From here, one trail is routed three miles southwest to Kaiser Ridge and Upper and Lower Twin Lakes in the Kaiser Wilderness, a great hike. Another trail heads north for three miles to Rattlesnake Creek, then enters the western slopes of the Ansel Adams Wilderness, with this portion featuring a series of canyons, streams, and very few people.

㉔ Portal Forebay

Location: On Forebay Lake in Sierra National Forest; map F4, grid b9.

Campsites, facilities: There are 14 sites for tents or small RVs up to 16 feet long. Picnic tables and fire grills are provided. Vault toilets are available. There is no piped water. Groceries are available nearby at Mono Hot Springs. Leashed pets are permitted.

Reservations, fees: No reservations; $8 per night. Open June through September.

Contact: Sierra National Forest, Pineridge Ranger District, (559) 855-5360 or fax (559) 855-5375.

Directions: From the town of Shaver Lake, drive 21 miles north on Highway 168 to the town of Lakeshore. From Lakeshore, drive northeast on Kaiser Pass Road/Forest Service Road 80 for about 13.5 miles to the campground entrance.

Trip notes: This small, primitive camp is set along the shore of little Forebay Lake at 7,200 feet. The camp is pretty and provides a good hiking option, with a trailhead near the camp that is routed up Camp 61 Creek and then to Mono Creek, with a ford of Mono Creek required about two miles in. Another side trip is visiting Mono Hot Springs about five miles to the east, just off the road to Lake Edison.

㉕ Smalley Cove

Location: On Kerckhoff Reservoir near Madera; map F4, grid c3.

Campsites, facilities: There are five sites for tents or RVs. Piped water, fire grills, picnic tables, and vault toilets are provided. Five group picnic sites are available. Supplies can be purchased in Auberry. Pets are permitted.

Reservations, fees: No reservations; $10 per night, $1 pet fee. Open year-round.

Contact: PG&E Building and Land Services, (916) 386-5164 or fax (916) 386-5388.

Directions: From Highway 99 in Madera, drive 19 miles east on Highway 145. Turn right (south) on County Road 206 to Friant. From Friant, drive

19 miles northeast on Millerton Road and Auberry Road to Auberry. From Auberry, drive 8.5 miles north on Powerhouse Road to the camp.

Trip notes: Kerckhoff Reservoir can get so hot that it might seem you could fry an egg on the rocks. Campers should be certain to have some kind of tarp they can set up as a sun screen. The lake is small and remote, and the use of motors on boats is prohibited. Most campers bring rafts or canoes, and there is a good swimming beach near the picnic area and campground.

26 Rock Creek

Location: In Sierra National Forest; map F4, grid c6.

Campsites, facilities: There are 19 sites for tents or RVs up to 32 feet long. Fire grills and picnic tables are provided. Piped water and vault toilets are available. Leashed pets are permitted.

Reservations, fees: No reservations; $12 per night. Open April through October.

Contact: Sierra National Forest, Mariposa-Minarets Ranger District, (559) 877-2218 or fax (559) 877-3108.

Directions: From the town of North Fork (south of Bass Lake), drive east and south on Mammoth Pool Road/County Road 225, which becomes Minarets Road/Forest Service Road 4S81 and will veer north to the campground. The total distance from North Fork is about 27 miles.

Trip notes: Piped water is the big bonus here. It's easier to live with than the no-water situation at Fish Creek (campground number 27), the other camp in the immediate area. It is also why this camp tends to fill up on weekends. A side trip is the primitive road that heads southeast out of camp, switchbacks as its heads east, and drops down the canyon near where pretty Aspen Creek feeds into Rock Creek. The elevation at camp is 4,300 feet. Note that the best camp in the immediate region is at Mammoth Pool.

27 Fish Creek

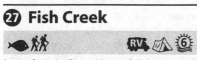

Location: In Sierra National Forest; map F4, grid c6.

Campsites, facilities: There are seven sites for tents or RVs up to 16 feet long. Picnic tables, fire grills, and vault toilets are available. There is no piped water. Leashed pets are permitted.

Reservations, fees: No reservations; $10 per night. Open April through October.

Contact: Sierra National Forest, Mariposa-Minarets Ranger District, (559) 877-2218 or fax (559) 877-3108.

Directions: From the town of North Fork (south of Bass Lake), drive east and south on Mammoth Pool Road/County Road 225, which becomes Minarets Road/Forest Service Road 4S81 and will veer north to the campground. The total distance from North Fork is about 23 miles.

Trip notes: This is a small, primitive camp set along Fish Creek at 4,600 feet in the Sierra National Forest. It's a nearby option to Rock Creek (campground number 26), both set on the access road to Mammoth Pool Reservoir.

28 Billy Creek

Location: On Huntington Lake in Sierra National Forest; map F4, grid c7.

Campsites, facilities: There are 57 sites for tents only and 20 sites for tents or RVs up to 25 feet long. Picnic tables, fire grills, and piped water are provided. Vault and flush toilets are available. A small grocery store is nearby. Leashed pets are permitted.

Reservations, fees: Reserve via phone at (877) 444-6777 ($8.65 reservation fee) or website www.reserveusa.com; $14 to $15 per night. Open June through September.

Contact: Sierra National Forest, Pineridge Ranger District, (559) 855-5360 or fax (559) 855-5375.

Directions: From the town of Shaver Lake, drive 21 miles north on Highway 168. Turn left on Huntington Lake Road and drive about five miles west to the campground.

Trip notes: Huntington Lake is at an elevation of 7,000 feet in the Sierra Nevada, and this is one of several camps here. The lake is four miles long and a half mile wide, with 14 miles of shoreline, five resorts, boat rentals, and a trailhead for hiking into the Kaiser Wilderness. This camp is located on the north side of the lake's western end, where Billy Creek feeds the lake. Of the camps at the lake, this one is located closest to town.

㉙ Catavee

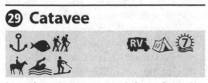

Location: On Huntington Lake in Sierra National Forest; map F4, grid c8.

Campsites, facilities: There are 26 sites for tents or RVs up to 25 feet long. Picnic tables, fire grills, and piped water are provided. Vault toilets are available. Horseback riding facilities and a small grocery store are nearby. Leashed pets are permitted.

Reservations, fees: Reserve via phone at (877) 444-6777 ($8.65 reservation fee) or website www.reserveusa.com; $14 per night. Open June through October.

Contact: Sierra National Forest, Pineridge Ranger District, (559) 855-5360 or fax (559) 855-5375.

Directions: From the town of Shaver Lake, drive 21 miles north on Highway 168. Turn left on Huntington Lake Road and drive a half mile to the campground.

Trip notes: Catavee Camp is one of three camps in the immediate vicinity, set on the north shore at the eastern end of Huntington Lake. The camp sits near where Bear Creek enters the lake. Huntington Lake is a scenic, high Sierra lake at 7,000 feet, where visitors can enjoy fishing, hiking, and sailing. Sailboat regattas take place here regularly during the summer. Nearby resorts offer boat rentals and guest docks, and a boat ramp is nearby. Tackle rentals and bait are also available. A trailhead near camp accesses the Kaiser Wilderness.

㉚ Kinnikinnick

Location: On Huntington Lake in Sierra National Forest; map F4, grid c8.

Campsites, facilities: There are 35 sites for tents or RVs up to 22 feet long. Picnic tables, fire grills, and piped water are provided. Flush toilets and horseback riding facilities are available. A grocery store is available nearby. Leashed pets are permitted.

Reservations, fees: Reserve via phone at (877) 444-6777 ($8.65 reservation fee) or website www.reserveusa.com; $14 per night. Open June through August.

Contact: Sierra National Forest, Pineridge Ranger District, (559) 855-5360 or fax (559) 855-5375.

Directions: From the town of Shaver Lake, drive 21 miles north on Highway 168. Turn left on Huntington Lake Road and drive a half mile to the campground.

Trip notes: Flip a coin; there are three camps in the immediate vicinity of Huntington Lake and, with a boat ramp nearby, they are all favorites. Kinnikinnick is located on the lake's north shore at the eastern end, set between Catavee and Deer Creek (campground numbers 29 and 31). The elevation is 7,000 feet.

㉛ Deer Creek

Location: On Huntington Lake in Sierra National Forest; map F4, grid c8.

Campsites, facilities: There are 34 sites for tents or RVs up to 22 feet long. Picnic tables, fire grills, and piped water are provided. Flush toilets and horseback riding facilities are available. A grocery store and propane gas are nearby. Leashed pets are permitted.

Reservations, fees: Reserve via phone at (877) 444-6777 ($8.65 reservation fee) or website www.reserveusa.com; $14 to $15 per night. Open June through September.

Contact: Sierra National Forest, Pineridge Ranger District, (559) 855-5360 or fax (559) 855-5375.

Directions: From the town of Shaver Lake, drive 21 miles north on Highway 168. Turn left on Huntington Lake Road and drive a half mile to the campground.

Trip notes: This is one of the best camps at Huntington Lake, set near lakeside with a boat ramp nearby. It is located on the north shore of the lake's eastern end. Huntington Lake is four miles long and a half mile wide, with 14 miles of shoreline, five resorts, boat rentals, and a trailhead for hiking into the Kaiser Wilderness.

㉜ College

Location: On Huntington Lake in Sierra National Forest; map F4, grid c8.

Campsites, facilities: There are 11 sites for tents or RVs up to 22 feet long. Piped water, fire grills, and picnic tables are provided. Vault toilets are available. Horseback riding facilities, grocery store, and propane gas are available nearby. Leashed pets are permitted.

Reservations, fees: Reserve via phone at (877) 444-6777 ($8.65 reservation fee) or website www.reserveusa.com; $14 per night. Open June through September.

Contact: Sierra National Forest, Pineridge Ranger District, (559) 855-5360 or fax (559) 855-5375.

Directions: From the town of Shaver Lake, drive 21 miles north on Highway 168. Turn left on Huntington Lake Road and drive a half mile to the campground.

Trip notes: College is a beautiful site located along the shore of the northeastern end of Huntington Lake, at 7,000 feet elevation.

㉝ Rancheria

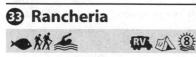

Location: Near Huntington Lake in Sierra National Forest; map F4, grid c8.

Campsites, facilities: There are 150 sites for tents or RVs up to 22 feet long. Picnic tables, fire grills, and piped water are provided. Flush toilets are available. A grocery store and propane gas are available nearby. Leashed pets are permitted.

Reservations, fees: Reserve via phone at (877) 444-6777 ($8.65 reservation fee) or website www.reserveusa.com; $14 to $15 per night. Open year-round.

Contact: Sierra National Forest, Pineridge Ranger District, (559) 855-5360 or fax (559) 855-5375.

Directions: From the town of Shaver Lake, drive 20 miles north on Highway 168 to the campground.

Trip notes: This is the granddaddy of the camps at Huntington Lake, and some say the best in the area. It is located along the shore of the lake's eastern end. A bonus here is the nearby Rancheria Falls National Recreation Trail, which provides access to beautiful Rancheria Falls. Another side trip is the 15-minute drive to Bear Butte (the access road is across from the campground entrance) at 8,598 feet, providing a sweeping view of the lake below. The elevation at camp is 7,000 feet.

㉞ Badger Flat Group Camp

Location: On Rancheria Creek in Sierra National Forest; map F4, grid c9.

Campsites, facilities: This campground will accommodate groups of up to 100 people in tents or RVs up to 25 feet long. Fire grills and picnic tables are provided. Vault toilets and horseback riding facilities are available. There is no piped water. A grocery store is nearby. Leashed pets are permitted.

Reservations, fees: Reserve via phone at (877) 444-6777 ($8.65 reservation fee) or website www.reserveusa.com; $100 per night per group. Open June through September.

Contact: Sierra National Forest, Pineridge Ranger District, (559) 855-5360 or fax (559) 855-5375.

Directions: From the town of Shaver Lake, drive 21 miles north on Highway 168. Turn northeast on Kaiser Pass Road/Forest Service Road 80 and drive six miles to the campground.

Trip notes: Badger Flat is a primitive site along Rancheria Creek at 8,200 feet, located about five miles east of Huntington Lake. It is a popular horse camp and a good jump-off spot for wilderness trekkers. A trail that passes through camp provides two options: 1) Head south for three miles to enter the Dinkey Lakes Wilderness, or 2) Head north for two miles to enter the Kaiser Wilderness.

⑤ Badger Flat

Location: On Rancheria Creek in Sierra National Forest; map F4, grid c9.

Campsites, facilities: There are 15 sites for tents or RVs up to 22 feet long. Fire grills and picnic tables are provided. Vault toilets and horseback riding facilities are available. No piped water is available. Leashed pets are permitted.

Reservations, fees: No reservations; $8 per night.

Contact: Sierra National Forest, Pineridge Ranger District, (559) 855-5360 or fax (559) 855-5375.

Directions: From the town of Shaver Lake, drive 21 miles north on Highway 168. Turn northeast on Kaiser Pass Road/Forest Service Road 80 and drive seven miles to the campground.

Trip notes: This camp is a good launching pad for backpackers. It is set at 8,200 feet along Rancheria Creek. The trail leading out of the camp is routed into the Kaiser Wilderness to the north and Dinkey Lakes Wilderness to the south.

⑥ Bolsillo

Location: On Bolsillo Creek in Sierra National Forest; map F4, grid c9.

Campsites, facilities: There are three tent sites. Piped water, picnic tables, and fire grills are provided. Vault toilets are available. Supplies can be purchased in Mono Hot Springs. Leashed pets are permitted.

Reservations, fees: No reservations; no fee. Open June through September.

Contact: Sierra National Forest, Pineridge Ranger District, (559) 855-5360 or fax (559) 855-5375.

Directions: From the town of Shaver Lake, drive 21 miles north on Highway 168. Turn northeast on Kaiser Pass Road/Forest Service Road 80 and drive for 15 miles to the campground entrance on the right.

Trip notes: This tiny camp has many first-class bonuses, including piped water. It is set at 7,400 feet along Bolsillo Creek, just three miles by car to Mono Hot Springs and seven miles to Lake Edison. A trailhead out of camp provides the chance for a three-mile hike south, climbing along Bolsillo Creek and up to small, pretty Corbett Lake on the flank of nearby Mount Givens, 10,648 feet.

⑦ Millerton Lake State Recreation Area

Location: Near Madera; map F4, grid d1.

Campsites, facilities: There are 138 sites for tents or RVs up to 31 feet long and two group sites available. Fire grills and picnic tables are provided. Piped water, showers, flush toilets, sanitary disposal station, and boat ramps are available. Some facilities are wheelchair accessible. Supplies can be purchased in Friant. Leashed pets are permitted.

Reservations, fees: From March 10 through September 10, reserve via phone at (800) 444-PARK/7275 ($7.50 reservation fee) or website www.cal-parks.ca.gov; $12 to $16 per night, $1 pet fee. Open year-round.

Contact: Millerton Lake State Recreation Area, (559) 822-2332 or fax (559) 822-2319.

Directions: From Highway 99 in Madera, drive 22 miles east on Highway 145 (six miles past the intersection with Highway 41) to the campground on the right.

Trip notes: As the temperature gauge goes up in the summer, the value of Millerton Lake increases at the same rate. The lake is set at 578 feet in elevation in the foothills of the San Joaquin Valley, and the water is like gold here. The campground and recreation area are set on a peninsula along the north shore of the lake; there are sandy beach areas on both sides of the lake with boat ramps available near the campgrounds. It's a big lake, with 43 miles of shoreline, from a narrow lake inlet extending to an expansive main lake body. The irony at Millerton is that when the lake is filled to the brim, the beaches are covered, so ideal conditions are actually when the lake level is down a bit, typically from early summer on.

38 Squaw Leap Walk-In

Location: On the San Joaquin River near Madera; map F4, grid d3.

Campsites, facilities: There are five family sites and two group sites for tents. All are walk-in sites. Fire grills and picnic tables are provided. Vault toilets and a hitching post are available. There is no piped water. Supplies can be purchased in Auberry. Pets are permitted.

Reservations, fees: No reservations; no fee. Open year-round.

Contact: Bureau of Land Management, Caliente Field Office, (805) 391-6000 or fax (805) 391-6040.

Directions: From Highway 99 in Madera, drive 19 miles east on Highway 145. Go right on Road 206 to the town of Friant. From Friant, drive 19 miles northeast on Millerton/Auberry Road to Auberry. From Auberry, drive two miles north on Powerhouse Road. Turn left at the Squaw Leap Management Area sign at Smalley Road. Drive four miles to the campground on the right.

Trip notes: Not many folks know about this spot. It's a primitive setting, but it has some bonuses. For one thing, there's access to the San Joaquin River if you drive to the fishing access trailhead at the end of the road. From there, you get great views of the San Joaquin River Gorge. The camp is a trailhead for two excellent hiking and equestrian trails. Beautiful wildflower displays are available in the late winter and spring.

39 Swanson Meadow

Location: Near Shaver Lake in Sierra National Forest; map F4, grid d6.

Campsites, facilities: There are 12 sites for tents or RVs up to 22 feet long. Fire grills and picnic tables are provided. Vault toilets are available. There is no piped water at this site. A grocery store is nearby. Leashed pets are permitted.

Reservations, fees: No reservations; $8 per night. Open May through October.

Contact: Sierra National Forest, Pineridge Ranger District, (559) 855-5360 or fax (559) 855-5375.

Directions: From Highway 168 just south of the town of Shaver Lake, drive three miles east on Dinkey Creek Road to the campground.

Trip notes: This is the smallest and most primitive of the camps near Shaver Lake; it is used primarily as an overflow area if lakeside camps are full. It is located about two miles from Shaver Lake at an elevation of 5,600 feet.

40 Dorabelle

Location: On Shaver Lake in Sierra National Forest; map F4, grid d6.

Campsites, facilities: There are 68 sites for tents or RVs up to 30 feet long. Picnic tables, fire grills, and piped water are provided. Vault toilets are available. A grocery store is nearby. Leashed pets are permitted.

Reservations, fees: Reserve via phone at (877) 444-6777 ($8.65 reservation fee) or website www.reserveusa.com; $12 per night. Open May through September.

Contact: Sierra National Forest, Pineridge Ranger District, (559) 855-5360 or fax (559) 855-5375.

Directions: From Highway 168 south of the town of Shaver Lake, turn east onto County Road N257/Dorabelle Road and drive a half mile to the campground.

Trip notes: This is one of the few Forest Service camps in the state that is set up more for RVers than for tenters. Shaver Lake is a popular lake for vacationers, and it is well stocked with trout during the summer months. Boat rentals and bait and tackle are available at the nearby marina. This is also a popular snow-play area in the winter. The elevation is 5,400 feet.

41 Camp Edison

Location: On Shaver Lake; map F4, grid d6.

Campsites, facilities: There are 252 sites for tents or RVs, 43 with full hookups. Piped water, cable TV, electrical connections, fire grills, and picnic tables are provided. Flush toilets, showers, sanitary disposal station, coin laundry, marina, boat ramp, and horseback riding facilities are available. Some facilities are wheelchair accessible. Leashed pets are permitted.

Reservations, fees: Reservations are accepted; $18 to $25 for two people per night, $2 pet fee per night. Open year-round with limited winter services.

Contact: Camp Edison, (559) 841-3134 or fax (559) 841-3193.

Directions: From the town of Shaver Lake, drive a mile north on Highway 168 to the campground entrance road.

Trip notes: Camp Edison is the best camp at Shaver Lake, set on a peninsula along the lake's western shore, with a boat ramp nearby. The lake is located at 5,370 feet in the Sierra, a pretty area that has become popular for its calm, warm days and cool water. Boat rentals and bait and tackle are available at the nearby marina. Newcomers with youngsters will discover that the best area for swimming and playing in the water is on the east side of the lake. Though more distant, this part of the lake offers sandy beaches rather than rocky drop-offs.

㊷ Buck Meadow

Location: On Deer Creek in Sierra National Forest; map F4, grid e8.

Campsites, facilities: There are five sites for tents only and five sites for tents or RVs up to 22 feet long. Picnic tables, fire grills, and vault toilet are available. There is no piped water. Leashed pets are permitted.

Reservations, fees: No reservations; no fee. Open June through September.

Contact: Sierra National Forest, Kings River Ranger District, (559) 855-8321 or fax (559) 855-2666.

Directions: From Highway 168 just south of Shaver Lake, turn east on Dinkey Creek Road and drive about 12 miles. Turn right on McKinley Grove Road and drive eight miles to the campground.

Trip notes: This is one of the three little-known, primitive camps in the area. It's set at 6,800 feet

along Deer Creek, about seven miles from Wishon Reservoir, a more popular destination.

㊸ Gigantea

Location: On Dinkey Creek in Sierra National Forest; map F4, grid e7.

Campsites, facilities: There are 10 sites for tents or RVs up to 16 feet long. Picnic tables are provided. Vault toilets and fire grills are available. There is no piped water. Supplies can be purchased in Dinkey Creek. Leashed pets are permitted.

Reservations, fees: No reservations; no fee. Open June through September.

Contact: Sierra National Forest, Kings River Ranger District, (559) 855-8321 or fax (559) 855-2666.

Directions: From Highway 168 just south of Shaver Lake, turn east on Dinkey Creek Road and drive about 12 miles. Turn right on McKinley Grove Road and drive six miles to the campground.

Trip notes: This primitive campground is set along Dinkey Creek adjacent to the McKinley Grove Botanical Area, which features a relatively little-known grove of giant sequoias. The campground is set on a short loop spur road, and day visitors are better off stopping at the McKinley Grove Picnic Area. The elevation is 6,500 feet.

㊹ Dinkey Creek

Location: In Sierra National Forest; map F4, grid d7.

Campsites, facilities: There are 128 sites for tents or RVs up to 22 feet long. Piped water, fire grills, and picnic tables are provided. Flush toilets and horseback riding facilities are available nearby. Supplies can be purchased in Dinkey Creek. Leashed pets are permitted.

Reservations, fees: From Memorial Day through Labor Day, reserve via phone at (877) 444-6777 ($8.65 reservation fee) or website www.reserveusa.com; $16 per night; 14-day stay limit. Open from May through September.

Contact: Sierra National Forest, Kings River

Ranger District, (559) 855-8321 or fax (559) 855-2666.

Directions: From Highway 168 just south of the town of Shaver Lake, turn east on Dinkey Creek Road and drive 14 miles to the campground.

Trip notes: This is a huge Forest Service camp set along Dinkey Creek at 5,700 feet. It is a popular camp for anglers who take the trail and hike upstream along the creek for small-trout fishing in a pristine setting. Backpackers occasionally lay over here before driving on to the Dinkey Lakes Parking Area, for hikes to Mystery Lake, Swede Lake, South Lake, and others in the nearby Dinkey Lakes Wilderness.

⑮ Trapper Springs

Location: On Courtright Reservoir in Sierra National Forest; map F4, grid e9.

Campsites, facilities: There are 75 sites for tents or RVs up to 22 feet long. Piped water, fire grills, and picnic tables are provided. Vault toilets are available. A boat ramp is nearby. This campground is wheelchair accessible. Leashed pets are permitted.

Reservations, fees: No reservations; $15 per night, $1 pet fee. Open June through September.

Contact: Sierra National Forest, Kings River Ranger District, (559) 855-8321 or fax (559) 855-2666.

Directions: From Highway 168 just south of the town of Shaver Lake, turn east onto Dinkey Creek Road and drive 12 miles. Turn right on McKinley Grove Road and drive 14 miles. Turn north onto Courtright Road and drive 12 miles to the campground.

Trip notes: Courtright Reservoir is a great destination, with excellent camping, boating, fishing, and hiking into the nearby John Muir Wilderness. The lake is set at an elevation of 8,200 feet, with a 15 mph speed limit making the lake ideal for fishing, canoeing, and rafting. This camp is on the west side of the lake. A trailhead located a mile north of camp by car heads around the north end of the lake to a fork; to the left is routed into the Dinkey Lakes Wilderness, and to the right is routed to the head of the lake, then follows Dusy Creek in a long climb into spectacular country in the John Muir Wilderness.

⑯ Marmot Rock Walk-In

Location: On Courtright Reservoir in Sierra National Forest; map F4, grid e9.

Campsites, facilities: There are 14 walk-in sites for tents only. There is no piped water here, but water is available three miles away at Trapper Springs Campground. Fire grills and picnic tables are provided. Vault toilets and a boat ramp are available. Leashed pets are permitted.

Reservations, fees: No reservations; $12 per night, $1 pet fee. Open June through September.

Contact: PG&E Building and Land Services, (916) 386-5164 or fax (916) 386-5388; Sierra National Forest, Kings River Ranger District, (559) 855-8321 or fax (559) 855-2666.

Directions: From Highway 168 just south of the town of Shaver Lake, turn east onto Dinkey Creek Road and drive 12 miles. Turn right (east) on McKinley Grove Road and drive 14 miles. Turn north on Courtright Reservoir Road and drive 10 miles to the campground on the south shore.

Trip notes: Courtright Reservoir is in the high country at 8,200 feet. Marmot Rock Walk-In is set at the southern end of the lake, with a boat ramp nearby. This is a pretty Sierra lake that provides options for boaters and hikers. Trout fishing can also be good here. Boaters must observe a 15 mph speed limit, which makes for quiet water.

⑰ Upper Kings River Group Camp

Location: On Wishon Reservoir; map F4, grid e9.

Campsites, facilities: There is a group site that will accommodate up to 50 people. Picnic tables and fire pits are provided. Piped water and vault toilets are available. Leashed pets are permitted.

Reservations, fees: Reservations are required; $125 per night with a two-night minimum, $1 pet fee per night. Open May through

October, weather permitting.

Contact: PG&E Building and Land Services, (916) 386-5164 or fax (916) 386-5388.

Directions: On Highway 168 just south of the town of Shaver Lake, turn east on Dinkey Creek Road and drive 12 miles. Turn right on McKinley Grove Road and continue to the Wishon Dam. The campground is located near the base of the dam.

Trip notes: Wishon Reservoir is a great place for a multiday camping trip. When the lake is full, which is not often enough, the place has great natural beauty, set at 6,500 feet and surrounded by national forest. The fishing is fair enough on summer evenings, and a 15 mph speed limit keeps the lake quiet. A side trip option is hiking from the trailhead at Woodchuck Creek, which within the span of a one-day hike takes you into the John Muir Wilderness and past three lakes—Woodchuck, Chimney, and Marsh.

⑱ Deer Creek Point Group Site

Location: On Pine Flat Lake; map F4, grid f5.

Campsites, facilities: There are two group sites (for 50 people each) that will accommodate tents or RVs. Piped water, fire grills, picnic tables, and vault toilets are provided. Boat rentals are available within five miles of camp. Leashed pets are permitted.

Reservations, fees: Reservations are required; $50 to $75 per night per group. Open April through September.

Contact: US Army Corps of Engineers, Pine Flat Field Office, (559) 787-2589 or fax (559) 787-2773.

Directions: From Fresno, take Belmont Avenue east; it will merge into Trimmer Springs Road. Continue on Belmont/Trimmer Springs approximately eight miles past the community of Piedra. Look for the Island Park Campground sign on the right. Turn right there and continue past the Island Park camp about a half mile to the Deer Park Group Site campground entrance.

Trip notes: When Pine Flat Lake is full, or close to full, it is very pretty, set in the foothills east of

Fresno at 961 feet elevation. The lake is 21 miles long with 67 miles of shoreline and 4,270 surface acres. Right: a big lake with unlimited potential. Because the temperatures get warm in spring here, then smoking hot in summer, the lake is like Valhalla for boating and water sports.

⑲ Pine Flat Recreation Area

Location: On Pine Flat Lake; map F4, grid f5.

Campsites, facilities: There are 52 sites for tents or RVs. Piped water, fire grills, and picnic tables are provided. Flush toilets, dump station, playground, and a wheelchair-accessible fishing area are available. A grocery store, coin laundry, and propane gas are nearby (within a mile). Leashed pets are permitted.

Reservations, fees: No reservations; $11 per night. Open year-round.

Contact: Fresno County Parks Department, (559) 488-3004.

Directions: From Fresno, take Belmont Avenue east; it will merge with Trimmer Springs Road. Continue on Belmont/Trimmer Springs to Pine Flat Road. Turn right on Pine Flat Road and drive three miles to the signed campground entrance on the right.

Trip notes: This is a county park that is open all year, but the lake levels, temperatures, and fishing are best in the spring and early summer. By June, the lake is best for water sports, highlighted by great waterskiing. There are several resorts on the lake that offer boat and ski rentals, as well as bait and tackle. Note: Pine Flat can be subject to drawdowns in late summer due to irrigation demands.

⑳ Island Park

Location: On Pine Flat Lake; map F4, grid f5.

Campsites, facilities: There are 52 designated sites for tents or RVs and 60 overflow sites with picnic tables available. Piped water, fire grills, and picnic tables are provided at designated sites. Flush toilets, showers, boat ramp, fish cleaning station, and a dump station are available. Some facilities are wheelchair accessible. There is a seasonal store at the campground entrance. Boat rentals are available within five miles. Leashed pets are permitted.

Reservations, fees: No reservations; $16 per night, $8 for each additional vehicle.

Contact: US Army Corps of Engineers, Pine Flat Field Office, (559) 787-2589 or fax (559) 787-2773.

Directions: From Fresno, take Belmont Avenue east. Belmont Avenue will merge into Trimmer Springs Road. Continue on Belmont/Trimmer Springs approximately eight miles past the community of Piedra. Look for the Island Park sign on the right. Turn right at the sign and continue about a quarter mile to the signed park entrance.

Trip notes: This is one of several campgrounds available at Pine Flat Lake, a popular lake set in the foothill country east of Fresno. The fishing for white bass is often excellent in late winter and early spring and, after that, conditions are ideal for water sports, especially waterskiing. The elevation is 1,000 feet.

⑤ Lakeridge Camping and Boating Resort

Location: On Pine Flat Lake; map F4, grid f5.

Campsites, facilities: There are 108 sites for tents or RVs up to 32 feet long. Rest rooms, hot showers, picnic tables, coin laundry, convenience store, ice, pay phone, petting zoo, and house boat rentals are available.

Reservations, fees: Reservations are recommended; $16 per night for tent sites and $20 per night for RV sites with hookups (for two people).

Contact: Lakeridge Camping and Boating Resort, PO Box 250, Piedra, CA 93649; (559) 787-2260.

Directions: From Fresno, drive east on Belmont Avenue (it will merge with Trimmer Springs Road). Continue on Trimmer Springs Road to Sunnyslope Road. Drive southeast on Sunnyslope Road to the resort at 30547 Sunnyslope Road.

Trip notes: Pine Flat Lake is a big lake with seemingly unlimited recreation potential. It is in the foothills east of Fresno at 961 feet elevation, covering 4,270 surface acres with 67 miles of shoreline. The lake's proximity to Fresno has made it a top destination for boating and water sports enthusiasts. Fishing for white bass can also be excellent in the spring and early summer. Note: The one downer is that there are only a few sandy beaches.

㊿ Kirch Flat

Location: On the Kings River in Sierra National Forest; map F4, grid f7.

Campsites, facilities: There are 17 sites for tents or RVs up to 22 feet long and a group camp that will accommodate up to 50 people. Fire grills and picnic tables are provided. Vault toilets are available. There is no piped water. Leashed pets are permitted.

Reservations, fees: No reservations, no fee for family camping. To reserve the group site, call the Trimmer Ranger Station, (209) 855-8321; group camp fee is $25 per night, with a 50-person maximum. Open year-round.

Contact: Sierra National Forest, Kings River Ranger District, (559) 855-8321 or fax (559) 855-2666.

Directions: From Trimmer, drive 18 miles east on Trimmer Springs Road to the campground entrance.

Trip notes: Kirch Flat is located on the Kings River, about five miles from the head of Pine Flat Lake. This campground is a popular takeout spot for rafters running the Middle Kings, putting in at Garnet Dike dispersed camping area and then making the 10-mile run downstream to Kirch Flat, a Class III run. The camp is set in the foothill country at 1,100 feet in elevation, where the temperatures are often hot and the water cold.

㊳ Black Rock

Location: On Black Rock Reservoir in Sierra National Forest; map F4, grid f8.

Campsites, facilities: There are seven sites for tents only and a trailer site. Piped water, fire grills, and picnic tables are provided. Vault toilets are available. Leashed pets are permitted.

Reservations, fees: No reservations; $8 per night. Open May through September.

Contact: Sierra National Forest, Kings River Ranger District, (559) 855-8321 or fax (559) 855-2666.

Directions: From Trimmer, drive east on Trimmer Springs Road for about 20 miles. Turn northwest onto Black Road and drive 10 miles to the campground.

Trip notes: Little Black Rock Reservoir is a relatively little-known spot that can provide a quiet respite compared to the other big-time lakes and camps in the region. The camp is set near the outlet stream on the west end of the lake, created from a small dam on the North Fork Kings River at 4,200 feet elevation.

54 Lily Pad

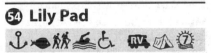

Location: Near Wishon Reservoir in Sierra National Forest; map F4, grid f9.

Campsites, facilities: There are six sites for tents only and 10 sites for tents or RVs up to 16 feet long. Piped water, picnic tables, and fire grills are provided. Vault toilets are available. Groceries, boat rentals, boat ramp, and propane gas are available nearby. This campground is wheelchair accessible. There is also a group campsite available nearby called Upper Kings River; it will accommodate up to 50 people. Leashed pets are permitted.

Reservations, fees: No reservations for single sites; $15 per night, $1 pet fee.

Contact: Sierra National Forest, Kings River Ranger District, (559) 855-8321 or fax (559) 855-2666.

Directions: From Highway 168 south of the town of Shaver Lake, turn east on Dinkey Creek Road and drive 12 miles. Turn right (east) on McKinley Grove Road and drive 16 miles to the campground.

Trip notes: This is the smallest of the three camps at Wishon Reservoir. It is set along the southwest shore at 6,500 feet, about a mile from

both the lake and a good boat ramp. A 15 mph speed limit ensures quiet water, making this an ideal destination for families with canoes or a raft.

55 Wishon Village

Location: Near Wishon Reservoir; map F4, grid e9.

Campsites, facilities: There are 26 sites for tents only and 96 RV sites with full hookups. Picnic tables, piped water, fire pits, electrical connections, and sewer hookups are provided. Restrooms, hot showers, coin laundry, country store, ice, boat ramp, motorboat rentals, bait and tackle, and propane gas are available. Leashed pets are permitted.

Reservations, fees: Reservations are recommended; $12 to $22 per night for two people, $2 for each additional person up to a six-camper limit per site. Open May through October.

Contact: Wishon Village, (559) 865-5361.

Directions: From Highway 168 just south of the town of Shaver Lake, turn east onto Dinkey Creek Road and drive 12 miles. Turn right on McKinley Grove Road and drive about 15 miles to 66500 McKinley Grove Road.

Trip notes: This privately operated mountain park is set on the North Fork of the Kings River near the shore of Wishon Reservoir. Trout stocks often make for good fishing in early summer, and anglers with boats love the 15 mph speed limit which keeps jet skis and the like off the water. Backpackers and hikers can find a great trailhead at the south end of the lake at Coolidge Meadow, where a trail awaits that is routed to the Woodchuck Creek drainage and numerous lakes in the John Muir Wilderness. The elevation is 6,500 feet.

56 Mill Flat

Location: On the Kings River in Sequoia National Forest; map F4, grid g8.

Campsites, facilities: There are five sites for tents only. Picnic tables and fire grills are provided. Vault toilets are available. No piped water is available. Leashed pets are permitted.

Reservations, fees: No reservations; no fee. Open year-round.

Contact: Sequoia National Forest, Hume Lake Ranger District, (559) 338-2251 or fax (559) 338-2131.

Directions: From Trimmer, drive about 17 miles east on Trimmer Springs Road/Forest Service Road 11S12. Cross the river and drive a mile along the south side of the Kings River on Forest Service Road 11S12, parallel to the Keller Ranch. At the junction with the second bridge, turn right onto a dirt road (Forest Service Road 12S01) and drive about 2.5 miles to the campground on the south side of the river. Trailers are not recommended.

Trip notes: This camp is on the Kings River at the confluence of Mill Flat Creek. It's a very small, primitive spot that gets very hot in the summer. Rafters sometimes use this as an access point for trips down the Kings River. A side trip from this camp is driving east on the Forest Service access road for five miles to its end point at the Kings River National Recreational Trail, then making the challenging seven-mile hike to the overlook of spectacular Garlic Falls. Try it in the spring, when temperatures are still cool and snowmelt from the high country is under way.

---

57 Camp 4

Location: On the Kings River in Sequoia National Forest; map F4, grid g8.

Campsites, facilities: There are five sites for tents only. Picnic tables and fire grills are provided. Vault toilets are available. There is no piped water. Leashed pets are permitted.

Reservations, fees: No reservations; no fee. Open year-round.

Contact: Sequoia National Forest, Hume Lake Ranger District, (559) 338-2251 or fax (559) 338-2131.

Directions: From Trimmer, drive about 17 miles east on Trimmer Springs Road/Forest Service Road 11S12. Cross the river and drive a mile along the south side of the Kings River on Forest Service Road 12S01. At the junction with the second bridge, turn right onto a dirt road/Forest Service Road 12S01 and drive about 1.5 miles to the campground on the south side of the

river. Camp 4 is a mile from Mill Flat. Trailers are not recommended.

Trip notes: This is one in a series of camps set on the Kings River upstream from Pine Flat Lake, a popular access point for rafters. The weather gets so hot that many take a dunk in the river on purpose; nonrafters best be assured that they'd better bring a cooler stocked with ice and drinks. See the trip notes for Mill Flat (campground number 56) for information on a great hike to Garlic Falls.

58 Camp 4½

Location: On the Kings River in Sequoia National Forest; map F4, grid g7.

Campsites, facilities: There are five sites for tents only. Picnic tables and fire grills are provided. Vault toilets are available. There is no piped water. Leashed pets are permitted.

Reservations, fees: No reservations; no fee. Open year-round.

Contact: Sequoia National Forest, Hume Lake Ranger District, (559) 338-2251 or fax (559) 338-2131.

Directions: From Trimmer, drive about 17 miles east on Trimmer Springs Road/Forest Service Road 11S12. Cross the river and drive a mile along the south side of the Kings River on Forest Service Road 12S01. At the junction with the second bridge, turn right onto a dirt road (Forest Service Road 12S01) and drive about 0.7 of a mile to the campground. Trailers are not recommended.

Trip notes: We found five sites here, not "four and a half." This campground is small, primitive, and usually hot. It is one in a series of camps located just east of Pine Flat Lake along the Kings River, primarily used for rafting access. See the trip notes for Kirch Flat (campground number 52) and Mill Flat (campground number 56) for more information.

59 Sunset

Location: In Kings Canyon National Park; map F4, grid h9.

Campsites, facilities: There are 184 sites for

tents or RVs up to 30 feet long. Piped water, fire grills, and picnic tables are provided. Flush toilets, evening ranger programs, and horseback riding facilities are available (only in the summer). A grocery store and Laundromat are nearby. Showers are available in Grant Grove. Leashed pets are permitted, except on trails.

Reservations, fees: No reservations; $12 per night. Open late May to mid-September.

Contact: Kings Canyon National Park, (559) 565-3341 or fax (559) 565-3730.

Directions: From Wilsonia in Kings Canyon National Park, drive a half mile north on Highway 180 to the campground entrance.

Trip notes: This is the biggest of the camps that are located just inside the Kings Canyon National Park boundaries at Wilsonia, 6,600 feet in elevation. The nearby Grant Grove of Giant Sequoias is the main attraction, with many short, easy walks among the sequoias, each breathtakingly beautiful. They include the Chicago Stump Trail, Boole Tree Trail, Big Stump Trail, Sunset Trail, North Grove Loop, General Grant Tree, Manzanita and Azalea Loop, and Panoramic Point and Park Ridge Trail. Seeing the General Grant Tree is a rite of passage for newcomers; after a half-hour walk you arrive at a sequoia that is 2,000 years old, 107 feet in circumference, and 267 feet tall.

⑥⓪ Azalea

Location: In Kings Canyon National Park; map F4, grid h9.

Campsites, facilities: There are 113 sites for tents or RVs up to 30 feet long. Piped water, fire grills, and picnic tables are provided. Flush toilets, dump station, evening ranger programs, and horseback riding facilities are available. Some campsites and rest room facilities are wheelchair accessible. A grocery store is nearby. Showers are available in Grant Grove. Leashed pets are permitted, except on trails.

Reservations, fees: No reservations; $12 per night. Open year-round.

Contact: Kings Canyon National Park, (559) 565-3341 or fax (559) 565-3730.

Directions: From the Kings Canyon National Park, entrance drive 3.3 miles north on Highway

180 to the campground.

Trip notes: This camp is tucked just inside the western border of Kings Canyon National Park. It is set at 6,600 feet near the Grant Grove of giant sequoias. For information on several short, spectacular hikes among the giant sequoias, see the trip notes for Sunset (campground number 59). Nearby Sequoia Lake is privately owned; no fishing, no swimming, no trespassing. To see the spectacular Kings Canyon, one of the deepest gorges in North America, reenter the park on Highway 180 at Cedar Grove.

⑥① Crystal Springs

Location: In Kings Canyon National Park; map F4, grid h9.

Campsites, facilities: There are 66 sites for tents or RVs up to 22 feet long. Piped water, fire grills, and picnic tables are provided. Flush toilets, horseback riding facilities, and evening ranger programs are available. Showers are available in Grant Grove. Groceries and propane gas are available nearby. Leashed pets are permitted, except on trails.

Reservations, fees: No reservations; $14 per night. Open mid-May to late September.

Contact: Kings Canyon National Park, (559) 565-3341 or fax (559) 565-3730.

Directions: From the Kings Canyon National Park entrance, drive three-quarters of a mile north on Highway 180 to the campground.

Trip notes: Directly to the south of this camp is the Grant Grove and its giant sequoias (for details, see Sunset, campground number 59). But continuing on Highway 180 provides access to the interior of Kings Canyon National Park, and this camp makes an ideal jump-off point. From here you can drive east, passing Cedar Grove, cruising along the Kings River, and finally coming to a dead-end loop, taking in the drop-dead gorgeous landscape of one of the deepest gorges in North America. One of the best hikes, but also the most demanding, is the 13-mile round-trip to Lookout Peak, out of the Cedar Grove area of Highway 180. It involves a 4,000-foot climb to 8,531 feet, and with it, a breathtaking view of Sierra ridges, Cedar Grove far below, and Kings Canyon.

62 Princess

Location: On Princess Meadow in Sequoia National Forest; map F4, grid h9.

Campsites, facilities: There are 50 tent sites and 40 sites for tents or RVs up to 22 feet long. Picnic tables, fire grills, and piped water are provided. Vault toilets and a dump station are available. A grocery store is nearby in Hume Lake (four miles away). Leashed pets are permitted.

Reservations, fees: Reserve via phone at (877) 444-6777 ($8.65 reservation fee) or website www.reserveusa.com; $12 per night. Open May through September.

Contact: Sequoia National Forest, Hume Lake Ranger District, (559) 338-2251 or fax (559) 565-3730.

Directions: From Fresno, drive east on Highway 180 for about 60 miles to the fork of Highway 180 north. Veer left and drive six miles on Highway 180 north to the campground on the right.

Trip notes: This mountain camp is at 5,900 feet. It is popular because of its proximity to both Hume Lake and the star attractions at Kings Canyon National Park. Hume Lake is just four miles from the camp and the Grant Grove entrance to Kings Canyon National Park is only six miles away to the south, while continuing on Highway 180 to the east will take you into the heart of Kings Canyon.

63 Eshom Creek

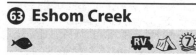

Location: On Eshom Creek in Sequoia National Forest; map F4, grid i8.

Campsites, facilities: There are 17 sites for tents or RVs up to 22 feet long and seven multi-family units. Piped water, picnic tables, and fire grills are provided. Vault toilets are available. Leashed pets are permitted.

Reservations, fees: No reservations; $10 per night. Open May through September.

Contact: Sequoia National Forest, Hume Lake

Ranger District, (559) 338-2251 or fax (559) 565-3730.

Directions: From Highway 99, drive east on Highway 198 through Visalia to Highway 245. Turn left (north) on Highway 245 and drive to Badger. From Badger drive eight miles northeast on County Road 465 to the campground.

Trip notes: The campground at Eshom Creek is located just two miles outside the boundaries of Sequoia National Park, an ideal alternative to the camps in the park. It is set along Eshom Creek, at an elevation of 4,800 feet. Most Eshom Creek campers head straight into the national park, with a trailhead at Redwood Saddle (just inside the park boundary) providing a route to see the Redwood Mountain Grove, Fallen Goliath, Hart Tree, and Hart Meadow in a sensational loop hike.

64 Sierra Lake Campground

Location: Near Visalia; map F4, grid i8.

Campsites, facilities: There are 10 sites for tents only and 25 RV sites, 12 with full hookups. Picnic tables, fire grills, piped water, electrical connections, and sewer hookups are provided. Rest rooms, showers, laundry room, store, dump station, and a full-service restaurant are available. Leashed pets are permitted.

Reservations, fees: Reservations are recommended; $12 to $22 per night, $1 pet fee. Open April through October.

Contact: Sierra Lake Campground, PO Box 68, Badger, CA 93603; (559) 337-2520.

Directions: From Highway 99, drive east on Highway 198 through Visalia to the town of Lemon Cove. Turn left on Highway 216 and go a half mile. Turn right (north) on Dry Creek Road and drive 16 miles to Mountain Road 453/Stagecoach Drive. Turn right and drive 1.5 miles to the campground on the right.

Trip notes: This secluded, privately managed, 106-acre park offers a 10-acre lake stocked with trout. The park is about a 30-minute drive from Kings Canyon and Sequoia National Parks and has three restaurants within three miles of the camp.

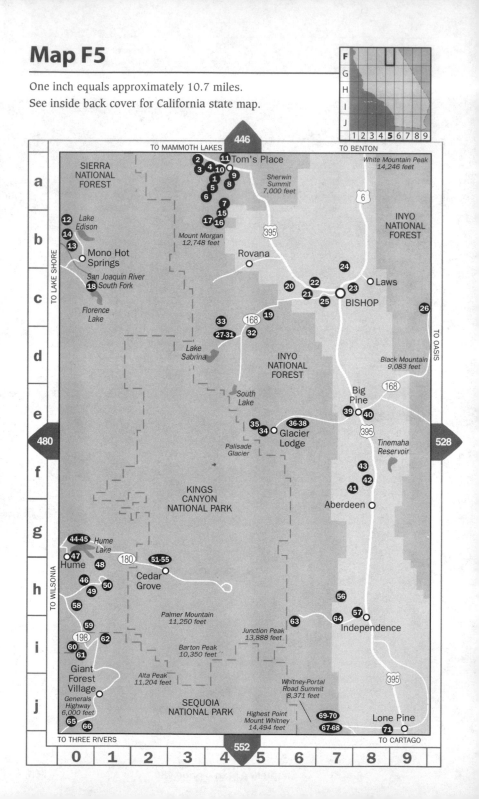

Chapter F5 features:

❶ Iris Meadow

Location: Near Crowley Lake in Inyo National Forest; map F5, grid a3.

Campsites, facilities: There are 14 sites for tents or RVs up to 22 feet long. Piped water, fire grills, and picnic tables are provided. Flush toilets are available. Supplies can be purchased in Tom's Place, three miles away. Leashed pets are permitted.

Reservations, fees: No reservations; $12 per night. Open June through August.

Contact: Inyo National Forest, White Mountain Ranger District, (760) 873-2500 or fax (760) 873-2563.

Directions: From the junction of US 395 and Highway 203 (the Mammoth Lakes turnoff), drive 15 miles south on US 395 to Tom's Place. Turn south on Rock Creek Road and drive three miles to the campground.

Trip notes: Iris Meadow, at 8,300 feet elevation on the flank of Red Mountain (11,472 feet), is the first in a series of five Forest Service camps set near Rock Creek Canyon on the road leading from Tom's Place up to pretty Rock Creek Lake. Rock Creek is stocked with trout, and nearby Rock Creek Lake also provides fishing and boating for small boats that can be hand launched. This camp also has access to a great trailhead for wilderness exploration.

❷ McGee Creek RV Park

Location: Near Crowley Lake; map F5, grid a3.

Campsites, facilities: There are 35 sites for tents or RVs, many with partial or full hookups. Piped water, fire grills, and picnic tables are provided. Flush toilets and hot showers are available. Leashed pets are permitted.

Reservations, fees: Reservations are accepted; $13.50 to $16.50 per night. Open April through mid-October.

Contact: McGee Creek RV Park, (760) 935-4233.

Directions: From the junction of US 395 and Highway 203 (the Mammoth Lakes turnoff), drive south on US 395 for 6.5 miles to the turnoff for the frontage road that runs parallel to the west

side of US 395. Continue south on that road for about 1.5 miles to McGee Creek Road. Turn right and you'll see the park entrance.

Trip notes: This is a popular layover spot for folks visiting giant Crowley Lake. Crowley Lake is still a of the better lakes in the Sierra for trout fishing, with good prospects for large rainbow trout and brown trout, though the 20-pound brown trout that once made this lake famous are now mainly a legend. Beautiful Convict Lake provides a nearby side trip option. The elevation is 7,000 feet.

❸ McGee Creek

Location: In Inyo National Forest; map F5, grid a3.

Campsites, facilities: There are 28 sites for tents or RVs up to 22 feet long. Piped water, fire grills, and picnic tables are provided. Flush toilets are available. Leashed pets are permitted.

Reservations, fees: Reserve via phone at (877) 444-6777 ($8.65 reservation fee) or website www.reserveusa.com; $12 per night. Open May through September.

Contact: Inyo National Forest, White Mountain Ranger District, (760) 873-2500 or fax (760) 873-2563.

Directions: From the junction of US 395 and Highway 203 (the Mammoth Lakes turn off), drive south on US 395 for 6.5 miles to the turnoff for the frontage road that runs parallel to the west side of US 395. Continue south on that road for about two miles to McGee Creek Road. Turn right (southwest) and drive 1.5 miles to the campground.

Trip notes: This is a Forest Service camp at elevation 7,600 feet set along little McGee Creek, a good location for fishing and hiking. The stream is stocked with trout, and a trailhead is available just up the road. From here you can hike along upper McGee Creek and into the John Muir Wilderness.

❹ Crowley Lake

Location: Near Crowley Lake; map F5, grid a4.

Campsites, facilities: There are 47 sites for

tents or RVs. Fire grills and picnic tables are provided. Pit toilets and a Dumpster are available. No piped water is available. A grocery store and boat ramp are nearby on Crowley Lake. Leashed pets are permitted.

Reservations, fees: No reservations; no fee. Open April 20 through October 15, weather permitting.

Contact: Bureau of Land Management, Bishop Resource Area, (760) 872-4881 or fax (760) 872-2894.

Directions: From Bishop, drive north 30 miles on US 395 to the Hilton Creek/Crowley Lake exit. Turn left on Crowley Lake Road and continue through the town of Hilton Creek to Old Highway 395. Turn north on Old Highway 395 and drive five miles to the signed campground entrance on the left.

Trip notes: This large BLM-managed camp is across US 395 from the south shore of Crowley Lake. Crowley is the trout fishing capital of the eastern Sierra, with the annual opener (the last Saturday in April) a great celebration. Though the trout fishing can go through a lull in midsummer, it can become excellent again in the fall when the lake's population of big brown trout heads up to the top of the lake and the mouth of the Owens River. The surroundings are fairly stark; the elevation is 7,000 feet.

⑤ Big Meadow

Location: Near Crowley Lake in Inyo National Forest; map F5, grid a4.

Campsites, facilities: There are five sites for tents only and six sites for tents or RVs up to 22 feet long. Picnic tables, fire grills, and piped water are provided. Flush toilets are available. Supplies can be purchased in Tom's Place, four miles away. Leashed pets are permitted.

Reservations, fees: No reservations; $12 per night. Open June through August.

Contact: Inyo National Forest, White Mountain Ranger District, (760) 873-2500 or fax (760) 873-2563.

Directions: From the junction of US 395 and Highway 203 (the Mammoth Lakes turnoff), drive 15 miles south on US 395 to Tom's Place. Turn south on Rock Creek Road and drive four miles to the campground.

Trip notes: This is a smaller, quieter camp in the series of campgrounds along Rock Creek. Giant Crowley Lake and tiny Rock Creek Lake provide nearby side trips. The elevation is 8,600 feet.

⑥ Palisade

Location: Near Crowley Lake in Inyo National Forest; map F5, grid a3.

Campsites, facilities: There are two sites for tents only and three sites for tents or RVs up to 22 feet long. Picnic tables, fire grills, and piped water are provided. Flush toilets and horseback riding facilities are available. Supplies can be purchased in Tom's Place, five miles away. Leashed pets are permitted.

Reservations, fees: No reservations; $12 per night. Open from May through September.

Contact: Inyo National Forest, White Mountain Ranger District, (760) 873-2500 or fax (760) 873-2563.

Directions: From the junction of US 395 and Highway 203 (the Mammoth Lakes turnoff), drive 15 miles south on US 395 to Tom's Place. Turn south on Rock Creek Road and drive five miles to the campground.

Trip notes: This shoe might just fit. Palisade, a tiny campground, provides a pretty spot along Rock Creek at 8,600 feet in elevation, with many side trip options. The closest is fishing for small trout on Rock Creek, with Crowley Lake toward the high plateau country to the east and pretty Rock Creek Lake up the road to the west.

⑦ East Fork

Location: Near Crowley Lake in Inyo National Forest; map F5, grid a4.

Campsites, facilities: There are 133 sites for tents or RVs up to 22 feet long. Picnic tables, fire grills, and piped water are provided. Flush toilets and horseback riding facilities are available. Supplies can be purchased in Tom's Place and at Rock Creek Lake Resort. Leashed pets are permitted.

Reservations, fees: Reservations are accepted for sites 16–57 and 102–127; reserve via phone at (877) 444-6777 ($8.65 reservation fee) or website www.reserveusa.com; $12 per night. Open May through September.

Contact: Inyo National Forest, White Mountain Ranger District, (760) 873-2500 or fax (760) 873-2563.

Directions: From the junction of US 395 and Highway 203 (the Mammoth Lakes turnoff), drive 15 miles south on US 395 to Tom's Place. Turn south on Rock Creek Road and drive five miles to the campground access road on the left.

Trip notes: This is a beautiful, popular campground set along East Fork Rock Creek at 9,000 feet elevation. The camp is only three miles from Rock Creek Lake, where there's an excellent trailhead.

❽ Aspen Group Camp

Location: Near Crowley Lake in Inyo National Forest; map F5, grid a4.

Campsites, facilities: There are five sites for tents or RVs up to 16 feet long. Piped water, fire grills, and picnic tables are provided. Flush toilets are available. Supplies can be purchased in Tom's Place, three miles away. Leashed pets are permitted.

Reservations, fees: Reserve via phone at (877) 444-6777 ($8.65 reservation fee) or website www.reserveusa.com; $40 group fee per night. Open May through September.

Contact: Inyo National Forest, White Mountain Ranger District, (760) 873-2500 or fax (760) 873-2563.

Directions: From the junction of US 395 and Highway 203 (the Mammoth Lakes turnoff), drive 15 miles south on US 395 to Tom's Place. Turn south on Rock Creek Road and drive three miles to the campground.

Trip notes: This small group campground set on Rock Creek is used primarily as a base camp for anglers and campers heading to nearby Crowley Lake or venturing west to Rock Creek Lake. The elevation at the camp is 8,100 feet.

❾ F. M. D. Holiday

Location: Near Crowley Lake in Inyo National Forest; map F5, grid a4.

Campsites, facilities: There are 48 sites for tents or RVs up to 22 feet long. Piped water, fire grills, and picnic tables are provided. Vault toilets are available. Groceries can be purchased nearby. Leashed pets are permitted.

Reservations, fees: No reservations; $12 per night.

Contact: Inyo National Forest, White Mountain Ranger District, (760) 873-2500 or fax (760) 873-2563.

Directions: From the junction of US 395 and Highway 203 (the Mammoth Lakes turnoff), drive 15 miles south on US 395 to Tom's Place. Turn south on Rock Creek Road and drive a half mile to the campground on the left.

Trip notes: During peak weekends, this campground is used as an overflow area. It is near Rock Creek, not far from Crowley Lake. The elevation is 7,500 feet, with surroundings far more stark than the camps to the west on Rock Creek Road.

❿ French Camp

Location: On Rock Creek near Crowley Lake in Inyo National Forest; map F5, grid a4.

Campsites, facilities: There are six sites for tents only and 80 sites for tents or RVs up to 22 feet long. Picnic tables, fire grills, and piped water are provided. Flush toilets are available. Groceries can be purchased nearby. Leashed pets are permitted.

Reservations, fees: Reservations are accepted for sites 1–30 and 73–86; reserve via phone at (877) 444-6777 ($8.65 reservation fee) or website www .reserveusa.com; $12 per night. Open April through September.

Contact: Inyo National Forest, White Mountain Ranger District, (760) 873-2500 or fax (760) 873-2563.

Directions: From the junction of US 395 and Highway 203 (the Mammoth Lakes turnoff), drive 15 miles south on US 395 to Tom's Place. Turn south on Rock Creek Road and drive a quarter mile to the campground on the right.

Trip notes: French Camp is just a short hop from US 395 and Tom's Place, right where the high Sierra turns into high plateau country. Side trip opportunities include boating and fishing on giant Crowley Lake and, to the west on Rock Creek Road, visiting little Rock Creek Lake 10 miles away. The elevation is 7,500 feet.

⑪ Tuff

Location: Near Crowley Lake in Inyo National Forest; map F5, grid a4.

Campsites, facilities: There are 15 sites for tents only and 19 sites for tents or RVs up to 22 feet long. Picnic tables, fire grills, and piped water are provided. Flush toilets are available. Leashed pets are permitted.

Reservations, fees: Reserve via phone at (877) 444-6777 ($8.65 reservation fee) or website www.reserveusa.com; $12 per night. Open April through September.

Contact: Inyo National Forest, White Mountain Ranger District, (760) 873-2500 or fax (760) 873-2563.

Directions: From the junction of US 395 and Highway 203 (the Mammoth Lakes turnoff), drive 15.5 miles south on US 395 to the camp just beyond Tom's Place.

Trip notes: Easy access off US 395 makes this camp a winner, though it is not nearly as pretty as those up Rock Creek Road to the west of Tom's Place. The fact that you can get in and out of here quickly makes it ideal for campers planning fishing trips to nearby Crowley Lake. The elevation is 7,000 feet.

⑫ Vermillion

Location: On Lake Edison in Sierra National Forest; map F5, grid b0.

Campsites, facilities: There are 11 tent sites and 20 sites for tents or RVs up to 16 feet. Piped water, picnic tables, and fire grills are provided. Vault toilets are available. A boat ramp and horseback riding facilities are nearby. Supplies

can be purchased in Mono Hot Springs. Leashed pets are permitted.

Reservations, fees: Reserve via phone at (877) 444-6777 ($8.65 reservation fee) or website www.reserveusa.com; $12 per night. Open June through September.

Contact: Sierra National Forest, Pineridge Ranger District, (559) 855-5360 or fax (559) 855-5375.

Directions: From the town of Shaver Lake, drive 21 miles north on Highway 168 to Kaiser Pass Road. Go northeast on Kaiser Pass Road/Forest Service Road 80; it becomes Edison Lake Road at Mono Hot Springs. Continue north on Kaiser Pass/Edison Lake Road for five miles past Mono Hot Springs to the campground on the west shore of Lake Edison.

Trip notes: Lake Edison is a premium vacation destination. The 15 mph speed limit on the lake guarantees quiet water, and trout fishing is often quite good in early summer. A day trip option is to hike the trail from the camp which travels along the north shore of Lake Edison for five miles to Quail Meadows, where it intersects with the Pacific Crest Trail in the John Muir Wilderness. The elevation is 7,700 feet.

⑬ Mono Hot Springs

Location: On the San Joaquin River in Sierra National Forest; map F5, grid b0.

Campsites, facilities: There are four tent sites and 26 sites for trailers, tents, or RVs, with horse pastures across from the campground. Picnic tables and fire grills are provided. Piped water and vault toilets are available. Supplies can be purchased in Mono Hot Springs. For those heading into the wilderness, there is also a free campground at the Mono Creek Trailhead for overnight horse camping.

Leashed pets are permitted.

Reservations, fees: Reserve via phone at (877) 444-6777 ($8.65 reservation fee) or website www.reserveusa.com; $12 per night. Open May through September.

Contact: Sierra National Forest, Pineridge Ranger District, (559) 855-5360 or fax (559) 855-5375.

Directions: From the town of Shaver Lake, drive 21 miles north on Highway 168. Turn northeast on Kaiser Pass Road/Forest Service Road 80; it becomes Edison Lake Road at Mono Hot Springs. Continue north beyond Mono Hot Springs about three miles to the campground entrance sign on the left.

Trip notes: How well do you speak horse? Yep, don't be surprised if you meet Mr. Ed at this camp which is used primarily by horses, not people, to carry vacationers into the adjacent backcountry. The campground is set in the Sierra at 6,500 feet in elevation along the San Joaquin River directly adjacent to the Mono Hot Springs Resort. There is a trail from the camp that forks either to Lake Edison or into the backcountry of the Ansel Adams Wilderness. It's a good idea to bring an apple along with you to this camp. Horsies like that.

⓮ Mono Creek

Location: Near Lake Edison in Sierra National Forest; map F5, grid b0.

Campsites, facilities: There are 14 sites for tents or RVs up to 16 feet long. Picnic tables, fire grills, and piped water are provided. Vault toilets are available. Horseback riding facilities and a boat ramp are nearby. Supplies can be purchased in Mono Hot Springs. Leashed pets are permitted.

Reservations, fees: Reserve via phone at (877) 444-6777 ($8.65 reservation fee) or website www.reserveusa.com; $10 per night. Open June through August.

Contact: Sierra National Forest, Pineridge Ranger District, (559) 855-5360 or fax (559) 855-5375.

Directions: From the town of Shaver Lake, drive 21 miles north on Highway 168. Drive northeast on Kaiser Pass Road/Forest Service Road 80; it becomes Edison Lake Road at Mono Hot Springs. Continue north on Edison Lake Road, three miles past Mono Hot Springs to the campground.

Trip notes: Here's a beautiful spot along Mono Creek that offers a good alternative to nearby Lake Edison. The camp, set at 7,400 feet, is about a mile upstream from the dam at Lake Edison

and has good evening trout fishing. For side trips, the Mono Hot Springs Resort is three miles away, and there are numerous trails nearby that access the backcountry.

⓯ Pine Grove

Location: Near Crowley Lake in Inyo National Forest; map F5, grid b4.

Campsites, facilities: There are five sites for tents only and six sites for tents or RVs up to 22 feet long. Picnic tables, fire grills, and piped water are provided. Flush toilets and horseback riding facilities are available. Supplies can be purchased in Tom's Place and at the Rock Creek Lake Resort. Leashed pets are permitted.

Reservations, fees: No reservations; $12 per night. Open May through September.

Contact: Inyo National Forest, White Mountain Ranger District, (760) 873-2500 or fax (760) 873-2563.

Directions: From the junction of US 395 and Highway 203 (the Mammoth Lakes turnoff), drive 15 miles south on US 395 to Tom's Place. Turn south on Rock Creek Road and drive seven miles to the campground.

Trip notes: Pine Grove is one of the smaller camps in the series of campgrounds along Rock Creek. Of the five camps in this canyon, this one is the closest to Rock Creek Lake, just a two-mile drive away. The elevation is 9,300 feet.

⓰ Rock Creek Lake

Location: In Inyo National Forest; map F5, grid b4.

Campsites, facilities: There are 28 sites for tents or RVs up to 22 feet long. Picnic tables, fire grills, flush toilets, and piped water are provided. Supplies can be purchased in Tom's Place and at the Rock Creek Lake Resort. Leashed pets are permitted.

Reservations, fees: No reservations; $12 per night. Open June through September.

Contact: Inyo National Forest, White Mountain Ranger District, (760) 873-2500 or fax (760) 873-2563.

Directions: From the junction of US 395 and Highway 203 (the Mammoth Lakes turnoff), drive 15 miles south on US 395 to Tom's Place. Turn south on Rock Creek Road and drive seven miles to the campground.

Trip notes: Rock Creek Lake, set at an elevation of 9,600 feet, is a small but beautiful lake that features cool, clear water, small trout, and a great trailhead for access to the adjacent John Muir Wilderness. When this camp fills, a nearby alternative is Mosquito Flat. Note that at times, especially afternoons in the early summer, winds out of the west can be cold and pesky at the lake.

⑰ Rock Creek Lake Group Camp

Location: In Inyo National Forest; map F5, grid b3.

Campsites, facilities: There is a group site for tent camping that can accommodate 20 to 50 people. Picnic tables, fire grills, flush toilets, and piped water are provided. Supplies can be purchased in Tom's Place and at the Rock Creek Lake Resort. Leashed pets are permitted.

Reservations, fees: Reserve via phone at (877) 444-6777 ($8.65 reservation fee) or website www.reserveusa.com; $40 per night. Open mid-June through October.

Contact: Inyo National Forest, White Mountain Ranger District, (760) 873-2500 or fax (760) 873-2563.

Directions: From the junction of US 395 and Highway 203 (the Mammoth Lakes turnoff), drive 15 miles south on US 395 to Tom's Place. Turn south on Rock Creek Road and drive seven miles to the campground.

Trip notes: This group camp is an alternative to Rock Creek Lake. It is also set on Rock Creek Lake at 9,700 feet.

⑱ Jackass Meadow

Location: On Florence Lake in Sierra National Forest; map F5, grid c0.

Campsites, facilities: There are 44 sites for tents or RVs up to 16 feet long. Picnic tables and fire grills are provided. Vault toilets, piped water, and wheelchair-accessible fishing pier are available. Leashed pets are permitted.

Reservations, fees: Reserve via phone at (877) 444-6777 ($8.65 reservation fee) or website www.reserveusa.com; $10 per night. Open June through September.

Contact: Sierra National Forest, Pineridge Ranger District, (559) 855-5360 or fax (559) 855-5375.

Directions: From the town of Shaver Lake, drive 21 miles north on Highway 168. Turn northeast on Kaiser Pass Road/Forest Service Road 80 and drive to Florence Lake Road (two miles south of the town of Mono Hot Springs). Turn south and drive five miles to the campground.

Trip notes: Jackass Meadow is a pretty spot adjacent to Florence Lake, near the Upper San Joaquin River. There are good canoeing, rafting, and float-tubing possibilities, all high-Sierra style. The elevation is 7,200 feet.

⑲ Big Trees

Location: On Bishop Creek in Inyo National Forest; map F5, grid c5.

Campsites, facilities: There are nine sites for tents or RVs. Piped water, flush toilets, fire grills, and picnic tables are provided. Horseback riding facilities are available. Supplies can be purchased in Bishop. Leashed pets are permitted.

Reservations, fees: No reservations; $12 per night. Open Memorial Day through Labor Day.

Contact: Inyo National Forest, White Mountain Ranger District, (760) 873-2500 or fax (760) 873-2563.

Directions: From Bishop on US 395, turn west on Highway 168 and drive 11 miles to the campground access road on the left. Turn left and drive two miles on a dirt road to the campground.

Trip notes: This is a small Forest Service camp on Bishop Creek at 7,500 feet in elevation. This section of the stream is stocked with small trout by the Department of Fish and Game. Both South Lake and Lake Sabrina are about 10 miles away.

⑳ Horton Creek

Location: Near Bishop; map F5, grid c6.

Campsites, facilities: There are 54 sites for tents or RVs. Fire grills and picnic tables are provided. Pit toilets and a Dumpster are available. There is no piped water. Leashed pets are permitted.

Reservations, fees: No reservations; no fee. Open May through September.

Contact: Bureau of Land Management, Bishop Field Office, (760) 872-4881 or fax (760) 872-2894.

Directions: From Bishop, drive 8.5 miles north on US 395. Turn west on Round Valley Road and drive five miles to the campground on the left.

Trip notes: This is a little-known, primitive BLM camp set along Horton Creek, northwest of Bishop. It can make a good base camp for hunters in the fall, with wild, rugged country to the west. The Inyo Mono Ecology Center is nearby. The elevation is 5,000 feet.

㉑ Brown's Millpond Campground

Location: Near Bishop; map F5, grid c6.

Campsites, facilities: There are 60 sites for tents or RVs, many with water and electric hookups. Piped water, fire grills, and picnic tables are provided. Flush toilets, showers, and coin laundry are available. Leashed pets are permitted.

Reservations, fees: Reservations are accepted; $12 to $15 per night. Open March through November.

Contact: Brown's Millpond Campground, (760) 873-5342.

Directions: From Bishop, drive six miles north on US 395. Turn west at the Millpond Recreation Area sign and drive a mile to the campground on the left.

Trip notes: This privately operated camp is adjacent to the Millpond Recreation Area which offers ball fields, playgrounds, and a swimming lake.

㉒ Pleasant Valley County Park

Location: Near Pleasant Valley Reservoir; map F5, grid c6.

Campsites, facilities: There are 200 sites for tents or RVs. Fire grills and picnic tables are provided. Piped water and pit toilets are available. Leashed pets are permitted.

Reservations, fees: No reservations; $6 per night. Open year-round.

Contact: Inyo County Parks Department, (760) 878-0272 or (800) 447-4696.

Directions: From Bishop, drive seven miles north on US 395. Turn right on the campground entrance road. Or seven miles northwest of Bishop on US 395 go north on Pleasant Valley Road and drive a mile to the campground on the right.

Trip notes: This county park is near long, narrow Pleasant Valley Reservoir, created by the Owens River. It is east of the Sierra range in the high desert plateau country; the elevation is 4,200 feet.

㉓ Shady Rest Trailer Park

Location: In Bishop; map F5, grid c7.

Campsites, facilities: There are 25 sites for tents or RVs. Piped water and full hookups are provided. Flush toilets, showers, cable TV, and coin laundry are available. Leashed pets are permitted.

Reservations, fees: Reservations are recommended; $16 to $18 per night for two people, $2 for each additional camper. Open year-round.

Contact: Shady Rest Trailer Park, (760) 873-3430.

Directions: In Bishop on US 395 heading north, turn right on Yaney Street and drive three-quarters of a mile to the campground at 399 East Yaney Street.

Trip notes: This is an option for folks who want to find a layover in the Bishop area without going to much trouble to find it. Possible side trips include the Indian Cultural Center in Bishop and the Pleasant Valley Reservoir, about a 15-minute drive from Shady Rest.

㉔ Highlands RV Park

Location: Near Bishop; map F5, grid b7.

Campsites, facilities: There are 103 RV sites with full hookups. Piped water and picnic tables are provided. Flush toilets, showers, dump station, cable TV, propane gas, and coin laundry are available. Groceries can be purchased nearby (about three blocks away). Leashed pets are permitted.

Reservations, fees: Reservations are recommended; $22 per night. Open year-round.

Contact: Highlands RV Park, (760) 873-7616.

Directions: From Bishop, drive two miles north on US 395/North Sierra Highway to the campground on the right at 2275 North Sierra Highway.

Trip notes: This is a privately operated RV park near Bishop that is set up for US 395 cruisers. Possible side trips include the Indian Cultural Center in Bishop or Pleasant Valley Reservoir, about 10 miles northwest. The elevation is 4,300 feet.

㉕ Brown's Town Schober Lane Camp

Location: Near Bishop; map F5, grid c7.

Campsites, facilities: There are 150 sites for tents or RVs, many with water and electric hookups. Piped water, fire grills, and picnic tables are provided. Flush toilets, showers, cable TV, museum, store, and a snack bar are available. Leashed pets are permitted.

Reservations, fees: Reservations are accepted; $12 to $17 per night. Open March through November.

Contact: Brown's Town Schober Lane Camp, (760) 873-8522; website www .sierraweb.com.

Directions: From Bishop, drive a mile south on US 395 to Schober Lane and exit left to the campground entrance. The campground is virtually at the corner of US 395 and Schober Lane.

Trip notes: This privately operated campground, a of several in the vicinity of Bishop, is the only a in the area that accepts tents. It's all shade and grass, and it's next to the golf course.

㉖ Grandview

Location: Near Big Pine in Inyo National Forest; map F5, grid c9.

Campsites, facilities: There are 26 sites for tents or RVs up to 22 feet long. Fire grills and picnic tables are provided. Vault toilets are available. There is no piped water. Leashed pets are permitted.

Reservations, fees: No reservations; no fee. Open May through October.

Contact: Inyo National Forest, White Mountain Ranger District, (760) 873-2500 or fax (760) 873-2563.

Directions: From Big Pine on US 395, turn east on Highway 168 and drive 13 miles. Turn north on Forest Service Road 4501/White Mountain Road and drive 5.5 miles to the campground.

Trip notes: This is a primitive and little-known camp, and the folks who find this area earn their solitude. It is located in the White Mountains east of Bishop at 8,600 feet along White Mountain Road. The road borders the Ancient Bristle Cone Pine Forest to the east and leads north to jump-off spots for hikers heading up Mount Barcroft (13,023 feet) or White Mountain (14,246 feet, the third highest mountain in California). A trail out of the camp leads up to an old mining site.

㉗ Sabrina

Location: Near Lake Sabrina in Inyo National Forest; map F5, grid d4.

Campsites, facilities: There are 18 sites for tents or RVs. Piped water, vault toilets, fire grills, and picnic tables are provided. A boat ramp and boat rentals are available. Supplies can be purchased in Bishop. Leashed pets are permitted.

Reservations, fees: No reservations; $11 per night. Open June through August.

Contact: Inyo National Forest, White Mountain Ranger District, (760) 873-2500 or fax (760) 873-2563.

Directions: From Bishop on US 395, drive 17 miles west on Highway 168 to the campground.

Trip notes: You get the best of both worlds at this camp. Set at 9,000 feet on Bishop Creek, the trails that are available here are routed into the high country of the John Muir Wilderness, and you're also just a half mile from Lake Sabrina, a beautiful high Sierra lake. Take your pick. Whatever your choice, it's a good one.

㉘ Forks

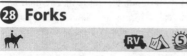

Location: Near South Lake in Inyo National Forest; map F5, grid d4.

Campsites, facilities: There are eight sites for tents or RVs. Piped water, flush toilets, fire grills, and picnic tables are provided. Horseback riding facilities are available at North Lake. Supplies can be purchased in Bishop. Leashed pets are permitted.

Reservations, fees: No reservations; $12 per night. Open May through September.

Contact: Inyo National Forest, White Mountain Ranger District, (760) 873-2500 or fax (760) 873-2563.

Directions: From Bishop on US 395, drive 13 miles west on Highway 168 to the campground.

Trip notes: After a visit here, it's no mystery how the Forest Service named this camp. It is located at the fork in the road, which gives you two options: you can turn south on South Lake Road and drive along the South Fork of Bishop Creek up to pretty South Lake, or you can keep driving on Highway 168 to another beautiful lake, Lake Sabrina, where hikers will find a trailhead that accesses the John Muir Wilderness. The elevation is 7,800 feet.

㉙ Creekside RV Park

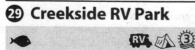

Location: On the South Fork of Bishop Creek; map F5, grid d4.

Campsites, facilities: There are four sites for tents only and 45 sites for RVs with full or partial hookups. Piped water, flush toilets, hot showers, coin laundry, grocery store, fish cleaning facilities, and propane gas are available. Leashed pets are permitted.

Reservations, fees: A deposit is required with each reservation; $17 to $25 per night, $1 pet fee. Open May through October.

Contact: Creekside RV Park, (760) 873-4483 or fax (760) 872-1966.

Directions: From Bishop on US 395, turn west on Highway 168 and drive 15 miles. Turn south on South Lake Road and drive two miles to the campground on the left at 1949 South Lake Road.

Trip notes: This privately operated park in the high country is set up primarily for RVs. A lot of folks are surprised to find it here. North, Sabrina, and South Lakes are in the area. The elevation is 8,400 feet.

㉚ Bishop Park Camp

Location: Near Lake Sabrina in Inyo National Forest; map F5, grid d4.

Campsites, facilities: There are 20 family sites and a group campsite for tents or RVs up to 22 feet long. Piped water, flush toilets, fire grills, and picnic tables are provided. Horseback riding facilities are available at North Lake. Supplies can be purchased in Bishop. Leashed pets are permitted.

Reservations, fees: No reservations; $12 per night or $42 group fee per night. Open May through October.

Contact: Inyo National Forest, White Mountain Ranger District, (760) 873-2500 or fax (760) 873-2563.

Directions: From Bishop on US 395, turn west on Highway 168 and drive 15 miles to the campground.

Trip notes: Bishop Park Camp is one in a series of camps that is located along Bishop Creek. It is about two miles from Lake Sabrina, an ideal jump-off spot for a backpacking expedition into the John Muir Wilderness. The elevation is 8,400 feet.

㉛ Intake

Location: On Sabrina Creek in Inyo National Forest; map F5, grid d4.

Campsites, facilities: There are five walk-in sites for tents only and 10 sites for tents or RVs. Piped water, flush toilets, fire grills, and picnic tables are provided. Supplies can be purchased in Bishop. Leashed pets are permitted.

Reservations, fees: No reservations; $12 per night. Open April through October.

Contact: Inyo National Forest, White Mountain Ranger District, (760) 873-2500 or fax (760) 873-2563.

Directions: From Bishop on US 395, turn west on Highway 168 and drive 14 miles to the campground entrance.

Trip notes: This small camp, set at 7,500 feet at a tiny reservoir on Bishop Creek, is about three miles from Lake Sabrina where a trailhead leads into the John Muir Wilderness. Nearby North Lake and South Lake provide side trip options.

㉜ Four Jeffrey

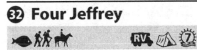

Location: Near South Lake in Inyo National Forest; map F5, grid d5.

Campsites, facilities: There are 106 sites for tents or RVs up to 22 feet long. Piped water, flush toilets, fire grills, and picnic tables are provided. Supplies can be purchased in Bishop. Leashed pets are permitted.

Reservations, fees: No reservations; $12 per night. Open mid-April through October.

Contact: Inyo National Forest, White Mountain Ranger District, (760) 873-2500 or fax (760) 873-2563.

Directions: From Bishop on US 395, turn west on Highway 168 and drive 13 miles. Turn south on South Lake Road and drive a half mile to the campground.

Trip notes: This is by far the largest of the Forest Service camps in the vicinity. There are three lakes in the area: North Lake, Lake Sabrina, and South Lake. The camp is set on the South Fork of Bishop Creek at 8,100 feet, about four miles from South Lake.

㉝ North Lake

Location: On Bishop Creek near North Lake in Inyo National Forest; map F5, grid c4.

Campsites, facilities: There are 11 tent sites. Piped water, vault toilets, fire grills, and picnic tables are provided. Horseback riding facilities are available. Supplies can be purchased in Bishop. Leashed pets are permitted.

Reservations, fees: No reservations; $12 per night. Open June through September.

Contact: Inyo National Forest, White Mountain Ranger District, (760) 873-2500 or fax (760) 873-2563.

Directions: From Bishop on US 395, turn west on Highway 168 and drive 17 miles. Turn north on Forest Service Road 8S02 and continue for two miles to the campground.

Trip notes: This prime trailhead camp in the high country (9,500 feet) takes care of a lot of the "up" that hikers usually have to contend with when entering the nearby John Muir Wilderness. The camp is set on the North Fork of Bishop Creek near North Lake and close to a trailhead that accesses numerous lakes in the John Muir Wilderness and eventually connects with the Pacific Crest Trail.

㉞ Big Pine Creek

Location: In Inyo National Forest; map F5, grid c5.

Campsites, facilities: There are five sites for tents only and 25 sites for tents or RVs. Piped water, fire grills, and picnic tables are provided. Vault toilets are available. Leashed pets are permitted.

Reservations, fees: Reserve via phone at (877) 444-6777 ($8.65 reservation fee) or website www.reserveusa.com; $11 per night. Open May to mid-October.

Contact: Inyo National Forest, White Mountain Ranger District, (760) 873-2500 or fax (760) 873-2563.

Directions: From US 395 in Big Pine, turn west on Glacier Lodge Road and drive nine miles to the campground.

Trip notes: This is another good spot for backpackers to launch a multiday trip. The camp is set along Big Pine Creek at 7,700 feet, with trails near the camp that are routed to the numerous lakes in the high country of the John Muir Wilderness.

35 First Falls Hike-In Camp

Location: In Inyo National Forest; map F5, grid e5.

Campsites, facilities: There are five tent sites. Fire grills and picnic tables are provided. Pit toilets are available. There is no piped water. Leashed pets are permitted.

Reservations, fees: No reservations; no fee. Open May to mid-October.

Contact: Inyo National Forest, White Mountain Ranger District, (760) 873-2500 or fax (760) 873-2563.

Directions: From US 395 in Big Pine, turn west onto Glacier Lodge Road and drive 8.5 miles. Park and hike two miles to the campground.

Trip notes: This high country hike-in camp is the first step for backpackers heading into the John Muir Wilderness. It is set at 8,300 feet on the South Fork of Big Pine Creek, with nearby Mount Alice (11,630 feet) looming to the west.

36 Palisade Group Camp

Location: On Big Pine Creek in Inyo National Forest; map F5, grid e6.

Campsites, facilities: There are two group sites for tents or RVs. Piped water, fire grills, and picnic tables are provided. Vault toilets are available. Leashed pets are permitted.

Reservations, fees: Reserve via phone at (877) 444-6777 ($8.65 reservation fee) or website www.reserveusa.com; $32 per night. Open May to mid-October.

Contact: Inyo National Forest, White Mountain Ranger District, (760) 873-2500 or fax (760) 873-2563.

Directions: From US 395 in Big Pine, turn west on Glacier Lodge Road and drive 8.5 miles to the campground.

Trip notes: This trailhead camp at 7,600 feet is popular for groups planning to rock climb the Palisades. This climbing trip is for experienced mountaineers only; it's a dangerous expedition where risk of life can be included in the bargain. Safer options include exploring the surrounding John Muir Wilderness.

37 Sage Flat

Location: On Big Pine Creek near Big Pine in Inyo National Forest; map F5, grid e6.

Campsites, facilities: There are 28 sites for tents or RVs. Piped water, fire grills, and picnic tables are provided. Vault toilets are available. Leashed pets are permitted.

Reservations, fees: Reserve via phone at (877) 444-6777 ($8.65 reservation fee) or website www.reserveusa.com; $11 per night. Open mid-April to mid-November.

Contact: Inyo National Forest, White Mountain Ranger District, (760) 873-2500 or fax (760) 873-2563.

Directions: From US 395 in Big Pine, turn west on Glacier Lodge Road and drive 8.5 miles to the campground.

Trip notes: This camp, like the others in the immediate vicinity, is set up primarily for backpackers who are getting ready to head out on multiday expeditions into the nearby John Muir Wilderness. Your hike from here will begin with a steep climb from the trailhead at 7,400 feet elevation. The camp is set along Big Pine Creek, which is stocked with small trout.

38 Upper Sage Flat

Location: On Big Pine Creek in Inyo National Forest; map F5, grid e6.

Campsites, facilities: There are 21 sites for tents or RVs. Piped water, fire grills, and picnic tables are provided. Vault toilets are available. Leashed pets are permitted.

Reservations, fees: Reserve via phone at (877) 444-6777 ($8.65 reservation fee) or website www.reserveusa.com; $11 per night. Open May to mid-October.

Contact: Inyo National Forest, White Mountain Ranger District, (760) 873-2500 or fax (760) 873-2563.

Directions: From US 395 in Big Pine, turn west on Glacier Lodge Road and drive 8.5 miles to the campground.

Trip notes: This is a in a series of Forest Service camps in the area set up primarily for backpackers taking off on wilderness expeditions. Several trails are available near the camp that lead into the John Muir Wilderness. Even starting at 7,600 feet, expect a steep climb.

㊷ Baker Creek County Campground

Location: Near Big Pine; map F5, grid e7.

Campsites, facilities: There are 70 sites for tents or RVs. Fire grills and picnic tables are provided. Piped water and pit toilets are available. Supplies can be purchased about 1.5 miles away in Big Pine. Leashed pets are permitted.

Reservations, fees: No reservations; $5 per night.

Contact: Inyo County Parks Department, (760) 878-0272 or fax (760) 873-2241.

Directions: From Big Pine, drive a half mile north on US 395. Turn left on Baker Creek Road and drive a mile to the campground on the left.

Trip notes: Because this is a county-operated RV park, it is overlooked by many who usually consider only camps on reservations systems. That makes this a good option for cruisers touring the eastern Sierra on US 395. It's ideal for a quick overnighter, with easy access from Big Pine. The camp is set along Baker Creek at 4,000 feet in the high plateau country of the eastern Sierra.

㊸ Glacier View County Campground

Location: Near Big Pine; map F5, grid e8.

Campsites, facilities: There are 40 sites for tents or RVs. Piped water, fire grills, and picnic tables are provided. Flush toilets are available. Supplies can be purchased in Big Pine. Leashed pets are permitted.

Reservations, fees: No reservations; $5 per night. Open April through October.

Contact: Inyo County Parks Department, (760) 878-0272 or fax (760) 873-2241.

Directions: From Big Pine, drive a half mile north on US 395 to the campground on the right.

Trip notes: This is one of two county camps near the town of Big Pine, providing US 395 cruisers with two options. The camp is set along the Big Pine Canal at 3,900 feet.

㊹ Goodale Creek

Location: Near Independence; map F5, grid f7.

Campsites, facilities: There are 62 sites for tents or RVs. Fire grills and picnic tables are provided. Pit toilets and a trash bin are available. There is no piped water. Leashed pets are permitted.

Reservations, fees: No reservations; no fee. Open April 20 through September.

Contact: Bureau of Land Management, Bishop Resource Area, (760) 872-4881 or fax (760) 872-2894.

Directions: From Independence, drive 12 miles north on US 395. Turn left on Aberdeen Road and drive two miles to the campground on the left.

Trip notes: This obscure BLM camp is set along little Goodale Creek at 4,100 feet. It is a good layover spot for US 395 cruisers heading north.

㊺ Tinnemaha Creek County Park

Location: Near Big Pine; map F5, grid f8.

Campsites, facilities: There are 55 sites for tents or RVs. Fire grills and picnic tables are provided. Pit toilets are available. There is no piped water. Leashed pets are permitted.

Reservations, fees: No reservations; $5 per night. Open year-round.

Contact: Inyo County Parks Department, (760) 878-0272 or fax (760) 873-2241.

Directions: From Independence, drive 19.5 miles north on US 395. Turn left on Fish Springs Road and drive a half mile. Turn right on Tinnemaha Road and drive two miles to the campground on the left.

Trip notes: This primitive, little-known (to out-of-towners) county park campground is located on Tinnemaha Creek at 4,400 feet.

㊸ Taboose Creek County Campground

Location: Near Big Pine; map F5, grid f8.

Campsites, facilities: There are 55 sites for tents or RVs. Fire grills and picnic tables are provided. Piped water and pit toilets are available. Supplies can be purchased in Big Pine or Independence. Leashed pets are permitted.

Reservations, fees: No reservations; $5 per night. Open year-round.

Contact: Inyo County Parks Department, (760) 878-0272 or fax (760) 873-2241.

Directions: From Big Pine, drive 11 miles south on US 395. Turn left on Taboose Creek Road and drive a mile to the campground.

Trip notes: The eastern Sierra is stark country, but this little spot provides a stream (Taboose Creek) and some trees near the campground. The easy access off US 395 is a bonus. The elevation is 3,900 feet.

㊹ Hume Lake

Location: In Sequoia National Forest; map F5, grid g0.

Campsites, facilities: There are 60 tent sites and 14 sites for tents or RVs up to 22 feet long. Picnic tables, fire grills, and piped water are provided. Flush toilets are available. A grocery store is nearby. Leashed pets are permitted.

Reservations, fees: Reservations are recommended for weekends and holidays; reserve via phone at (877) 444-6777 ($8.65 reservation fee) or website www.reserveusa.com; $14 per night. Open May through August.

Contact: Sequoia National Forest, Hume Lake Ranger District, (559) 338-2251 or fax (559) 781-4744.

Directions: From Fresno, drive east on Highway 180 for about 60 miles to the Y at Highway 180 north. Bear left on Highway 180 north and drive six miles to the Hume Lake Road junction. Turn south and drive three miles to Hume Lake.

Trip notes: For newcomers, Hume Lake is a surprise: a pretty lake, small enough to hike around, with good trout fishing, especially near the dam. Another surprise is the adjacent religious camp center. The nearby entrances to Kings Canyon National Park add a bonus. The elevation is 5,200 feet.

㊺ Aspen Hollow Group Camp

Location: Near Hume Lake in Sequoia National Forest; map F5, grid g0.

Campsites, facilities: This is a group campsite for up to 75 people with picnic tables, fire grills, and piped water. Vault toilets are available. A grocery store is nearby. Leashed pets are permitted.

Reservations, fees: Reserve via phone at (877) 444-6777 ($8.65 reservation fee) or website www.reserveusa.com; $75 to $112.50 per night. Open May through August.

Contact: Sequoia National Forest, Hume Lake Ranger District, (559) 338-2251 or fax (559) 781-4744.

Directions: From Fresno, drive east at Highway 180 for about 60 miles to the Y at Highway 180 north. Bear left on Highway 180 north and drive six miles to the Hume Lake Road junction. Turn south and drive about three miles to the Aspen Hollow Group Camp entrance, 1.5 miles past the campground at Hume Lake.

Trip notes: This large group camp is set at 5,200 feet, near Hume Lake. Entrances to Kings Canyon National Park are nearby.

Special note: This camp is closed for reconstruction. Call for status.

46 Ten Mile

Location: On Ten Mile Creek in Sequoia National Forest; map F5, grid h0.

Campsites, facilities: There are 10 sites for tents or RVs up to 22 feet long. Picnic tables and fire grills are provided. Vault toilets are available. There is no piped water. A grocery store is nearby. Leashed pets are permitted.

Reservations, fees: No reservations; no fee. Open May through September.

Contact: Sequoia National Forest, Hume Lake Ranger District, (559) 338-2251 or fax (559) 781-4744.

Directions: From Grant Grove in Kings Canyon National Park, drive six miles north on Highway 180 to the Hume Lake Road junction. Turn south and drive about seven miles around Hume Lake and up Ten Mile Road to the campground.

Trip notes: This is one of three small, primitive campgrounds along Ten Mile Creek above Hume Lake. This one is about four miles from the lake at 5,800 feet in elevation. It provides an alternative to camping in nearby Kings Canyon National Park.

---

47 Logger Flat Group Camp

Location: On Ten Mile Creek in Sequoia National Forest; map F5, grid g0.

Campsites, facilities: This is one group campsite for up to 50 people with picnic tables and fire grills. Piped water and vault toilets are available. A grocery store is nearby. Leashed pets are permitted.

Reservations, fees: Reserve via phone at (877) 444-6777 ($8.65 reservation fee) or website www.reserveusa.com; $37.50 to $75 per night.

Contact: Sequoia National Forest, Hume Lake Ranger District, (559) 338-2251 or fax (559) 781-4744.

Directions: From Grant Grove in Kings Canyon National Park, drive six miles north on Highway 180 to the Hume Lake Road junction. Turn south and drive about seven miles around

Hume Lake and up Ten Mile Road to the campground.

Trip notes: This is the group site alternative to Landslide. For more information, see the trip notes for Landslide (campground number 48).

---

48 Landslide

Location: On Ten Mile Creek in Sequoia National Forest; map F5, grid h1.

Campsites, facilities: There are six sites for tents only and three sites for tents or RVs up to 16 feet long. Picnic tables and fire grills are provided. Vault toilets are available. There is no piped water. A grocery store is nearby. Leashed pets are permitted.

Reservations, fees: No reservations; no fee. Open May through September.

Contact: Sequoia National Forest, Hume Lake Ranger District, (559) 338-2251 or fax (559) 781-4744.

Directions: From Grant Grove in Kings Canyon National Park, drive six miles north on Highway 180 to the Hume Lake Road junction. Turn south and drive seven miles around Hume Lake and up Ten Mile Road to the campground. Landslide is on the right, 1.5 miles beyond Ten Mile Campground.

Trip notes: If you want quiet, you got it; few folks know about this camp. If you want a stream nearby, you got it; Landslide Creek runs right beside the camp. If you want a lake nearby, you got it; Hume Lake is about two miles away. If you want a national park nearby, you got it; Kings Canyon National Park is nearby. Add it up: You got it. The elevation is 5,800 feet.

---

49 Buck Rock

Location: Near Big Meadows Creek in Sequoia National Forest; map F5, grid h0.

Campsites, facilities: There are five primitive sites for tents or RVs up to 16 feet long. Picnic tables and fire grills are provided. Vault toilets are available. There is no piped water. Leashed pets are permitted.

Reservations, fees: No reservations; no fee.

Open June through September.

Contact: Sequoia National Forest, Hume Lake Ranger District, (559) 338-2251 or fax (559) 781-4744.

Directions: From Grant Grove in Kings Canyon National Park, drive seven miles southeast on Generals Highway. Turn left on Big Meadows Road/Forest Service Road 14S11 and drive four miles to the camp.

Trip notes: This is a remote camp that provides a little-known option to nearby Sequoia and Kings Canyon National Parks. If the national parks are full and you're stuck, this camp provides an insurance policy. The elevation is 7,500 feet.

50 Big Meadows

Location: On Big Meadows Creek in Sequoia National Forest; map F5, grid h1.

Campsites, facilities: There are numerous sites along Big Meadows Creek and Big Meadows Road for tents or RVs up to 22 feet long. Picnic tables and fire grills are provided. Vault toilets are available. There is no piped water. Leashed pets are permitted.

Reservations, fees: No reservations; no fee. Open June through September.

Contact: Sequoia National Forest, Hume Lake Ranger District, (559) 338-2251 or fax (559) 781-4744.

Directions: From Grant Grove, drive seven miles southeast on Generals Highway. Turn left on Big Meadows Road/Forest Service Road 14S11 and drive five miles to the camp.

Trip notes: This primitive, high mountain camp (7,600 feet) is beside little Big Meadows Creek. Backpackers can use this as a launching pad, with the nearby trailhead (one mile down the road to the west) leading to the Jennie Lake Wilderness. Kings Canyon National Park, only a 12-mile drive away, is a nearby side trip.

51 Sentinel

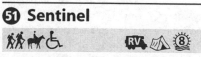

Location: In Kings Canyon National Park; map F5, grid g2.

Campsites, facilities: There are 83 sites for tents or RVs. Piped water, fire grills, and picnic tables are provided. Flush toilets, evening ranger programs, showers, and a dump station are available. Some facilities are wheelchair accessible. A grocery store, coin laundry, showers, restaurant, and horseback riding facilities are nearby. Leashed pets are permitted.

Reservations, fees: No reservations; $12 per night. Open April through October, weather permitting.

Contact: Kings Canyon National Park, (559) 565-3341 or fax (559) 565-3730.

Directions: From Cedar Grove in Kings Canyon National Park, drive west on Highway 180 about a quarter mile to the campground.

Trip notes: This camp provides a nearby alternative to Sheep Creek (campground number 52). They both tend to fill up quickly in the summer. It's a short walk to Cedar Grove, the center of activity in the park. The elevation is 4,600 feet.

52 Sheep Creek

Location: In Kings Canyon National Park; map F5, grid g2.

Campsites, facilities: There are 111 sites for tents or RVs. Piped water, fire grills, and picnic tables are provided. Flush toilets, showers, and a dump station are available. A grocery store, coin laundry, showers, restaurant, and horseback riding facilities are available nearby. Leashed pets are permitted.

Reservations, fees: No reservations; $12 per night. Open June through September.

Contact: Kings Canyon National Park, (559) 565-3341 or fax (559) 565-3730.

Directions: From Cedar Grove in Kings Canyon National Park, drive a half mile west on Highway 180 to the campground.

Trip notes: This is one of the camps that always fills up quickly on summer weekends. It's a pretty spot and just a short walk from Cedar Grove. The camp is set along Sheep Creek at 4,600 feet.

53 Canyon View Group Camp

Location: In Kings Canyon National Park; map F5, grid g2.

Campsites, facilities: There are four group sites for tents accommodating a minimum of 20 people and a maximum of 40 people per site. Piped water, fire grills, and picnic tables are provided. Flush toilets and a dump station are available. A grocery store, coin laundry, showers, restaurant, and horseback riding facilities are nearby (within 1.5 miles). Leashed pets are permitted.

Reservations, fees: Reservations must be made by mail. Write to Canyon View Group Sites, PO Box 948, Kings Canyon National Park, CA 93633; $7 to $16 per night. Phone (559) 565-3792 for information. Open June through August, weather permitting.

Contact: Kings Canyon National Park, (559) 565-3341 or fax (559) 565-3730.

Directions: From Cedar Grove in Kings Canyon National Park, drive east on Highway 180 to the campground (a half mile past the ranger station).

Trip notes: If it weren't for this spot, large groups wishing to camp together in Kings Canyon National Park would be out of luck. Reservations are a must. The elevation is 4,600 feet.

54 Canyon View

Location: In Kings Canyon National Park; map F5, grid g2.

Campsites, facilities: There are 37 sites for tents. Piped water, fire grills, flush toilets, and picnic tables are provided. Showers, horseback riding facilities, grocery store, restaurant, and a coin laundry are nearby. Leashed pets are permitted.

Reservations, fees: No reservations; $12 per night. Open June through August, weather permitting.

Contact: Kings Canyon National Park, (559) 565-3341 or fax (559) 565-3730.

Directions: From Cedar Grove in Kings Canyon National Park, drive east on Highway 180 to the campground (a half mile past the ranger station).

Trip notes: This is another of several camps in the Cedar Grove area of the Kings Canyon National Park. The access road leads to dramatic views of the deep Kings River Canyon, one of the deepest gorges in North America. The elevation is 4,600 feet.

55 Moraine

Location: In Kings Canyon National Park; map F5, grid g2.

Campsites, facilities: There are 120 sites for tents or RVs. Piped water, fire grills, picnic tables, and flush toilets are provided. Showers, horseback riding facilities, grocery store, restaurant, and a coin laundry are nearby. Leashed pets are permitted.

Reservations, fees: No reservations; $7 to $12 per night. Open June through September, weather permitting.

Contact: Kings Canyon National Park, (559) 565-3341 or fax (559) 565-3730.

Directions: From Cedar Grove in Kings Canyon National Park, drive east on Highway 180 to the campground (one mile past the ranger station).

Trip notes: This is the last in the series of camps in the Cedar Grove area of Kings Canyon National Park. This camp is used only as an overflow area. Hikers should drive past the Cedar Grove Ranger Station to the end of the road at Copper Creek, a prime jump-off point for a spectacular hike. The elevation is 4,600 feet.

56 Oak Creek

Location: In Inyo National Forest; map F5, grid h7.

Campsites, facilities: There are 21 sites for tents or RVs. Piped water, fire grills, and picnic tables are provided. Flush toilets are available. Supplies and a coin laundry are available in Independence. Leashed pets are permitted.

Reservations, fees: Reservations accepted; phone (877) 444-6777; $11 per night. Open June through September.

Contact: Inyo National Forest, Mount Whitney

Ranger District, (760) 876-6200 or fax (760) 873-2458.

Directions: From Independence, drive two miles north on US 395. Turn left (west) on North Oak Creek Drive and drive three miles to the campground on the right.

Trip notes: Oak Creek is a in a series of little-known camps located west of Independence that provides a jump-off spot for backpackers. This camp is set at 5,000 feet, with a trail from camp that is routed west (and up) into the California Bighorn Sheep Zoological Area, a rugged, stark region well above the tree line. Caution: Plan on a long, butt-kicker of a climb up to the Sierra crest.

57 Independence Creek County Campground

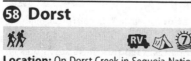

Location: In Independence; map F5, grid h7.

Campsites, facilities: There are 25 sites for tents or RVs. Piped water and picnic tables are provided. Pit toilets are available. Some facilities are wheelchair accessible. Supplies and a coin laundry are available in Independence. Leashed pets are permitted.

Reservations, fees: No reservations; $5 per night. Open year-round.

Contact: Inyo County Parks Department, (760) 878-0272 or fax (760) 873-2241.

Directions: In Independence, drive west on Market Street to the campground about half a mile outside the town limits.

Trip notes: This unpublicized county park is often overlooked among US 395 cruisers. It is set at 3,900 feet along Independence Creek.

58 Dorst

Location: On Dorst Creek in Sequoia National Park; map F5, grid h0.

Campsites, facilities: There are 218 family sites for tents or RVs and five group sites. Piped water, fire grills, and picnic tables are provided. Flush toilets, dump station, and evening ranger programs are available. A grocery store and a coin laundry are nearby. Leashed pets are permitted.

Reservations, fees: Reserve via phone at (800) 365-CAMP/2267; $16 per night (includes reservation fee). For group sites, reservations must be made by mail; write to Dorst Group Site, Box C, Lodgepole, Sequoia National Park, CA 93262. Open June through August.

Contact: Sequoia National Park, (559) 565-3341 or fax (559) 565-3730 for general and weather information.

Directions: From Giant Forest Village in Sequoia National Park, drive 14 miles northwest on Generals Highway. Due to steep curves on Generals Highway, vehicles over 22 feet are not advised on this road. An alternate route is to take Highway 180 into Kings Canyon National Park, and then turn south on Generals Highway just after entering the park.

Trip notes: Things that go bump in the night swing through Dorst all summer long. That's right, Mr. Bear, a whole bunch of them, make food raids like UPS drivers on pick-up routes. There are so many bears raiding food here that some years rangers keep a running tally. That's why keeping your food in a bear-proof locker is not only a must, it's the law. The camp is set on Dorst Creek at 6,700 feet, near a trail that is routed into the backcountry and through Muir Grove. It is one in a series of big, popular camps in Sequoia National Park.

59 Stony Creek

Location: In Sequoia National Forest; map F5, grid i0.

Campsites, facilities: There are 22 sites for tents and 20 sites for RVs up to 22 feet long. Piped water, fire grills, and picnic tables are provided. Flush toilets are available. A grocery store and coin laundry are nearby. Leashed pets are permitted.

Reservations, fees: Reserve via phone at (877) 444-6777 ($8.65 reservation fee) or website www.reserveusa.com; $8 per night. Open June through August.

Contact: Sequoia National Forest, Hume Lake Ranger District, (559) 338-2251 or fax (559) 781-4744.

Directions: From Grant Grove in Kings Canyon

National Park, drive 13 miles southeast on Generals Highway to the campground on the right.

Trip notes: Stony Creek Camp provides a good option if the national park camps are filled. It is set at creekside at 6,400 feet elevation. Sequoia and Kings Canyon National Parks are nearby.

60 Fir Group Campground

Location: Near Stony Creek in Sequoia National Forest; map F5, grid i0.

Campsites, facilities: This is a group campsite for up to 100 people with piped water, picnic tables, and fire grills provided. Vault toilets are available. A grocery store and coin laundry are nearby. Leashed pets are permitted.

Reservations, fees: Reserve via phone at (877) 444-6777 ($8.65 reservation fee) or website www.reserveusa.com; $75 to $112.50 per night. Open June through August.

Contact: Sequoia National Forest, Hume Lake Ranger District, (559) 338-2251 or fax (559) 781-4744.

Directions: From Grant Grove in Kings Canyon National Park, drive 14 miles southeast on Generals Highway to the campground on the left.

Trip notes: This is the second of two large group camps in the area set along Stony Creek.

61 Cove Group Camp

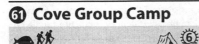

Location: Near Stony Creek in Sequoia National Forest; map F5, grid i0.

Campsites, facilities: This is a group campsite for up to 50 people. Piped water, picnic tables, and fire grills are provided. Vault toilets are available. A grocery store and coin laundry are available nearby. Leashed pets are permitted.

Reservations, fees: Reserve via phone at (877) 444-6777 ($8.65 reservation fee) or website www.reserveusa.com; $37.50 to $75 per night. Open June through August.

Contact: Sequoia National Forest, Hume Lake Ranger District, (559) 338-2251 or fax (559) 781-4744.

Directions: From Grant Grove in Kings Canyon National Park, drive 14 miles southeast on Generals Highway to the campground on the left.

Trip notes: This large group camp is located beside Stony Creek. The elevation is 6,500 feet.

62 Lodgepole

Location: On the Marble Fork of the Kaweah River in Sequoia National Park; map F5, grid i1.

Campsites, facilities: There are 250 sites for tents or RVs. Piped water, fire grills, and picnic tables are provided. Flush toilets, showers, dump station, horseback riding facilities, gift shop, and evening ranger programs are available. A grocery store, deli, pay showers, propane gas, and a coin laundry are nearby. Leashed pets are permitted.

Reservations, fees: Reserve via phone at (800) 365-CAMP/2267; $16 per night (includes reservation fee). Open year-round, with limited winter services.

Contact: Sequoia National Park, (559) 565-3341 or fax (559) 565-3730 for general and weather information.

Directions: From Giant Forest Village in Sequoia National Park, drive five miles northeast on Generals Highway. Due to steep curves on Generals Highway, vehicles over 22 feet are not advised between Giant Forest Village and Potwisha Campground. An alternate route is to take Highway 180 through the Kings Canyon National Park entrance and then turn south on Generals Highway just after entering.

Trip notes: This giant, pretty camp on the Marble Fork of the Kaweah River is typically crowded. A bonus here is an excellent trail-head nearby that leads into the backcountry of Sequoia National Park. The elevation is 6,700 feet.

63 Onion Valley

Location: In Inyo National Forest; map F5, grid i6.

Campsites, facilities: There are 29 sites for

tents only. Piped water, flush toilets, fire grills, and picnic tables are provided. Leashed pets are permitted.

Reservations, fees: Reservations are accepted; reserve via phone at (877) 444-6777 ($8.65 reservation fee) or website www.reserveusa.com; $11 per night. Open mid-June through September.

Contact: Inyo National Forest, Mount Whitney Ranger District, (760) 876-6200 or fax (760) 876-6202.

Directions: From US 395 in Independence, drive 15 miles west on Onion Valley Road to the campground at the road's end.

Trip notes: Onion Valley is one of the best trailhead camps for backpackers in the Sierra. The camp is set at 9,200 feet, and from here it's a 2,600-foot climb over the course of about three miles to awesome Kearsage Pass (11,823 feet). From there you can camp at the Kearsage Lakes, explore the Kearsage Pinnacles, or join up with the John Muir Trail and venture to your choice of many high Sierra lakes. A $4 Forest Service map and a free wilderness permit are your passports to the high country from this camp.

(64) Gray's Meadow

Location: On Independence Creek in Inyo National Forest; map F5, grid h7.

Campsites, facilities: There are 52 sites for tents or RVs. Piped water, fire grills, and picnic tables are provided. Flush toilets are available. Supplies and a coin laundry are available in Independence. Leashed pets are permitted.

Reservations, fees: Reservations are accepted; reserve via phone at (877) 444-6777 ($8.65 reservation fee) or website www.reserveusa.com; $11 per night. Open April through October.

Contact: Inyo National Forest, Mount Whitney Ranger District, (760) 876-6200 or fax (760) 876-6202.

Directions: From US 395 in Independence, turn west on Onion Valley Road and drive five miles to the campground on the right.

Trip notes: Gray's Meadow is one of two adjacent camps set along Independence Creek, which is stocked with small trout by the Department of Fish and Game. The highlight in the immediate area is the trailhead at the end of the road at Onion Valley Camp. For US 395 cruisers looking for a spot, this is a pretty alternative to the camps in Bishop.

(65) Potwisha

Location: On the Marble Fork of the Kaweah River in Sequoia National Park; map F5, grid j0.

Campsites, facilities: There are 44 sites for tents or RVs up to 30 feet long. Piped water, picnic tables, and fire grills are provided. Flush toilets, dump station, and evening ranger programs are available. Rest rooms and some campsites are wheelchair accessible. Leashed pets are permitted.

Reservations, fees: No reservations; $12 per night. Open year-round.

Contact: Sequoia National Park, (559) 565-3341 or fax (559) 565-3730 for general and weather information.

Directions: From Visalia, drive east on Highway 198 to the Foothills Visitor Center at Ash Mountain Center and then drive four miles northeast on Generals Highway. Vehicles of 22 feet or longer are not advised on Generals Highway from Potwisha to Giant Forest Village.

Trip notes: This pretty spot on the Marble Fork of the Kaweah River is one of Sequoia National Park's smaller drive-to campgrounds. From Buckeye Flat, located a few miles east of the camp, a trail runs along Paradise Creek. Hike with plenty of water here; it can be very hot and dry in the summer.

(66) Buckeye Flat

Location: On the Middle Fork of the Kaweah River in Sequoia National Park; map F5, grid j0.

Campsites, facilities: There are 28 tent sites. Picnic tables, fire grills, and piped water are provided. Flush toilets are available. Leashed pets are permitted.

Reservations, fees: No reservations; $12 per night. Open April through Labor Day weekend, weather permitting.

Contact: Sequoia National Park, (559) 565-3341 or fax (559) 565-3730 for general and weather information.

Directions: From Visalia, drive east on Highway 198 to the Foothills Visitor Center at Ash Mountain Center and then drive six miles northeast on Generals Highway. Vehicles of 22 feet or longer are not advised on Generals Highway from Potwisha to Giant Forest Village.

Trip notes: In any big, popular national park like Sequoia, the smaller the campground, the better. Well, Buckeye Flat is one of the smaller ones here, set on the Middle Fork of the Kaweah River with a trail just south of camp that runs beside pretty Paradise Creek.

⑥⑦ Lone Pine

Location: Near Mount Whitney in Inyo National Forest; map F5, grid J7.

Campsites, facilities: There are 43 sites for tents or RVs. Piped water, vault toilets, fire grills, and picnic tables are provided. Supplies are available in Lone Pine. Leashed pets are permitted.

Reservations, fees: Reservations are accepted for 60 percent of the sites. Reserve via phone at (877) 444-6777 ($8.65 reservation fee) or website www .reserveusa.com; $10 per night. Stays are limited to 14 days. Open year-round.

Contact: Inyo National Forest, Mount Whitney Ranger District, (760) 876-6200 or fax (760) 876-6202.

Directions: From Lone Pine, drive six miles west on Whitney Portal Road to the campground on the left.

Trip notes: This is an alternative for campers preparing to hike Mount Whitney or start the John Muir Trail. It is set at 6,000 feet, 2,000 feet below Whitney Portal (the hiking jump-off spot), providing a lower elevation location for hikers to acclimate themselves to the altitude. The camp is set on Lone Pine Creek, with decent fishing and spectacular views of Mount Whitney.

⑥⑧ Whitney Portal

Location: Near Mount Whitney in Inyo National Forest; map F5, grid j7.

Campsites, facilities: There are 44 sites for tents or RVs up to 16 feet long. Piped water, flush toilets, fire grills, and picnic tables are provided. Supplies are available in Lone Pine. Leashed pets are permitted.

Reservations, fees: Reservations are accepted for 60 percent of the sites. Reserve via phone at (877) 444-6777 ($8.65 reservation fee) or website www.reserveusa.com; $12 per night. Stays are limited to seven days. Open mid-May to mid-October.

Contact: Inyo National Forest, Mount Whitney Ranger District, (760) 876-6200 or fax (760) 876-6202.

Directions: From Lone Pine, drive 13 miles west on Whitney Portal Road to the campground on the left.

Trip notes: This camp is home to a world-class trailhead, regarded as the number one jump-off spot for the hike to the top of Mount Whitney (at 14,495 feet the highest spot in the Continental US) as well as the start of the 211-mile John Muir Trail from Mount Whitney to Yosemite Valley. Hikers planning to summit must have a wilderness permit, available at the Forest Service office in Lone Pine. The camp is set at 8,000 feet, and virtually everyone staying here plans to make the trek to the Whitney summit, a climb of 6,500 feet over the course of 10 miles. The trip includes an ascent over 100 switchbacks (often snow covered in early summer) to top Wotan's Throne and reach Trail Crest (13,560 feet). Here you turn right and take the Summit Trail, where the ridge is cut by huge notch windows providing a view down more than 10,000 feet to the little town of Lone Pine. When you sign the log book on top, don't be surprised if you see my name in the registry.

⑥⑨ Whitney Portal Group Camp

Location: In Inyo National Forest; map F5, grid j7.

Campsites, facilities: There are three group sites for tents. Piped water, flush toilets, fire grills, and picnic tables are provided. Supplies are available in Lone Pine. Leashed pets are permitted.

Reservations, fees: Reserve via phone at (877) 444-6777 ($8.65 reservation fee) or website www.reserveusa.com; $30 group fee per night. Open mid-May to mid-October.

Contact: Inyo National Forest, Mount Whitney Ranger District, (760) 876-6200 or fax (760) 876-6202.

Directions: From Lone Pine, drive 13 miles west on Whitney Portal Road to the campground on the right.

Trip notes: This is the spot for groups planning to hike to the top of Mount Whitney. Permits and reservations are required to climb and camp. The elevation is 8,100 feet. See the trip notes for Whitney Portal (campground number 68) for more information.

⑦⓪ Whitney Trailhead Hike-In

Location: In Inyo National Forest; map F5, grid j7.

Campsites, facilities: There are 10 tent sites at this walk-in campground. Piped water, pit toilets, fire grills, and picnic tables are provided. Supplies are available in Lone Pine. Leashed pets are permitted.

Reservations, fees: No reservations; $6 per night. Stays are limited to one night only. Open mid-May to mid-October.

Contact: Inyo National Forest, Mount Whitney Ranger District, (760) 876-6200 or fax (760) 876-6202.

Directions: From Lone Pine, drive 13 miles west on Whitney Portal Road and then hike about a quarter mile to the camp.

Trip notes: If Whitney Portal (campground number 68) is full (common for this world-class trailhead), this camp provides a hike-in option (elevation 8,000 feet). Reservations for the summit hike are required. That accomplished, this hike-in camp is an excellent choice for spending a day here to become acclimated to the high altitude. The trailhead to the Mount Whitney summit (14,495 feet) is nearby. Mount Whitney is the beginning of the 211-mile John Muir Trail, which ends in Yosemite Valley.

⑦① Portagee Joe County Campground

Location: Near Lone Pine; map F5, grid j8.

Campsites, facilities: There are 15 sites for tents or RVs. Piped water, pit toilets, fire grills, and picnic tables are provided. Supplies and a coin laundry are available in Lone Pine. Leashed pets are permitted.

Reservations, fees: No reservations; $6 per night. Open year-round.

Contact: Inyo County Parks Department, (760) 878-0272 or fax (760) 873-2241.

Directions: In Lone Pine, drive a half mile west on Whitney Portal Road to Tuttle Creek Road. At Tuttle Creek Road turn south and drive 0.1 of a mile to the campground.

Trip notes: This small, little-known county park provides an option for both Mount Whitney hikers and US 395 cruisers. It is about five miles from Diaz Lake (campground number five, Chapter G5), set on a small creek at 3,750 feet. Very few out-of-towners know about this spot, a nice insurance policy if you find yourself stuck for a campsite in this region.

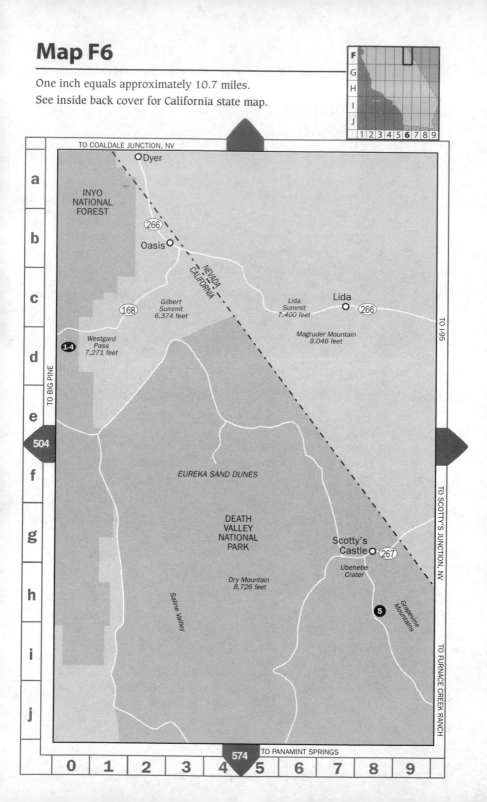

Map F6

One inch equals approximately 10.7 miles.
See inside back cover for California state map.

TO COALDALE JUNCTION, NV

Dyer

INYO
NATIONAL
FOREST

266

Oasis

NEVADA
CALIFORNIA

168

Gilbert
Summit
6,374 feet

Lida
Summit
7,400 feet

Lida

266

TO I-95

Magruder Mountain
9,046 feet

1-4

Westgard
Pass
7,271 feet

TO BIG PINE

504

EUREKA SAND DUNES

DEATH
VALLEY
NATIONAL
PARK

TO SCOTTY'S JUNCTION, NV

Scotty's
Castle

267

Ubehebe
Crater

Dry Mountain
8,726 feet

Saline Valley

5

Grapevine Mountains

TO FURNACE CREEK RANCH

574

TO PANAMINT SPRINGS

0   1   2   3   4   5   6   7   8   9

Chapter F6 features:

1 Piñon Group Camp

Location: Near Big Pine in Inyo National Forest; map F6, grid d0.

Campsites, facilities: There are five sites for tents or RVs. Picnic tables and vault toilets are provided. There is no piped water. Leashed pets are permitted.

Reservations, fees: Reserve via phone at (877) 444-6777 ($8.65 reservation fee) or website www.reserveusa.com; $20 group fee per night.

Contact: Inyo National Forest, White Mountain Ranger District, (760) 873-2500 or fax (760) 873-2563.

Directions: From Big Pine on U.S. 395, head east on Highway 168 for 13 miles to the camp.

Trip notes: Piñon Group Camp is the first of four group camps set in the immediate area along Highway 168. It is a remote and stark setting at 7,200 feet elevation, at the foot of the White Mountains on the east side of the Owens Valley. Most campers here will head to the Ancient Bristle Cone Pine Forest (turn north on White Mountain Road and drive eight miles to Schulman Picnic Area), where the oldest tree in the world, about 4,000 years old, has been documented. (It is unmarked so some idiot won't cut it down.) The road up here, by the way, provides sweeping views to the west of the Sierra. Hikers can get a similar view by taking the trail out of Cedar Flat to Black Mountain (9,038 feeet), about a five-mile tromp one way, with the trail quite faint, often invisible, over the last mile.

2 Poleta Group Camp

Location: Near Big Pine in Inyo National Forest; map F6, grid d0.

Campsites, facilities: There are eight sites for tents or RVs. Picnic tables and vault toilets are provided. There is no piped water. Leashed pets are permitted.

Reservations, fees: Reserve via phone at (877) 444-6777 ($8.65 reservation fee) or website www.reserveusa.com; $20 group fee per night.

Contact: Inyo National Forest, White Mountain Ranger District, (760) 873-2500 or fax (760) 873-2563.

Directions: From Big Pine on U.S. 395, turn east on Highway 168 and drive 13 miles to the campground.

Trip notes: This is one of four camps in the immediate area, so take your pick. For side trip possibilities, see the trip notes for Piñon Group Camp (campground number one).

3 Juniper Group Camp

Location: Near Big Pine in Inyo National Forest; map F6, grid d0.

Campsites, facilities: There are five sites for tents or RVs. Picnic tables and vault toilets are provided. There is no piped water. Leashed pets are permitted.

Reservations, fees: Reserve via phone at (877) 444-6777 ($8.65 reservation fee) or website www.reserveusa.com; $20 group fee per night.

Contact: Inyo National Forest, White Mountain Ranger District, (760) 873-2500 or fax (760) 873-2563.

Directions: From Big Pine on U.S. 395, head east on Highway 168 for 13 miles to the camp.

Trip notes: Juniper Camp is a nearby option to Poleta Camp for group campers. See the trip notes for Piñon Group Camp (campground number one) for side trip details.

④ Fossil Group Camp

Location: Near Big Pine in Inyo National Forest; map F6, grid d0.

Campsites, facilities: There are 11 sites for tents or RVs. Picnic tables and vault toilets are provided. There is no piped water. Leashed pets are permitted.

Reservations, fees: Reserve via phone at (877) 444-6777 ($8.65 reservation fee) or website www.reserveusa.com; $20 group fee per night.

Contact: Inyo National Forest, White Mountain Ranger District, (760) 873-2500 or fax (760) 873-2563.

Directions: From Big Pine on U.S. 395, head east on Highway 168 and drive 13 miles to the campground.

Trip notes: Fossil Group Camp is a primitive Forest Service group camp set at 7,220 feet in elevation, one of four in the immediate vicinity. See the trip notes for Piñon Group Camp (campground number 1) for side trip options.

⑤ Mesquite Spring

Location: In Death Valley National Park; map F6, grid i8.

Campsites, facilities: There are 30 sites for tents or RVs. Picnic tables are provided. Piped water, flush toilets, and a sanitary dump station are available. Facilities are wheelchair accessible. Leashed pets are permitted.

Reservations, fees: No reservations; $10 per night. Visitors may pay entrance fee and obtain a park brochure at the Furnace Creek, Grapevine, Stovepipe Wells, or Beatty Ranger Stations.

Contact: Death Valley National Park, (760) 786-2331 or fax (760) 786-3283.

Trip notes: Mesquite Spring is the most remote and often the prettiest campground in Death Valley, providing you time it right. If you are a lover of desert beauty, then you must make this trip in late winter or early spring, when all kinds of very tiny wildflowers bring the stark, valley floor to life.

Map G1

One inch equals approximately 10.7 miles.
See inside back cover for California state map.

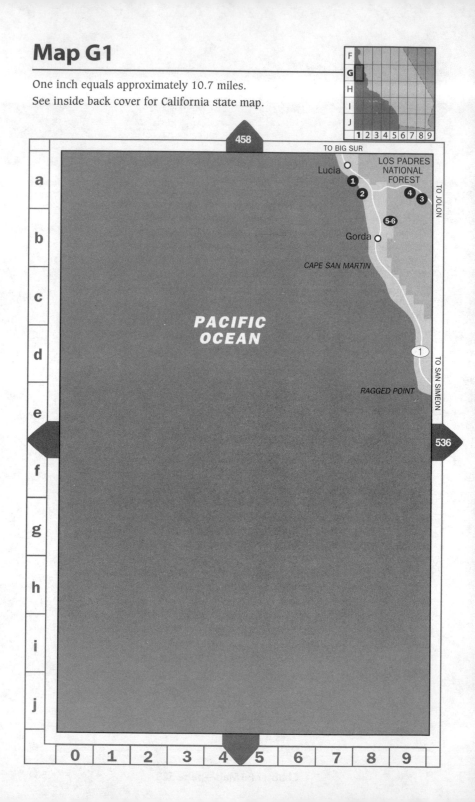

❶ Limekiln State Park

Location: On the Pacific Ocean; map G1, grid a7.

Campsites, facilities: There are 42 sites for tents or RVs up to 21 feet long or trailers up to 15 feet long. There is a limit of one vehicle per campsite; extra passenger vehicles are allowed in parking areas only if space permits. Piped water, rest rooms, showers, dump station, grocery store, bait, and firewood are available. Leashed pets are allowed, except on trails.

Reservations, fees: Reserve via phone at (800) 444-PARK/7275 ($7.50 reservation fee) or website www.cal-parks.ca.gov; $20 to $22 per night, $6 for each extra vehicle. Open year-round.

Contact: Limekiln State Park (under California Land Management), (831) 667-2403; California State Parks, Monterey District, (831) 649-2836.

Directions: From Big Sur, drive 26 miles south on Highway 1 to the park on the left.

Trip notes: This camp provides a great layover spot in the Big Sur area of Highway 1. It is designed primarily for RVs, with drive-in campsites set up both near the beach and the redwoods, take your pick. Several hiking trails are available, including one that is routed past some historic lime kilns, which were used in the late 1800s to make cement and bricks. Want more? Got more? A short rock hop on a spur trail (just off the main trail) leads to dramatic 100-foot Limekiln Falls, a gorgeous waterfall. This camp was originally called Limekiln Beach Redwoods and was privately operated. No more.

❷ Kirk Creek

Location: Near the Pacific Ocean in Los Padres National Forest; map G1, grid a8.

Campsites, facilities: There are 33 sites for tents or RVs. Piped water, picnic tables, and fire grills are provided. Flush toilets are available.

Leashed pets are permitted.

Reservations, fees: No reservations; $16 per night, $5 per night for bicyclists. Open year-round.

Contact: Parks Management Company, (805) 927-4622; Los Padres National Forest, Monterey Ranger District; (831) 385-5434 or fax (831) 667-2886.

Directions: From the little town of Lucia, drive four miles south on Highway 1 to the campground on the right.

Trip notes: This pretty camp is set along Kirk Creek near where it empties into the Pacific Ocean. A trail from camp branches north through the Ventana Wilderness, which is sprinkled with little-used, hike-in, backcountry campsites. For gorgeous scenery without all the work, a quaint little cafe in Lucia provides open-air dining on a cliff-top deck, with a dramatic sweeping lookout over the coast.

❸ Ponderosa

Location: In Los Padres National Forest, map G1, grid a9.

Campsites, facilities: There are 23 sites for tents or RVs up to 32 feet long. There is no potable water, but picnic tables and fire grills are provided. Vault toilets are available. Leashed pets are permitted.

Reservations, fees: No reservations; $10 per night. Open year-round.

Contact: Parks Management Company, (805) 927-4622; Los Padres National Forest, Monterey Ranger District, (831) 385-5434 or fax (831) 667-2886.

Directions: From Highway 1 four miles south of Lucia, turn left on Nacimiento-Ferguson Road and drive about 12 miles to the campground on the right.

Trip notes: As soon as you turn off Highway 1, you leave behind the crowds and enter a land that is largely unknown to people. This camp is set at 1,500 feet elevation in Los Padres National Forest, not far from the border of the Ventana Wilderness (good hiking and backpacking) and the Hunter Liggett Military Reservation (wild pig hunting is allowed there with a permit). It is one in a series of small camps on Nacimiento-Ferguson Road.

❹ Nacimiento

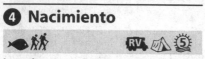

Location: In Los Padres National Forest; map G1, grid a9.

Campsites, facilities: There are nine sites for tents and eight sites for tents or RVs. Picnic tables and fire grills are provided. Vault toilets are available. Leashed pets are permitted.

Reservations, fees: No reservations; $5 per night.

Contact: Parks Management Company, (805) 927-4622; Los Padres National Forest, Monterey Ranger District, (831) 385-5434 or fax (831) 667-2886.

Directions: From the little town of Lucia, drive four miles south on Highway 1 to Nacimiento Road. Turn east and drive about eight winding miles to the campground.

Trip notes: This little-known spot is set near the Nacimiento River at 1,600 feet elevation. Most campers will head up Nacimiento-Ferguson Road to camp on a Friday night and get up Saturday morning to head off on a hiking or backpacking trip in the nearby Ventana Wilderness.

❺ Plaskett Creek

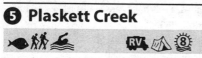

Location: Overlooking the Pacific Ocean in Los Padres National Forest; map G1, grid b8.

Campsites, facilities: There are 43 sites for tents or RVs. Piped water, picnic tables, and fire grills are provided. Flush toilets are available. Leashed pets are permitted.

Reservations, fees: No reservations; $16 per night, $5 for bicyclists. Open year-round.

Contact: Parks Management Company, (805) 927-4622; Los Padres National Forest, Monterey Ranger District, (831) 385-5434 or fax (831) 667-2886.

Directions: From the town of Lucia, drive 9.5 miles south on Highway 1 to the campground on the left.

Trip notes: This is a premium coastal camp for Highway 1 cruisers, set at 200 feet elevation along little Plaskett Creek above the Pacific Ocean. It gets overlooked by many for two reasons: it is not listed with a reservation service, and it is farther south of Big Sur than most are willing to drive. A little cafe in Lucia provides open-air dining with a dramatic lookout over the coast.

❻ Plaskett Creek Group Camp

Location: Overlooking the Pacific Ocean in Los Padres National Forest; map G1, grid b8.

Campsites, facilities: There are three group sites for tents or RVs. Piped water, picnic tables, and fire grills are provided. Vault toilets are available. Leashed pets are permitted.

Reservations, fees: Reserve via phone at (877) 444-6777 ($8.65 reservation fee) or website: www.reserveusa.com; $50 group fee per night. Open year-round.

Contact: Parks Management Company, (805) 927-4622; Los Padres National Forest, Monterey Ranger District, (831) 385-5434 or fax (831) 667-2886.

Directions: From the little town of Lucia, drive 9.5 miles south on Highway 1 to the campground on the left.

Trip notes: This is one of two prime coastal camps in the immediate area along Highway 1, which is one of the prettiest drives in the West. The camp is for small groups and is set beside little Plaskett Creek. For a premium day trip, drive north five miles to Nacimiento-Ferguson Road, turn east, and drive into Los Padres National Forest and to the border of the Ventana Wilderness. Coastal views and hikes are first-class.

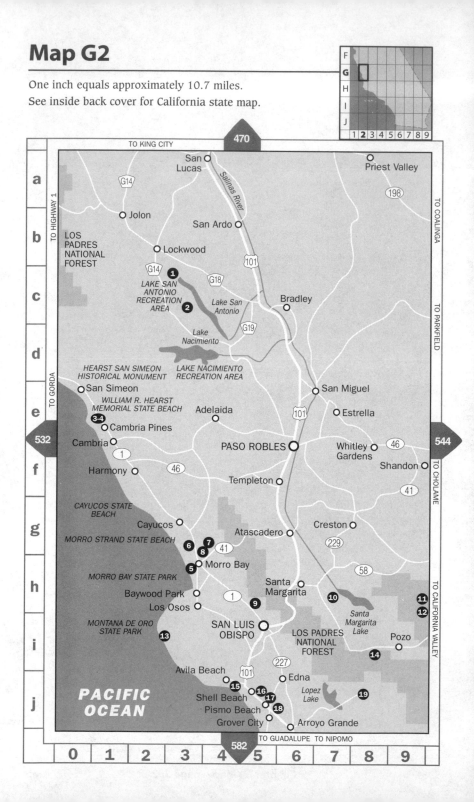

Map G2

One inch equals approximately 10.7 miles.
See inside back cover for California state map.

PACIFIC OCEAN

Chapter G2 features:

1 North Shore

Location: On Lake San Antonio; map G2, grid c3.

Campsites, facilities: There are 236 sites for tents or RVs, some with full or partial hookups. Piped water, fire grills, and tables are provided. A dump station, rest rooms, showers, boat ramp, boat rentals, stables, playground, recreation room, laundry facilities, and a grocery store are available. Leashed pets are permitted.

Reservations, fees: Reservations are accepted; $16 to $22 per night, $1 pet fee. Open year-round.

Contact: North Shore, (805) 472-2311.

Directions: From King City on US 101, turn south onto County Road G18 and drive 24 miles to the Lockwood intersection. Continue straight on County Road G18/Jolon Road and drive about 10 miles to the camp entrance road on the right.

Trip notes: Lake San Antonio makes a great year-round destination for adventure. It is a big, warm-water lake, long and narrow, set at an elevation of 900 feet in the foothills north of Paso Robles. The lake is 16 miles long, covers 5,500 surface acres, and has 60 miles of shoreline, making it an ideal place for fun in the sun. It is one of the top lakes in California for bass fishing, best in spring and early summer. It also provides the best wintering habitat in the region for bald eagles, and eagle-watching tours are available from the south shore of the lake. Of course, the size of the lake, along with hot temperatures all summer, make waterskiing and water sports absolutely first-class.

2 South Shore

Location: On Lake San Antonio; map G2, grid c3.

Campsites, facilities: There are three campgrounds with 482 campsites for tents or RVs, many with full or partial hookups. Piped water, fire grills, and tables are provided. A dump station, rest rooms, showers, boat ramp, boat rentals, playground, recreation room, laundry facilities, grocery store, and a visitor information center are available. Leashed pets are permitted.

Reservations, fees: Reservations are accepted; $16 to $22 per night, $1 pet fee. Open year-round.

Contact: South Shore, (805) 472-2311.

Directions: From King City, drive 29 miles south on US 101. Take County Road G19/Nacimiento Lake Road exit and drive 12 miles to County Road G14 /Interlake Road. Turn right and drive nine miles to the campground entrance road (San Antonio Road).

Trip notes: Harris Creek, Redondo Vista, and Lynch are the three campgrounds set near each other along the south shore of Lake San Antonio, a 16-mile reservoir that provides good bass fishing in the spring and waterskiing in the summer. In the winter months the Monterey County Department of Parks offers a unique eagle watch program here which includes boat tours. See the trip notes for North Shore (campground number 1) for more details about the lake.

❸ Washburn

Location: In San Simeon State Park; map G2, grid e1.

Campsites, facilities: There are 70 sites for tents or RVs up to 31 feet long. Fire grills and picnic tables are provided. Piped water and chemical toilets are available. A grocery store, coin laundry, and propane gas can be found nearby in Cambria. Leashed pets are permitted.

Reservations, fees: Reservations required for the March through September season only. Reserve via phone at (800) 444-PARK/7275 ($7.50 reservation fee) or website www.cal-parks.ca.gov; $10 to $12 per night, $1 pet fee. Open year-round.

Contact: Washburn, (805) 927-2035 or (805) 927-2020.

Directions: From Cambria, drive three miles north on Highway 1 to the park entrance. This campground is just beyond San Simeon Creek Campground on the park entrance road.

Trip notes: This camp is primarily used as an overflow area if the San Simeon Creek Campground is jammed to the rafters. It sits on the hill above the other camp and offers an ocean view, but is less developed. That's good or bad depending on your viewpoint.

❹ San Simeon Creek

Location: In San Simeon State Park; map G2, grid e1.

Campsites, facilities: There are 133 sites for tents or RVs up to 35 feet long. Fire grills and picnic tables are provided. Piped water, flush toilets, coin-operated showers, and a dump station are available. A grocery store, coin laundry, and propane gas can be found nearby in Cambria. Leashed pets are permitted.

Reservations, fees: Reserve via phone at (800) 444-PARK/7275 ($7.50 reservation fee) or website www.cal-parks.ca.gov; $17 to $19 per night, $1 pet fee. Open year-round.

Contact: San Simeon Creek, (805) 927-2035 or (805) 927-2020.

Directions: From Cambria, drive three miles north on Highway 1 to the park entrance.

Trip notes: Hearst Castle is only five miles northeast, so San Simeon Creek is a natural for visitors planning to take the tour (for a tour reservation, phone 800-444-7275). The camp is set across the highway from the ocean, with easy access under the highway to the beach. San Simeon Creek, while not exactly the Mississippi, runs through the campground and adds a nice touch. The best hike in the area is from Leffingwell Landing to Moonstone Beach, featuring sweeping views of the coast from oceantop bluffs and including a good chance to see passing whales.

❺ Morro Bay State Park

Location: In Morro Bay; map G2, grid h3.

Campsites, facilities: There are 20 RV sites with water and electrical connections and 115 sites for tents or RVs up to 31 feet long. Some sites are wheelchair accessible. Fire grills and picnic tables are provided. Piped water, flush toilets, coin-operated showers, dump station, museum exhibits, and nature walks and programs are available. A coin laundry, grocery store, propane gas, boat ramp, mooring, rentals, and food service are available in Morro Bay. The museum and food service areas are wheelchair accessible. Leashed pets are permitted.

Reservations, fees: Reserve via phone at (800) 444-PARK/7275 ($7.50 reservation fee) or website www.cal-parks.ca.gov; $17 to $18 per night, $1 pet fee.

Contact: Morro Bay State Park, (805) 772-7434 or fax (805) 772-5760; California State Parks, San Luis Obispo District, (805) 549-3312 or fax (805) 541-4799.

Directions: On Highway 1, drive to the south

end of Morro Bay and follow the signs to the park entrance.

Trip notes: Reservations are strongly advised at this popular campground. This is one of the premium stopover spots for folks cruising north on Highway 1. The park offers a wide range of activities and exhibits covering the natural and cultural history of the area. Activities include beach walks, kayaking in Morro Bay, fishing the nearby ocean on a party boat, touring Hearst Castle, or visiting the Morro Bay Wildlife Refuge. A "morro" is a small volcanic peak, and there are nine of them along the local coast. The top hike at the park climbs one of them, Cabrillo Peak, and rewards hikers with sensational coastal views.

❻ Morro Strand State Beach

Location: Near Morro Bay; map G2, grid g3.

Campsites, facilities: There are 23 sites for tents and 81 sites for RVs up to 24 feet long. Piped water, fire grills, and picnic tables are provided. Flush toilets and cold, outdoor showers are available. Supplies and a coin laundry are available in Morro Bay. Pets are permitted.

Reservations, fees: Reserve via phone at (800) 444-PARK/7275 ($7.50 reservation fee) or website www.cal-parks.ca.gov from Memorial Day to Labor Day; $17 to $18 per night, $1 pet fee.

Contact: Morro Strand State Beach, (805) 772-7434 or fax (805) 772-5760; California State Parks, San Luis Obispo District, (805) 549-3312 or fax (805) 541-4799.

Directions: This campground is within the Morro Bay city limits, just off Highway 1. The exit to the campground is signed.

Trip notes: A ton of Highway 1 cruisers plan to stay overnight at this state park. And why not? It is set along the ocean near Morro Bay, a pretty spot year-round. Side trips include the Morro Bay Wildlife Refuge, the Museum of Natural History, or an ocean fishing trip out of Morro Bay. See the trip notes for Morro Bay State Park (campground number five) for more information.

❼ Rancho Colina RV Park

Location: In Morro Bay; map G2, grid g4.

Campsites, facilities: There are 57 RV sites with full hookups. Picnic tables are provided. Rest rooms, showers, laundry facilities, and a recreation room are available. Supplies can be purchased nearby. Leashed pets are permitted.

Reservations, fees: Reservations are accepted; $20 per night. Open year-round.

Contact: Rancho Colina RV Park, (805) 772-8420.

Directions: From Morro Bay on Highway 1, drive one mile east on Atascadero Road/Highway 41 to 1045 Atascadero Road.

Trip notes: This privately operated RV park is one of several camping options in the Morro Bay area. Folks who park here typically stroll the boardwalk, exploring the little shops. For recreation activities, see the trip notes for Morro Bay State Park (campground number five).

❽ Morro Dunes Trailer Park and Camp

Location: In Morro Bay; map G2, grid g3.

Campsites, facilities: There are 43 sites for tents and 139 RV sites. Picnic tables, fire grills, piped water, electrical connections, cable TV and, in most cases, sewer hookups are provided. Rest rooms, showers, laundry facilities, store, wood, ice, and a dump station are available. Propane gas can be obtained nearby. Leashed pets are permitted.

Reservations, fees: Reservations are accepted; $15 to $25 per night. Open year-round.

Contact: Morro Dunes Trailer Park and Camp, (805) 772-2722 or fax (805) 772-5319.

Directions: From Highway 1 in Morro Bay, drive west on Atascadero Road/Highway 41 for a half mile to 1700 Embarcadero/Atascadero Road.

Trip notes: A wide array of side trip possibilities and great natural beauty make Morro Bay an attractive destination. Most visitors will walk the boardwalk, try at least one of the coastal restaurants, and then head to Morro Bay State Park for hiking or sea kayaking. Other folks will head straight to the port for fishing, or just explore the area before heading north to San Simeon for the Hearst Castle tour. See the trip notes for Morro Bay State Park (campground number five) for more information.

⑨ El Chorro Regional Park

Location: Near San Luis Obispo; map G2, grid h5.

Campsites, facilities: There are 44 sites for tents or RVs with full hookups and some undesignated overflow sites. Fire grills and picnic tables are provided. Piped water, flush toilets, and a playground are available. Supplies and a coin laundry are nearby in San Luis Obispo. Leashed pets are permitted.

Reservations, fees: No reservations; $18 to $21 per night, $2 pet fee. Groups may reserve six or more sites at $18 per night.

Contact: El Chorro Regional Park, (805) 781-5219.

Directions: From San Luis Obispo, drive 4.5 miles north on Highway 1 to the park entrance on the right side of the highway.

Trip notes: Located north of Morro Bay on the way to San Simeon and Hearst Castle, this can be a prime spot for RV travelers. Note that the campground isn't in the state park reservation system, which means there are times when coastal state parks can be jammed full and this regional park may still have space. Morro Bay, located six miles away, provides many possible side trips. Note that there's a men's prison about one mile away. For some people, this can be a real turnoff.

⑩ Santa Margarita KOA

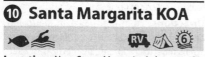

Location: Near Santa Margarita Lake; map G2, grid h7.

Campsites, facilities: There are 54 sites for tents or RVs. There are also 11 cabins. Picnic tables, fire grills, piped water and, in some cases, electrical connections and sewer hookups are provided. Rest rooms, showers, swimming pool, playground, coin laundry, store, dump station, and propane gas are available. Leashed pets are permitted.

Reservations, fees: Reservations are accepted; $20 to $26 per night, $34 to $42 per cabin per night. Open year-round.

Contact: Santa Margarita KOA, (805) 438-5618.

Directions: From San Luis Obispo, drive eight miles north on US 101 to the Highway 58/Santa Margarita exit. Drive through the town of Santa Margarita and turn right on Entrada. Within one mile, Entrada turns into Pozo Road. Continue six miles on Pozo Road to Santa Margarita Lake Road. Turn left and drive a half mile to the campground on the right.

Trip notes: Santa Margarita Lake should have a sign at its entrance that proclaims, "Fishing Only!" That's because the rules here do not allow waterskiing or any water contact, including swimming, wading, using float tubes, and windsurfing. The excellent prospects for bass fishing, along with the prohibitive rules, make this lake a favorite among anglers. Santa Margarita Lake covers nearly 800 acres, most of it long and narrow and set in a dammed-up valley in the foothill country at an elevation of 1,300 feet, just below the Santa Lucia Mountains.

⑪ Selby

Location: At the Carrizo Plain, northeast of San Luis Obispo; map G2, grid h9.

Campsites, facilities: This is a primitive camping area with no designated sites. A portable toilet is available. No piped water is provided and no trash facilities are available; please pack out your garbage. Leashed pets are permitted.

Reservations, fees: No reservations; no fee.

Contact: Bureau of Land Management, Bakersfield Field Office, 3801 Pegasus Drive, Bakersfield, CA 93308; (661) 391-6000.

Directions: From Bakersfield, take Highway 58 west for about 30 miles to McKittrick (where Highway 33 merges with Highway 58). Stay on Highway 58/33 for about another 10 miles, turn west on Seven-Mile Road, and drive seven miles (six miles will be on gravel road). Turn left on

Soda Lake Road and drive about six miles to the Selby camping area, located on your right.

Trip notes: The Carrizo Plain is California's largest nature preserve, but due to its remote location, primitive setting, and lack of recreational lakes and streams, it remains largely unknown and is explored by few people. The feature attraction is to visit Soda Lake in the winter to see flocks of the endangered sandhill crane; the lake is a nesting area for the huge bird with a seven-foot wingspan. Selby is a primitive camping area at the base of the Caliente Mountain Range, known for its scorching hot (hey, "Caliente") temperatures during the summer months. The top hiking destination in the region is Painted Rock, a 55-foot rock with Indian pictographs.

⑫ KCL

Location: At the Carrizo Plain, northeast of San Luis Obispo; map G2, grid h9.

Campsites, facilities: This is a primitive camping area with no designated sites. A portable toilet is available. No piped water is provided and no trash facilities are available; please pack out your garbage. Leashed pets are permitted.

Reservations, fees: No reservations; no fee.

Contact: Bureau of Land Management, Bakersfield Field Office, 3801 Pegasus Drive, Bakersfield, CA 93308; (661) 391-6000.

Directions: From Bakersfield, take Highway 58 west for about 30 miles to McKittrick (where Highway 33 merges with Highway 58). Stay on Highway 58/33 for another 10 to 12 miles, turn west on Seven-Mile Road, and drive seven miles. Turn left on Soda Lake Road and drive six miles to the entrance of the Carrizo Plains Natural Area. Continue about 15 miles to the KCL camping area located on your right.

Trip notes: KCL is the name of the old ranch headquarters in the Carrizo, of which remains an old broken-down barn, a water wagon, and not much else. At least there are some trees here (in comparison, there are almost none at nearby Selby camp). The Carrizo Plain is best known for providing a habitat for many rare species of plants, in addition to furnishing the winter nesting sites at Soda Lake for the awesome migration

of giant sandhill cranes. Occasionally these huge birds will fly down the valley and are visible here.

⑬ Montaña de Oro State Park

Location: Near Morro Bay; map G2, grid i2.

Campsites, facilities: There are 50 sites for tents or RVs up to 27 feet long, four walk-in environmental sites, and two group sites that can each accommodate 25 campers. Fire grills and picnic tables are provided. Pit toilets, horse camping facilities, and a nature trail are available. There is no piped water, but potable trucked water is available. Supplies and a coin laundry are nearby. Leashed pets are permitted.

Reservations, fees: Reserve via phone at (800) 444-PARK/7275 ($7.50 reservation fee) or website www.cal-parks.ca.gov; $7 to $10 per night for individual sites, $10 to $17 per night for the group camps, $17 to $50 per night for horse camping, and a $1 pet fee.

Contact: Montaña de Oro State Park, (805) 528-0513 or (805) 549-3312.

Directions: From Morro Bay, drive two miles south on Highway 1. Turn on South Bay Boulevard and drive four miles to Los Osos. Turn right on Pecho Valley Road and drive five miles to the park.

Trip notes: This sprawling chunk of primitive land includes coastline, 7,300 acres of foothills, and Valencia Peak at 1,345 feet in elevation. But there's no water—and that stops a lot of people from ever venturing here. The camp is perched on a bluff with stunning views of the ocean and cliffs. The nearby Bluffs Trail is one of the best easy coastal walks anywhere; it offers stunning ocean views, rock cliffs and, in the spring, tons of wildflowers over the course of just 1.5 miles. Another hiking option at the park is to climb Valencia Peak, a little butt-kicker of an ascent that tops out at 1,373 feet, providing more panoramic coastal views.

⑭ Hi Mountain

Location: In Los Padres National Forest; map G2, grid i8.

Campsites, facilities: There are 11 sites for tents or RVs up to 16 feet long (trailers not recommended). There is no piped water. Fire grills and picnic tables are provided. Vault toilets are available. Leashed pets are permitted.

Reservations, fees: No reservations; no camping fee, $ 5 per day per parked vehicle or Adventure Pass ($30 annual fee). Open year-round (road may be closed during heavy rains).

Contact: Los Padres National Forest, Santa Lucia Ranger District at (805) 925-9538 or fax (805) 349-0888.

Directions: From San Luis Obispo, drive eight miles north on US 101. Turn east on Highway 58 and drive four miles (four miles past Santa Margarita). Turn southeast on Pozo Road and drive for 16 miles to the town of Pozo. Turn on Hi Mountain Road and drive four miles to the campground.

Trip notes: At an elevation of 2,800 feet, this is the highest point in the Santa Lucia Wilderness. A mile west you can drive to the Hi Mountain Lookout, with awesome 360-degree views from the 3,180-foot summit. A mile to the east is a primitive road; turn south and drive to its end and a trailhead. From here, you can hike along Trout Creek for six miles to a little-known backpack camp called Buckeye.

---

⑮ Avila Hot Springs Spa and RV Park

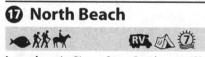

Location: On San Luis Obispo Bay; map G2, grid j4.

Campsites, facilities: There are 25 sites for tents and 50 RV spaces, many with full or partial hookups. Picnic tables and some fire grills are provided. Rest rooms, showers, swimming pool, hot mineral pool, spa, cable TV, dump station, recreation room, arcade, massage service, golf course, grocery store, and group barbecue pits are available. Leashed pets are permitted.

Reservations, fees: Reserve via phone at (800) 332-2359; $18 to $28 per night. There is an extra charge for use of the pool and spa facilities. Open year-round.

Contact: Avila Hot Springs Spa and RV Park,

(805) 595-2359 or fax (805) 595-7914.

Directions: From San Luis Obispo, drive nine miles south on US 101 to the Avila Beach Drive exit. Continue to 250 Avila Beach Drive.

Trip notes: The hot mineral pool here is a featured attraction. Nearby recreation options include Avila State Beach and Pismo State Beach.

---

⑯ Pismo Coast Village

Location: In Pismo Beach; map G2, grid j5.

Campsites, facilities: There are 400 RV sites with full hookups, satellite TV, picnic tables, and fire grills. Rest rooms, showers, playgrounds, swimming pools, laundry facilities, store, firewood, ice, recreation room, propane gas, recreation programs, restaurant, and a miniature golf course are available. Leashed pets are permitted.

Reservations, fees: Reserve via phone at (800) 458-1881; $22 to $36 per night. Open year-round.

Contact: Pismo Coast Village, (805) 773-1811.

Directions: In Pismo Beach, drive to 165 South Dolliver Street/Highway 1.

Trip notes: This big-time RV park gets a lot of use by Highway 1 cruisers. Its location is a plus, being set near the ocean. Pismo Beach is famous for its clamming, sand dunes, and beautiful coastal frontage.

---

⑰ North Beach

Location: In Pismo State Beach; map G2, grid j5.

Campsites, facilities: There are 103 sites for tents or RVs up to 31 feet long. Fire grills and picnic tables are provided. Piped water, hot showers, flush toilets, and a dump station are available. Horseback riding facilities, grocery store, coin laundry, and propane gas are nearby. Leashed pets are permitted.

Reservations, fees: Reserve via phone at (800) 444-PARK/7275 ($7.50 reservation fee) or website www.cal-parks.ca.gov; $14 to $18 per night, $1 pet fee.

Contact: North Beach, (805) 489-2684 or (805) 549-3312.

Directions: This campground is within Pismo Beach city limits, just off Highway 1. The exit is signed.

Trip notes: Plan on needing a reservation and having plenty of company when you come to North Beach. This is an exceptionally popular state beach, as an ultimate destination or as a stopover for folks cruising Highway 1. The adjacent dune area makes for great walks or, for kids, great rolls. The clamming on minus low tides is legendary.

⑱ Le Sage Riviera

Location: Near Pismo State Beach; map G2, grid j5.

Campsites, facilities: There are 60 RV sites. No tent camping is permitted. Picnic tables, piped water, electrical connections, and sewer hookups are provided. Rest rooms, showers, and laundry facilities are available. Stores, restaurants, and golf courses are nearby. Leashed pets are permitted.

Reservations, fees: Reservations are accepted; $23 to $32 per night. Open year-round.

Contact: Le Sage Riviera, (805) 489-5506 or fax (805) 489-2103

Directions: From Pismo Beach, drive two miles south on Grand Avenue or Dolliver Street to 319 North Highway 1.

Trip notes: This is a year-round RV park that can serve as headquarters for folks who are interested in visiting several nearby attractions, including neighboring Pismo State Beach and Lopez Lake, 10 miles to the east.

⑲ Lopez Lake Recreation Area

Location: Near Arroyo Grande; map G2, grid j8.

Campsites, facilities: There are 356 sites for tents or RVs of any length, many with full or partial hookups. Picnic tables and fire rings are provided. Rest rooms, showers, playground, laundry facilities, store, ice, snack bar, boat ramp, mooring, boat fuel, tackle, boat rentals, and a water slide are available. Leashed pets are permitted.

Reservations, fees: Reservations are accepted; phone (805) 489-8019; $13 to $21 per night, $2 pet fee, $4 boat launch fee. Open year-round.

Contact: Lopez Lake Recreation Area, (805) 489-1122.

Directions: From Arroyo Grande on US 101, take the Grand Avenue exit. Turn east and drive through Arroyo Grande. Turn northeast on Lopez Drive and drive 10 miles to the park.

Trip notes: Lopez Lake has become an example of how to do something right, with special marked areas set aside exclusively for waterskiing, jet skiing, and windsurfing, and the rest of the lake designated for fishing and low-speed boating. There are also reserved areas for swimming. That makes it perfect for just about everyone and, with good bass fishing, the lake has become very popular, especially on spring weekends when the bite is on. Lopez Lake is set amid oak woodlands southeast of San Luis Obispo. The lake is shaped something like a horseshoe, is 940 acres when full, and gets excellent weather most of the year.

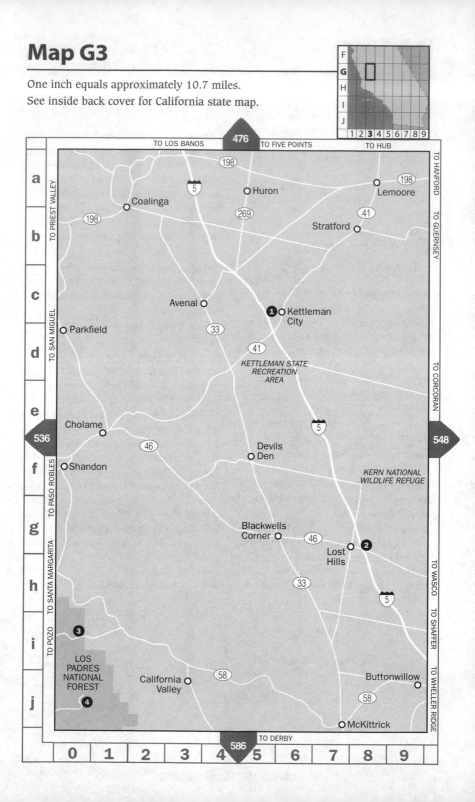

Chapter G3 features:

❶ Kettleman City RV Park

Location: Near Kettleman City; map G3, grid c5.

Campsites, facilities: There are 65 RV sites and unlimited tent sites. Picnic tables, piped water, and full or partial hookups are provided. There are eight sites with telephone hookups, available on request. Rest rooms, showers, playgrounds, video game room, pool, meeting room, coin laundry, store, dump station, dog run, restaurant, snack bar, horseshoeing services, horseback riding facilities, and propane gas are available. There is also a two-acre RV sales lot at the park. Leashed pets are permitted.

Reservations, fees: Reservations are accepted; $6 to $17 per night. Note: Overnight campers receive a 10 percent discount at the camp restaurant. Open year-round.

Contact: Kettleman City RV Park, (559) 386-4000.

Directions: From Interstate 5 near Kettleman City, take the Highway 41 exit. Drive a half mile north on Highway 41. Turn left on Hubert Way, then right on Cyril Place to 452 Cyril Place.

Trip notes: Being stuck in Kings County looking for a place to park an RV is no picnic. Unless, that is, you are lucky enough to know about Kettleman City RV Park. It's literally the "only game in town"; in fact, it's the only camp in the entire county. Visitors will find access to miles of open paths and roads for hiking or running.

❷ Lost Hills KOA

Location: Near Kern National Wildlife Refuge; map G3, grid g8.

Campsites, facilities: There are 10 sites for tents only, 80 RV sites, and one cabin. Picnic tables, piped water, satellite TV, and full hookups are provided. Rest rooms, showers, swimming pool, laundry facilities, store, video room, and propane gas are available. Some facilities are wheelchair accessible. Restaurants are nearby. Leashed pets are permitted.

Reservations, fees: Reserve via phone at (800) 562-2793; $20 to $26 per night; $36 per night cabin fee. Open year-round.

Contact: Lost Hills KOA, (661) 797-2719.

Directions: Drive to the junction of Interstate 5 and Highway 46. If you are coming from the south, make a left turn on Highway 46 into the park entrance. Coming from the north, make a right turn on Highway 46 into the park entrance.

Trip notes: The pickings can get slim around these parts when you're cruising north on Interstate 5 so if it's late, you'll likely be happy to find this KOA camp. The nearby Kern National Wildlife Refuge, about a 15-minute drive away, offers a side trip possibility. It's a waterfowl reserve that attracts ducks, geese, and other waterfowl in the fall and winter months.

❸ La Panza

Location: In Los Padres National Forest; map G3, grid i0.

Campsites, facilities: There are 16 sites for tents or RVs up to 16 feet long. Fire grills and picnic tables are provided. Vault toilets are available. There is no piped water. Leashed pets are permitted.

Reservations, fees: No reservations; $3 camping fee per night during deer season, $5 daily fee per vehicle or show your Adventure Pass ($30 annual fee). Open year-round.

Contact: Los Padres National Forest, Santa Lucia Ranger District, (805) 925-9538 or fax (805) 681-2781.

Directions: From San Luis Obispo, drive eight miles north on US 101. Turn east on Highway 58 and drive four miles (two miles past Santa Margarita). Turn southeast on Pozo Road and drive for 16 miles to the town of Pozo. Continue 11.5 miles east past Pozo on County Road M3093 to the campground.

Trip notes: This primitive spot is located at 2,400 feet in the La Panza Range, an oak woodland area that is crisscrossed by numerous trails and streams. From camp, if you drive west on the access road for one mile to a junction, turn left on Road M3093, and drive three miles to Pozo Summit, you will arrive at one of the better trailheads for the Maghesna Mountain Wilderness to the south. From here, the trail is routed on a ridge for two miles to the wilderness boundary, then heads east across Pine Mountain and Castle Crags. Water is scarce.

❹ Stony Creek Hike-In

Location: In Los Padres National Forest; map G3, grid j0.

Campsites, facilities: There are six sites for tents. Fire grills and picnic tables are provided. Vault toilets are available. There is no piped water, so bring plenty of your own. Leashed pets are permitted.

Reservations, fees: No reservations; no camping fee, $5 per day per parked vehicle, or Adventure Pass ($30 annual fee). Open year-round.

Contact: Los Padres National Forest, Santa Lucia Ranger District, (805) 925-9538 or fax (805) 681-2781.

Directions: From Arroyo Grande on US 101, take the Grand Avenue exit. Turn east and drive through Arroyo Grande. Turn northeast on Lopez Drive and drive 1.5 miles. Turn right on Huasna Road and drive 11 miles east. Continue east on County Road M2023/Huasna Road for 10 miles. Turn north (left) on Forest Service Road 30S02 and drive 2.5 miles to the trailhead. Hike in 2.5 miles past the locked gate to the campground.

Trip notes: Just about nobody goes out here. It is a small, primitive spot set along little Stony Creek at 1,800 feet elevation. This is deep in the Los Padres National Forest on the southern flank of Garcian Mountain in the La Panza Range. You're not going to see Bigfoot around here, but you won't likely see any other folks either. The access road/trail runs for four miles right along Stony Creek.

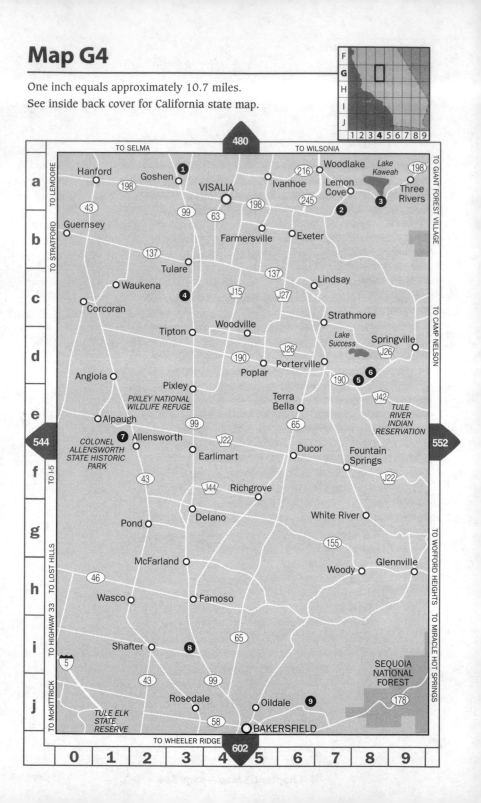

Map G4

One inch equals approximately 10.7 miles.
See inside back cover for California state map.

Chapter G4 features:

1 Goshen-Visalia KOA

Location: West of Visalia; map G4, grid a3.

Campsites, facilities: There are 30 sites for tents only, 48 RV sites, and 38 sites for tents or RVs. Piped water and full or partial hookups are provided. Rest rooms, showers, swimming pool, laundry facilities, playground, recreation room, store, dump station, and propane gas are available. Leashed pets are permitted.

Reservations, fees: Reservations are accepted; $18 to $26 per night.

Contact: Goshen-Visalia KOA, (559) 651-0544 or (800) 322-2336 in California.

Directions: From Visalia, drive five miles west on Highway 198 to the Plaza exit. Turn right on Plaza and drive five miles to Goshen Road. Turn left on Goshen Road and drive a quarter mile to the campground entrance.

Trip notes: This is a layover spot for Highway 99 cruisers. If you're looking for a spot to park your rig for the night, you can't get too picky around these parts.

2 Lemon Cove–Sequoia

Location: Near Lake Kaweah; map G4, grid a7.

Campsites, facilities: There are 55 sites for tents or RVs, as well as group camping facilities. Picnic tables, piped water, and full or partial hookups are provided. Rest rooms, showers, playground, swimming pool, laundry facilities, recreation room, cable TV, store, dump station, and propane gas are available. Leashed pets are permitted.

Reservations, fees: Reservations are accepted; $15 per night.

Contact: Lemon Cove–Sequoia, (559) 597-2346.

Directions: From Visalia, drive east on Highway 198 to its intersection with Highway 65. Continue for eight miles on Highway 198 to the camp on the left.

Trip notes: This is a privately run, year-round campground set on the outskirts of Visalia, about eight miles off Highway 99. It may not be the most beautiful spot on earth, but if you're stuck looking for a spot for the night and find this campground, it will look like paradise. Lake Kaweah is 17 miles east on Highway 198.

3 Horse Creek Recreation Area

Location: On Lake Kaweah; map G4, grid a8.

Campsites, facilities: There are 80 sites for tents or RVs. Piped water, fire grills, and picnic tables are provided. Flush toilets, showers, paved boat ramp, and a dump station are available. Some facilities are wheelchair accessible. Nearby are a grocery store, coin laundry, boat and water ski rentals, ice, snack bar, and propane gas. Leashed pets are permitted.

Reservations, fees: No reservations; $8 to $14 per night.

Contact: US Army Corps of Engineers, (559) 597-2301.

Directions: From Visalia, drive 25 miles east on Highway 198 to Lake Kaweah's south shore.

Trip notes: Lake Kaweah is a big lake, covering nearly 2,000 acres with 22 miles of shoreline. In the spring when the lake is full and the surrounding hills are green, you may even think you have found Valhalla. With such hot weather in the San Joaquin Valley, it's a boater's heaven, ideal for water-skiers, with good bass fishing in the coves and enough room for the jet skiers to stay clear. The camp is set on the southern shore of the lake. One problem is that the water level drops a great deal during late summer, as thirsty farms suck up every drop they can get, killing prospects of developing beaches for swimming and wading. The elevation is 300 feet.

❹ Sun and Fun RV Park

Location: Near Tulare; map G4, grid c3.

Campsites, facilities: There are 60 RV sites. Picnic tables, fire grills, piped water, and full hookups are provided. Rest rooms, showers, dump station, playground, swimming pool, spa, laundry facilities, and a recreation room are available. Some facilities are wheelchair accessible. A golf course, restaurant, and store are nearby. Leashed pets are permitted.

Reservations, fees: Reservations are accepted; $21 per night.

Contact: Sun and Fun RV Park, (559) 686-5779.

Directions: From Tulare, drive three miles south on Highway 99 to the Avenue 200 exit west. Drive a short distance to 1000 Avenue 200. From Tipton, drive 10 miles north on Highway 99. Exit on Avenue 200, bearing right over the freeway to the campground entrance.

Trip notes: This RV park is just off Highway 99, exactly halfway between San Francisco and Los Angeles. Are you having fun yet? Anybody making the long drive up or down the state on Highway 99 will learn what a dry piece of life the San Joaquin Valley can seem. That's why the swimming pool at this RV park can be a lifesaver.

❺ The Last Resort

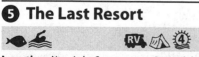

Location: Near Lake Success; map G4, grid d8.

Campsites, facilities: There are 250 sites for tents or RVs, 50 with full or partial hookups. Picnic tables and, in some cases, fire grills are provided. Rest rooms, showers, recreation room, playground, swimming pool, fishing facilities, laundry room, store, dump station, firewood, dog-walking area, and propane gas are available. Quiet, well-mannered, leashed pets are permitted.

Reservations, fees: Reservations are accepted; $14 to $23 per night. Open year-round.

Contact: The Last Resort, (559) 784-3948.

Directions: From Porterville on Highway 65, turn east on Highway 190 and drive five miles to 27798 Highway 190.

Trip notes: This campground is in a parklike setting with trees and flowers. It is two miles from Lake Success. A small, stocked fishing pond is available, and pet geese and ducks are often wandering around. For information on Lake Success, see the trip notes for Tule Recreation Area, (campground number six).

❻ Tule Recreation Area

Location: On Lake Success; map G4, grid d8.

Campsites, facilities: There are 104 sites for tents or RVs up to 30 feet long. Piped water, fire grills, and picnic tables are provided. Flush toilets, dump station, and a playground are available. Nearby are a grocery store, boat ramp, boat and water ski rentals, bait, tackle, and propane gas. Leashed pets are permitted.

Reservations, fees: No reservations; $14 per night, $2 launch fee.

Contact: US Army Corps of Engineers, (559) 784-0215 or fax (559) 784-5469.

Directions: From Porterville, drive eight miles east on Highway 190 to Lake Success and look for the campground entrance on the left.

Trip notes: Lake Success is a big lake with many arms, providing 30 miles of shoreline and making the place like a dreamland for boaters on hot summer days. The lake is set in the foothill country, at an elevation of 650 feet, where day after day of 100-degree summer temperatures are common. That is why boating, waterskiing, and jet skiing are so popular—anything to get wet. In the winter and spring, trout fishing and bass fishing are also big. No beaches are developed for swimming due to fluctuating water levels, though the day-use area has a decent sloped stretch of shore that is good for swimming. The wildlife area along the west side of the lake is worth exploring, and there is a nature trail below the dam.

❼ Colonel Allensworth State Historic Park

Location: Near Earlimart; map G4, grid e1.

Campsites, facilities: There are 15 sites for tents or RVs up to 30 feet long. There is also a 51-site overflow area. Piped water, fire grills, and picnic tables are provided. Rest rooms with hot showers and a visitor center are available. A grocery store is 12 miles away in Delano. Leashed pets are permitted.

Reservations, fees: No reservations; $10 per night, $1 pet fee. Open year-round.

Contact: California Department of Parks and Recreation, San Joaquin District Office, (559) 822-2332; Colonel Allensworth State Historic Park ranger station; (661) 634-3795.

Directions: From Fresno, drive south on Highway 99 about 60 miles to Earlimart. Turn right (west) on Avenue 56 and drive eight miles to the Highway 43 turnoff. Turn left on Highway 43 and travel south two miles to the park exit on the right. Drive 100 yards into the park directly ahead.

Trip notes: What you have here is the old town of Allensworth, which has been restored as a historical park dedicated to the African-American pioneers who founded it with Colonel Allen Allensworth, the highest ranking army chaplain of his time. One museum is available at the school here and another at the colonel's house with a 30-minute movie on the history of Allensworth.

❽ KOA Bakersfield

Location: North of Bakersfield; map G4, grid i3.

Campsites, facilities: There are 12 tent sites and 62 RV sites. Picnic tables, piped water, and full or partial hookups are provided. Rest rooms, showers, swimming pool (summer only), laundry room, store, dump station, and propane gas are available. Leashed pets are permitted.

Reservations, fees: Call for space available; $22 to $27 per night. Open year-round.

Contact: KOA Bakersfield, (661) 399-3107.

Directions: From Bakersfield, drive 12 miles north on Highway 99 to the Shafter–Lerdo Highway exit. Drive a mile west on Lerdo Highway to 5801 Lerdo Highway.

Trip notes: If you're stuck in the southern valley and the temperature feels like you're sitting in a cauldron, well, this spot provides a layover for the night near the town of Shafter. It's not exactly a hotbed of excitement.

❾ Kern River County Park

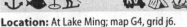

Location: At Lake Ming; map G4, grid j6.

Campsites, facilities: There are 50 sites for tents or RVs. Picnic tables, fire grills, and piped water are provided. Flush toilets, showers, dump station, playground, and a boat ramp are available. A grocery store is nearby. Leashed pets are permitted.

Reservations, fees: No reservations; $12 per night, $3 pet fee. Open year-round.

Contact: Kern County Parks Department, (661) 868-7000 or (661) 872-3179.

Directions: From Bakersfield, drive east on Highway 178. Turn left (north) on Alfred Harrell Highway and follow the signs to Lake Ming. Turn left on Lake Ming Road and follow the signs to the campground on the right.

Trip notes: Lake Ming is a little lake covering just 107 surface acres and, with the weather so hot, the hot jet boats can make it a wild affair here. It's become a popular spot for southern valley residents, only a 15-minute drive from Bakersfield. It is so popular for water sports that every year the lake is closed to the public for about three weeks for private boat races and waterskiing competitions. The elevation is 450 feet.

Special note: Sailing and windsurfing are permitted on the second weekend of every month and on Tuesday and Thursday afternoons. All motorized boating, including waterskiing and jet skiing, is permitted on the remaining days. All boats are required to have a permit; boaters may purchase one at the park. Swimming is not allowed.

Map G5

One inch equals approximately 10.7 miles.
See inside back cover for California state map.

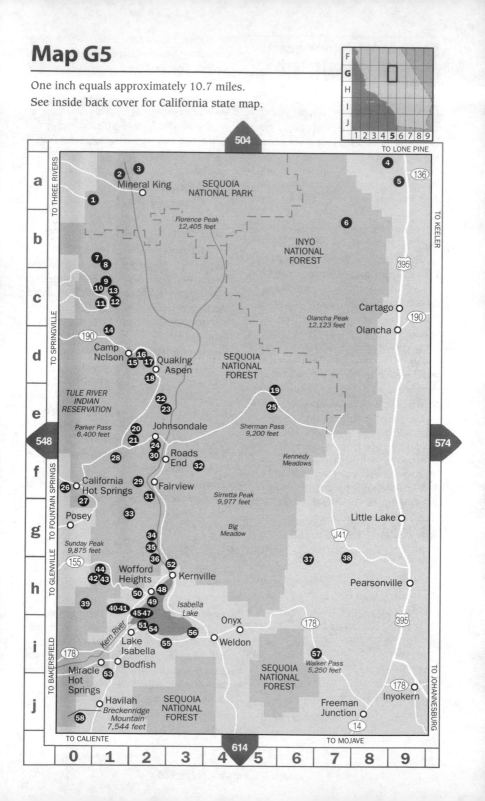

Chapter G5 features:

1 South Fork

Location: On the South Fork of the Kaweah River in Sequoia National Park; map G5, grid a0.

Campsites, facilities: There are 13 sites for tents only. Picnic tables and fire grills are provided. Pit toilets are available. There is no piped water. This is black bear habitat so proper food storage is required. Leashed pets are permitted, except on trails.

Reservations, fees: No reservations; $6 per night from May through October, no fee in other months.

Contact: Sequoia National Park, (559) 565-3341 or fax (559) 565-3730.

Directions: From Visalia, drive to Three Rivers on Highway 198. Turn east on South Fork Road and drive 13 miles to the campground.

Trip notes: The smallest developed camp in Sequoia National Park might just be what you're looking for. It is set at 3,650 feet on the South Fork of the Kaweah River, just inside the southwestern border of Sequoia National Park. A trail heads east from the camp and traverses Dennison Ridge, eventually leading to Hockett Lakes, a long, demanding overnight trip.

❷ Atwell Mill

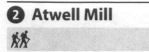

Location: On Atwell Creek in Sequoia National Park; map G5, grid a1.

Campsites, facilities: There are 21 tent sites; no trailers are permitted. Picnic tables, fire grills, and piped water are provided. Pit toilets are available. A small grocery store is nearby. Leashed pets are permitted.

Reservations, fees: No reservations; $6 per night. Open from May to September (depending on road and weather conditions).

Contact: Sequoia National Park, (559) 565-3341 or fax (559) 565-3730.

Directions: From Visalia, take Highway 198 to Three Rivers. Continue north for three miles on Highway 198. Turn right on Mineral King Road and drive 20 miles on a steep and winding road to the campground. Mineral King Road is quite rough—RVs and trailers are not recommended.

Trip notes: This small, pretty camp in Sequoia National Park is located on Atwell Creek near the East Fork of the Kaweah River, at an elevation of 6,650 feet. A trail at camp is routed south for a mile down to the Kaweah River, then climbs out of the canyon and along Deer Creek for another two miles through the East Fork Grove, an outstanding day hike.

❸ Cold Springs

Location: On the East Fork of the Kaweah River in Sequoia National Park; map G5, grid a2.

Campsites, facilities: There are 40 tent sites; no trailers are permitted. Picnic tables, fire grills, and piped water are provided. Pit toilets are available. A grocery store is nearby. Leashed pets are permitted.

Reservations, fees: No reservations; $6 per night. Open from May to September.

Contact: Sequoia National Park, (559) 565-3341 or fax (559) 565-3730.

Directions: From Visalia, take Highway 198 to Three Rivers. Continue to drive three miles north on Highway 198. Turn right on steep and winding Mineral King Road and drive 25 miles to the campground.

Trip notes: This high country camp at Sequoia National Park is set at 7,500 feet on the East Fork of the Kaweah River. There is a stellar hiking trail from here, with the trailhead located just west of the camp. The hike is routed south along Mosquito Creek, climbing over the course of about three miles to the pretty Mosquito Lakes, a series of four small, beautiful lakes set on the north flank of Hengst Peak (11,127 feet elevation).

❹ Tuttle Creek

Location: Near Mount Whitney; map G5, grid a8.

Campsites, facilities: There are 84 sites for tents or RVs and one group picnic area. There is no piped water, but pit toilets, fire grills, trash bin, and picnic tables are provided. Supplies are available in Lone Pine. Leashed pets are permitted.

Reservations, fees: No reservations; no fee. Open from early March through October.

Contact: Bureau of Land Management, Bishop Field Office, (760) 872-4881.

Directions: From Lone Pine, drive 3.5 miles west on Whitney Portal Road. Turn south on Horseshoe Meadow Road and drive 1.5 miles. Turn west on Tuttle Creek Road (a winding, dirt road) and drive directly into the campground.

Trip notes: This primitive BLM camp is set at the base of Mount Whitney along Tuttle Creek at 5,100 feet and is shadowed by several impressive peaks (Mount Whitney, Lone Pine Peak, and Mount Williamson). It is often used as an overflow area if the camps farther up Whitney Portal Road are full (see Whitney Portal, chapter F5, campground number 68).

❺ Diaz Lake

Location: Near Lone Pine; map G5, grid a9.

Campsites, facilities: There are 200 sites for

tents or RVs. Piped water, fire grills, and picnic tables are provided. Flush toilets, solar shower, and a boat ramp are available. Supplies and a coin laundry are available in Lone Pine. Leashed pets are permitted.

Reservations, fees: Reservations are accepted; $7 per night. Open year-round.

Contact: Inyo County Parks Department, (760) 876-5656.

Directions: From Lone Pine, drive two miles south on US 395 to the entrance on the right.

Trip notes: Diaz Lake is set at 3,650 feet in the Owens Valley, where it is often overlooked by visitors to nearby Mount Whitney. It's a small lake, just 85 acres, and it is popular for trout fishing in the spring, when a speed limit of 15 mph is enforced. In summer when hot weather takes over and the speed limit is bumped to 35 mph, you can say *adios* to the anglers and *hola* to water-skiers. A 20-foot limit is enforced for boats.

❻ Horseshoe Meadow

Location: Near the John Muir Wilderness in Inyo National Forest; map G5, grid b7.

Campsites, facilities: There are several walk-in sites and a few drive-in equestrian sites. Vault toilets, piped water, picnic tables, fire grills, pack station, and horseback riding facilities are available. Leashed pets are permitted.

Reservations, fees: No reservations; $6 per night for walk-in sites, $12 for equestrians. Open from mid-May through mid-October.

Contact: Inyo National Forest, Mount Whitney Ranger District, (760) 876-6200 or fax (760) 876-6202.

Directions: From Lone Pine, drive 3.5 miles west on Whitney Portal Road. Turn left on Horseshoe Meadows Road and drive 19 miles to the end of the road.

Trip notes: This is a trailhead camp, remote and obscure, for backpackers heading into the adjacent John Muir Wilderness. The camp is set at 10,000 feet near the wilderness border, with several trails leading out of camp. The best heads west through Horseshoe Meadow and along a creek, then rises steeply for four miles to Cottonwood Pass where it intersects with the Pacific Crest Trail. From here backpackers can hike north on the PCT for one mile to Chicken Spring Lake to set up camp, a demanding but rewarding overnighter.

❼ Hidden Falls

Location: On the Tule River in Mountain Home State Forest; map G5, grid b1.

Campsites, facilities: There are eight walk-in sites for tents only. Picnic tables, fire grills, and piped water are provided. Pit toilets are available. Leashed pets are permitted.

Reservations, fees: No reservations; no fee. Open from June to October.

Contact: Mountain Home State Forest, (559) 539-2855 (summer) or (559) 539-2321 (winter).

Directions: From Porterville, drive 19 miles east on Highway 190 (a mile past the town of Springville). Turn left (north) onto Balch Park Road and drive about 23 miles to the Mountain Home State Forest sign on the right. Continue on Balch Road, following the signs to the State Forest Headquarters where free forest maps are available. The campgrounds are well signed from this point. The total trip from the Highway 190/Balch Road turnoff to the campground is about 30 miles. Alternate route: After driving three miles on Balch Park Road, turn right (east) on Bear Creek Road and drive 25 miles to the campground. This is not a good road for trailers and RVs.

Trip notes: This small, quiet camp, set at 6,000 feet along the Tule River near Hidden Falls, is one of the prettier camps in Mountain Home State Forest. It is remote and overlooked by all but a handful of insiders who know its qualities.

❽ Moses Gulch

Location: On the Tule River in Mountain Home State Forest; map G5, grid b1.

Campsites, facilities: There are 10 sites for tents. Piped water, fire grills, and picnic tables are provided. Vault toilets are available. Leashed pets are permitted.

Reservations, fees: No reservations; no fee.

Contact: Mountain Home State Forest, (559) 539-2855 (summer) or (559) 539-2321 (winter).

Directions: From Porterville, drive 19 miles east on Highway 190 (a mile past the town of Springville). Turn left (north) onto Balch Park Road and drive about 23 miles to the Mountain Home State Forest sign on the right. Continue on Balch Road, following the signs to the State Forest Headquarters where free forest maps are available. (The campgrounds are well signed from this point.) The total trip from the Highway 190/Balch Road turnoff to the campground is about 31 miles. Alternate route: After driving three miles on Balch Park Road, turn right (east) on Bear Creek Road and drive 26 miles to the campground. This is not a good road for trailers and RVs.

Trip notes: Obscure Moses Gulch sits in a canyon below Moses Mountain (9,331 feet) to the nearby north. Mountain Home State Forest is surrounded by Sequoia National Forest. A trailhead at the eastern end of the state forest provides access both north and south along the North Fork of the Middle Fork Tule River for a scenic hike. The cost? Free.

❾ Frazier Mill

Location: In Mountain Home State Forest; map G5, grid c1.

Campsites, facilities: There are 46 sites for tents and a few RV sites. Piped water, fire grills, and picnic tables are provided. Vault toilets are available. Leashed pets are permitted.

Reservations, fees: No reservations; no fee. Open from June to October.

Contact: Mountain Home State Forest, (559) 539-2855 (summer) or (559) 539-2321 (winter).

Directions: From Porterville, drive 19 miles east on Highway 190 (a mile past the town of Springville). Turn left (north) onto Balch Park Road and drive about 23 miles to the Mountain Home State Forest sign on the right. Continue on Balch Road, following the signs to the State Forest Headquarters where free forest maps are available. (The campgrounds are well signed from this point.) The total trip from the Highway 190/Balch Road turnoff to the campground is

about 35 miles. Alternate route: After driving three miles on Balch Park Road, turn right (east) on Bear Creek Road and drive 17 miles to the campground. This is not a good road for trailers and RVs.

Trip notes: The prime attractions here are the obscurity, remoteness, and abundance of old-growth giant sequoias. A Forest Information Trail is nearby. The Wishon Fork of the Tule River is the largest of the several streams that pass through this forest. You can't beat the price.

❿ Shake Camp

Location: In Mountain Home State Forest; map G5, grid c1.

Campsites, facilities: There are 11 sites for tents or RVs. Piped water, fire grills, and picnic tables are provided. Vault toilets are available, and a public pack station with corrals is located nearby. Leashed pets are permitted.

Reservations, fees: No reservations; no fee. Open from June to October.

Contact: Mountain Home State Forest, (559) 539-2855 (summer) or (559) 539-2321 (winter).

Directions: From Porterville, drive 19 miles east on Highway 190 (a mile past the town of Springville). Turn left (north) onto Balch Park Road and drive about 23 miles to the Mountain Home State Forest sign on the right. Continue on Balch Road, following the signs to the State Forest Headquarters where free forest maps are available. (The campgrounds are well signed from this point.) The total trip from the Highway 190/Balch Road turnoff to the campground is about 36 miles. Alternate route: After driving three miles on Balch Park Road, turn right (east) on Bear Creek Road and drive 21 miles to the campground. This is not a good road for trailers and RVs.

Trip notes: This is a little-known spot for horseback riding. Horses can be rented for the day, hour, or night. The camp is set at 6,500 feet and there's a trailhead here for trips into the adjoining Sequoia National Forest and beyond to the east into the Golden Trout Wilderness. Hikers should note that the Balch Park Pack Station, a commercial outfitter, is located nearby, so you can expect horse traffic on the trail.

⑪ Balch County Park

🚶♿   🚐 ⛺ 🏕️⑥

Location: In Mountain Home State Forest; map G5, grid c1.

Campsites, facilities: There are 71 sites for tents or RVs up to 30 feet long. Piped water, fire grills, and picnic tables are provided. Flush toilets are available. Leashed pets are permitted.

Reservations, fees: No reservations; $12 per night, $1 pet fee. Open from May to October 25.

Contact: Balch County Park, (559) 733-6612 or (559) 539-3896.

Directions: From Porterville, drive 19 miles east on Highway 190 (a mile past the town of Springville). Turn left (north) onto Balch Park Road and drive three miles to Bear Creek Road. Turn east (right) and drive 15 miles to the campground (trailers not recommended). Alternate route: After turning north onto Balch Park Road, drive 40 miles to the park.

Trip notes: Secluded? Hard to reach? Yes, and that's just what folks want here. Mountain Home State Forest has eight campgrounds, all surrounded by state land and Sequoia National Forest. A nearby grove of giant sequoias is a featured attraction. The elevation is 6,500 feet.

⑫ Methuselah Group Camp

🚶   🚐 ⛺ 🏕️⑥

Location: In Mountain Home State Forest; map G5, grid c1.

Campsites, facilities: This group site can accommodate 20 to 100 people in tents or RVs. Fire grills and some picnic tables are provided. Vault toilets are available. There is no piped water, so bring your own. Leashed pets are permitted.

Reservations, fees: Reservations are required; no fee. Open from June to October.

Contact: Mountain Home State Forest, (559) 539-2855 (summer) or (559) 539-2321 (winter).

Directions: From Porterville, drive 19 miles east on Highway 190 (a mile past the town of Springville). Turn left (north) onto Balch Park Road and drive about 23 miles to the Mountain

Home State Forest sign on the right. Continue on Balch Road, following the signs to the State Forest Headquarters where free forest maps are available. (The campgrounds are well signed from this point.) The total trip from the Highway 190/Balch Road turnoff to the campground is about 40 miles. Alternate route: After turning north onto Balch Park Road, drive 40 miles to the campground.

Trip notes: This is one of the few free group camps available anywhere in California. Remember to bring water. The elevation is 5,900 feet. Mountain Home State Forest is best known for its remoteness, old-growth giant sequoias (hence the name of this camp, Methuselah), trails that provide access to small streams, and horseback trips into the surrounding Sequoia National Forest.

⑬ Hedrick Pond

Location: In Mountain Home State Forest; map G5, grid c1.

Campsites, facilities: There are 14 sites for tents or RVs. Piped water, fire grills, and picnic tables are provided. Vault toilets are available. Leashed pets are permitted.

Reservations, fees: No reservations; no fee. Open from June through October.

Contact: Mountain Home State Forest, (559) 539-2855 (summer) or (559) 539-2321 (winter).

Directions: From Porterville, drive 19 miles east on Highway 190 (a mile past the town of Springville). Turn left (north) onto Balch Park Road and drive about 23 miles to the Mountain Home State Forest sign on the right. Continue on Balch Road, following the signs to the State Forest Headquarters where free forest maps are available. (The campgrounds are well signed from this point.) The total trip from the Highway 190/Balch Road turnoff to the campground is about 35 miles. Alternate route: After driving three miles on Balch Park Road, turn right (east) on Bear Creek Road and drive 16 miles to the campground. This is not a good road for trailers and RVs.

Trip notes: Mountain Home State Forest is highlighted by giant sequoias, and Hedrick Pond provides a fishing opportunity, being stocked occasionally in summer with rainbow trout. This camp is set at 6,300 feet, one of eight camps in the immediate region. See Methuselah Group Camp (campground number 12) for a full array of recreation options.

⑭ Wishon

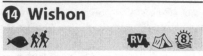

Location: On the Tule River in Sequoia National Forest; map G5, grid d1.

Campsites, facilities: There are nine sites for tents only and 26 sites for tents or RVs up to 22 feet long. Picnic tables, fire grills, and piped water are provided. Vault toilets are available. Leashed pets are permitted.

Reservations, fees: Reserve via phone at (877) 444-6777 ($8.65 reservation fee) or website www.reserveusa.com; $12 per night. Open year-round.

Contact: Sequoia National Forest, Tule River Ranger District, (559) 539-2607 or fax (559) 539-2067.

Directions: From Porterville, drive 25 miles east on Highway 190. Turn left on County Road 208/Wishon Drive and drive 3.5 miles. This camp is located at the bottom of a canyon.

Trip notes: Wishon Camp is set at 4,000 feet on the Middle Fork of the North Fork Tule River, just west of the Doyle Springs Summer Home Tract. Just down the road to the east, on the left side, is a parking area for a trailhead. The hike here is routed for a mile to the Tule River and then runs along the stream for several miles, including four miles to Mountain Home State Forest.

⑮ Coy Flat

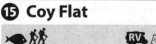

Location: In Sequoia National Forest; map G5, grid d1.

Campsites, facilities: There are 20 sites for tents or RVs up to 22 feet long. Piped water, fire grills, and picnic tables are provided. Vault toilets are available. Leashed pets are permitted.

Reservations, fees: Reserve via phone at (877) 444-6777 ($8.65 reservation fee) or website www.reserveusa.com; $10 per night. Open

from mid-April through mid-November.

Contact: Sequoia National Forest, Tule River Ranger District, (559) 539-2607 or fax (559) 539-2067.

Directions: From Porterville, drive 34 miles east on Highway 190 to Camp Nelson. Turn right on Coy Flat Road and drive one mile.

Trip notes: Coy Flat is set on Bear Creek, a small fork of the Tule River at 5,000 feet in elevation. The road out of camp is routed five miles to the Black Mountain Grove of redwoods, with some giant sequoias set just inside the border of the neighboring Tule River Indian Reservation. From camp, a hiking trail (Forest Trail 31S31) is routed east for two miles through the Belknap Camp Grove of sequoias and then turns and heads south for four miles to Slate Mountain, where it intersects with the Summit National Recreation Trail, a steep butt-kicker of a hike that tops out at over 9,000 feet.

⑯ Belknap

Location: On the South Middle Fork of Tule River in Sequoia National Forest; map G5, grid d2.

Campsites, facilities: There are 15 sites for tents or RVs up to 22 feet long. Trailers are prohibited in this area. Piped water, fire grills, picnic tables, and vault toilets are available. A grocery store is nearby. Leashed pets are permitted.

Reservations, fees: Reserve via phone at (877) 444-6777 ($8.65 reservation fee) or website www.reserveusa.com; $12 per night, $5 for an extra vehicle. Open from mid-April through mid-November.

Contact: Sequoia National Forest, Tule River Ranger District, (209) 539-2607 or fax (209) 539-2067.

Directions: From Porterville, drive 34 miles east on Highway 190 to Camp Nelson. Turn right on Nelson Drive and drive a mile to the camp.

Trip notes: The groves of sequoias in this area are a highlight wherever you go. This camp is set on the South Middle Fork of Tule River near McIntyre Grove and Belknap Camp Grove, and a trail from camp is routed east for three miles through Wheel Meadow Grove to the junction with the Summit National Recreation Trail at Quaking Aspen Camp. The elevation is 5,000 feet.

⑰ Quaking Aspen Group Camp

Location: At the headwaters of the South Middle Fork Tule River in Sequoia National Forest; map G5, grid d2.

Campsites, facilities: There are three group sites for up to 12 people, two group sites for up to 25 people, and two group sites for up to 50 people, all suitable for tents only. Piped water, fire grills, picnic tables, and vault toilets are available. A grocery store is nearby. Leashed pets are permitted.

Reservations, fees: Reserve via phone at (877) 444-6777 ($8.65 reservation fee) or website www.reserveusa.com; $18 to $75 group fee per night, depending on group size. Open from mid-May to mid-November.

Contact: Sequoia National Forest, Tule River Ranger District, (559) 539-2607 or fax (559) 539-2067.

Directions: From Porterville, drive 34 miles east on Highway 190 to Camp Nelson. Continue about 11 miles east on Highway 190 to the campground.

Trip notes: For groups, here is an alternative to nearby Peppermint. See the trip notes for Peppermint (campground number 22) for recreation options. The elevation is 7,000 feet.

⑱ Quaking Aspen

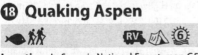

Location: In Sequoia National Forest; map G5, grid d2.

Campsites, facilities: There are 32 sites for tents or RVs up to 22 feet long. Piped water, fire grills, picnic tables, and vault toilets are available. A grocery store is nearby. Leashed pets are permitted.

Reservations, fees: Reserve via phone at (877) 444-6777; $12 per night, $5 for an extra vehicle. Open from May to November 15.

Contact: Sequoia National Forest, Tule River Ranger District, (559) 539-2607 or fax (559) 539-2067.

Directions: From Porterville, drive 34 miles east on Highway 190 to Camp Nelson. Continue 11 miles east of Camp Nelson on Highway 190 to the campground.

Trip notes: Quaking Aspen sits at a junction of Forest Service roads at 7,000 feet in elevation, near the headwaters of Freeman Creek. A trailhead for the Summit National Recreation Trail runs right through camp, a popular trip on horseback, heading deep into Sequoia National Forest. Another trail, ideal for day hikes, is routed east along Freeman Creek and reaches the Freeman Grove of sequoias in four miles.

⑲ Troy Meadows

Location: On Fish Creek in Sequoia National Forest; map G5, grid e5.

Campsites, facilities: There are 10 sites for tents only and 63 sites for tents or RVs up to 22 feet long. Piped water, fire grills, and picnic tables are provided. Vault toilets are available. Leashed pets are permitted.

Reservations, fees: No reservations; $5 per night. Open from May to November.

Contact: Sequoia National Forest, Cannell Meadow Ranger District, (760) 376-3781 or fax (760) 376-3795.

Directions: From the town of Brown on Highway 14, drive four miles north. Turn left (west) on Nine Mile Canyon Road and drive 31 miles northwest (the road becomes Sherman Pass Road) to the campground.

Trip notes: Obscure? Yes, but what the heck, it gives you an idea of what is possible out in the boondocks. The camp is set at 7,800 feet right along Fish Creek. An information station is available two miles northwest. You are advised to stop there prior to any backcountry trips. Note that off-highway vehicles (OHVs) are allowed in this area. Also note that the Jackass National Recreation Trail is available a short drive to the east; it runs north aside Jackass Creek to its headwaters just below Jackass Peak (9,245 feet).

㉒ Long Meadow Group Camp

Location: In Sequoia National Forest; map G5, grid e2.

Campsites, facilities: One group site for tents or RVs up to 16 feet long can accommodate up to 25 people. Fire grills and picnic tables are provided. Vault toilets are available. There is no piped water, so bring your own. Leashed pets are permitted.

Reservations, fees: Reserve via phone at (877) 444-6777 ($8.65 reservation fee) or website www.reserveusa.com; $18 to $75 per night, depending on group size. Open from June to September.

Contact: Sequoia National Forest, Hot Springs Ranger District, (611) 548-6503 or fax (611) 548-6236.

Directions: From Highway 99 in Earlimart, take the County Road J22/Avenue 56 exit and drive east for 39 miles to the town of California Hot Springs. Turn left on County Road M50/Parker Pass Road and drive 12 miles. Turn left on County Road M107/Western Divide Highway and drive four miles to the entrance.

Trip notes: Long Meadow is set on little Long Meadow Creek at an elevation of 6,500 feet, within a mile of the remote Cunningham Grove of redwoods one mile to the east. Note that Redwood Meadow (campground number 21) is located just one mile to the west, where the Trail of the Hundred Giants is a feature attraction.

㉑ Redwood Meadow

Location: Near Parker Meadow Creek in Sequoia National Forest; map G5, grid e1.

Campsites, facilities: There are 15 sites for tents or RVs up to 16 feet long. Piped water, fire grills, and picnic tables are provided. Vault toilets are available. Leashed pets are permitted.

Reservations, fees: Reserve via phone at (877) 444-6777 ($8.65 reservation fee) or website www.reserveusa.com; $12 per night. Open from June to September.

Contact: Sequoia National Forest, Hot Springs Ranger District, (661) 548-6503 or fax (661) 548-6236.

Directions: From Highway 99 in Earlimart, take the County Road J22/Avenue 56 exit and drive east for 39 miles to the town of California Hot Springs. Turn north left on County Road M50/Parker Pass Road and drive 12 miles. Turn left on County Road M107/Western Divide Highway and drive three miles to the entrance.

Trip notes: The highlight here is the half-mile Trail of the Hundred Giants, which is routed through a grove of giant sequoias and is usable by wheelchair hikers. The camp is set near Parker Meadow Creek at 6,500 feet elevation. If this camp is full, the Long Meadow (campground number 20) provides a nearby option. This is a popular place, so get here early.

㉒ Peppermint

Location: On Peppermint Creek in Sequoia National Forest; map G5, grid e2.

Campsites, facilities: There are 19 sites for tents or RVs up to 22 feet long. Picnic tables are provided. Vault toilets are available. There is no piped water, so bring your own. A grocery store is nearby. Leashed pets are permitted.

Reservations, fees: No reservations; no fee. A fire permit is required. Open from May to October.

Contact: Sequoia National Forest, Tule River Ranger District, (559) 539-2607 or fax (559) 539-2067.

Directions: From Porterville, drive 34 miles east on Highway 190 to Camp Nelson. Continue about 15 miles southeast on Highway 190 to the entrance road.

Trip notes: This is one of two primitive camps at Peppermint Creek, but the two are not directly connected by a road. Several backcountry access roads snake throughout the area, as detailed on a Forest Service map, and exploring them can make for some self-styled fortune hunts. For the ambitious, hiking the two-mile trail at the end of nearby Forest Service Road 21S05 can lead to a fantastic lookout at The Needles (8,245 feet). The camp elevation is 7,100 feet.

㉓ Lower Peppermint

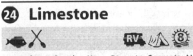

Location: In Sequoia National Forest; map G5, grid e2.

Campsites, facilities: There are 17 sites for tents or RVs up to 40 feet long. Piped water, fire grills, and picnic tables are provided. Vault toilets are available. Leashed pets are permitted.

Reservations, fees: No reservations; $12 per night. Open from June to October.

Contact: Sequoia National Forest, Hot Springs Ranger District, (661) 548-6503 or fax (661) 548-6236.

Directions: From the town of Lake Isabella, drive 35 miles north on Burlando Road and Sierra Way to the town of Johnsondale. Turn right on Forest Service Road 22S82/Lloyd Meadow Road and drive about 14 miles on a paved road to the campground.

Trip notes: This is a little-known camp in Sequoia National Forest, set along Peppermint Creek at 5,300 feet. This area has a vast network of backcountry roads, which are detailed on a Forest Service map.

㉔ Limestone

Location: On the Kern River in Sequoia National Forest; map G5, grid f2.

Campsites, facilities: There are 12 sites for tents only and 10 sites for tents or RVs up to 22 feet long. Fire grills and picnic tables are provided. Vault toilets are available. There is no piped water, so bring your own. Supplies and a coin laundry are available in Kernville. Leashed pets are permitted.

Reservations, fees: Reserve via phone at (877) 444-6777 ($8.65 reservation fee) or website www.reserveusa.com; $10 per night, $5 for an extra vehicle. Open from April through November.

Contact: Sequoia National Forest, Cannell Meadow Ranger District, (760) 376-3781 or fax (760) 376-3795.

Directions: From Kernville, drive 19 miles north on Kern River Highway/Sierra Way Road to the campground entrance.

Trip notes: Set deep in the Sequoia National Forest at 3,800 feet, Limestone is a small campground along the Kern River, fed by snowmelt from Mount Whitney. This stretch of the Kern is extremely challenging and sensational for whitewater rafting, with cold water and many of the rapids rated Class IV and Class V, for experts with guides only. The favored put-in is at the Johnsondale Bridge, and from here it's a 21-mile run to Kernville, where the river pours into Lake Isabella a few miles later. Two sections are unrunnable: Fairview Dam (mile 2.5) and Salmon Falls (mile 8) For nonrafters, South Creek Falls provides a side trip, one mile to the west.

㉕ Fish Creek

Location: In Sequoia National Forest; map G5, grid e5.

Campsites, facilities: There are 40 sites for tents or RVs up to 22 feet long. Piped water, fire grills, and picnic tables are provided. Vault toilets are available. A grocery store is nearby. Leashed pets are permitted.

Reservations, fees: No reservations; $5 per night. Open from May to November.

Contact: Sequoia National Forest, Cannell Meadow Ranger District, (760) 376-3781 or fax (760) 376-3795.

Directions: From US 395 15 miles north of China Lake, turn left on Nine Mile Canyon Road and drive 28 miles northwest (the road becomes Sherman Pass Road) to the campground.

Trip notes: This is a pretty spot set at the confluence of Fish Creek and Jackass Creek. The elevation is 7,400 feet. The nearby trails are used by off-highway vehicles and can make this a noisy campground during the day.

㉖ Leavis Flat

Location: On Deer Creek in Sequoia National Forest; map G5, grid f0.

Campsites, facilities: There are five sites for tents only and four sites for RVs up to 16 feet long. Piped water, fire grills, and picnic tables are provided. Vault toilets are available. A grocery store, coin laundry, and propane gas can be found nearby. Leashed pets are permitted.

Reservations, fees: Reserve via phone at (877) 444-6777; $10 per night. Open year-round.

Contact: Sequoia National Forest, Hot Springs Ranger District, (661) 548-6503 or fax (661) 548-6236.

Directions: From Highway 99 in Earlimart, take the County Road J22/Avenue 56 exit and drive east for 39 miles to the campground. Or from Highway 65 follow the California Hot Springs Resort signs from Ducor.

Trip notes: Leavis Flat is located just inside the western border of Sequoia National Forest along Deer Creek, at an elevation of 3,100 feet. The highlight here is the adjacent California Hot Springs.

㉗ White River

Location: In Sequoia National Forest; map G5, grid f0.

Campsites, facilities: There are eight sites for tents and four sites for RVs up to 16 feet long. Piped water, fire grills, and picnic tables are provided. Vault toilets are available. Leashed pets are permitted.

Reservations, fees: Reserve via phone at (877) 444-6777 ($8.65 reservation fee) or website www.reserveusa.com; $10 per night. Open from May to October.

Contact: Sequoia National Forest, Hot Springs Ranger District, (661) 548-6503 or fax (661) 548-6236.

Directions: From Highway 155 just west of Glennville, turn north on Linns Valley Road and drive about 2.5 miles. Turn left on County Road M10 and drive through Idlewild. Continue northeast on Forest Service Road 24S05 (dirt road) for six more miles.

Trip notes: White River is set at 4,000 feet, on the White River near where little Dark Canyon Creek enters it. A trail from camp follows downstream along the White River to the west for three miles, dropping into Ames Hole and Cove Canyon. The region's hot springs are about a 10-minute drive away to the north.

㉘ Holey Meadow

Location: On Double Bunk Creek in Sequoia National Forest; map G5, grid f1.

Campsites, facilities: There are 10 sites for tents or RVs up to 16 feet long. Piped water, fire grills, and picnic tables are provided. Vault toilets are available. Leashed pets are permitted.

Reservations, fees: Reserve via phone at (877) 444-6777 ($8.65 reservation fee) or website www.reserveusa.com; $10 per night. Open from June to October.

Contact: Sequoia National Forest, Hot Springs Ranger District, (661) 548-6503 or fax (661) 548-6236.

Directions: From Highway 99 in Earlimart, take the County Road J22/Avenue 56 exit and drive east for 39 miles to the town of California Hot Springs. Turn left on County Road M50/Parker Pass Road and drive 12 miles. Turn left on County Road M107/Western Divide Highway and drive a half mile to the entrance.

Trip notes: Holey Meadow is set at 6,400 feet on the western slopes of the Sierra. Parker Pass is located a mile to the west, and if you drive on the Forest Service road over the pass, continue southwest (four miles from camp) to Cold Springs Saddle, and then turn east on the Forest Service spur road, it will take you two miles to Starvation Creek and the Starvation Creek Grove.

㉙ Frog Meadow

Location: In Sequoia National Forest; map G5, grid f2.

Campsites, facilities: There are 10 sites for tents or RVs up to 16 feet long. Fire grills and picnic tables are provided. Vault toilets are available. There is no piped water. Leashed pets are permitted.

Reservations, fees: No reservations; no fee. Open from June to October.

Contact: Sequoia National Forest, Hot Springs Ranger District, (661) 548-6503 or fax (661) 548-6236.

Directions: From Highway 155 just west of Glennville, turn north on Linns Valley Road/County Road M3 and drive about four miles. Turn left onto County Road M9 and drive 4.5 miles to Guernsey Mill/Sugarloaf Lodge. Continue on Sugarloaf Road/Forest Service Road 23S16 for about seven miles. Turn left on Forest Service Road 24S50 (dirt road) to Frog Meadow and the campground.

Trip notes: This small, primitive camp, set near Tobias Creek at 7,500 feet, is in the center of a network of Forest Service roads that explore the surrounding Sequoia National Forest. The nearby feature destination is the Tobias Peak Lookout (8,284 feet), located two miles directly south of the camp.

⑳ Fairview

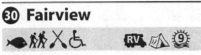

Location: On the Kern River in Sequoia National Forest; map G5, grid f2.

Campsites, facilities: There are 55 sites for tents or RVs up to 27 feet long. Piped water, fire grills, and picnic tables are provided. Vault toilets are available. Some sites are wheelchair accessible. Supplies and a coin laundry are available in Kernville. Leashed pets are permitted.

Reservations, fees: Reserve via phone at (877) 444-6777 ($8.65 reservation fee) or website www.reserveusa.com; $12 to $14 per night, $5 for an extra vehicle. Open from May to October.

Contact: Sequoia National Forest, Cannell Meadow Ranger District, (760) 376-3781 or fax (760) 376-3795.

Directions: From Kernville, drive 16 miles north on Kern River Highway/Sierra Road to the town of Fairview. The campground is located at the north end of town.

Trip notes: Fairview is one of six campgrounds set on the upper Kern River above Lake Isabella and adjacent to the Kern River, one of the prime rafting rivers in California. This camp is located at 3,500 feet. Many of the rapids are rated Class IV and Class V, for experts with guides only. The favored put-in is at the Johnsondale Bridge, and from here it's a 21-mile run to Kernville, where the river pours into Lake Isabella a few miles later. Two sections are unrunnable, Fairview Dam (mile 2.5) and Salmon Falls (mile eight).

㉛ Gold Ledge

Location: On the Kern River in Sequoia National Forest; map G5, grid f2.

Campsites, facilities: There are 37 sites for tents or RVs up to 22 feet long. Piped water, fire grills, and picnic tables are provided. Vault toilets are available. Supplies and a coin laundry are available in Kernville. Leashed pets are permitted.

Reservations, fees: Reserve via phone at (877) 444-6777 ($8.65 reservation fee) or website www.reserveusa.com; $12 to $14 per night, $5 for an extra vehicle. Open from May to September.

Contact: Sequoia National Forest, Cannell Meadow Ranger District, (760) 376-3781 or fax (760) 376-3795.

Directions: From Kernville, drive 10 miles north on Kern River Highway/Sierra Way Road to the campground.

Trip notes: This is another in the series of camps on the Kern River north of Lake Isabella. This one is set at 3,200 feet.

㉜ Horse Meadow

Location: On Salmon Creek in Sequoia National Forest; map G5, grid f3.

Campsites, facilities: There are 18 sites for tents only and 15 sites for tents or RVs up to 23 feet long. Piped water, fire grills, and picnic tables are provided. Vault toilets are available. Please pack out your garbage. Leashed pets are permitted.

Reservations, fees: No reservations; $5 per night. Open from June to November.

Contact: Sequoia National Forest, Cannell Meadow Ranger District, (760) 376-3781 or fax (760) 376-3795.

Directions: From Kernville, drive north on Sierra Way for about 20 miles to the sign that says "Highway 395/Black Rock Ranger Station." Make a sharp right on Sherman Pass Road and drive about 6.5 miles to Cherry Hill Road/Forest Service Road 22S12. There is a green gate with a sign that says "Horse Meadow/Big Meadow." Turn right and drive for about four miles. The road becomes dirt and continues for about another three miles (follow the signs) to the campground entrance road.

Trip notes: This is a little-known spot set along Salmon Creek at 7,600 feet. It is a region known for big meadows, forests, backcountry roads, and plenty of horses. It is located just west of the Dome Land Wilderness, and there is a series of three public pastures for horses in the area, as well as trails ideal for horseback riding. From camp one such trail follows along Salmon Creek to the west to Salmon Falls, a favorite for the few who know of it. A more popular overnight trip is to head to a trailhead about five miles east, which provides a route to Manter Meadows in the Dome Lands.

33 Panorama

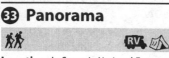

Location: In Sequoia National Forest; map G5, grid g1.

Campsites, facilities: There are 10 sites for tents or RVs up to 40 feet long. Fire grills and picnic tables are provided. Vault toilets are available. There is no piped water, so bring your own. Leashed pets are permitted.

Reservations, fees: No reservations; no fee. Open from June to September.

Contact: Sequoia National Forest, Hot Springs Ranger District, (661) 548-6503 or fax (661) 548-6236.

Directions: From Highway 155 just west of Glennville, turn north on Linns Valley Road/County Road M3 and drive about four miles. Turn left onto County Road M9 and drive about 4.5 miles to Guernsey Mill/Sugarloaf Lodge, and then continue on Sugarloaf Road 23S16 for about six miles to the campground (paved all the way).

Trip notes: This pretty spot is set at 6,800 feet in elevation in a region of Sequoia National Forest filled with a network of backcountry roads. A good side trip is to drive two miles south, turn left, and continue a short distance to a trailhead on the right side of the road for Portuguese Peak (a Forest Service map is strongly advised). From here, it's a one-mile butt-kicker to the top of Portuguese Peak, 7,914 feet in elevation.

34 Hospital Flat

Location: On the North Fork of the Kern River in Sequoia National Forest; map G5, grid g2.

Campsites, facilities: There are 40 sites for tents or RVs up to 22 feet long. Piped water, fire grills, and picnic tables are provided. Vault toilets are available. Supplies and a coin laundry are available in Kernville. Leashed pets are permitted.

Reservations, fees: Reserve via phone at (877) 444-6777 ($8.65 reservation fee) or website www.reserveusa.com; $12 to $14 per night, $5 for an extra vehicle. Open from May to September.

Contact: Sequoia National Forest, Cannell Meadow Ranger District, (760) 376-3781 or fax (760) 376-3795.

Directions: From Kernville, drive seven miles north on Kern River Highway/Sierra Way Road to the campground.

Trip notes: It's kind of like the old shell game, trying to pick the best of the camps along the North Fork of the Kern River. This one is seven miles north of Lake Isabella. The elevation is 2,800 feet. For information on rafting on the Kern River, see the trip notes for Fairview (campground number 30).

35 Camp 3

Location: On the North Fork of the Kern River in Sequoia National Forest; map G5, grid g2.

Campsites, facilities: There are 52 sites for tents or RVs up to 22 feet long. Piped water, fire grills, and picnic tables are provided. Vault toilets are available. Supplies and a coin laundry are available in Kernville. Leashed pets are permitted.

Reservations, fees: Reserve via phone at (877) 444-6777 ($8.65 reservation fee) or website www.reserveusa.com; $12 to $14 per night, $5 for an extra vehicle. Open from May to September.

Contact: Sequoia National Forest, Cannell Meadow Ranger District, (760) 376-3781 or fax (760) 376-3795.

Directions: From Kernville, drive five miles north on Kern River Highway/Sierra Way Road to the campground.

Trip notes: This is the second in a series of camps located along the Kern River north of Lake Isabella (in this case, five miles north of the lake). If you don't like this spot, Hospital Flat (campground number 34) is just two miles upriver and Headquarters (campground number 36) is just one mile downriver. The camp elevation is 2,800 feet.

36 Headquarters

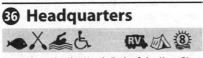

Location: On the North Fork of the Kern River in Sequoia National Forest; map G5, grid g2.

Campsites, facilities: There are 44 sites for tents or RVs up to 22 feet long. Piped water, fire grills, and picnic tables are provided. Vault toilets are available. Some facilities are wheelchair accessible. Supplies and a coin laundry are available in Kernville. Leashed pets are permitted.

Reservations, fees: Reserve via phone at (877) 444-6777 ($8.65 reservation fee) or website www.reserveusa.com; $12 to $14 per night, $5 for an extra vehicle. Open year-round.

Contact: Sequoia National Forest, Cannell Meadow Ranger District, (760) 376-3781 or fax (760) 376-3795.

Directions: From Kernville, drive three miles north on Kern River Highway/Sierra Way Road to the campground.

Trip notes: As you head north from Lake Isabella on Sierra Way, this is the first in a series of Forest Service campgrounds that you have your pick of, all of them set along the North Fork of the Kern River. The North Fork Kern is best known for offering prime white water for rafting. The elevation is 2,700 feet.

37 Long Valley

Location: Near the Dome Land Wilderness; map G5, grid g6.

Campsites, facilities: There are 13 tent sites. Nonpotable piped water, fire grills, and picnic tables are provided. Pit toilets are available. Please pack out your garbage. Leashed pets are permitted.

Reservations, fees: No reservations; no fee. Open year-round.

Contact: Bureau of Land Management, Barstow Field Office, (661) 391-6000 or fax (661) 391-6040.

Directions: From north of San Bernardino, drive north on US 395 to the junction of US 395 and Highway 14. Continue north for 11 miles to Pearsonville. At Pearsonville continue two miles north to Nine Mile Canyon Road (at the Kennedy Meadows sign). Turn left and drive 11 miles to the BLM Work Station. Turn left on the dirt road opposite the station and drive 14 miles to the campground.

Trip notes: This one is way out there in booger country. It's set at road's end in Long Valley, a mile from the border of the Dome Land Wilderness to the east, and the camp is used primarily as a jump-off spot for hikers. A trail from camp leads 2.5 miles west, climbing along a small stream and reaching the South Fork of the Kern River, in rugged and remote country. The elevation is 5,200 feet.

38 Chimney Creek

Location: On the Pacific Crest Trail; map G5, grid g7.

Campsites, facilities: There are 36 sites for tents or RVs up to 25 feet long. Nonpotable piped water, fire grills, and picnic tables are provided. Pit toilets are available. Please pack out your own garbage. Leashed pets are permitted.

Reservations, fees: No reservations, no fee. Open year-round.

Contact: Bureau of Land Management, Barstow Field Office, (661) 391-6000 or fax (661) 391-6040.

Directions: From north of San Bernardino, drive north on US 395 to the junction of US 395 and Highway 14, continue north for 11 miles to Pearsonville. At Pearsonville, continue two miles north to Nine Mile Canyon Road (at the Kennedy Meadows sign). Turn left and drive 11 miles to the BLM Work Station. Turn left on the dirt road opposite the station and drive three miles to the camp.

Trip notes: This BLM camp is set at 5,900 feet along the headwaters of Chimney Creek, on the southern flank of Chimney Peak (7,990 feet) two miles to the north. This is a trailhead camp for the Pacific Crest Trail, one of its relatively obscure sections. The PCT heads north from camp and in 10 miles it skirts the eastern border of Dome Land Wilderness.

㊴ Evans Flat

Location: In Sequoia National Forest; map G5, grid h0.

Campsites, facilities: There are 20 sites for tents or RVs up to 16 feet long. Fire grills and picnic tables are provided. A portable rest room is available. There is no piped water at this site, so bring your own. Four corrals with water troughs (though water for the troughs is not always available) and a pasture area are provided for horses. Leashed pets are permitted.

Reservations, fees: No reservations; no fee. Open from May to October.

Contact: Sequoia National Forest, Lake Isabella Ranger District, (760) 379-5646 or fax (760) 379-8597.

Directions: From Greenhorn Summit on Highway 155, turn south on Rancheria Road (paved, then dirt) and drive 8.3 miles to the campground.

Trip notes: Evans Flat is an obscure campground in the southwest region of Sequoia National Forest, about 10 miles west of Lake Isabella, with no other camps in the vicinity. You have to earn this one, but if you want solitude, Evans Flat can provide it. It is set at 6,200 feet, with Woodward Peak located a half mile to the east. A natural spring is located east of camp within walking distance.

㊵ Hungry Gulch

Location: On Lake Isabella, in Sequoia National Forest; map G5, grid h1.

Campsites, facilities: There are 78 sites for tents, RVs, or trailers up to 30 feet long. Piped water, fire grills, and picnic tables are provided. Flush toilets, showers, and a playground are available. Supplies and a coin laundry are available in Lake Isabella. Leashed pets are permitted.

Reservations, fees: Reserve via phone at (877) 444-6777 ($8.65 reservation fee) or website www.reserveusa.com; $14 per night, $5 for each additional vehicle. Open from April through September.

Contact: Sequoia National Forest, Greenhorn Ranger District, (760) 379-5646 or fax (760) 379-8597.

Directions: From the town of Lake Isabella, drive four miles north on Highway 155 to the campground.

Trip notes: Hungry Gulch is on the western side of Lake Isabella, but across the road from the shore. Nearby Boulder Gulch (campground number 46), located directly across the road, is an option. There are no boat ramps in the immediate area. For details about Lake Isabella, see the trip notes for Pioneer Point (campground number 41).

㊶ Pioneer Point

Location: On Lake Isabella, in Sequoia National Forest; map G5, grid h1.

Campsites, facilities: There are 78 sites for tents, RVs, or trailers up to 30 feet long. Piped water, fire grills, and picnic tables are provided. Flush toilets, showers, playground, and a fish cleaning station are available. A boat ramp is three miles from camp. Supplies and a coin laundry are available in the town of Lake Isabella. Leashed pets are permitted.

Reservations, fees: Reserve via phone at (877) 444-6777 ($8.65 reservation fee) or website www.reserveusa.com; $14 per night, $5 for each additional vehicle. Open year-round.

Contact: Sequoia National Forest, Greenhorn Ranger District, (760) 379-5646 or fax (760) 379-8597.

Directions: From the town of Lake Isabella, drive 2.5 miles north on Highway 155 to the campground.

Trip notes: Lake Isabella is the largest freshwater lake in Southern California, covering 38,400 acres, and with it comes a dynamic array of campgrounds, marinas, and facilities. It is set at 2,605 feet in the foothills east of Bakersfield, fed by the Kern River, and dominated by boating sports of all kinds . This camp is located at the lake's southwest corner, between the spillway and the main dam, with a boat ramp available a mile to the east. Another camp is nearby, Main Dam. Isabella is a first-class lake for waterskiing, but in the spring and early summer windsurfing is also excellent, best nearby just east of the Auxiliary Dam. Boat rentals of all kinds are available at several marinas.

㊷ Alder Creek

Location: In Sequoia National Forest; map G5, grid h1.

Campsites, facilities: There are 12 sites for tents or RVs up to 20 feet long. Fire grills and picnic tables are provided. Vault toilets are available. There is no piped water, so bring your own. Leashed pets are permitted.

Reservations, fees: No reservations; no fee. Open from May to November.

Contact: Sequoia National Forest, Greenhorn Ranger District, (760) 379-5646 or fax (760) 379-8597.

Directions: From Glennville, drive about eight miles east on Highway 155. Turn right on Alder Creek Road and drive three miles to the campground.

Trip notes: This primitive camp is located just inside the western border of Sequoia National Forest, an obscure spot that requires traversing a very twisty and, at times, rough road. It is set at 3,900 feet, just a quarter of a mile upstream from where Alder Creek meets Slick Rock Creek. There is a trail out of the camp that runs north for two miles along Slick Rock Creek.

㊸ Greenhorn Mountain Park

Location: Near Shirley Meadows; map G5, grid h1.

Campsites, facilities: There are 91 sites for tents or RVs up to 24 feet long. Piped water, fire grills, and picnic table are provided. Flush toilets and showers are available. Leashed pets are permitted.

Reservations, fees: Reservations are accepted for groups only; $8 per night, $2 pet fee.

Contact: For group reservations, phone Kern County Parks Department, (661) 868-7000. For general information, phone (760) 370-1739, or phone the Sequoia National Forest, Greenhorn Ranger District, (760) 379-5646 or fax (760) 379-8597.

Directions: From Wofford Heights (on the west shore of Lake Isabella), drive 10 miles west on Highway 155 to the park on the left side of the highway.

Trip notes: This county campground is located near the Shirley Meadows Ski Area, a small ski park open on weekends in winter when there is sufficient snow. Greenhorn Mountain Park covers 160 acres, set at 6,000 feet in elevation. The region is filled with a spiderweb network of Forest Service roads, detailed on a map of Sequoia National Forest. Lake Isabella is a 15-minute drive to the east.

㊹ Cedar Creek

Location: In Sequoia National Forest; map G5, grid h1.

Campsites, facilities: There are 10 sites for tents only. Piped water (from May to October only), picnic tables, and fire grills are provided, and rest rooms are available. Leashed pets are permitted.

Reservations, fees: No reservations; no fee. Open year-round.

Contact: Sequoia National Forest, Greenhorn Ranger District, (760) 379-5646 or fax (760) 379-8597.

Directions: From Glennville on Highway 155, drive nine miles east on Highway 155 to the campground. Or from Wofford Heights (on the west shore of Lake Isabella), drive 11 miles west on Highway 155 to the campground.

Trip notes: This is a little-known Forest Service camp set at 4,800 feet on the southwest flank of Sequoia National Forest, right along little Cedar Creek, with easy access off Highway 155. Greenhorn Mountain Park (campground num-

ber 43) and Alder Creek (campground number 42) provide nearby alternatives.

⑤ French Gulch Group Camp

Location: On Lake Isabella; map G5, grid h2.

Campsites, facilities: There is one large group campsite for up to 100 people with tents or RVs. Picnic tables, fire grills, and piped water are provided. Flush toilets and solar-heated showers are available. A grocery store, coin laundry, and propane gas are nearby. Leashed pets are permitted.

Reservations, fees: Reserve via phone at (877) 444-6777 ($8.65 reservation fee) or website www.reserveusa.com; $60 group fee per night. Open year-round.

Contact: Sequoia National Forest, Greenhorn Ranger District, (760) 379-5646 or fax (760) 379-8597.

Directions: From the town of Lake Isabella, drive three miles north on Highway 155 to the campground entrance on the right.

Trip notes: This is a large group camp on Lake Isabella, located at the southwest end of the lake about two miles north of Pioneer Point and the spillway. For recreation information, see the trip notes for Pioneer Point (campground number 41). The elevation is 2,700 feet.

⑥ Boulder Gulch

Location: On Lake Isabella; map G5, grid h2.

Campsites, facilities: There are 78 sites for tents, trailers, or RVs up to 45 feet long. Piped water, fire grills, and picnic tables are provided. Flush toilets, showers, playground, and a fish cleaning station are available. Some facilities are wheelchair accessible. Supplies and a coin laundry are available in the town of Lake Isabella. Leashed pets are permitted.

Reservations, fees: Reserve via phone at (877) 444-6777 ($8.65 reservation fee) or website www.reserveusa.com; $14 per night, $5 for each additional vehicle. Open from April through September.

Contact: Sequoia National Forest, Greenhorn Ranger District, (760) 379-5646 or fax (760) 379-8597.

Directions: From the town of Lake Isabella, drive four miles north on Highway 155 to the campground entrance.

Trip notes: Boulder Gulch lies fairly near the western shore of Lake Isabella, across the road from Hungry Gulch (campground number 40). Take your pick. Isabella is the biggest lake in Southern California and a prime destination point for Bakersfield area residents. Fishing for trout and bass is best in the spring. By the dog days of summer, when people are bowwowin' at the heat, water-skiers take over, along with folks just looking to cool off. Like a lot of lakes in the valley, Isabella is subject to drawdowns. The elevation is 2,650 feet. For more information, see the trip notes for Pioneer Point (campground number 41).

⑦ Main Dam

Location: On Lake Isabella; map G5, grid h2.

Campsites, facilities: There are 82 sites for tents, trailers, or RVs up to 30 feet long. Piped water, fire grills, and picnic tables are provided. Flush toilets and a dump station are available. Supplies and a coin laundry are available in the town of Lake Isabella. Leashed pets are permitted with proof of shots.

Reservations, fees: Reserve via phone at (877) 444-6777 ($8.65 reservation fee) or website www.reserveusa.com; $12 per night, $5 for each additional vehicle. Open May to September.

Contact: Sequoia National Forest, Greenhorn Ranger District, (760) 379-5646 or fax (760) 379-8597.

Directions: From the town of Lake Isabella, drive 1.5 miles northwest on Highway 155 to the campground.

Trip notes: This camp is located on the south shore of Lake Isabella just east of Pioneer Point and within a mile of a boat ramp. For recreation information, see the trip notes for Pioneer Point (campground number 41).

㊽ Camp 9

Location: On Lake Isabella; map G5, grid h2.

Campsites, facilities: There are 109 primitive sites for tents or RVs. Piped water, flush toilets, sanitary disposal station, boat launch, and a fish cleaning station are available. Supplies and a coin laundry are available nearby in Kernville. Leashed pets are permitted.

Reservations, fees: No reservations; $8 per night, $5 for each additional vehicle. Open year-round.

Contact: Sequoia National Forest, Greenhorn Ranger District, (760) 379-5646 or fax (760) 379-8597.

Directions: From Kernville, drive five miles south on Sierra Way to the north shore of Lake Isabella and the campground entrance.

Trip notes: This campground is primitive and sparsely covered, but it has several bonus features. It is set along the northwest shore of Lake Isabella, known for good boating, waterskiing in the summer, and fishing in the spring. Other options include great rafting waters along the North Fork of the Kern River (located north of the lake), a good bird-watching area at the South Fork Wildlife Area (along the northeast corner of the lake), and an off-road-motorcycle park across the road from this campground. The elevation is 2,650 feet.

㊾ Tillie Creek

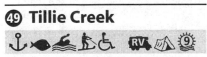

Location: On Lake Isabella; map G5, grid h2.

Campsites, facilities: There are 155 family sites and four group sites for tents or RVs up to 45 feet long. Piped water, fire grills, and picnic tables are provided. Flush toilets, showers, sanitary disposal station, playground, amphitheater, and a fish cleaning station are available. Four sites are wheelchair accessible. Supplies and a coin laundry are nearby in Wofford Heights. Leashed pets are permitted.

Reservations, fees: Reservations are required for group sites; reserve via phone at (877) 444-6777 ($8.65 reservation fee) or website www.reserveusa.com; $14 per night for family sites,

$5 for an extra vehicle; $75 to $120 per night for group sites. Open year-round.

Contact: Sequoia National Forest, Greenhorn Ranger District, (760) 379-5646 or fax (760) 379-8597.

Directions: From Wofford Heights on the west side of Lake Isabella, drive one mile southwest on Highway 155 to the campground.

Trip notes: This is one of two camps (the other is Live Oak) located near where Tillie Creek enters Lake Isabella, set on the northwest shore of the lake near the town of Wofford Heights. Lake Isabella is the largest freshwater lake in Southern California, covering 38,400 acres, and with it comes a dynamic array of campgrounds, marinas, and facilities. It is set at 2,605 feet in the foothills east of Bakersfield, fed by the Kern River, and dominated by boating sports of all kinds.

㊿ Live Oak North and South

Location: On Lake Isabella; map G5, grid h2.

Campsites, facilities: There are 150 family sites and a group site for tents or RVs up to 30 feet long. Piped water, fire grills, and picnic tables are provided. Flush toilets and showers are available. Supplies and a coin laundry are available in nearby Wofford Heights. Leashed pets are permitted.

Reservations, fees: Reservations are required for group sites; reserve via phone at (877) 444-6777 ($8.65 reservation fee) or website www.reserveusa.com; $14 per night for family sites, $5 for an extra vehicle; $150 per night for group site. Open from May through September.

Contact: Sequoia National Forest, Greenhorn Ranger District, (760) 379-5646 or fax (760) 379-8597.

Directions: From Wofford Heights on the west side of Lake Isabella, drive a half mile south on Highway 155 to the campground entrance road on your right.

Trip notes: This is one of two camps set in the immediate area on Lake Isabella's northwest side; the other is Tillie Creek. Live Oak is on the west side of the road, Tillie Creek on the eastern, lake side of the road. For recreation information, see the trip notes for Tillie Creek (campground number 49).

⑤ Auxiliary Dam

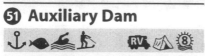

Location: On Lake Isabella; map G5, grid i2.

Campsites, facilities: There are a number of primitive, undesignated sites for tents or RVs. Piped water, flush toilets, and a dump station are available. Supplies and a coin laundry are available in the town of Lake Isabella. Leashed pets are permitted.

Reservations, fees: No reservations; no fee. Open year-round.

Contact: Sequoia National Forest, Greenhorn Ranger District, (760) 379-5646 or fax (760) 379-8597.

Directions: From the town of Lake Isabella, drive a mile northeast on Highway 178 to the campground entrance.

Trip notes: This primitive camp was designed to be an overflow area if other camps at Lake Isabella are packed. It's the only camp directly on the shore of the lake, and many people like it. In addition, a boat ramp is located just a mile north for good lake access, and the windsurfing prospects adjacent to the campground are the best of the entire lake. The winds come up and sail right over the dam, creating a steady breeze in the afternoon that is not gusty at all.

⑤ Rivernook Campground

Location: On the North Fork of the Kern River; map G5, grid h3.

Campsites, facilities: There are 54 sites for tents or RVs without hookups, 56 with partial hookups, and 15 RV sites with full hookups. Picnic tables and piped water are provided. Rest rooms, showers, dump station, and cable TV hookups are available. Leashed pets are permitted.

Reservations, fees: Reservations are accepted; $15 to $21 per night. Open year-round.

Contact: Rivernook Campground, (760) 376-2705.

Directions: From Kernville, drive a half mile north to 14001 Sierra Way.

Trip notes: This is a large, privately operated park set near Lake Isabella a few miles from the head of the lake. Boat rentals are available at one of the nearby marinas. An optional side trip is to visit Keysville, the first town to become established on the Kern River during the gold rush days. The elevation is 2,665 feet.

⑤ Hobo

Location: On the Kern River in Sequoia National Forest; map G5, grid i1.

Campsites, facilities: There are 25 sites for tents and 10 sites for RVs up to 16 feet long. Fire grills and picnic tables are provided. Water is provided some of the time; call ahead for details. Vault toilets and showers are available. Leashed pets are permitted.

Reservations, fees: Reservations are recommended; reserve via phone at (877) 444-6777 ($8.65 reservation fee) or website www.reserveusa.com; $10 per night for the first vehicle, $5 per night for each additional vehicle. There is no fee when there is no water at the camp. Open from May through September.

Contact: Sequoia National Forest, Greenhorn Ranger District, (760) 379-5646 or fax (760) 379-8597.

Directions: From the town of Lake Isabella, drive five miles southwest on Highway 178. Turn left on Borel Road and drive south for about a third of a mile to the intersection of Old Kern Road. Turn right and drive about two miles to the campground on your right.

Trip notes: Hobo is set along the lower Kern River, about 10 miles downstream of the dam at Lake Isabella. Rafters sometimes use this camp as a put-in spot for an 18-mile run to the take-out at Democrat Picnic Area, a challenging Class IV run. The elevation is 2,300 feet.

⑤ Paradise Cove

Location: On Lake Isabella; map G5, grid i2.

Campsites, facilities: There are 58 sites for

tents or RVs, some with picnic tables and fire grills provided. Flush toilets, showers, and a fish cleaning station are available. The rest rooms are wheelchair accessible. Supplies, dump station, and a coin laundry are available in Mountain Mesa. Leashed pets are permitted.

Reservations, fees: Reserve via phone at (877) 444-6777 ($8.65 reservation fee) or website www.reserveusa.com; $6 to $14 per night, $5 for each additional vehicle. Open year-round.

Contact: Sequoia National Forest, Greenhorn Ranger District, (760) 379-5646 or fax (760) 379-8597.

Directions: From the town of Lake Isabella, drive six miles northeast on Highway 178 to the campground entrance.

Trip notes: Paradise Cove is on the southeast shore of Lake Isabella. A boat ramp is located about two miles away to the east, near the South Fork Picnic Area. While the camp is not directly at the lakeshore, it does overlook the broadest expanse of the lake. This part of the lake is relatively undeveloped compared to the areas near Wofford Heights and the dam.

55 Lake Isabella RV Resort

Location: On Lake Isabella; map G5, grid i2.

Campsites, facilities: There are 91 tent and RV sites with full hookups. Picnic tables and fire grills are provided. Rest rooms, showers, swimming pool, clubhouse, billiards, cable TV, laundry facilities, and a fish cleaning station are available. Leashed pets are permitted.

Reservations, fees: Reservations are accepted; $13.50 to $17.50 per night. Open year-round.

Contact: Lake Isabella RV Resort, (800) 787-9920 or reserve online at www.lakeisabellarv.com.

Directions: From the town of Lake Isabella, drive six miles northeast on Highway 178 to the signed entrance on the right.

Trip notes: This quiet, privately operated park set up for RVs is located across the street from Lake Isabella. It is one of many camps at the lake, so plan on plenty of company. There is a free public boat ramp 200 yards away within

Sequoia National Forest and a full-service marina with watercraft rentals two miles west of the resort. For details on the immediate area, see the trip notes for the nearby Forest Service camps, Auxiliary Dam (campground number 51) and Paradise Cove (campground number 54). The elevation is 2,600 feet.

56 KOA Lake Isabella

Location: On Lake Isabella; map G5, grid i3.

Campsites, facilities: There are 104 sites for tents or RVs. Picnic tables, piped water, and full or partial hookups are provided. Rest rooms, showers, playground, swimming pool, laundry facilities, store, dump station, and propane gas are available. Leashed pets are permitted.

Reservations, fees: Reservations are accepted; $20 to $25 per night.

Contact: KOA Lake Isabella, (760) 378-2001.

Directions: From the town of Lake Isabella, drive 10 miles east on Highway 178 and look for the KOA sign on the left.

Trip notes: This KOA camp provides a good, clean option to the Forest Service camps on the southern end of Lake Isabella, Southern California's largest lake. It is set in South Fork Valley (elevation 2,600 feet), east of the lake off Highway 178. The nearest boat ramp is at South Fork Picnic Area (located about a five-minute drive to the west), where there is also a good view of the lake.

57 Walker Pass Walk-In

Location: On the Pacific Crest Trail southwest of Death Valley National Park; map G5, grid i7.

Campsites, facilities: There are two sites for tents and RVs with limited parking and nine walk-in sites for tents only. Water and pit toilets are available. No trash facilities are provided, so bring a garbage bag to pack out all refuse.

Reservations, fees: No reservations; no fee. A 14-day stay limit is enforced.

Contact: Bureau of Land Management, Bakersfield Field Office, 3801 Pegasus Drive, Bakersfield, CA 93308-6837; (661) 391-6000.

Directions: From Lake Isabella, drive east on Highway 178 and continue 14 miles past Onyx. At Walker Pass look for the campground on the right side of the road, where a sign is posted for the Pacific Crest Trail. It is a quarter-mile walk from the parking area to the campground.

Trip notes: Long-distance hikers on the Pacific Crest Trail treat this camp as if they were arriving at Valhalla. That's because it is set right on the trail and, better yet, piped water is available. Out here in the desert there aren't many places where you can act like a camel and suck up all the liquid you can hold. The camp is set at 5,200 feet, southwest of Death Valley National Park. And if you guessed it was named for Joe Walker, the West's greatest trailblazer and one of my heroes, well, right you are. If you arrive by car instead of on the PCT, use this spot as a base camp. Because of its desert remoteness very few hikers start trips from this location.

---

58 Breckenridge

🏕️ 💧7️⃣

Location: In Sequoia National Forest; map G5, grid j0.

Campsites, facilities: There are eight tent sites. Picnic tables and fire grills are provided and a portable rest room is available. There is no piped water, so bring your own. Leashed pets are permitted.

Reservations, fees: No reservations; no fee. Open from May to October.

Contact: Sequoia National Forest, Greenhorn Ranger District, (760) 379-5646 or fax (760) 379-8597.

Directions: From the town of Lake Isabella, on Highway 178 turn south on Caliente Bodfish Road and drive about 12 miles to the town of Havilah. Continue south on Caliente Bodfish Road for two more miles. Turn right on Forest Service Road 28S06 and drive 10 miles to the campground.

Trip notes: This is a popular spot for people to visit with sport utility vehicles. It is a tiny, primitive camp set at 7,100 feet near Breckenridge Mountain (a good lookout here) in a little-traveled southwest sector of the Sequoia National Forest. From camp, it's a two-mile drive south up to the lookout, with sweeping views afforded in all directions. There are no other camps in the immediate area.

Map G6

One inch equals approximately 10.7 miles.
See inside back cover for California state map.

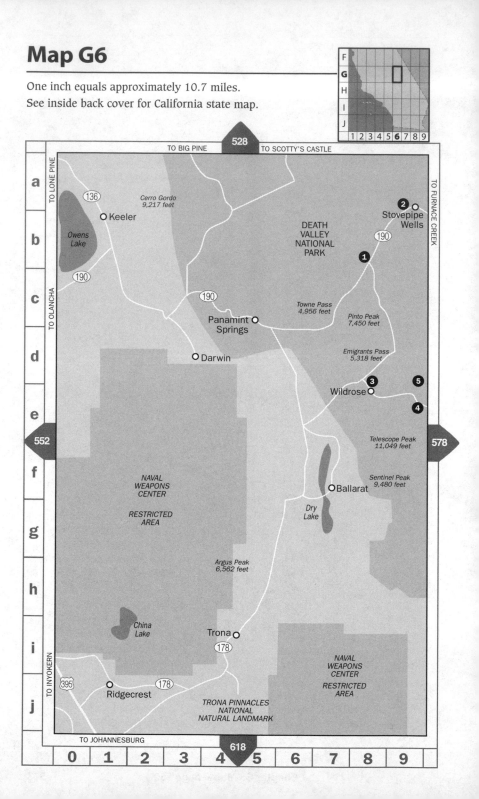

F G H I J
1 2 3 4 5 6 7 8 9

528
TO BIG PINE   TO SCOTTY'S CASTLE

TO LONE PINE

a

TO FURNACE CREEK

136
Cerro Gordo
9,217 feet

○ Keeler

DEATH
VALLEY
NATIONAL
PARK

2 ○ Stovepipe
Wells

b

Owens
Lake

190

1

190

TO OLANCHA

190

c

190

Towne Pass
4,956 feet

Pinto Peak
7,450 feet

Panamint
Springs ○

Emigrants Pass
5,318 feet

d

○ Darwin

3 **5**
Wildrose ○
4

e

552

Telescope Peak
11,049 feet

578

f

NAVAL
WEAPONS
CENTER

RESTRICTED
AREA

Sentinel Peak
9,480 feet

○ Ballarat

Dry
Lake

g

Argus Peak
6,562 feet

h

China
Lake

TO INYOKERN

i

Trona ○
178

NAVAL
WEAPONS
CENTER

RESTRICTED
AREA

j

395
○ Ridgecrest
178

TRONA PINNACLES
NATIONAL
NATURAL LANDMARK

TO JOHANNESBURG

618

0 1 2 3 4 5 6 7 8 9

❶ Emigrant

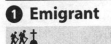

Location: In Death Valley National Park; map G6, grid b8.

Campsites, facilities: There are 10 sites for tents or RVs. Piped water and picnic tables are provided. Flush toilets are available. Leashed pets are permitted.

Reservations, fees: No reservations; no camping fee. There is a $10 entrance fee, which includes a park brochure (available at Furnace Creek, Grapevine, Stovepipe Wells, or Beatty Ranger Stations). Open May through October.

Contact: Death Valley National Park, (760) 786-2331.

Directions: In Stovepipe Wells Village, drive nine miles southwest on Highway 190. Turn left on Highway 178 and continue about 30 miles to the Wildrose site. Take the signed turnoff to the campground on the left.

Trip notes: The key here is the elevation, and Emigrant, at 2,000 feet, is out of the forbidding subzero elevations of Death Valley. That makes it one of the more habitable camps. From the camp a good side trip is to drive east on Highway 178 to the trailhead for Wildrose Peak, located on the left side of the road at the parking area for Charcoal Kilne. The trail here climbs 4.2 miles to the peak, with awesome views in the last two miles; the last mile is a butt-kicker.

❷ Stovepipe Wells

Location: In Death Valley National Park; map G6, grid b9.

Campsites, facilities: There are 10 sites for tents only and 200 sites for tents or RVs. Piped water is provided. Flush toilets, dump station, swimming pool, camp store, gasoline, and evening ranger programs are available on weekends. The rest rooms are wheelchair accessible. Leashed pets are permitted.

Reservations, fees: No reservations; $10 per night. There is a $10 entrance fee, which includes a park brochure (available at Furnace Creek, Grapevine, Stovepipe Wells, or Beatty Ranger Stations). Open May through October.

Contact: Death Valley National Park, (760) 786-2331

Directions: In Stovepipe Wells Village, drive to the north end of town on Highway 190 and make a right at the signed exit into the campground.

Trip notes: Stovepipe Wells is located on the major apex bordering Death Valley. An unusual trail is available off the highway within a short distance; look for the sign for the Mosaic Canyon Trail parking area. From here you can take the easy one-mile walk up a beautiful canyon, where the walls are marble and seem as if they are polished. Rock scramblers can extend the trip for another mile. The elevation is at sea level on the edge of dropping off into never-never land.

❸ Wildrose

Location: In Death Valley National Park; map G6, grid d8.

Campsites, facilities: There are 30 sites for tents or RVs. Picnic tables are provided. Piped water (April through November only) and pit toilets are available.Leashed pets are permitted.

Reservations, fees: No reservations; no camping fee. There is a $10 entrance fee, which includes a park brochure (available at Furnace Creek, Grapevine, Stovepipe Wells, or Beatty Ranger Stations). Open year-round.

Contact: Death Valley National Park, (760) 786-2331.

Directions: From Stovepipe Wells Village, drive 30 miles south on Highway 190 to Wildrose Canyon Road, turn left, and follow the signs to the campground.

Trip notes: Wildrose is set on the road that

heads out to the primitive country, eventually within range of Telescope Peak, the highest point in Death Valley National Park (11,049 feet). The elevation at the camp is 4,100 feet. A bonus here is the nearby Wildrose Ranger Station (it is often closed), which can provide the latest info on trail and road conditions in this remote region of the park.

❹ Mahogany Flat

Location: In Death Valley National Park; map G6, grid e9.

Campsites, facilities: There are 10 sites for tents only. Picnic tables and pit toilets are available. There is no piped water, so bring your own. The campground is accessible only by foot or four-wheel-drive vehicle. Leashed pets are permitted.

Reservations, fees: No reservations; no camping fee. There is a $10 entrance fee, which includes a park brochure (available at Furnace Creek, Grapevine, Stovepipe Wells, or Beatty Ranger Stations). Open year-round, weather permitting.

Contact: Death Valley National Park, (760) 786-2331.

Directions: From Stovepipe Wells Village, drive 38 miles south on Highway 190 to Wildrose Canyon Road, turn left, and drive to the end of the road and the camp.

Trip notes: This is one of two primitive, hard-to-reach camps (the other is Thorndike) set in Death Valley National Park's high country. It is one of the few shaded camps, offering beautiful piñon pines and junipers. What makes it popular, however, is the trail to Telescope Peak leading out from camp. Only the ambitious and well conditioned should attempt the climb, a seven-mile trip one way with breathtaking (literally) views of both Panamint Valley and Death Valley.

The elevation at the campground is 8,200 feet and Telescope Peak summits out at 11,049 feet, which translates to a climb of 2,849 feet.

❺ Thorndike

Location: In Death Valley National Park; map G6, grid d9.

Campsites, facilities: This backcountry campground is accessible only by foot or four-wheel-drive vehicle and has eight campsites for tents. Picnic tables and pit toilets are available. There is no piped water, so bring your own. Leashed pets are permitted.

Reservations, fees: No reservations; no camping fee. There is a $10 entrance fee, which includes a park brochure (available at Furnace Creek, Grapevine, Stovepipe Wells, or Beatty Ranger Stations). Open year-round, weather permitting.

Contact: Death Valley National Park, (760) 786-2331.

Directions: From Stovepipe Wells Village, drive 37 miles south on Highway 190 to Wildrose Canyon Road, turn left, and drive to the end of the road and the camp. (The road becomes extremely rough; four-wheel drive is required.)

Trip notes: This is one of Death Valley National Park's little-known camps. It is set in the high country at 7,500 feet. It's free, of course. Otherwise they'd have to actually send somebody out to tend to the place. Nearby are century-old charcoal kilns that were built by Chinese laborers and tended by Shoshone Indians. The trailhead that serves Telescope Peak (11,049 feet), the highest point in Death Valley, can be found in nearby Mahogany Flat (campground number four).

Special Note: For more camps in Death Valley National Park, see chapter G7.

Map G7

One inch equals approximately 10.7 miles.
See inside back cover for California state map.

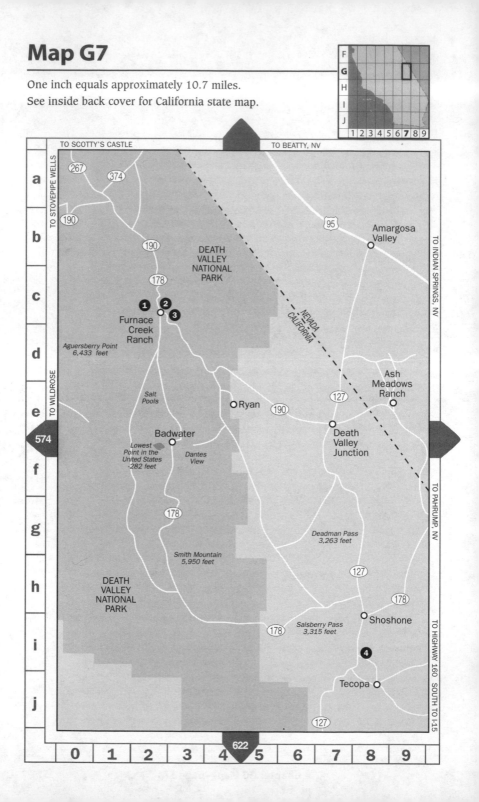

Chapter G7 features:

❶ Furnace Creek

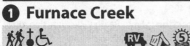

Location: In Death Valley National Park; map G7, grid c2.

Campsites, facilities: There are 136 sites for tents or RVs. Picnic tables and piped water are provided. Flush toilets, dump station, and evening ranger programs are available. The rest rooms are wheelchair accessible. Leashed pets are permitted.

Reservations, fees: Reservations are recommended. Reserve via phone at (800) 365-CAMP/2267; $10–16 per night (includes reservation fee). Open year-round.

Contact: Death Valley National Park, (760)786-2331.

Directions: From Furnace Creek Ranch, drive one mile north on Highway 190 to the signed campground entrance on the left.

Trip notes: This is a well-developed national park site that provides a good base camp for exploring Death Valley, especially for newcomers. The nearby visitors center and Death Valley Museum offer maps and suggestions for hikes and drives in this unique wildland. The elevation is 190 feet below sea level. This camp offers shady sites, a rarity in Death Valley. It's open all year, but keep in mind that the summer temperatures commonly exceed 100 degrees, making this area virtually uninhabitable in the summer.

❷ Sunset

Location: In Death Valley National Park; map G7, grid c2.

Campsites, facilities: There are 1,000 sites for tents or RVs; 16 are wheelchair-accessible sites near accessible rest rooms. Piped water and picnic tables are provided. Flush toilets, dump station, and evening ranger programs are available. Leashed pets are permitted.

Reservations, fees: No reservations; $10 per night. Open October through April.

Contact: Death Valley National Park, (760) 786-2331.

Directions: From Furnace Creek Ranch, drive a quarter mile east on Highway 190 to the signed campground entrance and turn left into the campground.

Trip notes: This is one of several options for campers in the Furnace Creek area of Death Valley, with an elevation of 190 feet below sea level. It is advised to make your first stop at the nearby visitors center for maps and suggested hikes (according to your level of fitness) and drives. Don't forget your canteen—and if you're backpacking, never set up a wilderness camp near water in Death Valley. A thirsty animal may think it has to fight you in order to get a drink. It'll probably win.

❸ Texas Spring

Location: In Death Valley National Park; map G7, grid c3.

Campsites, facilities: There are 92 sites for tents or RVs. There are also two group sites, each accommodating 70 people and 10 vehicles. Some sites are wheelchair accessible. Piped water and picnic tables are provided. Flush toilets, dump station, and evening ranger programs are available. Leashed pets are permitted.

Reservations, fees: No reservations; $10 per night. Open October to April.

Contact: Death Valley National Park, (760) 786-2331.

Directions: From Furnace Creek Ranch, drive a half mile east on Highway 190 to the signed campground entrance on the left.

Trip notes: Death Valley is kind of like an ugly dog. After awhile, once you get to know that dog, you'll love it more than anything. This campground, like the others near Furnace Creek Ranch, provides a chance for that kind of feeling to develop. The nearby visitors center and Death Valley Museum offer maps and suggestions for hikes and drives. The lowest point in the US, 282 feet below sea level, is located to the southwest. This camp has one truly unique feature: bathrooms that are listed on the National Historic Register.

❹ Tecopa Hot Springs County Campground

Location: North of Tecopa; map G7, grid i8.

Campsites, facilities: There are 300 sites for tents or RVs, 105 with electrical hookups. Some facilities are wheelchair accessible. Piped water, fire grills, and picnic tables are provided. Flush toilets, showers, dump station, coin laundry, groceries, and propane gas are available nearby. Leashed pets are permitted.

Reservations, fees: No reservations; $6.50 to $8 per night. Open year-round.

Contact: Inyo County Parks Department, (760) 852-4264.

Directions: From Death Valley Junction, drive about 35 miles south on Highway 127 to the park entrance on the left. From Baker drive north on Highway 127 for 57 miles to the park entrance.

Trip notes: This one is out there in no-man's-land, and if it weren't for the hot springs, all you'd see around here is a few skeletons. Regardless, it's quite an attraction in the winter, when the warm climate is a plus and the nearby mineral baths are worth taking a dunk in. The elevation is 1,500 feet. Nobody gets here by accident.

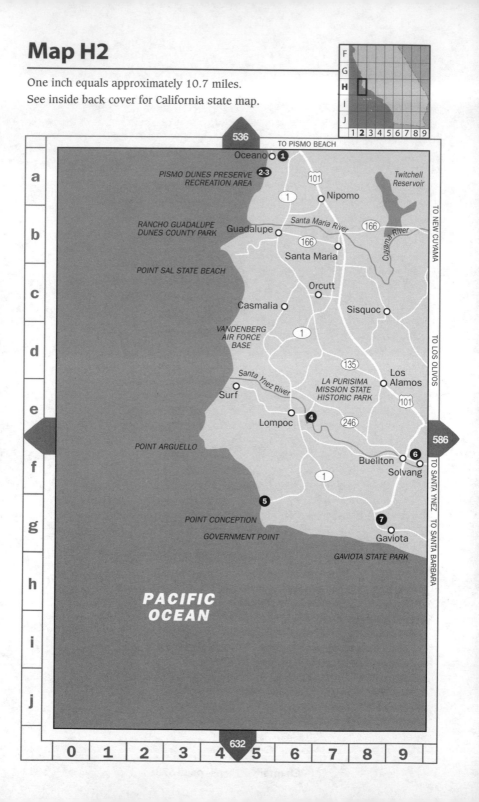

Map H2

One inch equals approximately 10.7 miles.
See inside back cover for California state map.

536
TO PISMO BEACH

Oceano ○ 1
PISMO DUNES PRESERVE 2-3
RECREATION AREA
101
Twitchell
Reservoir

a

1
○ Nipomo

RANCHO GUADALUPE
DUNES COUNTY PARK
Guadalupe ○
Santa Maria River
166
166

b

POINT SAL STATE BEACH
Santa Maria

○ Orcutt

c

Casmalia ○
Sisquoc ○

VANDENBERG
AIR FORCE
BASE
1

d

135
Los
Alamos ○

Surf ○
Santa Ynez River
LA PURISIMA
MISSION STATE
HISTORIC PARK
101

e

Lompoc ○ 4
246

586

POINT ARGUELLO
Buellton ○ 6
Solvang

f

1
5

g

POINT CONCEPTION
7
GOVERNMENT POINT
Gaviota ○

GAVIOTA STATE PARK

h

PACIFIC
OCEAN

i

j

0 1 2 3 4 5 6 7 8 9

632

TO NEW CUYAMA
TO LOS OLIVOS
TO SANTA YNEZ
TO SANTA BARBARA
Cuyama River

Chapter H2 features:

1 Oceano County Campground

Location: Near Arroyo Grande; map H2, grid a6.

Campsites, facilities: There are 24 sites for RVs with full hookups. Fire grills and picnic tables are provided. Flush toilets and showers are available. A playground, coin laundry, grocery store, and propane gas are available nearby. Leashed pets are permitted with proof of vaccinations.

Reservations, fees: No reservations; $21 per night, $2 pet fee. Open year-round.

Contact: Oceano County Campground, (805) 781-5219 or fax (805) 781-1102.

Directions: From Pismo Beach, drive south on US 101. Take the Arroyo-Grande Avenue exit west to Highway 1. Drive south on Highway 1 for 1.5 miles, turn right on Pier Avenue, and drive about half a block. Turn left on Pershing Avenue and continue to the campground on the right at 414 Pershing Avenue.

Trip notes: This county park often gets overlooked because it isn't on the state reservation system. That's other folks' loss and your gain. The location is a bonus, set near Pismo State Beach, the site of great sand dunes, clamming, and wide-open ocean frontage.

2 Oceano Dunes

Location: South of Pismo Beach; map H2, grid a5.

Campsites, facilities: There are 1,000 primitive sites for off-road vehicles. Vault toilets are provided. There is no piped water. Horseback riding facilities, grocery store, coin laundry, and propane gas are available nearby. Leashed pets are permitted.

Reservations, fees: Reserve via phone at (800) 444-PARK/7275 ($7.50 reservation fee) or website www.cal-parks.ca.gov; $6 per night. Open year-round.

Contact: Oceano Dunes, (805) 549-3433 or (805) 473-7230 or fax (805) 473-7234.

Directions: Heading north on US 101 in Arroyo Grande, take the Grand Avenue exit. Make a left at the signal and drive west on Grand Avenue for about four miles until the road ends at the beach camping area.

Trip notes: This is "National Headquarters" for all-terrain vehicles (ATVs)—you know, those three- and four-wheeled motorcycles that turn otherwise normal people into lunatics. They roam wild on the dunes here; that's the law, so don't go planning a quiet stroll. If you don't like 'em, you are strongly advised to go elsewhere. If this is your game, have fun and try to keep from killing yourself.

3 Oceano

Location: In Pismo State Beach; map H2, grid a5.

Campsites, facilities: There are 82 sites for tents, trailers, or RVs up to 36 feet long, 42 with partial hookups. There are also some primitive hike-in and bike-in sites. Picnic tables and fire grills are provided. Piped water, flush toilets, and coin-operated showers are available. Horseback riding facilities, grocery store, coin laundry, and propane gas are nearby. Leashed pets are permitted.

Reservations, fees: Reserve via phone at (800) 444-PARK/7275 ($7.50 reservation fee) or website www.cal-parks.ca.gov; $14 to $18 per night, $20 to $24 with hookup, $6 per night for hike-in/bike-in sites. Open year-round.

Contact: Oceano, (805) 549-3312.

Directions: From Pismo Beach, drive one mile south on Highway 1 to the campground entrance.

Trip notes: This is a prized state beach campground, with Pismo Beach and its sand dunes, clamming, and coastal frontage a centerpiece for the state park system. Its location on the central coast on Highway 1, as well as its beauty and recreational opportunities, makes it extremely popular. It fills to capacity most nights, and reservations are usually a necessity.

④ River Park

Location: In Lompoc; map H2, grid e6.

Campsites, facilities: There 34 RV sites with full hookups and a large open area for tents. Piped water, flush toilets, showers, dump station, fishing pond, and a playground are available. Supplies and a coin laundry are nearby. Leashed pets are permitted.

Reservations, fees: Reservations are accepted; $10 to $15 per night, $4 per night for hike-in/bike-in sites, $2 for dump station use, and $1 pet fee.

Contact: River Park, (805) 736-6565 or fax (805) 736-5195.

Directions: In Lompoc, drive to the junction of Highway 246 and Sweeney Road at the southwest edge of town and continue to the park at 401 East Highway 246.

Trip notes: Before checking in here you'd best get a lesson in how to pronounce Lompoc. It's "Lom-Poke." If you arrive and say, "Hey, it's great to be in Lom-Pock," they might just tell ya to get on back to Nebraska with the other cowpokes. The camp is set near the lower Santa Ynez River, which looks quite a bit different than it does up in Los Padres National Forest. A small fishing lake within the park is stocked regularly with trout. Side trip possibilities include the nearby La Purisima Mission State Historic Park.

⑤ Jalama Beach County Park

Location: Near Lompoc on the Pacific Ocean; map H2, grid g5.

Campsites, facilities: There are 110 sites for tents or RVs up to 35 feet long, including several group sites. Some sites have electrical hookups,

but there are no water hookups. Piped water, fire grills, and picnic tables are provided. Flush toilets, showers, dump station, and a grocery store are available. Note that the nearest gas station is 20 miles away. Leashed pets are permitted.

Reservations, fees: No reservations except for groups; $15 per night, $8 for an extra vehicle; $96 group fee per night, $2 pet fee.

Contact: Jalama Beach County Park, (805) 736-6316 or fax (805) 736-8020 or (805) 736-3504.

Directions: From Lompoc, drive about five miles south on Highway 1. Turn southwest on Jalama Road and drive 15 miles to the park.

Trip notes: This is a pretty spot set where Jalama Creek empties into the ocean, about five miles north of Point Conception and just south of Vandenberg Air Force Base. The area is known for its sunsets and beachcombing, with occasional lost missiles washing up on the beach.

⑥ Flying Flags RV Park

Location: Near Solvang; map H2, grid f9.

Campsites, facilities: There are 100 sites for tents and 256 RV sites with full or partial hookups. Picnic tables are provided. Rest rooms with wheelchair access, showers, playground, swimming pool, two hot therapy pools, laundry room, store, dump station, ice, recreation room, arcade, five clubhouses, and propane gas are available. A nine-hole golf course is nearby. Leashed pets are permitted.

Reservations, fees: Reservations are recommended; $17 to $25 per night for one or two people, $2 for each additional camper, $1 pet fee.

Contact: Flying Flags RV Park, (805) 688-3716 or fax (805) 688-9245.

Directions: From Santa Barbara, drive 45 miles north on US 101 to its intersection with Highway 246. Turn west on Highway 246 and drive about a half mile to the four-way stop. Turn left on Avenue of the Flags and drive about one block to the campground entrance on the left at 180 Avenue of the Flags.

Trip notes: This is one of the few privately operated parks in the area that welcomes tenters as well as RVers. Nearby side trips include the Santa Ynez Mission, located just east of Solvang. The town of Solvang is of unique interest, originally a small Danish settlement that has expanded since the 1920s yet managed to keep its cultural heritage intact over the years. The town is spotless, no trash of any kind in sight, and an example of how to do something right.

❼ Gaviota State Park

Location: Near Santa Barbara; map H2, grid g8.

Campsites, facilities: There are 55 sites for tents and RVs up to 27 feet long. Fire grills and picnic tables are provided. Piped water, flush toilets, coin-operated showers, and a boat hoist are available. A grocery store is nearby. Leashed pets are permitted.

Reservations, fees: No reservations; $15 to $16 per night, $1 pet fee.

Contact: Gaviota State Park, (805) 968-3294 or (805) 899-1400.

Directions: From Santa Barbara, drive 33 miles north on US 101 to the park entrance.

Trip notes: This is the granddaddy, the biggest of the three state beaches along Highway 1 northwest of Santa Barbara. Spectacular and beautiful, the park covers 2,800 acres, providing trails for hiking and horseback riding, as well as a mile-long stretch of stunning beach frontage. The ambitious can hike the beach to get more seclusion. Trails to Gaviota Overlook (1.5 miles) and Gaviota Peak (3.2 miles one way) provide lookouts with drop-dead gorgeous views. Want more? There is also a half-mile trail to the hot springs.

Special Note: Call to check status of the camping area before making the trip. The camp may be restricted to day-use only.

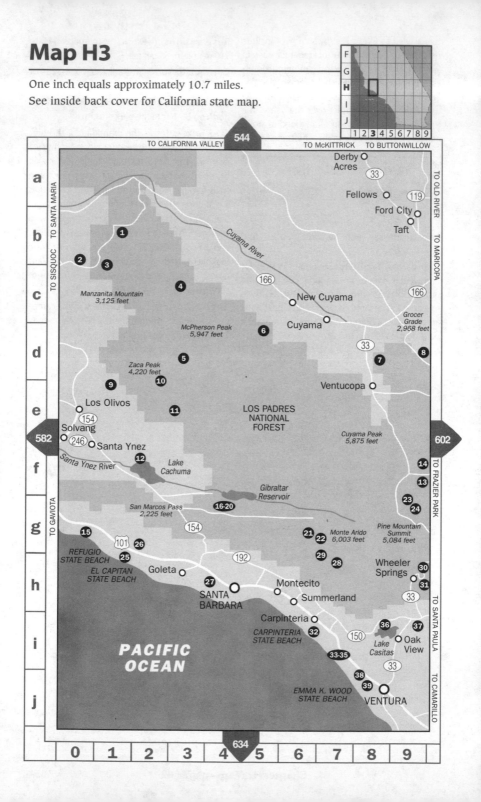

Map H3

One inch equals approximately 10.7 miles.
See inside back cover for California state map.

PACIFIC OCEAN

TO CALIFORNIA VALLEY
TO McKITTRICK TO BUTTONWILLOW
544

TO SANTA MARIA
TO SISQUOC
TO GAVIOTA

TO OLD RIVER
TO MARICOPA
TO FRAZIER PARK
TO SANTA PAULA
TO CAMARILLO

582
602
634

Derby Acres
Fellows
Ford City
Taft
(33)
(119)

Cuyama River
(166)
New Cuyama
Cuyama
Grocer Grade
2,968 feet
(166)
(33)

Manzanita Mountain
3,125 feet

McPherson Peak
5,947 feet

Zaca Peak
4,220 feet

Ventucopa

LOS PADRES NATIONAL FOREST

Cuyama Peak
5,875 feet

Los Olivos
(154)
Solvang
(246) Santa Ynez
Santa Ynez River
Lake Cachuma

Gibraltar Reservoir

San Marcos Pass
2,225 feet
(154)

Monte Arido
6,003 feet
Pine Mountain Summit
5,084 feet

REFUGIO STATE BEACH
(101)
EL CAPITAN STATE BEACH
Goleta
(192)

Wheeler Springs
(33)

SANTA BARBARA
Montecito
Summerland

Carpinteria
CARPINTERIA STATE BEACH
(150)
Lake Casitas
Oak View
(33)

EMMA K. WOOD STATE BEACH
Ventura

1 2 3 4 5 6 7 8 9
0 1 2 3 4 5 6 7 8 9
a b c d e f g h i j
F G H I J

Chapter H3 features:

---

❶ Wagon Flat

Location: On the North Fork of La Brea Creek in Los Padres National Forest; map H3, grid b12.

Campsites, facilities: There are three sites for tents. Fire grills and picnic tables are provided. Vault toilets are available. There is no piped water and no trash service. Leashed pets are permitted.

Reservations, fees: No reservations; no camping fee. An Adventure Pass ($30 annual fee) or $5 daily pass per parked vehicle is required. Open year-round, but access roads may be closed during and after heavy rains.

Contact: Los Padres National Forest, Santa Lucia Ranger District, (805) 925-9538 or fax (805) 681-2781.

Directions: From US 101 in Santa Maria, take the Betteravia Road exit. Drive eight miles southeast on Foxen Canyon Road. Bear left at the fork and continue southeast on Santa Maria Mesa Road. Turn left on Tepusquet Road and drive 6.5 miles. Turn right on Colson Canyon Road/Forest Service Road 11N04 and drive 10 more miles to the campground. Colson Canyon Road can be impassable when wet.

Trip notes: Not many folks know about this obscure spot, and if it's a hot, late summer day, they're probably better off for it. The camp is set at an elevation of 1,400 feet, in a hot, dry obscure region of Los Padres National Forest. The bright spot is little La Brea Creek, which runs by the camp.

❷ Colson

Location: In Los Padres National Forest; map H3, grid b0.

Campsites, facilities: There are five tent sites. Fire grills and picnic tables are provided. A pit toilet is available, but there is no trash service. Leashed pets are permitted.

Reservations, fees: No reservations; no camping fee. An Adventure Pass ($30 annual fee) or $5 daily pass per parked vehicle is required. Open year-round.

Contact: Los Padres National Forest, Santa Lucia Ranger District, (805) 925-9538 or fax (805) 681-2781.

Directions: From US 101 in Santa Maria, take the Betteravia Road exit. Drive eight miles southeast on Foxen Canyon Road. Bear left at the fork and continue southeast on Santa Maria Mesa Road. Turn left on Tepusquet Road and drive 6.5 miles. Turn right on Colson Canyon Road/Forest Service Road 11N04 and drive four miles to the campground. Colson Canyon Road can be impassable when wet.

Trip notes: Colson is set just a mile from the western border of Los Padres National Forest, making it far easier to reach than other Forest Service camps in this region. The camp is named after the canyon in which it sits, Colson Canyon. This area really has just two seasons when you should visit, spring and fall. In the summer, it's hot and dry, with no water available, and is scarcely fit for habitation. The elevation is 2,100 feet.

❸ Barrel Springs

Location: In Los Padres National Forest; map H3, grid c1.

Campsites, facilities: There are six tent sites. There is no piped water. Fire grills and picnic tables are provided. Vault toilets are available. Leashed pets are permitted.

Reservations, fees: No reservations; no camping fee. An Adventure Pass ($30 annual fee) or $5 daily pass per parked vehicle is required. Open year-round, but access roads may be closed during and after heavy rains.

Contact: Los Padres National Forest, Santa Lucia Ranger District, (805) 925-9538 or fax (805) 681-2781.

Directions: From Santa Maria on US 101, take the Betteravia Road exit. Drive eight miles southeast on Foxen Canyon Road. Bear left at the fork and continue southeast on Santa Maria Mesa Road. Turn left on Tepusquet Road and drive 6.5 miles. Turn right on Colson Canyon Road/Forest Service Road 11N04 and drive eight miles to the campground. Colson Canyon Road can be impassable when wet.

Trip notes: This small, primitive camp sits at 1,000 feet in elevation along La Brea Creek and is shaded by the oaks in La Brea Canyon. It is named after nearby Barrel Springs, which forms a small creek and feeds into La Brea Creek.

❹ Bates Canyon

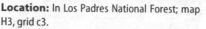

Location: In Los Padres National Forest; map H3, grid c3.

Campsites, facilities: There are six tent sites. Fire grills and picnic tables are provided. Vault toilets are available. There is no piped water. Leashed pets are permitted.

Reservations, fees: No reservations; no camping fee. An Adventure Pass ($30 annual fee) or $5 daily pass per parked vehicle is required. Open year-round.

Contact: Los Padres National Forest, Santa Lucia Ranger District, (805) 925-9538 or fax (805) 681-2781.

Directions: From Santa Maria, drive 50 miles east on Highway 166. Turn right on Cottonwood Canyon Road and drive 7.5 miles southwest to the campground.

Trip notes: This camp is located on the northeast flank of the Sierra Madre Mountains, along a small stream in Bates Canyon, at 2,900 feet in elevation. Note that the primitive access road out of camp to the south is often gated; it leads to the Sierra Madre Ridge, where a road contours right along the ridge on the border of the San Rafael Wilderness, passing from peak to peak.

❺ Nira

Location: On Manzana Creek in Los Padres National Forest; map H3, grid d3.

Campsites, facilities: There are 11 sites for tents or RVs up to 16 feet long. There is no piped water and no trash service. Fire grills and picnic tables are provided. Vault toilets and horse hitching posts are available. Leashed pets are permitted.

Reservations, fees: No reservations; no

camping fee. An Adventure Pass ($30 annual fee) or $5 daily pass per parked vehicle is required. Open year-round, but access roads may be closed during and after heavy rains.

Contact: Los Padres National Forest, Santa Lucia Ranger District, (805) 925-9538 or fax (805) 681-2781.

Directions: From US 101 in Santa Barbara, drive 22 miles northeast on Highway 154. Turn right on Armour Ranch Road and drive 1.5 miles. Turn right on Happy Canyon Road and drive 11 miles to Cachuma Saddle. Continue straight (north) on Sunset Valley/Cachuma Road/Forest Service Road 8N09 for six miles to the campground.

Trip notes: Nira is a premium jump-off spot for backpackers, set at 2,100 feet along Manzana Creek, on the border of the San Rafael Wilderness. A primary wilderness trailhead is available, routed east into the San Rafael Wilderness through Lost Valley, along Fish Creek, and to Manzana Creek (and beyond), all in just six miles, with a series of hike-in camps available as the trail enters the wilderness interior. Today's history lesson? This camp was originally an NRA (National Recovery Act) camp during the Depression, hence the name Nira.

⑥ Aliso Park

Location: In Los Padres National Forest; map H3, grid d5.

Campsites, facilities: There are 11 sites for tents or RVs up to 22 feet long. Fire grills and picnic tables are provided. Vault toilets are available. There is no piped water. Leashed pets are permitted.

Reservations, fees: No reservations; no camping fee. An Adventure Pass ($30 annual fee) or $5 daily pass per parked vehicle is required. Open year-round.

Contact: Los Padres National Forest, Mount Piños Ranger District, (661) 245-3731 or fax (661) 245-1526.

Directions: From Santa Maria, drive east on Highway 166 for 59 miles to Aliso Canyon Road. Turn right and drive south about six miles to the campground.

Trip notes: This primitive, quiet camp is set at the foot of the Sierra Madre Mountains at 3,200 feet, directly below McPherson Peak (5,747 feet). It is just inside the northeast boundary of Los Padres National Forest, making it easily accessible from Highway 166.

⑦ Ballinger

Location: In Los Padres National Forest; map H3, grid d8.

Campsites, facilities: There are 20 sites for tents or RVs up to 32 feet long. Fire grills and picnic tables are provided. Pit toilets are available. There is no piped water. Leashed pets are permitted.

Reservations, fees: No reservations; no camping fee. An Adventure Pass ($30 annual fee) or $5 daily pass per parked vehicle is required. Open year-round.

Contact: Los Padres National Forest, Mount Piños Ranger District, (661) 245-3731 or fax (661) 245-1526.

Directions: From Maricopa, drive southwest on Highway 166 about 14 miles to Highway 33. Turn south and drive about 3.5 miles to Ballinger Canyon Road/Forest Service Road 9N10. Turn left (east) and drive three miles to the campground.

Trip notes: Ballinger Camp is right inside the boundary of Los Padres National Forest in the Mount Piños Ranger District, just six miles east of Highway 33. Despite that proximity to a major roadway, this camp is obscure and gets little use. Why? Because there's nothing to do—no hiking, no fishing, no boating—except sit around and ask yourself, "Why am I here?"

⑧ Valle Vista

Location: In Los Padres National Forest; map H3, grid d9.

Campsites, facilities: There are seven sites for tents or RVs up to 22 feet long. Fire grills and picnic tables are provided. Vault toilets are available. There is no piped water. Leashed pets are permitted.

Reservations, fees: No reservations; no camping fee. An Adventure Pass ($30 annual fee) or $5 daily pass per parked vehicle is required. Open year-round.

Contact: Los Padres National Forest, Mount Piños Ranger District, (805) 245-3731 or fax (805) 245-1526.

Directions: From Maricopa, drive south on Highway 166 about nine miles to Cerro Noroeste Road. Turn left and drive 12 miles to the campground.

Trip notes: The view of Bakersfield Valley is the highlight of this primitive camp. It is set at 4,800 feet, near the boundary of Los Padres National Forest. Visitors have an opportunity to view condors here, and you can usually spot a few buzzards circling around. If you don't bring your own water, they might just start circling you. Little-known fact: this camp sits exactly on the border of Kern County and Ventura County. Wow.

---

9 Figueroa

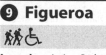

Location: In Los Padres National Forest; map H3, grid e1.

Campsites, facilities: There are 33 sites for tents. Fire grills, picnic tables, and vault toilets are provided. There is no piped water and no trash service. Leashed pets are permitted.

Reservations, fees: No reservations; no camping fee. An Adventure Pass ($30 annual fee) or $5 daily pass per parked vehicle is required. Open year-round.

Contact: Los Padres National Forest, Santa Lucia Ranger District, (805) 925-9538 or fax (805) 681-2781.

Directions: From Los Olivos on Highway 154, turn northeast on Figueroa Mountain Road and drive 12.5 miles to the campground.

Trip notes: This is one of the more attractive camps in Los Padres National Forest. It is set at 4,000 feet beneath an unusual stand of oak and huge manzanita trees, and offers a view of the Santa Ynez Valley. Nearby attractions include the Piño Alto Picnic Area, 2.5 miles away, offering a panoramic view of the adjacent wildlands with a half-mile, wheelchair-accessible nature trail. An exceptional view is also available from the nearby Figueroa fire lookout. Though it requires a circuitous 10-mile ride around Figueroa Mountain to get there, Nira (campground number five) to the east provides the best trailhead for the San Rafael Wilderness in this area.

---

10 Davy Brown

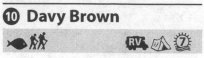

Location: On Davy Brown Creek in Los Padres National Forest; map H3, grid d2.

Campsites, facilities: There are 13 sites for tents and RVs up to 18 feet long. Fire grills and picnic tables are provided. Vault toilets are available. There is no piped water and no trash service. Leashed pets are permitted.

Reservations, fees: No reservations; no camping fee. An Adventure Pass ($30 annual fee) or $5 daily fee per parked vehicle is required. Open year-round.

Contact: Los Padres National Forest, Santa Lucia Ranger District, (805) 925-9538 or fax (805) 681-2781.

Directions: From US 101 in Santa Barbara, drive 22 miles northeast on Highway 154. Turn right on Armour Ranch Road and drive 1.5 miles. Turn right on Happy Canyon Road/County Route 3350 and drive 11 miles to Cachuma Saddle. Continue straight (north) on Sunset Valley/Cachuma Road/Forest Service Road 8N09 for four miles to the campground.

Trip notes: This is a pretty spot, set along little Davy Brown Creek at 4,000 feet, deep in Los Padres National Forest. The border of the San Rafael Wilderness and an excellent trailhead are located just two miles down the road (along Davy Brown Creek) to the northeast at Nira (see campground number five for hiking options).

---

11 Cachuma

Location: Near Cachuma Creek in Los Padres National Forest; map H3, grid e3.

Campsites, facilities: There are five tent sites. Fire grills and picnic tables are provided. Vault toilets are available. There is no piped water. Leashed pets are permitted.

Reservations, fees: No reservations; no

camping fee. An Adventure Pass ($30 annual fee) or $5 daily pass per parked vehicle is required. Open year-round.

Contact: Los Padres National Forest, Santa Barbara Ranger District, (805) 967-3481 or fax (805) 967-7312.

Directions: From US 101 in Santa Barbara, drive 22 miles northeast on Highway 154. Turn right on Armour Ranch Road and drive 1.5 miles. Turn right on Happy Canyon Road/County Route 3350 and drive 9.5 miles to the campground.

Trip notes: Yes, Cachuma is the sound you make when sneezing, but no, the camp, nearby stream, and famous lake were not named after such an event. This camp is set at 2,200 feet, along one of the major streams that feeds Lake Cachuma, just 10 miles downstream. A dirt road south of the camp follows the creek to the lake.

⑫ Lake Cachuma

Location: Near Santa Barbara; map H3, grid f2.

Campsites, facilities: There are 500 sites for tents or RVs, some with full hookups. Fire grills and picnic tables are provided. Flush toilets, showers, playground, general store, propane gas, swimming pool, boat ramp, mooring, boat fuel, boat rentals, bicycle rentals, ice, and a snack bar are available. Watercraft under 10 feet are prohibited on the lake. Leashed pets are permitted, but must be kept at least 50 feet from the lake.

Reservations, fees: No reservations; $14 to $18 per night, $8 for a second vehicle; $1 pet fee. Open year-round.

Contact: Lake Cachuma, (805) 688-4658 or (805) 686-5053.

Directions: From Santa Barbara, drive 20 miles north on Highway 154 to the campground entrance on the right.

Trip notes: Cachuma has become one of the best lakes in America for fishing for big bass, and the ideal climate makes it a winner for camping as well. Cachuma is set at 600 feet in the foothills northwest of Santa Barbara, a big, beautiful lake covering 3,200 acres. The rules are perfect for fishing: no waterskiing, jet skiing, swimming, canoeing, kayaking, or windsurfing is per-

mitted; for fishing boats there is a 5 mph speed limit in the coves and a 40 mph limit elsewhere. Yeah, let it rip on open water, then quiet down to sneak-fish the coves.

⑬ Reyes Creek

Location: In Los Padres National Forest; map H3, grid f9.

Campsites, facilities: There are 30 sites for tents only and six sites for tents or RVs up to 22 feet long. Fire grills and picnic tables are provided. Vault toilets are available. Leashed pets are permitted.

Reservations, fees: No reservations; no camping fee. An Adventure Pass ($30 annual fee) or $5 daily pass per parked vehicle is required. Open year-round.

Contact: Los Padres National Forest, Mount Piños Ranger District, (661) 245-3731 or fax (661) 245-1526.

Directions: From Ojai, drive 36 miles north on Highway 33. Turn right on Lockwood Valley Road and drive about three miles to Forest Service Road 7N11. Turn right and drive about 1.5 miles to the campground entrance on your right.

Trip notes: This developed Forest Service camp sits at the end of an old spur, Forest Service Road 7N11. The camp is set at 4,000 feet along Reyes Creek, which is stocked with trout in early summer. There is also a good swimming hole nearby. A trail is routed out of camp to the south and climbs three miles to Upper Reyes backpack camp, and beyond, up a ridge and down to Beartrap Creek and several trail camps along that creek.

⑭ Ozena

Location: In Los Padres National Forest; map H3, grid f9.

Campsites, facilities: There are 12 sites for tents or RVs up to 22 feet long. Fire grills and picnic tables are provided. Vault toilets are available. There is no piped water. Groceries and propane gas can be purchased about 30 minutes away. Leashed pets are permitted.

Reservations, fees: No reservations; no camping fee. An Adventure Pass ($30 annual fee) or $5 daily pass per parked vehicle is required. Open year-round.

Contact: Los Padres National Forest, Mount Piños Ranger District, (661) 245-3731 or fax (661) 245-1526.

Directions: From Ojai, drive 36 miles north on Highway 33. Turn right on Lockwood Valley Road and drive 1.5 miles to the campground.

Trip notes: This camp is set at 3,600 feet, about a mile from Reyes Creek and about four miles from Reyes Creek (campground number 13), the premium campground in this area.

⓯ Refugio State Beach

Location: Near Santa Barbara; map H3, grid g0.

Campsites, facilities: There are 85 sites for tents or RVs up to 30 feet long. There is one group site that can accommodate 80 tent or RV campers. Fire grills and picnic tables are provided. Piped water, flush toilets, coin-operated showers, grocery store, and food service are available. The campground, food service area, and grocery store are wheelchair accessible. Leashed pets are permitted, except on the beach.

Reservations, fees: Reserve via phone at (800) 444-PARK/7275 ($7.50 reservation fee for individual sites, $8.65 group reservation fee); $17 to $18 per night for individual sites, $120 per night for the group site, $1 pet fee. Open year-round.

Contact: Refugio State Beach, (805) 968-3294 or (805) 899-1400.

Directions: From Santa Barbara, drive 23 miles northwest on US 101 to the campground on the left.

Trip notes: Refugio State Beach is the smallest of the two beautiful state beaches located along Highway 1 north of Santa Barbara. The other is El Capitan, which also has a campground. As with all state beaches and private camps on Highway 1, reservations are strongly advised and often a necessity throughout the vacation season.

⓰ Fremont

Location: On the Santa Ynez River in Los Padres National Forest; map H3, grid g4.

Campsites, facilities: There are 15 sites for tents or RVs up to 16 feet long. Piped water, fire grills, and picnic tables are provided. Flush toilets are available. Groceries and propane gas are 15 minutes away. Leashed pets are permitted.

Reservations, fees: No reservations; $10 per night, $2 for a second vehicle. Open year-round.

Contact: Los Padres National Forest, Santa Barbara Ranger District, (805) 967-3481 or fax (805) 967-7312.

Directions: From Santa Barbara, drive about 10 miles northwest on Highway 154. Turn right on Paradise Road/Forest Service Road 5N18 and drive 2.5 miles to the campground on the right.

Trip notes: Traveling west to east, Fremont is the first in a series of Forest Service campgrounds along the Santa Ynez River. This one is located just inside the boundary of Los Padres National Forest at 900 feet in elevation, six miles east of Lake Cachuma to the west.

⓱ Los Prietos

Location: On the Santa Ynez River in Los Padres National Forest; map H3, grid g4.

Campsites, facilities: There are 37 sites for tents or RVs up to 22 feet long. Piped water, fire grills, and picnic tables are provided. Flush toilets are available. Leashed pets are permitted.

Reservations, fees: No reservations; $10 per night, $2 for a second vehicle. Open year-round.

Contact: Los Padres National Forest, Santa Barbara Ranger District, (805) 967-3481 or fax (805) 967-7312.

Directions: From Santa Barbara, drive about 10 miles north on Highway 154. Turn right on Paradise Road/Forest Service Road 5N18 and drive 3.8 miles to the campground.

Trip notes: Los Prietos is set along the Santa Ynez River at an elevation of 1,000 feet, just upstream from nearby Fremont (campground number 16) to the west. There are several nice hiking trails nearby; the best starts near the Los Prietos Ranger Station, heading south for two miles to Wellhouse Falls (get specific directions and a map at the ranger station).

⑱ Upper Oso

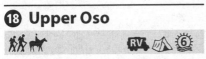

Location: Near the Santa Ynez River in Los Padres National Forest; map H3, grid g4.

Campsites, facilities: There are 28 sites for tents or RVs up to 22 feet long. Piped water, fire grills, horse corrals, and picnic tables are provided. Flush toilets are available. Leashed pets are permitted.

Reservations, fees: No reservations; $10 per night, $4 for a second vehicle. Open year-round, weather permitting.

Contact: Los Padres National Forest, Santa Barbara Ranger District, (805) 967-3481 or fax (805) 967-7312.

Directions: From Santa Barbara, drive about 10 miles north on Highway 154. Turn right on Paradise Road/Forest Service Road 5N18 and drive six miles. Turn left on Camuesa Drive/Forest Service Road 5N15 and drive 1.5 miles to the campground on the left.

Trip notes: This is one of the four Forest Service campgrounds located in the Santa Ynez Recreation Area. It is set in Oso Canyon at 1,100 feet, one mile from the Santa Ynez River. Note that at high water this campground can become inaccessible. A mile north of camp, a trailhead is available for a hike that is routed north up Oso Canyon for a mile, then three miles up to Happy Hollow, and beyond that to a trail camp just west of Little Pine Mountain, elevation 4,508 feet. A trailhead into the San Rafael Wilderness is nearby, and once on the trail, you'll find many primitive sites in the backcountry.

⑲ Paradise

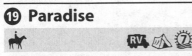

Location: On the Santa Ynez River in Los Padres National Forest; map H3, grid g4.

Campsites, facilities: There are 15 sites for tents or RVs up to 22 feet long. Piped water, fire grills, and picnic tables are provided. Flush toi-

lets are available. Horseback riding facilities, groceries, and propane gas can be found nearby. Leashed pets are permitted.

Reservations, fees: Reservations are requested; reserve via phone at (877) 444-6777 ($8.65 reservation fee) or website www.reserveusa.com; $10 per night, $5 for a second vehicle. Open year-round.

Contact: Los Padres National Forest, Santa Barbara Ranger District, (805) 967-3481 or fax (805) 967-7312.

Directions: From Santa Barbara, drive about 10 miles north on Highway 154. Turn right on Paradise Road/Forest Service Road 5N18 and drive three miles to the campground on the right.

Trip notes: Here is yet another option among the four camps along the Santa Ynez River. As you drive east it is the second camp you will come to, just after Fremont. The best hiking trailheads nearby are at Upper Oso Camp and the Los Prietos Ranger Station. Lake Cachuma is six miles to the west.

⑳ Sage Hill Group Camp

Location: On the Santa Ynez River in Los Padres National Forest; map H3, grid g4.

Campsites, facilities: There are five group areas with sites for tents or RVs up to 32 feet long. Piped water, fire grills, picnic tables, and flush toilets are available. Horse corrals are located in one group site. Leashed pets are permitted.

Reservations, fees: Reservations are required; reserve via phone at (877) 444-6777 ($8.65 reservation fee) or website www.reserveusa.com; $50 to $60 per group of 25 to 50 per night. Open year-round, weather permitting.

Contact: Los Padres National Forest, Santa Barbara Ranger District, (805) 967-3481 or fax (805) 967-7312.

Directions: From Santa Barbara, drive about 10 miles north on Highway 154. Turn right on Paradise Road/Forest Service Road 5N18 and drive five miles to the ranger station. Turn left and drive a half mile to the campground.

Trip notes: This is another in the series of camps located along the Santa Ynez River in Los

Padres National Forest. This one, set at 2,000 feet, was designed for large groups. A 3.5-mile loop trail starts at the back end of Sage Hill Group Camp. The first mile is a self-guided interpretive trail.

㉑ Mono Hike-In

Location: On Mono Creek in Los Padres National Forest; map H3, grid g6.

Campsites, facilities: There are five tent sites. Fire grills and picnic tables are provided. Vault toilets are available. There is no piped water. Leashed pets are permitted.

Reservations, fees: No reservations; no camping fee. An Adventure Pass ($30 annual fee) or $5 daily pass per parked vehicle is required. Open year-round, weather permitting.

Contact: Los Padres National Forest, Santa Barbara Ranger District, (805) 967-3481 or fax (805) 967-7312.

Directions: From US 101 in Santa Barbara, drive eight miles north on Highway 154. Turn right on East Camino Cielo/Forest Service Road 5N12 and drive 18 miles to the end of the paved road at Camuesa Road/Forest Service Road 5N15, which is a dirt road. Continue on Camuesa Road for five miles to Juncal Campground. Turn left and drive seven miles to Mono Hike-In.

Trip notes: Not many folks know about this spot. The camp is small and primitive, located at elevation 1,500 feet on little Mono Creek, complete with a great swimming hole. Also note that Little Caliente Hot Springs is one mile northeast of the campground. Mono Creek is a feeder to Gibralter Reservoir, a long, narrow lake with no direct access available.

㉒ P-Bar Flat

Location: On the Santa Ynez River in Los Padres National Forest; map H3, grid g7.

Campsites, facilities: There are four tent sites. Fire grills and picnic tables are provided. Vault toilets are available. There is no piped water. Leashed pets are permitted.

Reservations, fees: No reservations; no

camping fee. An Adventure Pass ($30 annual fee) or $5 daily pass per parked vehicle is required. Open year-round, weather permitting.

Contact: Los Padres National Forest, Santa Barbara Ranger District, (805) 967-3481 or fax (805) 967-7312.

Directions: From US 101 in Santa Barbara, drive eight miles north on Highway 154. Turn right on East Camino Cielo/Forest Service Road 5N12 and drive 18 miles to the end of the paved road at Camuesa Road/Forest Service Road 5N15, which is a dirt road. Continue on Camuesa Road for five miles to Juncal Campground. Turn left and drive four miles to P-Bar Flat.

Trip notes: The best thing or the worst thing, depending on how you look at it, about P-Bar Flat is a trailhead that is routed north into the remote wildlands of Los Padres National Forest. The camp is very small and primitive, set at 1,800 feet along the Santa Ynez River. The trail starts by heading up Horse Canyon and along a creek, but eventually is routed 10 miles to Hildreth Peak, elevation 8,066 feet, a 6,000-foot butt-kicker of a climb. A lot of guys in prison get less punishment.

㉓ Pine Mountain

Location: In Los Padres National Forest; map H3, grid f9.

Campsites, facilities: There are eight tent sites. Fire grills and picnic tables are provided. Vault toilets are available. There is no piped water. Leashed pets are permitted.

Reservations, fees: No reservations; no camping fee. An Adventure Pass ($30 annual fee) or $5 daily pass per parked vehicle is required. Open April through November.

Contact: Los Padres National Forest, Ojai Ranger District, (805) 646-4348 or fax (805) 646-0484.

Directions: From Ojai, drive 33 miles north on Highway 33. Turn right on Reyes Peak Road and drive 2.5 miles to the campground on the left.

Trip notes: Pine Mountain, along with nearby Reyes Peak (located a quarter mile to the east, see next listing), is a tiny, primitive campground in a pretty setting with a few trailheads close at hand. The two best nearby hikes lead to springs.

A trail is routed out of camp and into Boulder Canyon for a mile down the mountain, where it meets another trail that turns left and heads a quarter mile to McGuire Spring Trail Camp (piped springwater is available there). It's advisable to obtain a Forest Service map. The elevation is 6,700 feet.

㉔ Reyes Peak

Location: In Los Padres National Forest; map H3, grid g9.

Campsites, facilities: There are seven tent sites. Fire grills and picnic tables are provided. Vault toilets are available. There is no piped water. Leashed pets are permitted.

Reservations, fees: No reservations; no camping fee. An Adventure Pass ($30 annual fee) or $5 daily pass per parked vehicle is required. Open April through October.

Contact: Los Padres National Forest, Ojai Ranger District, (805) 646-4348 or fax (805) 646-0484.

Directions: From Ojai, drive 33 miles north on Highway 33. Turn right on Reyes Peak Road and drive five miles to the campground.

Trip notes: Reyes Peak is a primitive camp set at 6,800 feet. Three short hikes that you can access in the immediate vicinity lead to trail camps. The closest is from a trailhead located just to the west of camp, which provides a half-mile hike north to Raspberry Spring (a backcountry camp is available there); an easy trip. Nearby Pine Mountain (campground number 23) provides an alternative.

㉕ El Capitan State Beach

Location: Near Santa Barbara; map H3, grid g1.

Campsites, facilities: There are 142 sites for tents or RVs up to 30 feet long. The campground, picnic grounds, and grocery store are wheelchair accessible. Fire grills and picnic tables are provided. Piped water, flush toilets, coin-operated showers, dump station, and a grocery store are available. Leashed pets are permitted.

Reservations, fees: Reserve via phone at (800) 444-PARK/7275 ($7.50 reservation fee) or website www.cal-parks.ca.gov; $17 to $18 per night; $1 pet fee.

Contact: El Capitan State Beach, (805) 968-3294 or (805) 899-1400.

Directions: From Santa Barbara, drive 20 miles northwest on US 101 to the campground on the left.

Trip notes: This is one in a series of beautiful state beaches along the Santa Barbara coast. The water is warm, the swimming good, and folks, the park ranger asks that you "Please keep your bathing suits on." This is a perfect layover for Highway 1 vacationers, and reservations are usually required to assure a spot. Refugio State Beach to the north is another camping option.

㉖ El Capitan Canyon

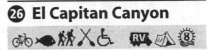

Location: Near Santa Barbara; map H3, grid g2.

Campsites, facilities: There are 150 sites with partial hookups for tents or RVs and 85 tent sites. Piped water, fire pits, and picnic tables are provided. Rest rooms, free hot showers, flush toilets, swimming pool, children's playground, live music, volleyball, horseshoes, croquet, small store, and firewood are available. Some facilities are wheelchair accessible. Leashed pets are permitted.

Reservations, fees: Reservations are recommended; $18 to $22 per night, $5 pet fee. Open year-round.

Contact: El Capitan Canyon, 11560 Calle Real, 93117; (805) 685-3887 or fax (805) 968-6772; website www.elcapitancanyon.com.

Directions: From Santa Barbara, drive about 20 miles northwest on US 101 to the El Capitan State Beach exit. Go straight on the frontage road paralleling the freeway for about 100 yards. Turn right at the sign for El Capitan Canyon on the mountain side of the freeway.

Trip notes: El Capitan Canyon, located on 65 acres in the coastal foothills north of Santa Barbara, offers campers the best of both worlds: There are 2,200 acres of public land near the camp with backcountry hiking and mountain biking trails, or for those who prefer the sand and surf, beach access is within walking distance and ocean kayaking and deep-sea fishing trips can be booked at the resort. In the summer months live entertainment is available, including a concert series and the "Blues and Barbecue" event every Saturday night.

27 Santa Barbara Sunrise RV Park

Location: Near Santa Barbara; map H3, grid h4.

Campsites, facilities: There are 33 sites for RVs with full hookups and patios and two tent sites. Rest rooms, showers, cable TV, and laundry facilities are available. A grocery store, golf course, tennis courts, and propane gas are nearby. Leashed pets are permitted.

Reservations, fees: Reservations are recommended; $25 to $30 per night for two people. Open year-round.

Contact: Santa Barbara Sunrise RV Park, (805) 966-9954, (800) 345-5018, or fax (805) 966-7950.

Directions: In Santa Barbara on US 101, take the Salinas Street exit going north or the Milpas Street exit going south and follow the blue camper signs to 516 South Salinas Street.

Trip notes: Motor home cruisers get a little of two worlds here. For one thing, the park is close to the beach; for another, the downtown shopping area isn't too far away, either.

28 Juncal

Location: On the Santa Ynez River in Los Padres National Forest; map H3, grid h7.

Campsites, facilities: There are seven tent sites. Fire grills and picnic tables are provided. Vault toilets are available. There is no piped water. Leashed pets are permitted.

Reservations, fees: No reservations; no camping fee. An Adventure Pass ($30 annual fee) or $5 daily pass per parked vehicle is required. Open year-round.

Contact: Los Padres National Forest, Santa Barbara Ranger District, (805) 967-3481 or fax (805) 967-7312.

Directions: From US 101 in Santa Barbara, drive eight miles north on Highway 154. Turn right on East Camino Cielo/Forest Service Road 5N12 and drive 18 miles to the end of the paved road at Camuesa Road/Forest Service Road 5N15, which is a dirt road. Turn left and drive five miles to the campground on the right.

Trip notes: We never did discover who Mr. Juncal was, but he got this campground, a road, and the dam at Jameson Lake named after him. As long as he wasn't a politician, that's okay with us. The camp is set on the Santa Ynez River at 1,800 feet, about two miles west of little Jameson Lake and four miles east of Middle Santa Ynez (campground number 29).

29 Middle Santa Ynez

Location: On the Santa Ynez River in Los Padres National Forest; map H3, grid h7.

Campsites, facilities: There are nine tent sites. Fire grills and picnic tables are provided. Vault toilets are available. There's no piped water. Leashed pets are permitted.

Reservations, fees: No reservations; no camping fee. An Adventure Pass ($30 annual fee) or $5 daily pass per parked vehicle is required. Open year-round, weather permitting.

Contact: Los Padres National Forest, Santa Barbara Ranger District, (805) 967-3481 or fax (805) 967-7312.

Directions: From US 101 in Santa Barbara, drive eight miles north on Highway 154. Turn right on East Camino Cielo/Forest Service Road 5N12 and drive 18 miles to the end of the paved road at Camuesa Road/Forest Service Road 5N15, which is a dirt road. Continue on Camuesa Road for five miles to Juncal Campground. Turn left and drive three miles to Middle Santa Ynez.

Trip notes: There are four camps bordering the Santa Ynez River between Gibraltar Reservoir to the west and little Jameson Lake to the east. Look 'em over and pick the one you like best. This one is set at an elevation 1,500 feet, about a half mile east of P-Bar Flat (campground number 22); see the trip notes for a trailhead there.

㉚ Holiday Group Camp

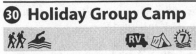

Location: On Matilija Creek in Los Padres National Forest; map H3, grid h9.

Campsites, facilities: There are eight sites for tents or RVs up to 22 feet long. Piped water, fire grills, and picnic tables are provided. Vault toilets are available. Leashed pets are permitted.

Reservations, fees: Reservations are required; reserve via phone at (877) 444-6777 ($8.65 reservation fee) or website www.reserveusa.com; $40 group fee per night. Open April through November.

Contact: Los Padres National Forest, Ojai Ranger District, (805) 646-4348 or fax (805) 646-0484.

Directions: From Ojai, drive nine miles northwest on Highway 33 to the campground entrance on the right.

Trip notes: This group site, set at 2,000 feet, is very near the North Fork of the Matilija. It's only three miles uphill from Matilija Reservoir. Note that Matilija Hot Springs are located downstream of the reservoir's dam.

㉛ Wheeler Gorge

Location: On Matilija Creek in Los Padres National Forest; map H3, grid h9.

Campsites, facilities: There are 73 sites for tents or RVs up to 16 feet long. Piped water, fire grills, and picnic tables are provided. Pit toilets are available. Leashed pets are permitted.

Reservations, fees: Reserve via phone at (877) 444-6777 ($8.65 reservation fee) or website www.reserveusa.com; $12 per night. Open year-round.

Contact: Los Padres National Forest, Ojai Ranger District, (805) 646-4348 or fax (805) 646-0484.

Directions: From Ojai, drive 8.5 miles north-west on Highway 33 to the campground on the right.

Trip notes: This developed Forest Service camp is set at 2,000 feet and is one of the more popular spots in the area. The North Fork of the Matilija runs beside the camp and provides some fair trout fishing in the spring and good swimming holes in early summer. Nearby Matilija Reservoir, three miles downhill, provides a side trip option.

㉜ Carpinteria State Beach

Location: Near Santa Barbara; map H3, grid i6.

Campsites, facilities: There are 85 sites for tents, 60 sites for RVs up to 21 feet long, and 40 sites for RVs up to 35 feet long. There are also two group sites, accommodating 40 or 65 campers, respectively. Piped water, fire grills, picnic tables, and in some cases, full hookups are provided. Flush toilets and coin-operated showers are available. A grocery store, coin laundry, and propane gas are nearby. Some areas are wheelchair accessible. Leashed pets are permitted, except on the beach.

Reservations, fees: Reserve via phone at (800) 444-PARK/7275 ($7.50 reservation fee) or website www.cal-parks.ca.gov; $17 to $29 per night; call for group site fees. Open year-round.

Contact: Carpinteria State Beach, (805) 684-2811; Channel Coast State Park District Office, (805) 899-1400.

Directions: From Santa Barbara, drive 10 miles south on US 101 to the Casitas Pass exit. Turn right on Casitas Pass Avenue and drive about a block to Carpinteria Avenue. Turn right and drive about three blocks to Palm Avenue. Turn left and drive less than a mile to the campground at the end of Palm Avenue.

Trip notes: First, plan on reservations, and then, plan on plenty of neighbors. This state beach is one pretty spot, and a lot of folks cruising up the coast like the idea of taking off their cowboy boots here for awhile. Other state beaches to the nearby north are El Capitan State Beach and Refugio State Beach, both with campgrounds.

㉝ Rincon Parkway

Location: On the Pacific Ocean north of Ventura; map H3, grid i7.

Campsites, facilities: There are 112 RV sites for self-contained vehicles up to 34 feet long. A sanitary disposal and supplies are available nearby. Leashed pets are allowed.

Reservations, fees: No reservations; $13 to $16 per night, $1 pet fee. Open year-round.

Contact: Ventura County Parks Department, (805) 654-3951.

Directions: From Ventura, drive six miles northwest on US 101 to the State Beaches exit. Turn north on West Pacific Highway and drive 4.5 miles to the campground.

Trip notes: This is basically an RV park located near the ocean. Emma Wood State Beach, San Buenaventura State Beach, and McGrath State Beach are all within 10 miles.

㉞ Hobson County Park

Location: On the Pacific Ocean north of Ventura; map H3, grid i7.

Campsites, facilities: There are 31 sites for tents or RVs up to 34 feet long. Piped water, fire grills, and picnic tables are provided. Flush toilets, coin-operated showers, and a snack bar are available. Leashed pets are permitted.

Reservations, fees: Reservations are accepted; $17 to $20 per night, $1 pet fee. Open year-round.

Contact: Ventura County Parks Department, (805) 654-3951.

Directions: From Ventura, drive six miles northwest on US 101 to the State Beaches exit. Turn north on West Pacific Highway and drive five miles to the campground.

Trip notes: This county park is located at the end of Rincon Parkway with easy access to the beach and offers many side trip possibilities. Emma Wood State Beach, San Buenaventura State Beach, and McGrath State Beach are all within 11 miles of the park.

㉟ Faria County Park

Location: On the Pacific Ocean north of Ventura; map H3, grid i7.

Campsites, facilities: There are 42 sites for tents or RVs up to 34 feet long. Piped water, fire grills, and picnic tables are provided. Flush toilets, playground, coin-operated showers, and a snack bar are available. Pets are permitted.

Reservations, fees: Reservations are accepted; $17 to $20 per night, $1 pet fee. Open year-round.

Contact: Ventura County Parks Department, (805) 654-3951.

Directions: From Ventura, drive six miles north on US 101 to the State Beaches exit. Turn north on West Pacific Highway and drive four miles to the campground.

Trip notes: This county park provides a possible base of operations for beach adventures. It is set along the ocean, with Emma Wood State Beach, San Buenaventura State Beach, and McGrath State Beach all within 10 miles of the park.

㊱ Lake Casitas Recreation Area

Location: North of Ventura; map H3, grid i8.

Campsites, facilities: There are 400 sites for tents or RVs up to 50 feet long, 150 with partial hookups and 14 with full hookups. Piped water, fire grills, and picnic tables are provided. Flush toilets, showers, two dump stations, seven playgrounds, grocery store, propane gas, ice, snack bar, water playground for children 12 and under, and a full-service marina (including boat ramps, boat rentals, slips, fuel, tackle, and bait) are available. Leashed pets are permitted.

Reservations, fees: Reservations should be made at least 14 days in advance and must be made 72 hours before arrival; reserve via phone at (805) 649-1122; $14 to $39 per night, $2 pet fee. Open year-round.

Contact: Lake Casitas Recreation Area, (805) 649-2233.

Directions: From Ventura, drive 11 miles north on Highway 33. Turn west on Highway 150 and drive about four miles to the campground entrance at 11311 Santa Ana Road.

Trip notes: Lake Casitas is known as Southern California's world-class fish factory, with more 10-pound bass produced here than anywhere, including the former state record, a bass that weighed 21 pounds, three ounces. The ideal climate in the foothill country (560 feet elevation) gives the fish a nine-month growing season, as well as providing excellent weather for camping. Casitas is located north of Ventura at an elevation of 285 feet in the foothills bordering Los Padres National Forest. The lake has 32 miles of shoreline with a huge number of sheltered coves, covering 2,700 acres. The lake is managed primarily for anglers. Waterskiing, jet skiing, and swimming are not permitted, and only boats between 11 and 24 feet are allowed on the lake.

37 Camp Comfort Park

Location: On San Antonio Creek; map H3, grid i9.

Campsites, facilities: There are 43 sites for tents or RVs up to 34 feet long. Fire grills, picnic tables, and in some cases, electrical connections are provided. Piped water, flush toilets, showers, and a playground are available. Supplies and a coin laundry are nearby. Leashed pets are permitted.

Reservations, fees: Reservations are accepted; $10 to $12 per night, plus $3 for a second vehicle, $1 pet fee.

Contact: Camp Comfort Park, (805) 646-2314.

Directions: From Ventura, take Highway 33 north to Highway 150. Turn west on Highway 150 and drive three miles to Creek Road. Turn right and drive one mile to the park.

Trip notes: This park gets missed by many. It's set in a residential area in the foothill country at 1,000 feet along San Antonio Creek in the Ojai Valley. Lake Casitas Recreation Area is 10 miles away.

38 Ventura River Camp

Location: On the Pacific Ocean near Ventura; map H3, grid j8.

Campsites, facilities: There are 61 sites including group areas for tents or RVs up to 40 feet long. Chemical toilets are available. There's no piped water. All conveniences are within a mile of the camp. Leashed pets are permitted.

Reservations, fees: Reservations are accepted for groups; $14 to $18 per night, $1 pet fee. Open year-round.

Contact: Channel Coast State Park District, (805) 654-4610 or (805) 899-1400.

Directions: From Ventura, drive three miles northwest on US 101 to the State Beaches exit. Drive under the freeway, making a left into the park.

Trip notes: This is an extremely popular state park, but you'd expect that with beachfront sites within such close driving range of Highway 101. Right? Right. Reservations? You'd better believe it. Day trips to the Channel Islands out of nearby Ventura Harbor provide a great adventure.

39 Emma Wood State Beach Group Camp

Location: On the Pacific Ocean north of Ventura; map H3, grid j8.

Campsites, facilities: There are four group sites for tents that can accommodate groups of 30 to 50 people. There are some additional sites for hikers and bicyclists. Picnic tables and fire grills are provided. Piped water, pit toilets, and cold showers are available. Supplies and a coin laundry are nearby. Leashed pets are permitted.

Reservations, fees: Reserve via phone at (800) 444-PARK/7275 ($7.50 reservation fee) or website www.cal-parks.ca.gov; $48 to $78 per night for group sites, $6 for hike-in/bike-in sites. Open year-round.

Contact: Emma Wood State Beach Group Camp, (805) 643-7532 or (805) 899-1400.

Directions: From Ventura drive two miles

north on US 101 to the California Street exit. Turn right and drive to Main Street. Turn left and drive 1.5 miles to the campground on the left.

Trip notes: This is more of a camping "area" than a campground with individual sites. And oh, what a place to camp: It is set along the ocean, a pretty spot with tide pools full of all kinds of little marine critters waiting to be discovered. It is also just a short drive from the town of Ventura and the Mission San Buenaventura. Reservations are a necessity.

Map H4

One inch equals approximately 10.7 miles.
See inside back cover for California state map.

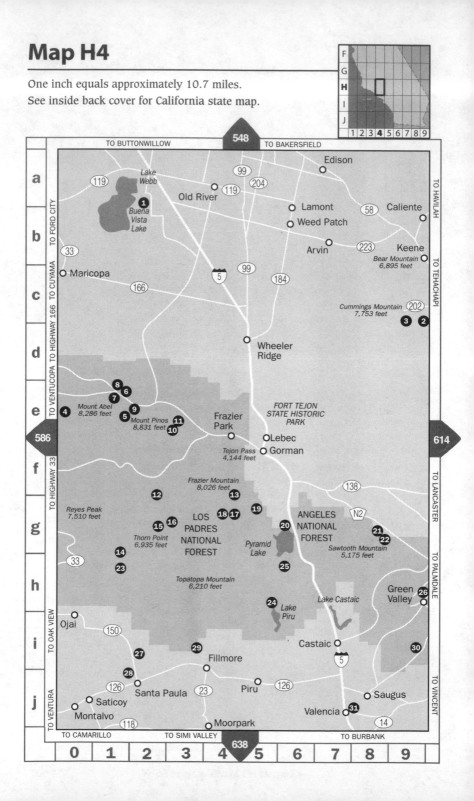

Chapter H4 features:

1 Buena Vista Aquatic Recreation Area

Location: Near Bakersfield; map H4, grid a2.

Campsites, facilities: There are 112 sites for tents or RVs, many with full hookups. Picnic tables and fire rings are provided. Rest rooms, showers, playground, three boat ramps, store, dump station, and propane gas are available. Leashed pets are permitted.

Reservations, fees: Reservations are accepted; phone (800) 950-7275; $18 to $26 per night, $3 pet fee. Open year-round.

Contact: Buena Vista Aquatic Recreation Area, (661) 763-1526.

Directions: From Interstate 5 near Bakersfield, drive two miles west on Highway 119. Turn south on Highway 43 and drive two miles to the campground at road's end.

Trip notes: Buena Vista is actually two connected lakes fed by the West Side Canal, little Lake Evans to the west and larger Lake Webb to the east. Be certain to know the difference between the two: Lake Webb (875 acres) is open to all boating except jet skis and similar personal watercraft, and fast boats towing skiers is a common, happy sight. Lake Evans (85 acres) is small, quiet, and has a strictly enforced 5 mph speed limit, an ideal lake for family water play and fishing. The elevation is 330 feet on the outskirts of Bakersfield.

2 Indian Hill Ranch Campground

Location: Near Tehachapi; map H4, grid c9.

Campsites, facilities: There are 225 sites for tents or RVs, 46 with full hookups and some with water and electric connections. Picnic tables and fire pits are provided. Flush toilets, showers, dump station, and five stocked fishing ponds are available (no fishing license is required). Leashed pets are permitted.

Reservations, fees: Reservations are accepted; $12 to $17 per night. Open year-round.

Contact: Indian Hill Ranch Campground, (661) 822-6613 or (800) 882-6613.

Directions: From Highway 58 near Tehachapi, take the Highway 202 exit. Head west on Highway 202 for 3.5 miles to Banducci Road. Turn left and drive a mile to Indian Hill/Arosa Road. Turn left and drive 1.5 miles to the campground.

Trip notes: This is a unique park with five ponds, all stocked with trout and catfish. The campground is open year-round and offers spacious, private sites with oak trees and a view of Brite Valley. The elevation is 5,000 feet.

❸ Brite Valley Aquatic Recreation Area

⚓ 🎣 🏃🏻‍♂️ 🏊🏻‍♀️ ♿ 🚐 🏕️ ⑦

Location: At Brite Lake; map H4, grid c9.

Campsites, facilities: There are 12 RV sites with water and electric connections, as well as several designated tent sites without hookups. Fire pits and picnic tables are provided. Rest rooms, showers, dump station, playground, three pavilions with electricity and tables, and a fish cleaning station are available. Supplies are available about eight miles away in Tehachapi. Leashed pets are permitted.

Reservations, fees: No reservations; $9 to $12 per night. Open late April to late October.

Contact: Brite Valley Aquatic Recreation Area, (661) 822-3228.

Directions: From Highway 58 near Tehachapi, take the Highway 202 exit. Head west on Highway 202 for 3.5 miles to Banducci Road. Turn left on Banducci Road and follow the signs for about a mile to the park on the right.

Trip notes: Brite Valley Lake is a speck of a water hole (90 acres) on the northern flanks of the Tehachapi Mountains, at an elevation of 4,000 feet. No gas motors are permitted on the lake, so it's perfect for canoes, kayaks, or inflatables. That makes the campground and lake ideal for a family camping experience. Fishing is fair for trout in the spring, catfish in the summer.

❹ Nettle Spring

🏃🏻‍♂️ 🚐 🏕️ ④

Location: In Los Padres National Forest; map H4, grid e0.

Campsites, facilities: There are nine sites for tents only and four sites for tents or RVs up to 22 feet long. Fire rings and picnic tables are provided. Vault toilets are available. There is no piped water. Leashed pets are permitted.

Reservations, fees: No reservations; no camping fee. An Adventure Pass ($30 annual fee) or $5 daily fee per parked vehicle is required. Open year-round.

Contact: Los Padres National Forest, Mount Piños Ranger District, (661) 245-3731 or fax (661) 245-1526.

Directions: From Maricopa, drive 14 miles south on Highway 166 to the Highway 33 exit. Turn south on Highway 33 and drive about 13 miles to Apache Canyon Road. Turn left and drive about 10 miles to the campground.

Trip notes: This remote camp is set near the end of a remain road in Apache Canyon. A mile east of camp, via the access road, is a primitive trailhead on the left side. This trail is routed four miles to Mesa Springs and a trail camp. The elevation is 4,400 feet.

❺ Campo Alto

🏃🏻‍♂️ 5% 🚐 🏕️ ⑥

Location: In Los Padres National Forest; map H4, grid e1.

Campsites, facilities: There are 17 sites for tents or RVs up to 22 feet long. Fire rings and picnic tables are provided. Vault toilets are available, but there is no piped water. Leashed pets are permitted.

Reservations, fees: No reservations; no camping fee. An Adventure Pass ($30 annual fee) or $5 daily fee per parked vehicle is required. Open May through October.

Contact: Los Padres National Forest, Mount Piños Ranger District, (661) 245-3731 or fax (661) 245-1526.

Directions: From Interstate 5, take the Frazier Park exit (just south of Lebec) and drive west on Lockwood Valley Road to the town of Lake of the Woods. Turn right on Cuddy Valley Road and go 15 miles west (it becomes Mil Potrero Highway). Turn south on Cerro Noroeste Road and drive nine miles to the campground.

Trip notes: Campo Alto means "High Camp," and you'll find that the name fits when you visit here. The camp is set high (8,200 feet) on Cerro Noroeste/Mount Abel in Los Padres National Forest. Don't show up thirsty, as there's no piped water. About half a mile from camp there is a trailhead on the southeast side of the road. From here, you can hike two miles to Grouse Mountain, and in another mile, reach remote, hike-in Sheep Camp.

❻ Marian

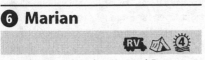

Location: In Los Padres National Forest; map H4, grid e1.

Campsites, facilities: There are seven sites for tents or RVs up to 16 feet long. Fire grills and picnic tables are provided and vault toilets are available. There is no piped water. Leashed pets are permitted.

Reservations, fees: No reservations; no camping fee. An Adventure Pass ($30 annual fee) or $5 daily fee per parked vehicle is required. Open May through October.

Contact: Los Padres National Forest, Mount Piños Ranger District, (661) 245-3731 or fax (661) 245-1526.

Directions: From Interstate 5, take the Frazier Park exit (just south of Lebec) and drive west on Lockwood Valley Road to the town of Lake of the Woods. Turn right on Cuddy Valley Road and continue 15.5 miles west on Cuddy Valley Road (which becomes Mil Potrero Highway) to the campground entrance. Proceed up the dirt entrance road one mile past the Caballo Campground to this camp.

Trip notes: Marian is extremely primitive, set on the outskirts of Los Padres National Forest at 6,600 feet in elevation, between Brush Mountain to the immediate northwest and San Emigdio Mountain to the immediate southeast. A primitive route out of camp leads three miles to the San Emigdio summit, 7,495 feet in elevation. A network of Forest Service roads provides access to a number of other camps in the area, as well as Mount Abel (8,250 feet) and Mount Piños (8,831 feet). If the access gate is locked, reaching this camp requires a two-mile hike; nearby Toad Spring (campground number seven) and Caballo (campground number eight) are smaller, but more easily accessible and better developed camps.

❼ Toad Spring

Location: In Los Padres National Forest; map

H4, grid e1.

Campsites, facilities: There are four sites for tents only and three sites for tents or RVs up to 16 feet long. Fire rings and picnic tables are provided and vault toilets are available. There is no piped water. Leashed pets are permitted.

Reservations, fees: No reservations; no camping fee. An Adventure Pass ($30 annual fee) or $5 daily fee per parked vehicle is required. Open May through October.

Contact: Los Padres National Forest, Mount Piños Ranger District, (661) 245-3731 or fax (661) 245-1526.

Directions: From Interstate 5, take the Frazier Park exit (just south of Lebec) and drive west on Lockwood Valley Road to the town of Lake of the Woods. Turn right on Cuddy Valley Road and continue 15.5 miles west on Cuddy Valley Road (which becomes Mil Potrero Highway) to the campground entrance.

Trip notes: Toad Spring is set at 5,700 feet near Apache Saddle, on the northwest flank of Mount Abel (8,250 feet). A primitive trail leads south out of camp and is routed four miles to a junction. From there it turns left (east) and takes you two miles to Mesa Springs and a trail camp.

❽ Caballo

Location: In Los Padres National Forest; map H4, grid e1.

Campsites, facilities: There are six sites for tents or RVs up to 16 feet long. Fire rings and picnic tables are provided. Vault toilets are available. There is no piped water. Leashed pets are permitted.

Reservations, fees: No reservations; no camping fee. An Adventure Pass ($30 annual fee) or $5 daily fee per parked vehicle is required. Open May through October.

Contact: Los Padres National Forest, Mount Piños Ranger District, (661) 245-3731 or fax (661) 245-1526.

Directions: From Interstate 5, take the Frazier Park exit (just south of Lebec) and drive west on Lockwood Valley Road to the town of Lake of the Woods. Turn right on Cuddy Valley Road and continue 15.5 miles west on Cuddy Valley Road (which becomes Mil Potrero Highway) to the campground entrance on the right.

Trip notes: Caballo is set at 5,800 feet on a small creek that is the headwaters for Santiago Creek, on the northern flank of Mount Abel. It is one of several primitive camps in the immediate area—a take-your-pick offer. But it's an offer not many folks even know about.

⑨ Mil Potrero Park

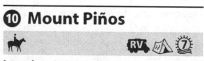

Location: Near Mount Piños; map H4, grid e2.

Campsites, facilities: There are 43 sites for tents or RVs. Fire rings and picnic tables are provided. Piped water, flush toilets, showers, and horse corrals are available. Leashed pets are permitted.

Reservations, fees: Reservations are required; $15 per night.

Contact: Mil Potrero Park, (661) 763-4246.

Directions: From Interstate 5, take the Frazier Park exit (just south of Lebec) and drive 6.5 miles on Frazier Mountain Park Road. Bear right on Cuddy Valley Road and drive five miles to Mil Potrero Highway. Turn right and drive 5.5 miles to Pine Mountain Village Center. Continue 1.3 miles to the park entrance on the left.

Trip notes: This is one of the rare RV parks that provides equal billing for tents. It is set at 5,300 feet, with national forest generally surrounding the area. Nearby side trips worth noting are to the Big Trees of Pleito Canyon, and also the drive on Forest Service roads to the summit of Frazier Mountain at 8,013 feet, where there is a lookout with drop-dead gorgeous 360-degree views.

⑩ Mount Piños

Location: In Los Padres National Forest; map H4, grid e3.

Campsites, facilities: There are 19 sites for tents or RVs up to 16 feet long. Piped water, fire grills, and picnic tables are provided. Vault toilets and horseback riding facilities are available. Leashed pets are permitted. A note of caution: the water wells have been known to run dry in

the summer, so bring your own water during the summer months.

Reservations, fees: No reservations; $8 per night. Open June through September.

Contact: Los Padres National Forest, Mount Piños Ranger District, (661) 245-3731 or fax (661) 245-1526.

Directions: From Interstate 5, take the Frazier Park exit (just south of Lebec) and drive west on Lockwood Valley Road to the town of Lake of the Woods. Turn right on Cuddy Valley Road and drive about seven miles. Turn left on Mount Piños Road and drive about six miles to the campground.

Trip notes: This camp is set at 7,800 feet, one of three camps on the eastern flank of Mount Piños (8,831 feet). It is a raptor breeding area, so if you run out of food, don't be surprised if the birds start circling overhead, eyeing you. A road to the top of Mount Piños for beautiful and sweeping views is available about two miles west. McGill (campground number 11) provides a nearby camping alternative.

⑪ McGill

Location: Near Mount Piños in Los Padres National Forest; map H4, grid e3.

Campsites, facilities: There are 73 family sites and two group sites for tents or RVs up to 16 feet long. Piped water, fire grills, and picnic tables are provided. Vault toilets are available. Leashed pets are permitted. A note of caution: the water wells have been known to run dry in the summer, so bring your own water during the summer months.

Reservations, fees: Reservations are required for group sites; reserve via phone at (877) 444-6777 ($8.65 group reservation fee); $8 per night for family sites, $50 to $65 for a group site. Open June through September.

Contact: Los Padres National Forest, Mount Piños Ranger District, (661) 245-3731 or fax (661) 245-1526.

Directions: From Interstate 5, take the Frazier Park exit (just south of Lebec) and drive west on Lockwood Valley Road to the town of Lake of the Woods. Turn right on Cuddy Valley Road and drive about seven miles. Turn left on Mount Piños Road and drive about six miles to the campground.

Trip notes: If you wanted a great panoramic lookout, you came to the right place. The camp is set at 7,400 feet, less than two miles by car from the top of nearby Mount Piños. A spectacular 360-degree view is available here, including a vantage point on clear days of the high Sierra, the San Joaquin Valley, the Channel Islands, and Antelope Valley. Frazier Mountain Park, which is about seven miles from camp, provides a nearby side trip.

⑫ Pine Spring

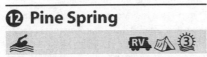

Location: Near San Guillermo Mountain in Los Padres National Forest; map H4, grid f2.

Campsites, facilities: There are eight sites for tents or RVs up to 22 feet long. Fire grills and picnic tables are provided. Vault toilets are available. There is no piped water. Leashed pets are permitted.

Reservations, fees: No reservations; no camping fee. An Adventure Pass ($30 annual fee) or $5 daily fee per parked vehicle is required. Open May through September.

Contact: Los Padres National Forest, Mount Piños Ranger District, (661) 245-3731 or fax (661) 245-1526.

Directions: From Interstate 5, take the Frazier Park exit (just south of Lebec) and drive west on Lockwood Valley Road to the town of Lake of the Woods. Continue southwest on Lockwood Valley Road (take the left fork) and drive about 12 miles to the campground entrance road on your left.

Trip notes: This primitive camp is set at 5,800 feet in elevation on a short spur road that deadends on the east flank of San Guillermo Mountain (6,600 feet). Pine Spring feeds the tiny headwaters of Guillermo Creek at this spot.

⑬ King's Camp

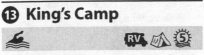

Location: Near Piru Creek in Los Padres National Forest; map H4, grid f4.

Campsites, facilities: There are three sites for tents only and four sites for tents or RVs up to 16 feet long. Fire grills and picnic tables are provided. Vault toilets are available. There is no piped water. Leashed pets are permitted.

Reservations, fees: No reservations; no camping fee. An Adventure Pass ($30 annual fee) or $5 daily fee per parked vehicle is required.

Contact: Los Padres National Forest, Mount Piños Ranger District, (661) 245-3731 or fax (661) 245-1526.

Directions: From Interstate 5, south of Gorman take the Gorman–Hungry Valley Road exit and drive 13 miles south on Hungry Valley Road/Forest Service Road 8N01 to the campground.

Trip notes: The Hungry Valley State Vehicular Recreation Area is located just five miles to the east. Figure it out: right, this is a primitive but well-placed camp for four-wheel-drive and off-road vehicles. The camp is near Piru Creek, off a short spur road, so it feels remote yet is close to one of California's top off-road areas. Note that this camp is subject to closure. Call before planning a trip.

⑭ Lions Canyon

Location: On Sespe Creek in Los Padres National Forest; map H4, grid g1.

Campsites, facilities: There are 22 sites for tents or RVs up to 16 feet long. Piped water, fire grills, and picnic tables are provided. Vault toilets and horseback riding facilities are available. Leashed pets are permitted.

Reservations, fees: No reservations; no camping fee; an Adventure Pass ($30 annual fee) or $5 daily fee per parked vehicle is required. Open April through November.

Contact: Los Padres National Forest, Ojai Ranger District, (805) 646-4348 or fax (805) 646-0484.

Directions: From Ojai, drive about 15 miles north on Highway 33. Turn right on Rose Valley Road and drive seven miles to the campground.

Trip notes: Lions Canyon is a pretty spot beside Sespe Creek, at an elevation of 3,000 feet in the southern end of Los Padres National Forest. Note that the camp's access road, Forest Service

Road 6N31, continues east and dead-ends at a great trailhead. From here you can hike along Sespe Creek, with the trail extending all the way (about six miles) to Willett Hot Springs at Sycamore Flat.

⑮ Thorn Meadows

Location: On Piru Creek in Los Padres National Forest; map H4, grid g2.

Campsites, facilities: There are five sites for tents or RVs up to 16 feet long. Fire grills and picnic tables are provided. There is no piped water. Vault toilets are available. Leashed pets are permitted.

Reservations, fees: No reservations; no camping fee. An Adventure Pass ($30 annual fee) or $5 daily fee per parked vehicle is required. Open May through September.

Contact: Los Padres National Forest, Mount Piños Ranger District, (661) 245-3731 or fax (661) 245-1526.

Directions: From Interstate 5, take the Frazier Park exit (just south of Lebec) and drive west on Lockwood Valley Road to the town of Lake of the Woods. Continue southwest on Lockwood Valley Road (take the left fork) and drive about 12 miles. Turn left on Mutau Flat Road/Forest Service Road 7N03 and drive seven miles to the campground entrance on your right.

Trip notes: The reward at Thorn Meadows is a small, quiet spot along Piru Creek at 5,000 feet, deep in Los Padres National Forest. A trail out of camp leads three miles up to Thorn Point, a magnificent 6,935-foot lookout. It is by far the best view in the area, worth the 2,000-foot climb.

⑯ Half Moon

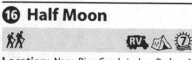

Location: Near Piru Creek in Los Padres National Forest; map H4, grid g3.

Campsites, facilities: There are 10 sites for tents or RVs up to 22 feet long. Fire rings and picnic tables are provided. Vault toilets are available. There is no piped water. Leashed pets are permitted.

Reservations, fees: No reservations; no camping fee. An Adventure Pass ($30 annual fee) or $5 daily fee per parked vehicle is required. Open May through October.

Contact: Los Padres National Forest, Mount Piños Ranger District, (661) 245-3731 or fax (661) 245-1526.

Directions: From Interstate 5, take the Frazier Park exit (just south of Lebec) and drive west on Lockwood Valley Road to the town of Lake of the Woods. Continue southwest on Lockwood Valley Road (take the left fork) and drive about 12 miles. Turn left on Mutau Flat Road/Forest Service Road 7N03 and drive eight miles to the campground entrance on your left.

Trip notes: Half Moon is a primitive camp set along Piru Creek at 4,700 feet. Adjacent to camp, Forest Service Road 7N13 follows the creek for a few miles, then dead-ends at a trailhead that continues along more remote stretches of this little stream. Hikers should also consider hiking to nearby Thorn Point for a beautiful lookout; see the trip notes for Thorn Meadows (campground number 15) for more information.

⑰ Twin Pines

Location: On Alamo Mountain in Los Padres National Forest; map H4, grid g4.

Campsites, facilities: There are five tent sites. Fire rings and picnic tables are provided. Vault toilets are available, but there is no piped water. Leashed pets are permitted.

Reservations, fees: No reservations; no camping fee. An Adventure Pass ($30 annual fee) or $5 daily fee per parked vehicle is required. Open May through October.

Contact: Los Padres National Forest, Mount Piños Ranger District, (661) 245-3731 or fax (661) 245-1526.

Directions: From Interstate 5 south of Gorman, take the Gorman–Hungry Valley Road exit (the northern exit for the Hungry Valley Recreation Area). Drive about 21 miles south on Hungry Valley Road/Forest Service Road 8N01, which becomes Alamo Mountain Road (a rough, dirt road). This road leads to the campground.

Trip notes: Twin Pines Camp is set at 6,600 feet on Alamo Mountain, a small, remote, and primitive spot. It is known best by four-wheel-drive cowboys rumbling around the area. The access road is remarkably twisty and often rough, to be avoided by most, but it is exactly what a modern-day cowboy yearns for. This camp provides an alternative to the Hungry Valley State Vehicular Recreation Area to the nearby northeast.

⑱ Dutchman

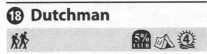

Location: On Alamo Mountain in Los Padres National Forest; map H4, grid g4.

Campsites, facilities: There are 10 sites for primitive camping. Fire grills are available, but there is no piped water. Leashed pets are permitted.

Reservations, fees: No reservations; no camping fee. An Adventure Pass ($30 annual fee) or $5 daily fee per parked vehicle is required. Open May through September.

Contact: Los Padres National Forest, Mount Piños Ranger District, (661) 245-3731 or fax (661) 245-1526.

Directions: From Interstate 5 south of Gorman, take the Gorman–Hungry Valley Road exit (the northern exit for the Hungry Valley Recreation Area). Drive about 23 miles south on Hungry Valley Road/Forest Service Road 8N01, which becomes Alamo Mountain Road (a rough, dirt road); this road leads to the campground.

Trip notes: Dutchman is a do-it-yourself camp, set near the top of Alamo Mountain at 6,800 feet. Nearby camping options are Cottonwood (campground number 26) and Twin Pines (campground number 17). Anybody venturing into this area is strongly advised to have a map of Los Padres National Forest.

⑲ Hard Luck

Location: On the Smith Fork of Piru Creek in Los Padres National Forest; map H4, grid g5.

Campsites, facilities: There are eight sites for tents or RVs up to 22 feet long. Fire grills and picnic tables are provided. Vault toilets are available. There is no piped water. Leashed pets are permitted.

Reservations, fees: No reservations; no

camping fee. An Adventure Pass ($30 annual fee) or $5 daily fee per parked vehicle is required. Open April through October.

Contact: Los Padres National Forest, Mount Piños Ranger District, (661) 245-3731 or fax (661) 245-1526.

Directions: From Interstate 5 south of Gorman, take the Gorman–Hungry Valley Road exit (the northern exit for the Hungry Valley Recreation Area). Drive about 10 miles south on Hungry Valley Road/Forest Service Road 8N01. Turn left on Canada de los Alamos and drive three miles to the campground entrance on your right. Turn right and drive three miles to the campground.

Trip notes: This camp is popular with dirt bikers, but there is no longer direct access to Hungry Valley State Vehicular Recreation Area from the campground. It is a primitive Forest Service camp set on the Smith Fork of Piru Creek at an elevation of 2,800 feet. Reaching Pyramid Lake to the southeast takes about 15 minutes.

⑳ Los Alamos

Location: Near Pyramid Lake in Angeles National Forest; map H4, grid g6.

Campsites, facilities: There are 93 family sites and several group sites for tents or RVs. Piped water, fire pits, flush toilets, and picnic tables are provided. A boat ramp is at the Emigrant Landing Picnic Area. Leashed pets are permitted.

Reservations, fees: For group reservations and fees, phone (805) 248-6575; no camping fee for family sites; an Adventure Pass ($30 annual fee) or $5 daily fee per parked vehicle is required. Open April through October.

Contact: Angeles National Forest, Saugus Ranger District, (661) 296-9710 or fax (661) 296-5847.

Directions: From Gorman, drive eight miles south on Interstate 5. Take the Smokey Bear Road exit. Drive west about three-quarters of a mile and follow the signs to the campground.

Trip notes: Los Alamos is set at an elevation of 2,600 feet near the southern border of the Hungry Valley State Vehicular Recreation Area and about 2.5 miles north of Pyramid Lake. Pyramid Lake is a big lake, covering 1,300 acres with 20 miles of shoreline, and is extremely popular for waterskiing and fast boating, as well as for windsurfing (best at the northern launch point), fishing (best in the spring and early summer and in the fall for striped bass), and swimming (best at boat-in picnic sites).

㉑ Sawmill

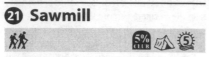

Location: On the Pacific Crest Trail in Angeles National Forest; map H4, grid g8.

Campsites, facilities: There are eight tent sites. Picnic tables, fire pits, and vault toilets are provided. There is no piped water. Leashed pets are permitted.

Reservations, fees: No reservations; no camping fee. An Adventure Pass ($30 annual fee) or $5 daily pass per parked vehicle is required. Open May through October, weather permitting.

Contact: Angeles National Forest, Saugus Ranger District, (661) 296-9710 or fax (661) 296-5847.

Directions: From Castaic, turn northeast on Lake Hughes Road and drive 27 miles to the town of Lake Hughes. Turn left on Pine Canyon Road and drive 10 miles to Bushnell Summit Road. Turn left and drive two miles to the campground on the left.

Trip notes: This is a classic hiker's trailhead camp. It is set at 5,200 feet, right on the Pacific Crest Trail and just one mile from the junction with the Burnt Peak Canyon Trail. For a good day hike head southeast on the Pacific Crest Trail for one mile to the Burnt Peak Canyon Trail, turn right (southwest), and hike just over a mile to Burnt Peak, elevation 5,788 feet. Note that this camp is inaccessible after the first snow. Nearby Upper Shake (campground number 22) provides an alternative.

㉒ Upper Shake

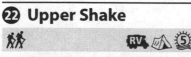

Location: Near the Pacific Crest Trail in Angeles National Forest; map H4, grid g8.

Campsites, facilities: There are 13 sites for tents or RVs up to 22 feet long. Fire pits, vault toilets and picnic tables are provided. There is

no piped water. Leashed pets are permitted.

Reservations, fees: No reservations; no camping fee. An Adventure Pass ($30 annual fee) or $5 daily fee per parked vehicle is required. Open May through October, weather permitting.

Contact: Angeles National Forest, Saugus Ranger District, (661) 296-9710 or fax (661) 296-5847.

Directions: From Castaic, turn northeast on Lake Hughes Road and drive 27 miles to the town of Lake Hughes. Turn left on County Road N2/Pine Canyon Road and drive about 5.5 miles to the entrance road on the left.

Trip notes: Upper Shake, like nearby Sawmill (campground number 21), is right on the Pacific Crest Trail. The elevation is 4,300 feet. Hikers who plan on heading to Burnt Peak are better off departing from Sawmill (less than two miles to the west). This camp, instead, is used primarily as a jump-off point for those heading east on the PCT; Lake Hughes is the nearest destination, less than four miles away, and a mile after that is Lake Elizabeth. The camp is inaccessible after the first snow.

㉓ Rose Valley

Location: In Los Padres National Forest; map H4, grid h1.

Campsites, facilities: There are nine sites for tents or RVs up to 16 feet long. Piped water, fire grills, and picnic tables are provided. Vault toilets and horseback riding facilities are available. Leashed pets are permitted.

Reservations, fees: No reservations; no camping fee. An Adventure Pass ($30 annual fee) or $5 daily pass per parked vehicle is required.

Contact: Los Padres National Forest, Ojai Ranger District, (805) 646-4348 or fax (805) 646-0484.

Directions: From Ojai, drive about 15 miles north on Highway 33. Turn right on Sespe River Road/Rose Valley Road and drive 5.5 miles to the campground entrance.

Trip notes: The short walk to Rose Valley Falls, a 300-foot waterfall that provides a happy surprise, makes this camp a sure-thing winner in late winter and spring. The walk to the waterfall is just a half-mile round-trip; note that there are two views of it, a long-distance view of the entire waterfall, and then at the base, a view of just the lower tier. It is one of the scenic highlights in this section of Los Padres National Forest. The camp is set at 3,400 feet next to Rose Valley Creek, about two miles from Sespe Creek.

24 Lake Piru Recreation Area

Location: On Lake Piru; map H4, grid h5.

Campsites, facilities: There are 235 sites for tents or RVs with electrical hookups. Five additional RV sites have full hookups. Fire pits and picnic tables are provided. Piped water, flush toilets, showers, dump station, snack bar, ice, bait, boat ramp, temporary mooring, boat fuel, motorboat rentals, and tackle are available. Leashed pets are permitted.

Reservations, fees: Reservations can be made Monday through Thursday from 8 A.M. to 4 P.M., seven days in advance; $16 to $22 per night, $1 pet fee. Open year-round.

Contact: Lake Piru Recreation Area, (805) 521-1500.

Directions: From Ventura, drive east on Highway 126 for about 30 miles to the Piru Canyon Road exit. Drive northeast on Piru Canyon Road for about six miles to the campground.

Trip notes: Things can get crazy at Lake Piru, but it's usually a happy crazy, not an insane crazy. This is a lake set up for waterskiing, with lots of fast boats. All others be forewarned: the rules prohibit boats under 12 feet and jet skis. The lake, shaped something like a teardrop, covers 1,200 acres when full and is set at an elevation of 1,055 feet. Bass fishing can be quite good in the spring before the water-skiers take over.

25 Oak Flat

Location: Near Pyramid Lake in Angeles National Forest; map H4, grid h6.

Campsites, facilities: There are 27 sites for tents or RVs up to 32 feet long. There is no piped water. Fire pits, vault toilets, and picnic tables

are provided. Leashed pets are permitted.

Reservations, fees: No reservations; no camping fee. An Adventure Pass ($30 annual fee) or $5 daily fee per parked vehicle is required. Open year-round.

Contact: Angeles National Forest, Saugus Ranger District, (661) 296-9710 or fax (661) 296-5847.

Directions: From Castaic, drive six miles north on Interstate 5. Turn left on Templin Highway, driving under the freeway, and continue northwest for three more miles to the campground.

Trip notes: Oak Flat is just a short drive from Pyramid Lake, at 2,800 feet near the southwestern border of Angeles National Forest. Pyramid is surrounded by national forest, quite beautiful, and is a favorite destination for folks with powerboats, especially those towing water-skiers. The lake covers 1,300 acres and has 20 miles of shoreline. Fishing for striped bass can be good in the spring and fall, but in summer warfare can practically break out between low-speed fishermen and high-speed skiers. For more information on Pyramid Lake, see the trip notes for Los Alamos (campground number 20).

26 Cottonwood

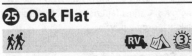

Location: Near the Warm Springs Mountain Lookout in Angeles National Forest; map H4, grid h9.

Campsites, facilities: There are 22 sites for tents or RVs up to 22 feet long. There is no piped water. Fire pits, vault toilets, and picnic tables are provided. Supplies are available less than four miles away in the town of Lake Hughes. Leashed pets are permitted.

Reservations, fees: No reservations; no camping fee. An Adventure Pass ($30 annual fee) or $5 daily fee per parked vehicle is required. Open year-round.

Contact: Angeles National Forest, Saugus Ranger District, (661) 296-9710 or fax (661) 296-5847.

Directions: From Castaic, turn northeast on Lake Hughes Road and drive 25 miles to the campground on the right.

Trip notes: Cottonwood Camp is set at 2,680

feet in remote Angeles National Forest along a small stream. The camp is located on the north flank of Warm Springs Mountain. A great side trip is to the Warm Springs Mountain Lookout (4,023 feet), about a five-mile drive. Drive south on Forest Service Road 7N09 for three miles, turn right (west) on Forest Service Road 6N32, and drive for 1.5 miles to Forest Service Road 7N13. Turn left (south) and drive a mile to the summit.

27 Steckel County Park

Location: On Santa Paula Creek; map H4, grid i2.

Campsites, facilities: There are 75 sites for tents or RVs. Fire pits and grills, picnic tables, and in most cases, electrical connections are provided. Piped water, flush toilets, dump station, and a playground are available. Some facilities are wheelchair accessible. Supplies and a coin laundry are nearby. Leashed pets are permitted.

Reservations, fees: Reservations are recommended; $12 per night for two people, $5 fee for additional campers 12 years of age or older, $1 to $3 for each additional child under 12, and $1 pet fee. Open year-round.

Contact: Steckel County Park, (805) 933-3200; Ventura County Parks Department, (805) 654-3951.

Directions: From Ventura, drive 14 miles east on Highway 126, turn northwest on Highway 150, and drive four miles to the park.

Trip notes: You either know about this spot or you don't. You either have this book or you don't. Other than the locals, few people are familiar with this park. It is a pretty spot set along little Santa Paula Creek in the foothill country.

28 Mountain View RV Park

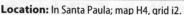

Location: In Santa Paula; map H4, grid i2.

Campsites, facilities: There are 31 sites for self-contained vehicles. Cable TV and a swim spa are available. A coin laundry, restaurant, and shopping center are nearby. Leashed pets are permitted.

Reservations, fees: Call for available space; $19 to $22 per night. Open year-round.

Contact: Mountain View RV Park, (805) 933-1942.

Directions: From Ventura, drive 11 miles east on Highway 126. Take the Peck Drive exit and drive a short distance to Harvard Boulevard. Turn right and drive to 714 West Harvard Boulevard.

Trip notes: The town of Santa Paula is known for its excellent weather and nearby recreation options. They include Steckel County Park, Los Padres National Forest, and the beaches at Ventura. Lake Casitas and Lake Cachuma, both known for big Florida bass, are within reasonable driving range.

29 Kenny Grove County Park

Location: Near Fillmore; map H4, grid i3.

Campsites, facilities: There are 17 sites for tents and 33 RV sites with partial hookups. Fire grills and picnic tables are provided. Piped water, flush toilets, and a playground are available. Supplies and a coin laundry are nearby. Leashed pets are permitted.

Reservations, fees: Reservations are accepted; $11 to $14 per night, $2 for a second vehicle, $1 pet fee.

Contact: Kenny Grove County Park, (805) 524-0750 or call the Ventura County Parks Department, (805) 654-3951.

Directions: From Ventura, drive 22 miles east on Highway 126. Take the Old Telegraph Road exit near the town of Fillmore and turn left. Drive to Seventh Street, turn right, and drive two miles to the park.

Trip notes: A lot of folks miss this spot, a county park tucked away among orchards and eucalyptus groves. It's just far enough off the highway to allow for some privacy.

30 Streamside

Location: On Bouquet Canyon Creek in Angeles National Forest; map H4, grid i9.

Campsites, facilities: There are nine tent sites. There is no piped water. Picnic tables, fire pits, and vault toilets are provided. Leashed pets are permitted.

Reservations, fees: No reservations; no camping fee. An Adventure Pass ($30 annual fee) or $5 daily fee per parked vehicle is required. Open April through September.

Contact: Angeles National Forest, Saugus Ranger District, (661) 296-9710 or fax (661) 296-5847.

Directions: From Castaic, drive six miles south on Interstate 5. Take the Magic Mountain Parkway exit and drive east to Valencia Boulevard. Turn left and drive about two miles to Bouquet Canyon Road. Turn north on Bouquet Canyon Road and drive about 14 miles to the campground on the left.

Trip notes: Streamside Camp is one of three Forest Service camps (Big Oak and Bouquet are the others) clustered along pretty Bouquet Canyon Creek at elevation 2,300 feet. This stream is typically stocked with trout twice a month in late spring and early summer. The creek and campgrounds are just downstream of Bouquet Reservoir, which provides stream flows in warm weather. Do not drink the water from Bouquet Canyon Creek under any circumstances.

Special note: This campground is subject to closure at any time. Definitely call prior to making your trip.

31 Valencia Travel Village

Location: In Valencia; map H4, grid j7.

Campsites, facilities: There are 280 RV sites with full hookups, plus 200 tent sites. A market and deli, three swimming pools, spa, lounge, billiards, video and games arcade, playground, shuffleboard, horseshoes, volleyball courts, laundry facilities, fire pits, propane, and a dump station are provided. Some facilities are wheelchair accessible.

Reservations, fees: Reservations are recommended; $20 to $25 per night. Weekly and monthly rates are available upon request. Open year-round.

Contact: Valencia Travel Village, 27946 Henry Mayo Road (Highway 126), Valencia, CA 91355; (661) 257-3333.

Directions: From Los Angeles, take Interstate 405 to Interstate 5, pass Magic Mountain Parkway, and exit at Highway 126. Turn left (north) and drive about one mile to the camp on the left.

Trip notes: This huge RV park is located in the scenic San Fernando foothills, just five minutes from Six Flags Magic Mountain. Lake Piru and Lake Castaic are only 15 minutes away. The camp was built on a 65-acre horse ranch.

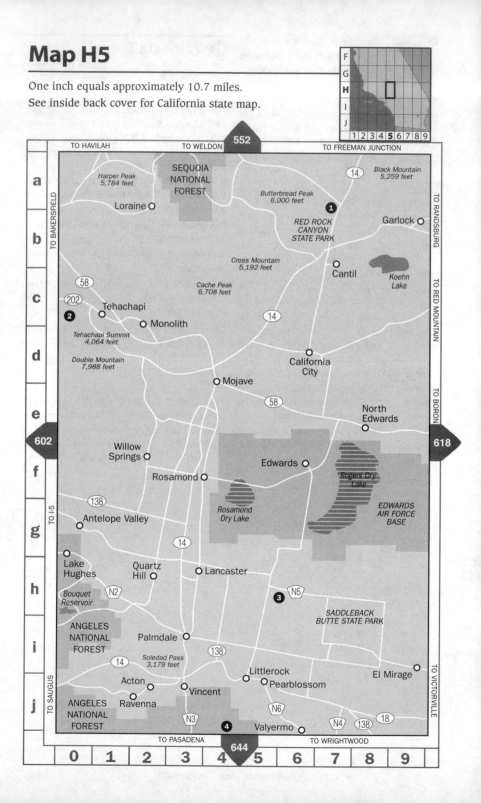

1 Red Rock Canyon State Park

Location: Near Mojave; map H5, grid a7.

Campsites, facilities: There are 50 sites for tents or RVs up to 30 feet long. Piped water, fire grills, and picnic tables are provided. Pit toilets, dump station, exhibits, and a nature trail are available. Two campsites are wheelchair accessible. Leashed pets are permitted.

Reservations, fees: No reservations; $10 per night, $5 for an extra vehicle, $1 pet fee. Open year-round.

Contact: Red Rock Canyon State Park, (661) 942-0662, (818) 880-0350, or fax (661) 940-7327.

Directions: From Highway 58 in the town of Mojave, turn northeast on Highway 14 and drive 25 miles to the park on the left.

Trip notes: This unique county park is one of the prettiest spots in the region year-round. What makes it worthwhile in any season is the chance to see wondrous geologic formations, most of them tinted red. A great, easy hike here is the two-mile walk to Red Cliffs Natural Preserve, where there are awesome 300-foot cliffs and columns, painted red by the iron in the soil (this area is closed from February to May to protect nesting raptors). For those who don't hike, a must is driving up Jawbone Canyon Road to see Jawbone and Last Chance Canyons. Hikers have it better. The elevation is 2,600 feet.

2 Tehachapi Mountain Park

Location: West of Mojave; map H5, grid c0.

Campsites, facilities: There are 61 sites for tents or RVs and a group campsite. Piped water, showers, fire grills, and picnic tables are provided. Pit and vault toilets and overnight corral facilities for equestrian groups are available.

Leashed pets are permitted.

Reservations, fees: No reservations; $8 per night, $2 pet fee. Open year-round.

Contact: Kern County Parks Department, (661) 822-4632.

Directions: In Tehachapi on Tehachapi Boulevard, take the Cury Street exit south and drive about three miles. Turn left on Highline Road and drive two miles. Turn left on Water Canyon Road and drive three miles to the park.

Trip notes: This county park is overlooked by most out-of-towners. It is a pretty spot covering 570 acres, set on the slopes of the Tehachapi Mountains, with elevations in the park ranging from 5,500 to 7,000 feet. This park is not only popular in spring, but also in winter, with the elevations sometimes high enough to get snow, offering a rare chance at winter sports. Chains are often required in the winter.

3 Saddleback Butte State Park

Location: Near Lancaster; map H5, grid h5.

Campsites, facilities: There are 50 sites for tents, trailers, or self-contained RVs up to 30 feet long. A group camp is available for up to 40 people. Sites are wheelchair accessible. Piped water, picnic tables, fire grills, flush toilets, and a dump station are available. Leashed pets are permitted.

Reservations, fees: No reservations for single sites; the group camp may be reserved via phone at (800) 444-PARK/7275 ($7.50 reservation fee) or website www.cal-parks.ca.gov; $10 per night for individual sites, $45 per night for the group site. Open year-round.

Contact: Saddleback Butte State Park, (661) 942-0662 or (818) 880-0350.

Directions: From Highway 14 at Lancaster, turn east on Avenue J and drive 17 miles to the park entrance on the right.

Trip notes: This 3,000-acre park was originally

established to preserve ancient Joshua trees. In fact, it used to be called Joshua Tree State Park, but folks kept getting it confused with Joshua Tree National Park, so it was renamed. The terrain is sparsely vegetated and desertlike, with excellent hiking trails up the nearby buttes. The best hike is the Saddleback Loop, a five-mile trip that features a 1,000-foot climb to Saddleback Summit at 3,651 feet, with fantastic views in all directions, including the Antelope Valley California Poppy Preserve, the surrounding mountains, and the Mojave Desert. The elevation is 2,700 feet.

❹ Basin

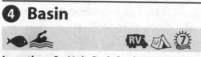

Location: On Little Rock Creek in Angeles National Forest; map H5, grid j4.

Campsites, facilities: There are 15 sites for tents or RVs up to 20 feet long. Piped water, fire pits, vault toilets, and picnic tables are provided. A grocery store is nearby. Leashed pets are permitted.

Reservations, fees: No reservations; $10 per night, $3 per additional vehicle. Open year-round.

Contact: Angeles National Forest, Valyermo Ranger District, (661) 944-2187 or fax (661) 944-4698.

Directions: From Highway 14 near Palmdale, turn east on Highway 138 and drive a short distance to Cheeseboro Road. Turn right and drive six miles to the campground.

Trip notes: If the camps at nearby Little Rock Reservoir (one mile to the north) are full, this camp provides an ideal alternative. It is set along Little Rock Creek at 3,400 feet, just south of a designated Off-Road-Vehicle Area. The entire area near Little Rock has been renovated; in addition to Basin Camp, there are two other new camps. Campsites are assigned at the entrance to Little Rock during the summer months. Nearby Little Rock Reservoir covers just 150 acres and, with a 5 mph speed limit, provides a quiet spot for fishing and swimming.

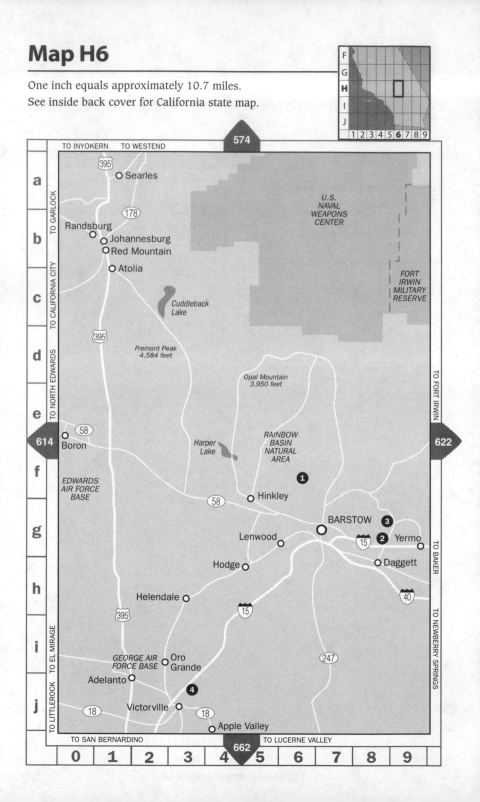

Map H6

One inch equals approximately 10.7 miles.
See inside back cover for California state map.

574

TO INYOKERN   TO WESTEND

a

(395)

○ Searles

b

Randsburg ○

○ Johannesburg
○ Red Mountain

TO GARLOCK

TO CALIFORNIA CITY

(178)

○ Atolia

*U.S.
NAVAL
WEAPONS
CENTER*

c

*Cuddleback
Lake*

*FORT
IRWIN
MILITARY
RESERVE*

d

(395)

*Fremont Peak
4,584 feet*

*Opal Mountain
3,950 feet*

TO NORTH EDWARDS

e

614

(58)
○ Boron

*Harper
Lake*

*RAINBOW
BASIN
NATURAL
AREA*

622

TO FORT IRWIN

f

*EDWARDS
AIR FORCE
BASE*

❶

(58)   ○ Hinkley

g

Lenwood ○

BARSTOW ○ **❸**

(15) **❷** Yermo ○

TO BAKER

Hodge ○

○ Daggett

h

Helendale ○

(15)

(40)

i

(395)

TO EL MIRAGE

(247)

TO NEWBERRY SPRINGS

j

*GEORGE AIR
FORCE BASE*   Oro ○
Grande

Adelanto ○

❹

(18)   Victorville ○   (18)

○ Apple Valley

TO LITTLEROCK

TO SAN BERNARDINO

662

TO LUCERNE VALLEY

0   1   2   3   4   5   6   7   8   9

1 Owl Canyon

Location: Near Barstow; map H6, grid f6.

Campsites, facilities: There are 31 sites for tents or RVs. Fire grills, picnic tables, and vault toilets are provided. There is limited piped water. Leashed pets are permitted.

Reservations, fees: No reservations; $6 per night.

Contact: Bureau of Land Management, (909) 697-5200; California Desert Information Center, (760) 252-6060.

Directions: From Barstow on Highway 58, drive eight miles north on Camp Irwin Road. Turn left on Fossil Beds Road and drive two miles to the campground.

Trip notes: The primary attraction of Owl Canyon camp is that the surrounding desert is sprinkled with exposed fossils of ancient animals. Guess they couldn't find any water, heh, heh. Well, if people try hiking out here without a full canteen, there may soon be some human skeletons out here, too. The sparse BLM land out here is kind of like an ugly dog you learn to love: after a while, when you look closely, you learn it has a heart of gold. The BLM country in this region is best visited in the winter, of course, when hiking allows a new look at what appears, at first, to be a wasteland. The beauty is in the detail of it—tiny critters and tiny flowers seen against the unfenced vastness, with occasional fossils to be discovered. The elevation is 2,600 feet.

2 Barstow Calico KOA

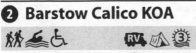

Location: Near Barstow; map H6, grid g8.

Campsites, facilities: There are 78 sites for tents or RVs, many with full or partial hookups. Picnic tables and fire grills are provided. Piped water, flush toilets, showers, sanitary dump station, playground, swimming pool, recreation room, grocery store, propane gas, ice, and a laundry room facilities are available. Some facilities are wheelchair accessible. Leashed pets are permitted.

Reservations, fees: Reservations are accepted; $17 to $24 per night. Open year-round.

Contact: Barstow Calico KOA, (760) 254-2311 or fax (760) 254-2247.

Directions: From Barstow, drive seven miles northeast on Interstate 15 north. Take the Ghost Town Road exit, drive left under the freeway, and then immediately turn left again onto the frontage road. Drive about a quarter mile to the campground on the right.

Trip notes: Don't blame us if you end up way out here. Actually, for vacationers making the long-distance grind of a drive on Interstate 15, this KOA can seem like the promised land. It's clean, and a nightly quiet time ensures that you have a chance to get rested. But hey, as long as you're here, you might as well take a side trip to the Calico Ghost Town, located about 10 miles to the northeast at the foot of the Calico Mountains. Rock hounding and hiking are other nearby options. The elevation is 1,900 feet.

3 Calico Ghost Town Regional Park

Location: Near Barstow; map H6, grid g8.

Campsites, facilities: There are 247 sites for tents or RVs, 47 with full hookups. Cabins and a bunkhouse are also available. Piped water and fire grills are provided. Flush toilets, showers, and a sanitary dump station are available. Groceries, propane gas, and laundry facilities are available nearby. Leashed pets are permitted.

Reservations, fees: Reservations are requested; $18 to $22 per night for tent or RV sites (scout camping is available at $3 per night). The cabin fee is $28 per night with a refundable $25 deposit, the bunkhouse fee is $5 per camper per night, $1 fee for off-road vehicles. Open year-round.

Contact: Calico Ghost Town Regional Park, (760) 254-2122.

Directions: From Barstow, drive seven miles northeast on Interstate 15. Take the Ghost Town Road exit and drive north for three miles to the park on the left.

Trip notes: Let me tell you about this ghost town: There are probably more people here now than there have ever been. In the 1880s and 1890s it was a booming silver mine town, and there are still remnants of that. Alas, it now has lots of restaurants and shops. Recreation options include riding on a narrow gauge railroad, touring a silver mine, and watching an old-style play with villains and heroes. Whatever you do, don't take any artifacts you may come across, such as an old nail, a jar, or anything; you will be doomed with years of bad luck. No foolin'.

---

❹ Shady Oasis Victorville KOA

Location: Near Victorville; map H6, grid j3.

Campsites, facilities: There are 136 sites for tents or RVs, many with full or partial hookups.

Piped water, picnic tables, and fire grills are provided. Flush toilets, showers, recreation room, swimming pool, playground, grocery store, propane gas, and a laundry room are available. Some facilities are wheelchair accessible. Leashed pets are permitted.

Reservations, fees: Reservations are accepted; $19 to $28 per night. Open year-round.

Contact: Shady Oasis Victorville KOA, (760) 245-6867.

Directions: From Victorville, drive north on Interstate 15 to Stoddard Wells Drive. Turn south and drive a short distance to the campground at 16530 Stoddard Wells Drive.

Trip notes: Most long-distance trips on Interstate 15 are grueling endurance tests with drivers making the mistake of trying to get a decent night's sleep at a roadside rest stop. Why endure the torture, especially with a KOA located way out here, in Victorville of all places? Where the heck is Victorville? If you are exhausted and lucky enough to find the place, you won't be making any jokes about it. By the way, if you visit, keep your eyes open for the ghost of Roy Rogers, the legendary cowboy singer. He lived just minutes away from this park, where he sat happily in his living room with his horse, Trigger, whom he had stuffed. Happy trails to you, until we meet again.

621

Map H7

One inch equals approximately 10.7 miles.
See inside back cover for California state map.

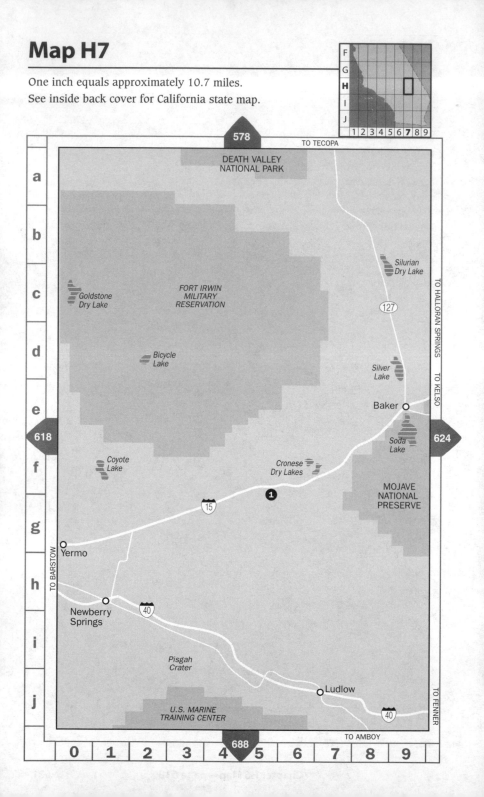

Chapter H7 features:

① Afton Canyon

Location: Near Barstow in the East Mojave National Scenic Area; map H7, grid f5.

Campsites, facilities: There are 22 sites for tents or RVs. Fire rings, picnic tables, and vault toilets are provided. There is limited piped water. Leashed pets are permitted.

Reservations, fees: No reservations; $6 per night.

Contact: California Desert Information Center, (760) 252-6060.

Directions: From Barstow, drive 40 miles east on Interstate 15 to Afton Canyon Road. Turn right and drive three miles to the campground.

Trip notes: This camp is set at elevation 1,400 feet in a desert riparian habitat along the Mojave River. Remember, rivers in the desert are not like rivers in cooler climates. There are lots of desert tamarisk trees and no fish worth eating. This is one of several Bureau of Land Management tracts in the East Mojave National Scenic Area. Side trip options include the Rainbow Basin Natural Area, Soda Springs, and the Calico Early Man Site.

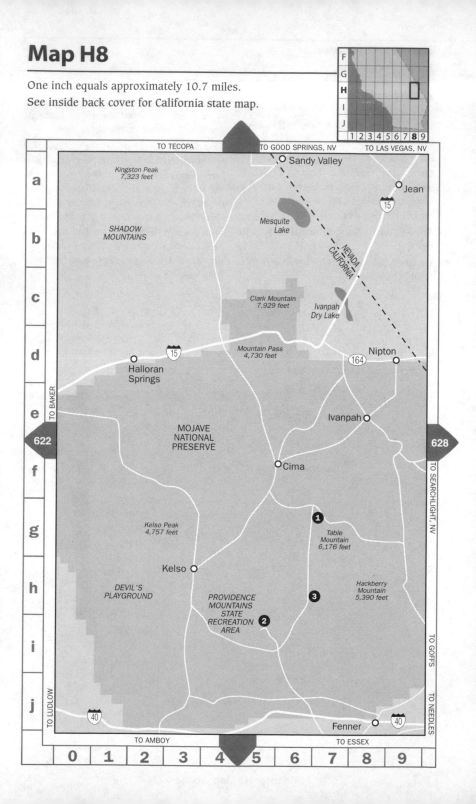

Map H8

One inch equals approximately 10.7 miles.
See inside back cover for California state map.

Chapter H8 features:

1 Mid Hills

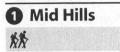

Location: In the Mojave National Preserve; map H8, grid g7.

Campsites, facilities: There are 26 sites for tents or RVs up to 22 feet long. Piped water, fire grills, picnic tables, and vault toilets are provided. Leashed pets are permitted.

Reservations, fees: No reservations; $10 per night. Open year-round.

Contact: Mojave National Preserve, (760) 733-4040.

Directions: From Interstate 40 near Essex, take the Essex Road exit and drive 10 miles north to Black Canyon Road. Turn north and drive about nine miles on pavement and 10 miles on rough, dirt road to the campground on the right.

Trip notes: This is a primitive campground set among the junipers and piñon trees in a mountainous area at 5,500 feet. It is one in a series of little-known camps sprinkled about the vast desert that is now managed by the National Park Service. The primary attraction here is the remoteness, as well as the nearby Providence Mountains State Recreation Area (campground number two) and winter hikes to obscure landmarks. The best hike in the region is to Teutonia Peak, elevation 5,755 feet, a four-mile round-trip that tops out on the rounded domelike top and provides 360-degree views across this vast desert landscape.

2 Providence Mountains State Recreation Area

Location: Near Mitchell Caverns; map H8, grid h5.

Campsites, facilities: There are six sites for tents. RVs up to 32 feet long can park in the parking lot. Fire grills, flush toilets, piped water, and picnic tables are provided. Leashed pets are permitted.

Reservations, fees: No reservations; $12 per night, $1 pet fee.

Contact: Providence Mountains State Recreation Area, (661) 942-0662.

Directions: From Interstate 40 near the town of Essex, turn northwest on Essex Road and drive 17 miles to the park at road's end.

Trip notes: This remote desert park, set at 4,300 feet, offers guided tours of Mitchell Caverns ($6 tour fee) every day from mid-September through mid-June. It's a good idea to make a reservation for the tour; phone (805) 942-0662. The cavern tours are the reason most people visit and camp at this park, but there are additional recreational opportunities. From the campground the Nina Mora Overlook Trail is a short (quarter-mile) walk to a lookout of the Marble Mountains and the valley below. Another short hike with a great view is the steep, one-mile hike on the Crystal Springs Trail.

3 Hole-In-The-Wall

Location: In the Mojave National Preserve; map H8, grid h7.

Campsites, facilities: There are 35 sites for tents or RVs. Fire grills, picnic tables, vault toilets, and piped water are available. Leashed pets are permitted.

Reservations, fees: No reservations; $10 per night. Open year-round.

Contact: Mojave National Preserve, (760) 733-4040.

Directions: From Highway 40 near Essex, take the Essex Road exit and drive 16 miles north to Black Canyon Road. Turn north and drive 10 miles to the campground on the left.

Trip notes: This is the tiniest and least-known of the camps in the vast Mojave National Preserve; the campground is at 5,000 feet in elevation. They even truck in water here, a big bonus. An interesting side trip is to the Mitchell Caverns and Winding Stair Caverns in the nearby Providence Mountains State Recreation Area (see the trip notes for campground number two for more information). To get there, go back to Essex Road, turn right, and continue northeast for about six miles to the end of Essex Road. It's a good idea to reserve a space for the popular Mitchell Caverns tour. For reservations phone (805) 942-0662.

Map H9

One inch equals approximately 10.7 miles.
See inside back cover for California state map.

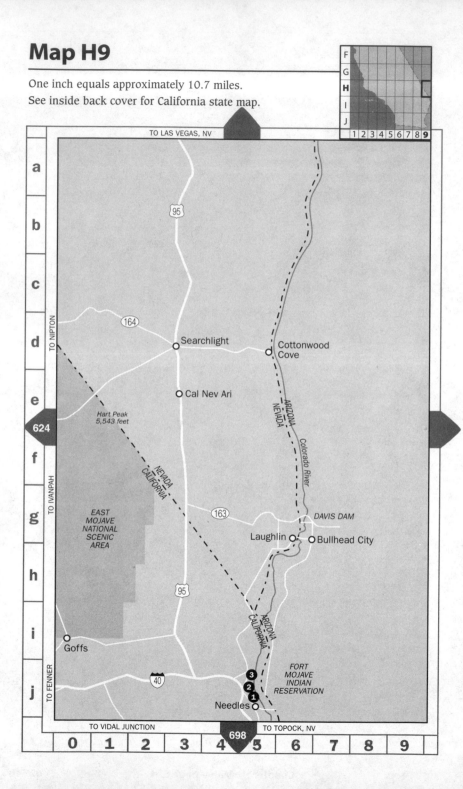

❶ Needles KOA

Location: Near the Colorado River; map H9, grid j5.

Campsites, facilities: There are 101 sites for tents or RVs, 30 with water and electric connections and 63 with full hookups. Flush toilets, showers, recreation room, swimming pool, playground, grocery store, snack bar, propane gas, and laundry facilities are available. Leashed pets are permitted.

Reservations, fees: Reservations are accepted; $17.95 to $22.95 per night. Open year-round.

Contact: Needles KOA, (760) 326-4207 or fax (760) 326-6329.

Directions: In Needles on Interstate 40, take the West Broadway exit, turning left on Needles Highway. Drive a short distance, turn left on National Old Trails Highway, and drive to the park on the right at 2005 Mira Vista Avenue.

Trip notes: Now quit your yelpin'. So it's hot. So it's ugly. So you're on your way home from Las Vegas after getting cleaned out. At least you've got the Needles KOA, complete with swimming pool, where you can get a new start. Side trips include venturing to the nearby Colorado River or heading north to Lake Mead. Of course, you could always go back to Las Vegas. Nah. Not enough money left.

❷ Needles Marina Park

Location: On the Colorado River; map H9, grid j5.

Campsites, facilities: There are 190 sites for RVs with full hookups and picnic tables. There are also six cabins. Flush toilets, showers, heated pool, whirlpool, recreation room, swimming pool, playground, boat ramp, boat slips, grocery store, gas, and laundry facilities are available. Leashed pets are permitted.

Reservations, fees: Reservations are accepted; $24 to $26 per night, $57 per night for cabins.

Contact: Needles Marina Park, (760) 326-2197 or fax (760) 326-4125.

Directions: From Interstate 40 in Needles, take the J Street exit to Broadway. Turn left, turn right on River Road, and drive a half mile to the park.

Trip notes: Bring your suntan lotion and a beach towel. This section of the Colorado River is a big tourist spot where the body oil and beer can flow faster than the river. There are a ton of hot bodies and hot boats, and waterskiing dominates the adjacent flat water section of the Colorado River. However, note that upstream of the Needles-area put-in is the prime area for waterskiing. Downstream is the chance for canoeing or kayaking. Meanwhile, there's also an 18-hole golf course adjacent to the camp, but most folks head for the river. Compared to the surrounding desert, why, this park is almost a golden paradise.

❸ Rainbo Beach Resort and Marina

Location: On the Colorado River; map H9, grid j5.

Campsites, facilities: There are 70 RV sites with full hookups and picnic tables. Rest rooms with showers, a coin laundry, and a recreation room are available. In the summer, a swimming pool and boat dock are also available. Leashed pets are permitted.

Reservations, fees: Reservations are accepted; $26 per night. Open year-round.

Contact: Rainbo Beach Resort and Marina, (760) 326-3101 or fax (760) 326-5085.

Directions: From Interstate 40 in Needles, drive 1.5 miles north on River Road to the resort on the right.

Trip notes: The big bonus here is the full marina, making this resort on the Colorado River headquarters for boaters and water-skiers. And headquarters it is, with tons of happy folks who are extremely well lubed, both inside and out. For boating details for the area, see the trip notes for Needles Marina Park (campground number two).

Southern California

Map I2

One inch equals approximately 10.7 miles.
See inside back cover for California state map.

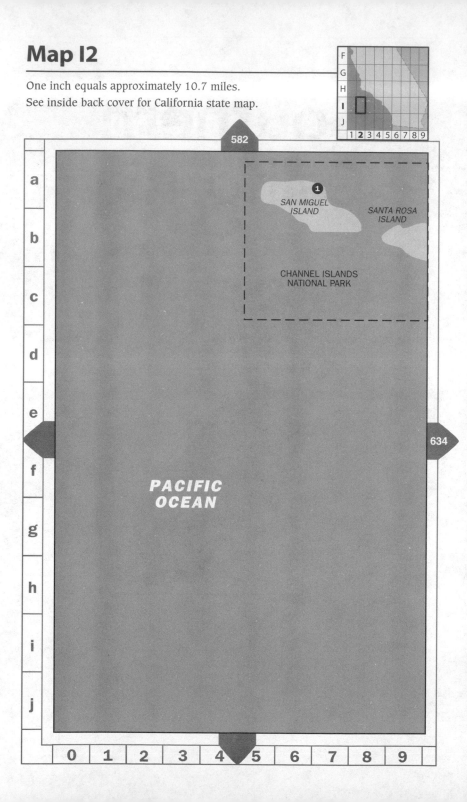

582

634

SAN MIGUEL
ISLAND

SANTA ROSA
ISLAND

CHANNEL ISLANDS
NATIONAL PARK

PACIFIC
OCEAN

Chapter 12 features:

1 San Miguel Island Hike-In

Location: In Channel Islands National Park; map 12, grid a6.

Campsites, facilities: There are nine primitive tent sites. Pit toilets, picnic tables, windbreaks, and food cabinets are provided. No piped water is available. No open fires are allowed; bring a camp stove for cooking. No pets are permitted.

Reservations, fees: Reserve by calling Island Packers at (805) 642-1393. After arranging transportation, you must obtain a permit number from the National Park Service. Phone (805) 658-5711 or write to Channel Islands National Park, 1901 Spinnaker Drive, Ventura, CA 93001. Camping is $2.50 per night; round-trip boat transportation is $90 for adults, $80 for children 12 and under.

Contact: For general and camping information, phone the park visitor center at (805) 658-5730. For camping and transportation information, phone Island Packers at (805) 642-1393. Ventura Visitors Bureau offers a free travel packet; phone (800) 333-2989.

Directions: From US 101 in Ventura, take the Victoria exit and follow the signs to Ventura Harbor. The boat ride is four hours one way.

Trip notes: There is no camping trip like this one anywhere in America. It starts with a four-hour boat ride, being dropped off at San Miguel Island, the most unusual of the five Channel Islands. It is small, distant, and extremely rugged, and is home to unique birds and much wildlife, including elephant seals and the largest sea lion rookery in California (located on the south side of the island). Only rarely do people take advantage of this island paradise, limited to no more than 30 people at any one time on the entire island. To reach the campground start from Cuyler Harbor, where you will be dropped off, and then hike up Nidever Canyon and take the right fork. Bring plenty of water, warm clothes, and be prepared for the chance of fog and wind; the boat typically will not return to pick you up for several days. That's why camping here is like staking out your own personal island wilderness.

Map I3

One inch equals approximately 10.7 miles.
See inside back cover for California state map.

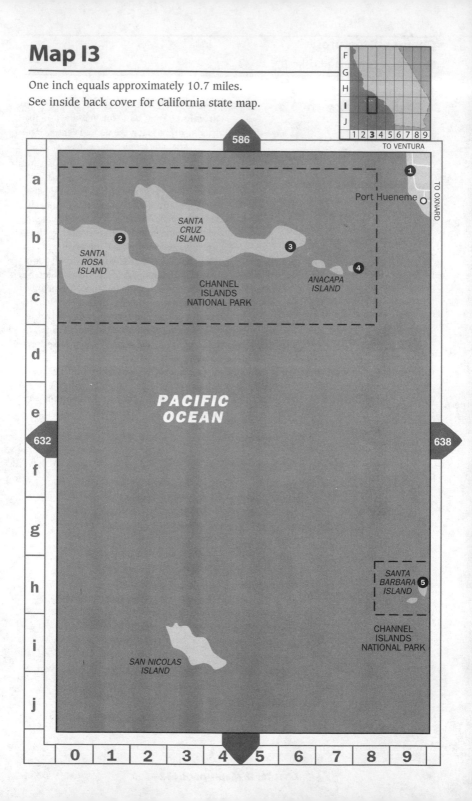

❶ McGrath State Beach

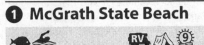

Location: On the Pacific Ocean south of Ventura; map 13, grid a9.

Campsites, facilities: There are 174 sites for tents or RVs up to 34 feet long. Piped water, fire grills, and picnic tables are provided. Flush toilets, coin-operated showers, dump station, horseshoes, and a visitor center are available. Supplies and a coin laundry are nearby. Leashed pets are permitted, but not on the beach.

Reservations, fees: Reserve via phone at (800) 444-PARK/7275 ($7.50 reservation fee) or website www.cal-parks.ca.gov; $17 to $18 per night, $1 pet fee. Open year-round.

Contact: McGrath State Beach, (805) 899-1400.

Directions: From Ventura, drive south on US 101. Take the Seaward Avenue/Harbor Boulevard exit, turn right, and continue four miles on Harbor Boulevard to the park.

Trip notes: This is a pretty spot just south of Pierpoint Bay. The north tip of the park borders the Santa Clara River Estuary Natural Preserve, where the McGrath State Beach Nature Trail provides an easy walk along where the freshwater of the Santa Clara River feeds into the estuary and then into the ocean. Ventura Harbor and the Channel Islands National Park Visitor Center are available for nearby side trips. Note: During most of the year, plan on making a camping reservation or don't plan to visit this park.

❷ Santa Rosa Island

Location: In Channel Islands National Park; map 13, grid b1.

Campsites, facilities: There are 15 primitive tent sites. Pit toilets, picnic tables, and windbreaks are provided. No piped water is available; you must bring your own. No open fires are allowed; bring a camp stove for cooking. No pets are permitted.

Reservations, fees: Reserve by calling Island Packers, (805) 642-1393. After arranging transportation, you must obtain a permit number from the National Park Service. To obtain a permit number, contact Channel Islands National Park, 1901 Spinnaker Drive, Ventura, CA 93001; (805) 658-5711. Camping is $2.50 per night; round-trip boat transportation costs $80 for adults and $70 for children 12 and under.

Contact: For general and camping information, phone the park visitor center, (805) 658-5730. For transportation information, phone Island Packers, (805) 642-1393. Ventura Visitors Bureau offers a free travel packet; to receive a packet, phone (800) 333-2989.

Directions: From US 101 in Ventura, take the Victoria exit and follow the signs to Ventura Harbor. The boat ride takes about 3.5 hours one way. Channel Islands Aviation offers a special flight to this island for campers who can't stomach the long boat ride. The flight takes 25 minutes and costs $150 round-trip. Phone (805) 987-1301 for information.

Trip notes: Santa Rosa, the second largest of the Channel Islands (the largest is Santa Cruz), is 10 miles wide and 15 miles long, and it holds many mysteries and adventures. A camping trip to Santa Rosa Island, available Friday through Sunday, will be an unforgettable experience even for those who think they've seen it all. Santa Rosa is especially good for kayakers, offering them a world-class adventure. The island is beautiful in the spring, when its grasslands turn emerald green and are sprinkled with wildflowers. There are many good hikes, the best being the Cherry Canyon Trail into the island's interior with the likely chance of seeing wild goats, and the Lobo Canyon Trail descending to a Chumash village site and on to a tide pooling area. Because the boat ride to Santa Rosa is longer than the trip to Santa Cruz, this island often receives fewer visitors than its nearby neighbor, which makes it even more special. Bring plenty of fresh water and, because of the chance of fog and wind, warm clothes.

❸ Santa Cruz Island

Location: In the Channel Islands; map I3, grid b6.

Campsites, facilities: There are 35 primitive campsites. Pit toilets, picnic tables, and fire rings are provided. No piped water is provided; you must bring your own. No pets are permitted.

Reservations, fees: Reserve through Island Packers, (805) 642-1393. After arranging transportation, you must obtain a permit number from the National Park Service. To obtain a permit number, contact Channel Islands National Park, 1901 Spinnaker Drive, Ventura, CA 93001; (805) 658-5711. Camping is $2.50 per night. Round-trip boat transportation is $54 for adults, $40 for children 12 and under.

Contact: Island Packers, (805) 642-1393.

Directions: From US 101 in Ventura, take the Victoria Avenue exit and follow the signs to the Ventura Harbor. The boat ride takes two hours one way.

Trip notes: This is the largest of the Channel Islands, perfect for camping and multiday visits. It covers 96 square miles, features a 2,450-foot mountain (Devil's Peak), and boasts an incredible array of flora and fauna, sheltered canyons, and sweeping ocean views. The camp is set in a eucalyptus grove in a valley, with a trailhead out of camp that hikers can take to reach the surrounding ridgeline. A great hike is from Pelican Bay to Prisoner's Harbor, a three-miler that is routed through the interior of the island to a beautiful beach. Herds of wild sheep are abundant, and kayaking through sea caves is outstanding, especially at the Painted Cave. This campground is the only one on the Channel Islands that is not managed by the National Park Service.

❹ Anacapa Island

Location: In Channel Islands National Park; map I3, grid c8.

Campsites, facilities: There are seven primitive tent sites. Picnic tables and pit toilets are provided. No piped water is available; you must bring your own. No open fires are allowed; bring a camp stove for cooking. No pets are permitted.

Reservations, fees: Reserve by calling Island Packers, (805) 642-1393. After arranging transportation, you must obtain a permit number from the National Park Service. To obtain a permit number, contact Channel Islands National Park, 1901 Spinnaker Drive, Ventura, CA 93001; (805) 658-5711. Camping is $2.50 per night; round-trip boat transportation is $48 for adults, $30 for children 12 and under.

Contact: For general and camping information, phone the park visitor center, (805) 658-5730. For camping and transportation information, phone Island Packers, (805) 642-1393. Ventura Visitors Bureau offers a free travel packet; to receive a packet, phone (800) 333-2989.

Directions: From US 101 in Ventura, take the Victoria exit and follow the signs to Ventura Harbor. The boat ride takes 75 minutes one way.

Trip notes: Little Anacapa, long and narrow, is known for its awesome caves, cliffs, and sea lion rookeries that range near huge kelp beds. After landing on the island, you face a 154-step staircase trail that leaves you perched on an ocean bluff. The trails from there, as well as from Inspiration Point and Cathedral Cove, provide vast views of the channel. The inshore waters are an ecological preserve loaded with marine life and seabirds and, with the remarkably clear water, this island makes a great destination for snorkeling and sea kayaking. Of the Channel Islands, the boat ride here is the shortest, only 75 minutes.

❺ Santa Barbara Island

Location: In Channel Islands National Park; map I3, grid h9.

Campsites, facilities: There are eight primitive tent sites. Pit toilets and picnic tables are provided. No piped water is available; you must bring your own. No open fires are allowed; bring a camp stove for cooking. No pets are permitted.

Reservations, fees: Reserve by calling Island Packers, (805) 642-1393. After arranging transportation, you must obtain a permit number from the National Park Service. To obtain a permit number, contact Channel Islands National Park, 1901 Spinnaker Drive, Ventura, CA 93001; (805) 658-5711. Camping is $2.50 per night;

round-trip boat transportation is $75 for adults, $65 for children 12 and under.

Contact: For general and camping information, phone the park visitor center, (805) 658-5730. For camping and transportation information, phone Island Packers, (805) 642-1393. Ventura Visitors Bureau offers a free travel packet; to receive a packet, phone (800) 333-2989.

Directions: From US 101 in Ventura, take the Victoria exit and follow the signs to Ventura Harbor. The boat ride takes 3.5 hours one way.

Trip notes: This is a veritable dot of an island, located well to the south of the four others that make up the Channel Islands. It is best known for its miles of hiking trails, solitude, snorkeling, swimming, and excellent viewing of marine mammals. It is a breeding ground for elephant seals, with dolphins, sea lions, and whales (in the winter), all common in the area. The snorkeling can be wonderful, as you dive amid playful seals. The only negative is the long boat ride, 3.5 hours from the mainland.

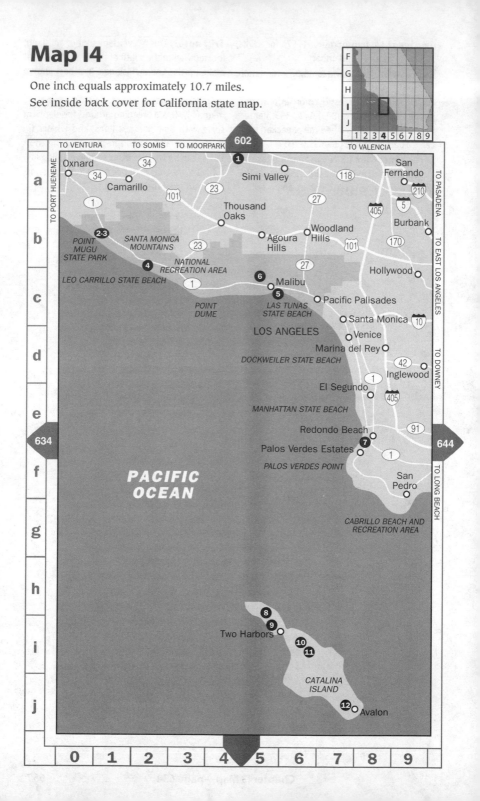

Map I4

One inch equals approximately 10.7 miles.
See inside back cover for California state map.

❶ Oak County Park

Location: In Simi Valley near Moorpark; map I4, grid a4.

Campsites, facilities: There is a large group tent area and 16 sites for RVs with partial hookups and an RV group area. Fire grills, picnic tables and, in some cases, electrical hookups are provided. Piped water, flush toilets, dump station, and a playground are available. Supplies and a coin laundry are located within one mile. Leashed pets are permitted.

Reservations, fees: Reservations are accepted; $17 per night, $1 pet fee.

Contact: Oak County Park, (661) 527-6886.

Directions: From Ventura, drive south on US 101 to Highway 23. Drive north on Highway 23 (which becomes Highway 118) for about 8.5 miles to the Collins Street exit. Drive east on Los Angeles Avenue about 1.5 miles to Quimisa Drive. Turn right into the park.

Trip notes: One of the frustrations of trying to find a camp for the night is that so many state and national park campgrounds are full from advance reservations, especially the state beaches. The county parks often provide a safety valve, and Oak County Park certainly applies. This is an oft-overlooked county park set in the foothill country of Simi Valley. The park has many trails offering good hiking possibilities. The camp is somewhat secluded, more so than many expect.

❷ Sycamore Canyon

Location: In Point Mugu State Park; map I4, grid b1.

Campsites, facilities: There are 54 sites for tents or RVs up to 31 feet long (up to eight campers per site). Picnic tables and fire grills are provided. Piped water, flush toilets, pay showers and a sanitary disposal station are available. Supplies can be obtained nearby. There is wheelchair access to trails, exhibits, picnic areas, and Sycamore Canyon Campground. Leashed pets are permitted, except on trails.

Reservations, fees: Reserve via phone at (800) 444-PARK/7275 ($7.50 reservation fee) or website www.cal-parks.ca.gov; $17 to $18 per night, $1 pet fee. Open year-round.

Contact: Sycamore Canyon, (818) 880 0350 or fax (818) 880-6165.

Directions: From Oxnard, drive 16 miles south on Highway 1 to the camp.

Trip notes: While this camp is across the highway from the ocean, it is also part of Point Mugu State Park, which covers 14,980 acres. That gives you plenty of options. One of the best is taking the Big Sycamore Canyon Loop, a long hiking route with great views that starts right at the camp. In all, it's a 9.5-mile loop that climbs to a ridge top and offers beautiful views of nearby canyons and long-distance vistas of the coast.

❸ Thornhill Broome State Beach

Location: In Point Mugu State Park; map I4, grid b1.

Campsites, facilities: There are 88 primitive sites for tents or RVs up to 31 feet long. Picnic tables are provided. Piped water and chemical toilets are available. Supplies can be obtained nearby. Leashed pets are permitted.

Reservations, fees: Reserve via phone at

(800) 444-PARK/7275 ($7.50 reservation fee) or website www.cal-parks.ca.gov; $10 to $12 per night, $1 pet fee. Open year-round.

Contact: Thornhill Broome State Beach, (818) 880-0350 or fax (818) 880-6165.

Directions: From Oxnard, drive 15 miles south on Highway 1 to the camp entrance.

Trip notes: Of the two campgrounds at Point Mugu State Park, this one is more attractive to those touring Highway 1 because it is on the ocean side of the highway (the other is on the east side of the highway). While the beachfront is pretty and you can always just lie there in the sun and pretend you're a beached whale, the park's expanse on the east side of the highway in the Santa Monica Mountains provides more recreation. That includes two stellar hikes, the 9.5-mile Big Sycamore Canyon Loop (see the trip notes for Sycamore Canyon, campground number 2) and the seven-mile La Jolla Valley Loop. In all, the park covers 14,980 acres, far more than the obvious little strip of beachfront.

❹ Leo Carrillo State Beach

Location: North of Malibu; map I4, grid b2.

Campsites, facilities: There are 127 sites for tents or RVs up to 31 feet long and under eight feet high. Picnic tables and fire grills are provided. Piped water, flush toilets, showers, and a dump station are available. Some facilities are wheelchair accessible. Supplies are available nearby. Leashed pets are permitted.

Reservations, fees: Reserve via phone at (800) 444-PARK/7275 ($7.50 reservation fee) or website www.cal-parks.ca.gov; $17 to $18 per night, $1 pet fee.

Contact: Leo Carrillo State Beach, (818) 880-0350 or fax (818) 880-6165.

Directions: From Santa Monica, drive 28 miles north on Highway 1 to the park. Or from Oxnard, drive 20 miles south on Highway 1 to the signed park exit on the left. Exit directly into the park.

Trip notes: There are two camping areas at this state park. One is located along the beach, near the ocean, and the other is in a nearby canyon. It's good either way. Reservations are

essential for the canyon sites. Beach sites are taken on a first-come, first-served basis. The Nicholas Flat Trail provides an excellent hike to the Willow Creek Overlook for beautiful views of the beach. In addition, a pedestrian tunnel is available that provides access to a wonderful coastal spot with sea caves, tunnels, and patches of beach.

❺ Malibu Creek State Park

Location: Near Malibu; map I4, grid c5.

Campsites, facilities: There are 63 sites for tents or self-contained RVs up to 24 feet long. Piped water, picnic tables, fire places (no wood fires allowed), hot showers, and rest rooms are provided. Some facilities are wheelchair accessible. Leashed pets are permitted, but only in the campground area.

Reservations, fees: Reserve via phone at (800) 444-PARK/7275 ($7.50 reservation fee) or website www.cal-parks.ca.gov; $17 per night.

Contact: Malibu Creek State Park, (818) 880-0350 or fax (818) 880-6165.

Directions: From US 101 northeast of Malibu, take the Las Virgenes exit and drive four miles west on Las Virgenes Canyon Road to the park entrance. If you're coming from Highway 1 in Malibu, turn east on Malibu Canyon Road and drive about five miles to the park entrance.

Trip notes: If you plan on staying here, be sure to get your reservation in early. This 6,600-acre state park is just a few miles out of Malibu between Highway 1 and US 101, two major thoroughfares for vacationers. Despite its popularity, the park manages to retain a natural setting, with miles of trails for hiking, biking, and horseback riding, and inspiring scenic views. It is an ideal spot for a break on a coastal road trip.

❻ Malibu Beach RV Park

Location: In Malibu; map I4, grid c5.

Campsites, facilities: There are 50 tent sites

and 140 RV sites with full or partial hookups. Picnic tables and barbecue grills are provided. Rest rooms, showers, hot tub, recreation room, playground, coin laundry, propane gas, ice, cable TV, sanitary dump station, and a grocery store are available. Some facilities are wheelchair accessible. Leashed pets are permitted, except in the tent area.

Reservations, fees: Reservations are accepted; $15 to $45 per night. Open year-round.

Contact: Malibu Beach RV Park, (310) 456-6052 or fax (310) 456-2532.

Directions: In Malibu at the intersection of Pacific Coast Highway/Highway 1 and Malibu Canyon Road, drive north on Pacific Coast Highway two miles to the RV park on the right.

Trip notes: This is one of the few privately developed RV parks that provides some sites for tent campers as well. It's one of the nicer spots in the area, set on a bluff overlooking the Pacific Ocean, near both Malibu Pier (for fishing) and Paradise Cove. Each site has a view of either the ocean or adjacent mountains. Get this: Hollywood is 10 miles to the east.

❼ Dockweiler Beach RV Park

Location: On the Pacific Ocean near Manhattan Beach; map I4, grid e8.

Campsites, facilities: There are 118 sites for RVs up to 35 feet long, 83 with full hookups. Picnic tables and barbecue grills are provided. Flush toilets, hot showers, sanitary disposal station, and coin laundry are available. Supplies can be purchased nearby. Leashed pets are permitted.

Reservations, fees: Reserve via phone at (800) 444-PARK/7275 ($7.50 reservation fee) or website www.cal-parks.ca.gov; $13 to $26.35 per night. Open year-round.

Contact: Dockweiler Beach, (800) 950-7275 or (310) 322-4951.

Directions: From Santa Monica, drive 12 miles south on Interstate 405 to the Imperial Highway West exit. Drive about 4 miles west on Imperial Highway to Vista del Mar and the park.

Trip notes: This layover spot for coast cruisers

is just a hop from the beach and the Pacific Ocean.

❽ Parson's Landing Hike-In

Location: On Catalina Island; map I4, grid h5.

Campsites, facilities: There are six tent sites, each accommodating a maximum of eight campers. Pit toilets, fire rings, barbecue pits, and limited water (2.5 gallons per campsite) are available. Firewood, charcoal, and lighter fluid must be obtained on the island, as US Coast Guard regulations prohibit combustible materials in passenger vehicles when crossing the channel. Pets are not permitted.

Reservations, fees: Reservations are required; $22 per night for the first person per site, $6.50 per night for each additional person up to a maximum of eight campers ($50 maximum per night per site). Check in at the visitor information booth to validate your camping permit. An adult round-trip ferry ride costs $25 to $36.

Contact: For ferry information or camp reservations phone (310) 510-2800 or (310) 510-0303.

Directions: From San Diego, San Pedro, or Long Beach, a ferry is available that will take you to Two Harbors. From Two Harbors travel by shore boat (check schedule) to Emerald Bay. Hike 1.5 miles to the campground.

Trip notes: This primitive campground is one of five on Catalina Island. It is set on the island's northern end, seven miles from the island's isthmus and the village of Two Harbors. If you want to try and avoid the crowds, this is the area to visit; forget Avalon and head instead to Two Harbors.

❾ Two Harbors

Location: On Catalina Island; map I4, grid i5.

Campsites, facilities: There are 52 sites, which can accommodate a total of 250 people. Chemical toilets, cold showers, fire rings, barbecues, picnic tables, sun shades, and telephones are provided. A general store, restaurant and saloon, snack bar, tennis courts, volleyball, coin laundry, and hot showers are available in the town of Two Harbors. Firewood, charcoal, and lighter fluid must be obtained on the island, as US Coast Guard regulations prohibit combustible materials in passenger vehicles when crossing the channel. Pets are not permitted.

Reservations, fees: Reservations are requested; $18 to $36 per person per night. Check in at the visitor information booth to validate your camping permit. An adult round-trip ferry ride costs $25 to $36.

Contact: For ferry information or camp reservations, phone (310) 510-2800 or (310) 510-0303.

Directions: From San Diego, San Pedro, or Long Beach, a ferry is available that will take you directly to Two Harbors. If you are on the island at Avalon, take the bus to Two Harbors. Hike approximately a quarter mile from the village of Two Harbors to the campground.

Trip notes: This campground is only a quarter mile away from the village of Two Harbors. Nearby attractions include the Two Harbors Dive Station with snorkeling equipment, paddleboard rentals, and scuba tank fills to 3,000 psi. There are guided tours of the island and a scheduled bus service between Two Harbors and Avalon; the bus stops at all the interior campgrounds. An excellent hike is the nine-mile round-trip from Two Harbors to Emerald Bay, featuring a gorgeous coast and pretty valleys.

⑩ Black Jack Hike-In

Location: On Catalina Island; map I4, grid i6.

Campsites, facilities: There are enough sites to accommodate up to 75 campers. Water, chemical toilets, fire rings, barbecue pits, and a public phone are available. Firewood, charcoal, and lighter fluid must be obtained on the island, as US Coast Guard regulations prohibit carrying any combustible materials in passenger vehicles when crossing the channel. Pets are not permitted.

Reservations, fees: Reservations are recommended; $18 to $36 per person per night. An adult round-trip ferry ride costs $25 to $36.

Contact: Black Jack Hike-in, (310) 510-2800 or (310) 510-0303.

Directions: From San Pedro or Long Beach, a ferry is available that can take you to Avalon or Two Harbors. From either Avalon or Two Harbors, take the shuttle bus to Black Jack Junction and then hike one mile in from the junction to the campground.

Trip notes: This camp is named after Mount Black Jack (2,008 feet) and is a great place to hunker down for a spell. It's also the site of the old Black Jack Mine. The camp is set at 1,500 feet in elevation. If you stand in just the right spot, you can see the mainland, but L.A. will seem like a million miles away.

⑪ Little Harbor Hike-In

Location: On Catalina Island; map I4, grid i6.

Campsites, facilities: There are enough sites to accommodate 150 campers. Chemical toilets, cold showers, barbecue pits, fire rings, picnic tables, phones, and shuttle bus service are available. Firewood, charcoal, and lighter fluid must be obtained on the island, as US Coast Guard regulations prohibit carrying any combustible materials in passenger vehicles when crossing the channel. Pets are not permitted.

Reservations, fees: Reservations are recommended; $18 to $36 per person per night. An adult round-trip ferry ride costs $25 to $36.

Contact: Little Harbor Hike-in, (310) 510-2800 or (310) 510-0303.

Directions: From San Diego, San Pedro, or Long Beach, a ferry is available that will take you to Two Harbors. You then hike seven miles to the campground.

Trip notes: Many folks consider this to be the pick of the campgrounds on the island. It is a gorgeous place; small wonder that some big Hollywood flicks have been shot here. There is plenty to do: You can swim, dive, fish, or go for day hikes. A Native American historic site is nearby. Two Harbors has several excellent hikes; the best is the nine-mile excursion to Emerald Bay.

⑫ Hermit Gulch

Location: On Catalina Island; map I4, grid j7.

Campsites, facilities: There are 60 tent sites. Piped water, hot showers, flush toilets, picnic tables, fire rings, barbecue pits, and a public phone are available. Firewood, charcoal, and lighter fluid must be obtained on the island, as US Coast Guard regulations prohibit carrying any combustible materials in passenger vehicles when crossing the channel. Some camping equipment is available for rent. Pets are not permitted.

Reservations, fees: Reservations are requested; $18 to $36 per person per night, children under six are free. An adult round-trip ferry ride costs $25 to $36.

Contact: Hermit Gulch, (310) 510-8368.

Directions: A ferry from San Pedro or Long Beach will take you to Avalon. From Sumner Avenue in Avalon, walk up Avalon Canyon. Follow the "Avalon Canyon Road" sign and walk 1.25 miles. The camp is across from the picnic grounds.

Trip notes: This is the closest campground to the town of Avalon, the gateway to Catalina. If you're making a tourist trip, there are a ton of things to do here: Visit Avalon's underwater city park, play the nine-hole golf course, or visit the famous casino. Fishing can be excellent, including angling for white seabass, yellowtail, and, in the fall, even marlin. What can work best of all is going for a good hike. The best hiking experience in the Avalon area is found by taking the shuttle bus to the Airport in the Sky and from there hiking along Empire Landing Road. The route traces the island's curving, hilly northern shore, providing great views of secluded beaches, coves, and rock formations, and also offers a chance to see wildlife, at times even buffalo.

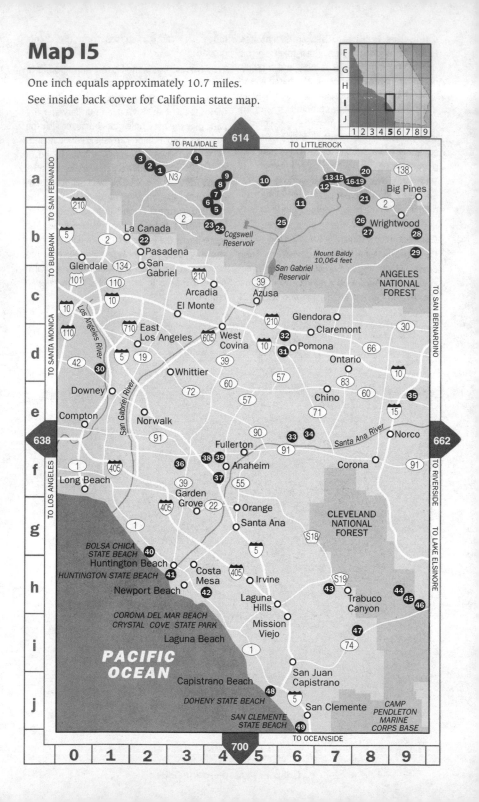

Map I5

One inch equals approximately 10.7 miles.
See inside back cover for California state map.

F G H I J
1 2 3 4 5 6 7 8 9

614
TO PALMDALE
TO LITTLEROCK

a

3 2 1
N3
4
9
8
7
6 5
13-15
16-19
20
12
10
138
21
2
11
Big Pines

TO SAN FERNANDO
TO PALMDALE

b

210
2
La Canada
22
Pasadena
2
23 24
Cogswell
Reservoir
25
26 Wrightwood
27
28
29

TO BURBANK

c

5
134
Glendale
101
110
San
Gabriel
210
Arcadia
El Monte
Azusa
39
San Gabriel
Reservoir
Mount Baldy
10,064 feet
ANGELES
NATIONAL
FOREST

TO SANTA MONICA
TO SAN BERNARDINO

d

10
10
710 East
Los Angeles
605
West
Covina
39
32
31 Pomona
Glendora
Claremont
210
Ontario
66
30
Whittier
57
83
60
10

TO SANTA MONICA

Los Angeles River
42
5 19
30
72
60
57
71
Chino

e

110
Downey
Compton
Norwalk
91
90
San Gabriel River
33 34
Santa Ana River
Norco
15
35

638
662
TO SANTA MONICA
TO RIVERSIDE

f

1
405
Long Beach
36
38 39
Anaheim
37
55
Fullerton
91
Corona
91

TO LOS ANGELES
TO LAKE ELSINORE

g

1
39
Garden
Grove
405
22
Orange
Santa Ana
5
S18
CLEVELAND
NATIONAL
FOREST

h

BOLSA CHICA
STATE BEACH
40
Huntington Beach
HUNTINGTON STATE BEACH
41
Costa
Mesa
42
Newport Beach
405
Irvine
Laguna
Hills
5
S19
43
44
45
46
Trabuco
Canyon

i

CORONA DEL MAR BEACH
CRYSTAL COVE STATE PARK
Laguna Beach
Mission
Viejo
1
47
74

j

PACIFIC
OCEAN
Capistrano Beach
DOHENY STATE BEACH
48
5
San Juan
Capistrano
San Clemente
CAMP
PENDLETON
MARINE
CORPS BASE
SAN CLEMENTE
STATE BEACH
49

700
TO OCEANSIDE

0 1 2 3 4 5 6 7 8 9

Chapter 15 features:

1 Mount Pacifico

Location: On the Pacific Crest Trail in Angeles National Forest; map 15, grid a2.

Campsites, facilities: There are 10 tent sites. Picnic tables, fire pits, and vault toilets are provided. There is no piped water, so bring your own. Leashed pets are permitted.

Reservations, fees: No reservations; an Adventure Pass ($30 annual fee) or $5 daily pass per parked vehicle is required. Open April through September.

Contact: Angeles National Forest, Los Angeles River Ranger District, (818) 790-1151 or fax (818) 790-5392.

Directions: From Interstate 210 north of Pasadena, drive north on the Angeles Crest Highway/Highway 2 for 29 miles. Turn left on Angeles Forest Highway/County Road N3 and drive about 12 miles. At the intersection with Santa Clara Divide Road/County Road 3N17, look for the Mill Creek Summit sign. Turn right and drive about five miles to Mount Pacifico Road. Turn left on the dirt road and drive five miles to the campground. At Mill Creek Summit, the gate is locked from November 15 to May 15 and it will be necessary to walk from the gate. When Santa Clara Divide Road is impassable due to weather conditions, it will be necessary to walk from Alder Saddle.

Trip notes: This is one of the great primitive camps in Angeles National Forest. It is set near the top of Mount Pacifico at an elevation of 7,134 feet, with the Pacific Crest Trail running right through the camp. The views are outstanding, especially to the north of the sparse Antelope Valley and beyond. From here, the PCT is routed through a series of ravines and draws and up short ridges, pleasant but not inspiring.

② Lightning Point Group Camp

Location: Near Mount Gleason in Angeles National Forest; map I5, grid a2.

Campsites, facilities: There are six group sites and 26 horse corrals. Piped water, picnic tables, and fire pits are provided. Flush toilets are available. Leashed pets are permitted.

Reservations, fees: Reservations are required; reserve via phone at (877) 444-6777 ($8.65 reservation fee) or website www.reserveusa.com; $40 group fee per site per night. The entire camp can accommodate 230 campers and is available for a fee of $240 per night. Open April through September.

Contact: Angeles National Forest, Tujunga Ranger District, (818) 899-1900 or fax (818) 896-6727.

Directions: From Interstate 210 north of Pasadena, take the Angeles Crest Highway/Highway 2 exit and drive north for nine miles. Turn left onto Angeles Forest Highway/County Road N3 and drive about 12 miles to the Santa Clara Divide Road intersection. Turn left and drive 10 miles to the campground entrance road on the left.

Trip notes: Lightning Point is set at 6,200 feet, high on the southwest flank of Mount Gleason, just a mile away from the summit (6,502 feet). This camp offers a one-mile interpretive trail and is also near a trailhead at Messenger Flats (campground number three) for a short hike to the top of Mount Gleason.

③ Messenger Flats

Location: Near Mount Gleason in Angeles National Forest; map I5, grid a2.

Campsites, facilities: There are 10 tent sites. Piped water (except in winter), picnic tables, fire pits, and vault toilets are provided. Two horse corrals are available. Leashed pets are permitted.

Reservations, fees: No reservations; $8 per night. Open year-round, but subject to snow closure from mid-November through February.

Contact: Angeles National Forest, Tujunga Ranger District, (818) 899-1900 or fax (818) 896-6727.

Directions: From Interstate 210 north of Pasadena, take the Angeles Crest Highway/Highway 2 exit and drive nine miles north. Turn left onto Angeles Forest Highway/County Road N3 and drive about 12 miles to the intersection with Santa Clara Divide Road. Turn left and drive 11 miles to the campground.

Trip notes: Messenger Flats is an ideal camp for many, located a half mile east of Mount Gleason (6,502 feet). The Pacific Crest Trail is routed through this camp, featuring a one-mile hike with a climb of 600 feet to reach Gleason's summit. The camp is at 5,900 feet, set in a flat area about a quarter mile east of an electronic transmitter at Messenger Peak.

④ Monte Cristo

Location: On Mill Creek in Angeles National Forest; map I5, grid a3.

Campsites, facilities: There are 19 sites for tents or RVs up to 32 feet long. Piped water, fire pits, vault toilets, and picnic tables are provided. There are two sites with wheelchair-accessible rest rooms. Leashed pets are permitted.

Reservations, fees: No reservations except for wheelchair sites; $8 per night, $3 for each additional vehicle. Open year-round.

Contact: Angeles National Forest, Tujunga Ranger District, (818) 899-1900 or fax (818) 896-6727.

Directions: From Interstate 210 north of Pasadena, take the Angeles Crest Highway/ Highway 2 exit and drive north for nine miles. Turn left onto Angeles Forest Highway/County Road N3 and drive about nine miles to the campground.

Trip notes: This is a Forest Service camp on Mill Creek at 3,600 feet, just west of Iron Mountain. The camp is situated under sycamore trees, which provide great color in the fall. In most years Mill Creek flows eight months out of the year.

❺ Bandido Group Camp

Location: Near the Pacific Crest Trail in Angeles National Forest; map I5, grid a4.

Campsites, facilities: There are 25 sites for tents or RVs up to 16 feet long. The camp will accommodate up to 120 people. Piped water, fire pits, vault toilets, and picnic tables are provided. Corrals and a water trough are available. Leashed pets are permitted.

Reservations, fees: Reservations are required; $25 per night per site. Groups can reserve half of the campground for $100 per night (60-person maximum) or the entire campground for $175 per night (120-person maximum). Open April through November.

Contact: Angeles National Forest, Los Angeles River Ranger District, (818) 790-1151 or fax (818) 790-5392.

Directions: From Interstate 210 north of Pasadena, take the Angeles Crest Highway/Highway 2 exit and drive north for 29 miles to the intersection with Santa Clara Divide Road at Three Points (there is a sign). Turn left and drive two miles to the campground on the left.

Trip notes: This is a base camp for groups preparing to hike off into the surrounding wilderness. A trail out of the camp heads north and intersects with the Pacific Crest Trail a little over one mile away at Three Points, a significant PCT junction. Before heading out most visitors check in first with rangers at the earby Chilao Visitor Center, two miles west of Three Points on Highway 2. The elevation is 5,100 feet.

❻ Horse Flats

Location: Near the San Gabriel Wilderness in Angeles National Forest; map I5, grid a4.

Campsites, facilities: There are 25 sites for tents or RVs up to 22 feet long. Piped water, fire pits, vault toilets, and picnic tables are provided. A grocery store is nearby. Leashed pets are permitted.

Reservations, fees: No reservations; $10 per night. The entire campground can be reserved for $200 per night for a maximum of 215 people. Open April through November.

Contact: Angeles National Forest, Los Angeles River Ranger District, (818) 790-1151 or fax (818) 790-5392.

Directions: From Interstate 210 north of Pasadena, take the Angeles Crest Highway/Highway 2 exit and drive north for 29 miles to the intersection with Santa Clara Divide Road at Three Points (there is a sign). Turn left and drive three miles to the signed campground.

Trip notes: This is one of four options in the immediate area: Chilao (campground number eight), Bandido Group Camp (campground number five), and Coulter Group Camp (campground number nine) are the other three camps; the latter two are for groups. Horse Flats is set at 5,500 feet along a national recreation trail and is close to the Chilao Visitor Center. Several trails into the San Gabriel Wilderness are nearby.

❼ Sulphur Springs Group Camp

Location: Near the Pacific Crest Trail in Angeles National Forest; map I5, grid a4.

Campsites, facilities: This is essentially a group camp, with 10 sites available for tents or RVs up to 16 feet long during deer hunting season. If reserved for a group, the campground will hold up to 80 people. Piped water, fire pits, vault toilets, and picnic tables are provided. Leashed pets are permitted.

Reservations, fees: No reservations for individual sites; reservations are required for groups; $6 per night for individual sites, $100 group fee per night (maximum of 80 people). Open April through November.

Contact: Angeles National Forest, Los Angeles River Ranger District, (818) 790-1151 or fax (818) 790-5392.

Directions: From Interstate 210 north of Pasadena, take the Angeles Crest Highway/Highway 2 exit and drive north for 29 miles to the intersection with Santa Clara Divide Road at Three Points (there is a sign). Turn left and drive five miles to the campground entrance road on the right (it will seem like the continuation of the road you're on).

Trip notes: This group camp is on the South Fork of Little Rock Creek, a short distance from a trailhead for the Pacific Crest Trail. It is set at 5,100 feet amid pines and is a popular jump-off point for group hikes. The nearby Chilao Visitor Center is a must-stop for newcomers.

8 Chilao

Location: Near the San Gabriel Wilderness in Angeles National Forest; map I5, grid a4.

Campsites, facilities: There are 110 sites for tents or RVs up to 22 feet long. Piped water, fire pits, vault toilets, and picnic tables are provided. A dump station is available at Charlton Flat Picnic Area. Leashed pets are permitted.

Reservations, fees: No reservations; $12 per night for individual sites, $30 per night for reserved double sites. Open May through October.

Contact: Angeles National Forest, Los Angeles River Ranger District, (818) 790-1151 or fax (818) 790-5392.

Directions: From Interstate 210 north of Pasadena, take the Angeles Crest Highway/Highway 2 exit and drive 26 miles northeast to the signed campground entrance road on the left.

Trip notes: This popular trailhead camp gets a lot of use. And it's easy to see why, with the Chilao Visitor Center (any questions?) located nearby and a national recreation trail running right by the camp. Access to the Pacific Crest Trail is two miles north at Three Points, and

parking is available there. The elevation is 5,200 feet.

9 Coulter Group Camp

Location: Near the San Gabriel Wilderness in Angeles National Forest; map I5, grid a4.

Campsites, facilities: There is one large group campsite that will accommodate up to 50 people. No RVs are permitted. Piped water, picnic tables, fire pits, and vault toilets are provided. Leashed pets are permitted.

Reservations, fees: Reservations are requested via phone at (877) 444-6777 ($8.65 reservation fee) or website: www.reserveusa.com; $100 group fee per night. Open May through October.

Contact: Angeles National Forest, Los Angeles River Ranger District, (818) 790-1151 or fax (818) 790-5392.

Directions: From Interstate 210 north of Pasadena, take the Angeles Crest Highway/Highway 2 exit and drive north for 26 miles to the signed campground. (Coulter Campground is between Little Pines Loop and Manzanita Loop, at the high end of either loop, through locked gates.)

Trip notes: This specially designated group camp is actually within the Chilao Camp. For details, see the trip notes for Chilao (campground number eight). The elevation is 5,300 feet.

10 Buckhorn

Location: Near Snowcrest Ridge in Angeles National Forest; map I5, grid a5.

Campsites, facilities: There are 40 sites for tents or RVs up to 16 feet long. Piped water, fire pits, vault toilets, and picnic tables are provided. Leashed pets are permitted.

Reservations, fees: No reservations; $12 per night. Open May through September.

Contact: Angeles National Forest, Los Angeles River Ranger District, (818) 790-1151 or fax (818) 790-5392.

Directions: From Interstate 210 north of Pasadena, take the Angeles Crest Highway/Highway

2 exit and drive 34 miles northeast to the signed campground entrance.

Trip notes: This is a prime jump-off spot for backpackers in Angeles National Forest. The camp is set among huge pine and cedar trees, along a small creek near Mount Waterman (8,038 feet). A great day hike begins here, a tromp down to Cooper Canyon and the PCT; hikers will be rewarded by beautiful Cooper Falls on this three-hour round-trip. Want a weekend trip? Got it: The High Desert National Recreational Trail leads north from camp into the backcountry, over Burkhart Saddle, and west around Devil's Punchbowl County Park to South Fork Campground. Then it heads south to the Islip Trailhead, east past Eagle's Roost, and south again for the last mile back to Buckhorn (campground number 10). It's a 20-mile hike, with the South Fork Camp situated 10 miles out, perfect for a weekend trip.

⑪ Deer Flat Group Camp

Location: Near Crystal Lake in Angeles National Forest; map I5, grid a6.

Campsites, facilities: There are nine group sites that will accommodate up to 20 campers each. Piped water, picnic tables, fire pits, and vault toilets are provided. A grocery store and visitor information center are nearby. Leashed pets are permitted.

Reservations, fees: Reservations required via phone at (877) 444-6777 ($8.65 reservation fee) or website www.reserveusa.com; $40 per night for a single site, $600 per night for all nine sites. Open year-round.

Contact: Angeles National Forest, Los Angeles River Ranger District, (818) 790-1151 or fax (818) 790-5392.

Directions: From Interstate 210, take the Azuza Canyon exit. Drive 25 miles north on San Gabriel Canyon Road/Highway 39 to the Crystal Lake Recreation Area and the campground.

Trip notes: This is an ideal spot to bring a troop of Boy or Girl Scouts. It is located about a mile from little Crystal Lake, a small lake with decent shoreline bait-dunking for trout. A nearby trail leads north from camp and in two miles intersects with the Pacific Crest Trail, though most just make it to the junction of the PCT, enjoy the views, and return.

⑫ Jackson Flat Group Camp

Location: Near the Pacific Crest Trail in Angeles National Forest; map I5, grid a7.

Campsites, facilities: There are five group sites that will accommodate 40 to 50 people each. Piped water, picnic tables, fire pits, and flush toilets are provided. Leashed pets are permitted.

Reservations, fees: Reservations are requested via phone at (877) 444-6777 ($8.65 reservation fee) or website www.reserveusa .com; $70 to $85 per night. Open June through September.

Contact: Angeles National Forest, Santa Clara/ Mojave Rivers Ranger District, (661) 296-9710 or fax (661) 296-5847.

Directions: From Interstate 15 near Cajon, take Highway 138 west. Turn west on Angeles Crest Highway/Highway 2 and drive five miles to Wrightwood. Continue for three miles to Big Pines. Bear left and continue on Angeles Crest Highway for two miles. Turn right opposite the sign for Grassy Hollow Campground and drive one mile to the campground.

Trip notes: This is a good spot for a group to overnight, assess themselves, and get information prior to heading out into the surrounding wildlands. The camp is set in the Angeles National Forest high country at 7,500 feet, at the end of a short spur road. The Pacific Crest Trail passes just north of camp and can be reached by a short connecting link trail.

⑬ Big Rock

Location: On Big Rock Creek in Angeles National Forest; map I5, grid a7.

Campsites, facilities: There are eight sites for tents. Fire pits, vault toilets, and picnic tables are provided. There is no piped water, so bring your own. Leashed pets are permitted.

Reservations, fees: No reservations; $5 per night. Open year-round.

Contact: Angeles National Forest, Santa Clara/ Mojave Rivers Ranger District, (661) 296-9710 or fax (661) 296-5847.

Directions: In Pearblossom on Highway 138, turn south on Longview Road and left on Avenue W/Valyermo Road and drive about 20 miles. Drive past the ranger station, turn right on Big Rock Road, and continue up the canyon (past the turnoff for South Fork Camp and past Camp Fenner) to the campground entrance road on the right.

Trip notes: This is a good spot for four-wheel-drive cowboys. It is a primitive Forest Service camp set at the head of Fenner Canyon along Big Rock Creek. Forest Service Road 4N11 to the southeast is a four-wheel-drive road that connects to a network of backcountry roads and hiking trails. A Forest Service map is essential. The elevation is 5,550 feet.

⑭ Sycamore Flat

Location: On Big Rock Creek in Angeles National Forest; map I5, grid a7.

Campsites, facilities: There are 11 sites for tents or RVs up to 22 feet long. Piped water, fire pits, vault toilets, and picnic tables are provided. Leashed pets are permitted.

Reservations, fees: No reservations; $8 per night. Open year-round.

Contact: Angeles National Forest, Santa Clara/ Mojave Rivers Ranger District, (661) 296-9710 or fax (661) 296-5847.

Directions: In Pearblossom on Highway 138, turn south on Longview Road and left on Avenue W/Valyermo Road and drive about 20 miles. Drive past the ranger station, turn right on Big Rock Road, and continue about two miles to the campground entrance.

Trip notes: Sycamore Flat is a developed camp located just inside the northern boundary of Angeles National Forest, set at 4,300 feet on the southwest flank of Piñon Ridge. While there are no trails leading out from this camp, a trailhead is available at South Fork (campground number 15), which is a little over one mile to the north, and an entry to a four-wheel-drive road is available at nearby Big Rock (campground number 13).

⑮ South Fork

Location: On Big Rock Creek in Angeles National Forest; map I5, grid a7.

Campsites, facilities: There are 21 sites for tents or RVs up to 16 feet long. There is no piped water, but picnic tables and fire rings are provided. Pit toilets are available. Leashed pets are permitted.

Reservations, fees: No reservations, no camping fee. Adventure Pass ($30 annual fee) or $5 daily fee per parked vehicle is required. Open year-around $8 per night. Open year-round.

Contact: Angeles National Forest, Valyermo Ranger District, (661) 296-9710 or fax (661) 296-5847.

Directions: In Pearblossom on Highway 138, turn south on Longview Road and left on Avenue W/Valyermo Road and drive about 20 miles. Drive past the ranger station, turn right on Big Rock Road, and continue about four miles up the canyon past the Sycamore Flat campground entrance to the South Fork campground entrance.

Trip notes: This is a developed camp located just inside the northern boundary of Angeles National Forest, set at 4,300 feet on the southwest flank of Piñon Ridge. While there are no trails leading out from this camp, a trailhead is available at South Fork, which is a little over one mile to the north, and an entry to a four-wheel-drive road is available at nearby Big Rock (campground number 13).

⑯ Apple Tree

Location: Near Jackson Lake in Angeles National Forest; map I5, grid a7.

Campsites, facilities: There are eight tent sites. Piped water, picnic tables, fire pits, and vault toilets are provided. Leashed pets are permitted.

Reservations, fees: No reservations; $8 per night April through October. From November through March, an Adventure Pass ($30 annual fee) or $5 daily fee per parked vehicle is required.

Open year-round.

Contact: Angeles National Forest, Santa Clara/Mojave Rivers Ranger District, (611) 296-9710 or fax (611) 296-5847.

Directions: From Interstate 15 near Cajon, take Highway 138 west. Turn west on Angeles Crest Highway/Highway 2 and drive five miles to Wrightwood. Continue for three miles to Big Pines. Bear right on Big Pines Highway/County Road N4 and drive two miles to the campground.

Trip notes: This is one of four camps set on Big Pines "Highway" near Jackson Lake. This "lake" is more of a pond and is located about a half mile to the west, just up the road. Lake and Peavine camps are located between Apple Tree and Jackson Lake, while Mountain Oak is located just beyond the lake. Any questions? Rangers can answer them at the nearby Big Pines Visitor Information Center and Ski Complexes. The elevation is 6,200 feet.

⑰ Mountain Oak

Location: Near Jackson Lake in Angeles National Forest; map I5, grid a7.

Campsites, facilities: There are 17 sites for tents or RVs up to 18 feet long. Piped water, fire pits, and picnic tables are provided. Flush toilets are available. Groceries and propane gas are nearby. Leashed pets are permitted.

Reservations, fees: No reservations; $10 per night. Open May through September.

Contact: Angeles National Forest, Santa Clara/Mojave Rivers Ranger District, (661) 296-9710 or fax (661) 296-5847.

Directions: From Interstate 15 near Cajon, take Highway 138 west. Turn west on Angeles Crest Highway/Highway 2 and drive five miles to Wrightwood. Continue for three miles to Big Pines. Bear right on Big Pines Highway/County Road N4 and drive three miles to the campground.

Trip notes: This is one of four camps within a mile of little Jackson Lake on Big Pines Highway. The others are Lake, Peavine, and Apple Tree. This camp is located about a quarter mile northwest of the lake. The elevation is 6,200 feet.

⑱ Lake

Location: On Jackson Lake in Angeles National Forest; map I5, grid a7.

Campsites, facilities: There are eight sites for tents or RVs up to 18 feet long. Piped water, fire pits, vault toilets, and picnic tables are provided. Leashed pets are permitted.

Reservations, fees: No reservations; $10 per night. Open May through October.

Contact: Angeles National Forest, Santa Clara/Mojave Rivers Ranger District, (661) 296-9710 or fax (661) 296-5847.

Directions: From Interstate 15 near Cajon, take Highway 138 west. Turn west on Angeles Crest Highway/Highway 2 and drive five miles to Wrightwood. Continue for three miles to Big Pines. Bear right on Big Pines Highway/County Road N4 and drive 2.5 miles to the campground.

Trip notes: This is a pretty setting on the southeast shore of little Jackson Lake. Of the four camps within a mile, this is the only one right beside the lake. The elevation is 6,100 feet.

⑲ Peavine

Location: Near Jackson Lake in Angeles National Forest; map I5, grid a7.

Campsites, facilities: There are four tent sites. Piped water, picnic tables, fire pits, and vault toilets are provided. A grocery store and propane gas are nearby. Leashed pets are permitted.

Reservations, fees: No reservations; $8 per night. Open May through October.

Contact: Angeles National Forest, Santa Clara/Mojave Rivers Ranger District, (661) 296-9710 or fax (661) 296-5847.

Directions: From Interstate 15 near Cajon, take Highway 138 west. Turn west on Angeles Crest Highway/Highway 2 and drive five miles to Wrightwood. Continue for three miles to Big Pines. Bear right on Big Pines Highway/County Road N4 and drive 2.5 miles to the campground.

Trip notes: This tiny camp is one of four in the immediate area, located just a half mile east of little eight-acre Jackson Lake. The elevation is 6,100 feet.

⑳ Table Mountain

Location: In Angeles National Forest; map I5, grid a8.

Campsites, facilities: There are 115 sites for tents or RVs up to 32 feet long. Piped water, fire pits, vault toilets, and picnic tables are provided. Leashed pets are permitted.

Reservations, fees: No reservations; $12 per night. Open May through September.

Contact: Angeles National Forest, Santa Clara/ Mojave Rivers Ranger District, (661) 296-9710 or fax (661) 296-5847.

Directions: From Interstate 15 near Cajon, take Highway 138 west. Turn west on Angeles Crest Highway/Highway 2 and drive five miles to Wrightwood. Continue for three miles to Big Pines. Turn right on Table Mountain Road and drive one mile to the campground.

Trip notes: This is a family campground that accommodates both tents and RVs. The road leading in is a paved two-lane county road, easily accessible by any vehicle. The nearby Big Pines Visitor Information Center, located one mile to the south, can provide maps and information on road conditions. The camp elevation is 7,200 feet. A rough road for four-wheel-drive rigs is available out of camp that leads north along the Table Mountain Ridge.

㉑ Blue Ridge

Location: On the Pacific Crest Trail in Angeles National Forest; map I5, grid a8.

Campsites, facilities: There are eight sites for tents or RVs up to 16 feet long. Fire pits, vault toilets, and picnic tables are provided. There is no piped water, so bring your own. Leashed pets are permitted.

Reservations, fees: No reservations; $5 per night. Open June through September.

Contact: Angeles National Forest, Santa Clara/ Mojave Rivers Ranger District, (661) 296-9710 or fax (661) 296-5847.

Directions: From Interstate 15 near Cajon, take Highway 138 west. Turn west on Angeles Crest Highway/Highway 2 and drive five miles to Wrightwood. Continue for three miles to Big Pines. Bear left and continue on Angeles Crest Highway for 1.5 miles. Turn left (opposite Inspiration Point) on Blue Ridge Road and drive three miles to the campground.

Trip notes: Blue Ridge is set high in Angeles National Forest at 8,000 feet and makes for a jump-off spot for a multiday backpacking trip. The Pacific Crest Trail runs right alongside the camp. Guffy (campground number 28), also located aside the PCT, provides an option two miles to the southeast, but it takes a four-wheel-drive vehicle to get there. There are a number of primitive four-wheel-drive routes in the area.

㉒ Millard

Location: Near Millard Falls in Angeles National Forest; map I5, grid b2.

Campsites, facilities: There are five tent sites. Piped water, picnic tables, fire pits, and vault toilets are provided. Leashed pets are permitted.

Reservations, fees: No reservations; no camping fee, an Adventure Pass ($30 annual fee) or $5 daily fee per parked vehicle is required. Open year-round.

Contact: Angeles National Forest, Los Angeles River Ranger District, (818) 790-1151 or fax (818) 790-5392.

Directions: From Interstate 210 north of Pasadena, take the Lake Avenue exit north to Loma Alta Drive. Turn west on Loma Alta Drive and drive to Chaney Trail Road (at the flashing yellow light). Follow the signs to the camp. It is a walk of several hundred feet from the parking lot to the campground.

Trip notes: This is a tiny and pretty camp, set near a creek amid oak and alder woodlands, that is best known as the launching point for some excellent hikes. The best is the half-mile hike to Millard Falls, where you actually rock hop your way upstream to Millard Falls, a 60-foot waterfall and a drop-dead beautiful sight. On weekends, there can be lots of foot traffic through the campground with hikers occasionally passing through on their way to the falls. Another trail out of camp leads to Inspiration Point and continues farther to San Gabriel Peak.

㉓ West Fork Walk-In

Location: On the West Fork of the San Gabriel River in Angeles National Forest; map I5, grid b4.

Campsites, facilities: There are seven tent sites. Picnic tables, fire pits, and vault toilets are provided. There is no piped water, so bring your own. Leashed pets are permitted.

Reservations, fees: No reservations; no camping fee, an Adventure Pass ($30 annual fee) or $5 daily fee per parked vehicle is required. Open April through October, weather permitting.

Contact: Angeles National Forest, Los Angeles River Ranger District, (818) 790-1151 or fax (818) 790-5392.

Directions: From Interstate 210 north of Pasadena, take the Angeles Crest Highway/Highway 2 and drive about 14 miles to Mount Wilson Road. Park in the lot there, walk in through the gate (on Red Box–Rincon Road) to the dirt road (not the paved one), and walk six miles to the camp or use the rock stairway on the east side of the parking lot and take that trail to the campground.

Trip notes: It takes a circuitous drive and a 4.5- to 6-mile hike to reach this camp, but for backpackers it is worth it. The camp is on the West Fork of the San Gabriel River amid pine woodlands, with two national recreation trails intersecting just south of here. The canyon is deep and the river is beautiful. The elevation is 3,000 feet.

㉔ Valley Forge Walk-In

Location: On the San Gabriel River in Angeles National Forest; map I5, grid b4.

Campsites, facilities: There are 17 tent sites. Piped water, picnic tables, fire pits, and vault toilets are provided. There is no piped water. Leashed pets are permitted.

Reservations, fees: No reservations; no camping fee, an Adventure Pass ($30 annual fee) or $5 daily fee per parked vehicle is required. Open April through October, weather permitting.

Contact: Angeles National Forest, Los Angeles River Ranger District, (818) 790-1151 or fax (818) 790-5392.

Directions: From Interstate 210 north of Pasadena, take the Angeles Crest Highway/Highway 2 and drive about 14 miles to Mount Wilson Road. Park in the lot there, walk in through the gate (on Red Box–Rincon Road) to the dirt road (not the paved one), and walk three miles to the campground.

Trip notes: Valley Forge is a good camp for anglers or hikers who are looking for a short backpacking trip. For hikers, a national recreation trail passes close to the camp. For fishermen, there are small but feisty trout. The elevation is 3,500 feet.

㉕ Coldbrook

Location: On the North Fork of the San Gabriel River in Angeles National Forest; map I5, grid b6.

Campsites, facilities: There are 22 sites for tents or RVs up to 22 feet long. Piped water, fire pits, vault toilets, and picnic tables are provided. The host is on site. Leashed pets are permitted.

Reservations, fees: No reservations; $8 per night, $3 for each additional vehicle. Open year-round.

Contact: Angeles National Forest, San Gabriel River Ranger District, (626) 335-1251 or fax (626) 914-3790.

Directions: From Interstate 210, take the Azuza Canyon exit. Drive 18 miles north on San Gabriel Canyon Road/Highway 39 to the campground entrance.

Trip notes: This roadside camp is set along the North Fork San Gabriel River, with little Crystal Lake located to the north. A secret waterfall is hidden off the road, about three miles north on Soldier Creek. To find it, park at the deep bending turn in the road at Soldier Creek, then hike uphill for less than a mile. It's just like a treasure hunt, and it's always a welcome surprise to find the waterfall. The elevation is 3,300 feet.

㉖ Lupine

Location: On Prairie Fork Creek in Angeles National Forest; map I5, grid b8.

Campsites, facilities: There are 11 tent sites. Picnic tables and fire pits are provided. Vault toilets are available. There is no piped water, so bring your own. Leashed pets are permitted.

Reservations, fees: No reservations; $5 per night. Open June through September.

Contact: Angeles National Forest, Santa Clara/ Mojave Rivers Ranger District, (661) 296-9710 or fax (661) 296-5847.

Directions: From Interstate 15 near Cajon, take Highway 138 west. Turn west on Angeles Crest Highway/Highway 2 and drive five miles to Wrightwood. Continue for three miles to Big Pines. Bear left and continue on Angeles Crest Highway/Highway 2 for 1.5 miles. Turn left (opposite Inspiration Point) on Blue Ridge Road (it's a rough, dirt road after the first three miles) and drive 10 miles to the camp.

Trip notes: This little-known, hard-to-reach camp, set at 6,500 feet along Prairie Fork Creek, is used most often by campers with four-wheel-drive rigs. A challenging butt-kicker hike on a primitive trail starts here. The trail is routed from the camp over Pine Mountain Ridge, down into a canyon, and then winding to the east up Dawson Peak—long, difficult, and completed by few.

㉗ Cabin Flat

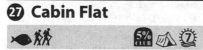

Location: On Prairie Fork Creek in Angeles National Forest; map I5, grid b8.

Campsites, facilities: There are 12 tent sites. Picnic tables, fire pits, and vault toilets are provided. There is no piped water, so bring your own. Leashed pets are permitted.

Reservations, fees: No reservations; $5 per night. Open June through September.

Contact: Angeles National Forest, Santa Clara/ Mojave Rivers Ranger District, (661) 296-9710 or fax (661) 296-5847.

Directions: From Interstate 15 near Cajon, take Highway 138 west. Turn west on Angeles Crest Highway/Highway 2 and drive five miles to Wrightwood. Continue for three miles to Big Pines. Bear left and continue on Angeles Crest Highway for 1.5 miles. Turn left (opposite Inspiration Point) on Blue Ridge Road and drive 12 miles to the campground (the road becomes a rough, dirt road after the first three miles).

Trip notes: It takes a four-wheel drive to get here, but that done, you're guaranteed solitude along little Prairie Fork Creek, deep in the Angeles National Forest. To get here, you will pass several other camps, including Guffy (campground number 28) and Lupine (campground number 26). A short trail runs beside the stream for about a quarter mile. The elevation is 5,400 feet.

㉘ Guffy

Location: On the Pacific Crest Trail in Angeles National Forest; map I5, grid b9.

Campsites, facilities: There are six tent sites. Picnic tables and fire pits are provided. Vault toilets are available. There is no piped water, so bring your own. Leashed pets are permitted.

Reservations, fees: No reservations; $5 per night. Open June through September.

Contact: Angeles National Forest, Santa Clara/ Mojave Rivers Ranger District, (661) 296-9710 or fax (661) 296-5847.

Directions: From Interstate 15 near Cajon, take Highway 138 west. Turn west on Angeles Crest Highway/Highway 2 and drive five miles to Wrightwood. Continue for three miles to Big Pines. Bear left and continue on Angeles Crest Highway for 1.5 miles. Turn left (opposite Inspiration Point) on Blue Ridge Road and drive six miles to the campground (it's a rough, dirt road after the first three miles).

Trip notes: A short trail right out of this camp connects with the Pacific Crest Trail, making Guffy a backpacker's special. The area is also popular for campers with four-wheel-drive rigs, with a number of primitive roads in the area. The elevation is 8,300 feet.

㉙ Manker Flats

Location: Near Mount Baldy in Angeles National Forest; map I5, grid b9.

Campsites, facilities: There are 21 sites for tents or RVs up to 16 feet long. Piped water, flush toilets, picnic tables, and fire grills are provided. Leashed pets are permitted.

Reservations, fees: No reservations; $8 per night, $3 for each additional vehicle. Open May through September.

Contact: Angeles National Forest, San Gabriel River Ranger District, (626) 335-1251 or fax (626) 914-3790.

Directions: From Ontario, drive six miles north on Highway 83 to Mount Baldy Road. Drive nine miles north on Mount Baldy Road to the campground.

Trip notes: This Camp is best known for its proximity to Mount Baldy, as well as for providing the trailhead to reach San Antonio Falls. The trail to San Antonio Falls starts at an elevation of 6,160 feet, three-tenths of a mile up the road on the left. From here, it's a 1.5-mile saunter on a ski park maintenance road to the waterfall, a pretty 80-footer. The wild and ambitious can continue six more miles and climb to the top of Mount Baldy (10,064 feet) for breathtaking 360-degree views. Making this all-day butt-kicker is like a baptism for Southern California hikers.

㉚ Del Rio Mobile Home and RV Park

Location: In Los Angeles; map I5, grid d1.

Campsites, facilities: There are 30 RV sites. Piped water, electrical connections, and sewer hookups are provided. A swimming pool, hot tub, and coin laundry are available. Leashed pets are permitted.

Reservations, fees: Reservations are accepted; $20 for two people per night, $1 for each additional camper (maximum of $24 for six or more people).

Contact: Del Rio Mobile Home and RV Park, (323) 560-2895.

Directions: From Interstate 710/Long Beach Freeway, take the Florence Avenue exit. Drive west on Florence Avenue to 5246 East Florence Avenue.

Trip notes: This privately operated, urban RV park is located about 15 minutes from downtown Los Angeles and 20 minutes from Long Beach.

㉛ Fairplex RV Park

Location: In Pomona; map I5, grid d6.

Campsites, facilities: There are 185 pull-through sites for RVs, 158 with full hookups and 27 with water and electric hookups. Rest rooms, showers, heated pool and spa, convenience store, dump station, and coin laundry are provided.

Reservations, fees: Reservations are accepted; $32.45 per night.

Contact: Fairplex RV Park, 2200 North White Avenue, Pomona, CA 91768; (909) 865-4318 or (909) 593-8915.

Directions: From Interstate 10 in Pomona, take the Fairplex exit and go left. At the bottom of the hill, turn right on McKinley Avenue. Take McKinley all the way to White Avenue and then turn left. The RV park is at 2200 North White Avenue.

Trip notes: This is what you might call an urban RV park. Then again, the L.A. County Fairgrounds are right across the street, and there's something going on there every weekend. Fishing at Bonelli Park is only 15 minutes away.

㉜ East Shore RV Park

Location: At Puddingstone Lake; map I5, grid d6.

Campsites, facilities: There are 25 walk-in tent sites and 519 RV sites. Piped water, electrical connections, and sewer hookups are provided. Rest rooms, showers, recreation room, swimming pool, grocery store, propane gas delivery, and coin laundry are available. Leashed pets are permitted.

Reservations, fees: Reservations are accepted; $24 to $27 per night, $2 pet fee. Open year-round.

Contact: East Shore RV Park, (909) 599-8355 , (800) 809-3778, or fax (909) 592-7481.

Directions: From Pomona, drive five miles west on Interstate 10. Take the Fairplex exit north to the first traffic light. Turn left on Via Verde and drive to the first stop sign. Turn right on Campers View and drive into the park.

Trip notes: Considering how close Puddingstone Lake is to so many people, the quality of fishing and waterskiing might be a surprise to newcomers. The lake covers 250 acres and is an excellent recreation facility. For the most part rules permit waterskiing between 10 A.M. and 4 P.M., making it an excellent lake for fishing for bass and trout (in season) during the morning and evening, and an excellent lake for waterskiing during the day. A ski beach is available on the north shore, and there is a large, sandy swimming beach on the southwest shore. The lake is just south of Raging Waters in San Dimas, and is bordered to the south by Bonelli Regional County Park.

33 Canyon RV

Location: Near Disneyland; map I5, grid e6.

Campsites, facilities: There are 120 sites for RVs up to 40 feet long, 42 with full hookups. Some tent sites are available. Fire grills and picnic tables are provided. Flush toilets, hot showers, dump stations, seasonal swimming pool, and a playground are available. A convenience store, coin laundry, and propane are also available. Restaurants are located nearby. Leashed pets are permitted.

Reservations, fees: Reservations are accepted; $17.50 to $25 per night, $1 pet fee. Open year-round.

Contact: Canyon RV, (714) 637-0210 or fax (714) 637-9317.

Directions: From Interstate 5 in Anaheim, drive east on Highway 91 for 13 miles. Turn left on Gypsum Canyon Road, go under the freeway, and drive about one block to the park entrance on the left.

Trip notes: In the mad rush to find a spot to park an RV in the area, this regional park is often overlooked. It is located near the Santa Ana River.

Side trip possibilities include Chino Hills State Park to the north, Cleveland National Forest to the south, and Lake Matthews to the southeast. The park is also close to Disneyland and Knott's Berry Farm.

34 Prado Regional Park

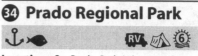

Location: On Prado Park Lake near Corona; map I5, grid e6.

Campsites, facilities: There are 35 sites for RVs with full hookups and 15 tent sites. Twenty-five sites are available for groups. Picnic tables, fire pits, rest rooms, coin laundry, and showers are provided. A snack bar, picnic area, boat ramp, and boat rentals are available. Leashed pets are permitted.

Reservations, fees: Reservations are accepted; $15 per night, $1 pet fee. Weekly, monthly, and senior rates are available. Group rates are $11 per unit, with a maximum of two units per site. (There is also a $10 reservation fee for groups.) Proof of insurance for all vehicles is required.

Contact: Prado Regional Park, (909) 597-4260.

Directions: From Riverside, take Highway 91 west to Highway 71. Turn north on Highway 71 and proceed four miles to Highway 83/Euclid Avenue. Turn right on Euclid Avenue and drive a mile to the park entrance on the right.

Trip notes: Prado Park Lake is the centerpiece of a recreation-oriented park that features an equestrian center, athletic fields, shooting range, and a golf course. The lake is small and used primarily for paddling small boats and fishing, which is best in the winter and early spring when trout are planted.

35 Rancho Jurupa County Park

Location: Near Riverside; map I5, grid e9.

Campsites, facilities: There are 80 sites for tents or RVs. Electrical connections, piped water, fire grills, and picnic tables are provided.

Flush toilets, showers, and a dump station are available. Leashed pets are permitted.

Reservations, fees: Reservations are accepted; $16 per night, $5-per-pole fishing fee, $2 pet fee. Open year-round.

Contact: Rancho Jurupa County Park, (909) 684-7032.

Directions: From Interstate 15 in Riverside, head west on Highway 60 for about three miles. Turn left on Rubidoux Boulevard and drive a half mile. Turn left on Mission Boulevard and drive about a mile to Crestmore Boulevard. Turn right and drive 1.5 miles to the park gate on the left.

Trip notes: Lord, it gets hot in the summertime, but there is shade and grass here. In the cooler weather during spring, this county park stocks a fishing pond. That is also the best time to explore the park's hiking and equestrian trails. Summer visitors will find that the nearest lake for swimming and water sports is Lake Perris, about a 20-minute drive away. The elevation is 780 feet.

㊱ Anaheim Vacation Park

Location: Near Knott's Berry Farm; map I5, grid f3.

Campsites, facilities: There are 222 RV sites with full hookups. Rest rooms, showers, satellite TV, phone hookups, playground, swimming pool, coin laundry, store, recreation room, and propane gas are available. A grocery store is nearby. Leashed pets are permitted.

Reservations, fees: Reservations are accepted; call for fees, $1 pet fee.

Contact: Anaheim Vacation Park, (714) 821-4311 or fax (714) 761-1743.

Directions: From Highway 91 in Anaheim, drive a mile south on Highway 39 to 311 North Beach Boulevard/Highway 39.

Trip notes: Some of the most popular RV parks in America are in this area, and it's easy to see why. Disneyland is nearby, and Knott's Berry Farm is within walking distance. Plus, where else are you going to park your rig?

㊲ Travelers World RV Park

Location: Near Disneyland; map I5, grid f4.

Campsites, facilities: There are 335 sites for tents or RVs with full hookups. Picnic tables, and fire grills provided. Rest rooms, showers, playground, adult lounge/game room, swimming pool, coin laundry, store, dump station, ice, recreation room, RV wash rack, and propane gas are available. Leashed pets are permitted.

Reservations, fees: Call for available space; $24 to $28 per night, $2 pet fee. Open year-round.

Contact: Travelers World RV Park, (714) 991-0100 or fax (714) 991-4939.

Directions: Heading south into Anaheim on Interstate 5, take a left at the Ball Road exit and drive to East Vermont Street. Make a right and proceed to Lemon Street. Make another right on Lemon Street and a right again at Ball Road and continue half a block to the campground on the right at 333 West Ball Road.

Trip notes: This is one of the premium and most popular RV parks for visitors to Disneyland and other nearby attractions. It is easy to see why, with the park located just a half mile from Disneyland. A shuttle-tour bus is a great bonus, with shuttles to Knott's Berry Farm, the Wax Museum, Universal Studios, Marineland, and the *Queen Mary*.

㊳ C. C. Camperland

Location: Near Disneyland; map I5, grid f4.

Campsites, facilities: There are 90 sites for tents or RVs. Picnic tables and full hookups are provided. Rest rooms, showers, solar-heated swimming pool, coin laundry, dump station, and ice are available. Leashed pets are permitted, except in the tent area.

Reservations, fees: Call ahead for available space; $20 to $28 per night for one or two people, $2 for each additional person. Open year-round.

Contact: C. C. Camperland, (714) 750-6747.

Directions: From Interstate 5 in Garden Grove,

drive south for 1.5 miles on Harbor Boulevard to the campground on the left at 2262 Harbor Boulevard.

Trip notes: Camperland is located nine blocks south of Disneyland, and that right there is the number-one appeal. Knott's Berry Farm is also close by.

㊴ Orangeland RV Park

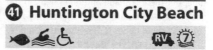

Location: Near Disneyland; map I5, grid f4.

Campsites, facilities: There are 212 RV sites with picnic tables, fire grills, and full hookups provided. Rest rooms, showers, playground, swimming pool, therapy pool, exercise room, coin laundry, store, car wash, shuffleboard court, billiards, dump station, ice, and a recreation room are available. Leashed pets are permitted.

Reservations, fees: Reservations are encouraged; $30 per night, $2 for each additional person, $1 pet fee. Open year-round.

Contact: Orangeland RV Park, (714) 633-0414 or fax (714) 633-0912.

Directions: In Anaheim on Interstate 5, turn east on Katella Avenue and drive two miles, passing Anaheim Stadium and the Santa Ana River, to the park at 1600 West Struck Avenue.

Trip notes: This park is located about five miles east of Disneyland. If the RV parks on West Street near Disneyland are filled, this is a viable alternative.

㊵ Bolsa Chica State Beach

Location: Near Huntington Beach; map I5, grid g2.

Campsites, facilities: This is a "destination" campsite (self-contained RVs can park for one-night stays, but they must leave by 12 P.M. the following day). The beach park provides fire rings, dressing rooms, cold showers, picnic areas, food service, bicycle trail, and a paved ramp for wheelchair access to the beach. Leashed pets are permitted.

Reservations, fees: Reserve via phone at (800) 444-PARK/7275 ($7.50 reservation fee) or website www.cal-parks.ca.gov; $20 per night. Open year-round.

Contact: Bolsa Chica State Beach, (714) 846-3460 or (949) 492-0802 .

Directions: From Huntington Beach, drive three miles north on Highway 1 to the park.

Trip notes: This is basically a beachfront parking lot, but a popular one at that. RV drivers typically park for the night and then say *adios* the next morning. Don't be so quick to leave. A great little walk is available at the adjacent Bolsa Chica State Reserve, a 1.5-mile loop that provides an escape from the parking lot and entry into the 530-acre nature reserve, complete with egrets, pelicans, and many shorebirds.

㊶ Huntington City Beach

Location: On the Pacific Ocean; map I5, grid h3.

Campsites, facilities: There are 160 sites for RVs up to 30 feet long. Piped water and fire rings are provided. Flush toilets and a dump station are available. Supplies are available within a mile. No pets are allowed.

Reservations, fees: Reservations are accepted in the winter months only; $15 per night. Open year-round.

Contact: Huntington City Beach, (714) 536-5280.

Directions: From Interstate 405 in Huntington Beach, take the Beach Boulevard exit and drive to Highway 1/Pacific Coast Highway. Turn north, drive to the intersection with First Street, and turn left into the campground parking area.

Trip notes: This is the other of the two popular beachside camps in the immediate area, both prime layovers for Highway 1 cruisers. Bolsa Chica State Beach provides an alternative if this camp is full. The best nearby adventure is the short loop walk at Bolsa Chica State Reserve; see the trip notes for Bolsa Chica State Beach (campground number 40) for more information.

㊷ Newport Dunes

Location: In Newport Beach; map I5, grid h4.

Campsites, facilities: There are 406 sites for

tents or RVs, all with full hookups. Picnic tables and fire grills are provided. Rest rooms, showers, swimming pool and spa, waveless saltwater lagoon, planned activities, coin laundry, grocery store, restaurant, fitness room, and marina with boat launch ramp are available. The facilities are wheelchair accessible. Kayaking, windsurfing, and sailing lessons and rentals are also available. Leashed pets are permitted.

Reservations, fees: Reserve via phone at (800) 288-0770; fees are a function of site size and location; $28 to $65 per night, except holidays when the fee is $46 to $95 per night. Open year-round.

Contact: Newport Dunes, (949) 729-3863.

Directions: From Laguna Hills, take Interstate 405 north to the Highway 55 exit. Turn south on Highway 55 and drive to the junction with Highway 73. Drive south five miles on Highway 73 to Back Bay Drive. Turn right on Back Bay Drive and drive about half a block to the resort entrance.

Trip notes: This privately operated park is set in a pretty spot on the bay, with a beach, boat ramp, and storage area providing bonuses. Corona del Mar State Beach to the west and Crystal Cove State Park to the south provide possible side trips. The park is five minutes' walking distance from Balboa Island, and is next to the largest estuary in California, the Upper Newport Bay Ecological Reserve.

43 O'Neill Regional Park

Location: Near Cleveland National Forest; map I5, grid h7.

Campsites, facilities: There are 90 sites for tents or RVs up to 35 feet long and several group camping areas. Piped water, fire grills, and picnic tables are provided. Flush toilets, showers, playground, and a dump station are available. A grocery store is nearby. Leashed pets are permitted.

Reservations, fees: No reservations are accepted, except for group sites; call for group fees; $12 per night for individual sites, $2 pet fee. Open year-round.

Contact: O'Neill Regional Park, (949) 858-9365.

Directions: From Interstate 5 in Laguna Hills, take the County Road S18/El Toro Road exit and drive east (past El Toro) for seven miles. Turn right onto Live Oak Canyon Road/County Road

S19 and drive about three miles to the park on the right.

Trip notes: This park is just far enough off the main drag to get missed by most of the RV cruisers on Interstate 5. It is set near Trabuco Canyon, adjacent to Cleveland National Forest to the east. Several roads near this park lead to trailheads into Cleveland National Forest. The elevation is 1,000 feet.

44 Falcon Group Camp

Location: In the Santa Ana Mountains in Cleveland National Forest; map I5, grid h9.

Campsites, facilities: There are three group camp sites for tents or RVs. Sage Camp accommodates 30 people and RVs up to 40 feet; Lupine Camp accommodates 40 people and RVs up to 20 feet, and Yarrow Camp accommodates 70 people and RVs up to 30 feet. Piped water, fire rings, pedestal grills, and picnic tables are provided. Pit toilets are available. A grocery store is within five miles. Leashed pets are permitted.

Reservations, fees: Reserve via phone at (877) 444-6777 ($8.65 reservation fee) or website www.reserveusa.com; $35 to $80 per group per night. Open May through October.

Contact: Cleveland National Forest, Trabuco Ranger District, (909) 736-1811 or fax (909) 736-3002.

Directions: From Interstate 15 in Lake Elsinore, take the Highway 74 exit and drive 12 miles west. Turn right on Forest Service Road 6S05 and drive about seven miles to the campground entrance on your left.

Trip notes: At an elevation of 3,300 feet, Falcon and Blue Jay (campground number 45) are adjacent to each other, with Blue Jay set up for individual campers and Falcon for groups. The campground is at the trailhead for the San Juan Trail and the Chiquito Trail, both of which lead into the backcountry wilderness and the Santa Ana Mountains.

45 Blue Jay

Location: In the Santa Ana Mountains in Cleveland National Forest; map I5, grid h9.

Campsites, facilities: There are eight sites for tents only and 43 sites for tents or RVs up to 22 feet long. Piped water, pedestal grills, and picnic tables are provided. Pit toilets are available and a grocery store is within five miles. Leashed pets are permitted.

Reservations, fees: No reservations; $15 per night with a two-vehicle maximum. Open May through September.

Contact: Cleveland National Forest, Trabuco Ranger District, (909) 736-1811 or fax (909) 736-3002.

Directions: From Interstate 15 at Lake Elsinore, take the Highway 74 exit and drive 12 miles west. Turn right on Forest Service Road 6S05 and drive about seven miles to the campground entrance on your left.

Trip notes: The few hikers who know of this spot like it and keep coming back, provided they time their hikes when temperatures are cool (nearby Upper San Juan Campground is also set near a great trailhead). The trailheads to the San Juan Trail and the Chiquito Trail, both of which lead into the backcountry wilderness and the Santa Ana Mountains, are adjacent to the camp. A Forest Service map is strongly advised. The elevation is 3,300 feet.

㊻ El Cariso North Campground

Location: Near Lake Elsinore in Cleveland National Forest; map I5, grid h9.

Campsites, facilities: There are 24 sites for tents or RVs up to 22 feet long. Piped water, fire rings, pedestal grills, and picnic tables are provided. Pit toilets are available. Leashed pets are permitted.

Reservations, fees: No reservations; $15 per night with a two-vehicle maximum. Open from April through November.

Contact: Cleveland National Forest, Trabuco Ranger District, (909) 736-1811 or fax (909) 736-3002.

Directions: From Interstate 5 in San Juan Capistrano, drive 24 miles northeast on Highway 74/Ortega Highway. Or from Interstate 15 in Lake

Elsinore, drive 12 miles west on Highway 74 to the campground.

Trip notes: This pretty, shaded spot at 3,000 feet is just inside the border of Cleveland National Forest with Lake Elsinore to the east. On the drive in there are great views to the east, looking down at Lake Elsinore and across the desert country. Hikers should head west to the Upper San Juan Campground.

㊼ Caspers Regional Park

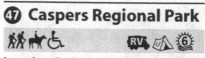

Location: On the San Juan River; map I5, grid i8.

Campsites, facilities: There are about 40 sites for tents or RVs and 30 additional sites for equestrian campers. Group sites are also available Picnic tables, barbecues, and piped water are provided. Flush toilets, showers, dump station, corrals, stables, 30 miles of trails, and a playground are available. Hikers must be accompanied by a ranger or group leader on the trails. Pets are not allowed.

Reservations, fees: Reservations are accepted; $12 per night, $4 per extra vehicle, $3 for each horse per night. Open year-round.

Contact: Caspers Regional Park, (949) 831-2174.

Directions: From San Juan Capistrano, drive 7.5 miles northeast on Highway 74 to the signed park entrance on the left.

Trip notes: Highway 74 provides easy access to this regional park. It is a popular spot for picnics and day hikes, and since the campground is not listed with any of the computer-based reservation services, it is overlooked by most out-of-town travelers. It is bordered to the south by the San Juan River and to the east by the Cleveland National Forest and the San Mateo Canyon Wilderness.

㊽ Doheny State Beach

Location: On Dana Point Harbor; map I5, grid j5.

Campsites, facilities: There are 120 sites for

tents or RVs. No hookups are provided. Fire grills and picnic tables are provided. Flush toilets, showers, dump station, exhibits, and food service (summer only) are available. Propane gas is nearby. Camping, picnic, food service, and exhibit areas are wheelchair accessible. Leashed pets are permitted in campground only, not on the beach.

Reservations, fees: Reserve via phone at (800) 444-PARK/7275 ($7.50 reservation fee) or website www.cal-parks.ca.gov; $18 to $24 per night, $1 pet fee. Open year-round.

Contact: Doheny State Beach, (949) 496-6172 or (949) 492-0802.

Directions: From San Juan Capistrano, drive three miles south on Interstate 5 to the Pacific Coast Highway/Doheny State Beach exit. Turn left at the second light onto Dana Point Harbor Drive. Drive one block and go left onto Park Lantern. The park entrance is one block away.

Trip notes: It's right in town, but you should still plan on a reservation or don't make a plan. It is set at the entrance to Dana Point Harbor, a pretty spot with easy access off the highway. San Juan Capistrano provides a nearby side trip. There are too many good things here not to expect a lot of folks to want to stay for the night.

㊾ San Clemente State Beach

Location: Near San Clemente; map I5, grid j6.

Campsites, facilities: There are 157 sites for tents or RVs, 72 with full hookups. Fire grills and picnic tables are provided. Flush toilets and showers are available. A grocery store, coin laundry, and propane gas are nearby. The camping area is wheelchair accessible. Leashed pets are permitted.

Reservations, fees: Reserve via phone at (800) 444-PARK/7275 ($7.50 reservation fee) or website www.cal-parks.ca.gov; $18 to $24 per night. Open year-round.

Contact: San Clemente State Beach, (949) 492-3156 or (949) 492-0802.

Directions: From Interstate 5 in San Clemente, take the Avenida Calafia exit. Drive west for a short distance to the park entrance.

Trip notes: Of the three local state beaches that provide easy access and beachfront camping, this one offers full hookups. The others are Doheny State Beach to the north and San Onofre State Beach to the south.

Map I6

One inch equals approximately 10.7 miles.
See inside back cover for California state map.

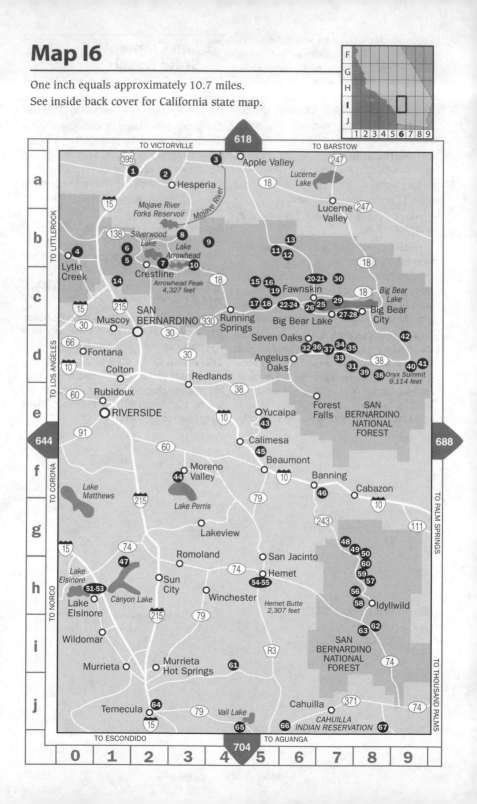

Chapter 16 features:

❶ Desert Willow RV Park

Location: In Hesperia; map I6, grid a1.

Campsites, facilities: There are 176 RV sites with full hookups. Rest rooms, hot showers, cable TV hookups, convenience store, groceries, ice, coin laundry, propane gas, swimming pool, indoor spa, recreation room, library, and cable TV are on the premises. Some facilities are wheelchair accessible. Leashed pets are permitted.

Reservations, fees: Reservations are accepted; $20 to $22 per night, $2 pet fee. Open year-round, with limited winter facilities.

Contact: Desert Willow RV Park, (760) 949-0377 or fax (760) 949-4334.

Directions: In Hesperia on Interstate 15, take the Main Street exit and drive west to 12624 Main Street West.

Trip notes: This is an RV park for Interstate 15 cruisers looking to make a stop. Silverwood Lake, a 1,000-acre recreation lake with fishing, boating, and water sports, is 16 miles to the south. The elevation is 3,200 feet.

❷ Hesperia Lake Campground

Location: In Hesperia; map I6, grid a2.

Campsites, facilities: There are 50 sites for tents, trailers, or RVs, 30 with electrical hookups. There are two tent-only group sites. Picnic tables, fire pits, rest rooms, and showers are provided. A playground, horseshoe pits, and a fishing pond are available. The facilities are wheelchair accessible. Leashed pets are permitted in the camp, but not around the lake.

Reservations, fees: No reservations; $12 to $15 per night, $2 pet fee.

Contact: Hesperia Lake Campground, (760) 244-5951.

Directions: From Interstate 15 in Hesperia, take the Main Street exit and drive 9.5 miles east (the road curves around and becomes Arrowhead Lake Road); the park is on the left.

Trip notes: This is a slightly more rustic alternative to Desert Willow RV Park in Hesperia. There is a small lake/pond for recreational fishing and there is a small fishing fee, but no fishing license is required. No boating or swimming is allowed, but youngsters usually get a kick out of feeding the ducks and geese that live at the pond.

❸ Mojave Narrows Regional Park

Location: On the Mojave River; map I6, grid a4.

Campsites, facilities: There are 110 sites for tents or RVs, 38 of which have hookups. Picnic tables and barbecue grills are provided. Piped water, flush toilets, showers, sanitary dump station, snack bar, bait house, boat rentals, horse rentals, and horseback riding facilities are available. A grocery store, propane gas, and coin laundry are available three miles from the campground. Leashed pets are permitted.

Reservations, fees: Reservations are accepted for full hookups; $10 to $15 per night, $1 pet fee. Fishing fees are charged when the river is stocked ($2 to $4). A fishing license is required for ages 16 and up. Open year-round.

Contact: Mojave Narrows Regional Park, (760) 245-2226.

Directions: From Interstate 15 south of Victorville, take the Bear Valley exit and drive east for six miles. Turn left on Ridgecrest, drive three miles, and make a left into the park.

Trip notes: Almost no one except the locals knows about this little county park. It is set at 2,000 feet and provides a few recreation options, including a stocked pond for fishing, horseback riding facilities, and trails. The river level fluctuates here, almost disappearing in some years in summer and early fall.

❹ Apple White

Location: Near Lytle Creek in San Bernardino National Forest; map I6, grid b0.

Campsites, facilities: There are 42 sites for tents or RVs up to 30 feet long. Piped water, flush toilets, picnic tables, and fire grills are provided. The rest rooms have sinks and electricity. A grocery store is nearby. Leashed pets are permitted.

Reservations, fees: No reservations; $8 to $10 per night, $15 for multifamily sites. Open year-round.

Contact: San Bernardino National Forest, Cajon Ranger District, (909) 887-2576 or fax (909) 887-8197.

Directions: From Los Angeles, take Interstate 10 past Ontario to the Interstate 15 north interchange. Drive 11 miles north on Interstate 15 to the Sierra Avenue exit. Turn left, go under the freeway, and continue north for about nine miles to the campground.

Trip notes: Nothing like a little insiders' knowhow, especially at this camp, set at 3,300 feet near Lytle Creek. Note that you can reach the Middle Fork of Lytle Creek by driving north from Fontana via Serra Avenue to the Lytle Creek area. To get to the stretch of water that is stocked with trout by the Department of Fish and Game, turn west on Middle Fork Road, which is 1.5 miles before the campground at Apple White. The first mile upstream is stocked in early summer.

⑤ West Fork Group Camps

Location: On Silverwood Lake; map I6, grid b1.

Campsites, facilities: There are three group camps here with piped water, flush toilets, showers, picnic tables, and fire grills. Picnic areas, fishing, hiking, swimming, boating, food service, and a grocery store are available. Leashed pets are permitted.

Reservations, fees: Reserve via phone at (800) 444-PARK/7275 ($7.50 reservation fee) or website www.cal-parks.ca.gov; $150 group fee per night, $1 pet fee. Open March through October.

Contact: Silverwood Lake State Recreation Area, (760) 389-2303 or (909) 657-0676.

Directions: From San Bernardino, drive north on Interstate 215/Interstate 15. Continue north on Interstate 15 to the Highway 138 exit in Cajon. Turn right and drive 13 miles east on

Highway 138 to the park.

Trip notes: This is a group camping option at Silverwood Lake. For information about Silverwood Lake, see the trip notes for Mesa Campground (campground number six).

⑥ Mesa Campground

Location: On Silverwood Lake; map I6, grid b1.

Campsites, facilities: There are 131 sites for tents or RVs up to 34 feet long. Piped water, flush toilets, showers, a sanitary dump station, picnic tables, fire rings, and fire grills are provided. The campground facilities, picnic areas, fishing, hiking paths, exhibits, swimming areas, boating, food service, and grocery store are wheelchair accessible. A boat ramp and boat rentals are available. Leashed pets are permitted.

Reservations, fees: Reserve via phone at (800) 444-PARK/7275 ($7.50 reservation fee) or website www.cal-parks.ca.gov; $17 to $18 per night, $1 pet fee. Open year-round.

Contact: Silverwood Lake State Recreation Area, (760) 389-2303 or (909) 657-0676.

Directions: From San Bernardino, drive north on Interstate 215/Interstate 15. Continue north on Interstate 15 to the Highway 138 exit in Cajon. Turn right and drive 13 miles east on Highway 138 to the park.

Trip notes: This state park campground is on the west side of Silverwood Lake at 3,355 feet in elevation, bordered by San Bernardino National Forest to the south and high desert to the north. The hot weather and proximity to San Bernardino make it a winner with boaters, who have 1,000 surface acres of water and 13 miles of shoreline to explore. It's a great lake for waterskiing (35 mph speed limit) and water sports (5 mph speed limit in coves), and fair for fishing (trout or bass, according to season) and windsurfing, with afternoon winds usually strong in the spring and early summer. The park has a modest trail system with both nature and bike trails. A bonus is that there are also some hike-in and bike-in campsites.

❼ Camp Switzerland

Location: Near Lake Gregory; map I6, grid b2.

Campsites, facilities: There are 10 sites for tents, 30 sites for RVs with full hookups, and two cabins. Piped water, flush toilets, coin-operated showers, and picnic tables are provided. Propane gas is available nearby. Leashed pets are permitted.

Reservations, fees: Reservations are accepted; individual sites are $18 to $21 per night, cabins start at $50 per night, $3 pet fee. Open year-round, weather permitting.

Contact: Camp Switzerland, PO Box 967, Crestline, CA 92325; (909) 338-2731.

Directions: From San Bernardino, drive 14 miles north on Highway 18 to the Crestline/Highway 138 exit. Drive two miles north on Highway 138, turn right on Lake Drive, and continue three miles to the signed campground entrance at the north end of Lake Gregory.

Trip notes: Well, it really doesn't look much like Switzerland, but this camp is set in a wooded canyon at 4,500 feet below the dam at little Lake Gregory. There are no lake views or even much of a sense that the lake is nearby. Surrounded by the San Bernardino National Forest, Lake Gregory covers just 120 acres, and while no privately owned boats are permitted here, boats can be rented at the marina (no motors are permitted). A large swimming beach is available on the northwest shore with a water slide and dressing rooms.

❽ Mojave River Forks Regional Park

Location: Near Silverwood Lake; map I6, grid b3.

Campsites, facilities: There are 30 sites for tents only, 25 RV sites with full hookups, and 25 sites for tents or RVs. Four group sites are also available. Picnic tables and fire grills are provided. Piped water, flush toilets, showers, and a sanitary dump station are available. A convenience store and recreation room are open in the summer. Leashed pets are permitted with proof of shots and/or current license.

Reservations, fees: Reservations are accepted for RV sites only; $13 to $19 per night, $2 pet fee. Open year-round.

Contact: Mojave River Forks Regional Park, (760) 389-2322.

Directions: From San Bernardino, drive north on Interstate 215/Interstate 15 to the Highway 138 exit. Drive nine miles east to Highway 173. Stay to the left and drive seven miles to the park. From Hesperia on Interstate 15, take the Hesperia exit and drive four miles east to Hesperia. Continue southeast on Highway 173 for nine miles to the park entrance.

Trip notes: The bonus here is the full hookups for RVs and the park's proximity to Silverwood Lake, which is only 15 minutes away but does not have any sites with hookups. The sites here are well spaced, but the nearby "river" is usually dry. The elevation is 3,000 feet.

❾ Dogwood

Location: Near Lake Arrowhead in San Bernardino National Forest; map I6, grid b4.

Campsites, facilities: There are 93 sites for tents or RVs up to 22 feet long. Piped water, flush toilets, sanitary dump station, picnic tables, and fire grills are provided. Some facilities are wheelchair accessible. A grocery store and coin laundry are nearby. Leashed pets are permitted.

Reservations, fees: Reserve via phone at (877) 444-6777 ($8.65 reservation fee) or website www.reserveusa.com; $15 per night, $20 for multifamily units. Open May through October.

Contact: San Bernardino National Forest, Arrowhead Ranger District, (909) 337-2444 or fax (909) 337-1104.

Directions: From San Bernardino, drive about 15 miles north on Highway 18 to Rimforest. Continue east on Highway 18 for 0.2 mile to Daley Canyon Road. Turn left on Daley Canyon Road, make an immediate right on the Daley Canyon access road, and turn left into the campground.

Trip notes: So close, but yet so far—that's the paradox between Lake Arrowhead and Dogwood.

The lake is just a mile away, but no public boating or swimming is permitted and only extremely limited access for shore fishing is permitted, with the lake ringed by gated trophy homes, each worth millions. The elevation is 5,600 feet. Any questions? The rangers at the Arrowhead Ranger Station, located about 1.5 miles down the road to the east, can answer them.

⑩ North Shore

Location: On Lake Arrowhead in San Bernardino National Forest; map I6, grid b3.

Campsites, facilities: There are 27 sites for tents or RVs up to 22 feet long. Piped water, flush toilets, picnic tables, and fire rings are provided. Some facilities are wheelchair accessible. A grocery store and a coin laundry are nearby. Leashed pets are permitted.

Reservations, fees: Reserve via phone at (877) 444-6777 ($8.65 reservation fee) or website www.reserveusa.com; $12 per night. Open May through November.

Contact: San Bernardino National Forest, Arrowhead Ranger District, (909) 337-2444 or fax (909) 337-1104.

Directions: From San Bernardino, drive about 17 miles north on Highway 18 to Highway 173. Turn left on Highway 173 and drive north for 1.6 miles to the traffic light. Turn right (still on Highway 173) and drive 2.9 miles to Hospital Road. Turn right and continue 0.1 mile to the top of the small hill. Turn left just past the hospital entrance and you will see the campground.

Trip notes: Of the two camps at Lake Arrowhead, this one is preferable. It is set at 5,300 feet near the northeastern shore of the lake, which provides decent trout fishing in the spring and early summer. To the nearby north, Deep Creek in San Bernardino National Forest is well worth exploring; a hike along the stream to fish for small trout or see a unique set of small waterfalls is highly recommended.

⑪ Big Pine Horse Camp

Location: In San Bernardino National Forest; map I6, grid b5.

Campsites, facilities: This camp is expressly for equestrians. There is one group camp that can accommodate up to 60 people and 15 cars. Piped water, vault toilets, picnic tables, and fire grills are provided. Leashed pets are permitted.

Reservations, fees: Reservations are required; reserve via phone at (877) 444-6777 ($8.65 reservation fee) or website www.reserveusa.com; $50 group fee per night.

Contact: San Bernardino National Forest, Big Bear Ranger Station, (909) 866-3437 or fax (909) 866-2867.

Directions: From San Bernardino, take Highway 30 (the sign says "Mountain Resorts") to Highway 330. Drive about 35 miles on Highway 330 to the dam on Big Bear Lake. Take the left fork (Highway 38) and drive about four miles to the town of Fawnskin. Turn left on Rim of the World Road (it becomes Forest Service Road 3N14, a dirt road, after a half mile) and drive seven miles. Turn left on Forest Service Road 3N16 and drive a mile to the campground on the right.

Trip notes: You might want to bring an apple or a carrot, or maybe some nose plugs. That's because this is a camp for the horse packers located adjacent to the Big Pine Flats Fire Station. A trailhead for the Pacific Crest Trail is located about two miles to the southeast of the camp via Forest Service Road 3N14. The elevation is 6,700 feet.

⑫ Ironwood Group Camp

Location: In San Bernardino National Forest; map I6, grid b6.

Campsites, facilities: There is one group camp that can accommodate up to 25 people and five cars (no trailers or RVs). Vault toilets, picnic tables, and fire grills are provided. There is no piped water. Leashed pets are permitted.

Reservations, fees: Reservations are required; reserve via phone at (877) 444-6777 ($8.65 reservation fee) or website www.reserveusa.com; $50 group fee per night. Open June through September.

Contact: San Bernardino National Forest, Big Bear Ranger Station, (909) 866-3437 or fax (909) 866-2867.

Directions: From San Bernardino, take Highway 30 (the sign says "Mountain Resorts") to Highway 330. Drive about 35 miles on Highway 330 to the dam on Big Bear Lake. Take the left fork (Highway 38) and drive about four miles to the town of Fawnskin. Turn left on Rim of the World Road (it becomes Forest Service Road 3N14, a dirt road, after a half mile) and drive six miles. Turn left on Forest Service Road 3N97 and drive two miles to the campground.

Trip notes: This is a primitive group camp that serves primarily as an overflow camp and nearby alternative to Hanna Flat (campground number 20). It is set at 6,700 feet, is somewhat isolated, and is close to a creek in a wooded area near a meadow. The last two miles of the access road can be rough going for cars.

⓭ Big Pine Flats

Location: In San Bernardino National Forest; map I6, grid b6.

Campsites, facilities: There are 17 sites for tents or RVs up to 30 feet long. Piped water, vault toilets, picnic tables, and fire grills are provided. Leashed pets are permitted.

Reservations, fees: No reservations; $10 per night. Open mid-May to mid-November.

Contact: San Bernardino National Forest, Big Bear Ranger Station, (909) 866-3437 or fax (909) 866-2867.

Directions: From San Bernardino, take Highway 30 (the sign says "Mountain Resorts") to Highway 330. Drive about 35 miles on Highway 330 to the dam on Big Bear Lake. Take the left fork (Highway 38) and drive about four miles to the town of Fawnskin. Turn left on Rim of the World Road (it becomes Forest Service Road 3N14, a dirt road, after a half mile) and drive seven miles to Big Pine Flats Fire Station and the campground on the right.

Trip notes: This pretty spot is set at 6,800 feet in San Bernardino National Forest and provides a little of both worlds: you are surrounded by wildlands near Redondo Ridge, yet you're not a long drive from Big Bear Lake to the south. Any questions? The firefighters at Big Pine Flats Fire Station, just across the road, can answer them.

⓮ San Bernardino– Cable Canyon KOA

Location: Near Silverwood Lake; map I6, grid c1.

Campsites, facilities: There are 155 tent and RV sites with full or partial hookups and picnic tables. There are also two camping cabins. Piped water, flush toilets, showers, coin laundry, playground, swimming pool, recreation room, grocery store, and propane gas are available. Some facilities are wheelchair accessible. Leashed pets are permitted.

Reservations, fees: Reservations are accepted; $19 to $28 per couple per night, cabins are $37 per night, $2 to $4 per extra camper per night. Open year-round.

Contact: San Bernardino–Cable Canyon KOA, (909) 887-4098.

Directions: From San Bernardino, drive 16 miles north on Interstate 215. Take the Devore exit, turn right on Devore Road, and drive to Santa Fe Road. Turn right and drive one block. Turn right on Dement Road (which becomes Cable Canyon Road) and continue to 1707 Cable Canyon Road.

Trip notes: This KOA camp provides space for tents as well as RVs. It is set at 2,200 feet and is virtually surrounded by national forest. Silverwood Lake to the east provides a nearby side trip. For information on Silverwood Lake, see the trip notes for Mesa Campground (campground number six).

⓯ Crab Flats

Location: Near Crab Creek in San Bernardino National Forest; map I6, grid c5.

Campsites, facilities: There are 29 sites for tents or RVs up to 15 feet long. Piped water, vault toilets, picnic tables, and fire rings are provided. Leashed pets are permitted.

Reservations, fees: No reservations; $8 per night. Open mid-May through October.

Contact: San Bernardino National Forest, Arrowhead Ranger District, (909) 337-2444 or fax

(909) 337-1104.

Directions: From San Bernardino, take Highway 30 to Highway 330 and continue on Highway 330 to Running Springs. Drive east on Highway 18 (two miles east of the town of Running Springs). Turn left on Green Valley Road and drive three miles to Forest Service Road 3N16 (a dirt road). Turn left and drive four miles. You will cross two creeks which vary in depth depending on season; high clearance is recommended but is not necessary if you are careful. After four miles, bear left at the intersection, and you'll see the campground entrance on your right.

Trip notes: Four-wheel-drive cowboys often make this a base camp, known as a staging area for off-road vehicles. It is a developed Forest Service camp set at a fork in the road at 6,200 feet. A challenging jeep road is available from here, heading west into Deep Creek Canyon. Note that Tent Peg Group Camp (campground number 17) is located just a half mile to the west on Forest Service Road 3N34 (a hiking trail is available there).

⑯ Green Valley

Location: Near Green Valley Lake in San Bernardino National Forest; map I6, grid c5.

Campsites, facilities: There are 37 sites for tents or RVs up to 22 feet long. Piped water, flush toilets, picnic tables, and fire rings are provided. A grocery store and coin laundry are nearby. Leashed pets are permitted.

Reservations, fees: Reservations may be made via phone at (877) 444-6777 ($8.65 reservation fee) or website www.reserveusa.com; $12 per night. Open May through September.

Contact: San Bernardino National Forest, Arrowhead Ranger District, (909) 337-2444 or fax (909) 337-1104.

Directions: From San Bernardino, take Highway 30 to Highway 330; continue on Highway 330 to Running Springs. Drive east on Highway 18 to Green Valley Road. Turn left and go four miles up the road to the campground (one mile past town of Green Valley Lake).

Trip notes: This camp is located along pretty

Green Valley Creek at an elevation of 7,000 feet. Little Green Valley Lake is located a mile to the west. The lake is stocked with trout by the Department of Fish and Game and is also a good spot to take a flying leap and belly flop.

⑰ Tent Peg Group Camp

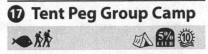

Location: Near the Pacific Crest Trail in San Bernardino National Forest; map I6, grid c5.

Campsites, facilities: There is one group camp that will accommodate 10 to 30 people and five cars. There is no piped water. Vault toilets, picnic tables, and fire rings are provided. A grocery store and coin laundry are five miles away. Leashed pets are permitted.

Reservations, fees: Reservations are required; reserve via phone at (877) 444-6777 ($8.65 reservation fee) or website www.reserveusa.com; $30 per night. Open May through October.

Contact: San Bernardino National Forest, Arrowhead Ranger District, (909) 337-2444 or fax (909) 337-1104.

Directions: From San Bernardino, take Highway 30 to Highway 330 and continue on Highway 330 to Running Springs. Drive east on Highway 18 (past the town of Running Springs), turn left on Green Valley Road, and drive three miles to Forest Service Road 3N16 (a dirt road). Turn left and drive four miles. You will cross two creeks which vary in depth depending on season; high clearance is recommended but not necessary if you are careful. After four miles, you will come to an intersection. Bear left on Forest Service Road 3N34 and drive west for one mile; the campground is on the left.

Trip notes: This camp would be a lot easier to reach with a helicopter than a vehicle. But that's why Tent Peg is a well-loved camp for the few who book it: a primitive camp for groups at 5,400 feet, complete with trailhead. A rough jeep road heads out of camp to the west and down into Deep Creek. In addition, there is a trailhead for a three-mile hike down the canyon to the south to Fisherman's Hike-In Group Camp (see campground number 18), set along Deep Creek. The trout are small but willing.

⑱ Fisherman's Hike-In Group Camp

Location: On Deep Creek in San Bernardino National Forest; map I6, grid c5.

Campsites, facilities: There is one group campsite that will accommodate 10 to 30 people. Vault toilets, picnic tables, and fire rings are provided. There is no piped water, so bring in your own. Please pack out your garbage. Leashed pets are permitted.

Reservations, fees: Reservations are required; reserve via phone at (877) 444-6777 ($8.65 reservation fee) or website www. reserveusa.com; $10 per night.

Contact: San Bernardino National Forest, Arrowhead Ranger District, (909) 337-2444 or fax (909) 337-1104.

Directions: From San Bernardino, take Highway 30 to Highway 330; continue on Highway 330 to Running Springs. Drive east on Highway 18 (two miles east of the town of Running Springs), turn left on Green Valley Road, and drive three miles to Forest Service Road 3N16 (a dirt road). Turn left and drive four miles. You will cross two creeks which vary in depth depending on season; high clearance is recommended but not necessary if you are careful. After four miles, you will come to an intersection. Bear left on Forest Service Road 3N34 and drive west for 1.3 miles to Forest Service Trail 2W07 on your left. Park and follow this hiking trail southwest for 2.5 miles to Deep Creek; the campground is on the other side of the creek.

Trip notes: Get here and you join the 5 Percent Club. Fisherman's Hike-In Group Camp is a beautiful, secluded, and wooded campground set deep in San Bernardino National Forest at 5,400 feet. Deep Creek runs alongside providing stream trout fishing and a beautiful setting. It's worth the significant effort required to get here. Once here, you will find a primitive route along the creek (which looks more like a deer trail than a hiking trail) that anglers use to tromp along the stream. The trout are small but well colored, and the first cast into the head of a pool often results in a strike.

⑲ Shady Cove Group Camp

Location: Near the Children's Forest in San Bernardino National Forest; map I6, grid c5.

Campsites, facilities: There are two group campsites which can accommodate a maximum of 30 at one site and 65 at the other. When reserved together, the two sites are allowed a maximum of 100 people with a limit of 15 cars (no trailers or RVs). Piped water, vault toilets, picnic tables, fire rings, and trash receptacles are provided. The camp is gated for safety; groups are given a key. Leashed pets are permitted.

Reservations, fees: Reservations are required; reserve via phone at (877) 444-6777 ($8.65 reservation fee) or website www. reserveusa.com; $50 to $100 per night. Open May through September.

Contact: San Bernardino National Forest, Arrowhead Ranger District, (909) 337-2444 or fax (909) 337-1104.

Directions: From San Bernardino, drive about 17 miles north on Highway 18 to the Arrowhead Ranger Station. Continue east on Highway 18 for seven miles (past the town of Running Springs). Turn south (right) on Keller Peak Road (just past Deer Lick Fire Station) and drive four miles to the Children's Forest. Bear left to the parking area. The sites are 100 yards from the parking area.

Trip notes: The highlight here is the adjacent short looped trail that is routed through the Children's Forest. The camp is excellent for Boy Scout and Girl Scout troops. The elevation is 7,500 feet.

⑳ Hanna Flat

Location: Near Big Bear Lake in San Bernardino National Forest; map I6, grid c6.

Campsites, facilities: There are 69 sites for tents and 19 sites for tents or RVs up to 15 feet long. Piped water, vault toilets, picnic tables, and fire grills are provided. Leashed pets are permitted.

Reservations, fees: Reservations are accepted via phone at (877) 444-6777 ($8.65 reservation fee) or website www.reserveusa.com; $15 per night, $5 for a second vehicle. Open May through September.

Contact: San Bernardino National Forest, Big Bear Ranger Station, (909) 866-3437 or fax (909) 866-2867.

Directions: From San Bernardino, take Highway 30 (the sign says "Mountain Resorts") to Highway 330. Drive about 35 miles on Highway 330 to the dam on Big Bear Lake. Take the left fork (Highway 38) and drive about four miles to the town of Fawnskin. Turn left on Rim of the World Road (it becomes Forest Service Road 3N14, a dirt road, after a half mile) and drive three miles to the campground on the left.

Trip notes: This is the largest, best maintained, and most popular of the Forest Service camps in the Big Bear Lake district. All the trees and vegetation provide seclusion for individual sites. It is set at 7,000 feet on the slopes on the north side of Big Bear Lake, just under three miles from the lake. Big Bear is a beautiful mountain lake covering over 3,000 acres, with 22 miles of shoreline and often excellent trout fishing and waterskiing. Note that a trailhead for the Pacific Crest Trail is located a mile by road north of the camp.

㉑ Gray's Peak Group Camp

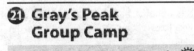

Location: Near Big Bear Lake in San Bernardino National Forest; map I6, grid c6.

Campsites, facilities: There is one group campsite that will accommodate up to 40 people and eight cars (limited use of trailers and RVs). There is no piped water. Vault toilets, picnic tables, and fire grills are provided. Leashed pets are permitted.

Reservations, fees: Reservations are accepted via phone at (877) 444-6777 ($8.65 reservation fee) or website www.reserveusa.com; $50 per night. Open June through September.

Contact: San Bernardino National Forest, Big Bear Ranger Station, (909) 866-3437 or fax (909) 866-2867.

Directions: From San Bernardino, take High-

way 30 (the sign says "Mountain Resorts") to Highway 330. Drive about 35 miles on Highway 330 to the dam on Big Bear Lake. Take the left fork (Highway 38) and drive about four miles to the town of Fawnskin. Turn left on Rim of the World Road (it becomes Forest Service Road 3N14, a dirt road, after a half mile) and drive 1.2 miles to Forest Service Road 2N13. Turn left and drive about a mile to the campground on the right.

Trip notes: The appeal of this primitive group camp is its proximity to Big Bear Lake, with the camp just three miles northwest of the lake, set at 7,200 feet. Gray's Peak (7,952 feet) is located about a mile south of the camp, but there is no direct access to the peak. The drive is not recommended for trailers or large RVs.

㉒ Siberia Creek Hike-In Group Camp

Location: In San Bernardino National Forest; map I6, grid c6.

Campsites, facilities: There is one group campsite that will accommodate up to 40 people. Fire rings are provided, but that's all. There is no piped water, so bring your own, and pack out your garbage. Leashed pets are permitted.

Reservations, fees: Reservations are requested; reserve via phone at (877) 444-6777 ($8.65 reservation fee) or website www. reserveusa. com; no camping fee. An Adventure Pass ($30 annual fee) or $5 daily pass per parked vehicle is required.

Contact: San Bernardino National Forest, Big Bear Ranger Station, (909) 866-3437 or fax (909) 866-2867.

Directions: From San Bernardino, take Highway 30 (the sign says "Mountain Resorts") to Highway 330. Drive about 20 miles on Highway 330 to just past Snow Valley Ski Area. Take the Camp Creek Trail turnoff and follow the signs to the trailhead. Park and hike three miles to the camp.

Trip notes: This is a primitive area that requires a fairly steep three-mile hike. Your reward is solitude at a camp that will hold up to 40 people. The camp is set near the confluence of Siberia Creek and larger Bear Creek. The latter is the major feeder stream into Big Bear Lake, and both provide a good opportunity to try sneak-fishing techniques for small rainbow trout. The elevation is 4,800 feet.

㉓ Bluff Mesa Group Camp

Location: Near Big Bear Lake in San Bernardino National Forest; map I6, grid c6.

Campsites, facilities: There is one group campsite that will accommodate up to 40 people and eight cars. There is no piped water. Pit toilets, picnic tables, and fire grills are provided. Leashed pets are permitted.

Reservations, fees: Reservations are requested; reserve via phone at (877) 444-6777 ($8.65 reservation fee) or website www.reserveusa. com; $50 group fee per night. Open June through September.

Contact: San Bernardino National Forest, Big Bear Ranger Station, (909) 866-3437 or fax (909) 866-2867.

Directions: From San Bernardino, take Highway 30 (the sign says "Mountain Resorts") to Highway 330. Drive about 35 miles on Highway 330 to the dam on Big Bear Lake. Bear right at the dam on Highway 18 and drive about four miles. Turn right on Mill Creek Road and drive about 1.5 miles to the sign at the top of the hill. Turn right on Forest Service Road 2N10 and drive three miles on the dirt road. Turn right on Forest Service Road 2N86 and drive a quarter mile to the campground.

Trip notes: Bluff Mesa Group Camp is one of several camps located south of Big Bear Lake. A highlight here is the trailhead (signed on the access road on the way in) for the half-mile walk to the Champion Lodgepole Pine, the largest lodgepole pine in the world: 400 years old, 112 feet tall, with a circumference of 20 feet. Many Forest Service roads are available nearby for self-planned side trips. The elevation is 7,600 feet.

㉔ Boulder Group Camp

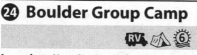

Location: Near Big Bear Lake in San Bernardino National Forest; map I6, grid c6.

Campsites, facilities: There is one group campsite that will accommodate up to 40 people and eight cars (limited use of trailers and RVs). There is no piped water. Pit toilets, picnic tables, and fire grills are provided. A grocery store and coin laundry are nearby. Leashed pets are permitted.

Reservations, fees: Reservations are required; reserve via phone at (877) 444-6777 ($8.65 reservation fee) or website www.reserveusa.com; $50 group fee per night. Open June through September.

Contact: San Bernardino National Forest, Big Bear Ranger Station, (909) 866-3437 or fax (909) 866-2867.

Directions: From San Bernardino, take Highway 30 (the sign says "Mountain Resorts") to Highway 330. Drive about 35 miles on Highway 330 to the dam on Big Bear Lake. Bear right at the dam on Highway 18 and drive about four miles to Mill Creek Road. Turn right on Forest Service Road 2N10 and drive about two miles. Turn right on Forest Service Road 2N10B and drive to the camp.

Trip notes: This is a primitive camp at 7,500 feet elevation, just far enough away from some prime attractions to make you wish you could move the camp to a slightly different spot. The headwaters of Metcalf Creek are hidden in the forest on the other side of the road, tiny Cedar Lake is about a half-mile drive north, and Big Bear Lake is about two miles north. You get the idea.

㉕ Holloway's Marina and RV Park

Location: On Big Bear Lake; map I6, grid c7.

Campsites, facilities: There are 100 RV sites with full hookups, two with partial hookups, and seven with no hookups. Picnic tables and fire grills are provided. Piped water, flush toilets, showers, sanitary dump station, cable TV, convenience store, ice, propane gas, coin laundry, playground, and a full marina with boat rentals are on the premises. Leashed pets are permitted.

Reservations, fees: Reservations are suggested; $25 to $40 per night.

Contact: Holloway's Marina and RV Park, (909) 866-5706 or (800) 448-5335.

Directions: From San Bernardino, take Highway 30 (the sign says "Mountain Resorts") to Highway 330. Drive about 17 miles to Highway 18 and bear right on Highway 18. Drive another 17 miles to the dam. Three miles past the dam, turn left on Edgemoor Road and drive to the park.

Trip notes: This privately operated park is a good choice at Big Bear Lake with boat rentals, ramp, and full marina available. Big Bear is the jewel of Southern California's mountains, covering over 3,000 surface acres with 22 miles of shoreline. Its cool waters make for excellent trout fishing, and yet, by summer, it has heated up enough to make for superb waterskiing. A bonus in the summer is that a breeze off the lake keeps the temperature in the mid-80s.

26 Holcomb Valley

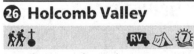

Location: Near the Pacific Crest Trail in San Bernardino National Forest; map I6, grid c6.

Campsites, facilities: There are 19 sites for tents or RVs up to 25 feet long. There is no piped water. Pit toilets, picnic tables, and fire grills are provided. Please pack out your garbage. Leashed pets are permitted.

Reservations, fees: No reservations; $10 per night. Open year-round, weather permitting.

Contact: San Bernardino National Forest, Big Bear Ranger Station, (909) 866-3437 or fax (909) 866-2867.

Directions: From San Bernardino, take Highway 30 (the sign says "Mountain Resorts") to Highway 330. Drive about 35 miles on Highway 330 to the dam on Big Bear Lake. Take the left fork (Highway 38) and drive about 10 miles. Turn left on Van Dusen Canyon Road/Forest Service Road 3N09 (a dirt road) and drive three miles. Turn left on Forest Service Road 3N16 to the campground on the right.

Trip notes: This camp is set near the Holcomb Valley Historic Area, 7,400 feet, in the mountains about four miles north of Big Bear Lake. On the way in on Van Dusen Canyon Road you will pass a trailhead for the Pacific Crest Trail (two

miles southeast of the camp.) From here you can make the two-mile climb southwest to Bertha Peak, 8,198 feet, overlooking Big Bear to the south.

27 Pineknot

Location: Near Big Bear Lake in San Bernardino National Forest; map I6, grid c7.

Campsites, facilities: There are 52 sites for tents and RVs up to 45 feet long. Piped water, flush toilets, picnic tables, and fire grills are provided. The facilities are wheelchair accessible. A grocery store and coin laundry are nearby. Leashed pets are permitted.

Reservations, fees: Reservations are accepted via phone at (877) 444-6777 ($8.65 reservation fee) or website www.reserveusa.com; $15 per night. Open mid-May through September.

Contact: San Bernardino National Forest, Big Bear Ranger Station, (909) 866-3437 or fax (909) 866-2867.

Directions: From San Bernardino, take Highway 30 (the sign says "Mountain Resorts") to Highway 330. Drive about 35 miles on Highway 330 to the dam on Big Bear Lake. Bear right at the dam on Highway 18 and drive about six miles to Summit Boulevard. Turn right, drive through the parking area, and make a left into the campground just before the gate to the slopes.

Trip notes: This popular, developed Forest Service camp is set just east of Big Bear Lake Village (located on the southern shore of the lake) about two miles from the lake. Of the camps at Big Bear, this is the closest one to supplies. The elevation is 7,000 feet.

28 Buttercup Group Camp

Location: Near the town of Big Bear Lake in San Bernardino National Forest; map I6, grid c7.

Campsites, facilities: There is one group campsite that will accommodate up to 40 people and eight cars (limited use of trailers or RVs). Piped water, portable toilets, picnic tables, and fire grills are provided. A grocery store and coin laundry are nearby. Leashed pets are permitted.

Reservations, fees: Reservations are requested; reserve via phone at (877) 444-6777 ($8.65 reservation fee) or website www.reserveusa.com; $75 group fee per night. Open June through September.

Contact: San Bernardino National Forest, Big Bear Ranger Station, (909) 866-3437 or fax (909) 866-2867.

Directions: From San Bernardino, take Highway 30 (the sign says "Mountain Resorts") to Highway 330. Drive about 35 miles on Highway 330 to the dam on Big Bear Lake. Bear right at the dam on Highway 18 and drive about six miles to Summit Boulevard. Turn right, drive through the parking area, and make a left into the campground just before the gate to the ski slopes.

Trip notes: This is a forested camp designed for large groups looking for a developed site near Big Bear Lake. It is about four miles from the southeast side of the lake, just outside the Snow Summit Ski Area. The elevation is 7,000 feet.

㉙ Serrano

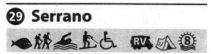

Location: On Big Bear Lake in San Bernardino National Forest; map I6, grid c7.

Campsites, facilities: There are 132 sites for tents or RVs up to 55 feet long. There are 30 sites that offer full hookups. Piped water, picnic tables, fire rings, rest rooms, hot showers, and a sanitary dump station are provided. Five sites are wheelchair accessible. There is a store nearby. Leashed pets are permitted.

Reservations, fees: Reserve via phone at (877) 444-6777 ($8.65 reservation fee) or website www.reserveusa.com; $15 to $25 per night. Open mid-April to mid-November.

Contact: San Bernardino National Forest, Big Bear Ranger Station, (909) 866-3437 or fax (909) 866-2867.

Directions: From San Bernardino, take Highway 30 (the sign says "Mountain Resorts") to Highway 330. Drive about 33 miles on Highway 330 to the dam on Big Bear Lake. Take the left

fork (Highway 38), drive about 2.5 miles east of Fawnskin, and watch for the Serrano Campground signs. The campground entrance is off North Shore Lane.

Trip notes: This campground opened in the 1990s and became the first National Forest campground to offer state-of-the-art rest rooms and hot showers. That is why it costs so much to camp here. Location is also a big plus, as this is one of the few camps at Big Bear within walking distance of the lakeshore. Another bonus is a paved trail that is wheelchair accessible. Want more? Big Bear is the jewel of Southern California lakes, the Lake Tahoe of the South, with outstanding trout fishing and waterskiing. Want even more? A trailhead for the Pacific Crest Trail is nearby, and Canada is only 2,200 miles away. The elevation is 7,000 feet.

㉚ Tanglewood Group Camp

Location: On the Pacific Crest Trail in San Bernardino National Forest; map I6, grid c7.

Campsites, facilities: There is one group campsite that will accommodate up to 40 people and eight cars (limited use of trailers or RVs). There is no piped water. Pit toilets, picnic tables, and fire grills are provided. Leashed pets are permitted.

Reservations, fees: Reservations are required; reserve via phone at (877) 444-6777 ($8.65 reservation fee) or website www.reserveusa.com; $50 group fee per night. Open June through September.

Contact: San Bernardino National Forest, Big Bear Ranger Station, (909) 866-3437 or fax (909) 866-2867.

Directions: From San Bernardino, take Highway 30 (the sign says "Mountain Resorts") to Highway 330. Drive about 35 miles on Highway 330 to the dam on Big Bear Lake. Take the left fork (Highway 38) and drive about 10 miles. Turn left on Van Dusen Canyon Road/Forest Service Road 3N09 and drive on the dirt road for four miles. Turn right on Forest Service Road 3N16, drive 1.7 miles, turn right on Forest Service Road 3N79, and drive one-half mile to the campground. Trailers are not recommended.

Trip notes: This primitive group camp is off an old spur road with the Pacific Crest Trail trailhead the primary highlight. It is set at 7,400 feet in a flat but wooded area northeast of Big Bear Lake. It is about a 10- to 15-minute drive from Big Bear City.

③ Skyline Group Camp

Location: In San Bernardino National Forest; map I6, grid d7.

Campsites, facilities: There is one group campsite that will accommodate up to 25 people. Piped water, vault toilets, and picnic tables are available. Leashed pets are permitted.

Reservations, fees: Reserve via phone at (877) 444-6777 ($8.65 reservation fee) or website www.reserveusa.com; $30 group fee per night.

Contact: San Bernardino National Forest, Mill Creek Ranger Station, (909) 866-3437 or fax (909) 866-2867.

Directions: From Redlands on Interstate 10, turn east on Highway 38 and drive 33.5 miles to Forest Service Road 1N02. Turn right and drive a mile to the campground, just behind Heart Bar.

Trip notes: Skyline Group Camp is set at an elevation of 6,900 feet near Big Meadows. A trailhead at the end of a short spur road about a half mile to the north off the main road provides access to a great butt-kicker of a trail about eight or nine miles (one way) that runs along Wildhorse Creek and up to Sugarloaf Mountain, elevation 9,952 feet. Insider's note: A trail camp is set on Wildhorse Creek, just past the midway point on the trail to Sugarloaf Mountain.

㉜ Council Group Camp

Location: Near the San Gorgonio Wilderness in San Bernardino National Forest; map I6, grid d6.

Campsites, facilities: There is one group campsite that will accommodate up to 50 people and 10 cars (no trailers or RVs). Piped water, vault toilets, picnic tables, and fire grills are provided. Leashed pets are permitted.

Reservations, fees: Reserve via phone at (877) 444-6777 ($8.65 reservation fee) or website www.reserveusa.com; $50 group fee per night.

Contact: San Bernardino National Forest, Mill Creek Ranger Station, (909) 866-3437 or fax (909) 866-2867.

Directions: From Interstate 10 in Redlands, drive 26 miles east on Highway 38 to the campground on the left.

Trip notes: This is a group camp in a pretty wooded area across the road from little Jenks Lake (there is a nice, easy walk around the lake) and a few miles north of the northern border of the San Gorgonio Wilderness. There are several other camps in the area.

㉝ South Fork

Location: Near the Santa Ana River in San Bernardino National Forest; map I6, grid d7.

Campsites, facilities: There are 24 sites for tents or RVs up to 30 feet long. Piped water, vault toilets, picnic tables, and fire grills are provided. Leashed pets are permitted.

Reservations, fees: No reservations; $9 per night, $5 for each additional vehicle. Open mid-May through mid-October.

Contact: San Bernardino National Forest, Mill Creek Ranger Station, (909) 866-3437 or fax (909) 866-2867.

Directions: From Interstate 10 in Redlands, drive 29.5 miles east on Highway 38 to the campground entrance road.

Trip notes: This is an easy-access Forest Service camp just off Highway 38, set at 6,400 feet near the headwaters of the South Fork Santa Ana River. It is part of the series of camps in the immediate area, just north of the San Gorgonio Wilderness. This one is a four-mile drive from little Jenks Lake. See the trip notes for Barton Flats (campground number 36) for more details.

㉞ Oso Group Camp

Location: Near the San Gorgonio Wilderness in San Bernardino National Forest; map I6, grid d7.

Campsites, facilities: This site will accommodate up to 100 people and 20 cars (limited use of trailers and RVs). Piped water, flush toilets, picnic tables, and fire grills are provided. Leashed pets are permitted.

Reservations, fees: Reserve via phone at (877) 444-6777 ($8.65 reservation fee) or website www.reserveusa.com; $75 to $100 per night. Open May through October.

Contact: San Bernardino National Forest, Mill Creek Ranger Station, (909) 866-3437 or fax (909) 866-2867.

Directions: From Interstate 10 in Redlands, drive 29 miles east on Highway 38 to the campground entrance road on the left.

Trip notes: Oso and Lobo Group Camps are set directly adjacent to each other at 6,600 feet elevation. Little Jenks Lake is located two miles away to the west, and the northern border of the San Gorgonio Wilderness is just a few miles to the south.

㉟ Lobo Group Camp

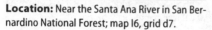

Location: Near the Santa Ana River in San Bernardino National Forest; map I6, grid d7.

Campsites, facilities: This site will accommodate up to 75 people and 15 cars (limited use of trailers and RVs). Piped water, flush toilets, picnic tables, and fire grills are provided. Leashed pets are permitted.

Reservations, fees: Reserve via phone at (877) 444-6777 ($8.65 reservation fee) or website www.reserveusa.com; $50 to $75 per night. Open April through October, weather permitting.

Contact: San Bernardino National Forest, Mill Creek Ranger Station, (909) 866-3437 or fax (909) 866-2867.

Directions: From Interstate 10 in Redlands, drive 29 miles east on Highway 38 to the campground entrance road on the left.

Trip notes: Lobo is right next to Oso Group Camp and is just north of the San Gorgonio Wilderness. The camp is about three-quarters of a mile from the Santa Ana River and a short drive to Jenks Lake. The elevation is 6,600 feet.

㊱ Barton Flats

Location: Near Jenks Lake in San Bernardino National Forest; map I6, grid d6.

Campsites, facilities: There are 47 sites for RVs up to 45 feet long. Piped water, flush toilets, showers, picnic tables, and fire grills are provided. The facilities are wheelchair accessible. Leashed pets are permitted.

Reservations, fees: Reserve via phone at (877) 444-6777 ($8.65 reservation fee) or website www.reserveusa.com; $15 per night, $20 for multifamily sites, $5 for each additional vehicle. Open mid-May through October.

Contact: San Bernardino National Forest, Mill Creek Ranger Station, (909) 866-3437 or fax (909) 866-2867.

Directions: From Interstate 10 in Redlands, drive 27.5 miles east on Highway 38 to the campground on the left.

Trip notes: This is one of the more developed Forest Service camps in San Bernardino National Forest. The camp is set at 6,300 feet near the northwest end of Jenks Lake, a small, pretty lake with good hiking and a picnic area. Barton Creek, a small stream, runs nearby although it may be waterless in late summer. The San Gorgonio Wilderness, located one mile to the south, is accessible via Forest Service roads to the wilderness area trailhead. Permits are required for overnight camping within the wilderness boundaries and are available at Forest Service ranger stations. For those driving in on Highway 38, stop at the Mill Creek Ranger Station in Redlands.

㊲ San Gorgonio

Location: Near the San Gorgonio Wilderness in San Bernardino National Forest; map I6, grid d7.

Campsites, facilities: There are 55 sites for RVs up to 43 feet long. Piped water, flush toilets, picnic tables, hot showers, and fire grills are provided. Leashed pets are permitted.

Reservations, fees: Reserve via phone at

(877) 444-6777 ($8.65 reservation fee) or website www.reserveusa.com; $15 per night, $20 for multifamily sites, $5 for each additional vehicle.

Contact: San Bernardino National Forest, Mill Creek Ranger Station, (909) 866-3437 or fax (909) 866-2867.

Directions: From Interstate 10 in Redlands, drive 28 miles east on Highway 38 to the campground.

Trip notes: San Gorgonio is one in a series of Forest Service camps along Highway 38 near Jenks Lake. See the trip notes for Barton Flats (campground number 36) for details.

38 Heart Bar Equestrian Group Camp

Location: In San Bernardino National Forest; map I6, grid d8.

Campsites, facilities: There is one group campsite with 46 corrals that will accommodate up to 65 people and 21 cars (limited use of trailers and RVs). Piped water (not potable), flush toilets, picnic tables, hot showers, and fire grills are provided. Leashed pets are permitted.

Reservations, fees: Reserve via phone at (877) 444-6777 ($8.65 reservation fee) or website www.reserveusa.com; $100 per night. Open May through November.

Contact: San Bernardino National Forest, Mill Creek Ranger Station, (909) 866-3437 or fax (909) 866-2867.

Directions: From Interstate 10 in Redlands, drive 33.5 miles east on Highway 38 to Forest Service Road 1N02. Turn right and drive 1.5 miles to the campground.

Trip notes: You might not meet Mr. Ed here, but bring an apple anyway. It's a horse camp on Heart Bar Creek, located less than a mile east of Heart Bar Family Camp. A good trail that leads into the San Gorgonio Wilderness starts four miles down the road at Fish Creek Meadows. It is routed west for three miles to Fish Creek and then up Grinnell Mountain to the north peak of the Ten Thousand Foot Ridge. A wilderness permit is required. The elevation is 7,000 feet.

39 Heart Bar Family Camp

Location: In San Bernardino National Forest; map I6, grid d8.

Campsites, facilities: There are 94 sites for tents or RVs up to 50 feet long. Piped water, vault toilets, picnic tables, and fire grills are provided. All facilities are wheelchair accessible. Leashed pets are permitted.

Reservations, fees: Reserve via phone at (877) 444-6777 ($8.65 reservation fee) or website www.reserveusa.com; $9 per night for single family sites, $18 for multifamily sites. Open May through November.

Contact: San Bernardino National Forest, Mill Creek Ranger Station, (909) 866-3437 or fax (909) 866-2867.

Directions: From Interstate 10 in Redlands, drive 33.5 miles east on Highway 38 to Forest Service Road 1N02. Turn right and drive a mile to the campground.

Trip notes: It's a good thing there is piped water at this camp. Why? Because Heart Bar Creek often isn't much more than a trickle and can't be relied on for water. The camp is set at 6,900 feet near Big Meadows, the location of the Heart Bar Fire Station. A challenging butt-kicker of a hike has a trailhead about a half mile away to the north off a spur road, midway between the camp and the fire station. The trail here is routed along Wildhorse Creek to Sugarloaf Mountain (9,952 feet, about eight or nine miles one way to the top). Insider's note: Just past the midway point on the trail to Sugarloaf Mountain is a trail camp on Wildhorse Creek.

40 Green Canyon Group Camp

Location: Near Green Springs in San Bernardino National Forest; map I6, grid d9.

Campsites, facilities: There is one group camp that will accommodate 40 people and eight cars (no trailers or RVs). There is no piped water. Pit toilets, picnic tables, and fire grills are provided. Leashed pets are permitted.

Reservations, fees: Reservations are required; reserve via phone at (877) 444-6777 ($8.65 reservation fee) or website www.reserveusa.com, $50 group fee per night. Open June through September.

Contact: San Bernardino National Forest, Big Bear Ranger Station, (909) 866-3437 or fax (909) 866-2867.

Directions: From Interstate 10 in Redlands, drive about 45 miles east on Highway 38 (1.5 miles past the town of Lake Williams) to the campground entrance road (Forest Service Road 2N93). Turn left, make another immediate left, and follow the road for a half mile; you'll see the campground sign on your left.

Trip notes: This primitive group camp provides an overflow area for Big Bear Lake campers who can't find a spot closer to the lake. It is set at 7,200 feet with a trail located to the southwest just off the road (look for the gate on the short spur road) that is routed along Green Canyon (and Green Canyon Creek) for 2.5 miles to Wildhorse Creek. There it intersects with a steep trail that heads west for three miles to Sugarloaf Mountain, 9,952 feet.

ⓣ Coon Creek Cabin Group Camp

Location: On the Pacific Crest Trail in San Bernardino National Forest; map I6, grid d9.

Campsites, facilities: There is one group camp that will accommodate up to 40 people and 14 cars (no trailers or RVs). There is no piped water. Vault toilets, picnic tables, and fire grills are provided. Leashed pets are permitted.

Reservations, fees: Reserve via phone at (877) 444-6777 ($8.65 reservation fee) or website www.reserveusa.com; $35 group fee per night. Open year-round.

Contact: San Bernardino National Forest, Big Bear Ranger Station, (909) 866-3437 or fax (909) 866-2867.

Directions: From Interstate 10 in Redlands, drive 33.5 miles east on Highway 38 to Forest Service Road 1N02. Turn right and drive five miles to the campground. (The access road is a dirt road.)

Trip notes: Backpackers call this the "Coon Creek jump-off" because it is set on the Pacific Crest Trail at 8,200 feet and provides a "jump-off" for a trek on the PCT. The camp is set on Coon Creek, but the creek often runs dry by summer. Note that in the off-season the access road, Forest Service Road 1N02, can be gated; campers must hike or cross-country ski to the camp.

ⓣ Juniper Springs Group Camp

Location: In San Bernardino National Forest; map I6, grid d9.

Campsites, facilities: There is one group camp that will accommodate up to 40 people and eight cars (limited use of trailers and RVs). Piped water, pit toilets, picnic tables, and fire grills are provided. Leashed pets are permitted.

Reservations, fees: Reservations are required; reserve via phone at (877) 444-6777 ($8.65 reservation fee) or website www.reserveusa.com; $50 per night. Open June through September.

Contact: San Bernardino National Forest, Big Bear Ranger Station, (909) 866-3437 or fax (909) 866-2867.

Directions: From Interstate 10 in Redlands, drive about 40 miles east on Highway 38 (1.5 miles past Onyx Summit) to the campground entrance road (Forest Service Road 2N01) on the right. Turn in on the dirt road and drive three miles. Make a right (opposite the sign that says 2N04 on your left) and drive into the campground.

Trip notes: This is a little-known group camp, set at 7,700 feet in a desert-like area about 10 miles east of Big Bear Lake. The reason it is little known is that there are not a lot of causes to camp here. You need to be creative. Got a Scrabble game? Want to watch the junipers grow? Or maybe watch the features of the land change colors as the day passes? You get the idea.

ⓣ Yucaipa Regional Park

Location: Near Redlands; map I6, grid e5.

Campsites, facilities: There are nine tent sites and 26 sites for trailers or RVs, 13 with full hookups. Piped water, rest rooms, picnic tables, showers, and fire rings are provided. A swimming lagoon, fishing ponds, water slides, and paddleboat rentals are available. The facilities are wheelchair accessible. Leashed pets are permitted.

Reservations, fees: Reservations are accepted; reserve via phone at (909) 790-3127; $10 to $18 per night. There are additional fees for fishing, swimming, and use of the waterslide. Open year-round.

Contact: Yucaipa Regional Park, (909) 790-3127.

Directions: From Redlands, drive east on Interstate 10 to the Yucaipa exit. Drive north on Yucaipa Boulevard to Oak Glen Road. Turn left and continue two miles to the park.

Trip notes: This is a great family-oriented county park, complete with water slides and paddleboats for the kids and fishing access and hiking trails for adults. Three lakes are stocked weekly with catfish and bass in the summer and trout in the winter, the closest thing around to an insurance policy for anglers. Spectacular scenic views of the Yucaipa Valley, the San Bernardino Mountains, and Mount San Gorgonio are possible from the park. Two museums are also nearby.

㊹ Lake Perris State Recreation Area

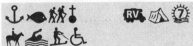

Location: On Lake Perris; map I6, grid f3.

Campsites, facilities: There are 261 sites for tents only, 265 sites for tents or RVs up to 31 feet long, seven primitive horse camps with corrals, and several group camps (by reservation only). There are no hookups in the group area. Picnic tables, fire grills, electric connections, and piped water are provided. Flush toilets, coin-operated showers, dump station, playground, grocery store, boat launch, mooring, and boat rentals are available. The exhibits, pathways, campgrounds, and picnic areas are wheelchair accessible. Leashed pets are permitted, except near the water.

Reservations, fees: For family camping, reserve via phone at (800) 444-PARK/7275 ($7.50 reservation fee) or website www.calparks.ca.gov; $8 to $16 per night, $1 pet fee. For group and horse camping, call the park contact number below. Open year-round.

Contact: Lake Perris State Park, (909) 940-5603 or (909) 657-0676.

Directions: From Riverside, drive about 11 miles east on Highway 60. Exit on Moreno Beach Drive, turn right, and drive four miles to Via Del Lago. Turn left on Via Del Lago into the park.

Trip notes: Lake Perris is a great recreation lake with first-class fishing for spotted bass and, in the summer, it's an excellent destination for boating and water sports. It is set at 1,500 feet in Moreno Valley, just southwest of the Badlands foothills. The lake has a roundish shape, covering 2,200 acres, with an island that provides a unique boat-in picnic site. There are large ski beaches on the northeast and southeast shores and a designated sailing cove on the northwest side, an ideal spot for windsurfing and sailing. Swimming is also excellent, best at the developed beach a short distance from the campground.

㊺ Bogart County Park

Location: In Cherry Valley; map I6, grid f5.

Campsites, facilities: There are 40 sites for tents or RVs and a group camping area. Fire grills and picnic tables are provided. Piped water, flush toilets, and a playground are available. Supplies are available in Beaumont. Leashed pets are permitted.

Reservations, fees: Reservations are required for groups only; reserve via phone at (800) 234-7275 (a reservation fee is charged); $12 per night. Open year-round.

Contact: Bogart County Park, (909) 845-3818.

Directions: From Interstate 10 in Beaumont, drive four miles north on Beaumont Avenue to 14th and Cherry Avenue; the park is located at 9600 Cherry Avenue.

Trip notes: This county park is overlooked by many vacationers on Interstate 10, and it is as pretty as it gets for this area. There are two miles of horse trails and some hiking trails provide a recreation option during the cooler months. The elevation is 2,800 feet.

㊼ Stagecoach RV Park

Location: In Banning; map I6, grid f7.

Campsites, facilities: There are 106 sites for tents or RVs, many with full hookups. Picnic tables and fire grills are provided. Cable TV, rest rooms, showers, playground, swimming pool, coin laundry, store, dump station, ice, recreation room, horseshoes, video arcade, and propane gas are available. Leashed pets are permitted.

Reservations, fees: Reservations are accepted; $13 to $18.50 per night. Open year-round.

Contact: Stagecoach RV Park, (909) 849-7513 or fax (909) 849-7998.

Directions: From Interstate 10 in Banning, take the Highway 243 exit and drive one block south on 8th Avenue. Turn left on Lincoln and drive two blocks. Turn right on San Gorgonio and drive a mile to the park at 1455 South San Gorgonio Avenue.

Trip notes: Banning may not seem like a hotbed of civilization at first glance, but this clean, comfortable park is a good spot to make camp while exploring some of the area's hidden attractions, including Agua Caliente Indian Canyons and the Lincoln Shrine. It is set at 2,400 feet, 22 miles from Palm Springs. A good side trip is to head south on curving "Highway" 240 up to Vista Point in the San Bernardino National Forest.

㊼ Palm View RV Park

Location: Near Lake Elsinore; map I6, grid g1.

Campsites, facilities: There are 45 sites for tents or RVs, some with full hookups. Rest rooms, fire rings, sanitary dump station, recreation area, swimming pool, and a pond are provided. Laundry facilities, store, ice, and firewood are available. Leashed pets are permitted.

Reservations, fees: Reservations are accepted; $18 to $20 per night. Group rates are available upon request. Open year-round.

Contact: Palm View RV Park, (909) 657-7791.

Directions: From the Los Angeles area, travel south on Interstate 15 and exit at the Highway 74/Central Avenue turnoff. Drive east on Highway 74 for four miles to River Road. Drive south on River Road about one mile to the park at 22200 River Road.

Trip notes: This privately operated RV park is located in a quiet valley between Lake Perris and Lake Elsinore at 700 feet elevation. The park's recreation area offers basketball, volleyball, horseshoes, tetherball, and a playground, which should tell you everything you need to know. For you wonderful goofballs, bungy jumping and parachuting is available in the town of Perris.

㊽ Black Mountain Group Camps

Location: Near Mount San Jacinto in San Bernardino National Forest; map I6, grid g7.

Campsites, facilities: There are two group camps here for tents or RVs up to 22 feet long. Each has a capacity of 50 people and 16 vehicles. Piped water, vault toilets, picnic tables, and fire grills are provided. Leashed pets are permitted.

Reservations, fees: Reserve via phone at (877) 444-6777 ($8.65 reservation fee) or website www.reserveusa.com; $60 per night. Open May through September.

Contact: San Bernardino National Forest, San Jacinto Ranger District, (909) 659-2117 or fax (909) 659-2107.

Directions: From Idyllwild, drive nine miles north on Highway 243. Turn right on Forest Service Road 4S01 (a narrow dirt road) and drive eight miles to the campground.

Trip notes: This is a beautiful scenic area, particularly to the north on the edge of the San Jacinto Wilderness and to the east in Mount San Jacinto State Park. The camp is set at 7,500 feet and has a trail that is routed out of the camp east for one mile to a junction with the Pacific Crest Trail. Here you can turn southeast and hike along Fuller Ridge for another mile to the border of Mount San Jacinto State Park. Note that Black Mountain Lookout is just a one-mile drive, located next to Boulder Basin (see campground number 49).

49 Boulder Basin

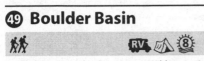

Location: Near the San Jacinto Wilderness in San Bernardino National Forest; map I6, grid g7.

Campsites, facilities: There are 34 sites for tents or RVs up to 22 feet long (trailers are not recommended). Piped water, vault toilets, fire grills, and picnic tables are provided. Leashed pets are permitted.

Reservations, fees: Reservations are accepted for half of the sites; reserve via phone at (877) 444-6777 ($8.65 reservation fee) or website www.reserveusa.com; $10 per night. Open May to mid-October.

Contact: San Bernardino National Forest, San Jacinto Ranger District, (909) 659-2117.

Directions: From Idyllwild, drive nine miles north on Highway 243. Turn right on Forest Service Road 4S01 (a very narrow dirt road) and drive six miles to the campground.

Trip notes: This camp is on the top of the world for these parts, 7,300 feet, adjacent to the Black Mountain Lookout with great views in all directions and highlighted by Tahquitz Peak (8,828 feet) 10 miles to the southeast. Boulder Basin is also located near the San Jacinto Wilderness (to the northeast) and makes a good trailhead camp for hikers. A trail starting at Black Mountain Lookout leads west, dropping steeply into a canyon and also into a designated scenic area.

50 Dark Canyon

Location: In the San Jacinto Mountains in San Bernardino National Forest; map I6, grid g8.

Campsites, facilities: There are 22 sites for tents or RVs up to 22 feet long. Piped water, vault toilets, fire grills, and picnic tables are provided. Leashed pets are permitted.

Reservations, fees: Reservations are accepted for half of the sites; reserve via phone at (877) 444-6777 ($8.65 reservation fee) or website www.reserveusa.com; $10 per night. Open May to mid-October.

Contact: San Bernardino National Forest, San Jacinto Ranger District, (909) 659-2117.

Directions: From Idyllwild, drive seven miles north on Highway 243. Turn right on Forest Service Road 4S02 and drive three more miles on a narrowing road to the camp.

Trip notes: This pretty setting is on the slopes of the San Jacinto Mountains at 5,800 feet in elevation. Hikers can drive to a trailhead less than a mile north of camp at the end of Forest Service Road 4S02. The trail leads east for three miles into Mount San Jacinto State Park to Deer Springs, where there is a trail camp and a junction with the Pacific Crest Trail. A wilderness permit is required.

51 Elsinore West Marina

Location: On Lake Elsinore; map I6, grid h0.

Campsites, facilities: There are 195 sites for tents or RVs with full hookups. Picnic tables are provided. Rest rooms, showers, sanitary dump station, horseshoes, clubhouse, convenience store, telephone hookups, cable TV hookups, boat ramp, and boat rentals are available. Leashed pets are permitted.

Reservations, fees: Reservations are accepted; $20 per night.

Contact: Elsinore West Marina, (909) 678-1300 or (800) 328-6844.

Directions: From Interstate 15 in Lake Elsinore, take Highway 74 and drive four miles west to the park at 32700 Riverside Drive.

Trip notes: This privately operated RV park is located just a half mile from Lake Elsinore. A nearby alternative RV park is Roadrunner (see next listing), which used to be owned by the same folks. For information about Lake Elsinore, see the trip notes for Lake Elsinore Recreation Area (campground number 53) and Roadrunner (campground number 52).

52 Roadrunner

Location: On Lake Elsinore; map I6, grid h0.

Campsites, facilities: There are 102 sites for

RVs with full hookups and 60 sites for tents only. Picnic tables are provided. Piped water, cable television, telephone hookups, coin laundry, sanitary dump station, and a boat ramp are available. Leashed pets are permitted.

Reservations, fees: Reservations are accepted; $20 per night.

Contact: Roadrunner, (909) 674-4900.

Directions: From Lake Elsinore on Interstate 15, turn west on Highway 74 and drive about four miles. Look for Roadrunner on the left side of the road, just a half mile past the city park.

Trip notes: The Roadrunner, a privately operated park, features 600 feet of lakefront property along Lake Elsinore. This lake is best known for waterskiing, with hot weather to match, but only poor to fair for fishing, with some bluegill, crappie, and catfish. Boat ramps are located at both the north and south ends of the lake.

53 Lake Elsinore Recreation Area

Location: On Lake Elsinore; map I6, grid h0.

Campsites, facilities: There are 400 sites for tents or RVs up to 40 feet long. Piped water, electrical connections, fire grills, and picnic tables are provided. Flush toilets, showers, dump station, playground, coin laundry, and a grocery store are available. The camping and picnicking areas are wheelchair accessible. Leashed pets are permitted.

Reservations, fees: No reservations; $15 to $20 per night.

Contact: The city of Lake Elsinore, (909) 674-3124 or fax (909) 245-9308.

Directions: From Interstate 15 in Lake Elsinore, drive three miles west on Highway 74 to the park entrance.

Trip notes: The weather is hot and dry enough in this region to make the water in Lake Elsinore more valuable than gold. Elsinore is a huge, wide lake, where water-skiers, jet skiers, and windsurfers can find a slice of heaven. This camp is set along the north shore, where there are also several trails for hiking,

biking, and horseback riding. There is a designated area near the campground for swimming and water play, with a gently sloping lake bottom a big plus here. If you like thrill sports, hang gliding and parachuting are also available at the lake and, as you scan across the water, you can often look up and see these daredevils soaring overhead.

Special note: This campground, formerly state run, is now administered by the city of Lake Elsinore. Renovations are planned; call ahead for status.

54 Casa del Sol RV Resorts

Location: In Hemet; map I6, grid h5.

Campsites, facilities: There are 358 RV sites. Piped water, electrical connections, cable TV, telephones, and sewer hookups are provided. Rest rooms, showers, swimming pool, recreation room, exercise room, billiard room, hot tub, and coin laundry are available. Leashed pets are permitted.

Reservations, fees: Reservations are accepted; $22 per night. Open year-round.

Contact: Casa del Sol RV Resorts, (909) 925-2515.

Directions: From Interstate 215 south of Perris, turn east on Highway 74 and drive about 14 miles to Hemet (the highway becomes Florida Avenue in Hemet). Turn south on Kirby Avenue and continue to the campground on the corner of Kirby and Acacia at 2750 West Acacia Avenue.

Trip notes: Hemet is a retirement town, so if you want excitement, the three lakes in the area are the best place to look for it: Lake Perris to the northwest, Lake Skinner to the south, and Lake Hemet to the east.

55 Mountain Valley RV Park

Location: In Hemet; map I6, grid h5.

Campsites, facilities: There are 170 RV sites.

Piped water, cable TV, electrical connections, and sewer hookups are provided. Rest rooms, showers, swimming pool, enclosed hot tub, coin laundry, recreation room, shuffleboard, and telephone hookups are available. A grocery store and propane gas are nearby. Leashed pets are permitted.

Reservations, fees: Reservations are accepted; $25 per night, $1 pet fee. Open year-round.

Contact: Mountain Valley RV Park, (909) 925-5812.

Directions: From Interstate 215 south of Perris, turn east on Highway 74 and drive about 14 miles to Hemet (the highway becomes Florida Avenue in Hemet). Turn right on Lyon Avenue and drive to 235 South Lyon Avenue. The park is at the corner of Lyon and South Acacia Avenues.

Trip notes: This is one of two RV parks in the Hemet area. Three lakes in the area provide side trip possibilities: Lake Perris to the northwest, Lake Skinner to the south, and Lake Hemet to the east.

56 Idyllwild County Park

Location: Near San Bernardino National Forest; map I6, grid h7.

Campsites, facilities: There are 90 sites for tents or RVs up to 34 feet long (30 for RVs only). Fire grills and picnic tables are provided. Flush toilets and showers are available. A grocery store, coin laundry, and propane gas are nearby. Leashed pets are permitted.

Reservations, fees: Reservations are accepted via phone at (800) 234-PARK/7275 ($7.50 reservation fee); $15 per night. Open year-round.

Contact: Idyllwild County Park, (909) 659-2656.

Directions: From Highway 243 in Idyllwild, drive a half mile west on Riverside County Playground Road (follow the signs) to the campground.

Trip notes: This park is set at 5,300 feet in elevation, surrounded by Mount San Jacinto State Park, San Jacinto Wilderness, and the San Bernardino National Forest lands. That provides plenty of options for visitors. The top hike in the region is the ambitious climb up the western slopes to the top of Mount San Jacinto (10,786 feet), a terrible challenge of a butt-kicker that provides one of the most astounding views in all the land. (The best route, however, is out of Palm Springs, taking the aerial tramway, which will get you to 8,500 feet in elevation before hiking out the rest.)

57 Stone Creek

Location: In Mount San Jacinto State Park; map I6, grid h8.

Campsites, facilities: There are 10 tent sites and 40 sites for tents or RVs up to 24 feet long. Fire grills and picnic tables are provided. Piped water and pit toilets are available. Supplies and coin laundry are nearby. Leashed pets are permitted.

Reservations, fees: Reserve via phone at (800) 444-PARK/7275 ($7.50 reservation fee) or website www.cal-parks.ca.gov; $10 to $11 per night, $1 pet fee. Open year-round.

Contact: Mount San Jacinto State Park, (909) 659-2607 or (760) 767-5311.

Directions: From Idyllwild, drive six miles north on Highway 243 to the park entrance.

Trip notes: This is a wooded camp, 5,900 feet in elevation, located off the main road along Stone Creek just outside the national forest boundary. It is less than a mile from the Fern Basin and less than three miles from Dark Canyon (campground numbers 59 and 50). The best trailhead in the immediate area is on the road just beyond Dark Canyon.

58 Idyllwild

Location: In Mount San Jacinto State Park; map I6, grid h8.

Campsites, facilities: There are 11 sites for tents only and 22 sites for tents or RVs up to 24 feet long. Fire grills and picnic tables are provided. Piped water, flush toilets, and showers are available. Supplies and coin laundry are nearby. Leashed pets are permitted.

Reservations, fees: Reserve via phone at

(800) 444-PARK/7275 ($7.50 reservation fee) or website www.cal-parks.ca.gov; $12 to $15 per night, $1 pet fee. Open year-round.

Contact: Mount San Jacinto State Park, (909) 659-2607 or (760) 767-5311.

Directions: In Idyllwild, drive to the north end of town on Highway 243 to the park entrance.

Trip notes: This is a prime spot for hikers and one of the better jump-off points for trekking in the area, set at 5,400 feet. A trail leading from the camp goes into the backcountry of Mount San Jacinto State Park and the San Jacinto Wilderness. The trail connects with the Pacific Crest Trail and then climbs on to Mount San Jacinto (10,786 feet) and its astounding lookout.

⑤⑨ Fern Basin

Location: Near Mount San Jacinto State Park in San Bernardino National Forest; map I6, grid h8.

Campsites, facilities: There are 22 sites for tents or RVs up to 15 feet long. Piped water, vault toilets, fire grills, and picnic tables are provided. Leashed pets are permitted.

Reservations, fees: Reservations are accepted for half of the sites; reserve via phone at (877) 444-6777 ($8.65 reservation fee) or website www.reserveusa.com; $10 per night. Open May through September.

Contact: San Bernardino National Forest, San Jacinto Ranger District, (909) 659-2117 or fax (909) 659-2107.

Directions: From Idyllwild, drive seven miles north on Highway 243. Turn right on Forest Service Road 4S02 and drive one mile to the campground.

Trip notes: This is a nearby alternative to Stone Creek (you'll pass it on the way in) and Dark Canyon (another three miles in). Hikers and backpackers should head north on Forest Service Road 4S02 for three-plus miles until it dead-ends at the Seven Pines Trailhead. That trail is routed east into Mount San Jacinto State Park, where it connects to the Pacific Crest Trail. Wilderness permits are required for overnight backpackers. The elevation is 6,300 feet.

⑥⓪ Marion Mountain

Location: In San Bernardino National Forest; map I6, grid h8.

Campsites, facilities: There are 24 sites for tents or RVs up to 15 feet long. Piped water, vault toilets, fire grills, and picnic tables are provided.

Reservations, fees: Reservations are accepted for half of the sites; reserve via phone at (877) 444-6777 ($8.65 reservation fee) or website www.reserveusa.com; $10 per night. Open May to mid-October.

Contact: San Bernardino National Forest, San Jacinto Ranger District, (909) 659-2117 or fax (909) 659-2107.

Directions: From Idyllwild, drive seven miles north on Highway 243. Turn right on Forest Service Road 4S02 and drive two miles to the campground.

Trip notes: You get good lookouts and a developed campground at this spot. Nearby Black Mountain (see Boulder Basin, campground number 49, for more information) is a good side trip, including a drive-to scenic lookout point. In additon, there are several trailheads in the area; the closest trail heads up the slopes to Marion Mountain and east into adjacent Mount San Jacinto State Park. The elevation is 6,400 feet.

⑥① Lake Skinner Recreation Area

Location: On Lake Skinner; map I6, grid i4.

Campsites, facilities: There are 257 sites for tents or RVs, many with full hookups. Picnic tables and fire grills are provided. Rest rooms, showers, playground, grocery store, ice, bait, dump station, swimming pool (in the summer), boat ramp, mooring, boat rentals, and propane gas are available. Leashed pets are permitted.

Reservations, fees: Reservations are requested; $15 to $18 per night, $2 pet fee. Open year-round.

Contact: Lake Skinner Recreation Area, (909) 926-1541.

Directions: From Interstate 15 in Temecula, take the Rancho California exit and drive 9.5 miles northeast to the park entrance.

Trip notes: Lake Skinner is set within a county park at an elevation of 1,470 feet in sparse foothill country, where the water can sparkle, and covers 1,200 surface acres. Unlike nearby Lake Elsinore, which is dominated by fast boats and water-skiers, no water contact sports are permitted here; hence no waterskiing, no swimming, no windsurfing. Afternoon winds make for great sailing, there is good fishing for trout or striped bass in the spring, and the recreation area provides hiking and horseback riding trails.

(62) Hurkey Creek County Park

Location: Near Lake Hemet; map I6, grid i8.

Campsites, facilities: There are 105 family sites and 104 group sites for tents or RVs up to 35 feet long. Fire grills and picnic tables are provided. Piped water, flush toilets, and showers are available. A dump station is available for a fee at nearby Lake Hemet. Leashed pets are permitted.

Reservations, fees: Reservations are recommended; reserve via phone at (800) 234-PARK/ 7275 (a reservation fee is charged); $15 per night, $2 pet fee. Open year-round.

Contact: Hurkey Creek County Park, (909) 659-2050.

Directions: From Palm Desert, drive about 32 miles southwest on Highway 74 to the campground entrance on your right.

Trip notes: This large county park is located just east (across the road) of Lake Hemet, beside Hurkey Creek (which runs in winter and spring). The highlight, of course, is the nearby lake (see next listing), known for good fishing in the spring. No swimming is permitted. The camp elevation is 4,800 feet.

(63) Lake Hemet

Location: Near Hemet; map I6, grid i8.

Campsites, facilities: There are 1,000 sites for tents or RVs. Piped water, fire grills, picnic tables and, in some cases, electrical connections are provided. Flush toilets, showers, dump station, playground, pond, boat ramp, boat rentals, grocery store, coin laundry, and propane gas are available. Leashed pets are permitted.

Reservations, fees: No reservations; $12 to $15.25 per night, $1 pet fee. Open year-round.

Contact: Lake Hemet, (909) 659-2680.

Directions: From Palm Desert, drive 32 miles southwest on Highway 74 to the camp entrance.

Trip notes: Lake Hemet covers 420 acres, is set at 4,335 feet, and is located near San Bernardino National Forest just west of Garner Valley. It provides a good camping/fishing destination, with stocks of 75,000 trout each year, a lot for a lake this size, and yep, catch rates are good. The lake also has bass and catfish. Boating rules prohibit boats under 10 feet or over 18 feet, canoes, sailboats, inflatables, and swimming; that leaves rowboats, and that's about it.

(64) Indian Oaks Trailer Ranch

Location: In Temecula; map I6, grid j2.

Campsites, facilities: There are 63 RV sites with full hookups, 16 with water and electricity hookups, 20 tent sites, and several group camping sites. Showers, rest rooms, coin laundry, propane, and a dump station are provided. Horseshoes, shuffleboard, and a recreation room are available. Leashed pets are permitted.

Reservations, fees: Reservations are recommended; $13 to $18 per night (maximum of two adults and two children per site), $4 per night for each additional person.

Contact: Indian Oaks Trailer Ranch, 38120 East Benton Road, PO Box 922, Temecula, CA 92593; (909) 676-5301.

Directions: From Riverside, take Interstate 215 south into Temecula and take the Temecula/Rancho California Road exit east. Drive nine miles out of town, past the Lucky shopping center, and then turn right on East Benton Road. Drive for 3.5 miles until you see the large sign for the camp.

Trip notes: This camp, once a Native American campground, is located in a 25-acre valley that is peppered with giant oak trees that are rumored to be 600 years old. Scenic hiking trails and picnic areas are located in and near the camp, and Lake Skinner is only three miles away for fishing. Plus, you can always visit the many wineries in the area.

65 Dripping Springs

Location: Near the Agua Tibia Wilderness in Cleveland National Forest; map I6, grid j4.

Campsites, facilities: There are 24 sites for tents or RVs up to 32 feet long. Piped water, fire rings, barbecue grills, and picnic tables are provided. Vault toilets are available. Supplies are available nearby in Temecula. Leashed pets are permitted.

Reservations, fees: No reservations; $12 per night, $2 for each additional vehicle. Open year-round.

Contact: Cleveland National Forest, Palomar Ranger District, (760) 788-0250 or fax: (760) 788-6130.

Directions: From Interstate 15 in Temecula, drive 11 miles east on Highway 79 to the campground.

Trip notes: This is one of the premium Forest Service camps available, set just inside the national forest border near Vail Lake and adjacent to the Agua Tibia Wilderness. The Dripping Springs Trail is routed south out of camp, starting at 1,600 feet and climbing to near the peak of Agua Tibia Mountain, 4,779 feet.

66 Oak Springs RV Resort

Location: Near Temecula; map I6, grid j6.

Campsites, facilities: There are 30 tent sites, 60 sites with full hookups, and 20 sites with partial hookups for RVs up to 45 feet long. A bunkhouse and a tepee are also available. Piped water, barbecues, and picnic tables are provided. Rest rooms, coin-operated hot showers, sanitary dump station, propane gas, coin laundry, heated swimming pool, children's playground, miniature golf, volleyball, basketball, baseball, horseshoes, shuffleboard, badminton, Ping-Pong, exercise room, horse corrals, private lake, and a small store are available. Paddleboat, kayak, and bicycle rentals are also available. The facilities are wheelchair accessible. Leashed pets are permitted.

Reservations, fees: Reservations are recommended; $15 to $22 per night. Group and monthly rates are available; call for details. Open year-round.

Contact: Oak Springs RV Resort, 38901 Reed Valley Road, Aguanga, CA 92536; (909) 767-1636, (888) 787-7275, or fax (909) 767-1612.

Directions: From Temecula, drive southwest on Highway 79 for 17.5 miles. Turn left on Highway 371 and drive three miles. Turn right on Reed Valley Road and drive four miles to the resort at 38901 Reed Valley Road.

Trip notes: This campground is set on 250 acres in an ideal location for hiking, biking, and fishing. A trailhead at the camp leads into 200,000 acres of wilderness in the neighboring San Bernardino National Forest. There is also a stocked lake, giving anglers the chance to catch trophy-size bass, bluegill, and catfish. The nearby Temecula wine country makes a good side trip.

67 Kamp Anza RV Resort

Location: Near Anza; map I6, grid j8.

Campsites, facilities: There are 116 sites for tents or RVs, many with full hookups. Horse-camping facilities are available. Picnic tables and fire grills are provided. Rest rooms, showers, playground, fishing pond, swimming spa, horseshoe pits, coin laundry, store, dump station, ice, recreation room, and propane gas are available.

Reservations, fees: Reservations are accepted; $12 to $18 per night, $12.50 per night per horse, $5 for an extra vehicle. Open year-round.

Contact: Kamp Anza RV Resort, (909) 763-4819.

Directions: From Palm Desert, drive west on Highway 74 for 24 miles. Turn left on Highway 371 and drive west to the town of Anza. Turn left on Kirby Road and drive one mile. Turn left on Wellman Road and drive one mile. Turn right on Terwilliger Road and drive to the park at 41560 Terwilliger Road.

Trip notes: This is a year-round RV park set at 4,100 feet, with many nearby recreation options. Lake Hemet is 11 miles away, with hiking, motorbiking, and jeep trails nearby in San Bernardino National Forest.

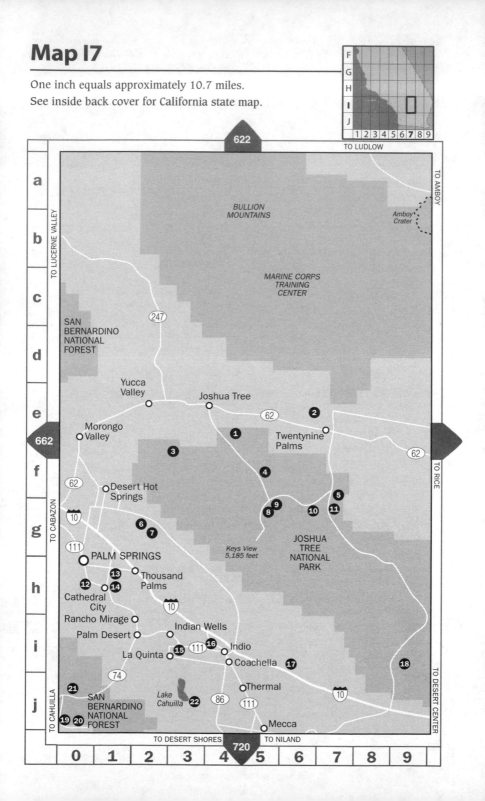

Chapter 17 features:

① Indian Cove Campground

Location: In Joshua Tree National Park; map I7, grid e4.

Campsites, facilities: There are 101 sites for tents or RVs up to 32 feet long. Adjacent to this campground is a group camp with 13 tent-only sites that will accommodate 15 to 60 people each. Drinking water is available at the Indian Cove Ranger Station. Pit toilets, picnic tables, and fire grills are provided. Gas, groceries, and laundry services are available in Joshua Tree, which is about 10 miles from camp. Leashed pets are permitted, but not on trails.

Reservations, fees: Reserve via phone at (800) 365-CAMP/2267; $10 per night for family sites, $20 to $35 per night for group sites.

Contact: Joshua Tree National Park, (760) 367-5500 or fax (760) 367-6392.

Directions: From Joshua Tree, drive about nine miles east on Highway 62 to Indian Cove Road. Turn right and drive three miles to the campground.

Trip notes: This is one of the campgrounds that is near the northern border of Joshua Tree National Park. The vast desert park, covering 1,238 square miles, is best known for its unique granite formations and scraggly looking trees. If you had to withstand the summer heat here, you'd look scraggly too. Drinking

water is available at the Indian Cove Ranger Station.

② Knott Sky RV Park

Location: Near Joshua Tree National Park; map I7, grid e6.

Campsites, facilities: There are 39 RV sites, 24 with full hookups (water, electricity, sewer, and cable TV) and 15 with partial hookups (water and electric only). An additional tent area for dispersed camping can accommodate about 50 people. Picnic tables and pedestal fire grills are provided. Piped water, flush toilets, showers, coin laundry, sanitary dump station, and a playground are available. Obtain supplies half a mile away in Twentynine Palms. Security gates are locked at night (from sunset to 6 A.M. in the summer and from 10 P.M. to 6 A.M. the rest of the year). Leashed pets are permitted.

Reservations, fees: Reservations are accepted; $7.50 to $17 per night. Open year-round.

Contact: Twentynine Palms City Parks, (760) 367-9669, (760) 367-5773, or fax (760) 367-4890.

Directions: From Twentynine Palms, drive a mile west on Highway 62, turn right on El Sol Avenue, and drive two miles to the signed park entrance.

Trip notes: What the heck, unlike the camps in the nearby national park to the south, this one has showers. And if you've spent any amount of time at Joshua Tree, you're probably in need of one. Whoo-eee! So turn that water on and dive in. The elevation is 2,000 feet.

③ Black Rock Campground

Location: In Joshua Tree National Park; map I7, grid f3.

Campsites, facilities: There are 100 sites for tents or RVs up to 32 feet long. One site is wheelchair accessible (campsite no. 61). Picnic tables and fire grills are provided. Piped water, flush toilets, and a sanitary disposal station are available. Leashed pets are permitted, but not on backcountry trails.

Reservations, fees: Reserve via phone at (800) 365-CAMP/2267; $10 per night. Open May through October, weather permitting.

Contact: Joshua Tree National Park, (760) 367-5500 or fax (760) 367-6392.

Directions: From the junction of Interstate 10 and Highway 62, drive about 22.5 miles north on Highway 62 to Yucca Valley. Turn right (south) on Joshua Lane and drive about five miles to the campground.

Trip notes: This is the fanciest darn campground this side of the galaxy. Why, they actually have piped water. Course, they charge you for it. The camp is set at the mouth of Black Rock Canyon, 4,000 feet elevation, which provides good winter hiking possibilities amid unique (in other words, weird) rock formations. Show up in summer and you'll trade your gold for a sip of water. The camp is set near the excellent Black Rock Canyon Visitor Center and a trailhead for a four-mile round-trip hike on the Hiking and Riding Trail to a rock wash and back. If you scramble onward, the route continues all the way to the top of Eureka Peak, 5,518 feet, an 11-mile round-trip. But hey, why not just drive there?

④ Sheep Pass Group Camp

Location: In Joshua Tree National Park; map I7, grid f5.

Campsites, facilities: There are six sites for tents. Picnic tables and fire grills are provided. Pit toilets are available. There is no piped water, so bring plenty along. Leashed pets are permitted.

Reservations, fees: Reserve via phone at (800) 365-CAMP/2267; $20 to $35 fee per night. Open year-round.

Contact: Joshua Tree National Park, (760) 367-5500 or fax (760) 367-6392.

Directions: From Twentynine Palms, drive south on Utah Trail for about 16 miles to the campground on the south (left) side of the road.

Trip notes: Several campgrounds are in this stretch of high desert. Ryan campground is just a couple miles down the road from this one and provides a nearby option with an excellent trailhead for a trek to Ryan Mountain, the best hike in the park (see the trip notes for Ryan, campground number eight). For details on this area, see the trip notes for White Tank (campground number 11) and other nearby camps. Temperatures are routinely over 100 degrees here in the summer.

⑤ Belle

Location: In Joshua Tree National Park; map I7, grid f7.

Campsites, facilities: There are 18 sites for tents or RVs up to 27 feet long. Picnic tables and fire grills are provided. Pit toilets are available. There is no piped water, so bring your own. Leashed pets are permitted.

Reservations, fees: No reservations; no fee. Open year-round.

Contact: Joshua Tree National Park, (760) 367-5500 or fax (760) 367-6392.

Directions: From Twentynine Palms, drive eight miles south on Utah Trail to Cottonwood Springs Road. Turn left on Cottonwood Springs Road (heading toward Interstate 10) and drive about 1.5 miles to the campground.

Trip notes: This camp is at 3,800 feet in rocky high country. It is one of six camps in the immediate area. For more details, see the trip notes for White Tank (campground number 11) and the other nearby camps.

❻ Sam's Family Spa

Location: Near Palm Springs; map I7, grid g2.

Campsites, facilities: There are 180 RV sites with full hookups and picnic tables. There is a separate area with fire grills. Rest rooms, showers, playground, swimming pool, wading pool, four hot mineral pools, sauna, coin laundry, store, and a restaurant are available. Leashed pets are permitted.

Reservations, fees: No reservations; $33 per night. Open year-round.

Contact: Sam's Family Spa, (760) 329-6457 or fax (760) 329-8267; website: samsfamilyspa.com.

Directions: From Interstate 10, take the Palm Drive exit and travel three miles north on Palm Drive. Turn right (east) on Dillon Road and drive 4.5 miles to 70-875 Dillon Road on the right.

Trip notes: Hot mineral pools attract swarms of winter vacationers to the Palm Springs area. This park, set 10 miles outside of Palm Springs, provides an alternative to the more crowded spots. The elevation of Sam's Family Spa is 1,000 feet. For information on the tramway ride to Desert View west of Palm Springs, or the hike to Mount San Jacinto, see the trip notes for Sky Valley East and West (campground number seven).

❼ Sky Valley East and West

Location: Near Palm Springs; map I7, grid g2.

Campsites, facilities: There are 614 RV sites. Piped water, cable TV hookups, electrical connections, and sewer hookups are provided. Rest rooms, showers, four swimming pools, nine natural hot mineral whirlpools, two laundry rooms, two large recreation rooms, social director, shuffleboard, tennis, horseshoes, crafts room, and walking trails are available. A grocery store and propane gas are nearby. Some facilities are wheelchair accessible. Leashed pets are permitted.

Reservations, fees: Reservations are accepted; $15 to $32.50 per night. Open year-round.

Contact: Sky Valley East and West, (760) 329-2909 or fax (760) 329-9473.

Directions: From Interstate 10, take the Palm Drive exit and travel three miles north on Palm Drive. Turn right on Dillon Road and drive 8.5 miles to 74-711 Dillon Road.

Trip notes: This park is a wonderful spot for family fun and relaxation. Also note that one of the best adventures in California is just west of Palm Springs, taking the tramway up from Chino Canyon to Desert View, a ride/climb of 2,600 feet for remarkable views to the east across the desert below. An option from here is then hiking the flank of Mount San Jacinto, including making the ascent to the summit (10,804 feet), a round-trip butt-kicker of nearly 12 miles.

❽ Ryan

Location: In Joshua Tree National Park; map I7, grid g5.

Campsites, facilities: There are 31 sites for tents or RVs up to 27 feet long. Picnic tables and fire grills are provided. Pit toilets are available. There is no piped water, so bring plenty along. Hitching posts are available (bring water for the horses). Leashed pets are permitted.

Reservations, fees: No reservations; no fee.

Contact: Joshua Tree National Park, (760) 367-5500 or fax (760) 367-6392.

Directions: From Twentynine Palms, drive south on Utah Trail about 20 miles to the signed campground entrance on the left.

Trip notes: This is one of the high desert camps in the immediate area (see also Jumbo Rocks, campground number 10). Joshua Tree National Park is a forbidding paradise, huge, hot, and waterless (most of the time). The unique rock formations look like some great artist made them with a chisel. The elevation is 4,300 feet. The best hike in the park starts here, a three-mile round-trip to Ryan Mountain, a 700-foot climb to the top at 5,470 feet. The view is simply drop-dead gorgeous, not only of San Jacinto, Tahquitz, and San Gorgonio peaks, but of several beautiful rock-studded valleys as well as the Wonderland of Rocks.

⑨ Hidden Valley

Location: In Joshua Tree National Park; map I7, grid g5.

Campsites, facilities: There are 39 sites for tents or RVs up to 27 feet long. Picnic tables and fire grills are provided. Pit toilets are available. There is no piped water, so bring plenty along. Leashed pets are permitted.

Reservations, fees: No reservations; no fee. Open year-round.

Contact: Joshua Tree National Park, (760) 367-5500 or fax (760) 367-6392.

Directions: From Joshua Tree on Highway 62, turn south on Park Boulevard and drive 14 miles southeast to the campground.

Trip notes: Set at 4,200 feet in the high desert country, this is one of several camping options in the area. A trailhead is available two miles from camp at Barker Dam, an easy one-mile loop that features the Wonderland of Rocks. The hike takes you next to a small lake with magical reflections of rock formations off its surface.

⑩ Jumbo Rocks

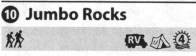

Location: In Joshua Tree National Park; map I7, grid g6.

Campsites, facilities: There are 125 sites for tents or RVs up to 27 feet long. Picnic tables and fire grills are provided. Pit toilets are available. There is no piped water, so bring plenty along. Leashed pets are permitted.

Reservations, fees: No reservations; no fee. Open year-round.

Contact: Joshua Tree National Park, (760) 367-7511 or fax (760) 367-6392.

Directions: From Twentynine Palms, drive south on Utah Trail for about nine miles to the campground on the left (south) side of the road.

Trip notes: Joshua Tree National Park covers more than 1,238 square miles. It is striking high desert country with unique granite formations that seem to change color at different times of the day. This camp is one of the higher ones in the park at 4,400 feet, with adjacent boulders and rock formations that look as if they have been strewn about by an angry giant.

⑪ White Tank

Location: In Joshua Tree National Park; map I7, grid g7.

Campsites, facilities: There are 15 sites for tents or RVs up to 27 feet long. Picnic tables and fire grills are provided. Pit toilets are available, but there is no piped water, so bring plenty along. Leashed pets are permitted.

Reservations, fees: No reservations; no fee.

Contact: Joshua Tree National Park, (760) 367-7511 or fax (760) 367-6392.

Directions: From Twentynine Palms, drive eight miles south on Utah Trail to the intersection with Cottonwood Springs Road. Turn left on Cottonwood Road (heading toward Interstate 10) and drive three miles to the campground.

Trip notes: Joshua Tree National Park is a unique area where the high and low desert meet. It looks kind of like high plains country. Winter is a good time to explore the beautiful boulder piles and rock formations amid scraggly Joshua trees. There are several trails in the area, with the best located near Black Rock Campground (campground number three), Hidden Valley (campground number nine), and Cottonwood (campground number 18). The elevation is 3,800 feet.

⑫ Happy Traveler RV Park

Location: In Palm Springs; map I7, grid h0.

Campsites, facilities: There are 139 RV sites with full hookups and picnic tables. Rest rooms, showers, recreation room, swimming pool, hot tub, and coin laundry are available. Leashed pets are permitted.

Reservations, fees: Reservations are accepted; $29 per night. Open year-round.

Contact: Happy Traveler RV Park, (760) 325-8518 or fax (760) 778-6708; email: happytrav@aol.com.

Directions: In Palm Springs, drive one mile south on Palm Canyon Drive. Turn right on Mesquite Avenue and go to 211 West Mesquite.

Trip notes: Are we having fun yet? They are at Happy Traveler, which is within walking distance of Palm Springs shopping areas.

⑬ Outdoor Resorts

Location: Near Palm Springs; map I7, grid h1.

Campsites, facilities: There are 1,213 RV sites with full hookups. Rest rooms, showers, eight swimming pools, 14 tennis courts, 10 whirlpools, a 27-hole golf course, two clubhouses, a health club with three saunas, a snack bar, a beauty salon, coin laundry, store, shuffleboard, and planned activities are available. Some facilities are wheelchair accessible. Leashed pets are permitted.

Reservations, fees: Reservations are accepted; $40 to $55 per night. Open year-round.

Contact: Outdoor Resorts, (760) 324-4005 or (800) 843-3131 (California only).

Directions: From Cathedral City, drive two miles north on Date Palm Drive to Ramon Road. Turn left and drive to 69-411 Ramon Road.

Trip notes: This is the RV park that was voted the "Most Likely to Succeed As a City." It's huge, it's flat, and it offers many activities. If you still can't think of anything to do, you can always compare tires. The park is located four miles from Palm Springs. Note that one of the best adventures in California is just west of Palm Springs, taking the tramway up from Chino Canyon to Desert View, a ride/climb of 2,600 feet for remarkable views to the east across the desert below. An option from here is then hiking the flank of Mount San Jacinto, including making the ascent to the summit (10,804 feet), a round-trip butt-kicker of nearly 12 miles.

⑭ Palm Springs Oasis RV Resort

Location: Near Palm Springs; map I7, grid h1.

Campsites, facilities: There are 140 RV sites with full hookups. Rest rooms, showers, cable TV hookups, two swimming pools, whirlpool, 18-hole golf course, tennis courts, coin laundry, and propane gas are available. Leashed pets are permitted.

Reservations, fees: Reservations are accepted; $22 to $30 per night. Open year-round.

Contact: Palm Springs Oasis RV Resort, (760) 328-4813, (800) 680-0144, or fax (760) 328-8455.

Directions: In Cathedral City, drive to 36-100 Date Palm Drive. The camp is on the corner of Gerald Ford Drive and Date Palm Drive.

Trip notes: This popular wintering spot is for RV cruisers looking to hole up in the Palm Springs area for awhile. Palm Springs is only six miles away.

⑮ Indian Wells RV Roundup

Location: In Indio; map I7, grid i3.

Campsites, facilities: There are 381 RV sites, most with full hookups. Picnic tables and fire grills are provided. Rest rooms, showers, cable TV hookups, three swimming pools, two therapy pools, fitness room, horseshoes, shuffleboard courts, putting green, planned activities, ice, dog run, barbecue, and coin laundry are available. Leashed pets are permitted.

Reservations, fees: Reservations are accepted; $18 to $25 per night. This is an adult-oriented park.

Contact: Indian Wells RV Roundup, (760) 347-0895, (800) 789-0895, or fax (760) 775-1147.

Directions: In Indio on Interstate 10, take the Jefferson exit. As you exit, stay in the right lane and turn right at the light. Follow Jefferson Street south for three miles. The park is on the left at 47-340 Jefferson Street.

Trip notes: Indio is a good-sized town located midway between the Salton Sea to the south and Palm Springs to the north. In the summer, it is one of the hottest places in America. In the winter, it is a favorite for "snowbirds," that is, RV and trailer owners from the snow country who migrate south to the desert for the winter.

⑯ Outdoor Resorts Motorcoach

Location: In Indio; map I7, grid i4.

Campsites, facilities: There are 292 sites for RVs only. Full hookups and cable television are provided. Rest rooms, showers, swimming pool, tennis court, sauna, whirlpool, coin laundry, and an 18-hole golf course are available. Some facilities are wheelchair accessible. Leashed pets are permitted.

Reservations, fees: Reservations are accepted; $45 per night.

Contact: Outdoor Resorts Motorcoach, (760) 775-7255, (800) 371-9988 (California only), (800) 892-2992 (outside California), or fax (760) 347-0875.

Directions: From Palm Springs, take Interstate 10 east to the Jefferson exit. Stay in the right lane as you exit and then turn right at the light on Jefferson. Drive through the intersection at Highway 111 and continue one block south to 48th Avenue. Turn left and drive to the park on the left side of the road at 80-394 48th Avenue.

Trip notes: For owners of tour buses, motor coaches, and lavish RVs, it doesn't get any better than this in Southern California. This is the sole RV-only park in California, and it is set close to golf, shopping, and restaurants. Jeep tours of the surrounding desert canyons and organized recreation events are available.

⑰ Corn Springs

Location: Near Indio; map I7, grid i6.

Campsites, facilities: There are 14 sites for tents or RVs and one group site. Picnic tables and fire rings are provided. Piped water and pit toilets are available. Leashed pets are permitted.

Reservations, fees: No reservations; $4 per night.

Contact: Bureau of Land Management, Palm Springs South Coast Field Office, 63-500 Garnet Avenue, PO Box 2000, North Palm Springs, CA 92258; (760) 251-4800.

Directions: From Indio on Interstate 10, drive 60 miles east to Corn Springs Road. Exit right on Corn Springs Road and drive eight miles to the campground.

Trip notes: Just think: If you spend a night here, you can say to darn near anybody, "I've camped someplace you haven't." I don't know whether to offer my condolences or congratulations, but Corn Springs offers a primitive spot in the middle of nowhere in desert country. What the heck, if you are stuck for a spot while cruising Interstate 10, this will seem like paradise. The side trip to Joshua Tree National Park to the north is also well worth the adventure, as is the tramway ride available west of Palm Springs for an incredible view of the desert (see the trip notes for Outdoor Resorts, campground number 13, for more information). On the other hand, if it's a summer afternoon, tell me, just how do you spend the day here when it's 115 degrees?

⑱ Cottonwood

Location: In Joshua Tree National Park; map I7, grid i9.

Campsites, facilities: There are 62 sites for tents or RVs up to 27 feet long. There is a group campground adjacent to this one (Cottonwood Group Camp) that has three sites for up to 25 people each. Group site number two is wheelchair accessible. Piped water, picnic tables, and fire grills are provided. Flush toilets are available. Leashed pets are permitted.

Reservations, fees: No reservations for individual sites; $8 per night. Reserve group sites via phone at (800) 365-CAMP/2267; $25 group fee per night. Open year-round.

Contact: Joshua Tree National Park, (760) 367-5500 or fax (760) 367-6392.

Directions: From Indio, drive 35 miles east on Interstate 10. Take the Twentynine Palms exit (near Chiriaco Summit) and drive seven miles north on the park entrance road to the campground.

Trip notes: If you enter Joshua Tree National Park at its southern access point, this is the first camp you come to. The park visitor center, where maps are available, is a mandatory stop. This park is vast, high desert country, highlighted by unique rock formations, occasional scraggly trees, and vegetation that manages to survive the bleak, roasting summers. This camp is set at 3,000 feet. A trailhead is available here for an easy one-mile nature trail, where small signs have been posted to identify different types of vegetation. You'll notice, however, that they all look like cacti (the plants, not the signs, heh, heh).

⑲ Tool Box Spring

Location: In San Bernardino National Forest; map I7, grid j0.

Campsites, facilities: There are six tent sites. Vault toilets, fire grills, and picnic tables are provided. No piped water is available. Leashed pets are permitted.

Reservations, fees: No reservations; no camping fee. An Adventure Pass ($30 annual fee) or $5 daily fee per parked vehicle is required. Open year-round.

Contact: San Bernardino National Forest, San Jacinto Ranger District, (909) 659-2117 or fax (909) 659-2107.

Directions: Traveling southeast just past Lake Hemet on Highway 74, you'll see Forest Service Road 6S13 (paved, then dirt) on the right. Turn right and drive about four miles. Turn left on Forest Service Road 5S13 and drive 4.5 miles to the camping area.

Trip notes: This is an extremely primitive campground that provides an alternative to Thomas Mountain Camp, located two miles southwest, also on the ridge of Thomas Mountain. The difference is that this camp has a little creek, created from Tool Box Spring, that runs nearby, though it turns into a trickle in the summer. A primitive trail runs right through the camp, descending to the valleys (and trailheads on roads) on each side of the ridge, not exactly a stellar

hike. In the winter, call for road conditions to determine accessibility. The elevation is 6,500 feet.

⑳ Thomas Mountain

Location: In San Bernardino National Forest; map I7, grid j0.

Campsites, facilities: There are six tent sites. There is no piped water, but vault toilets, fire grills, and picnic tables are provided. Leashed pets are permitted.

Reservations, fees: No reservations; no camping fee. An Adventure Pass ($30 annual fee) or $5 daily fee per parked vehicle is required. Open year-round.

Contact: San Bernardino National Forest, San Jacinto Ranger District, (909) 659-2117 or fax (909) 760-659-2107.

Directions: Traveling southeast just past Lake Hemet on Highway 74, you'll see Forest Service Road 6S13 (paved, then dirt) on the right. Turn right and drive about four miles. Turn left on Forest Service Road 5S13 and drive three miles to the camp.

Trip notes: If you don't want to be bugged by anything but a few bugs, this is the place. It's a small, primitive camp set just east of the summit of Thomas Mountain, 6,800 feet. There are no trails, no streams, no nuthin' in the immediate area; the closest hike is the trail to nowhere out of Tool Box Spring (see the trip notes for campground number 19). After you have purged your soul out here, you might consider a side trip to Lake Hemet, located four nautical miles (and a heck of a lot longer by car) to the north. The road in can be closed in winter.

㉑ Piñon Flat

Location: Near Cahuilla Tewanet Vista Point in San Bernardino National Forest; map I7, grid j0.

Campsites, facilities: There are 18 sites for tents or RVs up to 22 feet long. Piped water, vault toilets, fire grills, and picnic tables are provided. The facilities are wheelchair accessible. Leashed pets are permitted.

Reservations, fees: No reservations; $7 per night. Open year-round.

Contact: San Bernardino National Forest, San Jacinto Ranger District, (909) 659-2117 or fax (909) 659-2107.

Directions: From Palm Desert, drive 14 miles southwest on Highway 74 to the camp.

Trip notes: The Cahuilla Tewanet Vista Point is just two miles east of the camp and provides a good, easy side trip, along with a sweeping view to the east of the desert. A primitive trail is available two miles away to the southeast via Forest Service Road 7S01 off a short spur road (look for it on the left side of the road). This hike crosses a mix of sparse forest and high desert terrain for 10 miles, passing Cactus Spring five miles in. Desert bighorn sheep are sometimes spotted in this area. The elevation is 4,000 feet.

㉒ Lake Cahuilla County Park

Location: Near Indio; map I7, grid j3.

Campsites, facilities: There are numerated, primitive sites and 60 RV sites (50 with electric and water hookups and 10 with no hookups). There is also a group area with collapsible horse corrals and equestrian trails. Fire grills and picnic tables are provided. Rest rooms, showers, dump station, playground, swimming pool, and an unpaved, beach boat launch are available. No gas motors are allowed. Leashed pets are permitted.

Reservations, fees: Reservations are accepted ($6.50 reservation fee); $12 to $16 per night, $2 pet fee. Monthly rates are available. Closed Tuesday, Wednesday and Thursday.

Contact: Lake Cahuilla County Park, (760) 564-4712 or fax (760) 564-2506.

Directions: From Interstate 10 in Indio, take the Monroe Street exit and follow Monroe Street south for seven or eight miles to Avenue 58. Turn right and continue three miles to the lake.

Trip notes: Lake Cahuilla covers just 135 acres, but those are the most loved 135 acres for miles in all directions. After all, water out here is as scarce as polar bears. The park provides large palm trees and a 10-acre beach and waterplay area, excellent for swimming. Believe it or not, sometimes the water gets too warm from the summer heat to swim in, like a big hot tub. Only cartop boats are permitted, and a speed limit of 10 mph is enforced. A new equestrian camp is now available, complete with corrals. A warning: The wind can really howl through here, and temperatures well over 100 degrees are typical in the summer. If it weren't for this lake, they might as well post a sign on Interstate 10 that says, "You are now entering Hell."

Map I9

One inch equals approximately 10.7 miles.
See inside back cover for California state map.

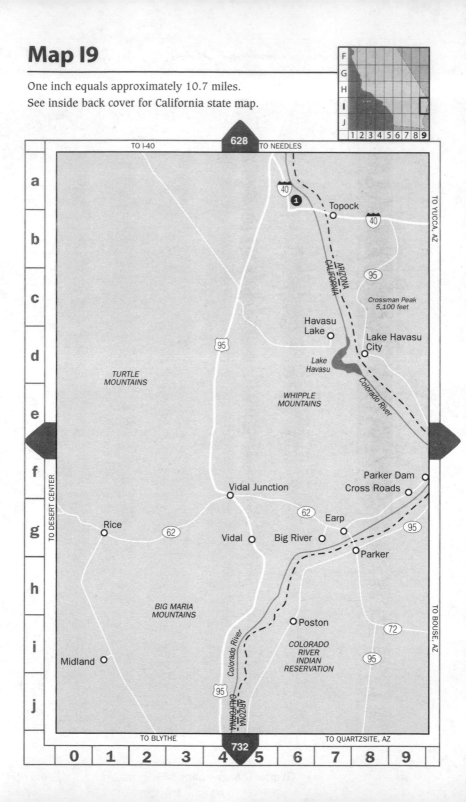

❶ Moabi Regional Park

Location: On the Colorado River; map 19, grid a6.

Campsites, facilities: There are more than 600 sites for tents or RVs, most with full hookups. Picnic tables and fire grills are provided at most sites. Flush toilets, showers, laundry facilities, store, ice, playground, two sanitary dump stations, and a boat ramp are available. Leashed pets are permitted.

Reservations, fees: Reservations are accepted Monday through Thursday, 8 A.M. to 4 P.M.; $12 to $20 per night, $1 pet fee. Open year-round.

Contact: Moabi Regional Park, (760) 326-3831 or fax (760) 326-3272.

Directions: From Needles, drive approximately 11 miles east on Interstate 40. Turn left on Park Moabi Road and continue a half mile to the park entrance.

Trip notes: The adjacent Colorado River provides the main attraction, the only thing liquid around these parts that isn't contained in a can or bottle. The natural response when you see it is to jump in the water and everybody does so, with or without a boat. You'll see lots of wild and crazy types having the times of their lives on the water. The boating season is a long one here, courtesy of that desert climate.

Map J5

One inch equals approximately 10.7 miles.
See inside back cover for California state map.

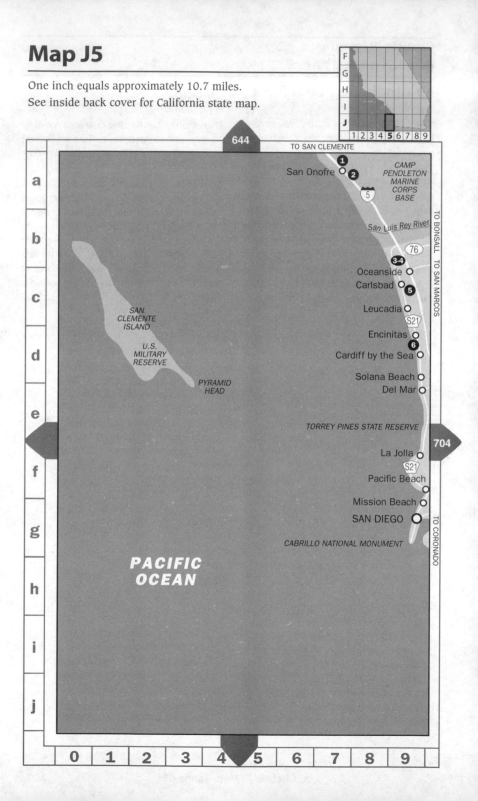

① San Onofre State Beach: Bluff Area

Location: Near San Clemente; map J5, grid a7.

Campsites, facilities: There are 221 sites for tents or RVs. Piped water, fire grills, and picnic tables are provided. Cold showers and flush toilets are available. A grocery store, coin laundry, and propane gas are nearby. Leashed pets are permitted.

Reservations, fees: Reserve via phone at (800) 444-PARK/7275 ($7.50 reservation fee) or website www.cal-parks.ca.gov; $17 to $18 per night, $6 for an extra vehicle. $1 pet fee. Open May through October.

Contact: San Onofre State Beach, (949) 492-4872, (949) 492-0802, or fax (949) 492-8412.

Directions: From San Clemente, drive three miles south on Interstate 5. Take the Basilone exit and drive to the park.

Trip notes: This state park is one of three parks set along the beach near San Clemente, located just off the busy Coast Highway. The others are San Clemente State Beach and Doheny State Beach, both situated to the north. This area is one of the most popular in California for surfing. A drawback: it sits in the shadow of the San Onofre Nuclear Power Plant.

② San Onofre State Beach: San Mateo Camp

Location: Near San Clemente; map J5, grid a7.

Campsites, facilities: There are 162 sites for tents or RVs, 70 with electric and water hookups. A dump station, hot showers, fire grills, and flush toilets are provided. A grocery store, propane gas, and coin laundry are nearby. Leashed pets are permitted.

Reservations, fees: Reserve via phone at (800) 444-PARK/7275 ($7.50 reservation fee) or website www.cal-parks.ca.gov; $17 to $24 per night, $1 pet fee. Open May through October.

Contact: San Onofre State Beach, (949) 492-0802, or fax (949) 492-8412.

Directions: From Interstate 5 at the southern end of San Clemente, take the Cristianitos exit and drive inland 1.5 miles to the park entrance.

Trip notes: Folks cruising the Coast Highway yearn for spots just like this, but the only catch is that you'd better have a reservation during the vacation season or run the risk of finding yourself out of luck. State parks with oceanside camps and beach access like this one are beautiful and in demand. Just offshore, the abundant kelp forests provide habitat for kelp bass and other fish, including sheepshead, barracuda, and yellowtail. Charter fishing trips are available to this area out of Oceanside to the south.

③ Paradise by the Sea RV Park

Location: In Oceanside; map J5, grid b9.

Campsites, facilities: There are 102 RV sites with full hookups. Flush toilets, showers, cable TV hookups, swimming pool, whirlpool, clubhouse, banquet room, coin laundry, RV supplies, telephone, and a small grocery store are available. Boat rentals are nearby. Leashed pets are permitted with proof of vaccination.

Reservations, fees: Reservations are recommended; $25 to $31 per night, $1 pet fee. Open year-round.

Contact: Paradise by the Sea RV Park, (760) 439-1376 or fax (760) 439-1919.

Directions: From Interstate 5 in Oceanside,

take the Highway 78/Vista Way exit. Drive west for a half mile. Turn right on South Coast Highway and go to 1537 South Coast Highway.

Trip notes: This is a classic oceanfront RV park, but no tenters need apply. It's an easy walk to the beach. For boaters, Oceanside Marina to the immediate north is the place to go. Oceanside is an excellent headquarters for deep-sea fishing, with charter trips available to Catalina Island, the kelp forests to the north offshore Camp Pendleton and San Onofre, as well as along the coast from Carlsbad and points south; contact Helgren's Sportfishing, (760) 722-2133, to arrange charters. Camp Pendleton, a huge Marine Corps training complex, is located to the north.

❹ Casitas Poquitos

Location: In Oceanside; map J5, grid b9.

Campsites, facilities: There are 140 RV sites with full hookups. Picnic tables and patios are provided. Flush toilets, showers, cable TV hookups, playground, coin laundry, recreation room, swimming pool, whirlpool, billiard room, propane gas, and a general store are available. Leashed pets are permitted.

Reservations, fees: Reservations are recommended; $23 to $29.90 per night, $1 pet fee. Open year-round.

Contact: Casitas Poquitos, (760) 722-4404.

Directions: From Interstate 5 in Oceanside, take the Oceanside Boulevard exit. Drive west for a half mile. Turn left on South Coast Highway and go to the park at 1510 South Coast Highway.

Trip notes: There are three options for RV cruisers in the Oceanside area, and this is one of them. It's a short distance to the beach. For details on the area, see the trip notes for Paradise by the Sea RV Park (campground number three).

❺ South Carlsbad State Beach

Location: Near Carlsbad; map J5, grid c9.

Campsites, facilities: There are 221 sites for tents or RVs up to 35 feet long. Picnic tables and fire grills are provided. Piped water, flush toilets, showers, and a dump station are available. Some facilities are wheelchair accessible. Supplies and a coin laundry are available in Carlsbad. Leashed pets are permitted.

Reservations, fees: Reserve via phone at (800) 444-PARK/7275 ($7.50 reservation fee) or website www.cal-parks.ca.gov; $17 to $21 per night, $1 pet fee. Open year-round.

Contact: South Carlsbad State Beach, (760) 438-3143 or (619) 642-4200.

Directions: From Carlsbad, drive four miles south on Pacific Coast Highway to the camp entrance.

Trip notes: No reservation? Then likely you can forget about staying here. This is a beautiful state beach and, as big as it is, the sites go fast to the coastal cruisers who reserved in advance. The nearby Agua Hedionda Lagoon provides a unique boating experience, where boaters must show proof of insurance coverage of at least $300,000 before they are allowed to roar around the quiet waters at speeds of up to 50 mph. Afternoon winds make this one of the best places in Southern California for windsurfing.

❻ San Elijo State Beach

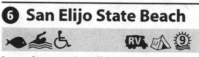

Location: In Cardiff by the Sea; map J5, grid d9.

Campsites, facilities: There are 171 sites for tents or RVs up to 35 feet long. Picnic tables and fire grills are provided. Piped water, flush toilets, showers, dump station, and a small store are available. Some of the campsites and the store are wheelchair accessible. Leashed (maximum of six feet) pets are permitted, but not on the beach.

Reservations, fees: Reserve via phone at (800) 444-PARK/7275 ($7.50 reservation fee) or website www.cal-parks.ca.gov; $17 to $23 per night, $1 pet fee. Open year-round.

Contact: San Elijo State Beach, (760) 753-5091 or (619) 642-4200.

Directions: From Cardiff by the Sea, drive a half mile northwest on County Road S21 to the park entrance.

Trip notes: Here is another in the series of popular state beaches along the San Diego

County coast. This one is located along a beautiful beach just north of the small town of Cardiff by the Sea. As at all state beaches, reservations are usually required to get a spot between Memorial Day weekend and Labor Day weekend.

Nearby San Elijo Lagoon at Solana Beach is an unexpected ecological preserve. Though near a developed area, there are numerous white egrets, as well as occasional herons and other marine birds.

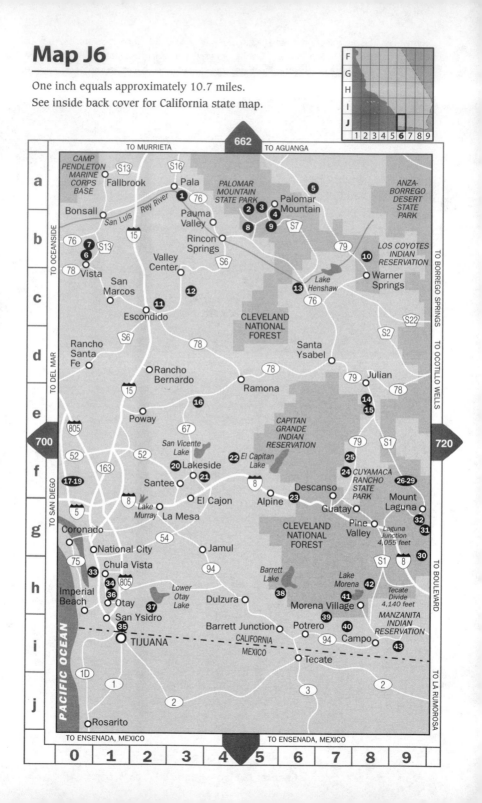

Map J6

One inch equals approximately 10.7 miles.
See inside back cover for California state map.

Chapter J6 features:

1 Rancho Corrido

Location: Near the Pala Mission; map J6, grid a3.

Campsites, facilities: There are 210 sites for tents or RVs (110 with water, electric, and cable TV hookups) and 100 tent sites. Picnic tables, fire pits, and, in some cases, sewer connections are provided. Flush toilets, showers, dump station, clubhouses, gazebos, playground, small store, rifle range, propane gas, fishing pond, and coin laundry are available. Leashed pets are permitted.

Reservations, fees: Reservations are preferred; $19 to $24 per night, $3 pet fee. Call for group rates. Open year-round.

Contact: Rancho Corrido, (760) 742-3755 or fax (760) 742-3245.

Directions: From Interstate 15, take the Highway 76 exit and drive east past the town of Pala. Continue east on Highway 76 for four miles to the camp at 14715 Highway 76.

Trip notes: This RV layover is located 10 miles east of Interstate 15, the main drag. A fishing pond is available for catch-and-release fishing only. It is a short drive to the Pala Indian Reservation and the Pala Mission to the east. The

Palomar Observatory is 20 miles to the east, another possible side trip.

❷ Palomar Mountain State Park

Location: Near the Palomar Observatory; map J6, grid a5.

Campsites, facilities: There are 31 sites for tents or RVs up to 21 feet long. Fire grills and picnic tables are provided. Piped water, flush toilets, and showers are available. Some facilities are wheelchair accessible. Leashed pets are permitted.

Reservations, fees: Reservations accepted for group sites only; reserve via phone at (800) 444-PARK/7275 ($7.50 reservation fee) or website www.cal-parks.ca.gov; $15 to $16 per night for individual sites, group fees are $45 to $60 per night, $1 pet fee. Open year-round.

Contact: Palomar Mountain State Park, (760) 742-3462 or (760) 767-5311.

Directions: From Interstate 15, turn east on Highway 76 and drive about 25 miles to County Road S6 (which brings you to the top of Palomar Mountain). At the top of the mountain turn left, go about 50 feet, turn left again on State Park Road/County Road S7, and drive about 3.5 miles to the park entrance.

Trip notes: This developed state park is a short drive from the Palomar Observatory. There are four other campgrounds in the immediate area that are a short distance from the observatory. The elevation is 4,700 feet. This camp offers hiking trails and some fishing in Doane Pond (great for youngsters learning to fish). There are three excellent hikes, the Observatory Trail (4.5 miles), Boucher Trail (4 miles), and Lower Doane Valley Trail (3 miles). The view from Boucher Lookout is stunning, at 5,438 feet looking out over the valley below. At the Palomar Observatory you'll find the 200-inch Hale telescope, America's largest telescope.

❸ Fry Creek

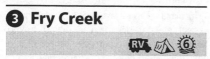

Location: Near the Palomar Observatory in Cleveland National Forest; map J6, grid a5.

Campsites, facilities: There are 12 tent sites and eight sites for tents or RVs up to 16 feet long. Piped water, fire pits, and picnic tables are provided. Vault toilets are available. A grocery store is nearby. Leashed pets are permitted.

Reservations, fees: No reservations; $12 per night. Open May through October.

Contact: Cleveland National Forest, Palomar Ranger District, (760) 788-0250 or fax (760) 788-6130.

Directions: From Interstate 15, head east on Highway 76 and drive about 25 miles to County Road S6 (the road that goes up to Palomar Mountain). At the top of the mountain, turn left and drive about nine miles to the campground entrance on the left. The road is not recommended for trailers.

Trip notes: A small, seasonal stream, Fry Creek, runs near the camp. The elevation is 5,200 feet. On a clear night, you can see forever from Palomar Mountain. Literally. That's because the Palomar Observatory, just a short distance from this forested camp, houses America's largest telescope. With the 200-inch Hale telescope, it is possible for scientists to see 100 billion galaxies.

❹ Observatory

Location: Near the Palomar Observatory in Cleveland National Forest; map J6, grid a5.

Campsites, facilities: There are 42 sites for tents or RVs up to 22 feet long (a few sites will accommodate RVs up to 28 feet long). Fire grills, picnic tables, and piped water are provided. Vault toilets are available. Leashed pets are permitted.

Reservations, fees: No reservations; $12 per night, double sites are $20 per night. Open May through October.

Contact: Cleveland National Forest, Palomar Ranger District, (760) 788-0250 or fax (760) 788-6130.

Directions: From Interstate 15, head east on Highway 76 and drive about 25 miles to County Road S6 (the road that goes up to Palomar Mountain). At the top of the mountain, turn left and drive about 8.5 miles to the campground entrance on the right.

Trip notes: This popular Forest Service camp is used primarily as a layover spot for campers visiting the nearby Palomar Observatory, housing the largest telescope in America. There are four other camps in the immediate area. The elevation is 4,800 feet. The trailhead for the Observatory Trail starts at this camp. This two-hour hike from the campground to the observatory includes one short, steep climb through woodlands, highlighted by a vista deck with a beautiful view of Mendenhall Valley, and then onward to the top and to the telescope viewing area.

⑤ Oak Grove

Location: Near Temecula Creek in Cleveland National Forest; map J6, grid a6.

Campsites, facilities: There are 81 sites for tents or RVs. Piped water, fire grills, and picnic tables are provided. Flush toilets are available. Propane gas and groceries are nearby. Leashed pets are permitted.

Reservations, fees: No reservations; $15 to $20 per night. Open year-round.

Contact: Cleveland National Forest, Palomar Ranger District, (760) 788-0250 or fax (760) 788-6130.

Directions: From Aguanga, drive 6.5 miles southeast on Highway 79 to the camp entrance.

Trip notes: Oak Grove camp is on the northeastern fringe of this section of Cleveland National Forest at 2,800 feet. Easy access from Highway 79 makes this a popular camp. The Palomar Observatory is located just five miles up the mountain to the west, but there is no direct way to reach it from the campground. Lake Henshaw is located about a half-hour drive to the south. A boat ramp and boat rentals are available there.

⑥ Sunrise Terrace RV Park

Location: Near Vista; map J6, grid b0.

Campsites, facilities: There are 32 RV sites with full hookups. Flush toilets, showers, coin laundry, telephones, and cable TV are available. There is a grocery store within four blocks. Leashed pets are permitted.

Reservations, fees: Reservations are accepted; $20 per night. Open year-round.

Contact: Sunrise Terrace RV Park, (760) 724-6654.

Directions: From Interstate 15 northbound, take the Gopher Canyon Road exit. Turn left on East Vista Way. Turn right on East Taylor and drive to 817 East Taylor Street. From Interstate 15 southbound, turn right on Gopher Canyon Road and then make a left on East Vista Way. Turn right again on East Taylor Street and drive to 817 East Taylor Street.

Trip notes: This rural country park provides an overnight spot for highway cruisers. Seasonal rentals are accepted. Guajome County Park (see campground number seven) is located nearby to the northwest, providing a small lake, marsh, and short loop hike around the lake. The San Diego Wild Animal Park is located about 20 miles southeast via Highways 15 and 78.

⑦ Guajome County Park

Location: In Oceanside; map J6, grid b0.

Campsites, facilities: There are 35 RV sites with water and electrical hookups. Picnic tables and fire grills are provided. Flush toilets, showers, dump station, and a playground are available. A grocery store and propane gas are nearby. Leashed pets are permitted.

Reservations, fees: Reservations are accepted; reserve via phone at (619) 565-3600 ($3 reservation fee); $14 per night, $1 pet fee. Open year-round.

Contact: San Diego County Parks Department, (619) 694-3049.

Directions: From Oceanside, drive seven miles east on Highway 76/Mission Avenue. Turn right on Guajome Lakes Road/Santa Fe Road and drive to the entrance.

Trip notes: Guajome means "home of the frog" and, yep, so it is with little Guajome Lake and the adjacent marsh, both of which can be explored with a delightful two-mile hike. The lake provides a bit of fishing for warm-water species, mainly sunfish and catfish. Because of the wetlands available, a huge variety of birds will stop here on their migratory journeys, making this a favorite area for bird-watching. There are also trails available for horseback riding.

8 Crestline Group Camp

Location: Near the Palomar Observatory in Cleveland National Forest; map J6, grid b5.

Campsites, facilities: There is one group campsite for tents only. Piped water, fire grills, and picnic tables are provided, and vault toilets are available. A grocery store is nearby. Leashed pets are permitted.

Reservations, fees: Reservations are required; reserve via phone at (877) 444-6777 ($8.65 reservation fee) or website www.reserveusa.com; $75 group fee per night. Open May through October.

Contact: Cleveland National Forest, Palomar Ranger District, (760) 788-0250 or fax (760) 788-6130.

Directions: From Interstate 15, head east on Highway 76 and drive about 20 miles to County Road S6 (the road that goes up to Palomar Mountain). Turn left and drive 6.5 miles. The campground is at the junction of County Roads S6 and S7.

Trip notes: This Forest Service camp is designed expressly for large groups planning to visit Palomar Observatory. For adventure information, see the trip notes for Palomar Mountain State Park (campground number two). The elevation is 4,800 feet.

9 Oak Knoll

Location: Near the Palomar Observatory; map J6, grid b5.

Campsites, facilities: There are 46 sites for tents or RVs, many with full or partial hookups. Flush toilets, showers, playground, swimming pool, clubhouse, baseball diamond, coin laundry, propane gas, and groceries are available.

Leashed pets are permitted.

Reservations, fees: Call ahead for available space; $15 per night, $1 pet fee. Open year-round.

Contact: Oak Knoll, (760) 742-3437.

Directions: From Interstate 15, turn east on Highway 76 and drive about 20 miles to County Road S6 (the road that goes up to Palomar Mountain). Turn left and drive one block to the campground.

Trip notes: The camp is set at 3,000 feet in San Diego County foothill country, among giant old California oaks. It is located at the western base of Palomar Mountain, and to visit the Palomar Observatory and its awesome 200-inch telescope requires a remarkably twisty 10-mile drive up the mountain. A good side trip is driving to the Boucher Lookout in Palomar Mountain State Park. Trailheads for excellent hikes on Palomar Mountain include the Observatory Trail, starting at Observatory (campground number 4) and the Doane Valley Loop (starting in Palomar Mountain State Park).

10 Indian Flats

Location: Near the Pacific Crest Trail in Cleveland National Forest; map J6, grid b8.

Campsites, facilities: There are 17 sites for tents. Piped water, fire grills, and picnic tables are provided. Vault toilets are available. Leashed pets are permitted.

Reservations, fees: No reservations; $10 per night. Open year-round.

Contact: Cleveland National Forest, Palomar Ranger District, (760) 788-0250 or fax (760) 788-6130.

Directions: From Warner Springs on Highway 79, drive two miles northwest on Highway 79. Turn right on Forest Service Road 9S05 and drive six miles to the campground.

Trip notes: Indian Flats is a remote campground, set at 3,600 feet just north of Pine Mountain. A highlight here is that the Pacific Crest Trail passes only two miles down the road to the south. A two-mile hike south on the PCT will take you down into a canyon and the home of Agua Caliente Creek.

⑪ Dixon Lake Recreation Area

Location: Near Escondido; map J6, grid c2.

Campsites, facilities: There are 45 sites for tents or RVs, some with full hookups. Picnic tables, fire grills, and piped water are provided. Flush toilets, showers, boat rentals, bait, ice, snack bar, and a playground are available. Pets are not permitted.

Reservations, fees: Reservations are accepted; $12 to $16 per night. Open year-round.

Contact: Dixon Lake Recreation Area, (760) 741-3328 or (760) 741-4680.

Directions: In Escondido, drive four miles northeast on El Norte Parkway to La Honda Drive. Turn left and drive to 1700 North La Honda Drive at Dixon Lake.

Trip notes: Little Dixon Lake is the centerpiece of a regional park in the San Diego foothills at an elevation of 1,405 feet. No private boats are permitted, and a 5 mph speed limit for rental boats keeps things quiet. The water is clear, with fair bass fishing in the spring, and trout fishing in the winter and early spring. A pretty and easy hike is available on the Jack Creek Nature Trail, a one-mile walk to a 20-foot waterfall.

⑫ Woods Valley Kampground

Location: Near Lake Wohlford; map J6, grid c3.

Campsites, facilities: There are 59 RV sites and 30 sites for tents or RVs. Picnic tables, fire grills, electrical connections, piped water, and, in some cases, sewer hookups are provided. Flush toilets, showers, dump station, swimming pool, kid's fishing pond, hay rides, small farm, playground, supplies, and coin laundry are available. Leashed pets are permitted, except no pit bulls are welcome.

Reservations, fees: Reservations are accepted; $20 to $26 per night, $3 pet fee. Open year-round.

Contact: Woods Valley Kampground, (760) 749-2905.

Directions: From Escondido on Interstate 15, turn east on County Road S6 and drive northeast to Valley Center. Turn right on Woods Valley Road and drive two miles east to 15236 Woods Valley Road.

Trip notes: This privately operated park is set up primarily for RVs and is located a short drive from Lake Wohlford to the south. Lake Wohlford has a 5 mph speed limit, which guarantees quiet water; canoes, inflatables, sailboats, and boats under 10 feet and over 18 feet are prohibited. It provides fair fishing for bass, bluegill, and catfish, best in late winter and spring.

⑬ Lake Henshaw Resort RV

Location: Near San Ysabel; map J6, grid c6.

Campsites, facilities: There are 164 sites for tents or RVs, many with full hookups. There are also 17 cabins with linens and kitchenettes. Flush toilets, showers, swimming pool, whirlpool, clubhouse, playground, dump station, coin laundry, propane gas, boat and motor rentals, boat launch, bait and tackle shop, restaurant, and groceries are available. A golf course is 10 miles away. Leashed pets are permitted.

Reservations, fees: No reservations are accepted; $14 to $16 per night, cabin fees are $45 to $60 per night. Open year-round.

Contact: Lake Henshaw Resort RV, (760) 782-3487, (760) 782-3501, or fax (760) 782-9224.

Directions: From Santa Ysabel, drive seven miles north on Highway 79. Turn left on Highway 76 and drive four miles to the campground on the left.

Trip notes: Lake Henshaw is the biggest lake in San Diego County, yet it only has one camp. It's a good one, with the cabin rentals a big plus. The camp is located on the southern corner of the lake, at 2,727 feet near Cleveland National Forest. Swimming is not permitted and a 10 mph speed limit is in effect. The fishing is best for catfish, especially in the summer, and at times decent for bass, with the lake-record bass weighing 14 pounds, four ounces.

⑭ William Heise County Park

Location: Near Julian; map J6, grid e8.

Campsites, facilities: There are 43 sites for tents only, 40 sites for tents or RVs, and several group sites. Fire grills and picnic tables are provided. Piped water, flush toilets, showers, coin laundry, dump station, and a playground are available. Supplies are available seven miles away in Julian. Leashed pets are permitted.

Reservations, fees: Reservations are accepted; phone (619) 565-3600; $12 to $14 per night, $1 pet fee. Open year-round.

Contact: San Diego County Parks Department, (619) 694-3049.

Directions: From Highway 78 west of Julian, turn south on Pine Hills Road and drive two miles. Turn left on Frisius Drive and drive two miles to the park.

Trip notes: This is a beautiful county park, set at 4,200 feet, that offers hiking trails and a playground, all amid pretty woodlands with a mix of oak and pine. A great hike starts right at camp (at the tent camping area) and is signed "Nature Trail." It joins with the Canyon Oak Trail and, after little more than a mile, it links up with the Desert View Trail. Here you will reach an overlook with a beautiful view of Anza-Borrego Desert and the Salton Sea. The area surrounding the park is filled with recreation options. They include Cleveland National Forest to the immediate south, Lake Cuyamaca and Cuyamaca Rancho State Park to the southeast, and the vast Anza-Borrego Desert State Park to the east.

⑮ Pinezanita Trailer Ranch

Location: Near Julian, map J6, grid d8.

Campsites, facilities: There are a total of 230 campsites, 40 for tents and 190 for RVs; 160 of the RV sites have partial hookups (electricity and sewer). There are also a few furnished cottages. Piped water, picnic tables and fire rings are provided. Rest rooms with showers, a general store, ice, propane, a fishing pond, and a dumping station are available. Leashed pets are permitted.

Reservations, fees: Reservations accepted; campsites are $17 per night per vehicle (two people), cottages are $110 to $125 per night for two people (no children or pets in the cottages), $2 each additional camper, $2 per hookup and $2 pet fee. Open year-round.

Contact: Pinezanita Trailer Ranch, PO Box 2380, Julian, CA 92036-2380; (760) 765-0429; email: stanley@ix.netcom.com.

Directions: From San Diego, drive east on Interstate 8 to the junction with Highway 79. Turn north on Highway 79 and drive 20 miles to the campground on the left.

Trip notes: Set at an elevation of 4,680 feet in dense pine and oak, this camp has had the same owners, the Stanley family, for over 30 years. The fishing pond is a great attraction for kids (no license is required), but there's no swimming allowed. The pond is stocked with blue gill and catfish, some of which are 12 inches or longer. Two possible side trips include Lake Cuiamaca, five miles to the south, and William Heise County Park, about 10 miles to the north as the crow flies.

⑯ Dos Picos County Park

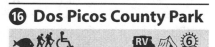

Location: Near Ramona; map J6, grid e3.

Campsites, facilities: There are 14 tent sites and 50 RV sites with water and electrical hookups. Picnic tables and fire grills are provided. Flush toilets, showers, and a playground are available. Supplies and a coin laundry are one mile away in Ramona. Leashed pets are permitted.

Reservations, fees: Reservations are accepted; reserve via phone at (619) 565-3600; $10 to $14 per night, $1 pet fee. Open year-round.

Contact: San Diego County Parks Department, (619) 694-3049.

Directions: From Interstate 8 in El Cajon, drive 22 miles north on Highway 67. Make a sharp right on Mussey Grade Road and drive two miles to the park.

Trip notes: As a county park, this camp is often missed by folks relying on less complete guides. The park is quite picturesque, with plenty of shade trees and a small pond. Several nearby recreation options are in the area. San Vicente Lake is about 15 miles away, a prime bass lake open Thursday through Sunday from September through June. The elevation is 1,500 feet.

⑰ De Anza Harbor Resort

Location: On Mission Bay; map J6, grid f0.

Campsites, facilities: There are 243 RV sites with full hookups and patios. Flush toilets, showers, playground, dump station, coin laundry, recreation room, bike rentals, boat ramp, propane gas, and a grocery store are available. Leashed pets are permitted.

Reservations, fees: Reservations are recommended; $18.50 to $72 per night. Open year-round.

Contact: De Anza Harbor Resort, (619) 273-3211 or fax (619) 274-0362.

Directions: From southbound Interstate 5 in San Diego, take the Clairemont exit to Mission Bay Drive. Turn left and drive to North Mission Bay Drive. Turn right on De Anza Road and drive to 2727 De Anza Road.

Trip notes: Location means everything in real estate and campgrounds, and this private park passes the test. It is set on a small peninsula that is surrounded on three sides by Mission Bay, Sea World, and the San Diego Zoo. A beach and golf course are adjacent to the park. Mission Bay has 27 miles of shoreline, expansive beach frontage, and fantastic boating for waterskiing, windsurfing, or ocean access for deep-sea fishing. Note that a 5 mph speed limit is enforced on the northern bay, and on the entire bay after sunset.

⑱ Campland on the Bay

Location: On Mission Bay; map J6, grid f0.

Campsites, facilities: There are 750 tent and RV sites, most with full or partial hookups. Picnic tables and fire grills are provided. Flush toilets, showers, phone hookups, swimming pools, hot tub, recreation hall, playground, dump station, coin laundry, grocery store, RV supplies, propane gas, boat ramp, boat docks, boat and bike rentals, and groceries are available. Leashed pets are permitted.

Reservations, fees: Reservations are accepted; $23 to $52 per night, $3 pet fee. Open year-round.

Contact: Campland on the Bay, (800) 422-9386, (619) 581-4200 or fax (619) 581-4264. Be prepared for a 20-minute wait to make reservations.

Directions: From southbound Interstate 5 in San Diego, take the Balboa-Garnet exit. Drive straight on Mission Bay Drive to Grand Avenue. Turn right and drive one mile. Turn left on Olney Avenue and drive a short distance to the campground entrance. From northbound Interstate 5 in San Diego, take the Grand-Garnet exit. Stay in the left lane and turn left on Grand Avenue. Turn left on Olney Avenue as above.

Trip notes: No kidding, this is one of the biggest campgrounds on this side of the galaxy. With space for both tenters and RVers, you can usually find a spot to shoehorn your way into. It is set on Mission Bay, a beautiful spot and a boater's paradise. Waterskiing, windsurfing, or ocean access for deep-sea fishing are preeminent. Note that a 5 mph speed limit is enforced on the northern bay, and on the entire bay after sunset. Sea World, located just north of San Diego, offers a premium side trip.

⑲ Santa Fe Travel Trailer Park

Location: In San Diego; map J6, grid f0.

Campsites, facilities: There are 129 RV sites with full hookups. No tent camping is allowed. Flush toilets, showers, playground, swimming pool, dump station, cable TV, and coin laundry are available. Leashed pets are permitted.

Reservations, fees: Reservations are recommended; $29.50 per night, $2 pet fee. Open year-round.

Contact: Santa Fe Travel Trailer Park, (619) 272-4051 or fax (619) 272-2845.

Directions: In San Diego from Interstate 5, take

the Balboa-Garnet exit (southbound). Drive straight (south) on West Mission Bay Drive for a short distance to Damon Street (second light). Go left and follow it to Santa Fe Street. Turn left and drive to 5707 Santa Fe Street.

Trip notes: This camp is a short drive from a variety of side trips, including the San Diego Zoo, Sea World, golf courses, beaches, sportfishing, and Tijuana.

⑳ Santee Lakes Regional Park

Location: Near Santee; map J6, grid f3.

Campsites, facilities: There are 152 sites for RVs with full hookups. There are 50 sites (out of the total 152) which can be used for tents. Some barbecue grills are provided. Flush toilets, showers, dump station, boat rentals, playground, swimming pool, grocery store, snack bar, recreation center, and coin laundry are available. Leashed pets are permitted in the campground, but not in the park.

Reservations, fees: Reservations are accepted; $15-26 per night, $1 pet fee. Open year-round.

Contact: Santee Lakes Regional Park, (619) 448-2482.

Directions: From Interstate 8 in El Cajon, drive two miles north on Highway 67 to the town of Santee. Turn left on Mission Gorge Road and drive 2.5 miles to Carlton Hills Drive. Turn right and drive to Carlton Oaks Drive. Turn right and drive a mile to the park on the right.

Trip notes: This small regional park is located 20 miles east of San Diego. Quiet, low-key boating is the name of the game here. Rowboats, pedal boats, and canoes are available for rent. The camp is set at 400 feet.

㉑ Rancho Los Coches RV Park

Location: Near Lake Jennings; map J6, grid f3.

Campsites, facilities: There are four tent areas and 142 RV sites with full hookups. Flush

toilets, showers, dump station, and coin laundry are available. A grocery store is one mile away. Leashed pets are permitted.

Reservations, fees: Reservations are recommended; $23 per night.

Contact: Rancho Los Coches RV Park, (619) 443-2025 or fax (619) 443-8440.

Directions: From El Cajon, drive east on Interstate 8 to the Los Coches Road exit. Go under the freeway, turn right on Highway 8 Business, and drive to the park entrance on the left at 13468 Highway 8 Business.

Trip notes: Nearby Lake Jennings provides an option for boaters and anglers and also has a less developed camp located on its northeast shore. Vista Point on the southeastern side of the lake provides a side trip. For more information, see Lake Jennings County Park (campground number 22).

㉒ Lake Jennings County Park

Location: On Lake Jennings; map J6, grid f4.

Campsites, facilities: There are 35 sites for tents only, 13 sites for tents or RVs, and 63 RV sites, most with full hookups. Picnic tables and fire grills are provided. Flush toilets, showers, playground, and a dump station are available. A grocery store is nearby. Leashed pets are permitted.

Reservations, fees: Reservations are accepted; phone (619) 565-3600; $12 to $16 per night, $1 pet fee. Open year-round.

Contact: San Diego County Parks Department, (619) 694-3049.

Directions: From San Diego, drive 16 miles east on Interstate 8. Take Lake Jennings Park Road north to the park entrance.

Trip notes: While this lake wasn't named after my friend Waylon (he's got a camp named after him in Littlefield, Texas), he wouldn't disown it if it were. It is a nice little backyard fishing hole and recreation area set at 700 feet, with easy access from Interstate 8. The highlights here are evening picnics, summer catfishing, and a boat ramp and rentals. Only one camp is available right at the lake, and this is it.

㉓ Alpine Springs RV Resort

Location: Near Lake Jennings; map J6, grid f6.

Campsites, facilities: There are 300 sites for tents or RVs, some with full or partial hookups. Picnic tables are provided. Flush toilets, showers, dump station, coin laundry, recreation room, and a swimming pool are available. No pets over 15 pounds are permitted.

Reservations, fees: Reservations are accepted; $18 to $20 per night. Open year-round.

Contact: Alpine Springs RV Resort, (619) 445-3162.

Directions: From Interstate 8 just east of Alpine, take the East Willows exit. Cross over the freeway and drive a third of a mile to 5635 Willows Drive.

Trip notes: This is one of the few RV parks in the area that welcomes tent campers. It is set in the foothill country in Alpine, eight miles from Lake Jennings to the west. See the trip notes for Lake Jennings County Park (campground number 22) for more information. Other nearby lakes include larger El Capitan to the north and Loveland Reservoir to the south.

㉔ Paso Picacho

Location: In Cuyamaca Rancho State Park; map J6, grid f7.

Campsites, facilities: There are 85 sites for tents or RVs. Fire grills and picnic tables are provided. Piped water, flush toilets, coin-operated showers, and a dump station are available. Supplies are available nearby in Cuyamaca. Leashed pets are permitted.

Reservations, fees: Reserve via phone at (800) 444-PARK/7275 ($7.50 reservation fee) or website www.cal-parks.ca.gov; $15 to $17 per night, $1 pet fee. Open year-round.

Contact: Cuyamaca Rancho State Park, (760) 765-0755.

Directions: From Julian, drive 11 miles south on Highway 79 to the park entrance.

Trip notes: This camp is set at 4,900 feet in Cuyamaca Rancho State Park, best known for Cuyamaca Peak, 6,512 feet. The trail up to the summit starts at the southern end of the campground, a 6.5-mile tromp (alas, on a paved road closed to traffic) with a climb of 1,600 feet in the process. The view from the top is breathtaking, with the ocean, desert, and Salton Sea all within range. Park headquarters features exhibits about the area's Native Americans, gold mining, and natural history. That's where I learned that Cuyamaca means "place beyond the rain."

㉕ Green Valley Falls

Location: In Cuyamaca Rancho State Park; map J6, grid f7.

Campsites, facilities: There are 81 sites for tents or RVs. Piped water, fire grills, and picnic tables are provided. Flush toilets and coin-operated showers are available. Some of the campgrounds, picnic areas, and exhibits are wheelchair accessible. A grocery store and propane gas are nearby. Leashed pets are permitted.

Reservations, fees: Reserve via phone at (800) 444-PARK/7275 ($7.50 reservation fee) or website www.cal-parks.ca.gov; $15 to $17 per night, $1 pet fee. Open year-round.

Contact: Cuyamaca Rancho State Park, (760) 765-0755.

Directions: From San Diego, drive approximately 40 miles east on Interstate 8 to Highway 79. Turn north and drive seven miles. Turn left on Green Valley Road, the entrance road into the park.

Trip notes: Green Valley Falls is the southernmost camp in Cuyamaca Rancho State Park. It is set at 3,900 feet, with Cuyamaca Mountain (6,512 feet) looming overhead to the northwest. A trailhead is available (look for the picnic area) at the camp for an easy 1.5-mile round-trip to Green Valley Falls and back, routing you out to the Sweetwater River, with a spur trail taking you down to a pretty but modest waterfall. Newcomers should visit the park headquarters, where exhibits detail the natural history of the area.

26 Horse Heaven Group Camp

Location: Near the Pacific Crest Trail in Cleveland National Forest; map J6, grid f9.

Campsites, facilities: There are three group sites for tents or RVs. Piped water, fire grills, and picnic tables are provided. Vault toilets are available. Supplies can be purchased in Mount Laguna. Leashed pets are permitted.

Reservations, fees: Reserve via phone at (877) 444-6777 ($8.65 reservation fee) or website: www.reserveusa.com; $60 to $150 per group per night.

Contact: Cleveland National Forest, Descanso Ranger District, (619) 445-6235 or fax (619) 445-6235.

Directions: From San Diego, drive about 50 miles east on Interstate 8 to the Laguna Junction exit. Drive about 11 miles north on Sunrise Highway to the town of Mount Laguna. Continue north for two miles on Sunrise Highway/Laguna Mountain Road to the campground entrance road on the left.

Trip notes: Horse Heaven is set on the northeastern border of Cleveland National Forest at 5,500 feet, near Mount Laguna in the Laguna Recreation Area. The Pacific Crest Trail passes near the camp. Laguna and El Prado Group Camp (campground numbers 27 and 28) provide nearby options. Side trip possibilities include visiting Little Laguna Lake to the immediate west, and Desert View Picnic Area to the south at Mount Laguna.

27 Laguna

Location: Near Little Laguna Lake in Cleveland National Forest; map J6, grid f9.

Campsites, facilities: There are 75 sites for tents only, 25 RV sites, and 20 sites for tents or RVs. Piped water, fire grills, and picnic tables are provided. Vault toilets are available. A grocery store and propane gas are nearby. Leashed pets are permitted.

Reservations, fees: Some sites are available by reservation only; reserve via phone at (877) 444-6777 ($8.65 reservation fee) or website www.reserveusa. com; $12 per night. Open year-round.

Contact: Cleveland National Forest, Descanso Ranger District, (619) 445-6235 or fax (619) 445-6235.

Directions: From San Diego, drive about 50 miles east on Interstate 8 to the Laguna Junction exit. Drive about 11 miles north on Sunrise Highway to the town of Mount Laguna. Continue north for 2.5 miles on Sunrise Highway/Laguna Mountain Road to the campground entrance road on the left.

Trip notes: Laguna is set on Little Laguna Lake, one of the few lakes in America where "Little" is part of its official name. That's because for years everybody always referred to it as "Little Laguna Lake," and it became official. Yep, it's a "little" lake all right, a relative speck, with the camp on its eastern side at an elevation of 5,550 feet. A trailhead for the Pacific Crest Trail is located a mile north on the Sunrise Highway/Laguna Mountain Road. Big Laguna Lake, which is actually a pretty small lake, is located one mile to the west.

28 El Prado Group Camp

Location: In Cleveland National Forest; map J6, grid f9.

Campsites, facilities: There are five group sites for tents or RVs. Piped water, fire grills, and picnic tables are provided. Vault toilets are available. Supplies can be purchased in Mount Laguna. Leashed pets are permitted.

Reservations, fees: Reserve via phone at (877) 444-6777 ($8.65 reservation fee) or website: www.reserveusa.com; $48 to $150 per group per night. Open May through September.

Contact: Cleveland National Forest, Descanso Ranger District, (619) 445-6235 or fax (619) 445-6235.

Directions: From San Diego, drive about 50 miles east on Interstate 8 to the Laguna Junction exit. Drive about 11 miles north on Sunrise Highway to the town of Mount Laguna. Continue north for 2.5 miles on Sunrise Highway/Laguna Mountain Road to the campground entrance road on the left.

Trip notes: El Prado Group Camp is located directly adjacent to Laguna (campground number 27) and is a group camp option to Horse Heaven Group Camp. The elevation is 5,500 feet.

㉙ Agua Dulce Group Camp

Location: Near the Pacific Crest Trail in Cleveland National Forest; map J6, grid f9.

Campsites, facilities: There are seven group sites for tents. Piped water, fire grills, and picnic tables are provided. Vault toilets are available. A grocery store is nearby. Leashed pets are permitted.

Reservations, fees: Reserve via phone at (877) 444-6777 ($8.65 reservation fee) or website www.reserveusa.com; $60 to $75 per group per night. Open May through September.

Contact: Cleveland National Forest, Descanso Ranger District, (619) 445-6235 or fax (619) 445-6235.

Directions: From San Diego, drive approximately 50 miles east on Interstate 8 to the Laguna Junction exit. Drive about eight miles north on Sunrise Highway/Laguna Mountain Road to the campground entrance road on the left.

Trip notes: This is one of three camps (two are group camps) south of the town of Mount Laguna. Little Agua Dulce Creek runs nearby, and the Desert View Picnic Area, located two miles to the northwest, provides a side trip option. The Pacific Crest Trail passes nearby, running past the Burnt Rancheria Camp. The elevation is 5,000 feet.

㉚ Cibbets Flat

Location: On Troy Canyon Creek in Cleveland National Forest; map J6, grid g9.

Campsites, facilities: There are 23 sites for tents or small RVs. Piped water, fire grills, and picnic tables are provided. Vault toilets are available. Leashed pets are permitted.

Reservations, fees: No reservations; $10 per night (two vehicle maximum). Open May through September.

Contact: Cleveland National Forest, Descanso Ranger District, (619) 445-6235 or fax (619) 445-6235.

Directions: From San Diego, drive about 53 miles east on Interstate 8 to the Kitchen Creek/Cameron Station exit. Turn north on Kitchen Creek Road and drive 4.5 miles to the campground entrance on the right.

Trip notes: Cibbets Flat is located at the southern flank of the Laguna Mountains, near Troy Canyon Creek. It is an obscure, fairly remote camp that passes as a staging area for the Pacific Crest Trail. A trailhead for the PCT is located a mile southeast of camp, mostly used by hikers heading north across the Laguna Mountains. The elevation is 4,000 feet.

㉛ Burnt Rancheria

Location: Near the Pacific Crest Trail in Cleveland National Forest; map J6, grid g9.

Campsites, facilities: There are 64 sites for tents only and 45 sites for tents or RVs. Piped water, fire grills, and picnic tables are provided. Vault toilets are available. Supplies are nearby in Mount Laguna. Leashed pets are permitted.

Reservations, fees: Some sites are available by reservation only, reserve via phone at (877) 444-6777 ($8.65 reservation fee) or website www.reserveusa.com; $10 per night (two vehicle maximum). Open May through September.

Contact: Cleveland National Forest, Descanso Ranger District, (619) 445-6235 or fax (619) 445-6235.

Directions: From San Diego, drive approximately 50 miles east on Interstate 8 to the Laguna Junction exit. Drive about nine miles north on Sunrise Highway/Laguna Mountain Road to the campground entrance on the right.

Trip notes: Burnt Rancheria is set high on the slopes of Mount Laguna in Cleveland National Forest, at an elevation of 6,000 feet. The Pacific Crest Trail runs right alongside this camp. It is quiet and private with large, roomy sites. Desert View Picnic Area, a mile to the north, provides a good side trip. Agua Dulce and Wooded Hill Group Camps are located less than two miles away.

32 Wooded Hill Group Camp

Location: Near the Pacific Crest Trail in Cleveland National Forest; map J6, grid g9.

Campsites, facilities: There are 22 sites for tents or RVs. Piped water, fire grills, and picnic tables are provided. Vault toilets are available. A grocery store is nearby. Leashed pets are permitted.

Reservations, fees: Reserve via phone at (877) 444-6777 ($17.35 reservation fee); $165 group fee per night. Open May through September.

Contact: Cleveland National Forest, Descanso Ranger District, (619) 445-6235 or fax (619) 445-6235.

Directions: From San Diego, drive approximately 50 miles east on Interstate 8 to the Laguna Junction exit. Drive about eight miles north on Sunrise Highway/Laguna Mountain Road to the campground entrance road on the left.

Trip notes: This camp is set right alongside Agua Dulce Camp, on the southern flank of Mount Laguna. The Pacific Crest Trail passes right by Burnt Rancheria (campground number 31), located a mile up the road to the northwest. The elevation is 6,000 feet.

33 International Motor Inn RV Park

Location: Near Imperial Beach; map J6, grid h0.

Campsites, facilities: There are 42 RV sites with full hookups. Picnic tables and patios are provided. Flush toilets, showers, swimming pool, whirlpool, and coin laundry are available. Leashed pets are permitted.

Reservations, fees: Reservations are accepted; $25.42 per night. Open year-round.

Contact: International Motor Inn RV Park, (619) 428-4486.

Directions: From Interstate 5, take the Via de San Ysidro exit and drive south on Calle Primera to the park at 190 East Calle Primera, next to Motel 6.

Trip notes: Easy access from Interstate 5 is a big plus here, but be advised to call ahead for available space. For nearby side trips, head west to Imperial Beach, south to Tijuana, or east to Otay Lake with its mega-sized bass and catfish.

34 Chula Vista Marina and RV Park

Location: In Chula Vista; map J6, grid h1.

Campsites, facilities: There are 237 RV sites with full hookups. Flush toilets, showers, TV hookups, playground, heated swimming pool and spa, game room, marina, fishing pier, free boat launch, coin laundry, propane gas, and groceries are available. Some facilities are wheelchair accessible. Leashed pets are permitted.

Reservations, fees: Reservations are recommended; $28.50 to $47.50 per night, $1 pet fee. Open year-round.

Contact: Chula Vista Marina and RV Park, (619) 422-0111 or fax (619) 422-8872.

Directions: From Interstate 5 in Chula Vista, take the J Street Marina Parkway exit and drive west a short distance to Sandpiper Way. Turn left and drive to 460 Sandpiper Way.

Trip notes: This RV park is close to San Diego Bay, a beautiful, calm piece of water where waterskiing is permitted in designated areas. An excellent swimming beach is available at Point Loma, and conditions in the afternoon for windsurfing are also excellent.

35 La Pacifica RV Park

Location: In San Ysidro; map J6, grid i1.

Campsites, facilities: There are 177 RV sites with full hookups and individual lawns and patios. Flush toilets, showers, heated swimming pool, whirlpool, recreation room, dump station, coin laundry, and propane gas are available. All facilities are wheelchair accessible. Leashed pets are permitted.

Reservations, fees: Reservations are recommended; $24 per night. Open year-round.

Contact: La Pacifica RV Park, (619) 428-4411.

Directions: From Interstate 5 in San Ysidro, drive east on Dairymart Road to San Ysidro Boulevard. Turn left and drive to 1010 San Ysidro Boulevard.

Trip notes: This RV park is less than two miles from the Mexican border, with regular Mexicoach bus service from the park to downtown Tijuana and back. Do this trip just once and you will find out how two miles can be the equivalent of a million miles.

36 San Diego Metropolitan KOA

Location: In Chula Vista; map J6, grid h1.

Campsites, facilities: There are 64 tent sites, 206 RV sites with full hookups, and a few cabins. Picnic tables and barbecue grills are provided. Flush toilets, showers, playground, dump station, coin laundry, swimming pool, whirlpool, bike rentals, propane gas, and groceries are available. Some facilities are wheelchair accessible. Leashed pets are permitted.

Reservations, fees: Reservations are accepted; $28 to $35 per RV or tent site per night, $38 to $46 per night for cabins. Open year-round.

Contact: San Diego Metropolitan KOA, (619) 427-3601 or fax (619) 427-3622; email: mbell@cts.com; website: www.koakampgrounds.com.

Directions: From Interstate 5 in Chula Vista, take the E Street exit and drive three miles east. Turn north on Second Street and drive to 111 North Second Street.

Trip notes: This is one in a series of parks set up primarily for RVs cruising Interstate 5. Chula Vista is located between Mexico and San Diego, allowing visitors to make side trips east to Lower Otay Lake, north to the San Diego attractions, south to Tijuana, or "around the corner" on Highway 75 to Silver Strand State Beach. Nearby San Diego Bay is beautiful with excellent waterskiing (in designated areas), windsurfing, and a great swimming beach at Dana Point.

37 Sweetwater Summit Regional Park

Location: At Lower Otay Lake; map J6, grid h2.

Campsites, facilities: There are 60 sites for tents or RVs with partial hookups. Twenty-two of the sites have horse corrals. Picnic tables and fire grills are provided. Piped water, flush toilets, showers, and a dump station are available. Leashed pets are permitted.

Reservations, fees: Reservations are accepted; reserve via phone at (619) 565-3600; $12 to $16 per night, $1 pet fee. Open year-round.

Contact: San Diego County Parks Department, (619) 694-3049.

Directions: From San Diego, drive southeast about 10 miles on Interstate 805 to Bonita Road. Go east on Bonita Road to San Miguel Road. Proceed on San Miguel Road another two miles to the park entrance on the left.

Trip notes: Otay Lake is set at an elevation of 490 feet near Chula Vista, just north of the California/Mexico border, and covers 1,265 surface acres with 13 miles of shoreline. It is surrounded by foothills, and while there are a few trails in the area, most people come here for one thing: the giant bass. It can make a fisherman's brain gears squeak to imagine the five-fish limit that Jack Neu caught here, 53 pounds, 14 ounces, and would you believe I was with him on that record day? I still get a chuckle over how he told everyone he was using plastic worms when he caught them on crawdads. Most fishermen are born honest, believe it or not, but after a few fishing trips, they get over it. The camp is located at the southern tip of Lower Otay Lake. A paved boat ramp, boat rentals, tackle, snack bar, and groceries are available on the west shore of the lake. The lake and its facilities are open Wednesdays, Saturdays, and Sundays, February through mid-October.

38 Barrett Lake Mobile Home and RV Park

Location: North of Tecate; map J6, grid h5.

Campsites, facilities: There are 40 RV sites with full or partial hookups. Flush toilets, showers, picnic tables, dump station, coin laundry, clubhouse, cable TV, and two swimming pools are available. Leashed pets are permitted.

Reservations, fees: Call ahead for available space; $14 per night; group rate of $12 per night per RV applies to groups of six or more RVs. Open year-round.

Contact: Barrett Lake Mobile Home and RV Park, (619) 468-3332 or fax (619) 468-3208.

Directions: From San Diego, drive 40 miles on Highway 94 to Barrett Lake Road on the left. Drive north on Barrett Lake Road to the campground at 1250 Barrett Lake Road.

Trip notes: This is just enough off the beaten path to get missed by a lot of folks. It is set near Barrett Lake amid the surrounding Cleveland National Forest (but you can't see Barrett Lake from the camp). The lake is only about 10 miles north of the Mexican border, and here's a tip: It provides the best fishing of any lake in the western US for bass and crappie, thanks to a great program, but access is restricted on a lottery basis only. For information, call the San Diego City Lakes Program, (619) 668-2050.

39 Potrero County Park

Location: Near the Mexican border; map J6, grid h7.

Campsites, facilities: There are 32 sites for tents or RVs. Picnic tables, fire grills, electrical hookups, and piped water are provided. Flush toilets, showers, playground, and a dump station are available. Supplies can be purchased in Potrero. Leashed pets are permitted.

Reservations, fees: Reservations are accepted; reserve via phone at (619) 565-3600; $10 to $12 per night, $1 pet fee. Open year-round.

Contact: San Diego County Parks Department, (619) 694-3049.

Directions: From San Diego, drive 42 miles east on Highway 94 to Potrero Valley Road. Drive north one mile on Potrero Valley Road to Potrero Park Road. Continue east on Potrero Park Road one mile to the park entrance.

Trip notes: If you are looking for a spot to hole up for the night before getting through customs, this is the place. It is just a heartbeat away from the customs inspection station in Tecate. A good side trip is to the nearby Tecate Mission Chapel, where you can pray that the guards do not rip your car up in the search for contraband. But why waste energy worrying? It's a lot easier just to live clean, be clean.

40 Lake Morena RV Park

Location: Near Campo; map J6, grid i7.

Campsites, facilities: There are 27 RV sites with full hookups and 17 with partial hookups. Picnic tables are provided. Flush toilets, showers, propane gas, and coin laundry are available. Leashed pets are permitted.

Reservations, fees: Reservations are recommended; $18 per night. A deposit is required on three-day weekends. Open year-round.

Contact: Lake Morena RV Park, (619) 478-5677 or fax (619) 478-5031.

Directions: From San Diego, drive approximately 53 miles east on Interstate 8. Take the Buckman Springs Road/County Road S1 exit and drive 5.5 miles south. Turn right on Oak Drive and drive 2.5 miles. Turn left on Lake Morena Drive and drive to 2330 Lake Morena Drive.

From Campo on Highway 94, turn north on County Road S1 and drive five miles to Oak Drive. Turn left on Oak Drive, turn left on Lake Morena Drive, and continue to the park at 2330 Lake Morena Drive.

Trip notes: This camp is near the southern side of Lake Morena, a great lake for bass fishing and off-season vacations. It is one of the three camps near the lake and the best for RVs. Lake Morena, at 3,200 feet, is a large reservoir in the San Diego County foothills and is known for big bass. The lake record weighed 19 pounds, two ounces. The lake has a paved ramp and rowboat rentals.

41 Lake Morena County Park

Location: Near Campo; map J6, grid h7.

Campsites, facilities: There are 90 sites for tents or RVs, some with partial hookups. Picnic tables and fire grills are provided. Piped water, flush toilets, and showers are available. A grocery store, boat ramp, and rowboat rentals are nearby. Leashed pets are permitted.

Reservations, fees: Reservations are accepted; phone (619) 565-3600; $10 to $16 per night, $1 pet fee. Open year-round.

Contact: San Diego County Parks Department, (619) 565-3600.

Directions: From San Diego, drive approximately 53 miles east on Interstate 8. Take the Buckman Springs Road/County Road S1 exit and drive 5.5 miles south. Turn right on Oak Drive and follow signs to the park. Turn left on Lake Morena Drive and drive to 2330 Lake Morena Drive.

Trip notes: Yes, Lake Morena is located out in the boondocks, but it's well worth the trip. If you like to fish for bass, don't miss it. The county park camp is set on the southern shore, at an elevation of 3,200 feet. The lake is just south of Cleveland National Forest and only seven or eight miles from the California/Mexico border. When full, it covers 1,500 acres, but water levels can fluctuate a great deal here. Catch rates for bass can be excellent, and some bass are big; the lake record weighed 19 pounds, two ounces. Boat rentals are available nearby.

㊷ Boulder Oaks

Location: Near Lake Morena in Cleveland National Forest; map J6, grid h8.

Campsites, facilities: There are six sites for tents only, 12 sites for tents or RVs, and 14 equestrian sites. Picnic tables, fire grills, and piped water are provided. Vault toilets are available. A grocery store is nearby. Leashed pets are permitted.

Reservations, fees: Equestrian sites are available by reservation only; reserve via phone at (877) 444-6777 ($8.65 reservation fee) or website www.reserveusa.com; $10 per night. Open year-round.

Contact: Cleveland National Forest, Descanso

Ranger District, (619) 445-6235 or fax (619) 445-6235.

Directions: From San Diego, drive approximately 55 miles east on Interstate 8 to the Kitchen Creek/Cameron Station exit. Turn right on the southern frontage road and drive about one mile to the campground.

Trip notes: Boulder Oaks is easy to reach, just off Interstate 8, yet is a very small camp with an important trailhead for the Pacific Crest Trail running right by it. The elevation is 3,500 feet, set in the southern end of Cleveland National Forest and the Laguna Mountains.

㊸ Outdoor World RV Park and Campground

Location: In Campo; map J6, grid i9.

Campsites, facilities: There are 138 sites for RVs, 122 with full hookups and 16 with partial hookups. There are also some primitive tent camping sites. A clubhouse, pool table, rest rooms, showers, horseshoes, fire rings, and a group camping area are provided.

Reservations, fees: Reservations are recommended; $10 to $15 per night. Weekly and monthly rates are also available.

Contact: Outdoor World RV Park and Campground, 37133 Highway 94, Campo, CA 91906; (619) 766-4480.

Directions: From San Diego, take Interstate 8 to the Boulevard/Campo exit. Turn right and drive three-quarters of a mile to the Olde Highway 80/Highway 94 exit. Turn right and drive to the fork where Olde Highway 80 and Highway 94 split. Make a left turn and drive 3.5 miles to the signed campground turnoff at Shasta Way.

Trip notes: The town of Campo is centrally located for a wide variety of recreation possibilities. Some 10 miles to the north is Mount Laguna, with hiking trails available. Some 30 minutes to the south is the nearest point of entry to Mexico, at Tecate. Fishing at Lake Morena or Lake Cuyamaca is also a possibility, as is soaking in nearby hot springs.

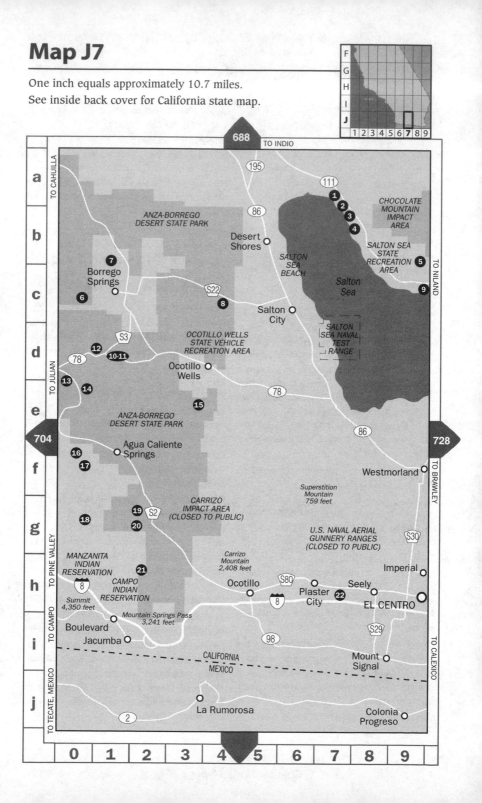

Map J7

One inch equals approximately 10.7 miles.
See inside back cover for California state map.

Chapter J7 features:

❶ Headquarters

Location: In the Salton Sea State Recreation Area; map J7, grid a7.

Campsites, facilities: There are 25 sites for tents or RVs up to 32 feet long. Piped water, fire grills, and picnic tables are provided. Sixteen sites have electrical connections and sewer hookups. Rest rooms, showers, dump station, grocery store, and propane gas are available nearby. There is wheelchair access to the camping, picnicking, boating, fishing, and exhibit areas. Leashed pets are permitted.

Reservations, fees: Reserve via phone at (800) 444-PARK/7275 ($7.50 reservation fee) or website www.cal-parks.ca.gov; $13 to $20 per night, $1 pet fee. Open year-round.

Contact: Salton Sea State Recreation Area, (760) 393-3052/3059 or (760) 767-5311.

Directions: From Mecca, drive 10 miles southeast on Highway 111 to the entrance.

Trip notes: This is the northernmost camps on the shore of the giant Salton Sea, that vast, shallow, and unique lake. It is set at the recreation area headquarters, just south of the town of Desert Beach at an elevation of 220 feet below sea level. Corvina fishing can be quite good at this lake. The best time to visit is from October through May. Summer is like visiting the devil, and spring and fall can be quite windy. If winds are hazardous, a red beacon on the northeast shore of the lake will flash. If you see it, get to the nearest shore.

❷ Mecca Beach

Location: In the Salton Sea State Recreation Area; map J7, grid a7.

Campsites, facilities: There are 110 sites for tents or RVs up to 30 feet long. Piped water, fire grills, and picnic tables are provided. Flush toilets, showers, groceries, and propane gas are available. Leashed pets are permitted.

Reservations, fees: No reservations; $13 per night, $1 pet fee. Open year-round.

Contact: Salton Sea State Recreation Area, (760) 393-3052/3059 or (760) 767-5311.

Directions: From Mecca, drive 12 miles southeast on Highway 111 to the entrance.

Trip notes: This is one of the camps set in the Salton Sea State Recreation Area on the northeastern shore of the lake. For details, see the trip notes for Headquarters (campground number one).

❸ Corvina Beach

Location: In the Salton Sea State Recreation Area; map J7, grid b7.

Campsites, facilities: There are 500 primitive sites for tents or RVs. Piped water is provided. Chemical toilets and a boat ramp are available. Groceries and propane gas are available nearby. Leashed pets are permitted.

Reservations, fees: No reservations; $7 per night, $1 pet fee. Open year-round.

Contact: Salton Sea State Recreation Area, (760) 393-3052/3059 or (760) 767-5311.

Directions: From Mecca, drive 14 miles southeast on Highway 111 to the entrance.

Trip notes: This is by far the biggest of the campgrounds on the Salton Sea. For details about the Salton Sea, see the trip notes for Headquarters (campground number one).

❹ Salt Creek Primitive Area

Location: In the Salton Sea State Recreation Area; map J7, grid b8.

Campsites, facilities: There are 150 primitive sites for tents or RVs. Chemical toilets are available, but there is no piped water. Leashed pets are permitted.

Reservations, fees: No reservations; $7 per night, $1 pet fee. Open year-round.

Contact: Salton Sea State Recreation Area, (760) 393-3052/3059 or (760) 767-5311.

Directions: From Mecca, drive 17 miles southeast on Highway 111 to the entrance.

Trip notes: Every camp has some claim to fame, however obscure. This one gets the award for the least likely place you want to visit on the Salton Sea. Why? No water. Even a water purifier won't work with the high-saline lake water, unless you're a corvina. For details on the Salton Sea State Recreation Area, see the trip notes for Headquarters (campground number one).

❺ Fountain of Youth Spa

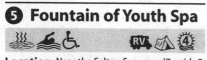

Location: Near the Salton Sea; map J7, grid c9.

Campsites, facilities: There are about 300 primitive sites and 546 RV sites with full hookups. Flush toilets, showers, natural artesian steam rooms, hydrojet pools, swimming pools, recreation centers, dump stations, coin laundry, barber shop, beauty parlor, masseur, church services, propane gas, and groceries are available. Leashed pets are permitted.

Reservations, fees: No reservations; $14 to $25 per night.

Contact: Fountain of Youth Spa, (760) 354-1340 or fax (760) 354-1558.

Directions: From Indio, drive 44 miles south on Highway 111 to Hot Mineral Spa Road. Or from Niland drive 15 miles north on Highway 111 to Hot Mineral Spa Road. Turn north on Hot Mineral Spa Road and drive about four miles to the park.

Trip notes: Natural artesian steam rooms are the highlight here, but I didn't seem to get any younger. This is a vast private park, set near the Salton Sea. See the trip notes for Red Hill Marina County Park (chapter J8, campground number one), located nearby, for side trip options.

❻ Culp Valley Primitive Camp Area

Location: Near Peña Springs in Anza-Borrego Desert State Park; map J7, grid c0.

Campsites, facilities: This is an open camping area in Anza-Borrego Desert State Park. It can be used for tents or RVs. Open fires are not allowed and there is no piped water, so bring your own. Leashed pets are permitted.

Reservations, fees: No reservations; $5 per vehicle per night. Open year-round.

Contact: Anza-Borrego Desert State Park, (760) 767-5311 or fax (760) 767-3424.

Directions: From Borrego Springs, drive 10 miles southwest on County Road S22.

Trip notes: Culp Valley is set near Peña Springs and offers a trailhead for a hike that is routed to the northeast to the high desert. An advisable side trip is to the Panorama Outlook, located at Borrego Palm Canyon (campground number seven), about a 15-minute drive north on County Road S22. The elevation is 3,400 feet.

❼ Borrego Palm Canyon

Location: In Anza-Borrego Desert State Park; map J7, grid b1.

Campsites, facilities: There are 52 RV sites with full hookups and 65 sites for tents or RVs. Piped water, fire grills, and picnic tables are provided. Flush toilets and showers are available. A grocery store, coin laundry, and propane gas are nearby. There are also five group tent camps that can accommodate 10 to 24 people each. Leashed pets are permitted.

Reservations, fees: Reserve via phone at (800) 444-PARK/7275 ($7.50 reservation fee) or website www.cal-parks.ca.gov; $14 to $21 per night, $36 group fee. Open year-round.

Contact: Anza-Borrego Desert State Park, (760) 767-5311 or fax (760) 767-3424.

Directions: From Borrego Springs, drive 2.5 miles west on County Road S22 and Palm Canyon Drive to the campground entrance.

Trip notes: This is one of the best camps in Anza-Borrego Desert State Park with two excellent hikes available. The short hike into Borrego Palm Canyon is like being transported to another world, from the desert to the tropics, complete with a small waterfall, a rare sight in these parts. The Panorama Outlook Trail also starts here. An excellent visitor center is available, offering an array of exhibits and a slide show. The elevation is 760 feet.

❽ Arroyo Salado Primitive Camp Area

Location: In Anza-Borrego Desert State Park; map J7, grid c4.

Campsites, facilities: This is an open camping area in the Anza-Borrego Desert State Park. It can be used for tents or RVs. Open fires are not allowed and there is no piped water, so bring your own. Leashed pets are permitted.

Reservations, fees: No reservations; $5 per vehicle per night. Open year-round.

Contact: Anza-Borrego Desert State Park, (760) 767-5311 or fax (760) 767-3424.

Directions: From Borrego Springs, drive about 16 miles east on County Road S22 to the camping area.

Trip notes: This camp is a primitive spot set along (and named after) an ephemeral stream, the Arroyo Salado. A few miles to the west is the trailhead for the Thimble Trail, which is routed south into a wash in the Borrego Badlands. The elevation is 800 feet.

❾ Bombay Beach

Location: In the Salton Sea State Recreation Area; map J7, grid c9.

Campsites, facilities: There are 200 sites for tents or RVs. Piped water and chemical toilets are available. Leashed pets are permitted.

Reservations, fees: No reservations; $3 to $20 per night, $1 pet fee. Open year-round.

Contact: Salton Sea State Recreation Area, (760) 393-3052/3059 or (760) 767-5311.

Directions: From Niland, drive 18 miles northwest on Highway 111 to the entrance.

Trip notes: All in all, this is a strange looking place, with the Salton Sea, a vast body of water, surrounded by stark, barren countryside. This camp is set in a bay along the southeastern shoreline, where a beach and nature trails are available. Nearby to the south is the Wister Waterfowl Management Area. Note that the Salton Sea is California's unique saltwater lake set below sea level, where corvina can provide a lively sport fishery.

❿ Yaqui Well Primitive Camp Area

Location: In Anza-Borrego Desert State Park; map J7, grid d1.

Campsites, facilities: This is an open camping area in Anza-Borrego Desert State Park. It can be used for tents or RVs. Pit toilets are available. Open fires are not allowed and there is no piped water, so bring your own. Leashed pets are permitted.

Reservations, fees: No reservations; $5 per vehicle per night. Open year-round.

Contact: Anza-Borrego Desert State Park, (760) 767-5311 or fax (760) 767-3424.

Directions: From Borrego Springs, drive about five miles south on County Road S3. Turn right on Yaqui Pass Road/County Road S3 and drive about six miles to the camping area on the right.

Trip notes: This camp is used primarily as an overflow area if the more developed Tamarisk Grove Camp is full. The Cactus Loop Trail, a 2.5-mile loop hike that passes seven varieties of cactus, starts at Tamarisk Grove. The elevation is 1,400 feet.

⑪ Yaqui Pass Primitive Camp Area

Location: In Anza-Borrego Desert State Park; map J7, grid d1.

Campsites, facilities: This is an open camping area in Anza-Borrego Desert State Park. It can be used for tents or RVs. There are no toilets. Open fires are not allowed and there is no piped water, so bring your own. Leashed pets are permitted.

Reservations, fees: No reservations; $5 per vehicle per night. Open year-round.

Contact: Anza-Borrego Desert State Park, (760) 767-5311 or fax (760) 767-3424.

Directions: From Borrego Springs, drive about five miles south on County Road S3. Turn right on Yaqui Pass Road/County Road S3 and drive about four miles to the camping area on the left.

Trip notes: This extremely primitive area is set beside rough Yaqui Pass Road at an elevation of 1,730 feet. The trailhead for the Kenyan Loop Trail is located to the immediate south. This spot is often overlooked because the Tamarisk Grove Camp nearby provides piped water and a feature trail.

⑫ Tamarisk Grove

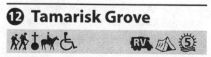

Location: In Anza-Borrego Desert State Park; map J7, grid d1.

Campsites, facilities: There are 27 sites for tents or RVs. Piped water, fire grills, and picnic tables are provided. Flush toilets and showers are available. Leashed pets are permitted.

Reservations, fees: Reserve via phone at (800) 444-PARK/7275 ($7.50 reservation fee) or website www.cal-parks.ca.gov; $14 to $15 per night, $1 pet fee. Open year-round.

Contact: Anza-Borrego Desert State Park, (760) 767-5311 or fax (760) 767-3424.

Directions: From Borrego Springs, drive 12 miles south on County Road S3 (which becomes Yaqui Pass Road) to the intersection with Highway 78.

Trip notes: They've got piped water here, and that's the number one reason this is one of the most popular camps in this desert park. It is one of three camps in the immediate area, so if this camp is full, primitive Yaqui Well to the immediate west and Yaqui Pass to the north on Yaqui Pass Road provide alternatives. The Cactus Loop Trail, with the trailhead just north of camp, provides a hiking option. This is a 2.5-mile loop that passes seven varieties of cactus, some as tall as people. The elevation is 1,400 feet.

⑬ Stagecoach Trails Resort

Location: Near Julian; map J7, grid d0.

Campsites, facilities: There are 286 RV sites with full hookups, most of which are pull-through. There is also a primitive camping area for tents with 75 horse corrals. Rest rooms, picnic tables, and fire rings are provided. A heated pool, hot showers, recreation room, banquet room, coin laundry, two dump stations, and propane gas are available. The facilities are wheelchair accessible. Pets are permitted.

Reservations, fees: Reservations are accepted; $12 to $20 per night, $3 per night per horse.

Contact: Stagecoach Trails Resort, 7878 Overland Stage Route, Julian, CA 92036; (760) 765-2197.

Directions: From San Diego, drive north on Interstate 15 to Highway 78 at Escondido. Drive east on Highway 78 to Santa Ysabel. Turn left on Highway 79 and drive 13 miles to County Road S2/San Felipe Road. Turn right on County Road S2 and drive 17 miles to Scissors Crossing. Turn right on Highway 78, drive 0.3 mile, then turn left back onto County Road S2. Drive about four miles to Stagecoach, just past mile marker 21, to the campground on the right.

Trip notes: You want space? You got space. That includes 600,000 acres of public lands bordering this RV campground, making Stagecoach Trails Resort ideal for those who love horseback riding. Seventy-five corrals at the campground let you know right away that this camp is very horse friendly. In addition, Stagecoach Trails Resort provides the perfect jumping-off place for trips into neighboring Anza-Borrego Desert State Park. The resort's name comes from its proximity to the old Wells Fargo Butterfield Stageline Route.

⑭ Butterfield Ranch

Location: Near Anza-Borrego Desert State Park; map J7, grid e0.

Campsites, facilities: There are 500 sites in all, with 300 full-hookup RV sites and 200 tent sites. Rest rooms, hot showers, sanitary dump station, playground, two swimming pools, whirlpool, coin laundry, cafe, recreation room, store, fish pond, and a petting farm are available. Leashed pets are permitted.

Reservations, fees: Reservations are accepted; $16 to $23 per night.

Contact: Butterfield Ranch, (760) 765-1463 or fax (760) 765-2083.

Directions: From San Diego on Interstate 8, drive 35 miles east to the town of Ramona. Turn east on Highway 78 and drive about 12 miles to County Road S2. Turn south and continue to the campground entrance.

Trip notes: Butterfield Ranch is an ideal layover spot for RV cruisers visiting nearby Anza-Borrego Desert State Park who want a developed park in which to stay overnight. Note that there is no gas available in Julian after 6 P.M. and that the nearest gas station is 36 miles to the east.

⑮ Fish Creek

Location: In Anza-Borrego Desert State Park; map J7, grid e3.

Campsites, facilities: There are eight sites for tents or RVs. Pit toilets are available, but there is no piped water, so bring your own. Leashed pets are permitted.

Reservations, fees: No reservations; $5 per vehicle per night.

Contact: Anza-Borrego Desert State Park, (760) 767-5311 or fax (760) 767-3424.

Directions: From Highway 78 in Ocotillo Wells, drive 12 miles south on Split Mountain Road to the campground.

Trip notes: This primitive camp is set just inside the eastern border of Anza-Borrego Desert State Park, at the foot of the Vallecito Mountains to the west. A few miles north of camp is the Elephant Trees Discovery Trail, a 1.5-mile hike highlighted by weird trees that are a variety of colors and mostly 5-10 feet tall with crumpled bark. Note that this is the closest camp to the Ocotillo Wells State Vehicular Recreation Area, which is located 12 miles to the north.

⑯ Vallecito County Park

Location: Near Anza-Borrego Desert State Park; map J7, grid f0.

Campsites, facilities: There are 44 sites for tents or RVs. Fire grills and picnic tables are provided. Piped water, flush toilets, and a playground are available. Leashed pets are permitted.

Reservations, fees: No reservations; $10 to $14 per night, $1 pet fee. Open October through June.

Contact: San Diego County Parks Department, (619) 565-3600 or (619) 694-3049.

Directions: From Julian, drive 12 miles east on Highway 78. Turn right (south) on County Road S2 and drive 18 miles to the park entrance on the right.

Trip notes: This nice county park in the desert gets little attention in the face of the other nearby attractions. These include the Agua Caliente Hot Springs, Anza-Borrego Desert State Park to the east, and Lake Cuyamaca and Cuyamaca Rancho State Park about 35 miles away. The elevation is 1,500 feet.

⑰ Agua Caliente County Park

Location: Near Anza-Borrego Desert State Park; map J7, grid f0.

Campsites, facilities: There are 104 RV sites with full or partial hookups and 36 sites for tents or RVs. Piped water, fire grills, and picnic tables are provided. Flush toilets, showers, swimming pool, therapy pool, and a playground are available. Groceries and propane gas are nearby. No pets are allowed.

Reservations, fees: Reservations are accepted; $10 to $14 per night. Open Labor Day through Memorial Day weekend.

Contact: San Diego County Parks Department, (619) 565-3600 or (619) 694-3049.

Directions: From San Diego, take Interstate 8 east to the town of Ocotillo. From there, take County Road S2 north for 25 miles to the park entrance on the right. From Julian, drive 12 miles east on Highway 78. Turn right on County Road S2 and drive 21 miles south to the park entrance road on the right.

Trip notes: Everything is hot here. The weather is hot, the coffee is hot, and the water is hot. And hey, that's what "Agua Caliente" means—hot water, named after the nearby hot springs. Anza-Borrego Desert State Park is also nearby. If you would like to see some cold water, Lake Cuyamaca and Cuyamaca Rancho State Park are about 35 miles away. The elevation is 1,350 feet.

⑱ Cottonwood

Location: In the McCain Valley Wildlife Management Area; map J7, grid g0.

Campsites, facilities: There are 29 sites for tents or RVs. Piped water, fire grills, and picnic tables are provided. Vault toilets are available. Leashed pets are permitted.

Reservations, fees: No reservations; $6 per night. Open year-round.

Contact: Bureau of Land Management, El Centro Resource Area, 1661 South Fourth Street, El Centro, CA 92243; (760) 337-4400 or fax (760) 337-4490.

Directions: From San Diego, drive approximately 70 miles east on Interstate 8 to the McCain Valley exit. Turn right, turn left on the southern frontage (county) road/Highway 98, and continue east for two miles to the intersection with McCain Valley Road. Turn left on McCain Valley Road and drive about 13 miles to the campground.

Trip notes: This camp is set on the western edge of the McCain Valley Wildlife Management Area. Like most Bureau of Land Management camps, it is little known and little used. The elevation is 4,000 feet.

⑲ Bow Willow

Location: Near Bow Willow Canyon in Anza-Borrego Desert State Park; map J7, grid g2.

Campsites, facilities: There are 14 sites for tents or RVs. Picnic tables and ramadas are provided. Piped water is limited and vault toilets are available. Leashed pets are permitted.

Reservations, fees: No reservations; $7 to $9 per night, $1 pet fee. Open year-round.

Contact: Anza-Borrego Desert State Park, (760) 767-5311 or fax (760) 767-3424.

Directions: From Interstate 8 in Ocotillo, turn north on County Road S2 and drive 14 miles to the gravel campground entrance road on the left.

Trip notes: Bow Willow Canyon is a rugged setting that can be explored by hiking the trail that starts at this camp. A short distance east of the camp, the trail forks to the south to Rockhouse Canyon. For a good side trip drive back to County Road S2 and head south over Sweeney Pass for the view at the Carrizo Badlands Overlook.

㉒ Mountain Palm Springs Primitive Camp Area

Location: In Anza-Borrego Desert State Park; map J7, grid g2.

Campsites, facilities: This is an open camping area in Anza-Borrego Desert State Park. It can be used for tents or RVs. Chemical toilets are available. Open fires are not allowed and there is no piped water, so bring your own. Leashed pets are permitted.

Reservations, fees: No reservations, $6 per vehicle per night. Open year-round.

Contact: Anza-Borrego Desert State Park, (760) 767-5311 or fax (760) 767-3424.

Directions: From Interstate 8 in Ocotillo, turn north on County Road S2 and drive 15 miles to the camp entrance road on the left.

Trip notes: A plus for this camping area is easy access from County Road S2, but no water is a giant minus. Regardless of pros and cons, only hikers will get the full benefit of the area. A trail leads south to Bow Willow Creek (and Bow Willow, campground number 19) and onward into Bow Willow Canyon. The Carrizo Badlands Overlook is located on the southeast side of Sweeney Pass, about a 10-minute drive south on County Road S2. The elevation is 950 feet.

㉑ Lark Canyon

Location: In the McCain Valley Wildlife Management Area; map J7, grid h2.

Campsites, facilities: There are 15 sites for tents or RVs. Fire grills and picnic tables are provided. Piped water and pit toilets are available. Leashed pets are permitted.

Reservations, fees: No reservations; $6 per night. Open year-round.

Contact: Bureau of Land Management, El Centro Resource Area, 1661 South Fourth Street, El Centro, CA 92243; (760) 337-4400 or fax (760) 337-4490.

Directions: From San Diego, drive approximately 70 miles east on Interstate 8 to the McCain Valley exit. Turn right, turn left on the frontage (county) road, and continue east for two miles to the intersection with McCain Valley Road. Turn left on McCain Valley Road and drive three miles to the campground.

Trip notes: This is a small camp that few know of, set at 4,000 feet in the McCain Valley National Cooperative and Wildlife Management Area. It is near a popular off-highway-vehicle area. Many dirt bikers use it as their base camp.

㉒ Rio Bend RV Park

Location: Near El Centro; map J7, grid h7.

Campsites, facilities: There are 228 sites with full hookups for RVs, and a group area with 42 sites with partial hookups. Picnic tables are provided. There is also a heated pool, spa, shuffleboard, volleyball, two small stocked lakes, golf course, and coin laundry. Telephone and cable television hookups are available. The park is wheelchair accessible. A small store is located nearby. Leashed pets are permitted.

Reservations, fees: Reservations are accepted; $13 to $25 per night.

Contact: Rio Bend RV Park, (760) 352-7061 or fax (760) 352-0055.

Directions: From El Centro, drive west on Interstate 8 for seven miles. Take the Drew Road exit and then drive south on Drew Road for one-quarter mile to the park, located at 1589 Drew Road.

Trip notes: This RV park is set at 50 feet below sea level near Mount Signal, about a 20-minute drive south of the Salton Sea. For some, this region is a godforsaken wasteland, but hey, that makes arriving at this park all the more like coming to a mirage in the desert. The park is usually well maintained, and management does what it can to offer visitors recreational options. It's hot out here, sizzling most of the year, but dry and cool in the winter, the best time to visit.

Map J8

One inch equals approximately 10.7 miles.
See inside back cover for California state map.

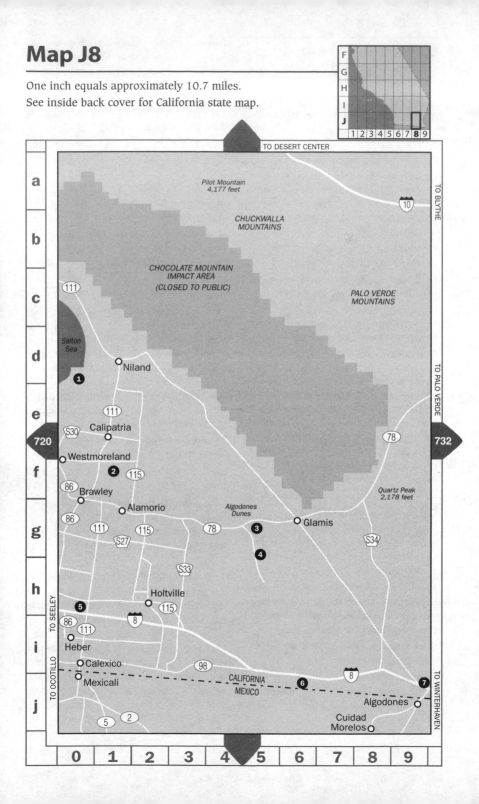

TO DESERT CENTER

TO BLYTHE

10

Pilot Mountain
4,177 feet

CHUCKWALLA
MOUNTAINS

CHOCOLATE MOUNTAIN
IMPACT AREA
(CLOSED TO PUBLIC)

PALO VERDE
MOUNTAINS

111

Salton
Sea

Niland

1

111

S30   Calipatria

720

Westmoreland

2   115

86   Brawley

86

111   115

Alamorio

Algodones
Dunes

S27

78

3

Glamis

4

S33

S34

Quartz Peak
2,178 feet

78

732

Holtville

5

115

8

86   111

Heber

Calexico

Mexicali

98

CALIFORNIA

MEXICO

6

8

7

Algodones

Cuidad
Morelos

TO SEELEY

TO OCOTILLO

TO PALO VERDE

TO WINTERHAVEN

5   2

❶ Red Hill Marina County Park

Location: Near the Salton Sea; map J8, grid d0.

Campsites, facilities: There are 115 sites for tents or RVs, 40 with hookups. Picnic tables, cabanas, barbecue pits, and piped water are provided. Flush toilets, showers, and a boat launch are available. Leashed pets are permitted.

Reservations, fees: No reservations; $7 to 12 per night with a 14-day limit.

Contact: Red Hill Marina County Park, (760) 348-2310.

Directions: From Niland, drive five miles south on Highway 111 to Sinclair Road. Turn right and drive to Garst Road. Go right and follow the road to the end (about 1.5 miles). Go left on Red Hill Road and follow it to the marina and campground.

Trip notes: This county park is near the south end of the Salton Sea. The Salton Sea, of course, is one of the weirdest places on Earth. Set 228 feet below sea level, it's a vast body of water covering 360 square miles, right, 35 miles long but with an average depth of just 10 feet. It's an extremely odd place to swim, bobbing around effortlessly in the highly saline water. Fishing is often good for corvina in the winter. Several wildlife refuges are in the immediate area, including two separate chunks of the Imperial Wildfowl Management Area, to the west and south, and the huge Wister Waterfowl Management Area, northwest of Niland. For side trip options, see the trip notes for Bombay Beach (chapter J7, campground number nine).

❷ Wiest Lake County Park

Location: On Wiest Lake; map J8, grid f1.

Campsites, facilities: There are 20 tent sites and 24 RV sites with full hookups. Picnic tables, fire grills, piped water, boat ramp, and a dump station are provided. Flush toilets and showers are available. A grocery store, coin laundry, and propane gas are nearby. Leashed pets are permitted.

Reservations, fees: No reservations; $7 to 12 per night.

Contact: Wiest Lake County Park, (760) 344-3712, (760) 339-4384, or fax (760) 339-4372.

Directions: From Brawley, drive approximately five miles north on Highway 111. Turn right on Rutherford Road and drive two miles to the park entrance on the right.

Trip notes: This is a developed county park along the southern shore of Wiest Lake, which adjoins the Imperial Wildfowl Management Area to the north. Wiest Lake is just 50 acres, set 110 feet below sea level, and a prized area with such desolate country in the surrounding region. Waterskiing and windsurfing can be excellent, although few take advantage of the latter. The Salton Sea, about a 20-minute drive to the northwest, is a worthy side trip.

❸ Gecko

Location: East of Brawley; map J8, grid g5.

Campsites, facilities: There are numerous dispersed sites for tents or RVs. Vault toilets and a trash bin are provided, but there is no piped water, so bring your own. Leashed pets are permitted.

Reservations, fees: No reservations; no fee. Open year-round.

Contact: Bureau of Land Management, El Centro Resource Area, 1661 South Fourth Street, El Centro, CA 92243; (760) 337-4400 or fax (760) 337-4490.

Directions: From Brawley, drive 27 miles east on Highway 78 to Gecko Road. Turn south on

Gecko Road and drive three miles to the campground entrance on the right.

Trip notes: There isn't a tree within a million miles of this camp. People who wind up here all have the same thing in common: they're ready to ride across the dunes in their dune buggies or off-road vehicles. Other recreation options include watching the sky and waiting for a cloud to show up. A gecko, by the way, is a harmless little lizard. I've had them crawl on the sides of my tent. Nice little fellows.

❹ Roadrunner

Location: East of Brawley; map J8, grid g5.

Campsites, facilities: There are dispersed sites for tents or RVs. Vault toilets and a trash bin are provided, but there is no piped water. Leashed pets are permitted.

Reservations, fees: No reservations; no fee. Open year-round.

Contact: Bureau of Land Management, El Centro Resource Area, 1661 South Fourth Street, El Centro, CA 92243; (760) 337-4400 or fax (760) 337-4490.

Directions: From Brawley, drive 27 miles east on Highway 78 to Gecko Road. Turn south on Gecko Road and drive five miles to the campground entrance at the end of the road.

Trip notes: This is the twin camp to Gecko (campground number 3) just a short ways down the road.

❺ Country Life RV

Location: Near El Centro; map J8, grid h0.

Campsites, facilities: There are six tent sites and 150 RV sites with full hookups. Flush toilets, showers, swimming pool, clubhouse, coin laundry, propane gas, and groceries are available. Some facilities are wheelchair accessible. Leashed pets are permitted.

Reservations, fees: Reservations are recommended; $15 to 18.50 per night. Open year-round.

Contact: Country Life RV, (760) 353-1040 or fax (760) 352-1948.

Directions: From Interstate 8 in El Centro, take the Highway 111 exit and drive a quarter mile north. Turn left on Ross Road and drive a short distance to the campground entrance.

Trip notes: You'd best have air conditioning. This is an RV parking lot on the desert flats about a 10-minute drive north of the Mexican border. Nearby side trips include the Salton Sea to the north, little Sunbeam Lake County Park to the west and, if you need to sober up, the Mexican border customs to the south.

❻ Midway

Location: In the Imperial Sand Dunes Recreation Area; map J8, grid j6.

Campsites, facilities: There are several primitive sites for tents or RVs. Pit toilets are available. No piped water is provided.

Reservations, fees: No reservations; no fee.

Contact: Bureau of Land Management, El Centro Resource Area, 1661 South Fourth Street, El Centro, CA 92243; (760) 337-4400 or fax (760) 337-4490.

Directions: From El Centro, drive east on Interstate 8 for about 40 miles to Sand Hills. Turn south on Gray's Wells Road and drive three miles. The road turns from pavement to dirt and then dead-ends; camping is permitted anywhere in this region.

Trip notes: This is off-road headquarters, a place where people bring their three-wheelers, four-wheelers, and motorcycles and act like lunatics without anybody even raising an eyebrow. That's because a large area has been set aside just for this type of recreation. As you drive in you will enter the Buttercup Recreation Area, which is part of the Imperial Sand Dunes Recreation Area. You do what you please, camp wherever you like, and nobody beefs.

❼ Pilot Knob RV Park

Location: Near the Colorado River; map J9, grid i9.

Campsites, facilities: There are 150 RV sites with full hookups and picnic tables. Flush toilets, showers, recreation room, swimming pool, spa, and coin laundry are available. Leashed pets are permitted.

Reservations, fees: Reservations are recommended; $15 per night. Open year-round.

Contact: Pilot Knob RV Park, (760) 572-5232 or fax (760) 572-5142.

Directions: From Interstate 8 in Winterhaven, take the Sidewinder Road exit and drive to the southern frontage road. Drive a half mile west on the frontage road to the campground on the left.

Trip notes: They don't call the town Winterhaven for nothing. Just try visiting in the summer and you'll find out why winter is preferred. This is a privately operated RV park that is a winter attraction for folks in the Pacific Northwest who are starting to rust from all the rain up there. The Colorado River and the Mexican border are to the nearby south.

Map J9

One inch equals approximately 10.7 miles.
See inside back cover for California state map.

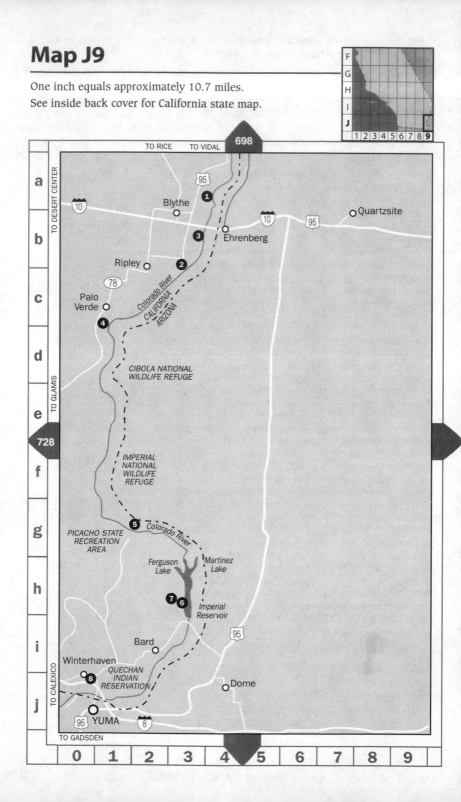

❶ Mayflower County Park

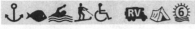

Location: On the Colorado River; map J9, grid a3.

Campsites, facilities: There are 28 tent sites and 152 RV sites with piped water and electrical hookups provided. Picnic tables and barbecues are provided. Flush toilets, showers, dump station, and a boat ramp are available. Leashed pets are permitted.

Reservations, fees: Reservations are accepted; $15 to $16 per night, $2 boat launch fee, $2 pet fee. Open year-round.

Contact: Mayflower County Park, (760) 922-4665.

Directions: From Blythe, drive 3.5 miles northeast on Intake Boulevard/US 95 to Sixth Avenue. Turn right on Sixth Avenue and drive three miles to the park entrance directly ahead.

Trip notes: The Colorado River is the fountain of life around these parts and, for campers, is the main attraction to this county park. It is a popular spot for waterskiing. There is river access here in the Blythe area. Note that this span of water is flanked by agricultural lands, although there are several developed recreation areas on the California side of the river south of Blythe near Palo Verde.

❷ McIntyre Park

Location: On the Colorado River; map J9, grid b3.

Campsites, facilities: There are 140 tent sites and 160 RV sites, with picnic tables, piped water, and electrical connections provided. Rest rooms, showers, dump station, propane gas, snack bar, grocery store, bait, ice, and a boat ramp are available. Some facilities are wheelchair accessible. Pets are not permitted.

Reservations, fees: Reservations are recommended; $16 to $25 per night. Open year-round.

Contact: McIntyre Park, (760) 922-8205.

Directions: From Blythe on Interstate 10, drive seven miles south on Intake Boulevard to the foot of 26th Avenue and the park entrance.

Trip notes: This RV park sits on the outskirts of Blythe on the Colorado River, with this stretch of river providing good conditions for boating, waterskiing, and other water sports. Fishing is an option, with a variety of fish providing fair results, including striped bass, largemouth bass, and catfish roaming the area.

❸ Riviera Blythe Marina

Location: Near the Colorado River; map J9, grid b4.

Campsites, facilities: There are 285 RV sites, many with full or partial hookups. Picnic tables are provided. Rest rooms, showers, swimming pool, spa, cable TV, coin laundry, store, card room, boat ramp, and propane gas are available. A golf course is within five miles. Leashed pets are permitted.

Reservations, fees: Reservations are accepted; $18 to $29 per night. Open year-round.

Contact: Riviera Blythe Marina, (760) 922-5350 or fax (760) 922-0599; website: www.destinyrv.com.

Directions: From Blythe, drive two miles east on Interstate 10 to the Riviera Drive exit. Follow it to 14100 Riviera Drive.

Trip notes: This RV park is set up for camper-boaters who want to hunker down for awhile along the Colorado River and cool off. Access to the park is easy off Interstate 10, and a marina is available, both big pluses for those showing up with trailered boats.

❹ Palo Verde County Park

Location: Near the Colorado River; map J9, grid c1.

Campsites, facilities: There are an undesignated number of sites for tents or RVs. Piped water, flush toilets, and a playground are available. A boat ramp is available at the Palo Verde Oxbow BLM site five miles west on the Colorado River (see the trip notes below for directions). A grocery store, coin laundry, and propane gas are available in Palo Verde. Leashed pets are permitted.

Reservations, fees: No reservations; no fee. Open year-round.

Contact: Palo Verde County Park, (760) 339-4384.

Directions: From Palo Verde, drive three miles south on Highway 78 to the signed campground exit on the left.

Trip notes: This is the only game in town, with no other camp around for many miles. It is set near a bend in the Colorado River, not far from the Cibola National Wildlife Refuge. To get to the boat ramp available at the Palo Verde Oxbow BLM site on the Colorado River, take the gravel road between mileposts 77 and 78 off Highway 78 and drive west for five miles to the river. This stretch of river is a good one for powerboating and waterskiing. The best facilities for visitors are available here and on the west side of the river between Palo Verde and Blythe, with nothing available on the east side of the river.

❺ Picacho State Recreation Area

Location: Near Taylor Lake on the Colorado River; map J9, grid g1.

Campsites, facilities: There are 58 sites for tents or small RVs. Picnic tables and fire grills are

provided. There are also several boat-in campsites available. Piped water, pit toilets, sanitary disposal station, solar showers, camp store, and a boat launch are available. Leashed pets are permitted.

Reservations, fees: No reservations except for group sites; $7 to $12 per night. Open year-round.

Contact: Picacho State Recreation Area, (760) 393-3059, (760) 996-2963, or (760) 767-5311.

Directions: From Highway 8 in Winterhaven, take the Winterhaven/Fourth Avenue exit. Turn left on Fourth Avenue and then turn right on County Road S24. Turn left on Picacho Road and drive under the railroad tracks. Continue on Picacho Road. When you cross the American Canal, the road becomes dirt. Continue north for 18 miles on the winding dirt road (not suitable for large RVs) to the campground. This takes about an hour.

Trip notes: To get here, you really have to want it. It's way out there, requiring a long drive north out of Winterhaven on a spindly little road. The camp is on the southern side of Taylor Lake on the Colorado River. The park is the best deal around for many miles, though, with a boat ramp, waterskiing, good bass fishing, and occasionally, crazy folks having the time of their lives. The sun and water make a good combination.

❻ Senator Wash Recreation Area

Location: Near Senator Wash Reservoir; map J9, grid h3.

Campsites, facilities: There are an undesignated number of sites for tents or self-contained RVs. There is no piped water in the camping areas. There are vault toilets at the north shore. A boat ramp, with adjacent piped water, flush toilets, and showers, is available a quarter mile from the south shore. Camping at the boat ramp is not allowed. Leashed pets are permitted.

Reservations, fees: No reservations; no fee. There is a maximum 14-day stay.

Contact: Bureau of Land Management, Yuma Field Office, (520) 317-3200 or fax (520) 317-3250.

Directions: From Yuma, Arizona, drive approximately 23 miles northeast on Imperial Highway/County Road S24 to Senator Wash Road. Turn left and drive about three miles to the campground on the left.

Trip notes: This campground is set in a large recreation area that borders the Colorado River. Specifically, it is nestled between Senator Wash Reservoir to the west and Squaw Lake (created by the Imperial Dam on the Colorado River) to the southeast. It is a vast, virtually unmonitored area, far less developed than that north from Palo Verde to Blythe. In other words, there's darn near nothing out here, except, that is, for this camping area and its nearby boat ramp.

❼ Squaw Lake

Location: Near the Colorado River; map J9, grid h3.

Campsites, facilities: There are 80 sites for tents or RVs. Picnic tables and fire grills are provided. Piped water, flush toilets, cold showers, and a boat ramp are available. Some facilities are wheelchair accessible. Leashed pets are permitted.

Reservations, fees: No reservations; $8 per vehicle of five or fewer people, $1 for each additional camper. There is a maximum 14-day limit. Open year-round.

Contact: Bureau of Land Management, Yuma Field Office, (520) 317-3200 or fax (520) 317-3250.

Directions: From Yuma, Arizona, drive approximately 23 miles northeast on Imperial Highway/County Road S24 to Senator Wash Road. Turn left and drive about three miles to the campground.

Trip notes: Take your pick. There are two camps near the Colorado River in this area (the other is Senator Wash, campground number six). This one

Is near Squaw Lake, created by the nearby Imperial Dam on the Colorado River.

❽ Sans End RV Park

Location: In Winterhaven; map J9, grid i0.

Campsites, facilities: There are 167 sites for RVs and a few sites for tents. Rest rooms, showers, recreation hall, pool table, coin laundry, and shuffleboard are available. Leashed pets are permitted.

Reservations, fees: No reservations; $20 per night.

Contact: Sans End RV Park, 2209 West Winterhaven Drive, Winterhaven, CA 92283; (760) 572-0797.

Directions: From Yuma, Arizona, take Interstate 8 west and then exit on Winterhaven Drive. Follow Winterhaven to the RV park at 2209 West Winterhaven Drive.

Trip notes: Sans End is only seven miles from Mexico, and lots of people who stay here like to cross the border for shopping and fun. The high season at this RV park is January to March, and no wonder, because it is blazing hot here in the summer. The Colorado River from Yuma to Winterhaven is nearby and provides recreational opportunities near Imperial Dam. Boat ramps are available in Yuma and Winterhaven. Some areas of this stretch of water are marshy wetlands that provide an opportunity for duck hunting in the fall and early winter. For anglers, there are some big catfish roaming these waters. Whatever you choose to do, remember this: The magic is always in the moment, so have fun. Life is no dress rehearsal.

Index

Index

Index

Acknowledgements

Michael Hodgson, author of *Facing The Extreme* (with Ruth Anne Kocour) and technical editor of Outdoor Retailer, reviewed all the equipment and technical information for this edition.

The following state and federal resource experts provided critical late-breaking information regarding changes in reservations services, fees, and recreation services:

Michael Dombeck, Linda Feldman, and Dick Patterson, U.S. Forest Service Headquarters, Washington, D.C.

Matt Mathes, U.S. Forest Service, Pacific Region headquarters, San Francisco, California

Andrea Patterson and Ken Colombini, California State Parks headquarters, Sacramento, California

Kathy Burdett, National Park Service, Washington, D.C.

Scott Gediman, Yosemite National Park

The following recreation resource experts reviewed and updated campground information in this edition:

Rosemary McCleod, Sequoia National Forest

Karen Finlayson and the Information Center Team, Eldorado National Forest

Charly Krause, Karen Rainey, and Pat Garrahan; Klamath National Forest

Joyce Hopkins, Kathy Turner, and Jamie; Lassen National Forest

Bill Tierney, Modoc National Forest

Molly Fuller and Debbie McIntosh, Mendocino National Forest

Sherleen Bloom, Plumas National Forest

Phil Bono and Jim Crossland, Six Rivers National Forest

Fred Ricktar, John Ellsworth, Debbie McLaughlin, Catherine Fink, and Jan Allison; Inyo National Forest

Debe Arndt, Susie Burkindine, and Mike Nowka; Sierra National Forest

Ed Hatakeda, Ron Armstrong, Anna Draper, and Hatcher; Shasta-Trinity National Forest

Elaine Owens and Ken Massa, Stanislaus National Forest

Andy Steele, Herta McClenahan, Mina Hernandez, Sylvia Crowe, and Patti Mahaffey; Tahoe National Forest

Ellen, Toiyable National Forest

John Bridgewater and Joe Duran,
Los Padres National Forest

Diane McComb, Angeles National Forest

Sandra Vandenberg and Bruce Lang,
San Bernardino
National Forest

Laura Lolly, Cleveland National Forest

Malinee Crapsey, Kings Canyon
and Sequoia National Parks

Russel Lesko, Lassen National Park

Carol Spears and Yvonne Menard,
Channel Islands National Park

Tim Wallace, Richardson Grove State Park

Jeff Lee, Henry Cowell Redwoods State Park

Ron Angier, Mount Tamalpais State Park

Steve Radosevich, California State Parks,
Santa Cruz District

Dave Gould, California State Parks,
Four Rivers District

Teri Roberts, Inyo County Parks

Brian, Bureau of Land Management,
Arcata Resource District

John B. Hervey, Bureau of Land Management, Caliente
Resource District

Frank Fonseca, U.S. Corps of Engineers,
Sacramento District

Adria Schulz, PG&E Land Projects, Sacramento

Editor in Chief	*Kyle Morgan*
Editors	*Holly Haddorff*
	Ronit Le Mon
	Carolyn Perkins
Production Coordinator	*Jan Shade*
Production Assistant	*Jean-Vi Lenthe*
	Mark Aver
Senior Research Editor	*Janet Connaughton*
Research Editor	*Hillary Connaughton*
Cover Photo	*Mark Gibson,*
	Mount Shasta

Leave No Trace

Leave No Trace, Inc., is a program dedicated to maintaining the integrity of outdoor recreation areas through education and public awareness. Foghorn Press is a proud supporter of this program and its ethics.

Here's how you can Leave No Trace:

Plan Ahead and Prepare
- Learn about the regulations and special concerns of the area you are visiting.
- Visit the backcountry in small groups.
- Avoid popular areas during peak-use periods.
- Choose equipment and clothing in subdued colors.
- Pack food in reusable containers.

Travel and Camp with Care
On the trail:
- Stay on designated trails. Walk single file in the middle of the path.
- Do not take shortcuts on switchbacks.
- When traveling cross-country where there are no trails, follow animal trails or spread out your group so no new routes are created. Walk along the most durable surfaces available, such as rock, gravel, dry grasses, or snow.
- Use a map and compass to eliminate the need for rock cairns, tree scars, or ribbons.
- If you encounter pack animals, step to the downhill side of the trail and speak softly to avoid startling them.

At Camp:
- Choose an established, legal site that will not be damaged by your stay.
- Restrict activities to areas where vegetation is compacted or absent.
- Keep pollutants out of the water by camping at least 200 feet (about 70 adult steps) from lakes and streams.
- Control pets at all times, or leave them at home with a sitter. Remove dog feces.

Pack It In and Pack It Out
- Take everything you bring into the wild back out with you.
- Protect wildlife and your food by storing rations securely. Pick up all spilled foods.

- Use toilet paper or wipes sparingly; pack them out.
- Inspect your campsite for trash and any evidence of your stay. Pack out all trash—even if it's not yours!

Properly Dispose of What You Can't Pack Out
- If no refuse facility is available, deposit human waste in catholes dug six to eight inches deep at least 200 feet from water, camps, or trails. Cover and disguise the catholes when you're finished.
- To wash yourself or your dishes, carry the water 200 feet from streams or lakes and use small amounts of biodegradable soap. Scatter the strained dishwater.

Keep the Wilderness Wild
- Treat our natural heritage with respect. Leave plants, rocks, and historical artifacts as you found them.
- Good campsites are found, not made. Do not alter a campsite.
- Let nature's sounds prevail; keep loud voices and noises to a minimum.
- Do not build structures or furniture or dig trenches.

Minimize Use and Impact of Fires
- Campfires can have a lasting impact on the backcountry. Always carry a lightweight stove for cooking, and use a candle lantern instead of building a fire whenever possible.
- Where fires are permitted, use established fire rings only.
- Do not scar the natural setting by snapping the branches off live, dead, or downed trees.
- Completely extinguish your campfire and make sure it is cold before departing. Remove all unburned trash from the fire ring and scatter the cold ashes over a large area well away from any camp.

For more information, call 1-800-332-4100.

About the Author

Tom Stienstra has made it his life work to explore the West—hiking, camping, fishing, and boating—searching for the best of the great outdoors and writing about it.

He is the outdoors writer for the *San Francisco Examiner,* which distributes his column on the New York Times News Service, and an associate editor for *Western Outdoor News.*

In the 1990s, he was twice named National Outdoor Writer of the Year (newspaper division) by the Outdoor Writers Association of America, and three times named California Outdoor Writer of the Year.

His books with Foghorn Outdoors are the best-selling outdoor guidebooks in the nation. They include:

Tom Stienstra's Outdoor Getaway Guide

California Hiking (with Ann Marie Brown)

California Fishing

California Boating and Water Sports

Pacific Northwest Camping

Easy Camping in Northern California

Epic Trips of the West: Tom Stienstra's 10 Best

FOGHORN OUTDOORS

Founded in 1985, Foghorn Press has quickly become one of the country's premier publishers of outdoor recreation guidebooks. Foghorn Press books are available throughout the United states in bookstores and some outdoor retailers. If you cannot find the title you are looking for, visit Foghorn's Web site at www.foghorn.com or call 1-800-FOGHORN.

The Complete Guide Series

- *Tom Stienstra's Outdoor Getaway Guide for Northern California* (448 pp) $ 18.95—5th Edition
- *California Hiking* (688 pp) $20.95—4th edition
- *California Fishing* (768 pp) $20.95—5th edition
- *California Boating and Water Sports* (552 pp) $19.95—2nd edition
- *California Waterfalls* (408 pp) $17.95—1st edition
- *The Outdoor Getaway Guide for Southern California* (344 pp) $14.95—1st edition
- *California Golf* (1056 pp) $24.95—8th edition
- *California Beaches* (640 pp) $19.95—2nd edition
- *Pacific Northwest Camping* (656 pp)$20.95—6th edition
- *Pacific Northwest Hiking* (648 pp) $20.95—3rd edition
- *Washington Fishing* (480 pp) $20.95—2nd edition
- *Tahoe* (678 pp) $20.95—2nd edition
- *Utah and Nevada Camping* (384 pp) $18.95—1st edition
- *Arizona/New Mexico Camping* (500 pp) $17.95—3rd edition
- *Colorado Camping* (480 pp) $16.95—2nd edition
- *Baja Camping* (288 pp) $14.95—2nd edition
- *Alaska Fishing* (448 pp) $20.95—2nd edition
- *Florida Camping* (672 pp) $20.95—1st edition
- *Florida Beaches* (680 pp) $19.95—1st edition
- *New England Hiking* (402 pp) $18.95—2nd edition
- *New England Camping* (520 pp) $19.95—2nd edition

The National Outdoors Series

- *America's Secret Recreation Areas—Your Recreation Guide to the Bureau of Land Management's Wild Lands of the West* (640 pp) $17.95
- *America's Wilderness—The Complete Guide to More Than 600 National Wilderness Areas* (592 pp) $19.95
- *The Camper's Companion—The Pack-Along Guide for Better Outdoor Trips* (458 pp) $15.95
- *Wild Places: 20 Journeys Into the North American Outdoors* (320 pp) $15.95

A book's page count and availability are subject to change.
For more information, call 1-800-FOGHORN,
email: foghorn@well.com, or write to:
Foghorn Press
P.O. Box 2036
Santa Rosa, CA 95405-0036